THE CLASSIC

The History of the NCAA Basketball Championship

THE CLASSIC
The History of the NCAA Basketball

PUBLISHED BY NATIONAL COLLEGIATE ATHLETIC ASSOCIATION, MISSION, KANSAS

Championship   by Ken Rappoport

IN COOPERATION WITH THE LOWELL PRESS, KANSAS CITY, MISSOURI

Library of Congress Cataloging in Publication Data

Rappoport, Ken.
The Classic.

Includes Index.
1. National Collegiate Athletic Association—History.
2. Basketball—United States—Tournaments—History.
I. Title.

GV885.49.N37R36   796'.06'273   78-73716   ISBN 0-913504-48-3

FIRST EDITION

To the one person who made this book possible:
The basketball player.
Long may he wave at the hoop.

Malcolm W. Emmons

CONTENTS

FOREWORD

Almost all of us at one time or another have tried to play basketball. We have set out to dribble, pass and shoot the uncomfortably large ball with hoped-for skill and grace. Unfortunately, all too often we have lost the dribble with an easy layup in sight or passed the ball to a spot where neither friend nor foe was waiting. A great portion of the American people thus have acquired some sense of the expertness required to play the game with precision—the way it is played when the best college teams in the nation gather for the National Collegiate Basketball Championship. That awareness of the astonishing skill demanded by the sport may be the substance of the sustained public interest that has made this NCAA championship the single most popular collegiate sports event.

Basketball is an intensely regional sport during the regular season. Once the NCAA championship season begins, however, millions of fans devoted to their respective teams become involved in the national playoff struggle and millions of more casual observers are caught up in the excitement. The atmosphere throughout the tournament competition becomes increasingly fervent until the Final Four are brought together in an electric, absorbing atmosphere to determine the national champion.

When the first NCAA basketball championship was played in 1939, relatively few people beyond the confines of Evanston, Illinois, took notice. It is a tribute to the farsightedness of the pioneers of the National Collegiate Basketball Championship that the tournament today symbolizes the special excitement of college athletics. Through four decades, the participating teams have thrilled millions of spectators with a superb level of talent and competitiveness; and in the final analysis, of course, it has been the players and coaches—Bob "Foothills" Kurland, Mr. Iba, the Grand Slam Kids, the Fabulous Five, the Wizard of Westwood and all the others—who have made the championship what it is.

Ken Rappoport has treated all of this with love and care. He has covered the administrative development of the tournament from eight teams in 1939 to an expanded bracket of 40 teams today. He has brought each championship season to life. Most importantly, however, he brings to the reader in human dimensions those players who have performed with discipline and perfection to reach the pinnacle of competitive success.

I believe the reader will enjoy this book thoroughly.

WALTER BYERS
Executive Director
NCAA

x

ACKNOWLEDGMENTS

Nobody can do a book alone, and I would be remiss if I did not name all the wonderful people who added the right touches to the canvas of this one. To the people at the NCAA national office, I can only express my gratefulness for initiating the project and certainly for their friendship and understanding in guiding me in the right direction. That must include Dave Cawood, NCAA director of public relations, for recommending me as an author; Wally Renfro, director of publishing, and Dave Seifert, publications editor, the two with whom I worked most closely on the manuscript; Dale Meggas, research assistant, for his help in locating data for the appendices; Ted Tow and Tom Jernstedt, assistant executive directors for publishing and events, respectively, for their advice and careful reading of the manuscript; and, of course, Walter Byers, executive director of the NCAA, who has guided the Association through 31 of the 40 years covered in this volume and who was responsible for obtaining approval of this project by the NCAA Executive Committee.

To Thomas Scott, longtime member and chairman of the NCAA tournament committee, I convey my deepest appreciation for his remarkable research work. As an administrator and expert on the NCAA basketball championship, Mr. Scott was an invaluable assistant. Large envelopes of information were flowing constantly from his home in Davidson, North Carolina, to mine in Old Bridge, New Jersey; and the gentlemanly Mr. Scott always was available for consultations, day or night, home or away. Dutch Lonborg, whose name also has been synonymous with the NCAA championship, gave a good deal of time to interviews, always with the gracious rejoinder, "please call me anytime." My thanks go out, too, to the many sports writers who did wonderful interviews with coaches: Larry Guest of the Orlando (Florida) Sentinel-Star with Ed Jucker; Earl Luebker of the Tacoma (Washington) News-Tribune with Phil Woolpert; Jack Tobin in Los Angeles, who contributed the extensive John Wooden tapes; Dick Otte of the Columbus (Ohio) Dispatch with Fred Taylor; Blaine Newnham of the Eugene (Oregon) Register-Guard with Howard Hobson, and Volney Meece of the Oklahoma City Times with Hank Iba.

My gratefulness also to the many coaches, players and sports information directors, too numerous to mention, who were gracious enough to help me.

And most importantly, I want to thank my extraordinary wife, Bernice, for her support, inspiration and understanding through the project.

KEN RAPPOPORT

PROLOGUE

"Basketball is here without a doubt to stay. Outside of college it is immensely popular; more so, in fact than it ever will be in college."
—R. B. Hyatt, Yale University, chairman of the Collegiate Basketball Rules Committee, 1909

"If attendance figures mean anything, if the number of participants is significant, basketball has become the great American sport. . . . It is entirely fitting that the prestige of college basketball should be supported, and demonstrated to the nation, by the colleges themselves . . . The National Collegiate Athletic Association Basketball Tournament should become a classic, a fitting annual climax in the program of this great American sport."
—William B. Owens, Stanford University, president of the National Collegiate Athletic Association, 1939

"There are other sports events that have earned the support and attention of large numbers of people, but no event has captured the emotion and excitement of the entire nation as has the National Collegiate Basketball Championship. It is the greatest single collegiate sports event of the year."
—Wayne Duke, commissioner of the Big Ten Conference, chairman of the NCAA tournament committee, 1978

College basketball had advanced a great distance in the 30 years between the report presented by R. B. Hyatt (only 17 years after the creation of the sport) and the prophesy issued by William Owens on the inauguration of the National Collegiate Basketball Championship in 1939. In the next 40 years, as Wayne Duke observed, the sport and the championship would grow into that grandest of events—an American sports classic.

Like many other American achievements, the NCAA basketball championship had a humble beginning. In large measure, it was the product of the efforts of one man with a dream; and ironi-

cally, it would sprout from ground cultivated by another basketball event—the National Invitation Tournament, which started in 1938.

Uncertainty was the hallmark of life in the 1930s, when the world swung from a preoccupation with the Great Depression to the compelling crisis of a world war. During this time, uniquely enough, sports seemed to reflect society.

The heavyweight boxing field was active and crowded until Joe Louis proved to be a knockout fighter in 1939. Davis Cup tennis was dominated first by the French, then by the British and finally by Don Budge and the United States team.

There were the uneasy Olympic Games at Berlin in 1936, where Adolf Hitler's extraordinarily rude conduct ruptured international relations.

And college basketball in America was going through growing pains. The excellence of the "City Game" long had been established, but the sport had not been nationally promoted until Ned Irish, a former newspaper man, began scheduling intersectional matches between popular local teams and well-known national schools at the nation's foremost arena at the time, Madison Square Garden. For the feature of the first date, the so-called "boy promoter" had a solid-gold hit when Notre Dame played the local heroes of New York University in one game of a doubleheader. This matchup, along with St. John's against Westminster of Pennsylvania, attracted 16,000 fans. The pattern of success was established.

The culmination of Irish's work was the planting of the National Invitation Tournament in the Garden in 1938. It began with six teams and eventually assumed proportions of a self-professed national championship.

Most members of the National Association of Basketball Coaches (NABC) looked with admiration at Irish's invention, but one in particular deplored its purpose. Harold G. Olsen, the idealistic basketball coach at Ohio State University, had nothing personal against Irish but did suggest that there was something radically wrong with "an

outside organization moving in and profiting from college athletics."

Olsen submitted that the colleges themselves could promote a basketball tournament that would be under their own wing, truly national in scope and a fitting climax to basketball each year. He reasoned that the proper body to handle such a postseason tournament was the National Collegiate Athletic Association and presented his proposal to that organization.

On October 3, 1938, the proposal was approved by the NCAA but with the condition that the coaches themselves handle the tournament. Thus, the first NCAA basketball championship was held in the spring of 1939 under the auspices of the NCAA but with the tender loving care of the NABC. In fact, the coaches selected the teams—one from each of the eight geographical districts comprising the NCAA.

Assembling the nuts and bolts required to stage a national tournament, Olsen discovered, was not the easiest of assignments. For example, determination of the playoff sites was an eleventh-hour judgment. Arthur C. "Dutch" Lonborg, the Northwestern University basketball coach who managed the 1939 finals, recalls that Olsen called him "two-and-a-half or three weeks" prior to the date of the finals to inquire if his school would host the championship game at Patten Gymnasium.

"I told him Northwestern would be happy to accept the finals," recalls Lonborg. "We had to scurry around to try and publicize it to draw a crowd."

There also was the problem of selecting teams to participate. There were complaints that the season had been over for several weeks and teams had not been practicing or that the athletes were participating in spring sports or that it would not be financially worthwhile. Nonetheless, the selections were made with the help of the various committees, whose membership lists read like a virtual Who's Who in college basketball, including such coaching luminaries of the day as Phog Allen of Kansas, Tony Hinkle of Butler, John Bunn of Stanford, Ozzie Cowles of Dartmouth, Vadal Peterson of Utah, Wisconsin's Doc Meanwell and Northwestern's Lonborg.

Finally, the four teams representing the Eastern districts gathered for regional competition at Philadelphia as did the four Western district teams in San Francisco. And on March 27, 1939, the two regional winners prepared to tip the ball in the first NCAA basketball championship. The thing had started; the wheels had been set in motion. It marked the electric combination of a sport that had captured the interest of a nation and a nation's

passion for competition. Moreover, the event was charged with that quality of participation which had become a tradition in collegiate athletics— pure enthusiasm for the game.

"I knew the tournament was going to be a great one," remarked Oklahoma A&M's (now Oklahoma State) legendary coach Henry Iba, whose teams would win back-to-back national championships in the 1940s. "The time was ripe for it. I'd been going to Madison Square Garden to play regular-season games; and everytime we'd go there, we'd break the attendance record by 200 or 300 people. . . . You knew good and well the NCAA was going to draw. You could see it coming."

Seeing was not believing the first year. The tournament lost $2,531, and the total attendance for all the regional and championship games was little more than 15,000—a far cry from the crowds pouring into the Garden for Irish's regular-season doubleheader extravaganzas. The coaches met, discussed the prospects and voted to turn the administration of the tournament over to the NCAA the following year. The rest is a history of four decades of growth and development into what Duke termed "the greatest single collegiate sports event of the year."

Never again did the event lose money. During the first 40 years of the championship, the gross receipts totaled $41.9 million; and the return in 1978 alone to the participating institutions in terms of expenses and shares of the net receipts ranged from more than $41,000 to more than $262,000. Olsen's concern that revenue from a national championship in collegiate basketball remain with the colleges has been satisfied.

Under the direction of the Association and its Basketball Committee, the tournament has grown from the original eight-team bracket (a format retained until 1951, when the number of entries was doubled) to the current 40-team format. Since the first regional game in March of 1939, 170 of the 256 institutions which sponsor Division I basketball have participated in the championship; and 22 different teams have won the right to say "We're No. 1."

Impressive figures, all. But the greatest testimony to the success and stature of this American sports classic may well be the people—those who have emerged as heroes and those who watched. More than five million people have jammed the arenas for the last 40 years watching such legends as Adolph Rupp, who coached four Kentucky teams to the championship; Branch McCracken, whose Indiana contingent won two titles 13 years apart, and John Wooden, the Wizard of Westwood, whose UCLA teams dominated the scene over a

ten-year period from the mid-1960s to the mid-1970s. In the last several years, the demand by the public for tickets has far outstripped the number of seats available. In 1974, for example, more than 172,000 tickets were requested for some 4,000 available seats. Television, of course, turned the games into a national love affair. Since 1969, based upon figures published by the National Broadcasting Company (NBC), more than 118 million homes have been tuned in to watch the drama of the final game of college athletics' premier event unfold.

Harold Olsen would be proud. Although the pioneers in developing the tournament were many, Olsen generally is given much of the credit for founding the event; he was the persistent missionary. After the financial failure the first year, Olsen pushed on undaunted. By the second year, he was ready to admit, "This is beginning to develop into what I had dreamed it might. We now have a truly national basketball tournament that is under the direct control of the colleges, and the caliber of schools that have entered is proof that the NCAA has administered affairs satisfactorily."

A man and his dream are a tough team to beat.

xiv

THE CLASSIC
The History of the NCAA Basketball Championship

THE EARLY YEARS
1939-1947

convention on the afternoon of April 4, 1938.

Taking note of the success of the National Invitation Tournament in New York and the NAIA tournament in Kansas City, Olsen pointed out, "There is quite a definite development along the line of invitational national college basketball championships. If there is to be a development of this kind, it would seem that the NABC, acting as an affiliate of the NCAA, might very well promote and manage such competition."

Olsen was among those assigned to investigate the feasibility of such an event. He and the others, Stanford's John Bunn and Phog Allen of Kansas, all came back with the same robust, positive reply. The trio proposed that the "NCAA assume responsibility for the conduct of a National Collegiate Basketball Tournament in the spring of 1939." On October 3, 1938, the NABC received notification that the NCAA "voted to approve the suggestion that a national tournament in basketball be held and that the matter be under the general supervision of the Basketball Rules Committee."

An eight-team format, with one representative from each of the NCAA's eight geographical districts, was used in the first tournament in 1939 on the campus of Northwestern University in Evanston, Illinois, and continued to be used until 1951 when the number of entries was doubled.

Olsen appointed a three- or four-man selection committee comprised of coaches, newspapermen and businessmen in each of the eight districts to select the best representative team from their area and conduct a playoff, if necessary.

In District 1—comprising Maine, New Hampshire, Vermont, Massachusetts, Rhode Island and Connecticut—the selection committee included Ozzie Cowles of Dartmouth, Wesley Fesler of Harvard and Sumner Dole of Connecticut State College. William Barber, a New York businessman, Everett Morris of the New York Herald Tribune and Jamison Swarts of the University of Pennsylvania represented District 2, composed of New York, New Jersey, Pennsylvania, Delaware and West Virginia. Roy M. Mundorff of the Georgia School of Technology, Kenneth Gregory of The Associated Press and Curtis Parker of Centenary College were in District 3. This area included Maryland, the District of Columbia, Virginia, North Carolina, South Carolina, Kentucky, Tennessee, Mississippi, Louisiana, Georgia, Alabama and Florida.

Dutch Lonborg of Northwestern, Tony Hinkle of Butler and Doc Meanwell of Wisconsin sat in jurisdiction in District 4, a Midwestern melange including Illinois, Ohio, Indiana, Michigan, Wisconsin and Minnesota. Allen, founder of the NABC and later an instrumental factor in having basketball included in the Olympic Games, served as chairman in District 5, the heart of Middle America that included Missouri, Kansas, Nebraska, Oklahoma, Iowa, North Dakota and South Dakota.

Clyde E. McBride of the Kansas City Star, George Edwards of Missouri and John C. Truesdale of Grinnell College made up the rest of the District 5 committee.

The Southwestern triumvirate of Texas, Arizona and Arkansas which formed District 6 was ruled over by James St. Clair of Southern Methodist, Dana X. Bible of Texas and George White of the Dallas News. Vadal Peterson, whose Utah team would win the NCAA championship in 1944, sat on the District 7 committee which oversaw Wyoming, New Mexico, Colorado, Utah and Montana. Joining him were W. A. Witte of Wyoming and Louis H. Mahoney of Denver.

Bunn, whose Stanford teams had revolutionized basketball in the 1930s with Hank Luisetti's one-handed shot, headed the District 8 committee whose jurisdiction included the Far West grouping of California, Washington, Oregon, Idaho and Nevada. Fred Bohler of Washington State College and Milton Gross of San Diego State were Bunn's colleagues on that panel.

Olsen, Allen and Bunn sat on the first Basketball Tournament Committee for 1939-40 along with William S. Chandler of Marquette and a New York businessman, H. H. Salmon. Their idea of a sound tournament was economy in all phases of the operation. "The committee was of the opinion that the number of games should be kept to a minimum and that sites for the playoffs and finals were important and should be selected to conserve travel time and to assure financial success," said one observer.

The first tournament, however, was not a financial success and after expenses showed a loss of $2,531. Because the NABC's treasury could not cover the loss, the group asked the NCAA to underwrite the deficit and assume full responsibility, financial and otherwise, for all future tournaments.

The second tournament, in 1940 at Kansas City, was highlighted by several "firsts." For the first time, the NABC was in attendance at the finals, and the annual convention of coaches since has been scheduled at the site of the NCAA championship. An all-tournament team and most outstanding player were selected for the first time; and, for the first time, the tournament showed a profit—$9,523.

The 1941 tourney followed the same format of the preceding two years, except that consolation games were played in both the Eastern and Western playoffs. In 1943, Madison Square Garden was the showcase for the NCAA finals and continued to be so through 1948. Due to increased seating and basketball popularity at the Garden, attendance increased from 24,372 in 1942 to 56,876 in 1943. Attendance at the 1943 finals was a record 13,300, and even that figure would be surpassed in subsequent years as the NCAA tournament flourished in the Garden, a hot house for basketball.

A revolutionary format change was made in 1946, when four teams were brought to the finals site in New York. It became the basis for the

Book 1

THE EARLY YEARS

1939-1947

currently accepted four-region format. For the eighth straight year, total attendance reached a new high—73,116. The number of people viewing the championship game was increased dramatically, however, when the finals were televised locally in New York City for the first time by WCBS-TV. The initial viewing audience was estimated to be 500,000.

An era in the history of the championship came to a close in 1947 when Arthur C. "Dutch" Lonborg of Northwestern began his long tenure as chairman of the tournament committee, replacing H. G. Olsen. Olsen had made his mark—college basketball had its championship.

THE TALL FIRS

"I talked to Bobby Anet before the game. Bobby was our sparkplug, our hard-driving guard. He was a great team leader and led our fast break. I told Bobby to make Ohio State call the first timeout and not to call any timeout until they were really tired. Well, Ohio State called five timeouts; and we didn't call any. After the game, I said to Bobby, 'Why didn't you call a timeout and rest a little when the game was pretty well in hand?' And he said to me, 'You told us not to call a timeout unless we were tired, and hell, we're not tired.'"—Howard Hobson, University of Oregon basketball coach

The basketball of Howard Hobson's playing days compared in excitement, as some said, to watching trees grow, but it was far different when he coached. His 1939 University of Oregon team was called the "Tall Firs" in deference to the size of his players, but in a sense it was a misnomer since they rarely stayed planted in one place very long. Speed was their essence and they made a run to glory that year, fast breaking to the first NCAA basketball championship with a dazzling energy hardly expressed anywhere in those awkward times.

This was no ordinary fast-breaking team, however. Leave it to Hobson, no ordinary man, to make sure of that.

"Our fast break was a little unusual in that we looked for it on every possession," Hobson says. "We used it all the time until the opportunity closed. It was a break that we always attempted after we gained possession, with the two guards handling the ball most of the time, the two forwards down ahead and the center trailing and coming in on the rebound."

This polished maneuver usually resulted in a two-on-one or three-on-two imbalance. It seemed one Oregon player always was open to shoot; and more often than not it was Laddie Gale, a forward who was one of the leading scorers in the old Pacific Coast Conference.

"I'd call it a controlled fast break," says Gale. "There was nothing reckless about it. We knew where we were going, and we knew where to expect our teammate to be; and when the situation would present itself, we were there. Prior to that, many who used fast breaks would just have five

men run down the floor, get a long pass or something and throw the ball up."

Commonly, the fast break is an offensive weapon, but this Oregon team used it on defense as well.

"It was a regular system as to how we did it," recalls John Dick, Oregon's other starting forward. "We had assignments for spots that we had to run back to on defense—one guy went to the deep hole, the other to the foul line, and so forth. We were constantly fast breaking going back as well as going down the court."

The gadfly for this historic team was Bobby Anet, a 5-8 playmaking guard with extraordinary confidence and leadership abilities. Anet worked in the backcourt with a longtime companion, Wally Johansen. The two had been together since junior high and played on a state championship team at Astoria High School coached by John Warren, who helped recruit many of the Oregon players.

Dick, the only junior on the senior-studded first team, was the perfect complement to Gale in the front court and kept up a running debate over respective sizes. "I was 6-4½ and Dick was 6-4½, and we constantly argued over who was taller," recalls Gale, laughing. "He always claimed that I was taller and I claimed that he was." Indeed, opponents generally were flabbergasted by the wall-to-wall stature of Oregon's front line. In the center of the group, and literally the Ducks' tower of strength, was Urgel "Slim" Wintermute, a skinny bundle of energy who was pushing 6-9.

By 1939 standards, that Oregon frontcourt was something to behold, since most teams rarely had

Wide World Photos

8

any one player with those Herculean dimensions, let alone three.

"A player the size of Wintermute was a novelty in the East," Hobson says. "The New York Times ran a picture of my players on page one during our trip to Madison Square Garden that year and called them, 'Giants from the Far West.' L. H. Gregory, sports editor of the Portland Oregonian, gave Hobson's team its colorful sobriquet of the "Tall Firs."

Behind the starting five were reserves that Hobson insisted "would have been starters for other teams," particularly Bob Hardy, set-shot ace Matt Pavalunas, Ted Sarpola (also off Warren's Astoria team) and Ford Mullen. Perhaps these players did not see as much game action as they wanted, but Hobson certainly made up for it with some of the most strenuous practice sessions in the land.

"We scrimmaged for two hours or more every day, and that didn't count all the preliminary stuff that led up to the scrimmage," says Dick, recalling those torturous practices under Hobson's steely gaze. "The emphasis was on running, so it seemed that when you got into a ball game, it was a piece of cake. We were always the best-conditioned team out there."

This was nothing new for many of the Oregon players. They had been schooled in their younger days by Warren, whom Gale called "a solid rock in the formation of all our players."

Warren's eye for talent was almost magical. During his time as a high school coach, he was able to sweep his area clean and ship all the rough diamonds to the University of Oregon, eventually polishing them himself as freshman coach and assistant to Hobson in the late 1930s.

While applauding the team's obvious offensive attributes, most observers, in Dick's mind, overlooked perhaps the Ducks' strongest point—defense.

"We had a defense that was not unlike what you see among some of your better teams today," Dick says. "We had the other teams so mixed up that

John Schick (white jersey) tips in two points for Ohio State in the first NCAA championship game. Oregon defeated Ohio State, 46-33.

they never knew whether we were playing a zone or a man-to-man defense—and they'd be hollering, 'zone, zone, zone,' while we were playing this team defense, really. I don't know how else to describe it but as a team defense. To play it, you had to have players who played together and were pretty close in their thinking and their attitudes. We were a very close team—on and off the floor."

Along with height, speed, shooting ability, defense and togetherness, there was one more ingredient that made the Oregon basketball team what it was: local pride. The team was made up essentially of native Oregonians. "We were proud of the fact that we were a Northwest team and had been recruited from our own area," says Gale.

The local loyalty started at the top with the coach. Hobson, a four-sport letterman at Franklin High School in Portland, captained the 1926 and 1927 Oregon basketball teams, during which time he laid the groundwork for his fast-breaking philosophy.

The controlled fast break was not the only innovation for the trailblazing Hobson. He also was among the first coaches in the country to chart players' court styles and habits.

"He was a very astute basketball coach," says Dick. "The thing I remember most about Hobby was his meticulous attention to detail. He kept the most voluminous records of everything that happened that you can imagine, in practices as well as games. He charted not only the number of shots taken by each player, but where on the floor they were taken. He had these little charts of the floor. He'd put the player's number where he took the shot and circle it if he made it. He did the same for rebounds, for turnovers, just about everything you could think of. He kept all of these statistics and analyzed them painstakingly.

"He was a very detailed planner. Before we'd leave on a trip, Hobby would give us an itinerary and we knew every minute from the time we left where we were going to be, right down to the hotels we were staying in, the trains we were riding in, the car numbers, the berth numbers, what we were going to eat—yeah, the menus for the whole trip."

Gale depicts Hobson as a worrisome martinet.

"He demanded discipline," says Gale. "There wasn't any goofing around. He was a worrywart and kept on top of what was going on all the time . . . and kept real good control."

There were no locker-room hysterics from Hobson, whose hallmark was a cool professional demeanor. As a lecturer, he was "more factual than anything," remembers Gale. "He'd have his outline on the blackboard and would quietly tell us what he thought we were doing right or wrong and what we should do. There were no inspirational speeches. It was very cut and dried."

From the beginning in 1939, Hobson was aware he had a championship-caliber team but didn't know he had championship-quality players until a unique barnstorming trip around the country early in the season.

"I believe the making of our team came in December of 1938 when we pioneered an Eastern trip for teams from the Northwest," Hobson notes. "We played 10 games in 22 days, traveling from Eugene to New York City by train.

"We lost our first game to a far inferior CCNY team by two points because of the interpretation of the rules by the officials," Hobson says. "We didn't score a field goal for 15 minutes in that game, and the officiating wasn't good. In fact, the Garden later apologized for it. They did a lot of things we didn't use or coach—they stepped on your feet, grabbed your pants and the officials allowed more contact on the screens. We were beaten badly in the first half, but it may have been the most important game for us that season. At the half, the boys were complaining about the officiating. I told them, 'I can sympathize with your feelings; but if I were you big fellows and they did those things to me, I'd at least protect myself.' Well, they went out there and played a great second half."

The sturdy character of the Oregon team blossomed with each succeeding stop. The Ducks, who had opened the trip against the Portland AAU Packards in Portland, also played St. Joseph's in Philadelphia, Miami (Ohio) in Cleveland, Canisius in Buffalo, Wayne State in Detroit, Bradley in Peoria, Western Illinois in Chicago, Drake in Des Moines and Stanford in San Francisco.

"Because of playing all through the rest of the country," points out Hobson, "we were ready for any kind of officiating on any kind of court."

Probably that was the key to Oregon's rousing NCAA tournament sweep of Texas, Oklahoma and Ohio State en route to the national championship. As Hobson points out:

"When we finally played Ohio State in the NCAA championship game in Evanston, Illinois, we were playing on a Big Ten court with two Big Ten officials. After the game, in fact, Ned Irish of Madison Square Garden came over and said, 'How could you put up with that officiating?' And I said, actually, I didn't even notice it. And that's true. We didn't. The Big Ten played rougher basketball than we did then, and the officials let the game be

9

very rough. But it really didn't bother us."

Nor did other disagreeable aspects in the NCAA finals concern the travel-toughened Oregon players. "The playing conditions were not good," points out Gale. "Everyone was right down on the court. The fans were on top of you. That was minor, though."

Looking back, the members of that Oregon team seem unanimous in their belief that victories in the PCC playoffs over Washington and California which got the Ducks into the national championships were far more difficult than the NCAA triumphs.

"Our toughest competition that year was on the Pacific Coast," notes Gale. "Washington was very strong that year and Cal was very strong, too. I remember in the Washington series (for the Northern Division championship), both teams used a fast-break offense that was dazzling."

Two straight victories over Washington in the Northern Division playoffs gave Oregon its second divisional title in two years; then the Ducks won the PCC championship by defeating Southern champion California twice.

"We had a real struggle with Washington every time we played them that year," remembers Dick. "And although we beat Cal two straight in the league playoffs, they were also tough for us. They were one of the few teams we played that was as big as we were . . . in fact, a little bigger."

Oregon thus qualified as one of the four teams in the Western regional of the first NCAA tournament. The other teams in that historic group included Oklahoma, Texas and Utah State. The winner of the Western playoffs went on to meet the champion of the East, whose field included Ohio State, Villanova, Brown and Wake Forest.

"All the teams except the University of Oklahoma were chosen on the basis of their outstanding records during the season by the committees in the eight districts," remembers John Bunn, the former Stanford coach who managed the Western playoffs. "Four teams in the fifth district were so evenly matched that a playoff for them was held in Oklahoma City. At the last moment, the University of Missouri had to pull out, so only Drake University, Oklahoma A&M (now Oklahoma State) and the University of Oklahoma participated, with the state university emerging the winner."

Games in the Western playoffs were held in the Sports Coliseum on Treasure Island, a man-made island in the center of San Francisco Bay and the site of the San Francisco International Exposition. Oregon was paired against Texas on the first night of play and Utah State played Oklahoma. Both Oregon and Oklahoma displayed a wide superiority over their opponents, the Ducks beating Texas, 56-41, and the Sooners routing Utah State, 50-39. In the finals, Oregon displayed a wider superiority over Oklahoma. Noted Bunn in the Basketball Guide: "Oregon's fast break, zone defense and phenomenal one-handed shooting were too much for the clever ball-handling and intricate, well-executed offensive system of the Oklahoma Sooners. After a cautious first quarter, the Oregonians pulled away steadily and won easily by the score of 55 to 37."

Along with Oregon's perfection at play, the officials put on a flawless performance in the Western playoffs as well. Noted Bunn in his managerial report: "Probably the most satisfactory feature of the whole occasion was the complete approval of the work of the officials. It is seldom that four teams so widely scattered can meet in competition without voicing a complaint or feeling a handicap in their play because of local rules interpretations. Lloyd Leith, Ernie Bailly, Dud DeGroot and Bill Hubbard, who handled all the games, are to be congratulated for their excellent and consistent work."

The teams had no complaint about their treatment by the management, either. Addressing his attention to details of hospitality, Bunn added these comments after the final Western game: "Trophies were awarded to the winners of the final and third-place games. Individual medals symbolic of the (San Francisco) Fair were given to each of the members of the teams which competed in the playoff. The full expenses of the four competing teams (a traveling squad of 15 each) were guaranteed by the management, and all were guests of the fair during their visit."

Prophetically, Bunn ended his report on a richly optimistic note, although at the time even he could not imagine the eventual stature of the NCAA tournament:

"Generous praise and hearty enthusiasm were expressed in the West and by the competing teams over the plan of the NCAA to conduct a basketball playoff each year between its member schools. Undoubtedly it will develop into the major basketball event of the season."

Judging by the crowds, this appeared at the time to be a long-shot statement. A total of 15,025 people—including 5,500 at the finals at Patten Gymnasium on the campus of Northwestern University—saw the NCAA tournament games that year. For the five dates, it was an average of 3,005 per game. In the West, about 6,000 fans witnessed the games. The crowds were much smaller in Philadelphia, where 2,036 showed up the first night and only 1,489 the second. Coupled with expenses,

the first tournament recorded a loss of $2,531.

While Oregon was winning the West with efficacy, Ohio State was doing the same in the East. The Buckeyes, champions of the Big Ten, displayed the greatest scoring punch ever seen at the University of Pennsylvania's arena, defeating Wake Forest, 64-52, in the semifinals and then Villanova, 53-36, in the Eastern championship game. Three records were set the first night: Ohio State rolled up the highest score in the 13-year history of the Palestra with its 64 points; the Buckeyes' Dick Baker broke the existing individual scoring record with 25 points, and the combined Ohio State-Wake Forest score, 116 points, established a record for total points scored in a game. In the final game, Ohio State captain James Hull broke Baker's record with 28 points. Hull's performance was all the more remarkable considering he was on the bench for seven minutes in the second half with an injury.

"It was the only injury I ever had in college," recalls Hull. "I took a rebound and a fellow came down and lit on my ankle. I was in so much pain, they had to carry me to my hotel. I was so bandaged, I felt I had all the tape in the drugstore on me."

The first night, Hull had complemented Baker nicely with an 18-point performance against Wake Forest. "Wake Forest had a very good shifting, man-to-man defense," Hull relates. "And they had one outstanding basketball player, Jim Waller. He was a left-hander and had a very accurate hook shot. In fact, right before half time he shot a hook shot in our game that was about a 35- or 40-footer. That was unheard of in those times."

Of Ohio State's two opponents in the Eastern playoffs, Wake Forest easily presented the stiffest challenge for the Buckeyes. Helped by Waller's shooting, the Deacons had a 29-23 advantage at the half. They held a slight advantage until late in the second half, when the Buckeyes caught fire behind Baker and Hull. In the finals, Ohio State mastered Villanova from the start, "dropping in shots from all angles," according to Eastern playoff manager H. Jamison Swarts.

Hull had a week to rest his tortured ankle before the NCAA finals, but apparently it was not enough time. "I don't mean to be a braggadocio, but had I been able to shoot my normal percentage from 18 to 20 feet out, from which I was accurate in those days, I think I could have kept our ball club in the game. But I was hurting. I could shoot, I could get

open against Oregon, but I wasn't as accurate as I usually was." Hull scored 12 points.

Hull also offers another explanation for Ohio State's 46-33 defeat in that championship game on March 27, 1939—a lack of motivation.

"Our ball club," he explains, "was so tired of basketball at the end of the Big Ten season that we were not even interested in playing in this tournament. I don't mean to take it lightly. It was just that it was a new tournament—unheard of. There was no publicity about it. And we didn't get any publicity in our town of Columbus until we won the Eastern championship. But, really, our sports editors in that area at that particular time were more interested in covering our state high school championships, and that got all the publicity in the papers. When we left to go east to play in the regionals, there was very little said other than Ohio State's going to the NCAA to play at the Palestra, that's all. It was not even in big print."

Remarkably, the Buckeyes did not even know about an NCAA tournament until after they won the Big Ten title—this despite the fact that their own coach, Harold Olsen, was the pioneering spirit behind the postseason tournament.

"Olsen never said a word to us about going to the NCAA tournament all season," says Hull. "Maybe he was afraid that we'd be looking ahead and fall flat on our faces in the Big Ten."

In contrast, Oregon's players were aware from the start that there would be a national championship to shoot for. It had served as an inspirational

University of Oregon

Coach Howard Hobson addresses students on the Oregon campus after returning home.

11

springboard for them, they say.

Olsen found himself in a rather awkward spot following Ohio State's victory in the Eastern finals. Hull remembers this postgame locker room scene:

"Olsen walked in and the first thing he said was, 'Gentlemen, this is a little embarrassing to me. But I do want to congratulate you . . .' And one of our players said, 'What do you mean embarrassing? We just won you the Eastern championship of the United States!' 'Well,' Olsen said, 'I'm chairman of that committee that organized this tournament, and here my team wins it. It's a little embarrassing!'"

As far as Ohio State was concerned, the tournament continued to keep a low profile right through the finale.

"We never even knew what teams were competing in the West," notes Hull. "In fact, after we won our Eastern tournament, there was very little said to us about whom we may even play. We were blind all the way through this thing. We knew practically nothing about Oregon. We had no idea they had all that height. We had nothing to practice against."

Obviously Hobson had done his homework better than Olsen in this regard. "We had some knowledge about Ohio State," remembers Dick. "We knew all about Hull, their leading scorer. We knew their starters were not very big compared to our team . . . and of course that gave us a tremendous advantage in the game. We controlled the boards, and the only big people they had were a couple of football players that they brought in off the bench. They were a little better than their starters on the boards, but they otherwise weren't very helpful to their cause."

Anet, a dwarfish counterpoint to Oregon's tall frontcourt players, was a virtual giant among them in the NCAA title game—"a beautiful guard," said Hull. "We had no idea how much speed he had." The diminutive Anet scored 10 points, third highest in the game, and directed the Oregon attack with his usual flair. The Oregon height did the rest.

"They played a zone defense with their three big guys, and we could usually get only one shot from the outside at the basket," says Hull. "But up until midway through the second half, the ball game was nip and tuck. They didn't really whip us until right at the very end. It was their height that killed us."

Sparked by Anet, Oregon had an 8-7 lead at the start, then outscored Ohio State by 10-4 to go up by 18-11. It was 21-16 at the half and just as reasonably close until the Ducks opened the throttle a little

Oregon fans crowd the train depot in Eugene to welcome home their victorious team.

13

more on their fast break. Despite the closeness of the score in the early going, however, Oregon's players never thought that Ohio State was in the game.

Recalls Gale: "Going to the dressing room at half time, Anet said to our coach, 'Hobby, you want us to lay off?' In other words, did he want us to keep the score down? He was pretty cocky. But really, there wasn't any problem. I don't mean to sound cocky myself, but there was no competition as far as we were concerned."

In Arthur C. "Dutch" Lonborg's account of the game in the Official Basketball Guide, the manager of the NCAA finals expressed similar admiration for the Ducks' power:

"Oregon placed a magnificent team on the floor for the title game. Despite a grueling 34-game campaign, in which the team traveled to New York and back, the five regulars played 39 minutes of the game. The fact that the team used the fast break most of the time shows the fine physical condition of the players. The Oregon team was unique in that the two guards, captain Bob Anet and Wally Johansen, were offensive guards and defensive forwards. Both were clever dribblers and were used to start the offense most of the time. Oregon's forwards and center were extremely tall and active and fit into the fast-break attack in fine style. On defense, Oregon used both zone and man-for-man.

"Ohio State experienced difficulty in penetrating Oregon's defense and relied largely upon a long-range attack. Captain Jim Hull, forward, and William Sattler, center, led the Buckeye attack with 12 and seven points, respectively. The shooting of the entire Ohio State team was below par and did not approach the accuracy shown during the Big Ten season."

While helping to break open the game, Anet also broke up the championship trophy with a hard slide into the audience. Dick, who scored a game-high 15 points, can still see the team's quarterback flying through the air with the greatest of ease:

"They had the big championship trophy sitting up on a table on the court edge where all the press and people were located and Anet dove for this loose ball and went right over the top of the table and clipped off the figure of a basketball player that was on top of that trophy. He ended up in the seats with the reporters. When they presented the trophy to us at the end, they had to hold the little figure on top . . . it was a two-handed presentation.

We had to bring the trophy back home in two pieces and then got a jeweler to mend it."

Winning a game of such importance with such clinical ease was a tribute to Oregon's toughness. The Ducks were playing on a so-called "neutral" Big Ten court but one that was obviously more familiar to the Buckeyes and a lot closer to home for them. Fan support was nil for Oregon as well. In fact, the Ducks might have had only one bona fide supporter in the crowd—Paul Jackson, a self-appointed mascot who had hitchhiked from the West Coast and almost beat the Oregon train there. Remembers Gale: "After we got there, about a half-day later, here comes Jackson. Slim Wintermute and I kept him in our room. We had a large bed that Primo Canera, the boxer, had slept in, and we put Jackson in the bottom of it. We more or less shanghaied him . . . and Hobby didn't know anything about it until the night of the game."

Unable to be at the game, the Oregon fans made sure to be at the train platform when the team arrived home for an uproarious celebration.

"As soon as we got into the state of Oregon, there would be people at the stations all along the line through the state," Gale remembers. "And Oregon is a pretty big state. When we got to Portland, we had a ticker-tape ride up and down Broadway and it was a hell of a reception. It was just like a big dream, but I can remember outstandingly that it seemed like the whole state of Oregon was at the train stations to meet us."

Hobson now has the perspective of history and the luxury of space to draw his own conclusions about that first NCAA tournament and determines that perhaps the logistics might have been better.

"I don't think that was a good site for the first tournament," he says, "although I'm not sure why they picked it. Tug Wilson, who was working with the NCAA then, was the athletic director at Northwestern and perhaps picked it for personal reasons. I think they could have gotten larger crowds in Chicago."

The loss of money did little to discourage the National Association of Basketball Coaches, but it did embarrass the group a bit. The coaches' treasury was too small to cover any such red ink, and they asked the NCAA if it would underwrite the deficit and assume full responsibility for all future tournaments. The NCAA did, but there was no way to imagine the success that would come its way due to this tournament.

POINT-A-MINUTE MEN

"They threw the ball to Curly Armstrong and he did a head and shoulder fake and hit Phog Allen's son right on the chin and knocked him flat. Curly reached down to him, motioned to the Kansas bench and said, 'Maybe you better sit with daddy.' Then the official called a foul on Curly, and Armstrong ruffled the official's hair up. Oh, hell, I'll never forget that. We did have a lot of fun."—Jay McCreary, Indiana forward

The night before Indiana played Kansas for the 1940 NCAA championship, Branch McCracken was given some helpful advice by two old friends.

"What kind of a defense do you plan to use against Kansas?" Stanford coach Everett Dean asked McCracken.

"The shifting man-to-man," the Indiana coach replied.

"Have you had them scouted?" Southern Cal coach Sam Barry interjected.

McCracken shook his head.

"Then take a tip from one of their victims and use a pressing, all-floor defense," Barry said.

Dean, who had coached McCracken at Indiana a decade before, concurred.

"He's right, Mac," Dean said. "If you let crack shots like Don Ebling, Bob Allen, Bill Hogben and Howard Engleman roam free back of that foul ring, the Kansas half of the scoreboard will be busier than a hound dog in hunting season."

Perhaps if Dean and Barry had not shown up in McCracken's hotel room on the eve of that game, college basketball might have had a different national champion that year. But the last-minute change of a defensive game plan helped Indiana defeat Kansas and enhance the nickname "Hurryin' Hoosiers."

"We pressed them the moment that ball changed hands," McCracken remembered later. "It took stamina and condition. It meant high speed for 40 minutes! But it wrecked Kansas' set shots and let us play our fireball game. After the game, Phog Allen, the Kansas coach, came up to me. He said, 'Say, Branch, where did you dig up so many speed merchants? Your fast break ran us to death."

Of course, the defense was not the most memorable hallmark of this wonderful Indiana team, also known as the "Laughing Boys" for its breezy, carefree court style. "They laughed all the way to the national championship," was the way one writer described them. More to the point, the Hoosiers quite literally ran all the way to the championship with their racehorse offensive style.

"McCracken taught us to get the ball, throw it to half court—and go," says guard Marv Huffman, the team captain who was named the first most outstanding player in the NCAA tournament. "As McCracken said, we were going to be the first ones down on both ends of the floor. And we were."

McCracken's run-and-shoot style almost became an obsession with him. "He hated pattern basketball," says John Wood, who played for McCracken in the late 1940s and early 1950s. "Everything was free lance. That was one of his favorite words. He always said the fans paid to see free-lance basketball."

McCracken certainly did not invent fast-break basketball—but he obviously improved on it. His teams were the quickest in the nation for many years. His better squads, such as the 1940 national champions, could bring the ball downcourt with such lightning speed that the ball often failed to hit the floor once on a dribble. McCracken had such faith in Indiana's speed and durability that he actually hoped to take close decisions into overtime, believing that no team in existence could beat his Hoosiers when depth and conditioning were most important.

McCracken did not invent aggressiveness, either—but he favored it to a high degree. When Indiana lost a game, McCracken first looked at the

personal fouls column. And if a player had a lofty number of points, but no fouls, the Indiana coach was likely to express an opinion that that particular player had not tried his best. Angry rival coaches more often than not accused McCracken of inspiring rough play.

"No, I don't," was McCracken's always cordial reply. Then a pause and a thoughtful final statement: "But I don't discourage it!"

On the floor, McCracken was oblivious to everything but his job and usually that meant battling the officials as well as opposing players. There are no such records, of course, but it is safe to assume that the Indiana coach was one of the all-time leaders in technical fouls. In one particular game against the University of Wyoming, McCracken became so engrossed in the game that he had not noticed that assistant coach Ernie Andrews had attached himself to his coattails in hopes of keeping the head coach out of foul trouble. Enraged at one call in particular, McCracken bounced off his seat and did not lose a step—dragging Andrews with him.

Though hot-tempered, McCracken was usually able to keep his wits about himself in such situations. Remembers Jay McCreary, a forward on the 1940 NCAA champions:

"In one game, Branch went right out on the floor after an official. He must have been about 19 steps from the bench. The official told him, 'Branch, for every step you take back to that bench, it's going to be a technical foul.' Quickly, Branch called out to his manager and his trainer and had them carry him off the floor."

In practices, McCracken was a bit more composed but just as effective.

"The scrimmages were killers," recalls McCreary. "We would start scrimmaging hard and quit two hours later, and wouldn't stop for anything—I mean nothing! We wouldn't even leave the floor for water. McCracken was a driver, but he drove himself. It was sort of an infectious thing. When the man ahead of you is driving, you don't feel so bad about working your fanny off. We did things to perfection. I mean, if we had a certain movement we had to go through, we went through it until we could do it in our sleep."

McCracken's needle was long and sharp when it came to making a point with his players, but the coach was human enough to take a jab or two himself once in a while and laugh about it. McCreary recalls this classic McCracken story:

"One day Mac was talking to us before we went out on the court and Curly Armstrong came in late. McCracken just looked at him and said, 'Well, I guess we can go and have practice now, by God, the great Armstrong is here!' Well, a couple of weeks later, during a practice session, Branch had to leave the floor for a phone call. While he was gone, Curly told us all to sit on the basketballs. And when Branch came back, Curly said, 'Well, I guess we can start practicing, the great McCracken is here!' He just broke everyone up, and Branch took off after him and they ran around the floor. All of a sudden, Branch stopped and said, 'Why am I chasing this guy? I'm the boss.' "

McCracken's sarcasm was part of his psychological approach to coaching.

"He was a master psychologist," says Jim Barley, who played for McCracken in the mid-1950s. "He was great at getting you up for a game. One way he would do it was by needling. He always knew who he could needle and how much. I remember one week, Mac started getting on Bobby Leonard (an all-America from the 1950s) about his defense. All week he hounded him about it. At the end of the week, we played Ohio State and they had Robin Freeman. He was a national sensation, and he was averaging about 30 points a game. But Leonard went out that night and held him to 12."

McCracken was equally successful at motivating his players with a pat on the back as well as a slap in the face.

Remembers Bob Dro, from the 1940 team:

"We were in Chicago to play the University of Chicago, and they really didn't have much. Before the game, Mac came up to me and said, 'Bob, this is your chance to make all-America. You can do it if you look good tonight. All the sports writers are here.' Later I found out that he had told that same thing to all the other starters."

One of McCracken's best psychological masterstrokes came when the Hoosiers were having problems at one point in the 1940 season. He arranged to "loosen up the players" one night by having a doctor friend of his invite them over to his house for a beer bust.

"We never knew that Branch had arranged it until about 15 years later," laughs McCreary. "We were at a reunion one time, sitting around and talking about how we had put one over on the coach and McCracken stops by. 'I know what you guys are talking about,' he said. And he told us exactly what happened. We were flabbergasted."

After that party, the Hoosiers went out to play their next game and "just beat the hell out of somebody," McCreary remembers.

McCracken was rarely that loose himself, though. His whimsical title, "The Head Coach of Worry," suited him well, but his nervousness manifested itself in weird ways. When he won (which was often), McCracken usually was affect-

ed, strangely enough, by insomnia, often pacing the floor for hours worrying about future games. Occasionally, enemies tried to take advantage of his jittery state. Once, a few days before an important game with Illinois, he received in the mail an oversized eight-ball with a note that read:

"Look behind this and you'll see the Indiana basketball team."

McCracken was a rugged, free-wheeling type, which helps to explain how he earned three varsity football letters at Indiana University, even though he had never seen a football game before he arrived at the Bloomington campus. He actually was recruited for basketball by Pete Straub of the Indiana Alumni Association, who discovered his talents at a high school in Monrovia, Indiana. When Straub arrived at the McCracken farm to talk to the promising youngster, he found Branch knee-deep in a swollen stream, snagging watermelons as they floated by. "A flash flood had washed away a field of melons from a farm upstream," recalls a friend, "and Branch felt there wasn't much sense in letting them go to waste. His only regret was that he couldn't catch them all."

Straub later found that McCracken could handle a basketball with equal agility. Branch enrolled at Indiana in the fall of 1927 and quickly established himself as one of the school's all-time top athletes. In his last two years, he was named to nearly every all-America team and, in his senior year, set a Big Ten season scoring record. After graduation and a fling at pro basketball, McCracken coached basketball at Ball State Teachers College in Muncie, Indiana, where he remained eight years and married the president's daughter. He was drafted for the Indiana coaching job when Everett Dean left after the 1938 season for Stanford.

At Indiana, McCracken's name became synonymous with fast-break basketball; but almost overlooked completely were his roles as a pioneer in breaking the color barrier, the use of air transportation for teams and the utilization of television for games. Perhaps McCracken's most important contribution was the breaking of the "color line" in Big Ten basketball—a move that also opened the doors to Blacks in other conference sports. Before McCracken stepped in, Blacks did not play Big Ten basketball prior to the 1947-48 season.

McCracken's offensive tempo, it is said, was established once and for all in a game against Minnesota early in his Indiana career. The Gophers had used their speed to run up a 29-13 lead at the half, and this scene took place in the Indiana locker room at intermission:

McCracken: "We've tried deliberate basketball against these fellows, and it doesn't work. This second half, let's drive. Let's run 'em right out of the field house."

A moment of silence, then. . .

Huffman: "Come on, gang. Let's go. Minnesota thinks they've got a fire-wagon outfit. We'll show them what speed really is."

Indiana did. The Hoosiers made a storybook comeback, outscoring the Gophers 20-1 and taking a 33-30 lead. Unfortunately for Indiana, there was no storybook ending, however. The Hoosiers lost the game, 46-44, when Minnesota scored just as the final gun went off. But McCracken gave up his slow-breaking attacks after that, expressing this vibrant philosophy:

"All we care about is getting the ball in the enemy basket in the shortest possible time. Our emphasis is on rolling up points. Our defense lies primarily in our offense. 'Go, go, go' is our watchword. Think of the ball as a red-hot potato that must be kept moving . . . and the faster the better."

McCracken's 1940 team was the epitome of his philosophy.

Going at full blast as it was, Indiana's 1940 team needed an inexhaustible supply of players who were not only talented, but able to play more than one position. As McCracken explained it. "You've got to have at least eight men who can play any position. That way you can substitute freely and give your players breathers. For instance, I might start Bob Dro as forward, yank him out for a rest and put him back in at guard. With eight versatile men, you can go at top speed all the time."

Four players shared the bulk of the playing time for the Hoosiers in 1940—center Bill Menke, forward Paul "Curly" Armstrong, Dro and Huffman. Four others were used as the significant interchangeable parts in this efficient machine—guard Herman Schaefer, center Bob Menke (Bill's brother) and forwards Tom Motter and Ralph Dorsey. In some games, as many as 21 players saw action.

Early in the season, shortly before McCracken's team was to meet Purdue, a friend took the coach to a fortune-telling gypsy in Indianapolis. The fortune-teller announced that Branch would have "a very successful year." Although he would have been the first to ridicule that sort of thing, he had to give the tea leaves interpreter her due after what happened that year. The Hoosiers beat the league-champion Boilermakers twice—the first time that had happened in the history of the rivalry. Indiana actually finished second to Purdue in the final Big Ten standings but was selected to go to the NCAA playoffs because of its victories over the Boilermakers. Before Indiana played Purdue for the second time, Huffman remembers that McCrack-

17

en called the team together and gave them a pep talk. "He said simply, 'If you're not going to win, we're not going to the playoffs.' So we said, 'Okay, we'll win—and we'll go!' And there was no doubt in our minds, all of us, that we were going to win the playoff berth. We were a very loose team. We all knew what we could do and we did it."

Springfield College was Indiana's opening-round opponent in the NCAA's Eastern playoffs, and Dro recalls that the Hoosiers "didn't know anything about them, other than they were supposed to be the best in the East." Despite the lack of information, Indiana had no trouble beating Springfield, 48-24, in the second game of the opening night doubleheader at the Butler University field house in Indianapolis. Duquesne, actually a better team than Springfield, edged Western Kentucky, 30-29, to advance to the finals.

Schaefer did most of the heavy work for Indiana, scoring 14 points as playoff manager Tony Hinkle observed that the Hoosiers were "one of the best offensive clubs ever to play in Butler University's giant field house." The opening game was far more interesting than Indiana's clinical triumph, according to Hinkle. "Duquesne and Western Kentucky brought the opening night crowd to its feet several times."

Indiana's 39-30 victory over Duquesne for the Eastern championship was fashioned with a bit more passion and a lot more work. The Hoosiers had played the Dukes earlier in the season and left Pittsburgh with a bitter taste in their mouths, something that could not be diminished even by a victory over the tough Eastern team. "We left that town mad," recalls McCreary, "because the Duquesne fans weren't too nice to us. Some people in their audience kept yelling all through our game there, 'What do they make in Indiana? Farm machinery!' That's what they'd say, like we were a bunch of farmers."

Duquesne had given Indiana plenty of trouble before succumbing in that first meeting. "Duquesne actually was one of the best teams in the country that year," remembers Dro. "They had an excellent player named Moe Becker and presented a tough zone defense. Their zone really disturbed us in our first meeting. But we were able to maneuver better in the second contest."

The Dukes were "rushed too hard and received no good shots," according to Hinkle's report in the Basketball Guide, and as a result Indiana held a 25-13 half-time lead. Duquesne rallied in the second half behind Moe Becker and Ed Milkovich, "but free throws by the Indiana quintet finally won the game." Hinkle, coach of Butler University at the time, attributed Indiana's victory to "fast-

breaking basketball, combined with the determination to play in the Kansas City finals of the national tournament."

Southern California was McCreary's personal preference as an opponent in the NCAA championship game because he had played his high school ball with Ralph Vaughn, one of the Trojan stars. But Southern Cal, widely applauded as one of the best college basketball teams in the country that year, was upset by Kansas, 43-42, in the dramatic Western finals at Kansas City. Forward Howard Engleman hit the winning basket on a set shot from the corner with 18 seconds remaining as Kansas scored "as thrilling an upset as can be found in fiction or the movies," according to Dan Partner of the Kansas City Star. "The thunder of 7,500 screaming voices boomed to the West Coast and back."

"The Trojans of 1940 were rated as perhaps the best basketball team in the country, and certainly they were considered to be the favorite in our game," recalls Ralph Miller, one of Kansas' leading players of that year. "They had a guy named Jack Morrison who was a very fine outside shooter. I remember immediately after Engleman hit our go-ahead basket, the Trojans called a timeout with about five or six seconds to play and still had a chance to win the game. They brought the ball up court with three men, and our defense was set to meet them at the half-court mark, because there were people in those days—including Morrison—who could shoot accurately from 50 feet. So as a result, their play situation was to come down with three men in a line and then make a wedge, just like wedge-blocking in football, right at the center circle, and then let Morrison shoot the ball from in back of that circle. I well remember the shot he took because I was up there defensing against them and got picked clean by that wedge. When he shot, I turned around and the ball was dead center . . . and I thought it was all over for us. But fortunately, the ball was about one-sixteenth of an inch too long and it hit the back of the rim, caromed out about 25 feet and the ball game was ours."

The victory over Southern California was all the more glittering for Kansas, since the Trojans had defeated NIT winner Colorado, 38-32, in the opening round of the Western championship. Kansas, meanwhile, had won its way into the Western finals by beating Rice.

At this point, Kansas was playing its best ball of the season. The Jayhawks had staged a driving finish to tie Oklahoma and Missouri for the Big Six championship; then had won the conference playoff and had defeated Oklahoma A&M (now Oklahoma State) in the NCAA's fifth district for a Western berth. The Jayhawks' whirlwind finish

had prompted a clever publicity man to take a picture of their leading players aboard a horse and dub the team "The Pony Express." However, their deliberate court style belied this appellation.

"They were unbelievably patient," says Huffman. "At one point in the first half of the championship game, we had them down something like 12 points, and they just held on to the ball, trying to work it inside with their set plays."

Allen once told McCracken that if he could control the ball 60 per cent of the game, Kansas could win. McCracken replied: "You can have it 90 per cent of the time as long as I outscore you."

And that was just about the story of the 1940 NCAA championship game: Kansas had the ball most of the time, but Indiana had most of the points and a 60-42 victory.

"Indiana came out with a fast-breaking attack, and we hadn't seen too much like that," notes Miller. "They picked us apart with no problem."

Indiana's fast break was as staggering as its pregame arrogance. "We all knew we were going to win it, really," says Huffman. "We made up our minds that we were going to play our best game—and we did."

The Hoosiers' national title highlighted a sublime and eventful period. They had taken a train to Kansas City and eaten gourmet food. "The menus were all in French," remembers Mary Jo McCracken, wife of the coach. "The kids had never seen anything like that before." They stayed in "a great, big hotel . . . that was really something special for us." And the afternoon of the championship game, they had convinced Mary Jo to take them to see a movie, much against the coach's wishes.

"Branch's feeling was that sitting in a dark theater would hurt your eyes," says McCreary, "and he was dead set against us seeing 'Gone With The Wind,' which had just opened. But Mary Jo took us to see the film. I remember, she was sitting in the middle of us, getting very emotional. And, smart aleck kids like we were, it was sort of funny to us. She was crying like a baby and we were laughing at her, and she said, 'Aw, shut up, you guys don't know what's going on, anyway.'"

During the intermission of the long film, however, Mrs. McCracken still had basketball on her mind. She made the players run around the block for exercise. When they got back to their hotel, McCracken was furious about their escapade and made them run around some more.

The scenes in the movie that they had witnessed were no more astonishing than the scene the Hoosiers watched as they went through their pregame warm-ups on the court. With the Kansas-oriented crowds cheering on their Jayhawks, Allen was already being honored and handed gifts. Remembers McCreary: "They read a telegram saying, 'We're behind you, Phog Allen.' They had golf clubs for him, and everything. And I asked McCracken, 'What the hell is going on?' He said, 'I don't know—we're just going to have to go out and win the ball game.'"

It was Armstrong who sounded the cry of battle for the Hoosiers. After listening attentively to the pregame ceremonies honoring Allen and his team, Armstrong hitched up his pants and said, "Now, isn't that something! Let's go out there and whip them before all their fans."

But the Hoosiers didn't immediately put Armstrong's words into action, falling behind, 10-4, after seven minutes had been played. "We called timeout at this point and just looked at each other, didn't say a word," says Huffman. "We just knew that we weren't playing ball. We weren't doing the job. We weren't blocking out good, and we weren't running fast enough. Then we went out there to do the job right and by half time, we had them down by 13 points (32-19)."

A Kansas City Star reporter described the "gale" caused by the visitors from Indiana:

"Kansas ran out of whirlwind finishes while Indiana finished in a howling gale and today the streamlined Hoosiers of the Big Ten Conference are National Collegiate basketball champions. On the sidelines were members of the National Association of Basketball Coaches and members of the Joint Basketball Rules Committee of the United States and Canada, meeting for the first time in history, and they were as astonished as the unschooled spectators at Indiana's breathtaking antics on the court. The valiant team from Lawrence missed the boat against coach McCracken's laughing boys from Bloomington."

The writer further applauded the Hoosiers for their "amazing" shooting percentage of 34.6, low by modern standards but extremely high for the time. Huffman earned the tourney's most outstanding player award by scoring 12 points in the finals, tying McCreary for the team high in that department, but was not so sure he deserved the top individual prize. "I was really surprised when I got it—shocked, as a matter of fact," he says. "I got whistled out of the ball game early. One of Bob Dro's fouls was given to me, and I went out on fouls with about 10 or 12 minutes left in the game. I remember McCracken argued fiercely about it but didn't win."

If Allen was dismayed at his team's loss in the NCAA finals, he could at least find solace in the artistic and financial success of the tournament as a whole. It was mostly through Allen's efforts that

19

the Western regionals and finals had been staged in Kansas City, and the cash customers repaid his faith in the area. They responded with an attendance of 25,880 for three nights of basketball at the Kansas City Municipal Auditorium. The gross from that gate, $22,228.65, erased the red ink from the year before. Combined with the Eastern playoffs, the five-night event attracted a crowd of 36,880, grossed $43,562.17 and netted a profit of $9,590.06. After all rental and travel expenses were paid, each of the competing institutions was given an appropriate slice of the net profits—from $250 for first-round losers to $750 for the finalists.

For the first time, the National Association of Basketball Coaches convention was held in conjunction with the finals, a ritual that has continued since. The general reaction to the scene by the nation's coaches was one of general enthrallment, according to an NABC bulletin:

"The Kansas City Municipal Auditorium, where Indiana and Kansas battled for the NCAA crown, is 'tops,' in the opinion of many who witnessed that memorable clash. The coaches were amazed at the beautiful entrance, its fine ramps, marvelous seats, and the unobstructed view of the game from all seats. For the benefit of those who were not in a position to attend, it might be explained that the court measured 94 x 50 feet, the floor was laid with blocks 2 x 4 inches, set on end, the lights were indirect, the lines were painted white and the backboards extended by wire. The seating capacity was 10,000. All in all, the coaches were highly impressed at the excellent arrangements."

The report further pointed out, "At the conclusion of the tournament, E. C. Quigley, master of ceremonies, presented trophies to the opposing captains. Fifteen medals went to the two finalists, as did gold watches to each team. It was a grand game played by two great teams before a tremendous crowd which enjoyed every second of it! May we have more!"

Some other "firsts" were established in that 1940 tournament—selection of a most outstanding player and an all-tournament team. Huffman was joined on the blue-ribbon team by teammates Bill Menke and McCreary, and Bob Allen and Howard Engleman of Kansas.

The spirit of James Naismith was nearly palpable during the championship game. Prior to the start of the contest, there was a dramatic ceremony honoring the founder of basketball, who had died on November 28, 1939. Following a brief description of the founding of the game, candles were lit and Naismith's picture was cast upon a screen. His three favorite expressions were then read:

"I want to build character in the hearts of young men.

"Do not fail to work for humanity and await your reward.

"Basketball is a game easy to play but difficult to master."

1941

ON, WISCONSIN!

The NCAA basketball tournament got off the ground in 1939, took its first steps forward in 1940 and by 1941 was believed to be solidly on its feet. Underscoring this optimism was the belief that the level of competition had at last achieved parity with the National Invitation Tournament, the initial "national championship" which flowered in Madison Square Garden.

More pointedly, interest in the NCAA tourney had reached feverish proportions. Full realization of this came when 48,055 paid their way in to see the five nights of playoff action in 1941. That was nearly 12,000 more than the previous season, when the NCAA finals featured two of the most traditional basketball powers in Indiana and Kansas. With all due respect to the NIT—the nation's oldest postseason basketball tournament by one year—the NCAA had "definitely become the World Series of basketball," according to one writer, and the artistry of the teams of 1941 did nothing to harm its image.

The finalists in this "World Series" at the Kansas City Municipal Auditorium gave the lusty 7,219 fans something to cheer about with the most exciting NCAA championship game in the tourney's young history. The result of this high-tension, low-scoring game was a 39-34 victory for Wisconsin over Washington State; and the reason for it was that Badger coach Bud Foster had done his homework better than his Cougar counterpart, Jack Friel.

Foster had the foresight to scout Washington State, sending assistant Fred Wegner ahead to Kansas City to watch the finals of the Western playoffs. In that game, Wegner watched Paul Lindeman score 14 points to lead the Cougars to an impressive 64-53 victory over heavily favored Arkansas. The information that Wegner supplied to Foster about the husky Washington State center inspired Wisconsin's defensive game plan for the NCAA finals.

"We did a little rigging," recalls Wegner. "Lindeman had such a tremendous game in the West-

ern playoffs that we had to stop him, whatever we did. So we double-teamed him. We had a guy behind him so he couldn't get on the boards and a guy dropping in front of him so he couldn't get passes."

Gene Englund, Wisconsin's all-America center, was a virtual wall behind the 6-7 Washington State star. And Johnny Kotz, Wisconsin's valuable forward, was one of those who dropped off to front the big man, virtually obscuring him from teammates. Lindeman, normally Washington State's high scorer, finished with three points—all free throws.

Wegner's scouting mission was unusual for the times, but not for Wisconsin's basketball team—which may have been one of the biggest reasons the Badgers were national champions that year. "We scouted our opponents very heavily," remembers Wegner, the one-man scouting operation. "We didn't go against any opponent blindly. I mean our team depended on it, because our kids really believed in our game plans."

The senior and acknowledged team leader, Englund was "a very tough competitor who really went after people and played with a lot of determination," according to Foster. It was Englund's magnetic force that eventually drove Wisconsin all the way, but the blending of strong heads and talents had been a mountainous challenge for Foster. The tough fiber of the 1940-41 team was formed on a two-game trip just before New Year's Eve during which the Badgers were crushed by Big Ten colleague Minnesota. Recalls Foster:

"We had a situation in that game where we didn't score a field goal in the second half, mainly because we seemed to have a little dissension on the team. Englund was a very strong offensive player and very determined and he took a lot on himself being a senior. I think probably the kids unconsciously resented him a little bit and probably, in that Minnesota game, decided they weren't going to give him the ball so much, and we got messed up. But I think the kids got a good lesson in that game. They found out if they wanted to win,

Wisconsin's Charles Epperson (38) narrowly misses a shot in the Badgers' championship win over Washington State.

they had better let Englund have the ball."

The Minnesota game was the last time Wisconsin lost, starting a 15-game winning streak that finished in glory at the NCAA finals. One of the Badgers' victims was Indiana, virtually the same team that had won the NCAA championship the year before. "They were expected to repeat in the Big Ten," Foster reflects, "and when we beat them down at Bloomington near the end of the season, we knew we had a championship-caliber team. That really put us in great mental condition."

When the Badgers won the Big Ten title with a 42-32 victory over Minnesota, it climaxed a dramatic uphill climb; the previous season, Wisconsin had finished a distant ninth in the conference standings. It was a year during which he had the players but not the chemistry, Foster says. Similar ingredients were there in 1940-41, and this time the coach mixed them like a master chemist, coming up with an explosive combination. The starting five of Englund at center, Kotz and Charlie Epperson at forwards and Ted Strain and Fred Rehm at guards "fit together very nicely and was a good machine," according to Foster. "We had a good frontline defense and big men who played well in the corners. Englund was a very strong rebounder and a man who could block out well and intimidate."

Wegner remembers that "it was not really a physically impressive team by today's standards, but a team that used each other's talents well. They just put emphasis on their patterns, played according to plan and things fell together. They didn't throw the ball away very much or make many errors. They had a good strong defense and good defensive rebounding."

In contrast to the fast-breaking style of the first two NCAA champions, Oregon and Indiana, Wisconsin used a much more prudent style of offense. "We used a patterned game," Foster explains, "which embraced pretty much setting up your offense and working for the percentage shot. We would only break on occasions when we had a steal or got one out in a hurry."

Foster's conservative style was an outgrowth of his association with Walter "Doc" Meanwell.

"To my mind, Meanwell was one of the early leaders of basketball," Foster says. "When he came out to the Midwest in 1911, he brought what was then known as the short-pass game, where he used a lot of pivoting, close ball-handling and return passing. And he was also one of the first men to use

University of Wisconsin

a shifting defense. I played my basketball under him, and a lot of his principles followed through with what I taught my teams."

This deep-seated basketball conservatism was even more entrenched after Foster had a harrowing experience early in his coaching career.

"We were playing Pittsburgh one year," Wegner remembers, "and got away from them pretty good. So we took the regulars out, and they all went for showers. But Pitt put on a rally, and I had to go into the showers and drag our first-string players back into the game. After that, we never thought a game was in the bag until it was over. That made us more conservative than ever."

The Badgers did not have the luxury of pulling regulars in the opening game of the NCAA's Eastern playoffs in 1941 at their own field house in Madison. Dartmouth's Ivy Leaguers gave Wisconsin an extremely tough battle and died hard, 51-50. Dartmouth led, 24-22, at the half and held an advantage for most of the second half before a burst of five points put the Badgers into a 47-44 lead they never lost. A field goal by Englund and two free throws by Kotz provided them with their winning points at the end.

"That was quite a game, and people still remember it around Madison," Foster says. "With a minute to go, we had a five-point lead and we did

22

tuck into a pretty tight defense and allowed them to come down the floor, and they hit a couple of long ones on us. But I never felt that we were in as much danger as the final score indicated, because we were getting control of the ball at the end."

From Kotz' view, the Wisconsin-Dartmouth game might have been the best of the entire tournament. "That was as close as you'll ever see a ball game—it was a fantastic game. We had never seen them before and didn't know how really good they were. That was the first time we saw the one-handed push shot. When they came into our arena, they had two guys who used it—George Munroe and Gus Broberg. They were tough, Dartmouth—a wonderful ball club."

Foster did not have much time to enjoy the victory, since his team was to meet the University of Pittsburgh the next night in the Eastern finals. The Panthers had defeated North Carolina in a desultory 26-20 contest in the other opening-round game. "We are rusty," Foster fretted after edging Dartmouth and looking forward with some anxiety to Pitt. H. C. Carlson, the Pitt coach, also had just cause to worry after an off-night of shooting by his team. As one obviously prejudiced Wisconsin writer expressed it, "Wisconsin meets Pitt tonight and practically everyone felt safe Friday night after watching the North Carolina-Pitt game. Don't forget that Pitt was missing shots last night at a terrific rate. I've never seen a good team, and Pitt's all of that, miss so many."

Aside from the obvious motivational factor of the Eastern championship, Wisconsin had the additional compulsion of revenge. Pitt had beaten the Badgers, 36-34, earlier in the season, one of only three losses handed the Big Ten team that year. Along with breeding contempt, the familiarity with the Pitt team was a helpful factor for Wisconsin the second time they met. "We knew a lot about them and what we had to do to beat them," says Kotz. "They had no business beating us the first time." Specifically, the Badgers had to control the boards by using their height advantage over the smaller Pitt team. This they did, and the Panthers fouled repeatedly in an overaggressive attempt to make up for their height disadvantage. This resulted in an abundance of free throws for Wisconsin, and the marked difference in this department (16 to 6) proved to be the difference in a 36-30 Badger victory. For the second straight night, Wisconsin had to rally from a half-time deficit (this time, 18-14). "Wisconsin had the stuff to come through in the stretch," wrote Henry J. McCormick in the Wisconsin State Journal, "and they won't ask any more than that of a champion."

The crowds and the clamor at the Eastern championships testified to the growing glamour of the NCAA event. According to a review in the Official Basketball Guide, "The Eastern regional drew around 10,000 people the first night and a capacity crowd of close to 13,000 the second night. It was marked by intense play but cordial relations among the players. Get-togethers sponsored by the committee helped to make things pleasant for the players and to cement friendly feelings." The guide added a revealing note about the artistic success: "Accustomed as it is to high-class basketball, Madison (Wisconsin) still ranked this as the finest exhibition of the sport it has seen."

The 1941 regionals were precedent-setting as well. This was the first time that third-place games were played in the NCAA regionals, and the appearance of Dartmouth marked the first Ivy League representative in the tournament.

When the Badgers arrived in Kansas City for the finals the following week, they were cast in the role of underdogs to Western champion Washington State. "The Badgers lack the manpower and the ability to reach the heights achieved by Indiana in the 1940 finals against Kansas," observed one newspaperman. "Wisconsin has as much speed as Washington State and more finesse at handling the ball, but it lacks the rugged strength of the only college team of the season to outscore Arkansas." The observer did hold out a ray of hope for the Big Ten champions, though: "Their only hope is to control the ball against Washington State, thus dictating the style of play."

The Badgers displayed a swaggering calm through all the pregame rhetoric, however. They reacted to the supposed awesome Cougar power with an arrogance that was an affront to a championship team.

While stopping in Chicago en route to Kansas City, Wisconsin reserve guard Ed Scheiwe had some time to talk to friends.

"Good luck," one called out, "I hope you win at Kansas City."

Scheiwe was almost indifferent in his reply. "Oh, hell, we've forgotten how to lose."

There was, however, good reason that the Badgers should hold some regard for their opponents. The Cougars had been the only team that season to beat Arkansas, a towering team that had been established as the tournament favorite.

"We were a big underdog to Arkansas," Washington State coach Jack Friel points out. "Everybody was. It was supposed to be the team to beat that year, definitely. It had beaten the Phillips Oilers and semipro teams like that. In fact, some coaching friends of mine told me flat out that we couldn't beat Arkansas."

23

Particularly worrisome to Friel was John Adams, the lean, high-scoring Arkansas forward who used a unique, two-hand overhead jump shot. "I had never seen it before," said Friel. Pregame hoopla touted an offensive duel between Adams and Washington State's Lindeman, but it never materialized. Adams, who according to one writer "leaped in the air like a kangaroo and propelled the ball straight at the basket with a two-handed push motion from his chest," scored his usual high quota with 22 points. Lindeman had to satisfy himself with only 14 points "and a spectacular floor game," but two other players had double figures in a balanced scoring effort that resulted in a shockingly easy 64-53 victory for Washington State in the Western finals at Kansas City.

"We got hot early," remembers Friel, "got a good lead and maintained it throughout. We had a great night shooting and the fast break really hurt them."

Washington State had handled Creighton just as easily in the opening round of the Western regionals, winning 48-39, while Arkansas was beating Wyoming, 52-40. "Ed Hickey was the coach of Creighton and he had a nice fast-breaking team," Friel says. "But they had a little trouble handling our big boy, Lindeman, on rebounds."

As was his custom, Adams received most of the attention and the applause in Arkansas' opener against Wyoming. After watching his 26-point performance, one writer observed that Adams was "practically unguardable and surprisingly accurate. On 11 occasions, gaunt John leaped into the air and whipped the ball through the mesh and added four more from the free-throw lane." Concluded the writer: "Wyoming, pride of the Rockies, brought forth a well-groomed but somewhat inexperienced quintet to face Arkansas . . . the boys from the Cowboy country had the will but they didn't have the physical qualifications to match the six-feet, four-inch average of the Razorbacks."

The Western finals proved without doubt to the same writer that the NCAA tournament had established itself as a solid gold hit. "Kansas City reared up and showed the basketball world it isn't necessary to have a home team on hand for an NCAA tournament to be a success," he said. "Washington State, Arkansas, Wyoming and Creighton furnished the necessary incentive in the way of cage attractions, and 17,836 enthusiastic fans responded to the extent of $16,027.95 in the course of the tournament play held in the modernistic, decorative Municipal Auditorium."

Wisconsin's home-court attraction in the Eastern playoffs was not lost to observers, though.

Feeling happy about winning the national championship are Wisconsin's Ted Strain, Gene Englund, Charles Epperson, Johnny Kotz and Fred Rehm.

About 23,000 fans watched the Badgers perform in the two nights at Madison.

"We were nearly filled to capacity the first night of the Eastern playoffs," Foster remembers, "and then after we won the first game, they sold everything they had. You couldn't buy a ticket for the Eastern championship game. They were offering all kinds of money for tickets, like four or five dollars. That was a lot then." The top ticket in the Eastern playoffs cost $1.10, according to Foster.

Many of those hard-core Wisconsin fans followed the team to the finals to join an already formidable group of alumni in the Kansas City area.

A "colorful crowd" of 7,219, which included the National Basketball Rules Committee and a reunion of the 1916 Wisconsin basketball team, applauded the Badgers and Cougars as the individual players were introduced beneath the glare of a huge spotlight. A moment later all stood at attention as a local military academy color guard marched onto the floor and the national anthem was played.

Wisconsin then went to work on its 15th straight victory with machine-like precision, the key being the domination of the barrel-chested Lindeman. "The Badgers bottled big Paul Lindeman and jammed in a tight cork in holding the 230-pound Cougar to three free throws and giving him only seven shots from the floor during the entire game," said one newspaper account. "This performance was a far cry from his exhibitions against Creighton and Arkansas last week."

The overemphasis on Lindeman allowed Kirk Gebert to shoot almost at will from the outside, and the 5-11 Cougar guard scored more than half his team's points with 21. Gebert's brilliant performance, "which kept the spectators electrified," kept Washington State within striking distance of Wisconsin all the way, but the rest of the Cougar offense was nonexistent. This was a result of a passionate defense and a possession-type game employed by the Badgers.

Continued the newspaper account: "The Badgers fulfilled their reputation as a slow-breaking, methodical team and handled the ball in a manner that reminded observers of Hank Iba's Oklahoma Aggies or Phog Allen's Kansas Jayhawks—quick, true passes with little wasted motion. With Washington (State), it was run and shoot, shoot, shoot. With Wisconsin, it was pass, pass, pass and shoot."

24

University of Wisconsin

25

After the Badgers took a 19-17 lead late in the first half, they never lost it. No more than seven points separated the teams the rest of the way, though, and the game was not really decided until the closing minutes. Holding a tenuous 34-32 margin with three minutes to go, the Badgers won the game by outscoring the Cougars, 5-2, on a field goal by Kotz, a free throw by Strain and a basket by reserve guard Bobby Alwin.

Kotz, who scored 12 points and was voted the tourney's most outstanding player, believes that Washington State had the stronger team—but Wisconsin had the better game plan and the good fortune of circumstance.

"I think they had a better ball club than us," says Kotz, "but I think what hurt them is that they had to stay in Kansas City that whole week leading up to the finals. They stayed there and practiced and roamed around all week. I think by the time the finals came, they were a little pooped. We came in a day ahead of time after spending the week at home, and I think we were better off for it."

Foster concurs with his player's assessment and further concludes that the Washington State basketball team might have been trapped by overcon-fidence: "They had done such a fine job against Arkansas the week before that they were the favorite sons of all the Kansas City fans. They made quite a bit of them that week. The papers praised them highly. They probably got a little cocky."

The Wisconsin victory was not fashioned without anxiety. During the first half, the condition of the unusually hard floor (a feature of the arena disliked by players) had caused havoc with Epperson's legs. "His legs were so stiff we had to carry him down the runway to the dressing room at halftime," recalls Wegner. "Then the trainer rubbed him down and he went back in the second half and played real well. But he had bad cramps for a while and was in terrible pain. We didn't know if he was going to make it."

He was able to walk with the championship trophy afterwards, however.

"That was something I'll never forget," says Wegner. "There were our players walking down the middle of the street back to our hotel, carrying this big trophy. It was about four feet high. I remember one of the guys said, 'Let's enjoy this because it'll be a long time before it happens again.' You know, he was right."

1942

A GENTLEMAN FROM INDIANA

"Gaining momentum each succeeding year, the 'World Series of Basketball' celebrated its fourth anniversary in 1942 with a tournament that included the greatest collection of collegiate cage personnel ever assembled in the 50-year history of the game. The hand-picked group of eight teams represented the best basketball had to offer from coast to coast, and there was not a team in the lot that did not have at least one of its members named as an all-America on one of the several selections."—The Official Basketball Guide, 1942

Except for Stanford's cardinal red uniforms and Dartmouth's green, it was hard to distinguish the two basketball teams in 1942. Both were called Indians and both employed the same flashy, one-handed shooting styles from long range with a maximum of passing and a minimum of dribbling. There was good reason for this, of course. Stanford coach Everett Dean and Dartmouth coach Osborne Cowles both learned their basketball in the Midwest. In fact, Cowles had played the game under Dean at Carleton College in Northfield, Minnesota. Thus, the 1942 NCAA championship game had taken on a deeper dimension: teacher vs. pupil.

Both teams reflected a quiet confidence as they were introduced in the spotlight's gleam at the lavish Kansas City Municipal Auditorium. The players stood stoically at attention as a naval color guard presented the flag and a military academy band played the National Anthem. Among those standing near the Stanford bench was a tormented Jim Pollard, contemplating a blow dealt by fate. Pollard, one of the leading players on the Stanford team, was in street clothes, benched by influenza. Pollard had scored a total of 43 points in the two Western regional playoff games to help Stanford beat Rice and Colorado.

Further crippling the Stanford hopes was an injury to Don Burness, another of the team's top shooters. Burness, who had watched the Western playoffs from the bench with an ankle injury, hobbled out to start the championship game; but it was obvious that he would be of little use to Stanford. He tried to play but was ineffective and left the game after only a few minutes.

Reporters had listened to the same monotonous soliloquy all season—that Stanford was strictly a five-man team and could not win with a part missing. Along with Pollard and Burness, the other theoretical essentials included Howie Dallmar, Ed Voss and Bill Cowden. However, Dallmar was not so sure about the theory, especially when a national title was at stake. "Certainly we felt down when Jim Pollard went to bed because of that sinus infection the day before we played Dartmouth," says Dallmar. "But we didn't worry about it very long. We had determination to win that national title, so we didn't worry too much about playing without Pollard."

With the absence of Pollard and Burness, Stanford-watchers suddenly discovered that the team had a bench. Most prominent of the reserves were Jack Dana and Fred Linari, who did most of the heavy work for the ailing stars. Then, too, Dallmar took it upon himself to become a team leader; he produced 15 points, a brilliant all-round floor game and an NCAA championship for Stanford. It is likely that no one expected Stanford's 53-38 rout, considering the adverse circumstances; and Dean was moved to admit, "I expect this is the best basketball team I have coached."

"It was defensively outstanding," Dean points out. "For a group of big boys, they were very active, handled themselves well, covered their men and used their arms excellently. Their reactions were really fast for big men. They were good enough to handle three defenses. They used a zone defense against Rice. When Colorado looked for a zone the next night, they used a shifting man-for-man.

Stanford's Jim Pollard.

Stanford University

27

Against Dartmouth, they used a combination. Bill Cowden, Ed Voss and Howard Dallmar stuck to their men; but the forwards in the front line shifted.

"Offensively, the boys reached their height in the tournament. They came through in adversity. Linari sparked our fast break against Dartmouth. Jack Dana played his best game of the year (14 points in the title game). Ed Voss was our second highest scorer of the tournament (38 points in the three games). Pollard, before he got sick, played his two best offensive games. Dallmar came through with points when Dartmouth was hottest to keep us in the running. Bill Cowden was as great as any guard I have seen. He held Colorado's great (Pete) McCloud to one field goal. Dartmouth's (George) Munroe got four off Bill in the first half and not one was a clean shot. He got only one in the second."

From many standpoints, the 1941-1942 Stanford team might have been the best in the school's history. The Indians won the Southern Division of the Pacific Coast Conference with consummate ease, beat Oregon State in a three-game playoff for the league championship and then won the national title with victories over Rice, Colorado and Dartmouth in the NCAA championship. Dean's champions won more games than any other Stanford team (28) and lost but four.

Forddy Anderson, Don Williams and Ken Davidson were staggering losses from a fine 1940-41 team, but this attrition was more than compensated by the emergence of Dallmar and Pollard and the spectacular improvement of Voss. Pollard had starred on the freshman team, and his ultimate success at Stanford and later in the pros took him a long way from his modest beginnings.

"Pollard was underprivileged socially and economically and was confined pretty much to the ghetto in his younger days," recalls a friend, Bob Burnett. "His family didn't have the education and employment to have any kind of standard of living. It was very much like a hand-to-mouth situation. Pollard went to Tech High in Oakland, and I mean he was lucky if he had a pair of pants. And if you speak to Jim Pollard today, he'll tell you it was a long, long trip to get where he got. He wasn't a typical Stanford boy who went there with a silver spoon in his mouth."

But Pollard had a rich source to tap—his basketball ability. Burnett, an assistant coach at Stanford in the 1940s and later head coach in the 1950s, reveres Pollard as "very quick, fast, lean—a whippet type of player. He could pass quick, play defense and rebound. He had great coordination and was a fine dribbler. Pollard was the catalyst of that team. He had great natural ability."

Burness' situation was similar to Pollard's in that his family could not pay for college, especially an expensive school like Stanford. But help came from Cliff Burnhill, an Oakland attorney and Stanford's No. 1 scout in those days, who saw to it that Burness received an athletic scholarship after improving his academic stature at a private school. This was all part of the essential backstage help provided by friends of Stanford. Remembering those days of recruiting intrigue, Burnett notes:

"We weren't allowed to go on campuses to recruit players. I couldn't go across the road to Palo Alto High School unless I was invited for a special occasion. The only time you could see a team play was on a neutral court, such as the Civic Center in San Francisco. Otherwise, you were not allowed to watch high school kids play. So we relied heavily on our alumni like Cliff Burnhill to help."

Dallmar's arrival at Stanford was preceded by a bit of a row. A nonpareil San Francisco prep star at Lowell High School, Dallmar originally had been recruited by the University of California and, in fact, took extension courses at that school in order to satisfy the admission requirements. However, after he became eligible for Cal, Dallmar changed

his plans and headed for Stanford. This switch of allegiances considerably irked California coach Nibs Price and the rest of the school's athletic administration, which thought Stanford perhaps had done some underhanded dealing to pry Dallmar away. An ensuing investigation by the league failed to support this contention, and Dallmar was merrily on his way to Palo Alto.

Price could well regret the loss of Dallmar, recognized as the Bay Area's No. 1 college prospect that season. Dallmar was a 6-4 center in high school who later became one of the nation's tallest college guards. Uniquely, he was one of five one-time centers in the king-sized Stanford lineup that averaged over 6-foot-4. Dallmar's backcourt mate was the 6-3 Cowden, while the 6-3 Burness played with Pollard at forward and Voss was a 6-5½ center.

"Because they all played center in high school, this meant they could alternate positions, which often left the defense mismatched," Dean points out. "It was a very remarkable team because not only was every man big, but they all had speed."

This inherent quality led to the natural inclination of the fast break, but the Indians were hardly imprudent with this device. They ran when they could. When they could not, they used a revolving offense, cutting off the post, working pivot plays around Voss.

"Most of our shots came off the screen," says Dallmar. "We pretty well divided the scoring, except for Cowden. He was our top defensive player. We were a very physical team and always very active. And when you get five active guys running and putting the ball up, you're going to get more rebounds and more second and third shots."

As Stanford showed in the NCAA finals of 1942, the team was not only well-balanced but also was deep. "Every player had his specialty," recalls Dean, "and they all worked together beautifully. It was not the kind of team any coach can normally expect to put together in one year."

The unique qualities of each player, especially the starters, excited and continually amazed Dean.

"Pollard could pass. He could always hit the pivot man. He was one of the first men to use the jump shot, but I think you'd have to give Hank Luisetti credit for inventing it. He also had great speed in driving."

Dean applauds Burness as the team's best shot and "a perfect passer—a great feeder and ball-handler off the post." Voss was skilled at passing off to cutters and at reverses off the pivot. Cowden was the tough workhorse, the defender. And Dallmar

"had a strong backboard game. He was a good shot and a great driver." Dallmar is most remembered for his broad-jump layups. "He would leave the floor at the foul line and land after the ball fell into the basket," says one observer.

These electric talents were galvanized by Dean, a man revered as "a gentleman from Indiana." To Burnett, "he was a very gentle soul and a religious man. He did not smoke, he did not drink, he did not swear. He was patient, thoughtful and sometimes too repetitious, and the boys would get a little nervous when he kept going over the same point. But they all respected him. From a coaching standpoint, he was a wonderful fundamentalist. He was a good teacher, but he was not an explosive guy. I was the antithesis of him. He loved to have me on the bench, I guess, because he'd give me a jab in the ribs which said, 'Come on, get on the officials,' because that was something that he just could not do. He didn't get a technical foul in his entire life."

Dallmar's reflections further enhance the Dean portrait: "I never heard him curse, and he never bawled out a player. He had a very soft manner. As a coach, he was a great tactician. He was the most super person that I've ever been associated with."

Even references to Dean in the unemotional print of biographical data make note of his nobility. One such encyclopedic note ran down his

Bill Cowden, co-captain of the 1942 NCAA champions from Stanford.

Stanford University

28

achievements and then made the editorial comment that Dean was retiring after 34 years of coaching "with the universal recognition of being one of the finest gentlemen in the game."

Dean was a four-year basketball star at Salem (Ind.) High School and a gifted three-year performer at Indiana University. ("He was a wonderful two-hand set shooter," remembers Burnett. "He won more milk shakes from me than I care to admit.") Dean coached at Carleton College from 1921 through 1924, winning 48 of 52 games, and then his coaching career gained momentum at Indiana. In 14 years, Dean coached the Hoosiers to 163 victories and ties for Big Ten titles in 1926, 1928 and 1936. Three years later, he was at Stanford; and despite the recent graduation of players like the great Luisetti, he continued a tradition of success.

Stanford lost only one game in the Pacific Coast Conference's Southern Division race in 1941-42, a 27-23 decision to a stalling Southern California team. "They slowed us down," Dean remembers. "It's always a great basketball tactic against a fast-break team, a great equalizer."

In the PCC playoffs, Oregon State extended Stanford to three games before the Indians won the championship and a ticket to Kansas City for the NCAA's Western playoffs. After Stanford's title-deciding 40-35 victory, a newspaper reported that the Indians had not allowed Oregon State "to set the defense. They dashed without hesitation for the bucket at every opportunity, shooting from any and every angle. The change of pace startled the Beavers into a temporary period of lethargy . . ." A sign of things to come in the NCAA playoffs manifested itself when Stanford won the PCC championship game with two starters crippled. Dallmar functioned with the noticeable effect of a charley horse, and a sprained ankle kept Burness on the side lines most of the game.

Burness was a spectator again when Stanford beat Rice, 53-47, in the first round of the NCAA's Western playoffs at Kansas City; and Dallmar remembers, "That was our toughest game out there. They came out at the start of the second half with a lot of points before we knew what hit us. They had two big guys, Bill Closs and Bob Kinney, who did a terrific job rebounding for them." A crowd of 8,200 at the Kansas City Municipal Auditorium watched Stanford utilize its superior height to control the ball throughout the first half and take what appeared to be a comfortable 33-21 margin. But Rice scored the first three baskets of the second half and, led by little Chet Palmer, eventually streaked into a 41-37 lead with a little more than eight minutes gone. Voss then became the dominating factor in the game. He kept Stan-

ford abreast of the Southwest Conference co-champions with two free throws and a field goal and later looped in a left-hander to put the Indians in front to stay with five minutes to go. Kinney and Closs fouled out for Rice at this point, and the PCC champions were able to control the ultimate flow of the game with their height advantage.

The superiority of the Stanford defense was evident in crucial stages of the game. The obvious lack of this important basketball weapon in youthful Buster Brannon's Rice team was duly noted by one writer in a review of the Western tournament: "Rice was willing to give a shot in order to get a shot in return and worried little about the essentials of defense."

Colorado, the Big Seven champion and a team that had lost only one game during the regular season, proved less of a challenge to Stanford in the Western finals. Actually, the Indians were surprised to be facing the Buffaloes at all in the championship game. "We thought we'd be seeing Kansas," Dallmar says. "Kansas was supposed to be the pretournament favorite. Even though Colorado had an outstanding record, everybody questioned its conference schedule. So they shook up a lot of people when they handled Kansas." Colorado, coached by a onetime pupil of Kansas coach Phog Allen, Forrest "Frosty" Cox, defeated the Jayhawks, 46-44, in the other opening-round game of the Western playoffs.

A team that depended on movement and split-second precision, Colorado never was able to get its rhythm started against Stanford. The Indians rushed to an early lead behind Pollard and kept up the pressure all the way en route to a near-flawless performance against the Buffaloes. After Stanford's efficient 46-35 victory for the Western championship, the Official Basketball Guide concluded that Stanford was "the greatest ever to appear in NCAA competition."

Stanford looked even better in the national championship game against Dartmouth, the Ivy League winner which had gained the finals with victories over Penn State and Kentucky in the Eastern playoffs at New Orleans. By game time, Dean was as familiar with Dartmouth's style as he was with his own, and not only because of his relationship with Big Green coach Ozzie Cowles. Dean had pregame scouting help from several of his West Coast coaching friends—"Hec" Edmundson of Washington, Jack Friel of Washington State, Howard Hobson of Oregon and "Slats" Gill of Oregon State all attended the coaches' rules meeting in New Orleans, where they saw Dartmouth win the Eastern title.

"I asked them to scout Dartmouth for me,"

29

30

Stanford University

Dean remembers. "Every one of them took time on the way home to come through Kansas City and give me the dope. Hobson spent two hours telling me about Dartmouth. Gill and Friel spent a day and a half in Kansas City, and Friel came out to practice to demonstrate what Dartmouth used. Edmundson stayed around for the title game and helped us. We knew something about Dartmouth after having played them twice in the preceding three years, but those coaches gave us details about the players that were invaluable."

Even with all that help, Dean did not find it easy balancing a basketball team on his hands for more than a week.

"We had to stay in a Kansas City hotel for eight days," Dean recalls. "It would have taken four days and four nights to go from Kansas City to San Francisco and return to Kansas City. This present-

Howard Dallmar of Stanford, most outstanding player in the 1942 tournament.

ed a big problem in training, discipline and getting results. Our schedule for the week was somewhat rugged because we were playing for the national collegiate championship and, at the same time, studying for final exams, some of which were in progress that very week. Some final exam questions, in fact, were sent to me to give exams to three players. The players were high-type men and cooperated to the fullest. Their mental attitude was perfect during the week and for the game. They came to play but seemed to worry about final exams as much as the game. This reflects the character of the team."

Dean's aim in preparing his team was "to maintain fresh mental and physical condition and hold moderate practices with one or two days off during the week."

Dean's overriding worries were Dartmouth's Jim Olsen, who had scored 19 points in Dartmouth's 44-39 victory over Penn State in the first round of the Eastern playoffs, and George Munroe, whose 20 points led the Big Green's 47-28 rout of Kentucky in the Eastern finals. Dean put the emphasis on defense in pregame drills leading up to the national finals. "Everett was on us all week to front our men, keep the ball away from their offense," said Dallmar. "The first two times I did not, and Dartmouth got the ball and scored. That was one of the few times I ever saw Everett angry. He called time out and got on me to work harder in the game—in effect, told me to get off my rear end."

Dallmar did and not only played defense like he was supposed to but scored points when he had to. With Pollard and Burness unavailable, Dallmar became Stanford's leading man with 11 points in the first half, helping forge a 24-22 lead at intermission. The sophomore guard scored four points in crucial stages of the second half, when Stanford broke the game open with a quick-paced last 10 minutes—"a rapid-fire, pile driver brand of basketball," according to United Press correspondent Webb Trout. Dallmar was named the outstanding player of the tournament, but he was a reluctant hero.

"Gosh, we were all high," Dallmar said in the bright glare of center stage. "Against Colorado and Rice, that Pollard was awfully hot. When he developed a touch of flu and a temperature, Jack Dana really went to work at forward against Dartmouth. And as far as Ed Voss is concerned, every time he went up against a highly publicized center, he outplayed his man. (Bob) Kinney (of Rice), (Bob) Doll (of Colorado) and (Jim) Olsen (of Dartmouth) all were supposed to be great, but big Ed was ahead of all of them, I thought. And we really needed a coordinator with Don Burness on the bench, and Bill Cowden was that. (Pete) McCloud was Colorado's star, but Bill held him to one field goal. For Dartmouth, George Munroe sank four quick field goals; but when Cowden took him over, he was held for the rest of the night." Munroe had one field goal in the second half and a total of 12 points.

Although Dartmouth was the Eastern champion, the general consensus in the Stanford camp was that Rice was a tougher team.

"Rice was the best team we faced," Dallmar said, "and we were fortunate to win. I guess we were lucky all around. We arrived at 1 a.m. Friday in Kansas City for the Western playoffs and had no chance for a regular practice. The floor was very hard, and it was the first time we had played against glass backboards. The only workout we had was 30 minutes of shooting before the game.

"Many of the boys had slight colds, but only Pollard was really stricken. After Kansas was eliminated, the local people seemed to choose us as their favorites, and that helped us a lot. With both of our regular forwards out of the final game, coach Dean told us to free lance—that is, don't wait for set plays but fast break and shoot as often as possible. We're happy it worked."

Dean was proud of everything except possibly the meager $93.75 check he brought home from the three games in Kansas City and the failure of his national champions to get gold watches for their reward. But, as Dean himself explains, a matter of circumstances forced this condition.

"The year before, Wisconsin was the Eastern champion and drew 15,000 in two nights in the Eastern finals at Madison. The Navy had taken over the biggest auditorium in New Orleans during the time of the 1942 Eastern playoffs, and the games had to be moved out to Tulane University's smaller gym. They made only $5,500 there. The NCAA paid the expenses of all eight teams. Stanford and Dartmouth, the finalists, came far distances and had to be kept in Kansas City a full week. The expenses were so large that the cuts were small."

While New Orleans was having moderate success with its Eastern tournament, Kansas City was packing in 12,372 at the Western playoffs. A week later, for the national finals, there were more than 6,000 persons seated in the Kansas City Municipal Auditorium, bringing the tournament total to 24,372. The figure was somewhat below that of 1941, but some of this attrition was attributed to the Second World War.

31

WAR-TIME PROSPERITY

Madison Square Garden in New York was a basketball mecca in the 1940s, "the Main Line," as one writer put it. It was the house that Ned Irish built and surely the Big Apple of everyone's eye in college basketball. The pulse of the world quickened with the fury of war, but even menacing global events failed to change the beat at America's most famous sports palace.

In 1943, it was business as usual on 8th Avenue and 49th Street; and that usually meant huge crowds to watch the nation's best collegiate teams. That year, when entertainment-hungry fans escaped from war news to the safe insanity of the basketball arena, the power and the glory belonged to a group of straight-shooters from the West, the University of Wyoming. Not only did the Cowboys win the NCAA championship, but they also further certified their greatness by beating the NIT champion as well in a game staged for the benefit of the Red Cross.

The unique double play left little doubt as to the No. 1 college basketball team that year, despite the opinion of some that Illinois should have laid claim to that distinction. The "Whiz Kids," as they were called, had gone through the Big Ten schedule undefeated; and at one point in the season, they were considered the top team in the country. But for some reason, they passed up postseason competition in both the NCAA and the NIT.

"I remember there was a lot of publicity about that," says Lew Roney, a guard on Wyoming's national champions. "Sports writers were still saying, even after we had won the NCAA championship, that Illinois was still the best team in the country. It kind of bugged us. They were good, no question about that . . . but we never really had a chance to find out how good."

While Illinois was an unknown quantity in tournament play, it was not hard to add up Wyoming's worth. The Cowboys' visibility was extremely high in the NCAA tournament games, which they won with a string of late rallies. In the Western regional, Wyoming came from behind to

beat Oklahoma, 53-50, and then Texas, 58-54; and in the NCAA finals, the Cowboys made a comeback to beat Georgetown, 46-34. The whipped cream on the season was a 52-47 triumph over NIT winner St. John's in the Red Cross game, which earned $26,000 for the war effort and a priceless amount of publicity for the Wyoming basketball team.

Except for Indiana import Milo Komenich and Nebraska refugee Don Waite, the Cowboys were a Wyoming product, the most notable being Kenny Sailors. Sailors was equally comfortable at forward, where he could unleash his lethal one-handed jump shot, or in the backcourt, where he dribbled as well as anyone in the country. This provided him with the unique stature of a playmaking forward, a rare bird in college basketball. Sailors styled his jump shot, it was said, after Stanford's demigod of the 1930s, Hank Luisetti; and his dribbling expertise provided a standard for others to shoot for in later years. "Bob Cousy, the great Boston Celtics star, made the statement many times that he patterned his play after Sailors," points out Larry Birleffi, a noted sportscaster of Wyoming basketball games. "He gave him the idea to jump-shoot. Kenny used to work so hard to perfect that jump shot. He was just tireless."

Sailors originally learned the eye-catching jumper out of necessity while at Laramie High School, shooting over zone defenses employed by C. H. "Okie" Blanchard at Casper High. Later, he was to perfect it at Wyoming under the care and feeding of Everett Shelton, an advocate of the one-handed shot. "We were the only team around in those days where everybody shot one-handed," says another Wyoming player from 1943, guard Floyd Volker. "You know, the Easterners all clicked their heels and shot two-handed. But we shot everything with one hand, even our free throws. They loved our style at Madison Square Garden. We were voted the most popular team to play there that year."

In the midst of all this flashy one-hand shooting

was Sailors, a virtual Harlem Globetrotter of his time. Sailors could really put on an exhibition with that ball," remembers Volker. "No team could press us because of his ball-handling abilities. No one or two men could get the ball from him, he was that good. We would spread out and just turn him loose and listen to the crowd applaud." Sailors was at the top of his game in the NCAA playoffs, where he earned the most valuable player award and hundreds of accolades. Some observers called him "the greatest basketball player" they had ever seen. Joe Cumminsky, sports editor of the New York PM, was one of many writers who applauded his extraordinary talents. "This Sailors can do everything with a basketball but tie a seaman's knot," he said, "and given a chance to dribble two steps, he'd probably be able to do that."

The term "enforcer" was not yet the vogue in basketball jargon, but Komenich was every inch such a figure at 6-foot-7, "a tremendous physical specimen," according to Roney. "He was a big, tough guy who could handle most anybody they had around then. He was tough as a shooter, too. He could shoot a left-handed hook that was really something. He controlled the inside, and few people ever beat us on the boards."

A big out-of-state catch, Komenich immediately found a home, literally and figuratively, in Laramie. "Shelton used to take care of his players like a father," says Birleffi, "and many of them slept in the basement of his house. Komenich had a bed right near the coal bin. Those were the days when athletic scholarships were not in use and coaches had to support their players, get them jobs and room and board."

Shelton did more than provide a rooming house for his players—he served as their chauffeur. "Ev always used to drive the team bus," recalls Roney, "and I must say it was an adventure. I remember one trip we made to Utah, I was sitting in the back of the bus with Komenich and here was a tire rolling down the road ahead of us. One of our tires had come off, and it was beating the bus. There was snow all over, and it must have been 15 degrees below zero; but we finally hitchhiked into a little town and stayed overnight."

Shelton was a one-man work force, "chief cook and bottlewasher," according to Roney. "Ev was also our baseball coach, and he was an assistant in football. Ev did everything. He probably took care of the gym, and everything else, for that matter."

The "Shelton Weave" was, of course, his most significant contribution to Wyoming basketball. "His style was ball control, screening, patterns, working in for the good shot," notes Birleffi. "He ran a very disciplined team . . . they never took a low-percentage shot."

"We did fast break on occasion," points out Roney. "Komenich could throw that ball a country mile. He'd get it off the board, and somebody would take off downcourt. But we really were a ball-control team. You didn't take too many bad shots with Ev."

The Hank Iba school of slow down no doubt influenced Shelton, a graduate of little Phillips University in Enid, Oklahoma. Shelton's teams were remarkably similar to those turned out by the Oklahoma A&M (now Oklahoma State) master when Shelton started coaching at Wyoming in 1940. "Shelton and Iba were a lot alike in that they were popular when they won but had a lot of critics when they lost," notes Birleffi. "It was because of their style. They used to control the ball and emphasize defense, and this sometimes wasn't the most exciting basketball in the world to watch."

But it usually was the most successful. Shelton showed exceptional ability from his first job as coach at Phillips University, where he had a 62-10 record in three years. When he left Wyoming following the 1959 season, Shelton had amassed an overall record of 623-313.

"Ev was one of the finest coaches I have ever known," says Bill Strannigan, one of several all-Americas turned out by Shelton and later a successful coach in his own right. "He did a lot of things that were ahead of his time, such as the weave and movement without the ball. Defensively, he was the finest coach I played for. It was quite a thrill for me to play on his first conference championship team (1941). He did all his own scouting and paid for a lot of it out of his own pocket because the basketball budget wasn't very big. He was the most dedicated coach I have known. But more importantly, he was a great man morally. You just had to respect him for his ideals. The thing that stands out in my mind about Ev was the fact that he never forgot his players. He was always there to give them a helping hand."

The Cowboys played in an intimidating little place nicknamed "Hell's Half Acre," a colorful gym with a balcony that seated about 5,000; and Birleffi remembers, "you never could get a ticket there—it was always packed." Shelton's eccentric side-line behavior injected a higher fever into the already electrified atmosphere. "He was pretty feisty," notes Roney. "He would really get on officials. And on the bench, nobody wanted to sit next to him because he'd get all excited during a game. He'd grab you on the leg and squeeze, or he'd hit you in the ribs. So when we sat on the bench, we always dove for the last chair, so we wouldn't have to sit next to him."

33

Wyoming basketball had attained a modest reputation in the 1930s, and Shelton built on that foundation of success in the 1940s and into the 1950s. His masterpiece, of course, was the 1942-43 team. The Cowboys played 33 games that year and lost only two, an exquisite achievement considering their demanding schedule. They had made one long, cross-country trip and engaged in an arduous AAU tournament featuring semipro teams in Denver shortly before springing into the NCAA playoffs. "We got beat in the semifinals of that AAU tournament," Roney recalls, "and that was really a big blow to us because we didn't think that anyone could beat us at that point. Phillips 66 went on to win the AAU title and that hurt our ego, because we had beaten them twice that year. As it turned out, though, it probably did us more good than harm to lose in the AAU. It gave us more incentive in the NCAA playoffs."

Along with the inspirational leadership of Sailors and the towering brilliance of Komenich, the Wyoming basketball team of 1942-43 had added combustibility in Jim Weir, a husky forward who supplied the needed frontcourt chemistry for a championship team. Usual starters along with those three were Roney and Volker in the backcourt, although the remaining parts were nicely interchangeable throughout any game. The top reserves included Jimmy Collins, Jimmy Reese, Earl "Shadow" Ray and Don Waite.

The Cowboys experienced few problems that year on their way to the championship of the Skyline Conference, beating Brigham Young in a three-game series at the end for the league title. Indefatigable, the Cowboys played in the AAU tournament in Denver before going to the NCAA's Western regional playoffs in Kansas City. "The papers said that we couldn't possibly do well in the NCAA because there was too much strain on us from all those games late in the season," recalls Volker, "but we didn't find it particularly tough."

Oklahoma, led by Gerry Tucker, and Texas, whose star was John Hargis, proved to be formidable opponents for Wyoming in the regionals. It was only after the Cowboys were able to get Tucker out of the game on fouls that they could subdue the Sooners. The Cowboys were unable to control Hargis, and the lanky forward set tournament scoring records; but a magnificent team performance pulled them through in the Western finals.

Although making a gallant comeback in the opening game against Oklahoma, the Cowboys' victory was a bit tainted because of the controversial foul situation surrounding Tucker. The Daily Oklahoman of Oklahoma City voiced the opinion, shared by some, that perhaps the officials were too

hasty in calling fouls on the Sooner star. "Tucker was the victim of some pretty weird officiating," said the newspaper. "Lloyd Leith, the Pacific Coast representative on the officiating staff, slapped three quick personals on Tucker for 'backing up' on his foe, Milo Komenich, the Wyoming giant. The fourth was called by Abb Curtis, the Southwest Conference arbiter. What made it ironical was that all the while the crowd was yelling at Leith to 'get him a saddle' over the way Komenich was using his hands, knees and elbows in his almost futile attempt to guard the big Sooner."

Shelton didn't help matters by intimating after the game to reporters that Wyoming had set out to trap Tucker into fouling out of the game. "We had an idea Tucker couldn't guard a big man and stay in the game, and we played it that way," Shelton said casually.

The newspapers also questioned the advisability of keeping Tucker in the game after he incurred his third foul. Of course, this second-guessing of coach Bruce Drake was even easier with the luxury of hindsight, since Tucker fouled out of the game with two minutes left in the first half. Komenich, who had been held to only three field goals by Tucker in the first half, scored nearly at will after intermission and wound up with 22 points.

While the Cowboys were beating the Sooners, Hargis was shooting down Washington with his accurate one-handers. The lanky Texas player scored 30 points—more than half his team's total figure—as the Longhorns beat the Huskies, 59-55, in the other opening-round game of the Western playoffs. Hargis added 29 points to his total in the finals against Wyoming, breaking the tournament scoring records for two and three games; but no doubt he would have traded his high individual achievement for the Western championship.

The Cowboys claimed the sectional title with an indispensable element that Shelton called the "sixth man," or the competitive spirit of the team. Sailors was in the middle of it all, "thrilling the crowd with his 'change of pace' dribble, and handling the ball as if it were a pea," according to Paul O'Boynick of the Kansas City Star. "Sailors had a knack of speeding down the floor, stopping suddenly and then continuing with his dribble. His work was on the brilliant side, but six other players figured in the final victory, namely Jimmy Weir, Milo Komenich, Volker, Roney, Collins and Waite." Komenich, once again, was the top scorer with 17 points. The broad-shouldered center had

Hy Gotkin (12) of St. John's attempts to defense Wyoming star Ken Sailors (4) in the 1943 championship game.

34

been the main reason that the Cowboys averaged 60 points a game during the regular season, a high figure for the day.

"Texas was definitely the tougher of the two teams we faced in the Western regional," remembers Volker, "but they didn't have the beef and the height to match us inside. They were a small team, a running team, but we beat them on the boards."

The symbolic end for the Longhorns came when Hargis, head down, walked off the court with his fifth foul late in the game. The audience acknowledged the most explosive scoring performance seen to that date in championship play and gave Hargis "one of the greatest ovations given a player in several years," according to O'Boynick.

The victory sent Wyoming into the national finals in New York against Georgetown, a dynamic, high-scoring team that had crushed NYU and beaten DePaul and its noted George Mikan in the Eastern championships. The Hoyas had experienced their best season in history under Elmer Ripley, an athletic giant of his age. "He was as knowledgeable in basketball as anyone alive then," says James "Miggs" Reilly, a forward on the 1942-43 Georgetown team. "He had been in the game all his life, and he knew talent very well."

"We had a tremendous ball-handling team," points out Reilly, acknowledged as "the best set shot on the team" in the school yearbook. "We moved exceptionally well. We were fairly unselfish. And we were pretty poised. We rarely lost the ball and if we got up by five or so, we rarely lost the lead."

John Mahnken was the indispensable part of the team at center, according to Reilly, "a very good, useful big man. He was ahead of his time. We would not have gone as far without him." The 6-8 Mahnken, only a freshman, led the Hoyas in scoring with a 15.4 average that year and was their leading rebounder as well. His age typified the Georgetown team, which was composed mostly of freshmen and sophomores. "We were an extremely young team," points out Reilly. "We were still coming then. If it hadn't been for the war, which dispersed us after that year, we would have been even better the next season." Along with Mahnken and Reilly, some of the other leading figures included guards Dan "Dutch" Kraus and Billy Hassett and forwards Andy Kostecka and Lloyd Potolicchio. "Kraus, an indefatigable player, was good defensively and an excellent shot, but his real forte was passing, dribbling and above all, setting up plays," noted the 1943 Georgetown University

35

yearbook. "Hassett and Kraus were the backbone of the team, setting up most of the plays, and never a pair teamed better." The yearbook called Kostecka the "best all-around shot on the club roster," and Potolicchio was termed a player with "a fighting heart who worked well with the team."

The Hoyas played one of their most formidable schedules in many years that season, encountering top-flight service teams as well as some of the toughest college opponents in the East. They had scored as much as 105 points in a game—mind-boggling at the time—and by the end of the regular season had a 19-4 record and an invitation to the NCAA's Eastern regional playoffs in Madison Square Garden. Playing their "fast and fancy, high-scoring brand of ball," according to one yearbook accolade, the Hoyas won a resounding 55-36 decision over NYU, the metropolitan area's best team that year. In the other opening-round game, DePaul defeated Dartmouth, 46-35, as Mikan, acknowledged as one of the nation's premier big men, scored 20 points.

DePaul was favored in the Eastern finals and looked every bit a championship team in the first half of the game, holding a 28-23 lead at intermission with the magnificent Mikan playing the role of bully. "Mikan grabbed everything inside," recalls Reilly, "and we just got off to a terrible start." But after intermission, the Hoyas began shooting over and around Mikan instead of at him and, led by Mahnken, wound up with an upset 53-49 victory. "We won that game," Reilly recalls, "because Mahnken went to the corners and banged in four shots in a row. We pulled Mikan deep and then Mikan had to come out and play him. And once we got Mikan away from the basket, we did all right."

After climbing that mountain, the Hoyas slipped and fell on their way to the ultimate basketball summit in the NCAA finals. "If we had been able to defense Sailors, we could have beaten Wyoming," Reilly points out. "But our inability to stop Sailors was what hurt us. I had seen the jump shot before, but never that effective. Billy Hassett had him most of the night, but I don't want to blame him for letting Sailors score. We switched, too. Sailors was quick and had a marvelous jump shot. He could feint, go to the basket, pull up. He hit especially well from the top of the circle."

Sailors scored 16 points that night, twice as many as anyone on the floor, in Wyoming's 46-34 victory—a relatively low-scoring game for both teams. The Cowboys, down by five points early in the game and losing throughout most of the first half, took command at intermission, 18-16, on a burst of three field goals, the last by the ubiquitous Sailors.

Georgetown took a five-point lead in the second half before Wyoming scored 11 straight points behind the driving force of Komenich and Collins. When Wyoming later held a 37-31 lead, Georgetown edged closer with a brief flurry. But the champions finished off the team from Washington, D.C., with a run of nine points in the final 90 seconds. Georgetown was severely handicapped because Kraus was obliged to sit out most of the game due to foul trouble; and when he did play late in the contest, it was with less than his usual brilliance.

"Jimmy Collins actually won the NCAA championship game for us," Komenich reflects. "We were down late in the game and Jimmy came in and hit four quick buckets. He was outjumping Weir, Volker and myself."

The Cowboys hardly had enough time to digest their sweet victory in the NCAA finals when they were served with another challenge, playing NIT winner St. John's (N.Y.) in the first Red Cross charity game. Designed as an exhibition contest to help the war effort, it nevertheless was seen by some as a game to decide a true national champion and received the expected attention with a monster crowd of 18,316 at Madison Square Garden.

Wyoming didn't even need a pep talk in the so-called "Champion of Champions" game, beating an excellent St. John's team in overtime, 52-47.

Once touched by the magic of the Garden, the NCAA tournament would be golden. With the help of those enormous New York crowds in 1943, more than twice the number of people witnessed the NCAA games than the previous year. The total attendance of 56,876 for five nights of NCAA playoff action (two in Kansas City and three in New York) exceeded the old record set in 1941 by nearly 9,000. Of the total NCAA playoff figure in 1943, the Garden was responsible for almost 44,000 of the fans, with 30,576 witnessing the Eastern playoffs and 13,300 witnessing the finals.

"Madison Square Garden definitely had a big impact on the tournament," points out Dutch Lonborg, a longtime chairman of the tournament committee. "We always made money there."

It was through the urging of Ned Irish and Garden associate John Goldna that the championship finals were shifted to New York for a six-year period starting in 1943 and played the big town again in 1950. "Ned and John would always come to the basketball coaches' meetings to talk to us about it," Lonborg remembers.

The total impact on the NCAA tournament of the "New York Experience"—the crowds, the exposure, the prestige—was plainly evident.

36

DESTINY'S STEPCHILDREN

The Second World War hit America's sports scene hard in the midsection but didn't knock it out. As a morale factor, the nation decided to keep athletics going during wartime as long as possible. Of course, there was a reduction of quality and a shortage of help in all fields.

Like everyone else, the University of Utah basketball team was affected. The Utes had begun the 1943-44 season without a home court, thanks to the Army, which had appropriated the field house. So coach Vadal Peterson did the next best thing—he appropriated the church gym. Then there was the matter of opponents. Utah's Skyline Conference had suspended operations, and Peterson had to scrounge for teams to play. It was said that his toughest job that season was not beating college teams but finding them. He found only three—Weber State, Idaho State and Colorado—and beat them all. The rest of Utah's regular-season victories were fashioned against service and industrial teams, many of which featured former college stars and all of which held a big advantage over the Utes in experience. Utah's best player, in fact, was only a freshman: Arnie Ferrin—"a 6-3½ collection of bones, bright red cheeks and a hank of blond hair," according to one writer—and the average age of the Utes was 18½ years.

That this exuberant team found itself in the NCAA tournament that year was a turn of fate. That the Utes won the national championship however, was no accident. Relative babies in the college basketball world at the start of the season, Utah's players grew up in a hurry while being thrown into the arena against the likes of the Salt Lake Air Base and the Fort Warren Army team.

"That definitely made us a better team that year," says Wat Misaka, one of the guards on Utah's 1944 national champions. "I learned a lot of things myself. I remember there was one former Long Island University player who played for the Salt Lake Air Base and pulled some tricks on me that I never had seen before or since.

"Playing against experienced ball players like that really toughened us," adds Misaka.

Choreographed by Peterson and his able assistant, Sherman "Pete" Couch, the Utes' rhythm was established by Ferrin, a great-grandson of a pioneer who struggled across the plains with Brigham Young to found Salt Lake City in 1847. "Ferrin was a money player," remembers John Mooney, sports editor of the Salt Lake Tribune. "He could rise to the heights in the big games." Ferrin was at his best in the NCAA finals against Dartmouth on March 28, 1944, at Madison Square Garden, scoring 22 points in Utah's overtime 42-40 victory. His long hair flying as he rushed downcourt, the blond bomber was the adored figure of the crowds and the favorite of the sports writers who voted for the tourney's most valuable player that year.

"Ferrin could jump into orbit," notes Joe Vancisin, who played for Dartmouth, "and it was obvious that the Utah team was built around him."

There was no doubt that the star forward was Peterson's pet, right or wrong, for better or worse. Usually it was for the better. "Peterson treated all the guys the same, with the exception of Arnie," says Mooney. "He was really tough on all of them and had one or two guys who were really his whipping boys, like Dick Smuin and Wat Misaka. Some of the guys would do something bad, and he would chew them out; and Arnie would do the same thing right back again, just for the hell of it, and Vadal wouldn't say anything. Ferrin made Vadal, as far as that was concerned, and I guess he knew it."

Somehow, whatever Ferrin did turned out right, anyway. Remembers Mooney:

"In one of the games, Smuin tried a running hook shot across the keyhole. It was never worth a damn, but it looked good. I think he shot 12 or 14 times that one game and didn't make a basket, and Vadal was so damned mad. Then Arnie would go out there, run across the keyhole and hook and, of course, Arnie would make 'em. One other time, Arnie had been fooling around, kind of holding the ball with both hands over his head, giving it a little

flip at the basket. He was about 6-foot-4, so he was taller than some of the guys he played. In this particular game, Utah was getting beat and the other team was sagging on the center and throwing up an awfully tight zone and Utah couldn't get in for a shot. So Arnie stationed himself outside the foul perimeter and put the ball over his head and flipped in about three or four. Then, of course, the other team came out of its zone and the Utes ran at them and beat them. After the ball game, Vadal was telling everybody how he and Arnie had developed this shot. But Arnie says he was doing it in practice one day and Vadal was screaming his head off at him for using the shot."

Like the rest of the Utah team, Ferrin was a local product, growing up in the shadow of the Salt Lake City skyline. The remainder of the top six players—"good Mormons who didn't drink or smoke," according to Mooney—included Smuin at the other forward position, Misaka in the backcourt along with Herb Wilkinson and Fred Lewis, and Fred Sheffield, a unique 6-1 center who was the NCAA's high-jump champion.

"They all played good defense," notes Mooney. "They usually took only high-percentage shots. Vadal was strong, a smart coach. He didn't relate well to his players, but as far as knowing basketball, he knew as much as anybody. Mr. Couch, his assistant, was a great scout. He could see a team and pick out weaknesses as well as anybody could in those days, and he was a hell of a guy and bridged the gap to the players."

Peterson developed a unique style at Utah in the 1930s, remembers Mooney. "He was one of the first guys to start shooting foul pitches with the one-handed push shot. I remember when I first went out to Utah in 1939, I did a feature story about the way we used to shoot between our legs and the push shot started by Peterson. Vadal had a theory that you could guide the ball better that way. And, of course, they all became a bunch of great one-hand shooters."

These Utah players did a lot of running as well as a lot of shooting. They worked hard to get free for their one-handers and played a sticky, aggressive defense. "There was rarely a rest where Peterson was concerned," recalls Misaka. "Vadal just believed in getting his athletes in condition and then staying with them all the way. That is the kind of pattern he followed his whole coaching career. He'd get about seven or eight guys playing, and the others would never get into the game. Of course, we were very adept at keeping our fouls to a minimum. We had to be, with the lack of depth we had. Peterson taught defense that way. He'd always tell us to get position first. That was his whole

Utah's Arnie Ferrin (22), shown here against Kentucky, was the most outstanding player in the 1944 championship. Utah defeated Dartmouth, 42-40, in overtime to win the title.

confidence. I know I considered myself a very clean-type player. I prided myself on not fouling very much."

Peterson brought one of two distinct styles to the Skyline Conference. The other belonged to Colorado's Frosty Cox. "Colorado was much more physical than Peterson's teams," Mooney points out. "They were using rolling screens, and they would put you up in the seats with a hard body check. Utah had a bunch of skinny kids, and there wasn't any of them that was built well enough to stand that kind of wear and tear in the pivot. But Utah was a terrific team to watch, from a fan's viewpoint. The Utes would come running down the floor, running like hell, and putting up those spectacular one-handed shots."

NCAA officials had their eyes on the Utah team that season and when it came time to give out bids for the tournament, they asked the Utes to appear in their Western regional in Kansas City. But when the NCAA refused to guarantee Utah's expenses, Peterson balked.

"Financially, the NIT was a better tournament at that time," remembers Ferrin, "and we declined the bid to the NCAA tourney." Mooney explains: "The NIT was where the money was then for the colleges. If the teams had their druthers, they took the NIT over the NCAA because they made more money there. The NCAA, when the games were held in Kansas City, was pretty small in comparison. You'd rather go to New York. There was more exposure there. If a guy like Ferrin had a good game in New York, he could make all-America."

Shortly after turning down the NCAA bid, Peterson got a phone call from Ned Irish, director of the NIT.

"We need an eighth team to complete the National Invitation roster," Irish said. "It'll be a tough field for your kids, but we thought maybe . . ." Before Irish had a chance to finish his sentence, Peterson accepted. "Mister," said the Utah coach, "we'll come anywhere we can get a decent game."

But the combination of the long train ride to New York—nearly 2,300 miles—the big city and Kentucky proved too much for the Utes in the NIT's first round. They lost, 46-38, and Peterson said disconsolately, "The kids were a little tight playing for the first time in the NIT, a little gawky-eyed at all the people. They're a young bunch. They only average 18 years. I wish we could

38

NCAA

play here again."

The Utah players were heartsick after that loss, Ferrin remembers. "We're sitting around thinking, how could that happen to us?" Their salvation, however, came shortly thereafter when a phone rang in Peterson's room. The call was from NCAA officials, who were in an exasperated state. Arkansas, the team that had accepted the bid Utah originally had turned down, was forced to withdraw after two of its leading players were seriously hurt in an automobile accident. Utah was asked to substitute, and the Utes agreed, after Peterson was assured that his financial demands would be met. Now jubilant at the new life afforded Utah, Ferrin said triumphantly, "We'll be back here in a week to play the Eastern NCAA champ."

"The coach kind of left it up to us to make the decision," recalls Misaka. "He called us together and said, 'Listen, you guys, we have this opportunity to go to the NCAA playoffs. But if we do go, that means packing up your bag right now, leaving New York. We haven't even had a chance to see the town. There's a few sights that you probably would like to see . . .' Most of us had never been to

New York before. He said if we went to Kansas City and lost, we'd have to go directly home from there and miss everything. And he seemed to be trying to talk us out of going, in a way. It was strange, but that was the feeling that all of us got. We were unanimous in our vote to attend the NCAAs. We said, the heck with it, let's give it a whirl. Financially, we had done okay in the NIT; and we had played Kentucky a respectable game, even though we didn't play our best. We weren't overwhelmed or embarrassed, or anything like that. From that standpoint, we had made a good showing for some green kids out of the West. So I guess Peterson was kind of satisfied with letting it go at that. But I was real proud of the kids, thinking back on it now, that we were unanimous in voting for the NCAA playoff bid—and not just mildly so."

And so the Utes got back on a train, this time headed for Kansas City and an unknown destiny. The trip required almost three days due to the erratic schedules caused by moving wartime troops. Utah made history the night of March 24 without firing a shot, becoming the first team to participate in both NIT and NCAA competition in

the same season. Utah, a team that had been invited to the NCAA tournament because of necessity, then took an easy 45-35 victory over Missouri, a team that had been invited for reasons of proximity. Utah's victory was a surprise to some, though, Misaka remembers. "I think they expected us to just show up, fill the spot and lose, and go on home and let the eventual winner of the Western regionals go on to New York. That's the kind of feeling we got, but it really helped us get up for the game." Ferrin scored 12 points for Utah and "dazzled Missouri with his speed and aggressiveness," according to one writer.

Iowa State, which had defeated Pepperdine, 44-39, despite Nick Buzolich's 22 points in the other Western semifinal game, was a stiffer challenge for Utah. One of Lou Menze's best teams, the Cyclones had won their first Big Six title in a decade with such players as Price Brookfield (transferred by the Navy from West Texas State), Jim Meyers and the Wehde twins, Roy and Ray. Utah's newly crowned "Blitz Kids" took an early lead, and Iowa State came back after the halftime intermission to catch up with them eight minutes into the second half. It wasn't until seven minutes were left in the game that Misaka's two straight field goals gave Utah the lead for good, and it wasn't until the end that Utah could be certain of a 40-31 victory. "The entire last half was bitterly waged by the finalists," reported Paul O'Boynick of the Kansas City Star, "but those blitz kids outscrapped the co-champions of the Big Six in the closing minutes. No more than five points ever separated the teams in the final half, which kept the crowd (6,000 in Kansas City's Municipal Auditorium) in an uproar. The score was knotted twice, and the lead changed hands as many times before Peterson's scrappy young aggregation spurted in the closing minutes to pull away to a safe margin." Ferrin was double-teamed and held to six points, but he controlled the ball, dribbling with either hand and passing cleverly to the open man. Sheffield, playing only part-time because of an injured ankle, and Misaka were the recipients of many of Ferrin's passes, scoring nine points each to lead the Utah offense. "Ferrin was brilliant at dribbling left-handed although he is right-handed," noted O'Boynick. "He goes southpaw to perplex rivals. He is versatile. When he lost his touch at the art of goalmaking against Iowa State, Ferrin took over guarding duties." About this latter aspect of Ferrin's multifaceted game, Peterson said in the glow of victory, "It was his able handling of defense that helped Utah to the championship."

Meanwhile, in the Eastern playoffs in New York, Ohio State had eliminated Temple, 57-47; and

Dartmouth, a unique melange of wartime transfers, had crushed subpar Catholic University, 63-38. For the regional championship, Dartmouth held off several Ohio State comebacks and beat the favored Buckeyes, 60-53. Earl Brown, who had played for George Keogan at Notre Dame, was a wartime coaching replacement for Osborne Cowles at Hanover and won a seventh straight Ivy League title with this pickup squad composed of Navy and Marine reservists. Uniquely, many of them were not at Dartmouth at the start of the season. "We went through the season with two distinct teams," recalls Vancisin, who was one of the few who stayed with Dartmouth from start to finish that year. "We started out the year strictly with Dartmouth guys like myself, Audley Brindley and John Monahan. Then the rest were shipped out to other schools and in came a new batch of cadets for our V-12 program." These included Harry Leggat, a Marine transfer from NYU, and Cornell's Bob Gale. By tournament time, the Navy's V-12 program had given Dartmouth another bonus in Dick McGuire, the St. John's star.

Ohio State had been favored to beat this fine team, perhaps because of Dartmouth's repeated failures in tournament play. But the Big Green endured in the Eastern finals as Brindley outplayed Buckeye star Arnie Risen and McGuire shackled high-scoring Don Grate. "Ohio State came in with one of its typical big, physical teams, with football players on it," Vancisin recalls. "We had seen the Buckeyes play Temple in the opener of the Eastern playoffs and knew that Risen was a threat. The game plan was to double-team him, put someone in front and in back of him."

While Utah's players were en route to New York by train, they were blissfully unaware that some melodrama would be added to the NCAA finals. St. John's had been making some history of its own in the NIT by defeating DePaul, 47-39, to win an unprecedented second straight title in that tournament. As NIT winners, the Redmen were to meet the eventual NCAA champion in the annual Red Cross game, a wartime benefit contest, and sat back to await the outcome of the Dartmouth-Utah finals. On the eve of the NCAA championship game, however, it was announced by the Department of the Navy that Dartmouth would not be permitted to play in the Red Cross game. As Ferrin remembers it, "Dartmouth got notice from their military people that they had been off-base as long as they could be; win or lose, they couldn't play in the Red Cross game. That became an interesting pressure for us in the NCAA finals. We didn't want to play the NIT champion as a loser. That would have been just terrible."

40

As it turned out, they didn't have to. Using a gambling defense that Peterson called a "pickup" to shut off Gale and Brindley and buoyed by Ferrin's high-powered offensive game, the Utes squeezed by Dartmouth on a shot by Wilkinson with three seconds left in overtime. Peterson's plan was to double-team Gale and Brindley with the ball, hoping that the other Dartmouth players would be reluctant to shoot. The strategy worked, although Utah never could pull away by more than four points. The Utes led, 36-32, with a minute left, but Gale tapped in a rebound to cut the deficit to two points; and with three seconds remaining, McGuire made a set shot for Dartmouth to send the game into overtime. On the verge of exhaustion, Ferrin kept the Utes even with the Big Green in the extra period, scoring four of his 22 points to help establish a 40-40 tie. As the final seconds ticked off, Wilkinson worked himself loose behind the free-throw circle and arched a one-hander toward the basket. The ball hung on the back of the rim for an instant, then dropped through for Utah's winning points.

"The game obviously could have gone either way," says Vancisin. "Our kid Brindley was a fine pivot man but rather frail, and as a result Utah hurt us on the boards. The thing that mostly sticks out in my mind about that game is that the coaches put a lot of strategic weight in the substitution system. They would send in subs all the time to stop the clock instead of calling timeouts, and there would always be players lined up at the scorer's table to get into the game."

A crowd of 15,000—largest in the history of the NCAA tournament for a single game—witnessed the dramatic finals, swelling the overall count for that year to a record 59,369, and this provided Harold Olsen with the luxury of self-indulgence. "Once again, the NCAA basketball tournament, held under war conditions, proved to be very successful, from the standpoint of both competition and attendance," the chairman of the NCAA Basketball Tournament Committee wrote in his annual report of tournament administration. He gave bouquets to tournament directors R. E. Peters in Kansas and A. B. Nixon, "assisted by J. W. St. Clair and Ned Irish," in New York. "While the representation of teams in the tournament was not as nationwide as usual, this fact did not seem to make much difference to the spectators."

The key, of course, was the participation of Madison Square Garden. Held there for the second year in a row, the NCAA playoffs continued to grow in the Garden hot house.

Ten days after the NCAA finals, 18,125 filled the famous arena to watch the Red Cross benefit contest, billed as the "Champion of Champions" game by promoters; and it was obviously Utah that many of them came to see. The splendid irony of the moment was evident to the patrons who cheered the charismatic Utes as they came on the floor for their warm-ups. Now they were no longer a mystery team. Even the fans in the upper reaches of the Garden's nose-bleed section knew the names of Ferrin, Sheffield, Smuin, Lewis, Wilkinson and Misaka, a group of Mormon youngsters who had fought against overwhelming odds just to be there. Now they had the chance to redeem themselves for their first-round loss in the NIT and to do it in style by beating the tourney champion.

"It got my adrenaline up," Misaka remembers, "and I'm sure it did for the rest of the players. We could hardly keep still."

The game earned $35,000 for the war effort, but that was nothing compared to what it earned in goodwill for the Utah basketball program. Ferrin provided the inspiration and the playmaking, while Misaka contributed the perspiration on defense; and when the first half ended in a 19-19 tie, there was no question who was the crowd's favorite. This was underscored at the start of the second half when the Utes were greeted by a deafening ovation. Buoyed by what amounted to a home-court atmosphere, Utah scored nine straight points midway through the second half and beat the favored Redmen, 43-36, to complete one of the most unique and stirring comebacks in sports history.

"I know Cinderella is really a cliche," says Mooney, "but actually there's no other way to describe that season. It was either a fluke, or the Good Lord was looking after that Utah team. Talk about chance. If possible, the NCAA could have gotten another good team like Texas Christian, say, for the Western regional to replace Arkansas; but they would have had to go to Washington to get them excused and they couldn't do that on the spur of the moment. Most of the good teams couldn't travel—so Utah was coming back on a train from the NIT and somebody at the NCAA got the bright idea to grab the Utes as they came through Omaha or Kansas City, or something. I guess they figured they had a ready-made team from the West there and it wouldn't cost them anything. It was just one of those strange turns of fate."

Mooney paused, reflecting on karma.

"It's funny, isn't it? If Arkansas' players had not gotten hurt in that car crash, and if the NCAA had not reconsidered Utah, then they would have never heard of Arnie Ferrin and the '44 Utes . . ."

41

A GIANT ARISES

"After watching the Oklahoma Aggies take their second straight NCAA basketball title, you find it hard to write about anything but Bob Kurland. You remember Bob when he first played in New York four years ago—a lanky, awkward seven-footer who galloped around the court with his shoulders bowed in an obvious effort to minimize his great height. He was only 17 then, lacking in coordination and skill and painfully embarrassed because of the publicity given his size. You remember him the next year as a goaltender, heavier, stronger, straighter... you remember him in last year's Champion of Champions game with DePaul, when he was guarded by 6-foot-9 George Mikan, the polished all-America, and how Mikan fouled out as Bob faked and feinted him and Kurland went on to lead his team to victory. Last Tuesday's performance is something you won't forget soon . . . at 21, Kurland still isn't a finished player, but he's a good, all-around player. It wasn't just his height, for Bob's best shots came on difficult hook shots; and he also played the role of feeder and defensive star. Of the Aggies' 16 baskets, Kurland scored nine and passed for three more . . . it was a grand farewell to the fans who have watched him develop. If anyone tries to talk about the 'evils' of basketball, you can tell him what a good game and a good coach have done for this boy who might have gone through life thinking of himself as a freak."—Hugh Fullerton of The Associated Press after the 1946 NCAA championship game in Madison Square Garden

The United States wrote off $25 billion in lend-lease aid to Great Britain after the Second World War, underscoring the euphoric level of prosperity that existed in America at the time. The era was the most affluent in the country's history to that point, and the college basketball world was one of the chief benefactors of this happy situation—in artistic as well as financial terms.

As the johnnies came marching home to join their destinies with the "American Dream," they replenished the nation's rosters, lending maturity and a new-found authority to the sport. Because the quality of basketball was thus upgraded sharply during this lush postwar period and the competition was painfully more intense, Oklahoma A&M's (now Oklahoma State) accomplishment takes a revered place in NCAA annals.

The Aggies enjoyed the distinction of winning two straight NCAA championships, in 1945 and 1946, thus becoming the first team in history to pull off that unique double play. And they did it in one of the toughest of basketball worlds, facing a flow of widespread incoming talent provided by

the end of the war.

"As kids, we really didn't realize the importance of winning those back-to-back championships and what a great accomplishment that was," says Bob "Foothills" Kurland, the highly decorated center on those Aggie teams. "In those days, you didn't have all the interest and coverage you have today. We just took it as a matter of course. Now that we look back on it, however, we realize it was pretty unusual." (Only four other schools in NCAA history have won titles in consecutive years—UCLA, San Francisco, Cincinnati and Kentucky.)

When Kurland arrived at Oklahoma A&M during the war years, he joined a growing program under the brilliant administration of Henry Iba, a coach renowned for his extraordinary patience. The Aggies' ascendancy had begun when Iba took over the coaching job in the 1930s and installed his deliberate system with the philosophy that it is not too bad to lose occasionally as long as you do not lose badly. Actually, Iba rarely lost at all. Before he arrived, the Aggies had lost all too frequently, never having reigned as Missouri Valley Confer-

ence champion. Iba's first year at Oklahoma A&M produced a .500 season, the school's best in 10 years but the worst he would have for two decades. When he retired as a college coach in 1970, Iba's 767 victories, including stops at Maryville (Missouri) Teachers College and Colorado, placed him third on the all-time winning list. Iba's success was based on a rigid system of ball control and defense, holding mistakes to a minimum. On offense, his teams ran set plays off constantly repeated patterns; and no one dared show any impatience.

"It was all pretty cut and dried, the way we played," Kurland remembers. "Once we set up the routine, as far as offense and defense go, we pretty much stuck with it. We were not an emotional team in the sense that we played on emotion. We played on a plan. We were never in a situation where it was dependent on emotion, where we had to 'get up' for a particular game. If things went wrong, we always looked at why the system wasn't working rather than criticize an individual or worry about the other team. We thought if we'd play our style, we'd win."

Kurland, one of the most publicized big men in the sport, melted into this total team concept despite his originality as a player. Before Kurland's arrival, Iba had great success without the help of a high-powered scorer. After Kurland left, Iba would continue along the same high road. But it was this well-coordinated seven-footer who provided him with his trip to the mountaintop with the two

Oklahoma State University

NCAA titles.

Kurland was not a natural shooter but worked hard to develop a variety of shots to go with his natural dunk. "I was only 17 and a big, clumsy kid when I started at Oklahoma A&M," Kurland recalls. "But coach Iba had the confidence that I could do the job and the patience to work with me. He instilled confidence in me to come ahead and work hard, and it took a heck of a lot of work to get to the point that we did."

At the top of his game, Kurland was the dominating factor on any court. He used his height and strength to control the backboards and to squash opponents' offensive manuevers. "Kurland made our type of game go," Iba says. "We knew he could get us the ball, so we never had to rush into a bad shot." Kurland was not especially known for his speed, but it did not matter in Iba's painstaking style of play. After grabbing a rebound, Kurland would pass the ball to a teammate; and while the big, red-haired center lumbered up court, the rest of the Oklahoma A&M team would nonchalantly set up a play. Then, with Kurland in position, the Aggies would either pass to him under the basket, cut off him for a layup or use his huge frame for a screen on a shot. While one of the country's leading scorers in the mid-1940s, Kurland perhaps made more of a name for himself on defense. An adept shot-blocker, Kurland perfected the goal-tending technique, knocking away a shot just before the ball reached the basket. It was the proficiency in this area by such big men as Kurland that led to the emergence of the goaltending rule.

An awesome, moon-faced giant out of Jennings (Missouri) High School, Kurland was wooed by many but won by Oklahoma A&M for the cost of a steak dinner, a bus ticket to Stillwater for a three-day tryout and a room-and-board scholarship. Kurland still remembers the steak dinner, and for good reason.

"Oklahoma A&M was in the Missouri Valley Conference at the time," says Kurland, "so they came to St. Louis for a game one weekend; and on a Sunday afternoon, I was invited to have dinner with the team. We went to a place on 'The Hill' in St. Louis and had our meal at a very fancy Italian restaurant. These were the Depression years as far as our family was concerned, and I had never seen a steak as big and as thick as the one that we got for dinner. That incident probably warmed me up to the players and to Mr. Iba as much as anything."

Later, Kurland went out to see the school and

43

Bob Kurland of Oklahoma A&M, the tournament's most outstanding player in 1945 and 1946, in the Aggies' 43-40 triumph over North Carolina in 1946.

was further impressed with the situation. "My interest then was getting the opportunity to go to college. Oklahoma A&M was a good engineering school, and I was interested in engineering at the time. Also, I had heard a lot of wonderful things about Iba from my high school coach. So, Oklahoma A&M had the assurance of a continued program, the integrity of Iba, an engineering school and, I think, it had the kind of people that I fitted in best with."

Kurland was bused to a three-day tryout in which he had to prove himself. He did. Iba offered him a scholarship but warned, "I don't know whether you'll play or not; but if you enroll and try to make the team and keep up your school work, you'll get room and board for four years."

The Kurland-Iba marriage was made in basketball heaven. In his freshman year, 1942-43, Kurland was used sparingly by Iba as Oklahoma A&M finished second in the league race. But in 1943-44, when the Missouri Valley Conference suspended its official schedule due to the war, Kurland was not only a regular but an all-America. The Aggies had a 26-4 record that season, losing only to service teams, and earned a trip to the National Invitation Tournament in New York. The following season, with the league still inoperative, the Aggies were even stronger. The new goaltending rule prevented Kurland from exercising that special talent, but in Iba's mind it made the seven-foot star a better all-around player. Kurland had a wonderful supporting cast in the 1944-45 season as well—Cecil Hankins, Weldon Kern, Doyle Parrack, J. L. Parks and Blake Williams. With a 23-4 record, the Aggies were invited to compete in the NCAA tournament. They beat Utah and Arkansas handily in the Western playoffs and then a splendid New York University team in the national finals.

"They were pretty mechanical games for us," Kurland says, reflecting on the 62-37 rout of defending NCAA champion Utah and the 68-41 decision over Arkansas in Kansas City. Kurland was described as "the answer to any coach's prayer" by Paul O'Boynick of the Kansas City Star. Writing about the Western championship game, O'Boynick said: "The Aggies controlled the sphere from the very start and put up such a strong defense that the Porkers were forced to shoot from long range, and the results weren't effective. It was the smooth and consistent play of the Aggies which amazed the fans. Those Cowboys made few, if any, wrong moves on the floor and with Kurland doing a great job of rebounding and passing off, the Aggies had all the answers."

Arkansas had done considerably better in the Western semifinals, edging Oregon, 79-76, in the

wildest-scoring tournament game to that point. The wide-open contest provided the highest score by both teams in championship history; the total of 155 beat the record of 119 set by the Dartmouth-North Carolina game in 1941. The patrons at the Kansas City Municipal Auditorium were "stunned" by the prolific point-making, according to O'Boynick. "The fans were busy trying to keep up with the big scoreboard. The teams maintained a 3.8 points-a-minute pace over the 40-minute period and through the first half averaged four points a minute with an 81 total."

Oklahoma A&M, which itself had far surpassed its scoring average in the Western playoffs, came down to earth in the NCAA finals at Madison Square Garden against a rugged NYU team. Howard Cann's players were no shrinking Violets when it came to playing hard-hitting basketball.

"It was an awfully, awfully rough game," recalls Iba about Oklahoma A&M's 49-45 triumph over NYU for the national title. "Howard Cann and I have talked about it a good many times. Dolph Schayes played against us, I remember; and with him in the ball game, it became almost a typical game like we played. They were trying to go under the basket all the time. They were very patient, too, even though they were the kind of ball club that had good shooters off the playgrounds of New York. When they got with us, they worked that ball pretty good. The ball game was close all the way. It was really and truly a rough game, physically. We had pretty good aggressiveness on the boards; and they did, too. I remember one of our kids, I think it was Parks, they knocked him clear under our bench. Because we'd been in the Garden so many times before, we had picked up some people who were for us and against New York University. Maybe it was Long Island University people or City College people, but I remember they got a chant for us going in the crowd. That helped make that ball game pretty rough. But, of course, the NYU Violets had real good backing in New York."

The NCAA final was a "typical Garden ball game," according to Iba. "When I say that, that's not explaining much to the public, but they were always hotly contested. In those days, when you got behind by four points, you didn't take a bad shot. See, there wasn't a whole lot of outside shooting overall. The team that did the best outside shooting was City College. But when you got down to the finals in New York City, you didn't take many chances.

The legendary Henry Iba, discussing strategy with his 1946 championship team from Oklahoma A&M.

"I'll tell you another way it was. There was a little different interpretation on the handling of a dribble. Anytime we got close to a team in New York, we'd always come up court slow 'cause if we tried to come up fast, they'd call us for palming the basketball. So we tried to do two things: release it to somebody rather than dribble and, if we did dribble, dribble it slow. There was a way you had to play when you went into New York; there wasn't any question about that."

As closely as the teams were matched, only the perfect execution of Oklahoma A&M's plays allowed the Aggies to survive. "The big thing in that ball game," says Iba, "is that it never got out of hand for us. You get some ball games that get out of hand, where you're behind eight or 10 points. That never did happen. That thing seesawed back and forth. And I remember we did an awfully good job of getting that ball to Kurland that night. That's the reason we won." (Kurland scored 22 points.)

Kurland was also given a "100 per cent rating" for his defensive play by one writer: "The Aggie giant planted himself in the right spot every time an NYU rally started; and during the highly exciting contest between the Eastern and Western division champions, Kurland saw to it that he and his Aggie teammates had possession of the ball at least three quarters of the entire playing time. The Aggies were too strong for the New York five, especially with their airtight defense. NYU's shots from the outside went amiss, and there were too many Oklahomans patrolling the inside to permit the Violet to crash through to the inside."

With less than four minutes remaining, only four points separated the teams. The same was true with one minute left, but NYU missed several shots near the end. "The Violet-clad forwards were pressing too hard, and passes usually safe and sure went wild in the excitement of trying to catch the tall Oklahoma aggregation," said one observer.

Kurland still winces at NYU's raw physical power. "That was a rough team—not so terribly tall, but physically rough. They had a kid named (Frank) Mangiapane, and he was a real tough kid.

45

Oklahoma State University

They played a hard, driving game; but if we beat them in any one area, we beat them on the backboards, where they weren't that tall."

The Violets, a "bunch of poor neighborhood kids who thought they could beat anybody," according to Mangiapane, had qualified for the title game with a dramatic 70-65 overtime victory over Ohio State in the Eastern playoffs at Madison Square Garden. They had beaten Tufts, 59-44, in the opening-round game but appeared to be hopelessly out of the Eastern championship game when Ohio State held a 62-52 lead with two minutes remaining. At this point, however, Buckeye star Arnie Risen fouled out, the New Yorkers halted the clock with continuous substitutions and Don Forman finally tied the score with a long set shot two seconds before the end of regulation play. The Buckeyes matched the Violets bruise for bruise in that contest, Mangiapane remembers. "They had a big, tough, physical team. It was a Big Ten tradition—I guess a carryover from their football teams. They always had some of their football players in the lineup."

NYU's style exemplified the "City Game" as much as any team in New York. The Violets were truly children of the playgrounds. It was easy to see that Howard Cann had recruited his players from New York schools. "It was continuous movement," explains Mangiapane. "We were more free-lance in our offensive approach, rather than use set plays all the time. We had those, too, but a lot of times we had freedom on the court. We liked to drive hard, pass off and we moved well without the ball. I guess you might call us 'loose.' "

Sid Tannenbaum was the acknowledged star of that NYU team, and Dolph Schayes was a diamond in the rough. Remembers Kurland: "Dolph came into the ball game and of course was a great high school player and had great potential. But he was young, and they had to use him at center. He was just not mature enough at that point to really carry the mail."

Attendance records continued to be set, thanks to the use of Madison Square Garden for the third straight championship game. A record crowd of 18,035 in the finals ("people with their feet nearly on the court and the top of the arena blacked out by smoke," says Kurland) boosted the overall attendance for the seventh national tournament to 67,780, a playoff record. Another full house was guaranteed by the wartime-inspired Red Cross benefit game between the NCAA and NIT winners, unofficially recognized as the "Champion of Champions" game. This one received more than the usual share of publicity because of the heralded battle between Kurland and DePaul's George

Mikan, literally and figuratively the two giants of the game in that period.

With the help of the 6-10 Mikan, DePaul had made a shambles of the NIT record book. The Demons set 10 team marks and Mikan accounted for 10 individual records, including a 53-point performance against Rhode Island, presaging his impending duel with Kurland.

The game was decided in the first half, when Kurland baited Mikan and lured him into foul trouble. The DePaul star lasted about 14 minutes before fouling out with only nine points. Kurland, cautiously playing with four fouls the rest of the way, wound up with 14 points.

The final score of 52-44 reflected not only the relative strengths of the teams but also indicated the distance that the NCAA championship had traveled since the trailblazing year of 1939. Harold Olsen and the rest of the tournament forefathers could beam with pride at their invention now that the NCAA winner was widely recognized as a true national champion. The NIT, for one, had no way to argue the point, since its champions had been beaten three straight times by the NCAA winner in the Red Cross benefit games. In the early years, the NIT had been recognized as the more prestigious tournament, basically because the money and publicity were in New York.

Ironically, it was Ned Irish's beloved Madison Square Garden that eventually helped push the NCAA tournament to the forefront. Enthralled by the magnetism of New York City, the NCAA held the championship game there for an extended period of time. The finals took place in Madison Square Garden seven times in an eight-year period, from 1943 through 1950, inspiring a growing legion of followers. As two-time champion, Oklahoma A&M was in the middle of this stunning growth. In 1946, the finals were televised for the first time by station WCBS-TV; and it was estimated that 500,000 persons watched on television as Oklahoma A&M defeated North Carolina, 43-40, in the championship game. Movies of the finals were made for the first time that year and were available to the participating teams to view at a later date.

As to format, the NCAA added a new wrinkle. The size of the field remained at eight, but for the first time four teams were brought to the site of the finals, introducing the third-place game. Ohio State, the beaten Eastern finalist, defeated Western finalist California, 63-45, for third place prior to the championship game. This doubleheader format obviously appealed to the fans, for they virtually tore down the gates to get into the Garden. The newly established energy of the NCAA tournament expressed itself with a record 18,479 watch-

46

ing the finals and a whopping total of 73,116 for all the playoff dates. For the first time in the eight-year history of the NCAA tournament, receipts were over $100,000. The two finalists received $4,500 each, the two teams playing for third place got $4,000 and the other four teams earned $3,000 apiece. This slicing of the pie differed from past practices in that it recognized the extra game played by the third-place competitors.

The 1945-46 tournament concluded a banner year for Oklahoma A&M. With the resumption of league play, the Aggies played fewer service teams and wound up with an even better record than the previous season, 28-2. They won all 12 of their Missouri Valley Conference games and then defeated Big Six champion Kansas, 49-38, to become District 5 representatives in the Western playoffs.

Bowling Green had provided Oklahoma A&M with a strong motivational factor by upsetting the Aggies early in the season. Iba says: "I remember Kurland getting everybody together in the back of the bus for a meeting after that one. I never asked him what he said, but it was the right thing." After that talk, Oklahoma A&M won 15 straight games, including the NCAA title.

Even Iba's deliberate style could not keep the scoring down on that team. The starters—Kern, Williams, Parks and Sam Aubrey—all made the Missouri Valley's all-conference team along with Kurland, a three-time all-America. That year, Kurland scored a school-record 58 points against St. Louis University and finished with an average of nearly 20 points a game. But it is likely that he contributed as many assists as baskets to a team that exemplified the perfect spirit of togetherness and discipline. "I don't think we had any tremendously outstanding athletes as such," Kurland says. "I had the advantage of size. We had better-than-average athletes but not great ones. But I've never seen a team before or since that could execute Mr. Iba's strategy as well."

In terms of style, the 1946 championship team was a duplicate of 1945. However, there were noticeable differences to Kurland. "In 1945, Parks and Williams were not that physically mature. They were better in the second year. And A. L. Bennett came back and played in the 1946 season. He really added to us as far as our guards were concerned. We had more total maturity in the 1946 season and the experience of having played through and felt the pressure of a tournament . . . and that's a big asset."

The 1946 team played without Hankins, whom Kurland calls "probably the best athlete we had and the backbone of that 1945 team. He could shoot, run, play well in all categories. He really rounded out the offense in terms of adding the ability to drive." And the Aggies not only welcomed Bennett into their fold, but Aubrey, perhaps the most dramatic element of the 1946 champions.

"Aubrey had been shot over in Italy," Kurland remembers, "and he came to school on crutches when I saw him in the spring of 1945. Nobody expected him to walk, much less play. But there he was in the lineup later that year. I think the highlight of that whole NCAA tournament as far as I was concerned was seeing Sam Aubrey, who was the first-string guard, standing there on that team that had won a national championship. That is the kind of thing you remember."

Even more memorable was Kurland's performance that year. The Aggies encountered little difficulty in beating Baylor, 44-29, and California, 52-35, in the Western playoffs in Kansas City before defeating North Carolina, 43-40, in a tense national final in New York. In all three games, the Aggie center was the difference; and his dominating play justifiably earned him the most outstanding player award in the tourney for the second straight year. "Kurland spun off the post, tipped in or jammed home semilong pokes for goals 12 times in 23 attempts for an amazing 52.1 percentage," exuded Dan Partner of the Kansas City Star after the Aggie star scored 29 points against California. Kurland, who had scored 20 against Baylor in the Western opener, also was applauded for other facets of his game by the Star writer: "In addition to his scoring, Bob hogged the rebounds and handled the ball flawlessly while passing off for numerous goals. He was the brightest of the many stars who performed in the event."

Iba is hoisted to the shoulders of players after one of his many wins at Oklahoma A&M.

Oklahoma State University

47

While Oklahoma A&M qualified with ease for the national finals, the same could not be said for North Carolina. The Tar Heels defeated New York University, 57-49, in a rugged game and then had to go into overtime to beat sturdy Ohio State, 60-57, in the Eastern finals. The Ohio State game had a strange beginning in that the two teams, featuring some of the nation's top scorers, played scoreless ball for the first 5:20. Ironically, it was the second straight overtime defeat in the Eastern finals for Ohio State and coach Harold Olsen. "We couldn't scout the Buckeyes; all we did was read about them in the newspapers," recalls Ben Carnevale, the North Carolina coach that year. "But we knew they were the Big Ten champions and had a lot of respect for them because of that. The Big Ten was always a tough league, and we knew that they played very physical basketball there."

Carnevale was more familiar with NYU. He had played there in the 1930s and knew coach Howard Cann's style. The Tar Heels, in addition, had played and beaten the Violets earlier in the season. "I really had mixed feelings about beating NYU twice that year," says Carnevale. "I once played for Cann and here I was, eight years later, coaching against him. He was like a dad to me. He was a tremendous person . . . a fine gentleman. And I loved him."

At North Carolina, Carnevale had a basketball team that some considered to be the finest in the history of the school. The Tar Heels had broken the all-time school record with 28 victories and surpassed the all-time scoring record with 1,784 points—a 56-point-per-game average, high for the day. Of their four defeats, three had come in overtime and one to a service team when the Tar Heels were lacking full strength. The team leaders included Horace "Bones" McKinney, a wiry, 6-6 center known as the Tar Heels' court jester for his devastating wit, and John "Hook" Dillon, a hook-shot artist of deservedly widespread repute. It was McKinney who provided some laughs in the NCAA finals, as was his custom; and it was Dillon who gave the Aggies a good scare.

During the game, McKinney attempted to rattle Kurland with his stream of steady, sarcastic chatter. "All-America?" he needled the Aggie center. "You're not even all-Madison Square Garden!" Late in the game, when a referee called a fourth foul on McKinney, he pleaded innocent in his own inimitable manner. "Mr. Ref, the other three fouls were correct," he said. "But you missed this one a mile. I didn't touch him. The sad part of this is that I've got another foul in my system and I'm going to have to commit it. But I figured I had that extra foul to give."

As McKinney had prophesied, he later fouled out. And when the fifth foul was called on him, he had this parting shot for the referee: "You called a good game except for that fourth foul. That was terrible."

The loss of McKinney cost the Tar Heels some size in the middle, but Dillon made up for that lack of height with the high arc of his famous hook shot. "Dillon came in and played the post instead of Bones and gave us a running fit," Iba says. "I remember I sent in my other center (Joe Halbert) to cover him. Kurland was having trouble covering that little fellow. I couldn't take a chance of losing Kurland on fouls, so I had to switch to a new defensive man." Dillon scored several of his team-leading 16 points near the end of the game, helping to change the momentum in North Carolina's favor. "The tempo of the thing had changed, no doubt about it," reflects Kurland. "Dillon almost sank our ship for us. Another five minutes and it might have been a different ball game."

Kurland, though, had his beefy hands in just about everything that night. Not only did he score 23 points and involve himself in all but four of Oklahoma A&M's field goals, he played a key, if inadvertent, role in a crucial little scenario near the end. Remembers Carnevale: "It got down to the last minute. We took a rebound and threw the ball downcourt. Kurland had his back to the play and didn't see the pass. But the ball accidentally hit him in the hand and dropped at his feet. He wasn't even looking for the pass! He just picked up the ball, fed it to one of his own players who was still in the area and they scored. It turned into a four-point play for them; and, of course, we only lost by three . . . so you can see what a difference that made."

In a game that close, there were obviously other crucial moments for Oklahoma A&M. Iba remembers one such point late in the contest:

"I think it was A. L. Bennett who had the ball out of bounds for us when the Tar Heels had a one-point lead. But he had it out of bounds on the press-row side of the Garden, where it was narrow to get the ball in. They were picking us up all the way downcourt; and Bennett didn't have anybody to throw the ball in to because we hadn't practiced, in those days, out-of-bounds plays with the push against us. I didn't teach him this; he did it himself. He didn't have anybody to throw to, so he just dropped down and rolled the ball on the floor. Everybody (on defense) was playing up around his man's shoulder and we just picked the ball up, went to the other end and I think we scored. If he'd tried to throw the ball in, we might not have won that game. From that day on, I used the roll-in from out of bounds."

48

1947
'THE FANCY PANTS AC'

"We weren't that well known. We were just a bunch of kids . . . just like when you put five or six or seven kids together, and it hits some magic spark. The combination was just there. We came out of no place. There was never a tradition at Holy Cross . . . we were the tradition. From that point on, everything that came after us was always being compared to this Cinderella team that came out of nowhere and didn't have any stars, big guns or highly recruited ballplayers."—George Kaftan, Holy Cross center

The 1947 NCAA tournament produced a fairly common geographical irony in that a coach schooled in Pennsylvania took a group of New York players to the national championship in New England. All of these regional elements were significant in adding up to an NCAA championship for Holy Cross that year, but one cannot dismiss the karma that brought them all together in the right place at the right time.

Coach Doggie Julian was a Pennsylvania product, a graduate of Bucknell and a coach at both Albright and Muhlenberg before moving to Worcester, Massachusetts. His basic style of play was similar to that of Duquesne, the dominant basketball power in western Pennsylvania during the 1930s and early 1940s. On defense, the Dukes played tight, aggressive man-to-man with zoning alternatives. On offense, they played a variation of the double post, with two big men serving as picks and screens for the other players to work around. It was this type of pattern Julian installed at Holy Cross when he arrived for the 1945-46 season; and he had instant success, winning 80 per cent of his games in his first year. By the end of his second year, he had won the NCAA championship.

"We had an open weave type of game, a give-and-go offense," points out Joe Mullaney, a guard who was one of several future coaches on that Holy Cross team. "We kept the middle open so that we could drive. Probably our wide-open offense wouldn't work today, because defenses are more sophisticated. But passing was our forte. We could kill a zone with our passing, and we could beat a man-to-man defense with our speed."

With none of the regulars taller than 6-4, it was a relatively small team, even for that time. George Kaftan was the top scorer and rebounder, and the other starters usually included Mullaney and Ken Haggerty in the backcourt and Dermie O'Connell and Frank Oftring in the frontcourt. On the bench were Bob Curran, Bob McMullan, Andy Laska and a freshman who thought he should be playing more—Bob Cousy. Often, though, the reserves were better than the starters on this team of extensive depth; and this forced Julian to devise a two-platoon system that kept the Crusaders happy and their opponents off-balance.

"The first team was very orthodox," remembers Mullaney, "but the second team was just the opposite. They would really go in and shake up the other team. Those guys would come flying out, and the tempo of the game would suddenly change. We had a bunch of players who could really handle the basketball. They called us the 'Fancy Pants AC.' That's what one of the headlines said in a Boston newspaper after one of our victories. We were a clever team, sometimes to the point of overdoing it. We would pass up shots just to pass off."

It was this exhilarating style of play that brought a basketball renaissance to New England, establishing the sport as a primary fan attraction in the area. Until the Holy Cross team of 1947 brought the NCAA title to the Eastern Seaboard for the first time, a general apathy prevailed in the New England sector, despite its historical significance as the birthplace of the game. For many years, New England basketball was largely colored by Dartmouth's Big Green. But despite four appearances in the NCAA tournament from 1939 through 1946, Dartmouth's excellent records were compiled in

its own basketball backwaters. Providence College won almost 70 per cent of its games in the 1930s under Albert McClellan but was relatively weak when compared to Dartmouth. Down the road at Kingston, Frank Kearney had a 28-year reign at Rhode Island during which his team won more than 400 games for a .770 percentage. But although Kearney's teams, led by such as Ernie Calverley, were exciting with their running and long lead passes, their schedule was not. It wasn't until 1938 that Rhode Island began to beat Providence, and the Rams never played Dartmouth.

When Julian arrived at Holy Cross, there was little tradition to build on, so he built his own.

"Prior to us coming up there," points out Kaftan, "Holy Cross was absolutely nothing in basketball. They didn't even have a home gym. They had always been good in football and baseball; but in basketball, there was really nothing that Holy Cross could be proud of before we won the title. And so we sort of hit the area like a ton of bricks. We became the darlings of New England."

Cousy, although not a dominating collegiate player, displayed the germ of a triple-threat talent that would eventually carry him to the heights in professional basketball with the Boston Celtics. Cousy's tricky dribbling, clever passing and outside shooting captured the fancy of the fans. And it was Julian who allowed him the opportunity to mature in this direction.

"Probably he wouldn't have had that freedom at other schools," notes Mullaney, "but Julian let him do his thing. He let all of us develop our individual skills with some flair; and that was, of course, to his advantage and ours."

In his freshman year, though, Cousy had difficulty breaking into the Crusaders' talented starting lineup. Even though he contributed greatly to the championship effort—and even more to the team's crowd appeal—the gifted backcourtman was not entirely happy at Holy Cross that season. In fact, at one point he wrote to Joe Lapchick at St. John's about a transfer. But the Redmen's coach advised against it, saying in part, "Doggie Julian is one of the finest basketball coaches in America, and some day you'll be proud you've played for him."

Cousy was one of many New Yorkers on that unique Holy Cross team, and how they all got to be in the same place at the same time was just a fortuitous set of circumstances.

"It was purely an accident that we all happened

Bob McMullan of Holy Cross looks for a teammate after stealing the ball from Oklahoma's Dick Reich (on floor). Holy Cross defeated Oklahoma, 58-47, to win the 1947 championship.

50

to wind up there for that championship season," says Cousy. "In my case, I didn't have much choice. I only had two offers when I got out of high school in New York, and they were from Holy Cross and Boston College. Boston College didn't have dormitories at that time and Holy Cross did. That narrowed my choice down to one."

Mullaney originally wanted to go to Notre Dame but was overruled by his father.

"Holy Cross had no basketball background," he says. "The only thing I knew about them was that they upset Boston College in football one year. And the only thing I remembered about the New England area was the big Coconut Grove fire in Boston. I had gone into service right out of high school. While coming home, I called my father, who said: 'You're going to Holy Cross—I don't want you hanging around.' My brother, Dave, was there, so it was natural that my father should want me to go, too. But I was really interested in going to Notre Dame. We had some family ties there, and I had had my eye on Notre Dame for a long time."

Mullaney was even less enthusiastic about playing for Holy Cross when he got there in 1945.

"I walked into their gym and saw a couple of 17-year-olds," he recalls, "and this team didn't look like it was going to be very good. I had been playing with some good, veteran teams in the service and the situation was a little disappointing to me."

The Holy Cross gym didn't make Mullaney feel any better. It was the relic of a past age, a genuine antique that better belonged in a museum than on a campus. "It was a joke," says Kaftan. "They used to try to hide it from the basketball players when they were recruiting them. A kid would say to Doggie, 'Let's go see the gym.' And Doggie would say, 'Let's go have something to eat.' Frankly, I don't know how all of us wound up at a school that didn't have a basketball program."

Because there was no adequate gym in which the Crusaders could play their home games, they actually had to play all their contests on the road. The Boston Garden was considered a home court of sorts, and it was here that the Crusaders became the adopted stepchildren of New England sports fans. Their drawing power was evident as early as Julian's first season, when a game with Rhode Island drew a sellout crowd of 13,900 at the Boston sports palace.

"I guess having no gym eventually worked to our advantage," says Kaftan, "because rather than have just the student fans or the surrounding area fans at our games, we drew from all of New England. We were adopted by the entire region, and this was a terrific psychological boost for us."

Although the Crusaders lost to Rhode Island

during the 1945-46 season, Julian learned the value of the fast break from the Rams. The next year began rather inauspiciously for Holy Cross. The Crusaders beat four opponents at the start but lost the next three games on a Christmas road trip against North Carolina State, Duquesne and Wyoming, three excellent teams. The Crusaders started to run a little against Wyoming, then began to crystalize in the next game against Toledo. In the subsequent three games, they averaged 77 points and from there went on through a 23-game winning streak to the NCAA championship. In the tournament at Madison Square Garden, they came from behind to beat Navy, 55-47; made a comeback to defeat CCNY, 60-45, and had to rally several times to whip Oklahoma, 58-47. As good as his offense was, Julian was always proud of the defense these tournament scores indicated.

"We peaked for the NCAA tournament," remembers Cousy. "Of course, that's very important when you get to that stage because all of the teams in it are capable of winning the championship. You don't reach that plateau without having some horses . . . so I think our motivation worked in our favor at the end. We had a good team. I don't know if we had a better team than the teams we beat, but we were emotionally charged."

No extensive scouting reports were needed to win the tournament games, as Cousy remembers. "We did a minimum of scouting. We obviously didn't have the sophisticated methods or the finances to pay for scouting reports. We used to get our information haphazardly—say, from a cab driver on the way to the game. I remember an instance in Indianapolis where we literally talked to the cab driver on the way in, and that information was the topic of our pregame discussions. We just didn't have those things available to us in terms of manpower or budget. Holy Cross was even poorer then in terms of being a very small, private school without the funds to put into an athletic program. I seem to recall that we knew something generally about Navy, and I assume we had something on City (CCNY) because it was a local team. We had a lot of alumni in the area who probably contributed. Other than being aware of Gerald Tucker's reputation, I don't recall that we had anything much on Oklahoma, either."

If Navy and CCNY had better scouting reports than Holy Cross it didn't help the Middies. As a matter of fact, it might have cost them their games in the Eastern regionals. As Mullaney recalls, "I was not the scorer on our team, so Navy coach Ben Carnevale put his high scorer, Kenny Shugart, on me in order to give him a breather defensively. I scored 18 points, possibly because Shugart didn't

kill himself guarding me. And Carnevale said afterwards, 'The one player who couldn't shoot had to kill me.' Then against CCNY, Nat Holman put his best defensive player on me because he apparently had seen my point production in the Navy game and was worried about me. 'We've got to watch for Mullaney,' he was quoted as saying in the newspapers. Well, Lionel Malamed came out to play me; and I scored something like three points... but Kaftan went wild with 30 points. They ended up being more concerned about me and it hurt them, because our real scorers went to work."

On Mullaney, Carnevale confirms: "Our scouting reports said he was the playmaker, not the shooter. So we didn't worry too much about him. But he hit several shots on us and killed us with them." Mullaney's field goals, many of them from distant points, helped the Crusaders erase an early 23-15 deficit.

In the Eastern finals, it was Kaftan who provided the spark for Holy Cross, both on the court and in the dressing room. CCNY, not unlike the Crusaders in style of play and team character, had defeated Big Nine champion Wisconsin, 70-56, in the other Eastern playoff opener but held little fear for the Crusaders, as Mullaney recalls. "They were a depleted team by that time," he says. "They had a holdover reputation; I don't think they were that powerful, really." The Beavers, however, were good enough to enjoy a 10-3 lead at the start of the game and to hold the Crusaders without a field goal for nearly eight minutes, keeping the nervous Julian at the edge of his seat and sometimes on top of it. "Holy Cross appeared outclassed for a big part of the first half," said Arthur "Dutch" Lonborg in his report as chairman of the tournament committee, although the Crusaders did hold a 27-25 lead at intermission. It was at the half that Kaftan, the team's clown prince, injected some humor into the tense situation. "I was sort of the guy on the team who would try to break up tension and get a couple of laughs going," Kaftan says. "Doggie was a highly nervous individual, and he used to lose his cool a lot. He was going crazy at this point, with us in a tight game. So I took a garbage can and rolled it right down the middle of the locker room and everybody started to laugh. We were okay after that."

Actually, the Crusaders were nearly perfect. Undaunted by the chants of "Allagaroo" that flooded Madison Square Garden for the hometown favorite Beavers, Holy Cross returned to great form behind Kaftan. "That was all you could hear was that 'Allagaroo' chant," Kaftan says, remembering a highly vocal crowd of 18,470. "It was awesome. The place was going crazy." The sight of Kaftan at work under the basket was just as awe-inspiring to Mullaney. "He didn't look like he could score that much," Mullaney says. "He was just a baby. He would score a bushel of points, and we would say, 'I don't ever remember him taking any shots.' And, actually, maybe he didn't. He was that kind of a player, had a great touch under the basket, tapping in the ball."

In playing Oklahoma for the national championship, the Crusaders faced a team that had just been through two arduous games in the Western regionals, not to mention an exhausting train trip to New York from Kansas City. Acknowledges Bruce Drake, the Oklahoma coach: "The travel hurt us before the NCAA finals more than anything. We spent 48 hours on a train and were just plain tired by the time we got into New York."

The Sooners obviously were just as wrung out from their torturous Western playoff triumphs. They withstood a late Oregon State attack to win, 56-54, in the opening round and then secured a berth in the NCAA finals by edging Texas, 55-54, in one of the most exciting games in tournament history. In that Western championship game, Texas trailed, 41-34, with seven minutes to play. But the Longhorns rallied, and Slater Martin's field goal tied the contest at 53 with just 55 seconds remaining. Al Madsen put Texas into a one-point lead with a free throw, but then Oklahoma won the game on a long shot by Ken Pryor with 10 seconds left.

"That was as exciting a game as you'll ever see," Drake recalls. "It was like someone had tapped me on the shoulder, you know, and said, 'Put Pryor in' . . . just like the Man Upstairs had done that. He had a two-handed jump shot, unusual for then, and he was a great dribbler. We had 16 seconds to get a shot off. Gerald Tucker was our all-America, and we knew that Texas would sag off on him. So my instructions were for Allie Paine, my guard, to count down the seconds out loud so Pryor could shoot in time. I told Paine to stay near the basket so he could get the followup, if need be."

Pryor remembers that the Sooners "didn't even call a timeout to set up the play. We just came on down the court. It wasn't free lance. We knew what play we were going to run. It was a set type of play. Actually, it didn't work exactly as we planned. The ball originally was supposed to go to someone else for the final shot. But the man I blocked for didn't get in the clear and Tucker couldn't find him. I was the safety valve on the play . . . and fortunately, I was clear. I got the ball from Tucker, dribbled two or three times and put in a little jump shot, a two-handed shot, both hands over my head."

53

University of Oklahoma

54

"Record-breaking crowds, hair-raising action and widely diverging types of basketball" were the ingredients of the ninth annual NCAA Western playoffs, according to George Shiebler, publicity chairman of the tournament committee. Shiebler pointed out that 17,571 spectators had "jammed the (Kansas City Municipal) Auditorium in the two nights to see a determined band of Oklahoma Sooners find the championship spurt that was needed to edge two top-caliber teams." Of the four games, two were decided by a single goal and one by a point. Along with Oklahoma's tenuous victories, Texas had barely squeezed into the Western finals with a 42-40 triumph over Wyoming on Martin's shot in the closing seconds. The Cowboys had led, 40-39, but unwisely elected to freeze the ball, three times declining golden scoring opportunities in the final four minutes.

The "widely differing styles or philosophies of basketball" were underscored in Shiebler's playoff

Oklahoma's Ken Pryor (29) hits the basket with 10 seconds to play that sent the Sooners into the 1947 finals. Pryor's shot gave Oklahoma a 55-54 win over Texas in the West regional finals.

report. Oklahoma, champion of the Big Six Conference, "was the representative of one of the last strongholds of defensive basketball," he said. Matched against that style was "the fast break of the Longhorns from Texas, thought by many to be the fastest team in basketball during the 1946-47 season" and, according to Pryor, "the best team in the country that year." Shiebler also praised the "nearly as fast Oregon State offensive attack and the midway style of Wyoming's Cowboys, kingpins of the Big Seven Conference."

In the case of Oklahoma, Shiebler would have been more correct in pointing out the Sooners' stunning offensive capabilities. "We were a high-scoring team for the day," says Pryor. "We liked to fast break a lot. As a matter of fact, the conditions were not the best for us at Kansas City, as I recall. They had a very hard floor there and because we liked to run, it really hurt our legs . . . just wore our players out."

Drake, termed an "offensive-minded" coach by Pryor, had invented a powerful weapon against tough defenses, called the "shuffle." As Drake remembers: "It actually was the result of playing Hank Iba (of Oklahoma A&M) twice every year. Playing a good defensive coach like that made you think about attacking more and how to break those tough defenses. A good defensive club always drops to the weak side, away from the ball, and makes it impossible to get the ball to the post man. We eliminated that by overloading to one side—leaving one man on the weak side. The shuffle was really a five-man offense. The defense doesn't know where the shot is coming from. It's a continuity of movement. We always knew where the ball was going to go, but the opponent didn't. We unveiled it against Minnesota one year after four years of study, and it worked very well."

Drake describes himself as a finicky coach, "a stickler for little things. Basketball was a chess game to me. I used to challenge the intelligence of my players."

"They used to say that with Iba's great defense and Drake's offense, you had the two best in those styles in that day," Pryor points out.

Drake went on to more euphoric levels in his 17-year career at Oklahoma, highlighted by his

team that played for the NCAA championship in 1947. Drake's best player that season was Tucker, a sweet-shooting big man with classic moves. "Nobody could cover him one-on-one," Drake says. "His fakes were out of this world. Doggie Julian put George Kaftan on him in the finals, and Tucker outscored him, 22-18, even though Kaftan was voted the most outstanding player. He pulled Kaftan off Tucker for a while, because he was afraid he might foul out trying to guard Gerry."

Most of the damage by Tucker was done in the first half of the championship game, when he scored 14 of his points to lead Oklahoma to a 31-28 lead. After that, Julian decided to use Bob Curran to defend against Tucker; and Cousy recalls that the Holy Cross big man "did a magnificent defensive job on him" in the second half. While holding the Sooner ace to but eight points after intermission, the Crusaders counterattacked with a quicker tempo that eventually broke open a close game at the end. The combatants fought through 11 ties and as many lead changes before Holy Cross knocked out Oklahoma with a 10-2 scoring burst in the final three minutes en route to a 58-47 victory.

"In that game," remembers Drake, "Holy Cross dropped off Dick Reich, one of our best shooters, to double-team Tucker. They gambled that Reich wouldn't hit—and he didn't. We lacked speed and Cousy stole the ball a couple of times. Holy Cross had more height and more speed; and, of course, the physical condition of our team was not the best because of that long trip from Kansas City."

Characteristically, the volcanic Julian erupted more than once during the game. Until the last few minutes, the uncertainty of the outcome had played havoc with his highly strung nervous system. "He was a very emotional guy," verifies Mullaney, "very emotional."

Julian's nervous condition had manifested itself before tipoff, as Kaftan recalls.

"He was so excited before the start of the game," notes Kaftan, "that he didn't know how to go about mentioning the names of his starting team. He had forgotten all the names, he was so nervous. In the locker room I remember he said, 'Dermy, you start, and George, you start, and Kaftan, you start, and O'Connell, you start, and Greek, you start.' So I was George, I was Kaftan and I was the Greek. And Dermy, of course, was Dermott O'Connell."

"But," adds Kaftan, "it was all right. We all knew who the starters had to be ourselves; we just got up, went out and played the ball game."

55

THE KENTUCKY YEARS 1948·1958

In the early 1950s, the tournament committee fired shots heard round the college basketball world. Pulling the trigger were Arthur C. "Dutch" Lonborg and Walter Byers. Those two guided the revamping of the format of the NCAA tournament into what is generally regarded today as the modern concept of the event.

Until 1951, the tournament was held on a limited, eight-team basis, one each from the eight NCAA districts. The winner of the Eastern championship met the Western champion for the national title. But this archaic system obviously needed to be junked in the face of the college basketball explosion in America in the early 1950s. There were too many good teams in the country and too few places to put them in the field. So, Lonborg, the chairman of the tournament committee, sat down with Byers, the executive director of the NCAA, and worked out a satisfactory plan. They doubled the field to 16 teams and later set up four regional tournaments. This action was greeted by a rousing vote of confidence from their peers.

"It relieved a lot of problems," Lonborg relates. "There would be occasions when we'd have a North Carolina State and a Kentucky—both great teams—and the selection committee from that district would call me and want me to tell them what to do. It happened more than once and I soon decided that was no go. I spent many long nights talking to chairmen, telling them I couldn't make a selection from Evanston (Illinois) or Lawrence (Kansas)."

Lonborg, once coach at Northwestern and manager of the first NCAA tournament there, was the athletic director at Kansas when he participated in the revolutionary concept of the 1950s. As far as many are concerned, that particular period had the most impact on the growth of the tournament. Of course, the popularity of the event later reached its zenith with the help of television.

"Everybody liked the idea right away," recalls Lonborg. "A lot of

teams didn't want to play off for district representation. With the new format, we got away from making tough decisions about which team to select. After Walter and I worked out the plan, we had the rest of the tournament committee check it out. Then we presented it to the coaches' convention, and everyone voted for it."

At the time of the new tournament concept, incidentally, Lonborg only had two teammates on the NCAA Basketball Committee—Asa Bushnell of the Eastern Collegiate Athletic Association (now Eastern College Athletic Conference) and Reaves Peters of the Missouri Valley Intercollegiate Athletic Association (now Missouri Valley Conference). The structure of this group also was destined to be swept up in the winds of change during the 1950s.

"We eventually went to a larger panel," Lonborg explains, "because the coaches' association recommended that they should have more representation on the committee—plus the fact that with more than eight teams in the tournament, the committee needed more manpower. The NCAA went along with the recommendation. The additional committeemen also were most helpful in recommending and selecting at-large teams. We got verbal suggestions from others, but we selected them on their record."

With the new format, the committee designated institutions to be hosts for the regional tournaments; and a committee member attended each site to make certain it was being conducted according to policy. "A lot of places were interested then in serving as tournament sites," Lonborg points out. The structure of the first 16-team tournament in 1951 included 10 automatic qualifying conferences and six at-large teams. About this first setup, Lonborg notes: "The automatic qualifying conferences were placed in the bracket, and the independents or at-large teams were drawn from a hat to see who they would play and placed in a bracket. There was no seeding."

As the field expanded to 16 in 1951 and then 22 in 1953, there were the inevitable growing pains.

There were numerous logistical problems, plus a crushing demand for tickets and hot discussions over who would pluck the plum of the championship game. Remembers Lonborg: "The real discussions came when we played the finals. Everyone wanted them. There were many coaches' meetings held in this regard."

Kansas City and Louisville were two of the more-favored finals sites of the 1950s. The Kansas City Municipal Auditorium hosted the event four times in that decade and Louisville's Freedom Hall twice.

"Kansas City was drawing well then," Lonborg remembers. "There was great enthusiasm there. But we finally outgrew Kansas City. They could seat only 10,500, and we had to go to larger places."

One of the favored arenas of the 1940s that would not get the NCAA's business in the 1950s was New York's Madison Square Garden. This was purely for economical reasons, as Lonborg explains:

"When we first moved out of the Garden for the 1949 tournament at the University of Washington, we just wanted a change. We had been at the Garden for six straight years. Washington always had good crowds, and we thought it would be a good place for the tournament. When we finally left the Garden for good in the early 1950s, it had nothing to do with the gambling scandals there. The main reason was the rental charge. It was very high. We figured we could make money on campuses. Schools would usually give us the gym for cost. It was more profitable for us to go to campuses at that time. There were some good, new arenas springing up that we could use, some nice field houses around the country."

Keeping pace with the tempo of the times, 1954 was another expansion year for the NCAA tournament. This time, the field was increased to 24 teams, adding an additional automatic qualifying league in the newly formed Atlantic Coast Conference and an at-large team. "One of the reasons for enlarging the tournament was that there were 150 institutions playing a major college schedule and a greater demand to participate in the championship," explains longtime committee member Tom Scott. "Each team's schedule was reviewed annually, and if necessary, they were reclassified."

In structuring the 1954 tournament, more thought was given to quality of play by permitting additional time between the regionals and the finals. This served a two-fold purpose, according to Scott. "The new format permitted the four regional winners more time to rest and prepare for the finals, as well as less loss of classroom time." First-round games were played on Monday and Tuesday, March 8 and 9; regionals on Friday and Saturday, March 12-13, and the final two rounds on Friday and Saturday, March 19 and 20. Previously, the championship semifinals and finals had been played on Tuesday and Wednesday following the Friday and Saturday regionals. Except for the finals in Kansas City's Municipal Auditorium, all games were played in campus facilities during the 1954 tournament.

The early 1950s served as the stage for a philosophical tug-of-war between academicians and athletics, and all interested parties eventually benefited from the smooth NCAA planning. Certain athletic camps supporting spring sports lobbied to have the basketball season shortened so that their efforts could take the spotlight. This the NCAA did in 1953 by rescheduling the basketball tournament. The basketball coaches wanted more rest for their teams in between the regionals and finals, and the NCAA acceded to these wishes. The academicians wanted more classroom time for the students. The NCAA solved this dilemma by proposing more regional sites "so there would be less travel for the students and so that they could be kept closer to home," explains Scott.

Book 2

THE KENTUCKY YEARS 1948-1958

By the same token, the NCAA was not hurting itself with the various regional tournaments. There, the pragmatic organization steered by the businesslike Byers made a public relations coup and found gold at the end of its rainbow.

"The going concern then," emphasizes Scott, "was to put all the energy into seeing the NCAA basketball tournament develop. That's why the committee arrived at the policy of the additional regions. It would expand interest. The NCAA's thought was to make more money for the membership. The change accomplished everything the committee wanted it to accomplish."

THE FABULOUS FIVE

The Kentucky Wildcats seemed dangerously carefree as they approached the 1948 NCAA finals with Baylor. Their very demeanor as they ambled onto the court at Madison Square Garden appeared to express the height of nonchalance. Adolph Rupp, the heavily jowled demigod of this terrifying basketball team, hadn't even bothered to get a scouting report on the enemy.

Before anyone had a chance to work up a sweat, Kentucky had scored 13 points to Baylor's one. There just wasn't anything that Baylor could do about 6-foot-7 Alex "The Nose" Groza, Kentucky's star center whose head seemed to threaten the mezzanine every time he outjumped a Baylor man. "He sucked in rebounds like a vacuum cleaner," said one writer. "He was swift afoot and dead-eyed." Nor were the Bears able to contain Ralph Beard or Wallace "Wah Wah" Jones, and Kentucky had its first NCAA championship with a clinically easy 58-42 conquest of the proud Southwest Conference winners.

"We were completely outmanned on the boards," recalls Baylor coach Bill Henderson. "Center Don Heathington was our tallest player at 6-4 or 6-5. They got the ball every time we shot and missed."

Henderson was warned by coaches beforehand not to run with the Wildcats but to "try to stop their fast break." In retrospect, he wishes he had listened more attentively to his colleagues' advice. "We were usually a deliberate team," he recalls, "but we went into that game trying to score early and then slow the game down. But we lost the battle of the boards and got behind right away. We later played deliberately, but it was too late then. If I had it to do over again, I would have played a more deliberate style all the way through."

Henderson's team was troubled not only by the Wildcats' awesome power but also seemed to be bothered just as much by the interpretation of the rules. Baylor was a team that used screens as its offensive foundation, but the Bears virtually had to eliminate that aspect of its game because of the sensitivity of Eastern officials in this area. "The Eastern interpretation of the rules was different than what we had seen all year," Henderson says. "Eastern officials would call fouls on us if we set up a screen and the opposing team ran into it. We had used the screening style all year, but now in the NCAA championship game we couldn't. It hurt our movement a lot." On the other hand, the officials allowed contact under the boards. "They were pretty loose about what happened under the boards," Henderson relates. "They let you battle under there. Of course, that was Kentucky's game. They had the height."

Haarlow and MacDonald had taken away Baylor's strongest suit and allowed Kentucky to play its best hand. For a team that had all the aces in the first place, that gave Kentucky the trump card in the 1948 championship game.

This was undoubtedly Rupp's best team, and it deserved an honored place on his burgeoning trophy shelf. College basketball's all-time No. 1 winner would say to his dying day on December 10, 1977, that the "Fabulous Five was the greatest basketball team of all time." The "Fabulous Five" is a misnomer of sorts, because the Kentucky team of this era had great depth; no fewer than 14 players put in some time in competition. But the true "Fabulous Five" consisted of Alex Groza at center, Wallace "Wah Wah" Jones and Cliff Barker at the forwards and Ralph Beard and Kenneth Rollins at the guards. That group, and those that followed, won three NCAA championships in four seasons, shared representation of the United States in capturing the 1948 Olympic Games title and compiled a won-lost record of 125-12.

Rollins, according to Rupp, "was the best defensive man I have ever seen play basketball." The coach applauded Beard as "the most terrific competitor of all time. I know of no one who tried harder to be a great basketball player than he did." Rupp felt that Groza "could hold his own with any center in the country at any time, and he proved that when he got into professional basketball."

University of Kentucky

Alex Groza, who led Kentucky to championships in 1948 and 1949.

Jones was "a rough, tough competitor who never backed off from anybody. He was quick and intelligent, and he had the size and weight to demand respect under the basket." Barker was a "tremendous ball handler," in Rupp's words.

These qualities, however, obviously were not so readily apparent to Rupp at the start. Actually, he could have assembled the "Fabulous Five" a full year earlier than he did. All the players were available. Rupp did start Barker several times during the 1946-47 season at forward, but the usual forwards were Joe Holland and Jack Tingle. Jones was a backup man to Groza at center and played some forward that year, but he didn't become a regular forward until the last four games. It wasn't until the 12th game of the 1947-48 season, after much experimentation, that the "Fabulous Five" played as a starting unit. The original group would live a short, spectacular life, playing only 28 games together in that brief span of less than a season. But in that meteoric time, they would become Rupp's most famous team.

While there seemed to be some reluctance on the part of fate to put these players into a starting unit, it was an irony of fate—or history—that made it possible for them to play together. Without World War II, the five players would not have been at Kentucky at the same time. Rollins, a sophomore in 1943, would have finished at Kentucky in 1945 while Beard and Jones were completing their high school careers. Barker, a freshman in 1940, would have graduated in 1943. Beard and Jones, though, would have been together throughout

their Kentucky playing days and Groza would have been with them for two years if the war hadn't intervened.

As an added touch of irony, most of the "Fabulous Five" were not especially coveted by Rupp at the beginning. Barker, for one, came back of his own accord after the war. "I wasn't so crazy about it at the time, because he wasn't a great prospect," Rupp said. "I had all these other kids coming back: Joe Holland, Jim Jordan—a transfer all-America from North Carolina—Dale Barnstable and Jim Line. So we had a fairly fine team. But Barker came back and soon convinced me that he would be in the starting lineup." During the war, Barker had been shot down over Germany, put in a concentration camp and held there for nearly two years. "He found a volleyball, found a hoop of some kind and shot baskets," Rupp remembered. "He had a lot of time to study about this thing when he was in that camp, and the first thing he thought about was coming back to Kentucky."

Beard and Jones came to Kentucky on football scholarships. The Wildcats, in fact, came close to losing Beard a couple of times. The first was in the summer of 1945 when the 5-10 guard played in the Kentucky-Indiana high school all-star game. Ed Diddle of Western Kentucky was the Kentucky stars' coach, and Beard was greatly impressed with the friendliness shown at Western. But he did enroll at Kentucky after he and Jones helped beat Indiana for the first time in the summer series. Later, Beard played three games of football at Kentucky but was "disillusioned," as he put it, after injuring both shoulders. He thought about transferring to Louisville at the time but was talked out of it by some coaching friends.

Groza at first wanted to go to Ohio State and follow in the footsteps of his famous football-playing brother, Lou. Kentucky was a second choice, Rupp said, but became the first choice for Groza when Ohio State didn't recruit him. "I just went up to talk to his family once," Rupp noted, "and that's how I got him. Groza was mad because Ohio State didn't ask him to come there. He didn't have any college offers, in fact. Finally, he settled on Kentucky because we were having a good time winning all these championships."

Uncommon basketball ability was part of the "Fabulous Five" power. But the compatibility of the parts was what made the unit run smoothly. The players complemented each other perfectly.

Dale Barnstable, Jim Line, Joseph Holland and

Johnny Stough were the top reserves on the 1947-48 team. And with Rollins and Holland out of eligibility the following year, Barnstable and Line became more prominent in the lineup. This combination, with Groza averaging 20.5 points a game—an exceptional average for those days—swept to a 32-2 record in 1948-49. Ranked No. 1 nationally by The Associated Press, the Wildcats climaxed their successful season by winning a second straight NCAA championship. This time, they defeated Oklahoma A&M (now Oklahoma State), 46-36, for the national title.

This extraordinary success story was not one of rags to riches. The foundation for this golden era had been built by Rupp many years before with rich Kentucky teams that thoroughly dominated the Southeastern Conference. But Rupp's fine records during these early years, impressive as they were, were not the measure of Kentucky's true contributions to the college basketball world. The Wildcats' greatest value lay in the way they helped move basketball toward a truly national game. Rupp, who had played under Phog Allen on the undefeated 1923 Kansas team and later coached successfully at Freeport (Illinois) High School, brought fast-breaking ideas to Lexington, where Johnny Mauer had been teaching a deliberate, ball-control game. More important, Kentucky sought to play the best teams from all sections of the country. Outside of Southeastern Conference play, the Wildcats always looked for bigger game. They played Notre Dame regularly; as early as 1933, they took on the Missouri Valley Conference champions; they scheduled the Big Ten's strongest teams, and they took on New York's best at Madison Square Garden.

A tough, outspoken leader whose trademark was a tired, brown suit, Rupp demanded and got the most he possibly could from his charges. The Wildcats were drilled in basic basketball and man-to-man defense but were always encouraged by Rupp to develop individual styles. However, a mistake meant a severe tongue-lashing and quick retirement to the bench. Rupp established a familiar and successful offensive pattern: always shoot when you're open. The Wildcats were trained to fire from comfortable places on the floor and shot with alarming skill. Most of Rupp's success was based on outstanding talent, but part of it was also the result of discipline.

Ironically, the man who won more games than any college basketball coach in history (an 880-190 record through 42 seasons) knew little about the sport as a youth. In fact, Rupp confessed once that he never heard of James Naismith, the inventor of basketball, until later in life when he entered Naismith's physical education class at the University of Kansas.

Once reminiscing about his youth, Rupp said: "I was born out on the plains of Kansas, and we never heard of anything. The only thing we knew on the farm was that we chopped wood and piled it high so that we had enough to burn for heat. When the chores were done at night, we had our evening meals and our devotions. We headed for bed around 8 o'clock in the evening and got up in the morning to do our chores and go to school."

Recreational activity on the farm was hampered by primitive facilities and equipment. Rupp played with a homemade ball "which was just a gunny sack stuffed with rags," he remembered. "Mother sewed it up and somehow made it round. You couldn't dribble it, though."

While the basketballs were falling apart in Rupp's hands, his fate was being galvanized in an awkward, little high school gymnasium in the Kansas town of Halstead (population 1,110). There, Rupp played on state championship teams in 1908 and 1909. Later, college basketball at Kansas refined Rupp's talents and enhanced his appreciation of the sport.

His arrival at Kentucky signaled a renaissance in the Blue Grass Country, to say nothing of the entire Southeastern Conference. Rupp introduced fast-break basketball the likes of which had not been seen before in that region, and his Wildcats never stopped running away with SEC titles. They won 27 under Rupp. His innovations gave Kentucky a 15-3 record in his first season (1930-31) when the Wildcats were part of the old Southern Conference, and Rupp never coached a losing season in his four glittering decades. All through these extravagant successes, Rupp showed a wildly superstitious nature. The legend of his brown suit persisted throughout his career and became one of the timeworn conversation pieces of college basketball lore. As Rupp explained it to one interviewer, "I once wore a blue suit to a game and we got the hell beat out of us. I figured I better go back to brown after that."

It was the color he contributed to college basketball, however, that caught everyone's eye. Rupp's immediate takeoff into basketball's higher stratosphere kindled some jealousy among his SEC peers, as most success does. But perhaps even more irritating to his colleagues was Rupp's philosophical approach. The man was dedicated to winning as the only reason for playing basketball. At the time of his greatest glories in the late 1940s and the 1950s, Rupp made this position clear enough with the statement that "I am not engaged in a popularity contest. I want to win."

63

Ironically, Rupp built championship teams at Kentucky despite a lack of big money. "I never had more than $10,000 a year to recruit," he said. "But at first I didn't need much money because everyone in the state wanted to come to Kentucky." Beard gave an indication of things to come when he led the Wildcats to a 46-45 victory over Rhode Island in the finals of the 1946 National Invitation Tournament. The following year, Kentucky lost in the NIT finals by four points to Utah; but the seeds of Rupp's greatest teams were starting to grow.

The early part of the 1947-48 season at Kentucky was marked by injuries. Jones, especially, was making a slow return to form after the football season and a sore foot. Finally, after mixing and matching his players for the first 11 games, Rupp stood in front of his team in the locker room at Miami University in Oxford, Ohio, on the night of January 5, 1948, and announced his newest starting lineup—Jones, Barker, Beard, Rollins and Groza. Rupp was unaware at the time, of course, that he was serving as midwife to the birth of a legend. But this strong Kentucky lineup went out and defeated Miami, 67-53; and after the same unit beat Michigan State, 47-45, in another road game, Rupp was convinced that he had found the right combination of complementary skills. Kentucky lost later in the season to Notre Dame, but the Wildcats suffered no further embarrassment that year. Nine victories took them through the regular season, including a revenge beating of Temple, the only other college team to beat the Wildcats that year. Four more victories in the SEC tournament sent them to New York for the NCAA competition, where they crushed Columbia, 76-53, and beat defending national champion Holy Cross, 60-52, in the Eastern regional. Columbia went down more easily than expected, considering the Lions had one of the best records in the country at 21-1 and wore the banner of Ivy League champions.

In the Eastern finals, Holy Cross was a little tougher for Kentucky, but not that much. Doggie Julian's Crusaders had swept into the NCAA field on the wings of an 18-game winning streak, carried for the most part by George Kaftan and Bob Cousy. Rollins drew the assignment of guarding Cousy, proclaimed as "the greatest" on a large bed sheet hanging from the Garden balcony.

"We studied his moves, and Dale Barnstable and I talked about what we would try to do," Rollins recalls. "We never knew which way he would go. Some players prefer to go one way. If they're right-handed, they might like to drive to their right and you can overplay them that way. But with Cousy, it didn't matter. So we made a concentrated effort to keep him in the center of the floor because

Kentucky forward Wallace "Wah Wah" Jones scores in the Wildcats' 46-36 win over Oklahoma A&M in 1949, despite the defensive efforts of Jack Shelton and Joe Bradley (22).

he did most of his scoring from the sides."

When Rollins was relieved by Barnstable near the end of the game, Cousy had only three points—all on free throws. Meanwhile, Groza controlled the boards over Kaftan and scored 23 points. After the game, someone brought the Cousy bedsheet to Rollins as a souvenir.

"I had a terrible night against them," Cousy remembers. "If I had had an average night, I think we would have been competitive and gone down to the wire and had a shot at them. But they had an outstanding team. In fact, they came back in the Boston Garden the following year and beat us by three points at home. We had an excellent team, also, but we couldn't stop Alex Groza. He was probably the most effective center in the game on the college level at the time. They just had a superior team. We were pleased that we gave them a battle."

This was no ordinary Holy Cross team that Kentucky had beaten, by the way. As defending national champions, the Crusaders had a seasoned squad that boasted a record of 23-3 going into the playoffs. But as one writer explained it, "the tremendous height advantage and superior shooting of the Kentuckians proved too much of a handicap for the flashy, fast-breaking Crusaders." The Eastern finals drew 18,472 at Madison Square Garden, one of the biggest crowds in NCAA tournament history.

The NCAA championship game was anticlimactic, because the Western regional at Kansas City had what appeared to be a comparatively weak draw. Baylor had made it to the finals with upsets over Kansas State and Washington. Remembers Baylor coach Bill Henderson: "We were the underdogs in both of our regional games. Kansas State actually was supposed to win everything. Kansas State was a very good team. We played a deliberate game and got ahead. We didn't stall. But you had the option in those days of either taking the ball out of bounds or shooting a free throw when you were fouled. We took the ball out and kept possession the latter part of the game and were able to beat Kansas State. Washington had a very tall team with an exceptionally big post man. We got behind by nine points. They played a zone; but in the first part of the second half, we caught up and they went into their man-to-man defense. They were awkward in this defense, due to their size. Then we played another delay game to preserve

64

that victory at the end."

Don Heathington, James "Red" Owen and Jackie Robinson were among the mainstays of the Baylor team that year. "We were a deliberate-type team," points out Henderson. "We had speed but no exceptional height. Robinson was the team leader. He played forward, brought the ball down, had exceptional speed and was a good ball handler." It had been a fairy-tale season for the Bears. They weren't even picked to win their own Southwest Conference but finished ahead of the favored Texas Longhorns. They followed that success with a 60-52 victory over Kansas State and a 64-62 decision over Washington in the NCAA Western playoffs, but the joy ended once Kentucky took the court at Madison Square Garden on March 23, 1948. Once again, it was Groza who was the dominating factor for the Wildcats, although they seemed a bit let down from the pressure game with Holy Cross. After Kentucky's 16-point victory in the finals before 16,174 at Madison Square Garden, Rupp called his Wildcats "the greatest team ever assembled in college sport." His eyes filled with tears, Rupp locked the dressing room door and told his players: "You've done everything you've been asked to do. You won your own SEC tournament. You won the NCAA championship. You've kept training and made sacrifices to do these things, and for all of it I thank you from the bottom of my heart." To Groza, who scored 14 points and policed the inside with his customary elan, Rupp said: "You undoubtedly played the greatest game at center that has ever been seen at the Garden." Groza was named the tourney's most outstanding player.

Kentucky's "Fabulous Five" were later selected to join players from the pro-level Phillips Oilers and other top American college teams to represent the United States in the Olympic Games that year. This team of riches swept through eight opponents in London, beating France, 65-21, in the finals.

Except for Rollins, it was the same Kentucky team that flexed its muscular power in the 1948-49 season. But Rupp still had the nagging doubt that he was not getting the best possible results from this talented team. A 42-40 loss to defending NIT champion St. Louis in the Sugar Bowl Tournament early in the year brought him to this realization. As good as the Wildcats were individually, they prided themselves on teamwork and balanced scoring. After that disconcerting loss to the Billikens, Rupp ordered a simple change in his team's makeup that had tremendous impact. He moved Barnstable to forward and put Barker at guard with one instruction: feed Groza. From this point on, Kentucky was a pivot-oriented team, with Groza the center of

attention. The year before, Groza had outscored Beard by merely 12 points; Jones was not far behind. But this year, Kentucky's big man would outscore the two of them combined, though the all-around play of the team seemed to benefit from the change. Barker developed into a passer of extraordinary skills. No longer were his passes just straight and a little harder than those of other players. He began to work more on trick passes—behind the back, looking one way and passing the other, putting a spin on the ball so it would bounce around the defensive player's reach. "I gained confidence in my passing," Barker once said, "but I lost confidence in my shooting." However, the change made Barker a more durable player—and more valuable in the Kentucky scheme of things. About his passes to Groza, Barker noted: "Usually, I didn't even look at him. I knew he'd catch the ball."

Bidding for a grand slam in postseason competition that season, Kentucky hurdled the Southeastern Conference tournament with relative ease but suffered a stunning 67-56 knockout blow by Loyola of Chicago in the first round of the NIT. "I was so furious after that," Rupp later remembered, "that I just sat up in my room until 2 o'clock in the morning wondering what happened. I kept telling myself, 'There's something wrong with this team. I tell them what to do and, dammit, they won't do it.' We had four fouls on this Loyola center and I kept yelling, 'Get the ball into Groza and foul him out.' And at the half, I just gave them hell because they didn't do that. In the second half, everybody on the bench kept hollering and finally, Groza fouled out. And when he fouled out, that ended the show." A less cocky, more determined Wildcat team went to work in the NCAA tournament after that. "I took the team home the next morning," said Rupp, "and we worked out. I mean, we really worked out! I spared no mercy."

Against Villanova, Groza collected 30 points as the Wildcats set an NCAA tournament scoring mark with an 85-72 decision in the first round of the Eastern regional. Against Illinois in the Eastern finals, Groza had 27 points in Kentucky's 76-47 rout. And against Oklahoma A&M in the NCAA finals, Groza scored 25 as the Wildcats won their second straight national championship with a 46-36 victory.

The Eastern regional was outstanding in that it brought together three of the nation's top six scorers in Groza, Villanova's Paul Arizin and Tony Lavelli of Yale. The games drew monster crowds totaling 33,177 for the two nights at Madison Square Garden. Rupp recalled that his team was "fired up" for Illinois because some of the players

from that Big Ten team were harassing his Wildcats through the early part of the game. "They kept saying to our kids, 'Who's going to ride in the front seat?' Well, we settled that in a hurry and gave them the worst licking they had in years."

The Western finals at Kansas City, meanwhile, were just as charismatic and considerably more competitive, at least in the opening round. Playing before a turnaway crowd of 10,200 at the Kansas City Auditorium, Hank Iba's Oklahoma A&M team edged Wyoming, 40-39, in clearly the most exciting game of the tournament that year.

Oklahoma A&M then disposed of Oregon State with relative ease in the Western finals, 55-30, and headed for Seattle, Washington, where the NCAA finals would be played on a college campus for the first time since 1941. The Aggies were sitting on the University of Washington campus waiting for Kentucky while the Wildcats were en route by train from New York. On the way, Rupp had time to map out a game plan with Harry Lancaster, his able and longtime assistant. Lancaster had scouted Iba's team, and his report put the burden squarely on Groza. Iba had said that his own center, 6-8 Bob Harris, was the best defensive center in the nation. But Lancaster told Rupp, "Get the ball to Groza. Harris can't handle him." Wah Wah Jones did an especially good job of feeding Groza in the championship game, driving across the circle to lure Harris out and then passing to the Kentucky center breaking under for layups. Groza wound up scoring 25 of his team's 46 points, and his final-game flourish broke the NCAA's tournament scoring record for three games. He scored 82 points and totaled the most field goals in three games (31) and the most free throws (20). These figures added up to a second straight most outstanding player award for the honored Kentucky big man.

"We had a very, very fine game in that second half and we broke it open," Rupp remembered. "Groza played a magnificent game, using the baseline to maneuver. That got him a lot of easy baskets against their center."

After Kentucky got off to an early 10-point lead, Rupp had his team loosen up and drop back on defense. But Iba's disciplined team never varied its deliberate patterns, never opened up on offense and never got close in the game. Defensively, the Aggies also came up short.

"I guess we missed enough setups in the first part of that ball game to have been way out in front," reflects Iba. "Groza was giving us trouble. We were having trouble covering him and some of their other big men, and they got loose inside. We let that ball game get away from us due to the fact that we didn't cover inside. We couldn't control their weight and height underneath, even with our two big men (Bob Harris and Jack Shelton). That was the turning point in the ball game. We were beaten from the free-throw line, as well. Kentucky had a real, real fine ball club."

The victory sent Rupp into a spasmodic dance of joy. He did a jig as his players hugged each other during the euphoric moments after the game. Rupp had every right to kick up his heels. In winning the NCAA tournament for the second straight year, the Wildcats had set several team and individual records. Along with Groza's marks, Kentucky also had the most points in one game (85 against Villanova) and the most for three games (207) among its NCAA tournament accomplishments for 1949. Fittingly, the Wildcats' second consecutive national title came against the only other team to have repeated as NCAA champions.

The city of Lexington had honored its basketball heroes before, but it was nothing like the welcome the Kentucky basketball team received on its triumphant return from Seattle on April 4, 1949. A crowd estimated at 25,000, the largest and most enthusiastic of all, turned out for "Wildcat Appreciation Day," which brought a partial holiday to most of the city and all of the schools. "The morning had a chilly tang, but the sunlight helped pep things up as a 37-unit parade formed for a march through an eight-block downtown area and then to the campus," notes Kentucky sports information director Russell Rice in his book on Wildcat basketball, "Big Blue Machine." "Main Street was a solid mass of humanity. Every store window from the first floor to the top was filled with faces; some of the more hardy souls climbed to dizzy perches to get a good view. Two men sat on a ledge atop the highest building, their legs dangling over the side."

The basketball used in the championship game was given special stature, sitting in a shiny car as the "NCAA Victory Ball." The main attraction, though, was still the handsome NCAA trophy. "Can you imagine how I'd have felt coming back to this celebration if we hadn't brought this hardware with us," Rupp said to an associate.

Rupp later retired the jersey numbers worn by Barker, Beard, Groza, Jones and Rollins, and this ceremonial salute eventually underscored their standing as the "Fabulous Five." The same numbers would be worn by Kentucky players again in later years, against Rupp's wishes, but not with the same luster.

THE GRAND SLAM KIDS

Nat Holman's basketball laboratory wasn't at all impressive—a 22-by-15-foot room in a tower of Lewisohn Stadium, site of football games and summer concerts at the sprawling concrete campus of the City College of New York. There was no secretary to open the day's mail, stacked on the only desk in the dwarfish room, and none of the usual heavyweight "assistants" and hangers-on who historically surround famous college coaches. One insufficient window adorned the ill-placed office of "Mr. Basketball," whose charismatic glitter compared favorably with stars in the sports world but who obviously did not share the same luxuries.

"On a summer morning, when the concert people are rehearsing, it's real nice in here," said the handsome Holman, his voice rolling broguishly. This was the relaxed Holman, a subdued, almost taciturn version of the leader of basketball champions. But it wasn't the complete Holman. Not by a long shot. The other half of this complex, rawboned man was the barnstormer, the New York street fighter who had learned to take care of himself by any means. It showed in his word-slurring language sometimes. In the heat of passionate teaching, Holman was all sound and fury.

"Sometimes I get violent," he said.

The volatile Holman was a tough kibitzer in practice sessions, tautly rearranging his players like a chess master. He scoured the floor for errors while the players prowled like big cats. He chewed them up in definitive notes in a little brown notebook: "Warner drifting from the pivot . . . Roman guilty of dribbling too much."

The players listened most attentively and danced to Holman's tune, no matter how high and strict the notes.

The demonstrative martinet was irreproachable in the arena, although hardly inconsiderate of feelings once he left a basketball court. If the players had immediate personal problems, they would direct them to Holman's assistant, Bobby Sands. Nevertheless, Holman had deep feelings for his team. For example, he never went into the locker room after practice because "kids like to be alone, like to have fun."

This was the gentle side of the whip hand. The rough-edged Holman yearned for polish and had an irrepressible will for self-improvement. He read biographies ranging from Henry Ford to Arturo Toscanini and Douglas MacArthur.

"They're organizers, too," he said.

In 53 years as player, coach and spectator, he estimated that he had been involved in more than 7,000 games, many of them as a professional touring with the Original Celtics. He played in makeshift places spiked with smoke and beer, in poorly lighted halls under exposed rafters.

He injected the Celtics' spirit into the CCNY bloodstream.

"The stories you read about champions getting weary of winning is so much nonsense," was a typical Holman remark. "No true champion ever wins so many contests that he doesn't mind losing one." This credo came from a man who defeated life's problems with much the same gusto that he tackled basketball opponents. His athletic talents elevated him from poor beginnings into a world of glamour, excitement and riches. He made the Original Celtics an artistic and financial success, then constructed CCNY into a national basketball power through innovations that became standards.

Among myriad accomplishments, Holman's most dramatic moment came in the 1949-50 season when his Beavers scored a "grand slam" by winning both major championships—the National Invitation Tournament and the NCAA championship. No other team has done it.

It was, after all, only an echo of the man's life. One of a Russian Jewish immigrant family of 10 children, his existence was a struggle to begin with. When Holman was born on New York City's Lower East Side in 1896, the game of basketball was also a baby. It had been invented a mere five years before by Dr. James Naismith.

The heart of the "Grand Slam Kids" was a group

consisting of Ed Warner, Ed Roman, Floyd Layne, Al "Fats" Roth and Irwin Dambrot. But Holman was the soul, providing determination and drive.

Naismith, of course, nailed up a peach basket to use as a target. And Holman was equally inventive at the age of eight, when he began playing basketball. He made his own ball—a sack stuffed with rags. By the time he was 12, he was playing with boys twice his age.

At 5-foot-11 and 165 pounds, Holman's body was compact but not especially big for basketball purposes. By necessity, therefore, he was forced to improvise equalizing tricks of ball handling and movement that later revolutionized the game. In neighborhood schoolyards, Holman was quick, aggressive and handled the ball exceptionally well.

"Nat can pass the ball to you through a keyhole," a teammate insisted.

He was applauded in public school and at Commerce High School, where he led the team to the New York City basketball title. Holman also excelled in football, soccer and baseball. He was a unanimous choice at goalie for the all-scholastic soccer team, too. Holman turned down an offer from the Cincinnati Reds to go into professional baseball and, instead, decided to attend the Savage School for Physical Education in New York. He worked his way through by playing professional basketball for $6 a night.

Because of his fast-growing reputation as a basketball expert, Holman was given the junior varsity coaching job at CCNY in 1917 when he graduated from the Savage School for Physical Education. Three years later, he was head coach.

In concert with his college duties, Holman took on another coaching job one year later. He joined the Original Celtics, a team of touring professionals which up to then had little distinction. Holman changed that, however.

While with the Celtics, he brought "brains" to basketball. He gave the pro game new life and respectability. Almost by himself, he turned the game from a simple, run-and-shoot style into a struggle of technology and tactics. He brought sophistication to the arena with erudite formations such as the pivot play, the sleeper play, fancy ball handling and the stall. The Holman originals made court trickery an instrument that gave the sport—and the Celtics—an upbeat tempo in the 1920s.

In 1930, he turned exclusively to coaching at CCNY and presided over an era of basketball prosperity at a school whose previous reputation was made on academics. It must be pointed out that, except for a rare season or two, Holman was hardly blessed with an overabundance of talent. Usually he developed ordinary performers into a well-coordinated team. His pet term was that he liked to have the players "mesh."

Holman's teams in 1923 and 1924 lost only one game each season, and the Beavers repeated that fancy accomplishment from 1931 through 1934. Their mark for that three-season period was 43-3.

"I want resourceful, flexible, thinking teams that are never stuck for an idea on what to do next," Holman warned his players; and he often got what he demanded.

Holman's improvisations manifested themselves throughout. His teams were characterizations of the man's playing style. They stressed ball handling and movement, "the two most essential parts of basketball." A losing season was rare in Holman's 37 years as head coach at CCNY. His record for that time was 421 victories against 190 defeats for a .689 lifetime percentage.

The golden years came after the Second World War, and Holman's fame guaranteed lecture tours, book-writing and a cult of worshippers.

And in the late summer of 1949, "Mr. Basketball" had a team that was the envy of America's coaches. Although his place among basketball greats was already guaranteed by previous accomplishments, Holman would take this team to unprecedented heights.

Holman boasted size and depth and promised the basketball world a superb collection of athletes "from my best freshman team ever." Roman was a 6-foot-6 center with an ambidextrous hook shot and a quick, one-handed set. His 220-pound frame seemed awkward and ill-suited for basketball, but few noticed the ungainliness while watching him score points.

Warner was a little man who played the big man's game. Holman, historically sparing in praise of his players, called him "the toughest bucket man in college ranks." Warner had timing and a deceptively fluid body motion that enabled him to juggle defensive men. He'd go to his left, fake right and come back left again and score the basket. The little star called it his "triple feint." He drove teams to distraction and forced opposing coaches to double- and triple-team him. Somehow, he managed to twist away from his shadows for a hook shot or curling layup.

Dambrot, "the perfect captain" in Holman's estimation, was the senior who gave the team direction. The coach called his rugged big man irreplaceable and opposing players found him immovable. Roth was a steadying influence in the backcourt, and Layne was considered one of the best defensive players in the country.

Holman gave the Beavers purpose with his fiery attitude. Every regular knew how to play all

69

70

corners of the court and the middle as well. Holman stressed that only a compact, fluid five-man effort could be successful.

It appeared that's what he had as the Beavers built a five-game winning streak at the start of the 1949-50 season and later won a crucial game over cross-town rival St. John's. But the finicky Holman hardly considered CCNY an outstanding team at this point. He scowled at the excessive dribbling and fancy passes. He fussed at practice sessions, halting play time and again by putting two fingers to his mouth and blasting through them. Seemingly, the whistle that dangled from his muscular neck was too much trouble for him to use.

After a seven-game winning streak later in the season, the Beavers began to scare people. One opponent, in fact, called on the services of a psychiatrist to get ready for a game with CCNY; but it didn't do any good. Holman smiled at last.

"The fast break," he announced happily, "is working to perfection."

Three losses in a five-game stretch late in the year sobered Holman again. However, when Roman fouled out of one of the games, the CCNY coach inserted the shorter Warner into the pivot position. It proved to be a life-saving move.

"All of a sudden, something dropped into place," said Holman, his gray-green eyes aglow. "You could see and almost feel them mesh into a team."

When the opposition began double-teaming Roman in the season's concluding games, Holman alternated him at center with Warner, who could outjump men six inches taller and score with more efficacy. Warner's point production increased, and CCNY finished the regular season by sweeping the other New York teams. As a result of their "Subway Conference" championship, the Beavers received one of the last bids for the NIT.

The Beavers, however, were expected to last no longer than the first round. The book on Holman's club was that it was "only a team of sophomores playing over their heads and will blow sky-high when the pressure is applied." It looked hopeless, but according to Holman, all the Beavers wanted was the opportunity to redeem their pride after losing five games during the season. "The kids," he said, "have grown up." Holman's "grown-ups" defeated San Francisco, Kentucky, Duquesne, and Bradley to win the NIT.

Five days after their NIT success, the Beavers took aim at the NCAA championship by defeating

Gene Melchiorre (23) and Bill Mann (11) of Bradley surround CCNY's Al Roth in fight for ball during the 1950 championship game.

Ohio State, 56-55, in the first round of the Eastern regional. They followed with a 78-73 triumph over North Carolina State in the Eastern finals and then claimed their second national title in less than two weeks, ironically by defeating Bradley again. The score of 71-68 in the NCAA championship game was a little closer than their 69-61 triumph over the Braves in the NIT.

Holman, typically, threw cold water on the stunning achievement.

"They still lose the ball so often it frightens me," he said.

But to earn their high marks, the CCNY players had done just about everything Holman had asked.

None of the NCAA tournament games was a soft touch for CCNY. Ohio State, a team devoted to fundamental basketball, employing a tight zone defense and a fast-paced offensive game, gave the Beavers trouble from start to finish. The Buckeyes entrusted their scoring to Dick Schnittker, who could shoot equally well with either hand, and rangy Bob Donham. Those two had their hands in just about everything the Buckeyes did and by the end of the first half, the teams were tied at 40-40. "This period was one of the most sensational ever contested on the (Madison Square) Garden court," marveled George Shiebler of the Eastern College Athletic Conference in the Official Basketball Guide. The Buckeyes put in 16 of their 31 field goal attempts and the Beavers hit 18 of 42. There were five ties and four lead changes in the first half, with the teams never more than five points apart.

In the second half, CCNY took an early three-point lead. Then Holman introduced a new strategy to counter the effect of the tough Ohio State zone, which had been clogging the middle and preventing the Beavers from driving through the area. CCNY held the ball, refusing to take a shot or make a move to the basket. The intent was to force the Buckeyes to come after the ball and open the middle to new lanes of attack. But Ohio State refused to take the bait and for five minutes nothing happened. CCNY then started to shoot over the zone, and the game accelerated a bit after that. Floyd Layne and Norm Mager, never known for their outside shooting, each hit seven times from long range.

Still, the game was close; and although CCNY held the lead, Holman's team seemed bent on giving it away at the end. With a minute left and the Beavers in command, 56-54, Dambrot found Warner all alone under the basket. Unsure whether to take an easy layup or dribble back out and freeze the ball, Warner stayed in the foul lane for more than three seconds, a violation of the rules; the ball was turned over to Ohio State. But

71

the Buckeyes were unable to capitalize on this turnover and with 20 seconds left, CCNY had possession of the ball and the lead. Once again, the Beavers stumbled into an error. This time Roman was called for charging into Bob Burkholder while driving for the basket. Burkholder converted the free throw to cut CCNY's lead to 56-55, and the Buckeyes had the ball out of bounds and a chance for the game-winning basket. With Schnittker and Donham out of the game on fouls, the Big Ten team was forced to go to Jim Remington for the final shot. He was not able to work free, finally tossing up a shot with five seconds left that was off the mark. Roth came down with the rebound and held the ball until the final buzzer sounded.

North Carolina State presented an entirely different look to CCNY. The Wolfpack played with wide-open, almost reckless frenzy behind the scoring proficiency of Sam Ranzino and Dick Dickey. The two had combined for 57 points as North Carolina State had run away from Holy Cross, 87-74, in the East's other opening-round game at the Garden. The Eastern finals followed much the same pattern as the CCNY-Ohio State meeting, with the teams going down to the last two minutes to decide the game. This time, CCNY nursed a three-point lead after the score had been tied 14 times. And again, the Beavers had forced the opposition's two big guns, Ranzino and Dickey, to foul out in the closing minutes. Roman, too, had fouled out; but CCNY still had an ace in the hole in Warner, who moved into the pivot and feinted his way to a pair of game-clinching layups.

And so it came down to the finals and once again, CCNY's opponent was Bradley. Ironically, the Braves were the last team to make the NCAA field. Bradley had been tied with Kansas in District 5, and a playoff game for that berth was postponed to allow the Braves to compete in the NIT. The day after their grueling loss to CCNY in the NIT finals, the Braves flew to Kansas City for a second chance against a strong Kansas team led by Clyde Lovellette. The rugged game was not decided until the last three minutes, when Paul Unruh scored three field goals in a 45-second span to earn a 59-57 victory for Bradley and a place in the NCAA's Western regional. There, the tired Braves had trouble before subduing UCLA and Baylor, a team that was a 14-point underdog.

Coach John Wooden, in his second year at UCLA, had seen his team win the Pacific Coast Conference title on a last-second, 50-foot shot by Ralph Joeckel against Washington State. The star of the Bruins was George Stanich, an Olympic high jumper in 1948 who could dunk the ball off a drive whenever he had an opening. The Braves were

trailing UCLA late in the second half before an energetic burst provided them with a 73-59 victory.

In the Western finals, Baylor was supposedly an easy mark for Bradley, a team that finished the regular season ranked No. 1 in The Associated Press poll. But the Southwest Conference team found itself close to a major upset in the final minute. The score was tied nine times in the game, and the lead changed on six occasions. With 3:33 remaining, Bradley led by eight points. But Don Heathington, who scored 26 points in the game, and Odell Preston and Gerald Cobb helped pare the Braves' margin to one point, 67-66, with nine seconds remaining. Five seconds later, Aaron Preece converted a free throw to give Bradley the Western championship, 68-66, in what the Braves' Unruh remembers as a "terrifically intense" game.

The next day, the travel-weary Bradley team went to New York for its fateful rematch with CCNY. Despite Bradley's generally tired condition, the majority opinion seemed to favor the Braves in the NCAA finals. It was generally thought that the team from Peoria, Illinois, considered by most to be the greatest in Bradley history, had more talent than CCNY. It was inconceivable to some that City could handle this team twice. "We always thought we were better," recalls Unruh. "We had a fast, quick ball club. Our fast break was a key part of our game and we had the players to handle it. We had five or six guys who gave us offense. We were a very well-rounded team, no weak spots."

The starting lineup usually included Unruh and Aaron Preece at forwards, Elmer Behnke at center and Gene "Squeaky" Melchiorre and Bill Mann in the backcourt. Joe Stowell, later a coach at Bradley, also was an integral part of this fine team. "Our group was composed mostly of service veterans who were a year or two older than the average college man," recalls Unruh. "Some of the guys like Melchiorre and Mann played for high-caliber service teams before they came to Bradley, and so we had a solid group of veteran players." Coach Forddy Anderson, who had replaced Bradley coaching legend A. J. Robertson in the late 1940s, was the perfect Pied Piper to guide the Braves' fortunes. "Anderson was just super," Unruh says. "He was at his prime then, a master tactician. He was highly organized, well disciplined. And we played very hard for him."

CCNY not only would be taking on the nation's No. 1 team but also would be trying to accomplish a feat that was without precedent. Four teams in

*Bradley's Bill Mann goes up for a shot in the Braves'
68-66 West regional title victory over Baylor.*

72

the previous 10 years had tried for a grand slam of both the NIT and the NCAA, and none had come this close. In the 1939-40 season, Colorado had won the NIT but had been beaten by Southern California in the NCAA's Western semifinals. That same year, Duquesne lost to Colorado in the NIT championship game and then was beaten by Indiana in the NCAA's Eastern finals. Utah had lost to Kentucky in the quarterfinals of the NIT before going on to win the NCAA title in 1943-44. And in 1948-49, Kentucky was favored to sweep both tourneys but never made it past the quarterfinals of the NIT. The Wildcats did, however, win the NCAA championship.

Despite the longshot odds, there was hope in the CCNY camp that the Beavers, outmatched or not, would find their way to victory. Even the usually cautious Holman seemed to exude a unique confidence. "The team just seemed to arrive in the Kentucky game during the NIT," said the CCNY coach. "I don't think they have been lucky, and I don't think they've just been hot. They simply found themselves."

The CCNY followers were equally as positive and a bit more fervent. Long before the game started, Madison Square Garden vibrated to the chants of "Allagaroo, Allagaroo," the Beavers' battle cry. As Nat Holman's team prepared to take the floor against Bradley, the robust, disconcerting sounds of "Allagaroo, garoo, garah; Allagaroo, garoo, garah; Ee-yah, Ee-yah, Sis, Boom, Bah" rolled out in waves and flooded the famous Garden.

Thus intoxicated, CCNY played at its highest pitch.

Although Bradley had switched from its man-to-man tactics of the first game to a zone defense, the NCAA finals were basically a rerun of the NIT championship game. The scoring was redistributed this time, though. Unruh and Behnke were shut off effectively, but Bradley's offensive punch was restored by Melchiorre, Preece and George Chianakas. There was beautiful balance in the CCNY attack, with Dambrot, Roman, Warner, Layne and Norm Mager all scoring in double figures.

Shooting successfully over the Bradley zone, CCNY moved to an early lead and finished the first half with a 39-32 advantage. When Bradley abandoned its zone in favor of a man-to-man defense, City turned to its running game and stretched its lead to as much as 10 points midway through the

73

NCAA

second half. With just a few minutes left, the score was 69-61, just as it had ended in the NIT; but Bradley turned to a full-court press that changed the game's momentum. The Braves' pressing defense already had caused many fouls, but now it caused turnovers. The Beavers, once quick and alert, had lost their snap and precision and soon lost most of their lead. With the suddenness and shock of a match struck in a dark room, Bradley was in contention in the last minute. Joe Stowell made a foul shot, and Melchiorre picked up a stray ball and drove for a layup. Less than 20 seconds later, the Bradley guard intercepted a pass and drove the length of the court to cut the CCNY lead to 69-68. Now with City trying to protect a tenuous one-point lead for a full 40 seconds, the ubiquitous Melchiorre picked off a wild pass and drove for the basket. This time he found his path guarded by an army of CCNY players.

"I had fouled out and watched the whole thing from the bench," remembers Unruh. "Melchiorre drove toward the middle, and the entire CCNY team converged on him. It was a hatchet job. The films later showed him being ripped apart. We all felt he was fouled, but there was no foul called."

As it was, though, Melchiorre's short jump-shot attempt from the free-throw line was intercepted by Dambrot, who somehow managed to retain control of the ball and fire a cross-court pass to Mager. The sprinting CCNY player laid the ball in the basket with less than 10 seconds showing on the clock, and the Beavers had a 71-68 victory.

"It was really a traumatic experience for us," Unruh says. "In fact, it still is. We've lived with that game to this day. It still hurts 30 years later."

The controversy of the final seconds of that championship game continued for weeks in Peoria, an emotionally distressed city, according to Bradley's basketball yearbook. "Peoria was heartbroken," the yearbook said. "It felt its team was the victim of injustice." Downtown and neighborhood theaters exhibited newsreels of the alleged foul. The marquee of the Madison Theater in town carried the following words: "Was Squeaky Fouled? You Be The Judge!"

"They were, I guess, what you would call a Cinderella team," says Unruh of CCNY. "We had reached our peak and tried to hang on. They came on like a whirlwind. They had had a mediocre season but came on hot as a firecracker at the end. They jelled, and we caught them at the wrong time."

Still, Unruh is not convinced that the better team won.

"It's a lesson of life, I guess. We all have victories and losses in life—and you have to learn to accept them all. But had the foul been called on Melchiorre, he probably would have made the free throws and there would have been a different NCAA champion."

It was, however, CCNY's show at the end and to the winner went all the spoils—including the outstanding player award to Dambrot, who scored a team-high 15 points in the championship game. The NCAA tournament that year, incidentally, was the most successful in history to that point in terms of attendance and income. Both the total attendance of 75,464 and the net income of $64,646 set records. These figures would continue to multiply in subsequent seasons, especially in light of the new format in 1951 which doubled the field to 16.

CCNY's meteoric flight, meanwhile, would be symbolic of an age past in college basketball. Never again would a team have the opportunity to win both the NIT and NCAA championships in one season. Oddly, though, the team that provided Holman with so much pride soon embarrassed him. Within a year of the "grand slam" season, some of the Beaver players were involved in scandal. They were accused of conspiring with gamblers to "shave points" in some of the winning games of 1949-50 with the purpose of keeping the final score within certain limits for betting.

Holman's spirit was broken when the scandal became public and the revelations were proven true. Always the most honest of basketball players, he was stunned by the immorality. College basketball eventually recovered fully from the point-shaving scandals, but it's probable that Holman never did.

SWEET KENTUCKY BABES

Shortly before the 1951 NCAA finals in snow-shrouded Minneapolis, Adolph Rupp probed Hank Iba for pregame advice. The conversation between the venerable coaches went something like this:

Rupp: "Tell me something about this Kansas State team."

Iba: "Now, Adolph, I can't tell you anything about them. It's the greatest basketball team that's ever been put together."

Rupp: "The greatest, for sure?"

Iba: "Yes, and you haven't got a chance to beat them. I don't know whether I've ever seen your team play, but you can't beat them."

Rupp: "The hell with that. We've got to find some way to beat them."

Iba was speaking from first-hand experience. His Oklahoma A&M (now Oklahoma State) Aggies had just been swallowed whole by the Wildcats, 68-44, in the finals of the Western regional at Kansas City. Now Kansas State would play Rupp's Kentucky team in the championship game on the campus of the University of Minnesota, and the Big Seven power exuded a noticeable swagger on the day of the game. Both teams ate their pregame meal in the same hotel dining room. While the Kentucky players sat in relative silence waiting to be served, the Kansas State players were talking and laughing, apparently relaxed and cocky.

"They're just whistling in the graveyard," an equally confident Rupp told his players.

Despite Rupp's optimism, however, the Kansas State team had his Wildcats down by two points at the half, 29-27. This was due in part to the indifferent play of Bill Spivey and the illness of Cliff Hagan. Spivey, the seven-footer who was just about everybody's all-America center that year, had problems in the first half with Kansas State's Lew Hitch in their heralded "battle of the pivot." Hitch, although five inches shorter than the much-honored Spivey, gave his adversary more than he bargained for and had outscored Spivey 10-4 as the Western champions raced to an early 19-13 lead. But then Rupp inserted Hagan into the

lineup, despite the fact that the 6-foot-4 forward had been sick with a sore throat and a fever in his hotel room two days earlier and carried the same disconcerting symptoms into the championship game at Williams Arena. With Hagan back in the lineup, it was not long before Kentucky began cutting away the Kansas State lead. At the half, Rupp gave his team an intoxicating pep talk, lit a fire under Spivey and overruled a doctor's orders for Hagan.

"He had a temperature of about 101½," Rupp remembered in later years, "and the doctor wouldn't let him play. I told the doctor, 'Hell, that's the right temperature to play.' I turned to Hagan and said, 'The hell with that . . . you start at forward.' Well, we just put Hagan in; and then after 10 minutes or so, we had a 20-point lead."

The second half belonged to Kentucky, now a savage team of seemingly limitless energy. The Southeastern Conference champions took control of the game shortly after intermission behind Spivey and Hagan and went on to win the championship, 68-58. Spivey scored 22 points and finished with 21 rebounds, and Hagan wound up with 10 points and several key rebounds.

"Spivey made the difference after he went to work," Rupp told reporters after the game. "Then, too, we opened up the middle more in the second half, sent the guards driving through and shooting more from the outside as well."

Most conspicuous of these shooters were Lucian Whitaker and Frank Ramsey, who scored nine points each for Kentucky. The gorgeous balance of the Wildcat offense was further emphasized by the eight-point performances of Shelby Linville and Bobby Watson.

"Rupp actually beat Kansas State with a delay game, although he never admitted it," Iba says. "I remember that because he never used a delay game. We had to go to a 'Doughnut Club' for breakfast the next morning, and I was giving him hell in the cab. He always said, 'I don't play a delay game.' They talk about the four-corners (delay)

now. Hell, he was runnin' it that night. He put Spivey in the middle and put one player in each corner, and they'd just pass that ball 'til they'd break somebody open. They talk about the four corners being new. It wasn't new back in those days, I'll tell you."

Kentucky's convincing decision was all the more golden because the Wildcats had beaten a team of enormous stature. Playing one of the nation's toughest schedules, Kansas State boasted victories over NIT winner Brigham Young and three other conference champions—Illinois, Oklahoma A&M and Arizona. In addition, Jack Gardner's fine team had scored big triumphs over Long Island University, Ohio State, Minnesota, Kansas and Purdue.

"In my own mind, Kansas State had the better ball club and could have beaten Kentucky on any other night," says Ernie Barrett, who played a leading role for the Big Seven team that season.

The 1950-51 Kansas State team was the culmination of hard work by Gardner, who had come to Manhattan, Kansas, in 1939, determined to build the Wildcats into winners. Thwarted by the Second World War, Gardner's rebuilding process was slow in developing. But by 1948, he had Kansas State at the top of the Big Seven Conference; and the Wildcats stayed among the nation's best teams until his departure five seasons later. Gardner, brought up on a deliberate style of basketball, began to adjust his thinking toward the fast break at Kansas State. But while embracing this system, Gardner always demanded that his teams discipline themselves to hold the ball whenever appropriate. He made elaborate checklists to anticipate what would happen in a game and charts to study what had happened. These scientific preparations resulted in a fine winning percentage at Kansas State and later at Utah. A milk-drinking fanatic who believed in its nerve-calming properties, Gardner would drink as much as four quarts during a game. Once as a prank his players added some milk of magnesia to his bottle and Gardner had, he said, "a very interesting evening."

Gardner used a two-platoon system at Kansas State in 1950-51, as was evidenced by nine players scoring more than 100 points and 11 seeing action in at least 23 games. Barrett, a 6-3 guard whom Gardner revered as "the finest competitor I have ever coached," was the leading scorer on this team of great balance, but not by much. Barrett had a 10.3 average to 9.6 for Jack Stone, who in turn held a whisker's edge over Jim Iverson's 8.9. Lew Hitch, Dick Knostman, Ed Head, Bob Rousey and John Gibson followed on their heels. These efficient components blended to give Kansas State a lofty 68.8 scoring average, one of the highest in the nation and 15.5 points per game better than its opponents. During a time when most teams were home-grown products, Kansas State's wide-ranging geographical mixture was an anomaly. Head and Stone were from Los Angeles; Rousey and Dick Peck from Anderson, Indiana; Hitch from Griggsville, Illinois; Glenn Channell from Dallas, Texas, and Iverson from Mitchell, South Dakota. Barrett and sophomore sensation Knostman were among the few home-state players.

Barrett was considered to be the gadfly of the Wildcats but only played slightly more than half the time, a good indication of the far-reaching depth of this Kansas State team that Gardner called the "best balanced" he ever coached. Barrett's talents helped Kansas State climb through the regionals, but an injury suffered against Oklahoma A&M in the Western title game virtually cut him out of the picture in the NCAA finals.

"I hurt my shoulder," Barrett recalls. "I started at Minneapolis the next Tuesday (three days later), but only thanks to coach Gardner. I couldn't raise my left arm at all—just about waist high." Barrett, who started along with Stone, Hitch, Head and Iverson in the championship game, played only about five minutes and scored but four points. He wanted to play more, but Gardner wouldn't allow it. "I begged Gardner to shoot me with Novocain. They do it all the time now, but he thought it might be injurious to my health or future."

Rupp's unprecedented third NCAA championship in four years was undoubtedly retributive for him. The year before, he had been involved in a distasteful episode where his defending national champions had won the Southeastern Conference title, yet ironically were not invited to the NCAA tournament.

"At that time," Rupp remembered, "there was one man who decided who would go in each district. In ours, it was Gus Tebell of the University of Virginia. North Carolina State was strong in their area, but the very fact that we had this fine bunch of boys back and had been Southeastern Conference champions two years in a row justified our going to the NCAAs. But Tebell finally cast his vote for North Carolina State. They went to the tournament and got beat in the first round." (Actually, North Carolina State did not lose in the first round. The Wolfpack managed to get by Holy Cross in the opening round of the Eastern regional before suffering a five-point defeat to CCNY in the Eastern finals.)

Kentucky, incidentally, went to the NIT that year and suffered considerably more embarrassment than North Carolina State. The Wildcats were humiliated, 89-50, by CCNY's "grand slam"

team. It was Rupp's worst defeat in 24 years of coaching. The rout elicited this classic, caustic comment by Rupp to his team in the dressing room: "I want to thank you, boys. You get me selected coach of the year and then bring me up here and embarrass the hell out of me."

There was no embarrassing Rupp the following year, however, as all the parts fit together with Spivey, the tower of strength, in the middle. Dale Barnstable and Jim Line were gone from the fine 1949-50 team that had won 25 of 30 games, but Rupp had 6-3 senior Walt Hirsch returning as a regular forward and 6-5 junior Shelby Linville ready to become a starter. At the guard positions, 5-10 Bobby Watson was back and a 6-3 freshman of great promise, Frank Ramsey, was made an immediate starter. Hagan, a 6-4 hook-shot artist, was on the freshman team and moved up to the varsity in midseason. Once there, he provided key scoring and rebounding in a reserve role. Hagan and Lucian "Skippy" Whitaker were the most useful members of a fine crop of reserves. In fact, Rupp had depth at every position with Read Morgan, Lou Tsioropoulos, Guy Strong, Dwight Price, Lindle Castle, Paul Lansaw and C. M. Newton.

The Wildcats achieved incredibly balanced scoring with their starters: Spivey averaged 19.2 points; Linville, 10.4; Watson, 10.4; Ramsey, 10.1, and Hirsch, 9.1. And with this unit in high gear, Kentucky lost only two games all season—by a total of five points. The first was a 43-42 overtime loss to St. Louis University in the Sugar Bowl tournament, and the last was a 61-57 upset by Vanderbilt in the Southeastern Conference playoffs. The loss to Vanderbilt, incidentally, did not knock Kentucky out of the NCAA tournament because the SEC regular-season champion, for the first time, received an automatic bid. Partly as an outgrowth of Rupp's fussing about being passed over the previous season, the NCAA had doubled its tournament field in 1951 to 16 teams.

Despite the losses to St. Louis and Vanderbilt, Kentucky's 1950-51 season was one of celebration from start to finish. The Wildcats won 32 games—including 21 straight at one point—and they did it playing one of the most representative schedules in the country. One of their biggest early victories was a 68-39 rout of Kansas. This battle for the No. 1 ranking in college basketball featured a heralded individual duel between Spivey and Clyde Lovellette of Kansas, a brilliant sophomore already being talked about as the season's all-America center. As an added element of drama, Rupp was pitted against his old coach, Phog Allen.

For several days before the big game, Spivey found newspaper clippings lauding Lovellette's prowess pasted on his locker door. He knew that Rupp had put them there as a bit of psychology; and by game time, Spivey said, "I was ready to jump through the ceiling." Spivey's intense emotion was equal to the high moment. The Kentucky center finished with 22 points to Lovellette's 10 and completely outplayed the Kansas sophomore in every phase of the game. Tears in his eyes, Lovellette fouled out with 13:33 left in the game. Rupp promptly pulled Spivey despite his pleas to "let me go back in." "I wanted them (the centers) to have exactly the same amount of playing time," the Kentucky coach said afterward.

Kentucky's loss to St. Louis later in the season dropped the Wildcats to No. 2 in the national polls behind undefeated Oklahoma A&M. In early February, however, after Oklahoma A&M had lost and Kentucky had won 11 straight games—including victories over DePaul and Notre Dame—the Wildcats were restored to the No. 1 position. By the time the SEC playoffs rolled around on March 1, the Wildcats had won 18 straight and clearly were playing their best ball of the season. Decisive victories over Mississippi State, Auburn and Georgia Tech preceded the finals against Vanderbilt, a team that Kentucky twice had beaten earlier in the season by a total of 57 points. There seemed no logical way that Vanderbilt could beat Kentucky. But it happened anyway, with the Commodores' spirit overcoming the Wildcats' talent. "Kentucky was outfought and it failed to move the ball," wrote Tom Siler in the Knoxville News-Sentinel. Dudley Green of the Nashville Banner called it "the greatest victory ever in Vanderbilt athletic history—football or basketball."

It was perhaps beneficial for Kentucky to lose at this point. The Wildcats had learned not to underestimate an opponent and entered the 1951 NCAA tournament as a grim and determined team. Their determination was enlarged somewhat by the absence of Hirsch, who was ineligible because he was in his fourth season of varsity play. His place in the lineup was taken by Hagan, fast showing the form that would make him a future all-America.

Kentucky's first opponent in the tournament was Louisville, one of the independent teams invited as an at-large entry in the newly enlarged NCAA setup. The Wildcats trailed their state rivals, 64-60, with 9:35 to go; but some clutch field goals by Whitaker helped pull Kentucky through, 79-68. Then, in the Eastern regional in New York, Kentucky got by St. John's without difficulty, 59-43. Afterward, St. John's player Al McGuire told Rupp, "We stopped Spivey, but we couldn't stop Watson or Ramsey." The Redmen held Spivey to a subpar

77

78

12 points but didn't anticipate Ramsey scoring 13 and Watson 12.

In the Eastern finals, Kentucky needed extraordinary performances from Spivey and Linville to beat Big Ten champion Illinois, 76-74. Spivey scored 28 points and collected 16 rebounds. Linville scored 14 points, including the winning field goal with 12 seconds left. "I said, 'Get the ball into Linville and let him work in there,'" Rupp recalled, "and he sure got some baskets in a hurry for us when we needed them."

The ball bounced right in every respect for Kentucky in this game. Illinois captain Don Sunderlage missed a driving shot at the end that hit the rim. The Wildcats considered themselves fortunate to win, since three of their starters—Spivey, Hagan and Whitaker—had fouled out. Kentucky's victory culminated one of the most captivating Eastern regionals in years. Illinois had drawn attention to itself earlier in the tournament by stopping Columbia's mammoth 31-game victory streak and stormed into the finals with an impressive triumph over North Carolina State behind Sunderlage, who set four individual records in the tourney. The Illinois star led all players with a record 83 points in four games. In addition, he set records for total free throws (27), total assists (22) and single-game assists (10).

Before Kansas State's humiliation of Oklahoma A&M in the finals, the Western regional was almost equally as feverish and artistic. Kansas State lost most of a 23-point lead before subduing Arizona, 61-59, then similarly lost the better part of a mountainous advantage before struggling past Brigham Young, 64-54. Against Oklahoma A&M, however, Kansas State would not buckle. The Wildcats had an early 20-5 lead as the Aggies went almost eight minutes before scoring from the field. It was 37-14 at intermission; Kansas State never had less than a 21-point lead thereafter, cresting at 28. It was on the wave of that impressive triumph over Oklahoma A&M that Kansas State sailed into the NCAA finals at Minneapolis, only to be brought down to earth by Kentucky.

Historically, it was not only a big year for Rupp's team, but also for the tournament. After 12 years of conducting the basketball tournament with a limited total of eight teams selected from each of the eight NCAA districts, the NCAA Executive Committee approved a revised plan to double the number of participating teams. The idea was generally prompted by the burgeoning growth of

Bill Spivey (77) and Frank Ramsey (30) of Kentucky battle Kansas State's John Gibson in the 1951 championship game.

college basketball across the face of America. Specifically, Kentucky's controversial shutout in the 1949-50 tournament was one of the main incidents that generated the revolutionary plan.

"The chairman of the selection committee in the Southern district (District 3) was having problems picking between Everett Case's North Carolina State team and Adolph Rupp's Kentucky team in the 1950 tournament," remembers Dutch Lonborg, who as chairman of the tournament committee at the time spent a lot of his waking hours talking to chairmen of the various selection committees around the country. "They didn't want to play off for the district championship; they both wanted to be in the NCAA tournament without having to go through that. Both had great teams that year, and the selection committee simply could not select the best team. That was the start of the new format. We went to two teams in each district then, mainly because of what was going on in the Southern district. The expansion permitted us to give automatic qualifications for the major conferences and a place for major independents. The increase in the number of teams made it possible for more good teams in the country to get into the tournament. A few teams did not get in, though, because some of them wanted to go to New York for the NIT."

Automatic qualification was based on a conference's winning percentage in earlier NCAA tournaments and was subject to an annual review. The 10 major conferences which first qualified for this expanded format in 1951 and their champions that year included: Southeastern (Kentucky), Big Ten (Illinois), Ivy League (Columbia), Southern (North Carolina State), Big Seven (Kansas State), Border (Arizona), Skyline (Brigham Young), Missouri Valley (Oklahoma A&M), Pacific Coast (Washington) and Southwest (Texas A&M). The six at-large teams deemed worthy of competition in this historic year included Louisville, St. John's, Connecticut, Villanova, San Jose State and Montana. The at-large teams, incidentally, were selected strictly on the basis of record, regardless of whether they were independents or conference members.

This dramatic change of format was one of the most significant chapters in the history of the NCAA championship. Of course, the field would be enlarged even more—in fact, doubled again by the 1970s—but the implications of the 1951 plan were obvious to all. With top conference representation, along with the cream of the independents, a truly representative national champion would be assured. By this point in time, the NCAA championship clearly had moved to the forefront as the nation's premier postseason tournament, surpass-

ing the venerable NIT.

"It is a foregone conclusion that under the new plan no deserving team will be on the outside looking in," wrote United Press sports editor Leo H. Petersen. "None of the top collegiate quintets will be shut out of the nation's No. 1 tournament as some have in the past because of the limited number of entries. That has happened in the past, when some coaches felt the NCAA tournament was too much of a 'closed shop' affair and thus passed it up for other postseason bids. Coaches generally, and many of them were critical of the old NCAA setup, acclaim the new tournament plan and believe the new system will produce a team which will be accepted without question as the intercollegiate basketball champion."

The expanded NCAA activity in 1951 necessitated the need for more playoff areas. The new format called for three first-round locations—Kansas City in the West and Raleigh, North Carolina, and New York in the East—along with the championship site in Minneapolis. Expansion triggered new records in attendance (110,645) and gross income (over $200,000).

Ironically, though, while the NCAA was making progress, college basketball in general was taking some backward steps with revelations of the gambling scandals. In New York, District Attorney Frank Hogan revealed that several college players had accepted bribes from professional gamblers to fix the scores of games. At first the scandals touched only players in the New York schools—CCNY, Long Island University, New York University and Manhattan. But later, although Adolph Rupp had once pontificated that "Gamblers couldn't touch my boys with a 10-foot pole," it was revealed that several Kentucky players were involved in the wrongdoing. The chain reaction later touched Bradley and Toledo as well, and there were more than 30 arrests of players and gamblers in 1951. When the grand jury ended its investigation of the sordid affair on April 29, 1952, Hogan had found 86 fixed games in 23 cities in 17 states. And hardly anyone was certain that all the guilty parties had been caught.

This explosion of notoriety shook the foundation of college basketball in America, jarring college officials into back-to-the-campus movements, limiting competition and forcing a closer scrutiny of players. Big-city arenas, such as New York's Madison Square Garden, suffered in the wake of the scandal. The NIT, for one, lost some of its luster. The Garden, thought by many to be a hothouse for festering the gambling element, wore a tarnished image among the college basketball set. Fan support dwindled and so did teams willing to compete at the world-famous arena.

Specifically because of the gambling scandals, all first-round and regional games eventually were moved to campus sites as a hedge against supposed "big-city corruption." However, in a concession to other obligations, the NCAA would not necessarily confine the finals to campus locations.

"This was primarily because off-campus sites were neutral and some had larger seating capacities than most college facilities," explains Lonborg. "In those cases, the additional seating meant more money for the NCAA and the teams."

There was some criticism of playing at campus sites because of the home-court advantage it afforded some teams. But the overall therapeutic effect was good, the NCAA's Executive Committee found. "Of course it is hard to legislate morals," says Lonborg, "but keeping the first rounds and regionals on campus probably helped in the area of gambling."

80

'STRATIFIED TRANSITIONAL MAN-FOR-MAN DEFENSE WITH THE ZONE PRINCIPLE'

For years, James Naismith and Phog Allen coexisted peacefully on one campus, although their philosophies were at opposite ends of the court. Naismith was rather wistfully indulgent and Allen respectful but condescending, each proud of what he had fashioned. Naismith, the low-key sportsman, advocated pure amateurism in college basketball. Allen, the fierce, far-sighted revolutionary, pioneered recruiting and intensive coaching. Naismith believed that basketball was a game which simply could not be coached, that the best thing to do was throw the ball up and let the boys have fun. Allen, conversely, felt that Naismith's invention lent itself to complicated strategies and sober achievements. They usually disagreed as well on the influence of rules—Naismith in defense of the old and Allen a standard-bearer for the newest innovations.

Clearly, Naismith had invented a game for fun and Allen had turned it to profit. However Allen's methods rubbed against Naismith, though, they were abundantly successful. Even Naismith would have to tip his hat to that.

Allen, who once played for Naismith at Kansas, later returned as coach of the Jayhawks and became as legendary as his predecessor. According to Kentucky demigod Adolph Rupp, Forrest C. Allen was "not only one of the greatest coaches that the game has ever developed, but also one of the finest leaders of men." Only Rupp's teams won more than Allen's mountainous total of 771 games. If Naismith, the inventor, is known as the "father of basketball," then Allen, the innovator, could justifiably be called the "father of basketball coaches." In his 48-year career, Allen produced a basketful of fine coaches from his extravagantly successful teams, including Rupp, Dutch Lonborg, John Bunn, Lou Menze, Dean Smith and Frosty Cox. In 39 seasons at Kansas, Allen's teams won 24

conference championships, two Helms Foundation national championships and the NCAA title in 1952. In addition to his remarkable coaching achievements, Allen founded the National Association of Basketball Coaches in 1927, was instrumental in including basketball in the Olympic Games and also was one of the leaders in the movement to start the NCAA tournament.

It is probable that Allen valued the NCAA championship his team won as much as any of his achievements, considering the steep emotional hill he had to climb to get to the mountaintop. The closest that Allen had come to winning the NCAA title was in 1940, when his Jayhawks were defeated by Indiana in the finals, 60-42. He nurtured a hope to return to the tournament, and this eventually became an all-consuming desire to win the championship after one happenstance during the 1946-47 season. Allen had reported for practice one afternoon wearing a suit and street shoes instead of the usual sweat clothes and gym shoes so he could leave in a hurry for a speaking engagement. During a drill, a player named Ted Bean was running the fast break and accidentally charged into Allen, knocking him back on his head.

"I saw it coming and tried to dodge and probably could have done so if I'd had sneakers as usual," Allen recalled. "But I slipped on my street shoes and Ted corked me. I knew it was going to be bad. As I was falling I remember a lot of things flashing before me, among them, General Patton's famous phrase, 'What a hell of a way to go.'"

Concerned players surrounded Allen, but the coach stoically brushed them away, refusing to let on how badly he had been hurt. "It was killing me . . . I called for several more patterns, then dismissed them. I must have sounded like an idiot at the talk that night; and how I drove there, I don't remember. Nor do I remember how I got home."

82

Things worsened for Allen after that and finally he decided to take a leave of absence. Howard Engleman, then a law student and a one-time Kansas all-America, took over the team for the rest of the 1946-47 season. As Allen boarded a train to California to recuperate, he wasn't sure that he would be back as Kansas coach; and associates were inclined to think the same way. It looked bad, Allen remembered.

"I went out there and swam in the cold ocean in the spring of 1947, ate well, slept well but had no coordination at all. I couldn't write my own name. My wife, Bess, kept asking me when I was going back. I told her, 'When I can write my own name.' That's how bad it was."

Allen had compounded his ailments with a professional mistake. As an osteopath, he had tried to treat himself. "It was a stupid thing to do," Allen noted. "Then one day I met a fellow osteopath, and he told me how silly I was and asked to let him help. The change was almost immediate. He worked over my neck and back, and in one day it looked better."

But if Allen was better, the situation at Kansas was still grim when he got back. "We were low on talent," he remembered. "Other schools, like Kansas State with Jack Gardner, had been loading up. Here we were struggling to finish in the first division of the league when we'd usually won it and even challenged for national honors."

There was a unique personal pressure on Allen as well. He felt he had to prove himself all over again. "I know what they were saying," he noted. "They were saying the old boy was gone, that he didn't have it anymore, that the game had passed him by, that he'd never come back. That's when I swore to go out and get me a team to win the national title and get to the Olympics in Helsinki, Finland, in 1952. I decided we'd do it or I'd die trying—and maybe take a couple of fellows with me."

A determined Allen went fishing for prospects and landed some big ones. By the 1951-52 season, he had a starting team that included one of the best centers in the game, 6-foot-9 Clyde Lovellette, and such fine players as Bob Kenney, Bill Hougland, Bill Lienhard and Dean Kelley. Junior college transfer John Keller and football player Charlie Hoag were the key reserves on this fine Kansas team that won the NCAA title that year. Later, the Jayhawks' top seven players participated on the unbeaten U.S. Olympic team at Helsinki where Allen, incidentally, served as assistant coach.

"It was touch and go at times, and we had luck along the way," Allen would remember with extreme pleasure in later years. "But we made it,

the whole bundle in one year—league title, NCAA title and the Olympics."

Lovellette, the one indispensable element of this explosive Kansas team, was lured to Lawrence by a hard recruiting campaign. He was stolen virtually from the shadow of Indiana University.

There were whimsical reports that Lovellette chose Kansas because Allen convinced him that the elevation of Mount Oread, no more than a bump on the campus landscape, would be good for his asthma. And there were more serious reports that Lovellette selected the school because Kansas had "paid the price" to lure him away from some 50 or 60 other schools vitally interested in the talented big man. But Lovellette says that "sincerity" was the only consideration.

"There were a lot of stories, including the one about asthma, which I had," an amused Lovellette recalls. "I was born in Indiana and already had gone down to talk to Branch McCracken (the Indiana coach), but Doc (Allen) stopped in one day and wanted me to see the school. So I came down with my mom and dad. Indiana was so big, about 16,000 students at the time compared to 7,000 at Kansas. The people (in Lawrence) were so friendly, the town was small and everybody was so sincere about wanting me to come that I went home and decided that was the place I wanted to go. The main thing is that they were more sincere than anybody else. People thought I got a lot of money. But I got a scholarship and an education, and I'm thankful for that."

In return, Lovellette gave Kansas its highest basketball status in history with a dazzling hook shot that helped him average more than 28 points a game in the 1951-52 season. About that devastating shot, teammate Lienhard notes: "His left elbow would come up and clear people out of the way. If they did get in his way, they only did it once." B. H. Born knows about that elbow. As a sophomore in 1951-52, the 6-9 Born faced the burly, aggressive Lovellette in practice sessions. He said the working-over he got from the Kansas star in drills helped immeasurably in making him an all-America in future years. At the end of the 1952 season, ballots were passed out for Kansas players to name their all-opponent team. Born put Lovellette on his. Told that was not cricket, Born replied: "I'm not changing. He's the toughest guy I'll ever run into, and he stays on my ballot."

An angular 6-5, Lienhard didn't pack as much weight on his frame as the mountainous Lovellette, but then he didn't have to. His was the outside game, the long-range shot. The 1951-52 Kansas press book called him the "finest one-handed set shooter in Kansas basketball history." Allen was

just as persuasive in bringing Lienhard to Kansas as he was Lovellette. Lienhard, in fact, had his heart set on Colorado until Allen made a trip to the home of the Newton (Kansas) high school star with Lovellette and Kenney in 1948.

"Doc told me he was building a team," Lienhard recalls, "and that 1952 was an Olympic year, and he wanted to know if I wanted to be a part of it."

Colorful nicknames were one of the trademarks of this national championship team. As he did on the court, Lovellette led the way in that area, too. Among his better-known appellations, the 245-pound Kansas star was called "Cumulus Clyde," "The Great White Whale of the Planks" and the "Monster of the Music Hall" (Hoch Auditorium, where Kansas played its home games). Lienhard was "Goose Neck," because of the peculiar twist of his wrist as he flicked his picturesque set or jump shot toward the basket. Allen gave the nickname of "Wormy" to Hougland because "of the way he worms in among the other people to get rebounds." Kelley was "George," again because of Allen. Asked by Kelley why the name, Allen replied, "You remind me of George Kell (baseball star) and your name's Kelley, so I find myself calling you George." Once during a team meeting, Allen addressed Kelley as "Dean" and Kelley broke up the session by replying, "No, Doc, I'm George, remember?" Allen, not usually given to laughter in the locker room, chuckled at Kelley's remark.

A team of formidable character, the 1951-52 Jayhawks were one of the most congenial ever gathered on a basketball court. Noticeably absent were the petty jealousies associated with a lot of big-time college teams. Abundantly present was a near-religious feeling of brotherhood. As Kenney said at a reunion many years later, "One of the most important things about the team of 1952 was that they came through it all lovin' each other."

"We were all from small towns—country kids who just wanted to play basketball," Lovellette remembers. "There was one thing about that ball club that you didn't find on most. There was no jealousy. If I scored 30 or 40 and Bill Lienhard got two or three, it didn't make any difference to him. And it wouldn't have made any difference if it had been the other way."

Dick Harp, an assistant under Allen in 1952 and later the head coach, underscores pride as another significant ingredient of the championship team. "The 1952 team wanted to win the national championship for Kansas because they believed there was no greater opportunity for a young man than to play basketball for KU," he says. "As long as I live, that team will be the greatest single thing I ever was associated with. They played and were coached in such a manner that they could use their experiences for guidelines the rest of their lives."

Among the more visual attributes of this fine Kansas team were its strong defensive orientation and its experience, perhaps the most important elements of all.

"The biggest reason for our success," stresses Lienhard, "was our defense. It was a pressing man-to-man, and at that time it was pretty revolutionary. It was something Harp developed. The defense did it . . . and, of course, Clyde, too."

About the team's veteran makeup, Hougland says, "Four of us—Lovellette, Lienhard, Kenney and I—entered the university at the same time. We were seniors that year, and we were playing our fourth season together. We knew what each other was going to do. Most of us were starters even as sophomores."

This was a team that had all its fun off the court. Once within the confines of an arena, basketball was serious business under the intrepid Allen.

"Phog was the kind of guy that kept us serious about the games," Lovellette points out. "After we had our nap in the afternoon, through the pregame meal of toast, tea and that celery stuff, all we thought about was the ball game. When we came in the dressing room, there might be some laughing and joking for a few minutes. But when Phog came in, that ceased. He liked 10 minutes of complete silence before talking to us."

And when he started talking to his players, Allen had a lot to say, none of it in simple terms. A stickler for conditioning and training, Allen drilled his teams with unique analogies of simians on the defense and a mongoose defeating a cobra. He developed a complex defense combining man-to-man and zone techniques that he eventually came to patent as the "Stratified Transitional Man-for-Man Defense with the Zone Principle." Other coaches were hard put trying to fathom the exact meaning of the phrase but had no trouble translating Allen's concepts and applying them successfully to their teams. Allen's authoritarian leadership extended to matters of diet, and he prescribed water by the quart as a staple for his charges—except during games. At times he would get mystical, proclaiming he could see the "victory light" shining in the eyes of his players.

Winning was very important to Allen, and the relatively infrequent times his teams lost left him disturbed sometimes to the point of distraction. Once after a loss to Creighton in Omaha, Nebraska, the disgusted Allen took his team to a diner for the postgame meal. There were only five stools in the place, so the players had to eat in shifts. Allen finished eating, went outside and boarded what he

83

thought was the team bus. Actually, the distracted coach had boarded a city bus; it drove off with him unwarily sulking inside. Inside the diner, the players witnessed the scene and broke out laughing. Finally, finished with their dinner, the players boarded the team bus. After a long wait, Allen solemnly walked up the street and got on.

"When he walked on that bus," Lienhard remembers, "you could hear a pin drop."

Fortunately for Allen and his players, there were not too many losing occasions to fret about during the 1951-52 season—only three, in fact. The Jayhawks' march through the Big Seven Conference was temporarily interrupted by consecutive losses in midseason to Kansas State and Oklahoma A&M (now Oklahoma State). The third loss was a two-point defeat by the noncollege Peoria Caterpillars in the finals of the Olympic trials in Madison Square Garden.

"We called that our midseason slump," says Hougland, recalling the brief down period of 1951-52. "We changed our defense about that time, and I think that may have hurt us a little. But you know how the Kansas-Kansas State series can be, and Mr. Iba (coach Hank Iba of Oklahoma A&M) had some fine teams about that time."

The resilient Jayhawks made up for those losses by beating both Oklahoma A&M and Kansas State later in the season, including a sweet-revenge victory over Jack Gardner's tough Wildcats when the Big Seven title was on the line. The Jayhawks seemed to explode with energy at this point of the season and carried the vitality into the NCAA tournament, where they won the title with victories over Texas Christian, St. Louis University, Santa Clara and St. John's.

The 1952 tournament, incidentally, marked another year of expansion and the beginning of the currently recognized format of four regions. St. John's won the Eastern regional at Raleigh, North Carolina, by beating North Carolina State, 60-49, and Kentucky, 64-57. Illinois won the Mideast at Chicago, beating Dayton, 80-61, and Duquesne, 74-68. Kansas took the Midwest at Kansas City with a 68-64 victory over Texas Christian and a 74-55 decision over St. Louis. Santa Clara was a surprising winner in the Far West at Corvallis, Oregon, defeating UCLA, 68-59, and Wyoming, 56-53. The four regional winners, as they do today, then advanced to the finals, held that year at the University of Washington Pavilion in Seattle.

As expected, expansion produced a larger total audience for the tournament. This time the crowd figure was up to 115,712, some 5,000 higher than the previous year's record. In addition, all of the championship games were televised for the first time, so millions more saw them in the comfort of their homes.

"There were two main reasons for the four first-round sites," explains Dutch Lonborg, the longtime chairman of the tournament committee. "First, there would be less travel for the teams involved. And second, there would be more income with the additional site. Walter Byers (NCAA executive director) asked me if I thought we could net $30,000 from each of the four regionals. I thought we could." Apparently the NCAA did even better than Lonborg had envisioned, grossing $248,621 for the tournament. The net income of $132,044 marked a record for tournament profit.

Artistically, the four-region system was widely accepted, remembers Lonborg. "In the old system, the winners of the East and the West would play in the finals and the losers would come along for the third-place game. But eventually, the losers didn't want to make the trip for that game. So we went to the four-region setup to make it more appealing. This was a major step for the tournament. It had greater crowd appeal, and the teams were happier."

In regional competition, Santa Clara's triumph in the Far West was clearly the tournament's major upset, although St. John's did turn quite a few heads by beating Kentucky in the East. Both UCLA and Wyoming were heavily favored to beat Santa Clara. Wyoming, in fact, had replaced its starting team when it held a runaway 14-3 lead at the start but then had to rush the front-line players back into the game when the youthful Broncos began catching up. LeRoy Esau of Wyoming put on a sensational shooting performance in the last four minutes when he sank six successive long-range shots in a desperate attempt to keep his team in contention. However, freshmen Herb Schoenstein, Jim Young and Ken Sears each contributed important baskets in the closing minutes to insure the Bronco triumph. Kentucky, meanwhile, had won 23 straight games before its upset by St. John's, a tough band of New York players coached by Frank McGuire.

The rest of the tournament largely went according to form, especially in Kansas City's Municipal Auditorium, where Lovellette took charge of everything. The Jayhawk center had two terrific nights. He scored 31 points against Texas Christian and collected a tournament record 44 points against St. Louis, hitting 16 of 24 shots (66.7 per cent). Ironically, Bob Zawoluk of St. John's had established a record earlier in the evening with 32 points against Kentucky before Lovellette erased it with his sweeping hook shot.

After Lovellette's sure touch had helped the

84

Charles Hoag of Kansas gets a shot away in the Jayhawks' 80-63 title win in 1952, despite the defensive efforts of Bob Zawoluk (30) and Ronnie MacGilvray (15) of St. John's.

Despite Allen's apprehensions, the Jayhawks landed safely in Seattle and later came down hard on Santa Clara and St. John's. Both times Lovellette scored 33 points as Kansas defeated Santa Clara, 74-55, in the Western final and then routed St. John's, 80-63, for the national championship.

Santa Clara, an extremely young team that hadn't even expected a bid to the tournament, was betrayed by its inexperience. Coach Bob Feerick's Broncos fell behind, 38-25, at the half and then buckled under the Kansas pressure shortly after intermission. St. John's, 61-59 conquerer of Illinois in the Eastern finals, was equally no match for Allen's team. At half time, Lovellette had 16 points and Kansas had a 41-27 lead. Just as significant as Lovellette's offensive performance in the first half was the defensive job he did on Zawoluk, holding the St. John's ace to six points. The Jayhawks were in front, 60-41, at the end of the third period; and Lovellette was on his way to a record-breaking performance with his 26th point. By game's end, the Kansas big man wound up with seven individual NCAA records, including total points in a four-game series with 141 and total rebounds with 69. He clearly was everyone's choice as the tourney's most outstanding player. Lovellette, too, was the leading candidate for the NCAA's all-tournament team, which was reinstituted after an 11-year absence. He was joined by teammate Dean Kelley, Zawoluk and Ron MacGilvray of St. John's and John Kerr of Illinois.

Lovellette's performance was all the more remarkable because of the physical beating he took in the title game from the aggressive St. John's team. Noted Bob Busby of the Kansas City Star, "The Redmen worked him over good, and the big boy had a busy evening freeing his arms for shots."

At one point during the title game, St. John's Solly Walker, called a "hatchet-man" by one writer, stuck a finger in Lovellette's eye. A timeout was called, and as the enraged Kansas center came to the bench, he blurted to Allen: "Dammit, Doc. I'm going to kill the ...!" Lovellette's mother was sitting near the bench and heard her son's profanity. She stepped in and reminded him how she'd tried to raise him as a "good Christian," and that such talk was terribly unbecoming. "Okay, mom," he replied, sheepishly. "I won't kill him, but I'm sure going to mark him up!" And he did. Walker quickly caught one of the famed Lovellette elbows and wasn't himself the rest of the evening.

85

Jayhawks to a regional championship, the big man lent a light touch to help Allen get over his fear of flying en route to the finals. Lovellette was sitting next to the Kansas coach on the flight to Seattle. The pilot of the plane, which was running low on gas, had been told to hold in a pattern until some bad weather had cleared. This made Allen nervous, but Lovellette reached over and took some fresh flowers from a vase on the wall, put them in his surprised coach's hands and quipped, "Relax, Doc! If we pile in, you've got on a good suit, you've got the flowers and they can take you right off to the funeral home." The laughter wiped out the tension.

HOOSIERS IN A HURRY

"In victory or in defeat, Branch was always the same. But that particular night in Kansas City, you could see the happiness in him. He loved to win, but he always wanted that NCAA title."—Bob Leonard, captain of Indiana's 1953 NCAA champions

Branch McCracken won the NCAA championship at Indiana in 1940 with a team that was relatively short on size but long on speed. McCracken, however, knew it would take more than a fast break to run away with the NCAA championship in the late 1940s and early 1950s. By then, the essential element was a good, king-sized center, a fact of college basketball life underscored by the successful teams at Oklahoma A&M (now Oklahoma State), Kansas, Kentucky and DePaul. To this end, McCracken made a big pitch for Clyde Lovellette.

In the fall of 1948, McCracken in fact thought he had sewed up the 6-9 Indiana high school phenom. Several days before Lovellette was to enroll as a freshman at Indiana, he mentioned that he would like to go home to Terre Haute to pick up some clothes.

"Go right ahead, son," said McCracken, "but hurry back."

That was the last McCracken heard of Lovellette until a wire service story reported 10 days later that the precocious youngster had enrolled at Kansas. In the subsequent years, Lovellette achieved all-America status and led the Jayhawks to the NCAA title in 1952. During this time, McCracken's Hoosiers—sometimes referred to as "McCracken's Midgets"—finished third, second and fourth in Big Ten competition.

"We had some mighty good material on those squads," notes Tom Miller, the longtime Indiana sports publicist. "Our '51 club, especially, had national championship quality at the guards and forwards, but we lacked one thing—a big man like Lovellette to grab the ball off the backboards. Most of the time, we had to use Bill Garrett, a great forward who was only 6-2, at center."

McCracken, an obsessive recruiter who drove upwards of 15,000 miles a year prospecting for talent among the 800-odd high school teams in the basketball-crazy state of Indiana, was still bemoaning the loss of Lovellette when he came upon Don Schlundt in South Bend. Schlundt, then a growing boy measured at a scant 6-6, was playing center for Washington-Clay Township High School and scoring points by the basketful. Impressed by Schlundt's size and agility, McCracken suggested a get-acquainted visit to the Indiana campus. Schlundt agreed.

In the spring of 1951, when Schlundt showed up at Bloomington, McCracken wisely eliminated any possibility of his escape a la Lovellette. Instead of waiting for September enrollment, McCracken induced Schlundt to enroll in summer school.

"You've made a wise decision," McCracken told Schlundt after his formal signing. "You're going to be mighty happy at Indiana."

And indeed he was. Schlundt eventually grew to 6-10 and became an irresistible, immovable force while helping the Hoosiers win the NCAA championship in 1953. As a relatively inexperienced but aggressive sophomore in the 1952-53 season, Schlundt established a Big Ten scoring record of 459 points in 18 games. Side-line observers who watched him spearhead Indiana's drive to the national title that year applauded his ambidextrous hook shot, usually deadly when fired within a radius of 15 feet of the basket. His raw power inside as an intimidator was equally astonishing. One of Schlundt's favorite maneuvers when he found traffic too congested under the basket was to raise his elbows—an action that was usually followed by the cracking of heads and the spectacle of reeling bodies. Pete Newell recalls such terrifying episodes from his days as coach at Michigan State.

"In one of our games against Indiana," he says,

"we used three men to guard Schlundt at various times. All three came back to the bench with lumps on their heads big enough to hang their hats on. That Schlundt really had a lethal pair of elbows."

Schlundt's startling metamorphosis from an ugly duckling to an eagle took place in a relatively quick span of time. It wasn't until he was 11 years old that he started playing basketball, and then there seemed little hope for a bright future. "I wasn't much good," Schlundt remembers. "Probably the only reason I got to play in my neighborhood was that I owned the ball." As a 14-year-old high school freshman, Schlundt stood only 5-9 and weighed 170 pounds when he reported for basketball tryouts. Coach Herschel Eaton at Washington-Clay told Schlundt quite bluntly that he was "too fat and too slow." Always fond of pies, cakes and doughnuts, Schlundt got fatter in his first year but still managed to make the team, serving as an obscure, third-string guard in the winter of 1948. A sudden change of metabolism, however, salvaged his basketball career. He grew seven inches—from 5-9 to 6-4—between the end of that basketball season and the start of the next.

"Nobody's ever figured out why," says Schlundt. "My dad is 6-1, but we've never had any exceptionally big men in our family. I guess Mother got the biggest surprise. She bought four pairs of slacks for me at a fire sale in April, figuring I'd be able to wear the pants all winter—but when she pulled them out of the closet in September, I couldn't get into them."

Schlundt, however, was able to get into the starting lineup at Washington-Clay without too much trouble. Coach Eaton moved him to center on the first team in a hurry.

"Schlundt was mighty awkward at first," Eaton recalled, "but he had two great assets—height and patience. He'd skip rope for half an hour to improve his footwork; then he'd practice his hook shot for hours. He'd stay around the gym until the janitor turned out the lights. He practiced in and out of season. After school closed in June, he worked on an outdoor court. There was hardly a day in Don's last three years in high school that he didn't shoot a basketball for at least an hour."

Schlundt continued to set an even tougher pace for himself after arriving at Indiana University. He worked on one-handed shots for at least half an hour before the Hoosiers' regular team-practice periods, firing at the basket 250 or more times from

varying angles while student managers served as retrievers. "That kind of practice was a lot of fun," Schlundt notes. "I did the shooting and they did the running." The graceful big man, who according to campus statisticians traveled about four miles during a game, kept in shape for this aspect of basketball with self-imposed hard running drills. To get in condition for a season, Schlundt would devote six afternoons a week during September and October to running Indiana's rugged four-mile cross-country course. On November 1, he usually started working out indoors, skipping rope for 20 minutes at a crack, much like a boxer.

"Don has to run," McCracken once explained, "because we play a running, fast-breaking game. When the other club misses a shot and one of our boys takes it off the backboard, it's usually Schlundt who makes the recovery. Ordinarily our forwards fast break down the floor, Schlundt clears the ball to one of our guards along the side lines and the guard tries to hit one of the forwards with a pass. But if the forwards are covered, the guards take the ball downcourt while Schlundt runs extra

Indiana University

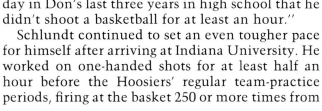

Don Schlundt (34) scored 29 points to lead Indiana past Louisiana State, 80-67, and into the 1953 finals against Kansas.

87

hard to get to his offensive post near the foul circle. Even after he gets there, he keeps running and faking, moving from side to side and waiting for a chance to grab a pass. Playing center in our type of game is no job for a lazy man."

Nor was playing guard. There, McCracken had an equally intense young man in Bob Leonard, who according to one writer close to the Indiana scene "would rather die than lose a basketball game."

Mary Jo McCracken, the coach's widow, remembers this typical story about the high-powered Leonard: "Bobby didn't make the Indiana all-star team after his senior year in high school. Mac and I went to the game, and Bob sat with us; and he and Mac never stopped talking basketball during the entire contest. Bobby already had announced that he was going to attend Indiana, and he and Mac really went over that all-star game. When the game ended, Bobby looked at Mac and said, 'Coach, I'm going to be the best basketball player that ever played for you. All you have to do is tell me what to do, and I'll do it.' He did that all the time he was at IU, and he came pretty near to accomplishing all that he said he would do."

Leonard, indeed, may have been McCracken's most alert and attentive pupil. Abundantly confident, he came to Indiana as a forward but only enjoyed a modicum of success at that position in his sophomore year. It wasn't until the 6-3 youngster was converted to guard in his junior year by McCracken that he played up to his potential. Many saw the move as the key to Indiana's championship season.

Leonard wasn't wooed by the Indiana coach until his senior season was over at Gerstmeyer Tech in Terre Haute, but McCracken didn't have a hard time selling him on Indiana. Leonard had long worshiped McCracken from afar. "He had a great personality," Leonard says. "He had a magnetism about him that drew people to him. He could walk in anywhere, and people would say with awe, 'That's Branch McCracken of IU.' "

Leonard was an average forward on an average Indiana team his sophomore year, but championship roots were growing. When flashy sophomore guard Sammy Esposito signed a bonus contract with the Chicago White Sox after the spring baseball season, McCracken talked to Leonard about moving to the backcourt.

"I worked all that summer on learning guard," Leonard recalls.

The first winter he was in the backcourt he made all-America, and well-known Chicago American sports writer Jim Enright called Leonard "pound-for-pound, dribble-for-dribble, pass-for-pass and shot-for-shot, without question the game's greatest individual player, in my book."

He was at the very least one of the most unselfish players in the game. Indiana fans remember fondly one night when Leonard, by himself under the basket with an easy shot, passed off to a nonplussed Schlundt to boost his teammate toward his record-breaking Big Ten scoring total in 1952-53.

The year came together in a hurry for this Hoosier team, considered McCracken's greatest and certainly one of the youngest ever to win the NCAA championship. The starters were composed of three juniors and two sophomores: Schlundt; Leonard; Dick Farley, an adhesive forward who usually shadowed the opposition's top scorer; Burke Scott, a clever playmaker who specialized in feeding under-the-basket passes to Schlundt, and Charley Kraak, a rugged forward who was considered the best rebounder in the Big Ten. Substitutes, equally as young, made vital contributions in almost every game and won an overtime battle from Northwestern on a last-second field goal by Paul Poff after all the starters had fouled out. That was the final link in the Hoosiers' chain of 17 straight victories and 20 consecutive conference triumphs over two seasons.

"We were a young club that got progressively better as the year went on," remembers Leonard. "McCracken brought us up at the end, just right for the NCAA."

McCracken's champions won 23 of 26 games and came very close to perfection that year. The Hoosiers lost two of their three nonconference games prior to the Big Ten race—71-70 at Notre Dame and 82-80 at Kansas State—but then were not defeated again until they had clinched the conference title. They were handed their third setback at Minnesota, 65-63, and then came home to end Iowa's late-season string of six victories before making their charge through the NCAA field. The Hoosiers defeated DePaul, Notre Dame, Louisiana State and Kansas to win their second NCAA championship in 14 years.

"Note that we came within five points of a perfect season," says Miller. "And all three of our defeats were the result of field goals scored with less than 30 seconds to play."

The Hoosiers gave convincing evidence of their right to the Big Ten crown that year by usurping the defending champion, Illinois, by a humbling 91-79 score. It was the highest point total ever recorded against the Illini, and it might have been higher had not the Hoosiers gone into their control game with an 82-62 lead with seven minutes remaining. Four juniors and three sophomores were the magic combination in what was then Indiana's 15th straight Big Ten victory. To do it,

these youngsters had to overcome the disadvantage of playing in the primitive and intimidating facilities of Illinois' Huff Gym. Remarkably, the youthful but poised Hoosiers made a shambles of a team which included four veterans of two conference championship seasons and four other members of the title-winning 1952 Illinois squad. The Illini never had lost a home game in which any of those eight seniors and juniors had played.

In retrospect, McCracken would point to the Illinois game as one of the important keys to the 1952-53 Indiana season.

"I believe the boys hit their peak at Champaign against Illinois," he said later. "We had some tough games after that, but the squad kept learning with every start and, of course, improving."

The resounding triumph at Illinois sent McCracken riding off the floor on the shoulders of his players, experiencing the joy of a league championship he had felt as a player on the 1928 Indiana team. That year, the Hoosiers had tied Purdue for the Big Ten title.

As outright Big Ten champions in 1952-53, the Hoosiers were one of 14 conference winners who received automatic berths to the NCAA tournament. Bouyed by the success of previous expansion years, the NCAA increased its field even more in 1952-53, this time from 16 to 22 teams. Four new conferences were added as automatic qualifiers in this scheme—the Rocky Mountain, Mid-American, Middle Atlantic and a New England designate. In addition, the NCAA made room for two more at-large teams. As the field boomed, the controls by necessity became tighter—the NCAA tying everything into a nice, neat bundle in hopes of keeping college sports in perspective and improving the overall quality of the event.

The organization issued new guidelines for its revolutionary format, with the main thrust aimed at "proper control of postseason competition . . . shortening of the basketball season . . . and encouraging the organization of formal conferences." The dates of the tourney were moved back by one week to insure an earlier finish of the season. Eligibility for the tournament was limited to members which participated in only one postseason tournament. And the increase of conference representation was thought to "have a direct effect of strengthening leagues and developing more closely knit and better-administered conferences."

Playoff sites dotted the face of America in a crazy-quilt pattern from the Eastern seaport of Philadelphia to the shores of Seattle, with stops in between in the nation's heartland. No fewer than four first-round sites were used; and there were four more regional points before the finals hit

Kansas City, Missouri, for the fourth time, the first since 1942. The far-flung NCAA tourney found itself with many of the familiar household names in college basketball, but the expanded field also allowed for such new faces as Lebanon Valley, Hardin-Simmons, Idaho State and Fordham. Indiana and Kansas, two of the more traditional names in the sport, waded through this 22-team field before meeting for the NCAA title.

The Hoosiers had to stand off a late rally by DePaul (playing on its unofficial home floor at Chicago Stadium) to win their first NCAA game in the Mideast regional at Chicago by a tight 82-80 score. Until they met Kansas in the finals, the DePaul game would be the toughest for the Hoosiers in the 1953 tournament. As George Bolinger of the Louisville Courier-Journal put it, "Indiana showed more overall ability and depth than the Demons but had a difficult time proving their superiority." Using what Bolinger called a "hatchet man" in Dan Lecos on Schlundt, the Demons were able to hold the high-scoring Hoosier to only nine points for the first 25 minutes. Then, after Lecos fouled out, Schlundt collected 14 more in the final 15 minutes to pace Indiana's winning drive. Notre Dame was a lot easier for Indiana in the regional finals the following night. Avenging their early-season defeat to the Irish, the Hoosiers won in convincing style, 79-66, as Schlundt scored 41 points. The high-powered performance by the Indiana center that night, the eve of his 20th birthday, broke his Indiana single-game scoring record and George Mikan's Chicago Stadium mark. The latter had been 37 points, scored by the DePaul star, ironically, against a wartime-weakened Indiana team in 1944.

Schlundt's explosive performance continued to have repercussions three nights later when Indiana encountered Louisiana State in the championship semifinals. Fearful of another Schlundt blitz—Don had poured in 18 points in the first 10 minutes against Notre Dame—LSU employed a tight defense designed to restrict the Indiana center's under-the-basket maneuvers. But this backfired on the Tigers. When LSU defenders clustered around Schlundt, Leonard fired away unmolested from just beyond the foul circle and sank his first six long shots. LSU thereupon reverted to a normal man-to-man defense, and Schlundt reverted to his normal scoring pace. At game's end, he had 29 points. Leonard, meanwhile, had 22 and McCracken crowed, "The Louisiana State game proved we were a well-balanced club."

The widespread regional contests had provided a wide spectrum of color and entertainment to followers of the NCAA tournament. Lebanon Val-

89

ley, an intriguing team relying largely on "five iron men," had beaten Fordham in the first round of the Eastern regional at Philadelphia before losing to LSU and the great Bob Pettit in the semifinals at Raleigh, North Carolina. LSU went on to defeat Holy Cross, 81-73, for the regional championship. Notre Dame had eliminated Pennsylvania, 69-57, in the Mideast semifinals, but the final score did not reflect the intensity with which that game had been played. Five minutes from the end, the score was 52-50 in favor of Notre Dame and the rivals had exchanged the lead on 13 occasions before the Irish broke open the game in the final quarter.

Washington and Seattle staged a virtual "hometown" battle in the semifinals of the Far West tournament at Corvallis, Oregon, with the Huskies winning, 92-70, as Bob Houbregs scored a tournament-record 45 points. Johnny O'Brien, the nation's leading scorer, had 24 points for Seattle. Washington then advanced to the championship round of four at Kansas City with a 74-62 whipping of Santa Clara. In the finals of the Midwest tournament at Manhattan, Kansas, the University of Kansas Jayhawks enjoyed an 11-point advantage, then had to hang on to beat Oklahoma A&M, 61-55, as Bertram Born scored 18 points.

Surprisingly, the Big Seven champions had less trouble with mighty Washington in the national semifinals at Kansas City, subduing the nation's No. 2 team, 79-53, with what Kansas City Star writer Bob Busby called the Jayhawks, "pressing, fire-wagon tactics." The Pacific Coast Conference champions, beaten only twice previously in 31 games, were favored by three points over Kansas. But the Huskies lost their heart after losing the great Houbregs on fouls early in the third period. Houbregs, fouling out of a game for only the third time in his career, scored a subpar 18 points; Born, meanwhile, stayed hot for Kansas with 25.

The national championship game made up for the lack of excitement in both of the semifinal games. There was even a rhubarb thrown in for good measure.

It was almost a home game for Kansas, one writer pointing out that "Kansans had bought up the rights to 10,000 seats in the hope that Phog Allen and his gang from nearby Lawrence would be there." Indiana University, meanwhile, had received an allotment of only 200 tickets; Hoosier students were lucky to scrape together a few hundred more from the undisposed quotas of LSU and Washington. Their voices at the Kansas City Auditorium were merely cries in a wilderness compared to the intimidating, stereophonic sound of the Kansas clan.

Indiana led, 21-19, after the first quarter; but in

the second, Schlundt acquired his third foul and then Farley his fourth. By that time, Kansas held a 39-33 advantage. Schlundt, who had sat down for a rest, came off the bench to help the Hoosiers forge a 41-41 tie at the half. In the first half, Leonard, hounded by Kansas' Dean Kelley, had been able to get only a half-dozen shots and hit but one of them. The night before, the Indiana guard had scored 18 points in the first half against LSU.

The teams were never more than two points apart during the third quarter, and it was near the end of this period that the rhubarb flared. It came when an official's whistle on Born brought the traditional wave-out from the scorer's table, signifying his fifth and last personal foul. Immediately there was consternation. All on press row had but four fouls for Born and evidently so did the Kansas book, for an immediate protest was launched by the Jayhawks. The scorer rechecked and counted four, which brought an instant firecracker reaction from McCracken, who charged the scorers and protested what he called "changing the book." "You had five on him and you changed it to four," McCracken shouted. "You know you did. We come out here and are supposed to be your guests. You're robbing us!"

As the big, white-haired McCracken vainly protested the scorer's change of decision, the partisan Kansas crowd meanwhile yelled almost in unison, "No, four, four!"

The scorers, "Big Six" Watkins and Harley Selvidge, held their ground; Born remained in the game. They said afterwards that they had miscounted when they waved Born out. To his dying day, McCracken never believed that. Later, Kansas coach Phog Allen censured the scorers and decried the incident, even if for the moment it had saved him the services of his finest player.

This was just one incident in the game between the hard-running teams, each of which relied on speed as the main strength of its attack. Schlundt and Leonard both drew technical fouls for making offensive remarks to the officials. And in the riotous last period, Indiana's Charley Kraak was charged with a technical after protesting a charging foul with 1:21 left. Angered with the foul, his fifth, Kraak slammed the ball on the court, giving Kansas three free throws and possession of the ball in a three-point game led by Indiana.

About that crucial moment, Kraak recalled in later years: "I just lost my cool and slammed the basketball on the playing floor so hard that it bounced nearly to the ceiling of the Kansas City

Dick Farley (31) shoots for Indiana in the Hoosiers' 69-68 decision over Kansas for the 1953 NCAA championship.

90

Auditorium. Naturally, a technical followed. I had the unpleasant experience of returning to a very hostile bench. To add to my despair, I recall watching Kansas running down the clock while behind by one point and attempting to find their best shooter for the final shot. The championship was hanging in the balance. On the bench, I watched that final shot hit the rim and bounce off. To this day, I wonder what my return to Indiana would have been like had the final Kansas shot gone in.''

Kraak's mistake set the stage for an excruciating finish. Kansas' Harold Patterson, who was fouled by Kraak on the play, converted only one of his two shots and Al Kelley missed on the technical. But the possession paid off for Kansas when Dean Kelley drove under Indiana's basket and sank a layup with 1:05 left to tie the score for the 14th and last time at 68-68.

With the clock showing the game 27 seconds from completion, Dean Kelley bumped Leonard in a mad flurry under the Indiana basket, giving the Hoosier captain two free throws. Leonard walked to the free-throw line with extreme trepidation. "I wanted to make the shots as much as anything I've ever wanted in my life," Leonard later said. "In fact, I had to make them!"

Leonard's first attempt was wide and the crowd yelled. The next one was good, and the Hoosiers had a 69-68 lead.

Indiana University

However, the game was not over. Allen called a timeout and told the Jayhawks how to win their second straight national championship: Freeze the ball for 22 seconds—each man counting them off to himself. "Then," said Allen, "pass the ball in to Al Kelley and let him shoot."

But when Kelley lined up for his shot, a forest of Hoosier arms barred his view of the net. He hurriedly passed into the corner to Jerry Alberts, whose frantic, off-balance attempt fell short. Thus Indiana won its second NCAA title by the smallest possible margin over the same school and on the same floor as when the Hoosiers had set the record, still standing at that time, for the final game's largest victory margin 13 years earlier.

"There were a lot of corks popping on the way back to the hotel," Leonard recalls. "The dressing rooms weren't done at that time at the Kansas City Auditorium, so we put on our sweat clothes and went to the hotel, only a block away. We had IU students out there—I think nearly 1,000 IU students—and they were carrying players on their shoulders all the way back to the hotel. It was really a great night for Indiana basketball."

Before the start of the championship game, there were apprehensions smoldering within Leonard. His usual swagger had slipped a bit after he watched Kansas upset Washington in the semifinals. "Washington was the favorite in the tournament," Leonard says, "and I remember going back to the hotel room after the game and talking to my roommate, Burke Scott. I said, 'We're going to have to come up with a fabulous ball game to beat Kansas tomorrow night for the NCAA championship.' Both ball clubs played the same style— we both usually pressed full-court for the entire game. It was one of those games where there was never more than two or three points separating the two ball clubs from start to finish."

After Leonard scored his dramatic tie-breaking point at the end, he was still apprehensive.

"Kansas came down the court and we put on an almost perfect defense. But we had been beaten three times that year on last-second shots, and when their last shot went up from the corner, I put my head to my hands, because I heard the gun— and I was waiting for the Kansas fans to go wild. But the shot hit the rim and came off. Dick White, our sixth man all year, got the rebound and with it the national championship."

So close to a national championship himself and yet so far, Allen consoled himself with a moral victory. His Jayhawks, a relatively short but scrappy team, had surprised almost everyone by coming as far as they did. "I'm as proud of this team as I can be," he said. "They've got great heart and have caught the fancy of the public. Indiana is nine deep and we're only six. That made a big difference, particularly when we lost Born. (The Kansas star eventually fouled out with 5:36 remaining.) Jerry Albert tried to keep their big boy (Schlundt) under control, but he wasn't able to do it." Schlundt eventually wound up with 30 points for the game, helping Indiana establish a new team scoring record with 310 points for the four games. However, it was not Schlundt who carried off the most outstanding player award, but Born, who had pushed the Kansas underdogs through to the finals with a magnificent performance that ended with 26 points in the championship game.

Although McCracken had insisted that Indiana wasn't "up to par" against Kansas in the finals, the Hoosiers did intimidate the Jayhawks with their wonderful speed. The Jayhawks, respectful of the Indiana quickness, didn't pick up as deep in enemy territory on the defense as they usually were accustomed to. In fact, the Kansas defenders seldom picked up the Hoosiers on the enemy side of the center line at all. Most of the time, particularly in the first half, the Jayhawks kept a slower pace than usual in bringing the ball downcourt. This no doubt was designed to slow up the game a little in an attempt to keep the Hoosiers off their usually frantic pace. However, when the Jayhawks had a fast-break opportunity off a rebound, they took advantage of it.

The running game, of course, was Indiana's trademark, the strongest expression of McCracken's basketball philosophy that carried over from the early 1940s when the team was first designated "The Hurryin' Hoosiers." That breakneck style had won many fans in the 1940 tournament and continued to elicit more applause in 1953. As Mary Jo McCracken remembers, "The same tournament manager who was there in 1940 was still in his post for the 1953 championship. He told us that people always remembered Indiana's running game after that 1940 victory, and he felt that our performance and brand of play in that NCAA turned the corner for the tournament and helped make it the popular success that it is now."

With Schlundt around to grab rebounds and trigger Indiana's ferocious offense, McCracken's fast break was at its classic best in 1952-53. Few opponents could keep the big man in check. "Before you start thinking about beating Indiana, you've got to figure out a way to stop that Schlundt," noted Notre Dame coach Johnny Jordan at the time, "and nobody's been able to do it yet."

THE PHILADELPHIA STORY

The 1954 NCAA basketball championship is not one which is immediately called to mind by fans of the game. Yet it actually proved to be one of the more newsworthy tournaments of the era.

For example, the 1954 tournament was the first in which the champion had to get by five opponents in order to win the title. Also, 1954 marked the first time the championship game was televised to a national audience. Finally, the winning team was able to capture the championship despite the fact that its strength rested largely in one player.

La Salle was that team, and Tom Gola was that single outstanding player. The Explorers' final conquest was a convincing 92-76 decision over Bradley before 10,500 fans at the Municipal Auditorium in Kansas City, a game that was close only until the early minutes of the second half. At that point, La Salle elected to employ a zone defense; and Bradley, resorting to outside shooting, failed to hit with any consistency. La Salle outscored Bradley, 30-14, in the third period to blow the game wide open and wound up setting a scoring record for the national finals.

In spite of its loss in the finals, Bradley had done well to make it that far. The Braves' regular-season record was only fair, yet they managed to upset highly favored Colorado, 76-64, and Oklahoma A&M (now Oklahoma State), 71-57, in the Midwest regional tournament at Stillwater, Oklahoma. Those upsets were only par for the course in the 1954 tournament, a stage for some of the biggest surprises in college basketball that season.

Two stunning upsets were witnessed in the Mideast regional at Iowa City. Notre Dame surprised Indiana's defending NCAA champions, 65-64, by holding high-scoring Don Schlundt to only one field goal and 10 points. The Fighting Irish's joy was short-lived, however, as their 18-game winning streak and dreams of a national championship were shattered by Penn State, the last club to be invited into the field, 71-63.

Events in the Far West were equally as titillating as Idaho State stopped Seattle's 26-game winning streak, 77-75; and Southern California squeezed by Santa Clara in double overtime, 66-65. In the latter game, most of the 10,000 fans at Corvallis, Oregon, cheered lustily as Santa Clara gambled by holding the ball for four minutes in the second overtime. When the clock showed only eight seconds remaining, the Broncos passed to Ken Sears, whose try for a winning basket was batted away. The loss was bitter for Santa Clara, playing in the Corvallis regional for the third straight year and thwarted a second time. In 1952, the Broncos reached the national semifinals.

In an Eastern first-round game at Buffalo, New York, La Salle nearly was upset by Fordham. Eddie Conlin, Fordham's fine rebounder, kept the Rams ahead most of the way. But Ken Loeffler, one of the most cerebral of coaches, cleverly used two time-outs in five seconds to engineer a tie; and La Salle won in overtime, 76-74. La Salle then exploded past North Carolina State, Navy, Penn State and Bradley for the NCAA title.

Ironically, this La Salle team was a reluctant NCAA tournament entrant. Most of the players had wanted to return to the National Invitation Tournament in New York, where the Explorers had enjoyed some success in recent years. As rank outsiders, they won the NIT in 1952, with freshman Gola sharing most valuable player honors with teammate Norm Grekin. In 1953, the Explorers suffered a heartbreaking, one-point loss to St. John's in the NIT quarterfinals despite widespread recognition as Loeffler's best team. The following year, the Explorers were coveted by both the NIT and NCAA but were committed to the latter's bid if offered because the 33-member Middle Atlantic Conference had agreed just that year to send its best representative. The NCAA call came after La Salle had defeated Fordham, 61-56, in a regular-season game that was not as close as the final score indicated.

However, despite a solid record, Loeffler honestly did not believe that his team deserved to be included in the NCAA tournament, or any other

tournament for that matter.

"Actually, we don't have any business being in a tournament," Loeffler said after a late-season victory over city rival St. Joseph's. "We aren't big enough to do any real damage. These kids have to outfox an opponent to win. They've got plenty of hustle, brains and desire to win. But we have only one outstanding player, Tom Gola. Our big problem this year was to keep Gola in the game, keeping him from tiring or fouling out. We accomplished this by constantly switching our offense and defense during the game. When we wanted Gola to take it easy, we'd go to a four-man screen with Tom on the inside line. Thus, he rested a bit on offense while the boys on the outside passed the ball around. On defense we used a zone to rest Gola, setting him in front of the basket to handle rebounds. We were lucky it worked."

If any one player was ever an indispensable part of a basketball team, it was Gola. At 6-foot-7, he had the strength and timing to rebound with the biggest centers; the ball-handling, passing and shooting ability to play backcourt with the best, and the speed and inside moves to play all-America forward. "If you were modeling your perfect ball player," noted one coach, "you would end up with a sure-fire description of Gola: good shooter, good rebounder, good dribbler, great on defense and a wonderful team man. Maybe you'd like to have him a little taller, but that's hardly necessary since he has opposed players up to seven feet tall and usually come out on top." Later, before La Salle's NCAA game with Fordham, Loeffler enhanced the Gola portrait with this absolute assessment: "He's not only the greatest college or pro player today but the greatest in basketball history. I know that I'm covering a lot of ground; but I go back 30 years in this game, and I'll take Tom Gola as the greatest."

Given that Loeffler was prejudiced, Gola was at the very least the prototype of the modern playground player. Even as a freshman, he displayed great poise and knowledge of the game, a thoroughly instinctive player who did whatever was needed to be done on a basketball court. Best of all, he had explosively quick hands—so marvelously quick, in fact, that he defensed, shot and passed with intuitive ease. If Gola was not the best player of all-time, as Loeffler claimed, conceivably he was the best in the country during the 1953-54 season and quite possibly as good as anyone from his era.

A genuine folk hero in Philadelphia, Gola meant more than just his 23 points and 22 rebounds a game to the La Salle team. "Playing with Gola gave everyone a lift," says Frank O'Hara, one of the guards on the 1954 NCAA champions. "He inspired all of us to play over our heads." Frank

Tom Gola of La Salle, the tournament's most outstanding player, drives past Navy's Ken McCally to the basket in La Salle's 64-48 victory over Navy for the championship of the East regional.

Blatcher, another of the La Salle guards that year, concurs. "You could write books about the guy. Not only was he completely unselfish, he was a hell of a steadying influence on the club."

La Salle needed every bit of Gola's magical court savvy in the 1953-54 season. When they headed into the season, it appeared the Explorers could use a miracle worker as well. Loeffler had lost a basketful of talent from the fine 1952-53 team, and it was questionable how far an all-America like Gola and a slick but small (5-9) playmaker like O'Hara could carry a club with nine sophomores. Compounding the problem of inexperience was La Salle's schedule, which included the Kentucky Invitational Tournament, the New York Holiday Festival, the bitter city games against St. Joseph's and Temple and the first road game at North Carolina State since a controversial 76-74 loss in the 1951-52 season. "We looked at that schedule," says O'Hara, "and agreed that we'd be pretty lucky to win half our games."

Gola and O'Hara, a fiery player who battled his way into the starting lineup despite Loeffler's reluctance to play "little men," were among the few players with any varsity experience. The supporting cast included a long line of untested sophomores. Among the best of these were Blatcher, Charlie Singley, Charlie Greenberg, Fran O'Malley and Bob Maples. Blatcher was a protege of Paul Arizin from South Philadelphia High School who would become the best outside shooter on the team, but his metamorphosis didn't happen overnight.

Remembering his early-season apprehension, Loeffler said later: "When we started the season, almost every one of our fellows lacked something. Some weren't good outside shooters. Others were weak on defense."

It seemed that Loeffler's fears were well-founded at the start of the season, when the Explorers lost three games before the new year rolled around. Two of the losses were to Niagara, and the second loss was especially stinging because it came in the semifinals of the Holiday Festival Tournament. Ned Irish and the Madison Square Garden crowd had been hoping for a La Salle-Duquesne final, since the Dukes were ranked No. 1 at that time. But the Explorers shot only 24 per cent from the field, losing 69-50, and Loeffler was criticized by the media for continuing to use a zone defense despite Niagara's brilliant outside shooting.

La Salle College

But there were some fragments of brilliance for La Salle. The Explorers had achieved some fame by beating John Wooden's unbeaten, 17th-ranked UCLA Bruins in the opening round of the Kentucky Invitational. And later, after the rout by Niagara, things began to pick up for Loeffler's team. Starting with a victory over Brigham Young in the consolation game of the Holiday Festival Tournament, the Explorers went on an 11-game winning streak, beating such teams as Manhattan, Dayton and North Carolina State. The victory over North Carolina State was especially sweet for Loeffler, who had been seeking revenge for what he thought was a home-town decision in his previous visit to the Raleigh, North Carolina, campus.

However, Loeffler had little to complain about once the Explorers got rolling in 1954. Blatcher, who scored 15 points to spark a second-half rally against Manhattan, feels that game was the turning point for La Salle. "We were starting to do the things that we had to do to win," he remembers. "Now there were seven or eight guys who knew that they could do the job. Kenny really knew the personnel and knew the right time to pick the right guy. As a club, we had pretty good balance. Kenny called us specialists."

La Salle's only other loss that season was a one-point defeat by Temple late in the season, and its possible therapeutic value cannot be dismissed by O'Hara. "In retrospect, they may have done us a favor," he says. "There would have been a lot more pressure if we had gone into the NCAA tournament with a long winning streak."

As it was, though, the Explorers had won 14 of their last 15 games and rode this crest into the tourney, highly confident. The Explorers drew Fordham as their first-round opponent in the Buffalo Auditorium and beat the Rams in what was considered one of the most dramatic games in tournament history. La Salle was losing by two points and called a timeout with four seconds left in regulation play. Gola took the ball inbounds and fed O'Malley with an "impossible" pass underneath the basket, and the 6-3 forward scored the tying point at the buzzer. La Salle then wrapped it up in overtime; and Gola noted later, "That Fordham game was the turning point for us. That's the game I'll never forget. They had the talent to beat us, and we were down with four seconds to go. But our guys had gained some confidence and poise by then. After we pulled it out, we were ready for anybody."

The scene was touched by an even more dramatic peripheral story than the final 76-74 score.

96

Blatcher did not know that his father had been taken seriously ill while the team was en route to Buffalo. He died while the game was in progress. "My dad and I had been very close," Blatcher recalls. "Suddenly that tournament took on so much more of a meaning to me because I know that he wanted to see us do well. Because of his death, basketball was secondary to me, but still important. There were things I wanted to see us do as a team and things I wanted to do as an individual."

Every hope eventually came true for Blatcher. First, there was an 88-81 victory over North Carolina State in the Eastern regional in Philadelphia. The Explorers stopped the Wolfpack's 10-game winning streak as Gola put on what Navy coach Ben Carnevale called "the greatest one-man show I've ever seen." Taking over with 2:20 left and La Salle leading, 71-69, Gola scored, passed off, blocked shots and grabbed rebounds to spark a late surge that clinched the game for the Philadelphia team. The Eastern finals were anticlimatic, with Gola, Bob Maples and Charlie Singley breaking open a close game with Navy in the third quarter. La Salle went on to beat Carnevale's team, 64-48.

Loeffler found himself coaching against his alma mater in the national semifinals at Kansas City, but Penn State put up little resistance, and La Salle went on to a 69-54 victory. After Bradley's exciting 74-72 triumph over Southern California in the opening of the semifinal doubleheader, the La Salle-Penn State game seemed pale by comparison. "The closing game was a somewhat lethargic affair that upon occasion drew slow hand claps from the audience, who desired more action," wrote Bob Busby in the Kansas City Star. Gola took only nine shots from the field. He made five and collected 19 points to share scoring honors with Blatcher, the game's only substitute for the winners.

"We weren't very interesting," Loeffler conceded, "but we did win. We did our part. Everything went the way we planned. Sure, Gola didn't score a lot in the beginning, but he accomplished what we wanted—he took care of two men from the defense." Gola took care of a few other things, too, such as rebounding. He collected 17 rebounds to lead everyone, and former Bradley star Paul Unruh later marveled at Gola's all-around abilities. "He makes plays a little man should make," noted Unruh, "and then turns around and does things only a big man usually does."

Bradley's victory in the first game of the semifinals, meanwhile, was just as remarkable as the rest of its roller-coaster season. Few had expected the Braves to reach the euphoric status of national finalists. Even the players were a little dazed by the

The 1954 champions from La Salle display their trophy.

heights they had reached. "We were fortunate to get as far as we did," noted one of the team members, Ed King. The Braves had finished the regular season with a 15-12 record, but some of the conquests by Forddy Anderson's team included such major basketball powers as Wake Forest, Notre Dame, Houston, Marquette and Tulsa. Bradley was the underdog in most of those games and would be through the NCAA tournament.

Bradley's first opponent in the NCAA tournament was Oklahoma City in the District 5 playoffs. The site of the game was the Bradley Field House and was determined by a phone call and a coin flip. The Braves won the toss, the home-court advantage and the game, 61-55. "That phone call has to list among the contributions to the many achievements of Bradley University," a school spokesman later stated. The Braves went on to the Western regional, where they defeated Colorado and Oklahoma A&M with uncommon fervor. The Braves' 71 points against Oklahoma A&M in the Western finals was the most points allowed by the Aggies that season. So unexpected was Bradley's victory that tickets were already printed up for the NCAA finals listing Oklahoma A&M as the winner of the Western regional.

It had been both a bizarre and a rewarding season for the Braves, who featured among others all-America Bob Carney, Jerry Hansen, Lee Utt and King, who eventually came back to become the dean of men at Bradley. Once when the Braves traveled to play the University of Arizona, three starters had to be held out of the lineup because of severe cases of sunburn suffered before the game. But despite a checkered and often confusing year, the inconsistent Braves nevertheless seemed to be playing their best ball of the season in the NCAA tournament. Loeffler recognized this after watching them beat Southern Cal in the national semifinals behind Carney's inspired play in the last minute. "They can be tough," a worried Loeffler said. "They battled Southern Cal all the way. Maybe a zone is the answer. I don't know. We'll have to see how things work out."

It was, indeed, a zone defense that helped La Salle beat Bradley in the championship game; and as Loeffler had prophesied, circumstances more than anything dictated its use. Gola picked up four fouls early, and the Explorers were forced to switch to a 2-3 zone with Gola in the corner to keep him from fouling out. On offense, Gola concentrated on setting up Singley and Blatcher, who scored 23 points each, and was able to play out most of the

La Salle College

97

game. Fittingly, it was Gola who gave the Explorers the lead for good at 49-47 with a three-point play. Gola, with a typical well-balanced game of 19 points and 19 rebounds, was voted the most outstanding player of the tournament. Many thought he was the player of the year, over the likes of LSU's Bob Pettit, Furman's Frank Selvy, Cliff Hagan and Frank Ramsey of Kentucky, Don Schlundt and Bob Leonard of Indiana, Togo Palazzi of Holy Cross and Duquesne's Dick Ricketts.

In later years, Loeffler would remember Gola's magical 1953-54 season: "He was greater than ever. He had to carry the rebounding load all by himself most of the time, and he was magnificent. Even when he was sick and should have been resting, he insisted on practicing and playing."

Almost as mystical to Loeffler was the rapidity with which his Explorers fused that season.

"Everybody worked together, and we got good results," he said. "You can pick out any player on the team and see where he helped. O'Hara started hitting with his outside shooting and gave our attack the balance I was afraid it would lack. Frank Blatcher, who was slow on defense, improved on that. We always knew Frank could shoot. Maybe he shot some bad ones sometimes; but when he started hitting, he was a nice guy to have on our side. Charlie Greenberg, Bob Maples and Charlie Singley all came through at different times. If one was weak, the other would pick up. They were all sophomores and bound to be inconsistent, but they certainly showed me one thing—guts. No team I've ever had gave out as much as these kids!"

To prove that their 1954 NCAA title was no fluke, the Explorers went all the way to the finals again the following season. There, they would meet a mountainous challenge in San Francisco's Bill Russell.

THE DONS AND THEIR INCREDIBLE JOURNEY

"The NCAA championship is something that has to be experienced to be believed. Almost as unbelievable was the present I got from Stan Watts that day. Watts, one of the great coaches in the game, gave me a brown paper sack after the championship in which was ensconced a fifth of bourbon. For a gentleman as abstentious as Mr. Watts to give me a bottle of bourbon was a highlight of that victory."—Phil Woolpert, University of San Francisco basketball coach

Bill Russell heard the questions about facing Tom Gola until they became a cliche; but he always had the same good-natured, thoughtful response: "I'm not worried about Gola. I'm just trying to help my team win." With his predictable, light-hearted candor, the big man of the San Francisco Dons usually would add, upon a moment's reflection, "But, man, that Gola would really give the coach an ulcer."

While all the pregame hoopla was going on for the 1955 NCAA championship game between Russell's Dons and Gola's La Salle Explorers, the general assumption was that the two stars would be matched against each other.

Even San Francisco coach Phil Woolpert thought so, until a last-minute change of plans.

"I had originally tinkered with the idea of Russell playing Gola," Woolpert says. "But I huddled with one of my former teammates, Scotty McDonald, along with Pete Newell, who had coached the University of California, and Billy Donovan, who had coached at Loyola University. The four of us sat down, and it was basically McDonald's idea to let K.C. Jones play Gola nose-to-nose."

Jones was only 6-1, while Gola, considered by many to be the best college basketball player in the nation, stood a full six inches taller. But the night before, in San Francisco's 62-50 victory over Colorado in the national semifinals, Jones had startled the Kansas City Municipal Auditorium crowd and his San Francisco teammates with his spectacular leaps around the basket. Woolpert and his friends reasoned that Jones might be able to handle Gola. And with Jones on Gola, Russell could stick around the basket and handle rebounds. Then, of course, should Gola take Jones inside, Russell would be there as always to help out and take away the layups.

The strategy worked perfectly, Woolpert points out with fatherly pride: "K. C. did a fantastic job. K. C. hounded Gola all over the court and did just truly an amazing job. The only problem was that he became a little overconfident and started to free lance a little bit late in the first half even though we had told him to play Gola nose-to-nose. Gola got the ball, charged down the court like a runaway locomotive and stuffed the ball as the gun went off to end the half. That triggered some comments from me at half time. For the rest of the game, K. C. restricted his defensive skills to taking care of Gola."

That he did with unique fervor, holding La Salle's leading man to 16 points. Jones further amazed everybody with his deadly outside shooting, collecting a game-leading 24 points. With that outstanding performance, the Dons dethroned the Explorers as national champions, 77-63.

But fine as Jones' play was, Russell remained the brightest star in San Francisco's galaxy. He commanded the middle and kept La Salle from driving inside while snaring 25 rebounds and batting away several shots. He was equally as frightening on offense. By half time, Russell had 18 points; and a Sports Illustrated writer noted, "Ken Loeffler's boys simply could not keep Russell's hands off the ball.

Particularly deadly were Russell's tap-ins. His leaps were timed perfectly. Russell would soar in the air just as a shot by a colleague floated in toward the basket and tip the ball into the basket while La Salle defenders impotently stretched and strained beneath." Russell finished with 23 points and got the supreme tribute from Kansas coach Phog Allen, who said after watching his skyrocketing performance, "I'm for the 20-foot basket."

Russell, an animated, likeable young man, called himself "the luckiest guy in the world" after that momentous occasion. Among the luckiest moments of his early life was the start he got as a basketball player at McClymonds High School in Oakland, California, where he came under the influence of coach George Powles. "He may not have known too much about basketball," Russell later said, "but he taught me a lot of other things—how important your heart and your attitude are."

Powles gave Russell a chance that other coaches may not have given an awkward youngster. At McClymonds, Russell was so awkward that his appearance on the basketball court often was the signal for jeers and catcalls from the crowd. But with Powles behind him, Russell stuck to the game, spending hours practicing the fundamentals. In his senior year at McClymonds, Russell had grown to a firm 6-6; but by the time he had rounded into form, it was too late to attract much notice from the colleges. A scholarship offer did come from the University of San Francisco, however, and Russell took it because the school was near home and small enough that he wouldn't get lost in the crowd. Russell, though, was a little apprehensive, as he relates in his book, "Go Up For Glory": "I felt a little less secure when so many people didn't even know there was a University of San Francisco. And even more insecure when I traveled across the bay three times and couldn't find the school. No one knew where it was. But I finally found it."

And when he did, he put it on the basketball map with his own bold stamp.

Russell established his trademark immediately in the Dons' opening game against California in 1953 when he blocked the first shot by the Bears' big center, Bob McKeen. Watching Russell attack the ball with his eagle-like ferocity, California coach Pete Newell was heard to say, "Now where in the world did he come from?" Whether he meant the rejection or the recruitment, the fact was that Newell was seeing the seed of a legend sprouting before his astonished eyes. Behind their nonpareil center, the Dons made a sharp turn in their basketball program. In Russell's sophomore year, they finished with a 14-7 record, highly

commendable considering San Francisco's longtime image as a loser. In his junior year, Russell had grown to a heady 6-10; his reputation had grown even bigger. By then, Russell was blocking shots and sucking up rebounds with computer-like efficiency and the Dons were winning games with startling efficacy. Led by the ubiquitous Russell, Phil Woolpert's team won the NCAA title in 1955 and then repeated as NCAA champion in 1956. As impressive as the two straight national championships was a monster winning streak that remained unchallenged until John Wooden's mighty UCLA teams broke it in the 1970s.

The Russell-led teams won the lion's share of the famous 60-game string that extended from December 1954 to December 1956. Of the 60 games, remarkably, there was only one where the issue was in doubt in the final minute. In the finals of the NCAA West regional at Corvallis, Oregon, in March 1955, the Dons had to hang on to turn back Oregon State, 57-56. No other team was within 10 points of them at the buzzer that season; and the following year, when they had a 29-0 record, a seven-point win over Marquette was the Dons' stiffest test. In the undefeated 1956 season, the Dons averaged only 72 points a game, pale by today's standards, but their opponents averaged merely 52. The figures were an expression of Woolpert's fierce dedication to defense, or as Russell was fond of calling it, "The Big D." In the NCAA final against Iowa in 1956, the Dons stretched their unbeaten streak to 55 games as Russell scored 26 points, came down with 27 rebounds and knocked away about a dozen Hawkeye shots in an 83-71 victory.

Summarizing the strength of those two golden teams, Woolpert emphasizes: "They had great defense at all times. Team awareness was consistent. We had a great bench, not in skill so much as in vocal and physical support. These teams had a great ability to overcome leads. Their play was relatively error-free at all times. Their pride in defense was truly amazing. They exhibited great pride and tremendous confidence, but they were unspoiled by the lack of any previous success. The tremendous floor leadership of K. C. Jones and the awesome talents of Bill Russell were the great contributing factors."

Every team needs a gadfly and the Dons had one in a 5-11 guard, Hal Perry. "He did a tremendous job all season for us," Woolpert says. "He was a boy who was continually needling everybody on the ball club, demanding better and better performances. He certainly was a great contributor to our overall season. He was as quick as anyone could be, a good dribbler and a fine jumper. He specialized in

99

100

20- to 25-foot shots. He was a good driver and had good court vision. He was as fine a defensive guard as there was, other than K. C. Jones."

If the Dons of 1955-56 had any shortcoming, Woolpert believes it was a lack of killer instinct. "We had a tendency to let up in intensity after the starters had amassed a comfortable lead. Then we would reinsert the starters and—this happened continually—the margin again would widen. This never failed. So we had a pretty good answer to the problem."

Russell, Jones and Perry were accompanied ably on their incredible journey by Stan Buchanan and Jerry Mullen, among others. Russell and Jones got most of the publicity, but Buchanan and Mullen got some of the big baskets for the Dons in the 1954-55 season. Recalls Woolpert: "When we played at Oregon State (in the NCAA West regional), they didn't guard Buchanan, figuring he couldn't hurt them. It was an insult. Then he hit two shots from the side lines, and they had to stop double-teaming Russell. Their information was wrong."

Buchanan, who started at the forward spot opposite Mullen, "was probably one of the most underrated basketball players in America," according to Woolpert. "He was 6-2 and did not have great physical skills, but he was one of the smartest

San Francisco's Stan Buchanan (15) and La Salle's Alonzo Lewis (5) battle for a rebound in the 1955 title game. Under the basket is San Francisco star Bill Russell (6), voted the tournament's most outstanding player.

and most effective players anyone could imagine. He did everything that was asked of him all season long. More often than not, he ended up defensing a 6-6, 6-7 or 6-8 forward. He would do a great job of keeping the ball away from that type of person, but he would do an even better job of blocking those oversized forwards away from the boards, obviously contributing a great deal to our ball club." About Mullen, Woolpert points out: "He had played solely zone defense in high school. But he developed; by the time he was a senior, he was second only to Russell as a defensive player. He was an excellent outside shooter and a good board man."

The true heart and soul of the Dons, of course, were Russell and Jones. Woolpert emphasizes that Jones was "truly without equal. He was one of the most underrated players in all of basketball. He was a tremendous leader and scored only when needed. He was one of the finest pure passers it was ever my pleasure to see." Woolpert, spare in his praise of Russell to the painful annoyance of his star player in the 1950s, is abundantly praising in a retrospective look: "He deserves all the superlatives that have been written about him. He was voted the best player of the half-century, and he will make it again when they consider the next era. He had fantastic pride and as much heart as anyone I've seen. He did not feel anyone could beat him; and that washed off on the other players, the coaches, the rooters and anyone associated with the team. He was a legend in the field of basketball. He had awesome physical talents but always wanted to improve."

The foundation for these great San Francisco teams was laid in the 1940s by Pete Newell. Newell had given the Dons a taste of prominence by winning the National Invitation Tournament in 1949. Just as important, Newell had infused the Dons with a system of tight, aggressive defense and a disciplined, patterned offense that was carried over into future seasons. The effects of Newell's teaching were measured in other ways than the NCAA championship he brought to the University of California in 1959. From his fine 1949 team at San Francisco, John Benington, Rene Herrerias and Ross Giudice carried Newell's successful methods into their own coaching careers. Giudice, for one, as freshman coach helped develop some of the great talents for the 1955-56 San Francisco teams—most notably Russell and Jones. Woolpert, Newell's successor at San Francisco in 1951, kept up the system. This was the prevailing style on the West Coast at the time, with roots tracing back to Loyola of Los Angeles, where Woolpert played for Scotty McDonald and where both McDonald and Newell played for James Needles.

Woolpert denies any association with greatness; rather, he appraises his success in terms of good schooling. "In all candor," he says, "I considered myself an average coach, a coach who during that time was blessed with great players—as must be any coach who is successful, in my opinion. My biggest asset at the time was my ability to teach defense and fundamentals. I reflect back to my coach in college, Jimmy Needles, who incidentally coached the 1936 Olympic team; and he certainly grounded me in good, solid basketball. I was never a chess player, as far as coaching was concerned. During a game, I was aware of situations but did not have the facile ability to make quick adjustments as some coaches are able to do. I attempted to overcome this by trying to imagine situations which might arise and having our players so well-grounded in fundamental basketball that we could adjust to any situation. And we did that reasonably well."

Woolpert's national champion Dons clearly were an extension of the man, whom Russell once described as "an excellent technician." As Woolpert likes to point out: "I did mold the team to my personality. I always considered myself more a leader than a driver, and I attempted through logic and example to indicate to the players what I wanted done. But I did want it done my way."

From the beginning under Woolpert, San Francisco's players worked hard. Woolpert's emphasis was on defense, yet the Dons drilled for hours on play patterns and timing. However, his success did not happen overnight. In his first three years, Woolpert's teams had a dismal 30-41 record. But in the fourth year, the hard work and some hard recruiting began to pay off. By the fifth year, Woolpert had a national champion. "My greatest reaction to winning the NCAA title in 1955 was numbness," he says, smiling. "We finally had done it. It was something I never had really figured on or counted on. And yet I knew or felt at the time that it was inevitable because of the team we had at the time. I thought it was a super team. I still do."

At the start of the 1954-55 season, however, Woolpert was one of the few aware of the power of this astonishing team. The Dons, while upgrading their program with the likes of Russell and Jones, still had to prove themselves in battle. In mid-December of that season, the players at the little Jesuit school still were relatively anonymous. Nobody looked toward the Dons for all-America candidates; and certainly no one, not even the fanatical

home-town followers, ever dreamed that the Dons would be playing in the NCAA finals at Kansas City in March. This San Francisco team did not have even a home to play in; the Dons rented the pavilion at nearby Kezar Stadium, borrowed the San Jose auditorium or used the Cow Palace when big-name schools like Stanford or California came to town.

Not until late December did reports begin to filter into the news about a rising college basketball power on the West Coast. After losing in the third game of the season, a 47-40 defeat by UCLA, the Dons began to win ball games. Actually, it was something that happened as a result of the loss to UCLA. "We went in there expecting to be beaten by 20 or 25 points," Jones said in later years, "there" being the tough UCLA home court in Westwood. Instead, it was a competitive game; and the Dons came out of it with a new awareness of their prodigious possibilities. More significantly, they came out of it with a new backcourt combination. "I inserted Hal Perry into a starting guard spot opposite Jones," points out Woolpert. "From that time on, that group did not lose a basketball game. While it was not all that inspired, it was a move that ended up being as successful as a move could be."

The Dons' confidence now matched that of their coach, and they put these feelings into action the rest of the season. One of the highest points came when they won the All-College Tournament in Oklahoma City, beating an exceptionally strong Wichita State team along the way. Woolpert remembers with evident relish: "Wichita State was certainly the favorite, or equal favorite, yet we ran away. In fact, in the third quarter the score was 53-26. We took out our first string and substituted the reserves. The score ended up 94-75. The first string was upset, not because they didn't get to play in the fourth quarter, but because the reserves allowed too many points."

That tournament would leave a lasting impression on the Dons, and for more reasons than just the winning of a championship. San Francisco by this time had six Black players on the team; and the day before the tournament started, the Dons attracted a lot of attention in the workouts. The floor was raised like a stage, with the seats below; and spectators were jeering them as "Globetrotters" and throwing pennies at them. Russell picked them all up and told Woolpert to keep them for him. "And that," said one observer, "may have been the toughest part of the tournament for the cool Dons."

Loose and confident the rest of the way, the Dons kept on winning and finished the regular season with a wonderful 23-1 record. But the slender Woolpert, nervous as usual, feared a letdown in the NCAA tournament. On the verge of meeting West Texas State in a preliminary Western regional first-round game in San Francisco, Woolpert felt that his team was "somewhat flat, having just completed our season. I was concerned about the game. My fears and suspicions were well-grounded because well into the first five minutes of the game, we were very listless and flat. West Texas was shooting the eyes out of the hoop." Russell had some bad falls in the early going as well, further compounding Woolpert's worries. "Russell went up to block a shot; and as he came down, a West Texas player submarined him and he came down quite heavily. He was pretty shaken up but went back into play. Two minutes after that, an occurrence of the same kind took place. He hit the floor very heavily, taking a great part of the blow on his head. We didn't know whether he would be able to continue. He did, however, and after some rest got back into the game. I was quite upset about it at the time and let the (other) coach know I didn't like what had happened."

The incidents served as a two-sided sword by which West Texas State died. "This ended up by arousing our team," remembers Woolpert, "and we turned what was a close game and a game of concern to me into quite a rout, 89-66."

The stage of the Western regional shifted to Corvallis, Oregon, where the Dons faced Utah in semifinal action. Russell's health, once again, was the center of concern for Woolpert in this game. He reconstructs the scene: "Russell didn't quite appear to be himself. Going down to the dressing room at half time, I heard Russell, behind me, coughing a great deal. As we got into the dressing room, he excused himself and went into the bathroom and came back out. He had coughed up some blood. This immediately concerned me. I called for a doctor. A local doctor came down, checked Bill out and said that if it were he, he would not play Russell again during the ball game. I accepted his advice and went back out to the floor. We probably had a 15- to 18-point lead. We began the second half without Russell, and the lead was steadily dwindling. It began to look quite serious. A couple of our alumni came down and urged me to have someone else look at Russell. Russell called over to me a couple of times and said he felt fine. I was adamant; but finally I agreed to let a doctor from San Francisco look Bill over. He told me that Bill had eaten some raw steak in his pregame meal, and that was what he had coughed up. We put him back into the game. Bill was a wild man, and we ended up coasting."

The Dons finished with a 78-59 victory over what Woolpert called "a great Utah team" and advanced to the regional finals against possibly a greater Oregon State club. It was certainly a taller team, at any rate. The Beavers, coached by Slats Gill, had the country's (and probably the world's) biggest basketball player in 7-3 Swede Halbrook. The impending matchup of the titanic Halbrook and the superlative Russell was the signal for pregame drum-beating, as Woolpert recalls.

"Upon our arrival in Corvallis, a newspaperman asked if he might pose Russell next to Halbrook. He wanted to use it as a publicity shot. We agreed and, as soon as we finished our workout, they brought in Halbrook dressed in civvies. They gave Halbrook the basketball and asked him to stand next to a wall and have the ball in his right arm, extended as high as he could. Then they asked Russell to reach as high on Halbrook's arm as he could. Bill ambled over, and, of course, he was 6-9⅝. Bill uncorked his left arm and it went up, and up and up, and he ended up by cupping his fingers on top of the basketball. Needless to say, that picture never was shown in any of the Corvallis newspapers. And as our players later said, we had beaten Oregon State right there."

San Francisco did beat Oregon State, but it wasn't quite that easy. "Early in the game," Woolpert remembers, "our fine captain, Jerry Mullen, severely sprained his ankle. He ended up playing intermittently throughout the game, far from his normal self. Coupled with an inspired Oregon State team, this led to a tough game for us. It was probably the turning point in the saga of this team because Oregon State had a last shot, just prior to the gun going off. The ball hit the back rim and came within an eyelash of dropping, which, of course, would have meant defeat for us; and I wouldn't be sitting here telling anyone about this."

As if the mountainous Halbrook wasn't enough of a handful for Russell, the San Francisco center had to take care of a 6-6 forward, Tony Vlastelica, at the same time. At the beginning of the game, these two double-teamed Russell in the middle, often leaving Buchanan open about 12 feet from the basket. But Buchanan was a reluctant shooter. Several times the Dons passed the ball out to their open man and he passed it back. When this had occurred once too often for Woolpert, the San Francisco coach called a timeout and insisted that Buchanan take the open shot. Twice down the floor, the Dons gave the ball to Buchanan and twice he shot and missed. But finally he started hitting;

and when he connected on three field goals in a row, Oregon State coach Slats Gill switched his team's defense back to a straight man-to-man, and the game stayed nervously close all the way to the end.

With 13 seconds left, San Francisco held a tenuous two-point lead, 57-55, when Oregon State's Jim O'Toole made a heads-up defensive play that for the moment knocked the Dons off balance. During a San Francisco huddle, Jones had broken from the bench and gone out on the floor before the timeout was over. But Woolpert had called Jones back for a final word. O'Toole, who had shadowed Jones all night, quickly jumped in front of him to block his move to the bench. Jones attempted to go around him, but O'Toole blocked him again; so Jones pushed him aside and was on his way to his coach when he heard the referee charge him with a technical foul. Oregon State made the shot, cutting the Dons' lead to one point, and then got the ball inbounds at midcourt. The Beavers moved the ball into the corner for Ron Robins' favorite two-handed shot, but the ball hit the back rim, went straight up in the air and came down in the hands of the 7-3 Halbrook and 6-1 Jones. Halbrook won the tap, but the ball went to Hal Perry; and San Francisco's little guard was swarmed under by Oregon State players. By the time the Beavers wrestled the ball away and went in for the layup that would have won the game for

La Salle College

Charles Singley of La Salle drives to the basket in the 1955 championship game, won by San Francisco, 77-63.

them, the buzzer had long since sounded, sealing San Francisco's 57-56 triumph.

After that ferocious game, the rest of the tournament was relatively tame for the Dons. In the national semifinals at Kansas City, they had little trouble subduing Colorado, a surprise team that had upset Bradley in the finals of the Midwest regional. The Big Seven champions held their own most of the first half, but the Dons opened a six-point lead in the final three minutes before intermission and went on to a 62-50 victory. Then came La Salle, the powerhouse from Philadelphia which had virtually wiped the court with its opponents in the Eastern regional, recording such stunning scores as 95-61 over West Virginia, 73-46 over Princeton and 99-64 over Canisius. The defending national champions also had beaten a good Iowa team in the national semifinals, although not as handily. Like Colorado, the Iowa Hawkeyes were surprise members of the Final Four, having survived a Mideast regional which included mighty Kentucky.

The Dons were "sitting around nice and loose during their pregame meeting," according to one observer, when Woolpert dropped a bombshell in Jones' lap. "K. C.," he said, "you've got Gola." Later, Jones recalled, "That just about blew my whole dinner." But it didn't spoil his appetite for basketball. At one point, he had held La Salle's glamour player without a field goal for 21 minutes; and this artistic effort expanded new avenues for the Dons, particularly in Russell's unapproachable territory near the basket. "We found that, because K. C. Jones was able to handle Gola and his movement in their five-man rotating offense, we were able to play Russell relatively close to the basket," says Woolpert. "We were able to win rather handily this way. We actually were coasting toward the end of the ball game."

Russell's Herculean performance of 25 rebounds and 23 points had sustained Loeffler's worst fears. Prior to the championship game, the La Salle coach had said of the San Francisco giant: "We just can't let that big guy get the ball. Once he gets his hands on it, he shoots. We can stop him only by keeping the ball away from him."

The center of attention in the game, Russell was also the center of an anecdote that Woolpert long has relished from that euphoric time in Kansas City.

"There was considerable concern about the gambling problems that were extant in New York City at the time. All the coaches were warned, and their players were warned of the danger. I dutifully and at some length cautioned our team. Because of the prominence of the NCAA competition, I ad-

La Salle's Tom Gola scores in the Explorers' regional championship over Canisius in the 1955 tournament.

vised them to report anyone or anything that might be suspicious, to let me know, and I would check it out. The morning of the first game—we had stayed in Kansas City overnight—Russell asked if he might see me after breakfast. I said sure, let's go outside. As we were walking along the street, he told me he had been approached by this rather unkempt, very suspicious-looking gentleman, that he asked him a great number of questions about the feeling of the team, the health of the players and so forth. I told Russell I surely wanted more information and hoped he could point out the individual to me. And he said, 'Here he is coming down the street.' Can you imagine who it was? Lo and behold, it was a reporter from Sports Illustrated!"

Appreciative San Franciscans began raising money to build an arena for the homeless Dons that year and by the end of the 1955 NCAA championship already had raised $350,000 toward a $700,000 gym the team could call its own. While the backers were thinking about constructing a home for the San Francisco basketball team, Woolpert was building another powerhouse for the 1955-56 season. The Dons had three holdovers from the 1955 NCAA champions—Russell, Jones and Perry. Mike Farmer, Carl Boldt and Gene Brown joined the veterans, giving the Dons a better-shooting team than the year before and, according to Woolpert, a "more poised and smart team, more efficient than the 1955 team. This team had a desire to prove the previous championship was not a fluke. The excellent play of newcomers Boldt and Farmer, along with the great play of Gene Brown, who substituted for Jones, was certainly outstanding. In fact, Gene played swingman all season long, and he never did anything but contribute plus situations for us. And there was the emergence of Russell as a team leader, another outstanding factor supplementing the fine work that K. C. Jones already had done. Bill took over and did a beautiful job."

Russell's leadership was especially needed in the NCAA tournament that year, since Jones was ineligible. As a sophomore, he had appeared only in the opening game before an emergency appendectomy sidelined him for the season. But that had cost him eligibility in the national tournament during his senior season. Thus he watched the NCAA action in 1956 from the bench, able to lend only moral support.

San Francisco's schedule in the 1955-56 season was harder, and perhaps it was a blessing. The Dons

NCAA

had little time to worry about their winning streak or defending their national title. As Jones would say later, "Every game was like a war, every loose ball a battle; and you're trying to stop a man from shooting; you get the ball, you run—there's no time for thinking about the end of the year."

If the Dons themselves had little time to savor their season, certainly their fans could. They were watching something wondrous unfold—the longest winning streak in college basketball history. Along the way, the Dons were responsible for breaking other formidable streaks. The Marquette Warriors had won 22 straight games before the Dons defeated them in the Chicago Invitational Tournament. "It was a tough basketball game, but we didn't appear to be playing our normal game. We finally won by seven points, which, incidentally, was the

lowest winning margin we had all season," Woolpert recalls. "I didn't know until after the end of the season that a member of our traveling party, and unknown to me, had taken the entire basketball team on a tour of a Chicago museum. They were gone for 4½ hours, up and down stairs and everything that goes with touring an outstanding museum. It was understandable why they were a little below par in their game, again not taking anything away from a great Marquette team."

The Dons broke the existing college basketball record of 39 straight victories against a fine California team, coached by Woolpert's famous predecessor and former teammate, Pete Newell. "We were gunning for our 40th straight win at Berkeley, a hotbed of basketball, and knew it was going to be tough," notes Woolpert with a grimace. "We were

behind by 10 points early in the game. I called a timeout, and we went into a full-court press and finally managed a lead. We were leading by four or five points early in the second half, and Newell called a timeout. His team held the ball for nine straight minutes. We had the lead and made no attempt to go after the ball. Players were sitting on the floor. It wasn't one of the more enjoyable games to watch." In any event, the Dons finally did win by nine points, 33-24.

With the Dons winning every one of their games in 1955-56 with cool expediency, Woolpert finds it hard to underscore a turning point. "Actually," he says, "the entire season was the turning point. Undefeated, a season of continual highs, no peaks and valleys. During the NCAA tournament, there was speculation that we would be missing K. C. Jones, his leadership and his great floor play. (But) Brown was truly outstanding, and he had a steady running mate in Perry."

San Francisco's winning streak extended to 51 as the regular season ended and the Dons swept into the NCAA tournament, now enlarged to 25 teams. As champions of the California Basketball Association, San Francisco had earned a first-round bye in the Western regional at Corvallis, Oregon. When the Dons finally went to work, they did an efficient job disposing of UCLA and Utah by 11 and 15 points, respectively. In the 72-61 decision over UCLA—obviously a sweet one since the Bruins had been the last team to beat the Dons—Brown started in Jones' place and scored a team-high 23 points. Utah, led by Art Bunte's 23 points, scored an unusually high 77 against San Francisco; but the Dons wound up with 92. Russell, who led San Francisco with 27 points, added another most outstanding player award to his burgeoning trophy case.

While San Francisco was winning the West, Iowa was qualifying for the second straight year for the Final Four. The Hawkeyes, led by Carl Cain, won their way into the championship round with an 89-77 victory over Kentucky in the finals of the Mideast regional. In the Midwest, speed and outstanding marksmanship had carried Southern Methodist to a convincing 84-63 victory over Oklahoma City. Temple, led by the superb Hal Lear, had won the East by virtue of a 60-58 triumph over stubborn Canisius.

Several streaks were on the line when these four regional winners held a summit meeting at Evanston, Illinois, for the NCAA championship of 1956. Doc Hayes had probably his best team at SMU, with Jim Krebs, Joel Krog and Larry Showalter; but the Dons ended the Mustangs' winning string at 19 by a smashing 86-68 score. The Dons almost made a farce out of the contest. With the radar-like out-

Iowa's Carl Cain takes a rebound away from Hal Perry of San Francisco in the 1956 championship game. San Francisco won the contest, 83-71, to take its second straight title.

side shooting of Perry and Brown threatening to tear the nets off the rims, and with the 6-7 Farmer left virtually unguarded while the Mustangs double-teamed Russell, the Dons stormed to a 40-19 lead. This left Russell with little to do except gather in rebounds, bat away some shots, intercept a few SMU passes and occasionally soar into the air and steer a misguided shot by a teammate into the basket. Despite the 18-point victory, Russell was not entirely happy with his game. It came as a surprise to some people, because he had scored 17 points and done just about everything in his power to make SMU helpless. "We didn't play too good a game—or at least I didn't," he said afterwards, looking solemn. "Farmer and Perry and the others did. But we won, and that's what we came for."

The SMU coach was much more impressed with the Dons' proficiency. "San Francisco can beat any basketball team I know of." He added thoughtfully, "San Francisco can beat the Russians."

Perhaps world supremacy was going a little too far in San Francisco's case, but Hayes at least had the U.S. collegiate basketball picture in sharp focus. Subsequent events showed that the Dons were every bit as good as Hayes' word when, on the following night, they defeated Iowa, 83-71, to cap a perfect season and become only the third team to win two successive NCAA titles. Once again, it was Russell leading the San Francisco charge. He scored 26 points, came down with 27 rebounds, knocked away nearly a dozen Iowa shots and so befuddled Bill Logan that the 6-7 Hawkeye center, who had scored 36 points in an 83-76 semifinal victory over Temple, abandoned all attempts to score under the basket and finished with only 12 points. The only thing that prevented Russell from winning the most outstanding player award a second straight year was the most spectacular shooting exhibition in NCAA tournament history, a 48-point spree by Temple's Lear which helped the Owls defeat SMU, 90-81, in the third-place game.

The versatile Dons were able to scrap their original game plan for the finals and still beat Bucky O'Connor's strong Iowa team rather handily. "We switched our game plan early because of a change in the starting lineup, the tremendous shooting of Iowa and a defensive breakdown on the part of our team," Woolpert remembers. "We were down early by 10 points, called a timeout and inserted a player by the name of Warren Baxter, a 5-8 guard who had played considerably as a substitute. When Warren moved in, we moved Brown to

Wide World Photos

defensive forward; and we ended up by not only overcoming Iowa's lead but going into a substantial lead of our own. The highlight was that this was the first time an all-Black team was on the floor at the same time, to my knowledge. When we moved Baxter into the game, we had five Black starters."

The Dons got off to a cold start and trailed, 15-4; but once Woolpert made his defensive adjustments, the tone of the game changed abruptly. The most crucial of the adjustments was putting Brown on Iowa's brilliant floor leader, Carl "Sugar" Cain. The Hawkeye star had gotten several easy baskets in the early going against Boldt to help Iowa open up its big lead. But once they got going, the Dons first led by 24-23 and then were in command at the half, 38-33. When the lead widened considerably after intermission, Woolpert went to his bench. "The biggest problem toward the end of the game," he says, "was to get all the personnel in the game. That was a must, as far as I was concerned, in any championship game. I always wanted all of our players to have a chance to participate. With a lead going into the final three minutes, due to a combination of factors, it was almost impossible for us to get the ball into play. I had benched our starters; and not only were we having trouble

getting the ball into play, the ball was being taken away from us and Iowa was scoring. I had to reinsert our starters to insure the victory."

Woolpert, who had been shaking his head sadly for two years while others persisted that this San Francisco team quite possibly was the greatest in college basketball history, finally acknowledged the supreme accolade.

"This team is the finest I've seen," he said after his second straight NCAA title. "I can say that in all honesty now. It has done everything asked of it. The difference—without a doubt—was Russell."

While Woolpert was applauding Russell, the rules committee of the NCAA was paying San Francisco's leading man perhaps his biggest compliment. In executive session, the committee was considering a new set of rules to prevent the inordinately agile and tall player from vaulting into the air and slapping the ball down into or away from the basket, which subsequently became known as goaltending. It was a problem which no one worried much about before Russell surfaced at San Francisco and, symbolically, was the coaches' way of saying goodbye to an era. Later, when the goaltending rule was passed, it was commonly acknowledged as the "Russell Rule."

A COOL 32

"The same night that we won easily over the University of San Francisco in the NCAA semifinals, North Carolina beat Michigan State in triple overtime. North Carolina was undefeated, but Michigan State should have won. Johnny Green blew two free throws late in the game to give North Carolina the victory. Frank McGuire, the North Carolina coach, always said he was sure his team was fated to win the championship after that game."—Wilt Chamberlain, University of Kansas center

Wilt Chamberlain, the Lord High Executioner of the Kansas basketball team, had a disquieting effect on the opposition. Mountainous in appearance at 7-foot-1, the stunning visual impact of his figure around the basket was enough to throw many teams off their game. "If Kansas gets the ball on the opening jump and passes in to Chamberlain for a dunk shot," pointed out an observer, "the impact is increased enormously. After Chamberlain blocks the first shot, the shock treatment is complete. Many good teams simply fall apart at this point; a great team is no longer great."

It was clearly Chamberlain's intimidation that led the Jayhawks through the Midwest regional and into the NCAA finals in 1957. The Chamberlain complex virtually hypnotized both Southern Methodist and Oklahoma City, who often were frozen when in the Great Man's presence. After Kansas' 73-65 victory over SMU, one coach pinpointed the unsettling effect Chamberlain had on the Mustangs: "I watched Larry Showalter go up once for a jump shot. Chamberlain wasn't even close to him. But he went up and took his eye off the basket, backboard and all."

A player who had maintained psychological and physical mastery over opposing teams, Chamberlain continued to display this paralyzing effect against San Francisco in the championship semifinals at Kansas City. After watching Chamberlain brutalize the Dons in the Jayhawks' 80-56 victory, North Carolina coach Frank McGuire knew he had to come up with something special to turn the psychological tables on the Kansas star in the finals. What he eventually conceived was perfect. First, in a move to disorient Chamberlain,

McGuire began the game by having the shortest player on his squad, Tommy Kearns, jump against the Kansas giant for the opening tipoff.

"I can still see the look of bewilderment and embarrassment on Chamberlain's face as Kearns lined up to jump against him," recalls McGuire. "Wilt looked 10 feet tall towering over Tommy, but they made such a ridiculous picture together that Chamberlain must have felt no bigger than his thumb. At least, that's the state of mind we wanted to get him into. North Carolina had to stop Chamberlain to win, and anything we could do to harass him would help. We wanted him thinking, 'Is this coach crazy? What other tricks does he have up his sleeve?' What I wanted was for Chamberlain to get a good shock."

The ludicrous picture Chamberlain made jumping against the 5-10 Kearns was nothing compared to his attempts to score against North Carolina's defense shortly thereafter. The Tar Heels gambled on letting the other Kansas players take shots while concentrating on holding down the great Chamberlain. They did this when it counted. Remembers McGuire:

"Joe Quigg played in front of Chamberlain, harassing him and trying to block any passes to him. We collapsed off the other men so that we surrounded Wilt. That is, the four other men were distributed in a zone defense, but the whole pattern was centered around Chamberlain. Each man was in a position to move in on Wilt. The weak-side men—those on the side away from the ball—always helped out Quigg. This gave Kansas opportunities for corner shots, but they couldn't or wouldn't take them. When a shot was taken by

Kansas, our boys didn't go in for the rebound; they went in for Chamberlain. He'd find two men in front of him and two behind him. We knew nobody could outrebound him, so we had to block him. The one man who was in the most disadvantageous position for blocking Chamberlain would go up for the rebound."

As Chamberlain was to say later, "I didn't get many shots off against that kind of defense." His teammates, meanwhile, "couldn't put a pea in the ocean," according to the Kansas center. The result was that Chamberlain did not score a point for the first five minutes of the game; and by then, North Carolina had a 9-2 lead. The Jayhawks did not shoot much better the rest of the first half, an embarrassing 27 per cent, while McGuire's more selective players were making shots with cool efficiency. By the half, the Tar Heels had shot a wondrous 65 per cent from the field, led by Lennie Rosenbluth's 14 points. North Carolina's high-powered scorer had missed only two shots before intermission, and the Tar Heels took a 29-22 lead into the dressing room.

Along with a defense geared to stop Chamberlain, McGuire's game plan that night in the Kansas City Municipal Auditorium also included an extremely high standard of shot selection. In the dressing room before the game, the North Carolina coach had warned his team against carelessness in this area. "I said I didn't care if we didn't take a single shot in the first half if the shot opportunity wasn't a good one. Against Chamberlain, this involved special consideration. We were not to shoot when he was under or near the defensive backboard, where he could block the shot or rebound it. Our job was to box him out from under the boards. Any shot we tried had to be a facing shot—that is, with the shooter facing the basket, where he could see Chamberlain."

When the game began, Kansas coach Dick Harp had produced a diamond-and-one defense with Chamberlain under the basket and Maurice King shadowing Rosenbluth, North Carolina's top scorer. "We'd come up against this before, when it was used as a spite defense to hold down Rosenbluth's scoring," McGuire notes. "That kind of defense couldn't beat us. We had five shooters, not one." When Carolina responded with outside shooting by Quigg and Pete Brennan, Kansas was forced to go back to a man-to-man defense. Then the 6-9 Quigg drew Chamberlain outside, and Rosenbluth moved inside for his 14 points.

McGuire's game plan had worked as close to perfection in the first half as he could have wished. "When you have the ball," he said, "the other team can't score. That was our object—to keep the

ball away from 'The Stilt' by slowing up our game and always keeping an eye on him."

The tempo of the second half was a repeat performance of the first, with the exception that North Carolina's shooting percentage—as was bound to happen—went down. And the Kansas percentage went up.

The Tar Heels also were hurt by foul trouble. Attempting to overload on Chamberlain, Quigg picked up four fouls and Rosenbluth and Kearns three each midway through the second half. Kansas rallied behind Chamberlain, Maurice King and Gene Elstun and took a 40-37 lead with 10:20 left. It was at this juncture, McGuire points out, that Kansas made a costly error in strategy.

"We were in a precarious position. We had played a triple overtime game the night before against Michigan State. The boys were tired. And we also had a bad foul situation. As I see it, Kansas should have pressed the foul situation and also our weariness. They had momentum after wiping out our half-time lead and going in front themselves. But instead of putting on the pressure, Kansas went into a stall for the next few minutes."

With a little less than seven minutes to go, Kansas made it a solid freeze; and McGuire remembers, "The local crowd in the jampacked Municipal Auditorium loved that. We had played ball control all night, and now their team was giving us a dose of our own bitter brew. The fans didn't realize that I loved it even more than they did. The slowdown gave us a chance to stay alive."

McGuire raised his hand to his team in a cautioning gesture, five fingers spread. Translation: "Let them hold the ball until there are five minutes to play."

"We stood at our end of the court and let Kansas play catch," says McGuire. "At five minutes, I waved my hand and the boys went after them. They'd given us time to get our second wind and provided us a safety margin in the foul column." Without meaning to, the Kansas players had dropped the whip hand.

North Carolina eventually did lose one man to fouls—the indispensable Rosenbluth. The Tar Heel star, who had been tossing up the softest, loveliest baskets imaginable, fouled out with 1:45 left after having scored 20 points. Kansas held a 46-43 lead at this point; and Chamberlain later recalled, "It looked like we had the championship in the bag."

"I remember looking up in the stands at some friends and thinking how groovy it was going to be to celebrate with them later," Chamberlain said in his autobiography. "I mean, one of our best free-throw shooters, Gene Elstun, was at the line, and if he made it, we'd be ahead by four points. Even if

University of North Carolina

they scored again, we'd get the ball back with a two-point lead and less than a minute to go. I was sure we could stall the game out. Well, Elstun misses the free throw, and the ball bounces damn near all the way to midcourt where they have a guy standing. They get a layup. A few seconds later, one of our guys blows an inbounds play and they get a free throw, and the game goes into overtime." The game thus ended tied, 46-46, and the team which played through three taut overtime periods the night before against Michigan State was faced with the same prospect again—this time without the services of its best shooter. North Carolina had won three overtime games during its perfect season, but never without Rosenbluth.

Ironically, it was Rosenbluth's replacement, Bob Young, who drove the lane for a Tar Heel lead at 48-46. But Chamberlain's jump shot tied it up, and these were the only points in the first overtime period. The teams went into the second extra period, locked in what was now a cautious, defensive chess game.

In the second period, both teams probed for perfect shots that never came; and the most excitement came when both benches charged the floor after a loose-ball wrestling match. The action picked up in the third overtime, when Kearns hit a field goal and two foul shots for North Carolina and Kansas came back to tie at 52-52 on a three-point play by Chamberlain and a free throw by King. McGuire ordered North Carolina to play for one shot. The Tar Heels stalled away two minutes, but then John Parker stole the ball from Quigg and Kearns deliberately fouled Elstun. He made one of two free throws for a 53-52 Kansas lead. Kearns drove for a shot but Chamberlain rejected it; Quigg rebounded and was fouled. It was a two-shot foul, and North Carolina called a timeout with six seconds left.

"I was nervous," Quigg later recalled. "All I could think about during the timeout period was making those two shots. But then things started flashing through my mind. I got to thinking about the season we had—undefeated through 31 games. And I thought to myself that I couldn't let the team down now—not at this stage, with the outcome of the game at stake. I thought about this being a chance of a lifetime—a chance to wind up the season undefeated and a chance to win the NCAA championship. Boy, I was glad it was a two-shot foul. If it had been a one-and-one situation—well, the pressure would have been greater."

North Carolina's Joe Quigg (41) looks to pass off as Ron Loneski of Kansas defenses him.

When the time came for Quigg to step to the free-throw line to shoot the most important shots of his career, he was brimming with self-assurance.

"I just had confidence in myself," he says. "Coach McGuire had just told me that I had missed a one-and-one situation earlier in the game and that here was a chance to make up for it."

Remembering assistant coach Buck Freeman's advice in the huddle to "follow through and end up on your toes," Quigg let go his first shot. "I knew it was in the moment it left my hands. You can just feel whether a shot is good or not. I took a deep breath and shot again—but the second one wasn't as hard to make. I had the range—and I knew I could make that one, after sinking the first one."

Now North Carolina had a 54-53 lead, but there were still six seconds to go. Kansas called a timeout to plot its strategy for the last shot. And here again, Quigg made the key play—this time on defense. When play resumed, Ron Loneski attempted to pass the ball in to Chamberlain, but Quigg blocked the pass. The ball bounced out to Kearns, who dribbled the clock away and in delight threw the ball toward the lights of the Municipal Auditorium as the final gun sounded.

The Tar Heels' conduct in the final moments of that pressurized game seemed to reflect the tone of their entire season. After the previous exhausting evening with Michigan State, under the acute pressure not only of a national championship game but their own 31-game winning streak and facing a great threat to peace of mind in Chamberlain, the Tar Heels kept their poise, played their style and won a game that few observers felt they could swing. "McGuire's Miracle," as some were to call North Carolina's perfect season, was in fact not without its mystical moments.

"There was something eerie about winning 32 straight," says McGuire. "We won several games we should have lost; we got breaks that were out of this world. I thought sure we would lose at least four games we won, and finally I almost hoped we could get beaten just to take the terrific pressure off the players. Well, not the players so much because they kept cool even if I didn't. But the students and the alumni and the people were generally feeling the strain. Strangers would come up to me and slip me a nutmeg, a lucky coin or a rabbit's foot to carry in my pocket, or a man might beg me to wear the same sports jacket to every game. Students were growing beards, they counted their steps from one class to another so they would take just the same number every day. One student got the idea he would jinx us if he moved his car. So he let it stand where it was and collected parking tickets until the season was over. What happened that year

III

couldn't happen again in a thousand years."

McGuire's team of destiny began shaping up in Rosenbluth's junior year, 1955-56, when the Tar Heels had an 18-5 record. By that time the so-called "Underground Railroad" was operating in full swing. The colorful and apropos nickname was applied by sports writers to the work of Harry Gotkin, the uncrowned czar of New York City recruiting. Gotkin was a good friend of McGuire's and channeled players from the New York area nonstop to the Chapel Hill station. Because of Gotkin's indefatigable work, McGuire's teams always had a strong New York-New Jersey accent. For instance, the nucleus of the 1957 NCAA champions consisted of five players from the New York metropolitan area—Lennie Rosenbluth, Bob Cunningham, Tommy Kearns, Joe Quigg and Pete Brennan. Overall, nine of the 12 players on the team were from that area.

It was not the easiest team in the world for a coach to orchestrate. Some of the players were headstrong and individualistic, but McGuire was able to apply the psychological masterstrokes and the proper coaching touches when needed; and when the canvas was complete, he had a 32-0 masterpiece. "It took a clutch ball club to accomplish that," he says. "Most coaches who saw our team during the year said that the greatest single factor distinguishing North Carolina was its poise. We made a point of keeping our mistakes to a minimum. We were careful not to walk or to throw bad passes. When we shot, it was a good shot. When we were forced into overtime games, the boys knew what had to be done."

The 6-5 Rosenbluth was far and away the best scorer on the team, averaging 28 points a game in 1956-57—or just about double that of the next best scorer, Brennan. Kearns, a confident, blue-eyed bandit of a guard who loved to steal the ball and drive in for layups, operated in the backcourt with defensive ace Cunningham. Quigg and Brennan, childhood friends off the sidewalks of New York, supplied most of the rebounding muscle. The top reserves were Tony Radovich, Bob Young and Danny Lotz.

"The players seemed to take the pressure far better than the fans or I did," notes McGuire. "Everybody was waiting for them to crack, but these kids wouldn't."

Until they had to sweat through two triple-overtime thrillers in the NCAA tournament, no game was tougher that season for North Carolina than the second game of the Atlantic Coast Conference playoffs against Wake Forest. As the Tar Heels struggled to beat Wake Forest, 61-59, one sports writer noted that the arena "nearly collapsed under the maddening pressure." Obviously, the Tar Heels did not. Trailing, 59-58, with 55 seconds to play, North Carolina went ahead to stay on a nifty three-point play by Rosenbluth.

North Carolina then won the ACC playoffs in style, crushing South Carolina, 95-75, and continued to look like the nation's No. 1 team with decisive triumphs over Yale, Canisius and Syracuse in the NCAA's Eastern regional.

Kansas was just as impressive in winning the Big Eight championship and then the NCAA's Midwest regional. The Jayhawks had finished their regular season with a 21-2 record, best in 20 years, with the highly visible Chamberlain the dominating figure. In the regional at Dallas, Chamberlain's profile was higher than ever. Preoccupied to the point of obsession with the Kansas center, Southern Methodist found it difficult to reach its splendid potential. Intensely aware of Chamberlain's frightening presence, the Mustangs' shooting was affected. SMU coach Doc Hayes had his players sandwiching Chamberlain tightly on defense, and this opened lanes for other Kansas players to drive through for easy shots. Gene Elstun and Ronnie Loneski were two players who especially took advantage of this situation to help give Kansas a big early lead. However, the Mustangs adjusted, giving the whole responsibility for Chamberlain to Jim Krebs and closing the lanes they had left open before. Krebs, fighting hard for rebounds and guarding Chamberlain closely, fouled him three times; but SMU gradually closed the wide gap. By the half, the Kansas lead was down to 33-32. "You had the feeling that Southern Methodist, working intelligently and calmly now and doing very well the things they had found they could do against Kansas, could win," observed Tex Maule and Jeremiah Tax in Sports Illustrated.

Indeed, SMU was in control for most of the second half; and Kansas showed signs of losing its composure. But with five minutes to play and SMU ahead by three points, Krebs fouled Chamberlain for the fifth time and left the game. SMU tried desperately to hoard the three-point lead by controlling the ball, but Kansas tied the game as the period ended and coasted through the five-minute overtime for a 73-65 victory. Chamberlain finished with 36 points and 22 rebounds; and as one writer pointed out, "the tournament was won for Kansas right there in the first game."

It wasn't official, however, until Kansas beat Oklahoma City, 81-61, in the finals. Oklahoma City, an exceptionally tall team with fine speed, clamped a rough, aggressive defense around Chamberlain; and the Kansas shooters—Elstun and King principally—were cold in the first half. But

they began to hit well in the second half, and the Oklahomans were forced to come out from under the basket and challenge the Jayhawks. That left Chamberlain free to move and shoot inside, and the game very quickly became a rout for Kansas. Despite a defense set up specifically to stop him and a highly unfriendly crowd that hooted and jeered him, Chamberlain played with considerable grace and self-assurance for a 19-year-old and scored 30 points.

Aside from the victories, the Dallas experience was not entirely pleasant for Chamberlain. From the moment of his arrival in the Southwestern capital, the heralded Kansas player felt harassed. Chamberlain voiced complaints that because of his color, he was shut off from all social activity in town. The team, in fact, had been forced to stay in a motel in Grand Prairie, Texas, about 30 miles from downtown Dallas. Antagonism was painfully evident in Chamberlain's case when someone burned a cross in a vacant lot across from the motel. In the game against SMU, there was more hostility directed Chamberlain's way. The crowd booed the Kansas player and hurled racial epithets at him. "I tried not to let it bother me much," he said later. "I figured I'd answer them on the basketball court." Chamberlain also got some racial abuse in the Oklahoma City game—and not only from the fans. One of the Oklahoma City players consistently called Chamberlain foul names and jabbed him and tripped him whenever possible. But later, Oklahoma City star Hubert Reed, who was white, apologized for the behavior of his teammate and the fans and that, according to Chamberlain, "more than offset all of the abuse."

While North Carolina and Kansas were predictably winning their regional tournaments, there was a surprising development in the Mideast, where Michigan State pulled off a spectacular 80-68 upset of Kentucky. And the Spartans did it the hardest way possible—storming back from a 12-point deficit at the half to rout the nation's third-ranked team. The Western championship game was a classic of defensive basketball engineered by two masters of the art, towel-chewing coach Pete Newell of California and gum-chewing coach Phil Woolpert of San Francisco. Both teams used fullcourt and midcourt presses, and guarding was so close that clear shots were almost impossible. In the game's last 19 minutes, the lead changed nine times and the score was tied three times before San Francisco finally won, 50-46. As he had done most of the season, Gene Brown led the Dons, scoring 20 points and playing flawless defense.

Faced with Chamberlain in the national semifinals at Kansas City, the Dons simply were not as efficient. Chamberlain blocked, dunked, ran and rebounded without flaw; and Kansas put San Francisco away by 24 points with a brilliant shooting exhibition of 60 per cent. The Kansans not only outshot the two-time defending national champions but also outdefensed them—a huge accomplishment, considering that the Dons were established as the country's best in that category.

By contrast, the other semifinal game was one of suspense down to the end—and then some. North Carolina and Michigan State were tied, 29-29, at the half; and they still were deadlocked, 58-58, at the end of regulation time as Johnny Green converted two free throws for the Spartans. At the end of the first overtime, it was 64-64, thanks to a short jump shot by North Carolina's Pete Brennan with three seconds remaining. The second extra period ended 66-66. This time, Green's tip-in with seven seconds left kept Michigan State's hopes alive. Thereafter, Lennie Rosenbluth stole the ball twice and scored on layups, and Tommy Kearns added two free throws to clinch the Tar Heels' dramatic 74-70 victory.

Kearns then sounded a warning for Kansas, speaking up briskly in a heavy fog of one-sided thinking that favored the Jayhawks in the championship game. "We're a chilly club," he said. "We play it chilly all the time. I mean we just keep cool. Chamberlain is not going to give us the jitters like he did to San Francisco and those other clubs."

As the irrepressible Kearns squared off against the Kansas center the following night in the memorable tipoff to trigger the national finals, the symbolism of David vs. Goliath was apparent. The game, as some were to point out later, even followed the lines of that old story.

113

Rich Clarkson

1958

THE FIDDLIN' FIVE

"We've got fiddlers, that's all. They're pretty good fiddlers; be right entertaining at a barn dance. But I'll tell you, you need violinists to play in Carnegie Hall. We don't have any violinists."—Adolph Rupp, University of Kentucky basketball coach

Since their NCAA championship in 1951, the Kentucky Wildcats had been on the periphery of the winner's circle. Adolph Rupp produced formidable teams throughout the 1950s, including one hawkish bunch that went undefeated in the 1953-54 season but declined an NCAA bid because three starters were ineligible. There was NCAA participation three straight seasons after that, with the same losing results, but always there was a persistent feeling that Kentucky was on the verge of breaking out. It finally happened for the Wildcats in 1958, although ironically this was possibly one of the weakest of Rupp's teams in that era. He had disparaged their talents and taunted them as "fiddlers" for their lack of fire, yet this team won an unprecedented fourth NCAA championship for Kentucky with players few people heard of and some nobody wanted.

"They weren't the greatest basketball players in the world," Rupp would say later. "All they could do was win."

Victories did not come easy, though, for the Wildcats that year. In fact, they lost six games and compiled their worst regular-season record since 1940-41. Incidentally, the six losses were the most by an NCAA champion at that point in the tournament's history, a dubious distinction that sat well with the character of their entire season. "They fiddled around enough to drive me crazy," Rupp once said of this enigmatic team. "They'd fool around and fool around; and then with maybe two or three minutes to go, they'd look over at the bench and see that the coach wasn't happy. And

then they'd get busy and win by one or two points. But in the meanwhile, they'd drive me crazy."

Typical of the season was an 85-83 triple-overtime victory over Temple, a game that seemed destined to go down as another loss in the Kentucky column. Kentucky's Vern Hatton had made a free throw with 49 seconds left and sent the game into overtime, tied 65-65. But the Wildcats seemed beaten when Temple's Guy Rodgers hit a 15-foot shot with three seconds to play in the first extra period. By the time Kentucky got a timeout, only one second showed on the clock. In the huddle, Rupp turned to Adrian Smith, who had fired an unsuccessful 60-footer near the end of regulation time. "Well, Smitty, I guess we'll have to let you shoot another." But assistant coach Harry Lancaster interceded: "Let's let Vernon try this one."

Temple's defense backed up, trying to protect against the long pass under the basket and the quick tip. Hatton took the inbounds pass near the side line at midcourt, wheeled toward the basket and let fly with both hands. The ball nicked the metal rim, bounced back and forth several times and then dropped through as Kentucky's Memorial Coliseum exploded in sound and fury. Near the end of the next overtime, Temple tied the score at 75. The third overtime, however, belonged to Hatton. He scored six points and helped the Wildcats beat one of the nation's strongest teams.

Kentucky's fallibility produced many more close games than Rupp's stout heart could take. At one juncture, after a characteristic one-point loss, Rupp noted: "This is the greatest record-setting basketball team in the history of the University of Kentucky. It just sets the wrong kind of records."

Indeed, the Wildcats lost three one-pointers during the regular season; and even though they had won the Southeastern Conference champion-

Plays such as this defensive action by Roy DeWitz (10), Bob Boozer (30) and Jack Parr (32) led Kansas State into the semifinals in 1958.

ship, few gave them a chance in the NCAA tournament.

"After winning the Southeastern Conference championship, people were congratulating me. But few thought we would get past the first round of the NCAA tournament," Rupp remembered. "They all told me how they thought we had a great year—they were sorry we couldn't go on—but they thought I had turned in a wonderful job. Well, in the first game, we beat Miami of Ohio by 20 points. And then in the second game, we played Notre Dame. And everyone said this is as far as you're going to go. There is no way you can beat Notre Dame. Even the administration told me that: 'You've had a great year, but then there's no way to beat Notre Dame.' I felt the same way, too. But, of course, we did . . .''

Of the many metaphors Rupp used to describe this team, the Kentucky coach likened the Wildcats more often than not to "barnyard fiddlers," alluding, no doubt, to the inconsistent quality of their play. Perhaps this was a barnyard mixture; at the very least, it was a group composed of many diverse personalities. Some had to be prodded and some had to be patted, and Rupp always seemed to know when to apply the proper psychological strokes. Hatton, for one, was a player who gave everything but could not perform under criticism. Thus Rupp only criticized him occasionally during a defensive drill, never in a game. Once during practice, Rupp angrily admonished Hatton to "play defense, you lazy thing!" Hatton walked off the court and announced that he was quitting, but Rupp appealed to his pride. "Vernon, I have been coaching for 30 years," he said, "and this is the first time I ever had a boy quit on me like this." Hatton, of course, rejoined the team after that and played with his accustomed fury.

On the other hand, John Crigler was motivated by little else than personal criticism. Once when the usually steady forward allowed his man to score the tying basket as the half ended against Auburn, Rupp told him in the dressing room: "John Lloyd, 150 years from now there will be no university, no field house. There will have been an atomic war, and it will all have been destroyed. But underneath the rubble, there will be a monument, which will be inscribed, 'Here lies John Lloyd Crigler, the most stupid basketball player ever at Kentucky, killed by Adolph Rupp,' because, boy, if you don't play better, I'm going to kill you."

Hatton and Crigler were two of the four starters returning from a Kentucky team that won 23 games in 1956-57. The others included forward Johnny Cox and center Ed Beck. Adrian Smith, a reserve who showed great promise the previous season, replaced Gerry Calvert at the other guard.

Hatton was perhaps the most interesting of these players. Confident, almost cocky, the 6-3 guard had an uncanny knack of coming through in clutch spots. "He was as courageous as any boy who ever played basketball," Rupp once pointed out. "He

had the most confidence in his ability of any boy I've had, and he was justified in it." The substance of Hatton's basketball philosophy was summed up in some advice his high school coach once gave him. "He always told me never to hide from the ball," Hatton notes. "When the game got tough, I always tried to get the ball. This carried through into college." Interestingly, Hatton's coach at Lafayette High School in Lexington, Kentucky, was none other than Ralph Carlisle, an all-conference forward for Rupp in the 1930s. Infused with the Carlisle philosophy, Hatton eventually disproved the judgment of a junior high school coach who called him "very, very clumsy." As a younger player, Hatton had been a forward, but Carlisle made a tall guard out of him with hard work. An all-America in his senior year at Lafayette, Hatton first agreed to attend Kentucky. But during the summer, he changed his mind and signed a letter of intent with Eastern Kentucky. When the news broke about Hatton's change of plans, Kentucky assistant coach Harry Lancaster pursued Hatton to Huntington, West Virginia, where the big guard was playing in an all-star game. Hoping to avoid Lancaster, Hatton stayed in the shower for an hour after the game. When he finally came out, there was the persistent Lancaster waiting for him.

"Boy," Lancaster said wearily, "you sure like to get clean, don't you?"

Not long after that, Hatton made another mid-course correction and turned his direction toward Kentucky.

With the exception of Cox, a junior from Hazard, Kentucky, who had led the Wildcats in scoring the year before with a 19.4 average, every starter was a senior. All things considered, Rupp probably thought Cox was most capable of realizing superstardom. Not only was Cox an excellent one-handed jump shooter from the top of the circle, he could hit sweeping hook shots and was a ferocious rebounder. Crigler, at the other forward, was one of those unselfish players Rupp always seemed to find room for in his lineup. A strong rebounder for his 6-3 stature, Crigler was capable of coming through occasionally with a high-scoring game. Beck had been a consistent scorer as a high school player in Fort Valley, Georgia. However, Rupp never encouraged his shooting abilities; and so the 6-7, 188-pounder began concentrating on rebounding and defense for Kentucky. Smith had been a high school star in Farmington, Kentucky, but at 5-10

Players from Seattle and Kentucky battle under the basket in the 1958 championship game. Included are Seattle's Charley Brown (45) and Jerry Frizzell (54) and Kentucky's John Crigler (32) and Johnny Cox (24).

and 150 pounds received no attention at first from Kentucky. In fact, Rupp said, "I once turned him down because I thought he was too little." Smith, however, grew taller in Rupp's estimation after he played junior college ball and averaged more than 27 points a game. "Smitty," said Rupp, "was a second Ralph Beard—ferocious in all respects."

The uneven year challenged Rupp's constitution, tested his coaching abilities and frayed his nerves. There were three losses before 1957 was out, including an opening-round defeat in Kentucky's own invitational tournament. The Wildcats, incidentally, lost two games in a row for the first time in 15 years. Throughout the checkered season, however, they had won when they had to and at the end assumed their familiar place atop the Southeastern Conference—winners for the 19th time. The Wildcats thus entered the NCAA tournament; to paraphrase a Rupp metaphor, his "fiddlers" had made it to the steps of Carnegie Hall. Many thought they would find the doors closed, though; and basketball society in general looked for a quick exit for the Wildcats—even though the Mideast regional was being played on Kentucky's home floor and the finals at nearby Freedom Hall in Louisville. But observers had underestimated the power of the home-court advantage and surely could not have known that Kentucky would be saving its best basketball for the last four games of the year.

With Cox scoring 23 points and three other players in double figures, Kentucky took a surprisingly easy 94-70 victory over Miami of Ohio. The Redskins had beaten Pittsburgh in a first-round Mideast game before falling so unceremoniously to the Wildcats. However easy their first conquest, the Wildcats seemed doomed to failure the next night against a strong Notre Dame team that had beaten Big Ten champion Indiana in the other Mideast semifinal game. Rupp's biggest concern was Tom Hawkins, Notre Dame's fine pivot man who had scored 31 points against Indiana. "He liked to get within 10 feet of the goal and use a tremendous hook shot," Rupp said with awe. "And they had a fine team otherwise."

Rupp, normally a swaggering leader, was betrayed by his nerves and reduced to a state of insecurity on the day of the game, the odds being what they were.

"I could not rest all that afternoon," he once told an interviewer. "I was in my office and I got ants all over me. I came home about 3 o'clock and was walking around the house. I couldn't sit still. I finally put my clothes on for the game and told my wife, 'I'm going over to the Coliseum.' She said, 'Why? You haven't even eaten yet. All you've done

117

is storm around the house. Sit down and relax.' I said, 'You don't relax on a day like this.' She said, 'All right. I'll get you something to eat.' My pregame meal was always two poached eggs and a piece of toast. I ate early, left for the Coliseum and then waited, waited and waited. . . .''

When Rupp arrived at the arena, he had instructed his team manager to keep his players in the dressing room. "I didn't want them to go out and see the first game (the Indiana-Miami third-place game). I wanted them to go to the squad room. And when they all got there, I wanted to talk to them." Particularly, Rupp was interested in rehearsing the game plan to stop Hawkins.

"I think it's okay," Rupp's chief assistant, Harry Lancaster, said finally.

"We'll soon find out," answered Rupp.

Few game plans work as efficiently as that one did. The Wildcats played a marvelous team defense, holding Hawkins to a subpar total of 15 points, and handed the Fighting Irish one of their worst defeats in history, 89-56.

When the Wildcats got to Louisville for the Final Four, Eastern champion Temple was working out on the floor of Freedom Hall. Temple's Guy Rodgers, still bemoaning the tough triple-overtime loss to Kentucky earlier in the season, walked over to Rupp, shook his hand and commented, "We're going to beat you this time."

"There's a possibility of that," Rupp responded.

Rodgers had led Temple through an exquisite season. The Owls that year had lost only to Kentucky in the triple-overtime thriller and to Cincinnati, which had the superb Oscar Robertson. The Temple-Kentucky rematch in the NCAA semifinals was a virtual instant replay of their earlier game that season. The Wildcats and Owls were as competitive as ever; with 24 seconds to go in the game, Temple held a 60-59 lead. At this point, Rupp called a timeout that would remain a vivid memory in later years.

"I told the boys that the thing they had to do was run and let either Smitty (Adrian Smith) or Hatton get a jump shot on one of the plays about 10 feet from the basket. And Smitty said, 'I don't want to take it.' Well, Hatton said, 'I'll take it—and I'll get it.' He had a lot of confidence in himself. But then Beck came up and changed my mind about that last play. He said, 'Coach, this (Tink) Van Patton, the center, won't shift on any of the plays. I believe I can pick off Van Patton and Rodgers or whoever else comes in there.' I said, 'You think you can?' He said, 'I know I can.' 'All right,' I said, 'forget what I told you then and let's go with Beck's play. We'll run a back screen. All four of you guys in front go up for the basket and get the rebound if we miss.

Kentucky's Ed Beck (34) blocks a shot by Seattle star Elgin Baylor in the 1958 championship game. Baylor was picked as the tournament's most outstanding player, but Kentucky won the championship.

Call a timeout then, and we'll think of something else.'''

Hatton took the inbounds pass, dribbled around Beck's screen and scored with 16 seconds left to give Kentucky a 61-60 lead. "All the coaches said that we got our points too quickly," chuckled Rupp. "Hell, you never get a basket too quick when you are one point behind with seconds to go. I want to be ahead!"

Rupp and Lancaster figured at this point that Temple would use a double screen to set up the last shot for Rodgers, who already had scored 22 points that night. They were right about the double screen—but they were wrong about the shooter. Temple set the shot up for "Pickles" Kennedy. However, as Kennedy came around the screen, Rodgers left his feet to throw the pass to him and tossed the ball high and out of bounds. The Kentucky-oriented crowd then made sure of the victory for the Wildcats by swallowing the ball. "We couldn't find that ball," remembered Rupp. "We tried to get that ball back in play, but we couldn't find it. No way."

Rupp then was able to scout Seattle, winner of the other semifinal game over heavily favored Kansas State. The Kentucky coach sat in as a guest color commentator for the Kansas State radio station during the first half of the contest. When he left, the score was 37-32 in favor of Seattle after a hotly competitive first half. Later he was surprised to find that the Chieftains had won so easily, 73-51. Lancaster had stayed to see the entire game and stormed into Rupp's hotel room in a frenzy.

"Coach, did you hear the score?" Lancaster asked Rupp.

"Yeah, I heard it."

"There's no way to beat this outfit," Lancaster continued. "They just made monkeys out of Kansas State. And it finally got to where they were hitting them in the back and taking the rebounds and making a joke out of things."

Rupp listened solemnly.

"There's no way we can beat them," Lancaster repeated.

The next morning, Rupp and Lancaster went over the scouting report on Seattle like seniors cramming for their final exams. Then came an unexpected assist.

"This fellow came to our door and said he had information we could use to beat Seattle," Rupp said. "His idea was different than our idea. So after

he left, Harry and I decided that we had to change our game plan. I told Harry, 'Wake these kids 30 minutes early and have them come in before we eat, and we'll have this chalk talk. We'll give them this new scouting report.'"

The advice Rupp had gotten from his visitor was to drive incessantly on Elgin Baylor, Seattle's great forward. "He's awfully weak defensively," the visitor told Rupp, "especially if you go to his right. He has to use his right hand. He'll grab you."

Baylor had been downright unmanageable for opposing teams while leading Seattle past Wyoming, San Francisco and California in the West regional. In the national semifinals, he had scored 23 points against Kansas State, the favorite in the Final Four, which had defeated mighty Cincinnati, 83-80, earlier in the tournament.

Shortly before the start of the championship game, John Crigler was told by Rupp to "drive and drive on Baylor." Seattle coach John Castellani made what many thought to be a tactical mistake by putting his star forward on Crigler. Everyone assumed that Baylor would be guarding Beck, who was averaging only 4.8 points a game. But Crigler had been ineffective against Temple the night before, and Castellani made a switch of defensive assignments. "We were shocked to see Baylor not

guard Beck," Rupp admitted later. But he also was delighted, for Crigler began to drive for the basket and quickly got three fouls on Baylor. When Baylor was finally taken off Crigler and put on Kentucky centers Beck and Don Mills, Hatton started driving down the middle, forcing Baylor to pick him up on the defensive switch. Baylor drew foul No. 4 trying to block a Mills hook shot, then could play only token defense against Hatton's slashing drives. Hatton finished with 30 points and long-shooting Johnny Cox had 24 as Kentucky won the national championship going away, 84-72, amidst the clamor of 18,803 fans, part of a tournament record turnout of 176,878.

Rupp never revealed the name of the mysterious stranger who had appeared at his door and offered the strategy to beat Seattle. The secret went with him to his grave. But it most certainly appeared to be a coaching colleague, quite possibly one on the West Coast, for in an interview late in his life, Rupp told a reporter:

"Seattle made a mistake the year before when they stole one of his boys and had him transfer. He never forgave the Seattle coach for that, and that's why he came in and told me the best way to beat them. And he was absolutely correct!"

Book 3
THE OHIO YEARS
1959·1963

A funny thing happened to Dutch Lonborg on the way to a legal practice. He was sidetracked by sports. The hopeful young barrister who was graduated from the School of Law at the University of Kansas in 1921 never practiced law, and he never regretted it. Lonborg coached for 29 years on the collegiate level, many of them at Northwestern, and served as director of athletics at Kansas for 14 years. His contribution to the NCAA basketball championship was just as significant. He served as chairman of the tournament committee for 13 years and left an indelible imprint of his leadership before retiring in 1960.

Even before his stewardship of the NCAA tournament through the crucial 1950s, Lonborg's life was interlaced with the event. As coach at Northwestern in 1939, Lonborg served judiciously as the tourney's first manager. His duties became more complicated—and his problems somewhat tougher—with his nomination as chairman of the tournament committee in 1947. Lonborg assumed that office in exploding times. With the revered "Dutch" helping to lead the charge, the NCAA tournament eventually grew up with expansion. Inevitably, as it is with all growing-up experiences, there was a little bit of pain along the way. The climate of the country had something to do with that.

"There were a few problems in 1958," Lonborg recalls. "The finals were held in Louisville—the first time they had been scheduled below the Mason-Dixon Line. Black players were housed with the whites and they were able to eat together and attend movies. But in Kansas City, the theater owners were not going to let the Iowa team in (because of Black players); but the Chamber of Commerce went to work and resolved the problem. There was also a small problem at Charlotte, North Carolina, in getting Blacks housed and into movies and restaurants. But it also was worked out. I think it was a big step toward integration."

Along with the racial difficulties, there were other giant headaches for the Lonborg administration. Lonborg remembers:

Book 3

THE OHIO YEARS 1959·1963

"We had one big problem with tickets in Louisville in 1958. I had asked them to hold 800 tickets for the coaches; but when I arrived, they had sold 400 of them. We went on radio broadcasts asking people who had bought them to return them, and we got a few back. We put chairs in the aisles, and everything worked out. I might add that the persons involved in selling the coaches' tickets were discharged.

"One of the other problems we had to solve was with the officiating. We had the conference commissioners work out a criss-cross formula, where officials would change locations for the playoffs. Those in the East went West, and vice versa."

This latter move was the NCAA's answer to criticism that teams were getting the benefit of "home-town" officiating.

Lonborg saw the NCAA field expand to 26 teams in his last year, 1960, before relinquishing his office to Bernie Shively of Kentucky. Lonborg's successor arrived in an uneasy era, the time of the second big point-shaving scandals in college basketball, and was touched by its tentacles. With the U.S. Senate enacting legislation making it a Federal offense to attempt to bribe the outcome of any sports contest, the NCAA kept a paternal watch over its own house. Pointedly, it was decided that all first-round and regional games in the NCAA tournament would be played in facilities owned and operated by educational institutions, hopefully as a safeguard against the gambling element indigenous to metropolitan areas. For the first time in eight years, there were no games in New York—at that time a hotbed of gambling activity in the nation.

There was a basketful of new administrative and policy changes in the conduct of the 1963 tournament, but by far the most significant was made in the area of television. A contract was worked out with Sports Network for national TV to run through 1968. Unquestionably, the tournament would reach its highest popularity in front of the cameras.

THE BEARS ARE GOLDEN

The plane carrying the national champions settled in cold and rainy San Francisco Airport and ran into a red-hot welcoming committee. As soon as the California basketball team stepped down to earth, the Bear hugs came.

Balloons soared, and banners snapped in the wind.

"You Did It," boldly proclaimed one sign in fire-engine red.

"Pete For President," stated another, referring to coach Pete Newell.

The pompon girls stirred up the 3,000 rooters. The Straw Hat Band strummed a bouncy tune and further incited the flock.

In his possession, each of the California players had a black-faced watch with "NCAA" engraved in gold. They also owned a piece of the NCAA's championship trophy, a memento of the 71-70 triumph over West Virginia for the NCAA championship of 1959.

As they squirmed through the pinching crowd and toward the team bus for the ride back to Berkeley, captain Al Buch exclaimed jubilantly: "They told us there'd be 500 here to meet us. They sure were wrong."

This local toast was just a slice of the nationwide applause for the new champions. Americans always adored underdogs and had identifiable heroes in California's Golden Bears.

"The West showed us how to play the game," said Joe Lapchick, the venerable and savvy coach of St. John's in New York.

Well, anyway, the Bears showed the rest of the country how they played the game as they knocked down reputations and rankings right and left en route to Louisville, Kentucky, for the championship of college basketball in late March.

They won it with unbending defense, unrattled professionalism and that archaic but real cliche, teamwork. It was also a coaching triumph, although Newell wouldn't relent readily to such immodest dialogue.

"Total unity and unselfishness epitomized this team," said Newell. "They took pride in team achievement rather than individual honor."

But as Newell soared to the top of his profession on March 21, the facts remained plain as the acid glare of Louisville's Freedom Hall: The title clearly was of Newell's making.

No one of the caliber of Oscar Robertson or Jerry West was numbered among the California talent. All-Americas simply weren't part of the makeup. The Bears couldn't even land a player on the all-Pacific Coast Conference team. They weren't rated any better than fourth in their conference before the start of the season and, in fact, couldn't crack the top 10 in any poll during the year.

But it was nothing tangible that made them champions, just a positive mental approach to the game. They felt they couldn't be beaten.

"Two incidents come to my mind that reflect the team's attitude," recalls Newell. "One happened during the season when we were behind by six points with slightly more than a minute to play. We pulled the game out, and afterward I was still shaking when I mentioned to Buch that I didn't think we would make it. He answered that it never occurred to him we would lose. He said it in a simple, matter-of-fact tone with no hint of conceit or false optimism. It indicated the confidence they had in each other. It gave me a clue as to why they were tough to beat.

"Another incident I remember concerned Bob Dalton, a skinny 6-foot-3 forward. I had a favorite expression for him. I would tell him that if we could buy him for what he was worth and sell him for what he thought he was worth, we could both retire. He was not a naturally gifted player but an effective, productive and competitive player. Well, in our NCAA semifinal game against Cincinnati and Oscar Robertson, I held off individual assignments until just prior to game time. I called Bob "Thunderbird." He was a scholarship kid who drove a Thunderbird, and this impressed me because I didn't know many people who could afford to drive one at the time.

"Anyway, Thunderbird got the call on the Big O and really lit up. All during warm-ups, I could see him getting himself up. At the tipoff, the players introduced themselves to each other with a handshake and name introduction. Bob said to Oscar, 'My name is Dalton, what's yours?' Anyone knows that you couldn't pick up a sports magazine or sports page without at least a reference to Oscar's great feats. A year later in Rome at the Olympics, Oscar wondered who that crazy guy was that guarded him that night and if he was putting him on. I still don't know if he had himself so high or if he was using psychology. I know he really loosened up our team with the question, and they all started to laugh."

This was the team that Newell steered to a national championship—a team with a lot of guys named "Joe." It was a team that took time to build.

From his first year in 1955, Newell steadily improved California clubs to Pacific Coast Conference title winners in 1957 and 1958. After winning a league playoff game with Oregon State in 1958, the Bears went to the West regional and defeated Idaho State, 54-43, before losing to Seattle and Elgin Baylor, 66-62.

The veterans came back for another shot the next year. Buch, a spectacular defensive guard who played his best offense in the crucial games, and Denny Fitzpatrick, one of the quickest and most deadly jump shooters in the West, comprised the starting backcourt. Dalton, who played the game with a fierce dedication, and junior college transfer Bill McClintock were front-line forwards. Darrall Imhoff secured the center job after tremendous improvement through his sophomore and junior years. An outstanding rebounder and jumper, the 6-10, 205-pound Imhoff proved to be the heart of the nation's leading defensive team. Jack Grout, a fine defensive player and bullish rebounder, was the top reserve. Dick Doughty backed up Imhoff.

No gaudy predictions were made for this team in September as Newell ran his players up and down the Berkeley hills for conditioning.

"The training of a team and the sacrifices bring it together; and under coach Newell, we prided ourselves in that," recalled Jim Langley, the fourth forward on California's deep bench. "I felt that our pride in our superior condition and the deepest affection and loyalty for our coach put us one-up on any team."

Newell's brood developed a distinct personality.

"I suppose that any successful team can say that it was exceptional," Langley recalled in later years. "It wasn't just that—it was the warmth. A team as close as we were, on or off the floor, and brought closer by the fact that we had no superstars, created a unique relationship."

The team inherited and carried its own peculiar language, useful on the floor to initiate plays.

The word "kabrood," for instance, was the backdoor play, the classic ploy whereby a player shakes loose of his defender and escapes to the basket, where the open man is promptly hit with a pass for a quick field goal. The indigenous language also extended to the social area—"tades" was the word for "dates" and a "lirg" was a "girl."

Buch was the only one of the group who didn't have to concern himself with "tades." He was the only married man and, consequently, was duly accorded the maturity to run the club as captain.

The aforementioned pompon girls, a psychological extension of the team, and the cacophonic Straw Hat Band were attached closely to the golden boys in sneakers. Lou Vienop, the head pompon girl who later became Mrs. Langley, was considerably more noted for her legs than Jim.

"But we would compare legs," said Langley. "I'd compare hers while she was pomponing and she would while I was playing. The Straw Hatters, too, traveled with us on the road through the worst conditions. The music and the support of the band were instrumental in picking up sagging spirits and pumping adrenaline."

The California superfans ate pregame meals with the team, then lent their palpable support in the arena while the Bears employed their glamourless techniques—discipline and defense.

Early-season losses on the road to Kansas State, the nation's No. 1-ranked team, and to St. Louis didn't cool the pompon passion or dull the hot music from the straw hat gallery. The nonconference contests were mere preliminaries to the serious business at hand—winning the PCC title for the third straight year.

The day after the California football team suffered a humiliating Rose Bowl loss, the California basketball team started on its yellow brick road with a 54-43 victory over Washington, the unanimous preseason favorite in the PCC. Fitzpatrick scored 21 points, and Imhoff held Washington star Doug Smar to five points. Slowed momentarily by a two-point upset loss to Oregon on the road, California staggered Washington for the second time in a week and established its place as a top conference contender. A desperate late-game rally fell short against Stanford on January 16, but that was the last time California lost.

Returning home, the Bears had perhaps their finest 40 minutes in a rematch with Stanford. Playing before a sellout crowd, California shot a marvelous 54 per cent from the floor as three Bears scored in double figures—Buch with 15, Fitzpatrick

with 14 and Imhoff with 13. Among them, they made 18 of 26 field goal attempts; and California held Stanford's John Arrillaga, Dick Haga and Paul Meumann to subpar games en route to a 67-46 triumph. The crowd cheered, the pompon girls bounced and the band played on.

Streaking California soon gave a new dimension to defense, heretofore established as a wave of the hand, an angry word and a dirty look in most circles. Within 18 days in February, the Bears beat seven teams, holding one in the 30-point range, two in the 40s and four in the 50s.

The Bears held Southern California without a field goal for 16 minutes at one point; Oregon couldn't score a point until almost 10 minutes into the game; Washington State never could recover from a 20-2 deficit at the start and wound up scoring only 37 points. Slow-gaited and stingy, the Bears made opponents dance to their tune. The result was a nation-leading average, holding opponents to about 50 points a game.

"Our methodical and well-executed patterns revealed Newell's discipline," said Langley.

Newell modestly throws the ball back to the players. "I don't want you to think that it was a nontalented team that was 'coached' to victory," remarks Newell. "On other clubs, my players would have had sectional and national honors, I am certain. But our style of ball was team-oriented and demanded a certain unselfishness which precluded, to an extent, the individual achievements."

The noble character of this team perhaps was best described in the simplest of terms by Frank McGuire, North Carolina's coach. He told Newell, "You are coaching as fine a group of young men as I have ever seen, on or off the court." Others agreed, but despite a mounting winning streak, glory was hard to win. National polls dismissed the Californians as no-name freaks, although the Bears were beginning to wipe out the top 20 one by one. The Establishment, as usual blinded by stars, pointed to the perennial Eastern powers and the teams of the Jerry Wests and Oscar Robertsons. Surely, it was reasoned, nobody had better single players.

It was true that California didn't have Jerry West or Oscar Robertson. Furthermore, the Bears didn't need them. None had a better "team"—in the pure sense—than California as the Golden Bears high-balled toward the spring of 1959, coasting on a winning streak that included No. 10 on February 28. That 65-45 triumph over Washington State clinched a tie for the PCC crown. A week later, the Bears were made champions when Washington lost to UCLA. A night later, on March 7, California took Oregon State, 55-52, to tie up its third straight

league crown in a nice, neat bundle.

This was the squad, then, that had dominated the Pacific Coast Conference: Dalton, who came to California as a tennis player; McClintock, who could not shoot outside; Imhoff, who could not shoot at all; Buch, who was slow and could not hit a jump shot, and Fitzpatrick, the best shooter of them all with a relatively low 13-point average. It did not seem like a championship team on paper, but it was different on a basketball court.

Their intangible ingredients that melded into athletic poetry made them six-point favorites in the West regional semifinals against Utah, the Skyline Conference winner. The Bears were, naturally, accompanied to San Francisco's Cow Palace by their band and effervescent pompon sidekicks, just as they had traveled with the team for thousands of miles to places like Santa Clara; Los Angeles; Pullman, Washington; Corvallis, Oregon, and Moscow, Idaho. Louisville at this point was still a dream—but a wide-awake one, at that.

After St. Mary's (California) of the West Coast Athletic Conference defeated Rocky Mountain Conference king Idaho State in the first game, California crushed high-scoring Utah, 71-53, with its typical steady, pressure game. The defensive play of Buch and his backcourt mates, Fitzpatrick and Bernie Simpson, held the high-powered Redskins to their lowest point total of the year. "Buch initiated one of the finest one-man presses I've seen all year," said one admirer. Buch also scored 15 points, a game high, as the Bears shot 45 per cent from the field in the first half and broke the game open early.

"Cal will eat St. Mary's for lunch," Utah coach Jim Rhead said when asked to predict the outcome of the West regional finale the following night.

Actually, the Bears dined on light food at midday and had St. Mary's for supper.

California's 14th straight triumph was fashioned typically—rarely spectacular but painstakingly solid. The intensity of the moment only made the PCC champions as good a defensive team as they had been all year. It resulted in a 66-46 triumph over the Gaels on March 14 before a lusty-throated, one-sided crowd of 12,937. Imhoff suffocated St. Mary's scoring and rebounding threat, Tom Meschery. The Gael star, who had controlled the boards in just about every game he had played that season, was outplayed by Darrall's dynamism— Imhoff grabbed 15 rebounds to Meschery's eight and doubled Meschery's five-point scoring total. Everything else went right for California, as well. The Bears, usually not a good foul-shooting team, made 18 of 20 free throws.

Once more, it was the California pressure cooker

that burned the opposition.

"We beat them to their favorite shooting spots and ran them out," noted Buch.

"We pressured their shooters," said Newell.

"We had a cold night, but their defensive pressure had a lot to do with that," pointed out Jim Weaver, the St. Mary's coach.

"We got behind, and the pressure caused us to force our position and our shots," added Meschery.

The pressure specialists were honed to "mathematical exactness," according to one sports writer, who watched the Bears that night with awe: "Throughout the whole team, there appears to be this exceptional balance."

The next stop for California's soldier-like players was Louisville, where they would try to contain a basketball superman—Cincinnati's Oscar Robertson. Although one of the Final Four teams in the NCAA tournament, the Bears still couldn't crack the top 10. While flying East, they were ranked a mere 12th in the country in the wire service polls and not considered by most to be in the same class with the other semifinalists—Cincinnati, West Vir-

ginia and Louisville. And California's upstarts were underdogs not only because of the poll rankings.

"Pressure will be paramount for the Bears, since the other clubs are so very close to Louisville," said an observer. "You can't get much closer to Louisville than the University of Louisville itself, and rugged Cincinnati is just across the Ohio River from the tournament city.

"To add to the picture, the home of the Mountaineers—Morgantown, West Virginia—is just 75 to 100 miles away; so rooters from that school will have an easy time of it insofar as travel is concerned. But California has a journey of some 2,200 miles to the Blue Grass country, an exhausting air trip that means the team must leave as soon as possible to recover its land legs in time for the tournament."

Newell discounted any advantage for the other three teams, however: "I firmly believe that our tournament experience and our ability to play our game without being thrown off will mean that the pressure at Louisville will not affect us. The thing I like about our club is the fact that when we have to do something, we do it."

Whatever it was that California was going to do, the team wasn't going to do it without the band and pompon girls. That was one of Newell's first thoughts after the Bears had won the West regional championship.

"They're an integral part of this team and we sure hope a way can be found to get them to Louisville, particularly since everybody from miles around will be rooting for the home club," said Newell.

A way was found for their trip. It was made possible by numerous donations from both private citizens and organized groups.

"Our goal is to outyell 12,000 fans at Louisville," said Tom Butler, an assistant band manager. "We'll try to neutralize Cincinnati all the way."

Their journey began at the Oakland International Airport on the Thursday before the Friday night game. It included a stop in Los Angeles, a long flight to Chicago and a 300-mile bus trip to Louisville, where the costumed group was given a police escort into Freedom Hall just nine minutes before California took the floor against Cincinnati.

The team itself had taken a more leisurely route to the Southern city, hitting town on Wednesday, March 18, to do some advance work for the semifinal game. The weather was about the same as

Courier-Journal and Louisville Times

California's Denny Fitzpatrick (21) slaps the ball away from Jerry West in the championship game. West was the tourney's most outstanding player, but California came away with the title.

126

San Francisco's when the players arrived, but the welcoming committee was much cooler. It consisted of a University of Louisville athletic assistant, a bus driver and Paul Christopolous, the California publicist. Christopolous said he was elated to finally see someone who would talk to him.

"They mention us around here like they would a fourth in bridge," said Christopolous. "About the warmest greeting I'd gotten all week was, 'California? Oh, yeah, they have a team in the tournament, haven't they?'"

The same mental climate existed among those trying to choose a winner who installed California as a longshot. Louisville was the favorite because of the home-court advantage.

Newell rather liked the underdog role because it minimized the pressure of winning. The handsome coach of the Bears, nevertheless, thought his team was being miscast.

"Heck, yes, I'll say it again and again," said Newell. "We're in a class with any of them. We've gone out against players of Oscar Robertson's caliber before and done a good job. I don't think his being on the court will psyche our boys."

Dalton was given the order to guard the nation's leading scorer. His job:

1. Prevent Robertson from getting the ball, and
2. Stop him from operating at will.

"Thunderbird" was targeted for subtle needling when word of his crucial assignment got out. Buch nudged Dalton gently one morning, waking him out of a deep sleep.

"What did you do to Oscar?" Buch asked, while Dalton was still sleep-dazed.

"He was lucky to get 10," he responded, falling off again.

With all the hullabaloo about Robertson and his 33-point average, it was sometimes forgotten that the Bearcats had other players, a squad that loved to run, shoot and rebound. Oscar's teammates included Ralph Davis and Bill Whitaker in the backcourt, strong boy Bob Weisenhahn at forward and center Dave Tenwick. Playmaker Mike Mendenhall was lost to the Bearcats for the playoffs because of an ineligibility ruling.

"Without Mendenhall, they're still very tough," said a California scout. "Cincinnati has the fastest team I've seen this year—tremendous speed and reactions, a bunch of real agile guys."

Cincinnati was made a six-point favorite over California in the second game of the semifinal doubleheader. Louisville took on West Virginia in the opener. A telegram, signed by 2,800 California students who could not attend the game, told the Bears: "Good luck."

Buch took the Bears out flying with a smashing layup off the opening tipoff, and they had a 14-6 lead after six minutes. But Robertson, although hounded by Dalton in front and bedeviled in back by a sagging California defense, managed to score four field goals and set up eight others. That gave Cincinnati a 33-29 lead at the intermission.

California, not shooting well in the first half, started to crowd the offensive boards in the second half. This aggressive play helped wipe out a 36-29 Cincinnati lead in a short time. McClintock muscled in with a followup shot for two points, Dalton scored a tip-in, Imhoff powered in a rebound shot off his own miss and Buch raced to the circle for a driving jump. Suddenly, California was in front.

Dalton snuffed out Robertson's field goal threats, allowing him only one more the rest of the game—and that, in good part, was the reason for California's 64-58 victory over the staggered Bearcats. Deliberate California broke away from a 54-54 tie with a clock-eating offense, moving the ball toward the tie-breaking shot. Imhoff took it after 93 seconds of stalling, the ball arching high from eight feet away on that characteristic, spinning hook shot of his. Then Cincinnati fouled Buch, and he sank two; Dalton was fouled, and he delivered both. That was it.

Long after the triumph, near-deserted Freedom Hall rang with the noise of the Straw Hatters, tooting happily in a pavilion once holding more than 18,000.

The California players were nearly as vociferous in their dressing room after the upset. The minute they came in, the boys started asking questions about what they had done to the Big O.

"How many did he get?" was asked repeatedly.

When Robertson's results were tabulated—five field goals and a relatively meager total of 19 points—some of the Californians yelled, "Tomorrow night we'll do the same thing to Jerry West."

West, like Robertson an all-America, had scored 38 points to lead West Virginia into the finals with a 94-79 triumph over Louisville—another upset.

After facing Robertson, Newell thought about stalling another high-powered player. He didn't especially like the prospect of facing two scoring machines on successive nights.

"West? I'm still trying to forget Robertson," the California coach said.

The Straw Hat Band and pompon girls spent Saturday morning in relaxation following an uncomfortable sleep on bunks in the University of Louisville gymnasium. Rafter-hanging sparrows had woken many before dawn of the big day.

In the afternoon, the troupe staged a rally in front of the team headquarters at the Sheraton-Sealbach Hotel. An overflow crowd rubbernecked

127

the proceedings, causing a traffic jam for five blocks. Pretty soon, the police broke up the sidewalk mob.

That evening, the California team had the bandsmen and girls as guests for dinner in the Gold Room of the Sealbach. West Virginia was the next item on the menu.

"They're tremendous, especially with that fast break," said Newell. "I really don't know what we'll do. But I said before we played Cincinnati that we had come this far with our defense, and we couldn't stop now."

Newell's no-star aggregation had sliced 30 points off Cincinnati's scoring average and was hoping to do the same thing against West Virginia, another offense-minded team. The Pacific Coast area favored the Bears, naturally, while the rest of the country felt that the Mountaineers would win the glamorous national trophy.

It was too close for comfort from the opening tipoff in the center of the giant arena to the electric ending. No lead was safe. California fought back from a 23-13 deficit with 10 minutes gone in the game to a 25-25 tie. The Bears scored heavily from the outside and had a 39-33 lead at the half despite 15 points by West.

West Virginia came out for the second half in a full-court press that eventually left both teams limp at game's end. Despite the pressure, California built its lead to 57-44 with McClintock, Imhoff and Fitzpatrick contributing key points. It looked well in hand for California, but it wasn't.

The Mountaineers made a dramatic comeback with 11:15 left in the game, inspiring the heated 18,619 fans to a fever pitch.

The usually poised Bears fell apart and began making turnovers, losing the ball for walking and on steals and getting tangled while trying to employ their renowned stalling technique. Led by West, the Mountaineers drove to within four points on three occasions—61-57, 63-59 and 65-61.

California walked and lost the ball again. The Bears threw the ball away once more and committed fouls on offense. Their lead dropped to three points with 3:07 left, and West Virginia seemed in command of the flow of the game. It was Mountaineer momentum.

Dalton gave California mild relief with a corner shot, and McClintock improved the margin to 69-64 with a rebound basket. But California's reserve guard, Bernie Simpson, walked with the ball. Then McClintock blocked a West shot. Newell was on the bench, leaning forward, chewing a towel.

Bucky Bolyard, a Mountaineer guard who was blind in one eye, was fouled and cut the California margin to 69-66 with two free throws. Bolyard then made a key steal, batting an inbounds pass toward West; the Mountaineer star was credited with a field goal on a goaltending call against Imhoff.

The score: 69-68 California with 51 seconds left.

"Stop 'em, stop 'em," players screamed from the California bench, then groaned when West tied up Imhoff for a jump ball.

The referee tossed up the ball, and Imhoff knocked it to Fitzpatrick. The Bears worked toward the basket methodically, and Imhoff went in for a layup. He missed the first try but banged it through after several tries in a crowd of players.

With seven seconds remaining, West Virginia's Willie Akers scored on a driving layup to cut California's lead to a single point, 71-70. It was all over, though. Bolyard fouled Fitzpatrick with two seconds left and the California player missed. But while the ball was being batted around under the basket, the game ended.

Everyone within reach got hugged and kissed, and the Straw Hatters struck up "Our Sturdy Golden Bear." Newell was carted around on broad, young shoulders like a rag doll.

The ecstasy reached the Berkeley campus minutes after the result was known in California. The school bells rang out "Cal Fights On." The bells served as a call for the college town to proceed to a victory rally at a theater. Auto horns honked, cars winked lights and a monstrous bonfire was lit only 20 minutes after California's stunning triumph.

"I'm proud of the fact that my team represents what I feel a college team should represent," said a champagne-splashed Newell. "We're an amateur team. In case anyone doubts it, the last five minutes of the finals should prove we're an amateur team."

Buch felt that their darkhorse posture helped the Bears. "On Friday night, there seemed to be a feeling that Cincinnati had drawn a bye," said the little captain. "That might have been good. That made us a little mad."

Asked what Newell had said early in the finals when the Bears trailed by 10 points, Buch said: "I couldn't say exactly because I was sort of nervous. In essence, he said West Virginia was making us play its type of game, that we were taking quick shots and not playing our usual game. So we just went out and did what the head man said, and it worked."

The flight back home was a joyride, the unlikely heroes carrying the NCAA hardware on board. A real home-town welcome waited. "It's raining in San Francisco," the pilot announced. It didn't matter. It was going to be a bright Sunday, anyway.

DEADEYE BUCKEYES

Midway through the 1960 NCAA championship game, the California Bears seemed to be in a state of shock after Ohio State put on one of the greatest shooting exhibitions in tournament history. The Buckeyes hit 15 of their first 16 field goal attempts and 16 of 19 for the first half when they took a commanding 37-19 lead. California coach Pete Newell herded his dismayed players into the dressing room and slammed the door.

"Men, we have to get more defensive rebounds," he said solemnly.

To which all-America center Darrall Imhoff replied:

"Coach, there have only been three; and I got all of them."

Fred Taylor had come to Cincinnati to appear on a radio show, and fellow guest Ed Jucker asked him the obvious question:

"What are the chances of scheduling some games with you?"

"I can't say yet," replied the Ohio State basketball coach. "Certainly, plenty of fans would be interested in it."

The coach of the Cincinnati Bearcats pursued his theme.

"People here think Columbus considers Cincinnati as being on the other side of the tracks," said Jucker. "They feel they don't get much from Columbus."

"I guess that's the way it appears to people on both sides," retorted Taylor. "As far as playing Cincinnati is concerned, I know we knocked heads once; both sides weren't happy with the results, but both were satisfied it was a good game."

And so the dialogue went in the early 1960s. Ohio State and Cincinnati, neighbors no more than 100 miles apart, never seemed to be able to get together on a basketball court—except, of course, at the NCAA national finals.

The state of Ohio dominated college basketball awareness from 1958 through 1963, with Cincinnati and Ohio State among the game's elite. During this era, their intrastate rivalry was sharpened to its keenest edge on the highest level. For five straight years—from 1959 through 1963—Cincinnati advanced to the Final Four of the NCAA tournament, an unprecedented achievement; Ohio State was there three times. The Buckeyes and Bearcats twice met for the national championship, in 1961 and 1962, with Cincinnati winning each time. In 1960, only an eight-point loss to California in the semifinals prevented Cincinnati from meeting Ohio State on another occasion for the NCAA title.

Jucker's fine team had a chance to make some special history for itself in 1963 but lost out on a third straight NCAA title to Loyola of Chicago by virtue of a missed free throw. That loss, however, did not diminish Cincinnati's overall accomplishment. Starting with the arrival of the superlative Oscar Robertson in 1957-58 and continuing through the national championship years, the Bearcats forged one of the college game's truly memorable dynasties. Their consecutive victories over Ohio State in the NCAA finals were no small accomplishment, for the Buckeyes in this era boasted some of the most talented players in the game's history, including Jerry Lucas, John Havlicek and Larry Siegfried.

Just as Oscar Robertson had been the trigger for a dynastic reign at Cincinnati, Ohio State's high fortunes paralleled the Bearcats at this precise time with some of the most sought-after collegians of the day. Lucas, Havlicek, Mel Nowell and Gary Gearhart had played together as Ohio's high school all-stars in their annual series with Kentucky and Indiana. The object of vigorous recruiting campaigns, they all decided to stay together at the home-state school. They joined Joe Roberts and Siegfried to help Ohio State win the NCAA championship in 1960.

Fred Taylor was the coach who took this splen-

130

Jon Brenneis, Sports Illustrated

did assortment of players to the NCAA summit; but it was Harold Olsen and Tippy Dye who laid the foundation of tradition at Ohio State, and it was Fred Stahl who began to assemble the team that won the national championship. Olsen, of course, was one of the founding fathers of the NCAA tournament and developed a considerable reputation for basketball excellence at Columbus. Dye enhanced this with players such as Dick Schnittker, Bob Donham and Neil Johnston; and Stahl had Paul Ebert, Robin Freeman and Frank Howard, not to mention Roberts and Siegfried.

Taylor had played for Dye and—though there was some Midwestern conservatism in his make-up—he preferred the running game. Fortunately, he had the crew to pull it off in 1960. The Buckeyes could run precise patterns, as well, to beat any kind of press or zone in case their fast-breaking and free-lancing offenses were stymied. Defensively, they simply were overpowering, especially the Nowell-Siegfried combination at guard. This was, as one observer pointed out, a blend of complementary talents and unselfish players with confidence carefully instilled by Taylor's thorough, driving leadership.

"The major attribute of the 1960 team," says Taylor, "was the balance between offense and defense. We had real good depth and excellent team speed. We didn't exactly 'live' by the fast break, but we certainly made good use of it. All things considered, it was a remarkably well-balanced and physically strong team. They worked hard, were exceptionally unselfish and played extremely well together as a team. I really believe that nobody cared who was the leading scorer. They all knew that on offense, if they passed the ball to a teammate—and then got open—they most likely would get it back."

The Buckeyes of 1960 had good overall size for that era. The guards were the 6-4 Siegfried and the 6-2 Nowell; Havlicek was the "small" forward at 6-5. The other forward—Roberts—and Lucas at center were in the 6-8 to 6-9 range. The first man off the bench, Dick Furry, also was about 6-8. The Buckeyes had more than adequate replacements in Gearhart, Richie Hoyt and Bobby Knight, who later made a bigger name for himself as a coach.

Lucas was one of the spiritual leaders of this poised team, an agile, nerveless kid of 19 who played constantly without changing his deadpan expression. When the Buckeyes went to their

131

Fans jammed the Cow Palace in San Francisco to see the 1960 NCAA championship game. Ohio State defeated defending champion California, 75-55, to win the title.

running game, which was often, Lucas usually trailed the leader and always managed to be hovering around the rim of the basket to stuff in a missed shot. On a team that boasted a flock of fine shooters, Lucas was unusually accurate. Taylor calls him his "most interesting" player of that era.

"He had such a detached approach to things, yet had such an outstanding attitude. He was extremely intelligent. And I seriously believe he didn't care about scoring points. He always said he would rather get a rebound than score a basket, and I think he meant it. He only had two goals that I know about—to be the nation's leading percentage shooter and the percentage rebound leader. He was overpowering at times, and he met both his goals. Points never mattered to Lucas. He knew he could be the leading scorer in almost any game he wanted—he was that dominant—but he would always sacrifice himself for the team. And he still put out as much in practice as anyone."

Then there was Havlicek, "one of the most remarkable people" Taylor had ever met. "He realized right away there would not be enough basketballs to go around offensively, so he was determined to make it at the defensive end. Eventually, he would be hurt if we did not give him the top defensive assignment. He relished the challenge—any challenge. And John was really people-oriented, very cool under any type of pressure and got along with absolutely everybody."

Siegfried had perhaps the biggest adjustment to make in 1960 of any Ohio State player. He had been the Buckeyes' leading scorer and most valuable player as a sophomore but just another member of a national championship team as a junior. "He realized the difference between an 11-11 season in 1959 and the championship," says Taylor. "He adjusted, though, and when the bell rang—every game—he took tremendous satisfaction in doing his job well."

Considering the wide array of talent at Ohio State in 1960, it is to Taylor's credit that the team concept worked to its utmost potential.

"I tried to mold the talent to the ultimate objective," he says. "The players had to come around to our way of thinking, which was that college would—and must—be far different from high school, where each had been the standout on his team. They had to come around to thinking and playing as a unit, to realize that this was the only way to play. We always tried to keep things in perspective, play each game as the most important one of the season. This was a very intelligent ball club and didn't need any gimmicks at all. They took instruction well, took pride in playing well, and even those who were least likely to play in a

game worked just as hard as the regulars in practice. They were not outgoing or demonstrative, but they were efficient."

The proof of this, of course, can be found in Ohio State's 1960 record. The Buckeyes won 25 games while losing only three en route to the Big Ten and NCAA championships. They peaked at tournament time, beating Western Kentucky, 98-79, and Georgia Tech, 86-69, in the Mideast regional. In the national semifinals, the Buckeyes battered New York University, 76-54, and then won the NCAA title by beating California's defending national champions at their own disciplined game, 75-55. If there ever had been doubt of the greatness of this Ohio State team, it was dispelled in the national finals when the Buckeyes shot 84 per cent from the floor during the first half and almost 70 per cent for the game as 13 players saw action.

The end result was the product of uncompromising devotion and attention to detail. With three sophomores in the starting lineup, the 1959-60 season had to be somewhat of a learning process. And as it turned out, the Buckeyes had learned their lessons well.

"If anything," Taylor remembers, "it took us a while to put it together at the defensive end of the floor. We had to convince the players that by applying good defensive pressure they could really help themselves offensively, create scoring opportunities through good, tough team defense."

This lesson was dramatized during one mild slump, points out Taylor:

"We had won a game from Butler, 99-66, and didn't play at all well. I told them so and added that we needed to get more serious about playing defense. Then we lost games at Utah and Kentucky, both times scoring more than 90 points but not playing enough defense to win. At Kentucky, we were ahead, 50-40, at half time. I told them it was sad when you can score 90 points on the road and not have it be enough to win. I told them they were putting their offense in serious difficulties and that they would have to play more defense to win consistently."

The Buckeyes not only played more defense, they played it with more sophistication. Specifically, it was their ability to switch alignments which caused the downfall of Georgia Tech in the finals of the Mideast regional at Louisville. Taylor sent his Buckeyes into a zone press (he called it a "rat" game) from the opening tipoff for the first time that year. That shook up Georgia Tech. Then, when the Bulldogs came out with an adjusted offense the second half expecting the same defense, the Buckeyes switched to a man-to-man and,

according to one newspaper account, "The Engineers were dead." Marveled Taylor at the conclusion of that 17-point victory, "You've got to admit these kids can kick the daylights out of a team when they have to."

Earlier, the Buckeyes had just plain kicked the daylights out of Western Kentucky by running the ball down the Hilltoppers' throats in an awesome display of speed in the second half. "We wanted to run against them because we felt we could keep it up longer than they could," points out Taylor. Trailing, 43-37, at intermission, Ohio State didn't really get going until the second half—actually the last six minutes. "We were four down with about six minutes to play," remembers Taylor, "and Jerry Lucas said, 'Let's keep running at them; they're getting tired.' Bobby Knight went into the game and hit a couple of long jumpers. Things started to come our way; and we actually won that game by 19 points, 98-79. And Knight said, 'I suppose that means we'll have whistle (conditioning) drills every day from now on.'"

Actually, Taylor was not so much worried about conditioning the body as he was the mind in preparation for New York University in the national semifinals at the Cow Palace in San Francisco. The Violets were an enigmatic team, difficult to prepare for. "NYU was a challenge," Taylor says. "They had Satch Sanders and a less-structured team that could score a bunch of points on what we call garbage—picking up a loose ball and stuffing it in the basket." No doubt Taylor concerned himself with the psychological implications of the game, hopeful that his Buckeyes would not take the Violets too lightly, since as an unknown quantity, NYU clearly was the dark horse of the 25-team 1960 NCAA tournament. Lou Rossini's team had pulled off a stunning 82-81 overtime victory over heavily favored West Virginia and Jerry West en route to the Eastern regional title.

"Our main concern for that game was coming off final exams," Taylor remembers. "Because of the exams, we only had three days to practice before the tournament finals."

As an additional concern, Havlicek had injured his finger in a freak household accident. "The Saturday before the tournament," remembers Taylor, "Havlicek was reaching for a paper towel in a dispenser in his dormitory and sliced the ends of two fingers on his left hand—nine stitches worth."

But Havlicek played—and played well—against NYU. The Buckeyes turned on their power at the start and rushed away from the Violets while the New York team fidgeted and fumbled. Lucas and Havlicek double-teamed Sanders, double-crossing NYU's offense. When the final buzzer mercifully

signaled the end of Ohio State's 76-54 rout, a brokenhearted Sanders said softly, "I guess you could say they were too much for us."

The other semifinal game between California and Cincinnati was much more competitive and far more intriguing. It featured the return of Oscar Robertson and a Cincinnati team determined to reverse its defeat at the hands of this same California squad the year before at the very same stage of the championship tournament. The Cincinnatians had brought their school band and hundreds of rooters with them to San Francisco, and they tore into the beautiful city with great confidence.

Within five seconds, the Bearcats had a basket. They scored again shortly thereafter and midway through the first half held a 20-11 lead. This was not to last, however, in the teeth of an exquisite California defense that was rated the best in the nation. As half time approached, the rugged defense began to pay off. The Bears caught and passed Cincinnati and left the floor leading, 34-30.

Despite California's continued defensive pressure in the second half, Cincinnati would not crack. With a minute and a half to go, California led by only three points. Here Cincinnati made a series of costly blunders that led to two quick baskets by California guard Earl Schultz and the game was over. California's 77-69 triumph was clearly a victory for defensive basketball, as taught by Pete Newell. "The ability to force Cincinnati into mistakes in ball handling saved the day," pointed out Jeremiah Tax in Sports Illustrated.

As the NCAA championship game was discussed in hotel lobbies the next day, many of the coaches were certain that California would beat Ohio State. So were the oddsmakers, who established the Golden Bears as five-point favorites. But few had taken into account the hard facts about this tall, rugged Ohio State team. Only three teams had beaten the Buckeyes that year—all on the road. Each time, the opposing team had been obliged to score 96 points; in two instances, the team had to make better than 53 per cent of its shots. The Buckeyes' 91-point scoring average during the season usually had produced wide margins over their opponents, and the added toughness of tournament play had not subdued their lust for points.

As for California's defense, widely applauded as the best in the nation, Taylor made intelligent plans to counteract it. "We sat up most of the night talking about California, deciding what we would do against them," he remembers. "We wanted to run our offense straight at Darrall Imhoff, the California center. Cal's defense tried to channel you down the middle where he could play defense, but we felt he had not really been tested there. So

133

California's Bill McClintock tips in a basket in the Bears' title-game loss to Ohio State, despite the efforts of Buckeye forward Joe Roberts (14).

we took it straight at him. In the first half, most of our baskets were either layups or short jumpers. It was no mystery why we were shooting better than 80 per cent. They were all good shots."

Along with their frontal assault, the Buckeyes made a defensive adjustment as well. Notes Taylor: "We felt that their one guard, Bobby Wendell, would have to prove to us that he could—or would—shoot from the outside. So we dropped off Mel Nowell from Wendell on defense and played him (Nowell) in the passing lanes and in front of their low-post people. Wendell obliged by going 0-for-6 from the field. That was the game plan, and I don't see how it could have worked better for us."

Not only did Ohio State shoot the proverbial eyes out of the basket in the first half, but also it beat California at its own game—defense. Lucas gave Imhoff room only when he was far away from the basket; in close, he was always between Imhoff and the ball. Still, very few in the noisy capacity audience at the Cow Palace—most of them, to be sure, California partisans—were ready to concede defeat to the Big Ten champions. Often enough in the past, California had come from far behind to win on the wings of its mistake-inducing press. Newell brought his team back into play in the second half with a crushing defense and within five minutes, Cal scored 10 points to Ohio State's five. Ironically, though, it was this fanatical defense that eventually proved to be Cal's undoing. Covering on the Ohio State man with the ball, the Bears were obliged to uncover a free man somewhere else. After a short period of fumbling, Ohio State began to find him. Two or three furiously quick breaks with more than five minutes to go destroyed California for good. When the flurry was over, Ohio State's shooting percentage was a remarkable 67.4 per cent; and its victory margin of 75-55 was the largest in the 22-year history of the NCAA finals.

There wasn't much frenzy at the winning moment, as Taylor remembers; and it was a long while before the impact of a national championship landed home. "We took the tournament just as we did every other game," says Taylor. "I was impressed that if the players were nervous, they didn't show it. They were calm, quiet, businesslike before the game—just as they always were."

Ohio State proved itself a worthy champion. The Buckeyes won their four games in a field that was widely acknowledged as the finest in the tourney's history to that point. The 1960 NCAA finals included the nation's top three ranked teams in Ohio State, California and Cincinnati. The 25-team starting field included all but three of the top twenty teams in the combined polls of the Associated Press and United Press International. The composite won-lost record of the four finalists (99-8) was the best in tournament history, bettering the old mark of 97-10 set in 1956. The starting field included the country's five highest-scoring teams, marking the first time so many of the top pointmakers had been gathered in one tournament. One of the national semifinal games matched the nation's No. 1 and No. 2 teams in California and Cincinnati—the order depending on which poll you read. And the national finals paired the country's top offensive unit in Ohio State against California's top-ranked defense.

While it was true that Ohio State's mighty offensive power had overcome California's defenses in another round of the offense-defense debate, it was just as certain that the Buckeyes knew how to handle themselves when the other team had the ball. For the most part, California was forced to take second-best shots and wound up with a subpar field goal percentage of 33.9. Afterwards, some vital truths surfaced about Ohio State's efficient defensive performance. Newell, it seemed, personally had presented Taylor with the weapon that killed him.

"I went to Newell last summer to learn how to coach basketball," Taylor acknowledged after the game. "My team last year had the worst defensive record in Ohio State's history. I had to do something and Pete's the best in the business at this. I asked him to help me and he did. He showed me everything. He confirmed some of my ideas, and he gave me the courage to try things I was afraid were too radical. Last year, my boys couldn't have caught Marilyn Monroe in a phone booth. Now look at them. I used most of Pete's ideas—and they paid off for us tonight."

135

THE BATTLE OF OHIO

"The thing was that nobody gave us a chance—the papers, the fans, even the other coaches. I remember a quote in the Kansas City papers from Johnny Bach, the Fordham University coach. He said Ohio State was like a Panzer outfit running across France. He said they were going to the beach, all the way to the beach. Well, the Ohio State Panzers didn't make it to the beach."—Ed Jucker, University of Cincinnati basketball coach

Lung for lung, Cincinnati's boosters were the wildest and brashest in college basketball. Whether in arenas during games or on the streets thereafter, they shouted, screamed, sung, stomped, clapped and tooted longer and louder than any of their competitors. "It's easy to tell when you're on the same block with Cincinnati fans," said one flinching coach. Another wasn't that conservative. "It's easy to tell when you're in the same state with Cincinnati fans," he said.

For six triumphant years, from 1958 through 1963, the backers of the Bearcats certainly had something to cheer about. In that period, their team went to the NCAA tournament every season and advanced to the round-of-four championship finals in all but the first year. Their unprecedented success included two national championships in 1961 and 1962 and the near-hit of a third in 1963.

The pinwheel for all this high goalmaking was Oscar Robertson, although ironically, the Cincinnati great himself never had the pleasure of playing on an NCAA championship team. Acknowledged by his peers as one of the finest all-around players in the game's history, Robertson gave the Cincinnati basketball team unique status immediately upon his arrival in the 1957-58 season. Before Robertson put on a Bearcat uniform, Cincinnati never had won a title in the Missouri Valley Conference, never had been highly ranked nationally and never had a Black player. In his first year, Robertson changed all that. Setting all kinds of scoring records and giving the Bearcats nonpareil playmaking, Robertson led Cincinnati to its first conference title, an NCAA tournament berth and No. 2 ranking in the country with a 25-3 season.

Observers of Cincinnati's 83-80 overtime loss to Kansas State in the Midwest regional that year saw something they would not witness too frequently during the rest of Robertson's career—an uncharacteristic loss of composure by the Bearcat guard. Robertson was shooting two free throws that would have meant the victory for Cincinnati, and his first attempt went in the net to tie the game. Teammate Wayne Stevens noticed an official counting as Robertson bounced the ball before his second shot and ran up to say, "Hurry up; he's counting on you." Robertson hurried his shot and missed, the game went into overtime and Kansas State won. (Although there is a rule that a player at the free-throw line must shoot within 10 seconds after receiving the ball, it seems as though it is rarely enforced.)

In 1958-59, Robertson led the nation in scoring for the second straight season, although his average dropped 2½ points from his 35-point figure of the previous year. During his junior year, the Bearcats won the Missouri Valley Conference championship and the NCAA's Midwest regional, only to fall to eventual champion California in the national semifinals. That season, the Bearcats were ranked fourth nationally and had a 26-4 record.

In 1960, they were 28-2, top-ranked by The Associated Press and again won the MVC title and the NCAA Midwest regional only to fall to California in the semifinals. Robertson won his third scoring title, totaled a record 2,973 points and 1,338 rebounds in his three years and graduated with 13 other NCAA records. In addition, he averaged seven assists a game. Coach George Smith's job was easy during Robertson's reign. For three years, the most notable player in college basketball controlled every game he played, aided by such fine

talents as Ralph Davis and Larry Willey; it would have been foolhardy for a coach to impose a system that would hamper Robertson's free-wheeling style. The Bearcats did not lose at home during Robertson's tenure, had a 79-9 record overall and were never out of the top five in national rankings. Suddenly, the Bearcats discovered a new-found ability to recruit Blacks at a school that previously had been disparaged as "Northern redneck" by some. When Robertson left after his three superlative years, part of his legacy was three excellent Black talents—Paul Hogue, Tom Thacker and Tony Yates—who would start for Cincinnati in 1960-61.

Possibly Smith thought it wise to step aside after Robertson's departure. Actually, he stepped up to the athletic director's chair and let longtime assistant Ed Jucker take over in the post-Robertson years, a period of assumed depression.

"Robertson took not only his 33-34 points a game but about 6,000 fans across town to the NBA Royals," says Jucker. "I told my kids what we had to do was to have five guys playing as one. Five playing as one could be an Oscar Robertson. We had no all-Americas and, as it turned out, had no players who went on to become established players in the NBA."

The enormity of Jucker's problem became immediately clear when his team lost three early games, including two in the conference.

"Cincinnati fans were used to 100-point games and run-and-shoot and the excitement that surrounds a singular star like Robertson," points out Jucker. "Then we came in with ball control and pressing, man-to-man defense. The fans had quite an adjustment. And to make it worse, we started poorly. We lost three of eight games. Before we could turn around, we were 0-2 in the league, the gym was only about half-full for our games at home and the fans were starting to shout, 'Let 'em shoot, Jucker!' One of my players even came up to me one day before practice and said, 'Maybe we ought to run, coach.' But I still felt the five-playing-as-one was the best system, and we stuck with it."

As it turned out, Jucker's system eventually was proven the best. At the start, Hogue, Thacker and Yates, along with Bob Wiesenhahn and Carl Bouldin, all seemed to be trying to wear Robertson's mantle. But as soon as Jucker convinced them that they had to be a complete team and forget trying to emulate an all-America player, things began to pick up noticeably at Cincinnati. The first sign of team togetherness surfaced against Dayton, when the

Bearcats were losing by 11 points nearly halfway through the game, yet came back to win by 10. Twenty-one games later, they still hadn't lost and were the NCAA champions with a 70-65 overtime victory over Ohio State.

"Defense was really the key," explains Jucker. "I put in a man-to-man pressing defense I felt our players could use. We were team oriented and stressed team defense. We also stressed ball control. The fans didn't like our style at first, but that was because we lost those three games early in the season. After we started winning, they didn't care how we won."

Jucker's players took great pride in playing error-free basketball. But that didn't apply only to turnovers. The Bearcats consistently were ranked among the country's leaders in the lowest number of personal fouls, despite their fierce style of pressure defense.

Jucker's defensive philosophy was basically a page taken from the book of Hank Iba of Oklahoma A&M (now Oklahoma State), who melded man-to-man and zone principles into the highest degree of efficiency. On offense, Jucker featured backdoor plays attributed to Pete Newell's California teams that beat Cincinnati in the 1959 and 1960 NCAA tournaments, plus variations that he developed or borrowed from other teams. In other words, whatever worked against Cincinnati, Jucker used to work for him.

137

John Havlicek of Ohio State gets a shot off over the defense of Cincinnati's Tom Thacker.

Malcolm W. Emmons

But without Jucker's religious devotion to team play, of course, nothing would have worked at all for Cincinnati in the 1960-61 season. He cracked down on the individual stylists, most notably Tom Thacker.

"Sometimes I had to keep my thumb on him a little," reflects Jucker. "I had to keep reminding him there was an easier, safer way to pass than behind the back."

The 6-foot-2 swingman was one of the most spectacular of the Cincinnati players during the early 1960s because, as Jucker says, "he could do so many things and do them with style. He was 6-2, but he could play guard or forward or jump over the basket. He could pass with a flair that delighted the crowd. He was a character—not so much of a ham, but I guess because of his great talents he was sort of a Harlem Globetrotter-type player. But he didn't pass behind the back to show off. He just did it because it came easy to him."

The toughest Bearcat in the 1960-61 season was Bob Wiesenhahn, 220 pounds of bruising muscle who averaged 10 rebounds a game. He got help up front from Paul Hogue, who, according to one observer, looked like "a 6-foot-9 bespectacled tree trunk." The tailor who cut the gray flannel blazers that the Bearcats wore while traveling added a fourth button to Hogue's coat. Three didn't look right on his massive frame. Thanks to Wiesenhahn and Hogue, Cincinnati was outrebounded only once during the regular season. In addition, Cincinnati had Carl Bouldin and Tony Yates, whom one West Coast coach called the finest pair of guards he had ever seen on the same team. Yates was the prime mover of this team, an intelligent backcourtman who played on all three Cincinnati teams that went to the NCAA's Final Four from 1961 through 1963. "Yates was the coach on the floor," notes Jucker. "He was a great leader and, all-around, our best player."

Cincinnati's inauspicious start in 1960 showed little promise of a Missouri Valley Conference winner, much less an NCAA champion. After one particularly embarrassing 17-point loss to St. Louis, Wiesenhahn recalled returning home and being taunted at the airport, "You guys are lucky you don't have to play Ohio State." The irony of that remark would not be lost to Wiesenhahn, nor the other Cincinnati players, later in the year when they did play the Buckeyes and beat them in the NCAA title game. An alarmed Jucker held a team meeting at this point in the season, said a prayer and told his players they could still win the MVC if they got tough. Not even Jucker was thinking about an NCAA title at the time; but after a loss to Bradley, the Bearcats got tough indeed and sprinted all the way to the NCAA championship without once tripping.

The only problems Jucker might have incurred en route to the national title in 1961 were usually peripheral. In this regard, his devotion to duty ironically once got him into trouble with the police. Cincinnati had finished its regular season and Jucker—aware that Ohio State probably would be in the NCAA tournament—drove to Columbus in a school station wagon with his family to scout the Buckeyes' last game of the year. But going through Wilmington, the last little town before reaching Columbus, he bumped into the car ahead of him at a red light.

"Bumped is not the right word, really," says Jucker. "I just touched him about like I might put a finger to your head. The guy pulled over to the curb and so did I. I got out and made sure there was no damage and then got back in my car and drove off."

A few miles out of town, however, the police pulled Jucker over and accused him of being a hit-and-run driver. The scenario began to take on the enigmatic qualities of an Alfred Hitchcock movie, with the perplexed Cincinnati coach forced to turn around and visit the local jail to explain things. Once Jucker arrived there, the script became more complicated.

"At the police station, I tried to identify myself and explain the importance of me getting to Columbus for the game. But it had no effect on the police sergeant. The problem was I didn't have my driver's license and didn't have papers to prove the school owned the car. The police had me make some long-distance calls back to various officials at the school; but since it was Saturday afternoon, I couldn't reach anybody. So I spent the afternoon in the Wilmington police station watching the Ohio State game on a small, snowy black-and-white TV set in the waiting room. My kids and me. That's how I scouted Ohio State."

They finally let Jucker go after he paid a $25 fine. And, yes, he lost his temper.

"I said a few things to the police sergeant," Jucker remembers. "I guess if he had been an official, I would have drawn a few technicals. I was visibly upset. There I was trying to get ready for my first shot at a championship, and I couldn't even see the game. It almost appeared as if the whole thing was rigged. But I'm sure it wasn't. Ohio State wouldn't have done that. They won 32 in a row,

Two of 1961's most dominating players, Jerry Lucas of Ohio State and Paul Hogue (22) of Cincinnati, battle under the boards during the 1961 championship game.

138

Malcolm W. Emmons

and they weren't worried about us."

Luckily for Jucker, his team's defense was better than his own. The Bearcats' exquisite defense, the most intriguing and unexpected basketball development of the year, was the reason they were able to sweep through the Midwest regional at Lawrence, Kansas. They defeated Texas Tech, 78-55, and then Kansas State, 69-64, while mighty Ohio State was sweating through the Mideast playoffs. Only by virtue of a late long shot by John Havlicek were the Buckeyes able to outlast stubborn Louisville, 56-55, in an earlier Mideast regional game.

A clue to what would happen in the finals came in Cincinnati's 82-67 victory over Western champion Utah in the second half of the semifinal doubleheader at Kansas City's Municipal Auditorium. The Bearcats' defense harassed Utah to distraction and simply ruined the Utes' famed fast break. Jucker was understandably delighted after that easy victory, as was the Cincinnati band, coeds and all, which oompahed its way into the dressing room to highlight an enthusiastic celebration. The euphoric scene was complete with kisses, hugs, cheers and singing of the alma mater. "Just one more," roared the team.

But that Cincinnati battle cry seemed like a voice in the wilderness when compared to the thunder and lightning of powerful Ohio State, everyone's No. 1 basketball team. Every opponent had pointed for the defending national champions that year, but none had beaten them. After the exhausting Mideast regional, Fred Taylor had taken his players back to Columbus for three days of furious practice. "Now they're head-hunting again," he announced, and the first available head they found belonged to St. Joseph's in the national semifinals. A surprise champion in the East, the Hawks from Philadelphia never had advanced this far in the NCAA tournament. When they won at Charlotte, North Carolina, their balding, insomniac coach, Jack Ramsay, forgot his limited budget and promised his underprivileged players new basketball shoes for Kansas City. Then, carried away with his new-found success, he bought them all hats, too. The night before the national semifinals, Ramsay had a nightmare that he was standing on the side lines trying to call a timeout, but no one would stop the game. It was an omen of things to come. Ramsay's nightmare became a reality the next day. His team played poorly and the Buckeyes won, 95-69. It was their 32nd straight victory dating back to the previous season.

The afternoon before the championship game on March 25, 1961, Taylor gave his team the scouting report on Cincinnati: "Much of their success is credited to their rebounding. Hogue and Wiesenhahn particularly will bomb the offensive boards and will push and shove to get up over you. Make Hogue foul." By game time, the seemingly impregnable Buckeyes were solid favorites.

"Ohio State was a prohibitive favorite," recalls Jucker. "There was one writeup that facetiously said that we had slipped out of town the night before the game to avoid the embarrassment. There was even some razzing by fans and some remarks in the press that we were going to finally find out that we shouldn't have been trying to play Ohio State. There had been some efforts for us to play Ohio State in regular-season games, but it never worked out. Ohio State was the Big Ten and we were Missouri Valley, and they sort of looked down on us. It was a very emotional game for us and for our fans."

The Municipal Auditorium had scheduled world-famous pianist Van Cliburn ("6-foot-4 and what a pair of hands," observed one coach) in an adjoining auditorium during the semifinals and came back with opera singer Rise Stevens the night of the finals, but the most memorable show still took place on the basketball court. It took 2½ hours to play the four-overtime third-place game between St. Joseph's and Utah, with the Hawks winning, 127-120. (St. Joseph's third-place position later was vacated due to the use of student-athletes who were declared ineligible subsequent to the tournament.) The 10,700 fans barely had settled down from that stirring contest when an equally remarkable game began to unfold for the national championship.

It was a beautiful basketball game between Cincinnati and Ohio State, played by both teams with the pure poise and aggressiveness demanded in a contest of such magnitude. The Bearcats maintained reasonable control of the backboards, took only the highest percentage shots and forced the game into a pattern they liked—a grudging defensive battle. Jerry Lucas of Ohio State was at his impassive and exquisite best, keeping the game close by hitting short one-handers. At the half, Ohio State's "prohibitive" favorites led by merely one point, 39-38. Jucker thought his team was in good shape.

"We made a long basket at the buzzer to close Ohio State's lead to one point. They had led us by five to seven most of the first half, so making that shot at half time gave us a lift. I didn't have to say much in the locker room. Our major concern was

Vic Rouse of Loyola drives toward the basket in the Ramblers' dramatic 1963 championship victory over Cincinnati.

140

Malcolm W. Emmons

that Paul Hogue, our center, had drawn three personal fouls very early in the game. The natural temptation was to pull him out for the first portion of the second half, but I decided to let him play."

It turned out to be a wise decision for Cincinnati. Hogue finished the game with those same three fouls and augmented Jucker's prime game plan, which was to slow down the Ohio State offense. Hogue and the rest of Cincinnati's burly frontcourt players virtually shut off the Ohio State fast break. The normally quick Buckeyes became fatally cautious and averaged only a shot a minute through the second half and the overtime period that followed.

"Our plan," remembers Jucker, "was to send a fourth man to the offensive boards and stop Ohio State's fast break. They were devastating when they'd get to running. They'd annihilate teams with it. Our plan was to make them slow down and have to set up on offense. And it worked."

Lucas did the only noticeable amount of damage for Ohio State, keeping the Buckeyes in the game with his 27 points. No one on the Cincinnati team was close to that output, but the Bearcats did make a lot of high marks collectively in the crucial area of turnovers. In a burst of early enthusiasm, Cincinnati made some charging fouls, then didn't make another after learning how closely the referees were watching for this violation. Jucker, in fact, counted only three turnovers in the entire game for this near-perfect team.

"When you think of playing that long with that much pressure in a game of that magnitude and only committing three turnovers, it becomes a source of great pride. But we needed that kind of game out of our kids to beat Ohio State."

Each team showed its nerve under pressure in the second half. With 11 minutes to play, Cincinnati led by six points, thanks to five jump shots by Bouldin ("best outside shooter," Taylor's scouting report on Cincinnati had said). Ohio State came back to take the lead by five points, only to lose it. The game was tied, 61-61, at the end of regulation time. With the help of Hogue's two free throws, Cincinnati quickly got ahead in overtime and didn't give Ohio State a chance to get even, winning 70-65 in a truly stunning upset. Larry Siegfried, the Ohio State battler, symbolized the Buckeye despair at the postgame ceremonies. Dismally clutching the huge second-place trophy to

his chest, Siegfried had thrown a towel over his head to hide himself from the crowd and cried.

Taylor offers no excuses for the loss except to say, "I suppose one of the toughest of times was sitting in what amounted to a broom closet waiting to play the national championship game." His reference, of course, is to the delay before the NCAA title game because of the extra-long third-place game between St. Joseph's and Utah. During this time, the Buckeyes sat fidgeting in their locker room, waiting for their game to start. Cincinnati players, meanwhile, had a more comfortable position while playing the waiting game—as spectators at the opener. If a psychological advantage existed between these two pregame extremes, then Cincinnati had it. Jucker thinks there is some validity to that thinking.

"Both teams stayed at the same hotel. We had to dress in our hotel rooms and walk across a parking lot to the gym. When we got there during the third-place game, I had our kids sit in the stands and watch. Fred Taylor had his kids go to the dressing room near the end of regulation, and there the Ohio State team sat in that tiny dressing room during all those overtimes. We remained in the stands and watched the game to conclusion. Whether Ohio State left their game in the locker, I don't know. But I'd think a team would be climbing the walls waiting that long for that big a game."

Vic Rouse of Loyola (40) tips in the winning basket in overtime in the 1963 championship game. This shot, one of the most dramatic in NCAA history, gave the underdog Loyola Ramblers a 60-58 decision over two-time defending champion Cincinnati.

NCAA

142

Cincinnati, a team of great composure in the national championship game, didn't take long to lose its cool shortly thereafter. The Bearcat players screamed, howled, pranced and danced as they received the NCAA championship trophy. Afterwards, the equally demonstrative Cincinnati fans turned their hotel "into a party," remembers Jucker. "It was a helter-skelter celebration. People got to drinking, and there were a few terse things said to the Ohio State people there; but that's all part of it." Jucker and his players flew home the next day, only to find the celebration enlarged. "There were thousands of people at the airport to greet us," he remembers, "and people lined the roads for a parade back to our gym. At the gym, there were 10,000 fans cheering and holding bumper stickers saying, 'Jucker for Governor.' They drove me and my family home from the gym in a fire truck with the sirens wailing and the bells clanging. My neighbors had a band playing and a banner across the front of our house that said, 'Juck The Giant-Killer.' At that time, we were living in North College Hills, a suburb. The mayor of that little town wanted to change the name of our street to Jucker Street. But we talked him out of it since we knew we were about to move to a home in another area."

It was a giddy experience for Jucker, a coach who had done what many considered the impossible—winning a national championship in his first year.

"I felt like a country boy," he says. "I was just happy to be involved in the NCAA tournament. I was awed by it all, the tournament and all the attention that went with it. I got along fine with the press and I didn't especially try to dodge saying anything that would appear on an opponent's bulletin board. I just tried to tell the truth, although I was accused of answering every question by saying, 'Say, that's a good question.' All I was doing was stalling, trying to think of a good answer, but not a deceptive answer. Through it all, I had a secret weapon—my kids playing together."

The following season, Jucker's remarkable piece of college basketball history repeated itself. This time, the Bearcats actually improved their record from 27-3 to 29-2. Wiesenhahn and Bouldin were gone, but they were replaced by Ron Bonham and George Wilson, two uncompromising sophomores whom Jucker brought along with care. It was perhaps an even more impressive team than the previous one. When Cincinnati won the Holiday Festival Tournament in Madison Square Garden early in the season, the New York audience called the Bearcats the finest team ever to play there.

Phil Pepe of the World-Telegram and Sun, for one, searched a week to find Cincinnati's Achilles'

heel. Then he watched a photographer set up a trick shot with the 6-foot-5 Bonham. The cameraman wanted Bonham's smallest teammates guarding him while the muscular forward posed shooting over their heads. Some Cincinnati players who seemed to be 6-1 or 6-2 got into the picture; and when the photographer asked for "one more shorty," he was told, "The next smallest we have is Fred Dierking at 6-6."

"That," said Pepe, "is their weakness. Not enough small players for pictures."

Cincinnati's two losses in 1961-62 came early in the season, by a total of three points. The Bearcats' conference championship came in a playoff with fifth-ranked Bradley, but to get there they had to salvage a near-loss to Drake. In the NCAA's Midwest regional, Hogue and Wilson blocked Paul Silas' first three shots for Creighton; Cincinnati went on to win comfortably, 66-46. The Bearcats held eighth-ranked Colorado to the same meager point total while winning the Midwest finals, 73-46; and sports writer Jay Simon of the Oklahoma City Daily Oklahoman remarked as he filled out his ballot for the all-tournament team, "In all honesty, I have to vote for the five Cincinnati starters." In the final tally, Hogue, Thacker and Wilson made the team.

A second straight national championship eventually belonged to this fine group of thoroughbreds but not until they survived a scare from UCLA in the national semifinals at Louisville, Kentucky. A sleeping giant soon to come awake with a fury on the college basketball scene, UCLA had surprised almost everyone by winning the West regional. But no one, not even UCLA coach John Wooden, gave the Bruins much of a chance to beat Cincinnati. Said Wooden upon arrival in Louisville: "I don't think we can beat Cincinnati at their slow-down game; and I don't much think we can beat them at our fast one, either." But the Bruins, who had beaten Utah State and Oregon State in the regionals, gave the Bearcats all they could handle. It started, predictably, with Cincinnati getting all the rebounds and most of the points. The defending national champions rushed out in front, 18-4. "The worst start I ever saw," Wooden would say later. But despite the inauspicious beginning for UCLA, Wooden kept his team at a good emotional pitch. "My players embraced the concept I always tried to get across—when you get behind, never hurry to catch up because hurrying usually makes you fall further behind. I kept telling this team, 'Just play your game.' If you're good enough, then things eventually will even out."

That's exactly what happened. UCLA's Gary Cunningham fired in one long jump shot after

144

Malcolm W. Emmons

Paul Hogue of Cincinnati, the tournament's most outstanding player in 1962, goes up to score in that year's championship game. Hogue led the Bearcats to their second straight title win over Ohio State.

another, and guards Walt Hazzard and John Green drove Yates and Thacker to distraction. Usually icily scientific Cincinnati did something it had not done in recent memory—it squandered a 14-point lead, and by half time the score was tied, 37-37.

It still was stubbornly and thrillingly tied in the closing minutes, with UCLA in possession of the ball. "We were holding the ball, and we were going to wait and go in for one shot," Wooden remembers. "Cunningham in particular had hit quite a few jump shots, and Green was hitting very well for us. We were going to work for a Cunningham jump shot. If he didn't get it, we would move Green into the short post for an inside shot."

But the Bruins never got it. Hazzard was called for charging—and turned the ball over to Cincinnati with 1:34 left. "We thought it was questionable," Wooden reflects. "Hazzard was not attempting to drive for the basket. It's one that might not have been called. Of course, Cincinnati was certain that he charged—that's usually the way those things go."

The Bearcats then froze the ball and called a timeout with 10 seconds left to set up their last shot. Jucker ordered a play designed to get the ball in to Hogue, the hottest hand on the court who had already scored 36 points. The strategy was no secret, least of all to Wooden. "We were confident they were going to go for Hogue underneath, or try to get it to Bonham for a shot with Hogue and Wilson following. But we had that covered well."

The only thing the Bruins weren't prepared for was a running, jumping 25-footer by Thacker that miraculously swished through the nets with three seconds left for a 72-70 Cincinnati victory. It was a low-percentage shot Wooden would have given an opponent every time. Thacker was not a good outside shot. In fact, he had missed six shots he had taken to that point; but that was the only option left to Cincinnati with Hogue and the others bottled up by UCLA.

Wake Forest—like UCLA an unexpected team in the Final Four—had left its magic back in the East regional. The Deacons, who surprised both Yale and St. Joseph's in overtime games after their cause appeared hopeless in regulation time, were overmatched in the national semifinals against Ohio

Captain Larry Siegfried symbolizes the frustration of Ohio State following the Buckeyes' loss to Cincinnati in 1961.

State. The mighty Buckeyes, who had dominated the Mideast regional as Cincinnati had dominated the Midwest, crushed Wake Forest, 84-68. The easy victory seemed to fortify a remark Deacon coach Bones McKinney had made about Ohio State on the eve of the semifinals: "I'd take most any player they've got and use him instead of mine."

There was, however, some payment the Buckeyes made for that triumph. Jerry Lucas, their most valuable player, injured his left kneecap in a freak fall during the game. Lucas was taken to the dressing room and for a long time was stretched out on a table, a towel wrapped with ice cubes around his knee. A large crowd formed at the door of the dressing room door and his wife, Treva, sent a message in. "Will he be able to play tomorrow?" she asked. "Will the sun come up in the East?" shot back a determined Lucas.

Lucas did play in the heralded rematch with

Malcolm W. Emmons

Cincinnati the following night—but he didn't play as well as he could have. Observers who had known Lucas at his best saw him limp late in the first half and saw the things he couldn't do—the drives, the cuts, the fierce rebounding that made him college basketball's best player that year. And they saw him score only 11 points while Paul Hogue was playing a better game for Cincinnati. Hogue, who wound up with 22 points, 19 rebounds and the tourney's most outstanding player trophy, from the start played like he was out to show Lucas he was better. In the first two minutes he put in a hook shot, blocked a Lucas shot and then sank another hook shot. He tore the ball off the backboards; and the rebounds he didn't get, Wilson did. The backboards, in fact, belonged to Cincinnati the rest of the way. "We only got one shot for so long it was pathetic," Ohio State coach Fred Taylor would say later. "Cincinnati wanted the basketball so badly they fought each other for it."

Rebounding wasn't Ohio State's only problem. The Buckeyes' usually efficient offense was slowed down by Cincinnati's painfully precise defense. Frustrated, the Buckeyes finally gave up their usual slashing style of attack and became hopelessly deliberate. "We must have movement," Taylor had written in his scouting report for the Cincinnati game. "We'll move the ball if we have to drop-kick it," an assistant had said. But in the last 10 minutes of the first half, Ohio State's vaunted offense could score only three baskets. Lucas, significantly, did not score in the final 15 minutes of the half. The Bearcats led, 37-29, at intermission and went on to win quite handily, 71-59. Not even Lucas' knee injury then could cast a shadow on Cincinnati's stunning achievement. Most of the coaches—and Ohio State's Taylor was among them—believed that even with Lucas at his best, the Buckeyes would have been no match that night for Jucker's team.

"Cincinnati played splendid defense, especially in the first half," Taylor said. "Their hustle and rebounding and Thacker's tremendous floor game and shooting beat us." Thacker finished with 21 points.

The following season, with only Hogue gone from the starting lineup, the Bearcats were once more a formidable, frightening team. Again they won the Missouri Valley Conference title, again led the country in defense and once more featured the deliberate, patterned team play taught by Jucker. The only thing they did not do in 1963 that they had done previously was win the national championship, although they literally came within inches of gaining an unprecedented third straight NCAA crown. Cincinnati beat Texas, Colorado

and Oregon State to get into the finals and for most of the game led Loyola of Chicago, at one time by as much as 15 points. But, unaccountably, the usually imperturbable Bearcats frittered away that big lead, made numerous errors and got into bad foul trouble; and the usually savvy Jucker didn't pull the right strings or press the right buttons. Even at that, the Bearcats still might have beaten George Ireland's team—and in fact had the game all but won in the closing seconds when they had the lead and a free-throw opportunity. Leading by a point with 12 seconds to play, the Bearcats had Larry Shingleton at the foul line with a one-and-one situation. Shingleton made the first shot and had only to sink the second for a certain victory. But he missed, Loyola tied the score in a desperation finish and went on to win in overtime, 60-58.

Up to the moment of that crushing climax, the college basketball world had all but belonged to the Bearcats. They had lost only one game all year, were ranked No. 1 in the country and had come into Louisville for the championship round of the NCAA tournament as the solid favorites. The town was alive with the prospect of seeing Jucker's stylists match up in the championship game with either Loyola or Duke, the speed entries in the Final Four. Oregon State simply did not figure to have a chance in the semifinal with the Bearcats, and this eventually was certified by Cincinnati's overwhelming 80-46 victory at Freedom Hall. The same night, Loyola whipped Duke, 94-75; and the Ramblers rolled into the national finals on the wings of an awesome performance in NCAA tournament competition. In earlier games, the nation's highest-scoring team had crushed Ohio Valley Conference champion Tennessee Tech by 69 points, then beat Southeastern Conference champion Mississippi State by 10 and Big Ten champion Illinois by 15.

The scores were indicative of Ireland's basketball theory, which was of a single-minded strategy: run and shoot. "The object of the game," Ireland would say, "is to put the ball in the basket." Loyola, of course, did it with greater regularity than any team in the country, hitting at a 91.8 clip.

Ireland had what he called "a good bunch of kids, relaxed but sensitive." The best of these included Jerry Harkness, Les Hunter ("he gets tears in his eyes when you correct him"), Ron Miller, Vic Rouse and John Egan. Chided for what some considered a weak schedule, the Ramblers wore the appellation of giant-killers as they tore through the NCAA tournament and prepared to meet Cincinnati, the biggest giant of them all. On the day of the championship game, Ireland sat in conference with his assistants and decided he had

146

a good chance against the Bearcats, despite what the experts and his coaching colleagues thought. "Can we board (outrebound) Cincinnati?" he asked, and answered himself. "I think we can. Can we press them? I think we can. We'll drive on them, drive for the basket. We'll make them play our game instead of standing around like they do. I think we can make them foul, and I don't think their big guy (George Wilson) is strong enough to handle ours (Hunter)."

The game began, though, as if the fastest guns in basketball were shooting with blanks. Ireland's players missed 13 of their first 14 shots, and Cincinnati steadfastly refused to let the Ramblers run. The Bearcats quickly moved out in front, 19-9; by half time, it was 29-21 in favor of Cincinnati. Loyola's shooting had been dreadful in the first half, eight baskets in 34 attempts.

"I'm not going to bawl you out," Ireland told his team in the locker room. "The ball's just not dropping for you. But it will. You're getting the shots, and it will. You're a better team than they are."

Cincinnati came out to make it a rout in the second half. The Bearcats sank five of six shots in one stretch. Then Bonham hit three in a row; and with 12 minutes to play, the nation's No. 1 team had the momentum and what many assumed to be an unapproachable 45-30 lead.

But, subtly, a change took place. Pressured perhaps as much as they ever had been, the Bearcats started turning over the ball on mistakes and, even worse, got into foul trouble. With 10:21 remaining and Cincinnati still holding a 45-33 lead, Wilson picked up his fourth foul. Jucker hurried in Dale Heidotting, his "bench." Heidotting was the only substitute in the game, and he was in for only four minutes. Cincinnati now virtually stopped shooting. Extra cautious because there were four fouls each on Thacker, Wilson and Yates, the Bearcats stalled. When they were afforded foul shots late in the game, they missed many of them. Their huge lead dwindled unbelievably. Time was still in Cincinnati's favor, however, when Harkness intentionally fouled Shingleton at the 12-second mark with the Bearcats in front, 53-52. Shingleton made the first of two free throws and grinned back at Yates as if to say, "We've got it now." But his

second shot dribbled off the rim to Hunter, who quickly got the ball downcourt to Harkness for the game-tying shot. There were still five seconds left in regulation, but Cincinnati did not call a timeout to set up a last shot. Jucker later said he tried but couldn't be heard above the din of the record crowd of 19,153 at pulsating Freedom Hall.

In the overtime, the teams were tied at 58-58 when Loyola, in possession of the ball with 2:15 to play, held for the final shot. The play was designed for Harkness, the Ramblers' best shooter, but Bonham would not let him get off the shot. Harkness passed off to Hunter in the middle who shot and missed—right into the hands of Rouse on the side. "I didn't tip it in," Rouse said later. "I grabbed it, tight, jumped up and laid it in. I'd missed a couple like that, and I wanted to be so sure. Oh, my, it felt good."

It felt better in the dressing room, where huge clusters of fans and the school band gathered around and everyone was claiming "No. 1, No. 1, No. 1" with raised fists.

There, but for a missed free throw, would have been Jucker. Shingleton was a disconsolate figure in the Cincinnati dressing room, hanging his head under the painful weight of the goat's mantle. Jucker knew his player was suffering and tried to comfort him as soon as he could. But first he was swept off to the interview room, and "it must have been a half-hour after the game before I could get to the player and talk to him."

In his retrospective view, Jucker refers to Shingleton only as the "player," because "I don't want to mention his name because I don't want to make it sound like he cost us the game."

"There he was in the dressing room," Jucker remembers, "absolutely crushed. I tried to tell him that he played a great game, which he did, and that you win and lose a game in 40 minutes, not with one free throw. In this case it was 45 minutes, and I told him that one play in that time doesn't lose a game. That's just sports. That's what makes it so great."

A teammate walked by.

"Hey, we won as a team and we lost as a team," he said.

Shingleton looked up. Jucker smiled. The Cincinnati players never had been closer.

Book 4
THE UCLA YEARS
1964·1975

If not for the farsightedness of Tom Scott, the NCAA tournament still might be a 25-team affair. But the relentless basketball visionary saw expansion as essential, and he sold the idea—with some difficulty.

Just as the expansion in the early 1950s was so important to the initial growth of the tournament, so were the giant steps taken in the 1970s during Scott's vibrant tenure. Scott was a member of the tournament committee from 1967 to 1975 and served as chairman for four years. During his stay on the committee, he initiated the enlargement of the tournament from 25 to 32 teams. Second representatives from conferences were added as at-large entries, a significant change of format.

"At first I questioned the consideration of a second conference team being eligible," notes Dutch Lonborg, the longtime committee chairman, "but that has proven to be a good move."

The 32-team format, in fact, was such a sparkling success that further expansion (to 40 teams) was undertaken by the committee.

Before the advent of the 32-team field in 1975, there was another important change of format during Scott's time on the committee. In 1969, acting on the recommendation of the National Association of Basketball Coaches, the committee shifted the days on which the championship finals were played from Friday-Saturday to Thursday-Saturday. Later, it became Saturday-Monday.

"One of the reasons we went to Thursday-Saturday was because it was the first time we had opened up the TV rights for bidding," says H. B. "Bebe" Lee, chairman of the committee from 1967 to 69. "Before that, Sports Network, Inc., had been doing it on its own; the major networks weren't interested. They became interested, however, and liked the idea of a day in between for preparation with the possibility of a national TV package." NBC got the rights to televise the NCAA championship in 1969 and has held them ever since.

One other significant change of format took place during Scott's

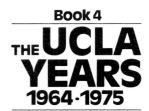

Book 4

THE UCLA YEARS 1964·1975

administration: the rotation of pairings between the regional champions. Beginning in 1973, the Eastern champion did not meet the Western champion each year—a break of policy that had been traditional since the start of the tourney in 1939. In 1973, the Eastern champion met the winner of the Midwest and the Mideast titlist played the Western champion.

The impact of television gave the NCAA tournament its biggest clout ever. In 1973, the championship game at the St. Louis Arena recorded the highest basketball rating in television history, college or professional. The contest between UCLA and Memphis State received a 20.5 figure on the ratings, which translated to 13,580,000 homes and roughly 39 million people. This came on top of an NBC report the previous year that "the 1972 tournament was the highest-rated basketball telecast of all time."

The television exposure turned the tournament into a financial bonanza through the gold-plated '70s, for the competing teams as well as the NCAA. For example, the four finalists in the 1973 tournament each earned $81,961.41. In 1978, the final four at St. Louis received in the neighborhood of $225,000 apiece—or an increase of 300 per cent.

1964·1965

TOAST OF THE COAST

"The Bruins are so quick that they press you from the time you leave the dressing room."—Howie Dallmar, Stanford University basketball coach

John Wooden, that grand master of homilies and hard-hitting basketball, could often lean on an epigram from "Piggie" Lambert in times of need.

"Expect mistakes," Wooden would say, echoing his former coach at Purdue. "If you're not making mistakes, then you're not doing anything. I'm positive that a doer makes mistakes."

In Wooden's book of basketball commandments, being a "doer" was everything. In other words, his philosophy was to "do" it to the opposition before they "did" it to him. So UCLA carried the fight to the enemy with an aggressive full-court press that became a basketball classic. Wooden stressed relentless pursuit of the enemy, a mistake-inducing defense. Speed was the ultimate clout against opponents. The conditioned stamina of Wooden's athletes worked to their advantage in this high-flying style.

"I told my players that I wanted them to be in better condition than any team we meet," said the ultrasuccessful UCLA coach. "Not as good, but better. I don't know whether we will be or not, but I want them to think in those terms."

The exasperating press promoted innumerable turnovers, but steals were only a small part of the defensive philosophy.

"Stealing the ball is only one of the side benefits," said Wooden. "We never go for steals. If you go for steals, you'll foul. We want our opponents to make the mistakes. We never try to take the ball away when a pass is made. We make the attempt to get the ball in the air. We are hoping to force the lob pass or the bounce pass."

The tactic injected a feeling of confidence in the Bruins and, conversely, brainwashed the enemy into an inferiority complex.

"We know when we're going to use it," Wooden said. "They don't."

The unnerving Bruin style once inspired this comment from an awe-stricken coach: "What do you do with the ball once you have an advantage?"

Before John Wooden took over at UCLA, West Coast basketball was considered less than golden by the snobbish East and Midwest fraternities. Even though San Francisco and California had won national titles in the 1950s, the hard-core cynics refused to budge an inch in their provincial thinking, pointing to only four title-winning coast teams in history. But in 1963-64, UCLA proved that it could play ball with the rest of the country. Better, in fact.

The Bruins won their first NCAA championship that year but didn't stop there. They won the next year, too; and before Wooden had retired at the end of the 1975 season, there was no college basketball coach to match his accomplishments and no sports dynasty that achieved his levels. The Bruins won 10 NCAA championships in 12 years under Wooden, including seven in a row between 1967 and 1973. This exquisite dynastic reign has been compared to those of the New York Yankees in baseball and the Boston Celtics in professional basketball; but in a way, Wooden's accomplishment was even more ethereal. While the Yankees and Celtics could put their best foot forward with the same stars, Wooden was forced to restructure several times around different players—and different types of players. He won with little men (Gail Goodrich and Walt Hazzard), big men (Lew Alcindor and Bill Walton) and in-between men (Sidney Wicks and Curtis Rowe). And while the Yankees and Celtics, any season, could win a championship merely by being the better team in a four-of-seven series, the NCAA tournament involves sudden-death games of Russian roulette in which a team cannot lose once en route to the title. One of UCLA's most coveted records under Wooden was a 38-game winning streak in NCAA

tournament competition, a standard of excellence that is hard to beat.

The UCLA dynasty began explosively the first year. Led by Walt Hazzard, Gail Goodrich, Keith Erickson, Jack Hirsch and Fred Slaughter, the Bruins raced through a 30-0 season that culminated with a smashing 98-83 victory over Duke in the national championship game. It was clearly a victory for the underdog as well as a coup for Wooden, whose team was considered too small to compete with the country's best. One national magazine, making preseason selections of the top teams, didn't even mention UCLA in the same class with the Michigans and Dukes. Wooden's dwarfish squad was listed among teams "not as good as the top 20 . . . (but) interesting. Some will upset their betters in games this season; others will be among next year's elite . . . they bear watching."

The magazine called Hazzard "one of the best offensive players in the nation and one of the worst defensive players on the Pacific Coast." Stanford was picked by most to win the championship of UCLA's conference, then known as the Athletic Association of Western Universities or Big Six (now the Pacific-10 Conference).

But Wooden wasn't buying the preseason talk. "We have no negative thinkers here," said the man who, except for his first year as a coach, had never had a losing season in his life as player or coach. "If we do have negative thinkers, they don't play very much. I'm a positive thinker myself."

Wooden had to be thinking positively when he looked over his team in the fall. He noticed that there were no giants in the audience. The lack of height obviously would be a shortcoming on most other teams. But most of these players were hand-picked—and not necessarily for size.

"I don't recruit players who are individual players and great scorers unless they have an awful lot of other qualities," explained Wooden. "I am interested in those who are defense-minded, team-oriented and not unmindful of the ability to score."

Erickson, at 6-5 as tall as any starter, didn't even excel at basketball particularly. But Wooden liked him because "he was a fierce competitor and a fine athlete. He wasn't a good basketball player, but he was willing to learn."

Goodrich, listed as 6-1, was a problem for Wooden at first.

"Gail was a very spirited player, and he wanted to handle the ball just as he did in high school,"

Malcolm W. Emmons

said Wooden. "Well, I didn't want Goodrich handling the ball that much because we had Hazzard on the team. And when Hazzard was in there, I wanted him handling the ball more often because he was such a great passer. I want the players to do their strengths. It took me a while; but Gail figured out that if he didn't have the ball, he'd have to work to get open. And if he got open, Hazzard would find him with the ball. Gail became a fine player away from the ball."

Wooden had his hands full with Hazzard, too.

"I discovered that Walt usually played his best when he was mad at me," said Wooden. "But I didn't make him mad very often; you can't do it too often. You have to be careful or it might backfire on you. I saved it for when I thought we really needed it."

Hazzard set the tempo for UCLA's smart offensive style. He switched on the fast break and supervised the stall, when needed. He was the player Wooden once called "hard to believe when on offense . . . there's nothing he can't do."

While Hazzard was the director of the band on offense, the Bruins had a virtuoso performer to key

their defense—Slaughter, a speedy 6-5 center whom Wooden in 1963-64 called "the key to our success."

Slaughter's biggest contribution to the UCLA game was his part in the zone press, a powerful weapon that helped the Bruins cut their usually taller opponents down to size. Slaughter's job was to meet the man with the ball up front, at the start of the press.

"I want my players thinking defense all over the court, and the zone press is one way of doing that," Wooden said. "Mainly, it is used to speed up the tempo of the game, to encourage the opponent to run with the ball when that might not be his best style of play. It is designed to alter the opponent's style."

Making people nervous was UCLA's main talent, it seemed.

"The press tries to create mistakes," said Wooden. "And it's only human nature that makes people hurry to correct those mistakes. And when you hurry, you get careless. We try to take advantage of that carelessness."

Hirsch also fit nicely into this scheme. He was 6-3, standing on tiptoe, and one of the smallest forwards in the country. But, oh, what poise.

"He never played a bad minute of basketball for me," Wooden noted about a fellow who was considered a misfit in high school. "When he went out of a game, we lost a lot at both ends of the floor."

Wooden, never an explosive locker room talker, calmly explained the facts of life without raising a syllable. He instilled team spirit in a quiet, unemotional manner, yet the Bruins were charged to a high emotional pitch before going out on the court. As one player put it:

"It's the way he tells us, for example, that no team can beat us, but that we beat ourselves. We hear that before every game. But after he says that, he'll stop talking and there's silence. He looks at everybody; then he says, in a low voice, 'Let's go.' That's what really psyches me up. We all feel like smashing right through the wall."

The players were polished beautifully for the 1963-64 season. Much of the game is reaction, not conscious thought, repeated Wooden. He devoted long hours on the practice floor to basics—dribbling drills, defensive drills, running without the ball, hitting spots on the floor, running the fast break without the ball.

It was book-taught basketball with Wooden reading the rules in firm, persuasive tones.

"I want you to be in balance when you shoot," crisply ordered Wooden, a church deacon who never cursed. "That's not your shot. You'd be better off closer in."

Wooden's men in motion, who also included two key reserves in Kenny Washington and Doug McIntosh, were prepared fully to run through the proverbial wall when Brigham Young came to Los Angeles on December 6 for the opening of the season. The Bruins showed they had learned their lessons well, blitzing the Cougars, 113-71, while 4,700 fans at the Sports Arena acknowledged that this was a very special UCLA team. The zone press, working to perfection, was beginning to shape the UCLA character. The Bruins received more applause later in the season when they thrashed second-ranked Michigan, 93-80, in the Los Angeles Classic, with Hirsch bottling up the great Cazzie Russell. "It was the greatest game I've ever seen my team play," Wooden said at the time. Illinois coach Harry Coombs, whose team was to play UCLA in the finals, concurred: "It was the best performance in a single game I've seen by a college team."

When the Bruins defeated the Illini the next night for the championship, the Los Angeles Herald-Examiner put in a plug for UCLA in the voting for the national polls. "Who's No. 1?" a headline in the newspaper asked.

The UCLA stock was pushed to No. 2, a shade behind Kentucky, while Wooden prepared his team for conference play, the part of the season he considered most important. The systematized coach approached practice sessions in much the same manner he came upon English compositions when he was a teacher in classrooms—with structural design. Basketball is quite logical, he explained in the most unemotional tones; and he marched the Bruins through precision drills while timing their exercises precisely from notes on three-by-five-inch cards. The "Wooden Man," as some have called him, rarely deviated from this religious arithmetic of style. "Almost all games are won on a practice floor," he would say. His work done in practice, Wooden was outwardly calm and serene on the bench during games. Assistant coach Jerry Norman made up for Wooden's often stoic appearance, doing enough yelling and squirming for both.

In January, UCLA was moved into the No. 1 position in both wire service polls as a result of a smashing victory over Washington State, coupled with Kentucky's first loss of the season. The Bruins remained the country's No. 1 team for the rest of the season, despite some close calls. California, under Rene Herrerias, broke the famed press and controlled the tempo, but Hazzard's foul-shooting at the end preserved a two-point victory; and Southern California extended the Bruins to 91-81 in the last regular-season game. Every time, UCLA's animated style beat back troublemakers. "Some-

153

how, some way, we know our pressure will get to 'em," said Hazzard.

Besieged by "No. 1" chants from their fans following their season-ending triumph over Southern Cal, the Big Six champions went through the traditional cord-cutting ceremonies with elan. Lifted off their feet, the Bruins didn't come down to earth again until Wooden's whip cracked in practice sessions for the NCAA's West regional. Some of the rest of the country still had a show-me attitude toward UCLA, which was No. 1 for the 12th straight week and finished as the mythical national champion in the final AP and UPI polls. Sports Illustrated, for one, cast aspersions on the Bruins' character: "UCLA will not go all the way because a team can no longer go through a season unbeaten . . . (and, besides) some weak rivals have inspired overconfidence." The magazine liked Duke. So did others.

"Most of the men in the business are saying that Duke would beat UCLA in a showdown," reported the Kansas City Star.

"We may not be the tallest on the court," retorted Wooden, "but we are the best conditioned team in the country."

In Corvallis, Oregon, UCLA's long-distance runners survived an upset try by Seattle to win the regional semifinals, 95-90. UCLA led, 49-39, at the half; but Seattle, equalizing the Bruins' quickness, came back with a rush to take a 75-73 lead with 7:58 to play on Rich Turney's jump shot. Then Slaughter put in four straight points to put UCLA on top again. Seattle got within a point, 81-80, with five minutes left but never caught the front-runners. A seven-point streak in the final 41 seconds gave the Bruins the game and a chance to meet San Francisco in the finals.

"Hardly anyone likes the Bruins," reported a newspaper story under a fat headline that read: "Only Few Pick Uclans To Win."

Wooden, meanwhile, was busy playing psychiatrist to his players.

"He shouted at me a lot in practice sessions," said Hazzard, "but I guess I needed it."

Washington, a moody sophomore, had to be handled differently. The outstanding reserve was sometimes "down on himself" when he felt he hadn't been playing well. His head drooped. But Wooden chucked him under the chin, making the player look at him while he was explaining the game. Wooden took Washington to a basket away from the rest of the team and showed him what he wanted in the way of a head fake if he were to play guard. Washington practiced it. Then after several trials, he drilled home a 22-foot shot. He grinned, applauding himself. He was ready to play again.

The complexities of the varied personalities became more profound in the pressure cooker of the NCAA tournament. But, no matter. Here was possibly the best-conditioned team in the country. And the Bruins were ready to run out from under their psyches, despite what the "experts" said about their talents.

UCLA's assertive character proved too much for San Francisco in the West finals. The Bruins trailed the Dons by 13 points at one time in the first half, then zone-pressed them into submission. UCLA outscored San Francisco, 17-8, at the start of the second half and suddenly led, 45-44, on Goodrich's short field goal with 14 minutes remaining. USF led for the last time at 48-47, but quick baskets by Erickson and Goodrich turned around the game's direction.

UCLA joined Duke, Michigan and Kansas State in the championship foursome at Kansas City. The Bruins, to no one's surprise, had few supporters despite the fact that they had beaten two of the other three teams there. Duke appeared to be the best of the lot, according to the Kansas City Star, and "Michigan looked best in the workouts."

Kansas State had a score to even with UCLA in the semifinals, having lost a three-point decision to the Bruins earlier in the year. Tex Winter's Wildcats were working on a 13-game winning streak, including upsets over ranked Texas Western (now Texas-El Paso) and Wichita State in the regional. Recalling his team's troubles with the UCLA press the previous December, Winter remarked: "I was just outcoached. We just weren't prepared to meet the kind of problems UCLA presented. However, I believe we're as good as any ball club that's going to be at the national finals." Still, Winter wasn't gambling on his luck. He had sent his "lucky" brown suit—the one he had worn on the current winning streak—to the cleaners on Monday of NCAA finals week and planned to have it back to wear for Friday night's showdown with UCLA at the Kansas City Municipal Auditorium. "If I hadn't had it cleaned," he said with a grin, "the suit would have been our biggest offensive threat in Kansas City."

The Wildcats, led by Big Eight player-of-the-year Willie Murrell, dominated much of the game. They led, 75-70, with slightly more than seven minutes left. It looked gloomy for the Bruins, but suddenly they came alive with the help of key baskets by Erickson and Goodrich. During this

The dominant player in UCLA's 1965 title verdict over Michigan was guard Gail Goodrich (25), who scored 42 points in the Bruins' 91-80 triumph. Here, Goodrich drives past George Pomey.

Rich Clarkson

156

Neil Leifer, Sports Illustrated

rally, UCLA got some added moral support. The UCLA song girls, delayed by airplane difficulties, arrived like a late cavalry charge. Their heroes were behind when they rushed onto the floor, bright and cheery in their blue-and-gold costumes. They got there just in time for the best part, for UCLA ripped off 11 points in three minutes and held the advantage to finish with a 90-84 decision.

In the locker room before the national championship game, Wooden's message consisted of only one question. "Who can remember," he asked his players, "which team finished second in the NCAA two years ago?"

The answer was Ohio State, but nobody knew it. "That one question," Gail Goodrich recalled in later years, "was all the coach really had to say—and he knew it."

So UCLA took the floor with a passion in the national finals against a run-and-shoot Duke team that had beaten Michigan by a convincing 91-80 score the night before. The Bruins came out like a team that wanted to prove something—and actually, that was exactly the case. Despite a 29-game winning streak and No. 1 posture in the national polls, UCLA was still an underdog in many eyes. Few were convinced that UCLA's boundless energy could overcome the height advantage of Duke, which boasted two 6-10 players in Jay Buckley and Hack Tison, along with all-America guard Jeff Mullins. A Kansas City sports writer expressed the popular opinion when he wrote in his pregame story: "The hard facts of life should come to the Bruins tonight. You can't beat the horses—and Duke has 'em."

Duke may have had the horses, as the writer pointed out, but UCLA had the thoroughbreds that night in Kansas City, particularly Kenny Washington. The Bruins were losing, 30-27, after eight minutes when Wooden sent Washington onto the floor to substitute for the foul-troubled Erickson. Playing for the first time before his father, a career Marine, Washington popped in two quick jumpers in the midst of a 16-point string. Hirsch took the ball away from the Blue Devils three times during that torrid stretch. Erickson came back, knocked down the shots of Mullins and turned them into UCLA baskets. Goodrich scored eight points. That was it. UCLA had a 43-30 lead and was on its way to a stunningly easy 98-83 conquest of the tough Atlantic Coast Conference champions. What the other 29 victories couldn't do, this one certainly did for UCLA.

"I can understand now why they went through

157

Freddie Goss (40) of UCLA goes against Michigan's Bill Buntin.

the season undefeated," said Duke coach Vic Bubas after the runaway officially made the Bruins No. 1.

"They really convinced me," said Mullins. "I didn't think they could do it with their size."

And from the Star, that final stronghold of disloyal opposition, came this report by Fritz Kreisler:

"Duke's Blue Devils are like the rest of the country now—they believe UCLA is for real."

That UCLA team scored more points and won more games than any Bruin squad in history up to that point. Almost a quarter of a million people enjoyed its talents. No one enjoyed it more than Wooden, however.

"The fact that this was my first NCAA championship team is reason enough for it to be my favorite, but there are other factors that make it particularly significant in my memory," he says. "Comparatively speaking, it was the shortest of all NCAA champions, it used the exciting press defense exceptionally well, it was a very colorful and fascinating team, it exemplified unselfishness to a remarkable degree and it came closer to realizing its full potential than any team I have ever seen."

For defense of the national championship in 1964-65, several changes had to be made at UCLA. Hazzard, Hirsch and Slaughter were gone from the title-winning team; and Wooden restructured around Goodrich, who took over for Hazzard as the playmaker. Freddie Goss was the other guard; and Edgar Lacey and Mike Lynn were bright sophomore forwards joining the likes of McIntosh, Erickson and Washington. "I think we'll be an entertaining team," Wooden told the press.

The Bruins were—but only after a 110-83 blitzing by Illinois in the season opener, which Wooden called "one of the worst beatings I ever took." That loss was a mixed blessing of sorts, for it took the pressure of the 30-game winning streak off the Bruins' backs. "Now you can just go out and play your game," Wooden confidently told his team.

Indeed, the Bruins did just that. The only other loss of the year was a five-point defeat by Iowa on the road two months later; and by the end of the season, UCLA's 28th victory meant a second straight NCAA title. This time, the Bruins beat a fine Michigan team with Cazzie Russell in the championship game.

To accommodate his new personnel that season, Wooden had made subtle variations in his zone press; but it was still the same unnerving, enigmatic defense for the opposition. At its heart was Erickson, whom Wooden calls "a tremendous competitor and one of the finest athletes I ever coached. He played an important position in our zone press. Erickson was not only the best I ever had (in that defensive setup), but the best I've ever seen. He was quick and he had speed. Sometimes you have quickness without the speed—but he had it all. But even with all that, he was a fiery competitor and had great judgment. We worked a tremendous amount of time with him on how to read the man with the ball, whether to move left or right or back or forward and how not to commit himself too soon. He was very aggressive, one who was not afraid to make a mistake. And if he did, he was quick to recover."

One West Coast coach made the observation that UCLA was every bit as strong as the previous year and even had the additional clout of more depth. The Bruins lived up to this high assessment by going through the conference season undefeated and burying Brigham Young, 100-76, in their first NCAA tournament game in the West regional. The Bruins won handily despite the fact they were playing on Brigham Young's home court, a situation that frankly distressed Wooden at the time.

"We went into that game well prepared," Wooden says, "but we were playing in the Brigham Young field house. That was wrong. There should never be a home team playing an NCAA game on its home floor. I had taken teams to Brigham Young, and Brigham Young gets tremendous support. There are great fans there, and they really get behind their team. Deep down, I was concerned about how we would respond to such a rabid home crowd. It's quite possible that the younger players felt the pressure." But the older players came through for Wooden, Goodrich getting 40 points and Erickson 28.

UCLA had a bit more trouble with Pete Peletta's San Francisco team in the regional finals. The Bruins were extended before winning, 101-93, and Wooden acknowledges that "San Francisco had an outstanding, well-balanced basketball team. There was no doubt in my mind when we went up there for the regional that San Francisco would be the team to beat, even though we were concerned about playing Brigham Young on its home floor. I felt San Francisco was a better team than Brigham Young."

Everything pointed to a classic showdown between UCLA and Michigan for the national championship. At least, that was the tone of conversation among the nation's basketball coaches as they

Bill Bradley couldn't lead the Princeton Tigers to the championship, but he scored a record 177 points in five games (including 58 against Wichita State) and was named the most outstanding player in the 1965 tournament.

158

Rich Clarkson

convened in Portland for the finals. One of the few dissenting voices came from Kentucky's Adolph Rupp, who believed that Princeton and all-America Bill Bradley would take it all. Few, if any, gave Wichita State a solid chance, although Iowa coach Ralph Miller commented about the Shockers' semifinal match with UCLA, "If Wichita can get off to a good start—by that, I mean hit well—they'll be in the game." Miller also felt Wichita State's star guard, 6-1 Kelly Pete, could contain the high-powered Goodrich. "Gail Goodrich is very good," said Miller, "but Pete is one of the best defensive players in the country. He certainly will not be embarrassed in this assignment."

As it was, it turned into one of the biggest mismatches in NCAA tournament history. UCLA had a 65-38 lead at half time and raced into the national finals with a resounding 108-89 victory over the Shockers behind Goodrich's 28 points and Lacey's 24 points and 13 rebounds. "Wichita," underscores Wooden, "was weaker than any of the teams we had played in the regional."

Wooden held Michigan in far higher esteem. In fact, he sounded awed by the prospect of facing the Wolverines in the national finals. The Big Ten champions had flattened Princeton, 93-76, in the other semifinal game, enhancing their image as the nation's top-ranked team. "It's hard to imagine a college team that strong," Wooden said of the aggregation that included prize players in Cazzie Russell and Bill Buntin. "I really doubt if any team in the pro ranks is bigger or stronger. There certainly are no thin men out there."

Wooden realized it would be foolish to try to slug it out with Michigan's heavyweights under the basket, so speed and maneuverability would be the key to the UCLA game plan.

"I was thinking of running them down," Wooden reflects. "They had a big, powerful team; they looked almost like football linemen. If we could run, maneuver and keep them off the boards, we thought we'd have a good chance for victory."

In many respects, the game at the Portland Coliseum—a shiny, modern edifice nicknamed "The Glass Palace"—was a repeat of UCLA's performance in the 1964 NCAA finals against Duke.

"The year before," Wooden remembers, "our starting center, Fred Slaughter, hadn't played too well; and I brought in McIntosh. He played extremely well. Now, one year later, McIntosh—our starting center—wasn't playing too well, and I

brought in Mike Lynn. And he did well."

There were, ironically, other startling similarities. Just as he had done against Duke in 1964, Kenny Washington came off the bench to play a vital role against Michigan in 1965 with 17 points. ("If we get this far every year," Wooden said at the time, "Kenny will take care of us.") And just as the team had done the previous year, the Bruins of 1965 turned their opponents into jittery, frantic losers with their terrifying press. Losing early in the game, a la 1964, the Bruins came back behind supersub Washington to take the lead. Then they finished the mighty Wolverines with a 14-2 scoring streak to take a 47-34 half-time lead. Michigan could get no closer than 11 points thereafter; and UCLA went on to win its second straight NCAA title, 91-80.

"Our press really took a great toll on them," notes Wooden. "I felt in the Michigan game, just as I had felt against Duke, that we had the game essentially won at the half. It was more than just the score. You could just tell by the general appearance and feelings of the teams. You can't tell your team you have them and it's all over, but I had the feeling we had them at the half. I think the running really got to them. I just felt that players as big as Michigan had were not going to be that maneuverable, and you could make them tire more easily. I remember when one of their big players was at the line. He was so tired, he took a deep breath and shot a free throw that was way short. It made me feel the toll had been taken."

Goodrich, a player who according to Wooden had made "an amazing improvement over the years," scored a championship-game record 42 points in the finals. But he lost out on the most outstanding player trophy because of Bill Bradley's incredible performance. Princeton's leading man established three individual tournament records, including most points scored in a game (58 against Wichita State in the national third-place game) and most points in a five-game tourney, 177. The vote for Bradley wasn't unanimous, however. Many in the UCLA camp thought Goodrich deserved the honor. Goodrich, himself, seemed unconcerned. Swigging a soft drink in the dressing room after the game, he said quietly, "I honestly wasn't sure when we went out there whether we could win. But after three minutes I knew we were going to take it."

160

TEXAS WESTERN STEALS IT

John Wooden's quest at UCLA for a third straight national title was knocked cold before the 1965-66 season started, when his team was crippled by injury, illness and graduation. That year belonged to a group of straight-shooters from the Southwest directed by a young coach with a penchant for speed and rock-hard defense. Texas Western (now Texas-El Paso) exploded across the college scene like a meteoric flash, never to be heard from again. But during that year, the Miners burned brightly under the stewardship of Don Haskins, who at 36 was one of the youngest coaches ever to win the NCAA tournament. Only a trio from the Big Ten were younger—Branch McCracken (31 when he guided Indiana to the first of two championships in 1940), Bud Foster (34 when he won with Wisconsin in 1941) and Fred Taylor (35 when Ohio State won in 1960).

Haskins, who had learned rugged defense and disciplined offense 15 years earlier at Oklahoma A&M (now Oklahoma State) with Hank Iba, brought a stunning team with him when he arrived at El Paso. The players included Dave "Big Daddy" Lattin, Bobby Joe Hill, Willie Cager, Orsten Artis, Nevil Shed and Willie Worsley. Lattin at 6-7 was the biggest man on the squad; but the Miners all could run, shoot and pass and play wonderful defense. Despite their short run, there was nothing fluky about their accomplishment. Going into the NCAA tournament, Haskins' team was ranked third in the nation by virtue of its 23-1 record. The Miners then came through with five victories, including decisions over such powerhouses as Cincinnati, Kansas, Utah and Kentucky in the championship game. This great finishing kick finally gave some credibility to the Miners, who generally had been given faint recognition for a supposedly weak schedule. "They opened the season with victories over lightweights," pointed out sports editor Jay Simon of the Daily Oklahoman, "but they finished with victories over four former champions that have won more national collegiate titles than almost any quartet you could

name. Any recognition Texas Western received until the end of the 1966 basketball season was given grudgingly. But when the nets were cut down at College Park, Maryland, at the conclusion of the 28th annual National Collegiate Championship, it was the Miners from El Paso who did the snipping."

The Miners earned that traditional rite by conquering a proud Kentucky team, 72-65, in a game that was not as close as the final score indicated. Texas Western's strong defense held Kentucky's heralded shooters 23 points below their season's average; and the Miners penetrated the Wildcats' zone at will with a free-wheeling attack directed by the dynamic Hill, a 5-10 bundle of energy. Hill made two key steals against Kentucky in the first half and converted them into easy baskets to set the tone of the game. In short, the Miners controlled the game without breaking it open. Years later, Rupp would say: "I still wake up in the middle of the night wondering what I could have done to help my boys win that game."

Actually, Rupp did have a built-in excuse, although few would deny that Texas Western was the superior team that night in Cole Field House. Before arriving at the national finals in College Park, some of Rupp's key players had been struck by illness while out in Iowa City for the Mideast regional. "I'm taking a bunch of sick boys to the championship finals," Rupp had announced, somewhat protectively. Particularly worrisome to Rupp was the illness to Larry Conley, the team leader, who complained of chest pains, a bad throat, fever and a generally weakened condition.

"Conley never practiced with us all week," Rupp said. "The doctors had him filled up with more pills than you can count. We worked on him all night before the national semifinals and finally got his fever broken. He started against Duke, and we beat them all right (83-79); but I had to take him out six times during the game because of his condition."

Center Thad Jaracz, although perhaps not as sick as Conley, also was under par with a bad cold, as

Rich Clarkson

were a few other Kentucky starters. "It was so ungodly warm out in Iowa City," Rupp had said, "they all caught strep throat. I caught it myself, and my voice was never very strong after that."

The thing that kept Rupp up most of the night before the championship game, however, was not his cold—but the specter of the Texas Western talent. "I knew that Texas Western had a good bunch of ball handlers; and they were fast, very fast. I knew they would be trouble." Nor did Rupp feel any more secure when a doctor told him after the semifinal victory over Duke: "Your team shot its load tonight. They'll never come back. Tonight you played well enough to beat Texas Western. But this team just won't be strong tomorrow night."

By comparison, the Miners had a healthy team and an easier semifinal game than Kentucky's, beating Utah, 85-78. All that kept the Utes in

Kentucky's players were hounded by Texas Western's defense all night in the 1966 championship game. This time, it's Kentucky's Larry Conley against Willie Worsley.

contention was Jerry Chambers, one of the most exciting players in that year's tournament. Chambers scored 38 points against the Miners, the most scored against them by a single player since Haskins arrived in El Paso five years before. When Texas Western's big men got into foul trouble, Haskins brought in Jerry Armstrong. The reserve came closer to stopping Chambers than the regulars had. Though the Miners won with relative ease, they were not especially happy.

"The officials called it like a girls' game," said Lattin, who fouled out. "Baby fouls," groaned Shed. "They called baby fouls."

Haskins also was mad at the officials—and at his players as well. His head splitting from a headache that steadily worsened as the tournament progressed, Haskins had been on his players' backs from the moment they landed in Washington, D.C., for the championship round. He yelled at Shed through much of practice and even benched Bobby Joe Hill once in disgust. "Isn't this the laziest bunch you've ever seen?" Haskins asked. There was no pretense with Haskins, a bear of a man who walked in a shuffle with his feet pointed out.

After the victory over Utah, the Texas Western coach went off to share some beers in his room with Bill Cornwall, an El Paso construction-supply engineer who was the team's good-luck charm. Cornwall missed only one Texas Western road trip all year—to Seattle—and that was the only game the Miners had lost that season.

The night before the NCAA championship game, Haskins sat up late with his friend and mused over his implausible circumstances. "Once in a lifetime," he said. "You know, this is a once in a lifetime." When it was pointed out that he was still young and the possibility existed of more cracks at the national championship, Haskins just shrugged and said:

"No. No chance. Mr. Rupp is 64 and made it a lot of times, but it's probably going to be just once in a lifetime for me."

Haskins made his one shot count the next day and used the casual approach to do it. Before the game, he let his players do as they pleased—no chalk talks or strategy sessions. Lattin, Texas Western's enforcer at center, slept most of the day, stirring only for meals and girl friends. Most of the other Texas Western players entertained guests and lolled around before boarding the team bus for the arena.

Haskins generally planned to stick with the game plan that had worked for him all season: a man-for-man on defense and a loose, free-lancing attack on offense. But he did have one surprise in store for Kentucky. Haskins introduced a three-guard lineup in order to get more speed against the fast Wildcats. Along with Hill and Artis, his regular backcourt starters, the Texas Western coach inserted Worsley in place of big Shed. All three played the entire game.

By comparison with the steely Miners, there seemed to be more emotion in the Kentucky locker room. Rupp asked: "Who's captain tonight?"

Someone suggested Pat Riley's name.

"It's his birthday tomorrow," Conley said.

"All right," Rupp said, "let's have a birthday present for him then."

They waited for the third-place game to be completed. Before long, Mike Harreld rushed into the Kentucky dressing room and said, "Duke beat Utah by two." Rupp then put on his legendary brown jacket and led his Wildcats out on the floor in hopes of winning his fifth NCAA championship. But it was a lost cause for Kentucky almost from the start.

Haskins had said all along that his team was capable of better defense than it had shown for weeks and in the finals proved that it was true. Kentucky's shooting was entirely inefficient in the face of the exquisite Miner defense, and even the shots the Wildcats made were salutes to the individual brilliance of Riley and Louie Dampier. The score was tied, 9-9, midway through the first half when Bobby Joe Hill made the moves that turned the game in Texas Western's favor. Hill first stole the ball from Tommy Kron, dribbled half the court and scored. Then he took it away from Dampier at midcourt and went in for another easy layup.

That flashy display by the Texas Western guard put the Miners in the driver's seat. Kentucky chased the lead the rest of the way but never caught it. At the end, Hill and Worsley just dribbled around until time ran out; and Haskins had his first NCAA title—a young coach at a school that had never before even challenged for a national title in any sport.

Haskins almost seemed embarrassed to stand in the spotlight in front of the redoubtable Rupp, an upstart for the moment overshadowing a legend.

"I'm just a young punk," Haskins said. "It was a thrill playing against Mr. Rupp, let alone beating him."

163

Page 164:
Harry Flournoy (44) of Texas Western outrebounds Kentucky's Pat Riley (42).

There would be celebrating into the night, of course, for the Texas Western fans, who had hungered much too long for this type of recognition. Bonfires burned through El Paso, orange bunting floated over the town and riot squads were called out to calm down the townspeople. But for once, they could scream "We're No. 1," and no one could take that away from them.

James Drake, Sports Illustrated

FIREHOUSE FOUR PLUS LEW

When Lew Alcindor first arrived at the UCLA campus in the fall of 1965, he instantaneously regretted his choice of schools. California was nearly 3,000 miles from his New York City home and represented a dramatic break with cozy, familiar surroundings.

"I was so homesick that I didn't unpack my bags for a week," he said. "I thought it would be nice if they could just transplant UCLA to Times Square."

He was also angered by apathy over the poverty in nearby Watts, the Negro ghetto. On campus, he heard racial slurs and cruel remarks about his unusual height, which was 7-foot-1.

The pain was all forgotten, however, when he played basketball.

Ignoring the pressure of his heralded first appearance, Alcindor scored 31 points to lead the freshmen over the varsity, 75-60, in a preseason game. Not incidentally, this was a varsity team going for its third straight national championship.

"UCLA is No. 1 in the country and No. 2 on its own campus," said one observer. The wisecrack was not far from the truth. If the varsity was good, the freshman team would be better in years to come. And the main reason, of course, was Alcindor.

Few players in the history of college basketball made their presence felt like the UCLA center. Controversial and often sullen off the court, "Mount Alcindor," as he was often called, was the Bruins' literal tower of strength on the court through three straight NCAA championship seasons. The Bruins played 90 games over that span and lost but two—by the total margin of four points. Alcindor averaged more than 26 points a game in that time, a figure that emphasized his wholly unselfish style of play. With his many talents, he could have scored 40 a game if he wished, most agreed.

Coach John Wooden, historically sparing in praise, uncharacteristically termed Alcindor "awesome."

"At times," Wooden said, "he even frightens me."

This "frightening" figure, also considered a monster by the opposition, had all-too-civilized beginnings.

Born in New York City in 1947, Ferdinand Lewis Alcindor Jr. at once was declared a basketball prospect by the doctor because of his size—12 pounds, 11 ounces and 22½ inches long. However, the baby's father and mother prepared him for other pursuits. He grew up in an atmosphere of contentment, charged with creativity. His mother, Cora, was a singer; his father studied classical music at Juilliard in New York while working at the less exotic occupation of bill collector.

The family moved from a tough Harlem neighborhood to the more pleasant surroundings of Upper Manhattan when Lew was three years old. Later he was a pupil at St. Jude's, a Catholic grammar school run by the Presentation Sisters. And his debut there was notable.

A teacher spotted Lew in the back of the room and said: "You, there, sit down!"

"But I am sitting down," responded Alcindor in that subdued, unemotional manner that would remain a lifelong trademark. Everyone else giggled, of course.

To say he was tall was a redundancy. Although he hardly gave basketball a thought for several years, he certainly was beginning to look like a basketball player in size. But finally his height was simply too good to be true—and so, in the fourth grade, he played in his first game.

He was 5-4 and not only towered over teammates but also was almost able to look the gym teacher in the eye. Alcindor learned this "new" game at the age of nine and had to be taught everything from scratch—the pushing, pulling and passion of that peculiarly indigenous New York style.

He provided clout for the St. Jude's grammar school program. Farrell Hopkins, his first coach, put him on a program of weight lifting for strength and rope skipping for speed, coordination and reflexes. His father played handball with him to further sharpen the youngster's timing. "Lew," his

Rich Clarkson

father said, "it's up to a man to improve himself."

Alcindor stayed overtime to learn. But at first, although he worked harder than any of his team-mates, he couldn't shoot layups.

Said Hopkins: "Look, Lewie, making layups is just a matter of practice. If you miss a layup at your height, you look ridiculous. You only give people something to laugh about."

Most of all, Alcindor didn't want people to laugh. They were already snickering at his height, which had leaped to outrageous proportions in the growing-up years. In the seventh grade, he was 6-6; in the eighth, 6-8. By the time he was ready to go to high school, the mark was 6-10.

Besieged by offers from hard-selling prep schools, Alcindor finally opted to go to Power Memorial High School. It wasn't a fast decision, for the 14-year-old prodigy had to consider the advances of many institutions whose assertive recruiting tech-niques matched any college's. He decided on Power, he said, because it was just a 20-minute train ride from his house and, more importantly, because his friends went there.

He found another "friend" at the school in coach Jack Donohue, who perhaps extended the most powerful influence on Alcindor's life style other than his parents. Donohue, who had been turning out winners at the midtown Manhattan school for years, immediately put a "no-talk" ban on his precocious freshman. The iron-willed Don-ohue closed the door on visitors, announcing that no one would reach the boy without his permis-sion. That included, of course, the most vital of publicity outlets—the newspapers. The New York writers simmered, but Donohue shrugged it off.

"It wasn't something that started with Lewie," Donohue insisted. "I always had the rule, but nobody realized it until Lewie came along. It wasn't so much for the newspapers as it was for the colleges. Without being imposed upon, he got as much publicity as he was going to get. I couldn't let him be subjected to all the scouts that wanted to talk to him."

Small wonder that they wanted to talk to him. After a modest first year, Alcindor stirred wide reaction as a sophomore while leading Power to the New York Catholic high school championship. He improved enormously from his freshman season in all facets of the game, using his exceptional 220-pound body to better advantage under Donohue's savvy tutelage. He leaned closer to the basket to utilize his height and perfected a hook shot which

Lew Alcindor (33) of UCLA scores against North Carolina's Bill Bunting (31) in the 1968 championship game.

could be delivered effectively with either hand.

It was estimated by admirers that Alcindor could have had a much healthier scoring average than his 26-point mark in his junior year. But under the Donohue philosophy, individual achievements were far less important than team unity. During that championship season, another unbeaten one for Power, Alcindor also averaged 18 rebounds and several phone calls a game. The callers, usually college scouts, were sidetracked to Donohue.

"The rule is this," said the coach: "No talking to Lew until his senior year."

The accolades were abundant. "Better than Wilt Chamberlain at this stage of his career," was the consensus, referring to the seven-foot super player who had been a high school sensation at Over-brook in Philadelphia.

The offers rolled into Alcindor in letter form from hundreds of colleges. Donohue took care of those until Alcindor played his final season at Power. That was some season.

During his senior year, the school's winning streak reached an astronomical 71. It was broken, however, with a three-point loss to DeMatha of Washington, D.C., in a struggle of high school titans. Alcindor took defeat hard, crying in the locker room. The Power star blamed himself be-cause he had scored "only" 16 points, but his coach soon lifted him out of his melancholy.

"Now, wait a minute," Donohue said in mock admonishment. "It's very selfish of you to say that you lost this game. What you're implying is that you won all the other games. If you want to take the blame for losing this game, then you have to take the credit for winning the other 71. Are you willing to take the credit, yes or no?"

"No," said Alcindor, and the problem was solved by a bit of amateur psychology.

Alcindor's final high school game was more artistic. He scored 32 points and had 22 rebounds, setting the New York City record for career points (2,067) and career rebounds (2,002), as Power defeated Rice High, 73-41, for another Catholic League championship. His success story prompted this comment from coach Gene Shue of the Baltimore Bullets: "I'll trade two first-round draft choices for him right now."

But the pros had a four-year wait for Alcindor's services. First he had to go to college; and for the talent-blessed Alcindor, it was a tortuous decision. The significance of that decision was reflected in the large body of 80 newsmen who appeared for his press conference in the Power gym May 4, 1965.

Alcindor's choice of schools was announced in a short statement: "This fall, I'll be attending UCLA." But the brevity of the announcement did

167

not mirror the agonizing thought process that went into it. The young man visited many campuses, crisscrossing America by plane and train. He was romanced by basketball stars and movie stars who had personal interest in special schools. However, Alcindor's faith in John Wooden, UCLA's preacher-like coach, at last made his decision easy. "And," added Alcindor, "UCLA has everything I want in a school."

Alcindor, however, had second thoughts when he hit the UCLA campus.

There were too many phonies and a heavy amount of bigotry in California, concluded Alcindor. People constantly were asking him how the weather was up there and other such inane questions in reference to his seven-foot-plus stature. Also, it didn't help that he was so far from home. He had never been away before.

But he liked playing basketball there, all right. Wooden, that master recruiter, had assembled a freshman team of high school all-Americas including Lucius Allen, Kenny Heitz, Kent Taylor and Lynn Shackelford. The talent-rich baby Bruins won 21 straight games, outscoring the opposition by an average of 113.2 to 56.6. Alcindor smashed the school's freshman scoring record by 150 points, averaging 33.1 a game along with a fancy 21.5 rebound mark.

He maintained high academic standards, as well, and waited restlessly to join the varsity in his sophomore year: "I just want to go out there and be able to do my thing and see if it is good enough."

While Alcindor waited offstage, the varsity fell off its high pedestal, "slumped" to an 18-8 season and relinquished the national title to Texas Western (now Texas-El Paso). The UCLA backers were as anxious as Alcindor himself to get him a shot in the big time.

They weren't disappointed, either, when the "Big A" made his debut in the 1966-67 season against Southern California. He ruined the Trojans with a school-record 56 points as UCLA defeated its fierce cross-town rival, 105-90.

The new hero was terribly nervous before his coming-out party, he later admitted. Alcindor said that he was not able to eat much before the game—"just scrambled eggs and orange juice for breakfast, then tea with honey for dinner. That's all I wanted."

During postgame interviews, Wooden sat next to Alcindor and patted his arm, saying: "Great start . . . keep it up."

"I'll try," said Alcindor, hardly smiling.

Alcindor was as good as his word, accepting his responsibility as the Bruins' main means of locomotion. He used his potential to full advantage in the Wooden scheme of team play. He helped knock down opponents left and right, frustrating every rigged defense—double-teaming, triple-teaming and pressing. He shrugged off illegal maneuvers, too—elbowing, gouging, bumping and foot-stomping. His rail-like appearance was deceptive, for his graceful body contained untapped power.

"He plays best when it gets tough," said Wooden. "I'm amazed that he can take that kind of play in there and still keep his poise. I don't think there's anyone who can handle him legally."

It brought to mind an outrageous moment in high school when an opponent bit Alcindor on the arm when he couldn't do anything else with him.

Alcindor's poetic motions built a UCLA winning streak, and the newspaper publicity grew in proportion. He said he didn't like to read his notices, however: "You read some of the things they say about you and get scared of yourself. I read all these things and I say, 'Is that me they're talking about?' "

It was, indeed. Alcindor was a big shot without vanity, though.

At the end of his sophomore season, UCLA had won 30 games without a loss, including the NCAA title with a 79-64 triumph over Dayton in the finals at Louisville. Alcindor was the architect, collecting all-America recognition that year and the most outstanding player trophy in the tournament. During the season, he averaged 29.7 points and 15.5 rebounds a game.

One sports writer datelined the NCAA championship game: "Lewisville, Kentucky." Another called UCLA "Lew-CLA," and still others recorded the event in nonstop superlatives.

Said one in particular about UCLA's blitz of Dayton: "It was a symphony with a fast-tempo beat, the kind of performance that was typical of UCLA's "Firehouse Four Plus Lew" all season long. And in the game that counted most of all, the Bruins made beautiful music together, proving once again that they are, indeed, unbeatable—so unbeatable, in fact, that they are likely to rule the college basketball world for a long time."

That prophecy did come true, of course, but not without the inevitable, crushing demands. At the end of Alcindor's terrifying reign in 1969, Wooden admitted that a great weight had been lifted from his shoulders—the proverbial uneasy crown worn by rulers. "In many ways, I was glad it had come to a close," Wooden says today. "I had put great pressure on myself, because deep down I felt with Alcindor we should win a national championship

The two-year rivalry between UCLA's Lew Alcindor (33) and Houston's Elvin Hayes (44) ultimately was won by UCLA, with semifinal victories over Houston in both 1967 and 1968.

Rich Clarkson

every year. Everyone else expected that, too. There shouldn't be that type of pressure on a coach. A coaching friend of mine once said he wished he could have a player like Alcindor. I said, 'I wouldn't wish that on you.' It was nothing against the individual. It was just the pressures that go with having a player like that.''

For all his traditionalism, Wooden was perfectly adaptable where Alcindor was concerned. In this young giant, Wooden recognized one of the most remarkable basketball talents ever to come along; and he designed his new set of players into a team that made the ultimate use of that talent. Indeed, the pragmatic Wooden worked as hard as his prodigy toward the fusion of a winning team—doing his homework on the patterns of a low-post offense which he had never used before. Complementing Alcindor were some terrific young players. In Allen and Mike Warren, Wooden had a pair of guards that appeared to rank with the great Walt Hazzard-Gail Goodrich tandem of past years. Warren had averaged 16 points and played a near flawless floor game the previous season as a sophomore. Allen was a quick, fluid guard of such consummate skills that he already was winning raves. Shackelford was a superlative shooter who had been nicknamed "The Machine" while shooting 62 per cent from the floor for the unbeaten freshman team, while Heitz was a peerless defensive performer. These two sophomores became frontliners perhaps against the better judgment of Wooden, who had problems at the forward position, but they soon proved their worth. Hustling Bill Sweek, a 6-3 sophomore who had been redshirted the previous season, and 6-7 junior college transfer student Jim Nielsen were among the top reserves; and Wooden, like a master chemist, made the best use of all these new ingredients. He used an old formula: The individual skills used to the greatest potential equaled team success. Because Shackelford could shoot so well and Heitz was a superlative driver, these two forwards were used to keep the defensive pressure off the low post. The guards, meanwhile, concentrated on working the ball in to Alcindor, which in turn often allowed them to get medium-range shots. Because Alcindor was always there in the middle, the forwards could overplay to the center on defense and give away the base line—something Wooden had never before allowed. Alcindor was the great intimidator at both ends of the court, the big hub around which the Bruins wheeled.

UCLA's 1966-67 team repeated the 1963-64 record, 30 victories in 30 games and an NCAA title. Early in the season, the Bruins routed a fine Duke team; and they had no close calls until their third

170

meeting with Southern Cal. Bob Boyd's stall almost worked, but UCLA finally won the game in overtime, 40-35. There was little opposition for UCLA in the NCAA's West regional. First the Bruins ran away to a stunning 55-18 half-time lead over Wyoming and crushed the Cowboys, 109-60. "One of the worst mismatches since the lions met the Christians," Jeff Prugh wrote in the Los Angeles Times. Wyoming coach Bill Strannigan called the Bruins "the greatest collegiate team I've ever seen" and added prophetically, "I think it will win three national championships."

"They were a bit awe-struck at seeing Alcindor," reflects Wooden, "and gave us no trouble at all." Strannigan, of course, gave credit where it was due—to Alcindor's stunning visual impact. But he also underscored the blinding quickness of the UCLA guards. "Besides Lew, they have other players, too," he noted.

It was Alcindor, however, who did most of the damage against a gallant University of the Pacific team in the regional finals. Alcindor, who often seemed to play with insouciance—almost "like he's not interested," as one writer put it—took command of the game with an unaccustomed ferocity. Goaded by an overly aggressive Pacific defense, Alcindor went to work with a fury and scored 38 points to help UCLA win, 80-64. Wrote Prugh in the Times: "Lew expressed himself emotionally more often Saturday night than in any game during his career at UCLA. He was visibly, and perhaps understandably, upset at all the body contact—and once he even broke into a smile late in the game when he was cited for a foul. Twice Lew came down with a rebound, elbows flailing violently. And once he shook off Pacific's 6-5 Robert DeWitt, who was struggling with him for a loose ball."

Since everyone had been pointing for Goliath all season, rugged physical battles had been nothing new for Alcindor. "I sort of prefer that Lew get worked up," said Wooden pointedly.

Preparing for the championship round in Louisville, Wooden was noticeably fearful of Houston's rebounding muscle in the national semifinals. "That's all coach Wooden and (assistant) Jerry Norman could talk about all week," recalls Shackelford. "They kept saying how Heitz and I were going to have to rebound and screen off. I was really up for the game. They claimed it was going to be our toughest game of the year by far and Houston was going to be the most physical team we

Lew Alcindor and Curtis Rowe (30) of UCLA battle Drake's Willie Wise (42) for a rebound in the Bruins' taut 85-82 semifinal victory in 1969.

Malcolm W. Emmons

UCLA

played. They were probably right. They were a bunch of monsters!"

Guy Lewis, the free-spirited Houston coach, had assembled a collection of muscular players who had been the terror of the Southwest, the most notable among them Elvin Hayes, the dynamic "Big E." Along with the 6-9 Hayes, the Cougars presented formidable bulk up front with 6-8 Don Cruse and 6-7 Melvin Bell as well as good backcourt size with 6-5 Don Chaney a key at both ends of the court. The Cougar concept was the antithesis of Wooden's basketball philosophy—both on and off the court. Lewis' players could do what they wanted off the court and did a lot of free-lancing on it. The Cougars even could wear facial hair, something Wooden repressed at UCLA. Also in stark contrast to UCLA, Houston's practice sessions were hardly the tightly structured affairs that Wooden ran. But Houston had a multitalented squad that played a tough zone defense and rebounded with the best teams in the nation.

Hayes was one of those rare birds who talked as good a game as he played; and his eloquence came over loud and clear before the national semifinals, when he issued a public challenge to Alcindor: "What I'm really looking forward to is a head-to-head situation with Alcindor. Any time I can get this situation, I'm going to. I don't think Lew can stay with me when he's on defense. I think I have some real fine moves. This is the game we've been waiting for, and I really believe we can beat them. This will be a game the UCLA players will remember for the rest of their lives."

It was, but not for the reasons Hayes thought. Alcindor refused to accept such a meaningless challenge as a grudge duel with Hayes and instead stuck to the UCLA game plan with his typical selfless play. "We play a team," Alcindor said. "We don't play one man. You lose playing one man." Significantly, that is precisely what happened to Houston that night. Although Lewis had vowed that his Houston team would play "its own game" and not gang up its defenses against Alcindor, the Cougars began sagging two—and sometimes three—defenders on the UCLA center. As a result, Shackelford had a chance to exhibit his considerable outside shooting talent and scored a team-high 22 points for the Bruins. With three other players in double figures, including Alcindor's 19 points, UCLA was able to win without too much pressure, 73-58. "They thought they were going to stop Alcindor and floated back," remembers Wooden,

Guard Mike Warren scores a layup in UCLA's 1968 championship win over North Carolina. The Tar Heels' Dick Grubar (13) is unable to stop Warren.

"but that left Shackelford open. Apparently they were going to make him prove he could shoot from the outside—and he did. Shackelford was too good a shooter to be left open like that."

Hayes was hardly a gracious loser, charging after the game that his teammates "choked" and adding that he had found Alcindor sadly lacking. Citing statistics that he had outscored the UCLA star, 25-19, and outrebounded him, 24-20, Hayes said with conviction: "I think I really outplayed him. I can't really say Alcindor should be the number one basketball player in the country." But it was significant that while Hayes arithmetically won the battle of statistics, it was Alcindor's team that won the battle because of his presence. Again and again, holding the ball high, poised, turning, looking, thinking, he would make the right play—shoot or pass to the open man. Houston quickly abandoned its plan of attacking Alcindor when the UCLA center blocked a couple of Hayes shots. The Cougars were forced to move outside with their offense, and this created a handicap. Their outside shooting had been poor all year and became even worse with Alcindor as a distraction. Alcindor, shrugging off Hayes' disparaging remarks, said that he had done only what he was supposed to do. "We thought we'd lose if they got a lot of inside shots. So my job was to make Hayes go outside. He's a good ball player, the best I've faced this year."

With all the sound and fury surrounding the UCLA-Houston meeting, the championship game was almost anticlimactic. Dayton had upset third-ranked North Carolina, 76-62, the previous night and had a fine forward in Don May; but the Flyers were overmatched against the Bruins. There were mismatches all over the court, in fact, most noticeably at center where sophomore Dan Sadlier, only 6-6, attempted to handle Alcindor with some help from his frustrated teammates. After UCLA's almost blasé 79-64 conquest of Dayton, the UCLA players said with admiration, and not patronizingly, that the Flyers were as well-coached a team as they had faced. But Dayton had taken nearly six minutes to score; and UCLA was in front, 20-4, soon after. The Bruins had a mountainous 70-46 lead when Wooden graciously removed Alcindor and Warren with more than five minutes left in the game, and there was a 29-point spread (76-47) just after Allen—the last Bruin starter—went to the bench. Wooden already had won an NCAA title with one of the smallest teams in tournament history; now he had won the title with one of the youngest. Moreover, UCLA became the first team to put together two perfect title-winning seasons and the second to win as many as three NCAA championships (Kentucky, at this point, was still

173

the leader with four). Wooden was pleased with all of those accomplishments but perhaps even more pleased to be able to keep alive his team concept with a player who was clearly head and shoulders above everyone. "From my earliest days of coaching, some have said I have been a 'nut' on team play; and when you get a superstar like Alcindor, with all the ability he had, you still want to keep that team-play concept. We were able to do that."

UCLA's dynastic aspirations were bolstered when Alcindor, who seriously had weighed leaving UCLA for Michigan, announced he would be back with the Bruins and was "looking forward to trying to do it again."

"Everywhere you go, you're going to find something you don't like," Alcindor said after the Dayton game. "There are things I don't like (at UCLA). But right now, that's where I am and I'm going to stay."

With Alcindor the exclamation point in their success story, the Bruins moved ahead full throttle the next season despite a no-dunk rule aimed at extra-tall players. The new law, which Wooden believed to be fired directly at Alcindor, had taken away his most devastating shot—but soon made him a better all-around player. The dunk shot was Alcindor's favorite weapon, as he swooped high like a massive bird and rammed the ball through the basket with fury. The no-dunk rule, which later came to be known as the "Lew Alcindor Rule," only fired the big man to more accomplishment in his junior and senior years. Sold on fundamental team basketball rather than individual achievement, Alcindor passionately wanted to become the consummate player. "I want to improve my game," said Alcindor, always the perfectionist, "and it will be a challenge for us now that we've won the national title. Everyone will be shooting for us."

Wooden's main concern in the 1967-68 season was personnel—he had too much of it, with Mike Lynn and Edgar Lacey coming back from suspension and injury, respectively. Those two fine forwards moved back into the lineup, sharing a frontcourt position and playing alongside Shackelford and the omnipresent Alcindor. Heitz was shifted to guard behind Warren and Allen.

On paper and on the court, the Bruins were a stronger team than the previous year. They ran their winning streak to 47 games before dropping a painful 71-69 decision to Houston at the Astrodome. Alcindor was outplayed by Elvin Hayes, but there were some performance-detracting factors for the "Big A." Although he gave no excuses for his subpar performance, Alcindor was in poor physical condition for his heralded battle with Hayes. He played with double vision because of a scratched eyeball and was weak from a recent hospital stay. After the game, Alcindor was further hurt by remarks from Hayes. In short, the Houston star said that Alcindor was not as good as his advance notices. Hayes' popoff sparked a feud between the two that resulted in a revenge match for UCLA later in the season.

"They had a lot to say about us, and I didn't think they were correct," said Alcindor, speaking specifically of Hayes' downgrading, personal remarks. "They were annoying and insulting. We want to teach those people some manners."

The next time they met was in the national semifinals of the NCAA tournament in the Los Angeles Sports Arena. The Bruins gained a measure of revenge—and a big slice of respectability—with a crushing 101-69 decision over Houston that established the Bruins' supremacy once and for all. Houston had been unbeaten in 31 games prior to that conclusive defeat and ranked No. 1 in the nation.

"We really haven't said anything publicly, but we're a vindictive team," Mike Warren said afterward. "We've been looking forward to this game a long time."

With Alcindor healthy this time, he was his old intimidating self on defense and made half of his 14 shots from the floor, five of six free throws and took down 18 rebounds. Hayes, humbled, scored but 10 points and most of the time "was about as anonymous as the janitor," according to one writer. UCLA kept tormenting Houston with its full-court press, fast breaks and accurate outside shooting. The Bruins' lead was 22 points by the half and reached a peak of 44 later in the game before Wooden brought in the reserves. "That's the greatest exhibition of basketball I've ever seen," admitted Houston coach Guy Lewis, clutching the polka-dot towel in which he had buried his face most of the game. "I feel like a dead man."

"I never had a team more eager to play in the tournament than we were to play Houston that night," remembers Wooden, "and we played just a flawless game."

Some deep thinking had gone into the UCLA game plan. "I never had gone into a game with the intention of playing a zone defense," points out Wooden. "I always used a man-to-man defense, with zone principles. But I decided to use a diamond-and-one." That put Warren at the top of the key, Allen and Lynn on the wings and Alcindor under the basket, leaving Shackelford free to shadow Hayes. "I told him to just play Elvin tight, not to worry too much about him after he got the ball, but not to let him have the ball, if he possibly could."

174

Shackelford did such a good job in this regard, said one observer, that "he and Hayes looked like two guys doing a soft-shoe routine." There was certainly no complacency in the Bruin camp the week before the game. "We worked all week on the diamond-and-one," recalls Shackelford. "This was one time I felt Wooden and Norman really were trying to get me up for a game. Even during the game, they were screaming and yelling at me not to let Hayes get the ball. When he finally did hit a basket—and we were way ahead—I thought Wooden and Norman were just going to go crazy. I thought they were going to come out there on the court and kill me for letting him score."

In retrospect, Wooden believes the surprise element, as much as anything, helped provide the killing blow for UCLA. "I don't think they expected a diamond-and-one defense against them, and their coach told me afterward that they never had come up against that kind of defense before. It caused some confusion, and perhaps this confusion helped us get off to such a good start. We built up momentum and picked up confidence. Hayes was discouraged, no question about it. Houston wanted to prove that the win in the Astrodome earlier in the year was no fluke. On the contrary, it showed it was a fluke. Subconsciously, I think a lot of our players were thinking about that earlier game. I know I had no concern, no worries about the second Houston game. And I could just tell by the general attitude that the players certainly were going to be ready to play."

Actually, the Bruins encountered greater difficulty in the regionals than in the championship round that year, holding off stubborn New Mexico State, 58-49, in Albuquerque, practically the Aggies' home territory. Alcindor saved the day for UCLA, scoring 28 points and snapping up 23 rebounds in a game in which the other Bruins did not shoot well. The next night, in the finals, they shot holes in Santa Clara's reputedly tough defense and won going away, 87-66. An important performer in UCLA's defensive effort was Mike Lynn, who allowed Santa Clara's best scorer, Bud Ogden, only one field goal and six of his 13 points in the decisive first half. "It was," said Wooden, "the finest game Lynn has played all year."

After the resounding victory over Houston in the national semifinals, the Bruins appeared to tower above everyone else in the country—and that included their opponents in the NCAA title game, North Carolina. Tar Heel coach Dean Smith had said as much, for public consumption. After the Eastern champion Tar Heels had beaten a good Ohio State team, 80-66, in the semifinals, Smith noted: "Obviously, Houston and UCLA are the two best teams in the country. And now, maybe we're third." Waiting for the UCLA-Houston game to start, Smith was asked which team he would rather play in the finals. The North Carolina coach answered flippantly but rather truthfully, "Getting hit by a train or a truck, it doesn't make much difference." After Smith watched the UCLA "train" run over the Houston "truck," he added a postscript: "I hope we don't get embarrassed."

Smith reasoned that the Tar Heels would not be embarrassed if they controlled the tempo against UCLA. He planned to use his "four corners" offense, with Charlie Scott, Rusty Clark, Bill Bunting and Dick Grubar in the corners and Larry Miller roaming free in the middle. Once the Tar Heels got through the UCLA press—or if they got through the press—they could look for the high-percentage shot. That way, Smith figured, his team might be within striking distance of the Bruins at the end.

Contrary to his usual policy, Smith let his players watch the first half of the Houston-UCLA game. But the Tar Heels were not awed by either team. "Young men," Smith said, "are not as realistic as coaches. I know it will take a miracle—but I have confidence in them."

Smith's miracle never came about. Recognizing early that only Miller and Scott seemed willing to shoot, UCLA concentrated on those two; and the two Tar Heels managed merely 26 points between them. Alcindor, meanwhile, was scoring 34 for UCLA against North Carolina's man-to-man defense and grabbing 16 rebounds. Time after time, a teammate would lob a pass to the agile seven-footer under the basket, and Alcindor would drop the ball in over bewildered North Carolina players. And UCLA confidently took North Carolina in the championship game by a record margin of 23 points, 78-55. "We didn't play the perfect game, and you have to play the perfect game to beat them," said Smith, who called Alcindor "the greatest player who ever played the game" and UCLA "the greatest basketball team of all time."

A gauge of the caliber of this starting UCLA five emerged when four of the Bruin players were picked on the all-tournament team. Alcindor, winning the most outstanding player award for the second year, was joined by Allen, Warren and Shackelford. The UCLA player who was left out, Lynn, had hit eight of 10 shots against Houston and would have merited all-tournament consideration except for North Carolina's superlative Miller.

UCLA left little doubt as to which was the best team in the country that year, dominating the championship round as no team had before. In fact, after the victory over Houston in the semifi-

175

nals, the outcome of the championship game seemed such a foregone conclusion that they failed to sell out the Los Angeles Sports Arena. "I think our performance against Houston convinced people that we were going to be the champion," notes Wooden, "but they could be so wrong on that. North Carolina had a fine basketball team."

It was, however, the Houston game that weighed the most in everyone's thinking, including the UCLA players. Alcindor said after the conquest of North Carolina: "The game against North Carolina counted a lot, but the win over Houston was our most satisfying victory. Getting to play them again is something that we all prayed for. I guess you could say I definitely wanted to win that one more

than any game I've played since I've been at UCLA."

For Alcindor's last year, Wooden again faced the pressures of success; and this time they had mounted even higher than before. "I wanted to win three NCAA championships in a row," he says, "because with Alcindor I felt we had a chance to do that. We had our foot in the door—of course the door can be slammed on the foot—but we had gotten by the first two stages of it and had the third one coming up. I never talked about this to the outside, but I knew deep down that I put more pressure on myself."

Some familiar faces were conspicuously absent in the UCLA camp for the 1968-69 season. Jerry

Malcolm W. Emmons

Norman, the hard-working assistant who had assembled the Bruins' championship teams of the Hazzard, Goodrich and Alcindor years, left basketball to become a stockbroker. Lucius Allen, a peerless guard who was to inherit Mike Warren's playmaking role, was lost for academic reasons; and Wooden was understandably apprehensive about his backcourt situation. Sounding an alarm, he noted, "Whoever they are, they'll be the most inexperienced set of guards I've ever had at UCLA." Wooden moved to shore up what most certainly seemed to be the weakest part of the team. He had but one "true guard" in 6-1 Donnie Saffer; so he moved forwards Bill Sweek and Kenny Heitz to the backcourt, imported an intelligent junior college transfer in John Vallely and welcomed a redshirt into the ranks, sophomore Terry Schofield.

The frontcourt was certainly no problem for Wooden. In that area, he had what he called "the strongest front line in the history of college basketball." Emphasized Wooden: "We have experience, depth, height and good quickness among them." The returnees included Alcindor, Shackelford and Jim Nielsen. The newcomers were highly-regarded sophomores—6-6 Curtis Rowe, 6-8 Sidney Wicks and 6-9 Steve Patterson, a trio that eventually would become the nucleus of future UCLA national championship teams.

Wooden weighed a heavy psychological implication as he looked ahead to the season: the players' collective frame of mind. He was concerned especially about the intensity of the seniors, who possibly might not be as hungry after feeding so well on the rest of the college basketball world for two years. "After successes like we had," Wooden says, "seniors sometimes go down, and that was the problem I felt we had for the following year. I made lots of notes in this regard when we began practice for that 1968-69 season. I was alert to this factor and tried to make sure we kept the same intensity."

With Alcindor back at the old stand, it was business as usual for UCLA in 1968-69. Vallely became a pleasant surprise for the Bruins as the season clicked along. "By the middle of the year," notes Wooden, "the players were calling Vallely our money man. He was the one they wanted to get the jump shot in the play where you had to have the basket." UCLA went through 23 games without a serious challenge, although Purdue's Rick Mount and Notre Dame's Austin Carr had good individual

The defensive play of UCLA's Kenny Heitz (22) on high-scoring Rick Mount of Purdue proved to be a decisive factor in the 1969 championship game.

games against the Bruins. Then, with the Pacific-8 Conference title and an NCAA tournament berth locked up, the Bruins had a short cold spell. They struggled to beat California in overtime in what Wooden called their toughest game in three years. Then came two equally tough games with Southern Cal—the second one of which they lost by two points when the Trojans played an exasperating slowdown game. That was the only time UCLA was beaten in the 1968-69 season, although the Bruins did have a frighteningly close call before subduing Drake in the national semifinals of the NCAA championship at Louisville.

Although the Bruins had appeared "kind of sluggish" to Wooden and he feared overconfidence in playing the regional at Pauley Pavilion—their home court—they beat New Mexico State by 15 points in the opening round of the West regional and then crushed Santa Clara by 38. Afterward, Wooden's fears had dissolved. "We're playing like we should," he said after watching his ferocious zone press at work in the regional finals. "We're hungrier now. If we play this well next week, we're going to be mighty, mighty tough."

Against Drake, the Bruins proved they could be tough but also showed they could be human. What started as an apparent runaway (7-0 after 3½ minutes) soon turned into a grim battle in which the Bruins had to claw, scratch and pick their way out of near-disaster. John Wooden and his team had come down to the last two games of the NCAA tournament with so many honors pressing against them, they hardly could keep track of them all. Drake, on the other hand, might have felt slighted by the fact that it had received little attention despite its 24-4 record, its Missouri Valley playoff victory over Louisville and its Midwest regional championship. The Bulldogs, who had not been ranked nationally until the final week of the season, appeared to take out their frustration on UCLA. Willie McCarter and Gary Zeller did the critical shooting for Drake, and Dolph Pulliam led a tough defense that so harassed the Bruins they could not see Alcindor well enough to get the ball in to him. Only Vallely's hot shooting in the second half saved UCLA. Because of him, the Bruins still led, 83-74, with a little over a minute left. But then Drake scored eight straight points to cut UCLA's lead to one point before Shackelford was fouled near the end. He made two free throws for UCLA's final 85-82 margin, and Wooden sighed, "I feel like I've had a reprieve. If John Vallely had not shot so well, we probably would have lost." The UCLA guard wound up with 29 points, and Wooden said it was the best game he ever played at UCLA. Alcindor, on the other hand,

"didn't play one of his better games," according to Wooden, but still managed to score 25 points and grab 21 rebounds. "Against the man-to-man defense," said Wooden, "I felt he should have gotten open better. Maybe it was our inability to get him the ball."

Whatever deficiencies Wooden thought Alcindor had in the semifinals the big man made up for in the national championship game against Purdue. Playing 36 minutes, Alcindor scored 37 points and took down 20 rebounds. Purdue, never in the game, did not have the quickness of Drake; and its man-to-man coverage of Alcindor was a disaster. The same team which had embarrassed proud North Carolina, 92-65, behind exciting Rick Mount in the semifinals was just a prosaic bunch against UCLA. Almost as important to the Bruins as Alcindor in the finals was the play of Kenny Heitz, the 6-3 guard with eyeglasses and wispy arms and legs who had the job of guarding the ubiquituous Mount. It wasn't easy for Heitz. Mount, one of the college game's best pure shooters, had scored 36 points against North Carolina. Against UCLA he fired in his first two field goal attempts from the corner before the championship game was minutes old. "I was scared to death, frankly," said Heitz. But the Bruin guard recovered nicely and shadowed Mount with uncommon ferocity the rest of the way. Mount did finish with 28 points, but he hit on only 12 of 36 shots—missing 14 in a row at one point—and most of his points came in the second half when they did not mean much. By then, UCLA had pulled ahead comfortably en route to a historic 92-72 victory that put the Bruins in a class by themselves in college basketball. UCLA's unprecedented third straight national title and equally unmatched achievement of a fifth championship in six years were clearly personal triumphs for Wooden and Alcindor. Five different schools—including UCLA itself—had won two NCAA titles in a row, but they all tripped on the way to a third. Only San Francisco in the middle 1950s and Cincinnati in the early 1960s really had

178

come close to reaching that goal.

Alcindor was the first "big man" Wooden ever had, and the ardent champion of the fast-break attack was happy to "have the challenge of change." Wooden displayed a legendary talent to adjust his philosophies to his players' abilities, one of the keys to his remarkable success.

When the championship game was over, Alcindor was decorated with more honors—the first player ever to win the tournament's most outstanding player award three years in succession. The achievement bettered such back-to-back winners as Oklahoma A&M's (now Oklahoma State) Bob Kurland (1945-46), Kentucky's Alex Groza (1948-49) and Ohio State's Jerry Lucas (1960-61). Alcindor also leaped past Lucas and West Virginia's Jerry West into third place on the NCAA tournament's all-time scoring ladder, finishing with 304 points behind Houston's Hayes (358) and Cincinnati's Oscar Robertson (324).

It was enough to make a father proud, and Ferdinand Lewis Alcindor Sr., watching the game from the stands, broke into a big grin and moved into a seat in the middle of the UCLA band to play first trombone.

"You could hardly blame Ferdinand Lewis Sr. for blowing his own horn," remarked a sports writer. "He had just finished watching his son make college basketball history with what may have been his greatest all-around performance yet."

After the outstanding performance, Alcindor headed for the nearest basket, reached up and unlaced the net for a necklace. Wooden wished it could have been diamonds.

"Lew's unusual physical characteristics were a tremendous factor in the accomplishment of three straight championships," said the coach. "But it was his willingness to lend this ability toward the welfare of the team that really insured it."

Sitting atop a teammate in the crush of the traditional net-cutting ceremonies seemed like an odd place for Alcindor. After all, he always had been the one to carry the team on his shoulders.

1970·1971
THE BEAT GOES ON

"It will be fun coaching to win again, rather than coaching to keep from losing."—John Wooden, UCLA basketball coach

With Lew Alcindor only a towering memory at UCLA, the highly contemptuous have-nots of the college basketball world hoped to bring the Bruins down to earth in the 1969-70 season. "Lots of coaches and people said now without the big man I'd get my comeuppance," says Wooden. "There were plenty of people who felt that way. Other teams had deep pride, and they wanted to prove that they had something in their own right."

But if success bred contempt for UCLA, it also inspired more success. The graduation of the mountainous Alcindor did nothing to ebb the flow of victories at UCLA. Rather, it kindled more creativity in Wooden.

With Alcindor gone, Wooden reverted to an earlier game plan of his career—the high-post, running offense. "I feel more comfortable with this style," he said. "We used the low-post offense solely because of Alcindor and the personnel we had with him." In 6-9 Steve Patterson, Wooden had an ideally unselfish center to serve as the hub of this style. An articulate, engaging junior, Patterson had been redshirted for a year, playing every day in practice against Alcindor; and he had matured beautifully for the assignment. He would be the center of an exquisitely powerful frontline that included 6-8 Sidney Wicks and 6-6 Curtis Rowe, two lithe, aggressive forwards who had come storming out of the black ghetto of Los Angeles. Wicks, probably the most talented of all on this extremely well-balanced team, had been erratic as a sophomore but now could unleash his fierce driving game with the absence of the big man in the low-post position.

"Wicks finally understood what I wanted," points out Wooden, "and started playing the kind of game I knew he was capable of and working into our style very well. I consider Wicks one of the greatest competitors I had. He was never afraid to take a shot in the clutch, and he often made the big defensive play in the clutch. Also, he could bring the ball downcourt against pressure."

Traditionally, Wooden had depended on the backcourt men to control the ball and the tempo of the game; this job was put in the capable, experienced hands of John Vallely. Both Terry Schofield and Kenny Booker, a redshirt transfer from Long Beach City College and a converted forward, were ready to fill in. Up from the freshman team was an excellent outside shooter in Henry Bibby, a versatile long-range import from North Carolina. The 1969-70 Bruins could run, press and shoot with the best of Wooden's teams, yet many of their performances were strangely flat and uninspired. They won several close games but lacked the fire and passion of Wooden's past national champions. One writer pointed out that they seemed "unemotional to the point of nonchalance."

As was his custom at the start of the season, Wooden wrote his prediction for the year on a slip of paper, sealed it in an envelope and put it in a desk drawer. The figures he jotted down were "11-3," meaning that he thought the Bruins would have an 11-3 record in the Pacific-8 Conference. The games he picked to lose that year were with Oregon State, Washington and Southern California. Wooden was close—the Bruins had a 12-2 record, losing to Southern Cal and Oregon. But what he couldn't see in his crystal ball was the significance of the 78-65 defeat by Oregon up in Eugene. Until that point, the Bruins had been unbeaten in 21 games but hardly had played as a team. There had been what some players had called a "lack of communication" among themselves; this spilled onto the basketball court, where a lack of unity was evident despite an unbeaten record. The Bruins beat an average Minnesota team, 72-71, on a Bibby jump shot; Princeton,

76-75, on a Wicks jumper after Geoff Petrie and John Hummer almost helped the Tigers spring an upset, and Oregon State, 72-71, on a John Ecker hook shot after Wicks had fouled out. Wicks and Rowe were playing two-man basketball and, it seemed, so were Patterson and Vallely. The Bruins' style had been almost more cocky than confident, and the loss to Oregon in the 22nd game of the season certainly shook things up.

"The loss to Oregon—and what came after it—was the key to our season," Patterson would later explain. "There had been things beneath the surface that no one had talked about before—a communications breakdown. After we began winning and winning, it became accepted and we stopped communicating. The defeat at Oregon helped us reestablish our priorities."

It was Bibby, the sophomore, who had spoken out for team togetherness, expressing a strong desire to repeat as national champions. The Bruins understood this could not be accomplished without total commitment to each other. "In the end," Patterson remembers, "all of us agreed that any-

thing was worth sacrificing for a national title."

When the Bruins lost again, it was after they had clinched the Pacific-8 championship and a berth in the NCAA tournament; and it was a respected old foe that did it—Bob Boyd's Southern Cal team. But after that 87-86 upset, the Bruins came back the next night to beat the Trojans by 13 points in the last game of the regular season and continued to roll right through tournament play. First, Long Beach State went down, 88-65, as Bibby bombed over the 49ers' zone defense for 20 points and Wicks knifed inside for 20 more. "Jerry Tarkanian used nothing but zone defenses," Wooden recalls of the Long Beach coach, "and our team was well cut out to play against zone defensive teams. As a matter of fact, I think I would have enjoyed every team playing a zone against us, with Bibby and Vallely both capable of shooting from the outside and with Patterson capable of shooting from around the high-post area."

The next night, in the regional finals, Utah State gave UCLA trouble only for the first half—when the Bruins seemed too confident for their own good. "Subconsciously," said Wooden, "I'm sure our players underestimated them. They were a little too loose. I noticed it the day before in practice. All our adult followers were overconfident, so how could our young men help but be that, too? Everybody else said we'd beat Utah State by 50 points. I guess our players thought they'd win by 40 or so." In the second half, it was a different UCLA team. Prideful rather than cocky, the Bruins went to their strengths against a man-to-man defense—working the ball in to Wicks and Rowe, who simply outmuscled the Aggie inside men for short jump shots and layups. Wicks and Rowe combined for 52 points, and the Bruins won going away, 101-79.

Although Wooden's team was playing its best ball of the year, the UCLA coach approached the national finals with less confidence than in the Alcindor years. Of the possible opponents in the Final Four, Wooden indicated more respect and fear for New Mexico State than either Jacksonville or St. Bonaventure (now without injured star Bob Lanier). "They've been waiting for the opportunity to beat us for two years," said Wooden of New Mexico State, "since we put them out of the running for the championship. They had fine teams then—ones that could have gone all the way if they'd gotten past us—and they're a fine team now. They've got a lot of seniors, and that has to

Curtis Rowe (30) was a major factor in UCLA's 1970 and 1971 championships. Here, he stops Jacksonville's Mike Blevins (21) from passing.

180

UCLA

inspire them; and I'm very high on their coach, Lou Henson. He's one of the better coaches I know."

However, UCLA now seemed like a team on fire. "I think the players wanted to win the NCAA title that year, probably more than they ever had," reflects Wooden. "I think they were trying to prove they could do something like that without Alcindor. Our team was playing really well at this time. It seems as far as overall balance at tournament time was concerned, this particular year we were in good shape."

Later, Wooden would complain that he wasn't happy with his team's offense or defense in spots, especially the number of times his offense turned the ball over (20). But the simple fact remained that UCLA had beaten a fine New Mexico State team with Jimmy Collins and Sam Lacey by 16 points, 93-77.

"Going in," noted Henson, "I'd stated that we would have to do something about UCLA's front-line if we were going to beat them. But they have so much speed and quickness that there was no way we could cope with them in the corners, either Wicks or Rowe. They're a fine club, well balanced and well coached. If they have a weakness, I don't know what it is."

UCLA's only weakness, as far as newsmen were concerned, was in the area of public relations. Contrary to the liberal policies of other teams, Wooden refused to let his players talk to the press—a rule that he had enforced all year. As Vallely explained while stopping off at a drinking fountain on the way to the team bus one day: "We've gotten burned by the news media, and I guess the coach doesn't want it to happen again. Some writers twist things . . . we've had troubles all over." As Wooden explained it to newsmen, "My job is to keep the team spirit high. You guys always want to talk to some player, and that doesn't help our morale any. When one player is given too much publicity, it tends to create problems."

This presented a sharp contrast to the team the Bruins would meet in the national finals, the free-spirited, free-lancing Jacksonville Dolphins. A classic confrontation was shaping up between two distinctly different philosophies—those of John Wooden and Jacksonville's flamboyant Joe Williams. "It was the discipline of UCLA vs. the devil-may-care attitude of Jacksonville," noted one observer, "the Establishment vs. the Age of Aquarius."

At the very moment Wooden was declaring his interview ban, Jacksonville's goateed center, Artis Gilmore, was crying out to newsmen from the other end of the practice floor, "Hey, man, we'll talk to you." The remark symbolized the Dolphins' wide-open approach to everything. Williams imposed few restrictions on the Dolphins, from shooting the breeze to shooting the ball. Once asked if he kept any kind of rein at all on his players, the flashy, mod-dressing Williams replied, "They do what they want to do."

Wooden, on the other hand, had much more of a militaristic approach to the game; and Williams' liberal style at first offended him.

"We eventually became great friends," Wooden says, "but prior to that I must say I did not like him. He is the wildest dresser I think I have ever seen. His team practiced to music, and I felt while watching them they didn't have any discipline—I didn't like that at all. After seeing our teams work out the day before the championship game, one of the writers did a little story about the old against the new, the staid against the mod . . . how they practiced, sort of on their own, and how Williams dressed. I remember they said that I dressed 'with all the sartorial splendor of an undertaker.' My wife, Nell, read that. Up to that time, I never wore anything but dark suits; but from that time on, she got me some blue shirts and yellow shirts and I started wearing sport coats."

The color of Williams' clothes matched the colorful show his Dolphins put on in practice. One of their best acts was a Harlem Globetrotter-type routine in which they whipped the ball around artfully to the tune of "Sweet Georgia Brown." The Dolphins entertained everyone during their jazzy practice sessions prior to the national finals at College Park, Maryland—even the Bruins themselves, who sat in the front row and smiled. "Greatest thing I ever saw," said Steve Patterson.

Showmanship aside, Jacksonville had the kind of material to give the Bruins plenty of trouble, despite a close-call victory over injury-weakened St. Bonaventure in the semifinals. Gilmore, at 7-2, was being hailed as the new Alcindor; and the Jacksonville giant had more than adequate rebounding help up front in 7-0 Pembrook Burrows and 6-10 Rod McIntyre—a frontcourt that averaged a fantastic seven feet. In the backcourt were Vaughn Wedeking, the prime mover of the team, and Rex Morgan, 6-5 and dangerous all over the court. Gilmore and Morgan wore the suitable sobriquet of "Batman and Robin"—recognized as the dynamic duo of the college basketball world. Wooden certainly was cognizant of this factor in working up strategy for the title game.

"I had felt that we must keep the ball away from Gilmore underneath," remembers Wooden. "We talked about that a lot, and I wanted Morgan played tight on the side with Vallely guarding him.

Rich Clarkson

UCLA's Sidney Wicks goes high to block a shot taken by seven-footer Artis Gilmore of Jacksonville in the 1970 championship game. Wicks' defensive play against Gilmore turned the tide in favor of UCLA.

Wicks would guard Gilmore, and Patterson would play their other seven-footer. I felt we should front Gilmore, and we had Curtis Rowe floating back in case they tried to lob the ball over to him. Wicks didn't like that. He accepted it but said he could guard Gilmore from behind. But I didn't feel there was any way that Sidney could guard Gilmore alone, considering the height discrepancy."

The Bruins' usual angry attention to business was not evident at first, and the game plan faltered. "Gilmore was getting some baskets," remembers Wooden, "and they were hurting us." Wooden was forced to call a timeout and figure out a new strategy. During the huddle, Wicks inserted, "Let me get behind Gilmore."

"I knew it wasn't going to be any worse," says Wooden, "so we switched Sidney behind him. I had learned a lot about Sidney through the years, and I wanted him confident, so I said, 'Well, all right, you go behind him. Maybe I was wrong at the beginning. Now, you can do the job.' He liked to be built up, this I know. So Sidney went behind him, and he did a tremendous job."

Wicks, a full six inches shorter than the Jacksonville center, was sky-high in more ways than one. He quickly soared over Gilmore's mountainous frame to block some of his shots; and from that point on, the Dolphin star was not the intimidating force he had been in past games. In all, Wicks blocked five Gilmore shots, as well as accumulating 17 points and 18 rebounds in a feverish all-around game to help the Bruins wipe out a nine-point deficit and draw out to an 80-69 victory. In slaying the giant, Wicks had help from Patterson, who sagged back to harass Gilmore from the front. When Patterson left Burrows open, Rowe floated over to help out. Vallely, meanwhile, put a clamp on Morgan, holding him to merely 10 points and scoring 15 himself while handing out five assists. "Vallely played one of his best ball games," says Wooden. "He made some excellent passes off the fast break. His play and the play of Rowe in particular were sort of lost in the spectacular things that Wicks did."

During UCLA's time of trial early in the first half, Rowe was more or less conceded the medium jump shot by Jacksonville; he took advantage of it for most of his team-leading 19 points. The classic

Sidney Wicks of UCLA drives to the basket in the Bruins' 93-77 semifinal win over New Mexico State in 1970.

display of team performance included 17 points and 11 rebounds from Patterson, and Bibby played 38 minutes and contributed eight points and four rebounds from his backcourt position. Talk in the UCLA dressing room underscored the Bruins' feverish dedication to team play and fierce pride in this particular triumph. "Everybody was looking forward to playing without Lew Alcindor," noted Rowe. "Right now, if Alcindor was on the team, who would the reporters be talking to? Look around you. The reporters are with five people, and that's beautiful. Every time somebody mentions three titles in a row, they say Lew did it. Now we just proved that four other men on the team could play basketball—with the best of them."

Rowe added firmly: "This victory is much sweeter than last year's. It was a total team."

UCLA's fourth straight national championship and sixth in seven years emphasized the value of quickness and also was a measure of the development of Wicks, a player who, in Wooden's words, "could rise to the occasion." Wicks certainly did rise against Gilmore, unleashing the kind of defen-

Malcolm W. Emmons

sive fury that made Bill Russell and Lew Alcindor famous in past NCAA play. "It was just like playing against Lew in practice last year," said Wicks, "except that I never blocked any of his shots. No matter how well I did, Lew could always score on me." This was specifically the way Wicks blocked the great Gilmore: "Those jumpers he took—I let those go. I'm surprised he didn't take more of those shots. My job was to make him commit himself. I wanted to wait back and let him make the first move. If I'd gone up with him instead of waiting, I would have been at his mercy. So he went up, then I went up." Gilmore, who scored a subpar 19 points, noted that nobody ever had blocked that many of his shots in one game. "He caught me by surprise," said Gilmore. "He must have watched my moves on films, or something. He was right on me. I was taking my jumper too much when really I should have been using my body more before

184

Malcolm W. Emmons

Artis Gilmore of Jacksonville.

shooting." Perhaps Wicks never could actually be the dominating force that Alcindor was in a game, but he was good enough for Wooden that year. "I don't think I would trade him for anyone else in the country," said Wooden about a player who had turned from a bench warmer one year into the most outstanding player in the NCAA tournament the next.

Wicks had not evolved into a swan overnight. "I had a long uphill climb to make," he says. "At UCLA, it takes a while to fit into the system. But I decided I had to make the personal sacrifices. So for the first time, I came to practice in shape. I'd never really done that before. I was disappointed because I didn't play much the year before. But this time I was in a better frame of mind."

Wooden, now elevated to still another level in his profession, received Presidential certification for his latest triumph when Richard Nixon made a congratulatory phone call to his home. As Wooden remembers it, he and his family were all set to go out to dinner when the phone rang. "The operator kept me waiting a while, and my family was hungry. I finally said, 'I'm going to have to go—my family's waiting. Will this be very long?' And the operator said that this was the President of the United States calling. I choked up a little at that point and replied, 'Oh, in that case, I'll wait.'" Nixon apologized for not being able to offer his congratulations in person, "but there was this postal problem, or something," Wooden recalls. "Then he talked to my grandchildren and was very gracious to them. I know he fell out of favor and he resigned from the Presidency, but I still have a warm feeling for what he did." Wooden's son, James, brought the coach down to earth afterwards when he asked, "Did the President pay for the call?"

Vallely was the only UCLA player gone when the next season started, bright with hope. Bibby was given the job as the ball handler, while Booker and Schofield, a bright, sensitive senior who wrote poetry, shared the other backcourt position. "I started Booker a little more than Schofield," says Wooden, "because he was the stronger defensive player. Schofield was a better offensive threat. I preferred to start the defensive player and bring the offensive player in a little later."

Bibby did all that was asked by Wooden, although his added responsibilities as playmaker threw off his shooting a little. Wicks and Rowe, eyeing fat professional contracts, were at the top of their games. But even at that, the Bruins seemed to have forgotten old lessons. They grew blase on

occasion, and there were some close calls during the 1970-71 season. Bibby pulled out a game against Oregon at Eugene, Wicks against Oregon State in Corvallis and Booker against Southern Cal—and the Bruins lost at Notre Dame when they couldn't stop Austin Carr. In addition, there were close conference victories against Washington at home and Stanford on the road. Wooden sensed the general lack of fire in his team. At one point of the season, he said: "We're not sharp. We're not hungry—not at all."

Yet at the end of the regular season, the seemingly lackluster Bruins had surpassed even Wooden's expectations. In his traditional preseason prophecy, he had predicted a 12-2 record for his team in the conference, but the Bruins happily went undefeated in 14 Pac-8 games. Because of the uncertainty at guard and very little bench strength, many believed this season to be Wooden's finest coaching performance.

Close calls continued to be a trademark of this championship season in the NCAA tournament when the Bruins managed to escape with a 57-55 victory over Long Beach State in the West regional finals at Salt Lake City, Utah. Easy winners over Brigham Young and the heralded Kresimir "The Wild Giraffe" Cosic in its opening game, UCLA was extended to the limit before beating Jerry Tarkanian's team. Almost always residing on the edge of disaster all season, the Bruins seemed about to topple over when the 49ers held a commanding 44-33 lead with 14 minutes to go. "The Bruins' outside shooters were so cold," noted one writer, "it appeared they'd spent the night in Siberia, not sunny Salt Lake." Another dispiriting blow to UCLA was Wicks' foul trouble. The Bruin forward had suffered four personals and was sitting on the bench. "At that moment," said Wooden, "I thought that Mrs. Wooden and I could leave for Houston a day early and just have a good time as spectators at the national finals."

But Wooden then made what many believed to be the most crucial move of the game. He pulled Schofield, who was 6-3, and inserted 6-6½ John Ecker into the lineup. That left only one guard—Bibby—to work along with Ecker, Rowe, Larry Farmer and Patterson. "Putting Ecker in made us stronger defensively," noted Wooden at the time, "and defense is what has sustained us this season." You couldn't notice the difference at first. Ecker didn't score a point and didn't get a rebound, but the Bruins slowly began to come together—and Long Beach State began to come apart.

"John played very well for us," Wooden remembers. "If you just look at the statistics, as people are apt to do, you'd say he didn't do

anything. But I would say his being in the game was very instrumental in the fact that we were able to pull the game out."

With six minutes to play, UCLA finally pulled into a tie at 50-50 on a long shot by Bibby. Not long after, Long Beach State's leading player, Ed Ratleff, fouled out—and with him went an immeasurable amount of poise. With 3:07 remaining and the score tied, 53-53, Long Beach State went into a delay game, seeking only the good shot. But Dwight Taylor, who had replaced Ratleff, cast off a low-percentage shot from the corner that missed. It was UCLA's turn to hold the ball this time, and the Bruins stalled until there were 25 seconds left.

"I felt now, at this point of the game, we had the better end of it," says Wooden, "and if it went into overtime I thought we were going to be in better shape. I thought now if we were to play it safe, we couldn't lose it—and we might win it."

Wicks, now quarterbacking the Bruins with his customary élan, made four foul shots in a row in the final 25 seconds for the deciding points; Wooden acknowledged afterwards that no victory in recent memory had come any harder than that 57-55 decision. "This is the best defensive team we've played this year," he said.

In retrospect, Wooden still sweats out that game. "It was a rough, tough ball game," he says. "There seemed to be a little bit of feeling between the teams, perhaps because of the proximity of the schools and perhaps because we had knocked them out in previous tournaments when they felt they had a real fine team. We were a little sluggish and didn't get the outside shooting I had hoped for against the type of zone they used. And then Tarkanian changed the zone, too. We were looking for his 1-2-2; he came up with a 2-3, and it did cause us considerable trouble. Tarkanian felt, as many others did, that our outside shooting definitely was suspect. In a 2-3 zone, you give up a little more on the outside shooting, but you're definitely stronger underneath; he wanted to be stronger underneath against Wicks and Rowe and Patterson."

The Bruins did better against Kansas' zone in the national semifinals in Houston. The Jayhawks' defense couldn't react nearly as fast as Long Beach's, and Bibby and Patterson often found themselves in the corners and at the top of the key alone—without so much as a hand in their faces. The jump shots went up and in—in the first half UCLA hit seven attempts from 15 feet and out— and the Bruins had a 32-25 lead at intermission. UCLA's fine outside shooting forced Kansas coach Ted Owens to revert to a man-to-man defense which really played to the Bruins' strong suit— quickness. UCLA's starting five bolted into a 68-53

lead before Wooden put in his reserves; and the Jayhawks made the final score respectable before losing, 68-60. Once again, the Bruin defense was outstanding, "taking Kansas out of the things it wanted to do," according to Wooden. And once again, it was Wicks who was the maestro of this band. During the game, he exhorted his teammates ("Henry, slow it up," and, "Steve, get over there"). He shouted at the man guarding him, 6-10 Dave Robisch, as he dribbled the ball up the court ("Look out, here I come"). At one point, Wicks hollered to Robisch, "Halt." His opponent did. There were "bravos" from the UCLA partisans

among the NCAA record crowd of 31,428 in the gaudy splendor of the Houston Astrodome. And there were cries of dismay from the Jayhawk fans, who watched Wicks cleanly block Robisch's first shot of the night, much the way he had against Jacksonville's Artis Gilmore a season before. Wicks drove and leaped for a team-high 21 points and consistently and calmly broke Kansas' press with Robisch hovering over him like an octopus.

In the national finals, UCLA faced another zoning team in Villanova[1], coached by Jack Kraft and led by Howard Porter and Hank Siemiontkowski. It was UCLA's ability to shoot from the

Neil Leifer, Sports Illustrated

Coach John Wooden of UCLA with Bruin players Sidney Wicks and Curtis Rowe, key factors in the Bruins' success in 1970 and 1971.

Malcolm W. Emmons

outside that propelled the Bruins into a 45-37 half-time lead; but then, ironically, they almost let the game slip away by a reluctance to shoot at the start of the second half. Wooden ordered his team into a stall with hopes of drawing the Wildcats out of their zone. "If we made them play us man-to-man," explained Wooden, "I felt we could beat Villanova man-for-man. If we had let them stay in their zone, I was afraid we might have hit a cold spot and started missing our shots for three or four minutes."

Wooden's strategy was inspired by an additional motive. He was trying to underscore one of his pet peeves—the lack of a clock to prevent stalling in the college game. "I've always wanted a 30-second clock," Wooden said later in the dressing room. "Maybe now the rules committee will think a little bit more about putting one in."

An NCAA tournament record crowd of 31,765, however, didn't like the maneuver—"You're the national champions," shouted many in the audience, "play ball!"—but the stall achieved its purpose. However, Wooden knew something else could happen if the Bruins went into their delay game—his team could lose its momentum. And that's exactly what happened.

Villanova, shocked by Patterson's 20 points in the first half, inexorably began cutting into UCLA's lead, which had reached as high as 12 points in the second half. The Wildcats did it uncharacteristically, with a man-to-man defense that got them the ball. At 5:09, Porter's sweeping hook shot brought Villanova within four points at 58-54. At 2:38, another Porter specialty—a base-line, turn-around jump shot—moved the Wildcats within three of the Bruins at 61-58.

But then UCLA's championship form surfaced, as the Bruins came up with what probably was the key play of the game. Bibby worked free underneath on a pick by Patterson, took a Wicks pass from the corner and put in a layup for a 63-58 UCLA lead. Porter came back with a 15-footer, but 63-60 was as close as Villanova got the rest of the way. The Bruins held on to win, 68-62, for their closest championship victory to that point. Previous to that six-point margin, UCLA's closest calls in final games were a pair of 11-pointers, over Michigan in 1965 and Jacksonville in 1970. But despite the tenuous margin, Wooden emphasized

Steve Patterson, shown here in the 1970 championship game against Jacksonville, scored 29 points against Villanova in the 1971 title game.

that he hadn't been concerned. "I didn't feel, in any way, that we would lose it," he said. Nor did Bibby—an outstanding tournament player throughout his UCLA career. "We knew it wasn't easy this time," he said. "But we've played so many games the same way this year, we knew how to handle it. We knew we could just hold out, be patient and play good basketball."

Standing in an unusual spotlight was Patterson, who had suffered through an erratic year prior to the NCAA finals. He had shot poorly most of the season and tossed his niftiest passes to the opposition. In fact, Wooden benched him for almost the whole game against Oregon State for lethargic play. Another time, he didn't start because he was late for the team dinner. And in the national semifinals against Kansas, he played as if he had been in a trance, managing just six points. But in the championship game, the sensitive, prideful Patterson showed up inspired against Villanova and scored a game-high 29 points, 12 more than anyone on the UCLA team. A mini-family celebration followed, Patterson's parents vaulting over the edge of the four-foot-high Astrodome floor, tearfully hugging their son and dancing around and around in circles with him.

Patterson looked up at the scoreboard, saw his name in red and yellow lights with a big "29" next to it and shook his head back and forth.

"I might as well die tonight," he said. "I can never do something like that again."

Emergence of the sleeping giant pointed up the basic strength of the UCLA team. As Villanova coach Jack Kraft would later emphasize:

"You hold down Wicks and Rowe as well as we did and that third guy kills you. It just shows you what a good club can do."

187

[1]Villanova's second-place finish later was vacated, due to the use of a student-athlete who was declared ineligible subsequent to the tournament.

Malcolm W. Emmons

1972 · 1973
THE WALTON GANG

"We played them (UCLA) the only way we could and hoped to stay close. We were close a long time. We were not close at the end. No one ever is."—Bob Gaillard, University of San Francisco basketball coach

If not for an uncharacteristic loss of composure in the 1974 NCAA tournament, UCLA would have blazed more new trails in college basketball. The inexplicable letdown happened against North Carolina State in the national semifinals at basketball-crazy Greensboro, North Carolina, and John Wooden is still trying to figure that one out. "It seems inconceivable," says the UCLA coaching great, "that we could dissipate a seven-point lead in overtime."

The 80-77 double-overtime loss to the eventual national champion certainly was not a source of embarrassment for Wooden, but it was hardly reminiscent of UCLA's lionhearted teams of past seasons—particularly those two NCAA champions inspired by the peerless Bill Walton in 1972 and 1973. Particularly distressing about this 1973-74 UCLA team was its obvious lack of passion. To the coach's consternation and regret, the Bruins had proven an old theory of their master. "When you have one group playing together for three years, and they've been successful," points out Wooden, "it's been my experience that the senior year is always the most difficult. The team always seems to peak in its junior season, and then there's usually a letdown as seniors. The 1973-74 team definitely did not come up to playing as close to its potential as it did the year before." Wooden blames himself in part. "I was never satisfied with my own work with the team that particular year. It's really up to a coach to motivate a team. Sometimes I was able to take care of that, but not that particular year."

Wooden had one of his most talented teams in

Bill Walton of UCLA (32), the game's dominant player in the early 1970s.

history at that point in time, its main source of power flowing from the ebullient Walton, an intense redhead who played basketball with child-like enthusiasm and professional-like skill. In his three years at UCLA, Walton's statistics always were impressive, but more to the point was the completeness of his game. In this regard, Wooden once appraised Walton thusly: "He does so many things that don't show up in a box score. Like intimidation. How do you measure that? I know that when we had Lewis Alcindor, the other teams had a lower shooting percentage. It went back up during the next couple of years but now, with Bill, it will go down again. Our opponents for the year are hitting less than 40 per cent, and he is greatly responsible for that—not only because of the shots he blocks, but because they are always looking for him, just as they used to for Lewis all the time."

In deference to the great Alcindor, observers called Walton "the greatest Caucasian center ever to play this game," and Wooden might second that motion. "Alcindor was the most valuable player I ever coached," he reflects, "and Walton was the second-most valuable player. Walton could do more things well than Alcindor; but some of the things that Alcindor did, he did so well that I felt he was the most valuable player I ever had. Both were excellent team players, which was what made them so great. And both had great maneuverability."

Walton, at times moody and grim in his dealings with the news media, was conversely an animated, bright figure on the court. Walton's game was characterized by his zest for basketball. He was everywhere—tipping in missed shots, leaping out of nowhere for blocks, chasing loose balls and calling signals for UCLA's tough 2-2-1 zone press. Typically, the favorite maneuver of this graceful seven-footer was one that involved the entire team—the

fast break. Walton was extremely adept at triggering the break after gathering in a rebound in his large, bony hands. He could rocket a pass to midcourt almost before his high-topped, size 15 leather sneakers hit the floor. While trailing the play, Walton—ever demonstrative—was apt to smile and clap his hands, just as if he were a fan sitting in the stands at Pauley Pavilion.

"On defense, I make a point of knowing where all my guys are, all the time," Walton said, in explaining his playing philosophy, "so when I get the ball, even while facing the basket, I am thinking about the fast break. I know Henry (Bibby) is over here, and Keith (Wilkes) is close by and Larry (Farmer) is at least within 10 feet of me. When I'm trailing the play and see everything materialize in front of me—wow! That pleases me the most."

In honor of this precocious center from San Diego, the Bruins immediately were dubbed "The Walton Gang" upon his emergence as a lustrous sophomore in 1971-72. Wooden planted Walton at the low post and had the perfect high-post complement for him in Keith Wilkes, a player the coach reveres as "one of the best forwards I ever had. He was an ideal youngster to work with and a player with no particular weakness. He rebounded well, was an outstanding defensive player, a good outside shooter and just did everything very, very well." The point man in Wooden's revamped offense was Greg Lee, a slick, deceptive passer—and like Walton and Wilkes, only a sophomore. The forward opposite Wilkes on this exceptionally young team was a junior, Larry Farmer, a quick jumper and rebounder whom Wooden called "a good, all-around player without being spectacular in any one area." The team leader was Henry Bibby, the experienced guard who had provided inspiration and perspiration for two straight national championship teams. And off the bench came three players who could have started most anywhere else—Larry Hollyfield, Tommy Curtis and Swen Nater. The 6-11 Nater, though playing backup to Walton, made the United States Olympic team; and before leaving camp, he impressed some foreign coaches so much that they asked Southern California coach Bob Boyd, a visitor to the camp, "How do we stop him?" Boyd's answer: "I can't tell you. We only see the other guy, Walton." Wooden says about Nater: "I knew he was going to be tremendous for us, if nothing more than to help in the development of Bill Walton. I know Walton made the remark that Nater was as tough as anyone he played against."

There wasn't a serious challenge all season, which saw another NCAA championship and a third perfect record for UCLA, 30-0. The awesome Bruins wreaked devastation among their foes, winning by an average of 33 points to obliterate the major-college record of 27.2 set by Kentucky's 1953-54 team, not to mention the 26.2 spread by Lew Alcindor's junior-year team at UCLA in 1967-68. The 1971-72 Bruins also outrebounded their opponents by 18.6 a game—far superior to the edge compiled by any previous Wooden team. Through it all, Walton caught everyone's eye and inspired everyone's applause. "That kid," said Stanford coach Howie Dallmar, "destroys you. He's better than Bill Russell at their comparative age and development." Santa Clara's Carroll Williams was even more effusive in his praise: "He's the best college basketball player I've ever seen. He's better at both ends of the court than Lew Alcindor was—he dominates like no college player in the history of the game. And that includes Bill Russell, whom I played against."

Head and shoulders above the rest of the teams in the country thanks to Walton, the Bruins blasted through the NCAA tournament which now was being referred to laughingly as "the UCLA Invitational." Weber State tried a 2-1-2 zone; but the Bruins destroyed that while hardly taking a deep breath and beat their first West regional opponent with ease, 90-58. "They sagged very deep," remembers Wooden, "and gave us some of the shortest perimeter shots we ever had. I think they were so afraid of Walton underneath that they left us the easy shots at the top of the key. If we couldn't hit those, we couldn't hit any shots."

Long Beach State went down fighting, literally, in the regional. The Bruins hammered out a 73-57 victory in one of the most emotional and bitter games they had to play in NCAA championship competition. The 49ers had been seething for a year after blowing a big lead over UCLA in the previous season's tournament, and they were waiting to redeem themselves. The Long Beach fans prepared banners to demean UCLA; and the Long Beach players were verbally demeaning as well, calling the Bruins "mere mortals, just another team." Ed Ratleff, the 49ers' leading man, sounded this warning to the nation's top-ranked team: "We're going to take it to 'em. They're going to know they've had a game."

Warlike conditions persisted throughout. Both Ratleff and UCLA's Bibby spent considerable time on the floor as a result of the pushing and shoving. At one point, Walton left the game briefly, holding his ribs, after an alleged blow by Long Beach center Nate Stephens. Healthy blows apparently were exchanged by both sides. Later, Long Beach coach Jerry Tarkanian was to say: "Ratleff is black and blue. His arms are sore—he's sorer than he has ever

Tommy Curtis (22) tries to stop Florida State's Greg Samuel (3) in the 1972 championship game.

Malcolm W. Emmons

been after a game. And he says he's never been knocked down so many times." Ratleff claimed that UCLA "was protected" by the officials, that "they were fouling us a lot, and we didn't get any of the calls." Wooden scoffs at such a notion. "There's a tendency for a team to say that after they've been knocked out of the NCAA tournament by another team a couple of years in a row," reflects Wooden. "They get the feeling that the referees are helping out the other team. Actually, we felt the opposite way. We were winning so much, we felt that we didn't get the protection because the officials felt subconsciously we didn't need it."

At one point, an angered Wooden left his seat and met with Long Beach assistant coach Dwight Jones in front of the scorer's table to complain about the "disgraceful and unethical" conduct of the Long Beach players. He carried his appeal to a higher court—one of the officials, who told Wooden, "I'll watch for it."

On the other hand, there wasn't much to watch in terms of the competition. UCLA had an early 17-7 lead, and it wasn't much of a contest after that. Bibby fired away at the 49ers' 2-3 zone for 23 points, mostly from the corners; Walton got 19 from the interior. As the usually stoic Bruins stood at courtside waiting for the presentation of the regional championship trophy, they betrayed their emotions. They slapped hands, embraced and laughed frequently. They threw cups of water at each other, while Wooden pretended not to notice. But when some of the water splashed on trainer Ducky Drake, Wooden growled, "Cut it out." The Bruins pretended not to notice him; and Tommy Curtis crowed, "Ooohhh, it's so good."

In the national semifinals at the Sports Arena in Los Angeles, Wooden faced his former assistant, Denny Crum. Crum's Louisville team featured an outstanding guard in Jim Price and a tough man-to-man defense. But the Cardinals were no match for UCLA, particularly Walton, who scored 33 points and swept off 21 rebounds. Thanks largely to a player that Crum himself had recruited for UCLA, the Bruins were easy 96-77 victors. In style, this game was almost a repetition of the Long Beach State game the week before—fists up, elbows out and no holds barred. There were swings taken and a good deal of physical abuse; when it was over, the Louisville players hollered "foul"—just as the ones from Long Beach had. "Walton is strong, but you can't touch him," said Al Vilcheck, the 6-9 Louis-

ville center who had a bitterly frustrating night with Walton. "The officials put him in a cage. We need neutral officials. Walton and UCLA got all the calls."

Wooden did not particularly enjoy meeting Crum in a tempestuous situation like that. As the UCLA coach says: "I was fond of Denny. As a general rule, I would prefer not to play teams coached by ex-players, or by my friends."

In the NCAA championship game, Florida State proved to be the most troublesome team that UCLA faced all season. The Seminoles, hungry from three years of NCAA probation, had upset Adolph Rupp's last Kentucky team in the Mideast regional and had beaten a solid North Carolina

team led by Bob McAdoo in the national semifinals. Hugh Durham had rounded up a bunch of brilliant Black players, flamboyant with Afro hairdos and all the proverbial moves. The Seminoles featured two powerhouse frontcourt players in Reggie Royals and Larry McCray, both 6-10, and a brilliant outside shooter in 6-4 Ron King. Unheralded at the start of the year, they had won 27 of 32 games and now insisted they could win one more. "No one knew us before," said Otto Petty, a cocky, 5-7 guard. "Now they know. We can play with anyone. They have the greatest coach in the world in Wooden and the greatest player in Walton, but we just might upset them."

The shadow of Florida State's probation for recruiting violations still hung over the team during tournament week in Los Angeles. The Seminoles, though having paid their debt to basketball society, were still the target of an angry blast from the president of the National Association of Basketball Coaches, Bill Wall of MacMurray College in Illinois. "I resent the fact that Florida State is here, and a lot of coaches do, too," Wall told a press conference. "Our coaches are amazed, disgusted and disillusioned at this. Their coach was caught with his fingers in the till not once, but twice." Florida State was stung by Wall's remarks and insisted on an apology from the NABC and Wall, saying it was "considering legal action." Said Durham: "Wall doesn't know what he's talking about. He doesn't know the facts, but I will not get down to his level to answer them. We've paid the price. We accepted punishment. We didn't debate it in the press or in public. Now we just want to play."

An NCAA spokesman concurred with Durham,

192

Larry Hollyfield (53) beats Florida State's Ron Harris (10) to the basket.

saying as far as it was concerned, Florida State once again "enjoys full rights and privileges."

Wooden later consoled the beleaguered Durham. "I'm sorry about this," he told his coaching colleague on the eve of the championship game. "I want you to know that we don't feel the same way (as Wall)."

"It won't affect us in any way," said the outspoken Petty. "That's off the court. We've got a job to do."

And the Seminoles did that job pretty well at first. A team that many had pictured as just a run-and-gun, "renegade" outfit, Florida State showed everyone a thing or two—most notably, discipline. The Seminoles' size and quickness were evident, too; and at one point they had a 21-14 lead—the largest anyone had held over UCLA all season. McCray gave Walton all he could handle, but the Florida State center got into foul trouble first and UCLA pulled out to a 67-51 lead. Then the Bruins held off a late challenge, led by the hot-shooting King, for an 81-76 victory. "Hugh Durham tended to mix up his defenses," recalls Wooden, "so we were ready for that. But where they could play us pretty well was with their quickness. Durham's feeling was a lot like mine as far as basketball went. He preferred quickness over size. Of course, that year they had both. That kind of a team could give us trouble."

Wooden had to summon Greg Lee off the bench to direct a keep-away tempo game the last five minutes and protect a 79-72 lead. "The most pleasing thing to me," says Wooden, "was that when we got behind early, we showed patience."

In one of the most bizarre of NCAA championship weeks, another shocking note was inserted by Walton's apparent lack of good taste. Wearing a dour expression at the postgame press conference, Walton flippantly dismissed UCLA's newest national title as inartistic. "I'm not that elated," he said, "because we didn't play that well. Florida State is an excellent team, but we didn't dominate the game like we know we can. If we had played our game the way we can, it would have been different. No excuses, but I don't like to back into things. I like to win convincingly." Then he added, "I felt like we lost it."

Wooden wisely intervened at this point, moving Bibby—the captain—in front of the microphone.

Malcolm W. Emmons

Ernie DiGregorio (15) of Providence dazzled the crowd in 1973 with his pinpoint passing and scoring.

Rich Clarkson

He got the predictable results as the cool Bibby handled the questions. "We made mistakes we shouldn't have made," he said, "but any team would like to be in our position right now."

UCLA, of course, would start the next season in the same No. 1 position, despite the loss of Bibby. Wooden admitted that his national champions probably would be harder for him to handle in 1972-73, owing to possible arrogance over their accomplishments. "I envision that will be true," he said. "But I'm happy to be in that situation. I can

194

UCLA

work with it. I have my own means of helping the players keep their feet on the ground." The indication was that Wooden planned to use a harder line to keep law and order among the Bruins. This was not especially good news for the UCLA players, since Wooden had used the whip often during 1971-72 despite the enormous enjoyment he had working with the team.

"One of the players asked me if I'd get off their backs if they lost a game," quipped Wooden.

This was not to happen in the 1972-73 season, although the Bruins did not win with the same authority as the previous season. The reason was that they had no outside shooter of Bibby's quality. As a result, the brunt of the scoring had to be done from close range, often on tips and rebounds by Walton, Wilkes and Larry Farmer. Larry Hollyfield was Bibby's replacement and was clearly his inferior as a long-range shooter and defensive player. At the same time, there was sporadic play at the point guard position, which was shared by Tommy Curtis and Greg Lee. However, UCLA had few other weaknesses. Indeed, with all the experienced players on the team, along with such outstanding new players as Dave Meyers, Andre McCarter and Pete Trgovich, Wooden reflects, "I expected to have a better team than the year before."

When the season began, the Bruins had won 45 games in a row and hoped to surpass the national major-college record streak of 60 set by the great San Francisco teams of the 1950s. In short order, the Bruins broke their own school record of 47 established by the Lew Alcindor teams of the late 1960s. Then, late in January 1973, UCLA reached another milestone by winning its 61st straight game—a surprisingly easy 82-63 conquest of Notre Dame at South Bend, Indiana. It never was close, and the only tense moments occurred when Notre Dame fans pelted the officials with coins and when Wooden leaped off the bench in the second half and angrily scolded Irish coach Dick "Digger" Phelps for what he thought was unnecessary roughness by forward John Shumate. Later, Wooden sent a note of apology to Phelps for his "hasty" action.

By the time the NCAA tournament came around in March, the Bruins still were achieving new standards of excellence, having built their mammoth winning streak to 71. In their first game of the West regional, they found an opponent reflective of their own racehorse style in Arizona State. "Their style of ball made it tough for us,"

Bill Walton hit 21 of 22 shots in the 1973 championship game against Memphis State.

notes Wooden. "They came down, put the ball up, had a good fast break and could break a press pretty well. And if they are hitting well with their outside jumpers, they really can put a lot of pressure on you. I really was concerned about this particular game." Wooden's fears seemed well founded in the early going when Arizona State led, 21-16. But then Larry Hollyfield began hitting with unusual consistency to lead the Bruins into a 51-37 half-time lead. In the first five minutes of the second half, UCLA stretched its lead to 63-41; it was all over. "We ran a backdoor play for Hollyfield," remembers Wooden, "and he got a number of easy baskets in that manner." Hollyfield wound up with a career-high 20 points, 18 of them in the game-breaking first half.

A 54-39 victory over San Francisco in the regional finals did not indicate the degree of difficulty UCLA had in subduing the Dons. San Francisco, upset winner in the semifinals over Long Beach State, was getting a second chance at UCLA after being humbled by the Bruins earlier in the season. Mindful of that 92-64 thrashing earlier in the year, San Francisco coach Bob Gaillard wisely slowed the tempo in this rematch. At one point, the Dons had the frustrated Bruins down 16-9. Wooden remembers: "They slowed down very well. But Greg Lee, a pretty good shooter, was reluctant to shoot; and with the type of defense they were playing, we were getting a lot of opportunities. So I brought in Tommy Curtis. He took the shots when he had them, and he happened to hit real well for us. That was important in our staying in the ball game in the first half. Also, Larry Farmer did an aggressive job on the boards. Larry was a fine defensive player and helped us in that respect, too." Eight minutes into the second half, with San Francisco's Phil Smith firing away, the Dons still were within striking distance of UCLA at 31-28. But then Walton took command of the game—blocking shots, scrambling for loose balls, rebounding on missed shots, hitting on a hook and a tip-in. Suddenly UCLA had a 40-28 lead, and the Dons were doomed. "They play like pros," said Gaillard about the indomitable Bruins.

Indiana, led by Quinn Buckner, wasn't close at the end in the national semifinals at St. Louis; but the Hoosiers certainly gave it that old college try before succumbing to UCLA, 70-59. It began as one of the sorriest mismatches in NCAA history with Walton and Company running away to an 18-point lead at half time. But then the Bruins—whose trademark had been poise—lost some of it, surrendered 17 straight points and led only 57-55 with less than six minutes to play and Walton in foul trouble. "You bet I was worried at this point,"

Wooden would say later. "We had it salted away, and then we got into a fix by making some very foolish mistakes." It took some clutch shooting by Curtis and some daring steals by Hollyfield to turn the direction of the game in UCLA's favor.

Providence, aching for a chance to play UCLA in the national championship game, slipped along the way. The Friars' chances went down in the thud of a fall by Marvin Barnes, who came off the boards badly in the eighth minute of the semifinal game with Memphis State and injured his right knee. With the loss of the nation's leading rebounder came an eventual loss to the Tigers. "With Barnes, we would have won," said Providence guard Ernie DiGregorio, a little ball of fire who had helped the Friars win 17 straight games prior to the national semifinals. "Now we'll never know if we could have beaten the Bruins."

Actually, no one could have beaten the Bruins the way Walton played in the championship game. Driving one-on-one, whirling, hooking, guiding teammates' high lob passes into the basket, Walton scored 44 points—breaking Gail Goodrich's NCAA title game record of 42 for UCLA in 1965. But what was even more remarkable was that he missed just one shot in 22 attempts. He also blocked shots and made deft passes and forced Memphis State into an outside shooting game that eventually proved to be its undoing. And UCLA conquered a good Memphis State team, 87-66, for its seventh straight NCAA championship.

"He's about as physical a big man as I've ever seen," Memphis State coach Gene Bartow said about Walton. "He did so many things so well that we just couldn't stop him. He's super—the best collegiate player I've ever seen. We played him wrong. We tried three or four things, but I guess we didn't try the right one. If you let him have the ball, he'll kill you."

Unquestionably the college player with the highest profile of his time, Walton was the subject of rumors that he might sign with a National Basketball Association team before finishing his career at UCLA. But he quieted these rumors when he turned down a reported $2 million offer from the Philadelphia 76ers. Wooden also put to rest rumors that he might retire after the 1972-73 season. Troubled by heart problems and "a trying season because of the pressure of the long winning streak," Wooden nevertheless decided to stay on—at least for another year. It was not, however, with the best wishes of his wife.

"I hope," Nell Wooden said, "this will be his last season, and I intend to try to do all I can to make it his last."

195

DAVID AND GOLIATH

It wasn't John Wooden's last year, as Nell Wooden would have wished, but it was certainly one of his most frustrating. All good things came to an end for UCLA during the 1973-74 season, including two of the most cherished, and possibly untouchable, streaks in college basketball. UCLA's Herculean winning streak had soared to 88 games before it was broken by Notre Dame in the frenzy and fury of South Bend, Indiana. Also, the Bruins' remarkable NCAA tournament string of 38 victories was cut by a revengeful North Carolina State team in the national semifinals at Greensboro, North Carolina. In both instances, similarities marked the UCLA performance—the Bruins were unable to hold big leads near the end. The passion of the previous two seasons had gone out of the UCLA character, it seemed to Wooden.

"At the beginning of the year," Wooden says, "I did feel we would lose some games. When we lost the winning streak at Notre Dame, I felt it was possible that was what we needed—that we might come back and get the act together and go the rest of the way. We did come back strong the next few games, but I'm not particularly surprised that we lost some games that year."

UCLA played one of its toughest nonconference schedules in history that season, including highly touted Maryland, San Francisco, the same North Carolina State team that had gone undefeated in 1972-73 but had been banned from postseason play and a home-and-home series with Notre Dame. In the face of this challenging schedule, Wooden was confronted by frustrating team problems. Wooden, himself, felt he had lost the whip hand over the Bruins, that he had become "complacent" and had relaxed disciplines. "We had a number of players who had become vegetarians," Wooden remembers, "and it made it difficult to have a team menu. I let the players eat in the cafeteria, and that took away from the camaraderie. It was catch-as-catch-can, and we didn't eat together. I felt that hurt the team somewhat." Then, too, some of the UCLA players became caught up in the national wave of transcendental meditation. "I allowed players to practice it," notes Wooden, "and that was making them late for basketball practice. There were just some things that were not in our best interest."

Wooden would change all of that the following season, when he would have a better grip on his team. But in 1973-74, the combination of varied elements proved to be UCLA's undoing. It did take a while, though, before the Bruins faltered. They won their first 13 games of the season, including an impressive 84-66 trouncing of previously unbeaten North Carolina State in neutral St. Louis. In the season's 14th game, UCLA seemed well on its way to victory No. 89, holding a 70-59 lead over Notre Dame with three minutes to go. But then it all turned around, as UCLA began making uncustomary mistakes and Notre Dame began taking advantage of them. Led by John Shumate, Adrian Dantley and Dwight Clay, the Fighting Irish—cheered on by their fierce, raucous fans—scored the game's last 12 points and, in a dramatic knockout, floored UCLA, 71-70.

The Bruins would make Notre Dame pay for that embarrassment on national television later in the season, when in a return match at Pauley Pavilion in Los Angeles they would defeat the Irish by 18 points. However, they were strangely inconsistent that year, later losing two disciplined games to lowly Oregon and hungry Oregon State on successive nights in Corvallis and Eugene. The lost weekend cost the Bruins their No. 1 ranking—and suddenly, they were in a dogfight for the Pacific-8 title. That fight did not end until the last game of the regular season, when UCLA beat Southern Cal, 82-52, as Walton played one of his more authoritative games and Andre McCarter and Marques Johnson provided strong support in substitute roles. At the same time, the Atlantic Coast Confer-

David Thompson of North Carolina State soars high to take a rebound in the Wolfpack's dramatic semifinal overtime decision against UCLA in 1974.

Malcolm W. Emmons

Rich Clarkson

ence championship was being decided in Greensboro, with top-ranked North Carolina State beating Maryland, 103-100, in overtime, in one of the best college games of the year.

Both UCLA and North Carolina State then won their NCAA regional tournaments—the Bruins pressed a bit more than the Wolfpack—and headed for their long-awaited rematch in the glamorous setting of the national semifinals. The magnitude of this game did not go unnoticed by either of the other two coaches in the final four, Marquette's Al McGuire and Ted Owens of Kansas. At a party Friday night before the semifinal doubleheader, McGuire said he was just happy to be playing in the "B-class division" against Kansas while Owens expressed pleasure at coaching in the "preliminary." Their game, sadly, lived down to these feelings, with Marquette winning a colorless 64-51 duel. The UCLA-North Carolina State game, however, lived up to everyone's expectations. In many eyes, the national championship truly was decided then, in North Carolina State's double-overtime 80-77 victory before a passionate Wolfpack-oriented crowd in the Greensboro Coliseum.

It was a game for the ages. Not only did the contest bring together the nation's No. 1 and No. 2 ranked teams, but its main matchups included four of the finest college players in the country—UCLA's Walton vs. North Carolina State's Tom Burleson and Wilkes against Wolfpack star David Thompson, a regal, high-jumping forward of many dimensions. And there was no hiding some traces of bitterness that remained over the bad beating that UCLA had administered North Carolina State's proud team earlier in the season. "A real whippin'," UCLA's Tommy Curtis called that one; and Wooden added psychological fuel on the eve of the national semifinals: "I want State to dwell on that 18-point margin."

North Carolina State coach Norm Sloan kept his verbal distance, but Wolfpack forward Tim Stoddard wasn't afraid to speak. "We know they aren't 18 points better than us," he said, "but what's more important is that they know it."

The Bruins, however, were 11 points better than North Carolina State as far into the game as the second half—two times, in fact—and managed to blow that commanding lead. A raging Burleson battled the magnificent Walton on even terms, and Thompson flew through the air with the greatest of ease while scoring time and again with his patented "Alley Oop" shot; suddenly, the never-say-die

UCLA's Keith Wilkes (52) goes inside to score against Tim Stoddard of North Carolina State.

Wolfpack was back in the game. With the diminutive Monte Towe directing the North Carolina State rally, tearing down the lane or firing football-type passes from midcourt, the Wolfpack scored 10 straight points to cut UCLA's 57-46 lead to 57-56. Minutes later, North Carolina State went into the lead at 63-61 when Thompson, practically vanishing into the rafters, made still another sky-lob basket and a three-point play. After 40 minutes of thrills, spills, bungled leads and concentrated fury, the game went into overtime, tied at 65-65.

It seemed like North Carolina State's game to win in the first overtime when Stoddard stole a pass from UCLA's Greg Lee, enabling the Wolfpack to hold the ball for the last shot. Thompson drove for the payoff shot with 10 seconds to go. But instead of shooting, he passed off to Burleson, whose short spin shot bounced off the rim. Then it seemed like UCLA's game to win in the second overtime, after Walton and Wilkes took the Bruins to a 74-67 lead with 3:27 remaining. But North Carolina State would not quit. The Wolfpack players pressed tighter, opened up the floor and got every offensive rebound they needed. Just like that, UCLA's lead was cut to one.

After Dave Meyers missed a critical one-and-one foul shot with 1:16 left, Thompson leaped one more time, banked a jumper over Wilkes and the Wolfpack was ahead to stay, 76-75. Thompson and Towe then each delivered two free throws for the clinching points. How State succeeded was simple enough. In the beginning, the Wolfpack forced the Bruins to start their offense farther out than they liked; State also stopped UCLA's backdoor plays as Thompson held his onetime nemesis, Wilkes, to five baskets in 17 attempts while scoring 28 points himself. Throughout the game, Burleson prevented Walton from dominating; and the tiny Towe, called "a lovable lightning bug" by one writer, buzzed around the UCLA guards until they got tired of swatting at him. In the end, it was the Wolfpack press that brought the ACC champions back. "We went to it simply because we were down," explained the 5-7 Towe. "We had to take the fight to 'em. We double-teamed and came up with some steals."

The championship game virtually was decided late in the first half with a play on which, ironically, Marquette took the lead. When Marquette's Marcus Washington was whistled for a charging foul after his driving score put the Warriors in front, 28-27, coach Al McGuire screamed too loudly over the call and was hit with a technical foul. Thompson put in three free throws for North Carolina State, and Burleson later twisted in for a layup to make the score 32-28 in favor of the

Wolfpack. Less than a minute later, after Burleson had scored again, the Warriors' Bo Ellis was called for goaltending a Wolfpack basket; and McGuire was up and on the court again. The Marquette coach was hit with another technical, which North Carolina State quickly converted. "The technicals sure gave us a lift," Thompson was to say later; and his team took a 39-30 lead into the dressing room at half time. The game really got out of Marquette's reach five minutes into the second half when North Carolina State built a 19-point lead. Along with the momentum-turning McGuire technicals, another key to North Carolina State's first NCAA title was the extraordinary backcourt play of Towe and Morris Rivers. Their ball handling was exceptional; and they pestered the Warriors with pressing tactics, particularly with a double team when the two found a Marquette guard isolated. "If anything created the turning point, it was our defense," North Carolina State coach Norm Sloan said, especially lauding Rivers and Towe after the Wolfpack's 76-64 victory. "Our guards have failed to receive the credit they've deserved this year."

UCLA literally regrouped after that fall from power. The following year, the Bruins presented an entire new face to the college basketball world. Four starters, including the peerless Walton and Wilkes, had graduated, but still "people thought we might have a pretty good team," according to Wooden. Basically, the UCLA coach relied on six players in 1974-75; as it turned out, six were enough to win another national championship for Wooden. It was his 10th and last.

The team leader was Dave Meyers, the only returning starter from 1972-73 and a player whom Wooden applauded for "his tremendous spirit and determination. He played the last half of the season hurt. But Dave had an outstanding year and was a great competitor."

Wooden also could use Marques Johnson, Richard Washington and Ralph Drollinger interchangeably in the front line. Pete Trgovich and Andre McCarter were the guards.

"I had to be careful with Marques," Wooden remembers, "because he had come back from hepatitis the year before, and I was under instructions not to permit him to get too tired. Now that's a very difficult situation for a coach. At practice, I was not able to give him the amount of work I would have liked because I was afraid he would get too tired; in games I was concerned about his

welfare and well-being, and in timeouts, I had to look at him and check him to make sure he wasn't getting too fatigued. And sometimes I had to take him out when he didn't want to come out. It made for a tough situation, but he accepted it extremely well. And he truly began to develop into the outstanding player I knew he would be."

Washington had only to overcome a lack of confidence, and he did this pretty well in his sophomore year. "Washington had improved tremendously from the year before," states Wooden. "He gained a lot of confidence in that one year. He was a fine pure shooter and a relaxed type of individual." Drollinger was not as natural a basketball player as Wooden would have liked, and Trgovich and McCarter lacked some of the qualities that the UCLA coach sought in his guards; but all of them worked hard at their games. "This team gave me about as much personal satisfaction and

Malcolm W. Emmons

Coach Al McGuire of Marquette, who was called for a pair of technical fouls in his team's 76-64 loss to North Carolina State for the 1974 championship.

200

Junior Bridgeman (10) of Louisville drives against UCLA's Ralph Drollinger in the 1975 semifinals. UCLA defeated the Cardinals in overtime, 75-74, in what UCLA coach John Wooden called "one of the greatest games in NCAA tournament history."

Malcolm W. Emmons

201

pleasure as any team I've had," says Wooden. "The 1975 team was comprised of as fine a group of young men as any group with whom I ever have had the privilege of working. They gave me no trouble either on or off the floor the entire season and were truly a pleasure to be around."

With UCLA's long reign as king of college basketball ended the year before by North Carolina State's ferocious team, and with the nation returning to more coast-to-coast balance, the Bruins no longer were held in as much awe as in previous seasons. But, at the end of the year, there was indomitable UCLA at the head of the Pacific-8 class, winning still another NCAA tournament berth. "They showed tremendous courage and determination in battling back from adversity time and again to win every game that really mattered," Wooden points out.

Meyers displayed as much courage as any on this gallant team, playing the second half of the season with a pulled groin muscle that not only slowed him but the entire team as well. "His injury hurt his maneuverability and hurt our team quite a bit," Wooden says. "He played a key position in our pressing defense and was not able to function to full capacity. It hurt us to the point where I nearly had to quit using our press—and our press was one of our strengths."

The road to the NCAA championship was rocky for UCLA. The Bruins had a tough time subduing both Michigan and Montana in regional games. Then after beating Arizona State to get into the Final Four, they managed to outlast Louisville, 75-74, in a brilliant overtime game in the national semifinals at San Diego. It could have gone either way, as one sports writer pointed out: "The key to the game was that the last team to get the ball won." Luckily for UCLA, the last player to handle the ball for them was Richard Washington, a cool customer. "We wanted to get Richard that shot," explains Wooden. "For one thing, he was the best pure shooter we had. Secondly, Richard was not affected by pressure. Fortunately for us, he got the shot and put it in just like he was capable of shooting . . . and I think everyone was more excited about it than Richard."

It had been a struggle of savage intensity from the beginning, pitting two teams of similar styles and equal talent; and when the contest was on the line, UCLA was up to taking it. Dave Meyers would say later: "I haven't been in that kind of game in a long time. Both gangs flailing away, no moaning or messing around. It seemed like two UCLAs, one and the same."

Fleet Louisville held nine-point leads on four occasions; but UCLA rallied behind Marques Johnson, who contributed some brilliant defensive plays and a key basket to save the game in regulation time for the Bruins. Then it was another overtime game in the national semifinals, the same situation in which the Bruins had been dethroned

by North Carolina State the previous year. "Nobody was thinking back," said Meyers. "We were just very lucky most of the game. Then it was time for bread and butter."

UCLA had plenty of both, it turned out. After Allen Murphy had scored seven points in overtime to run his game-leading total to 33 points and help Louisville take a 74-73 lead, Denny Crum's team went into a delay game. With 20 seconds to go, UCLA was forced to foul. Terry Howard had only to make both ends of his one-and-one to seal the victory for Louisville, but he missed. After UCLA's timeout to set up the last shot, Louisville lined up in a zone defense. The Bruins gave the ball to Johnson far outside; Washington faked toward the foul line, then drifted out along the baseline to receive Johnson's pass. The 6-9 sophomore lifted off, cocked and let go for the winning points. "It was a tremendous game," reflects Wooden. "Not because we won—it was a tremendous game for both teams. Tension-packed, well-played, no incidents, not unduly rough. The game was played more with finesse then with brute strength."

Wooden's appreciation of the artistry of this game was perhaps heightened even more by the knowledge that this would be his last week of college coaching. Only a few close friends and family realized the feelings that churned inside the 64-year-old Wooden as he watched the overtime death struggle with Louisville. There had been hints of his departure after the 1975 season. Some close coaching friends had reported that this would

Coach John Wooden of UCLA, who ended his career by directing the Bruins to their unprecedented 10th championship in 1975. This photo was taken during Wooden's last game, a 92-85 title decision over Kentucky.

be Wooden's last tournament. Though appearing to be in fine health, Wooden had not slept well and had been starting his traditional long morning walks as early as 5 a.m. A doctor advised him against becoming the coach of the 1976 Olympic team. Perceptive Bruin players were alerted before UCLA's final home contest when Wooden told them that this would be the last home game "for a few people in this room." Wooden says that he decided to retire when things "started bothering me that never had bothered me before."

"Maybe it wasn't true," reflects Wooden, "but people seemed to be critical and suspicious even though we had been winning as much as we had."

Facing the media after games was starting to be an ordeal, too, he says. "I thought, in going off the floor after the Louisville game, what a great game that was; in my opinion, one of the greatest basketball games in NCAA tournament history. I felt, had we lost that game, I would have dreaded to go before the wrath of the media . . . which certainly you should do and want to do. And here I found myself thinking about dreading it . . ."

Wooden spoke to the Bruins in the locker room immediately after the Louisville game. "I'm bowing out," he said in the vast quiet. His eyes went around the room and his voice cracked. "I don't want to. I have to." Then he walked away.

"I felt I had to make the announcement then," says Wooden. "If I would have waited until after the championship game to announce it, that wouldn't have been too good. Had we lost the championship game, I'm quite certain there would be comments like, 'He couldn't take losing two years in a row after winning all those years.' And if we had won, someone would have said, 'Well, he would have quit last year had he won.' So I felt that if I announced my retirement after the semifinal game, no one was going to say that the outcome of the championship had any bearing or influence on the fact that I decided to retire."

Nor was the retirement announcement made at that point as a motivational prop for the championship game, insists Wooden. "It never had anything to do with trying to psyche up my players for the championship game. That thought never en-

North Carolina State University

UCLA's Bill Walton and North Carolina State's David Thompson (44), the key players in the 1974 tournament. Thompson's Wolfpack ended UCLA's seven-year reign with an 80-77 overtime win in the semifinals.

Rich Clarkson

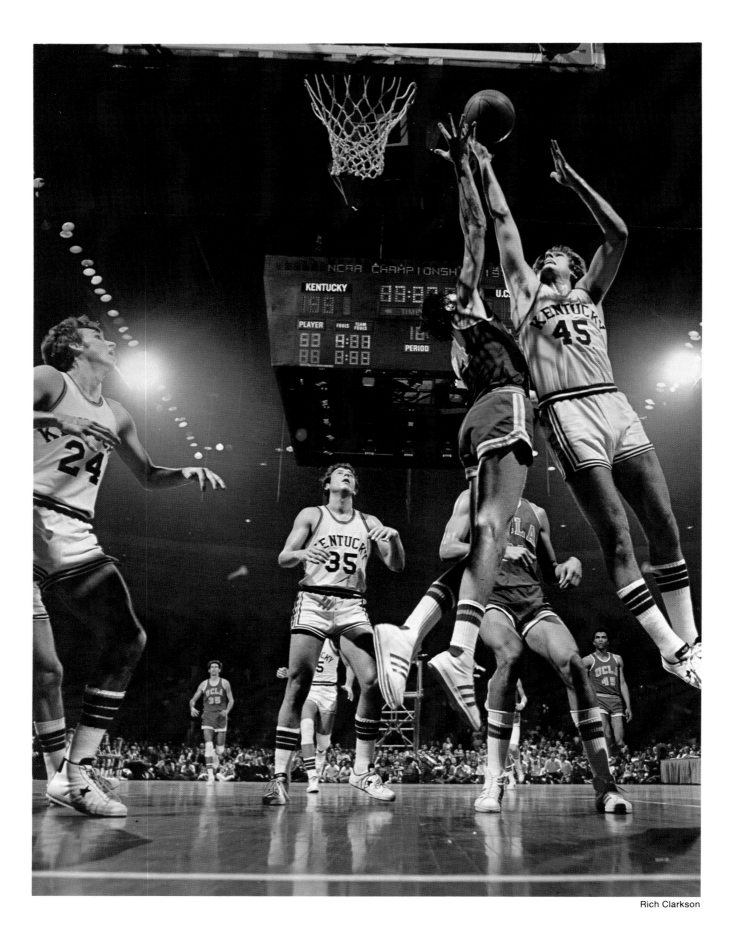

204

Rich Clarkson

Bob Guyette (45) of Kentucky goes up against UCLA's Dave Meyers.

tered my mind until someone mentioned it to me afterward."

To the finish, Wooden remained true to his unemotional image. In the locker room before the national finals against Kentucky, his pregame talk was predictable. "I didn't say anything special," remembers Wooden. "I pointed out that this had been one of the most gratifying years I had ever had in coaching and that the outcome of this championship game would not affect that in any way. Nothing that happened in this game would affect my feeling toward this particular team, because I had said that this team caused no particular problems on or off the floor. They came about as close to reaching their potential as any team I ever had. The last thing I told them before we went on the floor was to give it their best effort—to play so they could hold their heads up after the game. That way, they would never lose, even though they'd been outscored."

Whether or not Wooden's retirement announcement was intended to inspire UCLA, it certainly seemed to have that effect. The Bruins were in against a massive Kentucky team that had reached the championship game on muscle, giving Syracuse a fearsome 95-79 pounding in the national semifinals. But if the thin list of six Bruins who played in the national finals felt they couldn't handle the burly Wildcats, they didn't show it. Ralph Drollinger, playing what was probably the best game of his career, got 13 rebounds and 10 points in 16 minutes, while Washington scored 28, added 12 rebounds and found time to check Kentucky's ox-like centers, Rick Robey and Mike Phillips. "I even surprised myself," noted Washington, the tournament's most outstanding player.

After a furious first half in which there were 15 lead changes, the teams battled hard toward a compelling finish. When the ubiquitous Washington tipped in a missed shot by Johnson, the Bruins had an 80-77 lead. The Wildcats never got closer. At the end, it was 92-85 in favor of UCLA.

The fierceness of play inspired unusual passion among the participants. At one point, when the Bruins were ahead 76-75, Meyers went up for a jumper but fell into Kentucky's Kevin Grevey and was called for a foul. Screaming and pounding the floor, Meyers was hit with a technical foul, whereupon Wooden shouted "You crook!" at the referee and rushed onto the court.

At the end, though, Wooden could be only at

peace with the world. After the game, guard Andre McCarter, who had totaled 14 assists and scored a key late basket, embraced Wooden and said, "Coach, I hope you have a nice life."

Wooden's eyes sparkled a bit.

"I was obviously very happy, very tired, with no second thoughts of my retirement," Wooden says. "I felt then and feel today that it was the thing to do. I had done a lot of things in my time and had no regrets. Though a few years have passed, nothing has happened to make me feel that it was not meant for me to retire at that particular time."

205

Marques Johnson of UCLA.

Malcolm W. Emmons

THE **EMOTIONAL YEARS** 1976·1978

"The saddest thing about this tournament is that we can't handle all the people who want to see it. It's truly the championship of the United States. It has representation from all over the country, and it's a great thrill to see these people follow their teams. They travel thousands of miles and care nothing about expense. That is terrific loyalty, and I think it's great. This tournament is the greatest basketball attraction in the world right now."

A lot of people have to agree with Stan Watts, chairman of the NCAA Basketball Committee from 1975 to 1977. The NCAA championship game is one of the hottest tickets in town. It is one of the main reasons that the finals are gravitating toward bigger arenas, preferably in the metropolitan areas. Such cities as Indianapolis, Philadelphia, New Orleans and Seattle are scheduled as future tournament sites.

In this regard, the NCAA in 1978 cast aside an old formula of rotating sites in each of the country's four sections and threw open bids to any city able to support the championship game in the style to which it is accustomed. Cities now bid passionately for the NCAA finals, a solid gold plum that is worth millions of dollars to the local economy. To accommodate the growing attention, the NCAA also boosted the minimum size for arenas from 15,000 to 17,000.

"The problem with rotating the sites regionally was that very often there was not an arena available with the right specifications for the NCAA finals," explains Tom Scott, longtime committee member. "Now the NCAA has the pick of the best and biggest arenas in the country."

Watts had relatively smooth sailing during his brief administration. Automatic conference qualification—still a controversial issue—was one of the few issues that he confronted.

"One year Temple would have come into the tournament with a 9-18 record if they had won their postseason tourney," says Watts. "That's a little hard to justify."

Book 5

THE EMOTIONAL YEARS 1976-1978

It was perhaps just a situation that prompted the Basketball Committee to revamp the tournament when the decision to expand to 40 teams was made in the summer of 1978.

Under the direction of chairman Wayne Duke, commissioner of the Big Ten Conference, the committee adopted a policy of allowing 23 automatic qualifiers among conference champions. Of those 23 conference representatives, the 16 from the conferences with the best NCAA tournament records over the previous five-year period receive first-round byes. The remaining seven champions will join the 17 at-large teams (second conference representatives plus independents) in first-round action. In addition, teams will be seeded within each region in an attempt to give the field better balance.

1976
FAMILY AFFAIR

As a coach at Army early in his career, Bobby Knight developed his style—described by one writer as "a cross between Simon Legree and Father Flanagan." Knight produced uncompromising, compelling Cadet teams despite a lack of attractive basketball talent; and along the way there were outrageous stories of his behavior, hatching a fearful legend. But besides the splintered furniture, broken lockers and bruised egos, something good had come out of his hitch at West Point other than winning teams. Knight, it seemed, had developed good character in his charges.

Said a longtime associate: "Bobby is a disciplinarian, but he has a genuine interest in his players' welfare and has real affection for them. In return, he has their respect." Said a former player: "The greatest thing about him is that he cares so much about his players. He used basketball to make us better people."

At Indiana, Knight carried on his militaristic approach with "pride" the key word. His players were likened to soldiers, dressing in neat unison and wearing their hair at short length. Knight recruited only "coachable" players, he said. While other coaches may have offered enticements to recruits, Knight's players say he promised them only hair shirts, indentured servitude and unlimited practice. "And," noted an observer, "he always kept his promise."

Although Knight has been described as a "sensitive and kind man," these qualities rarely have extended to a basketball court. He is a driver of the most intense kind; his discipline is inspired by such as Ohio State football coach Woody Hayes and the late Gen. George S. Patton, two pretty tough customers.

However harsh, the system has worked. At Indiana, Knight became the demigod of a basketball cult. He has managed to assume complete command of the entire scene, a la Patton at the Rhine. When players don't go to class, they are left home from road trips. And when fans get too wild, Knight threatens to "lock the doors and play

without them if they don't behave." To Indiana fans, that would be tantamount to sending your son to bed without supper—they simply feed on basketball.

If Hoosierland was a hotbed of basketball before, the arrival of Knight enhanced the feeling even more. Typical of the intensity there was the season of 1975-76, when the strong and supple Hoosiers won the NCAA basketball championship. On game days, the state legislature adjourned early to make the first tipoff, day or night. Indianapolis clubs, men's and women's alike, met only on Indiana's nights off. Movie theaters were all but empty when the Hoosiers played. And the daily salutation in Bloomington was rarely "Good morning" but almost always "We're No. 1."

That fact was established right away when Indiana was given the No. 1 ranking in preseason polls, and it was certified at the end of the year by the Hoosiers' conclusive 86-68 victory over Michigan in the NCAA finals. That businesslike decision capped a splendid 32-0 season for the Hoosiers, matching the sublime perfection of North Carolina's work in 1956-57 as the best record by an NCAA champion.

"If we don't deserve to be national champions, then I don't know who does," said Indiana's superlative guard, Quinn Buckner, at the end of the perfect year. "We won all our games. What else can you do?"

The Hoosiers survived several pitfalls on the road to the championship—including a mild midseason slump that relegated Buckner to the bench. During this time, they struggled to beat Big Ten colleague Michigan twice.

"I had my troubles in midseason," Buckner admitted. "But I just kept trying. You've got to work harder when that happens, that's all."

Despite what Buckner called "peaks and valleys," Indiana made it through the Big Ten season undefeated, a performance that Michigan coach Johnny Orr called "unbelievable." What happened thereafter was even more impressive. The Hoo-

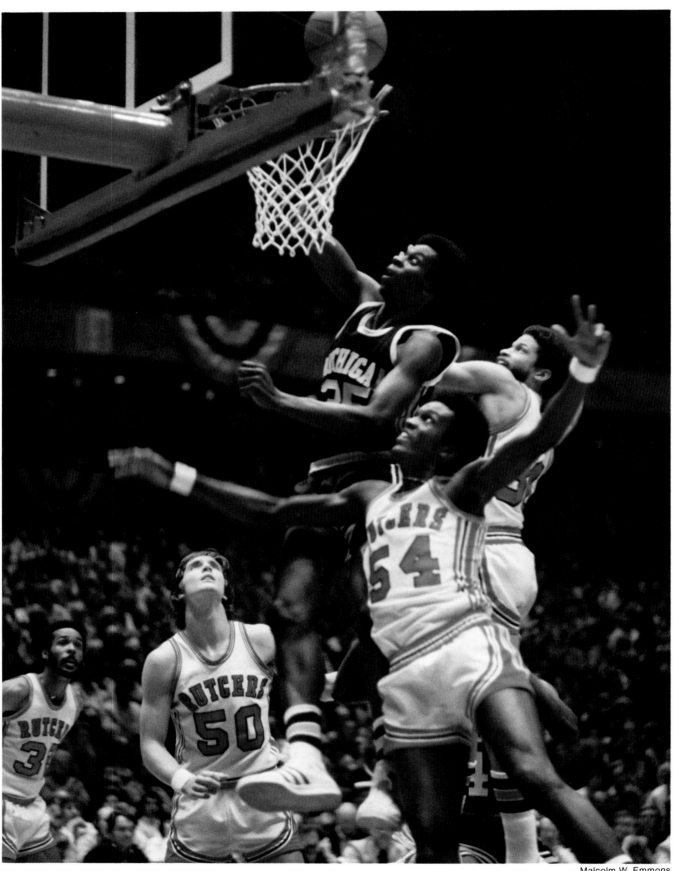

Malcolm W. Emmons

The play of Phil Hubbard helped Michigan defeat unbeaten Rutgers, 86-70, in the semifinals.

siers, playing in one of the toughest regional tourneys in NCAA history, defeated St. John's (New York), Alabama and Marquette to win the Mideast and advance to the gold-plated Final Four in Philadelphia.

"It was very physical all through the Big Ten and just as physical in the regionals," pointed out Indiana strongman Kent Benson. "It was as physical as I can remember."

Throughout the week of the NCAA finals, Knight demonstratively exhibited the total control he had over his Hoosiers. During workouts before the semifinal game with UCLA, a hand signal was all that was needed to put an end to frivolous byplay. He often monitored his player's answers to questions by reporters. The Indiana players bent to Knight's pressure, as one observer pointed out, "like pets looking for a caress." Because of Knight, Indiana had a remarkable ability to get emotionally ready for every game. Considering that the Hoosiers already had beaten UCLA by 20 points at the start of the season, they might have been excused for overconfidence. But Knight never let that happen to his team. "Frankly," said Knight, "UCLA does scare me. But then, so does any team we play. I'm sure that it will be a much tougher game than it was in St. Louis."

Despite Knight's fears, the Hoosiers handled UCLA in the semifinals almost as easily as they did on opening day. For a change, Benson and player-of-the-year Scott May took a back seat to two lesser lights—Tom Abernethy and Bobby Wilkerson. Abernethy scored 14 points and played a solid defensive game against Richard Washington, the player Knight feared most; and Wilkerson grabbed a career-high 19 rebounds as Indiana won convincingly, 65-51. "They made us feel helpless," said UCLA's Marques Johnson, "just like North Carolina State did two years ago."

Michigan, meanwhile, was making Rutgers feel helpless in the other semifinal game. The Scarlet Knights had arrived in Philadelphia with a 31-0 record and an exciting, racehorse style, playing as someone said "as if time was about to run out." There was criticism that Tom Young's team had played a light schedule, but he responded crisply: "Why do we have to apologize for being unbeaten?" Against Michigan, Rutgers looked quite beat-

Indiana's Kent Benson goes up to block a shot by Tom Staton of Michigan in the 1976 title game, the only time two teams from the same conference have played in the championship game.

able, however. The Scarlet Knights shot miserably, made mistakes right from the start and finally wound up an 86-70 loser to the beefy Wolverines. It set up a unique finale—the first time in NCAA tournament history that two teams from the same conference had met in the championship game.

"It'll probably be the last time in our lifetime that we see something like this," said Michigan coach Orr, a tall, balding man with droll wit. "Take a good look at it."

If familiarity bred contempt between these two fine Big Ten teams, it wasn't noticeable. Actually, it was more respect than anything else.

"A lot of people didn't believe me when I kept saying Michigan was probably the best team we've played all season," said Knight. "And don't forget, I said a long time ago they had a terrific shot at going to Philadelphia. Michigan is the toughest team we've played all season. They're physical, fast, and play defense and offense together. They take it to you on both ends of the floor. This should be a great, great ball game."

Pregame dialogue set the tone for a mellow atmosphere, despite the fierceness of this bitter conference rivalry. Orr underscored the rapport he had with Knight, reciting anecdotes about their relationship. Once, he said, Knight had called him on the telephone, saying it was the White House on the line and then, after having Orr completely fooled, gave it all away and admitted his deception. "He had me," the Michigan coach admitted, "but his voice finally got through to me. I said, 'President, hell. How could anyone from Ohio State ever

211

Malcolm W. Emmons

get to be President?' "

Knight, a particularly intriguing figure, could be aggressively warlike at times, yet given to periods of passivity—as he was on the eve of the NCAA title game. He revealed an infectious personality to the press, never raising his voice a decibel above the comfort level. Knight was modest, honest, comical and introspective.

"I just like to see my kids play as well as they can," he said. "It doesn't matter if we win or lose. If they reach their potential, that's all that matters."

The Wolverines perhaps figured they were due to beat Indiana after two Big Ten losses to the Hoosiers—especially after only a miracle rebound by Benson enabled Indiana to win one of the games. And certainly it seemed that way in the early part of the championship game, when Michigan controlled the tempo and went into the dressing room at half time leading, 35-29. To add to Indiana's early frustration, the 6-7 Wilkerson, one of the tallest and most able guards in the country, suffered a concussion in the early going and had to be carried from the court on a stretcher.

"When Bobby got hurt, we knew we had to go at it tougher," Buckner said afterward. "Bobby's a big part of our team. We did go at it."

Actually, the Hoosiers did not "go at it" until after the start of the second half. Benson, a blond giant with a pacifist temperament off the court and a killer instinct on, blamed his first-half timidity for the Hoosiers' uncharacteristic performance before intermission.

"I was a little tight in the first half," said Benson. "I knew I had to take the ball stronger to the hoop in the second half. It was just a matter of gathering myself."

Benson pulled himself together in the second half—and in the process, pulled Michigan apart. The all-America center took charge of things, scoring 15 of his 25 points and collecting six of his nine rebounds. With the help of their tower of strength in the middle, the Hoosiers went from a 51-51 tie with 10:15 left to a 73-59 lead at the 3:51 mark. The Hoosiers only had to run out the clock after that overpowering 22-8 burst and finished in front by an 86-68 score. May also had a high-powered game for Indiana in the second half, scoring 18 of his game-high 26 points and collecting all eight of his rebounds.

"Somebody had to help on the boards when Bobby Wilkerson got hurt," said May, "and that's what I had to do. At half time, we talked about keeping our game plan and outhustling them. That's what we did. No panic; we've been in that situation before."

In the end, Indiana clearly had won because of the leadership of Benson and May, its most impressive players. But it was also the little things that provided the Hoosiers with their third NCAA title: the long and late practices spent endlessly repeating the dull but demanding essentials. When Knight saw Wilkerson sprawled helplessly under the basket in the early part of the game, his first thought was, no doubt, "Who's my best replacement?" That turned out to be Jim Wisman, the same player whose jersey Knight almost tore off in a fit of anger during one game that season—ironically enough, against Michigan. This time, Wisman would not make Knight angry with his mistakes; rather, he would delight him with his perfection. He directed the Indiana offense with aplomb, following instructions to get the ball inside to the big men as Michigan, bruised by foul trouble, tried to play loose. Despite that effort, center Phil Hubbard and defensive specialist Wayman Britt fouled out of the game; and with their departures ultimately went Michigan's hopes.

"We couldn't get the running game going in the second half," pointed out Rickey Green, Michigan's high scorer with 18 points. "They were making their shots, and we couldn't get any rebounds. We've got to get the rebounds to run. I think we ran pretty well in the first half, and that was the difference."

Orr, finding himself losing to Indiana for the third time that season, could only throw up his hands helplessly. "They played a great second half," said Orr, tormented by mental exhaustion. "I don't know what more we could have done against them. Indiana was the best team here; you'd better believe it."

It was vindication for Knight, a resolute and fanatical man who at 35 became one of the youngest coaches to win the NCAA championship. "This was a two-year quest," he said, referring to the Hoosiers' bitter disappointment of the previous year, when they seemed destined to win the NCAA championship but had a 31-game winning streak stopped in a dramatic two-point loss to Kentucky in regional play.

But in 1975-76, the Hoosiers wouldn't allow themselves to be beaten. "No one knows better than I do what it means to these kids," said Knight. "I know how much work and effort has gone into it. This has been a somewhat strange season. We had stretches when we played basketball as well as it could be played, and then we'd suddenly go downhill. It was always up and down, until we got to the tournament and the chips were down. Then we played the game; we really did."

The Hoosiers had reached the end of their rainbow, finally, without getting hit by lightning.

212

1977
SEASHELLS AND BALLOONS

"The American idea is to win, unless you're playing against your grandmother. But even then you should try to win—unless you're mentioned in the will."—Al McGuire, Marquette University basketball coach

As the 1977 NCAA championship game ended in Atlanta, Hank Raymonds did a jig in front of the Marquette bench and grabbed coach Al McGuire in a bear hug. McGuire, his eyes filled with tears, broke away from his assistant coach and made his way through the sound and fury of the Omni into the Marquette dressing room. "I want to be alone," McGuire told reporters, wiping away tears with a towel. "I'm not afraid to cry."

The tough barroom philosopher, the street-corner aphorist, the self-acknowledged "street fighter," McGuire plainly had revealed a soft underbelly of sentimentalism after his Warriors had won the national title with a 67-59 victory over North Carolina. To the end, the colorful McGuire had entertained, enthralled and occasionally insulted the college basketball world with his outspoken dialogue and bizarre behavior. True to his code to the final moment, he ridiculed the involvement of grown men in a game, laughing at himself among others. But when it came time to finish his career as a basketball coach, there was McGuire directing his "guys in short pants" with the fervor that had marked his 20 passionate years on the side lines. And, eight seconds from the end, when the meaning of his first and last NCAA championship began sweeping over him, McGuire began sobbing on the bench. "It's seashells and balloons," McGuire would tell the press later, uttering a familiar phrase that defined the coach's personal euphoria.

If someone had suggested to McGuire in February that he would be standing in the winner's circle in March, the Marquette coach would have shrugged it off. Marquette had hit a bad late-season slump; and McGuire, as he was apt to say, thought it was "Tap City" for the Warriors. "When we lost our third game at home and were going on a

five-game road series with a 16-6 record, I'd given up." Lucky for Marquette, the players didn't. The Warriors won four of their last five games to finish with a 20-7 record, just barely good enough to get them into the NCAA tournament.

"Outside of a lucky suit, I don't know what caused it except maybe the subs coming through," McGuire said. "Subs win tournaments for you. The subs always must play over their capabilities."

Fulfilling McGuire's prophecy, the Warriors did indeed need superior performances from their bench to win in the NCAA's Midwest regional. Against Kansas State, sophomore Jim Dudley scored the go-ahead basket and contributed four key points as the Warriors came back from a 10-point deficit in the last 10 minutes to win, 67-66. And against Wake Forest, another sophomore, Bernard Toone, scored 18 points to lead an 82-68 victory in the Midwest finals. In both of those games, as well as a 66-51 triumph over Cincinnati in the first round, it was obvious that the Warriors had a special motivation for winning—McGuire's retirement announcement in the middle of the season. "No one has expressed it openly," said guard Jimmy Boylan, "but it would be nice for coach McGuire to end his career with an NCAA title." Added Boylan's backcourt partner, Butch Lee, "It would be a great way for him to go out."

But even at that point, Marquette seemed to be the least likely to succeed in the Final Four at Atlanta. The Warriors not only had lost the most games of any of the teams there but had been generally unimpressive in many of their victories. Rarely a team that won by big scores, the Warriors played tight, rugged defense and were methodical and patient on offense. "We usually get beat if the other team scores 70 or more," McGuire had said. The Warriors did just enough to win, usually

James Drake, Sports Illustrated

taking away what the opposition did best. They delighted in taking a racehorse offense and slowing it down, frustrating it, changing defenses, controlling the tempo until the opposition lost patience and began to force shots. Forward Bo Ellis and Lee, one of the country's most dynamic guards, were the leaders on the court; but there was no question who was the dominating figure on this team. "When you think of Marquette," said Lee, "you think of Al McGuire."

The first game of the championship weekend was a typical Marquette show—low scoring and high tension. The Warriors needed to play pre-

cisely their type of game to beat an unconventional North Carolina-Charlotte team that baffled basketball logic by using a 6-8 center to bring the ball downcourt. But even the magnificent Cedric "Cornbread" Maxwell couldn't do everything against the near-perfect Warriors. "We might have been a little tight," said Maxwell, whom coach Lee Rose called "the best all-around basketball player in the country."

Both teams, in fact, seemed tight at the beginning. The first five minutes of the opening semifinal game were no more than a sparring match between the two. Points were at a minimum until

Marquette's Butch Lee, the tournament's most outstanding player in 1977.

Marquette took charge behind center Jerome Whitehead and swept into a 23-9 lead. At this point, the highly vocal crowd at the Omni sensed that an execution was in progress. McGuire apparently was one of them, because at this juncture the overanxious Marquette coach attempted to put the 49ers away with his offensive team. He inserted Toone into the lineup with hopes that his terrific pointmaker could bomb out North Carolina-Charlotte with his long-range shots. Toone did make his first attempt but after that could hardly make any at all. The forward whom McGuire had called "probably the purest shooter in the country" suddenly fell flat, Marquette began making some crucial turnovers—and just like that it was a close game at the half, 25-22. Rose, the classy North Carolina-Charlotte coach, was still a bit disappointed despite his team's great comeback. "I think we came to Atlanta to play our worst half of the year," he said. "For some reason, we were very up-tight at first. We shot two or three air balls to start. The tremendous accomplishment it took to get here . . . maybe it was just overwhelming."

But the 49ers had some substance to them after all, as their second-half performance showed. Maxwell, apparently more relaxed, was his usual, ubiquitous self; and Lew Massey suddenly became a thorn in Marquette's side, hitting several shots.

A game of fluctuations, it rocked back and forth until a dramatic and controversial basket by the broad-shouldered Whitehead pulled it out for Marquette. With the score tied, 49-49, merely three seconds left and Marquette in possession of the ball, McGuire called a timeout and marched onto the court to the surprise of almost everyone. McGuire later explained: "I wasn't out there to do my Jimmy Durante act. I wanted to check the height of the clock." Clearly, McGuire was concerned that Lee's inbounds pass from the base line might hit the Omni's huge scoreboard above midcourt. If that happened, the ball would go to North Carolina-Charlotte under the Marquette basket with three seconds remaining. McGuire also was worried that Lee would hurl the ball too far, that it would sail out of bounds. As it turned out, neither of these things happened—but Marquette did get a lucky bounce when the ball finally touched Whitehead's straining fingers. The Marquette guard whipped the ball far downcourt. It glanced off Ellis' fingers, went through Maxwell's hands and finally was caught by Whitehead, who threw in a lunging layup as time ran out.

Nonetheless, it took several minutes for Marquette to claim its 51-49 victory because there was some question about the time of the basket. McGuire and several others raced to join referee Paul Galvan at the scorer's table. Had Whitehead's shot beaten the clock? "McGuire was going crazy," said Ken Angel, a North Carolina-Charlotte reserve. "I thought it was going to be a prizefight." Suddenly McGuire, ever the actor, emerged from the cluster with his arms spread in a sign of victory. A thunderous roar from the Marquette side finally signaled the end for North Carolina-Charlotte's gallant team. "I really didn't hear the horn," said Whitehead, who had carried the day for Marquette with 21 points and 16 rebounds. "There was too much noise. My mind was blank. All I was thinking about was getting the ball and putting it in." The 49ers were gracious in defeat. "I thought it was a good call," said Massey about the final basket. "If you judge by the horn, it was good. When the horn went off, I saw the ball land. What else can you say?"

That marvelous game was a tough act to follow, but somehow North Carolina and Nevada-Las Vegas managed to do it. The beginning of the second semifinal game held little competitive promise, but things picked up noticeably in the second half. North Carolina at first couldn't hold on to the ball, and Nevada-Las Vegas couldn't miss the basket. As a result, the aptly named Runnin' Rebels led by eight points several times. It appeared that the Tar Heels from the Atlantic Coast Conference were overmatched against a quick, brilliant-shooting team. But North Carolina was known for patience, a virtue that paid dividends for the Tar Heels all season long. Phil Ford, director of their exasperating four corners offense, worked for the final basket of the first half to trim Nevada-Las Vegas' lead to six points at 49-43. North Carolina coach Dean Smith kept the faith, if few others did. "I thought we were in good shape then," he said. "To play as badly as we did in the first half and only be down by six points at the half wasn't too bad." Besides, said Smith, "I didn't think their jump shots could keep going in."

Smith might have seemed like a cockeyed optimist to most people in the Omni. But there was more than optimism at work—there was thoughtful planning. The Tar Heels, who had been running with the Rebels for most of the first half, changed their strategy in the second half and slowed things down. The Rebels seemed to strangle in the grip of the Tar Heels' zone defense. One of the best shooting teams in the country, Nevada-Las Vegas was unable to make a field goal for a five-minute stretch in the second half. Meanwhile,

215

North Carolina was reeling off 14 points. In a flash, the Tar Heels had an eight-point lead and never lost their advantage. The ultimate winning point in North Carolina's 84-83 victory was a foul shot by John Kuester with seven seconds left.

"I think that Nevada-Las Vegas would do pretty well in the NBA," said Ford, grinning. He added, quite seriously, "But you have to give our team credit for not folding."

Playing catch-up against North Carolina at the end was not the easiest game in the world for Nevada-Las Vegas. "We were very unorganized," admitted forward Eddie Owens. "Whoever got it, shot it. We knew if they got a half-point lead, they would go into the four corners."

That would be McGuire's main worry in the national finals. "It's the Blue Plate special," McGuire said of North Carolina's famed slow-down offense. "Nobody does it any better."

The end of the trail loomed just around the corner for McGuire. In 13 years, the smooth talker off the sidewalks of New York had done more for the Marquette basketball program than anyone dared dream. His Warriors made 20-victory seasons a habit, playing to sellouts at home and generating tremendous national publicity for the urban Jesuit school in Milwaukee. Prior to the 1977 NCAA title game, Marquette had made continual visits to postseason tournaments, once winning the National Invitation Tournament and another time playing in the NCAA finals. But if McGuire was good for Marquette, his players tell you he was better for them. "It was his honesty," said George Thompson, the highest scorer in Marquette history. "He brought coaches out of closets. His style let coaches and players express themselves as people."

As was his custom, McGuire got lost when basketball wasn't in progress during the finals weekend. A motorcycle freak, he toured the Georgia countryside. A life freak, he explored Atlanta's nether regions incognito. He attended to business as well, of course. During the ritualistic press conference the day before the national championship game, McGuire luxuriously bathed in the spotlight. Characteristically, his comments were philosophical and extremely quotable.

On excitement: "The greatest excitement is winning. The next is losing, because it at least gives you some kind of feeling, even if it is nauseous."

On problem ball players: "I never had a problem with a ball player. I'm the only problem at Marquette."

North Carolina players surround Butch Lee of Marquette.

On pressure in sports: "People in golf think they've got pressure. Basketball's got much more. You put a 19-year-old kid in front of 15,000 people, they're shaking the basket, and the kid misses and he's a bum. A golfer has a chip shot so long (holding his hands 12 inches apart), and everyone has to be quiet."

On recruiting: "There are some distasteful things I have to do during my day, just as I'm sure there are some distasteful things you have to do in yours. I prefer to do mine early, so I don't blow the whole day."

On opposing coach Dean Smith: "He's a Jack Armstrong-type coach. He was born to be a college coach . . . not that he'll have any more kids in heaven than I do."

On playing North Carolina: "We have to cut the head off at the body. We'll have to short-stop Phil Ford. Ford's dynamite."

On his retirement: "That's all she wrote. It's curtains."

Just as Smith could not follow McGuire's act on Sunday, so did his North Carolina team fail to hold up to Marquette on Monday night. But typically, it was not easy for the Warriors. McGuire and his players had arrived at the Omni only 45 minutes before tipoff, with barely enough time to dress. Early in the game, the feverish Marquette coach kicked the scorer's table so hard that he limped the rest of the night. Minutes into the second half, as North Carolina stormed back from a 39-27 deficit and McGuire ranted and raved on the side line, his wife Pat stood in the stands pleading for him to sit down. But it was going to be all right for Marquette, even when North Carolina edged in front, 45-43,

with 13:48 left and soon thereafter went into its wicked four corners offense. The four corners turned out to be a double-edged sword for the Tar Heels, one by which they eventually met their demise.

Marquette sagged under the basket to take away the backdoor play which spun off the four corners. And, directed by Lee, the Warriors were patient on offense. Over the next 12 minutes, thanks in part to its own slowdown tactics, North Carolina was able to score only four points. Once Marquette regained the lead, the Warriors held it, even though there were some anxious moments at the end. With the Warriors leading, 53-49, with less than two minutes to play, Toone was poked in the eye accidentally by North Carolina's Mike O'Koren and reacted angrily by elbowing back. The officials awarded Toone a free throw for O'Koren's foul but also gave a technical foul to the Marquette forward—which meant two free throws for North Carolina. Toone missed his shot and Walter Davis made both for the Tar Heels, cutting Marquette's lead to 53-51 and setting up a jump-ball situation. Marquette won the tip, North Carolina started fouling and McGuire's ultimate victory was secure.

It was another frustration for Smith, who had guided North Carolina teams to the Final Four five times in 11 years, twice to the finals, but never had won the NCAA championship. As for McGuire, it was truly "seashells and balloons."

"I've always been an alley fighter," he said in his inimitable way. "I don't usually get into silk lace situations."

This time, however, the "alley fighter" went out in style.

1978
HAPPY ENDING

"We are expected to win—but I wouldn't want to be at a school where people didn't care."—Joe B. Hall, University of Kentucky basketball coach

It was a season without celebration for the Kentucky Wildcats. They had been haunted by tradition, pressured by their fanatical fans and driven unmercifully by their coach. "We've been under a tremendous amount of pressure to win the national championship this year," coach Joe B. Hall had said on the eve of the 1978 NCAA finals in St. Louis. "So much has been expected of us that there have been few rewards for this ball club. It's been a strange season. Being ranked No. 1 from the first eliminated almost any chance for success except for one accomplishment. We've got a lot of stored-up celebrating to do if we win the NCAA championship, I'll tell you."

This was the kind of pressure Hall and his team had lived under for four years, even though the Wildcats had won the National Invitation Tournament one season and finished as NCAA runner-up another year. Then, too, there had been three Southeastern Conference basketball championships to add to the burgeoning Kentucky showcase. But this was the last chance for the seniors to win an NCAA championship and fulfill the great expectations that everyone—including themselves—had held ever since they appeared on campus. As a result of that and Hall's constant goading, they had gone through the 1977-78 season with humorless determination.

"We want to save all the good times until after the season is over," said Rick Robey, an eloquent spokesman for the seniors. "During the season, you've got to be dedicated to succeeding. To be successful, you can't enjoy it during the work. Did I have more fun last season than this one? I'll answer that tomorrow night."

Even though Kentucky had lost but two games all season, the Wildcats were labeled the "Fold-Up Five" by some of their hard-line fans. "Why, even when we came home after winning the SEC cham-pionship, there was little noise," Hall said. "I would have given anything for someone to throw a firecracker or something."

On the other hand, Kentucky's opponent in the national finals had no such albatross around its neck. The Duke Blue Devils had no reputation to live up to and, as a result, had a relatively more relaxing season. The Atlantic Coast Conference champions, in fact, came into the title game at the Checkerdome "loose and having fun," according to the Duke people.

"We've just enjoyed the season so far," said Duke's brilliant floor leader, Jim Spanarkel. "You might as well enjoy basketball while you're playing it. So, preparing for the championship game, we've been very, very loose. I don't think there's a game so far this season where we've actually felt any pressure before game time. We have this philosophy: Five minutes before the game, we get serious. But it's only a 40-minute game; and if you worry about it, it only takes away from the fun of the game."

Duke coach Bill Foster, once an admitted "nervous type," encouraged the free and easy atmosphere. "Actually," he said, "the players have been able to relax me." Setting the tone of the wholly "loose" feeling expressed by Duke, Foster joked: "I didn't tell my players we were coming to St. Louis for the NCAA playoffs. I told them we were coming here to watch the Cardinals play."

As Kentucky eventually proved itself worthy of its No. 1 ranking, it also became obvious that Duke was No. 1 in the matters of harmony and brotherly love. On the floor, the Blue Devils believed in hugging, slapping palms and even holding hands before free throws. What's more, they laughed a lot. "It wasn't that way at first," said Foster. "It just developed. Our team spirit has been super. It's been a big part of our success."

220

Malcolm W. Emmons

Kentucky's Mike Phillips looks to pass off around the defensive efforts of Duke's Kenny Dennard.

Philosophies aside, there were other dramatic differences between the finalists of the 40th NCAA tournament—most noticeably the respective ages and styles of the teams. The Blue Devils were one of the youngest teams ever to appear in the tournament's final game. Their starting lineup consisted of a junior (guard Jim Spanarkel), two sophomores (center Mike Gminski and guard John Harrell) and two freshmen (forwards Eugene Banks and Kenny Dennard). Meanwhile, Kentucky's starting lineup featured three seniors in center Mike Phillips and forwards Jack Givens and Rick Robey, a junior in guard Truman Claytor and a sophomore in guard Kyle Macy. In addition, the first man off the bench was forward James Lee, a senior who generally was recognized as the best sixth man in college basketball that year.

The Blue Devils finished second to North Carolina in regular-season play in the Atlantic Coast Conference but came back to win the league tournament and the ACC's berth in the NCAA's Eastern regional. There, they defeated Rhode Island, Penn and Villanova to earn the trip to St. Louis. In their upset 90-86 victory over Notre Dame in the national semifinals, they showed just how good—and how bad—a young team can be. In the first half, the Blue Devils looked like world beaters while running up a 16-point lead. But when Notre Dame applied pressure in the second half, Spanarkel started throwing bad passes, Banks suddenly developed bad hands and Gminski was totally ineffective. Once, Banks let a pass go straight through his hands, then ran into a TV camera trying to retrieve the ball. The Blue Devils had an equally tough time holding on to the lead, just managing to hold off a rush by the Fighting Irish at the end.

In the matter of styles, most observers boiled it down to Kentucky's power game vs. the swiftness and finesse of the Duke attack. Although an oversimplification, the comparison had validity. With Robey and Phillips (both 6-10) and the 6-5 Lee and 6-4 Givens crashing the boards, getting layups and grabbing rebounds, Kentucky was well-fortified to win over most college teams in a battle based on strength. Although Hall didn't enjoy his team being called "physical," he did underscore the obvious: "We're not playing ballet."

But the Wildcats—although characterized as

James Lee of Kentucky and Bob Bender of Duke scramble for a loose ball in the 1978 championship game. Kentucky's Kyle Macy (4) looks on.

brutes—had more than one side. This was shown vividly as they won the Mideast regional with their inside, outside and all-around game. It was the Wildcat frontcourt players who helped Kentucky beat Miami of Ohio in one of the Mideast games, but it was the Wildcat backcourt that provided the impetus for a victory over Florida State and another in the finals over Michigan State.

The Mideast championship game was Macy's showcase, once the least publicized player in the Kentucky lineup was given the opportunity. Macy did not have the size of his bruising teammates or the style of the Spartans' Earvin "Magic" Johnson, but he did have the nerve when it counted. Macy's three-point play with 6:16 remaining broke a 41-41 tie, and his six straight one-and-one free throws in the last three minutes kept Kentucky in front for an eventual 52-49 victory over the Big Ten champions. Macy's performance in the Mideast finals was a dramatic contrast to the way he played two days earlier when the Wildcats defeated Miami, 91-69. In that game, Macy scored only two points while five of his teammates were hitting double figures. "Kyle hasn't even showed up yet," Hall prophetically would say later. "But Michigan State will

221

Malcolm W. Emmons

know he's there on Saturday."

Michigan State coach Jud Heathcote hardly gave Macy a second thought. He was more concerned about the brawny Wildcat frontline. "Even watching Kentucky kind of bruises you up a bit," Heathcote said before the finals in Dayton. "I hope it's a game, not a fight. If anyone ever came at me in a dark alley, I'd like to have those guys on my side."

Although Heathcote did not intend to be critical, he stirred up some controversy when he said, "There is no substitute for aggressiveness and intensity, and I think you achieve that by being physical." Hall bristled at that statement, equating the word "physical" with "dirty" basketball. "We don't give forearm shivers," he said, "but after all, we are athletes."

As it turned out, Heathcote need not have worried about Kentucky's muscle. It was Kentucky's hustle that beat him. The versatile Wildcats went to a change of style in the second half, after a lethargic first half during which Michigan State had built a 27-22 lead by sealing off Kentucky's inside game with a zone. Kentucky got back into the game, and eventually won, because of two major adjustments made in the dressing room at half time. First, Hall went to a 1-3-1 zone that spread his big men across the middle and

prevented the ubiquitous Johnson and his Spartan teammates from penetrating. Second, Hall told Robey to come outside and set screens to free Macy. After 10 minutes of the second half, the Wildcats had battled back to a 35-35 tie and clearly had things going their way.

Hall's offensive adjustments would have been wasted had his team not shot better in the second half, of course. The Wildcats' percentage leaped from 40 per cent in the first half to 57 in the second. Although Macy did not score every time Robey set a pick up for him, he did draw fouls—and therein was contained the story of the Mideast finals. Macy, a 90 per cent foul shooter who once hit 114 straight shots in a gym practice, made 10 of 11 in this game—including his seven big ones at the end that preserved Kentucky's tense victory. Macy, seemingly pressure-proof, was not bothered by the boisterous crowd or the two timeouts that Michigan State called when he was at the foul line with a one-point lead. In fact, he said, they made it easier for him. "The crowd made me concentrate more," he noted, "and the timeouts let me get a breather."

Robey was quick to underscore Kentucky's versatility. "We proved we can do it any way," he said after the game.

Foster believed this was true, especially after watching Kentucky defeat Arkansas, 64-59, in the national semifinals.

"Kentucky has been represented as a power team because of their big frontcourt players," said the Duke coach, "but I'm impressed with their quickness and their pressure defense. They overplay on defense very well and did a great job this way against Arkansas, one of the quickest teams you'll see."

Arkansas coach Eddie Sutton had thought that a closely officiated game would be to his advantage because it might limit the effectiveness of Kentucky's big men. He had hoped to get them into foul trouble, but instead just the opposite happened. The Razorbacks' two biggest starters, 6-11 Steve Schall and 6-7 Jim Counce, had four fouls each by half time, and Kentucky was ahead to stay, 32-30.

The Razorbacks had three of the best players in the country in Sidney Moncrief, Marvin Delph and Ron Brewer ("They are listed at 6-4, but they

Malcolm W. Emmons

Sidney Moncrief was one of the "triplets" who led
Arkansas in its national championship bid (Marvin Delph
and Ron Brewer were the other standouts).

222

Rich Clarkson, Sports Illustrated

224

Malcolm W. Emmons

Jay Shidler sets up the offense for Kentucky as Duke's Jim Spanarkel defends.

play bigger," Sutton had said) but no depth to match the loaded Kentucky bench. The Wildcats were bound to win a war of attrition and did just that, as their reserves outscored the Razorbacks, 19-3. Among the starters on both teams, only Givens played to form, scoring 23 points and grabbing nine rebounds for Kentucky.

Foul trouble did more than cost the Razorbacks players—it cost them their masterful style. Because of the fouls, the speedy Razorbacks spent most of the game in a zone defense instead of the stingy man-to-man that had propelled them into the national spotlight in 1977-78. It was not until they reverted to their favorite defense that they were able to make things interesting late in the game. The Hogs cut a nine-point Kentucky lead to one with 3:31 left. That was as close as Arkansas got, though. On the one opportunity the Southwest Conference power had to pull ahead, the usually reliable Moncrief—a 60 per cent shooter—missed a shot inside.

When the game was over, Robey repeated in the Kentucky locker room: "One more, one more, one more . . ."

Duke's fine basketball team remained Kentucky's final hurdle in its race against time for the long-sought-after national championship. The Blue Devils were the class team of a region that supposedly was the weakest of the four, but they had to fight to prove it. Duke, Villanova, Penn and Indiana brought a total of 28 losses into the tournament; and the Eastern regional was the butt of jokes, some calling it "the Least Regional" and "The Little Regional That Couldn't." The citizens of usually basketball-crazy Providence apparently agreed, leaving 1,096 seats empty in the Providence Civic Center for the regional finals.

Duke, which had played well only in spots in a 63-62 first-round victory over Rhode Island, wasn't entirely assertive against Penn in the regional semifinals, either. "Center Mike Gminski wandered through most of the semifinal looking as if he had lapsed into an irreversible coma," said one writer. That lasted until only 8:20 was left in the game and Duke was down by eight points. Then, Gminski slapped back three successive Penn shots and turned the game around, helping Duke come out with an 84-80 decision. Afterward, Penn coach Bob Weinhauer said that Duke was big but slow—a

mistaken concept that served to arouse the Blue Devils in the regional finals.

"The man did all that talking," Duke's Gene Banks was to say later. "He just went and made us mad."

The Blue Devils certainly played that way for the entire Eastern championship game. They took the opening tip against Villanova and didn't stop running until they had secured a 90-72 decision over the Wildcats. Spanarkel scored 22 points, had six assists and smartly directed the Duke attack. "I

Malcolm W. Emmons

Strong defense helped Kentucky to the 1978 championship. Here, James Lee blocks a shot.

225

Rich Clarkson

Jack Givens (21) of Kentucky scored 41 points in the Wildcats' 94-88 championship game decision over Duke.

think they underestimated our speed," Spanarkel said later without rancor.

Duke's speed was highly evident as well against Notre Dame in the national semifinals. The Blue Devils played brilliantly for 36 minutes, building a 45-29 lead before holding off Notre Dame's great comeback. When time finally did run out ("I was about to call for a mechanic to check the clock," Foster said after the game), the Blue Devils swarmed onto the court as if they had won the national title right there.

"We're No. 1 for sure next year," the exuberant Banks told his teammates in the shower.

"Wait a minute," Spanarkel replied. "We're not done with this year yet."

Duke's speed was the Blue Devils' most talked-about quality, but Kentucky still was considerably wary of their board strength headed by Gminski and Banks, the teenage terrors. "Duke enjoys contact," noted Robey. "They're a tough, all-around team."

The personalities of the combatants were demonstratively expressed at the start of the championship game. During the introduction of players, the exuberant Duke players ran out smiling and hugging. The soldier-like Kentucky players were grim, gritting their teeth. Foster skipped to shake Hall's hand; Hall stalked. But for all their easy, breezy spirit, the Blue Devils never were able to get the lead. The Wildcats attacked the Duke zone with fervor and shut off the Blue Devils' transition game from the start. The Blue Devils, who had stunned several previous tournament opponents with their fast break, got next to nothing from their running game against Kentucky.

Meanwhile, Givens' jump shot put holes in the Duke dream. Shooting from every conceivable angle, the left-handed forward scored 41 points, his career high and just three points shy of the championship-game record set by UCLA's Bill Walton in the same Checkerdome five years before. Givens scored 23 of his points in the first half to lead Kentucky to a 45-38 lead at intermission, then continued his one-man assault on the basket in the second half. "We always intend to get the ball inside to the big men," noted Givens, "but they were packing it in and left me open around the free-throw line. I took one shot in the second half, and it hit the side of the backboard and went

Senior Rick Robey exults in Kentucky's victory. The Wildcats were under pressure all year long as the championship favorite. But in the end, they were able to celebrate.

in. That's the kind of night I was having."

With the help of Givens' deadeye shooting, the Wildcats had a 66-50 lead with 12:42 left. When Hall began replacing his starters at the end, Duke made a frantic rally to cut the Wildcats' once-for-midable lead to 92-88. But the Kentucky regulars came back like a cavalry troop to preserve a 94-88 victory that was not as close as the score indicated.

When the game was over, there seemed to be more relief than satisfaction in the Kentucky dressing room. All season, Hall and his Wildcats were haunted by the specter that they might blow their final opportunity. Although ranked No. 1 for most of the season, the Wildcats were a target of constant chastisement and criticism from their coach. At one point in the season, Hall admitted that his players were "out of the doghouse" but pointedly explained, "They're still on a leash."

"We fussed a little bit," said Hall, "but I had to create some controversy to offset all the extravagantly good things that were being said about our team—that it could win both the National Basketball Association and National Football League titles. I had to change the players' thinking so they wouldn't believe that they already had won it."

The nightmarish season had dreamlike qualities at the end. Hall, the burden of the tough year finally lifted from his shoulders, stepped up to receive the NCAA championship trophy—the fifth in Kentucky history. The school band played the poignant "My Old Kentucky Home," and the fans sang the appropriate lyrics: "Weep no more my lady, weep no more for me."

At last Hall could smile. Even he had to admit that basketball was fun again.

227

Malcolm W. Emmons

APPENDICES
THE
RECORDS
1939 · 1978

CHRONOLOGICAL HISTORY

1938   Upon the recommendation of basketball coach H. G. Olsen of Ohio State, the incoming president of the National Association of Basketball Coaches, W. S. Chandler, was instructed by the NABC Convention to appoint a committee to explore the possibility of conducting a National Collegiate Basketball Championship. The committee was instructed to report its findings at the following year's convention. The committee was comprised of coaches John Bunn of Stanford, Forrest Allen of Kansas and Olsen.

The NCAA Executive Committee voted to approve the suggestion of the NABC that a national tournament be held and that the matter be under the general supervision of the NCAA Basketball Rules Committee. The NABC was responsible for the operation of the tournament.

The first NCAA tournament committee was elected for a one-year term. It was composed of H. G. Olsen (chairman), Forrest C. Allen, John Bunn, William S. Chandler of Marquette and H. H. Salmon, a businessman from New York City.

1939   The first Eastern playoff (Districts 1-4) was held at the University of Pennsylvania, and the first Western playoff (Districts 5-8) was held at Treasure Island in San Francisco.

The first NCAA basketball tournament finals were played at Patten Gymnasium on the campus of Northwestern University in Evanston, Illinois. Oregon defeated Ohio State, 46-33, to win the title. According to the format established, only the two regional winners advanced to the finals site (there was no third-place game). This first tournament finished with a deficit of $2,531.

The NABC agreed to provide each of its active or allied members in good standing with a complimentary ticket to the championship game, if present.

1940   The tournament came under the auspices of the NCAA effective with the 1940 championship, after the NABC voted to relinquish the administration of the competition.

The championship finals were held in Kansas City; Indiana defeated Kansas, 60-42. A ceremony honoring James Naismith, who invented the game of basketball in 1891 and died November 28, 1939, preceded the game.

For the first time, the NABC was in attendance at the finals. Its annual convention was, and has been since, scheduled at the site of the finals.

The first all-tournament team and most outstanding player selections were made. Howard Engleman and Bob Allen represented Kansas; Jay McCreary, William Menke and Marvin Huffman were selected from Indiana. Huffman was chosen as the most outstanding player. Although the selection of a most outstanding player continued, an all-tournament team was not selected again until 1952.

The net receipts for the tournament were $9,523, with the two finalists each receiving $750 in addition to expenses.

1943   The finals moved to Madison Square Garden in New York City. For the first time, total attendance for the tournament exceeded 50,000, with a total of 56,876 being recorded.

1946   For the first time, four teams advanced to the finals. Winners and runners-up from the East and West regionals came to Madison Square Garden. Oklahoma A&M (now Oklahoma State) defeated North Carolina, 43-40, to become the first team to win consecutive championships.

The championship trophy was named in honor of James W. St. Clair, chairman of the Basketball Rules Committee and a former member of the tournament committee. The trophy was donated by Ned Irish of Madison Square Garden. The championship trophy ceased to be referred to as the St. Clair trophy following the 1964 championship. NCAA policy now prohibits such designation of championship awards.

The finals were televised locally (New York City) for the first time by WCBS-TV. This initial viewing audience was estimated to be 500,000.

1947   Arthur C. "Dutch" Lonborg of Northwestern began his long tenure (13 years) as chairman of the tournament committee. Lonborg replaced H. G. Olsen.

The finals were held at Madison Square Garden for the fifth consecutive year. Holy Cross defeated Oklahoma, 58-47, to become the first independent team to win the NCAA championship.

1948   The tournament committee formulated a "Procedure for Guidance of NCAA Basketball Selection Committees," to be used in selecting teams for the tournament.

A new formula was devised for allocating the proceeds of the tournament, with 50 per cent going to the NCAA and 50 per cent to the participating institutions.

The NCAA Executive Committee voted to limit any district playoff to one game. Also, the Executive Committee voted to rotate the site of the finals among the various sections of the country, with specific locations to be recommended by the tournament committee.

1949   For the first time since 1941, the finals were played on a college campus, at the University of Washington. Kentucky defeated Oklahoma A&M (now Oklahoma State), 46-36, to become the second team to win consecutive titles. Alex Groza of Kentucky was selected as the most outstanding player for the second straight year, the second player to do so. Bob Kurland of Oklahoma A&M was the first (1945, 1946).

1950   City College of New York (CCNY) won both the NCAA championship and the NIT championship and holds the distinction of being the only team to do so.

1951   The NCAA championship field was expanded to 16 teams, with 10 conference champions qualifying automatically. Automatic qualifying conferences included: Eastern (Ivy), Big Ten, Southeastern, Southern, Border, Big Seven, Missouri Valley, Pacific Coast, Skyline and Southwest.

The format of the tournament continued to match the East winner against the West winner, and only two winners advanced to the finals. Regional losers played for third place at the finals site.

With the expansion of the field, it was necessary to adjust the formula for awarding shares of the net receipts. The new formula was as follows: two finalists, 16/144 each; two semifinalists, 14/144 each; four regional finalists, 11/144 each; eight first-round teams, 5/144 each.

1952 The number of regional sites was increased from two to four, with the four winners advancing to the finals. This regional format is still in use today.

The bracketing of teams was modified so that automatic qualifiers in the East did not play each other in the opening round. The East-West match-up continued.

Tournament games were televised regionally for the first time.

Selection of an all-tournament team was renewed. Players selected were Clyde Lovellette and Dean Kelley of Kansas, Bob Zawoluk and Ron MacGilvray of St. John's (New York) and John Kerr of Illinois. This was the first all-tournament team selected since 1939.

1953 The tournament bracket was increased from 16 teams to 22 teams, with 14 conferences receiving automatic qualification. Those conferences were the Eastern Intercollegiate (Ivy), Big Ten, Southeastern, Southern, Mid-American, Middle Atlantic, New England title designate, Big Seven, Missouri Valley, Southwest, Pacific Coast, Skyline Eight, Border and Rocky Mountain. The expanded format required four first-round sites and four regional sites.

1954 For the first time, the finals were televised nationally. La Salle defeated Bradley, 94-76, in Kansas City in the title game.

The tournament bracket was expanded again, this time to 24 teams. The Atlantic Coast Conference was added to the list of automatic qualifying conferences. At this time, 150 institutions were playing a major-college schedule.

Due to the problems encountered in the early 1950s with gambling, "game-fixing" and "point-shaving," all games except the finals were played in campus facilities.

A new format provided for first-round games March 8-9, regionals March 12-13 and the finals March 19-20. This gave the four regional winners more time to rest and prepare for the finals. Previously, the semifinals and finals had been played on Tuesday and Wednesday following the Friday and Saturday regionals.

The NCAA voted that national meets and tournaments conducted by the Association officially should be known as "National Collegiate Championship(s)."

1955 The first National Collegiate Basketball Championship handbook was printed, with information and policies concerning the event.

1956 The finals were played at Northwestern University, site of the first championship in 1939. Unbeaten San Francisco defeated Iowa, 83-71, to become the third institution to win back-to-back titles and the first to go undefeated (29-0).

Net income for the tournament exceeded $300,000 for the first time. The number of awards was increased from 14 to 15, with the champion and runner-up receiving watches, third- and fourth-place winners receiving plaques and all others receiving medals.

Hal Lear of Temple set two tournament records, scoring 48 points in the third-place game against Southern Methodist and totaling 160 points in five games.

The NCAA Council expressed serious concern about the reported increase in basketball gambling and the fact that some institutions were permitting their players to participate in highly organized summer basketball. The Council voted to circularize these beliefs to the membership, underscoring the dangers and institutional responsibilities in these areas.

1957 North Carolina became the second undefeated team (32-0) to win the title.

The largest media group to that point in the tournament's history was assembled for the finals in Kansas City. Coverage included an 11-station television network, 64 newspaper writers and live radio broadcasts by 73 stations in 11 states.

With the introduction of the College Division championship by the NCAA, the 19-year-old National Collegiate Basketball Championship became known as the University Division Championship.

Representatives of the NABC from the eight NCAA districts were appointed to assist the selection committee in determining at-large teams.

1958 Oscar Robertson of Cincinnati scored 56 points in the Midwest regional third-place game against Arkansas to set a national championship scoring record.

The tournament committee was increased from four to five members.

1959 In order to receive automatic qualification, institutions and conferences were required to operate their inseason basketball competition under eligibility rules at least as demanding as those of the NCAA.

Jerry West of West Virginia scored 160 points, which tied the five-game scoring record set by Temple's Hal Lear in 1956.

1960 The finals were held at the Cow Palace in San Francisco, where Ohio State defeated California, 75-55. The 20-point spread was the largest victory margin in a title game to that point in the tournament's history.

All but three of the nation's top 20 teams were in the tournament; and the composite won-lost record of the four finalists was the best in tournament history (99-8, .925), bettering the previous mark of (97-10, .907) in 1956.

Automatic qualifiers were reduced from 15 to 14 conferences as the Pacific Coast Intercollegiate Conference was dropped. Most of that conference's members transferred to the College Division. There were 11 at-large teams in the field. (This was a period in the tournament's history when the selection committee was free to choose from 23 to 25 teams for the competition.)

1961 Bernie A. Shively of the University of Kentucky assumed the duties as chairman of the tournament committee. He replaced Arthur C. "Dutch" Lonborg of the University of Kansas, who had served as chairman for 13 years.

Automatic qualification was granted to the Athletic Association of Western Universities (now the Pacific-10 Conference). Overall, the bracket totaled 24 teams—15 automatic qualifiers and nine at-large teams.

A system was implemented for selection, assignment and rotation of officials.

The officers submitted a preliminary report to the NCAA Executive Committee concerning the basketball gambling conspiracy.

Student-athletes representing St. Joseph's College (Pennsylvania) were declared ineligible subsequent to the tournament. Under NCAA rules, the team's and ineligible student-athletes' records were deleted, and the team's place in the final standings was vacated.

1962 The finals were held at Louisville, where Cincinnati defeated Ohio State for the second consecutive year, 71-59, to become the fourth team to win back-to-back titles.

All first-round and regional games were played in facilities owned and operated by educational institutions, because of the "point-shaving" scandals.

The U.S. Senate enacted legislation making it a Federal offense to attempt to bribe the outcome of any sports contest. Sixteen states were without antibribery legislation, and NCAA vice-presidents were urged to make every effort to develop antibribery laws in their states.

Procedures were outlined for naming an all-tournament team and most outstanding player for regionals and finals.

1963 For the first time, sites for finals competition were selected two years in advance.

For the semifinals and finals, officials were to be appointed and supervised by an officials supervisory committee composed of one member of the NCAA Basketball Rules Committee, one officials supervisor from a conference which did not have a team involved and one member of the University Division tournament committee, who served as chairman.

The Western Athletic Conference was added to the list of conferences receiving automatic qualification, and the Atlantic Coast Conference received a first-round bye for the first time. The Border Conference and the Mountain States Conference lost their automatic qualifying status.

Sunday competition in NCAA meets and tournaments was permitted in emergency situations if approved by the competing institutions.

The NCAA Council approved a proposal that University Division events be known as National Collegiate Championships and College Division events as National College Division Championships.

1964 The finals were played in Kansas City, where unbeaten UCLA won its first national championship by defeating Duke, 98-83. UCLA was the No. 1-ranked team in both wire service polls and the first top-ranked team to win the title since North Carolina in 1957.

A policy was adopted requiring any conference certified as an automatic qualifier to agree to make its championship team available for the tournament. In addition, the champion was obligated to compete unless it should decide to end its season at that time.

Responsibility for assigning officials to particular games was shifted from the tournament manager to the responsible tournament committee member. Officials were not to work games involving teams from their own conferences or booking agencies.

It was determined that season-end tournaments played to decide a conference's representative to the NCAA tournament would be considered as one game in determining the permissible 26 contests in a season.

1965 The finals were played at Memorial Coliseum in Portland, where UCLA defeated Michigan, 91-80, to become the fifth institution to win back-to-back titles.

The Ivy League, which lost its automatic qualification in 1956, had that status returned.

It was announced that beginning in 1967, all first-round games would be played on Saturday. In 1977, it became permissible to play first-round games on Sunday.

In an agreement with the NIT, the tournament committee agreed not to contact potential at-large entrants until 10 a.m. (local time) February 24.

A decision was made permitting the same officials to work first-round, regional and final tournament games.

Gail Goodrich of UCLA scored 42 points in the finals for a title-game record (held previously by Clyde Lovellette of Kansas, who scored 33 in 1952). Bill Bradley of Princeton scored 58 points against Wichita State in the national third-place game to break Oscar Robertson's single-game scoring record of 56, set against Arkansas in 1958. Bradley's 177 points in five games set an additional mark.

1966 Gross income for the tournament totaled $691,368 (including $180,000 from television), the highest in the tournament's history. Net income exceeded $500,000 for the first time.

The tournament committee announced that, beginning in 1967, it would become mandatory for the head basketball coach of each competing institution to participate in all official meetings connected with the tournament (first round through finals), as well as the awards ceremony.

The Yankee Conference lost its automatic qualifying status.

Televising was permitted of first-round and regional games at sites sold out 48 hours prior to game time (previously 72 hours) without geographical restrictions. The 72-hour restriction remained in effect for the finals.

Split officiating crews were to be used in first-round games whenever possible, with each of the competing teams having an official assigned by its regular-season officials booking office.

1967 H. B. "Bebe" Lee of Kansas State succeeded Bernie Shively as chairman of the tournament committee.

1968 The finals were played at the Sports Arena in Los Angeles, where UCLA became the first team to win back-to-back championships twice by defeating North Carolina, 78-55. The 23-point spread was the largest final-game winning margin in the tournament's history.

A conference commissioner (Paul Brechler of the Western Athletic Conference) was elected to the tournament committee, which increased its membership to seven persons.

The tournament committee recommended a Thursday night-Saturday afternoon format for the regionals and finals, starting in 1969 for a two-year period.

1969 The finals were played in Louisville, where UCLA won an unprecedented third consecutive title by defeating Purdue, 92-72. The Bruins went on to win seven consecutive championships.

The National Broadcasting Company was selected to televise the championship on the bases of revenue, exposure and promotional activities related to the tournament.

Fifteen conferences with automatic qualification and 10 at-large teams participated in the tournament.

Officials from the geographical areas of the teams competing in the East regional were assigned to the Midwest regional and vice versa. Comparable arrangements were made for officials assignments for the Mideast and West regionals.

The previous procedure of using Basketball Rules Committee district representatives and NABC-appointed district representatives to select at-large teams for the tournament was discontinued, and each advisory committee chairman was authorized to nominate three or four individuals to serve as a regional advisory committee.

Lew Alcindor of UCLA was selected as the most outstanding player for an unprecedented third consecutive year.

Total attendance for the tournament was 165,712; the gross income of $1,227,692, including $547,500 for television, was a record. The net income of $1,032,915 also was a record—the first time net income exceeded $1 million.

1970 Tom Scott of Davidson College replaced H. B. Lee as chairman of the tournament committee.

The tournament committee decided to continue the Thursday-Saturday format, which began in 1969 on an experimental basis. In addition, the committee chairman was authorized to represent the committee's interest in the sale of television rights for the games not televised by NBC.

1971 Total income for the tournament was $1,937,006, of which $726,000 was from television. This was a record, as was the net income of $1,555,478. Other record amounts were $207,514.94 for first-round receipts, $402,529.74 for the regionals and $382,876.26 for the finals.

Villanova, Western Kentucky and Long Beach State all had student-athletes who were declared ineligible subsequent to the tournament. Under NCAA rules, the teams' and ineligible student-athletes' records were deleted; and the teams' places in the final standings were vacated.

Fifteen automatic qualifiers and 10 at-large teams participated in the tournament.

A committee was appointed to study the possibilities of an

232

expanded bracket, potential regional alignment and the development of a rotation system for pairings at the finals.

Dates for the tournament were changed to meet the following schedule: first round, second Saturday in March; regionals, third Thursday and Saturday in March; finals, fourth Thursday and Saturday in March.

NBC recorded the largest audience for a basketball network telecast at the 1971 semifinals—a record 9,320,000 homes.

1972 The Pacific Coast Athletic Association was granted automatic qualification, bringing the total of such conferences to 16. Nine at-large teams also were selected to participate in the 1971 tournament.

NBC reported that the 1972 championship game was the highest-rated basketball telecast of all time.

Team place-standings and team and individual records for Long Beach State, Southwestern Louisiana and Minnesota were vacated, due to the use of ineligible student-athletes.

It was established that all future members elected to the tournament committee would be elected for three-year terms, rather than the previous six-year terms. A committee member could be reelected for a second three-year term.

1973 A new Saturday afternoon-Monday evening format replaced the Thursday-Saturday format for the finals. Regional play continued to take place on Thursday and Saturday.

Using a rotation plan, the East was bracketed against the Midwest and the Mideast against the West, which eliminated the East vs. West bracketing in effect since the tournament's inception in 1939. For 1974, the rotation bracketed East vs. West and Mideast vs. Midwest. The rotation system was to be conducted for those two years and then evaluated.

First-round byes were determined on the basis of evaluation of a conference's won-lost record over the past 10 years in National Collegiate Championship play.

Regional tournaments were permitted to be conducted in off-campus facilities in which a member institution played at least half of its home games. First-round games remained on campus.

An institution desiring to host a regional tournament was to agree that its team would participate only in the National Collegiate Basketball Championship following the conclusion of its regular season.

The membership of the tournament committee was decreased from seven to six with the elimination of a representative from the NABC.

Freshmen became eligible for varsity competition.

Specific criteria were established enabling conferences to apply for automatic qualification.

The tournament committee announced that an expanded 32-team bracket would be utilized beginning in 1975.

TVS, with the approval of NBC, agreed to televise those games not carried by NBC for a two-year period at a rights fee of $65,000 per year.

Student-athletes representing Southwestern Louisiana, Long Beach State and Austin Peay State were declared ineligible subsequent to the tournament, causing their records and team places to be vacated.

The championship game recorded the highest basketball television rating in history. The contest received a rating of 20.5 and was seen by 13,580,000 television homes. The total audience was 39 million people. For the first time, the championship game was televised in prime time.

Total attendance for the tournament was 174,049. Gross income—including $1,165,755 for television—set a record of $2,301,203. It was the first time tournament income had exceeded $2 million. Net income was $1,922,367.

Tickets for the 1974 finals were sold out April 1, 1973. This was the first time the finals were sold out a year in advance. Approximately 173,000 individual requests for tickets were received.

1974 With a bracket which scheduled East vs. West and Mideast vs. Midwest, the finals were played at Greensboro (North Carolina) Coliseum, where North Carolina State ended the seven-year reign of UCLA by defeating the Bruins in the semifinals, 80-77, in double overtime. The Wolfpack then defeated Marquette, 76-64, to win the championship.

Host institutions were permitted to retain 5 per cent of the net receipts for the use of their facilities on campus.

It was directed that the officials supervisory committee for the regionals and finals include a minimum of five individuals and be comprised of coaches, Basketball Rules Committee members, conference basketball supervisors and a tournament committee representative, with no more than two individuals from each category.

The NABC was authorized to conduct an experimental game with 11-foot baskets on Friday evening during finals weekend.

The tournament committee approved the recommendation of the Eastern College Athletic Conference that its membership be divided into four geographical areas, with a season-end tournament of the top four teams in each area beginning in 1975. The four winners were to receive automatic qualification. The Ivy League and Middle Atlantic teams were not affected.

1975 The finals were played at the San Diego Sports Arena, where UCLA won its 10th championship by defeating Kentucky, 92-85.

The tournament completed its first year with a 32-team bracket. Included were 20 automatic qualifying conferences (four teams from the ECAC) and 12 at-large teams. This also was the first year that a second conference team (other than the champion) could be selected as an at-large entry; if selected, it was to be placed in the bracket opposite the conference champion so they could not meet until the finals.

A provision was included in the tournament procedures declaring that after a 10-minute cooling-off period, dressing rooms were to be open to the news media and the coach was to proceed to the interview room.

Ticket price minimums were established for first-round and regional doubleheaders.

Third-place games in the regionals were eliminated, but it was determined that all teams that advanced to the regionals were to receive equal shares of the receipts.

The policy stating that an institution desiring to host a regional tournament must agree that its team would participate only in the NCAA tournament was relaxed to read that it must agree that its key administrative personnel would be available to conduct the tournament.

The first-round site policy was relaxed so that games could be played in off-campus facilities in which a member institution played at least half of its home games. Also, first-round or regional sessions could be conducted in off-campus facilities if hosted by an allied conference which has had a member institution play a regularly scheduled game in the facility during the year in which it would host the tournament.

It was determined that 30 per cent of the available tickets at the finals (after deducting tickets for the competing teams, NABC, NCAA, host institution and arena) should be scheduled for sale to the general public.

1976 Stan Watts of Brigham Young University was elected chairman of the tournament committee, replacing Tom Scott of Davidson College. Scott had served on the committee nine years, six as chairman.

Host institutions were permitted to retain 10 per cent (previously 5 per cent) of the net receipts for the use of

233

on-campus facilities. For off-campus facilities, the tournament committee was to negotiate satisfactory financial arrangements.

A new procedure was adopted for selecting and assigning officials: The tournament committee was to assign officials after the pairings were made, based upon a priority list of best officials supplied by the booking agencies. Officials were to be cross-assigned for all first-round games and whenever possible for regional and final sessions. Officials were to be evaluated by a committee (three to five members) representing coaches, Basketball Rules Committee, conference basketball supervisors and the tournament committee.

Jim Host and Associates began the first year of a three-year contract to establish the NCAA Radio Network. A total of 250 stations carried the 1974 games.

For purposes of automatic qualification, the requirement of conference competition was more clearly defined. Conference competition was defined as regular-season, round-robin type play among members of the conference, or a postseason tournament designed to determine the conference's champion and representative in NCAA competition.

1977   NBC reported that the championship game between Marquette and North Carolina marked the second time that more than 42 million persons viewed a television basketball game (the first was the 1975 final between Kentucky and UCLA).

The tournament committee voted that geographical rotation not be a determining factor in selecting future finals sites.

1978   The finals were played at the Checkerdome in St. Louis, where Kentucky won its fifth championship by defeating Duke, 94-88. Kentucky is the only team other than UCLA to win more than three championships.

Wayne Duke, commissioner of the Big Ten Conference, was elected chairman of the tournament committee, replacing Stan Watts.

NBC televised the four regional championship games and NCAA Productions televised all of the regional semifinals. NBC nationally televised a first-round doubleheader on Saturday and on Sunday, and NCAA Productions regionally televised all but one of the remaining games.

Complimentary tickets for all NCAA championships were eliminated.

The tournament committee voted that effective with the 1983 tournament, the facility in which the final session is conducted must have a minimum of 17,000 seats.

A policy was adopted requiring that five individuals be used in evaluating officials at each session. The high and low cards were to be discarded, and the remaining three cards averaged to determine the highest-rated official in each game.

A seeding process was used for the first time. A maximum of four automatic qualifying conference teams were seeded in each of the four regional brackets. These teams were seeded based on their respective conferences' won-lost percentages in tournament play during the past five years. At-large seeding in each region was based on current won-lost records, strength of schedule and eligibility status of student-athletes for postseason competition.

The tournament committee voted to expand the bracket for the 1979 championship to 40 teams. The expansion carried the following stipulations:

1. All eligible Division I allied conferences received automatic qualification, and the 16 conferences with the best won-lost record in tournament play over the past five years would receive byes into the second round.
2. Eight remaining byes were to be distributed among remaining automatic qualifying conferences, independents and second conference teams.
3. Each region was to include 10 teams. The lowest-seeded four teams within each region would play in first-round competition.
4. Twenty conference champions and three regional representatives from the ECAC were to comprise the automatic qualifiers, and the tournament committee would select the remaining 17 teams.

It was determined that commencing with the 1983 tournament, first-round games would be played on the third Saturday and Sunday in March, regional championships on the fourth Saturday and Sunday in March, the national semifinals on the next Saturday and the national championship game on the Monday following.

NCAA

BASKETBALL COMMITTEE

Committee Chairmen, 1940-1978

1940-47	Harold G. Olsen	Ohio State
1948-60	Arthur C. Lonborg	Northwestern, Kansas
1961-65	Bernie Shively	Kentucky
1966-70	H. B. Lee	Kansas State
1971-75	Tom Scott	Davidson
1976-77	Stan Watts	Brigham Young
1978-	Wayne Duke	Big Ten Conference

Committee Roster

Albus, Larry	St. Louis 1975-76; Metro-7 Conference 1977-78	1975-78
Allen, Forrest C.	Kansas	1940-41
Anderson, Ladell	Utah State	1978
Andreas, Lewis P.	Syracuse	1944-45; 1954-59
Brawner, Hoyt	Denver	1965-72
Brechler, Paul	Western Athletic Conference	1967-68
Brown, Robert	West Virginia	1957-62
Bunn, John	Stanford	1940
Bushnell, Asa S.	Eastern College Athletic Conference	1950-53
Carnevale, Ben	Navy 1964-66; New York University 1967-69	1964-69
Casale, Ernest	Temple	1970-76
Casey, Willis	North Carolina State	1975-78
Chandler, W. S.	Marquette	1940
Conboy, John	LaSalle	1977
Dean, Everett	Stanford	1948-50
Duke, Wayne	Big Ten Conference	1976-78
Eaves, Joel	Georgia	1971-74
Edmundson, C. S.	Washington State	1941-47
Edwards, George R.	Missouri	1942-50
Fisher, Waldo	Northwestern	1961-66
Geiger, Ferdinand	Pennsylvania	1978
Grover, B. T.	Ohio University	1941
Hallock, Wiles	Western Athletic Conference 1969-73; Pacific-8 Conference 1974-75	1969-75
Hickox, Edward W.	Springfield	1946-47
Holman, Nat	CCNY	1942
Karr, Ken	San Diego State	1976-78
Keene, Roy	Oregon	1957-61
Kelleher, E. A.	Fordham	1944-45
Lee, H. B.	Kansas State	1960-70
Lonborg, Arthur C.	Northwestern 1948-50; Kansas 1951-60	1948-60
McCoy, Ernest	Penn State	1959-64
Morgan, J. D.	UCLA	1968-74
Newell, Pete	California	1962-67
Nixon, Albert	New York University	1948-49
Nordgen, Nels	Chicago	1943
Olsen, Harold G.	Ohio State	1940-47
Peters, Reaves	MVIAA	1949-56
Peterson, Vadal	Utah	1953
St. Clair, James W.	Southern Methodist	1941-46
Salmon, H. H. Jr.	—	1940
Scott, Tom	Davidson	1966-75
Shelton, Everett	Wyoming	1954-58
Shively, Bernie	Kentucky	1959-65
Smith, Wilbur C.	Tulane	1943
Taylor, Fred	Ohio State	1967-73
Twogood, Forrest	Southern California	1961-63
Watts, Stan	Brigham Young	1974-77

More than a quarter-century of basketball leadership is pictured here with H. B. "Bebe" Lee (left), chairman of the NCAA tournament committee from 1966 to 1969; Arthur "Dutch" Lonborg, chairman from 1948 to 1960, and Tom Scott, chairman from 1970 to 1975.

APPENDIX C
FINANCIAL ANALYSIS

NCAA Basketball Championship
Financial Analysis

	First Round Net	Regionals Net	Finals Net	Receipts	Team & Game Expenses	Administrative Expenses	Net	Total Attendance
1939	$	$	$ (2,531)	$ 42	$ 2,573	$	$ (2,531)	15,025
1940		1,200	8,323	29,493	19,970		9,523	36,880
1941		9,286	1,652	31,120	20,182	1,895	9,044	48,055
1942		1,845	1,303	26,625	23,477	1,786	1,362	24,372
1943		716	11,001	55,387	43,869	1,318	10,200	56,876
1944		1,937	25,782	79,699	51,980	1,690	26,029	59,369
1945		3,007	26,768	89,847	60,081	2,099	27,667	67,780
1946		17,997	37,136	137,154	82,020	4,469	50,665	73,116
1947		16,974	43,542	153,337	92,821	2,881	57,635	72,959
1948	6,626	18,501	40,199	158,010	92,683	2,574	62,753	72,523
1949	9,130	43,822	22,559	151,003	75,491	14,664	60,848	66,077
1950	6,304	18,358	41,467	154,600	88,470	1,484	64,646	75,464
1951		87,493	22,447	222,497	112,558	4,945	104,994	110,645
1952		100,471	45,736	248,621	99,179	17,398	132,044	115,712
1953	20,810	106,955	42,792	319,571	149,014	10,683	159,874	127,149
1954	16,804	78,236	41,813	266,350	129,497	7,277	129,576	115,391
1955	19,053	111,326	50,219	295,842	115,244	5,825	174,772	116,983
1956	9,969	116,823	55,223	303,006	120,991	8,355	173,660	132,513
1957	14,588	114,115	58,318	301,477	114,454	10,197	176,826	108,891
1958	18,355	215,161	98,505	462,667	130,640	11,161	320,866	176,878
1959	27,693	223,345	123,370	508,755	134,347	11,319	363,089	161,809
1960	33,029	220,053	106,863	518,746	158,550	13,679	346,517	155,491
1961	33,758	229,677	103,322	514,692	147,935	11,077	355,680	169,520
1962	50,033	204,099	186,406	579,771	139,233	10,321	430,217	177,469
1963				TV 140,000				
	49,798	123,773	141,779	466,910	151,560	9,868	445,482	153,065
1964				TV 155,000				
	59,797	177,850	98,892	483,752	147,213	10,331	481,208	140,790
1965				TV 170,000				
	31,523	190,917	114,979	479,827	142,408	13,520	493,898	140,673
1966				TV 180,000				
	30,108	180,465	146,674	511,368	154,121	15,206	522,041	140,925
1967				TV 190,000				
	63,599	254,081	174,098	675,171	183,393	21,552	660,225	159,570
1968				TV 200,000				
	48,617	294,054	185,775	730,965	202,519	17,693	710,753	160,888
1969				TV 547,500				
	45,603	277,582	185,904	731,192	222,103	23,674	1,032,915	165,712
1970				TV 550,800				
	129,515	274,059	145,264	824,299	275,461	33,745	1,065,893	158,538
1971				TV 726,500				
	169,647	347,607	342,998	1,210,506	349,766	31,763	1,555,478	220,447

FINANCIAL ANALYSIS

	First Round Net	Regionals Net	Finals Net		Receipts	Team & Game Expenses	Administrative Expenses	Net	Total Attendance
1972				TV	743,500				
	57,167	376,939	236,400		997,938	323,899	31,528	1,386,011	166,341
1973				TV	1,165,755				
	52,244	425,829	310,599		1,135,448	342,471	36,365	1,922,367	174,049
1974				TV	1,240,999				
	53,586	420,100	238,758		1,073,235	359,240	38,828	1,916,161	173,331
1975				TV	2,530,000				
	252,866	364,024	278,811		1,442,857	546,618	47,252	3,378,987	193,051
1976				TV	2,590,000				
	263,753	470,934	331,551		1,696,455	599,129	48,023	3,639,303	216,165
1977				TV	4,041,062				
	286,063	703,972	331,083		2,071,976	714,289	47,226	5,378,825	239,402
1978				TV	4,690,683				
	357,888	450,939	460,939		1,924,473	285,305	81,126	6,088,955	233,362
				TV	19,861,799				
	2,217,925	7,274,522	4,916,719		33,194,738	7,204,754	664,797	33,924,464*	5,173,256

237

*Since 1941, the net receipts have been divided equally between the NCAA's general operating fund and the participating teams.

Attendance Figures

Year	Total Attendance	Dates	Average	Best at Finals	Best in Tourney
1939	15,025	5	3,005	5,500	Same as Finals
1940	36,880	5	7,376	10,000	Same as Finals
1941	48,055	5	9,611	7,219	12,500 (Madison Square Garden, Eastern Playoffs)
1942	24,372	5	4,874	6,500	Same as Finals
1943	56,876	5	11,375	13,300	Same as Finals
1944	59,369	5	11,874	15,000	Same as Finals
1945	67,780	5	13,556	18,035	Same as Finals
1946	73,116	5	14,623	18,479	Same as Finals
1947	72,959	5	14,592	18,445	Same as Finals
1948	72,523	5	14,505	16,174	18,472 (Madison Square Garden, Eastern Playoffs)
1949	66,077	5	13,215	10,600	18,499 (Madison Square Garden, Eastern Playoffs)
1950	75,464	5	**15,093	18,142	Same as Finals
1951	110,645	9	12,294	15,348	17,000 (Madison Square Garden, Eastern Playoffs)
1952	115,712	10	11,571	11,000	14,147 (Chicago Stadium, Mideast Regional)
1953	127,149	14	9,082	10,500	14,337 (Chicago Stadium, Mideast Regional)
1954	115,391	15	7,693	10,500	Same as Finals
*1955	116,983	15	7,799	10,500	18,499 (Madison Square Garden, East First Round)
1956	132,513	15	8,834	10,600	18,499 (Madison Square Garden, East First Round)
1957	108,891	14	7,778	10,500	16,589 (Madison Square Garden, East First Round)
1958	176,878	14	12,634	18,803	Same as Finals

Year	Total Attendance	Dates	Average	Best at Finals	Best in Tourney
1959	161,809	14	11,558	18,619 (Semis) 18,498 (Finals)	Same as Finals (Semis)
1960	155,491	16	9,718	14,500	Same as Finals
1961	169,520	14	12,109	10,700	18,893 (Freedom Hall, Louisville, Kentucky, Mideast Regional)
1962	177,469	14	12,676	18,469	Same as Finals
1963	153,065	14	10,933	19,153	Same as Finals
1964	140,790	14	10,056	10,864	12,400 (Reynolds Coliseum, Raleigh, North Carolina, East Regional)
1965	140,673	13	10,821	13,204	Same as Finals
1966	140,925	13	10,840	13,848	Same as Finals
1967	159,570	14	11,398	18,892	Same as Finals
1968	160,888	14	11,492	15,742 (Semis) 14,438 (Finals)	Same as Finals (Semis)
1969	165,712	15	11,047	18,669	Same as Finals
1970	158,538	16	9,909	14,380	Same as Finals
1971	**220,447	16	13,778	**31,428 (Semis) **31,765 (Finals)	Same as Finals
1972	166,341	16	10,396	15,063	15,247 (Marriott Fieldhouse, Brigham Young University, West Regional)
1973	174,049	16	10,878	19,301	Same as Finals
1974	173,331	16	10,833	15,829 (Semis) 15,742 (Finals)	Same as Semifinals
1975	193,051	16	12,066	15,151	Same as Finals
1976	216,165	16	13,510	17,540	Same as Finals
1977	239,402	16	14,962	16,086	21,965 (Brigham Young University West Regional)
1978	233,362	16	14,585	18,721	Same as Finals

—5,173,256 Total Attendance for Championship 1939-1978—

* The championship game (La Salle 92, Bradley 76) was televised nationally for the first time.

**Attendance records.

238

APPENDIX D
TOURNAMENT RECORDS

All-Time Scoring Leaders

Player, Institution (Years Competed)	g	fg	ft	tp	avg.
Elvin Hayes, Houston (1966-67-68)............	13	152	54	358	27.5
Oscar Robertson, Cincinnati (1958-59-60).......	10	117	90	324	32.4
Lew Alcindor, UCLA (1967-68-69).............	12	115	74	304	25.3
Bill Bradley, Princeton (1963-64-65)...........	9	108	87	303	33.7
Austin Carr, Notre Dame (1969-70-71)........	7	117	55	289	41.3
Jerry West, West Virginia (1958-59-60).........	9	97	81	275	30.6
Jerry Lucas, Ohio State (1960-61-62)..........	12	104	58	266	22.2
Bill Walton, UCLA (1972-73-74).............	12	109	36	254	21.2
Gail Goodrich, UCLA (1963-64-65)............	10	84	67	235	23.5
Marques Johnson, UCLA (1974-75-76-77).......	16	96	42	234	14.6
Tom Gola, LaSalle (1954-55)................	10	77	75	229	22.9
Cazzie Russell, Michigan (1964-65-66).........	9	81	64	226	25.1
Len Chappell, Wake Forest (1961-62)..........	8	72	77	221	27.6
Paul Hogue, Cincinnati (1960-61-62)..........	12	93	35	221	18.4
Jimmy Collins, New Mexico State (1968-69-70)...	11	91	37	219	19.9
Bill Russell, San Francisco (1955-56)..........	9	89	31	209	23.2
Richard Washington, UCLA (1974-75-76).......	13	94	21	209	16.1
Adrian Dantley, Notre Dame (1974-75-76)......	8	73	57	203	25.4
Eddie Owens, Nevada-Las Vegas (1975-76-77) ...	10	88	26	202	20.2
Jeff Mullins, Duke (1963-64)................	8	84	32	200	25.0

Leading Scoring Averages

Player, Institution	yr	g	fg-fga	ft-fta	rb	pf	tp	avg.
Austin Carr, Notre Dame	1970	3	68-118	22-26	24	5	158	52.7
Austin Carr, Notre Dame	1971	3	48-101	29-37	26	8	125	41.7
Dan Issel, Kentucky	1970	2	30- 53	12-16	21	6	72	36.0
Jerry Chambers, Utah	1966	4	55-108	33-40	56	11	143	35.8
Vann Williford, North Carolina State	1970	2	24- 46	23-29	23	4	71	35.5
Bill Bradley, Princeton	1965	5	65-114	47-51	55	20	177	35.4
Clyde Lovellette, Kansas	1952	4	53- NR	35-NR	NR	NR	141	35.3
Gail Goodrich, UCLA...........	1965	4	49- 88	42-48	14	14	140	35.0
Jerry West, West Virginia........	1960	3	35- 77	35-42	47	7	105	35.0
Bob Houbregs, Washington	1953	4	57- NR	25-NR	NR	NR	139	34.8
Elvin Hayes, Houston...........	1968	5	70-137	27-48	102	12	167	33.4
Mike Glenn, SIU-Carbondale......	1977	2	30- 45	5- 5	5	3	65	32.5
Johnny O'Brien, Seattle	1953	3	29- NR	38-NR	NR	NR	96	32.0
Hal Lear, Temple	1956	5	63- NR	34-NR	NR	NR	160	32.0
Jerry West, West Virginia........	1959	5	57- 96	46-71	73	15	160	32.0
Willie Smith, Missouri	1976	3	38- 79	18-27	17	9	94	31.3
Don Schlundt, Indiana	1953	4	37- NR	49-NR	NR	NR	123	30.8
Adrian Dantley, Notre Dame......	1975	3	29- 48	34-48	27	11	92	30.7
Henry Finkel, Dayton	1966	3	37- 61	18-21	48	13	92	30.7
Oscar Robertson, Cincinnati	1960	4	47- 94	28-40	47	12	122	30.5
Rick Mount, Purdue	1969	4	49-116	24-27	8	5	122	30.5

Eugene Banks of Duke, the Blue Devils' leading scorer in the 1978 title game with 22 points.

Top 20 Single Game Performances

Player, Institution vs. Opponent, Year	rd	fg	ft	tp
Austin Carr, Notre Dame vs. Ohio, 1970	1st	25	11	61
Bill Bradley, Princeton vs. Wichita State, 1965	C*	22	14	58
Oscar Robertson, Cincinnati vs. Arkansas, 1958	C	21	14	56
Austin Carr, Notre Dame vs. Kentucky, 1970..........	2nd	22	8	52
Austin Carr, Notre Dame vs. Texas Christian, 1971.....	1st	20	12	52
Elvin Hayes, Houston vs. Loyola, Ill., 1968	1st	20	9	49
Hal Lear, Temple vs. Southern Meth., 1956...........	C*	17	14	48
Austin Carr, Notre Dame vs. Houston, 1971	C	17	13	47
Dave Corzine, DePaul vs. Louisville, 1978	2nd	18	10	46
Bob Houbregs, Washington vs. Seattle, 1953	2nd	20	5	45
Austin Carr, Notre Dame vs. Iowa, 1970.............	C	21	3	45
Clyde Lovellette, Kansas vs. St. Louis, 1952	RC	16	12	44
Bill Walton, UCLA vs. Memphis State, 1973...........	F	21	2	44
Rod Thorn, West Virginia vs. St. Joseph's, Pa., 1963....	2nd	16	12	44
Oscar Robertson, Cincinnati vs. Kansas, 1960.........	RC	19	5	43
Jeff Mullins, Duke vs. Villanova, 1964...............	2nd	19	5	43
Willie Smith, Missouri vs. Michigan, 1976	RC	18	7	43
Johnny O'Brien, Seattle vs. Idaho State, 1953.........	1st	17	8	42
Bob Houbregs, Washington vs. Louisiana State, 1953 ...	C*	17	8	42
John Clune, Navy vs. Connecticut, 1954	1st	16	10	42
Jim Barnes, Texas-El Paso vs. Texas A&M, 1964	1st	16	10	42
Gail Goodrich, UCLA vs. Michigan, 1965	F	12	18	42

[Key: 1st—first round; 2nd—second round; RC—regional championships; C—regional consolation; C*—third place game; F—championship game.]

Leading Rebounder, Year-by-Year

Year	Player, Institution	g	rb	avg.
1951	Bill Spivey, Kentucky	4	65	16.3
1957	John Green, Michigan State	4	77	19.3
1958	Elgin Baylor, Seattle................	5	91	18.2
1959	Don Kojis, Marquette	3	56	18.7
1960	Howard Jolliff, Ohio	3	64	21.3
1961	Jerry Lucas, Ohio State	4	73	18.3
1962	Len Chappell, Wake Forest...............	5	86	17.2
1963	Nate Thurmond, Bowling Green............	3	70	23.3
1964	Paul Silas, Creighton	3	57	19.0
1965	Bill Bradley, Princeton	5	57	11.4
1966	Elvin Hayes, Houston................	3	50	16.7
1967	Elvin Hayes, Houston................	5	75	15.0
1968	Elvin Hayes, Houston................	5	97	19.4
1969	Lew Alcindor, UCLA................	4	64	16.0
1970	Sam Lacey, New Mexico State	5	90	18.0
1971	Sidney Wicks, UCLA	4	52	13.0
1972	Bill Walton, UCLA	4	64	16.0
1973	Bill Walton, UCLA	4	58	14.5
1974	Tom Burleson, North Carolina State	4	61	15.3
1975	Richard Washington, UCLA...............	5	60	12.0
1976	Phil Hubbard, Michigan	5	51	10.2
1977	Cedric Maxwell, North Carolina-Charlotte	5	64	12.8
1978	Eugene Banks, Duke.................	5	50	10.0

TOURNAMENT RECORDS

All-Time Rebounding Leaders

Player, Institution (Years Competed)	g	rb	avg.
Elvin Hayes, Houston (1966-67-68)	13	222	17.1
Lew Alcindor, UCLA (1967-68-69)	12	201	16.8
Bill Walton, UCLA (1972-73-74)	12	159	13.3
Sam Lacey, New Mexico State (1968-69-70)	11	157	14.3
Marques Johnson, UCLA (1974-75-76-77)	16	138	8.6
Jerry Lucas, Ohio State (1960-61)	8	137	17.1
Curtis Rowe, UCLA (1969-70-71)	12	131	10.9
Mel Counts, Oregon State (1962-63-64)	9	127	14.1
John Green, Michigan State (1957, 1959)	6	118	19.7
Artis Gilmore, Jacksonville (1970-71)	6	115	19.2
Sidney Wicks, UCLA (1969-70-71)	12	112	9.3
Paul Silas, Creighton (1962, 1964)	6	111	18.5
Bill Bradley, Princeton (1963-64-65)	9	108	12.0
Phil Hubbard, Michigan (1976-77)	8	96	12.0

Leading Rebounders—Average

Player, Institution	yr	g	rb	avg.
Nate Thurmond, Bowling Green	1963	3	70	23.3
Howard Jolliff, Ohio	1960	3	64	21.3
John Green, Michigan State	1959	2	41	20.5
Elvin Hayes, Houston	1968	5	105	21.0
John Green, Michigan State	1957	4	77	19.3
Paul Silas, Creighton	1964	3	57	19.0
Lew Alcindor, UCLA	1968	4	75	18.8
Don Kojis, Marquette	1959	3	56	18.7
Ollie Johnson, San Francisco	1965	2	37	18.5
James Ware, Oklahoma City	1965	3	55	18.3
Jerry Lucas, Ohio State	1961	4	73	18.3
Elgin Baylor, Seattle	1958	5	91	18.2
Paul Silas, Creighton	1962	3	54	18.0
Bill Walton, UCLA	1972	4	72	18.0
Sam Lacey, New Mexico State	1970	5	90	18.0
Mel Counts, Oregon	1963	3	53	17.7
Clyde Lee, Vanderbilt	1965	2	35	17.5
Len Chappell, Wake Forest	1962	5	86	17.2
Wayne Embry, Miami, Ohio	1958	3	51	17.0
John Fairchild, Brigham Young	1965	2	34	17.0

Best Single Game Performance

Player, Institution vs. Opponent, Year	rd	rb
Nate Thurmond, Bowling Green vs. Mississippi State, 1963	C	31
Jerry Lucas, Ohio State vs. Kentucky, 1961	RC	30
Toby Kimball, Connecticut vs. St. Joseph's, Pa., 1965	1st	29
Elvin Hayes, Houston vs. Pacific, 1966	RC	28
John Green, Michigan State vs. Notre Dame, 1957	2nd	27
Paul Silas, Creighton vs. Oklahoma City, 1964	1st	27
Elvin Hayes, Houston vs. Loyola, Ill., 1968	1st	27
Howard Jolliff, Ohio University vs. Georgia Tech, 1960	2nd	26
Phil Hubbard, Michigan vs. Detroit, 1977	2nd	26
Jerry Lucas, Ohio State vs. Western Kentucky, 1960	2nd	25
Elvin Hayes, Houston vs. Texas Christian, 1968	RC	25
Eddie Jackson, Oklahoma City vs. Creighton, 1964	1st	24
Paul Silas, Creighton vs. Memphis State, 1962	1st	24
Elvin Hayes, Houston vs. Louisville, 1968	2nd	24
Tom Burleson, North Carolina State vs. Providence, 1974	2nd	24
John Smyth, Notre Dame vs. Pittsburgh, 1957	RC	23
John Green, Michigan State vs. Louisville, 1959	RC	23
Dave Stallworth, Wichita State vs. Creighton, 1964	2nd	23
Cliff Anderson, St. Joseph's vs. North Carolina State, 1965	RC	23
Keith Swagerty, Pacific vs. Houston, 1966	RC	23
Lew Alcindor, UCLA vs. New Mexico State, 1968	2nd	23
Kresimir Cosic, Brigham Young vs. UCLA, 1971	2nd	23
Kent Benson, Indiana vs. Kentucky, 1975	RC	23

[Key: 1st—first round; 2nd—second round; RC—regional championships; C—regional consolation; C*—third place game; F—championship game.]

Tournament Records

INDIVIDUAL

Most Points, One Game
61, Austin Carr, Notre Dame (112) vs. Ohio (82), first round, 3/7/70

Most Points, Three-Game Series
158, Austin Carr, Notre Dame, 1970 (61 vs. Ohio, 52 vs. Kentucky, 45 vs. Iowa)

Most Points, Four-Game Series
143, Jerry Chambers, Utah, 1966 (40 vs. Pacific, 33 vs. Oregon, 38 vs. Texas El Paso, 32 vs. Duke)

Most Points, Five-Game Series
177, Bill Bradley, Princeton, 1965 (22 vs. Penn State, 27 vs. North Carolina State, 41 vs. Providence, 29 vs. Michigan, 58 vs. Wichita State)

Most Points, Career
358, Elvin Hayes, Houston, 1966-67-68

Most Field Goals, One Game
25, Austin Carr, Notre Dame (112) vs. Ohio (82), 44 attempts, first round, 3/7/70

Most Field Goals, Three-Game Series
68, Austin Carr, Notre Dame, 1970 (25 vs. Ohio, 22 vs. Kentucky, 21 vs. Iowa)

Most Field Goals, Four-Game Series
57, Bob Houbregs, Washington, 1953 (20 vs. Seattle, 12 vs. Santa Clara , 8 vs. Kansas, 17 vs. Louisiana State)

Most Field Goals, Five-Game Series
70, Elvin Hayes, Houston, 1968 (20 vs. Loyola, Ill., 16 vs. Louisville, 17 vs. Texas Christian, 3 vs. UCLA, 14 vs. Ohio State)

Most Field Goals, Career
152, Elvin Hayes, Houston, 1966-67-68

Most Free Throws, One Game
23, Bob Carney, Bradley (76) vs. Colorado (64), 26 attempts, second round, 3/12/54

Most Free Throws, Three-Game Series
34, Adrian Dantley, Notre Dame, 1975 (15 vs. Kansas, 5 vs. Maryland, 14 vs. Cincinnati)

Most Free Throws, Four-Game Series
49, Don Schlundt, Indiana, 1953 (13 vs. DePaul, 15 vs. Notre Dame, 13 vs. LSU, 8 vs. Kansas)

Most Free Throws, Five-Game Series
55, Bob Carney, Bradley, 1954 (9 vs. Oklahoma City, 23 vs. Colorado, 4 vs. Oklahoma State, 8 vs. Southern California, 11 vs. LaSalle)

Most Free Throws, Career
90, Oscar Robertson, Cincinnati, 1958-59-60

Most Rebounds, One Game
31, Nate Thurmond, Bowling Green (60) vs. Mississippi State (65), regional consolation, 1963

Most Rebounds, Three-Game Series
70, Nate Thurmond, Bowling Green, 1963 (20 vs. Notre Dame, 19 vs. Illinois, 31 vs. Mississippi State)

Most Rebounds, Four-Game Series
77, John Green, Michigan State, 1957 (27 vs. Notre Dame, 18 vs. Kentucky, 19 vs. North Carolina, 13 vs. San Francisco)

Most Rebounds, Five-Game Series
105, Elvin Hayes, Houston, 1968 (27 vs. Loyola, Ill., 24 vs. Louisville, 25 vs. Texas Christian, 13 vs. UCLA, 16 vs. Ohio State)

Most Rebounds, Career
222, Elvin Hayes, Houston, 1966-67-68

TEAM

Most Points, One Game
121, Iowa vs. Notre Dame (106), regional consolation, 3/14/70
121, Nevada-Las Vegas vs. San Francisco (95), first round, 3/12/77

Most Points, Both Teams, One Game
227, Iowa (121) vs. Notre Dame (106), regional consolation, 3/14/70

Most Points, Three-Game Series
317, Notre Dame, 1970, 105.7 per game (112-82 vs. Ohio, 99-109 vs. Kentucky, 106-121 vs. Iowa)

Most Points, Four-Game Series
400, UCLA, 1965, 100.0 per game (100-76 vs. Brigham Young, 101-93 vs. San Francisco, 108-89 vs. Wichita State, 91-80 vs. Michigan)

Most Points, Five-Game Series
505, Nevada-Las Vegas 1977, 101.0 per game (121-95 vs. San Francisco, 88-83

Duke's Mike Gminski defends against Jack Givens of Kentucky. Givens scored 41 points in the 1978 championship game.

Malcolm W. Emmons

vs. Utah; 107-90 vs. Idaho State, 83-84 vs. North Carolina; 106-94 vs. North Carolina-Charlotte)

Most Field Goals, One Game
52, Iowa (121) vs. Notre Dame (106), regional consolation, 3/14/70

Most Field Goals, Four-Game Series
162, UCLA, 1965 (44 vs. Brigham Young, 41 vs. San Francisco, 44 vs. Wichita State, 33 vs. Michigan)

Most Field Goals, Five-Game Series
218, Nevada-Las Vegas, 1977 (49 vs. San Francisco, 37 vs. Utah, 44 vs. Idaho State, 41 vs. North Carolina, 47 vs. North Carolina-Charlotte)

Most Free Throws, One Game
41, Utah (89) vs. Santa Clara (81), regional consolation, 3/12/60

Most Free Throws, Four-Game Series
108, Indiana, 1953 (29 vs. Notre Dame, 30 vs. DePaul, 30 vs. Louisiana State, 19 vs. Kansas)

Most Free Throws, Five-Game Series
146, Bradley, 1954 (23 vs. Oklahoma City, 38 vs. Colorado, 29 vs. Oklahoma State, 24 vs. Southern California, 32 vs. LaSalle)

Most Personal Fouls, One Game
39, Kansas (71) vs. Notre Dame (77), 3/15/75

Championship Results

Year	Champion	Score	Runner-Up	Third Place	Fourth Place
1939	Oregon	46-33	Ohio State	*Oklahoma	*Villanova
1940	Indiana	60-42	Kansas	*Duquesne	*Southern Cal.
1941	Wisconsin	39-34	Washington State	*Pittsburgh	*Arkansas
1942	Stanford	53-38	Dartmouth	*Colorado	*Kentucky
1943	Wyoming	46-34	Georgetown	*Texas	*DePaul
1944	Utah	42-40†	Dartmouth	*Iowa State	*Ohio State
1945	Oklahoma State	49-45	New York Univ.	*Arkansas	*Ohio State
1946	Oklahoma State	43-40	North Carolina	Ohio State	California
1947	Holy Cross	58-47	Oklahoma	Texas	CCNY
1948	Kentucky	58-42	Baylor	Holy Cross	Kansas State
1949	Kentucky	46-36	Oklahoma State	Illinois	Oregon State
1950	CCNY	71-68	Bradley	North Carolina St.	Baylor
1951	Kentucky	68-58	Kansas State	Illinois	Oklahoma State
1952	Kansas	80-63	St. John's, N.Y.	Illinois	Santa Clara
1953	Indiana	69-68	Kansas	Washington	Louisiana State
1954	LaSalle	92-76	Bradley	Penn State	Southern Cal.
1955	San Francisco	77-63	LaSalle	Colorado	Iowa
1956	San Francisco	83-71	Iowa	Temple	Southern Meth.
1957	North Carolina	54-53‡	Kansas	San Francisco	Michigan State
1958	Kentucky	84-72	Seattle	Temple	Kansas State
1959	California	71-70	West Virginia	Cincinnati	Louisville
1960	Ohio State	75-55	California	Cincinnati	New York Univ.
1961	Cincinnati	70-65†	Ohio State	Vacated¹	Utah
1962	Cincinnati	71-59	Ohio State	Wake Forest	UCLA
1963	Loyola, Ill.	60-58†	Cincinnati	Duke	Oregon State
1964	UCLA	98-83	Duke	Michigan	Kansas State
1965	UCLA	91-80	Michigan	Princeton	Wichita State
1966	Texas-El Paso	72-65	Kentucky	Duke	Utah
1967	UCLA	79-64	Dayton	Houston	North Carolina
1968	UCLA	78-55	North Carolina	Ohio State	Houston
1969	UCLA	92-72	Purdue	Drake	North Carolina
1970	UCLA	80-69	Jacksonville	New Mexico St.	St. Bonaventure
1971	UCLA	68-62	Vacated²	Vacated²	Kansas
1972	UCLA	81-76	Florida State	North Carolina	Louisville
1973	UCLA	87-66	Memphis State	Indiana	Providence
1974	North Carolina St.	76-64	Marquette	UCLA	Kansas
1975	UCLA	92-85	Kentucky	Louisville	Syracuse
1976	Indiana	86-68	Michigan	UCLA	Rutgers
1977	Marquette	67-59	North Carolina	Nev.-Las Vegas	N. Caro.-Charlotte
1978	Kentucky	94-88	Duke	Arkansas	Notre Dame

*Tied for third place.
†Overtime.
‡Three overtimes.

Year	Site of Finals	Coaches of Team Champions	Outstanding Player Award
1939	Evanston, Ill.	Howard Hobson, Oregon	None Selected
1940	Kansas City, Mo.	Branch McCracken, Indiana	Marvin Huffman, Indiana
1941	Kansas City, Mo.	Harold Foster, Wisconsin	John Kotz, Wisconsin
1942	Kansas City, Mo.	Everett Dean, Stanford	Howard Dallmar, Stanford
1943	New York City	Everett Shelton, Wyoming	Ken Sailors, Wyoming
1944	New York City	Vadal Peterson, Utah	Arnold Ferrin, Utah
1945	New York City	Henry Iba, Oklahoma State	Bob Kurland, Oklahoma State
1946	New York City	Henry Iba, Oklahoma State	Bob Kurland, Oklahoma State
1947	New York City	Alvin Julian, Holy Cross	George Kaftan, Holy Cross
1948	New York City	Adolph Rupp, Kentucky	Alex Groza, Kentucky
1949	Seattle, Wash.	Adolph Rupp, Kentucky	Alex Groza, Kentucky
1950	New York City	Nat Holman, CCNY	Irwin Dambrot, CCNY
1951	Minneapolis, Minn.	Adolph Rupp, Kentucky	None Selected
1952	Seattle, Wash.	Forrest Allen, Kansas	Clyde Lovellette, Kansas
1953	Kansas City, Mo.	Branch McCracken, Indiana	B. H. Born, Kansas
1954	Kansas City, Mo.	Kenneth Loeffler, LaSalle	Tom Gola, LaSalle
1955	Kansas City, Mo.	Phil Woolpert, San Francisco	Bill Russell, San Francisco
1956	Evanston, Ill.	Phil Woolpert, San Francisco	Hal Lear, Temple
1957	Kansas City, Mo.	Frank McGuire, North Carolina	Wilt Chamberlain, Kansas
1958	Louisville, Ky.	Adolph Rupp, Kentucky	Elgin Baylor, Seattle
1959	Louisville, Ky.	Pete Newell, California	Jerry West, West Virginia
1960	San Francisco, Calif.	Fred Taylor, Ohio State	Jerry Lucas, Ohio State
1961	Kansas City, Mo.	Edwin Jucker, Cincinnati	Jerry Lucas, Ohio State
1962	Louisville, Ky.	Edwin Jucker, Cincinnati	Paul Hogue, Cincinnati
1963	Louisville, Ky.	George Ireland, Loyola, Ill.	Art Heyman, Duke
1964	Kansas City, Mo.	John Wooden, UCLA	Walt Hazzard, UCLA
1965	Portland, Oregon	John Wooden, UCLA	Bill Bradley, Princeton
1966	College Park, Md.	Don Haskins, Texas-El Paso	Jerry Chambers, Utah
1967	Louisville, Ky.	John Wooden, UCLA	Lew Alcindor, UCLA
1968	Los Angeles, Calif.	John Wooden, UCLA	Lew Alcindor, UCLA
1969	Louisville, Ky.	John Wooden, UCLA	Lew Alcindor, UCLA
1970	College Park, Md.	John Wooden, UCLA	Sidney Wicks, UCLA
1971	Houston, Texas	John Wooden, UCLA	Vacated²
1972	Los Angeles, Calif.	John Wooden, UCLA	Bill Walton, UCLA
1973	St. Louis, Mo.	John Wooden, UCLA	Bill Walton, UCLA
1974	Greensboro, N.C.	Norm Sloan, North Carolina St.	David Thompson, N.C. State
1975	San Diego, Calif.	John Wooden, UCLA	Richard Washington, UCLA
1976	Philadelphia, Pa.	Bob Knight, Indiana	Kent Benson, Indiana
1977	Atlanta, Georgia	Al McGuire, Marquette	Butch Lee, Marquette
1978	St. Louis, Mo.	Joe Hall, Kentucky	Jack Givens, Kentucky

1. Student-athletes representing St. Joseph's College (Pennsylvania) were declared ineligible subsequent to the tournament. Under NCAA rules, the team's and ineligible student-athletes' records were deleted; and the team's place in the final standings was vacated.

2. Student-athletes representing Villanova University and Western Kentucky University were declared ineligible subsequent to the tournament. Under NCAA rules, the teams' and ineligible student-athletes' records were deleted (Howard Porter of Villanova was selected as the most outstanding player); and the teams' places in the standings (Villanova finished second and Western Kentucky finished third) were vacated.

Tournament Won-Lost Records

Team (Years Participated)	Years	Won	Lost	Pct.	1st	2nd	3rd	4th
Air Force (1960-62)	2	0	2	.000	0	0	0	0
Alabama (1975-76)	2	1	2	.333	0	0	0	0
Arizona (1951-76-77)	3	2	3	.400	0	0	0	0
Arizona State (1958-61-62-63-64-73-75)	7	7	8	.467	0	0	0	0
Arkansas (1941-45-49-58-77-78)	6	7	7	.500	0	0	3	0
Austin Peay (1974)¹	1	0	1	.000	0	0	0	0
Baylor (1946-48-50)	3	3	5	.375	0	1	0	1
Boise State (1976)	1	0	1	.000	0	0	0	0
Boston College (1958-67-68-75)	4	3	5	.375	0	0	0	0
Boston University (1959)	1	2	1	.667	0	0	0	0
Bowling Green (1959-62-63-68)	4	1	5	.167	0	0	0	0
Bradley (1950-54-55)	3	8	3	.727	0	2	0	0
Brigham Young (1950-51-57-65-69-71-72)	7	4	10	.285	0	0	0	0
Brown (1939)	1	0	1	.000	0	0	0	0
Butler (1962)	1	2	1	.667	0	0	0	0
California (1946-57-58-59-60)	5	11	5	.688	1	1	0	1
Canisius (1955-56-57)	3	6	3	.667	0	0	0	0
Catholic (1944)	1	0	2	.000	0	0	0	0
CCNY (1947-50)	2	4	2	.667	1	0	0	1
Central Michigan (1975-77)	2	2	2	.500	0	0	0	0
Cincinnati (1958-59-60-61-62-63-66-75-76-77)	10	20	9	.690	2	1	2	0
Colorado (1940-42-46-54-55-62-63-69)	8	8	10	.444	0	0	2	0
Colorado State (1954-63-65-66-69)	5	2	6	.250	0	0	0	0
Columbia (1948-51-68)	3	2	4	.333	0	0	0	0
Connecticut (1951-54-56-57-58-59-60-63-64-65-67-76)	12	4	13	.235	0	0	0	0
Cornell (1954)	1	0	2	.000	0	0	0	0
Creighton (1941-62-64-74-75-78)	6	6	7	.462	0	0	0	0
Dartmouth (1941-42-43-44-56-58-59)	7	10	7	.588	0	2	0	0
Davidson (1966-68-69-70)	4	5	5	.500	0	0	0	0
Dayton (1952-65-66-67-69-70-74)	7	9	9	.500	0	1	0	0
DePaul (1943-53-56-59-60-65-76-78)	8	9	11	.450	0	1	0	0
Detroit (1962-77)	2	1	2	.333	0	0	0	0
Drake (1969-70-71)	3	5	3	.625	0	0	1	0
Duke (1955-60-63-64-66-78)	6	15	6	.714	0	2	2	0
Duquesne (1940-52-69-71-77)	5	4	5	.444	0	0	1	0
East Carolina (1972)	1	0	1	.000	0	0	0	0
East Tennessee State (1968)	1	1	2	.333	0	0	0	0
Eastern Kentucky (1953-59-65-72)	4	0	4	.000	0	0	0	0
Florida State (1968-72-78)	3	4	3	.571	0	1	0	0
Fordham (1953-54-71)	3	2	3	.400	0	0	0	0
Fullerton State (1978)	1	2	1	.667	0	0	0	0
Furman (1971-73-74-75-78)	5	1	6	.143	0	0	0	0
Georgetown (1943-75-76)	3	2	3	.400	0	1	0	0

Players from Kentucky and Duke scramble for a loose ball in the 1978 title game, won by Kentucky, 94-88.

TOURNAMENT RECORDS

Team (Years Participated)	Years	Won	Lost	Pct.	1st	2nd	3rd	4th
Houston (1956-61-65-66-67-68-70-71-72-73-78)	11	14	16	.467	0	0	1	1
Idaho State (1953-54-55-56-57-58-59-60-74-77)	10	8	12	.400	0	0	0	0
Illinois (1942-49-51-52-63)	5	9	6	.600	0	0	3	0
Indiana (1940-53-54-58-67-73-75-76-78)	9	21	6	.778	3	0	1	0
Iowa (1955-56-70)	3	6	4	.600	0	1	0	1
Iowa State (1944)	1	1	1	.500	0	0	1	0
Jacksonville (1970-71-73)	3	4	3	.571	0	1	0	0
Kansas (1940-42-52-53-57-60-66-67-71-74-75-78)	12	20	13	.606	1	3	0	2
Kansas State (1948-51-56-58-59-61-64-68-70-72-73-75-77)	13	17	17	.500	0	1	0	3
Kentucky (1942-45-48-49-51-52-55-56-57-58-59-61-62-64-66-68-69-70-71-72-73-75-77-78)	24	42	21	.667	5	2	1	0
Lafayette (1957)	1	0	2	.000	0	0	0	0
La Salle (1954-55-68-75-78)	5	9	4	.692	1	1	0	0
Lebanon Valley (1953)	1	1	2	.333	0	0	0	0
Long Beach State (1970-77)[2]	2	1	3	.250	0	0	0	0
Los Angeles State (1974)	1	0	1	.000	0	0	0	0
Louisiana State (1953-54)	2	2	4	.333	0	0	0	1
Louisville (1951-59-61-64-67-68-72-74-75-77-78)	11	13	15	.464	0	0	1	2
Loyola, Ill. (1963-64-66-68)	4	7	3	.700	1	0	0	0
Loyola, La. (1954-57-58)	3	0	3	.000	0	0	0	0
Loyola Marymount (1961)	1	1	1	.500	0	0	0	0
Manhattan (1956-58)	2	1	3	.250	0	0	0	0
Marquette (1955-59-61-68-69-71-72-73-74-75-76-77-78)	13	23	14	.622	1	1	0	0
Marshall (1956-72)	2	0	2	.000	0	0	0	0
Maryland (1958-73-75)	3	5	3	.625	0	0	0	0
Massachusetts (1962)	1	0	1	.000	0	0	0	0
Memphis State (1955-56-62-73-76)	5	3	5	.375	0	1	0	0
Miami, Florida (1960)	1	0	1	.000	0	0	0	0
Miami, Ohio (1953-55-57-58-66-69-71-73-78)	9	3	11	.214	0	0	0	0
Michigan (1948-64-65-66-74-75-76-77)	8	15	8	.652	0	2	1	0
Michigan State (1957-59-78)	3	5	4	.556	0	0	0	1
Middle Tennessee State (1975-77)	2	0	2	.000	0	0	0	0
Minnesota (1972)[3]	1	1	1	.500	0	0	0	0
Mississippi State (1963)	1	1	1	.500	0	0	0	0
Missouri (1944-76-78)	3	3	3	.500	0	0	0	0
Montana (1975)	1	1	2	.333	0	0	0	0
Montana State (1951)	1	0	1	.000	0	0	0	0
Morehead State (1956-57-61)	3	3	4	.429	0	0	0	0
Murray State (1964-69)	2	0	2	.000	0	0	0	0
Navy (1947-53-54-59-60)	5	4	6	.400	0	0	0	0
Nevada-Las Vegas (1975-76-77)	3	7	3	.700	0	0	1	0
New Mexico (1968-74-78)	3	2	4	.333	0	0	0	0
New Mexico State (1952-59-60-67-68-69-70-71-75)	9	7	11	.389	0	0	1	0
New York University (1943-45-56-60-62-63)	6	9	9	.500	0	1	0	1

243

Malcolm W. Emmons

Team (Years Participated)	Years	Won	Lost	Pct.	1st	2nd	3rd	4th
Niagara (1970)	1	1	2	.333	0	0	0	0
North Carolina (1941-46-57-59-67-68-69-72-75-76-77-78)	12	23	14	.622	1	3	1	2
North Carolina-Charlotte (1977)	1	3	2	.600	0	0	0	1
North Carolina State (1950-51-52-54-56-65-70-74)	8	12	8	.600	1	0	1	0
Notre Dame (1953-54-57-58-60-63-65-69-70-71-74-75-76-77-78)	15	18	19	.486	0	0	0	1
Ohio (1960-61-64-65-70-72-74)	7	3	8	.273	0	0	0	0
Ohio State (1939-44-45-46-50-60-61-62-68-71)	10	21	9	.700	1	3	4	0
Oklahoma (1939-43-47)	3	4	3	.571	0	1	1	0
Oklahoma City (1952-53-54-55-56-57-63-64-65-66-73)	11	8	13	.381	0	0	0	0
Oklahoma State (1945-46-49-51-53-54-58-65)	8	15	7	.682	2	1	0	1
Oral Roberts (1974)	1	2	1	.667	0	0	0	0
Oregon (1939-45-60-61)	4	6	3	.667	1	0	0	0
Oregon State (1947-49-55-62-63-64-66-75)	8	10	11	.476	0	0	0	2
Pacific, Cal. (1966-67-71)	3	2	4	.333	0	0	0	0
Pennsylvania (1953-70-71-72-73-74-75-78)	8	7	9	.438	0	0	0	0
Penn State (1942-52-54-55-65)	5	6	7	.462	0	0	1	0
Pepperdine (1944-62-76)	3	2	4	.333	0	0	0	0
Pittsburgh (1941-57-58-63-74)	5	4	6	.400	0	0	1	0
Portland (1959)	1	0	1	.000	0	0	0	0
Princeton (1952-55-60-61-63-64-65-67-69-76-77)	11	8	15	.348	0	0	1	0
Providence (1964-65-66-72-73-74-77-78)	8	7	9	.438	0	0	0	1
Purdue (1969-77)	2	3	2	.600	0	1	0	0
Rhode Island (1961-66-78)	3	0	3	.000	0	0	0	0
Rice (1940-42-54-70)	4	2	5	.286	0	0	0	0
Rutgers (1975-76)	2	3	3	.500	0	0	0	1
St. Bonaventure (1961-68-70-78)	4	6	6	.500	0	0	0	1
St. John's, N.Y. (1951-52-61-67-68-69-73-76-77-78)	10	7	12	.368	0	1	0	0
St. Joseph's, Pa. (1959-60-62-63-65-66-69-71-73-74)[4]	10	5	14	.263	0	0	0	0
St. Louis (1952-57)	2	1	3	.250	0	0	0	0
St. Mary's, Cal. (1959)	1	1	1	.500	0	0	0	0
San Diego State (1975-76)	2	0	2	.000	0	0	0	0
San Francisco (1955-56-57-58-63-64-65-72-73-74-77-78)	12	20	10	.667	2	0	1	0
San Jose State (1951)	1	0	1	.000	0	0	0	0
Santa Clara (1952-53-54-60-68-69-70)	7	9	9	.500	0	0	0	1
Seattle (1953-54-55-56-58-61-62-63-64-67-69)	11	10	13	.425	0	1	0	0
South Carolina (1971-72-73-74)	4	4	5	.444	0	0	0	0
Southern California (1940-54-60-61)	4	4	6	.400	0	0	1	1
Southern Illinois-Carbondale (1977)	1	1	1	.500	0	0	0	0
Southern Methodist (1955-56-57-65-66-67)	6	7	8	.467	0	0	0	1
Southwestern Louisiana[5]	0	0	0	.000	0	0	0	0
Springfield (1940)	1	0	1	.000	0	0	0	0
Stanford (1942)	1	3	0	1.000	1	0	0	0
Syracuse (1957-66-73-74-75-76-77-78)	8	9	9	.500	0	0	0	1
Temple (1944-56-58-64-67-70-72)	7	8	7	.533	0	0	1	1
Tennessee (1967-76-77)	3	0	4	.000	0	0	0	0
Tennessee Tech (1958-63)	2	0	2	.000	0	0	0	0
Texas (1939-43-47-60-63-72-74)	7	6	10	.375	0	0	2	0
Texas A&M (1951-64-69-75)	4	1	5	.167	0	0	0	0
Texas Christian (1952-53-59-68-71)	5	4	5	.444	0	0	0	0
Texas-El Paso (1963-64-66-67-70-75)	6	9	5	.643	1	0	0	0
Texas Tech (1954-56-61-62-73-76)	6	3	7	.300	0	0	0	0
Toledo (1954-67)	2	0	2	.000	0	0	0	0
Trinity, Tex. (1969)	1	0	1	.000	0	0	0	0
Tufts (1945)	1	0	2	.000	0	0	0	0
Tulsa (1955)	1	1	1	.500	0	0	0	0
UCLA (1950-52-56-62-63-64-65-67-68-69-70-71-72-73-74-75-76-77-78)	19	53	13	.803	10	0	2	1
Utah (1944-45-55-56-59-60-61-66-77-78)	10	13	13	.500	1	0	0	2
Utah State (1939-62-63-64-70-71-75)	7	5	9	.357	0	0	0	0
Vanderbilt (1965-74)	2	1	3	.333	0	0	0	0
Villanova (1939-49-51-55-62-64-69-70-72-78)[6]	10	13	11	.542	0	0	1	0
Virginia (1976)	1	0	1	.000	0	0	0	0
Virginia Military (1964-76-77)	3	3	3	.500	0	0	0	0
Virginia Tech (1967-76)	2	2	2	.500	0	0	0	0
Wake Forest (1939-53-61-62-77)	5	9	5	.643	0	0	1	0
Washington (1943-48-51-53-76)	5	6	6	.500	0	0	1	0
Washington State (1941)	1	2	1	.667	0	1	0	0
Wayne State (1956)	1	1	2	.333	0	0	0	0
Weber State (1968-69-70-71-72-73-78)	7	3	8	.273	0	0	0	0
Western Kentucky (1940-60-62-66-67-70-76-78)[7]	8	6	9	.400	0	0	0	0
Western Michigan (1976)	1	1	1	.500	0	0	0	0
West Texas State (1955)	1	0	1	.000	0	0	0	0
West Virginia (1955-56-57-58-59-60-62-63-65-67)	10	8	10	.444	0	1	0	0
Wichita State (1964-65-76)	3	3	4	.429	0	0	0	1
Williams (1955)	1	0	1	.000	0	0	0	0

Team (Years Participated)	Years	Won	Lost	Pct.	1st	2nd	3rd	4th
Wisconsin (1941-47)	2	4	1	.800	1	0	0	0
Wyoming (1941-43-47-48-49-52-53-58-67)	9	4	14	.222	1	0	0	0
Xavier (1961)	1	0	1	.000	0	0	0	0
Yale (1949-57-62)	3	0	4	.000	0	0	0	0

1. Student-athletes representing Austin Peay were declared ineligible subsequent to the 1973 championship. Under NCAA rules, the team's (1-2) and ineligible student-athletes' records were deleted; and Austin Peay's team place in the final standings was vacated.

2. Student-athletes representing Long Beach State were declared ineligible subsequent to the 1973 championship. Under NCAA rules, the team's (6-3) and ineligible student-athletes' records for 1971, 1972 and 1973 were deleted; and Long Beach State's team places in the final standings were vacated.

3. Student-athletes representing Minnesota were declared ineligible subsequent to the 1972 championship. Under NCAA rules, the team's (1-1) and ineligible student-athletes' records were deleted; and Minnesota's team place in the final standings was vacated.

4. Student-athletes representing St. Joseph's were declared ineligible subsequent to the 1961 championship. Under NCAA rules, the team's (3-1) and ineligible student-athletes' records were deleted; and St. Joseph's team place (third) in the final standings was vacated.

5. Student-athletes representing Southwestern Louisiana were declared ineligible subsequent to the 1973 championship. Under NCAA rules, the team's (3-3) and ineligible student-athletes' records for 1972 and 1973 were deleted; and Southwestern Louisiana's team place in the final standings was vacated.

6. Student-athletes representing Villanova were declared ineligible subsequent to the 1971 championship. Under NCAA rules, the team's (4-1) and ineligible student-athletes' records were deleted; and Villanova's team place (second) in the final standings was vacated.

7. Student-athletes representing Western Kentucky were declared ineligible subsequent to the 1971 championship. Under NCAA rules, the team's (4-1) and ineligible student-athletes' records were deleted; and Western Kentucky's team place (third) in the final standings was vacated.

All-Tournament Teams

1940—Howard Engleman, Kansas; Jay McCreary, Indiana; William Menke, Indiana; Marvin Huffman, Indiana; Bob Allen, Kansas.

1952—Clyde Lovellette, Kansas; Bob Zawoluk, St. John's; John Kerr, Illinois; Ron MacGilvray, St. John's; Dean Kelley, Kansas.

1953—B. H. Born, Kansas; Bob Houbregs, Washington; Bob Leonard, Indiana; Dean Kelley, Kansas; Don Schlundt, Indiana.

1954—Tom Gola, La Salle; Chuck Singley, La Salle; Jesse Arnelle, Penn State; Roy Irvin, Southern California; Bob Carney, Bradley.

1955—Bill Russell, San Francisco; Tom Gola, La Salle; K.C. Jones, San Francisco; Jim Ranglos, Colorado; Carl Cain, Iowa.

1956—Hal Lear, Temple; Bill Russell, San Francisco; Carl Cain, Iowa; Hal Perry, San Francisco; Bill Logan, Iowa.

1957—Wilt Chamberlain, Kansas; Len Rosenbluth, North Carolina; John Green, Michigan State; Gene Brown, San Francisco; Pete Brennan, North Carolina.

1958—Elgin Baylor, Seattle; John Cox, Kentucky; Guy Rodgers, Temple; Charley Brown, Seattle; Vern Hatton, Kentucky.

1959—Jerry West, West Virginia; Oscar Robertson, Cincinnati; Darrall Imhoff, California; Don Goldstein, Louisville; Denny Fitzpatrick, California.

1960—Jerry Lucas, Ohio State; Oscar Robertson, Cincinnati; Mel Nowell, Ohio State; Darrall Imhoff, California; Tom Sanders, New York University.

1961—Jerry Lucas, Ohio State; Bob Wiesenhahn, Cincinnati; Larry Siegfried, Ohio State; Carl Bouldin, Cincinnati; Vacated.[1]

1962—Paul Hogue, Cincinnati; Jerry Lucas, Ohio State; Tom Thacker, Cincinnati; John Havlicek, Ohio State; Len Chappell, Wake Forest.

1963—Art Heyman, Duke; Tom Thacker, Cincinnati; Les Hunter, Loyola (Ill.); George Wilson, Cincinnati; Ron Bonham, Cincinnati.

1964—Walt Hazzard, UCLA; Jeff Mullins, Duke; Bill Buntin, Michigan; Willie Murrell, Kansas State; Gail Goodrich, UCLA.

1965—Bill Bradley, Princeton; Gail Goodrich, UCLA; Cazzie Russell, Michigan; Edgar Lacey, UCLA; Kenny Washington, UCLA.

1966—Jerry Chambers, Utah; Pat Riley, Kentucky; Jack Marin, Duke; Louie Dampier, Kentucky; Bobby Joe Hill, Texas-El Paso.

1967—Lew Alcindor, UCLA; Don May, Dayton; Mike Warren, UCLA; Elvin Hayes, Houston; Lucius Allen, UCLA.

Mike Gminski (43) scored 20 points and grabbed 12 rebounds for Duke in the 1978 championship game against Kentucky.

1968—Lew Alcindor, UCLA; Lynn Shackleford, UCLA; Mike Warren, UCLA; Lucius Allen, UCLA; Larry Miller, North Carolina.

1969—Lew Alcindor, UCLA; Rick Mount, Purdue; Charlie Scott, North Carolina; Willie McCarter, Drake; John Vallely, UCLA.

1970—Sidney Wicks, UCLA; Jimmy Collins, New Mexico State; John Vallely, UCLA; Artis Gilmore, Jacksonville; Curtis Rowe, UCLA.

1971—Steve Patterson, UCLA; Sidney Wicks, UCLA; Vacated.[2]

1972—Bill Walton, UCLA; Keith Wilkes, UCLA; Robert McAdoo, North Carolina; Jim Price, Louisville; Ron King, Florida State.

1973—Bill Walton, UCLA; Steve Downing, Indiana; Ernie DiGregorio, Providence; Larry Finch, Memphis State; Larry Kenon, Memphis State.

1974—David Thompson, North Carolina State; Bill Walton, UCLA; Tom Burleson, North Carolina State; Monte Towe, North Carolina State; Maurice Lucas, Marquette.

1975—Richard Washington, UCLA; Kevin Grevey, Kentucky; Dave Meyers, UCLA; Allen Murphy, Louisville; Jim Lee, Syracuse.

1976—Kent Benson, Indiana; Scott May, Indiana; Rickey Green, Michigan; Marques Johnson, UCLA; Tom Abernathy, Indiana.

1977—Butch Lee, Marquette; Mike O'Koren, North Carolina; Cedric Maxwell, North Carolina-Charlotte; Bo Ellis, Marquette; Walter Davis, North Carolina; Jerome Whitehead, Marquette.

1978—Jack Givens, Kentucky; Mike Gminski, Duke; Jim Spanarkel, Duke; Ron Brewer, Arkansas; Rick Robey, Kentucky.

*Institution's participation in tournament voided, due to use of student-athletes who were declared ineligible subsequent to tournament.

1. Also selected was John Egan of St. Joseph's (Pa.) Student-athletes representing St. Joseph's were declared ineligible subsequent to the tournament; under NCAA rules the team's and ineligible student-athletes' records were deleted, and the team's place in the final standings was vacated.

2. Also selected were Howard Porter (most outstanding player) and Hank Siemiontkowski of Villanova and Jim McDaniels of Western Kentucky. Student-athletes representing those institutions were declared ineligible subsequent to the tournament; under NCAA rules the team's and ineligible student-athletes' records were deleted, and the team's place in the final standings was vacated.

245

Malcolm W. Emmons

GAME-BY-GAME RESULTS

1939

First Round

Villanova

	fg	ft-fta	pf	tp
Lazorchak	3	0- 1	2	6
Montgomery	5	2- 3	0	12
Dubino	2	0- 0	1	4
Krutulis	6	2- 3	0	14
Nugent	1	0- 0	3	2
Robinson	0	0- 1	0	0
Sinnott	1	0- 0	1	2
Rice	0	0- 0	1	0
Yung	0	0- 0	2	0
Vigilante	1	0- 0	0	2
Totals	19	4- 8	10	42

Brown

	fg	ft-fta	pf	tp
Padden	2	2- 2	3	6
Wilson	2	1- 4	0	5
Platt	3	1- 2	3	7
Person	3	2- 3	0	8
Truman	0	1- 1	1	1
Mullen	0	1- 1	0	1
Campbell	0	0- 0	0	0
Fisher	1	0- 0	0	2
Totals	11	8-13	7	30

Half time: Villanova 17-7. Officials: Kearney and Schoenfeld.

Ohio State

	fg	ft-fta	pf	tp
Hull	7	4- 5	2	18
Baker	10	5- 7	1	25
Schick	1	0- 1	3	2
Dawson	1	0- 1	4	2
Lynch	3	3- 3	1	9
Mickelson	1	2- 2	3	4
Sattler	2	0- 4	3	4
Boughner	0	0- 0	2	0
Totals	25	14-23	19	64

Wake Forest

	fg	ft-fta	pf	tp
Waller	5	4- 5	4	14
Conway	3	1- 1	1	7
Owen	7	5- 9	0	19
Apple	4	2- 2	3	10
Sweel	0	1- 3	4	1
Carter	0	0- 0	1	0
Fuller	0	0- 1	0	0
Young	0	1- 1	3	1
Totals	19	14-22	16	52

Half time: Wake Forest 29-23. Officials: Sinnott and Brennan.

Oklahoma

	fg	ft-fta	pf	tp
McNatt	5	2- 3	3	12
Corbin	5	2- 2	2	12
Roop	1	3- 4	1	5
Zollner	1	0- 1	1	2
Richards	0	0- 0	0	0
Scheffler	1	3- 4	3	5
Kerr	0	1- 1	1	1
Mullen	0	0- 0	1	0
Mesch	3	1- 1	2	7
Snodgrass	3	0- 0	1	6
Walker	0	0- 0	0	0
Totals	19	12-16	15	50

Utah State

	fg	ft-fta	pf	tp
Bingham	1	4- 5	3	6
F. Morris	6	3- 5	3	15
James	0	1- 1	0	1
Reading	4	1- 2	1	9
C. Morris	1	0- 1	1	2
Agricola	0	2- 3	4	2
Lindquist	1	0- 0	0	2
Jacobson	1	0- 0	0	2
Totals	14	11-17	12	39

Half time: Oklahoma 25-14. Officials: Bailey and Hubbard.

Oregon

	fg	ft	pf	tp
Gale	2	2	1	6
Duke	6	1	3	13
Wintermute	7	0	0	14
Anet	1	2	0	4
Johansen	3	1	2	7
Sarpola	0	1	1	1
McNeely	0	0	1	0
Sandness	1	0	1	2
Hardy	1	0	1	2
Mullen	1	2	0	4
Pavalunas	1	1	1	3
Totals	23	10	11	56

Texas

	fg	ft	pf	tp
Hull	1	4	4	6
Granville	0	2	2	2
Tate	3	1	3	7
Moers	3	0	4	6
Nelms	1	0	0	2
Finley	2	2	0	6
Cooley	1	1	0	3
King	0	0	0	0
Houpt	0	0	0	0
Wiggins	1	2	0	4
Spears	2	1	3	5
Totals	14	13	16	41

Half time: Oregon 19-16. Officials: Leith and DeGroot.

Third Place

Utah State

	fg	ft-fta	pf	tp
Bingham	9	1- 1	3	19
Reading	1	1- 2	1	3
Morris	3	2- 2	3	8
Agricola	3	2- 3	4	8
Lindquist	1	1- 1	4	3
James	0	1- 1	2	1
Wilkins	0	0- 0	0	0
Morris	4	1- 1	1	9
Totals	21	9-11	18	51

Texas

	fg	ft-fta	pf	tp
Hull	3	4-10	2	10
Granville	2	3- 4	4	7
Tate	4	2- 3	1	10
Spears	1	4- 4	0	6
Nelms	3	1- 1	1	7
Cooley	2	0- 0	1	4
Finley	1	0- 0	0	2
Wiggins	0	2- 4	0	2
Moers	0	1- 1	3	1
Totals	16	17-27	12	49

Half time: 25-25. Officials: DeGroot and Hubbard.

1939 OREGON DUCKS—(l-r) Front Row: Wally Johansen, Slim Wintermute, Bobby Anet, Howard Hobson, Laddie Gale, John Dick; Back Row: Bob Hardy, Red McNeely, Jay Langston, Ford Mullen, Matt Pavalunas, Rob Officer, Ted Sarpola, Earl Sandness.

Semifinals

Ohio State

	fg	ft-fta	pf	tp
Hull	10	8- 8	1	28
Baker	2	0- 0	2	4
Schick	3	1- 1	3	7
Dawson	1	0- 2	1	2
Lynch	0	0- 1	3	0
Mickelson	1	0- 0	0	2
Stafford	1	0- 0	0	2
Sattler	3	2- 3	1	8
Maag	0	0- 0	0	0
Boughner	0	0- 0	0	0
Mees	0	0- 0	0	0
Scott	0	0- 0	0	0
Totals	21	11-15	11	53

Villanova

	fg	ft-fta	pf	tp
Lazorchak	2	0- 0	1	4
Montgomery	1	1- 3	4	3
Dubino	1	0- 3	3	2
Krutulis	2	1- 1	2	5
Nugent	7	2- 3	2	16
Duzminski	2	2- 3	3	6
Sinnott	0	0- 0	0	0
Rice	0	0- 0	0	0
Robinson	0	0- 0	0	0
Yung	0	0- 0	0	0
Totals	15	6-13	15	36

Half time: Ohio State 25-10. Officials: Kennedy and Walsh.

Oregon

	fg	ft-fta	pf	tp
Gale	3	5- 7	4	11
Hardy	0	3- 3	1	3
Sarpola	0	0- 0	0	0
Mullen	0	1- 2	0	1
Dick	6	2- 2	1	14
Wintermute	4	2- 2	1	10
Johansen	4	0- 1	3	8
Pavalunas	1	0- 0	1	2
Anet	1	4- 5	2	6
Totals	19	17-22	13	55

Oklahoma

	fg	ft-fta	pf	tp
McNatt	5	2- 3	1	12
Roop	1	1- 2	2	3
Walker	1	0- 1	0	2
Corbin	1	0- 0	0	2
Scheffler	2	2- 2	4	6
Mullen	0	0- 0	1	0
Kerr	3	3- 3	0	9
Mesch	1	0- 1	4	2
Zoller	0	0- 0	2	0
Snodgrass	0	1- 1	1	1
Totals	14	9-13	15	37

Half time: Oregon 21-14. Officials: Leith and Bailey.

Howard Hobson

Championship

Oregon	fg	ft-fta	pf	tp
Gale	2	4- 5	1	8
Dick	5	5- 5	3	15
Wintermute	2	0- 1	1	4
Anet	4	2- 3	3	10
Johansen	4	1- 2	1	9
Mullen	0	0- 0	0	0
Pavalunas	0	0- 0	0	0
Totals	17	12-16	9	46

Ohio State	fg	ft-fta	pf	tp
Hull	5	2- 2	2	12
Baker	0	0- 1	0	0
Schick	1	0- 0	1	2
Dawson	1	0- 0	4	2
Lynch	3	1- 3	3	7
Maag	0	0- 0	0	0
Scott	0	1- 1	1	1
Boughner	1	0- 0	0	2
Sattler	3	1- 2	0	7
Mickelson	0	0- 0	2	0
Stafford	0	0- 0	0	0
Totals	14	5- 9	13	33

Half time: Oregon 21-16. Officials: Getchell and Clarno.

1940

First Round

Duquesne	fg	ft	pf	tp
Kasperik	1	0	0	2
Milkovich	2	2	2	6
Lacey	4	0	2	8
Debnar	3	1	3	7
Widowitz	2	1	3	5
Becker	1	0	3	2
Totals	13	4	13	30

Western Kentucky	fg	ft	pf	tp
Ball	1	2	4	4
Fulks	0	0	2	0
Towery	6	1	4	13
Walters	4	4	0	12
H. Downing	0	0	1	0
Shelton	0	0	0	0
Woodard	0	0	0	0
A. Downing	0	0	0	0
Totals	11	7	11	29

Half time: Duquesne 14-12. Officials: Feezle and Burt.

Branch McCracken

Indiana	fg	ft	pf	tp
McCreary	2	0	0	4
Schaefer	6	2	0	14
W. Menke	2	0	2	4
Huffman	2	2	1	6
Dro	2	1	2	5
Armstrong	2	2	1	6
Francis	1	0	2	2
Zimmer	0	0	1	0
R. Menke	0	1	1	1
Gridley	1	0	1	2
Dorsey	1	2	2	4
Frey	0	0	0	0
Totals	19	10	13	48

1940 INDIANA HOOSIERS—(l-r) Front Row: Jim Gridley, Herm Schaefer, Bob Dro, Marvin Huffman, Jay McCreary, Paul "Curley" Armstrong, Ralph Dorsey; Back Row: Branch McCracken, Chet Francis, Bill Menke, Andy Zimmer, Bob Menke, Ralph Graham.

Springfield	fg	ft	pf	tp
Munro	0	4	4	4
Mortenson	1	1	0	3
Redding	3	1	3	7
Werner	1	0	4	2
Schmidt	2	0	0	4
Gray	0	1	2	1
MacVean	1	1	0	3
Kistner	0	0	1	0
Nover	0	0	1	0
Panatier	0	0	1	0
Totals	8	8	16	24

Half time: Indiana 30-11. Officials: Kennedy and Clamo.

Kansas	fg	ft-fta	pf	tp
Ebling	4	2- 3	0	10
Engleman	10	1- 1	1	21
Allen	0	0- 1	0	0
Miller	3	4- 8	4	10
Harp	3	1- 1	1	7
Hogben	0	0- 0	0	0
Johnson	0	0- 0	0	0
Voran	0	0- 0	0	0
Kline	1	0- 1	4	2
Hunter	0	0- 0	1	0
Totals	21	8-15	11	50

Rice	fg	ft-fta	pf	tp
Craddock	1	0- 0	2	2
Palmer	3	0- 0	3	6
Kinney	8	2- 6	3	18
Selman	0	0- 0	3	0
Carswell	4	1- 1	1	9
Gomez	2	1- 2	1	5
Pepper	2	0- 0	0	4
Zander	0	0- 0	0	0
Totals	20	4- 9	13	44

Half time: Kansas 24-14. Officials: DeGroot and Vidal.

Southern California	fg	ft-fta	pf	tp
Vaughn	5	0- 1	0	10
Morrison	3	4- 4	2	10
Sears	2	0- 1	4	4
Reising	2	1- 2	2	5
McGarvin	0	0- 1	3	0
Lambert	0	1- 2	2	1
Luber	1	0- 0	2	2
Lippert	2	2- 3	1	6
Totals	15	8-14	16	38

Colorado	fg	ft-fta	pf	tp
Doll	2	3- 5	2	7
Hendricks	3	1- 2	1	7
Grove	0	0- 1	0	0
Thurman	2	2- 3	0	6
Hamburg	2	0- 0	4	4
Schmidt	0	0- 0	0	0
Harvey	1	3- 4	4	5
McCloud	1	1- 1	0	3
Totals	11	10-16	11	32

Half time: 20-20. Officials: O'Sullivan and Curtis.

Third Place

Rice	fg	ft-fta	pf	tp
Craddock	9	0- 3	2	18
Gomez	2	2- 2	3	6
Pepper	0	0- 0	2	0
Kinney	4	0- 2	3	8
Selman	6	0- 1	2	12
Carswell	7	2- 3	1	16
Totals	28	4-11	13	60

Colorado	fg	ft-fta	pf	tp
Doll	5	0- 1	2	10
Hendricks	5	2- 2	0	12
Grove	0	0- 0	0	0
Harvey	4	2- 3	4	10
McCloud	2	1- 1	0	5
Thurman	5	4- 5	3	14
Hamburg	2	1- 1	2	5
Totals	23	10-13	11	56

Half time: 27-27. Regulation Score: 50-50. Officials: DeGroot and O'Sullivan.

Semifinals

Indiana	fg	ft	pf	tp
McCreary	0	0	3	0
Schaefer	2	4	3	8
W. Menke	4	2	4	10
Dro	2	1	2	5
Huffman	2	2	3	6
Zimmer	1	1	0	3
Dorsey	0	0	0	0
Armstrong	2	3	0	7
Totals	13	13	15	39

Marvin Huffman

Duquesne	fg	ft	pf	tp
Becker	2	2	4	6
Milkovich	4	2	4	10
Lacey	1	0	3	2
Debnar	0	2	2	2
Widowitz	3	1	3	7
Reiber	0	0	0	0
Kasperik	1	1	1	3
Totals	11	8	17	30

Half time: Indiana 25-13. Officials: Kennedy and Adams.

Kansas	fg	ft-fta	pf	tp
Ebling	2	4- 8	1	8
Engleman	3	0- 0	1	6
Allen	3	2- 2	2	8
Miller	2	2- 4	2	6
Harp	6	3- 4	3	15
Voran	0	0- 1	0	0
Kline	0	0- 0	0	0
Totals	16	11-19	9	43

Southern California	fg	ft-fta	pf	tp
Vaughn	2	2- 5	2	6
Morrison	0	0- 0	3	0
Sears	8	3- 4	2	19
McGarvin	3	0- 0	4	6
Lippert	4	0- 1	3	8
Lambert	0	1- 2	2	1
Luber	1	0- 1	0	2
Totals	18	6-13	16	42

Half time: Southern California 21-20. Officials: Curtis and Vidal.

247

Championship

Indiana	fg	ft-fta	pf	tp
Schaefer	4	1- 1	1	9
McCreary	6	0- 0	2	12
W. Menke	2	1- 2	3	5
Huffman	5	2- 3	4	12
Dro	3	1- 1	4	7
Armstrong	4	2- 3	3	10
Gridley	0	0- 0	0	0
R. Menke	0	0- 0	0	0
Zimmer	2	1- 1	1	5
Dorsey	0	0- 0	0	0
Francis	0	0- 0	1	0
Totals	26	8-11	19	60

Kansas	fg	ft-fta	pf	tp
Ebling	1	2- 5	0	4
Engleman	5	2- 3	3	12
Allen	5	3- 4	3	13
Miller	0	2- 2	4	2
Harp	2	1- 3	1	5
Hunter	0	1- 1	0	1
Hogben	2	0- 0	0	4
Kline	0	0- 0	0	0
Voran	0	1- 2	0	1
Sands	0	0- 0	0	0
Johnson	0	0- 0	0	0
Totals	15	12-20	11	42

Half time: Indiana 32-19. Officials: O'Sullivan and McDonald.

1941

First Round

Wisconsin	fg	ft-fta	pf	tp
Kotz	5	5- 9	0	15
Epperson	4	0- 0	0	8
Englund	6	6- 7	3	18
Timmerman	0	0- 0	1	0
Strain	0	1- 3	4	1
Alwin	0	0- 0	0	0
Rehm	2	5- 5	2	9
Totals	17	17-24	10	51

Dartmouth	fg	ft-fta	pf	tp
Broberg	9	2- 2	1	20
Munroe	7	1- 2	2	15
Else	0	0- 0	2	0
Olsen	1	0- 1	4	2
Shaw	0	0- 1	0	0
Horner	0	0- 0	0	0
Pearson	0	1- 1	4	1
Parmer	1	0- 0	3	2
Skaug	4	2- 3	3	10
Totals	22	6-10	19	50

Half time: Dartmouth 24-22. Officials: Chest and Risley.

Pittsburgh	fg	ft-fta	pf	tp
Straloski	3	0- 2	0	6
Kocheran	2	2- 2	2	6
Port	0	4- 7	2	4
Milanovich	1	1- 1	2	3
Klein	0	0- 0	1	0
Malarkey	3	1- 1	0	7
Paffrath	0	0- 0	3	0
Totals	9	8-13	10	26

North Carolina	fg	ft-fta	pf	tp
Rose	1	0- 1	3	2
Smith	0	0- 0	0	0
Paine	0	0- 1	2	0
Severin	1	1- 1	0	3
Glamack	4	1- 3	4	9
Pessar	1	0- 0	0	2
Howard	1	0- 0	2	2
Shytle	0	0- 0	0	0
Gersten	0	0- 1	0	0
Suggs	1	0- 1	0	2
Totals	9	2- 8	11	20

Half time: North Carolina 12-8. Officials: Haarlow and Boyle.

Washington State	fg	ft-fta	pf	tp
Gentry	1	1- 2	1	3
Butts	4	1- 2	1	9
Hooper	0	0- 0	0	0
Lindeman	12	2- 6	3	26
Zimmerman	1	0- 0	0	2
Gebert	2	0- 1	3	4
Hunt	0	0- 0	0	0
Gilbert	0	0- 0	0	0
Sundquist	2	0- 3	1	4
Mahan	0	0- 0	1	0
Totals	22	4-14	10	48

Creighton	fg	ft-fta	pf	tp
Fleming	3	1- 2	1	7
Jaquay	3	1- 2	0	7
Beisser	4	0- 0	3	8
Langer	0	0- 1	3	0
Haldeman	0	0- 1	3	0
Thynne	1	1- 1	1	3
Nolan	5	4- 5	2	14
Totals	16	7-12	12	39

Half time: Washington State 25-14. Officials: Curtis and Herigstad.

Arkansas	fg	ft-fta	pf	tp
J. Adams	11	4- 4	0	26
Carpenter	3	2- 3	2	8
Freiberger	2	3- 5	2	7
Pitts	4	0- 0	4	8
Wynne	0	0- 0	2	0
Hickey	1	1- 3	4	3
O. Adams	0	0- 0	0	0
Totals	21	10-15	14	52

Wyoming	fg	ft-fta	pf	tp
Krpan	0	1- 2	2	1
Bentson	0	0- 0	4	0
Gowdy	1	0- 2	2	2
Weir	2	0- 1	2	4
Muir	0	0- 0	0	0
Strannigan	3	2- 2	0	8
Sailors	6	5- 5	2	17
Butcher	0	0- 0	0	0
Rothman	3	2- 2	2	8
Totals	15	10-14	14	40

Half time: Arkansas 29-18. Officials: O'Sullivan and Cameron.

Third Place

Dartmouth	fg	ft-fta	pf	tp
Broberg	8	2- 4	1	18
Munroe	8	2- 4	0	18
Olsen	3	4- 6	3	10
Parmer	2	1- 1	0	5
Pearson	2	1- 1	0	5
Shaw	0	0- 0	2	0
Skaug	2	0- 1	1	4
Totals	25	10-17	7	60

North Carolina	fg	ft-fta	pf	tp
Rose	4	2- 3	1	10
Paine	0	0- 0	0	0
Pessar	0	0- 0	3	0
Severin	0	0- 0	3	0
Glamack	10	11-14	3	31
Howard	6	0- 0	1	12
Gersten	3	0- 0	0	6
Suggs	0	0- 0	1	0
Totals	23	13-17	12	59

Half time: Dartmouth 38-34. Officials: Haarlow and Risley.

Creighton	fg	ft-fta	pf	tp
Fleming	8	1- 1	1	17
Jaquay	2	0- 0	2	4
Thynne	1	0- 0	2	2
Beisser	6	2- 2	3	14
Langer	0	0- 0	0	0
Haldeman	1	3- 4	4	5
Nolan	1	1- 3	1	3
Totals	19	7-10	13	45

Wyoming	fg	ft-fta	pf	tp
Krpan	0	0- 0	0	0
Sailors	3	1- 3	2	7
Bentson	2	2- 2	2	6
Gowdy	0	0- 0	0	0
Weir	5	1- 4	1	11
Muir	0	0- 0	1	0
Strannigan	8	0- 3	1	16
Rothman	1	2- 2	0	4
Totals	19	6-14	7	44

Half time: Creighton 24-20. Officials: Cameron and Curtis.

Harold "Bud" Foster

John Kotz

Semifinals

Wisconsin	fg	ft-fta	pf	tp
Kotz	3	4- 4	1	10
Scott	0	0- 0	0	0
Epperson	2	3- 4	0	7
Englund	2	7- 8	4	11
Schrage	0	0- 0	0	0
Timmerman	0	0- 1	0	0
Strain	2	0- 2	3	4
Alwin	0	0- 0	0	0
Rehm	1	2- 2	0	4
Schiewe	0	0- 0	0	0
Totals	10	16-21	8	36

Pittsburgh	fg	ft-fta	pf	tp
Straloski	6	0- 1	4	12
Swacus	0	0- 0	0	0
Egan	0	0- 0	0	0
Kocheran	1	2- 2	0	4
Port	1	2- 3	4	4
Paffrath	1	1- 1	1	3
Milanovich	2	0- 0	3	4
Ziolkowski	0	0- 0	2	0
Artman	0	0- 0	0	0
Klein	0	0- 0	1	0
Malarkey	1	1- 1	3	3
Totals	12	6- 8	18	30

Half time: Pittsburgh 18-14. Officials: Boyle and Chest.

Washington State	fg	ft-fta	pf	tp
Gentry	4	1- 2	2	9
Butts	5	1- 1	1	11
Gilberg	3	0- 3	4	6
Zimmerman	0	0- 0	2	0
Lindeman	4	6- 9	2	14
Gebert	5	2- 2	1	12
Sundquist	2	2- 2	2	6
Hunt	1	0- 0	3	2
Akins	0	0- 0	0	0
Hooper	2	0- 0	4	4
Totals	26	12-19	21	64

Arkansas	fg	ft-fta	pf	tp
J. Adams	10	2- 5	1	22
Carpenter	2	1- 3	2	5
Freiberger	1	3- 5	3	5
Pitts	5	2- 4	2	12
Robbins	0	0- 1	3	0
Hickey	1	1- 2	2	3
Wynne	0	0- 1	2	0
O. Adams	2	2- 3	3	6
Totals	21	11-23	18	53

Half time: Washington State 37-25. Technical foul: Carpenter. Officials: Herigstad and O'Sullivan.

Championship

Wisconsin	fg	ft-fta	pf	tp
Epperson	2	0- 0	3	4
Schrage	0	0- 0	1	0
Kotz	5	2- 3	2	12
Englund	5	3- 4	2	13
Timmerman	1	0- 0	1	2
Rehm	2	0- 1	2	4
Strain	0	2- 2	1	2
Alwin	1	0- 0	0	2
Totals	16	7-10	12	39

Washington State	fg	ft-fta	pf	tp
Gentry	0	1- 2	1	1
Gilberg	1	0- 2	1	2
Butts	1	1- 1	1	3
Lindeman	0	3- 4	1	3
Zimmerman	0	0- 0	0	0
Gebert	10	1- 2	1	21
Hunt	0	0- 0	0	0
Sundquist	2	0- 1	3	4
Hooper	0	0- 0	0	0
Totals	14	6-12	8	34

Half time: Wisconsin 21-17. Officials: Haarlow and Cameron.

1942

First Round

Dartmouth	fg	ft-fta	pf	tp
Myers	4	1- 1	3	9
Munroe	3	0- 0	1	6
Olsen	8	3- 4	4	19
Shaw	0	0- 0	0	0
Pearson	1	1- 2	4	3
Parmer	0	0- 1	0	0
Skaug	2	3- 4	2	7
Totals	18	8-12	14	44

Penn State	fg	ft-fta	pf	tp
Gent	1	0- 0	0	2
Gross	3	3- 3	1	9
Baltimore	4	1- 1	0	9
Ramin	0	2- 3	1	2
Egli	5	2- 3	4	12
Grimes	0	0- 1	3	0
Hornstein	1	3- 4	2	5
Totals	14	11-15	11	39

Half time: Dartmouth 22-16. Officials: Adams and Pailet.

Kentucky	fg	ft-fta	pf	tp
White	0	1- 1	2	1
Allen	2	0- 0	2	4
Ticco	6	1- 2	0	13
Brewer	0	1- 1	3	1
King	2	2- 4	1	6
Staker	4	1- 2	3	9
England	1	2- 2	3	4
Akers	4	0- 0	0	8
Totals	19	8-12	14	46

Illinois	fg	ft-fta	pf	tp
Menke	7	1- 1	2	15
Hocking	0	0- 0	0	0
Smiley	5	3- 3	2	13
Fowler	0	0- 0	1	0
Mathisen	0	1- 1	0	1
Wukovits	2	0- 4	3	4
Phillip	2	2- 4	0	6
Vance	0	0- 0	3	0
Sachs	2	1- 2	2	5
Totals	18	8-15	13	44

Half time: Illinois 22-20. Officials: Coogan and Snyder.

1941 WISCONSIN BADGERS—(l-r) Front Row: Bob Alwin, Bob Sullivan, Fred Rehm, John Kotz, Gene Englund, Charles Epperson, Ted Strain, Harlo Scott, Ed Schiewe; Back Row: Morris Bradley, Walter Bakke, Ted Downs, Bob Roth, George Affeldt, Warren Schrage, Don Timmerman, Ted Deppe, John Lynch, Edward Jones, Harold "Bud" Foster, Fred Wegner.

1942 STANFORD INDIANS—(l-r) Bill Cowden, Howie Dallmar, Ed Voss, Jim Pollard, Don Burness, Everett Dean.

Stanford	fg	ft-fta	pf	tp
Dana	0	0- 1	1	0
Linari	0	0- 0	0	0
Pollard	12	2- 4	1	26
Voss	4	7- 8	3	15
Cowden	2	2- 4	3	6
Dallmar	3	0- 0	0	6
McCaffrey	0	0- 0	0	0
Totals	21	11-17	7	53

Rice	fg	ft-fta	pf	tp
Closs	3	2- 3	4	8
Zander	0	0- 0	1	0
Gomez	2	0- 0	3	4
Kinney	3	2- 3	4	8
McDonald	0	1- 2	0	1
Palmer	8	2- 2	3	18
Lambert	4	0- 0	0	8
Totals	20	7-10	15	47

Half time: Stanford 33-21. Officials: House and Herigstad.

Colorado	fg	ft-fta	pf	tp
McCloud	8	3- 4	0	19
Nuckolls	1	1- 1	2	3
Doll	2	2- 2	4	6
Huggins	2	1- 1	4	5
Putman	0	0- 0	0	0
Hamburg	4	1- 3	1	9
Kirchner	2	0- 0	3	4
Totals	19	8-11	14	46

Howie Dallmar

Kansas	fg	ft-fta	pf	tp
Miller	2	1- 2	4	5
Ballard	0	0- 0	0	0
Black	6	6- 8	2	18
Buescher	1	3- 4	2	5
Hall	1	0- 0	1	2
Evans	5	0- 0	2	10
Sollenberger	1	0- 0	0	2
Hunter	1	0- 2	1	2
Totals	17	10-16	12	44

Half time: Colorado 27-20. Officials: Curtis and Piluso.

Third Place

Penn State	fg	ft-fta	pf	tp
Gent	10	1- 1	1	21
Gross	0	4- 6	0	4
Baltimore	5	0- 0	2	10
Grimes	0	0- 0	0	0
Hornstein	1	0- 3	4	2
Ramin	0	0- 0	1	0
Egli	1	2- 3	4	4
Totals	17	7-13	12	41

Illinois	fg	ft-fta	pf	tp
Hocking	0	0- 0	1	0
Smiley	2	0- 0	1	4
Menke	3	2- 2	2	8
Parker	0	0- 0	1	0
Wukovits	1	4- 4	1	6
Mathisen	2	3- 3	0	7
Phillip	2	1- 2	1	5
Fowler	1	0- 0	0	2
Sachs	1	0- 0	3	2
Vance	0	0- 0	1	0
Totals	12	10-11	11	34

Half time: Penn State 26-21. Officials: Pailet and Coogan.

Everett Dean

Kansas	fg	ft-fta	pf	tp
Miller	4	3- 7	3	11
Kissell	0	0- 0	0	0
Ballard	0	0- 0	4	0
Walker	0	0- 0	0	0
Buescher	7	0- 0	1	14
Hall	0	0- 0	0	0
Black	6	4- 6	4	16
Hunter	1	0- 0	3	2
Evans	5	2- 2	4	12
Sollenberger	0	0- 0	0	0
Totals	23	9-15	19	55

Rice	fg	ft-fta	pf	tp
Closs	2	5- 9	2	9
Gomez	3	0- 1	3	6
Zander	0	1- 1	2	1
Kinney	2	2- 2	4	6
McDonald	1	0- 0	0	2
Palmer	11	3- 3	1	25
Lambert	1	2- 3	1	4
Totals	20	13-19	13	53

Half time: Rice 30-24. Officials: Piluso and Herigstad.

Semifinals

Dartmouth	fg	ft-fta	pf	tp
Myers	4	1- 2	2	9
Pogue	0	0- 0	0	0
Munroe	9	2- 4	2	20
Briggs	0	0- 0	0	0
Olsen	5	1- 3	2	11
Shaw	1	0- 0	0	2
Pearson	0	3- 3	1	3
Parmer	0	0- 1	2	0
Skaug	1	0- 1	4	2
McKernan	0	0- 0	0	0
Totals	20	7-14	13	47

Kentucky	fg	ft-fta	pf	tp
White	0	0- 0	2	0
Ramsey	0	0- 0	0	0
Allen	2	2- 4	2	6
Ticco	0	1- 1	1	1
Brewer	1	2- 4	1	4
King	1	2- 2	0	4
Staker	0	0- 0	4	0
England	1	0- 0	1	2
Akers	5	1- 2	3	11
Totals	10	8-13	14	28

Half time: Dartmouth 23-13. Officials: Snyder and Adams.

Stanford	fg	ft-fta	pf	tp
Dana	3	1- 2	1	7
Pollard	8	1- 1	2	17
Madden	0	0- 0	0	0
Voss	4	2- 5	3	10
Linari	0	0- 0	0	0
Eikelman	0	0- 0	1	0
Cowden	2	3- 5	2	7
McCaffrey	0	0- 0	0	0
Dallmar	2	1- 1	0	5
Oliver	0	0- 0	0	0
Totals	19	8-14	9	46

Colorado	fg	ft-fta	pf	tp
McCloud	1	1- 2	2	3
Huggins	0	0- 0	3	0
Nuckolls	0	0- 1	3	0
Putman	3	0- 0	1	6
Doll	3	5- 5	3	11
Hamburg	3	2- 2	2	8
Kirchner	3	1- 1	0	7
Totals	13	9-11	11	35

Half time: Stanford 22-15. Officials: Curtis and House.

Championship

Stanford	fg	ft-fta	pf	tp
Dana	7	0- 0	0	14
Eikelman	0	0- 0	0	0
Burness	0	0- 0	0	0
Linari	3	0- 0	0	6
Voss	6	1- 1	2	13
Madden	0	0- 0	0	0
Cowden	2	1- 2	3	5
McCaffrey	0	0- 0	0	0
Dallmar	6	3- 5	0	15
Oliver	0	0- 0	0	0
Totals	24	5- 8	5	53

Dartmouth	fg	ft-fta	pf	tp
Meyers	4	0- 1	1	8
Parmer	1	0- 0	0	2
Munroe	5	2- 2	1	12
Shaw	0	0- 0	0	0
Olsen	4	0- 0	0	8
Pogue	0	0- 0	0	0
Pearson	2	2- 2	3	6
McKernan	0	0- 0	0	0
Skaug	1	0- 0	2	2
Briggs	0	0- 0	0	0
Totals	17	4- 5	7	38

Half time: Stanford 24-22. Officials: Curtis and Adams.

1943

First Round

Georgetown	fg	ft-fta	pf	tp
Gabbianelli	2	1- 1	3	5
Potolicchio	3	0- 0	0	6
Reilly	1	2- 3	2	4
Duffey	1	1- 1	0	3
Feeney	1	0- 0	0	2
Mahnken	10	0- 0	1	20
Hassett	2	3- 3	1	7
Kraus	4	0- 0	1	8
Totals	24	7- 8	8	55

New York Univ.	fg	ft-fta	pf	tp
Fleishman	1	0- 0	1	2
Grenert	1	2- 3	1	4
Maher	4	1- 1	3	9
Leggat	1	0- 0	1	2
Danto	5	1- 2	1	11
Simmons	1	1- 3	0	3
Heiser	0	0- 0	0	0
Mele	2	1- 1	0	5
Totals	15	6-10	7	36

Half time: Georgetown 32-19. Officials: Burns and Nucatola.

DePaul	fg	ft-fta	pf	tp
Jorgenson	5	0- 0	3	10
Triptow	0	0- 0	0	0
Cominsky	3	3- 4	3	9
Danato	0	0- 0	0	0
Mikan	7	6- 7	3	20
Wiscons	0	0- 0	0	0
Starzyk	0	0- 1	4	0
Frailey	0	0- 0	0	0
Crowley	0	0- 0	0	0
Kelly	1	2- 2	2	4
Ryan	1	1- 1	0	3
Totals	17	12-15	15	46

Dartmouth	fg	ft-fta	pf	tp
Munroe	3	2- 4	0	8
Carroll	0	0- 0	0	0
Myers	1	3- 5	4	5
Brindley	5	0- 0	1	10
Olsen	2	3- 3	4	7
Skaug	0	2- 3	2	2
Monahan	0	0- 0	0	0
Coleman	1	1- 1	1	3
Briggs	0	0- 0	0	0
Totals	12	11-16	13	35

Half time: DePaul 26-14. Officials: Kennedy and Litwack.

Texas	fg	ft-fta	pf	tp
Overall	5	5- 7	4	15
Goss	0	0- 0	0	0
Hargis	10	10-12	3	30
Landon	1	0- 0	4	2
Wright	0	0- 0	1	0
Fitzgerald	1	0- 1	4	2
Cox	3	0- 0	0	6
Brahaney	1	2- 3	4	4
Kent	0	0- 0	1	0
Totals	21	17-23	21	59

249

250

1943 WYOMING COWBOYS—(l-r) Front Row: Don Waite, Earl Ray, Jim Reese; Back Row: Jim Collins, Floyd Volker, Milo Komenich, Ev Shelton, Lou Roney, Kenny Sailors, Jim Weir, Philip Badger (NCAA President).

Washington	fg	ft-fta	pf	tp
Ford	3	4- 7	2	10
Bird	3	0- 0	2	6
Gilbertson	2	0- 0	4	4
Sheafer	0	0- 0	4	0
Gilmur	2	1- 3	4	5
Nelson	0	0- 3	1	0
Morris	8	6- 9	2	22
Gissberg	2	2- 2	2	6
Taylor	1	0- 3	1	2
Brown	0	0- 0	0	0
Gronsdale	0	0- 0	0	0
Totals	21	13-27	22	55

Half time: Washington 33-28. Officials: Doubenmeier and O'Sullivan.

Wyoming	fg	ft-fta	pf	tp
Sailors	4	0- 2	2	8
Ray	0	0- 0	0	0
Weir	6	2- 4	3	14
Komenich	10	2- 4	2	22
Volker	3	0- 0	4	6
Waite	0	0- 0	0	0
Roney	0	1- 2	2	1
Collins	1	0- 0	1	2
Reese	0	0- 0	0	0
Totals	24	5-12	14	53

Oklahoma	fg	ft-fta	pf	tp
Reich	5	7- 9	1	17
Rousey	0	2- 2	0	2
Heap	1	1- 1	0	3
Pugsley	1	0- 0	0	2
Tucker	5	1- 4	4	11
McCurdy	0	0- 0	0	0
Marteney	1	0- 0	0	2
Paine	5	1- 2	4	11
Mitchell	1	0- 0	0	2
Totals	19	12-18	9	50

Half time: Oklahoma 25-22. Officials: Curtis and Leith.

Third Place

Dartmouth	fg	ft-fta	pf	tp
Munroe	2	2- 3	1	6
Carroll	0	1- 2	0	1
Myers	11	0- 3	3	22
Brindley	3	2- 3	0	8
Olsen	1	0- 0	3	2
Skaug	2	1- 1	4	5
Briggs	0	1- 1	0	1
Coleman	2	2- 2	3	6
Totals	21	9-15	14	51

New York Univ.	fg	ft-fta	pf	tp
Fleishman	3	0- 0	4	6
Grenert	3	4- 4	4	10
Leggat	0	1- 2	0	1
Maher	3	0- 2	4	6
Heiser	0	0- 0	0	0
Weissman	0	0- 0	0	0
Danto	2	1- 1	2	5
Rifkin	0	0- 0	0	0
Simmons	3	2- 2	0	8
Mele	4	5- 6	2	13
Totals	18	13-17	16	49

Half time: Dartmouth 25-19. Officials: Begovich and Soladara.

Oklahoma	fg	ft-fta	pf	tp
Heap	2	1- 2	2	5
Rousey	0	0- 0	1	0
Reich	6	1- 1	2	13
Pugsley	0	0- 0	0	0
Tucker	6	6- 8	0	18
Marteney	1	0- 0	0	2
McCurdy	0	0- 0	1	0
Paine	3	4- 4	4	10
Totals	18	12-15	10	48

Kenny Sailors

Washington	fg	ft-fta	pf	tp
Ford	1	0- 1	0	2
Gissberg	3	1- 4	2	7
Gilbertson	3	1- 3	2	7
Gilmur	1	0- 0	4	2
Morris	2	1- 2	4	5
Bird	2	0- 0	0	4
Taylor	7	2- 2	0	16
Totals	19	5-12	12	43

Half time: Oklahoma 24-21. Officials: Curtis and Doubenmeier.

Semifinals

Georgetown	fg	ft-fta	pf	tp
Gabbianelli	3	0- 0	1	6
Fenney	0	0- 0	2	0
Duffey	0	0- 0	0	0
Potolicchio	5	1- 3	1	11
Reilly	0	0' 0	0	0
Mahnken	8	1- 2	4	17
Hyde	1	0- 0	2	2
Hassett	2	7- 7	0	11
Kraus	1	4- 6	3	6
Totals	20	13-18	13	53

DePaul	fg	ft-fta	pf	tp
Jorgenson	6	2- 3	2	14
Frailey	0	0- 0	0	0
Cominsky	5	1- 3	3	11
Mikan	3	5- 8	1	11
Starzyk	3	1- 1	2	7
Kelly	2	2- 2	4	6
Ryan	0	0- 0	3	0
Totals	19	11-17	15	49

Half time: DePaul 28-23. Officials: Kennedy and Nucatola.

Ev Shelton

Wyoming	fg	ft-fta	pf	tp
Sailors	4	4- 6	3	12
Weir	6	1- 1	3	13
Waite	0	0- 0	1	0
Komenich	8	1- 4	2	17
Volker	3	1- 3	4	7
Roney	1	2- 3	3	4
Collins	2	1- 2	2	5
Totals	24	10-19	18	58

Texas	fg	ft-fta	pf	tp
Overall	5	4- 7	3	14
Hargis	11	7-11	3	29
Langdon	1	2- 3	2	4
Brahaney	1	0- 0	3	2
Fitzgerald	1	0- 0	4	2
Wright	1	1- 1	2	3
Cox	0	0- 0	3	0
Totals	20	14-22	20	54

Half time: Texas 33-27. Officials: O'Sullivan and Leith.

Championship

Wyoming	fg	ft-fta	pf	tp
Sailors	6	4- 5	2	16
Collins	4	0- 0	1	8
Weir	2	1- 3	2	5
Waite	0	0- 0	0	0
Komenich	4	1- 4	2	9
Volker	2	1- 2	3	5
Roney	0	1- 2	1	1
Reese	1	0- 0	0	2
Totals	19	8-16	11	46

Georgetown	fg	ft-fta	pf	tp
Reilly	1	0- 0	0	2
Potolicchio	1	2- 3	1	4
Gabbianelli	1	2- 3	3	4
Hyde	0	0- 0	0	0
Mahnken	2	2- 3	2	6
Hassett	3	0- 3	4	6
Finnerty	0	0- 0	0	0
Kraus	2	0- 1	3	4
Fenney	4	0- 0	1	8
Duffey	0	0- 0	0	0
Totals	14	6-13	14	34

Half time: Wyoming 18-16. Officials: Kennedy and Begovich.

1944

First Round

Dartmouth	fg	ft-fta	pf	tp
Gale	8	1- 1	1	17
Wilson	0	0- 0	0	0
Leggat	7	1- 5	4	15
Brindley	6	1- 1	2	13
Murphy	0	0- 0	0	0
McGuire	4	0- 0	2	8
Vancisin	3	0- 0	2	6
Monahan	0	2- 0	0	0
Goering	1	0- 0	0	2
Mercer	1	0- 0	1	2
Totals	30	3- 9	12	63

Catholic	fg	ft-fta	pf	tp
Mercak	6	0- 1	0	12
Szklarz	2	2- 5	1	6
Kingsbury	0	0- 0	0	0
Scanlon	4	3- 5	4	11
Rice	3	1- 3	0	7
Carlin	1	0- 0	1	2
Totals	16	6-14	6	38

Half time: Dartmouth 28-12. Officials: Adams and DeGroot.

Ohio State	fg	ft-fta	pf	tp
Grate	8	1- 2	3	17
Plank	0	0- 0	0	0
Dugger	2	0- 0	0	4
Caudill	3	0- 1	0	6
Risen	3	1- 3	3	7
Bowen	4	2- 5	3	10
Fink	0	1- 4	0	1
Huston	5	2- 2	2	12
Gunton	0	0- 0	0	0
Totals	25	7-17	11	57

Temple	fg	ft-fta	pf	tp
Koecher	5	2- 3	4	12
Joyce	7	2- 6	0	16
Budd	2	0- 0	3	4
Bramble	3	0- 0	0	6
Burns	0	0- 0	0	0
Fox	2	5- 6	3	9
Collins	0	0- 0	0	0
Totals	19	9-15	10	47

Half time: Ohio State 26-23. Officials: Dissinger and Menton.

Vadal Peterson

1944 UTAH UTES—(l-r) Front Row: Mas Tatsuno, Ray Kingston; Second Row: James Nance, Fred Lewis, Wat Misaka, William Kastelic; Back Row: Vadal Peterson, Fred Sheffield, Herb Wilkinson, Arnie Ferrin, Dick Smuin, Bob Lewis, Pete Couch.

Iowa State	fg	ft	tp
Ray Wehde	1	2	4
Roy Wehde	5	2	12
Meyers	5	1	11
Brookfield	4	2	10
Oulman	1	0	2
Block	1	0	2
Sauer	0	3	3
Totals	17	10	44

Pepperdine	fg	ft	tp
Ruby	2	1	5
Wandell	0	0	0
Nunn	2	0	4
Asher	0	0	0
Buzolich	9	4	22
Whaley	2	1	5
Witeck	1	1	3
Totals	16	7	39
Officials: Gibbs and Hess.			

Utah	fg	ft	tp
Ferrin	5	2	12
Smuin	3	1	7
Nance	0	0	0
Sheffield	3	1	7
Misaka	2	1	5
Wilkinson	3	2	8
F. Lewis	0	0	0
B. Lewis	3	0	6
Kingston	0	0	0
Totals	19	7	45

Missouri	fg	ft	tp
Crowder	3	1	7
Brown	1	0	2
C. Minx	2	1	5
Pippin	3	0	6
Toal	0	0	0
B. Minx	2	1	5
Collins	4	2	10
Heinsohn	0	0	0
Totals	15	5	35
Officials: Curtis and Piluso.			

Third Place

Temple	fg	ft-fta	pf	tp
Koecher	3	2- 2	4	8
Joyce	7	1- 2	1	15
Budd	2	0- 1	2	4
Bramble	3	0- 0	2	6
Fox	3	0- 0	1	6
Burns	4	0- 1	2	8
Rosen	3	1- 1	1	7
Collins	0	1- 2	0	1
Totals	25	5- 9	13	55

Catholic	fg	ft-fta	pf	tp
Mercak	1	1- 1	1	3
Szklarz	5	2- 2	0	12
Scanlon	4	4- 9	3	12
Kingsbury	0	0- 0	0	0
Rice	3	1- 1	2	7
Carlin	0	1- 4	2	1
Totals	13	9-17	8	35
Half time: Temple 24-21. Officials: Adams and Dissinger.				

Missouri	fg	ft	tp
Crowder	2	3	7
Brown	3	0	6
C. Minx	8	5	21
Toal	0	0	0
Pippin	5	2	12
Heinsohn	1	0	2
B. Minx	1	2	4
Glinkenbeard	0	0	0
Collins	3	3	9
Bellastatious	0	0	0
Totals	23	15	61

Pepperdine	fg	ft	tp
Ruby	2	1	5
Lewis	0	0	0
Nunn	2	0	4
Asher	2	2	6
Buzolich	8	7	23
Wandell	1	0	2
Whaley	3	0	6
Richardson	0	0	0
Witeck	0	0	0
Lawyer	0	0	0
Totals	18	10	46
Officials: Hess and Piluso.			

Arnie Ferrin

Semifinals

Dartmouth	fg	ft-fta	pf	tp
Gale	3	1- 1	2	7
Leggat	5	2- 4	2	12
Brindley	13	2- 3	3	28
McGuire	4	1- 3	1	9
Vancisin	0	0- 0	2	0
Monahan	2	0- 0	1	4
Totals	27	6-11	11	60

Ohio State	fg	ft-fta	pf	tp
Grate	3	1- 2	2	7
Dugger	3	2- 6	4	8
Gunton	0	0- 0	0	0
Risen	8	5- 6	0	21
Caudill	0	0- 0	1	0
Bowen	3	0- 0	1	6
Fink	0	0- 0	0	0
Huston	5	1- 1	3	11
Totals	22	9-15	11	53
Half time: Dartmouth 28-22. Officials: Menton and DeGroot.				

Utah	fg	ft	tp
Ferrin	3	0	6
Smuin	2	1	5
Sheffield	4	1	9
Misaka	4	1	9
Wilkinson	1	2	4
B. Lewis	3	1	7
Totals	17	6	40

Iowa State	fg	ft	tp
Ray Wehde	2	1	5
Block	2	1	5
Roy Wehde	2	0	4
Brookfield	3	0	6
Ewoldt	0	0	0
Oulman	2	1	5
Sauer	0	2	2
Meyers	2	0	4
Totals	13	5	31
Officials: Curtis and Gibbs.			

Championship

Utah	fg	ft-fta	pf	tp
Ferrin	8	6- 7	0	22
Smuin	0	0- 0	2	0
Sheffield	1	0- 0	1	2
Misaka	2	0- 0	1	4
Wilkinson	3	1- 4	0	7
Lewis	2	3- 3	2	7
Totals	16	10-14	6	42

Dartmouth	fg	ft-fta	pf	tp
Gale	5	0- 2	1	10
Mercer	0	1- 1	3	1
Leggat	4	0- 0	1	8
Nordstrom	0	0- 0	0	0
Brindley	5	1- 1	3	11
McGuire	3	0- 1	3	6
Murphy	0	0- 0	0	0
Vancisin	2	0- 0	3	4
Goering	0	0- 0	0	0
Totals	19	2- 5	14	40
Half time: Dartmouth 18-17. Regulation Score: 36-36. Officials: Osborne and Menton.				

1945

First Round

New York Univ.	fg	ft-fta	pf	tp
Grenert	5	2- 4	0	12
Forman	3	0- 2	1	6
Sarath	0	0- 1	2	0
Schayes	6	1- 3	1	13
Most	0	3- 3	1	3
Benanti	0	0- 0	0	0
Tanenbaum	7	3- 4	3	17
Mangiapane	2	2- 5	3	6
Walsh	1	0- 1	1	2
Totals	24	11-23	12	59

Tufts	fg	ft-fta	pf	tp
Skarda	7	1- 3	5	15
Moran	0	0- 0	3	0
Walz	2	0- 0	1	4
Burgbacher	3	2- 2	1	8
Johnson	1	1- 5	3	3
Cooney	0	0- 0	4	0
Cumiskey	6	2- 4	3	14
Totals	19	6-14	20	44
Officials: Beiersdorfer and Adams.				

Ohio State	fg	ft-fta	pf	tp
Grate	5	5- 9	3	15
Sims	1	0- 0	0	2
Dugger	0	0- 1	2	0
Caudill	5	4- 6	5	14
Snyder	0	0- 0	0	0
Risen	4	1- 3	5	9
Huston	2	1- 1	2	5
Amling	0	0- 4	4	0
Totals	17	11-24	21	45

Kentucky	fg	ft-fta	pf	tp
Tingle	5	1- 2	0	11
Schu	2	4- 5	4	8
Parker	0	0- 3	0	0
Campbell	2	2- 5	4	6
Vulich	0	2- 3	0	2
Parkinson	1	5- 6	3	7
Stough	1	1- 3	4	3
Sturgill	0	0- 0	3	0
Totals	11	15-27	18	37
Officials: Boyle and Melman.				

Arkansas	fg	ft	pf	tp
Richie	6	1	2	13
M. Schumchyk	7	6	4	20
Kearns	0	0	1	0
Kok	9	4	2	22
Jolliff	0	2	0	2
Flynt	3	3	3	9
F. Schumchyk	0	1	0	1
Wheeler	5	2	0	12
Totals	30	19	12	79

Oregon	fg	ft	pf	tp
Stamper	0	0	2	0
Berg	3	2	4	8
Wilkins	10	3	2	23
Smith	4	3	3	11
Hays	3	1	3	7
Bartelt	3	1	5	7
Hamilton	9	2	2	20
Totals	32	12	21	76
Half time: Arkansas 47-34. Officials: Lance and Smith.				

Henry Iba

Oklahoma A&M	fg	ft	pf	tp
Hankins	5	1	3	11
Wylie	0	0	1	0
Kern	2	3	2	7
Kurland	14	0	2	28
Halbert	0	0	1	0
Williams	4	0	3	8
Parks	1	0	1	2
Parrack	3	0	2	6
Johnson	0	0	0	0
Totals	29	4	15	62

1945 OKLAHOMA A&M AGGIES—(l-r) Front Row: D. W. Jones, Weldon Kern, J. L. Parks, Doyle Parrack, John Wylie; Back Row: Bill Johnson, Joe Halbert, Tug Wilson (NCAA President), Bob Kurland, Henry Iba, Blake Williams, Cecil Hankins, Buddy Milikan.

252

Utah	fg	ft	pf	tp
Dorton	3	1	0	7
Hamblin	2	1	2	5
Satterfield	4	6	2	14
Barnes	0	0	0	0
Howard	4	3	4	11
Keil	0	0	0	0
Totals	13	11	8	37

Half time: Oklahoma A&M 22-12. Officials: Curtis and McLarney.

Third Place

Kentucky	fg	ft-fta	pf	tp
Parker	6	2- 5	4	14
Allin	0	0- 0	0	0
Schu	10	1- 1	3	21
Tingle	0	0- 0	0	0
Campbell	3	1- 2	0	7
Vulich	4	5- 5	2	13
Parkinson	4	1- 2	2	9
Durham	0	0- 0	0	0
Stough	0	1- 1	1	1
Sturgill	0	1- 2	5	1
Totals	27	12-18	17	66

Tufts	fg	ft-fta	pf	tp
Skarda	8	4- 6	1	20
Matthews	0	0- 0	0	0
Moran	4	1- 1	2	9
Walz	0	1- 1	1	1
Andreason	0	0- 0	0	0
Burgbacher	4	2- 5	2	10
Johnson	0	1- 4	2	1
Cumiskey	3	2- 3	1	8
Cooney	1	5- 7	4	7
Beers	0	0- 0	0	0
Giordano	0	0- 0	0	0
Walker	0	0- 0	0	0
Dougherty	0	0- 0	0	0
Totals	20	16-27	13	56

Officials: Melman and Adams.

Oregon	fg	ft	pf	tp
D. Smith	0	1	0	1
Berg	3	3	5	9
Wilkins	9	3	3	21
Stamper	1	0	0	2
Hays	6	2	2	14
Allen	0	0	0	0
Hamilton	3	6	1	12
Kotnik	0	0	0	0
Hoffine	4	2	1	10
Totals	26	17	12	69

Utah	fg	ft	pf	tp
Dorton	11	2	4	24
Hamblin	1	3	4	5
Barnes	2	0	2	4
Satterfield	9	2	3	20
Keil	1	2	2	4
Howard	4	1	4	9
Totals	28	10	19	66

Half time: Utah 38-30. Officials: Curtis and Lance.

Semifinals

New York Univ.	fg	ft-fta	pf	tp
Grenert	2	2- 5	3	6
Benanti	0	0- 0	1	0
Forman	4	2- 2	2	10
Schayes	5	4- 8	4	14
Walsh	2	2- 3	5	6
Most	1	0- 1	2	2
Tanenbaum	5	3- 3	2	13
Mangiapane	7	3- 5	4	17
Goldstein	1	0- 0	2	2
Totals	27	16-27	25	70

Ohio State	fg	ft-fta	pf	tp
Grate	2	2- 3	4	6
Sims	2	3- 4	3	7
Snyder	0	0- 0	0	0
Dugger	1	2- 5	5	4
Caudill	3	1- 1	3	7
Risen	8	10-13	5	26
Huston	2	1- 3	5	5
Amling	5	0- 2	1	10
Totals	23	19-31	26	65

Regulation score: 62-62. Officials: Boyle and Beiersdorfer.

Bob Kurland

Oklahoma A&M	fg	ft	pf	tp
Hankins	8	6	1	22
Kern	3	0	2	6
Kurland	6	3	3	15
Halbert	0	0	1	0
Williams	2	3	2	7
Parks	1	0	1	2
Parrack	7	2	1	16
Wylie	0	0	0	0
Totals	27	14	11	68

Arkansas	fg	ft	pf	tp
Richie	2	0	0	4
Byles	1	0	1	2
M. Schumchyk	1	2	3	4
F. Schumchyk	0	0	1	0
Kearne	1	1	2	3
Kok	4	4	2	12
Jolliff	0	0	3	0
Flynt	5	1	2	11
Copeland	0	1	0	1
Wheeler	2	0	3	4
Totals	16	9	17	41

Half time: Arkansas 41-36. Officials: McLarney and Smith.

Championship

Oklahoma A&M	fg	ft-fta	pf	tp
Hankins	6	3- 6	3	15
Parks	0	0- 0	3	0
Kern	3	0- 4	3	6
Wylie	0	0- 0	0	0
Kurland	10	2- 3	3	22
Parrack	2	0- 1	3	4
Williams	1	0- 1	1	2
Totals	22	5-15	16	49

New York Univ.	fg	ft-fta	pf	tp
Grenert	5	2- 3	3	12
Forman	5	1- 2	1	11
Goldstein	0	2- 2	2	2
Schayes	2	2- 6	2	6
Walsh	0	0- 0	2	0
Tanenbaum	2	0- 0	2	4
Mangiapane	2	2- 4	3	6
Most	1	2- 3	2	4
Totals	17	11-20	17	45

Officials: Curtis and Adams.

1946

First Round

Ohio State	fg	ft-fta	pf	tp
Bowen	3	0- 0	4	6
Snyder	1	1- 2	4	3
Wells	2	0- 2	2	4
Kuhn	0	0- 0	0	0
Underman	5	4- 5	5	14
Elliott	0	1- 2	4	1
Huston	3	6- 8	3	12
Amling	3	0- 2	3	6
Totals	17	12-21	25	46

Harvard	fg	ft-fta	pf	tp
Gantt	1	2- 2	1	4
Swegan	1	0- 1	3	2
Clark	0	0- 0	0	0
Gray	2	7- 9	3	11
Davis	0	0- 0	0	0
Desci	1	5- 8	4	7
Mariaschin	5	1- 2	2	11
Petrillo	0	1- 2	1	1
McDaniel	0	0- 0	0	0
Champion	0	2- 6	4	2
Totals	10	18-30	18	38

Officials: Orwig and Nucatola.

North Carolina	fg	ft-fta	pf	tp
Paxton	6	1- 4	1	13
Dillon	7	1- 4	5	15
Anderson	1	2- 4	2	4
McKinney	4	3- 4	4	11
White	0	0- 0	5	0
Thorne	2	0- 0	1	4
Jordan	4	2- 2	5	10
Scholbe	0	0- 0	0	0
Totals	24	9-18	23	57

New York Univ.	fg	ft-fta	pf	tp
Forman	1	3- 4	2	5
Sarath	2	0- 2	1	4
Dolhon	1	0- 0	0	2
Goldstein	0	0- 0	0	0
DeBonis	5	3- 4	4	13
Schayes	2	5- 6	1	9
Kelly	0	0- 0	3	0
Tanenbaum	1	3- 3	3	5
Mangiapane	4	3- 7	4	11
Benanti	0	0- 0	0	0
Totals	16	17-26	18	49

Officials: Kennedy and Collins.

Oklahoma A&M	fg	ft-fta	pf	tp
Aubrey	0	0- 0	0	0
Bradley	3	1- 2	1	7
Bennett	0	0- 0	0	0
Kern	0	3- 5	2	3
Kurland	7	6-12	2	20
Halbert	0	0- 0	0	0
Williams	1	0- 1	5	2
Parks	4	1- 2	0	9
Bell	0	3- 3	1	3
Totals	15	14-25	11	44

Baylor	fg	ft-fta	pf	tp
Johnson	4	2- 3	4	10
Gonzales	0	0- 0	0	0
Robinson	1	3- 4	4	5
McCormick	0	1- 2	1	1
Devereaux	1	0- 0	1	2
Edwards	0	0- 0	5	0
Shearin	0	0- 0	5	0
Belew	2	0- 1	3	4
Hailey	3	1- 1	2	7
Totals	11	7-11	25	29

Half time: Oklahoma A&M 22-17. Officials: Oberhelman and Baker.

California	fg	ft-fta	pf	tp
LaFaille	3	2- 2	4	8
Wolfe	8	1- 2	0	17
Smith	2	0- 3	4	4
Walker	2	1- 6	3	5
Wray	4	0- 2	2	8
Hogeboom	3	2- 2	0	8
Totals	22	6-17	13	50

Colorado	fg	ft-fta	pf	tp
Walseth	3	1- 1	0	7
Beattie	2	1- 1	0	5
Fuller	1	0- 0	2	2
Ellis	3	0- 0	0	6
Hunt	0	0- 0	0	0
Knocke	4	1- 1	2	9
Putnam	2	1- 3	3	5
Huggins	2	4- 5	3	8
Robbins	1	0- 3	5	2
Allen	0	0- 0	0	0
Totals	18	8-14	15	44

Half time: California 23-18. Officials: Curtis and VanReen.

Third Place

New York Univ.	fg	ft-fta	pf	tp
Forman	0	3- 6	1	3
Sarath	0	0- 0	1	0
DeBonis	7	1- 1	3	15
Goldstein	0	0- 0	0	0
Benanti	0	0- 0	1	0
Schayes	1	0- 0	4	2
Kelly	10	2- 5	5	22
Regan	0	0- 0	0	0
Tanenbaum	3	4- 4	2	10
Mangiapane	6	3- 4	4	15
Totals	27	13-20	21	67

Henry Iba

1946 OKLAHOMA A&M AGGIES—(l-r) Joe Halbert, Joe Bradley, Sam Aubrey, Blake Williams, Eugene Bell, Mrs. James St. Clair, Bob Kurland, Paul Geyman, Henry Iba, Bob Crowe, A. L. Bennett, J. L. Parks, Weldon Kern.

Harvard	fg	ft-fta	pf	tp
Gantt	1	2- 3	4	4
Swegan	2	2- 4	1	6
Gray	9	4- 7	1	22
Desci	5	3- 4	3	13
Mariaschin	2	4- 6	4	8
Champion	3	0- 1	3	6
Petrillo	1	0- 0	0	2
Totals	23	15-25	16	61

Officials: Kennedy and Collins.

Colorado	fg	ft-fta	pf	tp
Fuller	0	0- 1	0	0
Walseth	4	3- 3	2	11
Huggins	6	1- 3	3	13
Stark	0	0- 0	0	0
Allen	0	0- 0	1	0
Knocke	1	5-11	0	7
Robbins	4	3- 5	1	11
Putnam	1	1- 2	3	3
Beattie	1	2- 2	3	4
Ellis	3	2- 3	4	8
Riley	1	0- 0	0	2
Hunt	0	0- 0	0	0
Totals	21	17-30	17	59

Baylor	fg	ft-fta	pf	tp
Belew	6	2- 6	4	14
Pulley	0	0- 0	1	0
Johnson	3	5- 6	3	11
Edwards	0	0- 0	5	0
Shearin	0	1- 1	5	1
Hailey	0	3- 3	4	3
Devereaux	0	0- 0	1	0
Robinson	5	5- 6	2	15
Totals	14	16-22	25	44

Half time: Colorado 25-22. Officials: Oberhelman and VanReen.

Semifinals

North Carolina	fg	ft-fta	pf	tp
Dillon	5	6-13	4	16
Anderson	3	0- 1	2	6
Scholbe	0	0- 0	1	0
Paxton	4	0- 2	3	8
McKinney	4	1- 3	5	9
White	2	3- 4	4	7
Thorne	1	0- 0	1	2
Jordan	4	4- 5	3	12
Totals	23	14-28	23	60

Ohio State	fg	ft-fta	pf	tp
Bowen	3	6- 6	4	12
Snyder	4	3- 7	3	11
Wells	0	0- 0	4	0
Underman	8	7- 8	4	23
Huston	3	3- 6	5	9
Johnston	0	0- 0	0	0
Amling	1	0- 1	5	2
Totals	19	19-28	25	57

Regulation Score: 54-54. Officials: Nucatola and Orwig.

Bob Kurland

Oklahoma A&M	fg	ft-fta	pf	tp
Aubrey	0	0- 0	0	0
Bennett	1	2- 2	1	4
Kern	2	0- 0	1	4
Geyman	0	0- 0	0	0
Kurland	12	5- 6	3	29
Steinmier	0	0- 0	0	0
Halbert	0	0- 0	0	0
Bell	1	2- 2	2	4
Bradley	1	1- 2	1	3
Williams	1	1- 1	0	3
Parks	2	1- 1	1	5
Totals	20	12-14	9	52

California	fg	ft-fta	pf	tp
LaFaille	4	2- 2	4	10
Wolfe	7	0- 1	2	14
Dean	0	0- 0	0	0
Smith	0	1- 3	3	1
Walker	2	2- 3	2	6
Wray	1	0- 0	2	2
Larner	0	0- 0	0	0
Hogeboom	0	2- 3	0	2
Totals	14	7-12	13	35

Half time: Oklahoma A&M 26-21. Officials: Baker and Curtis.

National Third Place

Ohio State	fg	ft-fta	pf	tp
Bowen	6	4- 4	2	16
Wells	0	0- 0	0	0
Lovett	0	0- 0	0	0
Snyder	3	4- 5	2	10
Underman	6	7- 8	4	19
Elliott	1	1- 1	1	3
Huston	2	1- 2	3	5
Johnston	0	0- 0	0	0
Amling	5	0- 1	4	10
Kuhn	0	0- 0	0	0
Totals	23	17-21	16	63

California	fg	ft-fta	pf	tp
LaFaille	9	4- 4	2	22
Wolfe	3	0- 0	0	6
Anderson	0	0- 0	1	0
Smith	2	0- 0	4	4
Walker	1	2- 7	4	4
Holcombe	0	1- 1	1	1
Dean	0	0- 0	0	0
Wray	0	1- 2	1	1
Bower	0	1- 1	2	1
Larner	0	0- 0	0	0
Hogeboom	2	2- 2	1	6
Riemke	0	0- 0	1	0
Totals	17	11-17	16	45

Officials: Orwig and Nucatola.

Championship

Oklahoma A&M	fg	ft-fta	pf	tp
Aubrey	0	1- 2	1	1
Bennett	3	0- 0	4	6
Kern	3	1- 3	2	7
Bradley	1	1- 2	1	3
Kurland	9	5- 9	5	23
Halbert	0	0- 0	0	0
Williams	0	2- 4	2	2
Bell	0	1- 1	1	1
Parks	0	0- 0	2	0
Totals	16	11-21	18	43

North Carolina	fg	ft-fta	pf	tp
Dillon	5	6- 6	5	16
Anderson	3	2- 3	3	8
Paxton	2	0- 0	4	4
McKinney	2	1- 3	5	5
White	0	1- 1	0	1
Thorne	1	0- 0	2	2
Jordan	0	4- 8	3	4
Totals	13	14-21	22	40

Officials: Kennedy and Collins.

1947

First Round

Holy Cross	fg	ft-fta	pf	tp
Kaftan	7	1- 7	2	15
O'Connell	1	0- 0	1	2
Oftring	2	1- 1	1	5
Mullaney	9	0- 0	4	18
Haggerty	3	1- 1	0	7
Laska	0	0- 0	0	0
Cousy	3	0- 0	2	6
McMullin	0	0- 1	1	0
Curran	0	2- 2	4	2
Totals	25	5-12	15	55

Navy	fg	ft-fta	pf	tp
Robbins	1	1- 1	0	3
Shugart	3	3- 4	0	9
Waldrop	6	3- 4	3	15
Barrow	5	1- 1	4	11
Dick	0	0- 1	2	0
Searle	1	2- 3	0	4
Durham	0	0- 0	1	0
Rensberger	0	0- 1	0	0
Sheehan	2	1- 3	0	5
Totals	18	11-18	10	47

Half time: Holy Cross 29-27. Officials: Orwig and Haarlow.

CCNY	fg	ft-fta	pf	tp
Trubowitz	0	0- 0	1	0
Dambrot	6	4- 5	1	16
Galiber	0	4- 6	4	4
Shapiro	0	1- 2	2	1
Malamed	6	1- 1	3	13
Jameson	5	0- 0	1	10
Farbman	2	2- 3	1	6
Finestone	4	1- 1	1	9
Brickman	0	0- 0	0	0
Schmones	3	1- 2	3	7
Finger	2	0- 0	1	4
Totals	28	14-20	18	70

Wisconsin	fg	ft-fta	pf	tp
Cook	5	3- 4	4	13
Menzel	5	5- 8	3	15
Mills	2	2- 3	4	6
Lautenbach	1	0- 0	2	2
Selbo	6	0- 0	3	12
Mader	0	0- 0	0	0
Hertz	1	0- 0	0	2
Rehfeldt	2	0- 2	1	4
Haarlow	0	1- 1	1	1
Krueger	0	1- 1	0	1
Falls	0	0- 0	0	0
Porkrzywinski	0	0- 0	0	0
Totals	22	12-19	18	56

Half time: Wisconsin 37-27. Officials: Kennedy and Anderson.

George Kaftan

Texas	fg	ft	tp
Hargis	3	3	9
Hamilton	0	0	0
Martin	4	1	9
Langdon	4	3	11
Cox	1	0	2
Wagner	3	0	6
Madsen	1	3	5
Totals	16	10	42

Wyoming	fg	ft	tp
Reese	3	4	10
Peyton	1	0	2
Todorovich	3	3	9
Pilch	1	0	2
Volker	5	1	11
Collins	2	2	6
Rogers	0	0	0
Totals	15	10	40

Officials: Ogden and Leith.

Oklahoma	fg	ft	tp
Reich	4	3	11
Courty	5	7	17
Jones	0	0	0
Tucker	7	3	17
Paine	2	0	4
Waters	2	1	5
Landon	0	2	2
Merchant	0	0	0
Totals	20	16	56

Oregon State	fg	ft	tp
Anderson	0	1	1
Samuel	0	0	0
Crandall	3	2	8
Carey	0	0	0
Torrey	3	0	6
Rocha	5	2	12
Peterson	2	1	5
Beck	8	4	20
Silver	1	0	2
Roelandt	0	0	0
Totals	22	10	54

Officials: Curtis and Shields.

Third Place

Wisconsin	fg	ft-fta	pf	tp
Cook	10	1- 1	2	21
Menzel	2	1- 1	3	5
Mills	0	2- 3	3	2
Selbo	3	2- 4	1	8
Lautenbach	2	2- 2	1	6
Rehfeldt	1	0- 0	0	2
Haarlow	2	2- 4	2	6
Totals	20	10-15	12	50

253

1947 HOLY CROSS CRUSADERS—(l-r) Front Row: Dermie O'Connell, Bob Cousy, Frank Oftring, Andy Laska; Second Row: Robert Curran, Ken Haggerty, Alvin "Doggie" Julian, Joe Mullaney, George Kaftan; Third Row: Albert "Hop" Riopel, Jim Riley, Charlie Bollinger, Bob McMullan, Charlie Graver, F. X. Dooley.

254

Navy	fg	ft-fta	pf	tp
Robbins	3	0- 0	0	6
Shugart	6	2- 2	1	14
Waldrop	5	1- 2	4	11
Barrow	2	1- 2	3	5
Dick	0	1- 1	4	1
Searle	3	1- 3	0	7
Woods	0	0- 0	0	0
Rensberger	0	0- 1	1	0
Eliopulos	1	0- 0	0	2
Sheehan	1	1- 2	1	3
Totals	21	7-13	14	49

Half time: Wisconsin 29-24. Officials: Kennedy and Andersen.

Oregon State	fg	ft	tp
Anderson	4	2	10
Peterson	3	0	6
Crandall	2	4	8
Carey	0	0	0
Rocha	3	3	9
Martin	0	0	0
Silver	2	0	4
Beck	8	4	20
Torrey	3	0	6
Totals	25	13	63

Wyoming	fg	ft	tp
Reese	7	3	17
Peyton	0	1	1
Rogers	0	0	0
Todorovich	3	5	11
Pilch	0	1	1
Collins	2	1	5
Doty	0	0	0
Volker	4	3	11
Bloom	0	0	0
Totals	16	14	46

Officials: Curtis and Shields.

Alvin "Doggie" Julian

Semifinals

Holy Cross	fg	ft-fta	pf	tp
Kaftan	11	8-12	2	30
O'Connell	2	1- 2	1	5
Oftring	2	3- 3	3	7
Mullaney	0	3- 5	2	3
Haggerty	2	0- 0	3	4
Cousy	2	1- 2	3	5
McMullen	1	1- 3	2	3
Laska	1	0- 0	1	2
Curran	0	1- 2	2	1
Totals	21	18-29	19	60

CCNY	fg	ft-fta	pf	tp
Trubowitz	2	0- 1	1	4
Dambrot	5	4- 7	3	14
Galiber	1	3- 5	4	5
Shapiro	2	1- 1	3	5
Malamed	1	1- 1	2	3
Jameson	1	1- 1	5	3
Farbman	0	1- 1	1	1
Benson	0	0- 0	1	0
Finestone	4	1- 2	4	9
Schmones	0	1- 1	1	1
Totals	16	13-20	25	45

Half time: Holy Cross 27-25. Officials: Haarlow and Orwig.

Oklahoma	fg	ft	tp
Reich	4	3	11
Courty	3	2	8
Pryor	1	0	2
Tucker	6	3	15
Paine	4	0	8
Merchant	0	1	1
Landon	2	2	6
Waters	1	2	4
Totals	21	13	55

Texas	fg	ft	tp
Hargis	3	3	9
Hamilton	0	1	1
Martin	8	2	18
Langdon	3	1	7
Madsen	1	4	6
Cox	1	0	2
Wagner	5	1	11
Totals	21	12	54

Officials: Leith and Ogden.

National Third Place

Texas	fg	ft-fta	pf	tp
Hargis	7	3- 6	3	17
Martin	7	0- 2	2	14
Langdon	4	1- 2	4	9
Madsen	2	2- 4	3	6
Cox	2	4- 6	2	8
Hamilton	0	0- 1	0	0
Wagner	0	0- 0	1	0
Totals	22	10-21	15	54

CCNY	fg	ft-fta	pf	tp
Jameson	4	2- 3	2	10
Finestone	6	2- 4	3	14
Galiber	1	0- 0	3	2
Dambrot	5	3- 5	3	13
Malamed	3	0- 3	3	6
Trubowitz	0	0- 0	1	0
Shapiro	1	0- 0	0	2
Farbman	0	1- 3	3	1
Schmones	1	0- 0	1	2
Totals	21	8-18	19	50

Half time: Texas 32-28. Officials: Orwig and Haarlow.

Championship

Holy Cross	fg	ft-fta	pf	tp
Kaftan	7	4- 9	4	18
O'Connell	7	2- 4	3	16
Oftring	6	2- 3	5	14
Mullaney	0	0- 0	2	0
Haggerty	0	0- 0	0	0
Laska	0	0- 0	0	0
Curran	0	0- 1	2	0
Reilly	0	0- 0	1	0
McMullin	2	4- 4	0	8
Cousy	0	2- 2	1	2
Bollinger	0	0- 0	0	0
Graver	0	0- 0	0	0
Totals	22	14-23	18	58

Oklahoma	fg	ft-fta	pf	tp
Reich	3	2- 2	3	8
Courty	3	2- 3	4	8
Tucker	6	10-12	3	22
Paine	2	2- 2	0	6
Landon	1	0- 1	4	2
Waters	0	0- 0	0	0
Day	0	0- 0	0	0
Pryor	0	1- 1	2	1
Merchant	0	0- 1	0	0
Totals	15	17-21	17	47

Half time: Oklahoma 31-28. Officials: Andersen and Kennedy.

1948

First Round

Kentucky	fg	ft	tp
Jones	9	3	21
Barnstable	2	1	5
Day	2	0	4
Barker	1	0	2
Line	2	1	5
Groza	7	3	17
Holland	2	0	4
Beard	6	3	15
Rollins	0	2	2
Jordan	0	1	1
Totals	31	14	76

Columbia	fg	ft	tp
Vogel	2	2	6
Moss	0	0	0
Lockwood	0	0	0
Gehrke	2	1	5
Skinner	2	5	9
Budko	7	3	17
Harwood	0	0	0
Marshall	1	2	4
Kaplan	5	2	12
Olsen	0	0	0
Totals	19	15	53

Officials: Begovich and Osborne.

Holy Cross	fg	ft	tp
Oftring	5	0	10
Cousy	9	5	23
O'Connell	0	1	1
Kaftan	7	1	15
Bollinger	1	0	2
Curran	2	1	5
McMullin	1	0	2
Mullaney	2	1	5
Totals	27	9	63

Michigan	fg	ft	tp
Suprunowicz	7	0	14
Wierda	0	0	0
McIntosh	4	2	10
Roberts	3	4	10
Bauerle	0	0	0
Harrison	2	3	7
Morrill	0	0	0
Elliott	2	0	4
Totals	18	9	45

Officials: Begovich and Osborne.

Wyoming	fg	ft	pf	tp
Doty	6	1	3	13
Peyton	9	2	2	20
Reed	1	1	5	3
Cotton	0	0	0	0
Collins	0	0	1	0
Larson	1	1	1	3
Pilch	1	5	5	7
Bloom	1	0	2	2
Totals	19	10	19	48

Kansas State	fg	ft	pf	tp
Harman	5	2	2	12
Weatherby	1	0	2	2
Howey	1	0	0	2
Langton	0	0	0	0
Thornton	0	0	1	0
Brannum	3	2	5	8
Clark	3	2	0	8
Dean	5	2	2	12
Krone	0	0	0	0
Shannon	4	6	2	14
Mahoney	0	0	1	0
Thuston	0	0	0	0
Totals	22	14	15	58

Officials: Curtis and Ferguson.

Washington	fg	ft	pf	tp
Vandenburgh	6	2	5	14
Arnason	0	0	1	0
White	4	3	3	11
Bird	0	0	1	0
Millikan	0	0	0	0
Nichols	6	5	5	17
Mallory	0	0	1	0
Jorgensen	3	0	1	6
Opacich	1	4	3	6
Taylor	3	2	2	8
Engstrom	0	0	1	0
Totals	23	16	23	62

Baylor	fg	ft	pf	tp
Owens	3	6	3	12
DeWitt	0	0	2	0
Preston	1	0	1	2
Hickman	3	0	2	6
Heathington	4	4	4	12
Johnson	9	2	0	20
Pulley	0	0	0	0
Robinson	3	6	3	12
Totals	23	18	15	64

Officials: Herigstad and Ogden.

Third Place

Michigan	fg	ft	tp
Suprunowicz	7	0	14
Mikulich	0	3	3
McCaslin	0	1	1
McIntosh	7	0	14
Wierda	1	0	2
Roberts	1	2	4
Wisniewski	1	0	2
Harrison	4	2	10
Elliott	5	5	15
Bauerle	0	1	1
Totals	26	14	66

Adolph Rupp

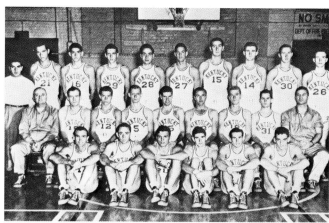

1948 KENTUCKY WILDCATS—(l-r) Front Row: Ray Thurman, Bill Smethers, John Schiffli, Roger Day, Mike Homa, Garland Townes; Second Row: Adolph Rupp, Jack Parkinson, Ralph Beard, Johnny Stough, Jim Line, Cliff Barker, Dale Barnstable, Al Cummins, Harry Lancaster; Back Row: Humzey Yessin, Albert Campbell, Walter Hirsch, Robert Henne, John Rousakis, Wallace Jones, Alex Groza, Joe Holland, Jim Jordan, Ken Rollins.

Columbia	fg	ft	tp
Vogel	7	4	18
Lockwood	0	1	1
Gehrke	1	2	4
Skinner	1	1	3
Olsen	1	1	3
Budko	3	3	9
Voydat	0	0	0
Marshall	2	1	5
Poch	1	0	2
Kaplan	2	0	4
Totals	18	13	49

Officials: MacDonald and Haarlow.

Wyoming	fg	ft	pf	tp
Doty	6	1	5	13
Larson	0	0	1	0
Peyton	3	1	2	7
Mankin	0	0	1	0
Reed	1	0	5	2
Cotton	0	0	0	0
Collins	0	0	1	0
Flinn	0	0	1	0
Pilch	8	8	3	24
Bloom	0	1	0	1
Totals	18	11	19	47

Washington	fg	ft	pf	tp
Vandenbugh	1	2	5	4
Carnovale	0	1	0	1
White	5	4	1	14
Arnason	0	0	2	0
Mallory	0	0	0	0
Nichols	7	8	5	22
Millikan	0	0	2	0
Jorgensen	2	0	0	4
Opacich	3	2	0	8
Taylor	2	0	3	4
Totals	20	17	18	57

Officials: Ferguson and Herigstad.

Semifinals

Kentucky	fg	ft	tp
Jones	4	4	12
Barker	2	0	4
Line	0	0	0
Groza	10	3	23
Holland	0	0	0
Beard	6	1	13
Rollins	3	2	8
Barnstable	0	0	0
Totals	25	10	60

Holy Cross	fg	ft	tp
Oftring	4	4	12
McMullan	0	0	0
Cousy	1	3	5
O'Connell	3	3	9
Kaftan	6	3	15
Bollinger	1	0	2
Curran	3	1	7
Formon	0	0	0
Mullaney	0	0	0
Laska	1	0	2
Totals	19	14	52

Officials: Begovich and Osborne.

Kansas State	fg	ft	pf	tp
Harman	3	6	4	12
Krone	0	2	0	2
Howey	3	3	5	9
Langton	1	1	3	3
Weatherby	0	0	2	0
Brannum	3	1	5	7
Clark	1	3	5	5
Dean	3	2	4	8
Shannon	1	4	1	6
Totals	15	22	29	52

Baylor	fg	ft	pf	tp
Owens	3	2	5	8
Kichman	0	0	2	0
DeWitt	3	0	5	6
Preston	1	3	1	5
Pulley	1	0	0	2
Heathington	3	9	2	15
Johnson	4	5	3	13
Robinson	5	1	4	11
Totals	20	20	22	60

Officials: Curtis and Ogden.

Alex Groza

National Third Place

Holy Cross	fg	ft	tp
Cousy	2	1	5
Oftring	4	3	11
Kaftan	4	3	11
Curran	2	1	5
Mullaney	3	0	6
Laska	2	0	4
Bollinger	1	0	2
Formon	0	0	0
McMullan	3	0	6
O'Connell	5	0	10
Dolan	0	0	0
Totals	26	8	60

Kansas State	fg	ft	tp
Harman	3	3	9
Howey	4	2	10
Brannum	1	2	4
Dean	5	2	12
Shannon	6	5	17
Weatherby	0	0	0
Mahoney	0	0	0
Clark	0	0	0
Langton	0	0	0
Krone	1	0	2
Thornton	0	0	0
Totals	20	14	54

Officials: Begovich and Osborne.

Championship

Kentucky	fg	ft	tp
Jones	4	1	9
Barker	2	1	5
Groza	6	2	14
Beard	4	4	12
Rollins	3	3	9
Line	3	1	7
Holland	1	0	2
Barnstable	0	0	0
Totals	23	12	58

Baylor	fg	ft	tp
Owens	2	1	5
DeWitt	3	2	8
Heathington	3	2	8
Johnson	3	4	10
Robinson	3	2	8
Pulley	0	1	1
Hickman	1	0	2
Preston	0	0	0
Srack	0	0	0
Totals	15	12	42

Officials: Haarlow and MacDonald.

1949

First Round

Illinois	fg	ft	pf	tp
Eddleman	5	1	4	11
Osterkorn	5	5	3	15
Green	4	2	2	10
Erickson	1	3	3	5
Marks	0	0	1	0
Foley	2	0	1	4
Kersulis	3	1	3	7
Sunderlage	7	1	5	15
Anderson	2	0	1	4
Totals	29	13	23	71

Yale	fg	ft	pf	tp
Anderson	7	5	4	19
Lavelli	10	7	3	27
Joyce	4	1	5	9
Fitzgerald	1	3	3	5
Nadherny	2	0	2	4
Johnson	0	1	0	1
Osbourn	1	0	0	2
Upjohn	0	0	0	0
Totals	25	17	17	67

Half time: Yale 35-31. Officials: Begovich and Chest.

Adolph Rupp

Kentucky	fg	ft	pf	tp
Jones	0	4	5	4
Line	9	3	5	21
Groza	12	6	4	30
Beard	0	3	3	3
Barker	6	6	3	18
Hirsch	1	0	3	2
Barnstable	2	1	2	5
Day	1	0	1	2
Totals	31	23	26	85

Villanova	fg	ft	pf	tp
Ricca	6	2	5	14
Raiken	3	0	5	6
Arizin	11	8	5	30
Wolf	0	2	3	2
Hannan	3	1	2	7
DelPurgatorio	2	0	2	4
Gecker	0	0	0	0
Weglicki	2	1	2	5
Dolan	1	0	0	2
Crossin	0	2	1	2
Totals	28	16	25	72

Half time: Kentucky 48-37. Officials: McDonald and Gentile.

Oklahoma A&M	fg	ft-fta	pf	tp
Parks	2	2- 4	4	6
McArthur	1	0- 0	0	2
Hobbs	0	0- 0	1	0
Shelton	5	6- 7	3	16
Pilgrim	0	0- 1	1	0
Harris	2	0- 1	4	4
Bradley	3	2- 4	2	8
Yates	1	0- 0	0	2
Jaquet	1	0- 0	5	2
Totals	15	10-16	20	40

Wyoming	fg	ft-fta	pf	tp
Doty	1	4-10	4	6
Bloom	3	3- 5	1	9
Livingstone	4	0- 1	3	8
Peyton	1	0- 1	1	2
Pilch	6	2- 4	5	14
Reed	0	0- 0	0	0
Totals	15	9-21	14	39

Half time: Wyoming 25-22. Officials: Curtis and Leith.

Oregon State	fg	ft-fta	pf	tp
Crandall	3	7- 7	4	13
Rinearson	0	1- 1	2	1
Petersen	5	0- 1	1	10
Sliper	1	0- 0	0	2
Fleming	1	0- 1	3	2
Snyder	0	0- 0	1	0
Watt	1	0- 0	2	2
Ballantyne	2	9-11	1	13
Torrey	3	0- 2	4	6
Harper	2	3- 4	2	7
Holman	0	0- 0	0	0
Catterall	0	0- 0	1	0
Totals	18	20-27	21	56

Arkansas	fg	ft-fta	pf	tp
Cathcart	2	2- 4	5	6
Horton	4	4- 6	5	12
Adams	0	0- 0	0	0
Ambler	2	0- 5	1	4
Price	0	0- 0	2	0
Coleman	0	2- 2	0	2
Kearns	1	1- 1	4	3
Williams	0	2- 2	2	2
Hudspeth	0	0- 0	2	0
Campbell	2	1- 3	3	5
Rankin	2	0- 0	0	4
Totals	13	12-23	24	38

Half time: Oregon State 21-17. Officials: Ogden and Ball.

255

1949 KENTUCKY WILDCATS—(l-r) Front Row: Adolph Rupp, Jim Line, Cliff Barker, John Stough, Ralph Beard, Joe B. Hall, Garland Townes, Harry Lancaster; Back Row: Dale Barnstable, Walt Hirsch, Wallace Jones, Alex Groza, Bob Henne, Roger Day, Humzey Yessin.

256

Third Place

Villanova	fg	ft	pf	tp
Ricca	5	3	5	13
Raiken	6	3	2	15
Arizin	7	8	3	22
Wolf	0	0	4	0
Hannan	12	1	2	25
Weglicki	1	1	0	3
Totals	31	16	16	78

Yale	fg	ft	pf	tp
Anderson	5	1	4	12
Lavelli	1	6	3	8
Joyce	1	1	4	3
Fitzgerald	6	0	0	12
Nadherny	4	0	1	8
Johnson	2	0	1	4
Osbourne	0	0	1	0
DeCoursey	1	1	2	3
Jackson	2	3	2	7
Upjohn	5	0	1	10
Totals	27	13	19	67

Half time: Villanova 33-31. Officials: McDonald and Chest.

Arkansas	fg	ft-fta	pf	tp
Cathcart	4	0- 1	4	8
Horton	7	2- 5	4	16
Ambler	5	3- 5	1	13
Coleman	1	0- 1	0	2
Kearns	7	0- 0	5	14
Williams	1	0- 0	1	2
Rankin	0	0- 0	0	0
Campbell	2	2- 2	4	6
Totals	27	7-14	19	61

Alex Groza

Wyoming	fg	ft-fta	pf	tp
Doty	1	2- 4	2	4
Larson	0	0- 1	0	0
Bloom	0	3- 3	2	3
Livingstone	3	0- 3	3	6
Reed	2	3- 3	3	7
Peyton	7	2- 3	0	16
Pilch	4	4- 4	3	12
Totals	17	14-21	13	48

Half time: Arkansas 33-23. Officials: Leith and Ogden.

Semifinals

Kentucky	fg	ft	pf	tp
Jones	4	1	3	9
Line	6	3	0	15
Groza	10	7	4	27
Beard	4	1	2	9
Barker	3	2	3	8
Hirsch	3	0	1	6
Barnstable	1	0	1	2
Totals	31	14	14	76

Illinois	fg	ft	pf	tp
Eddleman	3	0	1	6
Kersulis	3	3	2	9
Green	3	1	2	7
Osterkorn	2	1	5	5
Erickson	2	1	2	5
Foley	1	1	1	3
Gatewood	3	0	0	6
Marks	1	0	2	2
Cottrell	0	0	1	0
Anderson	0	0	1	0
Beach	1	0	0	2
Sunderlage	0	2	2	2
Totals	19	9	19	47

Half time: Kentucky 39-22. Officials: Begovich and Gentile.

Oklahoma A&M	fg	ft-fta	pf	tp
Shelton	3	7- 8	3	13
Hobbs	0	0- 0	0	0
Yates	0	0- 0	0	0
McArthur	0	0- 0	2	0
Pilgrim	0	0- 0	4	0
Harris	8	7- 7	1	23
Bradley	3	1- 1	1	7
Jaquet	0	0- 0	0	0
Allen	0	0- 0	1	0
Parks	2	4- 6	2	8
Smith	1	2- 2	1	4
Hayes	0	0- 0	1	0
Totals	17	21-24	16	55

Oregon State	fg	ft-fta	pf	tp
Petersen	2	0- 3	5	4
Catterall	0	1- 2	1	1
Sliper	0	0- 0	1	0
Fleming	1	0- 1	0	2
Snyder	1	0- 0	1	2
Watt	0	0- 0	1	0
Rinearson	0	0- 0	2	0
Crandall	4	3- 4	3	11
Harper	1	0- 1	1	2
Ballantyne	1	1- 1	2	3
Torrey	0	1- 1	0	1
Holman	1	2- 2	1	4
Totals	11	8-15	18	30

Half time: Oklahoma A&M 21-11. Officials: Curtis and Ball.

National Third Place

Illinois	fg	ft	pf	tp
Eddleman	5	1	5	11
Kersulis	3	1	2	7
Green	3	1	5	7
Anderson	0	0	1	0
Osterkorn	6	5	5	17
Erickson	3	0	4	6
Foley	2	3	4	7
Sunderlage	1	0	0	2
Totals	23	11	26	57

Oregon State	fg	ft	pf	tp
Crandall	6	6	4	18
Rinearson	1	0	1	2
Peterson	3	2	1	8
Snyder	1	2	2	4
Watt	3	0	2	6
Fleming	1	3	4	5
Ballantyne	3	2	4	8
Harper	1	0	3	2
Torrey	0	0	1	0
Totals	19	15	22	53

Officials: Lee and McCullough.

Championship

Kentucky	fg	ft	pf	tp
Jones	1	1	3	3
Line	2	1	3	5
Groza	9	7	5	25
Beard	1	1	4	3
Barker	1	3	4	5
Barnstable	1	1	1	3
Hirsch	1	0	1	2
Totals	16	14	21	46

Oklahoma A&M	fg	ft	pf	tp
Yates	1	0	1	2
Shelton	3	6	4	12
Harris	3	1	5	7
Bradley	0	3	3	3
Parks	2	3	5	7
Jaquet	0	1	0	1
McArthur	0	2	1	2
Pilgrim	0	2	1	2
Smith	0	0	1	0
Totals	9	18	21	36

Officials: Ogden and Curtis.

1950

First Round

CCNY	fg-fga	ft-fta	pf	tp
Layne	7-11	3- 4	2	17
Warner	3-16	2- 3	1	8
Roman	4- 9	0- 2	5	8
Galiber	0- 4	0- 0	1	0
Watkins	0- 0	0- 0	1	0
Roth	0- 1	0- 0	2	0
Mager	7-16	1- 2	5	15
Dambrot	3- 6	2- 4	2	8
Totals	24-63	8-15	19	56

Ohio State	fg-fga	ft-fta	pf	tp
Schnittker	9-19	8-11	5	26
Armstrong	0- 1	0- 0	1	0
Remington	0- 1	0- 0	0	0
Donham	4- 9	1- 3	5	9
Taylor	4-11	0- 2	0	8
Brown	1- 4	1- 1	1	3
Burkholder	1- 1	1- 2	1	3
Jacobs	2- 5	2- 3	2	6
Totals	21-51	13-22	15	55

Half time: 40-40. Officials: Boyle and Heft.

North Carolina St.	fg-fga	ft-fta	pf	tp
Ranzino	11-30	8-10	4	30
Cook	1- 3	0- 2	0	2
Dickey	8-17	9-13	3	25
Horvath	0- 2	1- 1	1	1
Cartier	6- 9	2- 4	4	14
Harand	1- 3	3- 4	2	5
Bubas	3- 3	0- 0	2	6
Terrill	2- 6	0- 4	1	4
Totals	32-73	23-38	17	87

Holy Cross	fg-fga	ft-fta	pf	tp
Cousy	11-38	2- 3	3	24
McDonough	2- 3	0- 1	3	4
McMullan	0- 4	0- 2	5	0
Mann	0- 1	0- 0	0	0
Formon	7-10	5- 6	1	19
Dilling	2- 6	2- 2	2	6
O'Neill	0- 0	0- 0	2	0
Laska	2-17	2- 2	1	6
Oftring	1- 3	1- 2	5	3
McLarnon	6-15	0- 1	4	12
O'Shea	0- 0	0- 0	4	0
Dieffenbach	0- 4	0- 0	2	0
Totals	31-101	12-19	32	74

Half time: North Carolina State 44-29. Officials: Meyer and Eisenstein.

Irwin Dambrot

Baylor	fg-fga	ft-fta	pf	tp
Hickman	0- 2	2- 2	4	2
Cobb	4- 9	4- 4	3	12
Heathington	7-16	7-12	3	21
Hovde	0- 0	0- 0	1	0
Preston	0- 7	0- 3	1	0
Carrington	0- 0	0- 2	0	0
DeWitt	2- 4	3- 3	5	7
Johnson	0- 0	0- 0	0	0
Srack	6-14	2- 4	1	14
Mullins	0- 0	0- 0	0	0
Totals	19-52	18-30	18	56

Brigham Young	fg-fga	ft-fta	pf	tp
Minson	8-23	3- 8	2	19
Nelson	5-23	3- 4	4	13
Hillman	0- 0	0- 0	2	0
Hutchins	8-22	3- 5	3	19
Jones	1- 4	0- 1	2	2
Romney	1- 4	0- 1	3	2
Whipple	0- 2	0- 1	4	0
Craig	0- 4	0- 0	5	0
Totals	23-82	9-20	25	55

Half time: Brigham Young 26-25. Officials: Lee and Gibbs.

Bradley	fg-fga	ft-fta	pf	tp
Mann	2- 6	3- 4	3	7
Preece	1- 3	1- 2	1	3
Chianakas	2- 4	0- 0	4	4
Melchiorre	6-12	7- 8	4	19
Schlictman	0- 1	1- 2	1	1
Unruh	5-14	3- 4	1	13
Behnke	3-13	4- 7	2	10
Kelly	0- 1	0- 0	1	0
Grover	7-14	2- 3	2	16
Totals	26-68	21-30	19	73

GAME-BY-GAME RESULTS

1950 CCNY BEAVERS—(l-r) Front Row: Mike Wittlin, Ed Roman, Joe Galiber, Nat Holman, Irwin Dambrot, Norman Mager, Seymour Levey; Second Row: Floyd Layne, Arnold Smith, Ed Warner, Al Roth, Herb Cohen; Third Row: Ronald Nadell, Arthur Glass, LeRoy Watkins, Ed Chenetz, Larry Meyer; Back Row: Al Ragusa, Bobby Sand.

UCLA	fg-fga	ft-fta	pf	tp
Norman	0- 6	0- 0	3	0
Joeckel	5-13	3- 5	2	13
Matulich	0- 0	0- 0	0	0
Sawyer	7-21	0- 2	1	14
Saunders	0- 0	0- 1	1	0
Kraushaar	2- 4	1- 1	5	5
Alba	0- 8	0- 2	2	0
Sheldrake	4-14	3- 5	5	11
Seidel	1- 3	0- 0	2	2
Johnson	0- 0	0- 0	0	0
Stanich	6-12	2- 6	5	14
Alper	0- 0	0- 0	1	0
Totals	25-81	9-22	27	59

Half time: 33-33. Officials: Morrow and Herigstad.

Third Place

Ohio State	fg-fga	ft-fta	pf	tp
Schnittker	6-10	5- 5	3	17
Jacobs	2- 7	6- 9	2	10
Armstrong	1- 1	0- 0	0	2
Donham	4-11	2- 5	3	10
Remington	1- 2	1- 2	2	3
Taylor	5-15	0- 1	3	10
Giacomelli	0- 1	1- 2	0	1
Brown	2- 6	1- 2	2	5
Karaffa	0- 0	1- 1	0	1
Burkholder	4-11	5- 5	1	13
Dawe	0- 0	0- 0	0	0
Totals	25-64	22-32	16	72

Holy Cross	fg-fga	ft-fta	pf	tp
McLarnon	3-12	0- 0	4	6
Cousy	6-23	2- 5	4	14
Dieffenbach	0- 1	0- 0	1	0
McMullan	0- 0	1- 2	2	1
O'Shea	0- 3	0- 0	3	0
O'Neill	0- 1	0- 0	0	0
Dilling	2- 7	2- 2	5	6
Formon	1-12	2- 2	4	4
Mann	0- 1	0- 0	0	0
Laska	0- 2	0- 0	1	0
McDonough	3- 9	4- 5	0	10
Oftring	5-11	1- 2	2	11
Totals	20-82	12-18	26	52

Half time: Ohio State 40-24. Officials: Eisenstein and Heft.

Brigham Young	fg-fga	ft-fta	pf	tp
Minson	5-11	3- 6	2	13
Nelson	12-25	6- 6	1	30
Hutchins	9-18	3- 6	5	21
Beem	5- 6	0- 0	1	10
Craig	0- 2	2- 2	1	2
Jones	0- 1	1- 1	1	1
Romney	0- 0	2- 4	2	2
Whipple	2- 3	0- 1	3	4
Totals	33-66	17-26	16	83

UCLA	fg-fga	ft-fta	pf	tp
Joeckel	1- 4	1- 1	4	3
Norman	0- 4	0- 0	2	0
Saunders	2- 6	2- 3	1	6
Sawyer	7-22	2- 2	4	16
Matulich	0- 0	0- 0	0	0
Kraushaar	2-11	2- 3	2	6
Alba	0- 7	0- 0	2	0
Johnson	1- 1	0- 0	0	2
Sheldrake	9-17	3- 3	2	21
Stanich	1-16	3- 4	5	5
Alper	1- 4	1- 2	2	3
Totals	24-92	14-18	24	62

Half time: UCLA 41-37. Officials: Gibbs and Morrow.

Semifinals

CCNY	fg-fga	ft-fta	pf	tp
Dambrot	5-14	3- 6	3	13
Warner	5-18	7-11	3	17
Roman	9-17	3- 4	5	21
Galiber	0- 0	0- 0	0	0
Nadell	2- 2	0- 1	2	4
Roth	2- 6	0- 0	5	4
Mager	4-11	1- 2	5	9
Layne	3-13	4- 5	2	10
Cohen	0- 0	0- 2	0	0
Totals	30-81	18-31	26	78

North Carolina St.	fg-fga	ft-fta	pf	tp
Ranzino	9-30	6- 9	5	24
Stine	1- 2	0- 0	0	2
Dickey	7-19	0- 0	3	14
Horvath	4- 4	6- 8	4	14
Bubas	0- 2	2- 2	4	2
Harand	0- 0	2- 2	2	2
Cartier	4- 8	3- 4	5	11
Cook	1- 3	0- 0	2	2
Totals	26-68	21-31	25	73

Half time: CCNY 38-37. Officials: Meyer and Boyle.

Nat Holman

Bradley	fg-fga	ft-fta	pf	tp
Mann	4- 7	5- 8	4	13
Chianakas	1- 5	0- 0	0	2
Schlictman	0- 0	0- 0	0	0
Melchiorre	4-11	3- 3	4	11
Unruh	2-11	3- 4	2	7
Behnke	1- 7	0- 1	0	2
Preece	4- 6	4- 6	3	12
Kelly	3- 7	2- 2	2	8
Grover	6-14	1- 1	2	13
Totals	25-68	18-25	17	68

Baylor	fg-fga	ft-fta	pf	tp
Hickman	3- 7	0- 0	3	6
Cobb	3- 8	1- 2	3	7
Carrington	0- 0	0- 0	0	0
Heathington	10-20	6- 6	5	26
Fleetwood	0- 0	0- 0	0	0
Preston	4-11	6- 7	4	14
Hovde	0- 0	0- 0	0	0
DeWitt	1- 6	2- 3	5	4
Johnson	0- 2	0- 0	0	0
Srack	3- 7	3- 3	3	9
Totals	24-61	18-21	23	66

Half time: Bradley 35-32. Officials: Lee and Herigstad.

National Third Place

North Carolina	fg-fga	ft-fta	pf	tp
Ranzino	5-25	11-15	2	21
Cartier	3-11	3- 4	3	9
Dickey	2-14	2- 3	3	6
Horvath	2- 8	1- 3	2	5
Harand	1- 3	2- 2	1	4
Terrill	1- 9	0- 2	0	2
Bubas	1- 7	4- 6	4	6
Totals	15-77	23-35	15	53

Baylor	fg-fga	ft-fta	pf	tp
DeWitt	2- 7	2- 3	5	6
Cobb	1- 1	1- 2	5	3
Fleetwood	0- 0	0- 0	1	0
Srack	5-17	1- 3	3	11
Preston	1- 7	3- 5	3	5
Harris	0- 0	0- 0	2	0
Heathington	3-14	1- 5	5	7
Hickman	4-14	0- 0	1	8
Johnson	0- 0	1- 2	0	1
Hovde	0- 0	0- 0	0	0
Carrington	0- 0	0- 0	1	0
Mullins	0- 0	0- 0	1	0
Totals	16-60	9-20	27	41

Half time: North Carolina State 21-20. Officials: Meyer and Morrow.

Championship

CCNY	fg-fga	ft-fta	pf	tp
Dambrot	7-14	1- 2	0	15
Roman	6-17	0- 2	5	12
Warner	4- 9	6-14	2	14
Roth	2- 7	1- 5	2	5
Mager	4-10	6- 6	3	14
Galiber	0- 0	0- 0	1	0
Layne	3- 7	5- 6	3	11
Nadell	0- 0	0- 0	1	0
Totals	26-64	19-35	17	71

Bradley	fg-fga	ft-fta	pf	tp
Grover	0-10	2- 3	3	2
Schlictman	0- 3	0- 0	2	0
Unruh	4- 9	0- 0	5	8
Behnke	3-10	3- 3	4	9
Kelly	0- 1	0- 2	0	0
Mann	2- 7	5- 5	5	9
Preece	6-11	0- 0	5	12
D. Melchiorre	0- 0	0- 0	0	0
G. Melchiorre	7-16	2- 4	4	16
Chianakas	5- 7	1- 3	4	11
Stowell	0- 0	1- 1	0	1
Totals	27-74	14-21	32	68

Half time: CCNY 39-32. Officials: Eisenstein and Gibbs.

1951

First Round

North Carolina St.	fg-fga	ft-fta	rb	pf	tp
Brandenburg	3- 6	2- 2	3	2	8
Cook	0- 2	0- 0	2	1	0
Kukoy	12-31	3- 4	10	2	27
Speight	5-16	6- 6	7	4	16
Goss	1-12	3- 7	17	5	5
Terrill	3- 8	1- 4	8	1	7
Yurin	1- 8	2- 3	9	2	4
Totals	25-83	17-26	56	17	67

Villanova	fg-fga	ft-fta	rb	pf	tp
Hennessey	6-19	4- 5	6	4	16
Mooney	2-13	4- 4	9	3	8
Gepp	1- 3	1- 1	7	3	3
Stanko	0- 0	0- 0	0	0	0
Brennan	4-12	1- 1	6	5	9
N. Maguire	0- 1	0- 0	1	1	0
Glassmire	3- 7	1- 3	5	5	7
J. Maguire	0- 2	0- 0	0	0	0
Stewart	8-21	3-11	15	5	19
Totals	24-78	14-18	49	26	62

Half time: Villanova 38-32.

Illinois	fg-fga	ft-fta	rb	pf	tp
Follmer	1- 6	1- 3	3	3	3
Bemoras	2- 7	4- 5	8	2	8
Peterson	1- 8	3- 3	8	5	5
Fletcher	6-18	1- 4	12	3	13
Sunderlage	9-19	7-10	9	1	25
Beach	10-17	2- 2	2	1	22
Baumgardner	1- 4	1- 1	2	0	3
Totals	30-79	19-28	44	15	79

Columbia	fg-fga	ft-fta	rb	pf	tp
Azary	5-14	3- 3	9	2	13
Reiss	4- 9	1- 1	2	3	9
Molinas	8-19	4- 5	15	4	20
Powers	4-12	1- 1	1	5	9
Stein	4-21	1- 1	4	4	9
Lewis	2- 6	4- 5	7	4	8
Brant	0- 2	1- 2	1	1	1
Maratos	0- 1	0- 0	1	0	0
Guittar	1- 1	0- 0	0	1	2
Rohan	0- 1	0- 0	0	0	0
Totals	28-86	15-18	40	24	71

Half time: Columbia 45-38.

St. John's, N.Y.	fg-fga	ft-fta	rb	pf	tp
Dombrosky	6-13	5- 5	10	0	17
McMahon	5-12	0 -0	5	5	10
Zawoluk	7-18	4- 5	18	3	18
McGuire	0- 0	0- 1	4	2	0
Mulzoff	2- 7	1- 1	3	5	5
MacGilvray	2- 8	5- 8	13	3	9
Noonan	0- 0	0- 0	0	0	0
McCool	0- 1	0- 0	0	0	0
Dunn	2- 4	0- 0	3	2	4
McAndrews	0- 0	0- 0	0	0	0
Giancontieri	0- 0	0- 0	0	1	0
O'Shea	0- 0	0- 0	0	0	0
Totals	24-63	15-20	56	21	63

Connecticut	fg-fga	ft-fta	rb	pf	tp
Yokabaskas	7-15	8-11	3	2	22
Widholm	2- 5	3- 3	6	5	7
Edel	5-12	2- 3	4	1	12
Clark	1- 6	0- 1	3	3	2
Gates	3-17	1- 3	1	2	7
Brouker	0- 2	0- 0	1	1	0
Fleischman	0- 2	0- 0	0	0	0
Silverstein	0- 1	0- 0	0	0	0
Kleckner	1- 3	0- 0	3	1	2
Demir	0- 0	0- 0	0	1	0
Totals	19-63	14-21	21	16	52

Half time: St. John's 34-19.

Kentucky	fg-fga	ft-fta	rb	pf	tp
Hagan	2- 8	4- 5	12	4	8
Linville	9-26	5- 5	10	5	23
Spivey	2- 9	6- 6	7	5	10
Tsioropoulos	1- 5	0- 0	9	1	2
Ramsey	4-17	6-10	15	3	14
Watson	3- 9	0- 0	2	1	6
Whitaker	8-15	0- 3	1	2	16
Totals	29-89	21-29	56	21	79

257

258

1951 KENTUCKY WILDCATS—(l-r) Front Row: Lindle Castle, Lucian Whitaker, Bobby Watson, Guy Strong, Ches Riddle; Second Row: Adolph Rupp, Cliff Hagan, C. M. Newton, Walt Hirsch, Paul Lansaw, Dwight Price, Harry Lancaster; Back Row: Frank Ramsey, Shelby Linville, Bill Spivey, Roger Layne, Lou Tsioropoulos, Read Morgan.

Louisville

	fg-fga	ft-fta	rb	pf	tp
Lochmueller	6-23	2-7	18	4	14
Brown	7-26	1-1	11	3	15
Wellman	0-1	0-0	0	2	0
Ford	0-0	0-0	0	0	0
Robison	5-10	0-3	3	5	10
Larrabee	2-5	0-3	6	3	4
Sullivan	3-6	0-0	4	2	6
Naber	6-8	3-5	3	5	15
Rubin	2-5	0-1	2	4	4
Dunbar	0-1	0-0	1	0	0
Totals	31-85	6-20	48	28	68

Half time: Kentucky 44-40.

Washington

	fg-fga	ft-fta	rb	pf	tp
Guisness	6-12	4-8	1	3	16
McClary	4-14	2-3	13	2	10
Enochs	1-1	0-0	5	1	2
Houbregs	5-18	1-2	13	3	11
Soriano	2-8	3-3	3	5	7
Ward	0-0	0-0	0	0	0
Henson	5-6	2-3	1	3	12
McCutchen	2-7	0-1	6	3	4
Cipriano	0-1	0-0	1	1	0
Team			8		
Totals	25-67	12-20	51	21	62

Texas A&M

	fg-fga	ft-fta	rb	pf	tp
DeWitt	6-16	2-2	8	3	14
Mikach	2-7	1-4	7	2	5
Martin	3-8	0-0	3	2	6
Davis	4-8	1-4	4	5	9
Williams	0-0	0-1	1	0	0
Farmer	0-0	0-0	1	0	0
Walker	1-13	1-1	3	3	3
Carpenter	0-1	0-0	1	2	0
McDowell	0-11	1-1	0	5	1
Heft	1-1	0-0	0	0	2
Team			6		
Totals	17-65	6-13	34	22	40

Half time: Washington 27-15.

Oklahoma A&M

	fg-fga	ft-fta	rb	pf	tp
Johnson	4-22	1-2	6	1	9
Sheets	0-4	0-0	1	1	0
Stockton	1-3	0-0	0	1	2
Miller	1-1	0-0	1	0	2
Rogers	1-5	2-2	4	4	4
Amaya	1-1	0-0	0	1	2
Darcey	1-2	1-1	6	4	3
Pager	3-9	3-3	5	3	9
McArthur	5-12	1-3	0	2	11
Smith	3-6	2-4	6	5	8
Team			6		
Totals	20-65	10-15	35	22	50

Montana State

	fg-fga	ft-fta	rb	pf	tp
Curry	5-13	1-3	0	0	11
Miller	4-9	0-0	3	2	8
Johnson	0-3	5-6	6	5	5
McCahill	0-3	0-0	5	1	0
McKethen	3-5	9-14	2	3	15
Saunders	0-0	0-0	0	0	0
Ward	1-5	0-1	2	5	2
Gleason	2-7	1-1	2	0	5
Team			11		
Totals	15-45	16-25	31	16	46

Half time: Oklahoma A&M 25-21.

Brigham Young

	fg-fga	ft-fta	rb	pf	tp
Richey	9-21	0-3	8	3	18
Minson	5-11	2-4	4	5	12
Hillman	0-3	2-5	1	1	2
Hutchins	10-23	2-4	12	1	22
Jarman	1-1	0-0	0	0	2
Christensen	3-11	1-2	4	3	7
Romney	1-11	3-4	7	2	5
Jones	0-1	0-0	0	0	0
Team			8		
Totals	29-82	10-22	44	15	68

San Jose State

	fg-fga	ft-fta	rb	pf	tp
Baptiste	0-1	0-1	1	0	0
Jensen	1-5	0-2	3	2	2
Giles	7-23	4-5	10	2	18
Schorr	2-4	1-1	0	1	5
Deming	0-3	0-1	2	1	0
Clark	3-11	2-2	6	2	8
Wilson	1-3	0-1	7	2	2
Crampton	5-11	0-0	7	1	10
Craig	5-9	1-1	2	4	11
Enzensperger	2-5	0-1	1	5	4
Prescott	0-0	1-1	0	0	1
Team			8		
Totals	26-75	9-16	47	20	61

Half time: Brigham Young 43-33.

Kansas State

	fg-fga	ft-fta	rb	pf	tp
Head	6-13	1-2	9	1	13
Peck	1-2	1-1	4	2	3
Schuyler	0-0	0-1	1	1	0
Stone	2-8	2-3	3	3	6
Gibson	0-0	1-1	0	1	1
Hitch	5-8	2-6	7	2	12
Knostman	0-7	2-3	2	1	2
Iverson	4-11	1-3	5	1	9
Upson	0-1	0-0	0	1	0
Barrett	3-13	1-1	8	1	7
Rousey	3-10	2-3	2	1	8
Team			7		
Totals	24-73	13-24	49	14	61

Arizona

	fg-fga	ft-fta	rb	pf	tp
Honea	7-19	1-1	5	4	15
Schuff	3-5	2-3	4	5	8
Carroll	0-0	0-1	0	3	0
Johnson, L.	3-9	3-3	2	4	9
Dillon	2-8	0-0	4	3	4
Howell	2-8	0-0	5	3	4
Kemmeries	2-4	0-0	0	0	4
Johnson, R.	6-17	3-4	8	4	15
Team			5		
Totals	25-70	9-15	33	26	59

Half time: Kansas State 36-20.

Second Round

Illinois

	fg-fga	ft-fta	rb	pf	tp
Follmer	2-8	2-2	4	2	6
Bemoras	3-10	1-1	12	2	7
Peterson	5-11	0-1	10	5	10
Fletcher	9-18	1-2	9	3	19
Sunderlage	9-17	3-3	0	1	21
Beach	8-20	1-1	5	1	17
Baumgardner	2-3	0-0	3	3	4
Totals	38-87	8-10	43	17	84

North Carolina St.

	fg-fga	ft-fta	rb	pf	tp
Speight	7-20	3-4	10	2	17
Kukoy	7-19	6-8	5	2	20
Goss	3-11	2-3	10	3	8
Yurin	0-1	0-0	1	0	0
Terrill	4-14	0-1	4	0	8
Morris	1-4	0-0	9	1	2
Brandenburg	4-5	1-4	3	0	9
Cook	1-4	0-0	2	0	2
Jackmowski	2-2	0-0	4	2	4
Totals	29-80	12-20	48	10	70

Half time: Illinois 40-29.

Kentucky

	fg-fga	ft-fta	rb	pf	tp
Hagan	1-8	2-4	11	3	4
Linville	4-9	1-5	2	5	9
Spivey	5-9	2-3	11	4	12
Watson	6-23	0-3	0	3	12
Ramsey	4-12	5-5	12	5	13
Whitaker	2-4	0-0	2	1	4
Tsioropoulos	1-5	1-2	4	2	3
Layne	1-2	0-1	1	1	2
Totals	24-72	11-17	49	18	59

St. John's, N.Y.

	fg-fga	ft-fta	rb	pf	tp
Dombrosky	1-5	2-3	5	4	4
McGuire	2-7	1-4	2	3	5
Zawoluk	6-24	3-5	10	3	15
McMahon	2-16	3-3	5	1	7
MacGilvray	4-11	2-4	11	2	10
Mulzoff	0-4	0-0	4	3	0
Dunn	0-0	0-0	0	0	0
Giancontieri	1-3	0-0	1	0	2
Noonan	0-0	0-0	0	0	0
McAndrews	0-0	0-0	0	0	0
O'Shea	0-0	0-0	0	0	0
McCool	0-0	0-0	0	0	0
Totals	16-70	11-19	38	16	43

Half time: St. John's 24-23.

Oklahoma A&M

	fg-fga	ft-fta	rb	pf	tp
Johnson	7-11	3-4	5	5	17
Rogers	0-1	0-0	0	0	0
Miller	1-4	2-4	6	5	4
Stockton	0-1	1-1	4	1	1
Sheets	0-0	0-0	0	3	0
Darcey	1-2	1-1	1	5	3
Pager	3-5	1-1	3	4	7
McArthur	6-8	5-6	0	2	17
Smith	4-6	4-5	1	2	12
Amaya	0-2	0-0	2	2	0
Team			6		
Totals	22-40	17-22	28	30	61

Washington

	fg-fga	ft-fta	rb	pf	tp
Guisness	1-5	2-4	3	5	4
Enochs	3-6	0-0	1	2	6
McClary	2-7	4-4	10	3	8
Ward	0-0	1-1	0	1	1
Stewart	0-0	0-0	0	0	0
Houbregs	6-18	7-7	9	5	19
Hensen	1-7	0-2	1	3	2
Soriano	1-4	1-1	4	1	3
McCutchen	3-7	2-3	5	2	8
Cipriano	3-8	0-2	0	4	6
Team			4		
Totals	20-62	17-23	31	29	57

Half time: Oklahoma A&M 36-23.

Kansas State

	fg-fga	ft-fta	rb	pf	tp
Head	5-11	1-2	12	3	11
Stone	4-13	3-9	6	1	11
Gibson	1-1	1-1	4	4	3
Hitch	3-6	0-1	11	2	6
Knostman	1-1	1-1	1	0	3
Iverson	3-9	1-2	2	0	7
Barrett	4-9	2-2	4	2	10
Rousey	5-9	3-3	3	2	13
Team			3		
Totals	26-59	12-21	46	14	64

Brigham Young

	fg-fga	ft-fta	rb	pf	tp
Richey	6-15	0-2	7	3	12
Minson	5-17	2-3	4	4	12
Hillman	4-10	1-3	1	5	9
Hutchins	5-13	0-1	7	4	10
Jarman	0-2	1-1	1	0	1
Christensen	0-0	0-0	1	3	0
Jones	1-2	0-0	1	2	2
Romney	1-9	6-8	5	4	8
Team			3		
Totals	22-68	10-18	30	25	54

Half time: Kansas State 39-21.

Third Place

St. John's, N.Y.

	fg-fga	ft-fta	rb	pf	tp
Dombrosky	4-9	0-0	4	3	8
McGuire	4-8	8-12	6	2	16
Zawoluk	4-9	1-2	9	3	9
McMahon	12-28	0-0	2	3	24
Mulzoff	0-4	1-1	2	2	1
Giancontieri	0-2	0-0	1	2	0
Dunn	2-4	1-2	3	1	5
MacGilvray	3-6	2-2	4	0	8
Noonan	0-1	0-0	0	0	0
McCool	0-0	0-0	0	0	0
O'Shea	0-0	0-0	0	0	0
Totals	29-71	13-19	31	16	71

North Carolina St.

	fg-fga	ft-fta	rb	pf	tp
Speight	4-20	4-4	9	2	12
Kukoy	6-19	10-10	5	4	22
Goss	6-8	1-2	8	2	13
Morris	2-7	0-0	4	5	4
Terrill	2-8	1-1	6	1	5
Brandenburg	0-2	1-1	4	0	1
Cook	0-2	2-2	0	0	2
Jackmowski	0-1	0-0	1	0	0
Stoll	0-0	0-0	0	0	0
Holt	0-0	0-0	0	0	0
Totals	20-67	19-20	37	14	59

Half time: North Carolina State 33-32.

Washington

	fg-fga	ft-fta	rb	pf	tp
Guisness	4-11	3-5	4	5	11
Ward	1-3	0-2	1	0	2
McClary	5-15	2-2	7	3	12
Enochs	0-3	0-0	1	1	0
Houbregs	11-25	1-4	7	2	23
Stewart	0-1	0-0	0	0	0
Soriano	3-6	2-2	0	2	8
McCutchen	6-12	0-3	10	4	12
Jefferson	0-0	0-1	0	0	0
Henson	3-9	1-1	6	2	7
Cipriano	2-2	1-1	0	2	5
Team			5		
Totals	35-87	10-21	41	21	80

Adolph Rupp

Brigham Young

	fg-fga	ft-fta	rb	pf	tp
Hillman	4- 8	2- 4	3	1	10
Rickey	1- 6	1- 2	3	2	3
Minson	7-23	3- 5	5	3	17
Malmrose	0- 1	0- 0	0	1	0
Hutchins	3- 8	3- 5	7	3	9
Jarman	0- 2	0- 0	0	0	0
Craig	1- 2	0- 0	3	2	2
Christensen	3- 5	0- 0	0	0	6
Dunn	1- 1	0- 0	1	1	2
Jones	4- 9	3- 3	3	4	11
Romney	1- 5	5- 5	5	3	7
Montgomery	0- 0	0- 0	0	0	0
Team			6		
Totals	25-70	17-24	36	20	67

Half time: 39-39.

Semifinals

Kentucky

	fg-fga	ft-fta	rb	pf	tp
Hagan	3- 9	2- 2	4	5	8
Linville	7-12	0- 0	4	4	14
Spivey	11-21	6-10	16	5	28
Watson	5-17	0- 0	8	4	10
Ramsey	2-19	1- 3	12	2	5
Tsioropoulos	0- 2	1- 2	1	1	1
Whitaker	4-11	2- 4	4	5	10
Newton	0- 0	0- 0	0	1	0
Totals	32-91	12-21	49	27	76

Illinois

	fg-fga	ft-fta	rb	pf	tp
Follmer	2- 3	2- 3	5	2	6
Bemoras	5- 8	2- 3	7	2	12
Peterson	3-11	2- 3	5	5	8
Fletcher	8-19	5-11	10	0	21
Sunderlage	6-15	8-11	3	2	20
Beach	2-12	3- 3	6	1	7
Baumgardner	0- 2	0- 1	1	4	0
Totals	26-70	22-35	37	16	74

Half time: Illinois 39-32.

Kansas State

	fg-fga	ft-fta	rb	pf	tp
Head	4- 9	1- 1	5	3	9
Gibson	0- 0	0- 2	3	0	0
Schuyler	2- 4	0- 1	0	1	4
Stone	5- 5	0- 0	1	2	10
Peck	0- 1	1- 1	1	2	1
Hitch	4-11	4- 6	8	2	12
Knostman	4- 8	3- 6	3	0	11
Iverson	3- 4	3- 3	2	0	9
Rousey	0- 1	1- 4	0	2	1
Barrett	1- 7	3- 3	4	4	5
Upson	3- 4	0- 0	1	2	6
Team			8		
Totals	26-54	16-27	36	18	68

Oklahoma A&M

	fg-fga	ft-fta	rb	pf	tp
Johnson	2-10	3- 3	5	4	7
McAfee	0- 1	0- 0	0	3	0
Miller	0- 2	0- 0	2	3	0
Stockton	0- 0	1- 1	1	0	1
Ward	1- 2	0- 0	0	1	2
Darcey	2- 5	0- 1	1	4	4
Pager	5-10	1- 2	2	3	11
Smith	0- 0	1- 1	1	2	1
Amaya	1- 2	0- 0	1	0	2
Rogers	2- 5	0- 0	0	2	4
McArthur	1-11	5- 5	2	2	7
Sheets	2- 4	1- 1	0	1	5
Team			10		
Totals	16-52	12-14	25	25	44

Half time: Kansas State 37-14.

National Third Place

Illinois

	fg-fga	ft-fta	rb	pf	tp
Bemoras	2- 7	1- 2	5	0	5
Beach	4-12	4- 4	4	2	12
Peterson	0-10	4- 5	7	5	4
Fletcher	5-11	4- 8	9	2	14
Sunderlage	4-11	9-10	6	4	17
C. Follmer	0- 2	6- 6	3	4	6
Baumgardner	0- 2	0- 0	0	2	0
Marks	0- 1	0- 0	0	0	0
Bredar	0- 0	0- 0	0	0	0
Schuldt	0- 0	0- 0	0	0	0
Gerecke	1- 1	1- 1	0	0	3
M. Follmer	0- 0	0- 0	0	0	0
Totals	16-57	29-36	34	19	61

Oklahoma A&M

	fg-fga	ft-fta	rb	pf	tp
Johnson	4-20	3- 6	7	3	11
Stockton	0- 3	0- 1	0	3	0
Darcey	1-10	0- 1	10	4	2
McArthur	7-16	3- 3	2	4	17
Sheets	0- 0	0- 1	0	4	0
Pager	2- 8	2- 4	5	1	6
Amaya	0- 0	0- 0	0	3	0
Miller	2- 7	2- 3	7	4	6
Rogers	2- 7	0- 0	7	4	4
Ward	0- 0	0- 0	0	1	0
McAfee	0- 0	0- 0	0	0	0
Totals	18-71	10-19	38	31	46

Half time: Illinois 31-22.

Championship

Kentucky

	fg-fga	ft-fta	rb	pf	tp
Whitaker	4- 5	1- 1	2	2	9
Linville	2- 7	4- 8	8	5	8
Spivey	9-29	4- 6	21	2	22
Ramsey	4-10	1- 3	4	5	9
Watson	3- 8	2- 4	3	3	8
Hagan	5- 6	0- 2	4	5	10
Tsioropoulos	1- 4	0- 0	3	1	2
Newton	0- 0	0- 0	0	0	0
Totals	28-69	12-24	45	23	68

Kansas State

	fg-fga	ft-fta	rb	pf	tp
Head	3-11	2- 2	3	2	8
Stone	3- 8	6- 8	6	2	12
Hitch	6-15	1- 1	9	3	13
Barrett	2-12	0- 2	3	1	4
Iverson	3-12	1- 2	0	3	7
Rousey	2-10	0- 0	2	3	4
Gibson	0- 2	1- 1	1	5	1
Upson	0- 1	0- 0	2	1	0
Knostman	1- 4	1- 2	3	1	3
Peck	2- 3	0- 1	0	0	4
Schuyler	1- 2	0- 1	1	2	2
Totals	23-80	12-20	30	23	58

Half time: Kansas State 29-27.

1952

First Round

Kentucky

	fg	ft	tp
Linville	6	0	12
Tsioropoulos	2	3	7
Whitaker	5	0	10
Neff	1	0	2
Evans	2	1	5
Hagan	9	2	20
Clark	0	0	0
Rose	2	2	6
Ramsey	4	3	11
Rouse	0	1	1
Watson	4	0	8
Totals	35	12	82

Penn State

	fg	ft	tp
Weidenhammer	1	0	2
Piorkowski	0	1	1
Williams	0	2	2
Sherry	4	2	10
McMahan	1	0	2
Arnelle	8	6	22
Haag	1	1	3
Sledzik	4	4	12
Totals	19	16	54

Half time: Kentucky 43-25.

St. John's, N.Y.

	fg	ft	tp
McMahon	3	5	11
Davis	5	0	10
Peterson	0	0	0
Giancontieri	0	1	1
Zawoluk	5	2	12
Walsh	1	4	6
Walker	1	0	2
MacGilvray	1	5	7
Duckett	5	1	11
McMorrow	0	0	0
Totals	21	18	60

1952 KANSAS JAYHAWKS—(l-r) Front Row: Dean Kelley, Ken Buller, John Thompson, Don Anderson, Dean Smith, Jack Rodgers, Allen Kelley; Second Row: Wayne Lauderback, La Vannes Squires, Everett Dye, Bob Godwin, Larry Davenport, Forrest "Phog" Allen, Bob Kenney, Wes Whitney, Wes Johnson, Dean Wells; Back Row: Dick Harp, John Keller, Bill Heitholt, Bill Hougland, B. H. Born, Clyde Lovellette, Bill Lienhard, Wally Beck, Charlie Hoag, Dean Nesmith.

259

North Carolina St.

	fg	ft	tp
Tyler	3	2	8
Speight	1	3	5
Brandenburg	0	1	1
Kukey	1	1	3
Cook	1	0	2
Thompson	3	0	6
Knapp	1	1	3
Goss	0	0	0
Terrill	4	0	8
Gotkin	5	3	13
Yurin	0	0	0
Applebaum	0	0	0
Totals	19	11	49

Half time: St. John's 28-25.

Illinois

	fg	ft	tp
C. Follmer	4	3	11
Bemoras	4	3	11
Peterson	1	4	6
Gerecke	0	0	0
Hooper	1	0	2
Christiansen	0	0	0
Kerr	5	3	13
M. Follmer	0	2	2
Bredar	5	9	19
Fletcher	4	4	12
Makovsky	0	4	4
Wright	0	0	0
Totals	24	32	80

Dayton

	fg	ft	tp
Grigsby	8	5	21
Horan	4	0	8
Donoher	2	0	4
Paxson	3	0	6
Sallee	0	0	0
Meineke	6	6	18
Taylor	0	0	0
Wovod	0	0	0
Boyle	0	1	1
Norris	1	1	3
Pedicord	0	0	0
Harris	0	0	0
Totals	24	13	61

Half time: Dayton 37-36.

Duquesne

	fg	ft	tp
Kennedy	8	0	16
Ricketts	6	2	14
Cerra	2	0	4
Tucker	4	3	11
Pacacha	3	4	10
Garay	1	2	4
Bailey	0	1	1
Totals	24	12	60

Princeton

	fg	ft	tp
Sisler	3	1	7
Tritschler	1	2	4
Emery	0	0	0
Cooper	1	2	4
De Voe	9	5	23
Zuravleff	5	1	11
Totals	19	11	49

Half time: Duquesne 28-24.

Kansas

	fg	ft	tp
Keller	1	1	3
Lienhard	1	1	3
Kenney	7	3	17
Lovellette	13	5	31
Born	1	0	2
Hougland	1	0	2
Hoag	2	0	4
A. Kelley	0	0	0
D. Kelley	1	2	4
Smith	1	0	2
Totals	28	12	68

Texas Christian

	fg	ft	tp
Fromme	1	1	3
Knox	2	0	4
Reynolds	3	2	8
Allen	1	0	2
McLeod	3	1	7
Ohlen	8	4	20
Ethridge	4	2	10
Swaim	3	1	7
Kilpatrick	1	1	3
Campbell	0	0	0
Totals	26	12	64

Half time: Kansas 34-24. Officials: Ogden and Morrow.

St. Louis

	fg	ft	tp
Kovar	1	0	2
Boushka	2	4	8
Sonnenberg	1	0	2
T. Lillis	3	1	7
J. Koch	1	0	2
B. Koch	1	2	4
Shockley	2	1	5
Steiner	2	4	10
McKenna	9	4	22
Totals	24	14	62

New Mexico A&M

	fg	ft	tp
Priddy	2	2	6
Tackett	8	5	21
Svilar	3	3	9
Blevins	1	1	3
Crouch	2	2	6
Coats	0	1	1
Clement	2	1	5
Dunn	1	0	2
Apodaca	0	0	0
Totals	19	15	53

Half time: St. Louis 35-26. Officials: Fraser and Holmes.

Forrest "Phog" Allen

260

Santa Clara

	fg	ft	tp
Young	7	1	15
Sears	3	3	9
Schoenstein	7	4	18
Peters	3	1	7
Brock	3	0	6
Benedetti	1	0	2
Garibaldi	4	1	9
Soares	1	0	2
Totals	29	10	68

UCLA

	fg	ft	tp
Norman	2	0	4
Hibler	3	2	8
Moore	2	2	6
Johnson	2	1	5
Livingston	4	6	14
Bragg	3	1	7
Porter	0	0	0
Bane	3	7	13
Evans	0	0	0
Costello	1	0	2
Totals	20	19	59

Half time: UCLA 35-31.

Wyoming

	fg	ft	tp
Samuelson	2	0	4
Radovich	4	5	13
Essu	4	1	9
Haag	1	0	2
Hughes	1	5	7
Rivers	4	3	11
Fowler	4	0	8
Burns	0	0	0
Eliopulos	0	0	0
Totals	20	14	54

Oklahoma City

	fg	ft	tp
Mayfield	2	0	4
Likens	4	2	10
Penwell	8	2	18
Short	3	2	8
Rose	3	0	6
Thompson	0	0	0
Couts	1	0	2
Totals	21	6	48

Half time: Wyoming 29-21.

Third Place

North Carolina St.

	fg	ft	tp
Tyler	2	2	6
Speight	5	5	15
Kukoy	1	0	2
Cook	1	0	2
Brandenburg	0	0	0
Thompson	8	5	21
Knapp	1	2	4
Yurin	0	3	3
Terrill	3	2	8
Gotkin	4	0	8
Applebaum	0	0	0
Totals	25	19	69

Penn State

	fg	ft	tp
Sherry	3	2	8
Weidenhammer	2	0	4
Williams	2	0	4
Piorkowski	2	1	5
Arnelle	8	6	22
McMahon	1	1	3
Haag	1	1	3
Sledzik	2	1	5
Makarewics	2	2	6
Blocker	0	0	0
Totals	23	14	60

Half time: N. C. State 42-36.

Dayton

	fg	ft	tp
Grigsby	6	2	14
Horan	3	1	7
Paxson	2	0	4
Sallee	0	2	2
Meineke	8	10	26
Donobar	0	1	1
Harris	1	3	5
Boyle	2	1	5
Norris	5	3	13
Totals	27	23	77

Princeton

	fg	ft	tp
Tritschler	11	0	22
Sisler	4	1	9
Ridgway	0	0	0
Marshall	0	0	0
Cooper	5	1	11
Hauptfuhrer	0	1	1
Sarbanes	0	1	1
Emery	1	4	6
Zuravleff	2	0	4
De Voe	2	3	7
Totals	25	11	61

Half time: Dayton 47-33.

Texas Christian

	fg	ft	tp
Fromme	4	4	12
Reynolds	5	1	11
Allen	0	0	0
Knox	0	1	1
McLeod	4	2	10
Ohlen	2	3	7
Ethridge	3	2	8
Swain	2	1	5
J. Taylor	0	0	0
Kilpatrick	3	1	7
T. Taylor	0	0	0
Totals	23	15	61

New Mexico A&M

	fg	ft	tp
Priddy	0	1	1
Vaughn	2	0	4
Coats	1	0	2
Tackett	5	4	14
Scott	3	0	6
Svilar	1	3	5
Crouch	2	1	5
Dunn	1	0	2
Blevins	0	0	0
Apodaca	1	1	3
Clement	1	0	2
Totals	17	10	44

Half time: TCU 25-18.

Oklahoma City

	fg	ft	tp
Likens	4	2	10
Short	7	8	22
Penwell	4	3	11
Rose	0	2	2
Thompson	2	4	8
Mayfield	0	2	2
Couts	0	0	0
Dalton	0	0	0
Rich	0	0	0
Bullard	0	0	0
Totals	17	21	55

UCLA

	fg	ft	tp
Moore	6	3	15
Norman	3	3	9
Hibler	1	2	4
Johnson	0	1	1
Livingston	5	3	13
Porter	1	1	3
Bane	1	1	3
Bragg	0	1	1
Evans	1	0	2
Davidson	1	0	2
Pounds	0	0	0
Costello	0	0	0
Totals	19	15	53

Half time: Oklahoma City 35-29.

Regional Championships

St. John's, N.Y.

	fg	ft	tp
McMahon	8	2	18
Davis	1	0	2
Walsh	1	2	4
Zawoluk	12	8	32
MacGilvray	1	3	5
Duckett	1	1	3
Walker	0	0	0
Totals	24	16	64

Kentucky

	fg	ft	tp
Tsioropoulos	0	0	0
Whitaker	3	3	9
Linville	1	2	4
Rouse	0	0	0
Hagan	9	4	22
Rose	1	0	2
Watson	1	2	4
Ramsey	5	4	14
Evans	1	0	2
Totals	21	15	57

Half time: St. John's 34-28.

Illinois

	fg	ft	tp
C. Follmer	2	8	12
Bemoras	7	2	16
Kerr	3	1	7
Peterson	4	0	8
Bredar	8	0	16
Fletcher	5	5	15
Makovsky	0	0	0
Totals	29	16	74

Duquesne

	fg	ft	tp
Kennedy	3	2	8
Ricketts	7	8	22
Ringer	0	0	0
Cerra	2	0	4
Nosworthy	1	1	3
Tucker	11	7	29
Pacacha	1	0	2
Bailey	0	0	0
Totals	25	18	68

Half time: Illinois 37-34.

Kansas

	fg	ft	tp
Keller	0	1	1
Kenney	2	2	6
Davenport	0	0	0
Lovellette	16	12	44
Born	0	1	1
Heitholt	0	0	0
Hougland	2	1	5
Hoag	2	3	7
Lienhard	0	0	0
Kelley	4	2	10
Smith	0	0	0
Squires	0	0	0
Totals	26	22	74

St. Louis

	fg	ft	tp
Kovar	3	4	10
Klostermeyer	0	0	0
Partington	1	0	2
Sonnenberg	3	2	8
Boushka	0	1	1
Shockley	0	0	0
B. Koch	1	1	3
T. Lillis	7	0	14
H. Lillis	0	0	0
Steiner	1	0	2
J. Koch	2	0	4
McKenna	4	3	11
Totals	22	11	55

Half time: 27-27.

Clyde Lovellette

Santa Clara

	fg	ft	tp
Young	5	4	14
Sears	5	4	14
Schoenstein	5	2	12
Brock	0	0	0
Peters	1	1	3
Benedetti	2	0	4
Garibaldi	2	1	5
Soares	1	2	4
Totals	21	14	56

Wyoming

	fg	ft	tp
Burns	1	2	4
Haag	2	0	4
Rivers	2	2	6
Radovich	7	4	18
Samuelson	1	3	5
Fowler	1	0	2
Esau	6	1	13
Rutz	0	0	0
Eliopulos	0	0	0
Hughes	0	1	1
Totals	20	13	53

Half time: Wyoming 27-24.

Semifinals

St. John's, N.Y.

	fg	ft	tp
McMahon	3	3	9
Davis	1	0	2
Walsh	2	0	4
Zawoluk	9	6	24
MacGilvray	2	2	6
Duckett	4	3	11
Walker	2	1	5
Totals	23	15	61

Illinois

	fg	ft	tp
C. Follmer	4	2	10
Bemoras	1	1	3
Peterson	2	0	4
Kerr	3	2	8
Bredar	7	0	14
Fletcher	5	4	14
Gerecke	3	0	6
Totals	25	9	59

Kansas

	fg	ft	tp
Kenney	3	1	7
Lienhard	0	0	0
Hoag	4	2	10
Keller	1	2	4
Lovelette	12	9	33
Born	1	2	4
D. Kelly	4	2	10
Heitholt	2	0	4
Davenport	0	2	2
Totals	27	20	74

Santa Clara

	fg	ft	tp
Sears	0	1	1
Young	3	2	8
Garibaldi	1	0	2
Gatzert	1	1	3
Schoenstein	6	1	13
Peters	1	1	3
Brock	3	1	7
Benedetti	1	0	2
Soares	7	2	16
Totals	23	9	55

Half time: Kansas 38-25.

National Third Place

Illinois

	fg	ft	tp
C. Follmer	6	5	17
Gerecke	2	3	7
Bemoras	0	3	3
Peterson	1	3	5
Kerr	10	6	26
Fletcher	1	2	4
Hooper	1	1	3
Bredar	1	0	2
Wright	0	0	0
Totals	22	23	67

Santa Clara

	fg	ft	tp
Sears	4	2	10
Gatzert	1	2	4
Young	6	6	18
Schoenstein	2	4	8
Soares	2	0	4
Peters	4	5	13
Benedetti	1	0	2
Garibaldi	0	0	0
Brock	2	1	5
Totals	22	20	64

Half time: Santa Clara 28-22.

Championship

Kansas	fg-fga	ft-fta	rb	pf	tp
Kenney	4-11	4- 6	4	2	12
Keller	1- 1	0- 0	4	2	2
Lovellette	12-25	9-11	17	4	33
Lienhard	5- 8	2- 2	4	4	12
D. Kelley	2- 5	3- 6	3	5	7
Hoag	2- 6	5- 7	4	5	9
Houghland	2- 5	1- 3	6	2	5
Davenport	0- 0	0- 0	0	1	0
Heitholt	0- 0	0- 0	0	0	0
Born	0- 0	0- 0	0	0	0
A. Kelley	0- 0	0- 0	1	0	0
Totals	28-63	24-35	42	25	80

St. John's, N.Y.	fg-fga	ft-fta	rb	pf	tp
McMahon	6-12	1- 4	2	4	13
Davis	1- 4	2- 3	2	4	4
Zawoluk	7-12	6-11	9	5	20
Duckett	2- 5	2- 2	2	4	6
MacGilvray	3- 8	2- 5	10	3	8
Walsh	3- 6	0- 0	4	3	6
Walker	0- 2	0- 0	2	4	0
McMorrow	1- 3	0- 0	0	3	2
Sagona	2- 2	0- 0	0	5	4
Giancontieri	0- 0	0- 2	1	0	0
Peterson	0- 1	0- 0	0	0	0
Totals	25-55	13-27	32	35	63

Half time: Kansas 41-27. Officials: Eisenstein and Ogden. Attendance: 11,302.

1953

First Round

Notre Dame	fg	ft	tp
Rosenthal	6	5	17
Bertrand	8	7	23
Lewinski	4	4	12
Stephens	3	2	8
Sullivan	1	0	2
McCloskey	4	2	10
Gibbons	0	0	0
Totals	26	20	72

Eastern Kentucky	fg	ft	tp
Davis	5	1	11
Mulcahy	2	0	4
Bingham	7	6	20
Floyd	0	2	2
Stanford	0	1	1
Geyer	2	3	7
Kearns	0	2	2
Holbrook	5	0	10
Totals	21	15	57

Half time: Notre Dame 34-29.

DePaul	fg	ft	tp
Lecos	2	3	7
Blum	4	2	10
Schyman	0	2	2
Johnson	4	5	13
Feiereisel	6	5	17
Lamkin	9	7	25
Totals	25	24	74

Miami	fg	ft	tp
Gunderson	5	5	15
Klitch	7	2	16
Griesinger	2	3	7
Walls	5	4	14
Yates	1	0	2
Doll	1	1	3
Knodel	4	1	9
Hedric	1	0	2
Welch	1	0	2
Bryant	1	0	2
Totals	28	16	72

Half time: DePaul 42-30.

Holy Cross	fg	ft	tp
Magilligan	1	1	3
Markey	5	7	17
Suprunowicz	0	2	2
Early	0	0	0
Kielley	7	0	14
Carroll	0	1	1
Nangle	1	1	3
Perry	5	7	17
Palazzi	11	8	30
Casey	0	0	0
Kasprzak	0	0	0
Totals	30	27	87

1953 INDIANA HOOSIERS—(l-r) Front Row: Bob Leonard, Charley Kraak, Don Schlundt, Dick Farley, Burke Scott; Second Row: Ron Fifer, Dick White, Jim DeaKyne, Branch McCracken, Paul Poff, Phil Byers, Ernie Andreas; Back Row: Ron Taylor, Jim Schooley, Goethe Chambers, Jack Wright.

Navy	fg	ft	tp
Clune	9	2	20
Hogan	1	0	2
Kniss	3	0	6
Sandlin	1	0	2
Cramer	0	0	0
Lange	11	6	28
Wigley	0	2	2
McCally	2	1	5
Van Scoyoc	2	1	5
Wells	1	2	4
Hoover	0	0	0
Totals	30	14	74

Half time: Holy Cross 44-37.

Lebanon Valley	fg	ft	tp
Finkelstein	3	3	9
Vought	3	2	8
Miller	4	4	12
Landa	7	7	21
Sorrentino	9	12	30
Totals	26	28	80

Fordham	fg	ft	tp
Larkin	7	0	14
Cunningham	4	0	8
Biggiano	1	2	4
McCabe	0	1	1
Conlin	7	2	16
Parchinski	8	0	16
Lyons	4	0	8
Woods	0	0	0
Totals	31	5	67

Half time: 32-32.

Seattle	fg	ft	tp
Moscatel	3	1	7
Doherty	3	1	7
J. O'Brien	17	8	42
Sanford	3	2	8
Glowaski	0	1	1
Pehanick	1	0	2
E. O'Brien	8	5	21
Totals	35	18	88

Idaho State	fg	ft	tp
Roh	7	6	20
Beckham	8	6	22
Bauer	6	5	17
Connor	4	2	10
Hays	2	3	7
R. Dakich	0	1	1
Totals	27	23	77

Half time: Seattle 43-35.

Hardin-Simmons	fg	ft	tp
Brunson	2	5	9
Covert	2	0	4
Green	10	7	27
Roberts	1	1	3
Hibler	4	0	8
Burks	2	1	5
Burroughs	0	0	0
Crow	0	0	0
Totals	21	14	56

Santa Clara	fg	ft	tp
Young	7	3	17
Sears	3	1	7
Schoenstein	1	0	2
Garibaldi	3	0	6
Soares	9	3	21
Gatzert	1	1	3
Mount	4	3	11
Benedetti	3	2	8
Simoni	1	2	4
Doyle	0	2	2
Totals	32	17	81

Second Round

Notre Dame	fg	ft	tp
Rosenthal	3	12	18
Bertrand	5	7	17
Lewinski	3	4	10
Stephens	8	3	19
Sullivan	1	1	3
Gibbons	0	2	2
Totals	20	29	69

Pennsylvania	fg	ft	tp
Heylmun	5	3	13
Leach	1	0	2
Beck	9	7	25
Lavin	0	0	0
Hoagland	4	1	9
Holt	2	4	8
Totals	21	15	57

Half time: Penn 31-30.

Indiana	fg	ft	tp
Farley	2	8	12
Kraak	3	0	6
White	3	4	10
DeaKyne	1	0	2
Schlundt	5	13	23
Scott	3	0	6
Poff	0	1	1
Leonard	9	4	22
Totals	26	30	82

Branch McCracken

DePaul	fg	ft	tp
Schyman	4	9	17
Rose	0	0	0
Johnson	4	1	9
Blum	4	2	10
Wylder	0	0	0
Feiereisel	9	9	27
Lamkin	6	3	15
Kieres	0	2	2
Lecos	0	0	0
Totals	27	26	80

Half time: Indiana 42-33.

Holy Cross	fg	ft	tp
Palazzi	14	4	32
Magilligan	2	3	7
Kielley	2	0	4
Nangle	2	2	6
Perry	5	6	16
Markey	5	4	14
Totals	30	19	79

Wake Forest	fg	ft	tp
Williams	6	7	19
George	1	0	2
Hemric	9	11	29
DePorter	1	3	5
Lyles	2	1	5
Lipstas	4	3	11
Totals	23	25	71

Half time: Holy Cross 43-32.

Louisiana State	fg	ft	tp
Belcher	8	1	17
Clark	2	0	4
Bridges	1	2	4
Pettit	13	2	28
Magee	8	7	23
McArdle	6	1	13
Totals	38	13	89

Lebanon Valley	fg	ft	tp
Vought	1	2	4
Finkelstein	7	3	17
Miller	7	12	26
Landa	5	8	18
Sorrentino	3	5	11
Gluntz	0	0	0
Totals	23	30	76

Half time: LSU 48-43.

Kansas	fg	ft	tp
A. Kelley	7	3	17
Squires	0	0	0
Patterson	1	7	9
Born	4	3	11
D. Kelley	2	3	7
Davenport	4	0	8
Reich	8	4	20
Smith	0	1	1
Anderson	0	0	0
Totals	26	21	73

Oklahoma City	fg	ft	tp
Short	7	3	17
Likens	5	4	14
Key	2	8	12
Rose	3	5	11
Couts	0	1	1
Bolin	0	0	0
Nath	2	0	4
Rich	1	1	3
Bullard	1	1	3
Totals	21	23	65

Half time: Kansas 47-26.

Oklahoma A&M	fg	ft	tp
Sheets	6	3	15
Fuller	0	0	0
Maloney	0	0	0
Stockton	1	2	4
Hendrick	0	0	0
Hicks	1	2	4
Mattick	13	9	35
Rogers	3	4	10
Roark	1	1	3
Totals	25	21	71

GAME-BY-GAME RESULTS

Texas Christian	fg	ft	tp
Warren	7	8	22
White	0	1	1
Allen	2	7	11
Ohlen	3	2	8
Brown	1	0	2
Lampkin	0	1	1
Brumbley	1	0	2
Swaim	1	1	3
Hill	1	2	4
Totals	16	22	54

Half time: TCU 31-28.

Washington	fg	ft	tp
McCutchen	3	4	10
Parsons	1	0	2
Apeland	0	0	0
McClary	5	0	10
Ward	0	0	0
Houbregs	20	5	45
Cipriano	4	4	12
Koon	6	1	13
Totals	39	14	92

Seattle	fg	ft	tp
Moscatel	1	0	2
Johansen	2	0	4
Kelly	2	1	5
Sanford	1	0	2
Glowaski	10	2	22
Pehanick	0	2	2
E. O'Brien	3	3	9
J. O'Brien	6	12	24
Totals	25	20	70

Half time: Washington 47-32.

Wyoming	fg	ft	tp
Jorgensen	4	5	13
Burns	3	1	7
Rivers	2	0	4
Wing	0	2	2
Sharp	7	9	23
Mulvehal	0	1	1
Moore	1	0	2
Kuska	0	0	0
Totals	17	18	52

Santa Clara	fg	ft	tp
Young	0	3	3
Sears	8	3	19
Schoenstein	4	2	10
Garibaldi	1	6	8
Soares	1	0	2
Gatzert	4	1	9
Mount	2	4	8
Benedetti	1	6	8
Totals	21	25	67

Half time: Santa Clara 26-24.

Third Place

Pennsylvania	fg	ft	tp
Heylmun	4	3	11
Vitetta	1	5	7
Leach	10	1	21
Beck	9	4	22
Hoagland	8	1	17
Holt	3	3	9
Gramigna	1	1	3
Totals	36	18	90

DePaul	fg	ft	tp
Blum	7	0	14
Schyman	3	3	9
Lecos	3	0	6
Johnson	1	1	3
Feiereisel	7	3	17
Lamkin	5	5	15
Kieres	3	0	6
Totals	29	12	70

Half time: Penn 44-34.

Wake Forest	fg	ft	tp
Lyles	7	3	17
Williams	10	3	23
George	4	2	10
Howard	1	0	2
DeVos	0	0	0
Hemric	11	7	29
DePorter	2	6	10
Totals	35	21	91

Lebanon Valley	fg	ft	tp
Gluntz	2	1	5
Landa	5	3	13
Kosier	0	1	1
Finkelstein	6	6	18
Sorrentino	5	5	15
Miller	1	4	6
Vought	6	1	13
Totals	25	21	71

Half time: Wake Forest 49-29.

Texas Christian	fg	ft	tp
Warren	3	1	7
Allen	2	1	5
Ohlen	12	4	28
Lampkin	1	0	2
Swaim	2	0	4
Brumbley	0	4	4
White	1	1	3
Hill	1	3	5
Totals	22	14	58

Oklahoma City	fg	ft	tp
Likens	9	3	21
Key	2	6	10
Bolin	1	0	2
Rose	1	3	5
Short	5	5	15
Bullard	0	1	1
Couts	0	1	1
Nath	0	1	1
Totals	18	20	56

Half time: Oklahoma City 25-24.

Wyoming	fg	ft	tp
Jorgensen	5	7	17
Mulvehal	5	4	14
Burns	1	1	3
Moore	1	0	2
Rivers	1	1	3
Wing	5	1	11
Sharp	3	8	14
Totals	21	22	64

Seattle	fg	ft	tp
Moscatel	1	0	2
Doherty	1	0	2
Sanford	2	2	6
Pehanick	0	1	1
Bissett	2	0	4
Glowaski	4	4	12
E. O'Brien	5	6	16
J. O'Brien	6	18	30
Malone	2	1	5
Johansen	1	0	2
Totals	24	32	80

Half time: Seattle 34-27.

B. H. Born

Regional Championships

Indiana	fg	ft	tp
Farley	0	2	2
White	0	1	1
Kraak	2	4	8
Schlundt	13	15	41
DeaKyne	0	1	1
Leonard	4	3	11
Poff	1	1	3
Scott	4	2	10
Byers	1	0	2
Totals	25	29	79

Notre Dame	fg	ft	tp
Rosenthal	6	7	19
Sullivan	1	1	3
Bertrand	3	2	8
Lewinski	8	3	19
Wise	0	0	0
Gibbons	0	2	2
Reynolds	0	1	1
Stephens	5	4	14
Totals	23	20	66

Half time: Indiana 42-32.

Louisiana State	fg	ft	tp
Clark	2	0	4
Belcher	6	5	17
Freshley	0	1	1
Pettit	12	5	29
McArdle	4	5	13
Magee	5	5	15
Bridges	1	0	2
Schultz	0	0	0
Totals	30	21	81

Holy Cross	fg	ft	tp
Palazzi	1	6	8
Magilligan	2	1	5
Early	3	0	6
Lewis	1	0	2
Kielley	3	1	7
Nangle	2	4	8
Perry	6	5	17
Markey	5	6	16
Suprunowicz	2	0	4
Totals	25	23	73

Half time: LSU 41-23.

Kansas	fg	ft	tp
Patterson	0	4	4
A. Kelley	4	5	13
Born	6	6	18
Alberts	0	1	1
Reich	2	4	8
Smith	0	0	0
D. Kelley	6	4	16
Davenport	0	1	1
Totals	18	25	61

Oklahoma A&M	fg	ft	tp
Haskins	0	0	0
Fuller	1	4	6
Stockton	0	0	0
Mattick	7	8	22
Hendrick	0	1	1
Roark	3	2	8
Reams	4	4	12
Hicks	2	2	6
Totals	17	21	55

Half time: Kansas 30-28.

Washington	fg	ft	tp
McCutchen	2	1	5
McClary	2	3	7
Parsons	1	2	4
Houbregs	12	10	34
Cipriano	6	3	15
Koon	3	3	9
Totals	26	22	74

Santa Clara	fg	ft	tp
Sears	7	9	23
Young	3	2	8
Gatzert	4	0	8
Mount	1	3	5
Schoenstein	2	2	6
Garibaldi	3	0	6
Soares	2	1	5
Benedetti	0	1	1
Totals	22	18	62

Half time: Santa Clara 32-28.

Semifinals

Indiana	fg	ft	tp
Kraak	2	5	9
Farley	4	2	10
DeaKyne	0	0	0
Schlundt	8	13	29
White	0	3	3
Leonard	9	4	22
Byers	0	0	0
Poff	0	0	0
Scott	2	3	7
Totals	25	30	80

Louisiana State	fg	ft	tp
Belcher	4	2	10
Clark	0	2	2
Freshley	0	1	1
Loughmiller	0	0	0
Pettit	10	9	29
Magee	6	5	17
McArdle	1	1	3
Bridges	1	3	5
Totals	22	23	67

Half time: Indiana 49-41. Officials: Ogden and Lightner.

Kansas	fg	ft	tp
Patterson	6	5	17
Smith	0	0	0
Alberts	0	0	0
A. Kelley	3	1	7
Davenport	0	2	2
Born	9	7	25
D. Kelley	8	2	18
Heitholt	1	0	2
Reich	3	2	8
Totals	30	19	79

Washington	fg	ft	tp
McCutchen	0	3	3
Halle	0	1	1
McClary	2	2	6
Parsons	0	1	1
Houbregs	8	2	18
Elliott	1	1	3
Cipriano	4	3	11
Apeland	1	0	2
Koon	3	2	8
Totals	19	15	53

Half time: Kansas 45-34. Officials: Conway and George.

National Third Place

Louisiana State	fg	ft	tp
Belcher	2	2	6
Bridges	1	0	2
Clark	5	4	14
Schultz	2	0	4
Pettit	14	8	36
McNeilly	0	0	0
Magee	0	0	0
Freshley	0	0	0
McArdle	3	1	7
Totals	27	15	69

Washington	fg	ft	tp
McCutchen	1	1	3
McClary	1	1	3
Elliott	0	1	1
Houbregs	17	8	42
Roake	0	4	4
Cipriano	11	2	24
Halle	1	1	3
Koon	1	0	2
Parsons	2	2	6
Totals	34	20	88

Half time: Washington 39-26.

Championship

Indiana	fg	ft-fta	pf	tp
Kraak	5	7-10	5	17
DeaKyne	0	0-0	1	0
Farley	1	0-0	5	2
Schlundt	11	8-11	3	30
White	1	0-0	2	2
Leonard	5	2-4	2	12
Poff	0	0-0	0	0
Scott	2	2-3	3	6
Byers	0	0-1	0	0
Totals	25	19-28	22	69

Kansas	fg	ft-fta	pf	tp
Patterson	1	7-8	3	9
A. Kelley	7	6-8	3	20
Davenport	0	0-0	0	0
Born	8	10-12	5	26
Smith	0	1-1	1	1
Alberts	0	0-0	1	0
D. Kelley	3	2-4	2	8
Reich	2	0-0	2	4
Totals	21	26-33	17	68

Half time: 41-41. Officials: Lightner and Shaw.

1954 LA SALLE EXPLORERS—(l-r) Front Row: Frank Blatcher, Bob Maples, Frank O'Hara, Tom Gola, Bob Ames; Back Row: Charles Greenberg, Fran O'Malley, Manny Gomez, John Yodsnukis, Charles Singley, John Moosbrugger.

1954

First Round

La Salle	fg	ft	tp
Maples	1	0	2
Blatcher	4	2	10
O'Malley	3	7	13
Gola	12	4	28
O'Hara	2	6	10
Greenberg	0	2	2
Singley	5	1	11
Totals	27	22	76

Fordham	fg	ft	tp
Lyons	5	2	12
Reese	5	2	12
Viggiano	0	0	0
Connors	0	0	0
Cunningham	1	0	2
Conlin	10	6	26
Parchinski	5	4	14
Larkin	2	4	8
Totals	28	18	74

Half time: La Salle 39-35.

Navy	fg	ft	tp
Clune	16	10	42
Hogan	5	1	11
McCally	0	0	0
McDonnell	0	0	0
Lange	8	2	18
Thompson	0	1	1
Wigley	0	6	6
Hoover	2	1	5
Sandlin	0	0	0
Wells	0	2	2
Slattery	0	0	0
Totals	31	23	85

Connecticut	fg	ft	tp
Patterson	7	7	21
Ahearn	2	2	6
Bushwell	2	1	5
Braveman	0	0	0
Quimby	8	3	19
O'Brien	0	0	0
Zima	2	2	6
Watson	2	2	6
Ruddy	4	4	12
Jones	2	1	5
Totals	29	22	80

Half time: Connecticut 40-38.

North Carolina St.	fg	ft	tp
Thompson	4	6	14
Tyler	5	5	15
Dickman	0	1	1
Shavlik	6	8	20
DiNardo	2	0	4
Molodet	6	0	12
Applebaum	3	3	9
Bell	0	0	0
Gotkin	0	0	0
Totals	26	23	75

George Washington	fg	ft	tp
Karver	7	7	21
John Holup	3	1	7
Morrison	1	0	2
Joe Holup	4	5	13
Ciriello	0	0	0
Devlin	6	8	20
Klein	1	1	3
Catino	3	1	7
Totals	25	23	73

Half time: N.C. State 46-39.

Notre Dame	fg	ft	tp
Fannon	5	5	15
Bertrand	6	4	16
Rosenthal	12	7	31
Stephens	3	4	10
Sullivan	3	2	8
Totals	29	22	80

Loyola, La.	fg	ft	tp
Baer	1	0	2
Stack	3	1	7
Reynoir	3	2	8
Gallmann	3	4	10
Conrad	1	0	2
O'Donnell	12	8	32
Rouzan	4	1	9
Totals	27	16	70

Half time: Notre Dame 37-24.

Penn State	fg	ft	tp
Sherry	2	1	5
Fields	1	3	5
Rohland	2	2	6
Blocker	2	0	4
Arnelle	4	5	13
Weidenhammer	4	2	10
Brewer	4	3	11
Haag	3	2	8
Totals	22	18	62

Toledo	fg	ft	tp
Martin	8	7	23
Maher	1	2	4
Spice	2	7	11
Pazdzior	2	1	5
Ray	1	5	7
Totals	14	22	50

Half time: Toledo 30-27.

Bradley	fg	ft	tp
Petersen	1	4	6
Carney	9	9	27
Riley	0	0	0
Estergard	4	3	11
King	3	3	9
Kent	2	1	5
Babetch	0	3	3
Totals	19	23	61

Oklahoma City	fg	ft	tp
Nath	2	0	4
Short	12	5	29
Rolin	1	5	7
Couts	1	0	2
Copp	4	0	8
Rich	0	2	2
Bullard	0	2	2
Jones	0	1	1
Totals	20	15	55

Half time: Bradley 27-25.

Santa Clara	fg	ft	tp
Mount	1	6	8
Young	5	2	12
Sears	8	5	21
Benedetti	3	3	9
Gatzert	3	1	7
Simoni	2	1	5
Schoenstein	4	3	11
Boudreau	0	0	0
Totals	26	21	73

Texas Tech	fg	ft	tp
Bolding	2	2	6
Reed	5	3	13
Carpenter	6	9	21
Blackmon	3	1	7
Ince	6	1	13
Blackshear	1	0	2
McKim	1	0	2
Sexton	0	0	0
Whatley	0	0	0
Totals	24	16	64

Half time: Texas Tech 36-35.

Idaho State	fg	ft	tp
Beckham	6	8	20
Roh	8	4	20
Bauer	4	4	12
Connor	3	3	9
Dakich	3	0	6
Hays	0	0	0
Belkow	3	4	10
Totals	27	23	77

Seattle	fg	ft	tp
Glowaski	2	4	8
Kelly	1	2	4
Pehanick	9	2	20
Bauer	10	2	22
Malone	4	2	10
Godes	2	0	4
Giles	0	0	0
Johansen	2	0	4
Casey	0	0	0
Sanford	1	1	3
Totals	31	13	75

Half time: Idaho State 32-31. Regulation Score: 66-66.

Ken Loeffler

Second Round

La Salle	fg	ft	tp
O'Malley	5	3	13
Singley	9	8	26
Gola	6	14	26
Maples	2	0	4
O'Hara	3	3	9
Blatcher	4	2	10
Greenberg	0	0	0
Totals	29	30	88

North Carolina St.	fg	ft	tp
Tyler	3	1	7
Thompson	5	9	19
DiNardo	2	1	5
Shavlik	10	4	24
Applebaum	4	1	9
Molodet	6	3	15
Scheffel	0	2	2
Totals	30	21	81

Half time: La Salle 36-35.

Navy	fg	ft	tp
Clune	7	7	21
Hogan	2	0	4
McCally	1	0	2
Lange	11	7	29
Hoover	2	1	5
Wigley	0	2	2
Wells	1	2	4
Sandlin	1	0	2
Totals	25	19	69

Cornell, N.Y.	fg	ft	tp
Rolles	0	2	2
MacPhee	0	0	0
Buncom	0	1	1
Mattes	2	3	7
Zelek	4	0	8
Morton	12	10	34
Bradfield	5	0	10
Wilens	1	3	5
Totals	24	19	67

Half time: Navy 40-32.

Penn State	fg	ft	tp
Sherry	1	9	11
Rohland	0	2	2
Brewer	2	1	5
Fields	4	1	9
Arnelle	10	4	24
Marisa	0	0	0
Haag	4	1	9
Weidenhammer	4	1	9
Blocker	4	1	9
Totals	29	20	78

Louisiana State	fg	ft	tp
Clark	4	2	10
Belcher	3	0	6
Jones	0	0	0
McNeilly	0	2	2
Pettit	13	8	34
Freshley	0	0	0
Magee	3	3	9
McArdle	2	5	9
Sebastian	0	0	0
Totals	25	20	70

Half time: Penn State 34-32.

Notre Dame	fg	ft	tp
Fannon	2	0	4
Bertrand	4	3	11
Weiman	0	0	0
McGinn	1	1	3
Rosenthal	9	7	25
Sullivan	4	2	10
Stephens	2	8	12
Totals	22	21	65

Indiana	fg	ft	tp
Kraak	2	3	7
Farley	2	9	13
Choice	1	1	3
White	0	0	0
Schlundt	1	8	10
Scott	9	2	20
Leonard	5	1	11
Totals	20	24	64

Half time: Notre Dame 37-32.

263

GAME-BY-GAME RESULTS

Bradley	fg	ft	tp
Petersen	1	0	2
Carney	7	23	37
Babetch	0	2	2
Gower	0	0	0
Hansen	0	1	1
Riley	0	0	0
Kilcullen	0	1	1
Estergard	1	5	7
King	3	3	9
Kent	7	3	17
O'Connell	0	0	0
Totals	19	38	76

Colorado	fg	ft	tp
Jeangerard	0	4	4
Coffman	0	2	2
Ranglos	1	3	5
Walter	1	2	4
Haldorson	2	7	11
Hannah	2	3	7
Mock	7	3	17
Harrold	6	1	13
Peterson	0	1	1
Abrames	0	0	0
Totals	19	26	64

Half time: Bradley 36-35.

264

Oklahoma A&M	fg	ft	tp
Fuller	2	2	6
Carter	2	3	7
Barnhouse	2	2	6
Maloney	0	0	0
Mattick	5	1	11
Hendrick	0	0	0
Bigham	5	2	12
Babb	2	5	9
Totals	18	15	51

Rice	fg	ft	tp
Bryan	0	0	0
Christensen	1	0	2
Lance	4	1	9
Schwinger	4	3	11
Durrenberger	3	4	10
Brashear	3	1	7
Robicheaux	3	0	6
Beavers	0	0	0
Totals	18	9	45

Half time: Rice 21-18.

Southern Cal.	fg	ft	tp
Pausig	3	0	6
Psaltis	4	3	11
Carr	5	1	11
Dunne	3	1	7
Findley	0	0	0
Irvin	9	7	25
Ludecke	0	0	0
Welsh	3	0	6
Hammer	3	1	7
Nagai	0	0	0
Totals	30	13	73

Idaho State	fg	ft	tp
Beckham	4	4	12
Roh	3	7	13
Bauer	3	2	8
Belkow	2	2	6
Dethlefs	0	0	0
Connor	3	3	9
Dakich	4	2	10
Hays	0	1	1
Totals	19	21	59

Half time: Southern California 33-25.

Tom Gola

Santa Clara	fg	ft	tp
Sears	5	1	11
Young	9	2	20
Boudreau	2	0	4
Robinson	0	0	0
Mount	0	1	1
Schoenstein	4	5	13
Benedetti	3	2	8
Gatzert	3	4	10
Simoni	2	0	4
Ball	0	2	2
Totals	28	17	73

Colorado A&M	fg	ft	tp
Gregory	0	0	0
Kinard	1	2	4
Caylor	5	1	11
Vanderhoef	1	0	2
Bartran	0	0	0
Stuehm	6	6	18
Hibbard	0	0	0
Pivic	0	1	1
Betz	2	2	6
Bryant	2	2	6
Cates	0	0	0
Savoini	1	0	2
Totals	18	14	50

Half time: Santa Clara 44-27.

Third Place

North Carolina St.	fg	ft	tp
Tyler	2	3	7
Thompson	9	8	26
Gotkin	0	0	0
Shavlik	3	2	8
Applebaum	0	6	6
Molodet	6	6	18
Stevenson	0	0	0
Totals	20	25	65

Cornell. N.Y.	fg	ft	tp
Rolles	3	3	9
MacPhee	3	3	9
Mattes	1	0	2
Zelek	5	2	12
Buncom	1	0	2
Morton	5	1	11
Bradfield	2	2	6
Wilens	1	1	3
Totals	21	12	54

Half time: N.C. State 35-29.

Indiana	fg	ft	tp
Kraak	3	4	10
Farley	0	8	8
Choice	1	3	5
L. Scott	2	1	5
Schlundt	9	11	29
Leonard	3	2	8
B. Scott	2	4	8
Totals	20	33	73

Louisiana State	fg	ft	tp
Belcher	4	1	9
Clark	2	2	6
McNeilly	1	0	2
Loughmiller	0	0	0
Pettit	10	7	27
Magee	3	3	9
Sebastian	1	7	9
Totals	21	20	62

Half time: LSU 33-31.

Rice	fg	ft	tp
Lance	9	5	23
Durrenberger	4	6	14
Christensen	1	0	2
Bryan	0	0	0
Pahmeier	0	0	0
Schwinger	6	2	14
Telligman	0	0	0
Brashear	3	0	6
Robicheaux	6	1	13
Beavers	2	0	4
Small	1	0	2
Totals	32	14	78

Colorado	fg	ft	tp
Jeangerard	5	3	13
Coffman	1	1	3
Ranglos	4	2	10
Walter	1	0	2
Owsley	0	0	0
Haldorson	3	2	8
Hannah	0	0	0
Mock	2	2	6
Peterson	0	3	3
Harrold	4	2	10
Totals	20	15	55

Half time: Rice 36-24.

Idaho State	fg	ft	tp
Beckham	9	3	21
Roh	3	9	15
Bauer	1	4	6
Belkow	4	0	8
Dakich	2	1	5
Connor	1	2	4
Hays	1	1	3
Totals	21	20	62

Colorado A&M	fg	ft	tp
Kinard	2	1	5
Caylor	3	0	6
Bartran	2	2	6
Vanderhoef	1	0	2
Stuehm	4	3	11
Hibbard	1	0	2
Betz	2	0	4
Pivic	5	3	13
Bryant	2	0	4
Savoini	2	0	4
Totals	24	9	57

Half time: Idaho State 26-21.

Regional Championships

La Salle	fg	ft	tp
O'Malley	1	3	5
Blatcher	2	1	5
Greenberg	0	0	0
Maples	5	3	13
Gola	8	6	22
O'Hara	0	3	3
Singley	5	6	16
Totals	21	22	64

Navy	fg	ft	tp
Clune	7	2	16
Hogan	3	1	7
Lange	1	1	3
Thompson	1	1	3
Wigley	0	4	4
Hoover	3	1	7
Sandlin	2	2	6
Wells	0	2	2
Totals	17	14	48

Half time: La Salle 22-21.

Penn State	fg	ft	tp
Weidenhammer	1	1	3
Sherry	4	6	14
Brewer	3	1	7
Arnelle	7	8	22
Rohland	0	0	0
Haag	4	4	12
Blocker	5	3	13
Totals	24	23	71

Notre Dame	fg	ft	tp
Fannon	3	2	8
Bertrand	3	4	10
McGinn	0	0	0
Rosenthal	8	4	20
Sullivan	3	3	9
Stephens	4	8	16
Weiman	0	0	0
Totals	21	21	63

Half time: Penn State 31-28.

Bradley	fg	ft	tp
Petersen	1	2	4
Carney	1	4	6
Babetch	0	1	1
Riley	0	0	0
Estergard	5	5	15
Kilcullen	0	2	2
King	5	13	23
Kent	6	0	12
Gower	2	2	6
O'Connell	1	0	2
Totals	21	29	71

Oklahoma A&M	fg	ft	tp
Fuller	1	0	2
Carter	1	3	5
Maloney	2	2	6
Mattick	6	7	19
Hendrick	0	3	3
Barnhouse	3	4	10
Babb	0	0	0
Reames	0	0	0
Bigham	5	2	12
Totals	18	21	57

Half time: Bradley 31-28.

Southern Cal.	fg	ft	tp
Psaltis	6	8	20
Pausig	0	2	2
Carr	2	5	9
Irvin	6	3	15
Ludecke	1	0	2
Welsh	3	7	13
Hammer	2	1	5
Totals	20	26	66

Santa Clara	fg	ft	tp
Sears	6	4	16
Young	8	4	20
Schoenstein	3	1	7
Mount	4	7	15
Benedetti	1	1	3
Gatzert	1	2	4
Simoni	0	0	0
Ball	0	0	0
Totals	23	19	65

Half time: Southern California 28-26. Regulation: 57-57. First Overtime: 65-65.

Semifinals

La Salle	fg	ft	tp
Singley	4	2	10
Maples	3	1	7
Blatcher	7	5	19
Gola	5	9	19
O'Malley	3	3	9
O'Hara	2	1	5
Totals	24	21	69

Penn State	fg	ft	tp
Weidenhammer	1	1	3
Haag	2	0	4
Fields	2	1	5
Brewer	3	0	6
Arnelle	5	8	18
Rohland	2	0	4
Blocker	2	0	4
Sherry	1	4	6
Edwards	2	0	4
Totals	20	14	54

Half time: La Salle 33-22. Officials: Enright and Ball.

Bradley	fg	ft	tp
Petersen	1	3	5
Gower	1	0	2
King	6	5	17
Kilcullen	0	0	0
Estergard	7	7	21
Utt	0	0	0
Carney	6	8	20
O'Connell	0	0	0
Kent	3	1	7
Babetch	1	0	2
Totals	25	24	74

Southern Cal.	fg	ft	tp
Pausig	5	2	12
Carr	1	1	3
Psaltis	2	0	4
Dunne	1	0	2
Irvin	9	5	23
Ludecke	1	0	2
Hammer	2	3	7
Welsh	6	7	19
Totals	27	18	72

Half time: Southern California 42-36. Officials: Anderson and Dean.

National Third Place

Penn State	fg	ft	tp
Weidenhammer...	4	4	12
Brewer	4	0	8
Sherry	2	3	7
Edwards	0	0	0
Arnelle	10	5	25
Haag	4	1	9
Fields	2	0	4
Rohland	1	1	3
Blocker	0	2	2
Totals	27	16	70

Southern Cal.	fg	ft	tp
Psaltis	4	3	11
Carr	1	2	4
Thompson	0	2	2
Pausig	2	1	5
Irvin	5	2	12
Ludecke	0	1	1
Hammer	2	4	8
Dunne	0	0	0
Welsh	3	12	18
Totals	17	27	61

Half time: Penn State 44-26. Officials: Ball and Enright.

Championship

La Salle	fg	ft-fta	pf	tp
Singley	8	7-10	4	23
Greenberg	2	1- 2	1	5
Maples	2	0- 0	4	4
Blatcher	11	1- 2	4	23
Gola	7	5- 5	5	19
O'Malley	5	1- 1	4	11
Yodsnukis	0	0- 0	5	0
O'Hara	2	3- 4	1	7
Totals	37	18-24	28	92

Bradley	fg	ft-fta	pf	tp
Petersen	4	2- 2	2	10
Babetch	0	0- 0	0	0
King	3	6- 7	4	12
Gower	0	1- 2	1	1
Estergard	3	11-12	1	17
Carney	3	11-17	4	17
Utt	0	0- 0	1	0
Kent	8	0- 2	2	16
Riley	1	1- 2	1	3
Totals	22	32-44	16	76

Half time: Bradley 43-42. Officials: Anderson and Dean.

1955

First Round

Marquette	fg	ft	tp
Hopfensperger...	1	0	2
Schulz	0	2	2
Rand	16	5	37
Wittberger	2	2	6
Walczak	4	8	16
Bugalski	7	4	18
O'Keefe	3	3	9
Totals	33	24	90

Miami, Ohio	fg	ft	tp
Keenon	7	1	15
Fox	1	2	4
Ellis	4	0	8
Barnette	9	4	22
Bryant	8	4	20
Klitch	3	2	8
Albers	0	0	0
Hedric	1	0	2
Totals	33	13	79

Half time: Miami 39-29.

Penn State	fg	ft	tp
Blocker	3	2	8
Edwards	2	0	4
Hoffman	1	0	2
Arnelle	6	8	20
Weidenhammer...	4	0	8
Fields	5	7	17
Totals	21	17	59

Memphis State	fg	ft	tp
Scott	2	1	5
Davis	4	4	12
McClain	2	0	4
Winn	1	0	2
Arnold	5	2	12
Fortner	1	0	2
Caldwell	8	2	18
Totals	23	9	55

La Salle	fg	ft	tp
Singley	6	1	13
Lewis	9	4	22
Blatcher	5	3	13
Ames	1	0	2
T. Gola	7	8	22
Fredricks	0	0	0
O'Malley	2	1	5
Greenberg	6	0	12
Maples	3	0	6
Totals	39	17	95

Bill Russell

West Virginia	fg	ft	tp
Hundley	8	1	17
Bergines	4	2	10
Mullins	1	0	2
Witting	0	3	3
White	7	5	19
Spadafore	1	0	2
Kishbaugh	1	2	4
Holt	1	0	2
King	1	0	2
Totals	24	13	61

Villanova	fg	ft	tp
Cirino	3	3	9
Weissman	1	1	3
Griffith	3	1	7
Devine	7	3	17
Schafer	4	14	22
Smith	5	5	15
Powers	0	1	1
Totals	23	28	74

Duke	fg	ft	tp
Mayer	2	0	4
Belmont	5	10	20
Turner	1	0	2
Morgan	4	5	13
Doherty	0	0	0
Tobin	10	2	22
Lakata	0	4	4
Lamley	3	2	8
Totals	25	23	73

Canisius	fg	ft	tp
Adams	5	4	14
Markey	0	0	0
Nowak	3	7	13
Coogan	0	0	0
Leone	2	0	4
Zatorski	1	0	2
Jas. McCarthy	1	0	2
Kelly	7	1	15
Brennan	0	0	0
Jn. McCarthy	8	3	19
Corcoran	2	0	4
Totals	29	15	73

Williams	fg	ft	tp
Buss	1	3	5
White	0	0	0
Dubroff	0	0	0
Wilson	5	8	18
Santos	0	0	0
Moro	9	9	27
Symens	0	0	0
Cullen	3	0	6
Smith	0	0	0
Evans	1	0	2
Jensen	0	2	2
Totals	19	22	60

Bradley	fg	ft	tp
Gower	2	6	10
Hansen	3	0	6
Babetch	6	9	21
Petersen	2	3	7
Albeck	2	5	9
Utt	6	2	14
Kent	1	0	2
Totals	22	25	69

Oklahoma City	fg	ft	tp
Lee	4	9	17
Bradshaw	4	5	13
Holloway	9	2	20
Nath	0	2	2
Bullard	0	1	1
Magana	3	2	8
Juby	1	2	4
Totals	21	23	65

Half time: Bradley 35-31.

Seattle	fg	ft	tp
Glowaski	7	3	17
Kelly	6	1	13
Fuhrer	1	0	2
Stricklin	9	2	20
C. Bauer	6	3	15
Cox	0	2	2
Malone	3	1	7
Martin	2	0	4
Totals	34	12	80

Idaho State	fg	ft	tp
Roh	7	1	15
Hicks	3	3	9
Dethlefs	0	1	1
Esterbrook	1	0	2
R. Bauer	6	1	13
Hays	2	1	5
Arnold	0	0	0
Connor	4	10	18
Totals	23	17	63

Half time: Seattle 34-27.

San Francisco	fg	ft	tp
Mullen	9	2	20
Buchanan	4	5	13
Lawless	0	1	1
King	1	0	2
Russell	14	1	29
Kirby	1	0	2
Jones	6	0	12
Perry	1	2	4
Zannini	1	0	2
Bush	1	0	2
Baxter	1	0	2
Totals	39	11	89

West Texas St.	fg	ft	tp
Overcast	0	0	0
Clifton	2	6	10
McClure	1	0	2
Burrus	6	0	12
Robinson	7	0	14
George	1	2	4
Scott	9	6	24
Totals	26	14	66

Half time: San Francisco 46-33.

Second Round

Marquette	fg	ft	tp
Hopfensperger...	3	7	13
Schulz	5	0	10
Wittberger	4	10	18
Rand	8	3	19
Bugalski	6	3	15
Walczak	2	0	4
Totals	28	23	79

Kentucky	fg	ft	tp
Brewer	7	2	16
Bird	2	0	4
Mills	2	0	4
Burrow	6	7	19
Rose	8	4	20
Calvert	4	0	8
Totals	29	13	71

Half time: Kentucky 38-36.

Iowa	fg	ft	tp
Davis	6	7	19
Cain	8	5	21
Schoof	2	2	6
Ridley	1	0	2
Martel	0	1	1
Logan	4	0	8
George	3	1	7
Scheuerman	1	0	2
Seaberg	6	1	13
Hawthorne	1	1	3
Totals	32	18	82

Penn State	fg	ft	tp
Weidenhammer...	2	0	4
Hoffman	6	2	14
Watts	1	0	2
Arnelle	3	5	11
Marisa	3	2	8
Fields	1	1	3
Blocker	2	1	5
Rohland	0	2	2
Ramsey	1	1	3
Hall	0	1	1
Totals	19	15	53

Half time: Iowa 39-25.

La Salle	fg	ft	tp
Singley	4	1	9
Blatcher	2	3	7
Lewis	4	1	9
Ames	1	0	2
T. Gola	9	6	24
Maples	1	4	6
Greenberg	4	2	10
O'Malley	2	2	6
Totals	27	19	73

Princeton	fg	ft	tp
Haabestad	6	3	15
DeVoe	3	5	11
MacKenzie	1	0	2
Batt	1	0	2
Dailey	0	0	0
Easton	2	2	6
Blankley	0	0	0
Davidson	3	2	8
Totals	16	12	46*

Half time: La Salle 33-22.

*T. Gola scored field goal for Princeton.

Phil Woolpert

GAME-BY-GAME RESULTS

266

Canisius	fg	ft	tp
Kelly	2	0	4
Nowak	8	11	27
Leone	1	2	4
Jn. McCarthy	7	14	28
Adams	4	2	10
Jas. McCarthy	0	0	0
Totals	22	29	73

Villanova	fg	ft	tp
Cirino	1	2	4
Devine	6	15	27
Schafer	8	6	22
Smith	1	2	4
Griffith	2	4	8
Weissman	3	0	6
Totals	21	29	71

Half time: 39-39.

Bradley	fg	ft	tp
Hansen	3	0	6
Gower	3	2	8
Petersen	2	4	8
Albeck	5	6	16
Babetch	6	6	18
Dickman	0	0	0
Kent	1	1	3
Utt	8	6	22
Totals	28	25	81

Southern Methodist	fg	ft	tp
Krog	5	2	12
McGregor	1	0	2
Scharffenberger	1	2	4
Showalter	2	0	4
Krebs	5	9	19
Miller	0	2	2
Barnes	8	4	20
Mills	2	3	7
Morris	3	3	9
Totals	27	25	79

Half time: Bradley 46-41.

Colorado	fg	ft	tp
Coffman	3	0	6
Jeangerard	3	1	7
Ranglos	3	1	7
Halderson	9	10	28
Hannah	0	0	0
Harrold	2	6	10
Mansfield	0	0	0
Mock	4	3	11
Totals	24	21	69

Tulsa	fg	ft	tp
Duncan	1	1	3
Patterson	7	7	21
Courter	2	6	10
Born	3	4	10
Evans	0	0	0
Hacker	3	7	13
Jobe	0	0	0
Stewart	1	0	2
Totals	17	25	59

Half time: Colorado 34-33.

Oregon State	fg	ft	tp
Vlastelica	7	0	14
Whiteman	3	3	9
Dean	2	3	7
Allord	1	0	2
Halbrook	9	3	21
Shadoin	5	0	10
Halligan	1	2	4
Toole	4	2	10
Jarboe	0	4	4
Fundingsland	1	0	2
Totals	33	17	83

Seattle	fg	ft	tp
Glowaski	4	3	11
Godes	6	4	16
Kelly	3	0	6
Vaughan	1	0	2
Stricklin	3	8	14
Fuhrer	2	3	7
Malone	3	1	7
Bauer	3	2	8
Cox	0	0	0
Totals	25	21	71

Half time: Oregon State 50-36.

San Francisco	fg	ft	tp
Buchanan	1	0	2
Mullen	7	10	24
Russell	5	3	13
Jones	4	5	13
Perry	6	2	14
Baxter	1	2	4
Wiebusch	2	0	4
Lawless	0	4	4
Zannini	0	0	0
Kirby	0	0	0
Totals	26	26	78

Utah	fg	ft	tp
Buckwalter	1	6	8
Berger	5	2	12
Bunte	4	4	12
Tonnesen	0	2	2
Jenson	3	0	6
Crowe	1	0	2
Condle	1	0	2
McCleary	1	4	6
Lewis	1	1	3
Berner	3	0	6
Totals	20	19	59

Half time: San Francisco 41-20.

Third Place

Villanova	fg	ft	tp
Schafer	6	8	20
Milligan	0	0	0
Griffith	3	0	6
Cirino	2	0	4
Weissman	3	1	7
Devine	4	6	14
Smith	5	3	13
Totals	23	18	64

Princeton	fg	ft	tp
Haabestad	10	3	23
Roberts	0	1	1
Davidson	4	5	13
Batt	3	2	8
DeVoe	3	0	6
MacKenzie	1	0	2
Easton	1	2	4
Totals	22	13	57

Half time: Princeton 34-32.

Kentucky	fg	ft	tp
Bird	8	1	17
Brewer	4	3	11
Mills	3	0	6
Burrow	9	4	22
Rose	3	1	7
Calvert	7	5	19
Adkins	1	0	2
Totals	35	14	84

Penn State	fg	ft	tp
Weid'ham'r	5	6	16
Edwards	2	0	4
Hoffman	5	0	10
Arnelle	8	9	25
Blocker	0	1	1
Rohland	0	0	0
Fields	0	3	3
Totals	20	19	59

Half time: Kentucky 40-28.

Tulsa	fg	ft	tp
Ducan	1	3	5
Patterson	13	10	36
Courter	4	6	14
Krouse	1	0	2
Yates	2	0	4
Born	2	0	4
Evans	0	0	0
Hacker	1	0	2
Stewart	0	1	1
Totals	24	20	68

Southern Methodist	fg	ft	tp
Krog	3	0	6
McGregor	0	2	2
Scharffenberger	1	0	2
Showalter	0	0	0
Krebs	5	5	15
Miller	6	1	13
Barnes	2	5	9
Mills	3	4	10
Morris	3	4	10
Totals	23	21	67

Half time: Tulsa 43-33.

Utah	fg	ft	tp
Buckwalter	2	2	6
Bergen	2	3	7
McCleary	6	2	14
Lewis	2	0	4
Bunte	13	9	35
Tonnesen	7	2	16
Jenson	3	4	10
Condle	2	1	5
Crowe	3	0	6
Berner	0	1	1
Pepple	2	0	4
Totals	42	24	108

Seattle	fg	ft	tp
Kelly	2	2	6
Glowaski	5	9	19
Godes	1	1	3
Vaughan	0	0	0
Sanford	1	0	2
Stricklin	5	4	14
Fuhrer	1	5	7
Bauer	7	7	21
Malone	1	7	9
Cox	0	4	4
Martin	0	0	0
Totals	23	39	85

Half time: Utah 58-38.

Regional Championships

La Salle	fg	ft	tp
Lewis	7	4	18
Singley	5	6	16
Blatcher	1	0	2
Ames	1	2	4
T. Gola	9	12	30
Greenberg	5	4	14
J. Gola	1	0	2
O'Malley	2	0	4
Maples	1	7	9
Totals	32	35	99

Canisius	fg	ft	tp
Kelly	0	2	2
Markey	2	11	15
Nowak	3	4	10
Coogan	2	0	4
Corcoran	0	1	1
Jas. McCarthy	1	2	4
Jn. McCarthy	5	7	17
Adams	4	0	8
Flynn	1	1	3
Totals	18	28	64

Half time: La Salle 43-30.

Iowa	fg	ft	tp
Cain	5	0	10
Davis	2	3	7
Schoof	3	2	8
Logan	11	9	31
George	1	1	3
Seaberg	5	2	12
Scheuerman	3	5	11
Johnson	1	1	3
Hawthorne	0	1	1
Totals	31	24	86

Marquette	fg	ft	tp
Schulz	5	12	22
Hopfensperger	5	6	16
Wittberger	7	2	16
Rand	7	3	17
Walczak	1	1	3
Bugalski	0	7	7
O'Keefe	0	0	0
VanVoore	0	0	0
Sevcik	0	0	0
Totals	25	31	81

Half time: Iowa 46-33.

Colorado	fg	ft	tp
Coffman	0	0	0
Jeangerard	12	5	29
Ranglos	3	4	10
Yardley	1	0	2
Halderson	7	9	23
Hannah	0	1	1
Harrold	4	10	18
Mansfield	1	2	4
Mock	2	2	6
Totals	30	33	93

Bradley	fg	ft	tp
Burnham	0	0	0
Hansen	2	0	4
Gower	3	0	6
Petersen	5	2	12
Albeck	6	4	16
Babetch	7	8	22
Dickman	1	0	2
Kent	2	0	4
Utt	6	3	15
Totals	32	17	81

Half time: Colorado 49-41.

San Francisco	fg	ft	tp
Mullen	0	2	2
Buchanan	2	0	4
Russell	11	7	29
Jones	2	7	11
Perry	2	0	4
Baxter	0	1	1
Wiebusch	1	4	6
Totals	18	21	57

Oregon State	fg	ft	tp
Halligan	2	1	5
Vlastelica	6	0	12
Halbrook	7	4	18
Jarboe	0	0	0
Toole	2	2	6
Whiteman	2	7	11
Robins	2	0	4
Totals	21	14	56

Half time: San Francisco 30-27.

1955 SAN FRANCISCO DONS—(l-r) Front Row: Hal Perry, Steve Balchios, Rudy Zannini, Warren Baxter; Second Row: Tom Nelson, Stan Buchanan, Bill Russell, Jerry Mullen, Jack King, Bob Wiebusch; Back Row: Phil Woolpert, K. C. Jones, Dick Lawless, Gordon Kirby, Bill Bush, Ray Healy.

GAME-BY-GAME RESULTS

Semifinals

La Salle	fg	ft	tp
O'Malley	1	4	6
Maples	1	2	4
Singley	5	6	16
Blatcher	2	1	5
Gola	8	7	23
Lewis	5	4	14
Greenberg	4	0	8
Totals	26	24	76

Iowa	fg	ft	tp
Davis	1	0	2
Schoof	3	0	6
Cain	8	1	17
Logan	7	6	20
Seaberg	5	5	15
Scheuerman	1	11	13
Totals	25	23	73

Half time: La Salle 45-36. Officials: Milner and Ogden.

San Francisco	fg	ft	tp
Wiebusch	1	0	2
King	1	2	4
Buchanan	0	6	6
Russell	10	4	24
Jones	3	2	8
Baxter	2	3	7
Bush	0	1	1
Perry	5	0	10
Zannini	0	0	0
Kirby	0	0	0
Totals	22	18	62

Colorado	fg	ft	tp
Jeangerard	1	2	4
Coffman	1	2	4
Ranglos	1	2	4
Yardley	1	2	4
Halderson	3	3	9
Hannah	2	5	9
Mock	2	0	4
Mansfield	0	4	4
Grant	1	0	2
Peterson	2	2	6
Totals	14	22	50

Half time: San Francisco 25-19. Officials: Fox and Mohr.

National Third Place

Colorado	fg	ft	tp
Jeangerard	5	4	14
Walter	0	0	0
Ranglos	6	6	18
Halderson	4	4	12
Hannah	1	4	6
Mock	3	7	13
Peterson	3	4	10
Grant	1	0	2
Totals	23	29	75

Iowa	fg	ft	tp
Davis	1	0	2
Schoof	2	2	6
Cain	4	6	14
Logan	5	7	17
George	0	3	3
Seaberg	1	2	4
Martel	1	0	2
Scheuerman	2	2	6
Totals	16	22	54

Half time: Colorado 35-28.

Championship

San Francisco	fg	ft-fta	pf	tp
Mullen	4	2- 5	5	10
Buchanan	3	2- 2	1	8
Russell	9	5- 7	1	23
Jones	10	4- 4	2	24
Perry	1	2- 2	4	4
Wiebusch	2	0- 0	0	4
Zannini	1	0- 0	0	2
Lawless	1	0- 0	0	2
Kirby	0	0- 0	1	0
Totals	31	15-20	14	77

La Salle	fg	ft-fta	pf	tp
O'Malley	4	2- 3	1	10
Singley	8	4- 4	1	20
Gola	6	4- 5	4	16
Lewis	1	4- 9	1	6
Greenberg	1	1- 2	4	3
Blatcher	4	0- 0	1	8
Maples	0	0- 0	0	0
Fredericks	0	0- 0	0	0
Totals	24	15-23	12	63

Half time: San Francisco 35-24.

1956

First Round

Connecticut	fg	ft	tp
Quinn	5	2	12
Ruddy	5	3	13
Narracci	0	0	0
Kaspar	9	5	23
O'Leary	0	0	0
Bushwell	7	10	24
O'Connor	0	0	0
Osborn	4	0	8
Burns	2	0	4
Totals	32	20	84

Manhattan	fg	ft	tp
Paulson	7	5	19
Murphy	2	2	6
Martinsen	3	0	6
Lombardo	4	2	10
Joseph	0	1	1
Powers	12	2	26
O'Connor	2	0	4
Cavanaugh	1	1	3
Totals	31	13	75

Temple	fg	ft	tp
Reinfeld	4	0	8
Fleming	1	2	4
Norman	1	0	2
Cohen	8	0	16
Lear	9	8	26
Rodgers	6	6	18
Totals	29	16	74

Holy Cross	fg	ft	tp
Liebler	10	0	20
Hughes	5	3	13
Heinsohn	7	12	26
Waddleton	1	0	2
Andreoli	1	2	4
Prohovich	2	0	4
Ryan	1	1	3
Totals	27	18	72

Half time: Temple 40-37.

Dartmouth	fg	ft	tp
Judson	7	4	18
Carruthers	2	2	6
Fraser	0	0	0
Francis	9	7	25
Donahoe	1	0	2
Julian	0	1	1
Blades	1	2	4
Booth	2	1	5
Totals	22	17	61

West Virginia	fg	ft	tp
Gardner	4	3	11
Hundley	8	2	18
Sharrar	3	2	8
Constantine	1	0	2
Kishbaugh	6	1	13
Vincent	1	5	7
Totals	23	13	59

Canisius	fg	ft	tp
Nowak	8	13	29
Kelly	5	4	14
Britz	0	0	0
Leone	2	0	4
Corcoran	1	2	4
Jas. McCarthy	0	0	0
Markey	5	2	12
Jn. McCarthy	5	6	16
Totals	26	27	79

1956 SAN FRANCISCO DONS—(l-r) Front Row: Warren Baxter, Hal Payne, Jack King, Hal Perry, Steve Balchios; Second Row: Phil Woolpert, Vince Boyle, John Koljion, Bill Russell, Bill Bush, K. C. Jones, Bill Mulholland; Third Row: Tom Nelson, Gene Brown, Mike Farmer, Carl Boldt, Mike Preaseau.

North Carolina St.	fg	ft	tp
Di Narde	4	5	13
Dickman	2	0	4
Pon	1	2	4
Seitz	0	0	0
Hopper	0	0	0
Shavlik	10	5	25
Stepanovich	1	2	4
Molodet	5	4	14
Maglio	5	4	14
Essler	0	0	0
Totals	28	22	78

Half time: Canisius 39-34. Regulation Score: 65-65. First O.T.: 69-69. Second O.T.: 71-71. Third O.T.: 71-71.

Wayne State	fg	ft	tp
Keller	3	0	6
Duncan	1	1	3
Porter	1	2	4
Brown	5	3	13
London	1	0	2
Straughn	9	9	27
Harvey	0	3	3
Kendrick	4	6	14
Totals	24	24	72

De Paul	fg	ft	tp
Heise	4	4	12
Sobieszczyk	5	5	15
Jaksy	2	6	10
Robinzine	6	3	15
Curtin	1	3	5
Henry	1	4	6
Totals	19	25	63

Half time: Wayne State 37-36.

Morehead	fg	ft	tp
Hamilton	9	5	23
Richards	0	0	0
Keleher	8	0	16
Jewell	0	2	2
Carroll	0	0	0
Swartz	12	15	39
Shimfessel	0	0	0
Tolle	3	2	8
Gaunce	6	7	19
Totals	38	31	107

Marshall	fg	ft	tp
Price	11	5	27
Greer	5	2	12
Ashley	2	2	6
Kirk	8	2	18
Underwood	9	0	18
Mayfield	0	0	0
Freeman	5	1	11
Totals	40	12	92

Seattle	fg	ft	tp
Sanford	4	2	10
Fuhrer	2	1	5
Godes	4	3	11
Bauer	6	8	20
Harney	0	0	0
Frizzell	0	1	1
Stricklin	3	2	8
Markey	4	5	13
Totals	23	22	68

Idaho State	fg	ft	tp
Siemen	8	0	16
Harris	8	0	16
Allain	2	7	11
Hicks	0	1	1
Horrocks	3	4	10
Dethlefs	3	2	8
Easterbrooks	1	0	2
Wells	0	2	2
Totals	25	16	66

Half time: Seattle 37-30.

Southern Methodist	fg	ft	tp
Showalter	2	0	4
Herrscher	0	0	0
Krog	7	5	19
Krebs	10	2	22
Mills	4	5	13
Morris	2	2	6
Miller	0	4	4
Totals	25	18	68

Texas Tech	fg	ft	tp
Elam	0	0	0
Carpenter	10	3	23
Scaling	1	4	6
Wilson	3	2	8
Cummings	5	2	12
Underwood	3	12	18
Totals	22	23	67

Half time: Texas Tech 35-33.

Oklahoma City	fg	ft	tp
Griffin	7	3	17
Bradshaw	5	1	11
Magana	3	0	6
Ratzlaff	0	0	0
Lee	5	5	15
Juby	2	2	6
Jeter	2	0	4
Holloway	1	9	11
Reed	10	7	27
Totals	35	27	97

GAME-BY-GAME RESULTS

Memphis State	fg	ft	tp
Swander	3	2	8
Doyle	0	2	2
Scott	7	9	23
Jones	1	0	2
Ballard	1	3	5
Fortner	5	5	15
Butcher	5	0	10
Hays	8	0	16
Totals	30	21	81

Half time: Memphis State 41-33.

Phil Woolpert

Second Round

Iowa	fg	ft	tp
Cain	8	12	28
Schoof	5	5	15
Logan	6	5	17
Seaberg	4	1	9
Scheuerman	6	2	14
George	0	3	3
Hawthorne	0	4	4
Martel	1	0	2
Paul	1	1	3
Schroeder	0	2	2
Totals	31	35	97

Morehead State	fg	ft	tp
Keleher	0	3	3
Hamilton	7	5	19
Richards	0	0	0
Jewell	0	2	2
Thompson	1	2	4
Swartz	8	4	20
Shimfessel	1	1	3
Gaunce	5	14	24
Tolle	2	2	6
Carroll	1	0	2
Totals	25	33	83

Kentucky	fg	ft	tp
Bird	5	0	10
Grawemeyer	3	1	7
Burrow	14	5	33
Calvert	5	4	14
Hatton	4	2	10
Brewer	1	0	2
Mills	0	1	1
Johnson	0	2	2
Cassady	1	1	3
Beck	1	0	2
Totals	34	16	84

Wayne State	fg	ft	tp
Keller	5	3	13
Duncan	4	1	9
Brown	5	4	14
Straughn	3	0	6
Porter	2	0	4
Kendrick	2	10	14
London	2	0	4
Halverson	0	0	0
Greenberg	0	0	0
Totals	23	18	64

Temple	fg	ft	tp
Fleming	0	0	0
Reinfeld	1	0	2
Norman	2	2	6
Cohen	5	0	10
Van Patton	0	0	0
Rodgers	1	5	7
Lear	18	4	40
Totals	27	11	65

Connecticut	fg	ft	tp
Osborn	4	3	11
Ruddy	8	3	19
O'Connor	0	0	0
Kaspar	1	2	4
Cherepy	1	0	2
Quinn	6	4	16
Bushwell	2	1	5
Burns	1	0	2
Totals	23	13	59

Half time: Temple 38-27.

Canisius	fg	ft	tp
Nowak	9	11	29
McMullen	0	0	0
Kelly	6	0	12
Britz	0	0	0
Coogan	0	0	0
Leone	2	0	4
Bartkowski	0	0	0
Markey	2	0	4
Corcoran	4	0	8
Jn. McCarthy	2	5	9
Totals	25	16	66

Dartmouth	fg	ft	tp
Judson	0	6	6
Donahoe	2	3	7
Carruthers	7	0	14
Erwin	0	0	0
Francis	7	5	19
Julian	1	0	2
Blades	1	0	2
Booth	3	0	6
Markman	0	2	2
Totals	21	16	58

Half time: Canisius 33-30.

Utah	fg	ft	tp
Buckwalter	3	4	10
Bergen	6	4	16
Koncar	0	0	0
Bunte	8	8	24
McCleary	1	2	4
Hale	3	4	10
Jenson	4	4	12
Crowe	2	1	5
Totals	27	27	81

Seattle	fg	ft	tp
Godes	4	1	9
Sanford	1	1	3
Gockel	0	2	2
Stricklin	7	2	16
Fuhrer	5	5	15
Markey	1	2	4
Bauer	3	7	13
Frizzell	5	0	10
Totals	26	20	72

Half time: Utah 44-38.

San Francisco	fg	ft	tp
Farmer	4	7	15
Boldt	0	0	0
Preaseau	1	1	3
Baxter	0	0	0
Russell	9	3	21
Perry	4	2	10
Brown	9	5	23
Totals	27	18	72

UCLA	fg	ft	tp
Burke	0	2	2
Herring	2	3	7
Halsten	1	4	6
Naulls	6	4	16
Johnson	0	1	1
Ranton	3	7	13
Taft	6	4	16
Totals	18	25	61

Half time: San Francisco 39-21.

Oklahoma City	fg	ft	tp
Griffin	6	8	20
Holloway	5	7	17
Lee	5	10	20
Reed	6	3	15
Bradshaw	3	1	7
Jeter	0	0	0
Juby	1	0	2
Magana	5	6	16
Totals	31	35	97

Kansas State	fg	ft	tp
Abbott	1	0	2
Powell	0	1	1
Stone	6	2	14
Parr	3	13	19
Kiddoo	3	3	9
Schneider	4	2	10
Vicens	4	7	15
Wallace	9	5	23
Totals	30	33	93

Half time: Kansas State 48-47.

Southern Methodist	fg	ft	tp
Herrscher	0	8	8
Krog	0	8	8
Scharffenberger	2	0	4
Showalter	4	1	9
Krebs	11	5	27
McGregor	1	0	2
Miller	3	1	7
Mills	3	5	11
Morris	4	5	13
Totals	28	33	89

Houston	fg	ft	tp
Evans	4	2	10
Foster	3	2	8
Helms	3	4	10
Tucker	3	0	6
Boldebuck	4	3	11
Dotson	5	0	10
Lopes	1	0	2
McElveen	3	0	6
Sells	2	7	11
Totals	28	18	74

Half time: SMU 47-31.

Third Place

Morehead State	fg	ft	tp
Jewell	0	4	4
Hamilton	6	0	12
Keleher	3	4	10
Richards	2	2	6
Swartz	12	6	30
Shimfessel	4	0	8
Gaunce	3	6	12
Tolle	4	5	13
Carroll	0	0	0
Totals	34	27	95

Wayne State	fg	ft	tp
Keller	9	2	20
Duncan	5	4	14
Greenberg	2	2	6
Kendrick	1	13	15
Brown	9	1	19
Straughn	3	0	6
Porter	1	0	2
Halverson	0	0	0
Hedden	1	0	2
Totals	31	22	84

Dartmouth	fg	ft	tp
Judson	4	0	8
Carruthers	6	4	16
Donahoe	1	0	2
Erwin	1	2	4
Fraser	1	0	2
Francis	6	2	14
Douglas	0	2	2
Julian	3	3	9
Booth	7	6	20
Blades	3	1	7
Markman	0	1	1
Jones	0	0	0
Totals	32	21	85

Connecticut	fg	ft	tp
Osborn	1	2	4
Ruddy	4	7	15
O'Connor	2	0	4
Kaspar	4	4	12
O'Leary	1	1	3
Cherepy	1	0	2
Quinn	2	1	5
Bushwell	3	2	8
Burns	5	1	11
Narracci	0	0	0
Dube	0	0	0
Totals	23	18	64

Half time: Dartmouth 46-34.

UCLA	fg	ft	tp
Herring	0	0	0
Burke	2	1	5
Naulls	14	5	33
Taft	5	10	20
Banton	3	0	6
Johnson	4	4	12
Halsten	5	6	16
Adams	0	0	0
Arnold	1	0	2
Totals	34	26	94

Hal Lear

Seattle	fg	ft	tp
Frizzell	8	5	21
Sanford	1	3	5
Fuhrer	3	7	13
Markey	1	6	8
Harney	3	1	7
Godes	2	2	6
Bauer	3	4	10
Stricklin	0	0	0
Rajicich	0	0	0
Totals	21	28	70

Half time: UCLA 40-34.

Kansas State	fg	ft	tp
Fischer	0	1	1
Jedwabny	2	0	4
Stone	6	8	20
Parr	7	7	21
Kiddoo	4	3	11
Schneider	2	0	4
Vicens	4	4	12
Wallace	6	4	16
Totals	31	27	89

Houston	fg	ft	tp
Evans	1	0	2
Foster	2	0	4
Helms	4	0	8
Tucker	2	2	6
Boldebuck	5	11	21
Dotson	6	2	14
Lopez	4	1	9
Sells	1	4	6
Totals	25	20	70

Half time: Kansas State 40-37.

Regional Championships

Temple	fg	ft	tp
Fleming	2	0	4
Reinfeld	0	1	1
Norman	3	7	13
Cohen	2	0	4
Van Patton	1	0	2
Rodgers	9	4	22
Lear	4	6	14
Totals	21	18	60

Canisius	fg	ft	tp
Kelly	5	0	10
Nowak	3	3	9
Leone	5	2	12
Jn. McCarthy	2	6	10
Markey	7	3	17
Totals	22	14	58

Half time: Canisius 30-29.

Iowa

Iowa	fg	ft	tp
Cain	12	10	34
Schoof	2	0	4
George	3	0	6
McConnell	0	0	0
Sebolt	0	0	0
Logan	6	2	14
Seaberg	2	5	9
Scheuerman	8	6	22
Totals	33	23	89

Kentucky	fg	ft	tp
Bird	9	5	23
Grawemeyer	2	1	5
Johnson	1	1	3
Burrow	13	5	31
Calvert	3	1	7
Hatton	2	0	4
Brewer	2	0	4
Cassady	0	0	0
Totals	32	13	77

Half time: Iowa 49-38.

San Francisco	fg	ft	tp
Boldt	6	1	13
Farmer	5	4	14
Preasseau	3	8	14
Nelson	0	0	0
Russell	12	3	27
Perry	2	0	4
Brown	7	4	18
Baxter	1	0	2
Totals	36	20	92

Utah	fg	ft	tp
McCleary	2	0	4
Bergen	2	2	6
Crowe	1	0	2
Bunte	8	7	23
Buckwalter	2	7	11
Jenson	9	3	21
Hale	1	6	8
Gaythwaite	1	0	2
Totals	26	25	77

Southern Methodist	fg	ft	tp
Herrscher	0	2	2
Krog	6	10	22
Showalter	8	4	20
Miller	1	6	8
Krebs	2	3	7
Lee	0	1	1
Mills	4	6	14
Morris	4	2	10
Totals	25	34	84

Oklahoma City	fg	ft	tp
Gilbert	1	2	4
Griffin	7	0	14
Holloway	3	0	6
Lee	2	4	8
Reed	7	7	21
Bradshaw	4	0	8
Magana	0	0	0
Wheeler	1	0	2
Totals	25	13	63

Half time: SMU 44-34.

Semifinals

Iowa	fg	ft	tp
Cain	8	4	20
Schoof	5	8	18
Logan	13	10	36
Seaberg	1	0	2
Scheuerman	1	2	4
Martel	1	1	3
Totals	29	25	83

Temple	fg	ft	tp
Reinfeld	1	0	2
Norman	1	0	2
Fleming	2	0	4
Cohen	3	0	6
Van Patton	1	0	2
Rodgers	12	4	28
Lear	15	2	32
Totals	35	6	76

Half time: Iowa 39-36.

San Francisco	fg	ft	tp
Boldt	3	1	7
Farmer	11	4	26
Preasseau	1	0	2
King	0	0	0
Russell	8	1	17
Perry	6	2	14
Brown	5	2	12
Baxter	4	0	8
Totals	38	10	86

Southern Methodist	fg	ft	tp
Showalter	4	0	8
Krog	3	0	6
McGregor	1	1	3
Krebs	10	4	24
Miller	1	0	2
Mills	1	9	11
Morris	4	2	10
Herrscher	1	2	4
Totals	25	18	68

Half time: San Francisco 44-32.

National Third Place

Temple	fg	ft	tp
Norman	8	1	17
Reinfeld	0	0	0
Fleming	2	1	5
Van Patton	2	2	6
Rodgers	6	2	14
Lear	17	14	48
Totals	35	20	90

Southern Methodist	fg	ft	tp
Krog	4	0	8
Showalter	4	0	8
Herrscher	2	1	5
Krebs	9	11	29
Morris	2	8	12
Mills	6	7	19
Totals	27	27	81

Half time: Temple 41-38.

Championship

San Francisco	fg	ft-fta	pf	tp
Boldt	7	2- 2	4	16
Farmer	0	0- 0	2	0
Preasseau	3	1- 2	3	7
Russell	11	4- 5	2	26
Nelson	0	0- 0	0	0
Perry	6	2- 2	2	14
Brown	6	4- 4	0	16
Baxter	2	0- 0	0	4
Totals	35	13-15	13	83

Iowa	fg	ft-fta	pf	tp
Cain	7	3- 4	1	17
Schoof	5	4- 4	3	14
Logan	5	2- 2	3	12
George	0	0- 0	0	0
Scheuerman	4	3- 4	2	11
Seaberg	5	7-10	1	17
Martel	0	0- 0	0	0
McConnell	0	0- 0	0	0
Totals	26	19-24	10	71

Half time: San Francisco 38-33.

1957

First Round

Syracuse	fg-fga	ft-fta	rb	pf	tp
Clark	12-16	2- 2	11	4	26
Cohen	9-22	6- 8	7	3	24
Snyder	4-14	3- 6	7	3	11
Breland	4-11	2- 2	4	1	10
Albanese	1- 8	2- 4	4	2	4
Cincebox	3- 7	0- 1	7	1	6
Loudis	0- 1	1- 2	0	0	1
Team			11		
Totals	33-79	16-25	51	14	82

1957 NORTH CAROLINA TAR HEELS—(l-r) Front Row: Ray Searcy, Gehrmann Holland, Danny Lotz, Karl Rosemond, Bob Cunningham, Tommy Kearns; Back Row: Frank McGuire, Joel Fleishman, Bob Young, Lennie Rosenbluth, Joe Quigg, Pete Brennan, Buck Freeman, John Lacey.

269

Connecticut	fg-fga	ft-fta	rb	pf	tp
Quinn	6-17	2- 2	2	0	14
Schmidt	5-12	4- 4	16	3	14
Cooper	9-15	1- 3	16	3	19
Davis	0- 0	0- 1	1	2	0
Osborne	1-10	6- 8	11	2	8
O'Connor	8-19	5- 6	5	2	21
Team			1		
Totals	29-76	18-24	52	12	76

Half time: Connecticut 37-35. Officials: Anderson and DeGravio.

West Virginia	fg-fga	ft-fta	rb	pf	tp
Hundley	4-20	9- 9	7	1	17
Smith	5-14	0- 2	10	3	10
Sharrar	1- 6	1- 2	8	3	3
Kishbaugh	5-11	2- 5	5	1	12
Vincent	3- 9	2- 3	7	1	8
Gardner	1- 5	2- 2	1	3	4
Clousson	1- 2	0- 1	5	3	2
Schertzinger	0- 1	0- 0	1	0	0
Team			9		
Totals	20-68	16-24	53	12	56

Canisius	fg-fga	ft-fta	rb	pf	tp
Nowak	8-13	3- 6	16	3	19
Springer	1- 6	0- 0	1	1	2
Leone	8-13	2- 2	12	4	18
Coogan	3-11	0- 1	5	3	6
Markey	2-13	1- 5	8	1	5
Mackinnon	1- 2	0- 0	1	0	2
Britz	5-15	2- 3	9	2	12
Team			4		
Totals	28-73	8-17	56	14	64

Half time: Canisius 34-18. Officials: Mihalik and Stevens.

North Carolina	fg-fga	ft-fta	rb	pf	tp
Rosenbluth	11-19	7-12	19	4	29
Young	0- 0	0- 0	1	3	0
Brennan	6-12	8-11	11	3	20
Quigg	5- 8	3- 4	1	2	13
Kearns	5-12	6- 9	4	3	16
Cunningham	4- 7	4- 4	7	3	12
Totals	31-58	28-40	43	18	90

Yale	fg-fga	ft-fta	rb	pf	tp
Lee	8-22	9- 9	4	5	25
Baird	0- 4	0- 0	4	3	0
Downs	5-15	3- 6	9	5	13
Bodman	1- 1	0- 0	2	0	2
Robinson	7-11	6- 9	17	5	20
Bab	0- 2	0- 0	0	1	0
Thompson	3- 5	0- 0	2	3	6
Sargent	2- 6	0- 2	0	5	6
Molumphy	1- 1	0- 1	0	1	2
Team			3		
Totals	27-67	18-27	41	28	74

Half time: 40-40.

Pittsburgh	fg	ft	tp
Pegues	3	8	14
Riser	6	8	20
Woznicki	0	0	0
Brautigam	2	2	6
Dorman	2	2	6
Markovich	0	1	1
Hursh	2	0	4
Hennon	11	9	31
Sawyer	0	2	2
Laneve	1	0	2
Totals	27	32	86

Morehead State	fg	ft	tp
Hamilton	5	10	20
Keleher	5	6	16
Yentes	0	1	1
Shimfessel	2	3	7
Hill	3	2	8
Thompson	1	5	7
Tolle	5	10	20
Carroll	3	0	6
Totals	24	37	85

Half time: Pittsburgh 46-44.

Notre Dame	fg	ft	tp
Hawkins	11	3	25
Smyth	7	9	23
McCarthy	8	6	22
Duffy	2	5	9
Devine	4	0	8
Sullivan	0	2	2
Totals	32	25	89

Miami, Ohio	fg	ft	tp
Brown	0	0	0
Ellis	3	1	7
Wingard	0	2	2
Miller	0	0	0
Babbs	0	1	1
Embry	9	7	25
Alberts	0	0	0
Thomas	7	1	15
Powell	10	3	23
Gentry	1	2	4
Crist	0	0	0
Knosher	0	0	0
Totals	30	17	77

Half time: Notre Dame 47-31.

GAME-BY-GAME RESULTS

270

Oklahoma City	fg	ft	tp
Lee	3	3	9
Holloway	9	0	18
Hill	3	1	7
Kelley	1	0	2
Bradshaw	2	0	4
Griffin	2	4	8
Reed	9	6	24
Gardner	0	0	0
Magana	1	0	2
Hanson	1	0	2
McGraw	0	0	0
Jeter	0	0	0
Totals	31	14	76

Loyola, La.	fg	ft	tp
Gaudin	10	11	31
Hall	0	2	2
Doll	0	0	0
Vogt	0	0	0
Schweiberger	2	0	4
Lorio	3	2	8
McLaughlin	3	2	8
Murret	0	0	0
Exsterstein	0	0	0
Hughes	1	0	2
Totals	19	17	55

Half time: Oklahoma City 38-16.

Idaho State	fg	ft	tp
Slemen	8	5	21
Hoge	0	0	0
Adlehardt	3	3	9
Allain	1	3	5
Cheney	0	0	0
Wells	0	0	0
Detmer	0	0	0
Hicks	8	7	23
Easterbrooks	4	2	10
Mauley	0	0	0
Totals	24	20	68

Hardin-Simmons	fg	ft	tp
Edmiston	2	2	6
Murray	0	0	0
Knight	0	5	5
Carlson	0	0	0
Capin	0	0	0
Tremaine	3	10	16
Cunningham	1	0	2
King	4	0	8
Groom	2	2	6
Benton	1	0	2
Lewis	4	2	10
Travis	1	0	2
Totals	18	21	57

Second Round

Lafayette	fg-fga	ft-fta	rb	pf	tp
Galtere	1- 9	6- 8	11	3	8
Sterlein	2- 6	0- 1	11	4	4
Mantz	5-11	6- 7	17	2	16
Murray	14-25	2- 5	6	0	30
Mack	1- 8	6- 9	3	5	8
Kohler	1- 4	1- 2	0	2	3
Jones	1- 2	0- 0	0	1	2
Totals	25-65	21-32	48	17	71

Syracuse	fg-fga	ft-fta	rb	pf	tp
Breland	0- 7	0- 2	7	3	0
Clark	13-20	8-10	13	3	34
Snyder	6-10	2- 5	14	4	14
Cohen	3-15	2- 3	4	3	8
Albanese	5-14	2- 3	4	3	12
Cincebox	3- 9	1- 4	9	0	7
Loudis	0- 0	0- 0	2	1	0
Totals	30-75	15-27	53	17	75

Half time: Syracuse 42-40. Officials: McPherson and Fillippi.

North Carolina	fg-fga	ft-fta	rb	pf	tp
Rosenbluth	15-30	9-11	10	2	39
Brennan	1- 8	4- 4	13	5	6
Quigg	4- 5	0- 2	9	4	8
Cunningham	2- 5	11-15	8	4	15
Kearns	8-11	3- 5	4	2	19
Young	0- 1	0- 0	1	2	0
Lotz	0- 0	0- 0	0	0	0
Searcy	0- 0	0- 0	0	0	0
Totals	30-60	27-37	45	19	87

Canisius	fg-fga	ft-fta	rb	pf	tp
Springer	2- 4	0- 0	1	1	4
Nowak	8-11	8-12	9	4	24
Leone	3-10	7- 9	6	5	13
Markey	5-11	2- 2	6	3	12
Coogan	5-11	0- 1	6	1	10
Britz	2-15	7- 7	5	4	11
Rojek	0- 0	1- 2	0	2	1
MacKinnon	0- 0	0- 0	0	0	0
Ruska	0- 0	0- 0	1	0	0
Shea	0- 0	0- 0	0	0	0
Totals	25-62	25-33	34	21	75

Half time: North Carolina 39-25. Officials: Conway and Pace.

Pittsburgh	fg-fga	ft-fta	rb	pf	tp
Pegues	7-15	1- 1	7	4	15
Riser	7-13	16-17	13	5	30
Laneve	0- 0	0- 1	1	0	0
Brautigam	4-11	5- 7	5	1	13
Hennon	11-29	2- 2	5	4	24
Dorman	2- 3	0- 0	2	5	4
Sawyer	1- 1	0- 0	1	0	2
Hursh	0- 2	1- 2	7	5	1
Lazor	0- 2	0- 0	0	0	0
Markovich	1- 2	1- 2	4	0	3
Totals	33-78	26-32	45	24	92

Kentucky	fg-fga	ft-fta	rb	pf	tp
Cox	7-18	12-14	9	2	26
Crigler	0- 4	2- 3	3	5	2
Mills	4-10	1- 4	9	4	9
Brewer	1- 3	8- 8	2	1	10
Beck	3- 4	3- 6	14	5	9
Calvert	9-17	0- 0	4	0	18
Hatton	10-23	4- 5	10	1	24
Smith	0- 2	0- 0	0	0	0
Collinsworth	0- 0	0- 1	1	0	0
Totals	34-81	30-41	52	18	98

Half time: Kentucky 50-42. Officials: Mihalik and Anderson. Attendance: 11,000.

Michigan State	fg-fga	ft-fta	rb	pf	tp
Ferguson	8-20	0- 0	10	4	16
Hedden	4-16	5-12	11	3	13
Green	8-21	4- 7	27	3	20
Quiggle	8-22	2- 3	7	3	18
Wilson	0- 2	0- 0	3	1	0
Scott	1- 2	2- 4	3	0	4
Anderegg	4- 8	6- 8	5	2	14
Totals	33-91	19-34	66	16	85

Notre Dame	fg-fga	ft-fta	rb	pf	tp
McCarthy	5-13	11-12	6	3	21
Hawkins	6-14	7- 7	10	3	19
Morelli	0- 3	0- 0	2	0	0
Smyth	11-22	3- 3	14	4	25
Duffy	3- 4	0- 0	1	5	6
Devine	3-14	4- 5	5	2	10
Gleason	1- 3	0- 1	0	3	2
Sullivan	0- 0	0- 0	2	1	0
Totals	29-73	25-28	40	21	83

Half time: Michigan State 37-36. Officials: Fox and DiGravio. Attendance: 11,000.

Kansas	fg-fga	ft-fta	rb	pf	tp
Elstun	4-12	1- 2	8	1	9
Loneski	4- 8	0- 0	7	0	8
Chamberlain	14-26	8-13	22	4	36
King	1- 7	2- 4	4	2	4
Parker	4- 7	0- 0	1	2	8
Johnson	3- 3	0- 0	2	2	6
Billings	0- 3	2- 2	0	0	2
Totals	30-66	13-21	44	11	73

Southern Methodist	fg-fga	ft-fta	rb	pf	tp
Showalter	4- 9	0-1	5	4	8
Herrscher	3-14	6-6	14	3	12
Krebs	8-28	2-2	6	5	18
Mills	5-11	0-2	2	0	10
Duncan	1-10	4-4	0	1	6
McGregor	5- 9	1-2	7	0	11
Totals	26-81	13-17	33	13	65

Half time: Kansas 33-32. Regulation Score: 59-59.

St. Louis	fg-fga	ft-fta	rb	pf	tp
Alcorn	4-13	8- 9	6	4	16
Mimlitz	9-21	2- 3	10	3	20
Todd	6-14	2- 2	2	2	14
Serkin	3- 9	0- 1	11	5	6
Burnett	0- 4	2- 2	11	3	2
Ferry	3- 5	0- 0	3	0	6
Rogers	1- 2	0- 0	0	1	2
Smith	0- 0	0- 1	0	1	0
Flood	0- 1	0- 0	0	0	0
Totals	26-69	14-18	43	19	66

Oklahoma City	fg-fga	ft-fta	rb	pf	tp
Holloway	4-11	5- 5	14	1	13
Lee	7-19	10-14	12	1	24
Reed	12-26	1- 5	12	3	25
Bradshaw	0- 9	2- 3	5	3	2
Magana	4-13	2- 2	6	3	10
Griffin	0- 1	0- 0	0	0	0
Hill	0- 0	1- 4	1	0	1
Jetter	0- 0	0- 0	1	0	0
Totals	27-79	21-33	51	11	75

Half time: Oklahoma City 37-32.

San Francisco	fg-fga	ft-fta	rb	pf	tp
Preaseau	4- 8	4- 4	3	2	12
Farmer	5-13	1- 1	8	4	11
Day	4-13	5- 6	7	4	13
Brown	6-14	6- 8	8	3	18
Dunbar	2- 4	1- 3	5	0	5
Mallen	3- 6	0- 0	3	3	6
Lillevand	0- 3	0- 0	0	0	0
Russell	0- 1	0- 0	2	0	0
Koljian	0- 3	1- 3	2	1	1
Radanovich	0- 2	0- 0	2	0	0
Mancasola	0- 1	0- 0	1	1	0
King	0- 0	0- 0	0	0	0
Totals	24-68	18-25	41	18	66

Idaho State	fg-fga	ft-fta	rb	pf	tp
Easterbrooks	1-11	3- 6	2	2	5
Siemen	4- 8	2- 2	10	0	10
Allain	4-10	4- 8	15	5	12
Hicks	1- 7	4- 4	4	5	6
Wells	5-10	1- 2	3	3	11
Adlehardt	2- 2	1- 5	3	0	5
Detmer	0- 1	2- 4	1	1	2
Hoge	0- 1	0- 0	2	0	0
Manley	0- 0	0- 0	0	0	0
Cheney	0- 0	0- 0	0	0	0
Totals	17-50	17-31	40	16	51

Half time: San Francisco 36-15. Officials: Ogden and Pryor.

Brigham Young	fg-fga	ft-fta	rb	pf	tp
Benson	7-15	3- 4	6	1	17
Rowe	3- 7	2- 2	5	0	8
Thacker	2- 4	1- 2	7	4	5
Anderson	2- 7	1- 3	8	2	5
Steinke	6-17	2- 2	6	1	14
Gustin	1- 3	2- 2	3	1	4
Jones	2- 3	0- 0	3	1	4
Wilkes	0- 0	2- 2	0	0	2
Jensen	0- 0	0- 0	0	0	0
Peterson	0- 1	0- 0	0	1	0
Totals	23-57	13-17	38	11	59

California	fg-fga	ft-fta	rb	pf	tp
Friend	11-25	3- 6	7	1	25
McKeen	2- 6	1- 2	6	0	5
Hagler	3- 8	3- 4	5	3	9
Robinson	8-14	2- 2	4	2	18
Arrillaga	3- 6	0- 1	4	1	6
Diaz	0- 4	0- 0	0	1	0
Grout	3- 4	0- 0	3	0	6
McIntosh	2- 4	0- 0	5	0	4
Buch	5- 8	2- 3	3	1	12
Kapp	0- 0	0- 0	1	0	0
Sterling	0- 0	1- 2	0	0	1
Simpson	0- 2	0- 0	1	0	0
Totals	37-81	12-20	39	9	86

Half time: California 40-35. Officials: Williamson and Morrow. Attendance: 4,688.

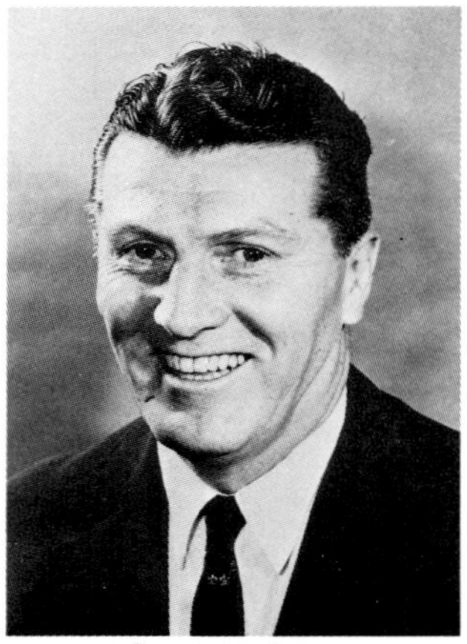

Frank McGuire

Third Place

Lafayette	fg-fga	ft-fta	rb	pf	tp
Galtere	4-13	3- 5	13	3	11
Sterlein	2- 2	4- 6	7	2	8
Mantz	8-15	6- 7	20	3	22
Murray	7-20	3- 3	3	2	17
Mack	3-10	9-14	6	4	15
Gustafson	0- 0	0- 0	1	1	0
Kohler	0- 0	0- 0	1	0	0
Jones	1- 4	1- 2	2	1	3
Totals	25-64	26-37	53	16	76

Canisius	fg-fga	ft-fta	rb	pf	tp
Nowak	1-10	13-16	8	1	15
Britz	11-23	3- 7	9	4	25
Leone	1- 8	2- 2	4	5	4
Coogan	7-12	0- 0	8	3	14
Markey	6-15	2- 2	10	4	14
Rojek	1- 2	0- 0	2	0	2
Mackinnon	3- 6	2- 2	2	1	8
Shea	0- 0	0- 0	2	2	0
Totals	30-76	22-29	45	20	82

Half time: Canisius 42-36. Officials: Pace and Filippi.

Notre Dame	fg-fga	ft-fta	rb	pf	tp
McCarthy	5-15	13-14	9	4	23
Hawkins	8-20	5- 9	14	1	21
Smyth	8-20	6- 8	23	3	22
Duffy	3- 4	2- 6	3	3	8
Devine	3-15	6- 6	1	4	12
Totals	27-74	32-43	50	15	86

Pittsburgh	fg-fga	ft-fta	rb	pf	tp
Pegues	4-12	5- 7	7	5	13
Riser	14-22	6- 9	10	4	34
Laneve	0- 0	0- 0	0	1	0
Dorman	0- 0	0- 0	0	0	0
Brautigam	2-10	1- 2	5	4	5
Hursh	4- 4	1- 3	9	4	9
Hennon	7-16	6- 6	5	4	20
Markovich	2- 3	0- 0	2	2	4
Totals	33-67	19-27	38	24	85

Half time: Notre Dame 38-36. Officials: Fox and DiGravio. Attendance: 12,300.

St. Louis	fg-fga	ft-fta	rb	pf	tp
Alcorn	10-19	0- 0	6	5	20
Mimlitz	6-17	5- 6	3	2	17
Todd	6-14	2- 3	4	1	14
Serkin	1- 5	1- 3	6	4	3
Burnett	0- 3	2- 2	7	0	2
Ferry	3-11	0- 1	3	4	6
Rogers	1- 4	0- 0	0	1	2
Smith	0- 1	0- 1	4	3	0
Flood	0- 3	0- 0	2	0	0
Hake	0- 0	0- 1	1	0	0
Redshaw	1- 1	0- 0	1	0	2
McCartney	1- 1	0- 0	0	0	2
Totals	29-79	10-17	37	20	68

Southern Methodist	fg-fga	ft-fta	rb	pf	tp
Showalter	1- 7	0- 1	6	0	2
Herrscher	4-10	6- 6	7	5	14
Krebs	9-24	15-18	9	3	33
Mills	6-15	3- 5	5	1	15
Duncan	4- 7	0- 0	4	0	8
McGregor	3- 7	0- 3	10	1	6
Eldridge	0- 1	0- 0	0	0	0
Brown	0- 0	0- 0	0	0	0
O'Kelley	0- 0	0- 0	2	0	0
Minton	0- 0	0- 0	0	1	0
Buddendorf	0- 0	0- 0	0	0	0
Knapo	0- 0	0- 0	0	0	0
Totals	27-71	24-33	43	11	78

Half time: Southern Methodist 36-28. Officials: Batmale and Mercer.

Idaho State	fg-fga	ft-fta	rb	pf	tp
Easterbrooks	2-10	4- 6	3	4	8
Adlehardt	0- 1	0- 0	4	0	0
Allain	4-10	2- 3	10	3	10
Hicks	6-20	0- 2	10	2	12
Wells	1- 7	16-19	2	3	18
Cheney	0- 2	0- 0	4	1	0
Detmer	1- 3	2- 2	0	1	4
Manley	0- 0	0- 0	0	2	0
Hoge	1- 4	0- 0	1	0	2
Totals	15-57	24-32	34	16	54

Brigham Young

	fg-fga	ft-fta	rb	pf	tp
Benson	6-12	10-12	3	4	22
Rowe	1-6	0-0	11	0	2
Thacker	3-8	2-2	11	2	8
Steinke	2-13	0-1	4	5	4
Anderson	9-16	9-13	6	3	27
Jensen	0-1	0-0	2	2	0
Miles	0-2	2-2	1	0	2
Gustin	0-1	0-0	0	0	0
Gravens	0-0	0-0	2	0	0
Wilkes	0-0	0-0	1	1	0
Totals	21-59	23-30	37	17	65

Half time: Brigham Young 34-23. Officials: Morrow and Williamson.

Regional Championships

Syracuse

	fg-fga	ft-fta	rb	pf	tp
Clark	5-13	1-2	12	5	11
Snyder	5-19	0-2	12	4	10
Cincebox	0-5	2-6	15	5	2
Breland	0-6	0-2	2	5	0
Cohen	9-23	7-11	13	3	25
Albanese	1-2	0-0	0	0	2
Loudis	3-6	0-0	2	3	6
Youmans	0-0	0-0	1	0	0
Schmelzer	1-1	0-0	0	2	2
Totals	24-75	10-23	57	27	58

North Carolina

	fg-fga	ft-fta	rb	pf	tp
Rosenbluth	8-18	7-11	9	2	23
Brennan	3-9	7-9	15	4	13
Lotz	0-2	1-2	6	0	1
Kearns	4-11	14-19	4	3	22
Cunningham	1-4	0-0	5	3	2
Quigg	1-3	4-4	8	4	6
Totals	17-47	33-45	47	16	67

Half time: North Carolina 37-28. Officials: Conway and McPherson.

Michigan State

	fg-fga	ft-fta	rb	pf	tp
Ferguson	5-15	5-6	12	3	15
Hedden	4-16	2-6	7	2	10
Anderegg	1-4	0-0	1	2	2
Markovich	0-0	0-0	1	1	0
Green	5-11	4-6	18	5	14
Bencie	2-5	1-2	5	1	5
Quiggle	9-22	4-4	4	4	22
Wilson	3-10	0-0	3	0	6
Lux	0-1	0-0	0	0	0
Scott	1-3	4-5	0	0	6
Totals	30-87	20-29	51	18	80

Kentucky

	fg-fga	ft-fta	rb	pf	tp
Cox	3-12	11-12	4	5	17
Crigler	5-11	0-1	9	2	10
Mills	0-2	2-4	4	2	2
Collinsworth	0-0	0-0	0	0	0
Beck	2-10	0-2	16	2	4
Calvert	8-18	2-3	6	4	18
Hatton	6-13	3-5	7	1	15
A. Smith	0-1	2-3	1	0	2
Brewer	0-1	0-0	0	0	0
Adkins	0-0	0-0	0	2	0
Totals	24-68	20-30	47	18	68

Half time: Kentucky 47-35. Officials: Anderson and Mihalik.

Oklahoma City

	fg-fga	ft-fta	rb	pf	tp
Holloway	1-7	0-0	10	5	2
Lee	5-12	9-12	4	4	19
Reed	12-34	2-3	13	3	26
Bradshaw	0-5	0-0	3	3	0
Magana	1-10	0-0	5	3	2
Griffin	3-8	0-0	1	1	6
Hill	0-1	0-1	2	0	0
Gardner	0-4	0-2	3	1	0
Kelley	0-0	0-0	0	0	0
Wallace	0-1	0-0	0	1	0
Hanson	3-4	0-0	2	4	6
Totals	25-86	11-18	43	25	61

Kansas

	fg-fga	ft-fta	rb	pf	tp
Elstun	2-7	2-3	10	0	6
Loneski	3-8	8-9	4	0	14
Chamberlain	8-17	14-22	15	2	30
King	5-12	3-4	3	3	13
Parker	4-4	2-2	4	0	10
L. Johnson	1-5	0-0	9	1	2
Billings	0-0	0-0	0	0	0
Hollinger	0-3	0-0	1	1	0
Dater	2-3	0-0	2	2	4
M. Johnson	0-0	0-0	0	0	0
Green	0-0	0-0	2	1	0
Kindred	0-3	2-2	1	0	2
Totals	25-62	31-42	51	10	81

Half time: Kansas 27-24. Officials: Haggert and Lightner.

San Francisco

	fg-fga	ft-fta	rb	pf	tp
Preaseau	0-7	5-6	6	2	5
Farmer	4-12	3-4	8	3	11
Day	4-9	1-5	9	4	9
Brown	8-16	4-5	4	3	20
Dunbar	0-3	5-8	3	1	5
Mallen	0-0	0-0	0	0	0
Totals	16-47	18-28	30	13	50

California

	fg-fga	ft-fta	rb	pf	tp
Friend	5-13	2-3	6	1	12
McKeen	3-5	0-1	6	4	6
Hagler	0-1	0-2	2	1	0
Robinson	6-13	4-4	6	3	16
Arrillaga	0-2	0-0	1	1	0
McIntosh	1-3	2-2	2	2	4
Diaz	0-1	4-5	2	3	4
Grout	1-3	0-1	2	0	2
Buch	0-2	2-2	1	1	2
Kapp	0-0	0-0	0	1	0
Totals	16-43	14-20	28	17	46

Half time: San Francisco 27-22. Officials: Pryor and Ogden. Attendance: 6,070.

Wilt Chamberlain

Semifinals

North Carolina

	fg-fga	ft-fta	rb	pf	tp
Rosenbluth	11-42	7-9	3	1	29
Cunningham	9-18	3-5	12	5	21
Brennan	6-16	2-4	17	5	14
Kearns	1-8	4-5	6	4	6
Quigg	0-1	2-3	4	5	2
Lotz	0-1	0-0	4	1	0
Young	1-3	0-1	2	1	2
Searcy	0-0	0-0	1	0	0
Team			5		
Totals	28-89	18-27	54	22	74

Michigan State

	fg-fga	ft-fta	rb	pf	tp
Quiggle	6-21	8-10	10	1	20
Green	4-12	3-6	19	2	11
Ferguson	4-8	2-3	1	5	10
Hedden	4-20	6-7	15	5	14
Wilson	0-3	2-2	5	1	2
Anderegg	2-7	3-6	3	2	7
Bencie	1-6	0-0	2	1	2
Scott	2-3	0-2	3	1	4
Team			7		
Totals	23-80	24-36	65	18	70

Half time: 29-29. Regulation Score: 58-58. First Overtime: 64-64. Second Overtime: 66-66. Officials: Ogden and Lightner.

Kansas

	fg-fga	ft-fta	rb	pf	tp
M. King	6-8	1-1	4	1	13
Elston	8-12	0-0	6	3	16
Chamberlain	12-22	8-11	11	0	32
Parker	1-1	0-0	3	0	2
Loneski	2-6	3-4	7	3	7
L. Johnson	1-3	0-0	8	0	2
Billings	0-1	0-0	0	0	0
Hollinger	1-1	0-1	0	0	2
Dater	1-1	0-0	2	2	2
Green	1-1	0-0	2	1	2
Kindred	0-0	0-2	2	0	0
M. Johnson	1-1	0-0	0	0	2
Team			1		
Totals	34-57	12-19	44	10	80

San Francisco

	fg-fga	ft-fta	rb	pf	tp
Day	3-14	3-8	7	2	9
Dunbar	2-8	0-0	4	1	4
Brown	5-14	0-0	2	2	10
Farmer	6-15	2-2	4	2	14
Preaseau	5-8	2-2	2	2	12
Mallen	0-2	0-0	1	1	0
Lillevand	1-3	0-0	0	1	2
Koljian	0-1	3-4	0	0	3
J. King	0-3	0-0	0	1	0
Russell	0-0	0-0	1	0	0
Radanovich	0-1	0-0	0	1	0
Mancasola	1-2	0-0	0	1	2
Team			4		
Totals	23-71	10-16	25	10	56

Half time: Kansas 38-34. Officials: Conway and Anderson.

National Third Place

Michigan State

	fg-fga	ft-fta	rb	pf	tp
Green	4-9	1-1	13	5	9
Ferguson	4-11	6-9	11	2	14
Hadden	4-10	1-2	5	5	9
Wilson	3-6	0-1	0	1	6
Lux	2-2	1-1	3	2	5
Anderegg	2-8	3-4	4	5	7
Scott	2-6	0-1	3	1	4
Bencie	0-5	0-0	4	1	0
Quiggle	2-6	2-2	4	1	6
Team			13		
Totals	23-63	14-21	60	23	60

San Francisco

	fg-fga	ft-fta	rb	pf	tp
Day	6-14	0-3	6	3	12
Dunbar	4-9	1-4	3	4	9
Brown	8-18	6-11	7	3	22
Farmer	4-12	8-9	2	1	16
Preaseau	2-6	4-4	6	4	8
J. King	0-2	0-0	0	0	0
Mallen	0-0	0-0	1	0	0
Lillevand	0-1	0-0	1	0	0
Team			9		
Totals	24-62	19-31	35	17	67

Half time: San Francisco 33-30. Officials: Ogden and Lightner.

Championship

North Carolina

	fg-fga	ft-fta	rb	pf	tp
Rosenbluth	8-15	4-4	5	5	20
Cunningham	0-3	0-1	5	4	0
Brennan	4-8	3-7	11	3	11
Kearns	4-8	3-7	4	1	11
Quigg	4-10	2-3	9	4	10
Lotz	0-0	0-0	2	0	0
Young	1-1	0-0	3	1	2
Team			6		
Totals	21-45	12-22	42	21	54

Kansas

	fg-fga	ft-fta	rb	pf	tp
Chamberlain	6-13	11-16	14	3	23
King	3-12	5-6	4	4	11
Elstun	4-12	3-6	4	2	11
Parker	2-4	0-0	0	4	4
Loneski	0-5	2-3	3	2	2
L. Johnson	0-1	2-2	0	1	2
Billings	0-0	0-0	0	0	0
Team			3		
Totals	15-47	23-33	28	14	53

Half time: North Carolina 29-22. Regulation Score: 46-46. First Overtime: 48-48; Second Overtime: 48-48. Officials: Conway and Anderson.

1958

First Round

Manhattan

	fg-fga	ft-fta	rb	pf	tp
Mealy	5-9	4-4	5	5	14
Wilbur	3-11	10-12	11	5	16
Brunone	2-2	2-5	2	5	6
McGorty	1-4	2-4	5	3	4
Powers	9-19	11-15	15	2	29
Burkoski	5-8	0-0	2	5	10
Koenig	1-2	4-7	2	3	6
Dougherty	1-2	0-0	1	1	2
Quarto	0-0	2-2	1	1	2
Schoenberger	0-0	0-0	0	0	0
Team			11		
Totals	27-57	35-49	54	29	89

West Virginia

	fg-fga	ft-fta	rb	pf	tp
West	5-12	0-1	4	5	10
Akers	2-3	4-4	4	5	8
Sharrar	2-11	10-16	9	5	14
Smith	7-14	4-5	7	4	18
Gardner	5-15	5-7	4	5	15
Retton	3-8	1-1	3	2	7
Clousson	0-0	3-7	2	3	3
Bolyard	4-7	1-1	3	3	9
Schertzinger	0-0	0-0	0	0	0
Team			10		
Totals	28-70	28-42	46	32	84

Half time: Manhattan 56-49. Officials: Nucatola and Bello.

Dartmouth

	fg-fga	ft-fta	rb	pf	tp
Carruthers	2-5	1-1	5	0	5
Larusso	10-13	4-5	10	3	24
Aley	4-9	2-2	4	4	10
Kaufman	10-20	4-10	4	2	24
Sosnowski	2-6	1-1	4	1	5
Farnsworth	0-1	0-0	2	0	0
Gavitt	1-8	0-0	4	0	2
Hanson	1-1	0-0	1	2	2
Douglas	0-0	0-1	1	1	0
Vendeweghe	1-3	1-2	5	3	3
Hobbie	0-1	0-0	0	0	0
Jones	0-0	0-0	0	0	0
Team			12		
Totals	31-67	13-22	52	16	75

Connecticut

	fg-fga	ft-fta	rb	pf	tp
Pipczynski	0-3	2-2	5	1	2
Kaspar	8-19	1-1	10	4	17
Cooper	1-7	3-3	6	2	5
Rose	7-18	3-3	4	2	17
O'Connor	4-9	1-3	1	3	9
Martin	1-2	0-0	2	3	2
Davis	2-4	1-2	7	1	5
Brown	0-2	1-2	0	0	1
Schmidt	0-3	2-4	0	0	2
Cross	1-1	2-2	0	0	4
Risley	0-2	0-0	1	0	0
Team			8		
Totals	24-70	16-22	44	16	64

Half time: Dartmouth 39-35. Officials: Nucatola and Bello.

Maryland

	fg	ft	tp
McNeil	2	2	6
Halleck	1	3	5
Nacincik	4	6	14
Bunge	4	3	11
Weingarten	0	2	2
Davis	11	2	24
Bechtle	1	2	4
Krukar	0	0	0
Young	3	6	12
Murphy	1	0	2
Danko	3	0	6
Totals	30	26	86

Boston College

	fg	ft	tp
Giersch	2	4	8
Harrington	0	7	7
Von Burg	0	3	3
McGrath	2	7	11
Manning	0	0	0
Magee	3	7	13
Schoppmeyer	0	0	0
Power	4	1	9
Lyons	3	0	6
Latkany	2	0	4
Bigelow	1	0	2
Totals	17	29	63

271

1958 KENTUCKY WILDCATS—(l-r) Front Row: Adolph Rupp, Adrian Smith, John Crigler, Ed Beck, Don Mills, Johnny Cox, Vernon Hatton, Harry Lancaster; Back Row: Jay Atkerson, Earl Adkins, Dick Howe, Phil Johnson, Bill Cassady, Lincoln Collinsworth, Harold Ross.

272

Pittsburgh	fg-fga	ft-fta	rb	pf	tp
Pegues	13-24	5- 9	5	5	31
Mills	0- 0	0- 1	1	5	0
Hennon	12-33	4- 5	7	4	28
Hursh	2- 4	4- 5	9	4	8
Dorman	2- 3	3- 3	7	4	7
Simpson	0- 2	0- 0	2	1	0
Maurd	0- 0	0- 0	1	0	0
Sawyer	1- 4	1- 3	13	3	3
Team			4		
Totals	30-70	17-26	48	27	77

Miami, Ohio	fg-fga	ft-fta	rb	pf	tp
Brown	7-11	3- 4	11	4	17
Thomas	3-10	4- 5	3	4	10
Embry	9-17	3-10	20	1	21
Hamilton	3-10	3- 7	2	3	9
Powell	5-19	5- 7	3	4	15
Wingard	2- 7	1- 2	7	0	5
Crist	1- 1	3- 4	1	0	5
Rowan	0- 0	0- 0	1	1	0
Team			8		
Totals	30-75	22-39	56	17	82

Half time: Pittsburgh 36-32. Officials: Elser and Betz. Attendance: 5,600.

Notre Dame	fg-fga	ft-fta	rb	pf	tp
Hawkins	12-22	6- 7	14	2	30
McCarthy	6-16	8- 8	21	1	20
Graney	4- 9	4- 5	11	5	12
Devine	5-16	1- 3	9	2	11
Duffy	3-10	1- 1	6	2	7
Reinhart	2- 8	2- 4	9	1	6
Gleason	1- 1	0- 0	1	1	2
Williams	1- 8	0- 0	8	2	2
Ireland	1- 3	0- 0	3	0	2
Bradtke	0- 2	2- 3	1	1	2
Team			3		
Totals	35-95	24-31	86	17	94

Tennessee Tech	fg-fga	ft-fta	rb	pf	tp
McDonald	5-17	1- 2	9	4	11
Puckette	0- 0	1- 3	3	5	1
Hagan	3-18	3- 5	9	5	9
Keller	3- 9	0- 0	1	1	6
Phelps	6-19	4- 4	10	4	16
Shearer	4- 6	3- 6	2	1	11
Gilley	0- 5	1- 2	0	1	1
Herron	2- 5	2- 3	2	1	6
Bruke	0- 0	0- 0	0	1	0
Vaughn	0- 5	0- 0	3	0	0
Team			5		
Totals	23-84	15-25	44	23	61

Half time: Notre Dame 40-28. Officials: Neff and Strauthers. Attendance: 6,500.

Oklahoma State	fg-fga	ft-fta	rb	pf	tp
Sutton	3- 6	1- 1	6	1	7
Crutchfield	2- 6	1- 1	5	3	5
Clark	7-12	12-12	14	3	26
Carberry	0- 5	5- 5	1	4	5
Adair	6-12	3- 4	1	2	15
Hale	0- 2	1- 1	3	2	1
Heffington	0- 2	0- 0	1	1	0
Fleming	0- 0	0- 0	1	0	0
Team			1		
Totals	18-45	23-24	31	17	59

Loyola, La.	fg-fga	ft-fta	rb	pf	tp
Gaudin	5-15	2- 3	8	3	12
Hall	1- 7	0- 1	9	4	2
Doll	3- 7	3- 4	9	5	9
McLaughlin	2- 4	4-10	4	2	8
Vogt	5-11	1- 2	4	2	11
Henneberger	0- 1	0- 0	0	0	0
Morris	0- 0	0- 0	0	1	0
Team			1		
Totals	16-45	10-20	35	17	42

Half time: Oklahoma State 27-20. Officials: Hays and Hamilton. Attendance: 5,000.

Idaho State	fg	ft-fta	pf	tp
Christian	2	2- 4	4	6
Sieman	7	4- 4	5	18
Bacher	8	5-10	4	21
Rodgers	5	1- 3	0	11
Germaine	5	6- 6	2	16
Morris	0	0- 0	0	0
Adelhardt	0	0- 0	0	0
Totals	27	18-27	15	72

Arizona State	fg	ft-fta	pf	tp
Burau	2	0- 3	2	4
Nealey	6	3- 6	2	15
Westbrooks	3	1- 1	4	7
Newman	8	3- 3	4	19
Youree	7	5- 6	4	19
Bowen	0	0- 0	0	0
Olsen	2	0- 0	3	4
Daugherty	0	0- 0	0	0
Totals	28	12-19	19	68

Adolph Rupp

Seattle	fg	ft-fta	pf	tp
Ogorek	5	8- 8	1	18
Frizzell	5	2- 2	1	12
Baylor	10	6- 7	2	26
Saunders	1	0- 1	1	2
Brown	5	1- 1	1	11
Plasecki	1	0- 1	2	2
Kootnekoff	2	0- 0	1	4
Humphries	4	1- 4	2	9
Petrie	2	0- 3	1	4
Totals	35	18-27	12	88

Wyoming	fg	ft-fta	pf	tp
Bertolero	10	2- 2	4	22
Carlson	0	1- 1	3	1
Hatten	5	2- 4	5	12
Eckhardt	2	0- 0	2	4
Windis	3	1- 1	1	7
Bora	0	1- 1	0	1
Campbell	1	0- 1	0	2
Gardner	0	0- 1	3	0
Whitefoot	0	2- 2	1	2
Totals	21	9-13	19	51

Half time: Seattle 51-25.

Second Round

Dartmouth	fg-fga	ft-fta	rb	pf	tp
Hobbie	0- 0	0- 0	0	0	0
Farnsworth	3- 5	0- 1	8	2	6
Vandeweghe	1- 5	2- 2	2	2	4
Carruthers	6-12	0- 0	7	2	12
Jones	0- 0	0- 0	0	0	0
Kaufman	8-20	6- 6	2	1	22
Hanson	0- 2	2- 2	1	1	2
Gavitt	0- 1	1- 2	5	1	1
Sosnowski	6-14	1- 5	7	2	13
Aley	2- 8	0- 0	3	3	4
Douglas	0- 0	2- 2	0	0	2
LaRusso	4-15	5- 6	15	4	13
Team			9		
Totals	30-82	19-26	59	18	79

Manhattan	fg-fga	ft-fta	rb	pf	tp
Quarto	1- 1	0- 0	1	1	2
Wilbur	2- 8	2- 3	8	3	6
Koenig	3- 4	0- 1	1	3	6
Schoenberger	0- 1	0- 0	0	0	0
Powers	4-13	4- 7	6	3	12
McGorty	6-16	0- 3	6	3	12
Burkoski	3- 7	3- 3	1	9	9
Mealy	3-15	1- 5	21	4	7
Brunone	3- 8	2- 3	8	2	8
Dougherty	0- 3	0- 0	1	1	0
Team			9		
Totals	25-76	12-25	60	19	62

Half time: Dartmouth 38-27.

Maryland	fg-fga	ft-fta	rb	pf	tp
Murphy	0- 2	0- 0	0	2	0
Danko	2- 3	5- 6	2	2	9
Young	1- 5	3- 6	5	2	5
Davis	8-15	2- 2	2	1	18
Nacincik	1- 4	1- 1	2	3	3
Halleck	0- 1	0- 0	4	2	0
McNeil	8-19	8- 9	13	2	24
Bunge	2- 8	1- 2	6	3	5
Team			3		
Totals	22-57	23-28	37	17	67

Temple	fg-fga	ft-fta	rb	pf	tp
Kennedy	8-11	2- 5	3	3	18
Rodgers	7-25	2-11	6	3	16
Van Patton	3-10	0- 3	11	4	6
Brodsky	4- 8	1- 1	5	3	9
Norman	6-12	2- 4	14	3	14
Fleming	4- 7	0- 0	4	2	8
Team			1		
Totals	32-73	7-21	46	18	71

Half time: Temple 39-32.

Notre Dame	fg-fga	ft-fta	rb	pf	tp
McCarthy	12-26	5- 6	11	1	29
Hawkins	10-24	11-14	11	3	31
Graney	1- 9	0- 1	10	8	2
Duffy	2- 4	5- 6	2	4	9
Devine	4- 9	6- 7	4	0	14
Ireland	0- 2	1- 1	6	3	1
Reinhart	3- 4	2- 2	6	2	8
Williams	0- 0	0- 0	0	0	0
Totals	32-78	30-37	50	21	94

Indiana	fg-fga	ft-fta	rb	pf	tp
Obremskey	7-15	4- 6	7	4	16
Thompson	4- 7	1- 1	3	4	9
Dees	9-27	10-11	16	2	29
Gee	2- 5	0- 0	2	3	4
Wilkinson	7-14	0- 2	3	5	17
Schlegemilch	1- 1	1- 2	0	1	2
Hinds	3- 4	0- 0	5	3	8
Radovich	1- 7	0- 1	6	4	2
Totals	34-80	18-28	42	26	87

Half time: Notre Dame 48-37. Officials: Meyer and Lannon.

Kentucky	fg-fga	ft-fta	rb	pf	tp
Cox	9-25	5- 5	15	0	23
Crigler	4-10	0- 0	10	4	8
Beck	2- 7	2- 2	8	5	6
A. Smith	6-16	6- 8	3	1	18
Hatton	5-16	4- 5	4	3	14
B. Smith	0- 0	0- 0	4	0	0
Collinsworth	2- 4	4- 4	5	0	8
Cassady	1- 1	0- 0	1	0	2
Johnson	1- 4	0- 0	3	2	2
Howe	0- 0	0- 0	0	0	0
Adkins	1- 2	0- 0	0	0	2
Mills	4-14	3- 5	12	4	11
Totals	35-99	24-29	61	19	94

Miami, Ohio	fg-fga	ft-fta	rb	pf	tp
Brown	3- 9	1- 1	9	4	7
Thomas	5-17	1- 1	8	2	11
Embry	8-22	10-13	15	4	26
Powell	5-16	2- 3	11	3	12
Hamilton	3- 7	2- 4	1	2	8
Wingard	0- 2	2- 2	6	2	2
Babbs	0- 0	0- 0	0	0	0
Rowan	0- 1	0- 0	1	0	0
Higgins	2- 3	0- 0	0	2	4
Miller	0- 0	0- 0	1	0	0
Crist	0- 1	0- 1	0	0	0
Totals	26-78	18-25	51	20	70

Half time: Kentucky 50-35. Officials: Mihalik and Mills. Attendance: 11,600.

Oklahoma State	fg-fga	ft-fta	rb	pf	tp
Crutchfield	0- 2	1- 1	1	1	1
Sutton	3- 5	2- 2	5	1	8
Clark	4- 7	12-15	13	2	20
Adair	5-11	1- 1	5	1	11
Carberry	3- 8	5- 7	8	3	11
Hale	3- 8	4- 4	4	3	10
Soergel	0- 0	0- 0	0	0	0
Heffington	1- 1	0- 0	0	0	2
Wade	0- 0	0- 0	0	0	0
Deutschendorf	1- 2	0- 0	0	0	2
Fleming	0- 1	0- 0	0	0	0
Walker	0- 0	0- 0	0	0	0
Totals	20-45	25-30	36	12	65

Arkansas	fg-fga	ft-fta	rb	pf	tp
Thompson	3- 9	1- 1	6	1	7
Dunn	3- 9	2- 3	4	4	8
Carpenter	2- 2	0- 1	2	5	4
Grim	5-16	3- 5	5	2	13
Grisham	3-13	0- 1	7	4	6
Rankin	0- 5	0- 0	2	2	0
Hankins	0- 1	0- 0	1	0	0
Rittman	0- 2	0- 0	0	1	0
Stolzer	1- 2	0- 2	2	1	2
Boss	0- 1	0- 0	0	0	0
Team			3		
Totals	17-60	6-13	32	20	40

Half time: Oklahoma State 37-23. Officials: Mercer and Milner.

Kansas State	fg-fga	ft-fta	rb	pf	tp
Abbott	0- 1	0- 0	2	3	0
Boozer	9-25	6-11	14	4	24
Parr	7-22	3- 4	12	4	17
DeWitz	4-10	7-10	9	1	15
Matuszak	2- 6	5- 7	4	5	9
Frank	5-10	2- 2	5	5	12
Fischer	1- 1	3- 4	2	5	5
Holwerda	0- 2	1- 2	0	0	1
Team			4		
Totals	28-77	27-40	52	24	83

GAME-BY-GAME RESULTS

Cincinnati	fg-fga	ft-fta	rb	pf	tp
Stevens	4-15	5-7	6	5	13
Robertson	12-20	6-8	14	5	30
Dierking	4-17	10-13	5	5	18
Davis	4-12	2-4	2	3	10
Mendenhall	3-10	3-3	3	2	9
Hornsby	0-0	0-0	0	0	0
Dykes	0-2	0-2	1	4	0
Whitaker	0-0	0-0	0	1	0
Willey	0-0	0-1	2	0	0
Nall	0-0	0-0	0	1	0
Team			4		
Totals	27-76	26-38	37	26	80

Half time: Cincinnati 40-39. Regulation Score: 74-74. Officials: Botmale and Kobe.

California	fg-fga	ft-fta	rb	pf	tp
Dalton	4-7	2-4	8	0	10
Sterling	2-7	2-3	6	1	6
McIntosh	4-11	2-2	14	3	10
Buch	2-11	1-3	0	0	5
Robinson	5-11	3-5	9	2	13
Fitzpatrick	1-3	1-1	1	2	3
Greut	0-1	0-0	1	0	0
Imhoff	1-2	1-1	2	2	3
Kapp	0-0	0-1	0	0	0
Schneider	1-1	2-2	0	0	4
Team			2		
Totals	20-54	14-22	43	10	54

Idaho State	fg-fga	ft-fta	rb	pf	tp
Christian	0-2	2-2	7	4	2
Siemen	7-14	0-0	9	2	14
Bacher	5-13	1-5	10	4	11
Germaine	3-5	4-6	2	4	10
Rodgers	1-16	0-0	7	2	2
Morris	1-2	0-0	0	2	0
Adelhardt	0-1	0-0	0	1	0
Griffin	1-2	0-0	0	0	2
Kugler	0-0	0-0	0	0	0
Team			5		
Totals	18-55	7-13	40	19	43

Half time: California 24-20. Officials: Lichty and Glennon. Attendance: 16,034.

Seattle	fg-fga	ft-fta	rb	pf	tp
Frizzell	4-8	0-0	7	2	8
Ogorek	2-10	3-6	8	4	7
Baylor	11-20	13-14	14	3	35
Brown	5-9	3-7	7	3	13
Piasecki	2-2	0-0	5	0	4
Harvey	1-3	0-0	2	0	2
Team			2		
Totals	25-52	19-27	45	12	69

San Francisco	fg-fga	ft-fta	rb	pf	tp
Farmer	5-14	0-1	7	5	10
LaCour	8-16	4-4	4	4	20
Day	4-14	5-6	10	1	13
Brown	7-18	5-6	10	5	19
Dunbar	1-7	0-0	2	1	2
Lillevand	1-2	1-1	1	0	3
Cunningham	0-1	0-1	1	1	0
Russell	0-2	0-0	0	1	0
Team			4		
Totals	26-74	15-19	39	18	67

Half time: San Francisco 33-31. Officials: McAlister and Morrow. Attendance: 16,034.

Third Place

Manhattan	fg-fga	ft-fta	rb	pf	tp
Quarto	1-1	0-0	0	2	2
Wilbur	3-5	2-2	2	5	8
Koenig	0-2	2-2	0	1	2
Powers	4-15	4-4	7	3	12
McGorty	5-11	0-0	6	5	10
Burkoski	0-3	0-2	2	2	0
Mealy	3-12	3-3	10	3	9
Brunone	3-6	6-8	5	1	12
Team			8		
Totals	19-55	17-21	40	22	55

Maryland	fg-fga	ft-fta	rb	pf	tp
Danko	0-1	2-2	1	2	2
Young	5-13	8-10	7	3	18
Davis	5-17	3-3	2	2	13
Nacincik	1-6	4-5	9	4	6
Bechtle	0-1	0-0	1	0	0
Halleck	1-3	4-4	4	1	6
Moore	0-2	0-0	2	0	0
McNeil	2-10	4-4	3	1	8
Bunge	2-6	2-3	7	3	6
Team			1		
Totals	16-59	27-31	37	16	59

Half time: Manhattan: 32-28.

Miami, Ohio	fg-fga	ft-fta	rb	pf	tp
Brown	2-10	1-1	16	2	5
Thomas	5-9	3-4	5	3	13
Embry	15-28	6-10	16	4	36
Hamilton	3-10	3-5	1	3	9
Powell	10-25	5-6	8	2	25
Wingard	0-3	0-1	8	1	0
Crist	1-2	0-0	3	0	2
Higgins	0-1	0-0	0	0	0
Miller	0-0	1-2	0	0	1
Totals	36-88	19-29	57	15	91

Indiana	fg-fga	ft-fta	rb	pf	tp
Obremskey	10-22	0-1	15	4	20
Thompson	6-19	3-4	15	3	15
Dees	8-15	9-9	14	3	25
Gee	2-10	2-3	2	4	6
Wilkinson	8-20	2-6	8	4	18
Hinds	0-6	0-0	3	0	0
Radovich	4-8	0-0	4	3	8
Schlegelmilch	3-5	0-0	3	2	6
Ball	0-1	0-0	1	0	0
Totals	41-106	16-23	65	23	98

Half time: Indiana 56-45. Officials: Meyer and Lennon. Attendance: 11,500.

Cincinnati	fg-fga	ft-fta	rb	pf	tp
Stevens	0-0	1-1	4	2	1
Robertson	21-36	14-16	7	3	56
Dierking	5-11	1-4	16	1	11
Mendenhall	3-6	10-10	1	2	16
Davis	3-9	1-1	2	5	7
Dykes	1-4	0-0	3	2	2
Willey	1-2	0-0	2	2	2
Whitaker	0-1	0-0	3	1	0
Nall	1-3	0-1	1	2	2
Apke	0-0	0-0	2	0	0
Team			9		
Totals	35-72	27-33	50	20	97

Arkansas	fg-fga	ft-fta	rb	pf	tp
Dunn	1-9	1-2	9	2	3
Thompson	6-13	0-1	2	3	12
Carpenter	3-11	3-4	9	4	9
Grisham	0-6	1-1	4	3	1
Grim	3-19	10-10	3	2	16
Rankin	3-10	0-0	1	1	6
Rittman	0-3	0-0	1	2	0
Stolzer	3-10	3-8	2	2	9
Hankins	3-6	0-1	3	5	6
Team			9		
Totals	22-87	18-27	43	24	62

Half time: Cincinnati 51-29.

Idaho State	fg-fga	ft-fta	rb	pf	tp
Christian	0-0	0-1	2	5	0
Sieman	7-14	3-3	9	2	17
Bacher	4-10	4-5	9	2	12
Germaine	3-4	3-3	1	3	9
Rodgers	3-12	1-1	3	4	7
Griffin	0-0	3-3	0	4	3
Morris	1-2	1-1	1	0	3
Adelhart	0-0	0-0	0	1	0
Team			4		
Totals	18-42	15-17	29	17	51

San Francisco	fg-fga	ft-fta	rb	pf	tp
Mallen	4-7	2-3	3	1	10
Russell	2-8	0-2	7	0	4
Farmer	4-11	7-8	5	3	15
Dunbar	0-3	0-0	4	3	0
Brown	3-8	4-5	5	0	10
Cunningham	3-4	2-2	1	0	8
LaCour	1-5	1-1	0	2	3
Day	2-2	0-0	1	2	4
Lillevand	0-2	1-2	2	0	1
Connolly	0-0	0-0	1	2	0
Robinson	0-0	0-0	1	0	0
Radanovich	1-1	0-0	1	1	2
Team			3		
Totals	20-51	17-23	34	14	57

Half time: San Francisco 26-21. Officials: Glennon and McAlister. Attendance: 16,034.

Regional Championships

Dartmouth	fg-fga	ft-fta	rb	pf	tp
Hobbie	0-0	0-0	0	0	0
Farnsworth	1-7	0-3	10	0	2
Vandeweghe	4-12	2-7	6	3	10
Carrathers	0-3	1-2	1	2	1
Jones	0-1	0-1	1	0	0
Kaufman	2-14	5-6	5	3	9
Hanson	0-0	0-0	0	0	0
Gavitt	2-6	0-0	2	1	4
Sosnowski	1-10	1-1	3	0	3
Aley	1-2	0-0	2	2	2
Douglas	0-0	0-0	1	0	0
LaRusso	7-22	5-7	21	5	19
Team			9		
Totals	18-77	14-27	61	16	50

Temple	fg-fga	ft-fta	rb	pf	tp
Kennedy	6-10	1-1	3	3	13
Rodgers	8-20	1-6	9	2	17
Van Patton	0-1	2-3	9	4	2
Peepe	0-0	0-0	0	1	0
Brodsky	6-12	4-4	8	4	16
Goss	0-0	0-0	0	0	0
Norman	6-14	2-6	9	3	14
Fleming	3-6	1-1	4	2	7
Franklin	0-0	0-0	0	0	0
Goldenberg	0-0	0-0	0	0	0
Team			0		
Totals	29-63	11-21	42	19	69

Half time: Temple 32-22.

Notre Dame	fg-fga	ft-fta	rb	pf	tp
McCarthy	7-18	3-3	8	2	17
Hawkins	7-24	1-4	16	4	15
Graney	1-6	2-3	5	4	4
Duffy	0-3	1-2	0	4	1
Devine	3-9	1-1	1	1	7
Ayotte	0-0	0-0	0	1	0
Williams	0-1	0-0	0	0	0
Reinhart	3-13	0-0	10	4	6
Ireland	0-0	0-0	0	1	0
Bradtke	0-0	2-2	1	1	2
Gleason	1-4	2-3	0	0	4
Totals	22-78	12-18	41	22	56

Kentucky	fg-fga	ft-fta	rb	pf	tp
Cox	6-18	2-3	13	2	14
Crigler	4-10	3-3	15	1	11
Beck	4-8	3-5	12	3	11
Hatton	11-22	4-5	9	2	26
A. Smith	4-10	8-8	3	3	16
Mills	1-1	1-2	0	0	3
Collinsworth	1-3	0-0	1	1	2
B. Smith	1-2	0-0	1	0	2
Johnson	0-2	0-0	3	0	0
Adkins	0-1	0-0	1	0	0
Ross	0-0	2-2	1	1	2
Cassady	0-1	2-3	1	1	2
Totals	32-78	25-31	60	14	89

Half time: Kentucky 43-31. Officials: Mihalik and Mills. Attendance: 12,000.

Kansas State	fg-fga	ft-fta	rb	pf	tp
Abbott	0-1	0-0	0	0	0
Boozer	12-16	2-5	9	3	26
Parr	5-14	3-5	10	4	13
DeWitz	3-6	0-2	2	4	6
Matuszak	6-7	2-2	5	4	14
Frank	4-11	2-2	8	4	10
Fischer	0-0	0-0	0	0	0
Holwerda	0-0	0-1	0	0	0
Long	0-0	0-0	0	0	0
Ballard	0-0	0-0	0	0	0
Team			2		
Totals	30-55	9-17	36	19	69

Oklahoma State	fg-fga	ft-fta	rb	pf	tp
Sutton	2-2	1-1	0	1	5
Crutchfield	2-8	2-2	1	3	6
Clark	8-22	8-12	8	4	24
Carberry	0-3	2-2	0	2	2
Adair	2-10	3-4	5	0	7
Hale	4-9	3-4	5	3	11
Heffington	0-0	0-0	1	1	0
Soergel	0-1	2-2	0	0	2
Walker	0-0	0-0	0	0	0
Team			1		
Totals	18-55	21-27	21	14	57

Half time: Kansas State 38-31. Officials: Batmole and Mercer.

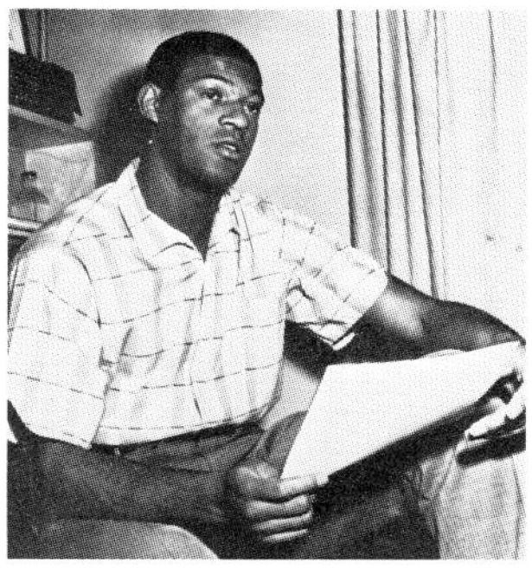

Elgin Baylor

California	fg-fga	ft-fta	rb	pf	tp
Dalton	1-6	1-2	4	5	3
Sterling	7-10	1-2	3	4	15
McIntosh	7-14	2-3	10	1	16
Buch	4-10	2-4	7	2	10
Robison	6-18	3-6	6	2	15
Grout	1-1	0-0	2	0	2
Fitzpatrick	0-3	1-1	0	0	1
Team			3		
Totals	26-62	10-18	35	14	62

Seattle	fg-fga	ft-fta	rb	pf	tp
Ogorek	3-9	2-2	7	4	8
Frizzell	1-2	1-1	1	3	3
Baylor	9-25	8-8	18	3	26
Brown	5-11	0-0	5	2	10
Harney	2-7	5-5	1	2	9
Piasecki	0-2	0-0	0	1	0
Saunders	4-7	2-3	8	1	10
Team			7		
Totals	24-63	18-19	47	16	66

Half time: California 37-29; Regulation Score: 60-60. Officials: Lichty and Morrow.

Semifinals

Kentucky	fg-fga	ft-fta	rb	pf	tp
Crigler	3-11	0-2	9	4	6
Cox	6-17	10-11	13	4	22
Collinsworth	0-0	0-0	0	1	0
Beck	3-9	2-2	15	2	8
Hatton	5-16	3-4	2	3	13
Smith	2-10	8-9	5	3	12
Team			5		
Totals	19-63	23-28	49	17	61

Temple	fg-fga	ft-fta	rb	pf	tp
Norman	7-17	2-3	6	3	16
Brodsky	2-5	0-2	14	2	4
Van Patton	1-1	1-2	3	4	3
Fleming	3-7	3-6	5	1	9
Rodgers	9-24	4-6	5	4	22
Kennedy	3-7	0-1	3	4	6
Team			5		
Totals	25-61	10-20	41	18	60

Half time: 31-31. Officials: Morrow and Mercer. Attendance: 18,586.

Seattle	fg-fga	ft-fta	rb	pf	tp
Ogorek	3-9	1-2	4	4	7
Frizzell	2-4	6-7	2	2	10
Petrie	0-0	0-0	0	0	0
Baylor	9-21	5-7	22	3	23
Humphries	0-0	0-0	0	0	0
Harney	0-4	0-0	2	1	0
Brown	5-6	4-5	13	2	14
Saunders	5-11	2-3	8	1	12
Piasecki	1-1	3-4	0	1	5
Kootnekoff	1-1	0-0	0	0	2
Team			5		
Totals	26-57	21-28	56	14	73

Kansas State	fg-fga	ft-fta	rb	pf	tp
Boozer	6-15	3-5	4	4	15
Frank	6-12	3-4	7	4	15
Abbott	0-4	0-0	2	1	0
Long	2-6	0-1	4	2	4
Fischer	0-1	0-0	0	1	0
Parr	2-11	0-1	8	1	4
Matuszak	3-8	1-3	7	1	7
DeWitz	2-7	2-3	0	2	6
Holwerda	0-2	0-0	1	2	0
Team			1		
Totals	21-66	9-17	33	18	51

Half time: Seattle 37-32. Officials: Conway and Mihalik.

National Third Place

Temple	fg-fga	ft-fta	rb	pf	tp
Norman	1-11	5-8	13	3	7
Brodsky	4-13	2-5	12	3	10
VanPatton	1-6	1-3	12	5	3
Fleming	2-3	3-3	6	4	7
Kennedy	8-16	7-9	0	0	23
Rodgers	7-17	3-3	4	2	17
Team			7		
Totals	23-66	21-31	54	17	67

Kansas State	fg-fga	ft-fta	rb	pf	tp
Boozer	6-19	7-9	12	4	19
Frank	3-9	2-3	11	2	8
Abbott	6-11	2-2	3	3	14
Parr	1-13	5-8	10	2	7
Matuszak	1-4	1-3	2	4	3
DeWitz	3-12	0-1	4	1	6
Holwerdia	0-1	0-0	0	0	0
Ballard	0-1	0-0	1	0	0
Douglas	0-1	0-0	1	3	0
Team			8		
Totals	20-71	17-26	51	22	57

Half time: Kansas State 39-28.

Championship

Kentucky	fg-fga	ft-fta	rb	pf	tp
Cox	10-23	4-4	16	3	24
Crigler	5-12	4-7	14	4	14
Beck	0-1	0-1	3	4	0
Mills	4-9	1-4	5	3	9
Hatton	9-20	12-15	3	3	30
Smith	2-8	3-5	6	4	7
Team			8		
Totals	30-73	24-36	55	21	84

Seattle	fg-fga	ft-fta	rb	pf	tp
Frizzell	4-6	8-11	5	3	16
Ogorek	4-7	2-2	11	5	10
Baylor	9-32	7-9	19	4	25
Harney	2-5	0-1	1	1	4
Brown	6-17	5-7	5	5	17
Saunders	0-2	0-0	2	3	0
Piasecki	0-0	0-0	0	0	0
Team			3		
Totals	25-69	22-30	46	21	72

Half time: Seattle 39-36. Attendance: 18,803.

1959

First Round

West Virginia	fg-fga	ft-fta	rb	pf	tp
West	11-17	3-9	15	3	25
Akers	3-8	1-3	6	2	7
Cloussen	1-6	4-5	9	2	6
Smith	6-9	2-2	6	3	14
Bolyard	1-9	3-6	9	1	5
Posch	0-1	0-0	0	1	0
Ritchie	5-7	5-5	5	1	15
Retton	3-3	1-3	1	0	7
Patrone	0-4	3-3	3	1	3
Goode	0-0	0-0	0	1	0
Visnic	0-0	0-0	0	0	0
Schertzinger	0-0	0-0	0	0	0
Team			9		
Totals	30-64	22-36	63	15	82

Dartmouth	fg-fga	ft-fta	rb	pf	tp
Vandeweghe	6-11	3-4	8	5	15
Larusso	5-13	2-3	7	5	12
Farnsworth	0-2	0-0	5	2	0
Sosnowski	6-8	1-4	4	4	13
Kaufman	6-15	1-1	1	4	13
Gavitt	2-4	0-0	1	1	4
Barnes	3-7	3-5	1	0	9
Berry	0-1	0-0	1	3	0
Fairbank	0-1	2-2	1	0	2
Team			6		
Totals	28-68	12-19	34	24	68

Half time: West Virginia 35-27. Officials: Mihalik and Anderson.

Boston University	fg	ft	tp
Cumings	5	5	15
Gates	4	2	10
Washington	1	6	8
Leaman	5	5	15
Stagis	1	2	4
O'Connell	1	4	6
Supriano	1	0	2
Totals	18	24	60

Connecticut	fg	ft	tp
Pipczynski	2	1	5
Davis	3	0	6
Kelly	0	0	0
Cooper	7	3	17
Rose	5	18	28
Risley	0	0	0
Countryman	1	0	2
Totals	18	22	58

Navy	fg-fga	ft-fta	rb	pf	tp
Bower	5-5	3-3	3	4	13
Egan	1-1	2-2	2	0	4
Brown	1-7	1-3	13	2	3
Metzler	7-10	6-8	12	4	20
Land	0-1	1-3	1	0	1
Johnson	5-10	6-9	4	1	16
Delano	2-7	4-6	4	0	8
Doyle	4-5	3-4	4	3	11
Team			4		
Totals	25-46	26-38	47	14	76

North Carolina	fg-fga	ft-fta	rb	pf	tp
Shaffer	2-5	2-2	3	5	6
Stanley	2-8	2-2	9	2	6
Moe	3-14	1-5	8	2	7
Lotz	1-2	3-3	5	3	5
Kepley	7-13	2-3	9	0	16
Donohue	0-1	0-0	0	1	0
Larese	3-15	2-2	5	5	8
Salz	5-12	4-4	5	5	14
Brown	0-0	0-0	0	0	0
Crotty	0-0	1-2	0	2	1
Team			2		
Totals	23-70	17-23	46	25	63

Half time: Navy 34-22.

Eastern Kentucky	fg-fga	ft-fta	rb	pf	tp
Upchurch	2-9	1-3	6	5	5
Moore	3-13	5-6	7	5	11
Kotula	3-7	1-2	2	3	7
Wood	2-8	1-1	2	3	5
Cole	4-15	3-4	5	3	11
Wierwille	1-4	5-8	7	4	7
Springate	2-7	3-3	4	2	7
Vencil	3-7	0-0	3	3	6
Slayback	0-0	0-0	0	0	0
Estepp	2-3	0-1	4	1	4
Totals	22-73	19-28	40	29	63

Louisville	fg-fga	ft-fta	rb	pf	tp
Goldstein	10-17	5-7	13	2	25
Turner	3-8	3-4	9	5	9
Sawyer	3-6	2-4	5	3	8
Andrews	2-15	3-7	7	4	7
Tieman	3-7	1-5	2	2	7
Kitchen	3-6	2-3	8	2	8
Stacey	0-0	0-0	0	1	0
Leathers	4-7	5-7	6	1	13
Totals	28-66	21-37	50	20	77

Half time: Louisville 38-31. Officials: Kaefer and Meyer. Attendance: 10,500.

Bowling Green	fg-fga	ft-fta	rb	pf	tp
McCampbell	2-11	0-2	7	1	4
Leach	5-18	4-5	15	0	14
Routson	0-3	1-1	4	4	1
Wade	4-10	0-2	5	2	8
Darrow	12-24	2-5	2	3	26
Parsons	1-4	0-0	5	4	2
Abele	1-3	0-0	2	0	2
McDonald	4-11	2-3	3	4	10
Kuzma	0-3	0-0	0	0	0
Williams	0-1	0-2	1	1	0
Burmeister	0-0	0-0	0	0	0
Harling	2-2	0-0	2	0	4
Totals	31-90	9-20	46	19	71

Marquette	fg-fga	ft-fta	rb	pf	tp
Mangham	6-12	4-4	8	3	16
Kojis	5-9	3-3	14	1	13
Moran	9-18	4-8	10	2	22
Kollar	2-5	4-5	3	1	8
McCoy	4-11	0-1	8	3	8
Suppelsa	0-0	0-0	1	0	0
Kakuska	1-2	0-1	1	2	2
Ripp	1-6	0-0	0	1	2
Plinska	3-8	2-4	6	2	8
Kersten	1-5	2-2	6	1	4
Carter	0-2	2-2	1	0	2
Rogan	2-2	0-0	0	0	4
Totals	34-80	21-30	58	16	89

Half time: Marquette 45-28. Officials: Sneed and Bell. Attendance: 10,000.

DePaul	fg	ft	tp
Salzinski	3	1	7
Cowsen	3	1	7
Flemming	3	2	8
Carl	6	4	16
Haig	7	5	19
Ruddy	0	0	0
Totals	22	13	57

Portland	fg	ft	tp
O'Donnell	0	1	1
Jolley	5	2	12
Bloedel	4	2	10
Panel	8	1	17
Armstrong	4	0	8
Altenhofen	3	2	8
Totals	24	8	56

Idaho State	fg	ft	tp
Munz	0	0	0
Griffin	0	3	3
Clock	3	0	6
Moulton	1	0	2
Rodgers	11	10	32
Morris	2	1	5
Griffith	1	2	4
Watkins	4	1	9
Cheney	0	1	1
Totals	22	18	62

New Mexico State	fg	ft	tp
Oliver	1	0	2
Kelly	3	7	13
Askew	0	0	0
Clark	5	2	12
Price	8	2	18
Robison	0	0	0
Rowen	1	3	5
Davis	3	5	11
Totals	21	19	61

Second Round

West Virginia	fg-fga	ft-fta	rb	pf	tp
Smith	2-11	3-4	5	2	7
Bolyard	4-10	2-4	5	3	10
Akers	3-10	7-8	6	4	13
Clousson	2-7	0-0	7	4	4
West	12-22	12-18	15	1	36
Ritchie	2-11	4-7	8	1	8
Ratton	1-4	2-2	2	4	4
Patrone	5-16	3-7	8	1	13
Posch	0-1	0-0	0	2	0
Team			9		
Totals	31-92	33-50	65	20	95

St. Joseph's, Pa.	fg-fga	ft-fta	rb	pf	tp
Clarke	6-9	3-4	13	5	15
McNeil	1-8	5-6	5	5	7
Spratt	6-10	5-7	10	5	17
Gallo	9-22	4-4	4	4	22
Egan	9-13	2-2	8	5	20
Reilly	1-4	2-2	3	2	4
Majewski	2-4	0-2	1	5	4
Hoffacker	0-0	1-2	0	1	1
Cooke	1-1	0-0	0	0	2
Coolican	0-0	0-0	0	0	0
Team			11		
Totals	35-71	22-29	55	32	92

Half time: St. Joseph's 48-42.

Navy	fg-fga	ft-fta	rb	pf	tp
Metzler	8-14	0-0	8	5	16
Johnson	1-4	0-0	1	0	2
Brown	4-10	0-0	14	1	8
Bower	1-11	6-6	10	1	8
Delano	2-2	4-6	2	4	8
Doyle	1-3	0-0	2	2	2
Land	0-1	0-0	1	1	0
Egan	0-0	0-0	1	0	0
Banyard	4-6	3-3	1	2	11
Team			5		
Totals	21-51	13-15	45	16	55

Boston University	fg-fga	ft-fta	rb	pf	tp
Washington	4-13	6-7	19	3	14
Cumings	6-15	2-3	6	1	14
Gates	3-9	3-4	3	2	9
Leaman	5-16	3-4	2	4	13
Stagis	3-13	2-2	5	0	8
O'Connell	1-3	0-0	0	1	2
Supriano	0-0	2-2	0	0	2
Team			3		
Totals	22-69	18-22	38	11	62

Half time: Boston University 32-30.

Kentucky	fg-fga	ft-fta	rb	pf	tp
Cox	3-15	4-5	7	5	10
Lickert	7-11	2-3	7	1	16
Mills	1-3	4-5	7	4	6
Coffman	4-12	5-6	3	5	13
Parsons	2-9	0-0	2	3	4
Johnson	2-4	0-0	4	0	4
Cohen	2-7	1-1	4	1	5
Slusher	1-6	1-1	3	3	3
Totals	22-67	17-21	37	22	61

Louisville	fg-fga	ft-fta	rb	pf	tp
Goldstein	7-12	5-7	13	4	19
Turner	4-10	5-7	8	2	13
Sawyer	2-10	3-5	10	2	7
Tieman	5-8	3-4	1	3	13
Andrews	5-9	5-5	2	0	15
Kitchen	1-2	5-5	2	2	7
Leathers	1-4	0-0	7	1	2
Totals	25-55	26-33	46	16	76

Half time: Kentucky 36-28.

Marquette	fg-fga	ft-fta	rb	pf	tp
Mangham	6-17	3-7	9	3	15
Kojis	7-17	3-6	21	3	17
Moran	3-15	3-4	5	4	9
Kollar	6-11	1-1	5	4	13
McCoy	6-18	1-1	10	2	13
Kersten	0-0	0-0	0	0	0
Ripp	0-2	0-0	1	0	0
Plinska	1-1	0-0	0	1	2
Team			7		
Totals	29-81	11-19	58	17	69

Michigan State	fg-fga	ft-fta	rb	pf	tp
Rand	1-5	1-2	5	2	3
Anderegg	10-19	3-7	8	1	23
Walker	9-21	2-3	8	2	20
Green	6-18	2-4	18	5	14
Olson	1-7	6-8	4	4	8
Fahs	2-6	0-1	1	0	4
Gowens	1-1	0-0	1	0	2
Team			6		
Totals	30-77	14-25	51	14	74

Half time: Michigan State 38-34.

Pete Newell

GAME-BY-GAME RESULTS

1959 CALIFORNIA GOLDEN BEARS—(l-r) Front Row: Bob Dalton, Jack Grout, Bernie Simpson, Al Buch, Denny Fitzpatrick, Jim Langley; Second Row: Jerry Mann, Earl Shultz, Dave Stafford, Wally Torkells, Ned Averbuck, Bobby Wendell; Third Row: Pete Newell, Tandy Gillis, Stan Morrison, Dick Doughty, Darrall Imhoff, Bill McClintock.

Kansas State

	fg-fga	ft-fta	rb	pf	tp
Frank	9-13	5- 6	4	2	23
Boozer	7-21	2- 3	12	1	16
Price	3-13	8-10	8	2	14
Matuszak	2- 6	2- 3	4	3	6
Douglas	7- 8	1- 1	6	3	15
Heinz	1- 5	4- 4	4	1	6
Guthridge	2- 4	0- 0	1	1	4
Long	0- 2	1- 2	1	1	1
Johnson	2- 2	0- 0	3	1	4
Holwerda	5- 8	1- 1	2	3	11
Balding	0- 0	0- 0	2	0	0
Graham	1- 1	0- 0	1	2	2
Team			15		
Totals	39-83	24-30	62	19	102

DePaul

	fg-fga	ft-fta	rb	pf	tp
Salzinski	2- 4	2- 2	1	3	6
Cowsen	3-18	1- 3	9	4	7
Flemming	3- 7	2- 4	11	4	8
Haig	3-11	3- 4	5	2	9
Carl	7-23	8-10	6	2	22
Ruddy	6-10	6- 7	6	5	18
Team			13		
Totals	24-73	22-30	51	20	70

Officials: Haggerty and Hayes.

Cincinnati

	fg-fga	ft-fta	rb	pf	tp
Robertson	12-24	10-13	10	4	34
Tenwick	2- 7	0- 0	1	4	4
Whitaker	3- 8	0- 1	3	1	6
Wiesenhahn	5- 8	2- 2	14	3	12
Davis	5-14	0- 3	2	0	10
Bouldin	2- 4	1- 1	6	3	5
Willey	0- 1	0- 0	3	3	0
Landfried	3- 5	0- 0	4	1	6
Team			8		
Totals	32-71	13-20	51	19	77

Texas Christian

	fg-fga	ft-fta	rb	pf	tp
Stevenson	4-16	7- 8	12	5	15
Nippert	2-11	5- 5	5	0	9
Kirchner	11-23	3- 7	18	4	25
King	1- 6	0- 0	1	5	2
Brunson	5-14	0- 0	2	1	10
Cobb	2- 5	0- 0	2	1	4
Tyler	3- 8	2- 2	1	3	8
Team			11		
Totals	28-83	17-22	52	15	73

Half time: Cincinnati 38-37. Officials: Lightner and Bussenius.

St. Mary's, Calif.

	fg	ft	tp
Sigaty	3	0	6
Doss	8	5	21
Meschery	8	3	19
Barry	4	5	13
B. Dold	4	3	11
Brennan	3	0	6
Claiborne	1	0	2
Womack	0	2	2
J. Dold	0	0	0
Tamm	0	0	0
Totals	31	18	80

Idaho State

	fg	ft	tp
Morris	4	2	10
Clock	1	3	5
Watkins	5	1	11
Rodgers	12	5	29
Griffith	1	2	4
Moulton	2	0	4
Griffin	4	0	8
Cheney	0	0	0
Link	0	0	0
Totals	29	13	71

Half time: St. Mary's 39-33.

California

	fg	ft	tp
Datson	6	1	13
McClintock	4	1	9
Imhoff	3	3	9
Buch	7	1	15
Fitzpatrick	4	4	12
Grout	1	0	2
Simpson	1	0	2
Doughty	3	0	6
Mann	0	0	0
Shultz	0	1	1
Langley	0	0	0
Gillis	1	0	2
Totals	30	11	71

Utah

	fg	ft	tp
Ruffell	4	0	8
Chestang	3	3	9
Pollard	4	1	9
Condie	4	0	8
Shores	0	2	2
Crisler	3	3	9
Rhead	0	1	1
Morton	1	2	4
Thomas	0	0	0
Cutler	0	0	0
Ancell	0	0	0
Van Wagenen	0	3	3
Totals	19	15	53

Third Place

Navy

	fg	ft-fta	tp
Metzler	7	4- 5	18
Bagnard	3	2- 5	8
Brown	4	3- 3	11
Bower	3	3- 5	9
Delano	1	4- 7	6
Doyle	2	2- 2	6
Egan	5	0- 1	10
Land	1	0- 1	2
Totals	26	18-29	70

St. Joseph's, Pa.

	fg	ft-fta	tp
Clarke	4	3- 4	11
McNeill	2	0- 0	4
Spratt	4	4- 6	12
Gallo	2	2- 2	6
Egan	8	2- 3	18
Hoffacker	0	0- 0	0
Cooke	2	0- 0	4
Majewski	0	1- 1	1
Totals	22	12-16	56

Half time: Navy 32-19.

Marquette

	fg-fga	ft-fta	rb	pf	tp
Mangham	2-13	0- 2	13	1	4
Kojis	7-19	1- 2	12	1	15
Moran	6-11	6-10	3	4	18
Kollar	4-11	2- 4	0	10	10
McCoy	3-10	1- 2	8	2	7
Kersten	0- 0	0- 0	0	0	0
Suppelsa	0- 0	1- 1	2	0	1
Ripp	1- 1	0- 0	0	0	2
Plinska	5-10	2- 3	4	3	12
Carter	0- 0	0- 0	0	0	0
Team			4		
Totals	28-75	13-22	49	12	69

Kentucky

	fg-fga	ft-fta	rb	pf	tp
Cox	5- 9	5- 5	7	1	15
Lickert	5-13	0- 2	8	3	10
Mills	11-19	2- 2	11	3	24
Coffman	13-18	2- 3	2	1	28
Parsona	3- 6	2- 2	0	0	8
Johnson	1- 2	1- 1	3	4	3
Cohen	2- 8	0- 0	5	2	4
Slusher	0- 0	0- 0	0	1	0
Robinson	0- 0	0- 0	1	0	0
Dardeen	2- 7	0- 0	2	0	4
Jennings	1- 1	0- 0	1	1	2
Team			4		
Totals	43-83	12-16	45	16	98

Half time: Kentucky 54-24.

Texas Christian

	fg-fga	ft-fta	rb	pf	tp
Stevenson	7-16	4- 6	14	2	18
Nippert	5-12	3- 5	11	3	13
Krichner	10-33	4- 6	24	2	24
Brunson	4-11	1- 1	0	2	9
King	2- 5	1- 1	1	1	5
Tyler	1- 4	0- 0	0	0	2
Cobb	0- 1	0- 0	1	0	0
Team			9		
Totals	29-82	13-19	60	10	71

DePaul

	fg-fga	ft-fta	rb	pf	tp
Ruddy	2- 4	1- 1	3	3	5
Cowsen	3-13	0- 1	8	4	6
Flemming	3- 7	1- 1	4	3	7
Haig	4-12	1- 2	4	3	9
Carl	10-18	4- 4	6	1	24
Salzinski	6-19	2- 5	6	1	14
Team			12		
Totals	28-73	9-14	46	17	65

Half time: TCU 37-33. Officials: Lightner and Bussenius.

Idaho State

	fg	ft	tp
Morris	8	3	19
Clock	4	1	9
Watkins	5	1	11
Griffin	4	1	9
Rodgers	7	5	19
Griffith	0	4	4
Moulton	0	0	0
Totals	28	15	71

Utah

	fg	ft	tp
Ruffell	3	1	7
Chestang	5	3	13
Pollard	8	5	21
Condie	5	1	11
Shores	3	0	6
Rhead	0	1	1
Crisler	1	1	3
Van Wagenen	0	2	2
Morton	0	1	1
Totals	25	15	65

Regional Championships

West Virginia

	fg-fga	ft-fta	rb	pf	tp
Smith	6-11	0- 1	1	0	12
Bolyard	2-11	1- 2	0	3	5
Akers	3-13	5- 5	8	4	11
Clousson	2- 4	4- 5	6	4	8
West	12-24	9-12	17	4	33
Ritchie	2- 5	8-10	9	4	12
Retton	0- 0	1- 3	0	2	1
Patrone	1- 4	2- 5	5	1	4
Posch	0- 0	0- 0	2	0	0
Team			9		
Totals	28-72	30-43	55	24	86

Boston University

	fg-fga	ft-fta	rb	pf	tp
Washington	2- 5	2- 4	10	5	6
Cumings	9-17	4- 9	13	1	22
Gates	7-14	4- 6	8	4	18
Leaman	3- 9	4- 4	3	4	10
Stagis	5-15	3- 6	7	5	13
Supriano	3- 7	2- 5	3	2	8
O'Connell	1- 7	3- 3	4	3	5
Chamberlain	0- 0	0- 0	0	2	0
Team			10		
Totals	30-74	22-37	58	26	82

Half time: 45-45.

Michigan State

	fg-fga	ft-fta	rb	pf	tp
Anderegg	8-21	3- 5	5	3	19
Walker	1- 9	1- 1	9	5	3
Green	11-21	7-12	23	3	29
Olson	6-15	4- 4	3	3	16
Rand	1- 7	0- 0	2	3	2
Fahs	0- 5	0- 1	1	2	0
Gowens	1- 1	1- 2	0	0	3
Stouffer	3- 5	0- 0	1	0	6
Team			5		
Totals	31-84	19-30	50	21	81

Louisville

	fg-fga	ft-fta	rb	pf	tp
Goldstein	7-15	7- 7	7	4	21
Turner	10-19	2- 3	6	4	22
Sawyer	6-12	2- 5	15	4	14
Tieman	0- 6	3- 3	4	2	3
Andrews	5- 9	3- 4	4	5	13
Kitchen	2- 4	1- 1	4	1	5
Leathers	3-10	4- 5	3	3	10
Team			9		
Totals	33-75	22-28	52	23	88

Half time: Michigan State 43-40. Officials: Mihalik and Andersen.

Cincinnati

	fg-fga	ft-fta	rb	pf	tp
Robertson	8-19	8- 9	17	4	24
Wiesenhahn	6-12	0- 1	9	5	12
Tenwick	5-16	12-15	9	4	22
Davis	6-16	1- 2	2	3	13
Whitaker	1- 4	2- 3	0	3	4
Landfried	2- 3	2- 3	10	1	10
Bouldin	0- 1	0- 0	0	0	0
Team			5		
Totals	30-73	25-33	52	20	85

Kansas State

	fg-fga	ft-fta	rb	pf	tp
Boozer	11-26	10-13	13	5	32
Frank	4-16	6-10	3	5	22
Price	1- 6	9-10	5	5	11
Matuszak	4- 7	0- 0	4	2	8
Douglas	1- 5	1- 1	4	5	3
Holwerda	3-11	0- 0	3	2	6
Heinz	1- 6	0- 1	8	1	2
Johnson	0- 2	0- 0	0	0	0
Guthridge	1- 3	1- 2	2	0	3
Team			13		
Totals	26-82	23-31	55	23	75

Half time: Kansas State 41-39. Officials: Lightner and Bussenius.

California

	fg	ft	tp
Dalton	3	7	13
McClintock	4	2	10
Imhoff	4	2	10
Buch	2	0	4
Fitzpatrick	9	3	21
Grout	2	0	4
Simpson	0	2	2
Shultz	0	2	2
Totals	24	18	66

St. Mary's, Calif.	fg	ft	tp
Doss	6	2	14
Sigaty	2	0	4
Meschery	2	1	5
B. Dold	1	1	3
Barry	6	2	14
Brennan	2	2	6
Womack	0	0	0
J. Dold	0	0	0
Totals	19	8	46

Half time: California 31-18.

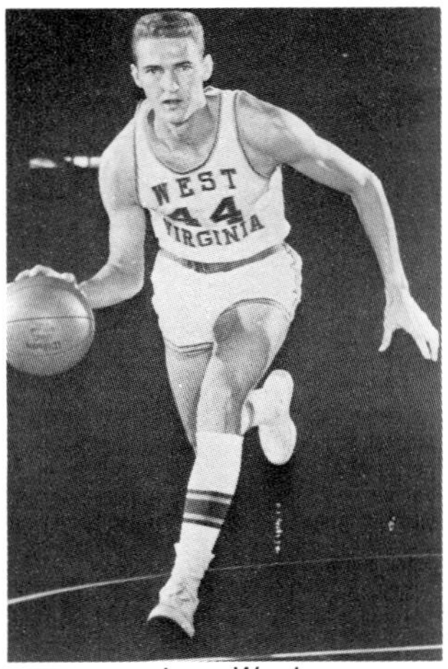

Jerry West

Semifinals

California	fg-fga	ft-fta	rb	pf	tp
McClintock	2-11	2- 4	11	1	6
Dalton	2- 4	3- 4	7	5	7
Imhoff	10-25	2- 5	16	4	22
Fitzpatrick	2- 9	0- 0	3	4	4
Buch	7-15	4- 6	6	2	18
Grout	2- 7	1- 2	2	1	5
Simpson	1- 2	0- 0	3	0	2
Team			8		
Totals	26-73	12-21	56	17	64

Cincinnati	fg-fga	ft-fta	rb	pf	tp
Robertson	5-16	9-11	19	4	19
Wiesenhahn	5-11	0- 0	3	1	10
Tenwick	2- 6	1- 1	4	1	5
Davis	6-15	1- 2	2	2	13
Whitaker	4- 7	0- 2	3	3	8
Landfried	0- 1	3- 5	4	3	3
Bouldin	0- 0	0- 1	0	1	0
Team			7		
Totals	22-56	14-22	42	15	58

Officials: Mihalik and Bell. Attendance: 18,619.

West Virginia	fg-fga	ft-fta	rb	pf	tp
West	12-21	14-20	15	3	38
Akers	2- 5	1- 2	8	5	5
Clousson	5- 5	2- 2	4	4	12
Smith	5- 9	2- 4	5	0	12
Bolyard	4-10	5- 7	3	1	13
Ritchie	2- 6	0- 2	5	1	4
Patrone	1- 4	0- 0	1	0	2
Retton	3- 4	0- 0	0	1	6
Schertzinger	0- 0	0- 0	0	0	0
Posch	1- 2	0- 0	0	0	2
Goode	0- 0	0- 0	0	0	0
Visnic	0- 0	0- 0	0	0	0
Team			8		
Totals	35-66	24-37	49	15	94

Louisville	fg-fga	ft-fta	rb	pf	tp
Goldstein	6-10	9- 9	9	4	21
Turner	8-16	2- 5	7	4	18
Sawyer	2- 6	3- 4	2	5	7
Tieman	1- 7	1- 1	0	0	3
Andrews	9-15	1- 1	2	3	19
Kitchen	3- 7	0- 0	5	4	6
Leathers	2- 8	1- 1	3	3	5
Geiling	0- 0	0- 0	0	1	0
Stacey	0- 0	0- 0	2	1	0
Team			7		
Totals	31-69	17-21	37	25	79

Half time: West Virginia 48-32.

National Third Place

Cincinnati	fg-fga	ft-fta	rb	pf	tp
Robertson	12-26	15-19	17	3	39
Wiesenhahn	4- 9	4- 5	10	3	12
Tenwick	2- 8	2- 4	6	2	6
Davis	11-25	2- 3	3	3	24
Whitaker	6- 8	3- 6	2	2	15
Landfried	1- 1	0- 1	5	2	2
Bouldin	0- 0	0- 0	1	0	0
Nall	0- 0	0- 0	0	1	0
Willey	0- 0	0- 0	1	1	0
Cetrone	0- 0	0- 0	0	1	0
Team			6		
Totals	36-77	26-38	51	18	98

Louisville	fg-fga	ft-fta	rb	pf	tp
Goldstein	8-15	5- 6	8	4	21
Turner	4-11	1- 2	12	4	9
Sawyer	0- 5	5- 5	9	4	5
Tieman	10-18	3- 4	1	4	23
Andrews	6-15	6- 6	4	3	18
Leathers	2- 4	2- 2	3	4	6
Kitchen	1- 2	0- 0	3	2	2
Geiling	0- 2	1- 1	0	0	1
Stacey	0- 0	0- 0	0	0	0
Mantel	0- 0	0- 0	0	0	0
Watkins	0- 0	0- 0	0	0	0
Team			6		
Totals	31-72	23-26	46	25	85

Half time: Louisville 53-49.

Championship

West Virginia	fg-fga	ft-fta	rb	pf	tp
West	10-21	8-12	11	4	28
Akers	5- 8	0- 1	6	0	10
Clousson	4- 7	2- 3	4	4	10
Smith	2- 5	1- 1	2	3	5
Bolyard	1- 4	4- 4	3	4	6
Retton	0- 0	2- 2	0	0	2
Ritchie	1- 4	2- 2	4	0	4
Patrone	2- 6	1- 2	4	1	5
Team			7		
Totals	25-55	20-27	41	16	70

California	fg-fga	ft-fta	rb	pf	tp
McClintock	4-13	0- 1	10	1	8
Dalton	6-11	3- 4	2	4	15
Imhoff	4-13	2- 2	9	3	10
Buch	0- 4	2- 2	2	3	2
Fitzpatrick	8-13	4- 7	2	1	20
Simpson	0- 1	0- 0	2	2	0
Grout	4- 5	2- 2	3	1	10
Doughty	3- 6	0- 0	1	3	6
Team			7		
Totals	29-66	13-18	38	18	71

Half time: California 39-33.

1960

First Round

Duke	fg	ft	tp
Hurt	8	0	16
Kistler	9	8	26
Youngkin	4	1	9
Frye	7	1	15
Mullen	2	2	6
Kast	1	0	2
Morgan	2	0	4
Beal	1	2	4
Bateman	1	0	2
Totals	35	14	84

Princeton	fg	ft	tp
Campbell	5	1	11
Burton	3	0	6
Swan	3	1	7
Brangan	8	0	16
Adams	6	2	14
Hyland	0	0	0
Brennan	1	0	2
Higgins	0	1	1
Pasalis	1	1	3
Totals	27	6	60

Half time: Duke 41-26.

West Virginia	fg-fga	ft-fta	rb	pf	tp
West	12-21	10-15	15	2	34
Ritchie	2- 6	3- 4	3	4	7
Akers	2- 6	1- 1	4	5	5
Warren	10-17	2- 2	5	0	22
Patrone	3- 4	2- 2	7	2	8
Posch	4- 5	2- 2	6	3	10
Miller	3- 7	0- 0	0	2	6
Popovich	0- 1	0- 0	0	1	0
Ward	0- 0	0- 0	2	0	0
Goode	1- 1	0- 0	1	1	2
Team			4		
Totals	37-68	20-26	47	20	94

Navy	fg-fga	ft-fta	rb	pf	tp
Brown	7-12	3- 3	11	3	17
Bower	5-15	3- 3	0	4	13
Metzler	11-18	5- 9	15	3	27
Hughes	4-11	3- 6	3	3	11
Tremaine	3-10	2- 2	4	4	8
Egan	3- 8	0- 2	0	2	6
Delano	2- 3	0- 0	1	0	4
Team			7		
Totals	35-77	16-25	41	19	86

Half time: West Virginia 44-32. Officials: Fox and Lemon.

New York Univ.	fg-fga	ft-fta	rb	pf	tp
Barden	8-15	7- 8	12	2	23
Filardi	0- 3	1- 3	4	2	1
Sanders	5-10	1- 2	15	3	11
Paprocky	5-12	0- 1	2	2	10
Cunningham	8-13	2- 2	6	2	18
Reiss	1- 5	6- 6	8	2	8
Loches	1- 1	0- 0	0	2	2
Lodinoff	0- 1	0- 0	0	1	0
Dinapoli	0- 0	0- 0	1	1	0
Murphy	0- 1	0- 0	3	1	0
Bigelow	0- 0	0- 0	0	0	0
Keith	0- 1	0- 0	0	0	0
Regan	2- 2	1- 1	0	0	5
Team			6		
Totals	30-64	18-23	57	18	78

Connecticut	fg-fga	ft-fta	rb	pf	tp
Sheldon	2-11	1- 1	4	2	5
Pipczynski	4-18	2- 3	16	3	10
Griffin	2-10	6- 8	9	4	10
Rose	6-20	3- 3	4	1	15
Uhl	2- 4	3- 3	3	4	7
Martin	1- 3	0- 1	1	0	2
Countryman	1- 2	0- 0	0	0	2
Madison	1- 3	0- 0	0	0	2
King	1- 2	0- 1	2	1	2
Risley	1- 1	2- 2	0	0	4
Kelly	0- 0	0- 0	0	0	0
Team			3		
Totals	21-74	17-22	42	15	59

Half time: New York University 40-31. Officials: Digravio and Fidgeon.

Notre Dame	fg-fga	ft-fta	rb	pf	tp
McCarthy	4-12	0- 1	3	2	8
Graney	8-19	4- 5	11	4	20
Dearie	9-18	3- 6	6	4	21
Crosby	1-10	0- 2	8	2	2
Schnurr	2-11	5- 6	0	1	9
McGann	1- 2	0- 0	0	0	2
Skrzycki	0- 0	0- 0	0	1	0
Bekelja	1- 1	2- 2	1	0	4
Team			2		
Totals	26-73	14-22	31	14	66

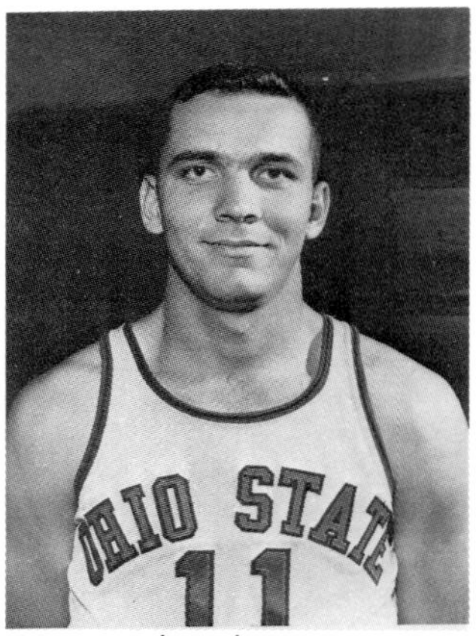

Jerry Lucas

Ohio	fg-fga	ft-fta	rb	pf	tp
Adams	2- 9	2- 4	10	2	6
Kruger	8-16	6- 6	7	3	22
Joliff	11-19	7-11	16	4	29
Whaley	3-10	0- 0	2	4	6
Bandy	5- 6	1- 1	3	2	11
Katz	0- 0	0- 0	0	0	0
Team			1		
Totals	29-60	16-22	39	15	74

Half time: Notre Dame 32-31.

Miami, Fla.	fg-fga	ft-fta	rb	pf	tp
Godfrey	3-12	2- 3	5	4	8
Applegate	4-12	5- 7	7	1	13
Manushaw	1- 5	2- 4	7	5	4
Hickox	7-16	3- 4	2	3	17
Cohen	2- 8	1- 3	1	3	5
Hammond	5-10	5- 5	3	0	15
Stavreti	1- 1	0- 0	0	0	2
Landis	0- 0	0- 0	1	0	0
Spisak	4- 6	1- 2	6	2	9
Nebel	3- 7	0- 0	3	1	6
Shapiro	1- 2	1- 2	0	2	3
Snider	0- 0	2- 2	0	0	2
Team			8		
Totals	31-79	22-32	43	21	84

Western Kentucky	fg-fga	ft-fta	rb	pf	tp
Ellison	7-17	1- 2	14	2	15
Todd	8-15	5- 6	16	3	21
Osborne	3- 6	4- 4	8	3	10
Rascoe	10-17	7-11	9	4	27
Parsons	3- 7	1- 4	1	1	7
Sarakatsannie	2- 4	0- 0	2	3	4
Talbott	5- 9	2- 2	3	0	12
Bicknell	2- 7	2- 3	3	0	6
McDaniel	0- 1	0- 0	0	0	0
Smith	1- 1	3- 4	6	2	5
Warren	0- 1	0- 0	0	1	0
Barnard	0- 0	0- 0	1	1	0
Team			7		
Totals	41-85	25-36	70	20	107

Half time: Western Kentucky 51-40.

California	fg	ft	tp
McClintock	7	1	15
Gillis	5	0	10
Imhoff	7	5	19
Wendell	3	0	6
Shultz	2	0	4
Doughty	3	0	6
Mann	0	2	2
Stafford	1	4	6
Alexander	0	3	3
Totals	28	15	71

Idaho State	fg	ft	tp
Griffith	0	0	0
Goodwin	4	4	12
Watkins	4	5	13
Swopes	3	4	10
Germaine	2	0	4
Kugler	1	0	2
Knackstedt	0	0	0
McNeley	1	1	3
Moulton	0	0	0
Totals	15	14	44

Half time: California 34-15.

New Mexico State	fg-fga	ft-fta	rb	pf	tp
Knighton	8-14	6- 9	7	5	22
Robison	4-13	3- 3	3	3	11
Price	3-12	5- 7	13	1	11
Knight	2-12	4- 4	9	4	8
Bowen	2- 6	0- 1	6	3	4
Canady	0- 2	0- 0	1	0	0
Logback	0- 1	0- 0	1	2	0
Clark	0- 2	1- 1	3	0	1
Bushmaier	1- 2	1- 4	2	2	3
Casanova	0- 0	0- 0	0	0	0
Team			8		
Totals	20-64	20-29	53	20	60

Oregon	fg-fga	ft-fta	rb	pf	tp
Herron	4-11	2- 4	6	4	10
Simmons	5-15	1- 3	10	4	11
Moore	2-11	1- 3	10	5	5
Rask	4-12	5- 7	6	2	13
Strickland	4- 8	4- 5	6	2	12
Warren	7- 9	1- 2	8	3	15
Knecht	1- 3	0- 1	0	1	2
Team			7		
Totals	27-69	14-25	53	21	68

Half time: New Mexico State 34-27. Officials: Combs and Soriano. Attendance: 2,106.

Utah	fg-fga	ft-fta	rb	pf	tp
Ruffel	0- 2	0- 0	5	0	0
Holmes	5-18	7- 8	17	2	17
McGill	8-20	11-18	10	2	27
Morton	8-11	2- 3	5	3	18
Cowan	3-10	1- 2	5	2	7
Rhead	4-12	3- 8	14	3	11
Team			12		
Totals	28-73	24-39	68	12	80

Southern California	fg-fga	ft-fta	rb	pf	tp
Rudometkin	13-24	5- 9	15	3	31
White	5-13	1- 1	6	5	11
Hanna	0- 0	0- 0	1	4	0
Pimm	6-20	4- 5	7	4	16
Kemp	3-15	1- 2	3	4	7
Hampton	1- 5	0- 1	7	4	2
Stanley	1- 4	0- 0	2	1	2
Appel	1- 1	2- 2	2	1	4
Ashby	0- 2	0- 0	1	0	0
Team			9		
Totals	30-84	13-20	53	26	73

Half time: Utah 44-34. Attendance: 9,909.

DePaul	fg-fga	ft-fta	rb	pf	tp
Cowsen	4- 9	4- 5	10	3	12
Salzinski	2- 8	2- 2	6	3	6
Flemming	6- 8	2- 2	8	3	14
Haig	3- 8	7- 8	2	3	13
Carl	9-20	6- 6	2	1	24
Ruddy	0- 2	0- 0	4	0	0
Team			8		
Totals	24-55	21-23	40	13	69

Air Force	fg-fga	ft-fta	rb	pf	tp
Norris	1- 3	3- 3	3	5	5
Ulm	9-15	2- 3	5	2	20
Vicellio	0- 1	0- 0	0	0	0
Long	1- 3	3- 3	2	4	5
Wolfswinkel	8-15	2- 2	3	4	18
Stover	2- 6	0- 0	1	0	4
Schaumberg	4-10	1- 2	7	0	9
Knipp	0- 2	0- 1	1	1	0
Lammers	1- 1	0- 1	0	0	2
Team			5		
Totals	26-56	11-15	27	16	63

Half time: DePaul 43-40.

Second Round

St. Joseph's, Pa.	fg-fga	ft-fta	rb	pf	tp
Callo	6-20	2- 2	5	5	14
Clarke	7-15	8-11	15	4	22
McNeill	4-12	0- 0	5	1	8
Egan	2-10	0- 3	6	2	4
Kempton	0- 7	2- 2	14	2	2
Majewski	0- 2	0- 0	0	0	0
Westhead	1- 1	0- 0	1	3	2
Reilly	2- 5	0- 0	1	1	4
Booth	0- 0	0- 0	0	0	0
Team			11		
Totals	22-74	12-18	58	18	56

Duke	fg-fga	ft-fta	rb	pf	tp
Mullen	0- 1	5- 7	2	0	5
Hurt	7-14	1- 2	6	2	15
Youngkin	9-15	4- 6	12	5	22
Frye	2- 9	2- 4	3	0	6
Kistler	2-11	2- 4	8	2	6
Menhort	1- 1	2- 3	2	2	4
Team			7		
Totals	21-51	16-26	40	11	58

Half time: Duke 27-20.

West Virginia	fg-fga	ft-fta	rb	pf	tp
Patrone	8-13	3- 5	10	4	19
Warren	1- 4	0- 0	2	2	2
Akers	2-11	4- 5	12	3	8
Ritchie	1- 6	3- 6	7	5	5
West	11-28	12-13	16	2	34
Posch	0- 1	0- 0	0	1	0
Popovich	5- 6	0- 0	3	2	10
Miller	1- 3	1- 4	1	4	3
Totals	29-72	23-33	51	23	81

1960 OHIO STATE BUCKEYES—(l-r) Front Row: Bobby Knight, Larry Siegfried, Richie Hoyt, Mel Nowell, John Havlicek, Jerry Lucas, Joe Roberts, Richard Furry, Howard Nourse; Second Row: Ernie Biggs, Fred Taylor, James Allen, Jack Landes, David Barker, John Cedargren, Nelson Miller, Gary Gearhart, Gary Milliken, Frank Truitt, Jack Graf.

New York Univ.	fg-fga	ft-fta	rb	pf	tp
Sanders	12-21	4- 7	19	3	28
Paprocky	5-13	5- 7	5	2	15
Filardi	4-20	5- 9	21	4	13
Barden	1- 4	1- 2	6	5	3
Cunningham	6-16	4- 8	2	4	16
Dinapoli	1- 6	3- 3	1	1	5
Loche	0- 2	0- 0	1	0	0
Reiss	1- 2	0- 0	0	1	2
Totals	30-84	22-36	55	20	82

Half time: West Virginia 41-40. Regulation Score: 77-77.

Ohio	fg-fga	ft-fta	rb	pf	tp
Adams	4-13	3- 9	9	3	11
Kruger	4-15	2- 2	8	3	10
Jolliff	9-20	2- 7	26	4	20
Whaley	3-11	3- 3	1	1	9
Bandy	2- 3	0- 0	2	5	4
Katz	0- 2	0- 0	0	2	0
Team			8		
Totals	22-64	10-21	54	18	54

Georgia Tech	fg-fga	ft-fta	rb	pf	tp
Denton	7-18	1- 1	11	2	15
Richards	2- 7	0- 1	6	3	4
Riley	0- 0	0- 0	0	3	0
Dews	1- 3	3- 5	4	3	5
Kaiser	7-22	11-11	6	3	25
Powell	0- 1	1- 2	2	0	1
Hoffman	0- 1	3- 7	5	1	3
Poteet	2- 4	0- 0	5	0	4
Gher	0- 3	0- 0	1	0	0
Team			8		
Totals	19-59	19-27	48	15	57

Half time: Ohio 33-23. Attendance: 16,524.

Western Kentucky	fg-fga	ft-fta	rb	pf	tp
Todd	3- 8	0- 0	7	4	6
Ellison	8-21	1- 2	7	4	17
Osborne	6-11	6- 7	9	1	18
Rascoe	4- 9	8-11	6	3	16
Parsons	6-11	5- 6	6	2	17
Talbott	0- 2	1- 1	2	0	1
Sarakatsannis	1- 4	0- 0	3	2	2
Cole	1- 2	0- 0	0	0	2
Team			6		
Totals	29-68	21-27	43	17	79

Half time: Western Kentucky 43-37. Attendance: 16,524.

Kansas	fg-fga	ft-fta	rb	pf	tp
Hightower	13-26	8-12	9	3	34
Gisel	2- 6	3- 3	2	1	7
Bridges	7-10	3- 7	14	4	17
Hickman	0- 4	11-11	6	2	11
Gardner	6-13	1- 2	7	4	13
Correll	2- 3	2- 2	2	1	6
Hoffman	0- 0	0- 0	1	0	0
Myers	1- 1	0- 0	0	1	2
Team			6		
Totals	31-63	28-37	47	16	90

Texas	fg-fga	ft-fta	rb	pf	tp
Hughes	0- 6	2- 3	8	2	2
Almanza	7-13	3- 5	6	3	17
Brown	0- 2	1- 1	4	5	1
Arnette	16-31	2- 3	7	4	34
Lasiter	6-12	2- 3	2	1	14
Clark	2- 6	2- 3	1	5	6
Skeete	1- 3	0- 1	4	1	2
Graham	0- 2	0- 0	0	3	0
Wilson	1- 1	3- 3	2	2	5
Team			8		
Totals	33-76	15-21	44	26	81

Half time: Texas 40-36. Officials: Kellogg and Fouts.

Cincinnati	fg-fga	ft-fta	rb	pf	tp
Robertson	12-25	5- 7	9	2	29
Willey	2- 2	2- 3	5	3	6
Hogue	9-12	0- 3	15	3	18
Davis	7-13	0- 0	2	0	14
Bouldin	4- 6	3- 3	1	1	11
Wiesenhahn	4- 8	1- 3	10	1	9
Sizer	2- 2	2- 2	0	1	6
Pomerantz	2- 7	0- 3	1	4	4
Calhoun	1- 2	0- 0	1	0	2
Bryant	0- 0	0- 0	0	0	0
Dierking	0- 1	0- 0	0	0	0
Reis	0- 0	0- 0	0	1	0
Team			11		
Totals	43-78	13-23	57	13	99

DePaul	fg-fga	ft-fta	rb	pf	tp
Cowsen	4-11	7- 8	6	4	15
Salzinski	2- 6	0- 1	4	3	4
Flemming	3- 7	0- 0	3	5	6
Haig	3- 7	0- 1	2	0	6
Carl	5-16	2- 5	3	1	12
Ruddy	4-12	2- 2	6	2	10
Meier	0- 0	0- 2	0	1	0
Bagley	3- 3	0- 0	1	1	6
Team			11		
Totals	24-62	11-19	36	17	59

Half time: Cincinnati 53-25. Officials: Murdock and Overstreet.

California	fg	ft	tp
Gillis	4	3	11
McClintock	6	1	13
Imhoff	7	2	16
Wendell	2	1	5
Shultz	6	4	16
Mann	0	0	0
Doughty	0	2	2
Stafford	1	0	2
Morrison	1	1	3
Pearson	0	1	1
Alexander	0	0	0
Averbuck	0	0	0
Totals	27	15	69

Santa Clara	fg	ft	tp
Bachich	2	0	4
Sobrero	2	1	5
Sheaff	2	1	5
Russi	7	6	20
Cristina	0	0	0
McGee	2	3	7
Lillevand	1	3	5
Keister	1	1	3
Marshall	0	0	0
Buoncristiani	0	0	0
Ramm	0	0	0
Totals	17	15	49

Half time: California 31-22.

Oregon	fg-fga	ft-fta	rb	pf	tp
Herron	3- 6	2- 5	5	4	8
Warren	2- 3	1- 2	1	2	5
Moore	7-13	5- 9	5	3	19
Rask	6-13	6- 8	8	4	18
Strickland	3- 7	1- 1	2	4	7
Simmons	0- 1	3- 6	4	3	3
Kimpton	0- 2	5- 6	2	0	5
Knecht	0- 0	0- 0	1	0	0
Robertson	0- 0	0- 0	0	0	0
Hayes	0- 0	0- 0	0	0	0
Granata	0- 0	0- 1	0	0	0
Team			12		
Totals	21-45	23-38	39	21	65

Utah	fg-fga	ft-fta	rb	pf	tp
Holmes	1- 2	5- 8	1	3	7
Morton	0- 1	4- 6	0	2	4
McGill	2- 3	2- 3	6	5	6
Rhead	2- 5	5- 8	6	4	9
Cowan	3- 7	2- 2	1	1	8
Ruffel	5- 8	0- 0	4	4	10
Crisler	2- 6	2- 2	1	4	6
Chestang	2- 6	0- 0	2	3	4
Ancell	0- 2	0- 0	0	0	0
Aufderheide	0- 1	0- 0	2	1	0
Lambert	0- 0	0- 0	1	0	0
Team			10		
Totals	17-41	20-29	33	27	54

Half time: Oregon 26-19. Officials: McAlister and Lawson. Attendance: 5,000.

Third Place

West Virginia	fg-fga	ft-fta	rb	pf	tp
West	12-28	13-14	16	3	37
Ritchie	3- 7	6- 9	10	1	12
Akers	2-13	3- 6	12	2	7
Patrone	9-13	5- 9	7	2	23
Warren	6-12	2- 2	4	1	14
Goode	0- 0	0- 0	1	0	0
Popovich	1- 1	0- 0	1	0	2
Posch	1- 4	5- 6	6	1	7
Visnic	1- 3	0- 0	0	1	2
Miller	1- 3	0- 0	0	0	2
Bode	0- 1	0- 0	0	0	0
Team			7		
Totals	36-85	34-46	63	14	106

St. Joseph's, Pa.	fg-fga	ft-fta	rb	pf	tp
Clarke	4-10	1- 1	6	5	9
Majewski	4- 9	4- 4	6	3	12
Gallo	13-26	3- 4	7	4	29
Westhead	2-13	4- 5	8	5	8
Kempton	4-10	0- 0	10	5	8
Egan	9-18	2- 2	10	5	20
McNeill	5-14	4- 4	4	2	14
Reilly	0- 3	0- 0	3	1	0
Coolican					
Team			7		
Totals	41-103	18-20	61	30	100

Half time: St. Joseph's 59-51.

Ohio	fg-fga	ft-fta	rb	pf	tp
Kruger	9-21	0- 1	11	3	18
Witte	2- 7	0- 2	5	3	4
Jolliff	10-20	3- 6	22	5	23
Adams	11-20	6-10	10	4	28
Bandy	1- 4	1- 2	0	4	3
Whaley	1- 8	1- 2	4	3	3
Wilcox	1- 5	0- 0	2	2	2
Katz	3- 7	0- 2	0	2	6
Team			11		
Totals	38-92	11-25	64	26	87

Ohio State (center column)

Ohio State	fg-fga	ft-fta	rb	pf	tp
Havlicek	7-15	3- 4	8	1	17
Roberts	2- 4	0- 0	3	1	4
Lucas	14-25	8-10	25	4	36
Nowell	6-11	3- 5	0	2	15
Siegfried	6-15	0- 1	7	2	12
Gearhart	2- 4	0- 0	3	5	4
Furry	1- 4	0- 0	2	2	2
Knight	3- 7	0- 0	1	2	6
Nourse	1- 1	0- 0	0	0	2
Hoyt	0- 0	0- 0	0	0	0
Barker	0- 0	0- 0	1	0	0
Team			2		
Totals	42-86	14-20	52	19	98

Western Kentucky	fg-fga	ft-fta	rb	pf	tp
Ellison	7-15	4- 5	7	2	18
Todd	5- 9	1- 2	6	5	11
Osborne	7-11	9-10	12	3	23
Parsons	8-13	7-10	1	4	23
Rascoe	4- 7	10-12	4	1	18
Sarakatsannis	2- 4	0- 0	1	1	4
Talbott	0- 1	0- 0	1	1	0
Team			7		
Totals	33-60	31-39	39	17	97

Half time: Ohio 43-42.

Texas	fg-fga	ft-fta	rb	pf	tp
Hughes	0- 4	0- 0	4	1	0
Almanza	2-13	1- 2	11	3	5
Clark	4- 8	3- 5	8	1	11
Arnette	13-27	3- 6	8	3	29
Lasiter	3-16	3- 3	10	3	9
Brown	0- 2	1- 1	2	0	1
Skeete	3- 8	0- 0	4	3	6
Wilson	0- 1	0- 0	1	1	0
Team			5		
Totals	25-79	11-17	53	15	61

DePaul	fg-fga	ft-fta	rb	pf	tp
Cowsen	4-11	8-11	17	2	16
Ruddy	1- 3	0- 0	3	1	2
Flemming	9-15	0- 0	11	1	18
Haig	2- 7	2- 3	2	4	6
Carl	7-18	5- 5	5	1	19
Salzinski	2- 4	0- 0	1	5	4
Flaiz	1- 3	0- 0	2	1	2
Team			5		
Totals	26-61	15-19	46	15	67

Half time: DePaul 39-37. Officials: Overstreet and Murdock.

Utah	fg	ft	tp
Ruffell	7	11	25
Holmes	3	4	10
McGill	3	8	14
Cowan	4	2	10
Morton	2	6	10
Rhead	4	4	12
Crisler	1	4	6
Chestang	0	2	2
Totals	24	41	89

Santa Clara	fg	ft	tp
Sobrero	3	2	8
Bachich	4	1	9
Sheaff	5	3	13
McGee	4	2	10
Russi	6	7	19
Lillevand	6	2	14
Keister	2	0	4
Buoncristiani	2	0	4
Totals	32	17	81

Half time: Utah 45-29.

Regional Championships

New York Univ.	fg-fga	ft-fta	rb	pf	tp
Sanders	6-14	10-12	16	2	22
Padrocky	4- 7	3- 5	4	2	11
Reiss	1- 4	0- 0	1	3	2
Barden	7-11	0- 0	5	3	14
Cunningham	4- 6	1- 3	3	1	9
Loche	2- 4	1- 3	0	2	5
Filardi	4- 6	3- 3	8	2	11
DiNapoli	0- 0	0- 0	0	0	0
Murphy	0- 0	0- 0	0	1	0
Regan	0- 1	0- 0	0	0	0
Lodinoff	0- 0	0- 0	0	0	0
Team			3		
Totals	28-53	18-26	40	16	74

Duke	fg-fga	ft-fta	rb	pf	tp
Mullen	1- 5	0- 1	0	3	2
Hurt	3- 9	1- 3	6	3	7
Youngkin	2- 5	4- 8	8	2	8
Frye	5-11	0- 0	2	3	10
Kistler	8-16	4- 5	8	4	20
Mewhart	1- 2	1- 2	4	1	3
Cantwell	1- 3	1- 2	0	2	3
Morgan	1- 2	2- 2	1	1	4
Kast	0- 2	2- 3	0	2	2
Albright	0- 1	0- 0	0	0	0
Bateman	0- 0	0- 0	0	0	0
Beal	0- 1	0- 0	1	0	0
Team			5		
Totals	22-57	15-25	38	19	59

Half time: New York Univ. 35-26. Attendance: 11,666.

Fred Taylor

Ohio State	fg-fga	ft-fta	rb	pf	tp
Havlicek	7-14	1- 3	10	3	15
Roberts	8-13	3- 4	9	2	19
Lucas	9-12	7-10	16	2	25
Nowell	3- 6	1- 1	2	4	7
Siegfried	6-11	2- 2	4	4	14
Gearhart	2- 4	0- 3	3	3	4
Hoyt	0- 1	0- 0	0	2	0
Furry	0- 1	0- 0	0	0	0
Knight	0- 0	0- 0	1	0	0
Cedargren	0- 0	0- 0	1	0	0
Nourse	0- 1	0- 0	1	0	0
Barker	1- 2	0- 0	0	0	2
Team			5		
Totals	36-65	14-23	52	20	86

Georgia Tech	fg-fga	ft-fta	rb	pf	tp
Denton	5-17	5- 6	6	4	15
Richards	2- 8	1- 1	3	5	5
Riley	2- 5	4- 4	15	4	8
Kaiser	11-24	5- 6	5	2	27
Dews	3- 6	3- 6	2	2	9
Hoffman	1- 5	1- 4	2	0	3
Gher	1- 1	0- 0	1	0	2
Poteet	0- 2	0- 0	0	0	0
Powell	0- 0	0- 0	1	0	0
Team			2		
Totals	25-68	19-27	37	17	69

Half time: Ohio State 41-35.

Cincinnati	fg-fga	ft-fta	rb	pf	tp
Robertson	19-30	5-10	14	2	43
Willey	4- 7	0- 0	6	4	8
Hogue	5-10	1- 2	10	4	11
Davis	4- 9	0- 1	3	0	8
Bouldin	0- 5	2- 3	7	3	2
Wiesenhahn	1- 6	5- 5	8	3	7
Sizer	0- 0	1- 1	0	0	1
Pomerantz	1- 1	0- 0	1	0	2
Team			1		
Totals	34-68	14-22	50	16	82

Kansas	fg-fga	ft-fta	rb	pf	tp
Hightower	8-24	6- 7	9	3	22
Gisel	1- 8	0- 0	3	0	2
Bridges	8-14	6- 7	9	4	22
Hickman	1- 5	0- 1	3	3	2
Gardner	6-15	0- 1	7	6	12
Correll	4- 5	3- 4	3	5	11
Team			7		
Totals	28-71	15-20	40	18	71

Half time: Kansas 42-40. Officials: Fouts and Kellogg.

California	fg-fga	ft-fta	rb	pf	tp
Gillis	2- 6	0- 0	1	4	4
McClintock	5-15	2- 6	15	1	12
Imhoff	5-12	8- 9	12	2	18
Shultz	5- 6	1- 2	7	3	11
Wendell	1- 6	2- 3	3	2	4
Doughty	3- 4	4- 5	5	3	10
Stafford	0- 2	5- 9	2	5	5
Mann	2- 3	0- 0	1	1	4
Morrison	1- 1	0- 0	1	0	2
Alexander	0- 0	0- 0	0	0	0
Team			7		
Totals	24-55	22-34	54	21	70

Oregon	fg-fga	ft-fta	rb	pf	tp
Herron	3-12	8-11	6	4	14
Simmons	1- 3	0- 1	2	3	2
Moore	3- 9	3- 3	1	3	9
Rask	7-10	1- 4	4	4	15
Strickland	0- 6	0- 0	4	2	0
Warren	1- 7	4- 5	8	4	6
Knecht	0- 0	3- 5	0	1	3
Kimpton	0- 1	0- 0	0	1	0
Robertson	0- 0	0- 0	1	1	0
Hayes	0- 0	0- 0	0	0	0
Team			6		
Totals	15-48	19-29	32	23	49

Half time: California 32-21. Officials: George and Ryan. Attendance: 7,000.

Semifinals

California	fg-fga	ft-fta	rb	pf	tp
McClintock	5-12	8-10	10	3	18
Gillis	5-10	3- 3	4	4	13
Imhoff	10-21	5- 5	11	4	25
Shultz	4- 7	3- 5	3	1	11
Wendell	0- 4	4- 7	3	2	4
Stafford	1- 4	2- 2	0	2	4
Doughty	1- 3	0- 0	2	1	2
Team			10		
Totals	26-61	25-32	43	17	77

Cincinnati	fg-fga	ft-fta	rb	pf	tp
Robertson	4-16	10-12	10	4	18
Willey	4- 9	1- 2	4	4	9
Hogue	5- 9	4- 6	11	5	14
Davis	4- 8	2- 2	2	1	10
Bouldin	4- 7	0- 0	0	4	8
Sizer	0- 0	0- 1	1	0	0
Wiesenhahn	5- 8	0- 0	9	3	10
Bryant	0- 1	0- 0	1	3	0
Pomerantz	0- 0	0- 0	0	0	0
Team			2		
Totals	26-58	17-23	40	24	69

Half time: California 34-30.

Ohio State	fg-fga	ft-fta	rb	pf	tp
Nowell	3- 8	0- 0	0	4	6
Gearhart	1- 3	1- 1	3	3	3
Havlicek	2- 8	2- 2	10	0	6
Cedargren	1- 1	0- 0	1	0	2
Lucas	9-15	1- 1	13	2	19
Furry	4- 7	2- 3	7	2	10
Hoyt	0- 0	2- 2	0	0	2
Roberts	3- 6	1- 2	7	0	7
Barker	1- 1	0- 0	0	0	2
Siegfried	7-11	5- 5	3	3	19
Knight	0- 0	0- 0	1	0	0
Nourse	0- 0	0- 0	0	0	0
Team			5		
Totals	31-60	14-16	48	14	76

New York Univ.	fg-fga	ft-fta	rb	pf	tp
DiNapoli	0- 0	0- 0	1	0	0
Paprocky	4-17	1- 2	0	3	9
Cunningham	4-14	6- 8	3	2	14
Loche	0- 3	1- 1	0	0	1
Murphy	1- 1	0- 1	0	0	2
Barden	2-11	4- 4	8	2	8
Sanders	4-13	0- 3	22	2	8
Reiss	0- 0	0- 0	1	1	0
Keith	0- 1	0- 0	0	0	0
Filardi	6-12	0- 1	6	3	12
Regan	0- 1	0- 0	0	1	0
Midoinoff	0- 1	0- 0	0	0	0
Team			3		
Totals	21-74	12-20	44	14	54

Half time: Ohio State 37-28.

National Third Place

Cincinnati	fg-fga	ft-fta	rb	pf	tp
Robertson	12-23	8-11	14	4	32
Willey	5- 8	0- 0	5	4	10
Hogue	7- 9	1- 5	19	2	15
Davis	3- 9	3- 3	1	0	9
Bouldin	7-11	0- 1	3	2	14
Bryant	1- 2	0- 0	1	0	2
Dierking	0- 2	0- 0	2	0	0
Wiesenhahn	4- 4	2- 2	5	4	10
Sizer	0- 4	1- 2	4	2	1
Pomerantz	1- 2	0- 0	0	0	2
Reis	0- 1	0- 0	1	0	0
Team			4		
Totals	40-75	15-24	56	15	95

New York Univ.	fg-fga	ft-fta	rb	pf	tp
Barden	3-12	1- 2	13	4	7
Filardi	1- 4	1- 1	4	3	3
Sanders	11-23	5- 6	11	4	27
Cunningham	4- 9	2- 3	0	2	10
Paprocky	6-13	3- 4	1	3	15
Loche	1- 2	2- 2	0	0	4
Murphy	0- 4	0- 0	2	0	0
Reiss	2- 4	1- 2	2	3	5
Team			3		
Totals	28-71	15-20	36	16	71

Half time: Cincinnati 39-25.

Championship

Ohio State	fg-fga	ft-fta	rb	pf	tp
Havlicek	4- 8	4- 5	6	2	12
Roberts	5- 6	0- 1	5	1	10
Lucas	7- 9	2- 2	10	2	16
Nowell	6- 7	3- 3	4	2	15
Siegfried	5- 6	3- 6	1	2	13
Gearhart	0- 1	0- 0	0	3	0
Cedargren	0- 0	1- 2	1	1	1
Furry	2- 4	0- 0	3	1	4
Hoyt	0- 1	0- 0	0	0	0
Barker	0- 0	0- 0	0	0	0
Knight	0- 1	0- 0	0	1	0
Nourse	2- 3	0- 3	3	1	4
Team			1		
Totals	31-46	13-19	35	13	75

California	fg-fga	ft-fta	rb	pf	tp
McClintock	4-15	2- 3	3	3	10
Gillis	4- 9	0- 0	1	1	8
Imhoff	3- 9	2- 2	5	2	8
Wendell	0- 6	4- 4	0	2	4
Shultz	2- 8	2- 2	4	4	6
Mann	3- 5	1- 1	0	0	7
Doughty	4- 5	3- 3	6	1	11
Stafford	0- 1	1- 2	0	1	1
Morrison	0- 0	0- 1	1	0	0
Averbuck	0- 0	0- 0	1	1	0
Pearson	0- 1	0- 0	0	0	0
Alexander	0- 0	0- 0	0	0	0
Team			7		
Totals	20-59	15-18	28	15	55

Half time: Ohio State 37-19.

1961

First Round

Princeton	fg-fga	ft-fta	rb	pf	tp
Swan	0- 0	1- 2	0	0	1
Whitehouse	3- 9	0- 4	8	5	6
Kaemmerlen	6-11	4- 7	10	2	16
Campbell	11-18	5- 7	4	3	27
A. Hyland	6- 7	4- 5	9	3	16
Higgins	3- 6	1- 5	5	5	7
Burton	2- 6	1- 3	5	1	5
Adams	1- 1	3- 3	2	1	5
D. Hyland	0- 0	0- 0	0	0	0
Pasaus	0- 0	0- 0	0	0	0
Brennan	0- 1	1- 2	0	0	1
Haarlow	0- 0	0- 0	0	0	0
Totals	32-59	20-38	43	20	84

George Washington

	fg-fga	ft-fta	rb	pf	tp
Markowitz	8-16	9-14	11	4	25
Ardell	0-3	1-3	3	4	1
Ingram	6-16	0-0	4	2	12
Feldman	5-22	1-5	5	3	11
Norton	3-7	4-4	1	4	10
Schweickhardt	1-3	2-2	6	2	4
Herron	1-2	0-0	1	0	2
Lockman	0-1	2-2	4	4	2
Wicline	0-0	0-0	0	0	0
Totals	24-70	19-30	35	23	67

Half time: Princeton 41-34.

St. Bonaventure

	fg	ft	tp
Crawford	16	2	34
Stith	11	7	29
McCully	2	2	6
Martin	8	1	17
Jirele	0	0	0
Fitzmaurice	0	0	0
Hannon	0	0	0
Herbert	0	0	0
Totals	37	12	86

Rhode Island

	fg	ft	tp
Lee	8	5	21
Ricereto	2	2	6
Koenig	3	3	9
Multer	9	5	23
Schachter	6	0	12
Weiss	1	1	3
Stenhouse	0	0	0
Smith	0	0	0
Logan	1	0	2
Totals	30	16	76

Half time: Rhode Island 43-38.

St. John's, N.Y.

	fg	ft-fta	tp
Jackson	9	8-8	26
Hall	7	2-3	16
Ellis	5	2-4	12
Kovac	2	3-4	7
Loughery	4	4-5	12
Burks	0	1-3	1
Marozas	0	0-1	0
Edelman	0	0-0	0
Goldy	0	0-0	0
Larranaga	0	0-0	0
O'Sullivan	0	0-0	0
Carroll	0	0-0	0
Sanders	0	0-0	0
Totals	27	20-28	74

Wake Forest

	fg	ft-fta	tp
Hart	12	4-6	28
Packer	1	3-3	5
Chappell	9	13-17	31
Hull	3	0-3	6
Wiedman	8	7-8	23
McCoy	0	0-0	0
Koehler	0	0-1	0
Steele	0	0-1	0
Fennell	0	0-0	0
Caldwell	0	0-0	0
Jensen	0	0-0	0
Zawacki	0	0-0	0
Wollard	2	0-0	4
Totals	35	27-39	97

Half time: St. John's 46-36.

Ed Jucker

Ohio

	fg-fga	ft-fta	rb	pf	tp
Adams	7-13	1-2	10	4	15
Kruger	11-20	2-4	8	4	24
Bunton	3-7	1-1	5	5	7
Katz	2-8	0-0	4	2	4
Whaley	5-12	10-13	4	3	20
Wilcox	0-1	0-1	2	0	0
Bolen	0-0	0-1	1	1	0
Team			7		
Totals	28-61	14-22	41	19	70

Louisville

	fg-fga	ft-fta	rb	pf	tp
Turner	7-20	10-11	8	3	24
Wasyer	1-6	1-1	7	1	3
Olsen	8-15	2-5	10	3	18
Stacey	3-7	5-8	3	4	11
Rubenstein	4-7	4-6	4	5	12
Frazier	3-4	0-0	7	4	6
Leathers	0-1	0-0	0	2	0
Armstrong	0-1	0-0	0	2	0
Ray	1-1	0-0	1	0	2
Team			3		
Totals	27-62	22-31	43	24	76

Half time: 30-30.

Xavier

	fg-fga	ft-fta	rb	pf	tp
Nicolai	2-7	1-3	9	5	5
McDermott	6-19	3-6	12	3	15
Thobe	9-16	1-3	8	4	19
Kirvin	7-18	0-2	6	4	14
Enright	5-13	0-1	2	3	10
Tepe	1-2	1-1	4	2	3
Team			11		
Totals	30-75	6-16	52	21	66

Half time: 33-33.

Marquette

	fg-fga	ft-fta	rb	pf	tp
Kojis	5-13	3-5	10	3	13
Glaser	1-12	6-8	5	1	8
Erickson	3-8	3-4	7	3	8
Nixon	4-12	0-0	2	4	8
Hornak	5-10	2-4	4	4	12
Jefferson	0-3	1-2	1	1	1
Scanlon	3-6	0-0	2	1	6
Chmielewski	2-3	0-0	0	0	4
Keidel	0-0	0-0	0	0	0
Team			8		
Totals	23-67	15-23	41	17	61

Houston

	fg-fga	ft-fta	rb	pf	tp
Thompson	0-4	3-4	2	1	3
Lemmon	1-3	0-0	0	1	2
Luckenbill	8-15	7-8	16	5	23
Thomson	6-10	1-3	7	1	13
Harger	0-0	0-0	1	1	0
Phillips	12-19	3-5	6	4	27
Thurman	0-1	0-0	2	1	0
Tuffli	0-0	1-2	3	0	1
Molchany	4-6	0-0	3	2	8
Bishop	0-0	0-0	1	0	0
Team			4		
Totals	31-58	15-22	45	16	77

Half time: Houston 42-18. Attendance: 4,200 (est.)

Seattle

	fg-fga	ft-fta	rb	pf	tp
Dunston	5-8	0-0	6	4	10
Mills	10-19	2-6	15	4	22
Brennan	1-4	0-0	6	3	2
Miles	8-21	8-9	3	2	24
Shaules	2-4	3-5	2	3	7
Stepan	1-2	0-0	0	0	2
Burton	0-0	0-0	0	1	0
Preston	1-2	1-2	4	0	3
Stautz	0-1	0-0	0	0	0
Team			3		
Totals	28-61	14-22	39	17	70

Arizona State

	fg-fga	ft-fta	rb	pf	tp
Payne	8-27	2-4	9	4	18
Cerkvenik	4-7	7-9	9	1	15
Hahn	5-10	3-6	12	2	13
Armstrong	6-21	0-0	7	5	12
Disarufino	3-10	1-2	10	4	7
McConnell	3-5	1-1	3	0	7
Dernovich	0-1	0-0	3	1	0
Team			4		
Totals	29-81	14-22	57	17	72

Half time: Seattle 39-28. Officials: Bussenius and Frivaldsky.

Southern California

	fg-fga	ft-fta	rb	pf	tp
Stanley	4-9	9-12	8	5	17
Ashby	1-3	0-2	4	3	2
Rudometkin	9-18	6-6	11	5	24
Appel	3-10	2-7	8	5	8
Edwards	5-7	0-0	5	1	10
Sloniger	0-0	2-2	0	0	2
Martin	5-10	4-5	5	3	14
Hillman	2-2	0-1	0	1	4
Team			6		
Totals	29-59	23-35	47	23	81

Oregon

	fg-fga	ft-fta	rb	pf	tp
Simmons	6-13	4-5	7	3	16
Warren	8-14	5-7	7	5	21
Moore	5-11	2-7	10	5	12
Hayes	1-6	1-1	4	1	3
Strickland	7-12	5-9	7	3	19
Mack	0-1	0-0	1	3	0
Kimpton	3-6	2-2	2	3	8
Jones	0-2	0-1	1	1	0
Team			6		
Totals	30-65	19-32	45	24	79

Half time: Oregon 36-27. Officials: Soriano and Barlow. Attendance: 4,709.

Second Round

St. Joseph's, Pa.

	fg	ft	tp
Lynam	4	3	11
Hoy	2	6	10
Majewski	0	2	2
Egan	7	5	19
Kempton	9	3	21
Wynne	1	1	3
Booth	0	2	2
Gormley	2	0	4
Totals	25	22	72

Princeton

	fg	ft	tp
Campbell	6	12	24
A. Hyland	3	1	7
Higgins	0	0	0
Kaemmerlen	7	4	18
Whitehouse	3	2	8
Adams	0	1	1
D. Hyland	2	1	5
Burton	2	0	4
Haarlow	0	0	0
Totals	23	21	67

Half time: St. Joseph's, Pa. 29-28.

Wake Forest

	fg-fga	ft-fta	rb	pf	tp
Hart	5-11	0-1	2	2	10
Hull	3-5	0-0	6	4	6
Packer	3-8	1-1	0	3	7
Wiedemann	4-14	6-9	7	4	14
Chappell	7-20	10-12	15	4	24
Koehler	1-1	0-0	0	2	2
Woolard	2-4	6-7	11	4	10
McCoy	1-4	3-4	4	0	5
Team			11		
Totals	26-67	26-34	56	23	78

St. Bonaventure

	fg-fga	ft-fta	rb	pf	tp
Jircle	2-4	1-1	3	4	5
McCully	1-7	2-6	8	2	4
Martin	3-10	1-1	6	5	7
Stith	8-21	13-16	12	2	29
Crawford	9-20	1-6	10	4	19
Ftizmaurice	1-2	3-4	3	5	5
Hannun	2-3	0-0	1	1	4
Team			4		
Totals	26-67	21-34	47	23	73

Half time: St. Bonaventure 37-36.

Ohio State

	fg-fga	ft-fta	rb	pf	tp
Havlicek	8-13	1-2	8	4	17
Hoyt	1-4	0-0	0	1	2
Lucas	2-7	5-7	18	1	9
Siegfried	6-12	2-2	5	2	14
Nowell	1-8	0-1	5	4	2
Knight	4-8	0-0	3	3	8
Gearhart	2-4	0-0	2	3	4
Team			4		
Totals	24-56	8-12	45	18	56

Louisville

	fg-fga	ft-fta	rb	pf	tp
Turner	9-20	7-8	15	1	25
Sawyer	1-6	2-5	7	4	4
Olsen	2-12	2-3	9	2	6
Stacey	6-15	3-6	1	2	15
Frazier	1-7	1-3	3	0	3
Rubenstein	1-3	0-0	2	1	2
Team			7		
Totals	20-63	15-25	44	10	55

Half time: Ohio State 26-25.

Kentucky

	fg-fga	ft-fta	rb	pf	tp
Newman	5-14	4-10	8	4	14
Lickert	11-23	6-7	16	1	28
Jennings	2-8	0-0	1	5	4
Pursiful	2-10	2-2	7	3	6
Parsons	2-7	3-4	9	4	7
Burchett	2-7	8-10	7	1	12
Feldhaus	0-0	0-0	0	0	0
Baesler	0-0	0-0	0	1	0
Team			11		
Totals	24-69	23-32	54	20	71

Half time: Kentucky 40-35.

Morehead State

	fg-fga	ft-fta	rb	pf	tp
Gibson	4-8	6-7	4	3	14
Pokley	2-2	1-3	15	3	5
Noe	4-10	5-5	11	5	13
H. Thompson	3-15	4-5	4	4	10
Williams	7-22	6-7	4	4	20
Cole	1-1	0-0	1	2	2
Team			3		
Totals	21-58	22-27	42	21	64

Half time: Kentucky 40-35.

Texas Tech

	fg-fga	ft-fta	rb	pf	tp
Patty	0-5	0-0	3	3	0
Hennig	3-11	1-3	2	2	7
Hudgens	9-20	8-10	6	1	26
Percival	3-7	0-3	9	4	6
Mounts	2-11	3-5	2	0	7
Gindorf	0-1	0-0	2	1	0
Mickey	0-0	2-3	0	0	2
Lemmons	2-2	1-1	0	1	5
Perkins	1-2	0-0	1	0	2
Varnell	0-1	0-0	0	1	0
Team			10		
Totals	20-60	15-25	35	13	55

Cincinnati

	fg-fga	ft-fta	rb	pf	tp
Wiesenhahn	9-21	3-5	18	2	21
Thacker	3-10	0-2	14	2	6
Hogue	10-17	4-5	8	3	24
Yates	2-4	0-0	5	0	4
Bouldin	6-12	0-0	3	12	
Sizer	2-3	0-1	2	1	4
Heidotting	2-5	0-0	3	3	4
Dierking	0-3	1-1	2	1	1
Shingleton	1-2	0-0	1	0	2
Calhoun	0-2	0-0	1	0	0
Reis	0-0	0-1	0	0	0
Altenau	0-1	0-1	0	2	0
Team			14		
Totals	35-80	8-16	68	18	78

Half time: Cincinnati 37-20. Officials: Filiberti and Bycort. Attendance: 8,500.

Kansas State

	fg	ft	tp
Comley	7	4	18
McKenzie	3	1	7
Price	2	8	12
Ewy	2	0	4
Peithman	2	2	6
Nelson	1	4	6
Brown	1	4	6
Heitmeyer	2	1	5
Wroblewski	3	1	7
Davidson	1	2	4
Roy	0	0	0
Baxter	0	0	0
Totals	24	27	75

279

Houston	fg	ft	tp
Molchaney	1	1	3
Thomson	5	4	14
Luckenbill	1	3	5
Thompson	1	6	8
Phillips	6	10	22
Harger	2	1	5
Thurman	2	0	4
Tuffil	0	1	1
Lemmon	1	0	2
Bishop	0	0	0
Pollan	0	0	0
Brown	0	0	0
Totals	19	26	64

Half time: Kansas State 33-29.

Loyola, Calif.	fg-fga	ft-fta	rb	pf	tp
Krallman	4-10	1- 2	5	4	9
Ryan	6-15	3- 3	9	3	15
Bento	7-11	1- 2	3	5	15
Quinn	8-20	1- 1	3	0	17
Grote	5-11	0- 2	5	2	10
Bowler	3- 4	1- 2	0	3	7
Simeon	1- 4	0- 1	3	0	2
Senske	0- 1	0- 0	0	0	0
Team			2		
Totals	34-76	7-13	30	17	75

Utah	fg-fga	ft-fta	rb	pf	tp
Rhead	8-12	7- 7	20	2	23
Ruffell	7-15	6- 8	8	3	20
McGill	12-21	5- 8	13	3	29
Morton	3- 7	2- 2	3	3	8
Rowe	1- 7	0- 0	2	0	2
Aufderheide	2- 2	0- 0	5	0	4
Crain	2- 3	1- 2	2	0	5
Thomas	0- 1	0- 0	1	0	0
Jenson	0- 0	0- 0	0	0	0
Cozby	0- 0	0- 0	0	0	0
Team			5		
Totals	35-68	21-27	59	11	91

Half time: Utah 49-42. Officials: Shelton and Gebhardt. Attendance: 3,332.

Arizona State	fg-fga	ft-fta	rb	pf	tp
Cerkvenik	2- 6	3- 3	18	4	7
Payne	4-11	1- 3	6	4	9
Hahn	9-17	2- 4	14	3	20
Armstrong	12-27	3- 6	4	1	27
Disarufino	3-11	0- 1	5	3	6
McConnell	4- 7	1- 1	8	2	9
Dernovich	0- 0	1- 2	1	1	1
Pryor	3- 6	1- 3	6	2	7
Daugherty	0- 1	0- 0	0	0	0
Engbretson	0- 0	0- 0	0	0	0
Team			8		
Totals	37-86	12-23	70	20	86

Southern California	fg-fga	ft-fta	rb	pf	tp
Stanley	4-12	3- 6	8	1	11
Martin	7-17	1- 1	6	4	15
Rudometkin	7-23	7- 8	13	2	21
Appel	4-11	2- 2	4	4	10
Edwards	3- 5	0- 4	5	1	6
Ashby	0- 2	0- 0	1	1	0
Sloniger	0- 5	4- 4	2	2	4
Bennedetti	1- 1	0- 0	0	0	2
Hillman	1- 1	0- 0	0	2	2
Parsons	0- 0	0- 0	0	0	0
Ledger	0- 0	0- 0	1	0	0
Carleton	0- 1	0- 0	0	1	0
Team			9		
Totals	27-78	17-25	49	18	71

Half time: Arizona State 42-32. Officials: Lichty and Glennon.

Jerry Lucas

Third Place

Princeton	fg-fga	ft-fta	rb	pf	tp
Campbell	11-25	2- 2	2	1	24
Hyland	5-12	3- 3	3	2	13
Burton	3- 7	1- 1	6	3	7
Kaemmerlen	4-11	5- 5	18	2	13
Whitehouse	3- 8	1- 4	4	2	7
Higgins	0- 2	1- 2	1	1	1
Adams	1- 2	0- 1	2	2	2
Hyland	0- 0	0- 0	0	0	0
Team			6		
Totals	27-67	13-18	42	13	67

St. Bonaventure	fg-fga	ft-fta	rb	pf	tp
Jircle	5- 7	1- 1	2	1	11
McCully	2- 4	0- 0	9	4	4
Martin	5- 9	0- 0	4	2	10
Stith	10-17	9-11	5	1	29
Crawford	7-14	2- 3	7	3	16
Hannon	7-12	1- 4	6	2	15
Fitzmaurice	0- 1	0- 0	0	1	0
Herbert	0- 3	0- 0	3	1	0
Patrovick	0- 0	0- 0	0	0	0
Ormsby	0- 1	0- 0	0	0	0
Team			5		
Totals	36-68	13-19	41	15	85

Half time: Princeton 42-31.

Morehead State	fg-fga	ft-fta	rb	pf	tp
Gibson	1- 2	0- 0	1	0	2
Pokley	3-10	1- 5	11	4	7
Noe	7-21	6- 9	10	2	20
Williams	1- 4	0- 1	1	0	2
H. Thompson	5-13	3- 4	6	3	13
Martin	1- 5	1- 2	3	2	3
Morgan	1- 3	0- 0	1	1	2
W. Thompson	5- 8	0- 2	5	1	10
Greene	0- 0	2- 2	3	0	2
Ellis	0- 2	0- 0	1	0	0
Cole	0- 1	0- 1	0	0	0
Team			6		
Totals	24-69	13-26	49	13	61

Louisville	fg-fga	ft-fta	rb	pf	tp
Turner	13-25	2- 2	13	3	28
Sawyer	7-11	2- 3	13	4	16
Olsen	9-21	2- 3	12	3	20
Stacey	4- 9	0- 1	1	1	8
Frazier	3- 6	1- 3	2	2	7
Leathers	0- 4	0- 1	0	0	0
Rubenstein	1- 1	0- 0	1	1	2
Peloff	0- 2	0- 0	4	3	0
Armstrong	0- 0	0- 0	1	1	0
Ray	0- 0	0- 0	2	1	0
Watkins	1- 2	0- 0	0	0	2
Team			9		
Totals	38-81	7-13	58	19	83

Half time: Louisville 47-23.

Texas Tech	fg	ft	tp
Patty	4	0	8
Hennig	2	7	11
Hudgens	11	2	24
Percival	5	0	10
Mounts	2	8	12
Gindorf	2	0	4
Totals	26	17	69

Houston	fg	ft	tp
Thomson	2	0	4
Luckenbill	6	3	15
Harger	2	1	5
Phillips	5	2	12
Thompson	2	0	4
Tuffli	1	0	2
Thurman	1	2	4
Lemon	5	1	11
Pollan	5	0	10
Bishop	0	0	0
Molchang	0	0	0
Totals	29	9	67

Half time: Texas Tech 36-27.

Loyola, Calif.	fg-fga	ft-fta	rb	pf	tp
Krallman	3- 6	2- 2	8	5	8
Ryan	4-11	2- 2	12	1	10
Bento	11-21	10-16	7	4	32
Quinn	3-10	2- 3	2	2	8
Grote	2- 7	7- 8	3	5	11
Senske	0- 0	0- 0	1	0	0
Simieon	0- 0	0- 0	3	0	0
Team			5		
Totals	23-55	23-31	41	17	69

1961 CINCINNATI BEARCATS—(l-r) Front Row: Jim Calhoun, Tony Yates, Carl Bouldin, Paul Hogue, Bob Wiesenhahn, Tom Thacker, Tom Sizer; Second Row: Ed Jucker, Larry Shingleton, Fred Dierking, Ron Reis, Dale Heidotting, Mark Altenau, Tay Baker.

Southern California	fg-fga	ft-fta	rb	pf	tp
Stanley	0- 3	0- 0	7	5	0
Martin	4- 8	3- 4	5	3	11
Rudometkin	8-15	8-10	12	2	24
Appel	10-22	2- 4	4	3	22
Sloniger	0- 5	4- 5	2	2	4
Parsons	2- 6	1- 2	4	3	5
Ashby	0- 0	1- 2	3	1	1
Hillman	0- 0	0- 0	0	2	0
Edwards	0- 0	0- 0	0	0	0
Carleton	0- 0	0- 0	0	0	0
Team			7		
Totals	24-59	19-27	44	21	67

Half time: Loyola 34-33. Officials: Shelton and Lichty.

Regional Championships

Wake Forest	fg-fga	ft-fta	rb	pf	tp
Hart	5-11	6- 6	3	5	16
Hull	4-10	1- 2	12	2	9
Packer	2- 6	0- 1	1	5	4
Wiedeman	5-13	1- 4	5	3	11
Chappell	11-18	10-14	16	3	32
McCoy	6- 6	2- 2	3	3	14
Woollard	0- 1	0- 0	0	0	0
Koehler	0- 2	0- 0	3	1	0
Caldwell	0- 1	0- 0	1	0	0
Fennell	0- 0	0- 0	0	0	0
Team			10		
Totals	33-68	20-29	53	23	86

St. Joseph's	fg-fga	ft-fta	rb	pf	tp
Lynam	3-11	9-12	2	4	15
Majewski	8-13	3- 4	9	4	19
Hoy	6-13	8-11	6	1	20
Egan	6-15	2- 3	9	4	14
Kempton	6-11	0- 1	2	5	12
Wynne	7-10	2- 2	4	4	16
Westhead	0- 0	0- 0	0	0	0
Booth	0- 0	0- 1	1	0	0
Team			4		
Totals	36-73	24-33	37	22	96

Half time: St. Joseph's 48-28.

Ohio State	fg-fga	ft-fta	rb	pf	tp
Havlicek	2-10	4- 5	10	2	8
Hoyt	1- 3	0- 0	2	2	2
Lucas	14-18	5-12	30	4	33
Nowell	5- 7	3- 5	1	3	13
Siegfried	8-14	4- 7	3	3	20
Knight	3- 4	1- 1	4	7	7
Gearhart	1- 2	0- 0	2	2	2
McDonald	0- 0	0- 1	2	2	0
Reasbeck	0- 0	0- 0	0	1	0
Miller	1- 1	0- 0	1	1	2
Lee	0- 0	0- 0	0	0	0
Team			10		
Totals	35-59	17-31	59	24	87

Kentucky	fg-fga	ft-fta	rb	pf	tp
Lickert	6-16	5- 6	3	1	17
Newman	7-12	17-22	7	1	31
Jennings	1- 3	2- 2	4	5	4
Pursiful	4-16	2- 2	5	5	10
Parsons	2-10	2- 3	3	3	6
Burchett	1- 4	0- 0	2	5	2
Feldhaus	1- 3	1- 2	1	2	3
McDonald	0- 3	1- 2	4	1	1
Baesler	0- 2	0- 1	0	0	0
Team			9		
Totals	22-69	30-39	35	23	74

Half time: Ohio State 36-28. Attendance: 17,494.

Kansas State	fg-fga	ft-fta	rb	pf	tp
Comley	7-19	2- 2	9	4	16
McKenzie	1- 4	1- 1	5	5	3
Price	3- 8	4- 6	6	4	10
Peithman	5-11	0- 0	1	4	10
Ewy	3- 5	1- 4	1	5	7
Wroblewski	3- 7	5- 5	2	2	11
Heitmeyer	0- 1	1- 2	1	2	1
Nelson	1- 5	2- 2	3	0	4
Davidson	0- 0	2- 2	0	0	2
Matusak	0- 0	0- 0	0	0	0
Team			8		
Totals	23-60	18-24	36	26	64

Cincinnati	fg-fga	ft-fta	rb	pf	tp
Wiesenhahn	8-12	6- 9	12	2	22
Thacker	5-11	6-10	12	4	16
Hogue	3- 6	2- 6	7	5	8
Yates	1- 5	6- 7	4	1	8
Bouldin	4-16	2- 4	2	0	10
Heidotting	2- 4	1- 1	5	5	5
Dierking	0- 1	0- 0	1	0	0
Sizer	0- 0	0- 0	0	0	0
Team			8		
Totals	23-55	23-37	51	17	69

Half time: 33-33. Officials: Filiberti and Lightner. Attendance: 10,000.

Utah	fg-fga	ft-fta	rb	pf	tp
Rhead	5-10	7- 9	10	3	17
Ruffell	12-17	0- 0	8	1	24
McGill	12-27	7- 8	18	3	31
Morton	4-15	1- 2	6	0	9
Rowe	1- 3	0- 0	4	2	2
Cozby	0- 1	0- 0	1	1	0
Aufderheide	1- 4	1- 1	2	1	3
Crain	1- 4	0- 0	2	0	2
Thomas	0- 1	0- 0	2	0	0
Team			2		
Totals	36-82	16-20	55	11	88

280

Arizona State	fg-fga	ft-fta	rb	pf	tp
Cerkvenik	3- 6	1- 3	7	0	7
Payne	6-17	0- 0	4	2	12
Hahn	6-15	2- 3	11	5	14
Armstrong	13-23	1- 2	6	4	27
Disarufino	5-12	2- 4	4	1	12
Pryor	0- 1	0- 1	3	0	0
McConnell	4-10	0- 0	6	3	8
Team			6		
Totals	37-84	6-13	47	15	80

Half time: Utah 46-28. Officials: Glennon and Gebhardt. Attendance: 5,059.

Semifinals

Cincinnati	fg-fga	ft-fta	rb	pf	tp
Wiesenhahn	5- 7	4- 6	5	4	14
Thacker	1- 7	5- 6	6	3	7
Hogue	9-16	0- 4	14	4	18
Bouldin	7-14	7- 8	3	0	21
Yates	4- 6	5- 7	5	2	13
Heidotting	3- 8	1- 1	6	1	7
Sizer	1- 1	0- 0	0	0	2
Dierking	0- 0	0- 0	1	1	0
Altenau	0- 0	0- 0	0	0	0
Shingleton	0- 0	0- 0	0	0	0
Calhoun	0- 0	0- 0	0	0	0
Team			5		
Totals	30-59	22-32	45	15	82

Utah	fg-fga	ft-fta	rb	pf	tp
Ruffell	6-11	2- 2	5	4	14
Rhead	2- 5	4- 6	10	4	8
McGill	11-31	3- 4	8	4	25
Morton	3- 9	1- 1	1	4	7
Rowe	1- 3	0- 0	1	2	2
Crain	2- 5	0- 1	5	4	4
Aufderheide	2- 3	2- 2	3	1	6
Cozby	0- 0	0- 0	0	0	0
Thomas	0- 0	1- 2	0	0	1
Jenson	0- 0	0- 0	0	0	0
Team			6		
Totals	27-67	13-18	39	23	67

Half time: Cincinnati 35-20. Officials: Wertz and Fox.

Ohio State	fg-fga	ft-fta	rb	pf	tp
Nowell	7-11	1- 1	0	2	15
Havlicek	5- 6	1- 2	9	2	11
Lucas	10-11	9-10	13	2	29
Hoyt	2- 6	0- 0	1	3	4
Siegried	8-11	5- 7	9	4	21
Knight	2- 5	1- 2	3	2	5
McDonald	1- 4	0- 0	2	1	2
Gearhart	0- 2	2- 2	1	2	2
Reasbeck	0- 1	0- 1	1	1	0
Lee	1- 1	0- 0	2	0	2
Miller	0- 0	0- 0	0	0	0
Landes	2- 2	0- 0	0	1	4
Team			9		
Totals	38-60	19-25	50	20	95

St. Joseph's, Pa.	fg-fga	ft-fta	rb	pf	tp
Lynam	2- 5	3- 4	0	0	7
Hoy	6-17	1- 1	2	2	13
Majewski	4-12	5- 7	4	1	13
Egan	3-15	2- 3	5	2	8
Kempton	5- 9	8- 8	8	3	18
Wynne	1- 9	2- 2	2	4	4
Booth	0- 3	2- 2	2	3	2
Gormley	1- 5	2- 2	1	3	4
Westhead	0- 1	0- 1	2	0	0
Bugey	0- 0	0- 0	0	0	0
Dickey	0- 0	0- 0	0	0	0
Team			9		
Totals	22-76	25-30	35	18	69

Half time: Ohio State 45-28. Officials: Glennon and Filiberti.

National Third Place

St. Joseph's, Pa.	fg-fga	ft-fta	rb	pf	tp
Majewski	5- 9	1- 2	11	3	11
Egan	17-33	8- 8	16	5	42
Kempton	7-12	2- 3	10	5	16
Lynam	9-18	13-14	2	2	31
Hoy	3-14	4- 4	3	1	10
Wynne	4-12	7- 9	10	5	15
Gormley	0- 2	0- 0	1	0	0
Booth	0- 0	2- 2	1	0	2
Westhead	0- 0	0- 0	0	0	0
Dickey	0- 1	0- 0	2	3	0
Team			7		
Totals	45-101	37-42	63	24	127

Utah	fg-fga	ft-fta	rb	pf	tp
Rhead	12-20	4-10	11	4	28
Ruffell	7-14	0- 0	5	3	14
McGill	14-23	6- 9	14	5	34
Morton	3-11	5- 9	6	3	11
Rowe	3- 8	0- 0	3	4	6
Crain	5-13	3- 3	8	5	13
Thomas	3- 7	0- 0	3	0	6
Aufderheide	1- 4	0- 1	3	3	2
Cozby	2- 3	2- 2	3	1	6
Jenson	0- 0	0- 0	0	0	0
Team			9		
Totals	50-103	20-34	65	28	120

Half time: St. Joseph's 48-41. Regulation Score: 89-89. 1st Overtime: 97-97. 2nd Overtime: 101-101. 3rd Overtime: 112-112. Officials: Wertz and Glennon.

Championship

Cincinnati	fg-fga	ft-fta	rb	pf	tp
Wiesenhahn	8-15	1- 1	9	3	17
Thacker	7-21	1- 4	7	0	15
Hogue	3- 8	3- 6	7	3	9
Yates	4- 8	5- 5	2	3	13
Bouldin	7-12	2- 3	4	4	16
Sizer	0- 0	0- 0	1	0	0
Heidotting	0- 0	0- 0	0	0	0
Team			6		
Totals	29-64	12-19	36	13	70

Ohio State	fg-fga	ft-fta	rb	pf	tp
Havlicek	1- 5	2- 2	4	2	4
Hoyt	3- 5	1- 1	1	3	7
Lucas	10-17	7- 7	12	4	27
Nowell	3- 9	3- 3	3	1	9
Siegfried	6-10	2- 3	3	2	14
Knight	1- 3	0- 0	1	1	2
Gearhart	1- 1	0- 0	0	1	2
Team			8		
Totals	25-50	15-16	32	14	65

Half time: Ohio State 39-38. Regulation Score: 61-61. Officials: Fox and Filiberti.

1962

First Round

Wake Forest	fg-fga	ft-fta	rb	pf	tp
Chappell	8-13	9-15	18	5	25
Christie	2- 5	0- 0	4	2	4
Woollard	2- 8	4- 5	11	3	8
Wiedeman	9-20	4- 5	6	2	22
Packer	5-14	5- 7	3	0	15
McCoy	6-12	3- 4	6	1	15
Hull	1- 1	1- 3	3	2	3
Team			5		
Totals	33-73	26-39	56	15	92

Yale	fg-fga	ft-fta	rb	pf	tp
Evans	5-11	2- 3	10	4	12
Kaminsky	10-18	3- 4	10	5	23
Goulding	1- 3	2- 2	2	5	4
Madden	5-10	4- 6	1	3	14
Lynch	5-14	2- 3	2	2	12
Schumacher	2- 5	1- 2	5	3	5
Derby	2- 7	0- 0	3	2	4
Polinsky	3- 3	0- 0	4	1	6
Ludlum	1- 1	0- 0	0	0	2
Team			4		
Totals	34-72	14-20	41	25	82

Half time: Wake Forest 46-42. Regulation Score: 76-76. Officials: Honzo and Eckman. Attendance: 9,214.

New York Univ.	fg-fga	ft-fta	rb	pf	tp
Kramer	4-16	7-10	7	3	15
Hairston	3- 7	1- 4	9	4	7
Galliard	2- 3	5- 9	8	3	9
Reiner	2-12	2- 2	8	2	6
Boose	5-11	4- 6	11	3	14
O'Neil	0- 0	0- 0	2	4	0
Williams	3- 7	0- 0	3	1	6
Filardi	1- 1	5- 6	2	3	7
Blaha	3- 5	0- 2	3	2	6
Jordan	0- 1	0- 0	2	0	0
Frontera	0- 0	0- 0	0	0	0
Patton	0- 1	0- 0	1	0	0
Team			3		
Totals	23-64	24-39	59	25	70

Massachusetts	fg-fga	ft-fta	rb	pf	tp
Leslie	3-10	1- 1	6	5	7
Twitchell	0-10	2- 4	10	4	2
Black	3- 7	4- 8	6	5	10
Bernard	6-18	1- 4	7	1	13
Mole	3-16	5- 7	4	5	11
Fohlin	2- 6	3- 4	14	5	7
R. Johnson	0- 1	0- 0	1	0	0
M. Johnson	0- 0	0- 0	1	0	0
Gventer	0- 0	0- 0	2	0	0
Team			9		
Totals	17-68	16-28	60	25	50

Half time: NYU 32-28. Officials: DiGravio and Lennon. Attendance: 9,214.

Villanova	fg-fga	ft-fta	rb	pf	tp
McMonagle	6-12	4- 5	11	4	16
O'Brien	4-14	3- 3	8	2	11
White	11-21	6-10	10	2	28
Leftwich	4-17	0- 0	3	4	8
Jones	13-17	1- 2	5	2	27
McGill	0- 0	0- 0	2	2	0
Walsh	0- 0	0- 0	0	0	0
Winterbottom	0- 0	0- 0	0	1	0
Brokars	0- 0	0- 0	1	0	0
Morris	0- 0	0- 0	0	0	0
Team			4		
Totals	38-81	14-20	44	17	90

West Virginia	fg-fga	ft-fta	rb	pf	tp
Ward	4-12	1- 2	8	5	9
Catlett	5-16	2- 3	7	2	12
Lowry	7-13	2- 2	13	2	16
Thorn	11-21	1- 3	13	2	23
Weir	3- 6	1- 2	5	1	7
Wolfe	0- 4	0- 0	2	0	0
Dubois	2- 2	2- 2	0	0	6
Shuck	0- 1	2- 2	1	1	2
Bode	0- 1	0- 0	0	1	0
Team			5		
Totals	32-76	11-16	54	14	75

Half time: West Virginia 42-39. Officials: Bonder and Gasser. Attendance: 9,214.

Bowling Green	fg-fga	ft-fta	rb	pf	tp
Chatman	1- 6	2- 2	8	0	4
Gilbert	3-12	0- 0	9	2	6
Thurmond	10-18	1- 3	14	4	21
Komives	5-15	1- 1	1	4	11
Dawson	4-10	1- 3	2	2	9
Carbaugh	0- 2	2- 3	4	1	2
Baker	1- 3	0- 1	3	1	2
Reynolds	0- 0	0- 0	0	0	0
Knepper	0- 0	0- 0	0	0	0
Team			4		
Totals	24-66	7-13	45	14	55

Butler	fg-fga	ft-fta	rb	pf	tp
Bowman	7-22	4- 6	11	1	18
Freeman	1- 4	0- 0	7	4	2
Blue	4- 8	8-11	12	2	16
Williams	5-13	3- 3	5	4	13
Haslam	3- 9	1- 1	8	1	7
Shook	0- 1	0- 0	1	0	0
Team			1		
Totals	20-57	16-21	45	12	56

Half time: Butler 28-25. Officials: Conley and Strauthers. Attendance: 5,500.

Western Kentucky	fg-fga	ft-fta	rb	pf	tp
Dunn	7-15	5- 7	10	4	19
Jackson	2- 8	2- 2	9	3	6
Todd	2- 5	6- 6	17	5	10
Carrier	11-17	4- 5	3	3	26
Rascoe	9-19	7- 8	5	3	25
Smith	1- 4	2- 2	3	3	4
Team			4		
Totals	32-68	26-30	51	21	90

Detroit	fg-fga	ft-fta	rb	pf	tp
DeBusschere	14-33	10-13	19	5	38
Munson	4-13	5- 6	12	1	13
Dzik	6-18	0- 1	16	5	12
Chickowski	0- 9	2- 3	1	3	2
Cech	6-21	2- 2	4	3	14
McDaniel	0- 0	2- 2	3	2	2
Johnson	0- 1	0- 0	2	1	0
Schoenherr	0- 1	0- 0	1	1	0
Barnes	0- 0	0- 0	0	0	0
Team			3		
Totals	30-96	21-27	61	21	81

Half time: Western Kentucky 43-39. Officials: Steiner and Chuckovitz. Attendance: 6,000.

Air Force	fg-fga	ft-fta	rb	pf	tp
Zoeller	2-11	4- 4	7	1	8
Judd	1- 5	0- 0	2	3	2
Knipp	7-16	5- 6	4	2	19
Schaumberg	3-11	4- 5	7	1	10
Viccellio	3- 3	7- 7	7	5	13
Hinman	1- 8	2- 2	2	3	4
Diffendorfer	5- 8	0- 2	5	3	10
Head	0- 3	0- 0	1	0	0
Team			10		
Totals	22-65	22-26	45	18	66

Texas Tech	fg-fga	ft-fta	rb	pf	tp
Mounts	5-10	6- 7	3	4	16
Percival	3- 9	2- 4	8	5	8
Hudgens	4-13	2- 6	12	3	10
Gindorf	8-18	4- 4	6	2	20
Hennig	5- 8	0- 1	4	5	10
Wall	1- 2	2- 3	1	0	4
Farley	0- 1	0- 0	1	0	0
Team			11		
Totals	26-61	16-25	46	19	68

Half time: Texas Tech 41-31. Officials: Fuller and Henderson.

Memphis State	fg-fga	ft-fta	rb	pf	tp
Neumann	7-16	9-12	8	5	23
Beckman	7-12	5- 6	5	4	19
Weaver	0- 0	0- 0	0	1	0
Randolph	0- 0	2- 2	0	1	2
Drewell	0- 0	0- 0	1	0	0
Kirk	5- 9	5- 6	6	5	15
Garber	5-16	3- 4	4	3	13
Parrish	1- 9	1- 2	4	3	3
Horton	3- 9	2- 2	2	3	8
Team			15		
Totals	28-71	27-34	45	25	83

281

Creighton	fg-fga	ft-fta	rb	pf	tp
Officer	3- 7	2- 2	8	5	8
Silas	11-31	5-10	24	3	27
McManamon	6- 9	5- 8	2	1	17
Dowling	0- 1	0- 0	0	0	0
Bakos	7-14	6- 8	11	5	20
Silvestrial	0- 0	0- 1	0	0	0
Millard	2- 7	0- 1	2	5	4
Wagner	4-16	3- 5	5	5	11
Jimenes	0- 3	0- 0	0	1	0
Forehand	0- 0	0- 0	0	0	0
Swassing	0- 0	0- 0	2	1	0
Team			30		
Totals	33-88	21-35	84	26	87

Half time: Memphis State 47-44. Officials: Gergens and Ceracino.

Seattle	fg-fga	ft-fta	rb	pf	tp
Butler	4- 8	0- 1	7	2	8
Dunston	3-10	1- 3	4	5	7
Tresvant	2- 3	0- 1	3	4	4
Miles	10-14	6- 8	6	1	26
Shaules	6-17	4- 6	4	4	16
Brennan	0- 0	2- 2	2	0	2
Preston	1- 1	0- 1	0	4	2
Smither	0- 0	0- 0	0	0	0
Stautz	0- 0	0- 0	0	0	0
Team			5		
Totals	26-53	13-21	32	20	65

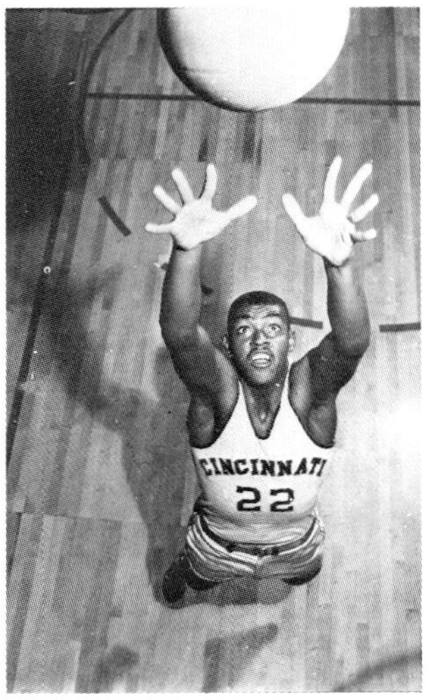

Paul Hogue

Oregon State	fg-fga	ft-fta	rb	pf	tp
Jacobson	0- 0	0- 0	5	1	0
Carty	8-15	11-12	11	0	27
Counts	6-19	8- 9	15	4	20
Pauly	5-18	1- 1	10	3	11
Baker	2- 8	0- 1	0	4	4
Hayward	2- 6	3- 3	0	3	7
Torgerson	0- 0	0- 0	1	1	0
Campbell	0- 1	0- 0	2	0	0
Team			4		
Totals	23-67	23-26	48	16	69

Half time: Seattle 29-23. Regulation Score: 59-59. Officials: Jones and Overly. Attendance: 9,702.

Utah State	fg	ft-fta	pf	tp
Johnson	7	2- 5	4	16
Green	9	9-11	2	27
Haney	6	3- 4	4	15
Goldsberry	1	0- 0	2	2
Hasen	7	0- 1	5	14
Nate	1	0- 1	1	2
Holman	0	2- 2	0	2
Totals	31	16-24	18	78

Arizona State	fg	ft-fta	pf	tp
Cerkvenick	6	2- 3	3	14
Caldwell	6	4- 5	4	16
Hahn	3	0- 2	4	6
Disarufino	1	0- 0	1	2
Armstrong	4	5- 6	2	13
Payne	4	0- 0	4	8
Senitza	2	2- 2	1	6
Becker	1	0- 3	0	2
Howard	0	0- 0	0	0
McConnell	3	0- 0	0	6
Totals	30	13-21	19	73

Half time: Arizona State 36-35.

Second Round

Villanova	fg-fga	ft-fta	rb	pf	tp
Jones	6-15	2- 3	4	1	14
Leftwich	3-13	3- 5	2	2	9
McMonagle	5-10	3- 3	8	3	13
O'Brien	6-13	0- 0	10	5	12
White	11-19	9-12	6	4	31
Walsh	0- 1	0- 0	1	0	0
Team			5		
Totals	31-71	17-23	36	15	79

New York Univ.	fg-fga	ft-fta	rb	pf	tp
Boose	4- 6	3- 4	4	4	11
Hairston	7-14	7- 9	12	4	21
Kramer	10-15	6- 6	10	4	26
O'Neill	3- 5	0- 2	1	1	6
Reiner	5- 8	2- 2	5	4	12
Williams	0- 0	0- 0	0	0	0
Filardi	0- 1	0- 0	0	0	0
Blaha	0- 0	0- 0	0	0	0
Jordan	0- 0	0- 0	1	0	0
Team			2		
Totals	29-49	18-23	35	17	76

Half time: New York University 42-40.

Wake Forest	fg-fga	ft-fta	rb	pf	tp
Christie	5-10	0- 1	10	3	10
Chappell	9-17	16-20	18	4	34
Woolard	4- 8	4- 4	11	5	12
Wiedeman	5-12	5- 6	4	3	15
Packer	8-14	1- 2	1	2	17
McCoy	3- 5	2- 2	4	1	8
Hull	0- 3	0- 0	4	1	0
Carmichael	0- 0	0- 0	0	0	0
Hassell	0- 0	0- 0	0	0	0
Team			1		
Totals	34-69	28-35	53	19	96

St. Joseph's, Pa.	fg-fga	ft-fta	rb	pf	tp
Wynne	10-26	9- 9	7	2	29
Boyle	6-13	4- 4	7	4	16
Dickey	2- 8	1- 2	4	5	5
Hoy	1- 6	4- 5	9	3	6
Lynam	6-12	3- 3	3	2	15
Gormley	5- 6	0- 0	0	3	10
Hoffman	0- 1	3- 6	5	5	3
Tiller	0- 0	0- 0	0	0	0
Booth	0- 2	1- 2	1	1	1
Courtin	0- 0	0- 0	0	0	0
Team			3		
Totals	30-74	25-31	39	25	85

Half time: St. Joseph's 41-36. Attendance: 11,700.

Kentucky	fg-fga	ft-fta	rb	pf	tp
Burchett	6-11	0- 0	9	4	12
Roberts	2- 4	3- 5	6	2	7
Nash	11-24	1- 1	10	5	23
Pursiful	12-21	2- 2	6	1	26
Baesler	3- 9	0- 1	4	1	6
Feldhaus	2- 4	1- 2	3	3	5
McDonald	0- 2	0- 0	0	0	0
Deeken	0- 1	0- 0	0	1	0
Ishmael	1- 1	0- 0	1	1	2
Rupp	0- 1	0- 0	0	0	0
Team			2		
Totals	37-78	7-11	41	18	81

Butler	fg-fga	ft-fta	rb	pf	tp
Bowman	4-11	1- 1	2	1	9
Freeman	2- 3	0- 0	3	1	4
Blue	7-14	5- 8	11	2	19
Williams	9-20	2- 3	3	2	20
Haslam	1- 9	1- 1	6	3	3
Shook	0- 1	0- 1	1	0	0
Engle	1- 8	3- 3	2	4	5
Braun	0- 0	0- 0	0	0	0
Krebs	0- 0	0- 0	0	0	0
Bultman	0- 0	0- 0	0	0	0
Totals	24-66	12-17	28	13	60

Half time: Kentucky 37-36. Officials: Honzo and Eckmann. Attendance: 8,300.

Ohio State	fg-fga	ft-fta	rb	pf	tp
Havlicek	7- 9	3- 3	5	4	17
McDonald	9-14	3- 6	5	0	21
Lucas	4-13	1- 1	13	4	9
Nowell	3- 9	4- 6	4	2	10
Reasbeck	6-11	0- 0	1	3	12
Doughty	1- 4	1- 2	1	0	3
Bradds	3- 7	4- 5	7	0	10
Taylor	1- 2	0- 0	0	0	2
Flatt	0- 0	0- 0	1	0	0
Frazier	0- 1	0- 1	0	1	0
Knight	1- 6	0- 0	1	2	2
Gearhart	3- 7	1- 2	2	2	7
Totals	38-83	17-26	40	18	93

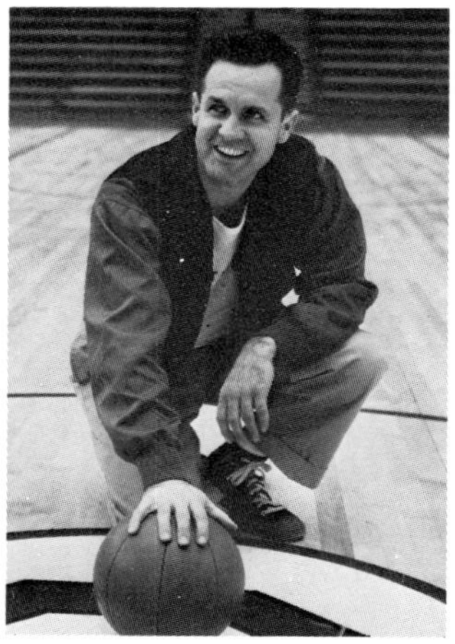

Ed Jucker

Western Kentucky	fg-fga	ft-fta	rb	pf	tp
Dunn	5-13	2- 2	11	3	12
Jackson	4- 9	3- 3	7	4	11
Todd	4- 9	4- 7	8	3	12
Carrier	4-13	0- 0	2	3	8
Rascoe	8-23	10-12	7	3	26
Ridley	1- 1	0- 0	2	0	2
Smith	1- 1	0- 0	0	1	2
Day	0- 0	0- 0	0	1	0
Caines	0- 0	0- 0	0	1	0
Castle	0- 0	0- 0	0	0	0
Totals	27-69	19-24	37	19	73

Half time: Ohio State 43-30. Officials: Bello and Eisenstein. Attendance: 8,300.

Creighton	fg-fga	ft-fta	rb	pf	tp
McManamon	1- 8	2- 4	8	5	4
Bakos	2-14	3- 4	12	5	7
Silas	3-14	9-12	7	4	15
Millard	2-13	1- 2	4	4	5
Wagner	2-11	3- 4	3	4	7
Silvestrini	2- 3	0- 0	3	1	4
Officer	2- 9	0- 0	1	1	4
Team			10		
Totals	14-72	18-26	48	24	46

Cincinnati	fg-fga	ft-fta	rb	pf	tp
Bonham	4-10	6- 7	5	2	14
Wilson	0- 3	3- 6	1	4	3
Hogue	10-14	4- 5	19	4	24
Yates	0- 7	2- 3	5	1	2
Thacker	5- 8	2- 3	13	1	12
Dierking	1- 3	0- 0	2	1	2
Sizer	1- 3	4- 6	1	3	6
Heidotting	0- 1	0- 2	1	1	0
Shingleton	0- 1	1- 2	1	0	1
Calhoun	1- 1	0- 0	1	0	2
Team			10		
Totals	22-51	22-34	59	17	66

Half time: Cincinnati 29-18.

Colorado	fg-fga	ft-fta	rb	pf	tp
Gilmore	4- 8	3- 4	9	2	11
Charlton	9-21	0- 0	6	0	18
Davis	8-11	1- 5	9	4	17
Lee	3- 7	2- 4	8	3	8
Whissen	2- 4	1- 3	4	2	5
Sparks	0- 1	1- 2	1	1	1
Mueller	2- 5	1- 1	5	2	5
Melton	1- 4	0- 0	1	0	2
Team			3		
Totals	29-61	9-19	46	14	67

Texas Tech	fg-fga	ft-fta	rb	pf	tp
Percival	3- 6	1- 2	5	3	7
Gindorf	4- 7	3- 3	1	3	11
Hudgons	5-13	2- 3	10	1	12
Mounts	7-20	5- 6	3	2	19
Hennig	1- 6	3- 3	5	5	5
Wall	3- 6	0- 0	0	2	6
Team			10		
Totals	23-58	14-17	34	16	60

Half time: Colorado 43-32. Officials: Filiberti and Korte. Attendance: 8,000.

Pepperdine	fg-fga	ft-fta	rb	pf	tp
Dinnel	3-10	2- 8	9	4	8
Smith	4- 9	0- 0	4	3	8
Tift	6-11	3- 7	9	3	15
Tinsley	6-15	1- 2	3	3	13
Warlick	9-21	5- 6	13	4	23
Bridges	0- 1	0- 0	2	0	0
Dougan	0- 1	0- 1	1	3	0
Team			6		
Totals	28-68	11-24	47	20	67

Oregon State	fg-fga	ft-fta	rb	pf	tp
Carty	4-15	6- 6	6	1	14
Pauly	7-18	1- 2	7	1	15
Counts	4-18	7- 8	21	5	15
Baker	6-14	3- 5	3	4	15
Hayward	0- 2	0- 0	0	0	0
Jacobsen	4- 9	2- 2	6	5	10
Torgerson	0- 0	0- 1	4	1	0
Campbell	0- 0	0- 0	0	0	0
Team			15		
Totals	25-76	19-24	62	17	69

Half time: Oregon State 35-30. Attendance: 9,816.

UCLA	fg-fga	ft-fta	rb	pf	tp
Cunningham	9-18	3- 4	7	4	21
Blackman	3- 8	2- 2	2	4	8
Slaughter	5- 7	0- 0	9	5	10
Hazzard	4-12	5- 8	8	0	13
Green	3-15	5- 8	7	2	11
Stewart	2- 5	4- 6	7	4	8
Hicks	1- 2	0- 0	0	2	2
Waxman	0- 2	0- 0	1	1	0
Rosvall	0- 0	0- 0	0	0	0
Team			12		
Totals	27-69	19-28	53	22	73

Utah State	fg-fga	ft-fta	rb	pf	tp
Green	9-20	8-12	16	4	26
Johnson	4- 9	2- 6	15	2	10
Haney	4-16	4- 9	14	4	12
Hasen	5-15	0- 1	0	4	10
Goldsberry	1- 3	0- 0	2	4	2
Nate	0- 0	0- 0	0	2	0
Holman	1- 6	0- 1	0	2	2
Team			9		
Totals	24-69	14-29	56	22	62

Half time: UCLA 43-30. Attendance: 10,186.

Third Place

St. Joseph's, Pa.	fg-fga	ft-fta	rb	pf	tp
Boyle	3- 6	3- 4	5	5	9
Wynne	8-18	8-11	8	5	24
Dickey	0- 2	0- 0	5	5	0
Hoy	7-15	4- 4	7	1	18
Lynam	1- 1	0- 1	0	3	2
Hoffman	2-11	5-12	19	1	9
Booth	2- 8	3- 4	0	1	7
Gormley	5-11	2- 2	4	3	12
Kelly	0- 1	0- 0	0	2	0
Courtin	1- 6	0- 0	0	3	2
Tiller	1- 3	0- 2	4	1	2
Team			5		
Totals	30-82	25-40	57	30	85

New York Univ.	fg-fga	ft-fta	rb	pf	tp
Kramer	4-11	4- 7	12	5	12
O'Neill	4- 6	5- 8	3	3	13
Hairston	10-15	5- 6	8	2	25
Boose	4-15	8-12	18	4	16
Reiner	5-10	7- 7	1	3	17
Blaha	1- 3	2- 3	3	5	4
Galliard	0- 1	4- 4	4	4	4
Williams	1- 1	0- 0	1	2	2
Filardi	0- 1	1- 2	1	0	1
Jordan	0- 0	0- 0	0	0	0
Patton	0- 0	0- 0	0	0	0
Frentera	0- 0	0- 0	0	0	0
Team			6		
Totals	29-63	36-49	57	28	94

Half time: St. Joseph's 51-40.

Western Kentucky	fg-fga	ft-fta	rb	pf	tp
Dunn	9-15	1- 1	9	3	19
Jackson	5-16	4- 4	4	1	14
Carrier	11-20	0- 1	8	4	22
Rascoe	14-22	1- 1	5	3	29
D. Smith	1- 4	0- 0	5	4	2
Totals	40-77	6- 7	31	15	86

Butler	fg-fga	ft-fta	rb	pf	tp
Bowman	9-18	3- 3	7	0	21
Freeman	4- 8	0- 0	5	2	8
Blue	8-14	2- 4	8	0	18
Williams	9-20	5- 8	3	2	23
Haslam	4- 8	1- 1	4	2	9
Engle	4- 5	0- 0	0	1	8
Pope	0- 2	0- 0	0	1	0
Totals	38-75	11-16	27	8	87

Half time: Western Kentucky 40-31. Regulation Score: 76-76. Officials: Bello and Eisenstein.

Creighton	fg-fga	ft-fta	rb	pf	tp
McManamon	8-19	2- 4	9	2	18
Officer	1- 3	0- 1	6	3	2
Bakos	5-12	0- 2	10	5	10
Silvestrini	2- 7	0- 1	11	1	4
Silas	3-16	6- 8	13	4	12
Swassing	0- 1	0- 0	0	0	0
Millard	3-10	6- 7	7	4	12
Wagner	2- 7	1- 1	2	4	5
Team			7		
Totals	24-75	15-24	65	23	63

Texas Tech	fg-fga	ft-fta	rb	pf	tp
Percival	4-14	1- 3	9	3	9
Gindorf	1- 3	0- 0	1	5	2
Hudgens	5-11	2- 5	6	5	12
Mounts	6-16	12-14	8	1	24
Hennig	4- 7	2- 4	8	4	10
Wall	1- 6	2- 4	3	3	4
Farley	0- 1	0- 1	1	0	0
Mickey	0- 0	0- 0	0	0	0
Team			8		
Totals	21-58	19-31	44	21	61

Half time: Creighton 34-30. Officials: Marick and Korte. Attendance: 9,000.

Pepperdine	fg-fga	ft-fta	rb	pf	tp
Dinnel	4-10	3- 5	6	1	11
Smith	1- 6	2- 4	6	2	4
Tift	10-17	2- 5	5	3	22
Tinsley	9-20	1- 1	6	4	19
Warlick	4-16	3- 5	12	5	11
Bridges	3- 9	0- 2	9	3	6
Dougan	1- 3	0- 0	6	1	2
Team			14		
Totals	32-81	11-22	64	19	75

1962 CINCINNATI BEARCATS—(l-r) Front Row: Larry Shingleton, Tony Yates, Larry Elsasser, Tom Thacker, Tom Sizer, Jim Calhoun; Second Row: Tay Baker, Bill Abernethy, Fred Dierking, George Wilson, Ron Reis, Paul Hogue, Dale Heidotting, Ron Bonham, Ed Jucker.

Utah State	fg-fga	ft-fta	rb	pf	tp
Johnson	1- 6	1- 1	3	4	3
Green	6-17	8-13	7	3	20
Haney	9-16	1- 1	8	2	19
Goldsberry	0- 0	0- 0	1	2	0
Holman	6-13	1- 1	1	1	13
Garn	3- 6	2- 2	4	0	8
Nate	1- 6	0- 2	4	1	2
Casey	0- 1	0- 1	2	3	0
Puzey	1- 1	0- 0	0	0	2
Watts	0- 0	0- 0	0	0	0
Hasen	1- 4	2- 2	1	2	4
Team			15		
Totals	28-70	15-23	46	18	71

Half time: Pepperdine 42-36.

Regional Championships

Wake Forest	fg-fga	ft-fta	rb	pf	tp
Chappell	9-23	4- 6	21	2	22
Christie	2- 4	2- 3	3	2	6
Woollard	9-15	1- 1	18	1	19
Packer	7-15	4- 4	1	2	18
Wiedeman	5-12	2- 4	3	2	12
Hull	0- 0	0- 0	0	0	0
McCoy	1- 2	0- 0	2	1	2
Team			2		
Totals	33-71	13-18	50	10	79

Villanova	fg-fga	ft-fta	rb	pf	tp
White	6-25	2- 4	14	2	14
O'Brien	7-10	0- 0	10	3	14
McMonagle	3-11	0- 1	6	4	6
Leftwich	4-13	2- 6	8	2	10
Jones	11-18	3- 3	5	2	25
McGill	0- 0	0- 0	0	0	0
Walsh	0- 0	0- 0	0	1	0
Winterbottom	0- 0	0- 0	0	0	0
Stefanic	0- 0	0- 0	0	0	0
Team			3		
Totals	31-77	7-14	46	14	69

Half time: Villanova 44-42. Attendance: 12,500.

Ohio State	fg-fga	ft-fta	rb	pf	tp
Havlicek	5-15	3- 4	10	3	13
McDonald	0- 0	0- 0	0	1	0
Lucas	12-21	9-10	15	3	33
Nowell	1- 5	3- 4	3	2	5
Reasbeck	4-11	0- 0	3	3	8
Doughty	4-12	0- 0	2	2	8
Bradds	0- 0	0- 1	0	0	0
Gearhart	1- 1	5- 7	4	0	7
Taylor	0- 0	0- 0	0	0	0
Flatt	0- 0	0- 0	0	0	0
Knight	0- 0	0- 0	0	0	0
Totals	27-65	20-26	37	14	74

Kentucky	fg-fga	ft-fta	rb	pf	tp
Burchett	3- 9	2- 4	3	5	8
Roberts	4- 8	0- 0	0	5	8
Nash	5-19	4- 6	9	1	14
Pursiful	8-17	5- 5	4	4	21
Baesler	2-10	3- 4	9	4	7
Feldhaus	1- 4	0- 2	2	2	2
McDonald	2- 2	0- 0	1	0	4
Deeken	0- 0	0- 0	0	0	0
Totals	25-69	14-21	28	21	64

Half time: Ohio State 41-37. Officials: Eckmann and Honzo. Attendance: 14,500.

Cincinnati	fg-fga	ft-fta	rb	pf	tp
Bonham	8-20	1- 2	7	3	17
Wilson	7-12	5- 8	7	2	19
Hogue	9-17	4- 4	12	3	22
Yates	1- 8	3- 3	6	1	5
Thacker	3- 8	0- 1	4	0	6
Sizer	1- 1	0- 0	1	2	2
Heidotting	0- 0	0- 0	0	1	0
Dierking	0- 0	0- 0	0	0	0
Shingleton	0- 1	0- 0	1	0	0
Calhoun	1- 1	0- 0	0	1	2
Reis	0- 0	0- 0	1	0	0
Team			6		
Totals	30-68	13-18	45	13	73

Colorado	fg-fga	ft-fta	rb	pf	tp
Gilmore	5- 6	5- 6	7	3	15
Charlton	4-16	3- 6	7	3	11
Davis	3- 8	0- 0	4	2	6
Lee	2- 5	0- 0	1	4	4
Millies	2- 4	0- 1	4	1	4
Whissen	2- 6	0- 0	0	4	4
Mueller	0- 1	2- 2	2	1	2
Sparks	0- 1	0- 1	1	0	0
Melton	0- 0	0- 0	0	0	0
Woodward	0- 0	0- 2	0	0	0
Zyzda	0- 0	0- 0	0	0	0
McCann	0- 0	0- 0	0	0	0
Team			9		
Totals	18-47	10-18	35	14	46

Half time: Cincinnati 41-29. Officials: Filiberti and Hale. Attendance: 9,000.

UCLA	fg-fga	ft-fta	rb	pf	tp
Cunningham	4- 9	4- 4	11	4	12
Blackman	3- 9	1- 1	5	1	7
Slaughter	2- 8	3- 5	10	0	7
Hazzard	6- 9	5- 5	4	5	17
Green	5-16	13-16	3	3	23
Waxman	5- 8	2- 2	5	0	12
Hicks	2- 2	0- 1	2	0	4
Stewart	1- 2	0- 0	1	1	2
Rosvall	1- 2	0- 0	0	0	2
Gower	0- 0	2- 2	1	0	2
Milhorn	0- 1	0- 0	0	0	0
Huggins	0- 0	0- 1	0	0	0
Team			8		
Totals	29-66	30-37	50	14	88

Oregon State	fg-fga	ft-fta	rb	pf	tp
Carty	4- 8	1- 5	5	2	9
Jacobson	2- 3	1- 2	5	1	5
Counts	11-25	2- 2	17	2	24
Baker	2-10	2- 3	2	4	6
Pauly	4- 8	2- 5	2	3	10
Rossi	1- 4	0- 0	2	3	2
Benner	0- 3	0- 0	3	2	0
Hayward	3- 9	0- 0	2	1	6
Campbell	0- 1	0- 0	2	1	0
Bastor	1- 3	1- 1	0	2	3
Torgerson	2- 3	0- 0	2	0	4
Team			8		
Totals	30-77	9-18	50	21	69

Half time: UCLA 44-30. Attendance: 9,816.

Semifinals

Wake Forest	fg-fga	ft-fta	rb	pf	tp
Chappell	10-24	7-11	18	5	27
Christie	0- 2	1- 1	4	2	1
Wollard	1- 3	1- 2	3	2	3
Wiedeman	5-16	3- 6	8	0	13
Packer	8-14	1- 2	5	3	17
Hull	0- 2	0- 0	2	2	0
McCoy	0- 1	2- 2	1	1	2
Carmichael	0- 0	0- 0	1	1	0
Hassell	1- 2	0- 0	0	0	2
Zawacki	0- 0	1- 3	0	0	1
Koehler	0- 1	0- 0	0	0	0
Brooks	0- 1	2- 2	1	1	2
Totals	25-66	18-29	43	17	68

Ohio State	fg-fga	ft-fta	rb	pf	tp
Havlicek	9-19	7- 9	16	3	25
McDonald	5-10	1- 2	5	3	11
Lucas	8-16	3- 4	16	1	19
Nowell	2-11	0- 0	2	2	4
Reasbeck	5- 7	0- 0	3	4	10
Gearhart	2- 5	0- 0	0	4	4
Doughty	2- 4	4- 4	5	1	8
Bradds	0- 0	0- 1	4	3	0
Knight	0- 2	0- 0	2	2	0
Flatt	0- 0	1- 2	0	0	1
Taylor	0- 0	0- 0	0	1	0
Frazier	1- 1	0- 0	0	0	2
Totals	34-75	16-22	53	24	84

Half time: Ohio State 46-34. Attendance: 18,274.

UCLA	fg-fga	ft-fta	rb	pf	tp
Blackman	2- 3	0- 0	2	5	4
Cunningham	8-14	3- 3	9	2	19
Slaughter	1- 4	0- 0	7	5	2
Green	9-16	9-11	7	1	27
Hazzard	5-10	2- 3	6	2	12
Waxman	2- 3	2- 3	3	1	6
Stewart	0- 0	0- 0	1	2	0
Totals	27-50	16-20	35	18	70

Cincinnati	fg-fga	ft-fta	rb	pf	tp
Bonham	8-14	3- 4	4	2	19
Wilson	1- 6	1- 2	4	1	3
Hogue	12-18	12-17	19	3	36
Thacker	1- 7	0- 0	4	3	2
Yates	4-10	2- 3	3	3	10
Sizer	1- 3	0- 0	1	3	2
Totals	27-58	18-28	33	17	72

Half time: 37-37. Attendance: 18,274.

National Third Place

Wake Forest	fg-fga	ft-fta	rb	pf	tp
Chappell	9-13	8-10	11	5	26
Christie	1- 8	0- 0	2	3	2
Wollard	4- 6	1- 3	12	3	9
Packer	10-19	2- 2	5	1	22
Wiedeman	7-13	4- 6	1	4	18
McCoy	0- 1	3- 3	2	3	3
Hull	0- 0	0- 1	2	1	0
Brooks	0- 0	0- 0	0	0	0
Hassell	1- 1	0- 0	0	0	2
Totals	32-61	18-25	35	20	82

UCLA	fg-fga	ft-fta	rb	pf	tp
Cunningham	5-17	7- 8	11	5	17
Blackman	4-10	3- 4	8	2	11
Slaughter	8-11	1- 1	10	1	17
Green	3-12	1- 3	4	5	7
Hazzard	5-17	5- 5	10	3	15
Waxman	1- 3	5- 6	8	0	7
Hicks	2- 4	0- 1	3	1	4
Stewart	1- 2	0- 0	1	2	2
Milhern	0- 1	0- 0	0	0	0
Totals	29-77	22-28	55	19	80

Half time: Wake Forest 38-36. Attendance: 18,469.

Championship

Ohio State	fg-fga	ft-fta	rb	pf	tp
Havlicek	5-14	1- 2	9	1	11
McDonald	0- 1	3- 3	1	2	3
Lucas	5-17	1- 2	16	3	11
Reasbeck	4- 6	0- 0	0	4	8
Nowell	4-16	1- 1	6	2	9
Doughty	0- 1	0- 0	2	2	0
Gearhart	1- 4	0- 0	4	3	2
Bradds	5- 7	5- 6	4	2	15
Totals	24-66	11-14	42	19	59

Cincinnati	fg-fga	ft-fta	rb	pf	tp
Bonham	3-12	4- 4	6	3	10
Wilson	1- 6	4- 4	11	2	6
Hogue	11-18	0- 2	19	2	22
Thacker	6-14	9-11	6	2	21
Yates	4- 8	4- 7	1	1	12
Sizer	0- 0	0- 0	0	0	0
Totals	25-58	21-28	43	10	71

Half time: Cincinnati 37-29. Attendance: 18,469.

1963

First Round

New York Univ.	fg-fga	ft-fta	rb	pf	tp
Kramer	13-23	11-14	6	1	37
Hairston	11-17	7- 9	0	4	29
Williams	5-10	1- 2	1	1	11
O'Neill	0- 3	2- 6	4	5	2
Patton	1- 4	0- 0	1	4	2
Jordan	1- 2	0- 0	0	1	2
Blaha	1- 2	6- 7	2	4	8
Groothuis	0- 1	2- 5	0	0	2
Team			8		
Totals	32-62	29-43	22	20	93

Pittsburgh	fg-fga	ft-fta	rb	pf	tp
Jinks	8-14	1- 2	1	4	17
Generalovich	5-16	3- 6	0	5	13
Krieger	0- 1	1- 1	0	5	1
Grgurich	2- 5	1- 1	3	2	5
Roman	6-19	4- 4	2	3	16
Ruby	2- 3	0- 1	0	4	4
Sheffield	6- 8	8- 8	2	1	20
Saver	2- 5	3- 4	1	4	7
Team			8		
Totals	31-71	21-27	17	28	83

Half time: New York Univ. 44-34. Officials: Stevens and DiGravio.

West Virginia	fg-fga	ft-fta	rb	pf	tp
Catlett	3- 5	1- 1	0	4	7
Wolff	0- 3	1- 1	3	0	1
Lowry	7-11	5- 7	1	3	19
McCormick	6-11	3- 3	4	4	15
Thorn	8-17	1- 3	2	0	17
Lantz	0- 1	2- 2	2	3	2
Maphis	2- 7	1- 3	1	0	5
Cluck	1- 2	0- 1	0	2	2
Ray	1- 4	7- 8	0	2	9
Weir	0- 0	0- 0	0	1	0
Team					
Totals	28-61	21-29	15	19	77

Connecticut	fg-fga	ft-fta	rb	pf	tp
Manning	4-13	1- 2	2	2	9
Kimball	8-14	3- 7	1	4	19
Slomcenski	1- 6	0- 1	0	5	2
Perno	4-14	8-10	4	2	16
Czucry	0- 2	2- 2	1	0	2
Coney	8-17	1- 3	0	3	17
Haines	0- 3	0- 0	0	1	0
Holteen	1- 6	4- 4	0	3	6
Team			5		
Totals	26-75	19-29	13	20	71

Half time: West Virginia 42-40. Officials: Eisenstein and Fox. Attendance: 9,236.

St. Joseph's, Pa.	fg-fga	ft-fta	rb	pf	tp
Wynne	5-16	4- 7	7	4	14
Boyle	6-13	4- 4	5	4	16
Hofmann	0- 1	0- 1	3	1	0
Lynam	8-16	2- 3	4	3	18
Courtin	9-19	3- 3	6	5	21
Tiller	2- 4	4- 6	10	1	8
Kelly	2- 6	0- 0	1	1	4
Hoy	0- 3	1- 3	0	1	1
Team			2		
Totals	32-77	18-27	38	20	82

283

Princeton	fg-fga	ft-fta	rb	pf	tp
Haarlow	5-9	0-1	4	1	10
Berling	1-1	0-0	0	1	2
Howard	2-2	3-4	7	4	7
Bradley	12-21	16-16	16	5	40
Hyland	8-16	4-4	7	3	20
Roth	0-2	0-2	5	5	0
Johnston	1-2	0-0	1	1	2
Niemann	0-1	0-0	1	2	0
Kingston	0-0	0-0	0	0	0
Team			4		
Totals	29-54	23-27	45	22	81

Half time: Princeton 33-31. Officials: Eckman and Bonder. Attendance: 9,236.

Bowling Green	fg-fga	ft-fta	rb	pf	tp
Gilbert	1-5	2-2	5	4	4
Junior	4-9	0-0	7	1	8
Thurmond	5-16	6-9	20	4	16
Haley	4-7	0-1	2	1	8
Komives	10-25	14-15	7	2	34
Chatman	1-2	1-1	2	2	3
Reynolds	2-4	0-0	2	0	4
Team			4		
Totals	27-68	23-28	49	14	77

Notre Dame	fg-fga	ft-fta	rb	pf	tp
Miller	1-7	1-1	5	3	3
Sahm	7-13	0-0	15	3	14
Jesewitz	1-8	4-7	10	4	6
Andreoli	7-22	3-3	3	2	17
Matthews	9-19	5-7	3	5	23
Erlenbaugh	1-3	3-3	4	2	5
Skarich	2-4	0-0	5	0	4
Team			5		
Totals	28-76	16-21	50	19	72

Half time: Bowling Green 42-40. Officials: Stout, Meyer. Attendance: 8,613.

Loyola, Ill.	fg-fga	ft-fta	rb	pf	tp
Harkness	9-17	1-4	12	1	19
Rouse	7-9	4-5	14	2	18
Hunter	6-8	5-5	6	1	17
Egan	5-13	8-10	5	2	18
Miller	7-14	7-8	7	0	21
Wood	2-3	2-2	5	1	6
Connaughton	2-2	2-4	3	0	6
Reardon	1-3	0-0	4	0	2
Rochelle	1-3	2-3	4	0	4
Team			6		
Totals	40-72	31-41	66	7	111

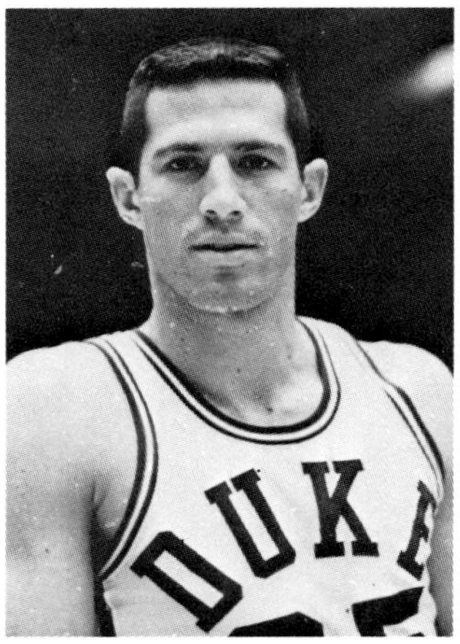

Art Heyman

Tennessee Tech	fg-fga	ft-fta	rb	pf	tp
Carnwell	4-6	0-0	4	4	8
Young	6-21	2-3	3	1	14
Adams	0-1	1-1	2	3	1
Rychener	2-10	0-0	4	5	4
Mason	4-15	2-2	2	4	10
Davenport	0-1	0-0	1	2	0
Nichols	0-5	0-0	2	2	0
Sexton	2-9	0-0	8	1	4
Wright	0-6	0-0	8	1	0
Hays	0-2	1-1	1	4	1
Underhill	0-1	0-0	1	0	0
Wood	0-5	0-1	2	0	0
Team			4		
Totals	18-82	6-8	42	27	42

Half time: Loyola 61-20. Officials: Soohy and Radabaugh. Attendance: 8,613.

Colorado State	fg-fga	ft-fta	rb	pf	tp
Etheridge	1-8	2-2	15	4	4
Sigafoos	6-10	0-1	4	4	12
Green	6-15	7-8	12	5	19
Matthews	8-13	1-3	4	1	17
Anderson	5-10	0-1	3	1	10
Foster	0-0	0-1	1	2	0
Ellis	2-4	1-1	2	1	5
Team			7		
Totals	28-60	11-17	48	18	67

Oklahoma City	fg-fga	ft-fta	rb	pf	tp
Jackson	4-10	2-6	10	3	10
Miller	2-3	0-0	3	1	4
Johnston	4-12	3-5	9	3	11
Koper	8-21	1-1	6	1	17
Hill	8-13	3-7	0	4	19
Gibbon	0-0	1-2	1	0	1
Stephens	0-1	0-1	2	4	0
White	3-7	0-2	3	0	6
Heusman	1-3	0-0	0	2	2
Hopkins	0-0	0-0	0	0	0
Team			10		
Totals	30-70	10-24	44	18	70

Half time: Colorado State 42-31. Officials: Lawson and Watson.

Texas Western	fg-fga	ft-fta	rb	pf	tp
Toren	1-2	3-4	0	3	5
Richardson	2-7	0-1	2	4	4
Barnes	2-4	6-9	6	5	10
Lesley	3-12	2-2	5	2	8
Brown	6-15	3-4	2	2	15
Vaughn	0-2	1-1	2	1	1
Campbell	1-2	2-3	5	2	4
Team			4		
Totals	15-44	17-24	26	19	47

Texas	fg-fga	ft-fta	rb	pf	tp
Fisher	0-1	0-1	2	5	0
Franks	4-6	1-1	6	3	9
Humphrey	8-11	2-4	10	2	18
Puryear	1-2	4-5	1	3	6
Gilbert	2-8	7-7	0	2	11
Clark	0-2	0-0	0	0	0
Fultz	7-10	2-3	5	3	16
Heller	1-1	1-1	2	1	3
Dugan	1-1	0-0	1	4	2
Smith	0-0	0-0	0	0	0
Weeks	0-1	0-0	2	0	0
Team			5		
Totals	24-43	17-22	34	23	65

Half time: 25-25. Officials: Fette and Carpenter. Attendance: 7,100.

Utah State	fg-fga	ft-fta	rb	pf	tp
Estes	12-22	8-8	9	4	32
Johnson	7-13	1-2	7	5	15
Collier	2-12	4-4	11	4	8
Hasen	6-12	0-0	2	5	12
Goldsberry	2-6	0-2	5	3	4
Angle	2-5	0-0	2	1	4
Casey	0-0	0-0	0	0	0
Team			4		
Totals	31-70	13-16	40	22	75

Arizona State	fg-fga	ft-fta	rb	pf	tp
Cerkvenik	1-5	5-7	10	3	7
Caldwell	13-22	5-6	9	4	31
Becker	8-18	1-2	19	4	17
Senitza	5-13	2-3	2	0	12
Dairman	4-15	0-0	8	3	8
Howard	1-2	1-3	0	0	3
Disarufino	0-0	1-2	0	0	1
Team			5		
Totals	32-75	15-23	53	14	79

Half time: Utah State 41-35. Regulation score: 67-67. Officials: Fouts and Filibarti.

Oregon State	fg-fga	ft-fta	rb	pf	tp
Pauly	6-10	1-3	5	3	13
Kraus	1-1	0-0	1	0	2
Counts	13-21	4-5	11	3	30
Peters	3-6	2-2	3	3	8
Baker	2-8	5-7	3	4	9
Jarvis	3-7	0-0	2	0	6
Rossi	0-0	0-0	0	1	0
Hayward	1-3	0-0	1	1	2
Team			5		
Totals	29-56	12-17	31	15	70

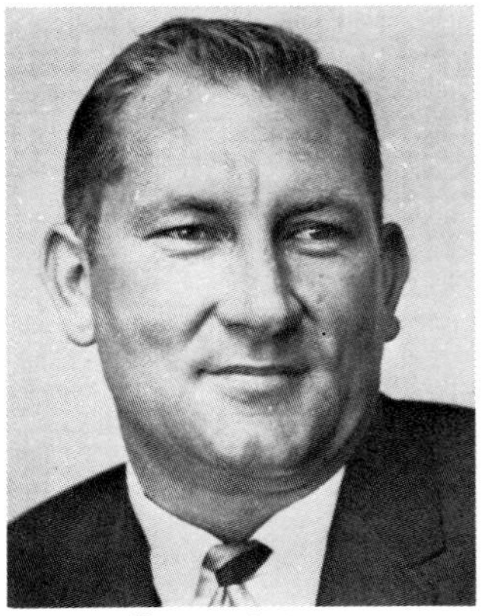
George Ireland

Seattle	fg-fga	ft-fta	rb	pf	tp
Smither	4-9	1-1	6	2	9
Dunston	2-7	1-2	6	4	5
Tresvant	6-11	4-4	8	3	16
Williams	4-8	0-0	2	3	8
Miles	11-19	6-9	5	3	28
Preston	0-1	0-0	0	0	0
Team			7		
Totals	27-55	12-16	34	15	66

Second Round

St. Joseph's, Pa.	fg-fga	ft-fta	rb	pf	tp
Boyle	9-11	5-6	8	4	23
Wynne	10-19	3-5	7	3	23
Hoffman	4-9	1-7	11	3	9
Lynam	6-8	8-12	1	3	20
Courtin	7-13	3-4	4	5	17
Tiller	2-3	1-2	1	1	5
Hoy	0-0	0-1	1	1	0
Kelly	0-0	0-0	1	0	0
Totals	38-63	21-37	34	20	97

West Virginia	fg-fga	ft-fta	rb	pf	tp
Catlett	2-5	1-1	2	5	5
Wolfe	2-5	1-1	7	5	5
Lowry	1-3	1-1	5	3	3
McCormick	10-18	3-5	2	3	23
Thorn	16-28	12-15	6	3	44
Shuck	1-1	0-0	3	1	2
Weir	0-1	0-0	0	1	0
Maphis	1-6	0-0	3	2	2
Ray	1-2	2-2	2	3	4
Totals	34-69	20-25	30	26	88

Half time: St. Joseph's 58-37.

Duke	fg-fga	ft-fta	rb	pf	tp
Heyman	6-21	10-14	13	2	22
Mullins	10-16	5-7	7	0	25
Buckley	4-8	2-5	16	5	10
Harrison	2-2	0-0	0	4	4
Schmidt	6-10	0-0	0	3	12
Herbster	3-3	0-0	1	2	6
Tison	1-2	0-0	4	3	2
Ferguson	0-2	0-0	1	0	0
Totals	32-64	17-26	42	19	81

New York Univ.	fg-fga	ft-fta	rb	pf	tp
Kramer	12-26	10-11	4	4	34
Williams	2-4	1-2	3	2	5
Hairston	8-13	2-4	11	4	18
O'Neill	3-9	0-0	4	3	6
Patton	2-5	0-1	5	4	4
Blaha	3-9	3-6	4	1	9
Jordan	0-1	0-0	1	0	0
Totals	30-67	16-24	32	18	76

Half time: Duke 32-27.

Loyola, Ill.	fg-fga	ft-fta	rb	pf	tp
Harkness	7-11	6-7	9	1	20
Rouse	8-24	0-0	19	4	16
Hunter	3-13	6-7	10	3	12
Egan	1-9	0-1	1	5	2
Miller	5-9	1-1	4	1	11
Wood	0-0	0-0	1	3	0
Team			4		
Totals	24-66	13-16	48	17	61

Mississippi State	fg-fga	ft-fta	rb	pf	tp
Mitchell	6-10	2-5	11	5	14
Gold	3-9	5-7	3	3	11
Brinker	3-6	3-5	7	4	9
Hutton	5-9	0-2	1	0	10
Stroud	3-15	1-1	3	2	7
Nichols	0-0	0-0	0	0	0
Team			10		
Totals	20-49	11-20	35	14	51

Half time: Loyola 26-19. Officials: Fox and Stevens.

Illinois	fg-fga	ft-fta	rb	pf	tp
Downey	7-20	6-9	12	4	20
Starnes	1-7	1-2	2	1	3
Burwell	8-16	5-9	11	1	21
Small	4-14	5-5	2	1	13
Brody	1-2	1-1	0	4	3
Thoren	5-9	0-0	12	2	10
Edwards	0-0	0-0	1	2	0
Team			9		
Totals	26-68	18-26	49	15	70

Bowling Green	fg-fga	ft-fta	rb	pf	tp
Junior	6-17	2-2	8	4	14
Gilbert	2-8	0-0	6	4	4
Thurmond	6-19	2-3	19	3	14
Haley	1-3	3-3	4	3	5
Komives	8-21	9-10	8	5	25
Chatman	2-5	1-1	3	3	5
Reynolds	0-1	0-0	0	0	0
Team			3		
Totals	25-74	17-19	51	22	67

Half time: Bowling Green 37-35. Officials: Fox and Mills.

Oklahoma City	fg-fga	ft-fta	rb	pf	tp
Miller	0-3	2-2	2	2	2
Jackson	5-11	1-2	11	3	11
Johnston	1-3	2-3	6	2	4
Koper	11-28	4-4	1	2	26
Hill	7-15	1-1	2	5	15
Heuman	2-3	0-0	2	2	4
Stephens	0-2	2-3	4	4	2
Gibbon	0-0	0-0	0	0	0
White	4-10	0-0	2	0	8
Snider	0-1	0-0	0	0	0
Team			10		
Totals	30-76	12-15	40	20	72

Colorado	fg-fga	ft-fta	rb	pf	tp
Mueller	4-6	3-5	5	3	11
Charlton	9-14	8-10	12	0	26
Davis	8-13	0-4	17	3	16
Lee	8-19	1-4	6	0	17
Parsons	0-6	5-7	5	2	5
Melton	1-3	1-2	1	1	3
Sparks	0-1	0-0	0	1	0
Joyce	0-0	0-0	0	1	0
Team			7		
Totals	30-62	18-32	53	11	78

Half time: Colorado 37-34. Officials: Bussenius and Soriano. Attendance: 5,500.

Cincinnati	fg-fga	ft-fta	rb	pf	tp
Bonham	9-23	6-11	4	1	24
Thacker	5-11	4-7	7	1	14
Wilson	8-20	9-12	12	2	25
Shingleton	0-3	1-2	4	2	1
Yates	2-6	3-3	2	4	7
Heidotting	1-1	0-0	0	1	2
Team			9		
Totals	25-64	23-35	38	11	73

Texas	fg-fga	ft-fta	rb	pf	tp
Franks	8-13	2-2	6	5	18
Fisher	2-6	0-0	3	2	4
Humphrey	4-4	1-1	5	4	9
Gilbert	4-10	5-5	1	2	13
Puryear	4-8	1-1	5	1	9
Fultz	6-9	1-2	8	4	13
Clark	0-0	1-1	0	0	1
Heller	0-1	0-0	0	1	0
Dugan	0-0	1-1	2	3	1
Smith	0-0	0-0	0	1	0
Weaks	0-0	0-0	0	0	0
Team			2		
Totals	28-51	12-13	32	23	68

Half time: Cincinnati 36-34. Officials: Varnell and Janzen.

Oregon State	fg-fga	ft-fta	rb	pf	tp
Kraus	1-3	1-2	9	4	3
Baker	10-17	1-1	0	0	21
Counts	9-22	4-5	4	5	22
Pauly	1-3	0-2	4	2	2
Peters	2-4	5-7	3	2	9
Jarvis	3-5	2-2	3	2	8
Campbell	0-1	0-0	1	0	0
Team			7		
Totals	26-55	13-19	30	16	65

San Francisco	fg-fga	ft-fta	rb	pf	tp
C. Thomas	8-10	5-7	8	4	21
Lee	4-14	4-4	9	4	12
Johnson	5-11	5-6	10	3	15
Moffatt	2-4	0-1	1	1	4
Brovelli	3-7	1-2	4	5	7
Brainard	1-4	0-0	1	1	2
H. Thomas	0-1	0-2	1	0	0
Belluomini	0-0	0-0	1	0	0
Team			6		
Totals	23-51	15-22	40	18	61

Half time: Oregon State 35-30.

Arizona State	fg-fga	ft-fta	rb	pf	tp
Caldwell	10-18	2-3	12	2	22
Cervanik	9-12	0-1	13	2	18
Becker	9-14	5-6	13	3	23
Senitza	5-7	3-4	1	3	13
Dairman	6-10	1-4	3	3	13
Howard	1-5	0-1	1	2	2
Disarufino	0-4	0-0	2	4	0
Orr	0-1	0-2	2	2	0
Jones	1-6	0-0	0	2	2
Owens	0-1	0-0	1	1	0
Sturgeon	0-1	0-0	1	0	0
Team			17		
Totals	41-79	11-21	65	25	93

UCLA	fg-fga	ft-fta	rb	pf	tp
Hirsch	8-17	3-4	4	5	19
Goss	3-10	2-3	5	0	8
Slaughter	4-9	6-7	5	4	14
Hazzard	4-11	5-7	5	2	13
Goodrich	1-8	1-2	1	0	3
Erickson	0-6	2-2	2	0	2
Waxman	2-5	1-3	1	2	5
Stewart	5-15	3-4	11	2	13
Milhorn	1-5	0-0	3	3	2
Team			12		
Totals	28-86	23-32	49	18	79

Half time: Arizona State 62-31.

Third Place

West Virginia	fg-fga	ft-fta	rb	pf	tp
Catlett	1-3	0-0	2	4	2
Wolfe	1-2	4-4	0	1	6
Shuck	1-3	2-4	2	2	4
McCormick	1-3	0-0	4	1	2
Thorn	13-24	7-7	9	0	33
Lowry	2-8	8-11	3	4	12
Lentz	6-9	0-1	10	3	12
Maphis	3-8	1-1	6	5	7
Weir	2-8	1-2	2	0	5
Totals	30-68	23-30	34	23	83

New York Univ.	fg-fga	ft-fta	rb	pf	tp
Kramer	6-13	17-20	14	4	29
Hairston	5-13	7-9	7	5	17
Williams	3-8	1-1	3	3	7
O'Neill	3-7	2-2	3	1	8
Patton	3-5	0-0	11	5	6
Jordan	0-2	0-0	3	1	0
Blaha	3-4	0-0	4	2	6
Frontera	0-0	0-0	0	0	0
Totals	23-52	27-32	45	21	73

Half time: West Virginia 39-36.

Vic Rouse

Les Hunter

Mississippi State	fg-fga	ft-fta	rb	pf	tp
Mitchell	5-14	13-16	8	4	23
Brinker	2-6	3-3	10	4	7
Shows	2-5	1-3	7	5	5
Hutton	5-11	4-7	3	1	14
Stroud	5-13	3-3	2	2	13
Williams	0-5	1-2	6	4	1
Posey	0-1	0-0	2	0	0
Nichols	1-1	0-1	4	0	2
Team			9		
Totals	20-56	25-35	51	20	65

Bowling Green	fg-fga	ft-fta	rb	pf	tp
Junior	3-12	3-3	5	3	9
Chatman	0-2	0-1	6	3	0
Thurmond	6-22	7-10	31	3	19
Haley	1-1	0-1	1	1	2
Komives	7-26	6-7	2	3	20
Reynolds	0-3	0-0	0	1	0
Gilbert	1-3	2-3	2	3	4
Chapman	0-3	0-0	3	3	0
Pepin	2-3	0-0	1	4	4
Baker	1-5	0-0	1	3	2
Team			8		
Totals	21-80	18-24	60	27	60

Half time: Mississippi State 34-26. Officials: Mills and Fox.

Oklahoma City	fg-fga	ft-fta	rb	pf	tp
Hill	8-19	5-8	4	4	21
Jackson	2-8	3-3	13	5	7
Johnston	1-6	3-3	2	2	5
Stephens	4-6	3-4	4	5	11
Koper	10-18	5-9	5	1	25
Hopkins	1-1	0-2	2	2	2
White	1-3	1-2	2	2	3
Neusman	0-2	1-2	2	2	1
Nygard	0-0	0-1	1	1	0
Gibbon	0-1	0-0	0	1	0
Miller	2-3	4-6	4	2	8
Snider	0-0	0-0	0	0	0
Team			8		
Totals	29-67	25-40	45	27	83

Texas	fg-fga	ft-fta	rb	pf	tp
Franks	5-8	2-3	4	5	12
Fultz	4-6	1-3	6	5	9
Humphrey	4-7	8-10	10	4	16
Gilbert	5-10	7-11	10	3	17
Puryear	5-11	3-4	4	4	13
Heller	6-7	0-1	3	2	12
Fisher	0-2	0-1	1	1	0
Clark	0-1	0-0	0	0	0
Weaks	0-1	1-1	1	1	1
Dugan	3-5	4-6	6	5	10
Team			7		
Totals	32-58	26-40	52	30	90

Half time: Texas 50-44. Officials: Varnell and Janzen. Attendance: 8,500.

San Francisco	fg-fga	ft-fta	rb	pf	tp
C. Thomas	5-14	5-6	9	4	15
Lee	1-4	3-4	3	3	5
Johnson	7-16	6-9	20	1	20
Moffatt	4-10	3-6	8	4	11
Brovelli	4-7	5-5	0	3	13
Brainard	0-2	4-6	1	2	4
H. Thomas	1-2	6-6	1	0	8
Team			7		
Totals	22-55	32-42	49	17	76

UCLA	fg-fga	ft-fta	rb	pf	tp
Waxman	6-16	1-2	8	2	13
Hirsch	2-9	2-3	8	4	6
Slaughter	2-6	0-2	11	5	4
Hazzard	4-11	5-5	4	4	13
Milhorn	3-10	0-0	1	1	6
Stewart	1-4	0-0	3	4	2
Erickson	1-2	0-0	2	1	2
Goodrich	6-9	5-7	3	5	17
Goss	4-8	2-2	2	0	10
Huggins	0-0	2-2	1	3	2
Team			3		
Totals	29-75	17-23	46	29	75

Half time: UCLA 35-30.

Regional Championships

Duke	fg-fga	ft-fta	rb	pf	tp
Heyman	3-14	10-15	10	2	16
Mullins	10-16	4-4	5	1	24
Buckley	4-9	2-3	18	2	10
Harrison	0-3	1-2	2	0	1
Schmidt	9-16	2-2	5	0	20
Herbster	0-2	2-2	0	1	2
Tison	0-1	0-0	1	0	0
Totals	26-61	21-28	41	6	73

John Egan

St. Joseph's, Pa.	fg-fga	ft-fta	rb	pf	tp
Boyle	2-17	0-1	10	5	4
Wynne	13-23	3-3	9	2	29
Hoffman	1-5	0-0	4	4	2
Courtin	7-16	0-0	4	1	14
Lynam	4-7	0-1	5	4	8
Tiller	0-2	2-2	5	3	2
Kelly	0-2	0-0	1	1	0
Totals	27-72	5-7	38	20	59

Half time: Duke 34-33.

Loyola, Ill.	fg-fga	ft-fta	rb	pf	tp
Harkness	13-23	7-11	7	3	33
Rouse	3-17	0-0	19	2	6
Hunter	4-9	4-4	15	4	12
Egan	3-11	7-8	4	3	13
Miller	6-15	3-4	11	2	15
Wood	0-1	0-0	1	0	0
Team			8		
Totals	29-76	21-27	65	14	79

Illinois	fg-fga	ft-fta	rb	pf	tp
Downey	9-22	2-5	6	4	20
Starnes	1-6	0-0	4	2	2
Burwell	5-15	0-1	5	4	10
Brody	3-8	0-1	5	3	6
Thoren	4-11	0-2	7	3	8
Edwards	2-4	1-2	0	2	5
Redmon	0-1	0-0	2	1	0
McKeown	1-4	2-3	0	1	4
Small	3-9	3-3	4	3	9
Team			14		
Totals	28-80	8-17	49	23	64

Half time: Loyola 38-30. Officials: Stevens and Lennon.

Cincinnati	fg-fga	ft-fta	rb	pf	tp
Bonham	8-18	6-7	2	3	22
Thacker	7-13	4-5	13	1	18
Wilson	6-11	3-7	10	3	15
Shingleton	1-2	2-4	0	1	4
Yates	2-11	1-3	4	4	5
Heidotting	1-1	1-1	1	1	3
Team			10		
Totals	25-56	17-27	40	15	67

Jerry Harkness

285

Colorado	fg-fga	ft-fta	rb	pf	tp
Charlton	9-17	5-5	12	3	23
Mueller	3-10	3-6	14	4	9
Davis	5-9	1-4	12	3	11
Parsons	4-11	1-5	0	3	9
Lee	2-7	0-1	0	2	4
Melton	2-2	0-0	0	2	4
Sparks	0-0	0-0	0	1	0
Woodward	0-0	0-0	0	0	0
Joyce	0-0	0-0	0	1	0
Price	0-0	0-0	0	0	0
Sponholtz	0-0	0-0	0	0	0
Saunders	0-0	0-0	0	0	0
Team			5		
Totals	25-56	10-21	43	19	60

Half time: Colorado 32-31. Officials: Soriano and Bussenius. Attendance: 8,500.

Oregon State	fg-fga	ft-fta	rb	pf	tp
Kraus	0-0	0-0	2	2	0
Pauly	9-14	3-6	6	3	21
Counts	11-20	4-4	13	3	26
Peters	4-7	6-6	5	4	14
Baker	6-9	3-3	1	4	15
Jarvis	1-3	3-3	1	5	5
Rossi	0-1	2-3	0	3	2
Torgerson	0-0	0-2	0	0	0
Team			13		
Totals	31-54	21-27	41	24	83

Arizona State	fg-fga	ft-fta	rb	pf	tp
Caldwell	6-19	5-10	7	3	17
Cerkvenik	5-12	6-10	7	5	16
Becker	6-16	1-3	16	3	13
Dairman	2-4	2-3	2	2	6
Senitza	4-15	0-2	1	3	8
Howard	2-3	3-4	4	3	3
Disarufino	1-1	0-0	0	3	2
Team			10		
Totals	24-69	17-31	47	22	65

Half time: Oregon State 43-38.

Semifinals

Cincinnati	fg-fga	ft-fta	rb	pf	tp
Bonham	3-12	8-9	5	3	14
Thacker	5-8	4-8	11	3	14
Wilson	8-9	8-12	13	2	24
Yates	5-9	2-3	5	1	12
Shingleton	1-2	0-0	2	1	2
Heidotting	0-0	1-2	2	1	1
Cunningham	2-3	0-0	1	1	4
Meyer	1-1	1-2	1	1	3
Smith	1-3	0-2	1	1	2
Elsasser	1-2	0-1	1	0	2
Abernethy	1-2	0-0	3	0	2
Totals	28-51	24-39	44	14	80

Oregon State	fg-fga	ft-fta	rb	pf	tp
Pauly	2-8	0-1	3	5	4
Kraus	1-6	1-1	3	3	3
Counts	8-14	4-4	9	5	20
Peters	1-5	2-2	4	4	4
Baker	0-9	0-1	2	0	0
Jarvis	1-6	3-4	0	3	5
Rossi	1-3	0-0	0	1	2
Campbell	0-2	1-1	2	2	1
Torgerson	1-2	0-0	0	0	2
Hayward	0-2	1-1	2	3	1
Benner	2-2	0-0	1	0	4
Totals	17-59	12-15	26	26	46

Half time: Cincinnati 30-27.

Semifinals

Loyola, Ill.	fg-fga	ft-fta	rb	pf	tp
Harkness	7-18	6-9	11	3	20
Rouse	6-12	1-2	6	4	13
Hunter	11-20	7-9	18	3	29
Egan	4-9	6-7	3	2	14
Miller	8-11	2-2	5	4	18
Wood	0-1	0-0	3	0	0
Rochelle	0-0	0-0	0	0	0
Reardon	0-0	0-0	0	0	0
Cannaughton	0-0	0-0	0	0	0
Team			5		
Totals	36-71	22-29	51	16	94

Duke	fg-fga	ft-fta	rb	pf	tp
Heyman	11-30	7-9	12	5	29
Mullins	10-20	1-3	9	4	21
Buckley	4-10	2-4	13	3	10
Schmidt	0-2	0-0	2	3	0
Harrison	0-3	2-3	3	0	2
Herbster	0-2	0-0	0	1	0
Ferguson	1-2	0-0	0	1	2
Jamison	0-0	0-0	0	1	0
Cox	0-0	0-0	0	0	0
Mann	0-1	0-0	0	0	0
Tison	5-12	1-3	8	3	11
Team			5		
Totals	31-82	13-22	52	21	75

Half time: Loyola 44-31.

National Third Place

Duke	fg-fga	ft-fta	rb	pf	tp
Tison	4-9	3-5	11	3	11
Mullins	4-13	6-8	10	2	14
Buckley	2-5	2-5	7	4	6
Schmidt	10-15	0-0	4	1	20
Heyman	7-14	8-13	7	3	22
Harrison	4-8	1-2	5	1	9
Herbster	0-0	1-2	0	0	1
Ferguson	1-1	0-0	0	0	2
Kitching	0-0	0-0	0	0	0
Jamison	0-0	0-0	0	2	0
Cox	0-0	0-0	0	0	0
Mann	0-0	0-0	0	0	0
Team			6		
Totals	32-65	21-35	50	16	85

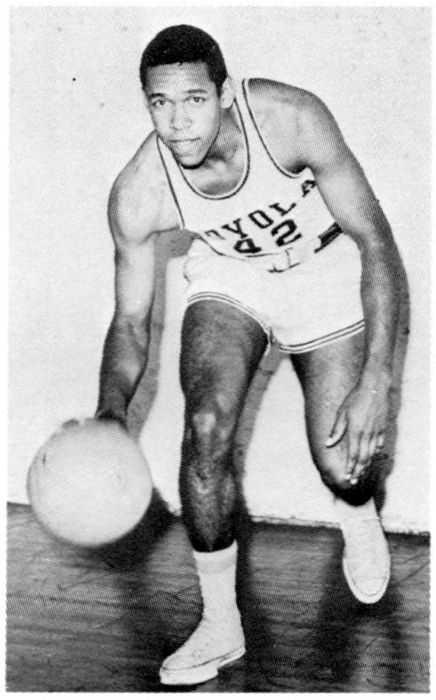

Ron Miller

Oregon State	fg-fga	ft-fta	rb	pf	tp
Pauly	5-15	2-2	11	4	12
Jarvis	3-12	1-1	6	5	7
Counts	9-30	7-10	18	2	25
Peters	3-9	2-2	6	4	8
Baker	3-11	1-1	3	2	7
Kraus	0-3	0-1	8	3	0
Benner	0-1	0-0	0	1	0
Hayward	2-6	0-0	1	3	4
Torgerson	0-0	0-0	1	0	0
Team			8		
Totals	25-87	13-17	62	24	63

Half time: Duke 34-23.

Championship

Loyola, Ill.	fg-fga	ft-fta	rb	pf	tp
Harkness	5-18	4-8	6	4	14
Rouse	6-22	3-4	12	4	15
Hunter	6-22	4-4	11	3	16
Egan	3-8	3-5	3	3	9
Miller	3-14	0-0	2	3	6
Team			11		
Totals	23-84	14-21	45	17	60

Cincinnati	fg-fga	ft-fta	rb	pf	tp
Bonham	8-16	6-6	4	3	22
Thacker	5-12	3-4	15	4	13
Wilson	4-8	2-3	13	4	10
Yates	4-6	1-4	8	4	9
Shingleton	1-3	2-3	4	0	4
Heidotting	0-0	0-0	1	2	0
Team			7		
Totals	22-45	14-20	52	17	58

Half time: Cincinnati 29-21. Regulation Score: 54-54.

1964

First Round

Villanova	fg-fga	ft-fta	rb	pf	tp
Moore	12-24	1-1	8	1	25
Sallee	1-5	0-0	7	3	2
Washington	5-13	4-7	19	1	14
Jones	7-22	3-3	6	0	17
Melchionni	6-11	1-1	2	1	13
Schaffer	1-3	1-1	5	3	3
Leftwich	0-2	3-4	2	1	3
Erickson	0-0	0-0	0	0	0
Winterbottom	0-0	0-0	0	0	0
Iorio	0-0	0-0	0	0	0
Totals	32-80	13-17	49	10	77

Providence	fg-fga	ft-fta	rb	pf	tp
Stone	5-12	4-4	4	0	14
Kovalski	4-9	0-0	9	5	8
Thompson	7-13	4-8	3	5	18
Benedict	8-14	0-0	4	2	16
Ahern	1-3	0-0	4	1	2
Blair	3-5	1-1	1	0	7
Dutton	0-0	0-0	4	0	0
Lasher	0-0	1-3	0	0	1
Stein	0-0	0-0	0	0	0
Totals	28-56	10-16	29	13	66

Half time: Villanova 34-28. Officials: Stevens and Honzo.

Connecticut	fg-fga	ft-fta	rb	pf	tp
Hesford	5-12	4-5	6	1	14
Kimball	6-21	0-4	17	1	12
Slomcenski	5-11	3-4	14	2	13
Perno	0-8	0-1	1	2	0
Ritter	0-1	0-0	1	0	0
DellaSala	7-13	0-1	8	1	14
Whitney	0-0	0-0	0	0	0
Totals	23-66	7-15	47	7	53

Temple	fg-fga	ft-fta	rb	pf	tp
Fitzgerald	5-13	0-1	9	2	10
Richardson	3-10	0-0	7	2	6
Williams	4-15	3-4	20	3	11
Kelley	7-14	2-2	4	3	16
Harrington	1-10	3-4	0	2	5
Bishop	0-0	0-0	1	1	0
Snethen	0-0	0-0	0	0	0
Totals	20-62	8-11	41	13	48

Half time: Temple 26-24. Officials: Bonder and Fox.

Princeton	fg-fga	ft-fta	rb	pf	tp
Bradley	12-22	10-11	12	3	34
Haarlow	7-17	1-1	7	1	15
Niemann	1-1	0-0	3	1	2
Roth	0-1	1-1	4	4	1
Howard	3-6	5-6	10	3	11
Steube	1-3	1-2	2	4	3
Kingston	0-0	0-0	3	0	0
Rodenbach	4-12	2-2	3	3	10
Kitch	1-1	0-0	0	0	2
Wright	2-2	0-0	0	0	4
Uhle	1-1	0-0	1	0	2
Berling	1-1	0-0	0	1	2
Totals	33-67	20-23	45	20	86

Virginia Military	fg-fga	ft-fta	rb	pf	tp
Schmaus	2-7	1-1	5	3	5
Gavsepohl	0-2	1-2	3	1	1
Watson	2-10	5-5	5	5	9
Kruszewski	8-17	3-4	5	4	19
Blair	6-20	8-12	4	4	20
Guy	1-2	2-3	5	1	4
Prosser	0-0	0-0	0	0	0
Hartung	0-1	0-0	0	0	0
Cooper	1-1	0-0	0	0	2
Totals	20-60	20-27	27	18	60

Half time: Virginia Military 36-35. Officials: Eisenstein and Reilo. Attendance: 9,211.

Ohio	fg-fga	ft-fta	rb	pf	tp
Hilt	5-8	4-10	15	4	14
Haley	6-12	5-5	5	3	17
Storey	5-13	3-5	6	2	13
Gill	2-3	1-2	4	3	5
Jackson	5-14	5-8	4	0	15
Davis	2-4	0-0	4	3	4
Weirich	1-1	1-1	2	0	3
Team			3		
Totals	26-55	19-31	43	15	71

Louisville	fg-fga	ft-fta	rb	pf	tp
Hawley	3-7	3-3	7	4	9
Reuther	11-22	5-7	7	4	27
Rothman	3-8	2-3	12	4	8
Rooks	2-7	1-1	1	3	5
Creamer	6-16	0-0	2	4	12
Finnegan	2-7	0-0	0	0	4
Clifford	1-3	2-3	7	2	4
Houston	0-1	0-0	0	2	0
Team			2		
Totals	28-71	13-17	38	23	69

Half time: Louisville 37-32. Officials: Allen and McPherson. Attendance: 8,500.

Loyola, Ill.	fg-fga	ft-fta	rb	pf	tp
Rouse	6-14	4-8	11	4	16
Miller	10-16	1-4	6	2	21
Hunter	5-10	3-6	22	4	13
Coleman	9-13	9-12	6	3	27
Egan	9-26	6-9	4	2	24
Wood	0-1	0-0	0	0	0
Manzke	0-0	0-0	0	0	0
Team			4		
Totals	39-80	23-39	53	15	101

Murray State	fg-fga	ft-fta	rb	pf	tp
Jennings	8-21	8-9	19	3	24
Varnas	10-15	1-1	10	3	21
Johnson	9-23	0-0	6	5	18
Pendleton	7-15	1-1	4	3	15
Schlosser	2-4	0-2	4	5	4
Goheen	3-5	1-1	2	4	7
Goerei	0-0	0-0	0	2	0
Walker	1-3	0-0	2	1	2
Team			6		
Totals	40-86	11-14	53	26	91

Half time: Loyola 54-43. Officials: Payak and Cochran. Attendance: 8,500.

Creighton	fg-fga	ft-fta	rb	pf	tp
Pointer	10-21	3-3	7	3	23
McGriff	10-15	5-8	10	5	25
Silas	7-15	1-6	27	4	15
Brown	4-12	1-1	0	2	9
Officer	1-10	1-1	7	0	3
Forehand	3-6	6-8	5	2	12
Apke	0-3	0-0	4	3	0
Miles	1-3	0-1	2	0	2
Totals	36-85	17-28	62	19	89

Oklahoma City	fg-fga	ft-fta	rb	pf	tp
Miller	2-6	2-3	2	4	6
Hunter	4-9	1-1	1	5	9
Jackson	5-10	2-3	24	3	12
Koper	9-18	8-11	4	2	26
Wells	9-15	1-4	6	5	19
Ware	1-4	0-3	5	1	2
Bagby	2-4	0-0	2	0	4
Snider	0-2	0-0	1	1	0
Harris	0-0	0-0	0	0	0
Totals	32-68	14-25	45	21	78

Half time: Creighton 47-38. Officials: Elliott and Covin. Attendance: 8,500.

Texas Western	fg-fga	ft-fta	rb	pf	tp
Stoglin	6-14	0-1	10	3	12
Banks	1-4	0-0	1	1	2
Barnes	16-23	10-13	19	3	42
Artis	2-7	3-4	2	1	7
Tredennick	0-1	0-1	0	1	0
Dibler	0-1	0-1	1	0	0
Flournoy	1-3	3-3	3	1	5
Team			6		
Totals	26-53	16-23	42	10	68

Texas A&M	fg-fga	ft-fta	rb	pf	tp
Gasway	1-2	0-0	5	3	2
Robinette	1-4	1-2	4	2	3
Beasley	6-12	1-1	4	3	13
Lenox	11-25	2-2	1	1	24
Timmins	3-7	0-0	1	2	6
Ferguson	0-0	0-0	0	2	0
Stringfellow	2-3	1-1	2	2	5
Norman	3-5	2-3	1	3	8
Timmerman	0-1	1-1	0	0	1
Team			8		
Totals	27-59	8-10	26	18	62

Half time: Texas A&M 35-32. Officials: Overby and Litchey. Attendance: 8,500.

Oregon State	fg-fga	ft-fta	rb	pf	tp
Eaton	3-6	2-5	4	4	8
Dreisewerd	2-3	0-1	1	3	4
Counts	6-17	15-18	19	4	27
Jarvis	4-9	0-2	2	5	8
Peters	3-11	0-1	7	5	6
Kraus	1-4	0-0	7	1	2
Baxter	0-0	0-0	0	1	0
Benner	0-0	0-0	0	0	0
Whelan	1-2	0-0	1	5	2
Team			7		
Totals	20-52	17-27	48	28	57

Seattle	fg-fga	ft-fta	rb	pf	tp
Vermillion	3-7	7-10	4	3	13
Turney	0-6	1-2	3	3	1
Tresvant	1-8	3-5	7	4	5
Williams	3-11	6-8	2	2	12
Heyward	5-9	4-8	4	4	14
Griffin	0-0	0-0	1	1	0
Wheeler	2-7	5-6	5	3	9
Phillips	2-8	3-4	6	2	7
Tebbs	0-0	0-0	0	0	0
Team			16		
Totals	16-56	29-43	48	22	61

Half time: Oregon State 34-31. Officials: Combs and Varnell. Attendance: 9,524.

Utah State	fg-fga	ft-fta	rb	pf	tp
Walker	7-16	4-6	8	4	18
Estes	14-29	10-11	8	3	38
Collier	9-21	4-5	13	5	22
Watts	5-8	1-4	2	4	11
Long	1-3	1-2	1	1	3
Hanson	0-2	0-0	0	0	0
Dittebrand	0-0	0-1	0	2	0
Angle	0-5	0-0	2	0	0
Team			13		
Totals	36-84	20-29	47	19	92

Arizona State	fg-fga	ft-fta	rb	pf	tp
Dairman	0-6	4-5	6	5	4
Caldwell	10-16	5-5	15	5	25
Becker	13-24	3-6	9	4	29
Senitza	2-9	3-4	4	5	7
Coppola	5-8	3-5	2	0	13
Myers	3-6	2-2	5	2	8
Hamilton	2-12	0-0	10	4	4
Jones	0-0	0-0	0	0	0
Harper	0-0	0-0	0	0	0
Team			12		
Totals	35-81	20-27	63	25	90

Half time: Arizona State 48-43. Officials: Soriano and Bussenius.

GAME-BY-GAME RESULTS

1964 UCLA BRUINS—(l-r) Front Row: Dennis Minishian, Gail Goodrich, Jack Hirsch, Rich Levin, Walt Hazzard, Kent Graham, Mike Huggins, Chuck Darrow; Second Row: Ducky Drake, Jerry Norman, Steve Brucker, Fred Slaughter, Doug McIntosh, Vaughn Hoffman, Keith Erickson, Kim Stewart, Kenny Washington, John Wooden.

Second Round

Connecticut	fg-fga	ft-fta	rb	pf	tp
Hesford	1- 2	1- 1	1	4	3
Perno	4-15	4- 5	3	2	12
Ritter	5- 9	0- 0	0	1	10
Kimball	6-11	4- 8	13	2	16
Slomcenski	1- 4	5- 5	8	1	7
DellaSala	2- 3	0- 0	3	1	4
Totals	19-44	14-19	28	11	52

Princeton	fg-fga	ft-fta	rb	pf	tp
Rodenbach	3- 6	0- 0	0	0	6
Haarlow	5-13	0- 0	7	0	10
Roth	0- 0	0- 0	0	1	0
Niemann	1- 1	0- 0	1	2	2
Bradley	6-15	10-12	10	3	22
Uhle	2- 5	0- 0	4	1	4
Howard	1- 3	0- 0	3	3	2
Steure	1- 4	0- 0	0	2	2
Kingston	1- 1	0- 0	0	1	2
Totals	20-48	10-12	25	13	50

Half time: Princeton 28-27. Officials: Tanksley and Scobey. Attendance: 12,400.

Duke	fg-fga	ft-fta	rb	pf	tp
Ferguson	0- 3	0- 0	2	4	0
Buckley	3- 8	3- 6	12	0	9
Tison	3- 6	7- 8	6	5	13
Harrison	1- 8	0- 0	1	2	2
Mullins	19-28	5- 6	12	1	43
Vacendak	3- 5	2- 3	6	0	8
Herbster	2- 3	0- 0	0	0	4
Marin	2- 5	4- 6	5	1	8
Totals	33-66	21-29	44	13	87

Villanova	fg-fga	ft-fta	rb	pf	tp
Melchionni	9-17	0- 2	3	4	18
Jones	6-20	6- 7	6	3	18
Moore	4-12	0- 0	3	3	8
Washington	2- 7	4- 4	11	5	8
Sallee	3- 7	0- 0	6	1	6
Erickson	5- 7	0- 2	2	2	10
Schaffer	2- 4	1- 1	4	3	5
Leftwich	0- 1	0- 0	0	1	0
Totals	31-75	11-16	35	22	73

Half time: Duke 49-33. Officials: Mihalik and Machock.

Michigan	fg-fga	ft-fta	rb	pf	tp
Tregoning	7-15	0- 0	14	5	14
Darden	4-10	1- 1	6	4	9
Buntin	9-23	8-10	13	4	26
Cantrell	3- 6	6- 8	3	2	12
Russell	8-15	5- 8	7	2	21
Pomey	0- 0	0- 0	1	1	0
Myers	1- 4	0- 0	3	1	2
Totals	32-73	20-27	47	19	84

Loyola, Ill.	fg-fga	ft-fta	rb	pf	tp
Miller	7-26	2- 5	7	2	16
Rouse	5-13	2- 3	14	2	12
Hunter	11-18	3- 6	6	5	25
Egan	3-15	4- 5	3	5	10
Coleman	7-14	3- 4	6	3	17
Wood	0- 1	0- 0	1	1	0
Manzke	0- 1	0- 0	0	0	0
Totals	33-88	14-23	37	18	80

Half time: Michigan 43-36. Officials: Bello and Fox. Attendance: 9,948.

Ohio Univ.	fg-fga	ft-fta	rb	pf	tp
Haley	7-14	1- 1	7	1	15
Hilt	4- 9	6- 7	9	4	14
Storey	8-15	3- 6	9	0	19
Jackson	11-22	3- 5	11	1	25
Gill	1- 1	1- 3	5	3	3
Davis	1- 5	5- 7	3	2	7
Weirich	0- 0	0- 0	0	0	0
Barry	0- 0	0- 0	0	0	0
Buck	0- 0	0- 0	0	0	0
Schoon	0- 0	0- 0	0	0	0
Brown	1- 2	0- 0	1	0	2
Totals	33-68	19-29	45	11	85

Kentucky	fg-fga	ft-fta	rb	pf	tp
Deeken	5-17	0- 1	14	4	10
Conley	7-16	3- 3	5	5	17
Nash	4-14	2- 3	9	3	10
Mobley	8-13	1- 1	5	3	17
Kron	0- 1	0- 0	1	0	0
Ishmael	1- 5	0- 0	1	1	2
Adams	0- 0	0- 0	0	1	0
Embry	5-12	1- 3	2	2	11
S. Harper	1- 2	0- 1	1	1	2
Totals	31-80	7-12	38	20	69

Half time: Ohio 40-24. Officials: Eisenstein and Honzo.

Kansas State	fg-fga	ft-fta	rb	pf	tp
Moss	0- 3	2- 2	4	0	2
Murrell	9-24	6- 8	11	2	24
Robinson	5- 6	4- 6	4	1	14
Suttner	5-10	6- 8	13	4	16
Simons	2- 7	2- 3	4	2	6
Williams	1- 2	0- 0	2	2	2
Team			10		
Totals	22-52	20-27	46	11	64

Texas Western	fg-fga	ft-fta	rb	pf	tp
Barnes	1- 5	2- 3	9	5	4
Artis	1-12	0- 1	4	2	2
Tredennick	0- 1	0- 0	0	0	0
Stoglin	5-12	2- 2	5	5	12
Flournoy	3- 5	1- 1	5	3	7
Banks	8-16	4- 6	6	2	20
Dibler	6-15	1- 1	4	1	13
Shockley	1- 2	0- 0	1	1	2
Team			7		
Totals	25-68	10-14	40	19	60

Half time: Kansas State 23-21. Officials: Filiberti and Fouts. Attendance: 10,811.

Wichita State	fg-fga	ft-fta	rb	pf	tp
Stallworth	7-17	8- 9	23	3	22
Bowman	5-10	6- 9	8	4	16
Leach	3- 5	8-10	3	3	14
Pete	4- 7	3- 4	7	5	11
Criss	1- 6	0- 0	1	5	2
Smith	1- 5	7- 7	5	3	9
Nosich	4- 5	0- 1	2	3	8
Davis	1- 1	0- 0	0	1	2
Rowland	0- 0	0- 0	0	0	0
Reimond	0- 0	0- 1	1	0	0
Team			2		
Totals	26-56	32-41	52	27	84

Creighton	fg-fga	ft-fta	rb	pf	tp
Silas	5-12	12-15	17	2	22
Pointer	3-10	1- 1	5	5	7
Officer	10-25	1- 3	3	4	21
McGriff	1- 7	4- 9	6	5	6
Brown	1- 8	1- 3	2	2	3
Forehand	1- 2	0- 0	0	2	2
Apke	0- 1	0- 1	3	4	0
James	0- 0	0- 2	0	1	0
Miles	3- 6	1- 2	4	3	7
Team			9		
Totals	24-71	20-36	49	28	68

Half time: Wichita 38-28. Officials: Marich and Lloyd. Attendance: 10,811.

San Francisco	fg-fga	ft-fta	rb	pf	tp
Lee	1- 3	1- 1	2	0	3
Mueller	4- 8	0- 2	4	5	8
Johnson	9-13	8- 9	17	3	26
Brovelli	4- 8	0- 0	1	0	8
Ellis	6-13	3- 4	4	1	15
Thomas	1- 4	0- 2	1	3	2
Brainard	1- 4	0- 2	4	1	2
Gumina	0- 0	0- 0	0	0	0
Team			6		
Totals	26-53	12-20	39	13	64

Utah State	fg-fga	ft-fta	rb	pf	tp
Walker	7-16	1- 2	4	3	15
Estes	6-19	9- 9	11	4	21
Collier	9-18	4- 6	14	3	22
Watts	0- 4	0- 0	1	5	0
Long	0- 6	0- 0	3	0	0
Dittebrand	0- 2	0- 0	3	0	0
Team			6		
Totals	22-65	14-17	42	15	58

Half time: San Francisco 29-25. Officials: Glennon and Watson. Attendance: 9,500 (Estimated).

UCLA	fg-fga	ft-fta	rb	pf	tp
Erickson	3-13	1- 4	13	5	7
Hirsch	8-12	5- 5	13	5	21
Slaughter	6-10	1- 3	13	5	13
Goodrich	6-22	7-11	6	4	19
Hazzard	9-14	8-11	7	3	26
McIntosh	1- 1	0- 1	1	1	2
Stewart	0- 1	0- 0	0	2	0
Washington	3- 4	1- 4	3	4	7
Huggins	0- 0	0- 0	0	0	0
Hoffman	0- 0	0- 0	0	0	0
Darrow	0- 0	0- 0	0	0	0
Team			6		
Totals	36-77	23-39	62	29	95

Seattle	fg-fga	ft-fta	rb	pf	tp
Tresvant	5-15	10-16	20	3	20
Vermillion	6- 9	3- 3	5	5	15
Wheeler	7-16	6-11	8	4	20
Williams	5-20	2- 4	13	5	12
Heyward	3- 8	3- 5	4	4	9
Phillips	2- 8	2- 2	4	4	6
Turney	2- 6	4- 4	2	5	8
Tebbs	0- 0	0- 0	0	1	0
Team			6		
Totals	30-82	30-45	62	31	90

Half time: UCLA 49-39. Officials: George and Magnusson. Attendance: 9,661.

Walt Hazzard

Third Place

Villanova	fg-fga	ft-fta	rb	pf	tp
Melchionni	8-20	1- 2	9	2	17
Jones	16-29	2- 3	7	1	34
Moore	1- 2	2- 2	0	1	4
Washington	1- 9	2- 2	13	3	4
Sallee	0- 0	0- 0	0	2	0
Erickson	2- 6	0- 1	4	0	4
Leftwich	4-11	1- 1	4	0	9
Schaffer	1- 4	0- 2	8	1	2
Winterbottom	0- 1	0- 0	0	0	0
Totals	33-82	8-13	45	10	74

Princeton	fg-fga	ft-fta	rb	pf	tp
Kingston	0- 1	0- 0	3	2	0
Rodenbach	1- 5	0- 0	0	3	2
Haarlow	3- 7	2- 3	4	1	8
Howard	0- 2	2- 3	4	0	2
Bradley	13-23	4- 6	13	3	30
Niemann	2- 5	0- 1	4	2	4
Steube	2- 5	2- 2	2	0	6
Roth	0- 0	0- 0	1	0	0
Uhle	2- 3	0- 0	0	1	4
Wright	3- 6	0- 0	4	1	6
Kitch	0- 0	0- 0	0	0	0
Totals	26-57	10-15	35	13	62

Half time: Villanova 42-30. Officials: Tanksley and Scobey.

Loyola, Ill.	fg-fga	ft-fta	rb	pf	tp
Miller	8-16	3- 6	5	2	19
Rouse	2- 8	4- 4	4	0	8
Hunter	10-22	7- 7	18	2	27
Egan	4-11	5- 5	4	5	13
Coleman	3-12	14-17	8	3	20
Wood	0- 1	0- 0	0	0	0
Manzke	4- 9	3- 3	2	2	11
Connaughton	0- 2	2- 2	1	2	2
Totals	31-81	38-44	42	16	100

Kentucky	fg-fga	ft-fta	rb	pf	tp
Deeken	5-11	2- 2	5	3	12
Conley	6-13	3- 5	7	4	15
Nash	11-27	1- 3	11	5	23
Mobley	8-13	5- 5	4	5	21
Embry	0- 4	0- 2	3	2	0
Ishmael	3- 7	0- 0	7	1	6
Kron	2- 4	1- 2	2	4	5
Adams	4- 5	1- 1	2	1	9
Sharper	0- 0	0- 0	1	0	0
Totals	39-84	13-20	38	28	91

Half time: Kentucky 45-43. Officials: Eisenstein and Fox.

Texas Western	fg-fga	ft-fta	rb	pf	tp
Barnes	6-15	3- 4	15	4	15
Artis	3-11	3- 3	13	1	9
Tredennick	0- 1	0- 0	0	1	0
Stoglin	1- 8	8- 8	6	1	10
Flournoy	0- 2	2- 3	4	3	2
Banks	4-12	5- 8	6	1	13
Dibler	7-18	0- 2	3	0	14
Team			8		
Totals	21-67	21-28	50	12	63

Creighton	fg-fga	ft-fta	rb	pf	tp
Silas	6-15	2-13	13	3	14
Pointer	4- 9	0- 1	4	3	8
Officer	5-13	1- 2	5	2	11
McGriff	5-11	2- 7	8	5	12
Brown	0- 2	0- 0	1	1	0
Forehand	2- 8	1- 1	6	0	5
Apke	0- 2	0- 2	3	0	0
James	0- 0	0- 0	0	0	0
Miles	0- 0	2- 2	0	0	2
Team			10		
Totals	22-60	8-16	49	19	52

Half time: Creighton 32-26. Officials: Marich and Lloyd. Attendance: 10,815.

Seattle	fg-fga	ft-fta	rb	pf	tp
Tresvant	8-14	2- 4	19	5	18
Vermillion	8-15	10-11	13	3	26
Wheeler	3-11	2- 3	12	5	8
Williams	3-16	8- 9	7	3	14
Heyward	3- 4	0- 1	1	5	6
Phillips	1- 2	0- 0	1	0	2
Tebbs	4- 9	1- 2	1	0	9
Turney	2- 4	0- 0	8	0	4
Griffin	0- 0	0- 1	1	0	0
Mathews	0- 0	1- 2	2	0	1
Team			7		
Totals	32-75	24-33	72	21	88

288

Utah State

	fg-fga	ft-fta	rb	pf	tp
Estes	6-18	2-3	6	2	14
Walker	9-21	3-3	5	4	21
Collier	8-20	6-8	8	2	22
Watts	3-8	0-5	5	4	6
Long	1-1	0-0	1	1	2
Dittebrand	3-9	1-4	8	5	7
Hansen	1-2	0-0	1	1	2
Angle	1-2	0-0	1	1	2
Hunsaker	1-3	0-0	2	2	2
Widmer	0-1	0-0	0	0	0
Jones	0-0	0-0	1	0	0
Lyons	0-1	0-0	0	1	0
Team			6		
Totals	33-86	12-23	44	23	78

Half time: Seattle 41-35. Officials: George and Magnusson. Attendance: 9,000. (Approx.)

Regional Championships

Duke

	fg-fga	ft-fta	rb	pf	tp
Ferguson	3-4	0-0	1	1	6
Buckley	5-7	2-3	6	3	12
Tison	4-8	6-7	8	3	14
Harrison	2-6	1-1	2	0	5
Mullins	14-23	2-2	8	1	30
Marin	2-3	0-0	0	5	4
Vacendak	7-7	0-1	3	1	14
Herbster	2-3	0-1	2	3	4
Kitching	1-6	0-1	2	1	2
Harscher	2-3	1-1	3	2	5
Mann	0-3	2-3	5	0	2
Cox	1-2	1-2	1	1	3
Totals	43-75	15-21	41	21	101

Connecticut

	fg-fga	ft-fta	rb	pf	tp
Hesford	3-6	1-1	3	2	7
Perno	2-7	1-3	3	2	5
Ritter	4-8	0-0	1	1	8
Kimball	6-21	6-8	14	3	18
Slomcenski	1-5	1-2	6	1	3
Whitney	0-3	1-3	0	1	1
DellaSala	3-5	1-1	1	3	7
Whitcomb	1-4	0-1	1	0	2
Libertoff	0-5	1-3	2	2	1
Capiga	1-4	0-0	1	3	2
Talbott	0-1	0-0	1	0	0
Stanek	0-0	0-1	0	0	0
Totals	21-69	12-23	32	18	54

Half time: Duke 62-27. Officials: Mihalik and Machock. Attendance: 12,400.

Michigan

	fg-fga	ft-fta	rb	pf	tp
Tregoning	1-3	1-2	3	2	3
Darden	3-5	0-0	7	3	6
Buntin	6-17	3-3	10	4	15
Cantrell	2-2	2-2	1	2	6
Russell	9-20	7-7	6	0	25
Pomey	3-7	0-0	2	1	6
Myers	2-10	2-2	7	1	6
Herner	0-1	2-3	0	0	2
Totals	26-65	17-19	36	13	69

Ohio Univ.

	fg-fga	ft-fta	rb	pf	tp
Haley	4-16	2-6	11	3	10
Hilt	8-15	2-3	9	1	18
Storey	6-12	0-0	3	2	12
Jackson	6-14	1-2	7	2	13
Gill	1-5	0-0	3	4	2
Davis	0-1	0-0	0	0	0
Weirich	0-2	0-0	0	1	0
Lashley	0-0	0-0	0	1	0
Schoon	0-0	0-0	0	1	0
Barry	0-0	2-2	0	0	2
Buck	0-0	0-0	0	0	0
Totals	25-65	7-13	33	15	57

Half time: Michigan 32-27. Officials: Bello and Honzo. Attendance: 8,706.

Kansas State

	fg-fga	ft-fta	rb	pf	tp
Moss	4-8	3-5	2	1	11
Murrell	11-24	6-10	10	1	28
Robinson	2-7	7-10	7	3	11
Suttner	7-11	2-4	6	5	16
Simons	6-14	2-3	6	5	14
Williams	3-3	2-2	6	4	8
Paradis	2-2	2-3	1	1	6
Team			2		
Totals	35-69	24-37	40	20	94

John Wooden

Wichita State

	fg-fga	ft-fta	rb	pf	tp
Stallworth	14-22	9-12	16	3	37
Bowman	4-6	4-5	8	5	12
Leach	3-10	1-1	5	5	7
Criss	4-9	1-1	1	5	9
Smith	2-3	0-0	3	4	4
Nosich	0-0	0-0	0	0	0
Davis	0-1	0-0	2	1	0
Rowland	0-0	0-0	0	0	0
Pete	7-12	3-3	5	2	17
Totals	34-63	18-22	40	25	86

Half time: Kansas State 46-33. Officials: Filibirti and Fouts. Attendance: 10,815.

UCLA

	fg-fga	ft-fta	rb	pf	tp
Erickson	3-10	1-6	10	4	7
Hirsch	5-11	4-5	7	3	14
Slaughter	4-9	1-4	8	4	9
Goodrich	6-18	3-5	4	1	15
Hazzard	9-19	5-5	3	3	23
McIntosh	0-1	3-5	4	1	3
Washington	2-4	1-4	3	1	5
Team			9		
Totals	29-72	18-34	48	17	76

San Francisco

	fg-fga	ft-fta	rb	pf	tp
Lee	2-5	2-2	4	4	6
Mueller	6-12	3-5	7	4	15
Johnson	6-9	10-11	13	2	22
Brovelli	5-8	1-1	2	4	11
Ellis	5-14	1-2	10	3	11
Thomas	0-0	0-0	2	2	0
Brainard	2-8	1-2	4	5	5
Gumina	1-1	0-0	1	1	2
Team			3		
Totals	27-57	18-23	46	25	72

Half time: San Francisco 36-28. Officials: Glennon and Watson. Attendance: 9,416.

Semifinals

UCLA

	fg-fga	ft-fta	rb	pf	ip
Goodrich	7-18	0-0	6	3	14
Slaughter	2-6	0-0	5	4	4
Hazzard	7-10	5-7	7	2	19
Hirsch	2-11	0-0	1	4	4
Erickson	10-21	8-9	10	2	28
McIntosh	3-5	2-3	10	3	8
Washington	5-11	3-4	11	1	13
Totals	36-82	18-23	45	19	90

Kansas State

	fg-fga	ft-fta	rb	pf	tp
Moss	3-9	1-1	5	3	7
Robinson	2-7	0-1	5	4	4
Simons	10-17	4-6	7	3	24
Suttner	3-9	0-5	10	2	6
Murrell	13-22	3-5	13	3	29
Paradis	5-9	0-1	1	0	10
Williams	1-1	2-3	1	2	4
Nelson	0-1	0-0	0	1	0
Gottfrid	0-0	0-0	0	1	0
Barnard	0-1	0-0	0	0	0
Totals	37-76	10-21	42	19	84

Half time: UCLA 43-41. Officials: Mahalik and Honzo. Attendance: 10,731.

Duke

	fg-fga	ft-fta	rb	pf	tp
Ferguson	6-11	0-1	0	0	12
Buckley	11-16	3-5	14	4	25
Tison	3-10	6-10	13	4	12
Harrison	6-15	2-3	2	2	14
Mullins	8-19	5-6	8	1	21
Marin	1-2	-0-	2	1	2
Vacendak	2-5	1-2	2	1	5
Herbster	0-0	0-0	0	0	0
Totals	37-78	17-27	41	13	91

Michigan

	fg-fga	ft-fta	rb	pf	tp
Buntin	8-18	3-3	9	5	19
Cantrell	6-10	0-0	4	2	12
Russell	13-19	5-6	8	5	31
Tregoning	3-11	2-2	6	4	8
Darden	2-6	1-1	9	5	5
Myers	2-5	0-0	5	2	4
Pomey	0-1	1-2	0	0	1
Herner	0-1	0-0	0	0	0
Totals	34-71	12-14	41	23	80

Half time: Duke 48-39. Officials: Fouts and Glennon. Attendance: 10,731.

National Third Place

Michigan

	fg-fga	ft-fta	rb	pf	tp
Buntin	9-18	15-17	14	2	33
Cantrell	8-17	4-5	3	2	20
Herner	0-3	0-0	1	3	0
Tregoning	6-13	4-5	8	1	16
Darden	8-16	1-3	14	3	17
Myers	3-10	1-2	6	1	7
Pomey	2-4	0-0	2	1	4
Clawson	1-3	1-2	2	0	3
Totals	37-84	26-34	50	13	100

Kansas State

	fg-fga	ft-fta	rb	pf	tp
Moss	4-9	3-3	3	5	11
Robinson	6-11	0-0	6	2	12
Simons	4-8	3-3	3	3	11
Suttner	7-15	6-8	5	4	20
Murrell	10-19	0-0	10	2	20
Williams	2-4	0-1	2	0	4
Nelson	2-6	1-1	2	2	5
Paradis	1-4	3-4	0	0	5
Gottfrid	1-1	0-0	2	3	2
Barnard	0-1	0-0	3	1	0
Poma	0-1	0-0	1	1	0
Hoffman	0-0	0-0	0	0	0
Totals	37-79	16-20	37	23	90

Half time: Michigan 52-47. Officials: Fouts and Honzo.

Championship

UCLA

	fg-fga	ft-fta	rb	pf	tp
Goodrich	9-18	9-9	3	1	27
Slaughter	0-1	0-0	1	0	0
Hazzard	4-10	3-5	3	5	11
Hirsch	5-9	3-5	6	3	13
Erickson	2-7	4-5	5	8	8
McIntosh	4-9	0-0	11	2	8
Washington	11-16	4-4	12	4	26
Darrow	0-1	3-4	1	2	3
Stewart	0-1	0-0	0	1	0
Huggins	0-1	0-1	1	2	0
Hoffman	1-2	0-0	0	0	2
Levin	0-1	0-0	0	0	0
Totals	36-76	26-32	43	25	98

Duke

	fg-fga	ft-fta	rb	pf	tp
Ferguson	2-6	0-1	1	3	4
Buckley	5-8	8-12	9	4	18
Tison	3-8	1-1	1	2	7
Harrison	1-1	0-0	1	2	2
Mullins	9-21	4-4	4	5	22
Marin	8-16	0-1	10	3	16
Vacendak	2-7	3-3	6	4	7
Herbster	1-4	0-2	0	0	2
Kitching	1-1	0-0	1	0	2
Mann	0-3	3-4	2	1	3
Harscher	0-0	0-0	0	0	0
Cox	0-1	0-0	0	0	0
Totals	32-72	19-28	35	24	83

Half time: UCLA 50-38. Officials: Mihalik and Glennon. Attendance: 10,864.

1965

First Round

Princeton

	fg-fga	ft-fta	rb	pf	tp
Bradley	7-22	8-9	9	2	22
Haarlow	5-13	1-2	9	2	11
Brown	0-4	0-0	5	1	0
Rodenbach	5-11	2-3	5	3	12
Walters	3-7	0-0	2	2	6
Hummer	4-5	1-3	13	1	9
Team			5		
Totals	24-62	12-17	48	11	60

Penn State

	fg-fga	ft-fta	rb	pf	tp
Avillion	5-11	1-2	8	4	11
Saunders	3-5	0-0	6	2	6
Clinton	5-21	2-5	16	4	12
Weiss	5-16	3-4	5	2	13
Reed	7-15	2-3	6	2	16
Mickey	0-1	0-0	3	1	0
Team			1		
Totals	25-69	8-14	45	15	58

Half time: Princeton 31-28. Officials: Eisenstein and Honzo.

St. Joseph's Pa.

	fg-fga	ft-fta	rb	pf	tp
Ford	6-14	2-3	4	4	14
Duff	5-11	0-1	6	1	10
Anderson	5-15	2-3	12	2	12
Oakes	3-9	0-1	3	4	6
Guokas	7-12	5-5	5	2	19
McKenna	2-2	2-2	4	1	6
Chapman	0-0	0-0	0	0	0
Team			3		
Totals	28-63	11-15	37	14	67

Connecticut

	fg-fga	ft-fta	rb	pf	tp
Hesford	7-12	0-1	6	1	14
Ritter	3-10	1-2	2	2	7
Kimball	9-15	3-3	29	3	21
Curran	0-0	0-1	0	2	0
Bialosuknia	5-18	3-4	1	3	13
Penders	2-6	2-5	4	2	6
Thompson	0-2	0-0	1	0	0
Team			3		
Totals	26-63	9-16	46	13	61

Half time: Connecticut 33-26. Officials: Stevens and Gentile. Attendance: 9,282.

Providence

	fg-fga	ft-fta	rb	pf	tp
Blair	5-11	8-9	9	4	18
Riordan	4-9	5-5	7	3	13
Westbrook	8-15	2-4	14	4	18
Benedict	10-18	1-1	2	1	21
Walker	6-13	2-3	5	5	14
Kinski	1-2	1-1	1	2	3
Lasher	0-1	0-0	1	0	0
Ahern	1-2	0-0	1	0	2
Dutton	0-1	0-0	1	0	0
Sarantopoulos	1-2	0-0	0	0	2
Cox	0-1	0-0	1	0	0
McLaughlin	0-0	0-0	0	0	0
Team			2		
Totals	36-75	19-22	42	19	91

Bill Bradley

West Virginia

	fg-fga	ft-fta	rb	pf	tp
Maphis	10-18	1-5	11	5	21
Camp.	0-10	0-1	11	5	0
Lentz.	5-13	0-0	11	2	10
Quertinmont	4-10	5-7	2	3	13
Lesher	4-8	4-4	9	1	12
Shaffer	3-8	1-2	1	2	7
Benfield	0-0	0-0	0	1	0
Ryczai	0-1	0-0	2	0	0
Palmer	1-2	2-2	2	1	4
Team			2		
Totals	27-70	13-21	51	20	67

Half time: Providence 49-29. Officials: Lennon and Fox. Attendance: 9,282.

Eastern Kentucky

	fg-fga	ft-fta	rb	pf	tp
Bodkin	8-17	5-5	6	3	21
Bradley	1-9	0-0	2	4	2
Tolan	4-8	3-6	5	3	11
Lemos	2-12	0-1	4	1	4
Walton	3-7	3-3	1	2	9
Bisbey	2-5	0-0	7	1	4
Clemons	0-2	0-0	1	1	0
Carr	0-0	0-0	0	0	0
Westerfield	0-1	0-1	0	0	0
Grabowski	0-2	0-0	0	0	0
King	0-2	1-1	0	1	1
Clark	0-3	0-0	3	0	0
Team			2		
Totals	20-68	12-17	31	17	52

DePaul

	fg-fga	ft-fta	rb	pf	tp
Palmer	4-5	3-3	13	2	11
Swanson	7-13	1-1	9	3	15
Mills	9-10	3-6	6	2	21
Meyer	9-16	2-2	7	2	20
Murphy	6-16	4-4	6	3	16
Modestes	0-1	0-0	4	0	0
Birgells	1-1	0-0	1	1	2
Flanagan	1-1	0-0	1	1	2
Gulley	2-2	2-3	0	0	6
Norris	2-4	2-2	1	0	6
Odishoo	0-0	0-0	0	1	0
Ortolano	0-1	0-0	0	0	0
Team			7		
Totals	41-70	17-21	55	15	99

Half time: DePaul 43-33. Officials: Scobey and Strauthers.

Ohio

	fg-fga	ft-fta	rb	pf	tp
Haley	4-9	3-5	5	3	11
Hilt	6-10	7-11	8	3	19
Schroeder	5-9	6-8	7	3	16
Hammond	6-12	3-4	7	1	15
Davis	0-3	0-0	3	0	0
Brown	2-5	0-1	0	3	4
Buck	0-2	0-0	2	2	0
Team			5		
Totals	23-50	19-29	37	15	65

Dayton

	fg-fga	ft-fta	rb	pf	tp
Sullivan	3-12	3-3	5	4	9
Cassidy	2-9	5-5	11	3	9
Finkel	10-13	7-9	11	5	27
Papp	6-16	5-6	6	1	17
Klaus	2-8	0-0	2	2	4
Wannemacher	0-1	0-0	0	4	0
Warrell	0-4	0-0	1	1	0
Team			7		
Totals	23-63	20-23	43	20	66

Half time: Dayton 30-20. Officials: Gardner and Fouty. Attendance: 7,500 (est.).

Notre Dame

	fg-fga	ft-fta	rb	pf	tp
Miller	6-16	6-11	8	3	18
Sahm	6-11	5-7	10	5	17
Jesewitz	6-16	5-6	20	5	17
Sheffield	8-15	1-2	3	4	17
Reed	7-25	2-4	15	5	16
McGann	5-9	3-3	3	3	13
Hardy	0-0	0-1	1	0	0
Monahan	0-0	0-0	0	1	0
Totals	38-92	22-34	59	27	98

Houston

	fg-fga	ft-fta	rb	pf	tp
Ballard	8-20	6-6	6	4	22
Jones	4-10	3-4	9	5	11
Lentz	6-7	6-11	12	3	18
Hamood	5-15	4-5	4	5	14
Margenthaler	6-10	1-2	2	2	13
Apolskis	3-3	4-6	4	5	10
Perry	2-2	1-2	2	2	5
Grider	0-0	0-0	0	0	0
Winch	0-3	2-2	0	1	2
Neumann	2-4	0-0	1	1	4
Totals	36-74	27-38	40	28	99

Half time: Notre Dame 49-40. Officials: Watson and Pryor. Attendance: 4,500.

Oklahoma City

	fg-fga	ft-fta	rb	pf	tp
Hopkins	1-7	5-7	9	4	7
Hunter	10-17	4-4	11	0	24
Ware	3-13	0-1	17	3	6
Gray	9-20	2-4	2	1	20
Wells	4-10	5-7	5	2	13
Totals	27-67	16-23	44	10	70

Colorado State

	fg-fga	ft-fta	rb	pf	tp
Wright	4-14	0-0	4	4	8
Key	1-2	0-0	4	1	2
Bustion	13-26	4-6	20	2	30
Vidakovich	6-13	1-1	1	4	13
Foster	1-4	1-4	3	2	3
Davidson	0-2	0-0	3	1	0
Westoby	6-9	0-0	1	2	12
Totals	31-70	6-11	36	16	68

Half time: Oklahoma City 36-32. Officials: Elliott and Hagerty. Attendance: 4,500.

Second Round

Providence

	fg-fga	ft-fta	rb	pf	tp
Westbrook	6-13	4-10	17	5	16
Walker	6-16	8-10	3	2	20
Blair	3-9	1-1	7	3	7
Benedict	11-17	0-0	3	2	22
Riordan	5-11	6-8	6	4	16
Lasher	0-1	0-0	0	0	0
Totals	31-67	19-29	36	16	81

St. Joseph's, Pa.

	fg-fga	ft-fta	rb	pf	tp
Ford	5-14	3-5	12	2	13
Duff	3-10	5-6	11	5	11
Anderson	5-14	5-6	12	5	15
Goukas	7-11	0-1	6	4	14
Oakes	6-17	0-2	4	3	12
McKenna	4-10	0-3	10	1	8
Chapman	0-0	0-0	2	2	0
Totals	30-76	13-23	55	22	73

Half time: St. Joseph's 40-34. Regulation Score: 61-61.

North Carolina State

	fg-fga	ft-fta	rb	pf	tp
Coker	4-10	0-3	8	3	8
Mattocks	3-14	1-2	4	2	7
Lakins	2-10	3-5	2	5	7
Moffitt	0-2	4-6	3	3	4
Biedenbach	1-7	0-2	3	1	2
Worsley	5-15	4-5	13	2	14
Gealy	0-0	0-0	1	0	0
Hodgdon	0-0	0-0	0	0	0
Moore	0-3	2-2	2	3	2
Taylor	0-0	0-0	3	1	0
Blondeau	1-3	0-0	1	1	2
Hale	1-1	0-0	0	0	2
Totals	17-66	14-25	38	20	48

Princeton

	fg-fga	ft-fta	rb	pf	tp
Bradley	10-18	7-9	14	4	27
Haarlow	4-9	2-2	3	4	10
Brown	2-6	0-2	13	3	4
Rodenbach	3-6	2-2	4	2	8
Walters	0-3	0-0	2	2	0
Hummer	5-12	3-4	10	3	13
Roth	1-1	0-0	2	0	2
Kingston	0-0	0-0	0	0	0
Koch	1-4	0-2	3	0	2
Shank	0-1	0-1	2	0	0
Adler	0-0	0-0	1	0	0
Totals	26-60	14-22	54	18	66

Half time: Princeton 27-16.

1965 UCLA BRUINS—(l-r) Front Row: Jerry Norman, Gail Goodrich, Jim Lyons, John Galbraith, Mike Serafin, Brice Chambers, Larry McCollister, Freddie Goss; Second Row: John Wooden, Ducky Drake, Rich Levin, Edgar Lacey, Doug McIntosh, Vaughn Hoffman, Bill Winkelholz, Mike Lynn, Keith Erickson, Kenny Washington, Bill Ureda.

Michigan

	fg-fga	ft-fta	rb	pf	tp
Tregoning	6-10	0-0	7	1	12
Darden	7-12	3-3	9	0	17
Buntin	12-21	2-5	11	1	26
Russell	5-14	4-4	9	2	14
Pomey	4-7	3-4	3	4	11
Myers	1-2	3-4	4	0	5
Thompson	1-2	0-0	2	1	2
Clawson	1-6	1-1	4	0	3
Ludwig	0-3	0-0	3	1	0
Brown	0-1	0-0	1	0	0
Bankey	0-0	0-0	0	0	0
Dill	4-9	0-1	2	1	8
Totals	41-87	16-21	56	8	98

Dayton

	fg-fga	ft-fta	rb	pf	tp
Sullivan	6-14	1-1	3	2	13
Cassidy	4-15	2-2	8	4	10
Finkel	11-18	0-2	12	4	22
Papp	7-16	1-1	4	0	15
Klaus	1-3	0-0	0	1	2
Wannamacher	2-4	0-0	2	2	4
Warrell	1-3	0-0	2	2	2
Johnson	1-2	0-0	1	0	2
Hrcka	0-0	0-0	0	0	0
Brooks	0-0	1-1	0	0	1
Inderriden	0-0	0-0	0	0	0
Samanich	0-0	0-0	0	0	0
Totals	33-75	5-7	30	15	71

Half time: Michigan 44-27.

Vanderbilt

	fg-fga	ft-fta	rb	pf	tp
Grace	4-9	3-3	4	5	11
Taylor	0-2	2-3	7	1	2
Lee	8-20	8-10	15	5	24
Miller	5-13	6-10	1	1	16
Thomas	7-10	4-4	6	0	18
Calvert	6-8	0-1	4	3	12
Green	0-2	0-0	5	3	0
Gibbs	0-0	0-0	0	0	0
Totals	30-64	23-31	42	18	83

DePaul

	fg-fga	ft-fta	rb	pf	tp
Palmer	10-18	8-11	19	5	28
Swanson	4-8	1-1	8	5	9
Mills	3-4	1-2	5	3	7
Murphy	9-25	3-4	7	2	21
Meyer	5-11	1-3	4	2	11
Flanagan	0-3	0-0	1	4	0
Birgells	1-3	0-0	1	2	2
Norris	0-3	0-0	1	0	0
Totals	32-75	14-21	47	24	78

Half time: Vanderbilt 39-32. Regulation Score: 76-76. Attendance: 11,500.

Wichita State

	fg-fga	ft-fta	rb	pf	tp
Smith	3-9	3-3	4	4	9
Thompson	8-22	2-3	7	3	18
Leach	4-13	3-6	8	4	11
Criss	4-6	1-1	2	4	9
Pete	12-16	7-12	12	4	31
Reed	2-4	3-5	7	3	7
Nosich	0-2	0-0	1	1	0
Davis	0-0	1-1	0	0	1
Team			6		
Totals	33-72	20-31	47	23	86

Southern Methodist

	fg-fga	ft-fta	rb	pf	tp
Smith	3-6	0-0	3	0	6
Ward	3-6	4-7	5	5	10
Hooser	9-16	2-3	9	5	20
Holman	3-10	2-2	5	5	8
Beasley	7-16	4-4	8	3	18
Begert	5-8	6-10	9	4	16
Wendorf	1-3	1-2	2	3	3
Carpenter	0-0	0-0	1	0	0
Team			6		
Totals	31-65	19-28	46	25	81

Half time: Wichita State 43-41. Officials: Marich and Korte. Attendance: 10,500.

Oklahoma State

	fg-fga	ft-fta	rb	pf	tp
Hassmann	9-20	0-0	7	3	18
King	3-6	4-4	11	2	10
Johnson	11-17	3-5	13	4	25
Hawk	2-9	2-3	6	3	6
Iba	2-3	3-5	3	4	7
Moulder	1-2	1-1	1	0	3
LaBrue	2-2	2-2	0	0	6
Feamster	0-0	0-0	1	0	0
Team			7		
Totals	30-59	15-20	49	16	75

Houston

	fg-fga	ft-fta	rb	pf	tp
Ballard	3-12	0-1	5	4	6
Jones	2-8	2-4	8	3	6
Lentz	3-9	0-0	9	1	6
Hamood	8-24	1-1	7	1	17
Margenthaler	3-8	1-1	1	1	7
Apolskis	3-5	2-5	1	3	8
Grider	0-1	2-3	1	0	2
Winch	2-4	1-1	0	2	5
Perry	1-1	0-0	2	1	2
Arning	0-0	0-0	0	1	0
Palmquist	0-1	1-3	2	0	1
Team			6		
Totals	25-73	10-19	42	17	60

Half time: Oklahoma State 33-22. Officials: Filiberti and Soriano. Attendance: 10,500.

San Francisco

	fg-fga	ft-fta	rb	pf	tp
Gumina	6-10	0-2	5	5	12
Mueller	5-14	3-4	12	4	13
Johnson	17-27	1-2	16	0	35
Thomas	1-4	1-1	2	4	3
Ellis	6-18	0-0	14	3	12
James	0-3	2-2	0	0	2
Blum	7-11	1-2	1	0	15
Esters	0-2	0-0	0	1	0
Gale	0-1	1-1	1	0	1
Team			6		
Totals	42-90	7-12	59	19	91

Oklahoma City

	fg-fga	ft-fta	rb	pf	tp
Hopkins	2-6	1-1	8	1	5
Hunter	5-16	2-2	3	1	12
Ware	6-18	5-6	22	3	17
Wells	4-15	5-7	6	3	13
Gray	8-15	4-6	0	5	20
Bolen	0-1	0-0	1	0	0
Castleberry	0-1	0-0	0	0	0
Morrison	0-0	0-0	0	0	0
Team			5		
Totals	25-72	17-22	45	13	67

Half time: 29-29.

UCLA	fg-fga	ft-fta	rb	pf	tp
Lacey	7-11	1- 3	13	3	15
Erickson	14-22	0- 1	9	4	28
McIntosh	1- 6	0- 2	9	3	2
Goodrich	16-27	8- 9	5	2	40
Goss	2-10	0- 0	2	5	4
Washington	0- 5	1- 1	4	5	1
Lynn	3- 9	2- 2	10	3	8
Hoffman	0- 1	0- 1	2	0	0
Chambers	0- 1	0- 0	1	0	0
Lyons	1- 2	0- 0	0	0	2
Levin	0- 0	0- 0	0	1	0
Team			11		
Totals	44-94	12-19	66	26	100

Brigham Young	fg-fga	ft-fta	rb	pf	tp
Kramer	5- 7	0- 1	4	2	10
Roberts	2-11	3- 4	6	0	7
Fairchild	8-17	7- 8	13	2	23
Gardner	5-10	4- 4	4	4	14
Nemelka	2-11	1- 5	1	2	5
Hill	2- 5	0- 3	7	4	4
Quinney	1- 5	2- 2	4	0	4
Congdon	2- 5	0- 1	1	1	4
Stanley	2- 3	0- 1	4	0	4
Raymond	0- 2	1- 2	4	1	1
Jimas	0- 1	0- 0	0	0	0
James	0- 3	0- 1	1	0	0
Team			7		
Totals	29-80	18-32	56	16	76

Half time: UCLA 51-40. Attendance: 10,766.

Third Place

North Carolina State	fg-fga	ft-fta	rb	pf	tp
Coker	2- 5	3- 5	4	1	7
Mattocks	6-12	2- 2	9	2	14
Lakins	12-22	9-11	14	4	33
Moffitt	5- 9	5- 6	3	2	15
Biedenbach	5- 7	4- 6	2	4	14
Worsley	6-11	0- 2	6	3	12
Blondeau	1- 3	0- 0	1	0	2
Gealy	0- 0	0- 0	0	0	0
Hale	0- 0	0- 0	0	0	0
Hodgdon	1- 2	0- 0	0	0	2
Moore	2- 4	0- 0	3	1	4
Taylor	0- 0	0- 0	1	1	0
Team			7		
Totals	40-75	23-32	50	18	103

St. Joseph's, Pa.	fg-fga	ft-fta	rb	pf	tp
Ford	8-20	5- 5	7	3	21
Duff	1- 4	1- 1	6	5	3
Anderson	12-22	2- 6	23	4	26
Goukas	5-12	4- 5	2	4	14
Oakes	3-14	2- 3	1	3	8
McKenna	1- 3	1- 1	3	0	3
Chapman	0- 2	0- 0	0	0	0
DiJulia	1- 2	0- 0	0	3	2
Brenner	1- 2	0- 0	3	1	2
Grundy	1- 1	0- 2	0	0	2
McFadden	0- 0	0- 1	0	0	0
Team			7		
Totals	33-82	15-24	52	23	81

Half time: North Carolina State 48-37. Officials: Pace and Payak.

DePaul	fg-fga	ft-fta	rb	pf	tp
Palmer	4-10	5- 6	18	4	13
Swanson	6-16	3- 4	7	3	15
Mills	4- 7	4- 6	7	3	12
Meyer	6-18	1- 1	1	3	13
Murphy	5-15	5- 5	5	2	15
Odishou	0- 2	1- 1	0	2	1
Totals	25-68	19-23	38	17	69

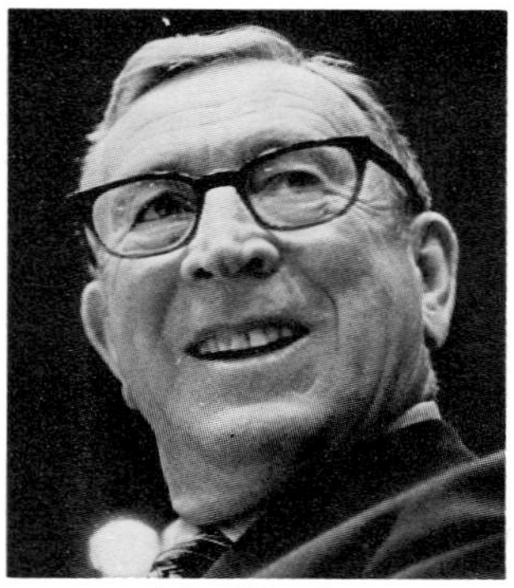
John Wooden

Dayton	fg-fga	ft-fta	rb	pf	tp
Sullivan	2- 8	4- 4	12	0	8
Cassidy	3- 9	2- 2	6	4	8
Finkel	11-16	4- 6	12	5	26
Papp	3- 9	5- 5	2	2	11
Klaus	4- 8	4- 6	6	3	12
Wannamacher	4- 7	2- 4	3	1	10
Totals	27-57	21-27	41	15	75

Half time: Dayton 39-34. Officials: Honzo and Stout.

Southern Methodist	fg-fga	ft-fta	rb	pf	tp
Ward	4-13	3- 7	9	4	11
Smith	4- 9	4- 5	9	3	12
Hooser	11-18	5- 8	22	5	27
Holman	3- 8	2- 3	4	4	8
Beasley	6-13	7- 8	3	0	19
Begert	1- 2	6-10	5	5	8
Wendorf	0- 1	0- 1	0	1	0
Marsh	1- 3	0- 0	0	1	2
Carpenter	1- 2	0- 0	0	1	2
Jones	0- 0	0- 0	0	0	0
Ramsey	0- 0	0- 0	0	0	0
Team			7		
Totals	31-69	27-42	59	24	89

Houston	fg-fga	ft-fta	rb	pf	tp
Ballard	7-16	0- 1	4	4	14
Jones	3- 7	1- 1	7	5	7
Lentz	2- 8	2- 3	9	3	6
Hamood	10-22	3- 5	5	1	23
Margenthaler	8-15	1- 2	3	4	17
Apolskis	2- 7	6- 8	8	5	10
Grider	1- 2	0- 1	2	0	2
Winch	1- 4	0- 0	3	1	2
Perry	0- 0	2- 2	1	0	2
Palmquist	0- 2	4- 7	1	4	4
Arning	0- 0	0- 0	0	1	0
Team			11		
Totals	34-83	19-30	54	28	87

Half time: Houston 50-47. Officials: Filiberti and Marich. Attendance: 12,500.

Brigham Young	fg-fga	ft-fta	rb	pf	tp
Quinney	10-18	4- 4	9	3	24
Kramer	8-11	2- 2	10	4	18
Fairchild	4-19	8-12	21	0	16
Gardner	5-15	6- 7	5	3	16
Nemelka	9-23	2- 3	6	4	20
Roberts	0- 2	0- 0	0	1	0
Congdon	1- 6	0- 1	1	5	2
Hill	2- 4	0- 0	3	1	4
Jimas	1- 1	0- 0	0	1	2
Team			7		
Totals	40-99	22-29	62	22	102

Oklahoma City	fg-fga	ft-fta	rb	pf	tp
Hopkins	5- 7	2- 3	6	4	12
Hunter	8-22	1- 2	12	3	17
Ware	6-12	6- 6	16	5	18
Wells	10-20	11-12	5	3	31
Gray	12-22	8- 9	2	3	32
Castleberry	1- 1	0- 0	0	1	2
Team			9		
Totals	42-84	28-32	50	19	112

Half time: Oklahoma City 62-46.

Regional Championships

Princeton	fg-fga	ft-fta	rb	pf	tp
Bradley	14-20	13-13	10	3	41
Haarlow	7-10	4- 5	7	2	18
Brown	5-10	4- 5	11	3	14
Rodenbach	3- 4	0- 0	1	4	6
Walters	2- 4	0- 0	0	3	4
Hummer	4- 4	5- 5	9	3	13
Roth	1- 1	0- 0	0	0	2
Kingston	1- 2	1- 3	1	1	3
Koch	1- 1	0- 0	2	0	2
Shank	1- 2	0- 0	1	1	2
Niemann	2- 2	0- 0	0	0	4
Adler	0- 0	0- 0	0	0	0
Team			4		
Totals	41-60	27-31	46	20	109

Providence	fg-fga	ft-fta	rb	pf	tp
Westbrook	6-12	1- 5	8	4	13
Walker	8-19	11-13	4	5	27
Blair	0- 0	0- 0	1	5	0
Benedict	4-17	2- 2	3	1	10
Riordan	4- 8	1- 2	5	2	9
Lasher	1- 4	4- 4	3	1	6
McLaughlin	0- 0	0- 0	0	0	0
Kinski	0- 0	0- 0	0	2	0
Ahern	1- 4	0- 1	0	0	2
Dutton	0- 3	0- 0	1	1	0
Sarantopoulou	1- 2	0- 0	0	0	2
Cox	0- 0	0- 0	1	0	0
Team			3		
Totals	25-69	19-27	29	21	69

Half time: Princeton 47-34.

Michigan	fg-fga	ft-fta	rb	pf	tp
Tregoning	5- 9	1- 3	6	1	11
Darden	6-14	2- 6	12	4	14
Buntin	11-25	4- 7	14	5	26
Russell	9-19	8-10	8	2	26
Romey	3- 4	0- 2	3	4	6
Myers	2- 3	0- 0	2	1	4
Dill	0- 0	0- 1	0	0	0
Totals	36-74	15-29	45	17	87

Vanderbilt	fg-fga	ft-fta	rb	pf	tp
Grace	2- 4	3- 5	12	4	7
Taylor	3- 7	0- 1	6	3	6
Lee	11-22	6- 7	20	4	28
Thomas	9-18	3- 3	3	5	21
Miller	8-16	1- 2	3	2	17
Green	1- 2	2- 2	3	0	4
Gibbs	0- 2	0- 1	2	2	0
Calvert	1- 2	0- 0	0	3	2
Totals	35-73	15-21	49	23	85

Half time: Vanderbilt 39-38. Officials: Lennon and Grossman. Attendance: 11,800.

Wichita State	fg-fga	ft-fta	rb	pf	tp
Smith	2- 2	8- 9	4	4	12
Thompson	2- 4	3- 3	2	2	7
Leach	5- 8	1- 3	2	4	11
Criss	2- 6	1- 1	3	3	5
Pete	6- 9	7- 9	9	0	19
Team			2		
Totals	17-29	20-25	22	13	54

Oklahoma State	fg-fga	ft-fta	rb	pf	tp
Hassmann	4- 9	1- 1	1	5	9
King	2- 3	2- 2	5	2	6
Johnson	3- 8	3- 3	3	3	9
Iba	2- 2	1- 2	2	3	5
Hawk	2- 6	3- 4	4	1	7
Moulder	3-10	0- 1	4	2	6
LaBrue	2- 4	0- 0	1	1	4
Team			2		
Totals	18-42	10-13	22	17	46

Half time: Wichita 31-22. Officials: Soriano and Korte. Attendance: 12,500.

UCLA	fg-fga	ft-fta	rb	pf	tp
Lacey	7-13	1- 2	7	4	15
Erickson	13-26	3- 6	11	4	29
McIntosh	2- 3	1- 1	6	1	5
Goss	6-15	1- 1	0	1	13
Goodrich	10-18	10-11	3	3	30
Lynn	2- 3	3- 4	1	4	7
Washington	1- 4	0- 1	1	2	2
Team			9		
Totals	41-82	19-26	38	19	101

San Francisco	fg-fga	ft-fta	rb	pf	tp
Gumina	6-12	4- 5	4	2	16
Mueller	4- 6	4- 5	4	5	12
Johnson	15-20	7-10	21	4	37
Ellis	7-13	2- 4	11	3	16
Thomas	3- 4	2- 2	0	1	8
James	1- 5	0- 0	0	2	2
Blum	1- 4	0- 0	1	2	2
Esters	0- 1	0- 1	2	1	0
Team			3		
Totals	37-65	19-27	46	20	93

Half time: UCLA 51-46. Attendance: 10,515.

Michigan	fg-fga	ft-fta	rb	pf	tp
Tregoning	6- 9	1- 1	2	10	13
Darden	6-13	1- 3	3	9	13
Buntin	7-13	8-10	4	14	22
Russell	10-21	8- 9	0	10	28
Pomey	2- 8	2- 2	4	3	6
Myers	1- 4	0- 0	1	4	2
Thompson	0- 1	2- 2	0	0	2
Dill	0- 0	3- 4	2	1	3
Ludwig	0- 0	0- 0	1	0	0
Clawson	2- 2	0- 1	0	1	4
Totals	34-71	25-32	17	52	93

Princeton	fg-fga	ft-fta	rb	pf	tp
Bradley	12-25	5- 5	5	7	29
Haarlow	4-10	1- 4	1	3	9
Brown	2- 6	0- 0	5	3	4
Walters	5-10	1- 2	1	3	11
Rodenbach	2- 5	2- 2	3	1	6
Hummer	4-10	4- 5	4	9	12
Koch	1- 4	1- 2	1	4	3
Kingston	0- 1	2- 2	1	2	2
Totals	30-71	16-22	21	32	76

Half time: Michigan 40-36. Officials: Korte and Magnuson.

Wichita	fg-fga	ft-fta	rb	pf	tp
Smith	4-11	0- 1	2	3	8
Thompson	13-19	10-11	6	2	36
Leach	6-14	0- 1	10	3	12
Pete	6-11	5- 5	6	5	17
Criss	4-13	0- 0	4	4	8
Reed	2- 3	1- 1	4	4	5
Davis	1- 2	0- 0	1	0	2
Trope	0- 1	0- 0	0	0	0
Nosich	0- 0	1- 3	0	0	1
Reimond	0- 1	0- 0	1	0	0
Team			4		
Totals	36-75	17-22	38	21	89

UCLA	fg-fga	ft-fta	rb	pf	tp
Lacey	9-13	6-10	2	13	24
Erickson	1- 6	0- 0	2	5	2
McIntosh	4- 5	3- 4	2	4	11
Goodrich	11-21	6- 8	2	5	28
Goss	8-13	3- 3	2	9	19
Washington	4-13	2- 4	1	7	10
Lynn	5- 9	0- 0	1	8	10
Chambers	0- 5	0- 0	1	2	0
Lyons	2- 3	0- 0	2	1	4
Levin	0- 1	0- 0	1	1	0
Galbraith	0- 0	0- 0	1	0	0
Hoffman	0- 0	0- 0	0	0	0
Totals	44-89	20-29	17	55	108

Half time: UCLA 65-38. Officials: Mihalik and Honzo.

National Third Place

Princeton	fg-fga	ft-fta	rb	pf	tp
Haarlow	4- 7	2- 3	0	3	10
Bradley	22-29	14-15	17	4	58
Brown	3- 5	1- 1	11	4	7
Rodenbach	7-14	2- 2	1	2	16
Walters	3- 5	0- 0	3	1	6
Hummer	3- 4	3- 3	4	3	9
Kingston	0- 1	0- 1	1	1	0
Shank	1- 2	0- 0	2	0	2
Koch	5- 6	0- 3	3	1	10
Neimann	0- 1	0- 0	1	2	0
Roth	0- 0	0- 0	2	0	0
Adler	0- 1	0- 0	0	0	0
Team			4		
Totals	48-75	22-28	49	21	118

Wichita	fg-fga	ft-fta	rb	pf	tp
Smith	3- 6	7- 9	5	4	13
Thompson	6-15	6- 7	3	4	18
Leach	5-10	0- 0	2	5	10
Pete	6-11	9-13	8	2	21
Criss	5- 9	0- 0	1	5	10
Reed	2- 7	0- 0	3	1	4
Nosich	1- 3	2- 2	1	0	4
Davis	1- 4	0- 1	0	0	2
Zafinos	0- 1	0- 0	0	0	0
Trope	0- 0	0- 0	0	0	0
Reimond	0- 0	0- 0	0	0	0
Team			8		
Totals	29-66	24-32	31	21	82

Half time: Princeton 53-39. Officials: Korte and Magnuson.

Championship

UCLA	fg-fga	ft-fta	rb	pf	tp
Erickson	1- 1	1- 2	1	1	3
Lacey	5- 7	1- 2	7	3	11
McIntosh	1- 2	1- 2	0	2	3
Goodrich	12-22	18-20	4	4	42
Goss	4-12	0- 0	3	1	8
Washington	7- 9	3- 4	5	2	17
Lynn	2- 3	1- 2	6	1	5
Lyons	0- 0	0- 0	0	1	0
Galbraith	0- 0	0- 0	0	0	0
Hoffman	1- 1	0- 0	1	0	2
Levin	0- 1	0- 0	1	0	0
Chambers	0- 0	0- 1	0	0	0
Team			6		
Totals	33-58	25-33	34	15	91

Michigan	fg-fga	ft-fta	rb	pf	tp
Darden	8-10	1- 1	4	5	17
Pomey	2- 5	0- 0	2	2	4
Buntin	6-14	2- 4	6	5	14
Russell	10-16	8-10	5	2	28
Tregoning	2- 7	1- 1	5	5	5
Myers	0- 4	0- 0	3	2	0
Brown	0- 0	0- 0	0	0	0
Ludwig	1- 2	0- 0	0	0	2
Thompson	0- 0	0- 0	0	0	0
Bankey	0- 0	0- 0	0	0	0
Clawson	3- 4	0- 0	0	2	6
Dill	1- 2	2- 2	1	1	4
Team			7		
Totals	33-64	14-18	33	24	80

Half time: UCLA 47-34. Officials: Mihalik and Honzo. Attendance: 13,204.

1966

First Round

Providence	fg-fga	ft-fta	rb	pf	tp
Blair	3- 8	3- 3	3	4	9
Benedict	5-14	0- 0	4	2	10
Walker	8-16	3- 6	6	4	19
Lasher	2- 8	0- 0	6	1	4
Riordan	2- 7	2- 3	10	4	6
McLaughlin	0- 1	0- 0	0	0	0
Team			3		
Totals	20-54	8-12	32	15	48

St. Joseph's Pa.	fg-fga	ft-fta	rb	pf	tp
Anderson	4-12	3- 7	14	1	11
Duff	7-13	5- 5	11	2	19
Ford	1- 4	2- 3	6	2	4
Guokas	5- 9	1- 1	5	2	11
Oakes	7-16	4- 5	2	1	18
McKenna	1- 3	0- 1	3	1	2
Team			4		
Totals	25-57	15-22	45	9	65

Half time: St. Joseph's 31-29. Officials: Eisenstein and Stevens. Attendance: 9,200.

Rhode Island	fg-fga	ft-fta	rb	pf	tp
Stephenson	1- 6	1- 2	4	4	3
Fitzgerald	4-10	2- 2	6	3	10
Chubin	5-20	13-14	10	3	23
Carey	3-13	0- 0	2	1	6
Cymbale	8-14	3- 4	3	2	19
Boehm	1- 4	0- 0	1	5	2
Johnson	1- 3	0- 1	2	2	2
Granat	0- 1	0- 0	0	0	0
Team			7		
Totals	23-71	19-23	35	20	65

Davidson	fg-fga	ft-fta	rb	pf	tp
Snyder	3- 6	5- 5	5	4	11
Squier	1- 5	0- 1	4	1	2
Knowles	15-27	9-11	20	3	39
Lane	7-14	2- 3	4	2	16
Youngdale	5- 8	1- 2	8	4	11
Hatcher	4- 6	1- 2	5	1	9
Light	1- 3	1- 2	4	1	3
Stone	2- 4	0- 0	1	0	4
Hyder	0- 0	0- 0	1	0	0
Clifton	0- 0	0- 0	0	0	0
Team			7		
Totals	38-73	19-26	59	16	95

Half time: Davidson 37-28. Officials: Allmond and Lennan. Attendance: 9,200.

Dayton	fg-fga	ft-fta	rb	pf	tp
May	3-11	6- 7	7	1	12
Torain	2- 6	0- 0	6	2	4
Finkel	9-15	7- 7	17	4	25
Waterman	5-16	3- 5	4	3	13
Hooper	1- 2	2- 2	3	3	4
Klaus	0- 0	0- 0	1	0	0
Team			3		
Totals	20-50	18-21	41	13	58

Miami, Ohio	fg-fga	ft-fta	rb	pf	tp
Peirson	4- 7	1- 2	4	4	9
Chamberlain	2- 4	1- 2	2	2	5
Patterson	1- 2	2- 2	3	5	4
Fisher	2- 4	1- 2	6	1	5
Snow	8-17	2- 2	2	1	18
Hallihan	1- 1	1- 3	0	0	3
Foster	1- 4	0- 1	0	1	2
Lukacs	0- 1	1- 1	0	0	1
Jackson	2- 2	0- 0	2	0	4
Team			4		
Totals	21-42	9-15	23	14	51

Half time: Dayton 32-25. Attendance: 7,013.

Western Kentucky	fg-fga	ft-fta	rb	pf	tp
D. Smith	12-21	5- 6	5	3	29
G. Smith	9-14	1- 1	15	4	19
Haskins	11-17	3- 5	9	2	25
Cunningham	7-14	2- 2	8	4	16
Chapman	2- 6	2- 2	5	4	6
Kaufman	4- 8	2- 3	1	0	10
Butler	0- 1	0- 1	0	0	0
Team			0		
Totals	45-81	15-20	43	17	105

Loyola, Ill.	fg-fga	ft-fta	rb	pf	tp
Wardlaw	9-18	2- 3	5	4	20
Coleman	5-14	0- 0	10	4	10
Bell	9-22	6- 8	6	4	24
Perez	1- 2	2- 2	0	0	4
Tillman	1- 4	1- 2	3	2	3
Manzke	0- 0	0- 0	0	0	0
Hogan	0- 0	0- 0	0	0	0
Smith	8-11	9- 9	16	3	25
Bukousky	0- 0	0- 0	0	0	0
Team			0		
Totals	33-71	20-24	40	17	86

Half time: Western Kentucky 49-43. Officials: Fouty and Tortorello. Attendance: 7,013.

Oklahoma City	fg-fga	ft-fta	rb	pf	tp
Gray	4-10	3- 3	0	5	11
Wells	7-19	4- 7	0	5	18
Ware	3- 7	4- 5	12	5	10
Hunter	9-15	3- 4	6	5	21
R. Koper	1- 1	0- 0	2	2	2
Lawrence	1- 2	7- 7	1	2	9
O'Brien	1- 2	0- 0	4	2	2
Vas	0- 0	0- 0	0	0	0
H. Koper	0- 3	1- 1	1	1	1
Bolen	0- 0	0- 0	0	1	0
Team			6		
Totals	26-59	22-27	32	28	74

Texas Western	fg-fga	ft-fta	rb	pf	tp
Flournoy	4- 7	1- 3	7	5	9
Lattin	8-15	4- 5	15	3	20
Shed	2- 4	0- 0	6	4	4
Artis	5-14	4- 4	7	1	14
Hill	8-18	8-14	4	3	24
Worsley	4- 7	6- 8	2	3	14
Armstrong	0- 1	0- 0	0	0	0
Cager	1- 3	2- 4	6	4	4
Myers	0- 0	0- 0	0	1	0
Baudoin	0- 0	0- 0	0	0	0
Palacio	0- 0	0- 0	0	0	0
Team			8		
Totals	32-69	25-38	55	24	89

Half time: Texas Western 43-37. Officials: Watson and Brown. Attendance: 9,045.

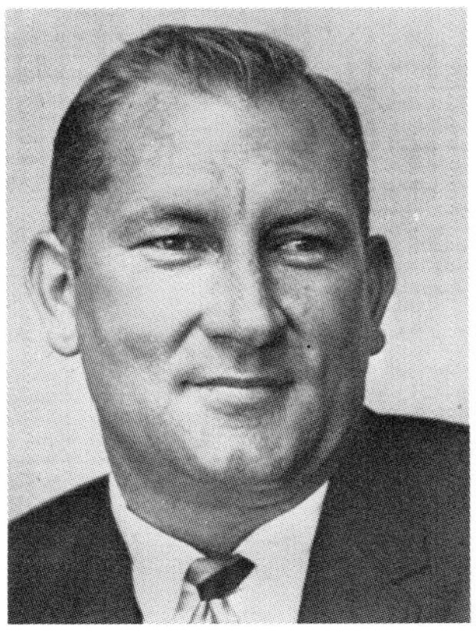

Don Haskins

Houston	fg-fga	ft-fta	rb	pf	tp
Ballard	4- 7	5- 5	3	1	13
Hamood	9-17	5- 7	1	1	23
Hayes	8-15	2- 5	12	5	18
Chaney	3-12	1- 2	11	1	7
Lentz	3-11	3- 4	6	2	9
Grider	2- 2	0- 1	3	0	4
Kruse	4- 9	0- 0	5	1	8
Apolskis	0- 1	0- 3	2	0	0
Team			4		
Totals	33-74	16-27	47	11	82

Colorado State	fg-fga	ft-fta	rb	pf	tp
Vidakovich	7-12	0- 0	5	4	14
Wright	8-16	1- 2	6	4	17
Rule	7-18	4- 6	7	5	18
Schlueter	3- 7	4- 5	19	4	10
Fines	5- 6	1- 1	1	4	11
Greene	1- 2	0- 0	0	0	2
Good	1- 2	0- 0	2	0	2
Montel	1- 5	0- 0	1	0	2
Robinson	0- 0	0- 0	0	0	0
Team			2		
Totals	33-68	10-14	43	21	76

Half time: Houston 44-35. Officials: Scott and Kortes. Attendance: 9,045.

Second Round

Davidson	fg-fga	ft-fta	rb	pf	tp
Snyder	9-22	7- 9	8	4	25
Youngdale	3- 9	4- 6	9	5	10
Lane	1- 7	3- 3	3	3	5
Squier	2-11	1- 1	3	1	5
Knowles	9-24	7- 9	11	3	25
Leight	1- 4	0- 1	4	1	2
Hatcher	2- 4	2- 4	5	1	6
Team			6		
Totals	27-81	24-33	49	18	78

Syracuse	fg-fga	ft-fta	rb	pf	tp
Penceal	4- 5	0- 1	0	0	8
Bing	9-20	2- 2	12	2	20
Boeheim	7- 9	0- 0	3	3	14
Harper	0- 2	1- 2	2	4	1
Dean	5-13	2- 2	12	4	12
Hickey	9-14	4- 6	8	2	22
Cornwall	4- 7	1- 1	3	1	9
Trobridge	0- 1	2- 2	2	2	2
Goldsmith	2- 4	0- 0	2	3	4
Reid	1- 3	0- 3	5	1	2
Nicoletti	0- 0	0- 0	3	2	0
Ableman	0- 1	0- 0	0	1	0
Team			7		
Totals	41-79	12-19	59	25	94

Half time: Syracuse 43-27.

Duke	fg-fga	ft-fta	rb	pf	tp
Verga	8-17	6- 6	4	1	22
Riedy	1- 5	3- 5	5	3	5
Marin	6-16	6- 8	15	2	18
Vacendak	6-14	1- 2	7	2	13
Lewis	6-12	2- 2	15	4	14
Chapman	1- 3	2- 3	5	4	4
Wendelin	0- 0	0- 0	0	1	0
Team			5		
Totals	28-67	20-26	56	17	76

St. Joseph's, Pa.	fg-fga	ft-fta	rb	pf	tp
Oakes	4-18	0- 0	1	1	8
Ford	2- 5	2- 4	6	1	6
Guokas	7-15	5- 5	4	5	19
Anderson	6-15	8-10	15	4	20
Duff	7-22	3- 5	8	3	17
McKenna	1- 8	2- 2	13	3	4
Chapman	0- 1	0- 0	0	0	0
Team			0		
Totals	27-84	20-26	47	17	74

Half time: Duke 37-33. Officials: McPherson and Wirtz.

Michigan	fg-fga	ft-fta	rb	pf	tp
Thompson	4- 9	0- 0	5	3	8
Bankey	0- 0	0- 0	0	0	0
Russell	7-15	10-12	6	3	24
Clawson	8-12	2- 2	2	2	18
Dill	1- 2	0- 0	1	1	2
Myers	4-15	2- 3	10	3	10
Darden	7-16	4- 5	12	1	18
Team			7		
Totals	31-69	18-22	43	13	80

Western Kentucky	fg-fga	ft-fta	rb	pf	tp
Chapman	11-23	0- 1	6	4	22
Kaufman	1- 2	0- 0	0	0	2
Haskins	5-16	5- 7	12	3	15
G. Smith	4-11	1- 3	13	4	9
D. Smith	3-10	1- 2	2	5	7
Cunningham	11-21	2- 4	6	0	24
Team			5		
Totals	35-83	9-17	44	16	79

Half time: Western Ky. 47-41. Officials: Eisenstein and Honzo.

Kentucky	fg-fga	ft-fta	rb	pf	tp
Dampier	14-23	6- 7	6	1	34
LeMaster	0- 2	0- 0	1	0	0
Kron	1- 6	1- 1	6	3	3
Conley	0- 5	1- 1	3	1	1
Riley	11-18	7- 8	8	3	29
Berger	1- 3	0- 0	0	4	2
Jaracz	7- 9	3- 3	7	3	17
Team			3		
Totals	34-66	18-20	34	15	86

Dayton	fg-fga	ft-fta	rb	pf	tp
Klaus	1- 1	0- 0	0	1	2
Finkel	15-26	6- 7	13	4	36
May	6-16	4- 5	3	3	16
Waterman	6-13	2- 4	9	3	14
Cassidy	0- 0	0- 0	0	0	0
Hooper	2- 7	1- 2	7	3	5
Torain	2-10	2- 2	4	3	6
Team			2		
Totals	32-73	15-20	38	17	79

Half time: Dayton 40-38. Officials: Allmond and Eckman. Attendance: 11,500.

Texas Western	fg-fga	ft-fta	rb	pf	tp
Shed	0- 2	0- 0	2	0	0
Flournoy	1- 5	0- 0	7	2	2
Lattin	10-15	9-10	8	3	29
Hill	7-18	3- 6	5	1	17
Artis	4- 8	3- 3	1	4	11
Cager	5- 5	5- 6	2	2	15
Worsley	1-10	2- 2	2	3	4
Team			5		
Totals	28-63	22-27	32	15	78

Cincinnati	fg-fga	ft-fta	rb	pf	tp
Rolfes	3- 9	4- 6	4	2	10
Howard	1- 9	3- 3	6	4	5
Krick	9-12	0- 0	9	4	18
West	7-12	5- 6	11	5	19
Foster	5- 9	1- 2	2	2	11
Rolf	4- 8	1- 1	7	1	9
Weidner	0- 0	0- 0	1	0	0
Calloway	2- 3	0- 0	1	0	4
Team			2		
Totals	31-62	14-18	43	18	76

Half time: Cincinnati 42-36. Regulation Score: 69-69. Officials: Filiberti and Bussenius.

Kansas	fg-fga	ft-fta	rb	pf	tp
Franz	9-15	1- 2	5	5	19
Lopes	4-10	3- 3	5	5	11
Wesley	9-17	5- 8	12	2	23
White	4-17	2- 2	7	4	10
Lewis	4-12	1- 1	7	1	9
Bohnenstiehl	1- 6	0- 0	7	1	2
Lochmann	1- 4	0- 1	6	2	2
Team			4		
Totals	32-81	12-17	53	20	76

Southern Methodist	fg-fga	ft-fta	rb	pf	tp
Begert	4-10	4- 7	9	4	12
Beasley	5-13	7- 9	9	2	17
Hooser	10-20	2- 4	7	4	22
Holman	3- 8	0- 1	10	1	6
Jones	2- 3	0- 0	0	1	4
Ramsay	2- 5	1- 1	3	2	5
Higgenbotham	1- 2	2- 2	1	0	4
Team			4		
Totals	27-61	16-24	43	14	70

Half time: 46-46. Officials: Varnell and Marich. Attendance: 8,000.

Houston	fg-fga	ft-fta	rb	pf	tp
Ballard	1- 8	0- 0	2	1	2
Lentz	1- 7	1- 1	3	2	3
Hayes	6-13	2- 4	10	4	14
Hamood	6-18	6- 8	4	3	18
Chaney	2- 8	2- 2	9	3	6
Kruse	4-10	0- 2	2	2	8
Grider	2- 5	2- 2	6	2	6
Apolskis	0- 1	3- 3	1	2	3
Team			7		
Totals	22-70	16-22	44	19	60

Jerry Chambers

Oregon State	fg-fga	ft-fta	rb	pf	tp
Petersen	6- 8	1- 2	10	5	13
Eaton	2- 5	2- 2	1	1	6
Fredenburg	3- 6	4- 7	5	2	10
White	4- 9	2- 4	8	1	10
Whelan	11-14	2- 5	6	3	24
Gunner	0- 0	0- 0	2	2	0
Team			3		
Totals	26-42	11-20	35	14	63

Half time: Houston 30-28. Officials: Jenkins and Overby. Attendance: 10,106.

Utah	fg-fga	ft-fta	rb	pf	tp
MacKay	4- 8	2- 5	9	3	10
Chambers	17-30	6- 8	11	1	40
Ockel	3- 6	4- 7	10	4	10
Tate	3-12	1- 3	9	1	7
Jackson	5- 9	0- 2	4	4	10
Black	1- 3	0- 0	1	0	2
Lake	1- 4	2- 2	1	1	4
Team			7		
Totals	34-72	15-27	52	14	83

Pacific	fg-fga	ft-fta	rb	pf	tp
Odale	3- 9	1- 2	4	3	7
Krulish	8-18	3- 4	10	5	19
Swagerty	6-22	4- 6	19	3	16
Fox	5-16	1- 2	6	4	11
Parsons	7-13	3- 5	9	3	17
Gilbert	0- 0	0- 0	0	1	0
Selim	2- 4	0- 0	1	0	4
Team			7		
Totals	31-82	12-19	56	19	74

Half time: Utah 49-41. Officials: Watson and Lawson. Attendance: 8,846.

Third Place

Davidson	fg-fga	ft-fta	rb	pf	tp
Snyder	3-14	0- 0	10	5	6
Youngdale	3- 3	2- 2	1	5	8
Lane	5-10	4- 4	4	1	14
Squier	4-10	0- 1	2	2	8
Knowles	10-19	8-11	10	4	28
Leight	1- 2	0- 0	1	4	2
Hatcher	1- 1	2- 2	4	0	4
Clifton	1- 3	2- 2	2	0	4
Stone	0- 1	2- 2	0	0	2
Team			9		
Totals	28-63	20-24	43	21	76

St. Joseph's, Pa.	fg-fga	ft-fta	rb	pf	tp
Ford	7-15	3- 4	7	1	17
Guokas	6-16	2- 2	9	2	14
Anderson	5-11	10-12	10	1	20
Duff	6-16	5- 6	8	2	17
McKenna	2- 9	0- 1	7	3	4
Oakes	2- 5	2- 3	2	1	6
Chapman	2- 6	3- 3	1	0	7
Brenner	1- 4	0- 0	2	1	2
Danches	2- 3	0- 0	2	2	4
Crundy	0- 2	1- 3	1	0	1
DeArgelis	0- 0	0- 0	0	2	0
Team			9		
Totals	33-87	26-34	58	15	92

Dayton	fg-fga	ft-fta	rb	pf	tp
Klaus	1- 7	0- 0	2	1	2
Finkel	13-20	5- 7	18	5	31
Brooks	0- 1	0- 0	1	1	0
May	6-25	3- 8	11	4	15
Waterman	3-10	1- 1	5	4	7
Cassidy	0- 4	0- 0	4	0	0
Hooper	2- 7	0- 0	2	3	4
Torain	4-15	1- 1	3	2	9
Team			4		
Totals	29-89	10-17	48	24	68

Western Kentucky	fg-fga	ft-fta	rb	pf	tp
Chapman	6-16	6- 8	8	3	18
Haskins	7-18	6- 6	17	1	20
Hicks	1- 6	0- 0	1	2	2
G. Smith	4- 6	3- 7	13	5	11
D. Smith	1-14	9-12	11	3	11
Cunningham	8-15	4- 4	12	1	20
Team			4		
Totals	27-75	28-37	66	15	82

Half time: Western Kentucky 41-29. Officials: Eisenstein and Allmond.

Cincinnati	fg-fga	ft-fta	rb	pf	tp
Rolfes	7-16	6- 7	6	2	20
Howard	5- 9	1- 2	7	3	11
Krick	1- 1	0- 0	1	2	2
West	4-17	4- 6	12	2	12
Foster	5-10	0- 0	3	0	10
Rolf	2- 5	3- 4	2	2	7
Couzins	1- 3	0- 0	0	1	2
Calloway	6- 7	0- 0	3	3	12
Weidner	3- 5	0- 0	3	3	6
Biedenharn	1- 1	0- 0	1	0	2
Team			2		
Totals	35-74	14-19	37	18	84

1966 TEXAS WESTERN MINERS—(l-r) Front Row: Bobby Joe Hill, Orsten Artis, Togo Railey, Willie Worsley; Second Row: David Palacio, Dick Myers, Harry Flournoy, Louis Baudoin; Third Row: Nevil Shed, Jerry Armstrong, Willie Cager, David Lattin, Don Haskins.

Southern Methodist	fg-fga	ft-fta	rb	pf	tp
Begert	7-11	4- 5	7	4	18
Beasley	2-12	4- 5	3	0	8
Hooser	8-11	5- 6	8	4	21
Holman	12-13	1- 1	2	0	25
Ramsay	2- 5	1- 1	6	2	5
Higginbotham	4- 9	4- 4	9	2	12
Jones	0- 1	0- 0	0	3	0
Team			2		
Totals	35-62	19-22	37	15	89

Half time: SMU 50-41. Officials: Varnell and Filiberti. Attendance: 8,100.

Houston	fg-fga	ft-fta	rb	pf	tp
Ballard	7-13	2- 4	7	3	16
Lentz	6-12	0- 0	6	2	12
Hayes	11-26	9-12	28	4	31
Chaney	3-12	0- 0	10	4	6
Hamood	9-20	0- 1	2	3	18
Apolskis	3- 5	1- 2	1	0	7
Grider	3- 7	4- 5	3	2	10
Ozug	1- 3	0- 0	3	0	2
Perry	0- 1	0- 0	0	1	0
Kruse	0- 1	0- 0	1	1	0
Team			2		
Totals	43-100	16-24	63	19	102

Pacific	fg-fga	ft-fta	rb	pf	tp
Krulish	7-19	3- 3	7	3	17
Odale	4-13	4- 7	8	2	12
Swagerty	11-23	4- 5	23	4	26
Fox	2-10	5- 7	5	5	9
Parsons	9-19	3- 3	11	4	21
Selim	2- 7	0- 1	8	0	4
Gilbert	1- 3	0- 0	1	1	2
Michelson	0- 0	0- 0	0	0	0
Team			4		
Totals	36-94	19-26	67	19	91

Half time: Houston 47-43. Officials: Watson and Lawson. Attendance: 7,250.

Regional Championships

Duke	fg-fga	ft-fta	rb	pf	tp
Verga	10-13	1- 3	1	2	21
Riedy	3- 6	6- 8	10	4	12
Marin	7-14	8-10	9	1	22
Vacendak	7-15	5- 7	3	3	19
Lewis	4-10	8- 8	13	3	16
Chapman	0- 0	1- 1	2	2	1
Liccardo	0- 2	0- 0	0	1	0
Team			5		
Totals	31-60	29-37	43	15	91

Syracuse	fg-fga	ft-fta	rb	pf	tp
Penceal	0- 1	0- 0	0	0	0
Bing	4-14	2- 2	8	4	10
Boeheim	6-10	3- 4	1	3	15
Harper	5-12	3- 3	10	5	13
Dean	4- 8	8- 9	7	4	16
Hickey	7-20	3- 3	7	4	17
Cornwall	5-10	0- 0	1	1	10
Goldsmith	0- 0	0- 0	0	0	0
Nicoletti	0- 0	0- 0	0	2	0
Team			6		
Totals	31-75	19-21	40	23	81

Half time: Duke 44-37. Officials: Wirtz and Stout.

Michigan	fg-fga	ft-fta	rb	pf	tp
Brown	0- 1	0- 0	1	0	0
Thompson	2- 6	2- 4	3	2	6
Bankey	1- 1	0- 0	1	1	2
Russell	10-25	9- 9	11	2	29
Clawson	5-14	1- 2	5	3	11
Dill	1- 3	0- 0	0	0	2
Myers	5-19	0- 0	11	3	10
Darden	8-16	1- 3	12	5	17
Team			4		
Totals	32-85	13-18	46	17	77

Kentucky	fg-fga	ft-fta	rb	pf	tp
Dampier	6-12	3- 4	6	3	15
Porter	0- 0	0- 0	0	0	0
Kron	6-14	2- 5	9	4	14
Conley	6-11	2- 6	8	4	14
Riley	13-27	3- 4	5	2	29
Jaracz	6- 8	0- 0	7	2	12
Team			7		
Totals	37-72	10-19	42	15	84

Half time: Kentucky 42-32. Officials: Eckman and Honzo. Attendance: 11,500.

292

Texas Western

	fg-fga	ft-fta	rb	pf	tp
Armstrong	0-0	0-0	1	0	0
Flournoy	3-7	5-6	8	5	11
Lattin	7-16	1-2	17	4	15
Hill	7-20	8-13	4	3	22
Artis	5-12	2-3	7	3	12
Cager	3-7	0-1	4	4	6
Worsley	1-4	1-1	1	0	3
Shed	3-5	6-9	4	2	12
Team			5		
Totals	29-71	23-35	51	21	81

Kansas

	fg-fga	ft-fta	rb	pf	tp
Franz	5-8	2-3	4	5	12
Lopes	7-15	3-4	6	4	17
Wesley	9-23	6-12	15	5	24
White	7-14	5-6	11	4	19
Lewis	1-3	4-4	1	5	6
Lochmann	0-0	0-0	3	1	0
Bohenstiehl	1-3	0-0	2	1	2
Wilson	0-0	0-0	0	0	0
Team			6		
Totals	30-66	20-29	48	25	80

Half time: Texas Western 38-35; Regulation Score: 69-69; First Overtime: 71-71; Second Overtime: 80-80. Officials: Marich and Bussenius. Attendance: 8,200.

Utah

	fg-fga	ft-fta	rb	pf	tp
MacKay	1-8	2-2	9	0	4
Chambers	13-31	7-8	10	4	33
Ockel	2-6	1-2	14	1	5
Tate	5-14	6-10	7	0	16
Jackson	5-10	0-1	11	3	10
Black	1-2	0-0	3	1	2
Team			7		
Totals	27-71	16-23	61	9	70

Oregon State

	fg-fga	ft-fta	rb	pf	tp
Petersen	2-13	1-1	4	4	5
Eaton	6-13	1-1	5	3	13
Fredenburg	7-14	1-1	9	2	15
White	9-18	2-2	14	4	20
Whelan	5-14	0-0	1	1	10
Gunner	0-4	1-2	3	2	1
Carlile	0-4	0-0	2	2	0
Team			4		
Totals	29-80	6-7	42	18	64

Half time: Utah 41-24. Officials: Jenkins and Overby. Attendance: 10,365.

Semifinals

Duke

	fg-fga	ft-fta	rb	pf	tp
Marin	11-18	7-10	7	2	29
Riedy	2-7	2-2	8	3	6
Lewis	9-13	3-3	6	3	21
Verga	2-7	0-0	3	1	4
Vacendak	7-16	3-3	3	5	17
Wendelin	1-4	0-1	2	4	2
Liccardo	0-1	0-0	0	0	0
Barone	0-0	0-0	0	1	0
Team			7		
Totals	32-66	15-19	36	19	79

Kentucky

	fg-fga	ft-fta	rb	pf	tp
Conley	3-5	4-4	1	0	10
Riley	8-17	3-4	8	5	19
Jaracz	3-5	2-3	4	5	8
Dampier	11-20	1-2	4	3	23
Kron	5-13	2-2	10	1	12
Tallent	1-2	2-2	1	0	4
Berger	1-4	5-6	5	1	7
Gamble	0-0	0-1	0	1	0
Team			8		
Totals	32-66	19-24	41	16	83

Half time: Duke 42-41. Officials: Honzo and Jenkins. Attendance: 14,253.

Texas Western

	fg-fga	ft-fta	rb	pf	tp
Hill	5-20	8-10	11	4	18
Artis	10-20	2-3	5	2	22
Shed	2-3	5-6	3	3	9
Lattin	5-7	1-1	4	5	11
Flournoy	3-6	2-2	9	5	8
Cager	2-5	1-1	0	3	5
Worsley	5-8	2-3	5	3	12
Armstrong	0-2	0-1	3	2	0
Totals	32-71	21-27	40	27	85

Utah

	fg-fga	ft-fta	rb	pf	tp
Tate	0-4	1-3	2	5	1
Jackson	3-9	2-2	1	2	8
Mackay	4-10	6-9	7	2	14
Ockel	1-1	3-3	9	3	5
Chambers	14-31	10-12	17	3	38
Black	3-8	2-4	2	3	8
Lake	1-1	0-0	0	3	2
Day	1-2	0-0	0	0	2
Totals	27-66	24-33	39	20	78

Half time: Texas Western 42-39. Officials: Bussenius and Wirtz. Attendance: 14,253.

National Third Place

Duke

	fg-fga	ft-fta	rb	pf	tp
Verga	7-13	1-1	3	2	15
Riedy	2-5	0-0	2	5	4
Marin	9-26	5-5	8	4	23
Vacondak	5-13	1-4	4	3	11
Lewis	5-7	4-5	11	1	14
Wendelin	2-4	0-2	0	1	4
Kennedy	0-0	0-0	1	0	0
Barone	1-2	0-0	1	1	2
Chapman	2-8	0-1	4	1	4
Kolodziej	1-1	0-0	0	1	2
Liccardo	0-2	0-2	3	0	0
Totals	34-81	11-20	37	19	79

Utah

	fg-fga	ft-fta	rb	pf	tp
Tate	1-8	2-5	2	1	4
Jackson	6-12	2-2	5	0	14
Mackay	4-10	5-6	8	4	13
Ockel	5-9	0-0	5	3	10
Chambers	11-16	10-12	18	3	32
Black	2-5	0-1	3	3	4
Day	0-1	0-0	0	0	0
Team			1		
Totals	29-61	19-26	42	14	77

Half time: Duke 41-37. Officials: Bussenius and Wirtz. Attendance: 14,253.

Championship

Kentucky

	fg-fga	ft-fta	rb	pf	tp
Dampier	7-18	5-5	9	4	19
Kron	3-6	0-0	7	2	6
Conley	4-9	2-2	8	5	10
Riley	8-22	3-4	4	4	19
Jaracz	3-8	1-2	5	5	7
Berger	2-3	0-0	0	0	4
Gamble	0-0	0-0	0	1	0
LeMaster	0-1	0-0	0	1	0
Tallent	0-3	0-0	0	1	0
Totals	27-70	11-13	33	23	65

Texas Western

	fg-fga	ft-fta	rb	pf	tp
Hill	7-17	6-9	3	3	20
Artis	5-13	5-5	8	1	15
Shed	1-1	1-1	3	1	3
Lattin	5-10	6-6	9	4	16
Cager	1-3	6-7	6	3	8
Flournoy	1-1	0-0	0	0	2
Worsley	2-4	4-6	4	0	8
Totals	22-49	28-34	35	12	72

Half time: Texas Western 34-31. Officials: Honzo and Jenkins. Attendance: 14,253.

1967

First Round
at Blacksburg, Virginia

Princeton

	fg-fga	ft-fta	rb	pf	tp
Heiser	12-22	2-2	5	3	26
Walters	0-5	0-0	3	1	0
Thomforde	2-2	10-11	6	4	14
Haarlow	8-23	2-2	11	3	18
Hummer	1-5	4-4	13	4	6
Brown	0-2	0-2	6	5	0
Lawyer	0-0	0-1	1	0	0
Lucchino	2-2	0-0	0	0	4
Team			5		
Totals	25-61	18-21	50	20	68

West Virginia

	fg-fga	ft-fta	rb	pf	tp
Holmes	1-4	1-2	6	2	3
Williams	9-18	3-4	3	3	21
Head	9-16	2-6	4	5	20
Reaser	1-7	1-2	1	4	3
Benfield	2-10	3-9	14	5	7
Ludwig	1-3	1-2	2	0	3
Grimm	0-0	0-0	1	0	0
Penrod	0-1	0-0	0	0	0
Hale	0-0	0-0	0	0	0
Harvard	0-0	0-0	0	0	0
Team			8		
Totals	23-59	11-25	39	19	57

Half time: Princeton 29-21.

at Kingston, Rhode Island

Boston College

	fg-fga	ft-fta	rb	pf	tp
Kissane	4-5	2-3	4	2	10
Evans	1-3	3-6	0	3	5
Kavancz	3-3	2-4	1	4	8
Adelman	5-7	6-7	1	1	16
Driscoll	0-2	2-3	2	2	2
Wolters	3-5	1-2	4	3	7
Kelleher	0-1	0-0	1	0	0
Team			8		
Totals	16-26	16-25	21	15	48

Connecticut

	fg-fga	ft-fta	rb	pf	tp
Penders	2-3	1-1	0	5	5
Corley	3-3	0-0	3	5	6
Holowaty	3-6	2-2	4	2	8
Ritter	2-4	0-0	0	0	4
Bialosuknia	5-15	5-5	2	3	15
Thompson	1-2	2-3	2	1	4
Curran	0-0	0-0	0	1	0
Team			5		
Totals	16-33	10-11	16	17	42

Half time: Boston College 14-13.

at Blacksburg, Virginia

St. John's, N.Y.

	fg-fga	ft-fta	rb	pf	tp
Swartz	0-7	2-4	5	3	2
Calzonetti	3-4	0-0	3	1	6
Bogad	5-12	4-5	6	2	14
Warren	4-8	4-4	9	3	12
Dove	7-17	7-9	13	3	21
Brunner	0-0	0-0	0	1	0
Jackson	1-1	0-0	0	0	2
Hill	0-1	0-0	0	0	0
Team			7		
Totals	20-50	17-22	41	10	57

Temple

	fg-fga	ft-fta	rb	pf	tp
Baum	4-9	2-2	4	4	10
Cromer	3-6	0-0	7	4	6
Brocchi	4-11	2-2	6	2	10
Brookins	9-14	3-6	3	0	21
Kefalos	1-8	2-3	2	0	4
Kehoe	0-1	0-0	0	5	0
Mast	1-1	0-0	0	1	2
Team			4		
Totals	22-50	9-13	26	16	53

Half time: St. John's 28-24.

Lew Alcindor

at Lexington, Kentucky

Dayton

	fg-fga	ft-fta	rb	pf	tp
May	10-18	6-9	20	3	26
Sadlier	3-6	0-0	4	3	6
Obrovac	0-4	1-2	6	1	1
Klaus	0-3	1-1	0	0	1
Hooper	2-5	5-5	1	5	9
Waterman	6-14	4-7	3	5	16
Torain	4-10	2-4	8	0	10
Team			7		
Totals	25-60	19-28	49	13	69

Western Kentucky

	fg-fga	ft-fta	rb	pf	tp
Chapman	5-10	2-3	5	5	12
Haskins	3-14	2-5	7	1	8
G. Smith	3-6	1-3	11	4	7
D. Smith	7-12	4-7	5	2	18
Kaufman	8-19	1-1	8	3	17
Hicks	0-0	0-0	0	0	0
Weaver	2-5	1-1	4	4	5
Fawcett	0-1	0-0	0	2	0
Team			5		
Totals	28-67	11-20	43	21	67

Half time: Western Kentucky 35-25. Regulation Score: 62-62.

at Lexington, Kentucky

Virginia Tech

	fg-fga	ft-fta	rb	pf	tp
Perry	5-12	2-2	6	3	12
Talley	10-15	4-7	19	3	24
Ware	8-11	1-2	9	4	17
Combs	7-20	4-5	3	4	18
Ellis	2-6	1-3	7	3	5
Brown	3-7	0-0	7	3	6
Mallard	0-2	0-0	0	0	0
Alavder	0-0	0-0	0	0	0
Team			3		
Totals	35-73	12-19	54	20	82

Toledo

	fg-fga	ft-fta	rb	pf	tp
Backensto	1-6	1-2	6	2	3
Brisker	7-17	1-1	9	3	15
Mix	5-16	8-11	14	3	18
Babione	4-9	0-0	5	4	8
Rudley	6-9	1-4	3	3	13
Miller	6-15	7-9	7	1	19
White	0-4	0-0	1	0	0
Team			2		
Totals	29-76	18-27	47	14	76

Half time: Toledo 46-43.

at Fort Collins, Colorado

Houston

	fg-fga	ft-fta	rb	pf	tp
Hayes	12-20	6-10	14	2	30
Bell	5-10	0-2	6	3	10
Chaney	5-17	1-2	1	5	11
Grider	2-3	2-3	0	2	6
Kruse	0-4	0-1	1	2	0
Lentz	1-3	0-1	3	1	2
Spain	0-0	0-0	2	0	0
Lewis	0-0	0-0	0	2	0
Team			8		
Totals	25-57	9-19	35	17	59

New Mexico State

	fg-fga	ft-fta	rb	pf	tp
Turner	2-5	3-4	4	3	7
Gambill	6-13	2-2	7	3	14
Evans	5-10	4-5	1	4	14
Landis	0-1	2-2	0	1	2
Collins	7-13	5-6	10	4	19
Morehead	0-0	0-0	1	2	0
Harris	1-2	0-1	2	0	2
Franco	0-1	0-0	0	0	0
Team			10		
Totals	21-45	16-20	35	17	58

Half time: New Mexico State 25-23.

at Fort Collins, Colorado

Texas Western

	fg-fga	ft-fta	rb	pf	tp
Lattin	4-6	9-13	14	4	17
Worsley	6-14	12-12	0	1	24
Cager	3-10	5-6	9	3	11
Palacio	1-7	5-8	6	4	7
John	0-2	0-0	0	0	0
Harris	1-6	1-1	3	2	3
Carr	0-4	0-0	1	2	0
Myers	0-0	0-1	0	0	0
Team			9		
Totals	15-49	32-41	42	16	62

294

Seattle	fg-fga	ft-fta	rb	pf	tp
T. Workman	5- 8	3- 6	4	0	13
Strong	2- 6	4- 5	3	5	8
Lott	2- 7	2- 4	7	4	6
Looney	7-18	1- 1	4	4	15
Wilkins	1- 4	0- 0	6	4	2
LaCour	2- 6	2- 3	5	4	6
Kreiger	0- 0	0- 0	1	2	0
Acres	0- 0	0- 0	0	2	0
Beil	2- 5	0- 0	2	3	4
Jackson	0- 1	0- 0	0	0	0
J. Workman	0- 0	0- 0	0	0	0
O'Brien	0- 0	0- 0	0	0	0
Team			10		
Totals	21-55	12-19	42	28	54

Half time: Seattle 23-20.

Second Round

at College Park, Maryland

North Carolina	fg-fga	ft-fta	rb	pf	tp
Miller	7-17	2- 2	10	4	16
Bunting	4- 8	1- 2	9	0	9
Clark	3-10	7- 9	9	5	13
Grubar	2- 5	12-16	7	4	16
Lewis	4-17	6- 9	10	3	14
Tuttle	0- 0	3- 4	0	1	3
Gauntlett	1- 3	0- 0	2	0	2
Brown	2- 4	1- 1	5	0	5
Team			13		
Totals	23-64	32-43	65	17	78

Princeton	fg-fga	ft-fta	rb	pf	tp
Heiser	8-20	2- 3	8	4	18
Walters	1- 5	0- 4	4	5	2
Thomforde	6-17	2- 2	7	5	14
Haarlow	1- 4	0- 1	2	1	2
Hummer	6-18	2- 5	9	4	14
Lucchino	2- 4	0- 0	1	2	4
Lawyer	3- 9	2- 2	4	5	8
Brown	3- 8	2- 4	7	2	8
Team			11		
Totals	30-85	10-21	53	28	70

Half time: North Carolina 29-28. Regulation Score: 63-63.

at College Park, Maryland

Boston College	fg-fga	ft-fta	rb	pf	tp
Adelman	5-14	7- 7	4	1	17
Kissane	1- 8	5- 6	5	3	7
Wolters	2- 9	5- 5	7	3	9
Kvancz	2- 7	3- 3	1	1	7
Evans	2- 7	6- 9	3	0	10
Driscoll	2- 8	1- 2	8	3	5
Hice	1- 1	4- 4	1	3	6
Kelleher	1- 1	0- 0	0	1	2
Team			2		
Totals	16-55	31-36	31	15	63

St. John's, N.Y.	fg-fga	ft-fta	rb	pf	tp
Bogad	7-16	7- 8	16	4	21
Warren	2- 8	0- 0	4	4	4
Dove	6-11	3- 4	10	5	15
Swartz	2- 5	0- 1	3	3	4
Calzonetti	5- 9	2- 2	4	1	12
Brunner	2- 3	0- 0	3	2	4
Hill	1- 1	0- 0	0	5	2
Team			4		
Totals	25-53	12-15	44	24	62

Half time: St. John's 24-22.

at Evanston, Illinois

Dayton	fg-fga	ft-fta	rb	pf	tp
May	2-10	5- 5	14	2	9
Sadlier	4- 4	2- 2	1	4	10
Obrovac	1- 2	1- 2	4	2	3
Hooper	6- 7	2- 2	0	0	14
Klaus	5- 7	2- 2	0	0	12
Waterman	2- 3	0- 0	0	0	4
Torain	0- 2	1- 1	3	2	1
Team					
Totals	20-35	13-14	25	10	53

Tennessee	fg-fga	ft-fta	rb	pf	tp
Widby	7-20	6- 7	4	2	20
Boerwinkle	4- 7	2- 3	9	5	10
Hendrix	5-11	0- 0	1	2	10
Hann	0- 4	1- 1	2	0	1
Justus	4- 9	2- 3	5	2	10
Bell	0- 1	1- 2	0	0	1
Coffman	0- 0	0- 0	0	0	0
Team			4		
Totals	20-52	12-16	27	11	52

Half time: Dayton 36-25.

at Evanston, Illinois

Virginia Tech	fg-fga	ft-fta	rb	pf	tp
Perry	2-12	3- 5	13	5	7
Talley	6-10	4- 4	11	2	16
Ware	1- 4	5- 8	8	4	7
Combs	11-24	7-10	4	2	29
Ellis	4- 9	0- 0	7	5	8
Brown	2- 4	4- 4	7	4	8
Mallard	1- 1	2- 2	0	0	4
Team			5		
Totals	27-64	25-33	55	22	79

Indiana	fg-fga	ft-fta	rb	pf	tp
Joyner	6-18	2- 7	10	4	14
Johnson	6-15	3- 4	14	3	15
DeHeer	2- 5	1- 1	11	3	5
Payne	7-19	4- 8	4	5	18
Russell	4-17	3- 7	7	3	11
Stenberg	1- 1	1- 1	0	1	3
Schneider	0- 3	0- 0	2	3	0
Pfaff	2- 3	0- 1	0	3	4
Turpen	0- 0	0- 0	0	0	0
Oliverio	0- 3	0- 0	2	0	0
Team			11		
Totals	28-84	14-29	61	25	70

Half time: Virginia Tech 35-31.

at Lawrence, Kansas

Southern Methodist	fg-fga	ft-fta	rb	pf	tp
Begert	7-10	2- 2	9	2	16
Beasley	4-13	1- 2	4	3	9
Phillips	8-14	2- 8	6	0	18
Jones	3- 6	0- 0	1	2	6
Holman	13-21	4- 4	5	2	30
Voight	2- 6	0- 0	4	2	4
Team			6		
Totals	37-70	9-16	35	11	83

Louisville	fg-fga	ft-fta	rb	pf	tp
King	10-13	0- 2	8	3	20
Beard	6-15	2- 7	9	2	14
Unseld	8-14	2- 2	12	4	18
Gilbert	2- 8	0- 0	3	1	4
Holden	11-17	1- 2	3	2	23
Daeken	1- 1	0- 1	1	0	2
Liedtke	0- 0	0- 0	0	1	0
Team			8		
Totals	38-68	5-14	44	13	81

Half time: Louisville 45-44.

at Lawrence, Kansas

Houston	fg-fga	ft-fta	rb	pf	tp
Hayes	9-18	1- 2	10	3	19
Bell	5-11	1- 4	7	0	11
Kruse	2- 4	2- 3	5	4	6
Grider	1- 2	2- 5	5	0	4
Chaney	8-16	4- 4	5	0	20
Lentz	2- 6	2- 3	1	0	6
Spain	0- 1	0- 0	1	0	0
Lewis	0- 3	0- 0	0	0	0
Team			15		
Totals	27-61	12-21	49	7	66

Kansas	fg-fga	ft-fta	rb	pf	tp
Franz	3-11	0- 0	2	4	6
Bohnenstiehl	5-13	2- 3	8	1	12
Vanoy	4- 5	5- 6	9	1	13
White	9-24	0- 0	3	4	18
Sloan	0- 1	0- 0	0	2	0
Harmon	2- 9	0- 0	3	4	4
Arndt	0- 0	0- 0	0	0	0
Team			11		
Totals	23-63	7- 9	36	16	53

Half time: Houston 32-29.

at Corvallis, Oregon

UCLA	fg-fga	ft-fta	rb	pf	tp
Heitz	3- 3	0- 0	0	5	6
Shackelford	5- 8	0- 0	7	2	10
Alcindor	12-17	5- 5	10	1	29
Allen	6-11	3- 3	5	1	15
Warren	4-11	2- 4	5	0	10
Chrisman	2- 2	2- 3	0	3	6
Nielsen	4- 6	0- 0	5	1	8
Saner	2- 3	0- 0	4	1	4
Sweek	4- 6	0- 2	5	2	8
Lynn	0- 1	0- 0	0	1	0
Sutherland	2- 4	1- 2	1	1	5
Saffer	4- 6	0- 0	2	0	8
Team			1		
Totals	48-78	13-19	45	18	109

1967 UCLA BRUINS—(l-r) Front Row: Don Saffer, Lucius Allen, Mike Lynn, Gene Sutherland, Mike Warren; Second Row: John Wooden, Jerry Norman, Joe Chrisman, Lynn Shackelford, Neville Saner, Lew Alcindor, Jim Nielsen, Kenny Heitz, Bill Sweek, Ted Henry, Ducky Drake.

Wyoming	fg-fga	ft-fta	rb	pf	tp
Hall	6-16	7-11	5	2	19
Asbury	8-20	4- 6	10	2	20
Von Krosigk	1- 7	2- 4	8	4	4
Wilson	2- 6	1- 1	3	3	5
Eberle	6-12	0- 1	5	4	12
Nelson	0- 2	0- 0	2	1	0
Team			7		
Totals	23-63	14-23	40	16	60

Half time: UCLA 55-18.

at Corvallis, Oregon

Pacific	fg-fga	ft-fta	rb	pf	tp
Krulish	10-14	4- 5	3	2	24
Jones	0- 1	0- 0	1	1	0
Swagerty	5- 9	9-12	8	4	19
Fox	7-15	0- 2	4	3	14
Parsons	4- 9	2- 4	4	2	10
DeWitt	0- 0	0- 0	1	1	0
Foley	1- 6	3- 5	8	2	5
Team			8		
Totals	27-54	18-28	37	15	72

Texas Western	fg-fga	ft-fta	rb	pf	tp
Cager	5-15	3- 3	10	3	13
Harris	3- 4	2- 2	9	4	8
Lattin	6-13	1- 1	5	5	13
Palacio	1- 7	0- 0	3	1	2
Worsley	6-22	1- 4	4	4	13
John	0- 1	0- 0	0	0	0
Myers	1- 1	0- 0	2	2	2
Carr	5- 8	2- 6	12	0	12
Team			6		
Totals	27-71	9-16	51	19	63

Half time: Pacific 36-33.

Third Place

at College Park, Maryland

Princeton	fg-fga	ft-fta	rb	pf	tp
Heiser	6-11	2- 2	1	1	14
Walters	4- 9	2- 3	4	2	10
Thomforde	9-14	4- 6	15	2	22
Hummer	3- 8	1- 1	7	1	7
Lucchino	3-12	0- 0	1	2	6
Lawyer	0- 0	1- 2	1	1	1
Brown	0- 3	0- 0	2	2	0
Pajcic	1- 2	0- 0	0	2	2
Adler	5- 7	0- 0	8	5	10
Koch	2- 6	0- 0	3	2	4
Dodd	1- 1	0- 0	1	0	2
Totals	34-73	10-14	44	18	78

St. John's, N.Y.	fg-fga	ft-fta	rb	pf	tp
Bogad	7-18	3- 4	11	2	17
Warren	1- 5	5- 5	6	0	7
Dove	4-11	4- 7	10	2	12
Swartz	2- 4	0- 0	5	2	4
Calzonetti	4- 8	0- 0	1	0	8
Brunner	0- 1	1- 2	2	1	1
Hill	1- 2	0- 0	0	0	2
Jackson	2- 6	1- 1	0	1	5
Rowland	1- 1	0- 1	3	2	2
Bettridge	0- 0	0- 0	0	1	0
Frey	0- 1	0- 1	0	0	0
Totals	22-57	14-21	38	11	58

Half time: Princeton 32-28.

at Evanston, Illinois

Indiana	fg-fga	ft-fta	rb	pf	tp
Joyner	5-10	0- 2	8	3	10
Johnson	2- 7	5- 7	4		9
DeHeer	4- 8	5- 8	16	3	13
Payne	2- 6	4- 5	2	3	8
Russell	3-11	4- 4	2	1	11
Pfaff	0- 1	1- 1	1	1	1
Schneider	0- 0	0- 0	0	1	0
Team			4		
Totals	16-43	19-25	43	17	51

Tennessee	fg-fga	ft-fta	rb	pf	tp
Widby	8-19	7- 9	9	4	23
Hendrix	2- 7	0- 2	1	5	4
Boerwinkle	1- 5	0- 1	7	4	2
Justus	3-12	7- 7	4	2	13
Hann	0- 1	2- 2	1	0	2
Bell	0- 1	0- 0	0	1	0
Coffman	0- 1	0- 0	0	1	0
Team			5		
Totals	14-46	16-21	27	17	44

Half time: 21-21.

at Lawrence, Kansas

Kansas	fg-fga	ft-fta	rb	pf	tp
Franz	4- 9	0- 0	5	5	8
Bohnenstiehl	5- 9	3- 3	6	2	13
Vanoy	4-10	2- 4	10	2	10
White	11-22	0- 0	5	2	22
Sloan	0- 3	2- 2	0	1	2
Arndt	1- 3	0- 0	4	1	2
Harmon	5- 9	3- 4	2	1	13
Team			3		
Totals	30-65	10-13	35	14	70

Louisville	fg-fga	ft-fta	rb	pf	tp
King	6-12	3- 4	5	3	15
Beard	7-17	3- 5	6	2	17
Unseld	6-14	4- 6	17	2	16
Gilbert	3- 5	0- 2	2	2	6
Holden	6- 9	2- 3	2	3	14
Liedtke	0- 0	0- 0	0	0	0
Team			8		
Totals	28-57	12-20	40	12	68

Half time: Kansas 39-38.

GAME-BY-GAME RESULTS

at Corvallis, Oregon

Texas Western	fg-fga	ft-fta	rb	pf	tp
Cager	2-4	2-5	2	3	6
Carr	4-5	0-0	5	5	8
Lattin	11-20	12-13	13	1	34
Myers	0-0	0-0	0	1	0
Worsley	3-9	2-6	3	3	8
Harris	1-4	2-2	5	1	4
Palacio	4-14	1-3	4	4	9
Team			4		
Totals	25-56	19-29	36	18	69

Wyoming	fg-fga	ft-fta	rb	pf	tp
Hall	8-14	5-8	6	1	21
Asbury	3-8	0-1	6	5	6
VonKrosigk	3-6	4-6	9	3	10
Wilson	2-3	0-0	3	5	4
Eberle	4-15	5-5	8	4	13
Nelson	5-14	3-3	2	2	13
Johnson	0-0	0-0	1	0	0
Team			11		
Totals	25-60	17-23	46	20	67

Half time: Texas Western 35-31.

Regional Championships

at College Park, Maryland

North Carolina	fg-fga	ft-fta	rb	pf	tp
Miller	6-16	10-12	5	2	22
Bunting	5-10	2-3	4	4	12
Clark	7-10	4-5	18	3	18
Grubar	1-2	1-1	3	3	3
Lewis	11-18	9-10	3	1	31
Gauntlett	1-1	0-0	0	0	2
Tuttle	1-1	0-0	0	1	2
Brown	2-4	0-0	3	2	4
Moe	0-0	0-0	0	0	0
Frye	1-1	0-1	0	0	2
Fletcher	0-0	0-0	0	0	0
Bostick	0-0	0-0	0	0	0
Team			5		
Totals	35-63	26-32	41	16	96

Boston College	fg-fga	ft-fta	rb	pf	tp
Adelman	4-12	1-2	6	2	9
Kissane	5-15	5-5	10	3	15
Wolters	2-8	2-2	7	4	6
Kvancz	5-8	1-1	1	4	11
Evans	3-8	2-5	3	2	8
Driscoll	7-17	3-4	10	2	17
Hice	3-7	0-1	2	4	6
Kelleher	0-1	0-0	0	0	0
King	1-2	0-0	1	1	2
Rooney	0-1	0-0	0	0	0
Pacynski	3-3	0-0	2	1	6
Gallup	0-0	0-0	0	1	0
Team			6		
Totals	33-82	14-20	48	24	80

Half time: North Carolina 44-42.

at Evanston, Illinois

Dayton	fg-fga	ft-fta	rb	pf	tp
May	9-24	10-11	16	1	28
Sadlier	3-6	0-1	7	4	6
Obrovac	1-2	1-1	0	3	3
Hooper	5-10	2-2	1	0	12
Klaus	0-1	0-0	0	1	0
Waterman	4-12	1-2	4	2	9
Torain	5-11	3-3	9	4	13
Team			7		
Totals	27-66	17-20	44	15	71

Virginia Tech	fg-fga	ft-fta	rb	pf	tp
Perry	6-12	2-5	2	5	14
Talley	4-5	1-1	10	4	9
Ware	3-7	2-3	8	4	8
Combs	7-23	2-3	8	0	16
Ellis	5-11	1-1	4	4	11
Brown	2-4	0-0	3	1	4
Mallard	1-2	2-2	2	0	4
Team			2		
Totals	28-64	10-15	39	18	66

Half time: Dayton 28-27. Regulation Score: 64-64.

at Lawrence, Kansas

Houston	fg-fga	ft-fta	rb	pf	tp
Hayes	14-27	3-6	11	3	31
Bell	5-11	1-2	8	4	11
Kruse	1-1	2-2	1	3	4
Grider	3-4	3-5	2	2	9
Chaney	3-15	4-4	10	2	10
Lentz	3-5	2-4	10	3	8
Spain	4-4	2-3	6	3	10
Lewis	0-1	0-0	0	0	0
Team			4		
Totals	33-68	17-26	52	20	83

Southern Methodist	fg-fga	ft-fta	rb	pf	tp
Begert	3-11	5-5	15	3	11
Beasley	8-16	2-2	4	3	18
Phillips	1-4	4-7	7	4	6
Jones	5-9	0-0	1	1	10
Holman	5-14	6-7	0	4	16
Higginbotham	0-0	0-1	0	0	0
Voight	4-10	6-8	4	2	14
Team			6		
Totals	26-64	23-30	37	17	75

Half time: Houston 39-33.

at Corvallis, Oregon

UCLA	fg-fga	ft-fta	rb	pf	tp
Heitz	4-6	1-1	3	3	9
Shackelford	3-12	0-1	4	2	6
Alcindor	13-20	12-14	14	4	38
Allen	5-8	3-6	6	3	13
Warren	4-8	4-6	2	1	12
Sweek	1-4	0-0	0	4	2
Saffer	0-0	0-0	0	0	0
Team			7		
Totals	30-58	20-28	36	17	80

Pacific	fg-fga	ft-fta	rb	pf	tp
Krulish	5-12	2-2	7	3	12
Jones	0-1	0-0	0	1	0
Swagerty	5-12	1-5	8	4	11
Fox	6-18	5-7	6	4	17
Parsons	1-3	5-6	6	2	7
DeWitt	3-9	0-3	13	2	6
Ferguson	1-3	0-0	0	1	2
Foley	4-6	1-2	4	4	9
Team			6		
Totals	25-64	14-25	50	21	64

Half time: Pacific 21-17.

Semifinals

Dayton	fg-fga	ft-fta	rb	pf	tp
May	16-22	2-6	15	2	34
Sadlier	4-7	0-1	0	0	8
Obrovac	0-0	0-1	1	4	0
Klaus	3-6	9-10	8	4	15
Hooper	1-7	3-4	4	1	5
Torain	4-14	6-8	11	5	14
Wannemacher	0-0	0-2	0	0	0
Waterman	0-0	0-0	0	0	0
Team			5		
Totals	28-56	20-31	44	13	76

John Wooden

North Carolina	fg-fga	ft-fta	rb	pf	tp
Miller	6-18	1-1	13	4	13
Bunting	1-3	1-1	5	4	3
Clark	8-14	3-5	11	4	19
Lewis	5-18	1-1	3	3	11
Grubar	2-7	3-3	2	4	7
Gauntlett	1-4	0-0	3	0	2
Brown	0-3	0-0	0	0	0
Tuttle	3-5	1-1	1	3	7
Team			5		
Totals	26-72	10-12	43	22	62

Half time: Dayton 29-23.

UCLA	fg-fga	ft-fta	rb	pf	tp
Heitz	0-0	1-1	0	1	1
Shackelford	11-19	0-1	8	1	22
Alcindor	6-11	7-13	20	1	19
Allen	6-15	5-5	9	2	17
Warren	4-10	6-7	9	0	14
Nielsen	0-3	0-0	3	5	0
Sweek	0-4	0-0	1	2	0
Saffer	0-0	0-0	0	0	0
Team			1		
Totals	27-62	19-27	51	12	73

Houston	fg-fga	ft-fta	rb	pf	tp
Hayes	12-31	1-2	24	4	25
Bell	3-11	4-7	11	4	10
Kruse	2-5	1-1	0	2	5
Grider	2-7	0-0	2	2	4
Chaney	3-11	0-2	4	4	6
Lentz	1-2	0-3	4	1	2
Spain	1-5	0-0	4	2	2
Lewis	0-0	0-1	0	1	0
Lee	2-3	0-0	1	0	4
Team			1		
Totals	26-75	6-16	51	20	58

Half time: UCLA 39-28.

National Third Place

Houston	fg-fga	ft-fta	rb	pf	tp
Hayes	10-23	3-5	16	3	23
Bell	0-2	0-2	7	2	0
Kruse	2-5	0-0	2	5	4
Chaney	6-13	7-8	8	0	19
Grider	2-6	2-3	3	1	6
Lentz	3-10	0-1	17	3	6
Spain	9-14	6-9	14	3	24
Lewis	0-1	0-0	0	1	0
Lee	0-1	0-1	5	1	0
Hamood	1-1	0-0	0	0	2
Benson	0-1	0-0	0	0	0
McVey	0-1	0-0	0	0	0
Team			4		
Totals	33-78	18-29	76	19	84

North Carolina	fg-fga	ft-fta	rb	pf	tp
Lewis	9-23	5-6	11	3	23
Miller	5-20	2-4	11	0	12
Clark	3-6	3-4	10	5	9
Moe	0-0	0-0	0	0	0
Gauntlett	2-7	2-3	1	2	6
Grubar	1-7	0-0	4	2	2
Bunting	1-8	2-7	4	2	4
Brown	0-5	0-1	1	2	0
Tuttle	1-4	0-0	1	2	2
Fletcher	1-3	0-0	2	1	2
Frye	0-1	0-0	0	0	0
Bostick	1-1	0-0	1	0	2
Team			6		
Totals	24-85	14-25	52	19	62

Half time: 42-23.

Championship

UCLA	fg-fga	ft-fta	rb	pf	tp
Heitz	2-7	0-0	6	2	4
Shackelford	5-10	0-2	3	1	10
Alcindor	8-12	4-11	18	0	20
Allen	7-15	5-8	9	2	19
Warren	8-16	1-1	7	1	17
Nielsen	0-1	0-1	1	3	0
Sweek	1-1	0-0	0	1	2
Saffer	2-5	0-0	1	4	4
Saner	1-1	0-0	2	2	2
Chrisman	0-0	1-2	1	2	1
Sutherland	0-0	0-0	0	0	0
Lynn	0-1	0-0	0	0	0
Team			7		
Totals	34-69	11-25	54	15	79

Dayton	fg-fga	ft-fta	rb	pf	tp
May	9-23	3-4	17	4	21
Sadlier	2-5	1-2	7	5	5
Obrovac	0-2	0-0	2	1	0
Klaus	4-7	0-0	0	1	8
Hooper	2-7	2-4	5	2	6
Torain	3-14	0-0	4	3	6
Waterman	4-11	6-7	9	0	14
Sharpenter	2-5	4-5	5	1	8
Samanich	0-2	0-0	2	0	0
Beckman	0-0	0-0	0	0	0
Inderrieden	0-0	0-0	0	0	0
Wannemacher	0-0	0-0	0	0	0
Team			8		
Totals	26-76	12-18	51	20	64

Half time: UCLA 38-20.

1968

First Round

at Kingston, Rhode Island

Boston College	fg-fga	ft-fta	rb	pf	tp
Steve Adelman	3-7	0-1	2	2	6
Bob Dukiet	5-6	2-4	3	5	12
Terry Driscoll	10-21	4-8	13	4	24
Jim Kissane	3-7	1-1	5	4	7
Jack Kvancz	6-12	0-0	2	1	12
Billy Evans	3-6	1-1	1	3	7
Steve Kelleher	5-10	0-0	3	3	10
Tom Verroneau	0-0	0-0	0	1	0
Pete Sollene	0-0	0-0	0	0	0
Ray LaGace	1-2	0-0	0	1	2
Tom Pacynski	6-8	1-3	5	4	13
Team			8		
Totals	42-79	9-18	42	28	93

St. Bonaventure	fg-fga	ft-fta	rb	pf	tp
Billy Kalbaugh	2-5	4-5	0	0	8
Bill Butler	12-19	10-13	11	4	34
Jimmy Satalin	4-12	1-1	2	4	9
Bob Lanier	12-15	8-12	15	4	32
John Hayes	7-12	5-8	4	2	19
Vinnie Martin	0-0	0-0	0	0	0
Team			9		
Totals	37-63	28-39	41	14	102

Half time: St. Bonaventure 54-46. Officials: Fidgeon and McNally. Attendance: 5,248.

at College Park, Maryland

Columbia	fg-fga	ft-fta	rb	pf	tp
Jim McMillian	7-16	3-4	8	0	17
Roger Walaszek	5-11	7-7	6	5	17
Dave Newmark	5-11	3-4	7	2	13
Heyward Dotson	10-14	12-14	10	5	32
Bill Ames	1-6	0-1	3	1	2
Larry Borger	0-0	0-0	0	2	0
Bruce Metz	0-0	0-0	1	0	0
George Thomas	0-0	0-1	0	0	0
Tom Garnevicus	0-0	0-0	0	0	0
Jon Schiller	1-1	0-0	0	0	2
Team			5		
Totals	29-59	25-31	40	15	83

La Salle	fg-fga	ft-fta	rb	pf	tp
Larry Cannon	6-17	2-4	3	3	14
Ed Szczesny	7-10	4-5	9	1	18
Stan Wlodarczyk	2-6	3-5	7	4	7
Bernie Williams	9-17	6-6	4	3	24
Roland Taylor	1-4	0-0	5	2	2
Dave Ervin	1-2	0-0	0	5	2
Frank Dunphy	1-2	0-2	2	2	2
Joe Markmann	0-0	0-0	0	0	0
Jerry Dugan	0-0	0-0	0	0	0
Team			4		
Totals	27-58	15-22	34	21	69

Half time: Columbia 45-34. Officials: DiTomasso and Hernjak. Attendance: 12,890.

at College Park, Maryland

Davidson	fg-fga	ft-fta	rb	pf	tp
Dave Moser	1-7	1-1	1	1	3
Wayne Huckel	2-8	2-5	4	1	6
Mike Maloy	9-12	5-7	10	1	23
Doug Cook	5-7	6-9	3	4	16
Jerry Kroll	4-9	8-9	7	3	16
Fox DeMoisey	0-0	0-0	0	0	0
Mike O'Neill	1-2	2-2	3	1	4
Rodney Knowles	4-13	3-3	6	2	11
Team			3		
Totals	26-58	27-36	37	13	79

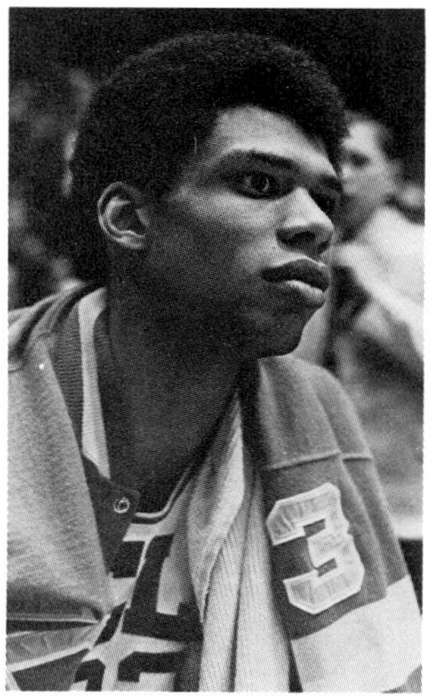

Lew Alcindor

St. John's, N.Y.	fg-fga	ft-fta	rb	pf	tp
John Warren	10-18	4- 6	9	2	24
Rudy Bogad	6-10	2- 2	8	5	14
Dan Cornelius	0- 1	0- 1	1	5	0
Carmine Calzonetti	4- 8	0- 0	0	2	8
Joe De Pre	4- 9	5- 5	10	4	13
Jim Smyth	1- 1	0- 0	1	0	2
Kit Frey	1- 3	1- 2	2	2	3
Mike Rowland	0- 1	0- 0	0	0	0
Ralph Abraham	3- 8	0- 2	5	3	6
Team			4		
Totals	29-59	12-18	40	23	70

Half time: Davidson 40-34. Officials: Fox and Honzo.

at Kent, Ohio

Bowling Green	fg-fga	ft-fta	rb	pf	tp
Walt Piatkowski	13-21	1- 3	5	4	27
Joe Henderson	0- 1	1- 2	0	3	1
Al Dixon	1- 7	4- 6	10	4	6
Al Hairston	7-14	4- 4	2	1	18
Dick Rudgers	3-13	3- 4	7	2	9
Carl Assenheimer	5- 7	0- 0	5	5	10
John Heft	0- 0	0- 2	0	0	0
Mark Hoffman	0- 0	0- 0	0	1	0
Team			9		
Totals	29-63	13-21	38	20	71

Marquette	fg-fga	ft-fta	rb	pf	tp
George Thompson	12-19	9-14	10	4	33
Brian Brunkhorst	8-20	4- 7	14	4	20
Pat Smith	0- 1	0- 3	4	5	0
Jim Burke	5- 7	1- 1	3	1	11
Brad Luchini	3- 9	2- 3	5	4	8
Blanton Simmons	0- 1	0- 0	0	1	0
Joe Thomas	0- 0	0- 0	1	1	0
Team			10		
Totals	28-57	16-28	45	20	72

Half time: Marquette 39-34. Officials: Wedge and Kaefer.

at Kent, Ohio

East Tennessee St.	fg-fga	ft-fta	rb	pf	tp
LeRoy Fisher	7-12	5- 6	12	2	19
Mike Kretzer	4- 8	0- 0	4	5	8
Ernie Sims	2- 9	1- 1	8	2	5
Richard Arnold	6- 9	4- 4	4	1	16
Harley Swift	7-23	8- 8	10	2	22
Worley Ward	2- 5	1- 1	6	3	5
Tim Fleming	2- 3	0- 1	0	0	4
Team			5		
Totals	30-69	19-21	49	15	79

Florida State	fg-fga	ft-fta	rb	pf	tp
Dick Danford	1- 3	1- 3	4	1	3
Jan Gies	4- 8	5- 5	6	1	13
Dave Cowens	5-12	1- 1	4	5	11
Jeff Hogan	4-11	2- 2	4	2	10
Darrel Stewart	6-13	0- 0	3	4	12
Randy Cable	1- 5	1- 1	0	0	3
Bob DePathy	3- 5	2- 3	3	0	8
Dale Klay	4- 7	1- 1	1	3	9
Team			6		
Totals	28-64	13-16	31	16	69

Half time: East Tennessee 37-30. Officials: Fouty and McPherson. Attendance: 7,300.

at Salt Lake City, Utah

Houston	fg-fga	ft-fta	rb	pf	tp
Don Chaney	4-10	4- 4	3	3	12
Vern Lewis	2- 6	1- 3	1	3	5
Elvin Hayes	20-28	9-15	27	1	49
Ken Spain	5-14	5- 9	15	2	15
Theodis Lee	4-10	5- 9	6	2	13
Carlos Bell	0- 0	0- 2	2	0	0
Neimer Hamood	0- 1	0- 0	0	0	0
Tom Gribben	0- 1	0- 0	2	0	0
Team			7		
Totals	35-70	24-42	63	11	94

Loyola, Ill.	fg-fga	ft-fta	rb	pf	tp
Walter Robertson	5-13	1- 4	4	4	11
Doug Wardlaw	2- 9	2- 2	3	4	6
Jim Tillman	5-11	0- 0	7	3	10
Corky Bell	8-15	2- 2	7	5	18
Wade Fuller	7-16	2- 4	11	5	16
Art Oates	1- 3	0- 0	2	3	2
Coak Cannon	0- 8	1- 1	7	4	1
Bill Baumgartner	0- 1	2- 2	1	1	2
Alan Miller	2- 8	0- 0	1	0	4
Mike Hogan	3- 5	0- 0	2	1	6
Team			6		
Totals	33-89	10-15	51	30	76

Half time: Houston 53-34. Officials: Payak and Scott.

at Salt Lake City, Utah

Weber State	fg-fga	ft-fta	rb	pf	tp
Justus Thigpen	2- 9	2- 3	1	1	6
Monte VreNon	5-10	2- 2	2	4	12
Dan Sparks	3- 6	3- 7	12	5	9
Nolan Archibald	4- 6	6- 8	11	4	14
Larry Bergh	3- 8	0- 0	2	3	6
Ted Bryant	2- 6	0- 1	3	1	4
Roger Reid	2- 4	0- 0	1	1	4
Richard Nielsen	1- 1	0- 1	1	2	2
Gary Strong	0- 0	0- 0	0	0	0
Gus Chatmon	0- 0	0- 0	0	0	0
Totals	22-50	13-22	33	21	57

New Mexico State	fg-fga	ft-fta	rb	pf	tp
Paul Landis	0- 0	0- 3	2	2	0
Robert Evans	3- 6	1- 1	7	1	7
Sam Lacey	8-13	4- 8	18	3	20
Jimmy Collins	8-19	5- 8	8	2	21
Richard Collins	7-16	4- 6	9	2	18
John Burgess	0- 1	0- 0	1	3	0
Hardy Murphy	0- 2	2- 3	2	1	2
Tom Las	0- 0	0- 0	1	1	0
Totals	26-57	16-29	48	15	68

Half time: New Mexico State 36-28. Officials: Evans and Webb. Attendance: 4,873.

East Regional

at Raleigh, North Carolina

North Carolina	fg-fga	ft-fta	rb	pf	tp
Dick Grubar	4- 7	1- 1	3	4	9
Bill Bunting	1- 5	2- 3	8	2	4
Charlie Scott	9-13	3- 4	3	3	21
Rusty Clark	9-13	0- 0	10	3	18
Larry Miller	9-18	9-14	16	4	27
Joe Brown	2- 5	0- 1	5	4	4
Ed Fogler	2- 5	0- 0	0	0	4
Gerald Tuttle	0- 2	0- 0	0	1	0
Ralph Fletcher	1- 3	2- 3	2	0	4
Jim Delaney	0- 0	0- 0	0	0	0
Jim Frye	0- 0	0- 0	1	1	0
Gra Whitehead	0- 0	0- 0	0	0	0
Team			5		
Total	37-71	17-26	53	22	91

St. Bonaventure	fg-fga	ft-fta	rb	pf	tp
Billy Kalbaugh	1- 3	1- 2	1	3	3
Bill Butler	10-22	3- 5	12	3	23
Jimmy Satalin	2-11	3- 4	5	5	7
Bob Lanier	10-24	3- 5	9	5	23
John Hayes	4- 8	2- 2	7	4	10
Vinnie Martin	0- 1	2- 5	4	1	2
Gene Fahey	1- 3	2- 2	1	0	4
Team			4		
Totals	28-72	16-25	43	21	72

Half time: North Carolina 40-30. Officials: Fouty and Stout. Attendance: 12,600.

at Raleigh, North Carolina

Davidson	fg-fga	ft-fta	rb	pf	tp
Dave Moser	4- 8	0- 0	8	0	8
Wayne Huckel	3-14	4- 5	2	4	10
Mike Maloy	4- 8	3- 4	10	1	11
Doug Cook	1- 2	2- 2	2	1	4
Jerry Kroll	2- 7	1- 4	4	3	5
Rodney Knowles	7-13	0- 0	7	5	14
Mike O'Neill	3- 7	3- 6	8	2	9
Jim Youngsdale	0- 0	0- 0	0	1	0
Team			4		
Totals	24-59	13-21	45	17	61

Columbia	fg-fga	ft-fta	rb	pf	tp
Jim McMillian	6-15	2- 3	12	5	14
Heyward Dotson	4- 6	7- 7	3	5	15
Roger Walaszek	0- 5	1- 3	3	2	1
Bill Ames	2- 4	0- 2	1	4	4
Dave Newmark	8-20	3- 3	9	1	19
Bruce Metz	1- 1	0- 1	2	0	2
Larry Borger	2- 2	0- 0	2	1	4
Team			2		
Totals	23-53	13-19	34	18	59

Half time: Davidson 32-28. Regulation Score: 55-55. Officials: Allen and Wirtz.

at Raleigh, North Carolina

St. Bonaventure	fg-fga	ft-fta	rb	pf	tp
Billy Kalbaugh	4-17	0- 1	3	4	8
Bill Butler	6-13	4- 5	11	4	16
Jimmy Satalin	3-12	2- 2	4	5	8
Bob Lanier	8-22	2- 4	13	5	18
John Hayes	5-11	5- 6	10	5	15
Vinnie Martin	0- 3	7- 8	1	1	7
Gene Fahey	0- 3	3- 4	2	3	3
Dick Ulasewicz	0- 1	0- 0	0	1	0
Jim Gagnier	0- 0	0- 0	0	0	0
Pete Wisniowski	0- 0	0- 0	0	0	0
Team			3		
Totals	26-82	23-30	47	28	75

Columbia	fg-fga	ft-fta	rb	pf	tp
Jim McMillian	7-13	5- 7	14	1	19
Heyward Dotson	8- 8	4- 7	3	4	20
Roger Walaszek	1- 4	1- 2	6	3	3
Bill Ames	6-10	3- 3	7	1	15
Dave Newmark	5- 8	6- 8	7	5	16
Bruce Metz	1- 5	0- 0	1	2	2
Jon Schiller	1- 1	0- 1	3	2	2
Larry Borger	3- 4	4- 5	2	0	10
Ken Brown	0- 0	2- 3	0	1	2
Bruce Fogel	0- 0	4- 4	3	0	4
Tom Garnevicus	0- 0	0- 0	0	2	0
George Thomas	1- 1	0- 0	1	1	2
Team			1		
Totals	33-54	29-40	48	22	95

Half time: Columbia 46-36. Officials: Wirtz and Stout.

at Raleigh, North Carolina

North Carolina	fg-fga	ft-fta	rb	pf	tp
Dick Grubar	3- 8	5- 6	1	5	11
Bill Bunting	1- 4	0- 0	4	4	2
Charlie Scott	8-15	2- 2	6	2	18
Rusty Clark	8-17	6- 7	17	3	22
Larry Miller	7-14	2- 5	6	2	16
Ed Fogler	0- 3	1- 2	0	0	1
Joe Brown	0- 1	0- 0	1	0	0
Gerald Tuttle	0- 0	0- 1	2	0	0
Team			1		
Totals	27-62	16-23	38	16	70

Davidson	fg-fga	ft-fta	rb	pf	tp
Dave Moser	0- 7	2- 2	7	4	2
Wayne Huckel	4- 8	4- 5	5	0	12
Mike Maloy	6-13	6- 6	13	1	18
Jerry Kroll	5-13	6- 6	5	5	16
Rodney Knowles	5-17	1- 2	12	4	11
Mike O'Neill	3- 7	1- 1	5	2	7
Team			1		
Totals	23-65	20-22	48	16	66

Half time: Davidson 34-28. Officials: Allen and Fouty. Attendance: 12,500.

Mideast Regional

at Lexington, Kentucky

Marquette	fg-fga	ft-fta	rb	pf	tp
George Thompson	4- 7	5- 5	2	5	13
Brian Brunkhorst	6-14	11-12	7	2	23
Pat Smith	0- 0	0- 2	5	4	0
Jim Burke	7-13	2- 2	1	1	16
Brad Luchini	6-11	7- 8	1	5	19
Joe Thomas	5-10	0- 2	7	3	10
Mike Curran	0- 1	0- 1	1	0	0
Blanton Simmons	0- 0	0- 0	0	0	0
Ron Rahn	2- 5	0- 0	3	2	4
Jeff Sewell	1- 1	2- 2	0	0	4
Team			5		
Totals	31-62	27-34	32	22	89

Kentucky	fg-fga	ft-fta	rb	pf	tp
Mike Pratt	8-13	2- 2	6	3	18
Thad Jaracz	1- 4	0- 0	2	1	2
Dan Issel	14-18	8-10	13	2	36
Mike Casey	8-19	3- 4	6	2	19
Steve Clevenger	2- 4	2- 2	1	3	6
Gary Gamble	3- 3	2- 3	1	4	8
Jim LeMaster	2- 3	2- 3	2	2	6
Tommy Porter	4- 5	0- 2	3	0	8
Randy Pool	1- 1	0- 0	2	3	2
Art Laib	0- 0	0- 0	0	1	0
Bill Busey	0- 0	0- 0	0	0	0
Phil Argento	0- 0	2- 2	0	1	2
Team			4		
Totals	43-70	21-28	40	22	107

Half time: Kentucky 53-40. Officials: DiTomasso and Fox. Attendance: 11,500.

at Lexington, Kentucky

East Tennesee St.	fg-fga	ft-fta	rb	pf	tp
LeRoy Fisher	6-16	1- 1	4	1	13
Mike Kretzer	10-15	3- 4	9	3	23
Ernie Sims	2- 9	1- 7	18	1	5
Richard Arnold	2-10	2- 2	1	3	6
Harley Swift	7-21	7- 7	6	4	21
Larry Woods	0- 1	2- 2	2	1	2
Worley Ward	0- 2	0- 0	3	1	0
George Walling	1- 2	0- 0	0	0	2
Bob Hall	0- 1	0- 0	0	1	0
Tim Fleming	0- 1	0- 0	0	1	0
Team			4		
Totals	28-78	16-23	47	16	72

Ohio State	fg-fga	ft-fta	rb	pf	tp
Steve Howell	10-17	2- 3	8	2	22
Bill Hosket	7-13	4- 7	20	5	18
Dave Sorenson	7- 9	0- 0	6	4	14
Bruce Schnabel	4- 8	1- 1	1	3	9
Denny Meadors	4-11	4- 7	3	3	12
Jody Finney	0- 0	0- 0	1	0	0
Dan Andreas	0- 0	0- 0	0	0	0
Ed Smith	2- 5	0- 0	5	0	4
Team			2		
Totals	34-63	11-18	46	17	79

Half time: Ohio State 37-27. Officials: Honzo and Allmond.

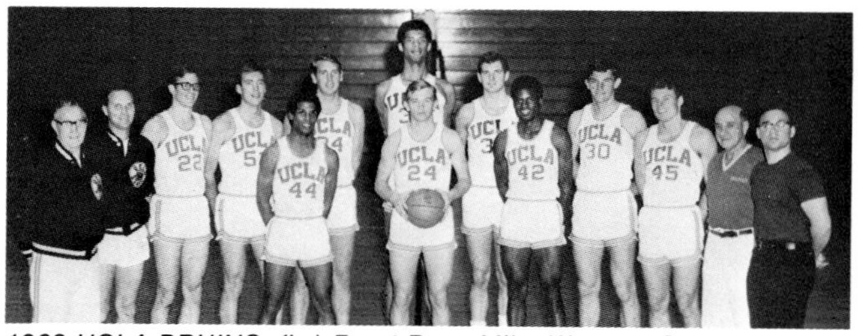

1968 UCLA BRUINS: (l-r) Front Row: Mike Warren, Gene Sutherland, Lucius Allen; Second Row: John Wooden, Jerry Norman, Kenny Heitz, Lynn Shackelford, Jim Nielsen, Lew Alcindor, Mike Lynn, Neville Saner, Bill Sweek, Ducky Drake, Frank Adler.

GAME-BY-GAME RESULTS

at Lexington, Kentucky

East Tennessee St.	fg-fga	ft-fta	rb	pf	tp
LeRoy Fisher	3- 7	1- 2	3	2	7
Mike Kretzer	11-17	4- 6	5	4	26
Ernie Sims	3- 5	1- 2	9	5	7
Richard Arnold	2- 4	1- 1	2	3	5
Harley Swift	3- 8	3- 3	0	3	9
George Walling	0- 0	0- 0	1	2	0
Tim Fleming	0- 0	0- 0	0	0	0
Worley Ward	1- 1	0- 0	0	0	2
Larry Woods	0- 0	1- 2	1	1	1
Willard Nickerson	0- 2	0- 0	0	0	0
Bob Hall	0- 1	0- 0	0	0	0
Team			2		
Totals	23-45	11-16	23	20	57

Marquette	fg-fga	ft-fta	rb	pf	tp
George Thompson	7-13	6- 8	5	1	20
Brian Brunkhorst	1- 3	3- 3	4	4	5
Pat Smith	2- 2	4- 6	4	2	8
Jim Burke	3- 6	4- 5	2	3	10
Brad Luchini	7-13	4- 5	6	1	18
Joe Thomas	4- 6	0- 0	3	1	8
Ron Rahn	0- 0	0- 0	1	0	0
Jack Burke	0- 0	0- 0	0	0	0
Mike Curran	0- 0	0- 0	0	0	0
Jim Langenkamp	0- 0	0- 0	0	0	0
Team			4		
Totals	24-43	21-27	29	12	69

Half time: Marquette 42-26. Officials: DiTomasso and Allmond.

at Lexington, Kentucky

Ohio State	fg-fga	ft-fta	rb	pf	tp
Steve Howell	9-18	2- 2	7	2	20
Bill Hosket	8-21	5- 5	12	4	21
Dave Sorenson	10-24	2- 5	7	1	22
Bruce Schnabel	0- 0	0- 0	0	0	0
Denny Meadors	3- 6	0- 0	2	1	6
Jody Finney	4- 9	1- 1	7	2	9
Ed Smith	2- 4	0- 1	4	0	4
Team			13		
Totals	36-82	10-14	52	10	82

Kentucky	fg-fga	ft-fta	rb	pf	tp
Mike Pratt	6-14	2- 3	7	2	14
Thad Jaracz	6-13	1- 1	7	3	13
Dan Issel	7-19	5- 6	8	2	19
Mike Casey	8-16	0- 0	8	4	16
Steve Clevenger	7-15	1- 2	3	1	15
Jim LeMaster	1- 2	0- 1	0	0	2
Gary Gamble	1- 2	0- 0	1	0	2
Team			13		
Totals	36-81	9-13	47	12	81

Half time: Ohio State 44-40. Officials: Honzo and Fox. Attendance: 11,500.

Midwest Regional

at Wichita, Kansas

Houston	fg-fga	ft-fta	rb	pf	tp
Elvin Hayes	16-31	3- 8	24	1	35
Theodis Lee	9-21	0- 2	9	4	18
Ken Spain	4-15	4- 5	11	2	12
Vern Lewis	4- 7	1- 1	3	3	9
Don Chaney	7-12	3- 6	3	4	17
Neimer Hamood	0- 0	0- 0	0	0	0
Team			9		
Totals	40-86	11-22	59	14	91

Louisville	fg-fga	ft-fta	rb	pf	tp
Wes Unseld	9-16	5- 9	22	4	23
Jerry King	5-13	0- 1	1	2	10
Marv Selvy	0- 2	0- 0	1	0	0
Butch Beard	9-23	3- 5	7	5	21
Fred Holden	4-11	1- 1	1	2	9
Ed Linonis	0- 4	1- 2	4	0	1
Denny Deeken	1- 2	0- 0	0	0	2
Mike Grosso	2- 7	1- 1	12	3	5
Gordon Minner	0- 0	0- 0	0	0	0
Bob Gorius	2- 2	0- 0	2	0	4
Team			4		
Totals	32-80	11-19	54	16	75

Half time: Houston 45-32. Officials: Brown and Filiberti. Attendance: 10,938.

at Wichita, Kansas

Texas Christian	fg-fga	ft-fta	rb	pf	tp
Mickey McCarty	8-23	1- 1	15	3	17
Tom Swift	6-12	1- 1	4	5	13
James Cash	5- 9	0- 0	5	2	10
Rick Wittenbraker	6-14	6- 8	6	1	18
Bill Swanson	0- 4	1- 2	5	0	1
Carey Sloan	0- 2	5- 5	3	2	5
Mike Sechrist	1- 3	0- 1	6	1	2
Jeff Harp	3- 5	5- 6	1	2	11
Randy Kerth	0- 3	0- 1	1	2	0
Team			8		
Totals	29-75	19-25	54	18	77

Kansas State	fg-fga	ft-fta	rb	pf	tp
Steve Honeycutt	7-17	5- 5	4	5	19
Jeff Webb	4-12	3- 6	12	4	11
Nick Pino	7-21	1- 5	8	2	15
Earl Seyfert	4- 9	2- 5	9	3	10
Eugene Williams	5- 9	2- 2	10	1	12
Fred Arnold	0- 1	0- 0	0	1	0
Ray Willis	0- 2	0- 0	2	0	0
Kent Litton	2- 3	1- 1	2	1	5
George Shupe	0- 0	0- 0	0	0	0
Team			6		
Totals	29-74	14-24	53	17	72

Half time: Kansas State 41-37. Officials: Bussenius and Wader.

at Wichita, Kansas

Kansas State	fg-fga	ft-fta	rb	pf	tp
Steve Honeycutt	8-22	2- 4	4	4	18
Jeff Webb	2- 7	0- 2	5	1	4
Earl Seyfert	4-11	0- 1	4	4	8
Eugene Williams	1- 3	4- 4	4	1	6
Fred Arnold	0- 1	0- 0	0	0	0
Ray Willis	1- 7	0- 1	4	2	2
Kent Litton	0- 1	0- 0	1	1	0
George Shupe	0- 1	0- 0	1	0	0
Greg Dickerson	1- 7	0- 0	2	1	2
Mike Barber	7-13	3- 8	10	3	17
Loren Peithman	0- 1	0- 0	0	0	0
Mitchell Third	2- 6	2- 4	7	0	6
Team			8		
Totals	26-80	11-24	50	17	63

Louisville	fg-fga	ft-fta	rb	pf	tp
Wes Unseld	9-14	7-10	19	1	25
Jerry King	6-13	0- 0	5	3	12
Mike Grosso	2- 6	2- 2	4	3	6
Butch Beard	9-13	3- 3	5	4	21
Fred Holden	6-10	4- 4	4	1	16
Marv Selvy	4- 6	0- 1	5	2	8
Ed Linonis	1- 1	0- 2	1	1	2
Denny Deeken	1- 5	1- 1	2	1	3
Gordon Minner	0- 1	0- 1	0	0	0
Bob Gorius	0- 0	0- 0	1	2	0
Gary Holland	0- 0	0- 0	0	0	0
Paul Callahan	0- 0	0- 0	0	0	0
Team			9		
Totals	38-69	17-24	55	18	93

Half time: Louisville 42-33. Officials: Filiberti and Wader.

at Wichita, Kansas

Houston	fg-fga	ft-fta	rb	pf	tp
Elvin Hayes	17-34	5-10	25	2	39
Theodis Lee	7-14	2- 3	7	2	16
Ken Spain	5-11	6- 7	16	2	16
Vern Lewis	0- 5	3- 5	3	1	3
Don Chaney	4-11	4- 5	6	4	12
Neimer Hamood	2- 4	0- 0	2	1	4
Tom Gribben	2- 6	2- 2	5	4	6
Carlos Bell	2- 4	3- 4	3	0	7
Larry Cooper	0- 0	0- 0	0	0	0
Kent Taylor	0- 0	0- 0	0	1	0
Team			9		
Totals	39-89	25-36	76	17	103

Texas Christian	fg-fga	ft-fta	rb	pf	tp
Mickey McCarty	3-12	2- 4	7	2	8
Tom Swift	3-14	3- 3	7	4	9
James Cash	4- 8	0- 0	14	3	8
Rick Wittenbraker	2-12	3- 5	6	3	7
Bill Swanson	2-10	0- 1	3	3	4
Carey Sloan	1- 7	2- 3	4	1	4
Mike Sechrist	0- 1	1- 1	1	3	1
Jeff Harp	4-11	0- 0	1	2	8
Randy Kerth	2- 2	1- 1	2	0	5
Tommy Gowan	5- 9	1- 1	2	1	11
Robert Nees	1- 4	0- 0	1	1	2
Jerry Chambers	0- 1	1- 1	0	0	1
Team			7		
Totals	27-91	14-20	55	23	68

Half time: Houston 59-26. Officials: Brown and Bussenius. Attendance: 11,004.

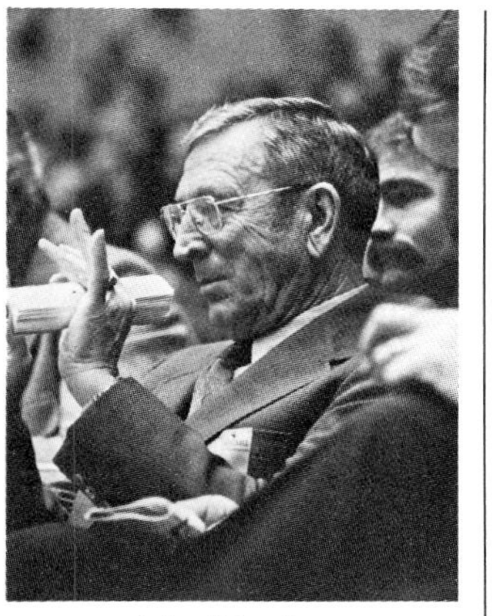

John Wooden

West Regional

at Albuquerque, New Mexico

UCLA	fg-fga	ft-fta	rb	pf	tp
Lew Alcindor	9-13	10-16	23	3	28
Mike Lynn	2- 7	0- 0	4	3	4
Lucius Allen	3-11	0- 0	3	5	6
Mike Warren	4- 6	2- 2	3	1	10
Lynn Shackelford	2- 7	3- 3	6	3	7
Kenny Heitz	1- 7	1- 3	2	4	3
Jim Nielsen	0- 1	0- 0	0	0	0
Bill Sweek	0- 0	0- 0	0	1	0
Team			9		
Totals	21-52	16-24	50	20	58

New Mexico State	fg-fga	ft-fta	rb	pf	tp
Robert Evans	4-13	6-10	3	4	14
Jimmy Collins	7-16	2- 5	6	1	16
John Burgess	2- 5	0- 3	5	4	4
Richard Collins	2- 6	1- 2	11	5	5
Sam Lacey	3-12	0- 0	5	5	6
Hardy Murphy	0- 1	0- 0	0	0	0
Paul Landis	1- 4	2- 4	3	0	4
Wes Morehead	0- 1	0- 1	1	0	0
Tom Las	0- 0	0- 0	1	2	0
Team			7		
Totals	19-58	11-25	42	21	49

Half time: 28-28. Officials: Jenkins and Smith.

at Albuquerque, New Mexico

Santa Clara	fg-fga	ft-fta	rb	pf	tp
Terry O'Brien	7- 7	4- 5	10	3	18
Bob Heaney	3- 7	1- 1	6	1	7
Bud Ogden	9-13	4- 7	7	4	22
Joe Diffley	1- 2	5- 9	5	2	7
Dennis Awtrey	5-11	3- 5	5	5	13
Kevin Eagleson	0- 2	0- 2	1	4	0
Chris Dempsey	4- 5	0- 0	3	2	8
Ralph Ogden	5- 9	1- 3	7	3	11
Team			5		
Totals	34-56	18-32	49	24	86

New Mexico	fg-fga	ft-fta	rb	pf	tp
Dave Culver	1- 2	5- 7	6	3	7
Ron Nelson	9-19	2- 3	1	5	20
Ron Becker	7-15	4- 5	4	5	18
Terry Schaafsma	0- 2	0- 0	0	1	0
Howard Grimes	3- 7	0- 3	7	4	6
Ron Sanford	3- 9	2- 3	3	5	8
Steve Shropshire	0- 2	1- 2	0	0	1
Keith Griffith	1- 4	0- 0	1	1	2
George Maes	1- 1	0- 0	0	1	2
Larry Jones	1- 3	0- 1	3	1	2
Leonard Lopez	2- 4	3- 5	4	3	7
Team			10		
Totals	28-68	17-29	39	29	73

Half time: Santa Clara 45-34. Officials: Overby and Dreight. Attendance: 15,345.

at Albuquerque, New Mexico

New Mexico State	fg-fga	ft-fta	rb	pf	tp
Robert Evans	4-10	2- 2	5	3	10
Paul Landis	5- 7	2- 4	2	1	12
Jimmy Collins	6-11	5- 6	1	2	17
Richard Collins	2- 7	2- 2	7	2	6
Sam Lacey	1- 9	3- 3	7	5	5
John Burgess	3- 3	5- 6	1	2	11
Hardy Murphy	0- 2	1- 1	1	1	1
Team			11		
Totals	21-49	20-24	35	16	62

New Mexico	fg-fga	ft-fta	rb	pf	tp
Ron Nelson	9-23	8- 8	2	0	26
Ron Sanford	11-17	1- 4	8	3	23
Ron Becker	1- 2	1- 2	3	4	3
Howard Grimes	1- 4	2- 5	9	5	4
Steve Shropshire	1- 1	0- 1	1	4	2
Keith Griffith	0- 0	0- 0	0	1	0
Larry Jones	0- 3	0- 0	1	2	0
Leonard Lopez	0- 4	0- 0	4	2	0
Team			8		
Totals	23-54	12-20	36	21	58

Half time: New Mexico 30-29. Officials: Smith and Dreight.

at Albuquerque, New Mexico

UCLA	fg-fga	ft-fta	rb	pf	tp
Lew Alcindor	6- 8	10-17	18	2	22
Mike Lynn	5- 9	0- 1	5	4	10
Lucius Allen	7-15	7- 7	8	3	21
Mike Warren	6-14	3- 3	5	3	15
Lynn Shackelford	1- 8	2- 2	6	0	4
Kenny Heitz	3- 8	1- 1	3	1	7
Gene Sutherland	0- 3	0- 0	1	0	0
Neville Saner	1- 3	0- 0	1	3	2
Jim Nielsen	2- 4	0- 0	3	4	4
Bill Sweek	1- 2	0- 0	1	3	2
Team			6		
Totals	32-74	23-31	57	23	87

Santa Clara	fg-fga	ft-fta	rb	pf	tp
Terry O'Brien	3- 6	1- 1	2	3	7
Bob Heaney	2-10	0- 1	1	2	4
Bud Ogden	4- 7	5-10	9	3	13
Joe Diffley	0- 3	2- 2	0	2	2
Dennis Awtrey	7-12	3- 4	10	4	17
Kevin Eagleson	0- 1	2- 3	0	4	2
Bob Stuckey	1- 5	3- 4	2	0	5
Kevin Donahue	0- 0	0- 0	1	0	0
Keith Paulson	0- 3	0- 0	1	1	0
Chris Dempsey	0- 4	1- 2	4	1	1
Ralph Ogden	5-11	1- 1	3	2	11
Ray Thomas	2- 3	0- 1	2	2	4
Team			10		
Totals	24-65	18-29	45	24	66

Half time: UCLA 51-34. Officials: Overby and Jenkins. Attendance: 15,010.

297

Semifinals

at Los Angeles, California

Ohio State	fg-fga	ft-fta	rb	pf	tp
Steve Howell	6-17	1- 2	3	2	13
Bill Hosket	4-11	6- 9	9	5	14
Dave Sorenson	5-17	1- 3	11	3	11
Bruce Schnabel	0- 1	0- 0	2	1	0
Denny Meadors	3-13	2- 2	3	3	8
Jody Finney	8-13	0- 2	4	2	16
Ed Smith	2- 6	0- 0	5	1	4
Dan Andreas	0- 0	0- 0	0	0	0
Craig Barclay	0- 1	0- 0	0	0	0
Jim Geddes	0- 0	0- 0	1	1	0
Team			11		
Totals	28-79	10-18	49	18	66

North Carolina	fg-fga	ft-fta	rb	pf	tp
Larry Miller	10-23	0- 1	6	2	20
Bill Bunting	4- 7	9-10	12	2	17
Rusty Clark	7- 9	1- 1	11	4	15
Charlie Scott	6-16	1- 4	5	3	13
Dick Grubar	4- 9	3- 3	6	0	11
Ed Fogler	1- 2	0- 0	0	1	2
Joe Brown	0- 4	0- 0	4	2	0
Gerald Tuttle	1- 1	0- 1	0	0	2
Team			10		
Totals	33-71	14-20	54	14	80

Half time: North Carolina 34-27. Officials: Bussenius and Jenkins.

at Los Angeles, California

Houston	fg-fga	ft-fta	rb	pf	tp
Theodis Lee	2-15	0- 0	4	4	4
Elvin Hayes	3-10	4- 7	5	4	10
Ken Spain	4-12	7-10	13	1	15
Don Chaney	5-13	5- 7	7	2	15
Vern Lewis	2- 8	2- 2	5	0	6
Neimer Hamood	3- 5	4- 6	0	2	10
Tom Gribben	0- 5	0- 1	5	1	0
Carlos Bell	3- 8	3- 4	5	0	9
Kent Taylor	0- 0	0- 0	0	0	0
Larry Cooper	0- 2	0- 0	1	0	0
Team			9		
Totals	22-78	25-37	54	14	69

UCLA	fg-fga	ft-fta	rb	pf	tp
Lynn Shackelford	6-10	5-5	3	4	17
Mike Lynn	8-10	3-3	8	4	19
Lew Alcindor	7-14	5-6	18	3	19
Mike Warren	7-18	0-0	5	3	14
Lucius Allen	9-18	1-2	9	1	19
Jim Nielsen	2-3	0-0	1	4	4
Kenny Heitz	3-6	1-1	1	1	7
Bill Sweek	1-1	0-1	0	0	2
Gene Sutherland	0-1	0-0	0	1	0
Neville Saner	0-2	0-0	1	2	0
Team			11		
Totals	43-83	15-18	57	23	101

Half time: UCLA 53-31. Officials: Honzo and Fouty. Attendance: 15,742.

National Third Place

at Los Angeles, California

Houston	fg-fga	ft-fta	rb	pf	tp
Theodis Lee	13-26	1-2	8	0	27
Elvin Hayes	14-34	6-8	16	4	34
Ken Spain	4-12	2-4	12	4	10
Vern Lewis	3-7	0-1	3	3	6
Don Chaney	4-15	0-1	8	5	8
Carlos Bell	0-0	0-0	0	1	0
Neimer Hamood	0-1	0-0	0	1	0
Tom Gribben	0-0	0-0	0	1	0
Team			7		
Totals	38-95	9-16	54	19	85

Ohio State	fg-fga	ft-fta	rb	pf	tp
Steve Howell	12-26	2-2	13	4	26
Bill Hosket	5-11	9-11	17	4	19
Dave Sorenson	8-13	3-4	9	2	19
Denny Meadors	3-11	3-4	5	0	9
Mike Swain	1-3	0-0	2	1	2
Jody Finney	5-11	3-3	3	3	13
Ed Smith	0-2	1-2	1	0	1
Team			8		
Totals	34-77	21-26	58	14	89

Half time: Ohio State 46-42. Officials: Bussenius and Jenkins.

Championship

at Los Angeles, California

UCLA	fg-fga	ft-fta	rb	pf	tp
Lynn Shackelford	3-5	0-1	2	0	6
Mike Lynn	1-7	5-7	6	3	7
Lew Alcindor	15-21	4-4	16	3	34
Mike Warren	3-7	1-1	3	2	7
Lucius Allen	3-7	5-7	5	0	11
Jim Nielsen	1-1	0-0	1	1	2
Kenny Heitz	3-6	1-1	2	3	7
Gene Sutherland	1-2	0-0	2	1	2
Bill Sweek	0-1	0-0	0	1	0
Neville Saner	1-3	0-0	2	2	2
Team			9		
Totals	31-60	16-21	48	16	78

North Carolina	fg-fga	ft-fta	rb	pf	tp
Larry Miller	5-13	4-6	6	3	14
Bill Bunting	1-3	1-2	2	5	3
Rusty Clark	4-12	1-3	8	3	9
Charlie Scott	6-17	0-1	3	3	12
Dick Grubar	2-5	1-2	0	2	5
Ed Fogler	1-4	2-2	0	0	4
Joe Brown	2-5	2-2	5	1	6
Gerald Tuttle	0-0	0-0	0	0	0
Jim Frye	1-2	0-1	1	0	2
Gra Whitehead	0-0	0-0	0	0	0
Jim Delany	0-1	0-0	0	0	0
Ralph Fletcher	0-1	0-0	0	0	0
Team			10		
Totals	22-63	11-19	35	17	55

Half time: UCLA 32-22. Officials: Honzo and Fouty. Attendance: 14,438.

1969

First Round

at Kingston, Rhode Island

St. Joseph's, Pa.	fg-fga	ft-fta	rb	pf	tp
John Connolly	1-5	1-1	4	2	3
Mike Dignazio	1-3	0-1	0	1	2
Mike Haver	3-10	8-12	4	3	14
Dan Kelly	6-15	4-5	3	1	16
Ed Leonarczyk	0-2	1-2	3	2	1
Tom Lynch	0-0	0-0	0	2	0
Bruce Marks	0-3	0-1	3	0	0
Frank McLaughlin	0-1	0-0	3	1	0
Eric Mitchell	2-3	2-2	5	3	6
Dave Pfahler	1-4	1-6	6	5	3
Jack Snyder	3-11	1-1	1	2	7
Team			4		
Totals	17-57	18-31	36	22	52

Duquesne	fg-fga	ft-fta	rb	pf	tp
Larry Abraham	0-0	0-0	0	0	0
Moe Barr	2-7	0-0	7	4	4
Tim Bradley	0-0	0-0	0	0	0
Ron Connolly	1-1	0-1	0	1	2
Jarrett Durham	9-13	1-1	8	4	19
George Gilbert	0-0	0-0	0	0	0
Willie Hines	1-4	3-3	1	2	5
Gary Major	2-10	4-4	7	4	8
Garry Nelson	7-14	3-7	18	4	17
Bill Zopf	5-9	0-0	6	3	10
Barry Nelson	0-1	7-9	5	4	7
Walt Zinn	0-0	2-2	0	1	2
Steve McHugh	0-1	0-0	0	0	0
Team			5		
Totals	27-60	20-27	57	27	74

Half time: Duquesne 29-21. Attendance: 2,200.

at Raleigh, North Carolina

Villanova	fg-fga	ft-fta	rb	pf	tp
Frank Gillen	1-5	1-1	4	3	3
Fran O'Hanlon	3-11	4-4	3	5	10
Johnny Jones	7-19	1-3	6	2	15
Jim McIntosh	4-5	2-2	8	3	10
Howard Porter	10-20	3-4	10	4	23
Leon Wojnowski	0-0	0-0	0	0	0
Frank McCall	0-1	0-0	0	0	0
Sammy Sims	0-0	0-0	0	1	0
Clarence Smith	0-1	0-0	1	0	0
Joe Walters	0-0	0-0	0	0	0
Bob Melchionni	0-1	0-0	0	0	0
John Fox	0-0	0-0	0	0	0
Team			4		
Totals	25-63	11-14	36	18	61

Davidson	fg-fga	ft-fta	rb	pf	tp
Dave Moser	3-5	4-5	5	4	10
Wayne Huckel	2-4	3-3	3	1	7
Mike Maloy	11-19	9-13	17	1	31
Doug Cook	7-15	2-3	5	3	16
Jerry Kroll	3-10	1-1	6	2	7
Mike O'Neill	2-4	0-0	0	0	4
Ron Stelzer	0-0	0-0	0	0	0
Duncan Postma	0-0	0-0	0	0	0
Rocky Crosswhite	0-0	0-0	0	0	0
Tony Orsbon	0-0	0-0	0	0	0
Steve Kirley	0-0	0-0	0	0	0
Jan Postma	0-0	0-0	0	0	0
Team			4		
Totals	28-57	19-25	40	11	75

Half time: Davidson 40-24. Officials: Allmond and Rooney.

at Raleigh, North Carolina

St. John's N.Y.	fg-fga	ft-fta	rb	pf	tp
Carmine Calzonetti	5-10	2-2	2	0	12
Ralph Abraham	3-4	4-5	10	4	10
John Warren	7-11	4-4	3	0	18
Dan Cornelius	3-7	3-3	3	3	9
Joe DePre	7-15	4-5	3	4	18
Bill Paultz	2-4	1-1	3	4	5
Jim Smyth	0-3	0-0	0	0	0
Richie Gilkes	0-0	0-1	1	1	0
Team			1		
Totals	27-54	18-21	26	16	72

Princeton	fg-fga	ft-fta	rb	pf	tp
Ed Stanczak	1-2	4-6	6	4	6
Chris Thomforde	5-16	2-3	14	4	12
William Sickler	0-2	2-2	2	0	2
John Hummer	13-16	2-5	10	4	28
Geoffrey Petrie	5-19	5-5	6	4	15
John Arbogast	0-0	0-0	3	0	0
Team			0		
Totals	24-55	15-21	41	16	63

Half time: St. John's 37-33. Officials: DiTomasso and Grossman. Attendance: 7,600.

at Carbondale, Illinois

Murray State	fg-fga	ft-fta	rb	pf	tp
Claude Virden	8-17	1-1	10	4	17
Hector Blondet	7-10	1-1	3	3	15
Ron Johnson	4-7	2-3	4	4	10
Jimmy Young	3-7	1-1	2	0	7
Frank Streety	0-4	2-2	1	2	2
Jim Stocks	3-5	3-4	3	5	9
Ron Romani	0-0	0-0	0	0	0
Steve Riley	1-1	0-1	1	0	2
Gary Wilson	0-0	0-0	0	0	0
Gary Steverson	0-1	0-0	0	0	0
Team			7		
Totals	26-52	10-13	31	18	62

Marquette	fg-fga	ft-fta	rb	pf	tp
George Thompson	9-20	5-5	5	2	23
Joe Thomas	4-8	1-1	6	0	9
Ric Cobb	4-6	2-9	8	2	10
Jeff Sewell	8-11	1-2	4	5	17
Dean Meminger	6-11	3-4	5	1	15
Ron Rahn	0-1	0-0	0	0	0
Jack Burke	1-2	0-0	0	2	2
Pat Smith	0-0	0-1	0	0	0
John Reider	0-0	0-0	0	0	0
Bob Black	0-0	1-2	0	0	1
Mike Curran	0-0	1-2	1	0	1
Hugh McMahon	2-2	0-0	2	0	4
Team			6		
Totals	34-61	14-26	37	12	82

Half time: Marquette 42-32. Officials: Weiler and Crowell.

at Carbondale, Illinois

Notre Dame	fg-fga	ft-fta	rb	pf	tp
Bob Arnzen	4-10	3-4	11	1	11
Dwight Murphy	4-9	3-4	6	5	11
Bob Whitmore	5-15	3-6	6	4	13
Jack Meehan	1-2	0-0	2	1	2
Austin Carr	1-6	4-6	3	1	6
Mike O'Connell	4-6	0-1	2	3	8
Tom Sinnott	2-3	0-0	1	3	4
Collis Jones	1-5	3-5	3	1	5
Sid Catlett	0-1	0-1	3	0	0
John Pleick	0-0	0-0	0	0	0
Team			7		
Totals	22-57	16-27	41	19	60

Miami, Ohio	fg-fga	ft-fta	rb	pf	tp
Glen Pryor	2-5	3-3	8	4	7
Walt Williams	7-21	1-1	7	2	15
Ray Loucks	3-8	3-5	14	4	9
Frank Lukacs	4-12	1-1	4	2	9
George Burkhart	2-4	3-4	1	2	7
Mike Wren	2-6	12-13	1	3	16
Team			10		
Totals	20-56	23-27	45	17	63

Half time: Miami, Ohio 34-31. Officials: Allen and Kingzett. Attendance: 9,600.

at Fort Worth, Texas

Texas A&M	fg-fga	ft-fta	rb	pf	tp
Ronnie Peret	2-5	6-8	8	4	10
Billy Bob Barnett	4-7	4-5	11	4	12
Steve Niles	6-6	5-6	16	2	17
Sonny Benefield	10-19	5-7	3	1	25
Mike Heitmann	2-7	5-5	3	2	9
Bill Brown	0-0	1-2	0	1	1
Bill Cooksey	3-6	1-3	3	1	7
Harry Bostic	0-0	0-0	2	1	0
Chuck Smith	0-0	0-0	2	0	0
Team			4		
Totals	27-50	27-36	52	16	81

Trinity, Tex.	fg-fga	ft-fta	rb	pf	tp
Larry Jeffries	6-18	2-4	6	3	14
Tom Fisher	3-9	2-2	3	1	8
Jim Bowles	3-7	1-4	8	5	7
Bill Stokes	4-11	0-1	4	5	8
John Lynch	4-16	2-2	1	3	10
Felix Thruston	6-9	2-2	7	4	14
Bill Summers	2-6	1-2	3	4	5
Tim Wattam	0-1	0-0	1	2	0
Team			3		
Totals	28-77	10-17	36	27	66

Half time: Texas A&M 42-34. Officials: Hamilton and Jeter. Attendance: 6,897.

at Fort Worth, Texas

Dayton	fg-fga	ft-fta	rb	pf	tp
Ken May	6-10	1-3	5	2	13
Dan Sadlier	6-14	2-4	6	3	14
Dan Obrovac	5-6	2-7	9	4	12
Jim Gottschall	0-2	0-0	1	2	0
Jerry Gottschall	1-7	0-0	2	3	2
George Janky	1-3	1-2	5	3	3
Steve Turnwald	3-7	0-0	2	2	6
Tom Crosswhite	0-1	0-0	1	0	0
Team			6		
Totals	22-50	6-16	37	19	50

Colorado State	fg-fga	ft-fta	rb	pf	tp
Cliff Shegogg	4-12	4-4	7	3	12
Archie Weems	2-6	1-1	5	5	5
Mike Davis	2-4	0-2	9	5	4
Lloyd Kerr	6-16	5-7	4	0	17
Floyd Kerr	3-7	5-7	8	0	11
Tom Meeker	0-0	0-0	1	0	0
Jeff Ash	1-3	0-0	1	2	2
Doug Peden	0-0	0-0	0	0	0
Jim Stockham	0-0	1-2	0	1	1
Team			3		
Totals	18-48	16-23	38	16	52

Half time: Colorado State 27-23. Officials: Lambert and Evans.

at Las Cruces, New Mexico

New Mexico State	fg-fga	ft-fta	rb	pf	tp
Jimmy Collins	9-22	0-0	3	3	18
Hardy Murphy	1-2	2-2	2	1	4
John Burgess	1-2	3-3	14	1	5
Jeff Smith	6-9	1-7	13	4	13
Sam Lacey	6-16	4-6	13	5	16
Chito Reyes	6-16	6-8	9	1	18
Herb Bowen	0-1	0-0	0	0	0
Team			8		
Totals	29-68	16-26	62	15	74

Brigham Young	fg-fga	ft-fta	rb	pf	tp
Lynn Parsons	4-8	1-1	3	1	9
Doug Howard	5-16	2-2	1	0	12
Kari Liimo	7-15	4-5	9	3	18
Marty Lythgoe	2-7	0-0	0	3	4
Paul Ruffner	4-13	3-4	13	5	11
Jim Miller	0-0	0-0	0	1	0
Scott Warner	3-9	2-5	4	4	8
Jon Dresser	0-1	0-0	0	0	0
Team			5		
Totals	25-69	12-17	35	17	62

Half time: New Mexico State 37-33. Officials: Corte and Marich. Attendance: 12,100.

at Las Cruces, New Mexico

Weber State	fg-fga	ft-fta	rb	pf	tp
Justus Thigpen	7-12	0-0	2	4	14
Sessions Harlan	6-9	3-5	4	4	15
Gus Chatmon	1-4	1-4	7	2	3
Larry Bergh	8-13	0-1	10	4	16
Willie Sojourner	7-11	8-10	12	3	22
Richard Nielsen	0-2	4-5	1	2	4
Gary Strong	0-4	1-3	4	1	1
Team			2		
Totals	29-55	17-28	42	20	75

Seattle	fg-fga	ft-fta	rb	pf	tp
Tom Little	7-22	5-10	6	5	19
Lou West	3-10	5-9	7	2	11
Sam Pierce	6-16	3-4	6	3	15
Don Edwards	0-0	1-1	5	3	1
Bill Jones	3-6	2-2	9	3	8
Jim Gardner	7-11	3-4	12	3	17
Tom Giles	1-4	0-0	1	1	2
Team			2		
Totals	27-69	19-30	48	20	73

Half time: Weber State 39-35. Officials: Ross and Murdock.

1969 UCLA BRUINS: (l-r) Front Row: Bill Sweek, John Vallely, Lee Walczuk, Terry Schofield, Don Saffer; Second Row: Bob Marcucci, Denny Crum, Lynn Shackelford, John Ecker, Curtis Rowe, Steve Patterson, Lew Alcindor, Sidney Wicks, George Farmer, Bill Seibert, Kenny Heitz, John Wooden.

East Regional

at College Park, Maryland

North Carolina	fg-fga	ft-fta	rb	pf	tp
Bill Bunting	6- 8	2- 2	9	5	14
Charlie Scott	9-19	4- 7	9	2	22
Rusty Clark	5- 9	5- 6	8	2	15
Lee Dedmon	4-10	2- 5	6	3	10
Ed Fogler	3- 8	3- 3	2	2	9
Jim Delany	0- 1	5- 5	0	1	5
Gerald Tuttle	0- 2	0- 1	1	0	0
Joe Brown	1- 4	2- 4	2	0	4
Team			6		
Totals	28-61	23-33	43	15	79

Duquesne	fg-fga	ft-fta	rb	pf	tp
Moe Barr	8-16	1- 3	9	1	17
Jarrett Durham	9-16	3- 3	5	3	21
Garry Nelson	5- 9	2- 2	5	5	12
Bill Zopf	6-11	1- 2	5	3	13
Gary Major	2- 5	1- 6	5	4	5
Barry Nelson	3- 8	0- 0	5	3	6
Wally Hines	2- 4	0- 1	3	1	4
Team			6		
Totals	35-69	8-17	43	20	78

Half time: Duquesne 37-31. Officials: Lawson and Overby.

at College Park, Maryland

St. John's, N. Y.	fg-fga	ft-fta	rb	pf	tp
Carmine Calzonetti	1- 4	1- 1	0	2	3
Ralph Abraham	2- 7	3- 3	9	4	7
John Warren	9-20	0- 1	5	4	18
Dan Cornelius	2- 4	3- 3	5	4	7
Joe Depre	8-15	0- 0	1	4	16
Bill Paultz	2- 3	0- 1	4	5	4
Jim Smyth	4-10	0- 0	2	2	8
Richie Gilkes	2- 2	2- 2	2	2	6
Team			3		
Totals	30-65	9-11	31	27	69

Davidson	fg-fga	ft-fta	rb	pf	tp
Dave Cook	6-10	7- 9	5	3	19
Jerry Kroll	3- 8	5- 6	10	3	11
Mike Maloy	11-19	13-13	12	3	35
Wayne Huckel	1- 3	0- 2	0	0	2
Steve Kirley	0- 0	0- 0	0	0	0
Dave Moser	2- 7	5- 6	7	2	9
Mike O'Neill	1- 2	1- 2	1	1	3
Team			3		
Totals	24-49	31-38	38	12	79

Half time: Davidson 35-26. Officials: Dreith and Jetter. Attendance: 13,166.

at College Park, Maryland

St. John's, N. Y.	fg-fga	ft-fta	rb	pf	tp
Carmine Calzonetti	2- 2	1- 1	0	0	5
Ralph Abraham	0- 2	3- 3	2	1	3
John Warren	6-13	1- 1	2	4	13
Dan Cornelius	0- 1	0- 0	2	0	0
Joe Depre	4-12	5- 6	6	2	13
Bill Paultz	9-16	6- 6	12	3	24
Jim Smyth	4- 9	2- 3	4	2	10
Richie Gilkes	1- 4	2- 2	3	2	4
John Devasto	0- 1	0- 0	0	1	0
Pete Lamantia	0- 0	0- 0	0	0	0
Neil Levane	0- 1	0- 0	0	0	0
Team			4		
Totals	26-61	20-22	35	15	72

Duquesne	fg-fga	ft-fta	rb	pf	tp
Moe Barr	3-10	1- 2	5	1	7
Jarrett Durham	8- 9	8-10	3	4	24
Garry Nelson	3- 9	0- 0	6	2	6
Bill Zopf	9-15	5- 6	8	3	23
Gary Major	5-10	3- 5	5	4	13
Barry Nelson	0- 2	0- 1	2	3	0
Wally Hines	1- 2	0- 1	2	0	2
Team			7		
Totals	29-57	17-25	38	17	75

Half time: Duquesne 44-37. Officials: Jetter and Lawson.

at College Park, Maryland

North Carolina	fg-fga	ft-fta	rb	pf	tp
Bill Bunting	7-12	8- 9	8	2	22
Charlie Scott	14-21	4- 5	6	1	32
Rusty Clark	8- 9	0- 1	4	4	16
Ed Fogler	4- 8	0- 1	1	2	8
Lee Dedmon	1- 2	0- 0	3	5	2
Jim Delany	0- 6	3- 4	2	2	3
Gerald Tuttle	1- 3	0- 0	2	2	2
Joe Brown	0- 4	2- 2	4	0	2
Team			5		
Totals	35-65	17-22	37	18	87

Davidson	fg-fga	ft-fta	rb	pf	tp
Doug Cook	7-13	4- 4	6	5	18
Jerry Kroll	6-15	4- 4	2	5	16
Mike Maloy	10-23	5- 7	13	3	25
Wayne Huckel	3-10	1- 1	8	1	7
Steve Kirley	2- 3	0- 0	5	2	4
Dave Moser	2- 6	0- 0	3	3	
Mike O'Neill	3- 9	4- 7	1	2	10
Ron Stelzer	0- 0	1- 2	1	0	1
Team			11		
Totals	33-79	19-25	50	21	85

Half time: North Carolina 40-39. Officials: Overby and Dreith. Attendance: 13,166.

Lew Alcindor

Mideast Regional

at Madison, Wisconsin

Kentucky	fg-fga	ft-fta	rb	pf	tp
Larry Steele	1- 6	2- 2	2	5	4
Mike Pratt	6-13	5- 6	5	5	17
Dan Issel	4- 8	5- 7	16	2	13
Phil Argento	8-15	0- 0	2	5	16
Mike Casey	7-14	10-10	5	5	24
Bob McCowan	0- 2	0- 0	1	4	0
Jim Dinwiddie	0- 0	0- 0	0	0	0
Terry Mills	0- 0	0- 0	0	0	0
Team			8		
Totals	26-64	22-25	39	26	74

Marquette	fg-fga	ft-fta	rb	pf	tp
George Thompson	7-16	8-13	4	1	22
Joe Thomas	3- 6	0- 0	2	5	6
Ric Cobb	7- 8	3- 7	14	1	17
Dean Meminger	6-15	8-13	6	2	20
Jeff Sewell	7- 9	1- 2	3	5	15
Jack Burke	0- 1	0- 0	0	2	0
Pat Smith	0- 1	0- 1	1	2	0
Ron Rann	0- 1	0- 0	1	1	0
Team			15		
Totals	30-57	21-38	46	19	81

Half time: Marquette 36-33. Officials: Herrold and Brown.

at Madison, Wisconsin

Miami, Ohio	fg-fga	ft-fta	rb	pf	tp
Glen Pryor	4- 5	1- 1	2	1	9
Walt Williams	4-15	3- 3	5	1	11
Ray Loucks	0- 3	1- 1	3	1	1
George Burkhart	0- 2	1- 2	2	1	1
Frank Lukacs	4-10	0- 0	2	3	8
Ron Snyder	0- 3	3- 4	2	3	3
Mike Wren	6-13	4- 4	1	2	16
Tom Slater	0- 0	0- 0	0	0	0
Gerald Sears	2- 8	0- 0	0	0	4
Terry Martin	8-15	2- 4	10	2	18
Bill Strauch	0- 0	0- 0	0	1	0
Team			4		
Totals	28-75	15-19	31	15	71

Purdue	fg-fga	ft-fta	rb	pf	tp
Larry Weatherford	3- 9	1- 2	7	1	7
George Faerber	8- 8	0- 2	14	1	16
Chuck Bavis	1- 1	0- 0	1	4	2
Rick Mount	12-20	8- 8	1	0	32
Bill Keller	9-15	1- 1	6	2	19
Tyrone Bedford	2- 5	0- 0	5	3	4
Jerry Johnson	2- 2	1- 1	5	4	5
Frank Kaufman	0- 1	3- 4	4	0	3
Ralph Taylor	0- 0	0- 0	0	0	0
Steve Longfellow	1- 1	0- 0	1	0	2
Ted Reasoner	0- 0	1- 2	0	0	1
Team			5		
Totals	38-62	15-20	49	15	91

Half time: Purdue 49-34. Officials: Filiberti and Bussenius. Attendance: 12,725.

at Madison, Wisconsin

Miami, Ohio	fg-fga	ft-fta	rb	pf	tp
Glen Pryor	2-10	7- 8	10	3	11
Ron Snyder	0- 6	1- 3	5	4	1
Terry Martin	4-13	2- 4	9	4	10
George Burkhart	4-10	2- 2	4	3	10
Frank Lukacs	2- 4	0- 0	3	2	4
Walt Williams	2- 4	0- 0	1	0	4
Tom Slater	1- 1	1- 2	1	0	3
Mike Wren	11-15	0- 2	5	2	22
Ray Loucks	3- 5	0- 0	2	2	6
Team			4		
Totals	29-68	13-21	44	20	71

Kentucky	fg-fga	ft-fta	rb	pf	tp
Larry Steele	5-10	2- 3	6	3	12
Mike Pratt	3- 8	2- 5	6	2	8
Dan Issel	12-17	12-12	10	4	36
Phil Argento	0- 4	3- 3	2	2	3
Mike Casey	1- 6	3- 4	4	3	5
Bob McCowan	3- 5	2- 2	2	2	8
Randy Pool	0- 2	0- 0	0	0	0
Team			6		
Totals	24-52	24-29	36	16	72

Half time: Kentucky 38-33. Officials: Herrold and Filiberti.

Midwest Regional

at Madison, Wisconsin

Marquette	fg-fga	ft-fta	rb	pf	tp
George Thompson	9-17	10-11	8	1	28
Joe Thomas	5-13	1- 2	13	3	11
Ric Cobb	2-10	3- 7	9	4	7
Dean Meminger	5-14	2- 6	14	1	12
Jeff Sewell	3- 9	2- 2	4	4	8
Jack Burke	3- 5	1- 1	2	3	7
Team			7		
Totals	27-68	19-29	55	16	73

Purdue	fg-fga	ft-fta	rb	pf	tp
Larry Weatherford	5-14	3- 3	3	0	13
George Faerber	3- 5	2- 3	8	4	8
Jerry Johnson	2- 6	0- 1	16	3	4
Rick Mount	11-32	4- 5	2	2	26
Bill Keller	6-11	5- 5	2	5	17
Tyrone Bedford	0- 1	0- 0	3	2	0
Frank Kaufman	0- 0	0- 0	0	3	0
Herman Gilliam	2- 3	3- 3	3	2	7
Team			5		
Totals	29-72	17-20	42	21	75

Half time: Purdue 35-30. Regulation Score: 63-63. Officials: Brown and Bussenius. Attendance: 13,025.

Midwest Regional

at Manhattan, Kansas

Drake	fg-fga	ft-fta	rb	pf	tp
Dolph Pulliam	4- 8	1- 1	6	4	9
Al Williams	1- 3	3- 4	3	4	5
Willie Wise	2-15	6- 9	16	3	10
Willie McCarter	12-24	0- 0	3	1	24
Don Draper	6-16	1- 1	3	2	13
Gary Zeller	3- 6	2- 2	0	3	8
Garry Odom	2- 2	4- 8	12	2	8
Ron Gwin	2- 2	0- 0	1	1	4
Rick Wanamaker	0- 0	0- 0	0	0	0
Al Sakys	0- 0	0- 0	0	0	0
Dale Teeter	0- 0	0- 0	0	0	0
Bob Mast	0- 0	0- 0	0	0	0
Team			6		
Totals	32-76	17-25	50	20	81

Texas A&M	fg-fga	ft-fta	rb	pf	tp
Mike Heitman	3-12	6- 8	4	1	12
Billy Bob Barnett	2- 8	2- 4	11	2	6
Steve Niles	5-10	2- 3	9	5	12
Sonny Benefield	2-14	4- 4	2	1	8
Ronnie Peret	1- 5	2- 4	9	5	4
Chuck Smith	5-12	0- 1	11	4	10
Bill Cooksey	4- 8	3- 4	6	2	11
Bill Brown	0- 2	0- 0	0	0	0
Harry Bostic	0- 0	0- 0	0	1	0
Team			7		
Totals	22-71	19-28	59	21	63

Half time: Drake 32-26. Officials: Stout and Bushkar.

at Manhattan, Kansas

Colorado	fg-fga	ft-fta	rb	pf	tp
Tim Wedgeworth	1- 9	2- 2	10	2	4
Mike Coleman	0- 5	1- 7	9	0	1
Cliff Meely	11-26	10-14	11	4	32
Gordon Tope	1- 6	1- 1	0	5	3
Dudley Mitchell	5-16	0- 0	2	3	10
Ted Erfert	0- 4	0- 0	4	2	4
Tim Richardson	1- 3	0- 0	3	3	2
Mickey Kern	0- 0	0- 0	1	4	0
Lloyd Hutchinson	0- 0	0- 0	0	0	0
Terry Jameson	0- 1	0- 0	0	0	0
Scoopy Smith	0- 0	0- 0	0	1	0
Ron Maulsby	0- 0	0- 0	0	0	0
Team			13		
Totals	21-70	14-24	53	24	56

Colorado State	fg-fga	ft-fta	rb	pf	tp
Archie Weems	0- 2	0- 0	4	4	0
Cliff Shegogg	9-18	2- 3	9	4	20
Mike Davis	3- 5	4- 5	10	5	10
Lloyd Kerr	4-17	4- 8	9	1	12
Floyd Kerr	4- 6	6- 9	3	1	14
Tom Meeker	1- 3	1- 3	3	1	3
Jim Stockham	1- 1	1- 2	0	2	3
Doug Peden	0- 0	2- 3	0	0	2
Team			9		
Totals	22-52	20-34	50	18	64

Half time: Colorado State 28-27. Officials: Honzo and DiTomasso. Attendance: 5,500.

299

GAME-BY-GAME RESULTS

300

at Manhattan, Kansas

Colorado	fg-fga	ft-fta	rb	pf	tp
Cliff Meely	12-23	2- 4	5	4	26
Lloyd Hutchinson	2- 3	3- 3	5	5	7
Ted Erfert	2- 6	0- 2	7	5	4
Gordon Tope	11-14	2- 2	3	1	24
Mickey Kern	0- 1	2- 2	1	2	2
Dudley Mitchell	6- 9	0- 1	1	0	12
Tim Wedgeworth	3- 7	1- 2	7	2	7
Tim Richardson	2- 5	3- 4	4	2	7
Mike Coleman	2- 2	2- 5	3	4	6
Scoopy Smith	1- 1	0- 1	2	0	2
Ron Maulsby	0- 0	0- 0	0	1	0
Terry Jameson	0- 1	0- 0	0	1	0
Team			5		
Totals	41-72	15-26	43	27	97

Texas A&M	fg-fga	ft-fta	rb	pf	tp
Mike Heitman	6-14	5- 6	4	3	17
Billy Bob Barnett	8-14	2- 5	8	5	18
Steve Niles	2- 8	5-13	12	4	9
Sonny Benefield	5-10	2- 2	3	3	12
Ronnie Peret	7-15	7- 9	12	3	21
Chuck Smith	0- 2	1- 2	2	1	1
Bill Cooksey	1- 4	2- 2	0	0	4
Bill Brown	0- 0	0- 0	0	1	0
Roddy McAlpine	0- 1	0- 0	0	1	0
Team			12		
Totals	29-68	24-39	53	21	82

Half time: Colorado 51-31. Officials: Stout and Bushkar.

at Manhattan, Kansas

Drake	fg-fga	ft-fta	rb	pf	tp
Dolph Pulliam	5-14	3- 4	3	4	13
Al Williams	2- 8	0- 0	5	3	4
Willie Wise	4-11	8-12	7	4	16
Willie McCarter	9-23	3- 3	5	4	21
Don Draper	5-11	1- 1	4	4	11
Garry Odom	4- 5	2- 3	6	1	10
Gary Zeller	4- 5	1- 2	3	2	9
Ron Gwin	0- 1	0- 0	1	0	0
Team			5		
Totals	33-78	18-25	39	22	84

Colorado State	fg-fga	ft-fta	rb	pf	tp
Archie Weems	2- 7	0- 0	9	4	4
Cliff Shegogg	1- 7	6- 6	2	5	8
Mike Davis	2- 4	9-10	16	4	13
Lloyd Kerr	5-15	2- 2	8	2	12
Floyd Kerr	8-17	5- 7	6	4	21
Jim Stockham	0- 0	0- 0	0	0	0
Tom Meeker	0- 0	0- 0	0	1	0
Doug Peden	7-10	5- 6	1	2	19
Team			10		
Totals	25-60	27-31	52	22	77

Half time: Drake 38-37. Officials: Honzo and DiTomasso. Attendance: 7,000.

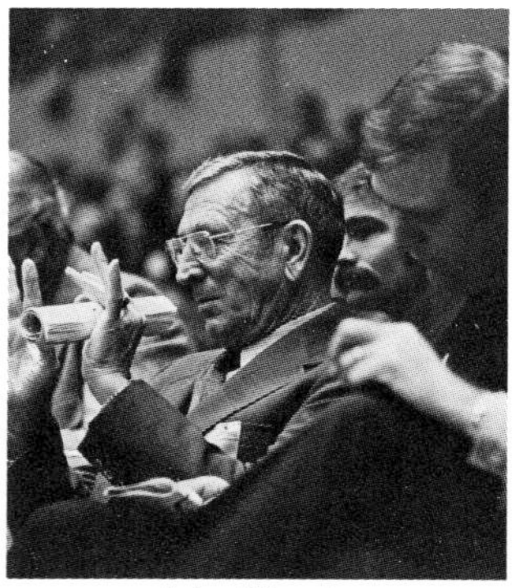

John Wooden

West Regional

at Los Angeles, California

UCLA	fg-fga	ft-fta	rb	pf	tp
Curtis Rowe	3-12	2- 2	7	2	8
Lynn Shackelford	4-10	0- 0	3	0	8
Lew Alcindor	8-15	0- 5	16	3	16
Kenny Heitz	4- 6	1- 1	4	3	9
John Vallely	5-12	0- 0	5	1	10
Sidney Wicks	0- 2	0- 0	0	0	0
Bill Sweek	1- 1	0- 2	0	1	2
Steve Patterson	0- 0	0- 0	0	1	0
Terry Schofield	0- 0	0- 0	0	0	0
Team			7		
Totals	25-58	3-10	42	11	53

New Mexico St.	fg-fga	ft-fta	rb	pf	tp
Jeff Smith	2- 4	3- 3	8	3	7
Chito Reyes	2- 5	1- 2	2	0	5
Sam Lacey	5-16	1- 1	11	4	11
Jimmy Collins	4-17	3- 3	4	1	11
John Burgess	0- 3	0- 1	2	0	0
Hardy Murphy	1- 2	0- 0	1	1	2
Herb Bowen	1- 1	0- 0	0	0	2
Team			5		
Totals	15-48	8-10	33	9	38

Half time: UCLA 21-17. Officials: Wirtz and Fouty. Attendance: 12,817.

at Los Angeles, California

Santa Clara	fg-fga	ft-fta	rb	pf	tp
Ralph Ogden	4-13	1- 1	6	3	9
Bud Ogden	7-13	4- 7	13	2	18
Dennis Awtrey	9-17	1- 1	7	5	19
Kevin Eagleson	2- 2	1- 3	2	4	5
Terry O'Brien	1- 3	3- 3	1	4	5
Chris Dempsey	1- 2	3- 5	8	0	5
Joe Diffley	1- 5	0- 1	5	0	2
Team			2		
Totals	25-55	13-21	44	18	63

Weber State	fg-fga	ft-fta	rb	pf	tp
Gus Chatmon	0- 1	0- 0	3	3	0
Larry Bergh	3- 5	2- 2	1	5	8
Willie Sojourner	2-14	8- 9	18	3	12
Justus Thigpen	7-16	2- 4	2	1	16
Sessions Harlan	4-10	3- 4	5	1	11
Gary Strong	4-10	0- 2	6	1	8
Richard Nielsen	0- 2	0- 0	0	0	0
Dave Sackolwitz	1- 2	2- 5	3	5	4
Team			4		
Totals	21-60	17-26	42	19	59

Half time: Santa Clara 29-19. Officials: McPherson and Payak.

at Los Angeles, California

New Mexico St.	fg-fga	ft-fta	rb	pf	tp
Jeff Smith	2- 5	0- 3	9	3	4
Chito Reyes	4-12	1- 1	4	2	9
Sam Lacey	3-10	2- 3	13	2	8
Jimmy Collins	8-15	3- 4	6	3	19
Lee Leonard	5- 9	0- 0	2	1	10
John Burgess	3-10	0- 1	11	1	6
Mike Banks	0- 1	0- 0	0	0	0
Team			2		
Totals	25-62	6-12	47	12	56

Weber State	fg-fga	ft-fta	rb	pf	tp
Larry Bergh	6-15	1- 1	4	2	13
Gus Chatmon	3- 6	0- 0	11	0	6
Willie Sojourner	4- 9	4- 6	11	3	12
Justus Thigpen	6-19	2- 2	2	2	14
Sessions Harlan	3- 8	0- 2	3	2	6
Dave Sackolwitz	0- 1	2- 2	1	1	2
Richard Nielsen	0- 2	3- 4	2	0	3
Gary Strong	1- 2	0- 0	2	0	2
Team			4		
Totals	23-62	12-17	40	10	58

Half time: New Mexico State 29-23. Officials: Wirtz and McPherson.

at Los Angeles, California

UCLA	fg-fga	ft-fta	rb	pf	tp
Lynn Shackelford	3- 7	0- 1	3	1	6
Curtis Rowe	3- 6	1- 2	5	1	7
Lew Alcindor	8-14	1- 3	7	2	17
John Vallely	5- 5	1- 2	3	2	11
Kenny Heitz	3- 6	0- 0	1	2	6
Bill Sweek	4- 7	4- 5	1	1	12
Sidney Wicks	3- 4	5- 8	2	1	11
Steve Patterson	4- 6	1- 1	5	4	9
Terry Schofield	1- 6	0- 0	2	0	2
John Ecker	2- 2	1- 1	1	0	5
Bill Seibert	0- 0	2- 2	3	1	2
George Farmer	1- 2	0- 0	0	0	2
Team			6		
Totals	37-65	16-25	39	15	90

Santa Clara	fg-fga	ft-fta	rb	pf	tp
Ralph Ogden	1-13	2- 4	7	2	4
Bud Ogden	3-10	3- 3	5	4	9
Dennis Awtrey	5- 9	4- 6	8	4	14
Kevin Eagleson	0- 0	0- 1	3	3	0
Terry O'Brien	0- 2	0- 1	1	2	0
Joe Diffley	1- 4	0- 0	2	2	2
Keith Paulson	2- 4	1- 3	1	0	5
Chris Dempsey	2- 3	1- 1	2	2	5
Bob Tobin	1- 2	0- 0	4	2	2
Tom Scherer	2- 5	0- 0	1	0	4
Gary Graves	1- 1	1- 1	1	1	3
Mitch Champi	2- 3	0- 0	2	3	4
Team			5		
Totals	20-56	12-20	42	25	52

Half time: UCLA 46-25. Officials: Fouty and Payak. Attendance: 12,812.

Semifinals

at Louisville, Kentucky

North Carolina	fg-fga	ft-fta	rb	pf	tp
Bill Bunting	7-13	5- 7	7	2	19
Charlie Scott	6-19	4- 6	6	3	16
Rusty Clark	7- 9	6-10	9	2	20
Ed Fogler	1- 4	0- 0	2	2	2
Gerald Tuttle	2- 4	0- 1	3	3	4
Jim Delany	0- 2	0- 0	1	4	0
Lee Dedmon	0- 1	0- 1	4	2	0
Joe Brown	1- 4	0- 0	1	0	2
Dale Gipple	0- 3	0- 0	1	0	0
Dave Chadwick	1- 2	0- 0	2	0	2
Richard Tuttle	0- 1	0- 0	0	0	0
Don Eggleston	0- 0	0- 0	0	0	0
Team			1		
Totals	25-62	15-25	37	18	65

Purdue	fg-fga	ft-fta	rb	pf	tp
Herman Gilliam	3-11	0- 0	8	0	6
George Faerber	3- 3	2- 2	9	3	8
Jerry Johnson	2- 5	1- 3	5	4	5
Rick Mount	14-28	8- 9	4	0	36
Bill Keller	9-19	2- 3	5	3	20
Frank Kaufman	0- 1	2- 3	6	4	2
Larry Weatherford	3- 6	1- 1	2	1	7
Tyrone Bedford	3- 3	0- 0	5	4	6
Ralph Taylor	1- 1	0- 1	3	0	2
Steve Longfellow	0- 1	0- 0	2	0	0
Ted Reasoner	0- 0	0- 0	0	1	0
Glenn Young	0- 0	0- 0	0	0	0
Team			2		
Totals	38-78	16-22	51	20	92

Half time: Purdue 53-30. Officials: Overby and Brown.

at Louisville, Kentucky

Drake	fg-fga	ft-fta	rb	pf	tp
Dolph Pulliam	4-14	4- 5	5	4	12
Al Williams	0- 1	0- 0	1	4	0
Willie Wise	5- 7	3- 4	16	3	13
Willie McCarter	10-27	4- 4	1	3	24
Don Draper	5-13	2- 2	1	2	12
Garry Odom	0- 2	0- 1	2	4	0
Rick Wanamaker	4- 7	1- 1	7	4	9
Gary Zeller	4-12	4- 6	3	3	12
Ron Gwin	0- 0	0- 1	1	3	0
Team			4		
Totals	32-83	18-24	41	30	82

UCLA	fg-fga	ft-fta	rb	pf	tp
Lynn Shackelford	2- 5	2- 3	2	4	6
Curtis Rowe	6- 9	2- 2	13	2	14
Lew Alcindor	8-14	9-16	21	3	25
Kenny Heitz	3- 6	1- 3	1	5	7
John Vallely	9-11	11-14	6	5	29
Sidney Wicks	0- 2	0- 0	1	1	0
Bill Sweek	0- 0	0- 0	0	1	0
Steve Patterson	0- 0	2- 2	0	0	2
Terry Schofield	0- 3	2- 4	0	0	2
Team			4		
Totals	28-50	29-44	48	21	85

Half time: UCLA 44-43. Officials: Fouty and DiTomasso. Attendance: 18,435.

National Third Place

at Louisville, Kentucky

Drake	fg-fga	ft-fta	rb	pf	tp
Dolph Pulliam	4-10	2- 3	3	4	10
Al Williams	8-13	0- 1	8	4	16
Willie Wise	6- 9	4- 4	9	3	16
Willie McCarter	12-20	4- 5	6	3	28
Don Draper	3- 8	0- 0	0	1	6
Gary Zeller	3- 9	1- 1	3	0	7
Garry Odom	2- 2	0- 0	3	3	4
Rick Wanamaker	5- 6	1- 2	4	2	11
Ron Gwin	1- 2	2- 2	0	1	4
Bob Mast	0- 0	0- 0	0	1	0
Dale Teeter	1- 1	0- 0	0	0	2
Jim O'Dea	0- 0	0- 0	0	0	0
Team			1		
Totals	45-80	14-18	37	22	104

North Carolina	fg-fga	ft-fta	rb	pf	tp
Bill Bunting	3- 6	1- 2	9	5	7
Charlie Scott	16-26	3- 6	4	2	35
Rusty Clark	2- 9	8-10	12	1	12
Ed Fogler	3- 7	1- 3	4	1	7
Lee Dedmon	5-10	1- 2	10	3	11
Gerald Tuttle	1- 3	2- 2	0	1	4
Joe Brown	0- 2	0- 0	2	1	0
Jim Delany	0- 2	2- 2	1	2	2
Dale Gipple	0- 0	1- 2	0	1	1
Dave Chadwick	1- 2	0- 0	2	0	2
Don Eggleston	0- 0	0- 0	0	0	0
Richard Tuttle	1- 1	1- 2	1	0	3
Team			2		
Totals	32-68	20-31	47	17	84

Half time: Drake 54-45. Officials: Overby and Fouty.

Championship

at Louisville, Kentucky

UCLA	fg-fga	ft-fta	rb	pf	tp
Lynn Shackelford	3- 8	5- 8	9	3	11
Curtis Rowe	4-10	4- 4	12	2	12
Lew Alcindor	15-20	7- 9	20	2	37
Kenny Heitz	0- 3	0- 1	3	4	0
John Vallely	4- 9	7-10	4	3	15
Bill Sweek	3- 3	0- 1	1	3	6
Sidney Wicks	0- 1	3- 6	4	1	3
Terry Schofield	1- 2	0- 0	0	0	2
Steve Patterson	1- 1	2- 2	2	0	4
Bill Seibert	0- 0	0- 0	1	0	0
George Farmer	0- 0	0- 0	0	1	0
John Ecker	1- 1	0- 0	0	0	2
Team			5		
Totals	32-58	28-41	61	19	92

Purdue	fg-fga	ft-fta	rb	pf	tp
Herman Gilliam	2-14	3- 3	11	2	7
George Faerber	1- 2	0- 0	3	5	2
Jerry Johnson	4- 9	3- 4	9	2	11
Rick Mount	12-36	4- 5	1	3	28
Bill Keller	4-17	3- 4	4	5	11
Frank Kaufman	0- 0	2- 2	5	5	2
Tyrone Bedford	3- 8	1- 3	8	3	7
Larry Weatherford	1- 5	2- 2	1	3	4
Ted Reasoner	0- 1	0- 1	1	2	0
Ralph Taylor	0- 0	0- 0	0	0	0
Team			5		
Totals	27-92	18-24	48	30	72

Half time: UCLA 50-41. Officials: DiTomasso and Brown. Attendance: 18,669.

1970

First Round

at Jamaica, New York

Davidson	fg-fga	ft-fta	rb	pf	tp
Brian Adrian	12-26	4- 5	7	3	28
Doug Cook	6-12	3- 6	6	2	15
Mike Maloy	5-12	3- 6	12	3	13
Jerry Kroll	4-10	4- 5	2	4	12
Steve Kirley	0- 4	2- 2	2	2	2
Eric Minkin	1- 3	0- 2	3	0	2
Ron Stelzer	0- 0	0- 0	0	0	0
Team			4		
Totals	28-67	16-26	36	14	72

St. Bonaventure	fg-fga	ft-fta	rb	pf	tp
Bob Lanier......	13-24	2- 3	15	5	28
Bill Kalbaugh	8-11	1- 1	3	3	17
Matt Gantt......	8-17	3- 4	16	4	19
Paul Hoffman	1- 4	3- 4	6	1	5
Greg Gary	4- 8	5- 5	4	4	13
Mike Kull.......	1- 4	1- 1	0	2	3
Team..........			5		
Totals	35-68	15-18	49	19	85

Half time: Davidson 36-34. Officials: Bushkar and Rooney. Attendance: 5,320.

at Princeton, New Jersey

Pennsylvania	fg-fga	ft-fta	rb	pf	tp
Dave Wohl......	5-15	1- 1	5	5	11
Steve Bilsky.....	7-16	8- 9	2	4	22
Corky Calhoun ...	5-17	5- 7	13	3	15
Robert Morse....	5-18	0- 0	2	1	10
James Wolf	1- 7	1- 4	10	4	3
Jim Murphy	0- 0	0- 0	0	1	0
Carl Robbins	0- 0	1- 3	3	2	1
John Koller......	0- 2	0- 0	1	0	0
Al Cotler	3- 5	1- 1	2	1	7
Team..........			10		
Totals	26-80	17-25	48	21	69

Niagara	fg-fga	ft-fta	rb	pf	tp
Marshall Wingate .	2- 3	1- 4	4	1	5
Calvin Murphy ...	13-24	9-10	5	3	35
Steve Schafer....	3- 8	1- 3	6	5	7
Mike Samuel	4- 8	1- 1	3	1	9
Bob Churchwell ..	6-12	2- 3	14	4	14
Mike Brown	0- 1	6- 7	4	2	6
Wayne Jones	1- 3	1- 2	5	2	3
Team..........			11		
Totals	29-59	21-30	52	18	79

Half time: Pennsylvania 35-34. Officials: DiTomasso and Grossman. Attendance: 7,500.

at Philadelphia, Pennsylvania

Temple	fg-fga	ft-fta	rb	pf	tp
Ollie Johnson	3-15	1- 1	10	1	7
John Richardson..	9-15	3- 6	14	4	21
Lee Tress.......	7-21	6- 8	21	4	20
Tom Wieczerak...	5-15	0- 0	1	5	10
Paul Collins	4-10	1- 2	6	4	9
Drew Nolan	0- 0	0- 0	1	3	0
Jim Feneli	1- 3	0- 0	2	1	2
Team..........			6		
Totals	29-79	11-17	61	22	69

Villanova	fg-fga	ft-fta	rb	pf	tp
Clarence Smith...	5-13	2- 5	13	1	12
Sammy Sims	5-12	2- 6	8	3	12
Howard Porter ...	7-15	4- 6	14	5	18
Fran O'Hanlon....	5-19	4- 6	7	4	14
Chris Ford	6-16	7- 8	7	1	19
H. Siemiontkowski .	1- 1	0- 0	0	0	2
Leon Wojnowski ..	0- 0	0- 0	0	0	0
Team..........			5		
Totals	29-76	19-31	54	14	77

Half time: Villanova 39-36. Officials: DiBonis and Folsom. Attendance: 8,708.

at Dayton, Ohio

Ohio	fg-fga	ft-fta	rb	pf	tp
Greg McDivitt....	2-13	4- 8	11	2	8
Dave Groff	7-13	3- 7	5	3	17
Craig Love.......	4-12	0- 0	13	4	8
John Canine.....	12-29	0- 0	4	3	24
Ken Kowall......	3- 7	1- 2	0	3	7
Doug Parker......	1- 4	2- 2	4	1	4
Tom Corde......	2- 6	0- 1	3	0	4
Gary Wolf	3- 5	0- 0	6	1	6
Larry Hunter	1- 3	0- 0	3	3	2
Mike Miller......	1- 1	0- 0	0	0	2
Bernard Rumpke..	0- 0	0- 0	0	0	0
John Glancy	0- 1	0- 0	0	0	0
Team..........			7		
Totals	36-94	10-20	56	20	82

Notre Dame	fg-fga	ft-fta	rb	pf	tp
Austin Carr	25-44	11-14	6	1	61
Collis Jones.....	9-19	6- 6	17	4	24
Jack Meehan	0- 1	2- 2	2	0	2
John Gallagher...	4- 8	1- 2	2	1	9
Jay Ziznewski ...	5-12	0- 1	10	2	10
Sid Catlett......	0- 1	0- 0	11	3	0
Tom Sinnott.....	2- 4	0- 1	6	2	4
Jim Hinge	1- 1	0- 0	0	0	2
Team..........			8		
Totals	46-90	20-26	62	13	112

Half time: Notre Dame 54-41. Officials: Donlin and Wortman.

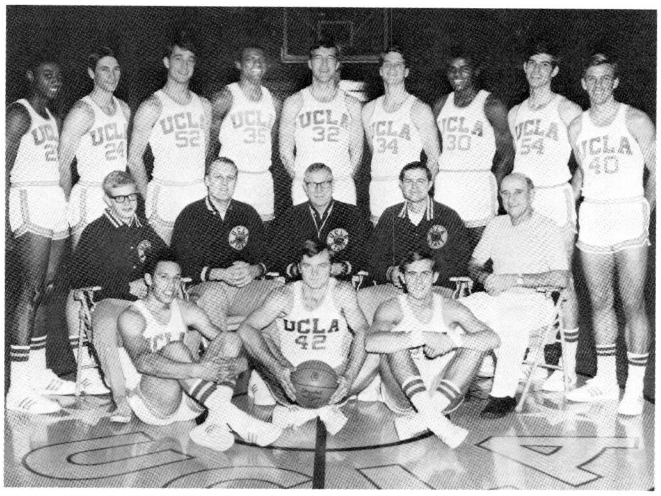

1970 UCLA BRUINS—(l-r) Front Row: Henry Bibby, Terry Schofield, Andy Hill; Second Row: George Morgan, Gary Cunningham, John Wooden, Denny Crum, Ducky Drake; Third Row: Kenny Booker, Rick Betchley, John Ecker, Sidney Wicks, Steve Patterson, Jon Chapman, Curtis Rowe, Bill Seibert, John Vallely.

at Dayton, Ohio

Western Kentucky	fg-fga	ft-fta	rb	pf	tp
Jerome Perry	6-15	0- 0	7	3	12
Clarence Glover ..	3-12	1- 2	6	4	7
Jim McDaniels ...	13-22	3- 4	7	5	29
Gary Sundmacker .	3- 7	2- 2	1	1	8
Jim Rose	6-11	4- 4	3	2	16
Walker Banks....	1- 4	1- 1	2	5	3
Danny Johnson...	3- 5	2- 2	6	3	8
Wayne Bright....	1- 4	0- 0	6	5	2
Paul Haskins	3- 4	4- 4	1	1	10
Terry Davis	0- 2	0- 0	1	0	0
Steve Eaton.....	0- 3	1- 2	0	0	1
Team..........			6		
Totals	39-89	18-21	46	29	96

Jacksonville	fg-fga	ft-fta	rb	pf	tp
Mike Blevins	2- 5	0- 1	2	0	4
Pembrook Burrows.	2- 4	0- 2	3	3	4
Artis Gilmore	11-20	8-13	19	2	30
Rex Morgan	7-12	10-13	6	1	24
Vaughn Wedeking .	9-15	1- 2	4	0	19
Chip Dublin	4- 4	1- 1	4	4	9
Greg Nelson.....	3- 8	5- 7	7	2	11
Rod McIntyre	1- 3	4- 4	3	3	6
Rusty Baldwin ...	1- 1	0- 0	0	1	2
Curtis Kruer.....	0- 1	0- 0	0	0	0
Ken Selke	0- 2	0- 0	3	0	0
Team..........			5		
Totals	40-75	29-43	56	16	109

Half time: Jacksonville 53-47. Officials: Waldo and Waddell. Attendance: 13,450.

at Fort Worth, Texas

Dayton	fg-fga	ft-fta	rb	pf	tp
Pat Murnen	1- 7	1- 2	1	2	3
George Jackson ..	2- 6	1- 3	11	0	5
George Janky....	3- 7	2- 3	9	3	8
Ken May	8-18	0- 0	9	4	16
Jerry Gottschall ..	9-17	2- 2	0	2	20
Steve Turnwald ..	0- 0	0- 0	1	1	0
Tom Crosswhite ..	5-11	0- 0	4	3	10
Al Bertke.......	1- 3	0- 0	0	1	2
Team..........			3		
Totals	29-69	6-10	38	16	64

Houston	fg-fga	ft-fta	rb	pf	tp
Melvin Bell......	0- 2	2- 2	3	0	2
Ollie Taylor	7-18	12-14	6	2	26
Dwight Davis	9-20	1- 1	14	3	19
Tom Gribben	4- 9	0- 0	6	2	8
Poo Welch	3- 4	1- 1	2	2	7
Jeff Hickman	0- 5	0- 0	4	1	0
Bob Hall........	4- 4	1- 1	3	0	9
Team..........			5		
Totals	27-62	17-19	43	10	71

Half time: Dayton 34-32. Officials: Hartsfield and Wilcoxen.

at Fort Worth, Texas

Rice	fg-fga	ft-fta	rb	pf	tp
Ted Melady	0- 2	1- 1	5	1	1
Don Snyder	0- 2	2- 2	0	1	2
Steve Wendel....	1- 6	0- 0	12	0	2
Gary Reist	7-23	4- 4	1	3	18
Tom Myer	10-23	1- 1	3	4	21
Jim Naples......	5- 8	3- 3	6	2	13
Don Sturr.......	3-10	2- 3	10	1	8
Terry Timmerman.	0- 1	0- 1	5	1	0
Chuck Nelson....	0- 2	0- 1	2	1	0
Dan McGuire	2- 7	2- 2	1	1	6
Leroy Marion	0- 1	1- 2	6	1	1
Dale Johnson	1- 1	3- 3	0	2	5
Team..........			3		
Totals	29-86	19-23	54	18	77

New Mexico State	fg-fga	ft-fta	rb	pf	tp
Charley Criss....	2- 6	3- 3	3	3	7
Jimmy Collins....	10-17	2- 3	2	2	22
Sam Lacey......	9-20	1- 1	20	0	19
John Burgess....	1- 6	0- 1	7	2	2
Jeff Smith	8-13	2- 2	7	2	18
Milton Horne	3- 5	0- 1	1	2	6
Chito Rayes.....	5-10	1- 1	7	2	11
Roy Neal	3- 8	1- 3	6	1	7
Bill Moore	2- 3	0- 0	1	0	4
Lonnie Lefevre ...	1- 2	0- 1	3	3	2
Tom McCarthy ...	0- 1	3- 4	0	1	3
Rudy Franco.....	0- 0	0- 0	1	0	0
Team..........			3		
Totals	44-91	13-20	61	18	101

Half time: New Mexico State 52-30. Officials: Lawson and Murdock. Attendance: 5,827.

at Provo, Utah

Weber State	fg-fga	ft-fta	rb	pf	tp
Kent Ross	3-12	2- 6	4	1	8
Jonnie Knoble....	4-14	3- 4	9	4	11
Willie Sojourner ..	5-11	3- 6	9	4	13
Sessions Harlan ..	4-10	7-10	6	2	15
Richard Nielsen ..	2- 8	0- 1	1	2	4
Dave Sackolwitz..	1- 6	0- 0	3	0	2
Bill Orr	3- 7	0- 1	0	0	6
Herm Pluim	0- 0	0- 0	1	1	0
Curt Nations.....	4- 9	0- 0	0	2	8
Jim Sivulich.....	1- 1	0- 0	1	2	2
Rick Camac	2- 3	0- 0	2	0	4
Mike Della Pia ...	0- 0	0- 0	0	1	0
Team..........			10		
Totals	29-81	15-28	46	19	73

Long Beach State	fg-fga	ft-fta	rb	pf	tp
Sam Robinson ...	4-10	2- 2	14	4	10
Billy Jankans....	7- 8	2- 3	6	4	16
George Trapp....	7-11	3- 3	6	3	17
Ray Gritton	4-10	0- 0	0	0	8
Shawn Johnson ..	7-11	2- 2	3	1	16
Dave McLucas ...	3- 4	0- 0	8	2	6
A. Montgomery...	2- 6	1- 2	4	1	5
Dwight Taylor....	2- 5	8-10	1	4	12
Bernard Williams .	0- 2	2- 2	0	2	2
Bob Sullivan.....	0- 1	0- 0	1	0	0
Team..........			12		
Totals	36-68	20-24	55	21	92

Half time: Long Beach State 37-28.

at Provo, Utah

Utah State	fg-fga	ft-fta	rb	pf	tp
Marvin Roberts...	11-20	8- 9	16	4	30
Nate Williams....	14-21	3- 4	10	5	31
Tim Tollestrup ...	5- 9	4- 6	9	3	14
Paul Jeppesen ...	1- 6	2- 3	3	2	4
Jeff Tebbs	0- 2	1- 2	4	3	1
John Ericksen....	1- 1	0- 0	0	5	2
Ron Hatch	2- 4	3- 4	2	1	7
Ed Epps	0- 0	0- 0	0	2	0
Terry Wakefield ..	1- 2	0- 0	0	0	2
Dick Wade	0- 0	0- 0	0	0	0
Chris Bean......	0- 0	0- 0	0	0	0
Team..........			7		
Totals	35-65	21-28	51	25	91

301

Texas-El Paso	fg-fga	ft-fta	rb	pf	tp
Bob Doyle	3-11	0- 1	2	2	6
Dick Gibbs	2-10	3- 4	10	1	7
Mike Switzer	5-13	8-10	8	5	18
Ples Vann	1- 6	2- 4	4	4	4
Nate Archibald ...	13-21	10-11	3	2	36
Scott English	0- 1	0- 2	0	0	0
Len Stewart	3- 7	2- 2	3	3	8
John Ruud	1- 2	0- 0	0	3	2
Team..........			8		
Totals	28-71	25-34	38	20	81

Half time: Utah State 45-33. Attendance: 10,403.

East Regional

at Columbia, South Carolina

Villanova	fg-fga	ft-fta	rb	pf	tp
Fran O'Hanlon....	5-11	4- 4	7	4	14
Sammy Sims	8-15	3- 5	14	1	19
Chris Ford	3- 8	5- 8	2	4	11
Clarence Smith...	6- 9	1- 1	12	1	13
Howard Porter ...	13-22	3- 3	18	3	29
H. Siemiontkowski .	2- 6	0- 0	1	1	4
Bob Gohl	1- 1	0- 3	1	0	2
John Fox	1- 3	0- 0	2	0	2
Joe McDowell....	1- 1	0- 0	0	1	2
Mike Daly	1- 1	0- 0	0	1	2
Leon Wojnowski ..	0- 1	0- 0	0	0	0
Team..........			4		
Totals	41-78	16-24	61	16	98

Niagara	fg-fga	ft-fta	rb	pf	tp
Marshall Wingate .	3- 9	5- 7	7	0	11
Mike Brown	3- 6	1- 2	1	3	7
Calvin Murphy ...	8-22	2- 3	7	4	18
Steve Schafer....	3- 9	0- 0	7	2	6
Mike Samuel	1- 5	0- 0	2	1	2
Wayne Jones	7-19	3- 3	8	3	17
Bob Churchwell ..	2- 9	6- 6	4	3	10
Peter Aiello	0- 0	0- 0	0	0	0
Joe Adomanis....	1- 1	0- 0	0	0	2
Orlander Harrison.	0- 0	0- 0	0	0	0
Paul Thornton....	0- 0	0- 0	0	0	0
Team..........			3		
Totals	28-80	17-21	39	16	73

Half time: Villanova 46-29. Officials: Scott and Jeter.

at Columbia, South Carolina

St. Bonaventure	fg-fga	ft-fta	rb	pf	tp
Matt Gantt......	7-18	1- 4	11	5	15
Greg Gary	6-11	0- 1	11	0	12
Bob Lanier......	10-23	4- 5	19	4	24
Paul Hoffman	6- 9	0- 1	9	1	12
Bill Kalbaugh	4- 8	5- 6	2	3	13
Mike Kull.......	1- 4	2- 3	0	2	4
Tom Baldwin	0- 1	0- 0	0	1	0
Team..........			1		
Totals	34-74	12-20	53	16	80

North Carolina St.	fg-fga	ft-fta	rb	pf	tp
Paul Coder	8-14	0- 1	6	3	16
Vann Williford	13-22	9-13	12	3	35
Rick Anheuser	3- 6	1- 2	10	4	7
Ed Leftwich	4-13	0- 1	5	3	8
Joe Dunning	0- 7	2- 2	3	3	2
Al Heartley	0- 1	0- 1	1	0	0
Team			1		
Totals	28-63	12-20	38	16	68

Half time: Saint Bonaventure 41-31. Officials: Jenkins and Shosid. Attendance: 12,316.

at Columbia, South Carolina

Niagara	fg-fga	ft-fta	rb	pf	tp
Steve Schafer	3- 6	1- 3	5	4	7
Wayne Jones	10-20	0- 1	12	1	20
Bob Churchwell	1-12	0- 0	10	5	2
Mike Brown	7-14	5- 5	4	5	19
Calvin Murphy	13-26	9- 9	7	5	35
Marshall Wingate	1- 2	3- 3	4	3	5
Mike Samuel	0- 2	0- 0	0	0	0
Orlander Harrison	0- 0	0- 0	1	0	0
Paul Thornton	0- 1	0- 0	0	3	0
Joe Adomanis	0- 0	0- 0	0	0	0
Team			4		
Totals	35-83	18-21	47	26	88

North Carolina St.	fg-fga	ft-fta	rb	pf	tp
Vann Williford	11-24	14-16	11	1	36
Rick Anheuser	12-15	4- 6	10	2	28
Paul Coder	10-20	4- 8	13	2	24
Joe Dunning	2- 3	2- 4	7	3	6
Ed Leftwich	4- 8	2- 3	2	4	10
Al Heartley	1- 5	2- 4	6	2	4
Jim Risinger	0- 1	0- 0	1	1	0
Team			3		
Totals	40-76	28-41	53	15	108

Half time: North Carolina State 57-48. Officials: Jenkins and Jeter.

at Columbia, South Carolina

St. Bonaventure	fg-fga	ft-fta	rb	pf	tp
Matt Gantt	7-20	5- 8	18	3	19
Greg Gary	10-17	0- 1	11	1	20
Bob Lanier	11-22	4- 4	14	2	26
Bill Kalbaugh	5- 9	5- 5	3	1	15
Paul Hoffman	3- 6	0- 1	4	3	6
Mike Kull	4- 6	3- 3	2	2	11
Team			6		
Totals	40-80	17-22	58	12	97

Villanova	fg-fga	ft-fta	rb	pf	tp
Chris Ford	7-14	1- 2	4	3	15
Sammy Sims	1- 5	3- 5	7	1	5
Howard Porter	6-14	2- 2	9	5	14
Fran O'Hanlon	10-15	0- 2	4	5	20
Clarence Smith	1- 8	0- 0	4	1	2
H. Siemiontkowski	3-13	4- 4	3	2	10
Joe McDowell	3- 7	0- 1	3	2	6
John Fox	1- 2	0- 0	0	0	2
Bob Gohl	0- 1	0- 0	0	1	0
Leon Wojnowski	0- 0	0- 0	0	0	0
Team			6		
Totals	32-79	10-16	40	20	74

Half time: Saint Bonaventure 46-30. Officials: Shosid and Scott. Attendance: 10,981.

Mideast Regional

at Columbus, Ohio

Kentucky	fg-fga	ft-fta	rb	pf	tp
Mike Pratt	7-15	0- 2	4	5	14
Tom Parker	4- 7	4- 5	6	4	12
Dan Issel	17-28	10-14	11	4	44
Jim Dinwiddie	5- 7	1- 1	2	1	11
Kent Hollenbeck	3- 5	1- 3	4	3	7
Terry Mills	5- 7	3- 5	5	3	13
Larry Steele	2- 3	4- 4	6	4	8
Stan Key	0- 0	0- 0	0	0	0
Team			6		
Totals	43-72	23-34	44	24	109

Notre Dame	fg-fga	ft-fta	rb	pf	tp
John Gallagher	2- 7	1- 2	5	2	5
Collis Jones	9-17	4-10	9	5	22
Jay Ziznewski	1- 3	1- 1	6	4	3
Jackie Meehan	3- 6	1- 2	0	0	7
Austin Carr	22-35	8- 8	8	2	52
Sid Catlett	0- 2	0- 1	5	5	0
Tom Sinnott	1- 2	2- 2	4	5	4
Mike O'Connell	1- 3	4- 5	0	2	6
Jim Hinga	0- 0	0- 1	0	1	0
Team			6		
Totals	39-75	21-32	43	26	99

Half time: Notre Dame 53-48. Officials: Filiberti and Marich.

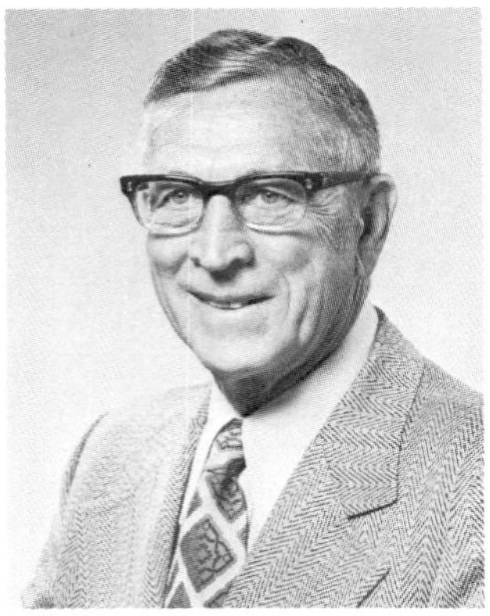

John Wooden

at Columbus, Ohio

Iowa	fg-fga	ft-fta	rb	pf	tp
Glenn Vidnovic	8-13	8-11	8	3	24
John Johnson	9-19	1- 3	8	3	19
Dick Jensen	1- 8	2- 3	4	3	4
Fred Brown	13-23	1- 2	4	3	27
Chad Calabria	7-12	7- 8	8	4	21
Ben McGilmer	4- 8	0- 2	3	4	8
Ken Grabinski	0- 0	0- 2	2	0	0
Team			9		
Totals	42-83	19-31	46	20	103

Jacksonville	fg-fga	ft-fta	rb	pf	tp
Mike Blevins	0- 1	0- 0	1	3	0
Pembrook Burrows	11-12	1- 2	9	3	23
Artis Gilmore	13-24	4- 7	17	5	30
Vaughn Wedeking	2- 8	1- 3	4	1	5
Rex Morgan	9-14	5- 9	4	4	23
Chip Dublin	2- 8	0- 0	2	5	4
Greg Nelson	6- 7	6- 6	9	1	18
Rod McIntyre	0- 1	1- 2	1	0	1
Rusty Baldwin	0- 1	0- 0	0	1	0
Team			4		
Totals	43-76	18-29	51	23	104

Half time: Jacksonville 50-49. Officials: Bussenius and Vidal. Attendance: 13,937.

at Columbus, Ohio

Iowa	fg-fga	ft-fta	rb	pf	tp
Glenn Vidnovic	7-14	10-10	11	1	24
John Johnson	14-31	3- 3	9	3	31
Dick Jensen	2- 2	1- 1	7	1	5
Fred Brown	8-16	0- 0	6	3	16
Chad Calabria	15-22	1- 2	8	3	31
Ben McGilmer	6- 9	0- 0	6	3	12
Tom Schulze	0- 1	0- 0	0	0	0
Jim Hodge	0- 0	2- 2	0	0	2
Ken Grabinski	0- 1	0- 1	0	1	0
Omar Hazley	0- 1	0- 0	1	0	0
Tom Miller	0- 1	0- 0	1	0	0
Team			3		
Totals	52-98	17-19	52	15	121

Notre Dame	fg-fga	ft-fta	rb	pf	tp
Collis Jones	12-24	0- 0	8	3	24
Austin Carr	21-39	3- 4	10	2	45
Sid Catlett	3-10	1- 1	6	2	7
Mike O'Connell	1- 3	0- 0	0	1	2
Jackie Meehan	1- 3	1- 1	1	0	3
Jay Ziznewski	2- 6	3- 4	10	2	7
Tom Sinnott	2- 5	6- 6	3	2	10
Jim Hinga	2- 5	2- 2	2	1	6
John Gallagher	1- 2	0- 0	2	0	2
Team			8		
Totals	45-97	16-18	50	13	106

Half time: Iowa 75-42. Officials: Filiberti and Vidal.

at Columbus, Ohio

Kentucky	fg-fga	ft-fta	rb	pf	tp
Tom Parker	8-18	5- 5	4	2	21
Mike Pratt	4-13	6- 9	13	5	14
Dan Issel	13-25	2- 2	10	5	28
Jim Dinwiddie	1- 2	0- 1	0	0	2
Kent Hollenbeck	4- 8	2- 2	7	3	10
Stan Key	0- 2	0- 0	1	1	0
Terry Mills	7-11	4- 4	3	5	18
Larry Steele	1- 4	1- 1	2	5	3
Mark Soderberg	2- 5	0- 0	3	0	4
Randy Noll	0- 1	0- 0	0	0	0
Team			1		
Totals	40-89	20-24	44	26	100

Jacksonville	fg-fga	ft-fta	rb	pf	tp
Vaughn Wedeking	4-13	4- 5	3	0	12
Mike Blevins	0- 1	0- 0	3	2	0
Pembrook Burrows	3- 4	2- 2	4	3	8
Artis Gilmore	10-20	4- 7	20	4	24
Rex Morgan	10-14	8- 9	3	4	28
Chip Dublin	6- 8	7- 8	2	4	19
Greg Nelson	5- 7	3- 5	7	1	13
Rod McIntyre	1- 2	0- 0	3	2	2
Team			3		
Totals	39-69	28-36	47	20	106

Half time: Jacksonville 52-45. Officials: Marich and Bussenius. Attendance: 13,865.

Midwest Regional

at Lawrence, Kansas

Drake	fg-fga	ft-fta	rb	pf	tp
Al Williams	10-19	4- 7	17	3	24
Jeff Halliburton	3- 8	5- 6	7	4	11
Tom Bush	3- 6	1- 2	7	4	7
Bobby Jones	7-15	1- 2	5	2	15
Gary Zeller	7-16	5- 7	3	3	19
Rick Wanamaker	4-10	0- 1	10	0	8
Carl Salyers	4- 4	0- 1	0	3	8
Team			6		
Totals	38-78	16-26	55	19	92

Houston	fg-fga	ft-fta	rb	pf	tp
Ollie Taylor	6-12	3- 5	9	3	15
Dwight Davis	9-19	6- 8	10	4	24
Bob Hall	1- 2	0- 0	2	2	2
Tom Gribben	2- 9	1- 1	7	5	5
Poo Welch	9-18	4- 4	3	3	22
Jeff Hickman	7-11	2- 3	4	3	16
Sonny Willis	0- 3	0- 1	2	1	0
Mars Evans	1- 1	1- 2	2	1	3
Melvin Bell	0- 0	0- 1	0	0	0
Team			4		
Totals	35-75	17-25	43	22	87

Half time: Drake 45-32. Officials: DiTomasso and Rooney.

at Lawrence, Kansas

Kansas State	fg-fga	ft-fta	rb	pf	tp
Bob Zender	3-10	1- 2	9	2	7
Jerry Venable	12-30	2- 8	14	3	26
David Hall	5-16	6-11	21	5	16
Jeff Webb	4-17	0- 0	1	4	8
Wheeler Hughes	2- 7	2- 4	3	4	6
Terry Snider	1- 4	0- 0	6	4	2
Jack Thomas	0- 0	0- 1	0	0	0
David Lawrence	0- 1	1- 3	4	0	1
Eddie Smith	0- 0	0- 0	0	0	0
Team			9		
Totals	27-85	12-29	67	22	66

New Mexico State	fg-fga	ft-fta	rb	pf	tp
John Burgess	0- 4	3- 3	10	3	3
Jeff Smith	3-10	2- 3	7	4	8
Sam Lacey	5-12	5- 7	11	3	15
Charley Criss	4- 9	5- 7	4	3	13
Jimmy Collins	8-19	7- 9	6	2	23
Bill Moore	0- 0	0- 0	1	0	0
Chito Reyes	2- 3	2- 2	2	1	6
Roy Neal	1- 1	0- 1	2	5	2
Milton Horne	0- 0	0- 0	1	1	0
Team			7		
Totals	23-58	24-32	51	22	70

Half time: New Mexico State 35-27. Officials: Cooper and Wirtz. Attendance: 10,200.

at Lawrence, Kansas

Houston	fg-fga	ft-fta	rb	pf	tp
Ollie Taylor	10-18	6-11	13	3	26
Dwight Davis	7-14	2- 3	9	4	16
Melvin Bell	0- 0	0- 0	0	1	0
Tom Gribben	6-16	5- 9	10	5	17
Poo Welch	5-18	4- 5	5	4	14
Jeff Hickman	7-12	2- 2	6	3	16
Sonny Willis	0- 3	1- 3	0	0	1
Bob Hall	2- 5	0- 0	4	1	4
Mars Evans	0- 2	0- 0	0	3	0
John Youngdale	2- 2	0- 0	0	0	4
Team			6		
Totals	39-90	20-33	53	24	98

Kansas State	fg-fga	ft-fta	rb	pf	tp
Bob Zender	7-13	1- 3	10	3	15
Jerry Venable	11-26	2- 4	10	5	24
David Hall	12-19	1- 3	19	4	25
Jeff Webb	7-13	0- 0	6	2	14
Wheeler Hughes	4- 8	1- 2	5	5	9
David Lawrence	2- 4	2- 6	5	3	6
Terry Snider	2- 4	3- 5	1	3	7
Eddie Smith	2- 6	2- 2	7	0	6
Jack Thomas	0- 0	1- 1	1	1	1
Mike Barber	0- 0	0- 0	0	0	0
Kent Kitton	0- 1	0- 0	1	0	0
Team			6		
Totals	47-94	13-26	71	26	107

Half time: Kansas State 51-46. Officials: Cooper and Rooney.

at Lawrence, Kansas

Drake	fg-fga	ft-fta	rb	pf	tp
Al Williams	4-15	1- 3	14	5	9
Jeff Halliburton	8-18	8- 8	9	3	24
Tom Bush	6- 8	1- 6	7	5	13
Gary Zeller	4-15	1- 1	1	5	9
Bobby Jones	5- 8	0- 0	1	5	10
Al Sakys	0- 2	2- 4	1	3	2
Rick Wanamaker	1- 4	1- 2	3	3	3
Carl Salyers	3- 5	0- 0	0	1	6
Lee Allen	1- 3	0- 0	0	2	2
Dale Teeter	0- 1	0- 0	1	0	0
Team			5		
Totals	32-79	14-24	42	32	78

New Mexico State	fg-fga	ft-fta	rb	pf	tp
John Burgess	0- 0	0- 0	7	2	0
Jeff Smith	2- 4	1- 3	3	5	5
Sam Lacey	7-12	6-10	24	2	20
Charley Criss	5-10	4- 7	0	4	14
Jimmy Collins	9-18	8-10	3	3	26
Roy Neal	2- 2	3- 4	4	1	7
Milton Horne	3- 6	7- 9	0	4	13
Chito Reyes	0- 1	2- 2	5	1	2
Team			8		
Totals	28-53	31-45	54	22	87

Half time: New Mexico State 47-35. Officials: DiTomasso and Wirtz. Attendance: 8,400.

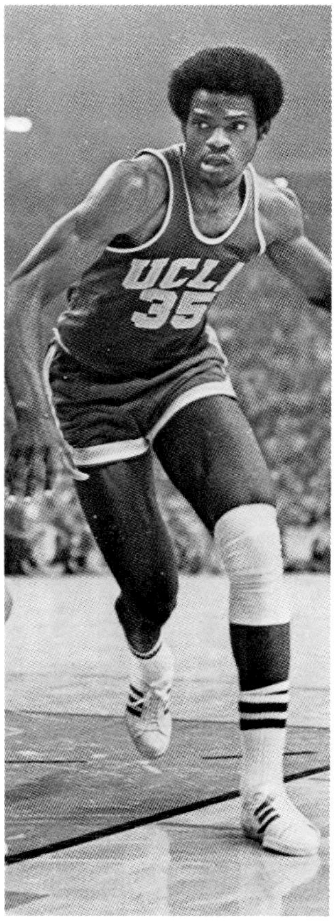

Sidney Wicks

GAME-BY-GAME RESULTS

West Regional

at Seattle, Washington

Utah State	fg-fga	ft-fta	rb	pf	tp
Nate Williams	10-22	4- 5	3	3	24
Marv Roberts	5-14	6- 9	16	1	16
Tim Tollestrup	3-11	1- 2	13	5	7
Paul Jeppesen	2- 8	4- 4	3	5	8
Jeff Tebbs	1- 8	1- 1	4	2	3
Ron Hatch	1- 4	0- 0	3	3	2
Ed Epps	3- 5	3- 3	2	1	9
Chris Bean	0- 1	0- 0	0	0	0
John Ericksen	0- 0	0- 0	1	1	0
Team			3		
Totals	25-73	19-24	48	21	69

Santa Clara	fg-fga	ft-fta	rb	pf	tp
Ralph Ogdon	5-15	2- 7	4	3	12
Bruce Bochte	1- 3	2- 4	8	4	4
Dennis Awtrey	9-16	6- 8	11	4	24
Kevin Eagleson	2- 5	1- 2	3	2	5
Jolly Spight	8-16	5- 7	9	4	21
Mart Peterson	1- 3	0- 0	2	3	2
Keith Paulson	0- 1	0- 0	0	0	0
Team			12		
Totals	26-59	16-28	49	20	68

Half time: Santa Clara 35-31. Officials: McPherson and Scott.

at Seattle, Washington

UCLA	fg-fga	ft-fta	rb	pf	tp
Sidney Wicks	8-14	4- 7	11	3	20
Curtis Rowe	5-11	5- 9	11	1	15
Steve Patterson	6-14	1- 1	12	4	13
John Vallely	6-15	2- 5	5	2	14
Henry Bibby	8-13	4- 5	6	2	20
Kenny Booker	0- 1	0- 0	0	1	0
John Ecker	1- 2	0- 0	1	0	2
Terry Schofield	1- 2	0- 0	1	0	2
Bill Siebert	0- 1	0- 0	0	0	0
Jon Chapman	1- 1	0- 0	1	0	2
Team			6		
Totals	36-74	16-27	54	13	88

Long Beach State	fg-fga	ft-fta	rb	pf	tp
Sam Robinson	7-13	4- 6	7	2	18
Billy Jankans	2-10	1- 3	7	5	5
George Trapp	10-18	0- 1	4	3	20
Ray Gritton	0- 2	0- 0	1	1	0
Shawn Johnson	5-12	3- 3	4	0	13
Dave McLucas	0- 0	0- 0	1	0	0
Dwight Taylor	1- 7	1- 2	0	3	3
Arthur Montgomery	3- 4	0- 0	1	5	6
Bernard Williams	0- 1	0- 0	1	2	0
Team			8		
Totals	28-67	9-15	34	21	65

Half time: UCLA 42-29. Officials: Stout and Huiot. Attendance: 5,500.

at Seattle, Washington

Long Beach State	fg-fga	ft-fta	rb	pf	tp
Sam Robinson	6-15	3- 4	6	2	15
Arthur Montgomery	1- 6	3- 3	9	3	5
George Trapp	6-16	5- 6	10	5	17
Ray Gritton	5-13	3- 3	3	0	13
Shawn Johnson	6-19	3- 3	8	1	15
Dave McLucas	2- 2	0- 0	5	3	4
Billy Jankans	7-12	1- 2	5	4	15
Dwight Taylor	0- 1	2- 2	1	1	2
Team			3		
Totals	33-84	20-23	50	19	86

Santa Clara	fg-fga	ft-fta	rb	pf	tp
Ralph Ogden	9-28	3- 4	7	4	21
Bob Tobin	2- 4	0- 0	6	1	4
Dennis Awtrey	15-17	7-11	13	2	37
Kevin Eagleson	0- 2	2- 3	3	4	2
Keith Paulson	1- 3	0- 0	2	1	2
Mart Peterson	1- 2	0- 0	0	0	2
Jolly Spight	4- 8	3- 3	4	3	11
Tom Lunceford	0- 1	0- 0	3	0	0
Bruce Bochte	4- 5	2- 2	1	3	10
Team			5		
Totals	36-70	17-23	44	18	89

Half time: Santa Clara 51-50. Officials: McPherson and Stout.

at Seattle, Washington

UCLA	fg-fga	ft-fta	rb	pf	tp
Sidney Wicks	10-14	6- 7	8	4	26
Curtis Rowe	9-17	8- 8	16	3	26
Steve Patterson	4-12	1- 2	9	2	9
Henry Bibby	4- 8	7- 9	7	4	15
John Vallely	5-13	4- 7	3	1	14
Kenny Booker	2- 4	0- 1	1	2	4
John Ecker	0- 0	1- 2	2	1	1
Terry Schofield	0- 0	0- 0	0	0	0
Jon Chapman	0- 2	0- 0	3	0	0
Bill Seibert	1- 1	2- 2	1	1	4
Rick Betchley	1- 2	0- 0	0	0	2
Andy Hill	0- 0	0- 0	0	0	0
Team			6		
Totals	36-73	29-38	56	18	101

Utah State	fg-fga	ft-fta	rb	pf	tp
Nate Williams	7-24	0- 0	11	4	14
Marv Roberts	14-35	5- 7	15	4	33
Tim Tollestrup	1- 4	4- 6	10	4	6
Jeff Tebbs	0- 4	0- 0	2	4	0
Paul Jeppesen	4- 6	4- 4	1	4	12
Ed Epps	6-13	0- 1	6	3	12
Ron Hatch	0- 4	2- 2	2	2	2
John Ericksen	0- 0	0- 0	0	0	0
Terry Wakefield	0- 0	0- 0	0	1	0
Dick Wade	0- 1	0- 0	1	0	0
Chris Bean	0- 0	0- 0	1	0	0
Team			5		
Totals	32-91	15-20	54	26	79

Half time: UCLA 51-44. Officials: Huiot and White. Attendance: 4,200.

Semifinals

at College Park, Maryland

Jacksonville	fg-fga	ft-fta	rb	pf	tp
Vaughn Wedeking	7-15	1- 1	6	4	15
Rex Morgan	6-15	5- 6	5	3	17
Pembrook Burrows	2- 4	1- 1	4	4	5
Rod McIntyre	0- 3	0- 0	3	1	0
Artis Gilmore	9-14	11-15	21	2	29
Chip Dublin	1- 3	9- 9	2	2	11
Gene Nelson	1- 7	10-12	7	3	12
Mike Blevins	1- 1	0- 0	0	1	2
Rusty Baldwin	0- 1	0- 1	0	1	0
Team			4		
Totals	27-63	37-45	52	21	91

St. Bonaventure	fg-fga	ft-fta	rb	pf	tp
Bill Kalbaugh	5- 8	2- 2	4	3	12
Paul Hoffman	4-14	2- 4	6	3	10
Greg Gary	2- 7	5- 8	13	5	9
Tom Baldwin	2-10	1- 2	4	5	5
Matt Gantt	8-17	0- 0	8	5	16
Mike Kull	4- 7	0- 0	0	5	8
Vic Thomas	7-17	1- 2	4	3	15
Paul Grys	1- 5	2- 2	1	2	4
Dale Tepas	0- 0	2- 2	1	0	2
Gene Fahey	1- 1	0- 0	0	1	2
Team			6		
Totals	34-86	15-22	47	32	83

Half time: Jacksonville 42-34. Officials: Scott and Marich.

at College Park, Maryland

UCLA	fg-fga	ft-fta	rb	pf	tp
Curtis Rowe	4- 7	7-11	15	0	15
Steve Patterson	5- 9	2- 2	6	3	12
Sidney Wicks	10-12	2- 5	16	3	22
John Vallely	7-19	9-10	4	3	23
Henry Bibby	8-13	3- 3	2	5	19
Kenny Booker	0- 1	0- 0	0	2	0
Rick Betchley	0- 0	0- 0	0	0	0
Terry Schofield	0- 0	0- 0	0	1	0
John Ecker	0- 0	0- 0	0	0	0
Bill Seibert	0- 1	0- 0	1	0	0
Andy Hill	0- 0	0- 1	0	1	0
Jon Chapman	1- 1	0- 0	1	0	2
Team			0		
Totals	35-63	23-32	45	18	93

New Mexico State	fg-fga	ft-fta	rb	pf	tp
Charley Criss	6-16	7- 9	2	5	19
Jimmy Collins	13-23	2- 3	0	3	28
John Burgess	1- 6	0- 0	2	2	2
Jeff Smith	4-11	2- 3	7	5	10
Sam Lacey	3- 9	2- 3	16	3	8
Chito Reyes	1- 6	0- 0	4	2	2
Roy Neal	2- 4	0- 0	6	2	4
Milton Horne	0- 4	2- 2	1	2	2
Bill Moore	1- 1	0- 0	1	0	2
Lonnie Lefevre	0- 0	0- 0	1	0	0
Rudy Franco	0- 0	0- 0	0	0	0
Tom McCarthy	0- 0	0- 0	0	0	0
Team			5		
Totals	31-80	15-20	45	24	77

Half time: UCLA 48-41. Officials: White and Wirtz. Attendance: 14,380.

National Third Place

at College Park, Maryland

St. Bonaventure	fg-fga	ft-fta	rb	pf	tp
Mike Kull	7-17	0- 0	2	2	14
Bill Kalbaugh	3- 9	0- 0	3	1	6
Paul Hoffman	2- 5	0- 1	4	3	4
Greg Gary	8-14	6- 7	11	4	22
Matt Gantt	6-16	2- 5	10	2	14
Dale Tepas	0- 1	0- 0	0	0	0
Vic Thomas	3- 7	2- 2	1	2	8
Tom Baldwin	1- 1	1- 1	0	0	3
Paul Grys	1- 1	0- 0	1	0	2
Team			2		
Totals	31-71	11-16	34	14	73

New Mexico State	fg-fga	ft-fta	rb	pf	tp
Charley Criss	4-16	2- 2	7	3	10
Jimmy Collins	9-22	0- 0	3	2	18
John Burgess	1- 2	0- 0	9	1	2
Jeff Smith	2- 5	3- 6	5	4	7
Sam Lacey	7-17	4- 6	19	0	18
Roy Neal	5- 7	2- 2	7	1	12
Chito Reyes	4- 7	2- 2	5	0	10
Milton Horne	1- 1	0- 0	0	1	2
Bill Moore	0- 0	0- 0	0	0	0
Team			2		
Totals	33-77	13-18	57	12	79

Half time: New Mexico State 36-30. Officials: White, Marich and Allmond.

Championship

at College Park, Maryland

Jacksonville	fg-fga	ft-fta	rb	pf	tp
Vaughn Wedeking	6-11	0- 0	2	2	12
Mike Blevins	1- 2	1- 2	0	1	3
Rex Morgan	5-11	0- 0	4	5	10
Pembrook Burrows	6- 9	0- 0	6	1	12
Artis Gilmore	9-29	1- 1	16	5	19
Greg Nelson	3- 9	2- 2	5	1	8
Chip Dublin	0- 5	2- 2	1	4	2
Rusty Baldwin	0- 0	0- 0	0	0	0
Rod McIntyre	1- 3	0- 0	3	4	2
Dan Hawkins	0- 1	1- 1	1	1	1
Ken Selke	0- 0	0- 0	0	0	0
Team			2		
Totals	31-80	7- 8	40	24	69

UCLA	fg-fga	ft-fta	rb	pf	tp
Curtis Rowe	7-15	5- 5	8	4	19
Steve Patterson	8-15	1- 4	11	1	17
Sidney Wicks	5- 9	7-10	18	3	17
John Vallely	5-10	5- 7	7	2	15
Henry Bibby	2-11	4- 4	4	1	8
Kenny Booker	0- 0	2- 3	0	0	2
Bill Seibert	0- 1	0- 0	1	1	0
John Ecker	1- 1	0- 0	0	0	2
Rick Betchley	0- 0	0- 1	0	0	0
Jon Chapman	0- 1	0- 0	1	0	0
Andy Hill	0- 0	0- 1	0	0	0
Terry Schofield	0- 0	0- 0	0	0	0
Team			3		
Totals	28-63	24-35	53	12	80

Half time: UCLA 41-36. Officials: Scott and Wirtz. Attendance: 14,380.

1971

First Round

at Morgantown, West Virginia

Duquesne	fg-fga	ft-fta	rb	pf	tp
Mickey Davis	7-16	2- 4	12	3	16
Barry Nelson	3- 6	0- 0	3	3	6
Garry Nelson	4- 9	3- 5	13	3	11
Jarrett Durham	3-11	4- 7	6	3	10
Mike Barr	1- 2	0- 0	2	3	2
Steve McHugh	5- 7	2- 2	3	3	12
Jack Wajdowski	4- 6	0- 0	1	2	8
Team			2		
Totals	27-57	11-18	42	20	65

Pennsylvania	fg-fga	ft-fta	rb	pf	tp
Bob Morse	10-22	4- 6	16	3	24
Phil Hankinson	2- 3	0- 0	3	0	4
Jim Wolf	1- 1	0- 0	4	3	2
Dave Wohl	7-17	5- 8	1	2	19
Corky Calhoun	4- 9	3- 3	5	3	11
Craig Littlepage	0- 3	0- 2	4	0	0
Steve Bilsky	2- 8	6- 6	3	3	10
Team			3		
Totals	26-63	18-25	39	14	70

Half time: Pennsylvania 32-28. Officials: Hartack and Grossman. Attendance: 13,861.

at Philadelphia, Pennsylvania

Villanova	fg-fga	ft-fta	rb	pf	tp
Howard Porter	9-20	8-11	18	4	26
Clarence Smith	5-12	3- 4	9	3	13
H. Siemiontkowski	9-20	5- 5	11	5	23
Chris Ford	2- 9	3- 3	9	4	7
Tom Ingelsby	6- 9	8-12	3	0	20
Joe McDowell	0- 0	0- 1	5	1	0
Bob Gohl	1- 1	0- 1	1	0	2
John Fox	1- 1	0- 0	0	1	2
Mike Daly	0- 0	0- 0	0	0	0
Team			3		
Totals	33-72	27-37	59	18	93

St. Joseph's, Pa.	fg-fga	ft-fta	rb	pf	tp
John Connolly	6-10	3- 3	5	5	15
Pat McFarland	6-20	2- 3	2	2	14
Mike Bantom	7-15	6- 8	14	4	20
Jack Snyder	4- 6	2- 2	2	4	10
Mike Moody	1- 6	2- 3	5	4	4
Jim McCollum	2- 9	2- 3	2	5	6
Eric Mitchell	3- 5	0- 1	3	2	6
Bruce Marks	0- 0	0- 0	0	0	0
Bob Sabol	0- 2	0- 0	1	0	0
Bob Haas	0- 0	0- 0	0	0	0
Jack Krutsick	0- 0	0- 0	0	0	0
Team			6		
Totals	29-73	17-23	40	26	75

Half time: Villanova 44-37. Officials: Diehl and Kaplan. Attendance: 9,137.

at Jamaica, New York

Fordham	fg-fga	ft-fta	rb	pf	tp
Charles Yelverton	11-24	8-14	19	2	30
William Mainor	8-15	3- 4	6	2	19
Kenneth Charles	8-16	2- 7	10	3	18
Bart Woytowicz	9-14	0- 0	13	4	18
George Zambetti	3- 3	0- 0	1	1	6
Thomas Sullivan	0- 2	2- 2	2	4	2
John Burik	2- 4	0- 1	2	4	4
Thomas Pipich	1- 2	2- 2	0	0	4
Robert Larbes	2- 3	0- 0	0	1	4
Steven Cain	0- 2	0- 0	0	0	0
Peter Carlesimo	0- 0	0- 0	0	0	0
Paul Griswold	0- 0	0- 0	0	0	0
Team			7		
Totals	44-85	17-30	60	21	105

Furman	fg-fga	ft-fta	rb	pf	tp
Don Jackson	4-12	3- 5	2	3	11
Bernard Collier	4- 8	3- 4	3	1	11
Jerry Martin	2- 6	1- 2	2	3	5
Lisco Thomas	10-20	1- 4	14	1	21
Charles Selvy	4- 6	1- 3	2	2	9
Steve Cockrum	4-10	5- 8	10	3	13
Steve Dougherty	0- 3	2- 3	3	5	2
David Whitener	0- 0	0- 0	1	1	0
Steven Ehlmann	0- 0	0- 0	1	0	0
John Campbell	1- 2	0- 0	0	0	2
Team			7		
Totals	29-67	16-29	45	19	74

Half time: Fordham 50-30. Officials: Bushkar and DeBonis. Attendance: 6,004.

GAME-BY-GAME RESULTS

304

East Regional

at Raleigh, North Carolina

Fordham	fg-fga	ft-fta	rb	pf	tp
William Mainor	4-15	2- 2	2	4	10
John Burik	2- 6	2- 2	5	1	6
Charles Yelverton	12-28	8- 8	9	3	32
Kenneth Charles	2- 8	2- 2	8	3	6
Bart Woytowicz	5-17	5- 6	8	0	15
Thomas Sullivan	2- 5	2- 7	6	3	6
Thomas Pipich	0- 1	0- 0	0	0	0
Robert Larbes	0- 0	0- 0	0	0	0
Peter Carlesimo	0- 0	0- 0	0	0	0
Paul Griswold	0- 0	0- 0	1	0	0
Steven Cain	0- 0	0- 0	0	0	0
George Zambetti	0- 0	0- 0	0	0	0
Team			9		
Totals	27-80	21-27	48	14	75

Villanova	fg-fga	ft-fta	rb	pf	tp
Tom Ingelsby	4- 9	4- 4	8	2	12
H. Siemiontkowski	7- 9	5- 5	8	3	19
Chris Ford	5-10	2- 4	5	3	12
Clarence Smith	5-11	1- 1	10	4	11
Howard Porter	11-17	3- 3	8	5	25
Joe McDowell	3- 4	0- 0	0	3	6
John Fox	0- 0	0- 0	0	0	0
Mike Daly	0- 0	0- 0	0	0	0
Bob Gohl	0- 1	0- 0	0	0	0
Team			0		
Totals	35-61	15-17	39	20	85

Half time: Villanova 47-36. Officials: Lawson and Bain.

at Raleigh, North Carolina

South Carolina	fg-fga	ft-fta	rb	pf	tp
John Roche	5-18	4- 5	5	2	14
Bob Carver	2- 5	0- 0	1	1	4
Rick Aydlett	3- 5	2- 2	3	5	8
Tom Owens	6-14	4- 7	10	2	16
Tom Riker	3-15	4- 4	9	2	10
John Ribock	1- 2	0- 1	3	5	2
Kevin Joyce	3- 8	2- 2	9	4	8
Danny Traylor	1- 2	0- 0	3	1	2
Casey Manning	0- 0	0- 0	1	0	0
Jimmy Powell	0- 0	0- 0	0	0	0
Dennis Powell	0- 0	0- 0	0	0	0
Team			3		
Totals	24-69	16-21	47	22	64

Pennsylvania	fg-fga	ft-fta	rb	pf	tp
Dave Wohl	5-15	10-11	3	3	20
Steve Bilsky	3- 8	2- 2	1	1	8
Corky Calhoun	3- 8	4- 4	7	3	10
Bob Morse	10-18	8-10	5	3	28
Jim Wolf	1- 2	4- 4	10	4	6
Phil Hankinson	2- 6	2- 2	7	1	6
Craig Littlepage	0- 0	0- 0	3	2	0
John Koller	0- 1	0- 0	0	0	0
Alan Cotler	0- 0	1- 2	0	0	1
Jim Haney	0- 0	0- 0	0	0	0
Bill Walters	0- 0	0- 0	0	0	0
Team			5		
Totals	24-58	31-35	41	17	79

Half time: South Carolina 37-36. Officials: Dreith and Wilcoxen. Attendance: 12,400.

at Raleigh, North Carolina

Fordham	fg-fga	ft-fta	rb	pf	tp
William Mainor	9-19	5- 5	6	4	23
John Burik	8-14	7- 7	2	0	23
Charles Yelverton	11-23	3- 3	10	5	25
Kenneth Charles	9-24	4- 4	10	4	22
Bart Woytowicz	0- 2	1- 1	3	5	1
Thomas Sullivan	2- 6	2- 2	6	0	6
Thomas Pipich	0- 0	0- 0	0	0	0
Peter Carlesimo	0- 0	0- 0	0	0	0
Robert Larbes	0- 0	0- 0	0	0	0
Steven Cain	0- 0	0- 0	0	0	0
George Zambetti	0- 0	0- 0	0	0	0
Team			4		
Totals	39-88	22-22	41	18	100

South Carolina	fg-fga	ft-fta	rb	pf	tp
John Roche	2- 9	4- 6	0	5	8
Bob Carver	1- 3	0- 1	3	2	2
Tom Owens	5-11	3- 5	13	4	13
Kevin Joyce	5-10	8- 8	8	3	18
Tom Riker	18-26	3- 5	11	2	39
Rick Aydlett	4-11	2- 2	6	3	10
Team			9		
Totals	35-70	20-27	50	19	90

Half time: South Carolina 48-42. Officials: Dreith and Lawson.

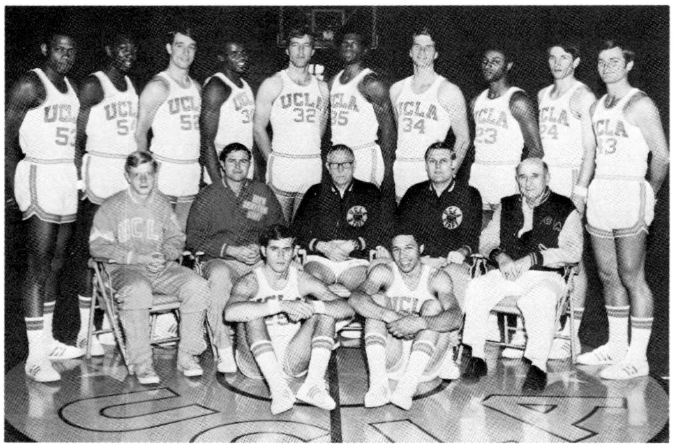

1971 UCLA BRUINS—(l-r) Front Row: Andy Hill, Henry Bibby; Second Row: George Morgan, Denny Crum, John Wooden, Gary Cunningham, Ducky Drake; Third Row: Larry Hollyfield, Larry Farmer, John Ecker, Curtis Rowe, Steve Patterson, Sidney Wicks, Jon Chapman, Kenny Booker, Rick Betchley, Terry Schofield.

at Raleigh, North Carolina

Villanova	fg-fga	ft-fta	rb	pf	tp
Tom Ingelsby	1- 3	6- 7	4	2	8
H. Siemiontkowski	10-15	0- 0	7	3	20
Chris Ford	2- 4	5- 9	5	0	9
Clarence Smith	7-11	1- 2	8	0	15
Howard Porter	16-24	3- 4	15	2	35
Joe McDowell	0- 1	0- 0	1	0	0
John Fox	0- 1	1- 1	0	0	1
Bob Gohl	1- 1	0- 0	1	1	2
Mike Daly	0- 0	0- 0	0	0	0
Team			3		
Totals	37-60	16-23	44	8	90

Pennsylvania	fg-fga	ft-fta	rb	pf	tp
Dave Wohl	3-10	0- 0	0	2	6
Steve Bilsky	1- 4	0- 0	0	2	2
Corky Calhoun	1- 7	0- 0	5	2	2
Bob Morse	2- 8	2- 2	2	1	6
Jim Wolf	3- 8	1- 1	8	3	7
Phil Hankinson	4- 9	0- 0	4	1	8
Craig Littlepage	1- 7	3- 5	4	2	5
Alan Cotler	2- 7	0- 0	2	2	4
John Koller	2- 4	0- 0	1	0	4
Jim Haney	0- 2	0- 0	2	0	0
Bill Walters	1- 1	1- 1	1	1	3
Team			5		
Totals	20-67	7- 9	34	16	47

Half time: Villanova 43-22. Officials: Wilcoxen and Bain. Attendance: 12,400.

at South Bend, Indiana

Jacksonville	fg-fga	ft-fta	rb	pf	tp
Chip Dublin	2- 5	1- 2	3	2	5
Harold Fox	9-18	1- 1	6	2	19
Artis Gilmore	3-10	6-10	22	1	12
Pembrook Burrows	0- 6	1- 3	8	3	1
Ernie Fleming	8-15	2- 2	8	4	18
Vaughn Wedeking	3- 8	1- 3	3	0	7
Rusty Baldwin	0- 0	0- 0	0	0	0
Mike Blevins	3- 3	0- 0	2	2	6
Greg Nelson	2- 2	0- 0	0	2	4
Team			7		
Totals	30-67	12-21	59	16	72

Western Kentucky	fg-fga	ft-fta	rb	pf	tp
Jim Rose	6-17	1- 2	7	2	13
Rex Bailey	3- 7	0- 1	6	3	6
Jim McDaniels	11-28	1- 4	13	4	23
Jerry Dunn	5-16	1- 4	10	5	11
Clarence Glover	8-21	0- 1	17	2	16
Gary Sundmacker	0- 0	0- 0	2	1	0
Chuck Witt	2- 7	1- 1	0	1	5
Team			3		
Totals	35-96	4-13	58	18	74

Half time: Jacksonville 44-30. Officials: Miller and Copeland.

at South Bend, Indiana

Marquette	fg-fga	ft-fta	rb	pf	tp
Dean Meminger	6- 9	9-12	2	2	21
Allie McGuire	4- 6	0- 1	1	2	8
Jim Chones	9-13	3- 6	14	0	21
Gary Brell	0- 2	0- 0	2	1	0
Bob Lackey	4- 8	0- 1	12	4	8
Kurt Spychalla	0- 0	0- 0	0	0	0
Guy Lam	0- 1	0- 0	0	0	0
Gary Grzesk	0- 0	0- 0	1	0	0
Mike Mills	0- 0	0- 1	0	0	0
Hugh McMahon	1- 3	0- 1	6	4	2
George Frazier	1- 1	0- 0	3	1	2
Team			1		
Totals	25-43	12-22	42	14	62

Miami, Ohio	fg-fga	ft-fta	rb	pf	tp
Jerry Sears	4- 8	8- 9	3	2	16
Tim Meyer	0- 5	0- 0	1	3	0
Tom Roberts	3- 6	0- 1	5	1	6
Darrel Dunlap	1- 6	3- 3	2	2	5
Ron Nickamp	4-10	0- 0	5	2	8
Mike Wren	1- 5	1- 3	0	2	3
Ken Byrd	0- 1	0- 0	1	0	0
Herb Hilgeman	0- 0	0- 0	0	0	0
Steve Handy	4- 9	1- 2	4	4	9
Team			2		
Totals	17-50	13-18	23	16	47

Half time: Marquette 23-21. Officials: Wedge and White. Attendance: 11,345.

Mideast Regional

at Athens, Georgia

Marquette	fg-fga	ft-fta	rb	pf	tp
Gary Brell	5-10	0- 0	8	0	10
Robert Lackey	1- 9	6- 8	9	4	8
Jim Chones	9-19	0- 2	10	3	18
Dean Meminger	4-11	3- 7	3	5	11
Allie McGuire	5-11	2- 3	0	4	12
Hugh McMahon	0- 1	0- 0	2	3	0
George Frazier	0- 1	0- 1	0	0	0
Gary Grzesk	0- 0	0- 0	1	0	0
Mike Mills	0- 0	0- 0	0	0	0
Team			13		
Totals	24-62	11-21	46	19	59

Ohio State	fg-fga	ft-fta	rb	pf	tp
Mark Wagar	0- 2	1- 3	2	1	1
Mark Minor	1- 5	0- 2	3	2	2
Luther Witte	5-13	3- 4	11	3	13
Allan Hornyak	4-15	3- 3	4	4	11
James Cleamons	7-13	7- 8	4	2	21
Robert Siekmann	4- 5	2- 2	4	4	10
David Merchant	1- 3	0- 0	1	1	2
Team			13		
Totals	22-56	16-22	42	17	60

Half time: Marquette 31-27. Officials: Herrold and Ross.

at Athens, Georgia

Kentucky	fg-fga	ft-fta	rb	pf	tp
Tom Parker	11-18	1- 1	5	4	23
Larry Steele	1- 5	2- 3	1	5	4
Tom Payne	7-18	1- 3	10	2	15
Jim Dinwiddie	2- 7	0- 0	2	2	4
Mike Casey	4-11	4- 5	6	2	12
Kent Hollenbeck	2- 2	3- 4	0	5	7
Jim Andrews	3- 5	2- 4	6	0	8
Terry Mills	0- 2	4- 5	1	1	4
Stan Key	3- 4	0- 0	3	2	6
Larry Stamper	0- 2	0- 0	2	0	0
Team			9		
Totals	33-74	17-25	45	23	83

Western Kentucky	fg-fga	ft-fta	rb	pf	tp
Jerry Dunn	3- 8	3- 5	7	4	9
Clarence Glover	8-16	2- 5	17	2	18
Jim McDaniels	12-21	11-11	11	4	35
Jim Rose	12-21	1- 1	3	3	25
Rex Bailey	3-10	3- 4	2	2	9
Gary Sundmacker	2- 2	1- 2	1	3	5
Chuck Witt	2- 4	0- 0	1	0	4
Danny Johnson	0- 0	2- 2	0	1	2
Terry Davis	0- 0	0- 0	0	0	0
Ray Kleykamp	0- 0	0- 0	0	0	0
Steve Eaton	0- 1	0- 0	0	0	0
Team			8		
Totals	42-83	23-30	50	19	107

Half time: Western Kentucky 51-38. Officials: Evans and Brown. Attendance: 10,615.

at Athens, Georgia

Kentucky	fg-fga	ft-fta	rb	pf	tp
Tom Parker	5-12	0- 1	3	4	10
Larry Steele	7-11	6- 9	2	4	20
Tom Payne	0- 1	1- 1	2	5	1
Jim Dinwiddie	0- 1	0- 0	0	1	0
Mike Casey	2- 8	4- 4	1	2	8
Kent Hollenbeck	5- 8	4- 4	0	3	14
Jim Andrews	6- 9	2- 2	5	0	14
Stan Key	0- 1	1- 2	1	2	1
Terry Mills	1- 1	0- 2	1	2	2
Larry Stamper	2- 3	0- 0	0	0	4
Clint Wheeler	0- 0	0- 0	0	0	0
Steve Penhorwood	0- 0	0- 0	0	0	0
Team			8		
Totals	28-55	18-25	23	23	74

Marquette	fg-fga	ft-fta	rb	pf	tp
Gary Brell	3- 9	1- 2	9	2	7
Robert Lackey	4- 7	2- 3	12	3	10
Jim Chones	11-16	5- 7	12	0	27
Dean Meminger	8-12	14-17	4	4	30
Allie McGuire	3-10	1- 2	1	5	7
George Frazier	1- 2	1- 2	4	1	3
Mark Ostrand	1- 1	0- 0	0	0	2
Gary Grzesk	0- 0	2- 2	0	4	2
Mike Mills	0- 0	1- 2	0	0	1
Guy Lam	0- 1	0- 0	0	0	0
Kurt Spychalla	1- 1	0- 0	0	0	2
Team			6		
Totals	32-59	27-37	48	19	91

Half time: Marquette 50-43. Officials: Herrold and Ross.

at Athens, Georgia

Ohio State	fg-fga	ft-fta	rb	pf	tp
Mark Minor	3- 8	1- 1	3	4	7
Mark Wagar	2- 6	3- 4	3	5	7
Luther White	10-19	3- 5	17	4	23
James Cleamons	4- 9	4- 6	7	4	12
Allan Hornyak	11-21	4- 4	3	1	26
Robert Siekmann	1- 2	1- 1	2	0	3
David Merchant	0- 2	0- 0	0	0	0
Team			6		
Totals	31-67	16-21	41	18	78

Western Kentucky	fg-fga	ft-fta	rb	pf	tp
Clarence Glover	2- 9	7- 9	22	2	11
Jerry Dunn	5-14	2- 5	15	4	12
Jim McDaniels	14-35	3- 6	6	4	31
Jim Rose	6-13	1- 1	6	4	13
Rex Bailey	7- 9	0- 1	0	2	14
Danny Johnson	0- 1	0- 0	0	1	0
Chuck Witt	0- 1	0- 0	1	0	0
Team			6		
Totals	34-82	13-22	56	17	81

Half time: Ohio State 40-34. Regulation Score: 69-69. Officials: Evans and Brown. Attendance: 10,521.

Midwest First Round

at Houston, Texas

Texas Christian	fg-fga	ft-fta	rb	pf	tp
Jim Ferguson	4-10	3- 4	4	3	11
Ricky Hall	8-12	2- 3	4	4	18
Simpson Degrate	9-16	4- 7	9	2	22
James Williams	8-12	2- 2	2	5	18
Eugene Kennedy	10-20	3- 3	16	4	23
John Hurdle	0- 0	0- 0	0	0	0
Jimmy Parker	1- 1	0- 0	0	0	2
Coco Villarreal	0- 1	0- 0	1	0	0
Steve Smith	0- 0	0- 0	0	0	0
Evans Royal	0- 1	0- 0	0	3	0
Ken Hough	0- 0	0- 0	1	0	0
Mark Stone	0- 0	0- 0	0	0	0
Team			3		
Totals	40-73	14-19	40	21	94

Notre Dame	fg-fga	ft-fta	rb	pf	tp
Austin Carr	20-34	12-15	6	1	52
Jackie Meehan	4- 8	0- 1	1	2	8
Collis Jones	10-19	6- 8	11	5	26
Sid Catlett	3- 8	1- 1	9	4	7
John Pleick	3- 6	1- 3	8	5	7
John Egart	0- 0	0- 0	0	0	0
Tom Sinnott	0- 0	2- 2	0	1	2
Bill Hinga	0- 0	0- 0	0	0	0
Jim Hinga	0- 0	0- 0	0	0	0
Doug Gemmell	0- 1	0- 0	0	0	0
Don Silenski	0- 0	0- 0	0	0	0
Team			8		
Totals	40-76	22-30	43	18	102

Half time: Notre Dame 56-42. Officials: Clark and Weiler.

at Houston, Texas

Houston	fg-fga	ft-fta	rb	pf	tp
Jerry Bonney	1- 5	0- 0	3	0	2
Poo Welch	9-18	5- 7	4	1	23
Dwight Davis	11-19	8-10	8	5	30
Bob Hall	4- 7	4- 5	13	3	12
Steve Newsome	2-11	1- 1	10	4	5
Sonny Willis	0- 1	0- 1	0	1	0
Larry Brown	0- 3	0- 0	1	1	0
Team			11		
Totals	27-64	18-24	50	15	72

New Mexico State	fg-fga	ft-fta	rb	pf	tp
Bill Moore	0- 2	0- 0	0	4	0
Alex Scott	13-22	1- 2	6	4	27
Jeff Smith	3- 9	2- 2	5	3	8
Harry Ward	8-22	5- 8	10	3	21
Chito Reyes	2- 6	1- 1	10	2	5
Elgren Green	0- 2	0- 0	1	0	0
Clint Davis	1- 3	0- 2	1	2	2
Roy Neal	2- 4	2- 4	2	1	6
Team			7		
Totals	29-70	11-19	42	19	69

Half time: New Mexico State 36-28. Officials: Shosid and Hale. Attendance: 10,514.

Midwest Regional

at Wichita, Kansas

Drake	fg-fga	ft-fta	rb	pf	tp
Al Sakys	7-13	1- 1	8	5	15
Bobby Jones	5-16	1- 2	9	0	11
Tom Bush	7-11	5-10	16	4	19
Leon Huff	7-19	1- 3	12	5	15
Jeff Halliburton	5-21	2- 3	11	5	12
Dave Wicklund	0- 0	0- 0	0	0	0
Carl Salyers	1- 2	2- 2	0	0	4
Jim Nordrum	1- 3	1- 3	5	0	3
Tony Johnson	0- 1	0- 2	2	0	0
Team			3		
Totals	33-86	13-26	66	19	79

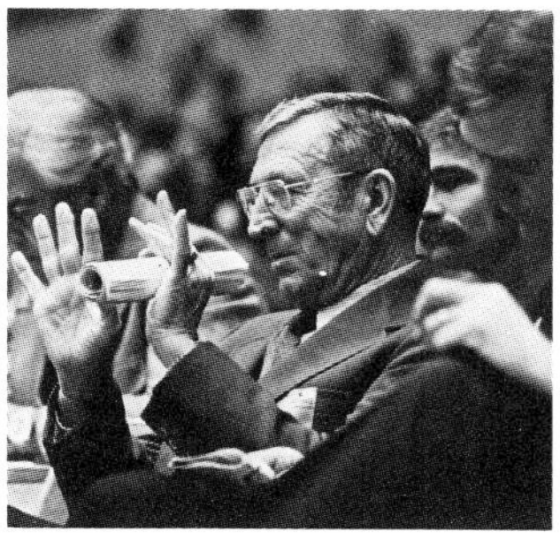

John Wooden

Notre Dame	fg-fga	ft-fta	rb	pf	tp
Austin Carr	11-27	4- 5	8	4	26
Jackie Meehan	4- 8	3- 4	4	5	11
Sid Catlett	2-11	3- 3	17	2	7
Collis Jones	7-26	5- 7	16	4	19
John Pleick	2- 4	0- 0	4	5	4
Tom Sinnott	1- 2	1- 2	2	1	3
Doug Gemmell	1- 4	0- 1	6	2	2
Team			3		
Totals	28-82	16-22	60	23	72

Half time: Drake 39-32. Regulation Score: 62-62. Officials: Diehl and Hermjek.

at Wichita, Kansas

Kansas	fg-fga	ft-fta	rb	pf	tp
Bud Stallworth	10-21	5- 7	8	2	25
Aubrey Nash	4- 7	1- 3	1	4	9
Roger Brown	1- 9	1- 2	7	4	3
Dave Robisch	10-23	9-14	16	3	29
Pierre Russell	3-10	0- 0	4	3	6
Bob Kivisto	0- 1	2- 3	0	0	2
Greg Douglas	0- 1	0- 0	1	0	0
Randy Canfield	2- 3	0- 0	4	3	4
Team			8		
Totals	30-75	18-29	49	19	78

Houston	fg-fga	ft-fta	rb	pf	tp
Dwight Davis	5-18	9-14	10	5	19
Steve Newsome	4-13	2- 2	11	4	10
Bob Hall	5- 8	3- 5	17	2	13
Jerry Bonney	1- 2	2- 2	1	2	4
Poo Welch	13-22	2- 2	5	4	28
Larry Brown	0- 1	0- 0	0	1	0
Sonny Willis	1- 3	0- 1	1	2	2
Gene Bodden	0- 1	1- 3	3	2	1
Team			10		
Totals	29-68	19-29	58	22	77

Half time: Houston 37-36. Officials: Honzo and Woolridge. Attendance: 10,550.

at Wichita, Kansas

Houston	fg-fga	ft-fta	rb	pf	tp
Poo Welch	13-30	12-18	4	3	38
Dwight Davis	8-14	2- 2	13	4	18
Steve Newsome	12-16	5- 9	8	5	29
Bob Hall	9-16	2- 3	15	2	20
Jerry Bonney	4- 6	0- 1	4	3	8
Sonny Willis	0- 0	2- 3	1	1	2
Gene Bodden	1- 2	2- 3	3	4	4
Team			7		
Totals	47-84	25-39	55	22	119

Notre Dame	fg-fga	ft-fta	rb	pf	tp
Austin Carr	17-40	13-17	12	3	47
Jackie Meehan	1- 7	0- 1	1	5	2
Sid Catlett	7-11	2- 3	10	1	16
Collis Jones	8-17	9- 9	22	4	25
John Pleick	1- 9	2- 2	5	3	4
Doug Gemmell	3-10	1- 1	3	4	7
John Egart	1- 1	0- 0	0	1	2
Tom Sinnott	1- 7	1- 3	6	5	3
Team			7		
Totals	39-102	28-36	66	25	106

Half time: Houston 62-50. Officials: Diehl and Hermjek.

at Wichita, Kansas

Drake	fg-fga	ft-fta	rb	pf	tp
Al Sakys	2- 4	0- 1	5	5	4
Tom Bush	6- 9	4- 6	15	5	16
Bobby Jones	5-14	0- 0	5	3	10
Jeff Halliburton	8-20	1- 4	7	3	17
Leon Huff	8-14	4- 5	4	5	20
Dave Wicklund	0- 1	1- 1	2	0	1
Jim Nordrum	1- 1	0- 0	1	0	2
Tony Johnson	0- 1	1- 2	0	0	1
Team			5		
Totals	30-64	11-19	44	23	71

Kansas	fg-fga	ft-fta	rb	pf	tp
Bud Stallworth	6-13	1- 3	3	5	13
Aubrey Nash	2- 4	2- 3	3	4	6
Dave Robisch	10-18	7- 9	10	3	27
Pierre Russell	0- 3	3- 5	5	5	3
Roger Brown	6-10	3- 5	9	1	15
Bob Kivisto	2- 4	5- 7	2	0	9
Randy Canfield	0- 0	0- 0	1	2	0
Mark Mathews	0- 0	0- 1	0	0	0
Team			4		
Totals	26-52	21-33	37	20	73

Half time: Drake 38-30. Officials: Honzo and Woolridge. Attendance: 10,550.

West First Round

at Logan, Utah

Weber State	fg-fga	ft-fta	rb	pf	tp
Willie Sojourner	4-10	1- 1	10	5	9
Bob Davis	3-16	0- 1	9	3	6
Brady Small	2-16	2- 2	2	3	6
Jonnie Knoble	3- 8	5- 9	5	3	11
Rich Cooper	5-11	5- 5	5	4	15
Kent Ross	7-13	3- 4	5	1	17
Greg Soter	0- 2	0- 0	0	0	0
Bill Orr	0- 1	2- 2	0	0	2
Team			5		
Totals	24-77	18-24	41	19	66

Long Beach State	fg-fga	ft-fta	rb	pf	tp
George Trapp	8-13	5- 5	5	5	21
Ed Ratleff	10-15	11-12	13	1	31
Chuck Terry	1- 6	1- 1	6	5	3
Eric McWilliams	0- 1	1- 2	3	1	1
Bob Lynn	4-10	4- 5	6	3	12
Bernard Williams	2- 6	3- 3	4	4	7
Dwight Taylor	0- 1	2- 2	0	1	2
Dave McLucas	0- 0	0- 0	0	0	0
Rich Ewasky	0- 0	0- 0	0	0	0
Roy Miller	0- 0	0- 0	0	0	0
Team			11		
Totals	25-52	27-30	48	20	77

Half time: Long Beach State 38-25. Officials: Sharwood and Herrold.

at Logan, Utah

Utah State	fg-fga	ft-fta	rb	pf	tp
Nate Williams	11-21	7- 8	6	5	29
Terry Wakefield	2- 6	0- 0	1	5	4
Lafayette Love	3- 6	1- 2	7	4	7
Robert Lauriski	9-16	2- 2	8	4	20
Marvin Roberts	2- 6	3- 4	3	5	7
Ed Epps	2- 4	3- 3	2	1	7
Jeff Tebbs	0- 2	0- 0	0	2	0
Bryan Pavlish	0- 0	0- 0	0	0	0
Pat Cooley	0- 0	0- 0	0	0	0
Walter Bees	0- 0	0- 0	0	0	0
Ron Hatch	2- 3	2- 2	1	2	6
Ken Thompson	1- 1	0- 0	1	1	2
Team			7		
Totals	32-65	18-21	36	29	82

Brigham Young	fg-fga	ft-fta	rb	pf	tp
Bernie Fryer	6- 8	13-15	5	2	25
Kresimir Cosic	10-19	10-12	11	4	30
Steve Kelly	7-10	4- 5	1	5	18
Jim Miller	1- 3	4- 8	6	4	6
Phil Tollestrup	4- 9	2- 4	2	3	10
Jay Bunker	1- 2	0- 0	1	1	2
Kalevi Sarkalahti	0- 0	0- 0	0	1	0
Dave Bailey	0- 0	0- 0	0	0	0
Clyde Baker	0- 0	0- 0	1	0	0
Craig Jorgensen	0- 0	0- 0	0	0	0
Veikko Vainio	0- 0	0- 0	0	0	0
Team			6		
Totals	29-51	33-44	33	20	91

Half time: Brigham Young 45-40. Officials: Brown and Overby. Attendance: 10,322.

West Regional

at Salt Lake City, Utah

Long Beach State	fg-fga	ft-fta	rb	pf	tp
George Trapp	8-18	7-10	6	3	23
Chuck Terry	9-19	0- 0	9	3	18
Bob Lynn	3- 9	0- 1	7	4	6
Ed Ratleff	5-13	3- 5	10	2	13
Bernard Williams	0- 3	0- 2	4	2	0
Eric McWilliams	3- 6	1- 1	2	5	7
Dwight Taylor	3- 5	5- 6	3	2	11
Team			5		
Totals	31-73	16-25	46	21	78

Pacific	fg-fga	ft-fta	rb	pf	tp
Jim McCargo	3- 9	5- 9	10	5	11
Bernard Dulaney	2- 9	0- 1	6	3	4
John Gianelli	5- 9	6- 8	17	4	16
Bob Thomason	7-22	5- 6	3	2	19
Robbie Sperring	4- 4	5- 6	4	2	13
Paul Scheidegger	1- 3	0- 0	2	1	2
John Joshua	0- 0	0- 0	1	0	0
Pete Jensen	0- 0	0- 0	1	2	0
Ossie Noble	0- 0	0- 0	0	0	0
Pat Douglass	0- 1	0- 0	0	1	0
Team			5		
Totals	22-57	21-30	49	20	65

Half time: Pacific 44-31. Officials: Jones and Stout.

at Salt Lake City, Utah

UCLA	fg-fga	ft-fta	rb	pf	tp
Curtis Rowe	5-11	3- 6	9	0	13
Sidney Wicks	6-16	2- 5	20	1	14
Steve Patterson	6-13	1- 3	11	4	13
Henry Bibby	6-13	3- 3	9	3	15
Kenny Booker	2- 6	0- 0	1	2	4
Terry Schofield	6-13	0- 2	6	3	12
Larry Farmer	5- 9	1- 3	6	0	11
John Ecker	1- 3	0- 0	0	0	2
Rick Betchley	3- 4	1- 1	0	0	7
Team			2		
Totals	40-88	11-23	64	13	91

Brigham Young	fg-fga	ft-fta	rb	pf	tp
Phil Tollestrup	0- 3	1- 2	1	2	1
Steve Kelly	9-16	6- 6	5	1	24
Kresimir Cosic	8-18	2- 2	23	3	18
Bernie Fryer	8-19	2- 6	4	3	18
Jim Miller	4-11	2- 5	5	3	10
Jay Bunker	1- 3	0- 0	5	4	2
Craig Jorgensen	0- 1	0- 0	1	0	0
Kalevi Sarkalahti	0- 0	0- 0	0	0	0
Dave Bailey	0- 1	0- 0	0	1	0
Team			2		
Totals	30-72	13-21	46	17	73

Half time: UCLA 41-32. Officials: White and Strauthers. Attendance: 15,032.

at Salt Lake City, Utah

Brigham Young	fg-fga	ft-fta	rb	pf	tp
Steve Kelly	6-21	4- 6	7	4	16
Phil Tollestrup	2- 7	4- 4	1	4	8
Kresimir Cosic	6- 9	2- 3	13	4	14
Bernie Fryer	6-15	5- 5	3	4	17
Jim Miller	7-14	0- 4	11	4	14
Jay Bunker	4- 7	0- 1	6	5	8
Kalevi Sarkalahti	2- 2	0- 0	1	1	4
Team			3		
Totals	33-75	15-23	45	26	81

Pacific	fg-fga	ft-fta	rb	pf	tp
Bernard Dulaney	4- 5	1- 1	1	3	9
Jim McCargo	2- 7	4- 6	11	4	8
John Gianelli	10-17	4- 6	13	5	24
Robbie Sperring	3- 4	2- 4	2	3	8
Bob Thomason	4-10	3- 5	2	2	11
Paul Scheidegger	2- 6	6- 8	5	1	10
Pat Douglass	4- 5	6- 6	3	1	14
John Joshua	0- 1	0- 0	1	0	0
Pete Jensen	0- 0	0- 0	3	1	0
Team			1		
Totals	29-55	26-36	42	20	84

Half time: Pacific 48-37.

at Salt Lake City, Utah

Long Beach State	fg-fga	ft-fta	rb	pf	tp
George Trapp	5-13	5- 6	16	3	15
Chuck Terry	4- 4	3- 4	6	3	11
Bob Lynn	3-10	1- 3	5	4	7
Bernard Williams	1- 7	0- 0	4	3	2
Ed Ratleff	8-14	2- 4	4	5	18
Eric McWilliams	0- 1	0- 0	2	2	0
Dwight Taylor	0- 2	2- 4	2	2	2
Team			2		
Totals	21-51	13-21	41	22	55

UCLA	fg-fga	ft-fta	rb	pf	tp
Curtis Rowe	3- 6	6-12	12	2	12
Sidney Wicks	5-13	8-12	15	4	18
Steve Patterson	2- 8	1- 1	5	2	5
Henry Bibby	4-18	3- 3	6	4	11
Kenny Booker	0- 4	0- 0	2	0	0
Terry Schofield	3- 9	0- 0	3	1	6
Larry Farmer	0- 3	1- 2	4	2	1
Rick Betchley	1- 1	2- 2	0	0	4
John Ecker	0- 0	0- 0	0	1	0
Team			4		
Totals	18-62	21-32	51	16	57

Half time: Long Beach State 31-27. Attendance: 14,003.

Semifinals

at Houston, Texas

Western Kentucky	fg-fga	ft-fta	rb	pf	tp
Clarence Glover	5-15	2- 4	20	4	12
Jerry Dunn	11-33	3- 6	8	5	25
Jim McDaniels	10-24	2- 4	17	5	22
Jim Rose	8-21	2- 3	8	2	18
Rex Bailey	5-11	2- 3	8	1	12
Chuck Witt	0- 1	0- 0	0	3	0
Gary Sundmacker	0- 0	0- 0	0	1	0
Team			8		
Totals	39-105	11-20	69	21	89

Villanova	fg-fga	ft-fta	rb	pf	tp
Clarence Smith	5-14	3-6	11	1	13
Howard Porter	10-20	2-3	16	4	22
H. Siemiontkowski	11-20	9-10	15	5	31
Tom Ingelsby	5-10	4-7	4	1	14
Chris Ford	3-6	2-2	1	4	8
Joe McDowell	2-3	0-3	3	1	4
Team			4		
Totals	36-73	20-31	54	16	92

Half time: Western Kentucky 38-35. Regulation Score: 74-74. First Overtime: 85-85. Officials: Bain and Brown.

at Houston, Texas

Kansas	fg-fga	ft-fta	rb	pf	tp
Dave Robisch	7-19	3-6	6	3	17
Pierre Russell	5-12	2-2	4	4	12
Roger Brown	3-8	1-3	9	4	7
Bud Stallworth	5-10	2-4	5	5	12
Aubrey Nash	3-9	1-2	3	1	7
Bob Kivisto	1-1	1-4	1	2	3
Randy Canfield	0-0	0-0	0	1	0
Mark Williams	0-1	2-2	0	2	2
Mark Mathews	0-0	0-0	0	0	0
Greg Douglas	0-0	0-0	1	0	0
Team			3		
Totals	24-60	12-23	32	22	60

UCLA	fg-fga	ft-fta	rb	pf	tp
Curtis Rowe	7-10	2-4	15	2	16
Sidney Wicks	5-9	11-13	8	2	21
Steve Patterson	3-11	0-0	6	2	6
Henry Bibby	6-9	6-6	4	3	18
Kenny Booker	1-2	1-2	5	3	3
Terry Schofield	1-3	0-1	0	3	2
Larry Farmer	0-2	0-1	2	1	0
Rick Betchley	0-0	0-1	0	0	0
John Ecker	0-1	2-2	1	0	2
Andy Hill	0-0	0-0	0	0	0
Jon Chapman	0-0	0-0	1	2	0
Team			5		
Totals	23-47	22-30	47	18	68

Half time: UCLA 32-25. Officials: White and Honzo. Attendance: 31,428.

National Third Place

at Houston, Texas

Western Kentucky	fg-fga	ft-fta	rb	pf	tp
Clarence Glover	3-8	4-5	13	5	10
Jerry Dunn	3-13	4-6	10	3	10
Jim McDaniels	14-30	8-10	19	4	36
Jim Rose	4-12	3-4	2	3	11
Rex Bailey	3-11	1-2	5	2	7
Gary Sundmacker	1-1	0-1	1	1	2
Chuck Witt	0-1	0-1	1	3	0
Steve Eaton	0-0	1-2	0	0	1
Danny Johnson	0-0	0-0	1	0	0
Team			4		
Totals	28-76	21-31	56	21	77

Kansas	fg-fga	ft-fta	rb	pf	tp
Dave Robisch	9-21	5-8	9	4	23
Pierre Russell	4-10	0-1	7	1	8
Roger Brown	7-16	2-3	16	3	16
Bud Stallworth	3-13	4-8	14	4	10
Aubrey Nash	4-14	2-3	7	3	10
Bob Kivisto	2-3	0-1	2	1	4
Randy Canfield	1-6	2-3	5	5	4
Team			7		
Totals	30-83	15-27	67	21	75

Half time: Western Kentucky 38-27. Officials: Honzo and White.

Championship

at Houston, Texas

Villanova	fg-fga	ft-fta	rb	pf	tp
Clarence Smith	4-11	1-1	2	4	9
Howard Porter	10-21	5-6	8	1	25
H. Siemiontkowski	9-16	1-2	6	3	19
Tom Ingelsby	3-9	1-1	4	2	7
Chris Ford	0-4	2-3	5	4	2
Joe McDowell	0-1	0-0	2	0	0
John Fox	0-0	0-0	0	0	0
Team			4		
Totals	26-62	10-13	31	14	62

UCLA	fg-fga	ft-fta	rb	pf	tp
Curtis Rowe	2-3	4-5	8	0	8
Sidney Wicks	3-7	1-1	9	2	7
Steve Patterson	13-18	3-5	8	1	29
Henry Bibby	6-12	5-5	2	1	17
Kenny Booker	0-0	0-0	0	0	0
Terry Schofield	3-9	0-0	1	4	6
Rick Betchley	0-0	1-2	1	1	1
Team			5		
Totals	27-49	14-18	34	9	68

Half time: UCLA 45-37. Officials: Bain and Brown. Attendance: 31,765.

1972

First Round

at Williamsburg, Virginia

Temple	fg-fga	ft-fta	rb	pf	tp
Ollie Johnson	7-16	2-4	8	1	16
Mike Jones	4-8	1-2	7	2	9
Joe Newman	3-13	2-3	5	4	8
Rick Trudeau	2-5	1-2	3	0	5
John Kneib	3-8	3-3	4	1	9
Paul Collins	1-2	0-0	1	0	2
Lee Tress	1-5	0-0	3	4	2
Team			7		
Totals	21-57	9-14	38	12	51

South Carolina	fg-fga	ft-fta	rb	pf	tp
Rick Aydlett	1-6	1-1	1	1	3
Tom Riker	9-14	5-8	5	2	23
Danny Traylor	5-5	1-3	10	4	11
Bob Carver	2-3	0-0	2	1	4
Kevin Joyce	6-14	0-1	7	1	12
Brian Winters	0-3	0-0	1	2	0
Team			4		
Totals	23-45	7-13	30	11	53

Half time: Temple 29-25. Officials: Phillips and Honzo. Attendance: 6,000.

at Princeton, New Jersey

Villanova	fg-fga	ft-fta	rb	pf	tp
Ed Hastings	2-7	5-7	5	3	9
Tom Ingelsby	8-18	2-2	5	2	18
H. Siemiontkowski	6-15	0-0	8	2	12
Chris Ford	11-19	2-5	4	1	24
Larry Moody	8-13	4-5	10	4	20
Bob Gohl	0-0	2-2	0	0	2
Dimitrus Alston	0-1	0-0	0	0	0
Joe McDowell	0-1	0-0	0	1	0
John Gaspar	0-1	0-0	0	0	0
Team			8		
Totals	35-75	15-21	40	13	85

East Carolina	fg-fga	ft-fta	rb	pf	tp
Al Faber	5-11	1-1	14	2	11
Jim Fairley	5-10	6-9	9	3	16
Dave Franklin	9-15	1-3	5	1	19
Jerome Owens	5-10	3-3	2	2	13
Earl Quash	2-6	1-2	2	3	5
Nicky White	2-7	0-0	2	2	4
Ernie Pope	0-1	0-0	1	0	0
Greg Crouse	0-2	0-0	1	0	0
Ray Peszko	0-1	2-2	1	0	2
Team			10		
Totals	28-63	14-20	47	13	70

Half time: Villanova 38-36. Officials: Wooldrige and Grossman. Attendance: 6,600.

at Jamaica, New York

Pennsylvania	fg-fga	ft-fta	rb	pf	tp
Corky Calhoun	8-9	3-9	6	1	19
Phil Hankinson	6-11	2-2	4	3	14
Bob Morse	9-16	1-1	9	3	19
Alan Cotler	3-4	0-0	1	2	6
Craig Littlepage	4-5	3-4	2	1	11
John Jablonski	1-1	0-1	0	0	2
Ron Billingslea	2-3	0-0	2	0	4
Bill Finger	0-0	1-2	0	0	1
Team			7		
Totals	33-49	10-16	31	10	76

Providence	fg-fga	ft-fta	rb	pf	tp
Ernie DiGregorio	8-15	1-2	2	2	17
Marvin Barnes	3-10	1-2	6	2	7
Charles Crawford	2-3	1-1	6	3	5
Donald Lewis	4-8	0-0	3	2	8
Nehru King	1-4	0-0	2	0	2
Francis Costello	8-18	4-5	4	4	20
Larry Ketvirtis	0-1	1-3	4	0	1
Team			2		
Totals	26-59	8-13	29	13	60

Half time: Providence 31-27. Officials: DeBonis and Folsom. Attendance: 6,007.

East Regional

at Morgantown, West Virginia

North Carolina	fg-fga	ft-fta	rb	pf	tp
Bill Chamberlain	3-6	4-5	4	1	10
Dennis Wuycik	4-11	8-10	5	3	16
Robert McAdoo	4-14	3-6	13	3	11
Steve Previs	5-8	3-4	5	3	13
George Karl	8-12	2-3	3	4	18
Kim Huband	2-5	4-4	4	3	8
Bobby Jones	1-3	3-4	9	2	5
Ray Hite	2-2	0-0	1	0	4
Don Johnston	0-1	0-0	2	2	0
Craig Corson	0-0	0-0	0	2	0
Bill Chambers	2-3	3-4	1	0	7
Team			5		
Totals	31-65	30-40	52	23	92

South Carolina	fg-fga	ft-fta	rb	pf	tp
Tom Riker	4-13	2-4	10	4	10
Rick Aydlett	2-4	2-2	4	4	6
Danny Traylor	3-6	3-4	2	4	9
Kevin Joyce	6-18	9-9	7	5	21
Bob Carver	2-6	2-2	2	3	6
Brian Winters	4-11	1-1	3	5	9
Rick Mousa	1-4	1-4	4	1	3
Casey Manning	0-3	3-3	2	0	3
Jimmy Powell	0-2	0-0	1	0	0
Billy Grimes	1-1	0-1	1	0	2
Team			8		
Totals	23-68	23-30	44	26	69

Half time: North Carolina 51-32. Officials: Bain and Lawson.

at Morgantown, West Virginia

Villanova	fg-fga	ft-fta	rb	pf	tp
Chris Ford	6-11	2-3	4	3	14
H. Siemiontkowski	6-11	10-12	11	1	22
Larry Moody	2-4	0-1	3	4	4
Tom Ingelsby	8-19	5-5	6	2	21
Ed Hastings	3-3	0-0	2	4	6
Joe McDowell	0-1	0-0	0	1	0
Bob Gohl	0-0	0-0	0	1	0
Team			4		
Totals	25-49	17-21	30	16	67

Pennsylvania	fg-fga	ft-fta	rb	pf	tp
Bob Morse	8-18	4-4	9	0	20
Phil Hankinson	10-19	2-2	6	2	22
Craig Littlepage	2-4	2-3	4	4	6
Corky Calhoun	8-11	5-5	7	4	21
Alan Cotler	3-7	3-4	1	3	9
Ron Billingslea	0-1	0-0	1	2	0
John Jablonski	0-2	0-2	0	2	0
Team			5		
Totals	31-62	16-20	33	17	78

Half time: Pennsylvania 38-31. Officials: Scott and Smith. Attendance: 10,430.

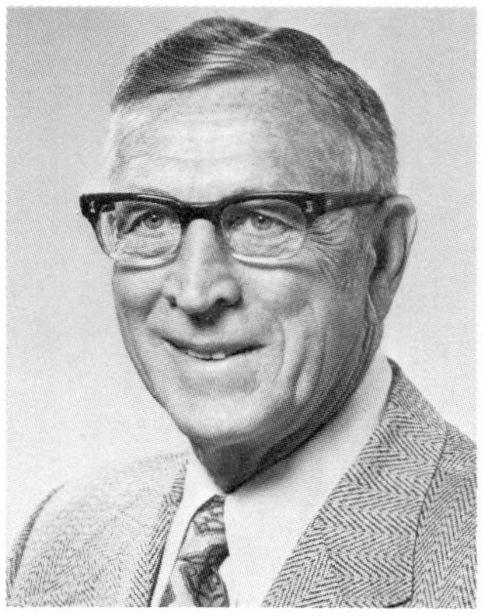

John Wooden

at Morgantown, West Virginia

Villanova	fg-fga	ft-fta	rb	pf	tp
Chris Ford	7-19	5-8	6	4	19
H. Siemiontkowski	11-22	4-5	10	2	26
Larry Moody	4-8	1-2	9	4	9
Tom Ingelsby	5-12	1-3	6	3	11
Ed Hastings	3-5	1-1	5	4	7
Joe McDowell	2-2	0-0	1	2	4
Bob Gohl	1-3	0-0	3	1	2
Mike Daly	0-0	0-0	1	1	0
Team			2		
Totals	33-71	12-19	43	21	78

South Carolina	fg-fga	ft-fta	rb	pf	tp
Tom Riker	14-22	8-11	16	1	36
Rick Aydlett	2-8	3-3	3	4	7
Danny Traylor	7-12	1-6	7	4	15
Kevin Joyce	6-12	7-8	7	1	19
Bob Carver	3-3	3-3	1	2	9
Brian Winters	1-2	0-0	0	2	2
Casey Manning	1-1	0-0	0	0	2
Rick Mousa	0-0	0-0	0	1	0
Team			3		
Totals	34-60	22-31	37	15	90

Half time: Villanova 43-38. Officials: Lawson and Smith.

at Morgantown, West Virginia

Pennsylvania	fg-fga	ft-fta	rb	pf	tp
Bob Morse	5-14	4-6	6	4	14
Phil Hankinson	5-19	2-2	9	5	12
Craig Littlepage	1-1	2-4	4	4	4
Corky Calhoun	3-8	1-2	7	2	7
Alan Cotler	2-7	6-6	1	4	10
Ron Billingslea	5-7	2-3	3	4	12
Whitey Varga	0-0	0-0	1	0	0
Team			4		
Totals	21-56	17-23	35	23	59

North Carolina	fg-fga	ft-fta	rb	pf	tp
Bill Chamberlain	2-6	3-3	2	1	7
Dennis Wuycik	7-12	4-5	4	4	18
Robert McAdoo	5-10	7-10	9	0	17
Steve Previs	1-3	0-0	5	1	2
George Karl	5-9	6-7	1	4	16
Kim Huband	2-3	3-3	2	4	7
Ray Hite	0-0	0-0	0	1	0
Bobby Jones	2-4	0-1	6	3	4
Craig Corson	0-0	0-0	1	0	0
Don Johnston	0-0	0-0	1	0	0
Bill Chambers	1-1	0-0	2	0	2
Team			2		
Totals	25-48	23-29	35	18	73

Half time: North Carolina 37-35. Officials: Bain and Scott. Attendance: 10,078.

Mideast First Round

at Knoxville, Tennessee

Marquette	fg-fga	ft-fta	rb	pf	tp
George Frazier	6-8	3-4	7	3	15
Bob Lackey	8-16	4-4	7	3	20
Larry McNeill	9-16	4-4	9	4	22
Marcus Washington	2-7	0-2	4	2	4
Allie McGuire	3-7	0-0	4	2	6
Kurt Spychalla	1-2	0-1	0	0	2
Mark Ostrand	1-2	0-0	0	0	2
Gary Grzesk	0-0	0-0	0	1	0
Mike Mills	1-1	0-0	2	0	2
Team			7		
Totals	31-59	11-15	40	15	73

Ohio	fg-fga	ft-fta	rb	pf	tp
Tom Riccardi	2-11	1-1	4	2	5
Bill Brown	4-6	2-2	4	1	10
Dave Ball	2-7	0-0	2	1	4
Tom Corde	2-7	1-3	2	0	5
Todd Lalich	4-8	2-4	6	4	10
Bob Howell	3-9	1-2	0	2	7
Denny Rusch	1-5	6-7	7	4	8
Denny Thompson	0-1	0-0	0	0	0
Team			8		
Totals	18-54	13-19	33	14	49

Half time: Marquette 38-20. Officials: Brodbeck and Ballaban.

1972 UCLA BRUINS—(l-r) Front Row: Les Friedman; Second Row: John Wooden, Ducky Drake, Gary Cunningham; Third Row: Tommy Curtis, Greg Lee, Larry Hollyfield, Jon Chapman, Keith Wilkes, Bill Walton, Swen Nater, Vince Carson, Larry Farmer, Gary Franklin, Andy Hill, Henry Bibby.

at Knoxville, Tennessee

Florida	fg-fga	ft-fta	rb	pf	tp
Rowland Garrett..	3-11	0-2	10	4	6
Lawrence McCray.	4-5	3-4	4	4	11
Reggie Royals...	4-6	4-6	8	5	12
Ron King	3-13	4-7	2	2	10
Greg Samuel	0-0	0-0	1	0	0
Ron Harris	5-11	3-4	8	1	13
Otto Petty	5-8	5-6	2	3	15
Larry Gay	3-3	0-1	3	0	6
Otis Cole	3-9	4-6	7	0	10
Team			12		
Totals	30-66	23-36	57	19	83

Eastern Kentucky	fg-fga	ft-fta	rb	pf	tp
Daryl Dunagan	3-10	8-10	15	3	14
Charlie Mitchell	10-18	3-5	4	4	23
Dan Argabright	7-10	0-1	2	5	14
George Bryant	4-16	3-4	4	3	11
Billy Burton	2-3	1-2	4	5	5
Roberts Brooks.	1-2	1-3	2	1	3
Wade Upchurch	1-2	1-2	1	1	3
Bobby Newell	1-2	0-0	0	1	2
Chuck Worthington	0-0	2-2	1	1	2
Charlie Brunker	2-7	0-0	1	3	4
Team			7		
Totals	31-70	19-29	41	27	81

Half time: Florida State 50-42. Officials: Bennett and Bennett. Attendance: 4,500.

Mideast Regional

at Dayton, Ohio

Marquette	fg-fga	ft-fta	rb	pf	tp
Allie McGuire	3-15	2-2	1	0	8
Larry McNeill	3-10	3-4	8	5	9
Bob Lackey	8-14	5-7	6	4	21
George Frazier	4-5	0-0	6	3	8
Marcus Washington	6-24	2-4	4	5	14
Mike Mills	3-5	1-1	7	1	7
Mark Ostrand	0-0	0-0	0	1	0
Kurt Spychalla	1-3	0-0	3	5	2
Guy Lam	0-2	0-0	0	0	0
Team			2		
Totals	28-78	13-18	37	24	69

Kentucky	fg-fga	ft-fta	rb	pf	tp
Tom Parker	3-5	6-8	9	3	12
Ronnie Lyons	6-16	5-7	8	1	17
Larry Stamper	7-10	3-5	11	2	17
Stan Key	4-5	6-6	5	0	14
Jim Andrews	5-11	7-7	16	3	17
Bob McCowen	0-0	0-0	0	1	0
Rick Drewitz	3-4	0-0	2	2	6
Team			2		
Totals	28-51	29-34	46	13	85

Half time: Marquette 34-33. Officials: Brown and Evans.

at Dayton, Ohio

Florida State	fg-fga	ft-fta	rb	pf	tp
Greg Samuel	0-1	1-1	0	1	1
Rowland Garrett	11-19	1-1	11	3	23
Reggie Royals	4-9	3-6	11	4	11
Ron King	5-11	1-3	5	1	11
Lawrence McCray.	1-2	0-1	8	1	2
Ron Harris	5-7	0-1	2	0	10
Otto Petty	0-8	2-3	1	1	2
Otis Cole	3-5	4-4	1	1	10
Team			3		
Totals	29-62	12-20	42	12	70

Minnesota	fg-fga	ft-fta	rb	pf	tp
Bob Nix	1-12	4-5	1	2	6
Keith Young	3-12	1-1	5	5	7
Dave Winfield	2-8	4-5	8	3	8
Clyde Turner	8-17	3-4	12	3	19
Jim Brewer	5-11	0-0	14	1	10
Bob Murphy	3-6	0-0	3	2	6
Team			3		
Totals	22-66	12-15	46	16	56

Half time: Florida State 35-29. Officials: Vidal and Filiberti. Attendance: 13,458.

at Dayton, Ohio

Minnesota	fg-fga	ft-fta	rb	pf	tp
Bob Nix	1-3	2-2	3	2	4
Keith Young	8-15	2-2	6	2	18
Dave Winfield	4-7	8-11	9	1	16
Clyde Turner	12-25	1-3	5	4	25
Jim Brewer	5-12	4-4	22	4	14
Bob Murphy	0-2	0-0	0	0	0
Team			2		
Totals	30-64	17-22	47	13	77

Marquette	fg-fga	ft-fta	rb	pf	tp
Allie McGuire	5-11	0-0	4	2	10
Larry McNeill	10-21	4-4	10	4	24
Mike Mills	2-8	3-5	9	3	7
Bob Lackey	3-15	7-8	12	4	13
Marcus Washington	9-24	0-0	8	0	18
Kurt Spychalla	0-1	0-0	1	0	0
Guy Lam	0-0	0-0	1	0	0
Mark Ostrand	0-1	0-0	0	0	0
Team			3		
Totals	29-81	14-17	47	14	72

Half time: Minnesota 47-39. Officials: Vidal and Evans.

at Dayton, Ohio

Kentucky	fg-fga	ft-fta	rb	pf	tp
Tom Parker	5-13	0-1	6	3	10
Ronnie Lyons	5-13	0-0	2	3	10
Larry Stamper	2-6	5-7	9	2	9
Stan Key	1-4	0-0	1	3	2
Jim Andrews	7-14	3-3	11	1	17
Bob McCowan	2-4	1-1	2	4	5
Rick Drewitz	0-0	1-1	0	0	1
Team			2		
Totals	22-54	10-13	33	16	54

Florida State	fg-fga	ft-fta	rb	pf	tp
Greg Samuel	1-2	1-1	1	0	3
Rowland Garrett	2-4	1-1	3	2	5
Reggie Royals	4-13	4-5	12	3	12
Ron King	9-19	4-4	8	0	22
Lawrence McCray	6-13	0-2	5	3	12
Ron Harris	3-7	0-0	5	3	6
Otto Petty	2-5	9-9	6	2	13
Otis Cole	0-1	0-0	0	0	0
Team			2		
Totals	27-64	19-22	42	13	73

Half time: Florida State 34-28. Officials: Brown and Filiberti. Attendance: 13,458.

Midwest First Round

at Las Cruces, New Mexico

Marshall	fg-fga	ft-fta	rb	pf	tp
Mike D'Antoni	9-22	8-11	9	3	26
Bill James	4-14	0-0	6	3	8
Tyrone Collins	4-18	3-3	6	3	11
Barry Driscoll.	2-7	3-6	7	3	7
Gary Orsini	2-3	0-4	4	5	4
Randy Noll	10-19	1-3	16	5	21
Russell Lee	11-29	2-3	16	4	24
John Sark	0-0	0-0	1	0	0
Team			3		
Totals	42-112	17-30	68	26	101

SW Louisiana	fg-fga	ft-fta	rb	pf	tp
Dwight Lamar	12-31	11-15	5	0	35
Steve Greene	0-1	0-0	1	1	0
Jerry Bisbano	7-12	5-7	7	3	19
Mike Haney	0-0	1-2	3	4	1
Wayne Herbert	1-1	0-0	0	0	2
Fred Saunders	0-1	3-4	9	5	3
Payton Townsend	3-6	3-5	5	2	9
Wilbert Loftin	5-6	0-1	11	4	10
Roy Ebron	14-22	5-7	20	3	33
Team			5		
Totals	42-80	28-41	66	22	112

Half time: Southwestern Louisiana 55-52. Officials: Copeland and Wortman.

at Las Cruces, New Mexico

Texas	fg-fga	ft-fta	rb	pf	tp
Eric Groscurth	3-6	4-5	11	4	10
Jack Louis	3-5	0-1	1	5	6
Joe Lenox	4-11	8-12	2	3	16
Jimmy Blacklock	0-0	2-2	1	0	2
B. G. Brosterhous	6-13	1-1	12	3	13
Harry Larrabee	3-6	9-11	5	2	15
Larry Robinson	9-16	5-6	14	2	23
Lynn Howden	0-0	0-0	0	1	0
Team			5		
Totals	28-57	29-38	51	20	85

Houston	fg-fga	ft-fta	rb	pf	tp
Randy Kightl	0-0	0-0	0	1	0
Donnell Hayes	2-6	0-0	4	4	4
Jerry Bonney	1-7	1-2	2	0	3
Dwight Jones	3-10	2-5	9	4	8
Sonny Willis	1-2	0-0	1	2	2
Clay Hoster	1-2	0-0	0	1	2
Larry Brown	0-1	1-2	0	2	1
Doug Worrell	0-2	0-0	1	2	0
Dwight Davis	11-22	3-7	7	5	25
Sidney Edwards	1-3	1-2	1	0	3
Steve Newsome	10-22	6-8	17	4	26
Team			8		
Totals	30-77	14-26	46	25	74

Half time: Texas 45-33. Officials: Shosid and Galvan. Attendance: 4,336.

Midwest Regional

at Ames, Iowa

Louisville	fg-fga	ft-fta	rb	pf	tp
Ron Thomas	8-12	3-10	13	4	19
Mike Lawhon	5-6	3-6	10	3	13
Al Vilcheck	5-6	3-6	10	3	13
Jim Price	10-15	5-6	2	2	25
Henry Bacon	5-9	1-2	6	0	11
Ken Bradley	2-6	2-2	5	1	6
Larry Carter	2-6	0-1	1	2	4
Totals	34-60	20-33	39	15	88

SW Louisiana	fg-fga	ft-fta	rb	pf	tp
Fred Saunders	2-10	0-1	11	4	4
Wilbert Loftin	5-7	2-2	10	4	12
Roy Ebron	3-10	5-5	12	4	11
Dwight Lamar	14-42	1-3	0	2	29
Jerry Bisbano	6-13	3-4	5	4	15
Payton Townsend	4-6	2-3	7	3	10
Mike Haney	1-5	1-2	5	1	3
Steve Greene	0-1	0-0	1	1	0
Totals	35-94	14-20	52	24	84

Half time: Southwestern Louisiana 44-39. Officials: Hernjack and Saar.

at Ames, Iowa

Texas	fg-fga	ft-fta	rb	pf	tp
Larry Robinson	10-14	2-3	3	3	22
Eric Groscurth	0-5	0-1	5	2	0
B. G. Brosterhous	4-8	2-5	4	4	10
Joe Lenox	6-12	2-3	2	4	14
Harry Larrabee	2-10	1-1	8	5	5
Jack Louis	2-5	0-1	5	1	4
Totals	24-54	7-14	27	19	55

Kansas State	fg-fga	ft-fta	rb	pf	tp
Ernie Kusnyer	5-9	2-5	6	3	12
Bob Zender	2-6	2-2	9	2	6
David Hall	4-6	5-6	12	3	13
Lon Kruger	4-9	3-4	3	1	11
Danny Beard	8-18	4-7	2	1	20
Larry Williams	1-4	0-0	4	2	2
Steve Mitchell	1-2	0-0	2	2	2
Totals	25-54	16-24	38	14	66

Half time: Kansas State 36-25. Officials: Stout and Grossman. Attendance: 10,000.

at Ames, Iowa

SW Louisiana	fg-fga	ft-fta	rb	pf	tp
Wilbert Loftin	6-10	1-1	9	4	13
Fred Saunders	1-5	1-1	7	2	3
Roy Ebron	8-12	3-4	12	2	19
Dwight Lamar	15-32	6-7	2	1	36
Jerry Bisbano	7-10	0-2	7	3	14
Payton Townsend	3-3	1-1	7	4	7
Mike Haney	0-1	0-1	5	2	0
Steve Greene	1-4	3-3	2	2	5
Denny Wright	1-2	1-1	1	2	3
Steve Caldwell	0-0	0-0	0	2	0
Totals	42-79	16-21	52	24	100

Texas	fg-fga	ft-fta	rb	pf	tp
Jimmy Blacklock	3-5	1-3	6	3	7
Eric Groscurth	6-11	9-10	9	3	21
B. G. Brosterhous	5-13	4-6	18	4	14
Joe Lenox	5-17	5-6	1	3	15
Harry Larrabee	1-4	2-4	4	1	4
Jack Louis	1-7	2-6	4	0	4
Steve Slaton	1-3	1-1	0	3	3
Jerry Brooks	0-1	0-0	0	0	0
George Stacy	0-0	2-2	0	0	2
Totals	22-60	26-38	42	17	70

Half time: Southwestern Louisiana 43-29. Officials: Saar and Stout.

at Ames, Iowa

Louisville	fg-fga	ft-fta	rb	pf	tp
Ron Thomas	6-10	6-10	14	4	18
Mike Lawhon	3-8	4-5	7	1	10
Al Vilcheck	4-9	0-0	7	5	8
Henry Bacon	4-10	0-3	5	3	8
Jim Price	11-16	3-4	0	1	25
Larry Carter	0-1	0-0	0	1	0
Bill Bunton	1-1	1-1	6	1	3
Ken Bradley	0-2	0-0	0	0	0
Totals	29-57	14-23	39	16	72

Kansas State	fg-fga	ft-fta	rb	pf	tp
Ernie Kusnyer	4-6	5-5	6	4	13
Bob Zender	2-6	0-1	4	1	4
David Hall	4-9	0-0	2	10	8
Lon Kruger	3-8	8-9	2	4	14
Danny Beard	4-9	0-1	2	4	8
Bob Chipman	0-1	0-2	0	1	0
Steve Mitchell	3-7	0-0	5	1	6
Larry Williams	6-8	0-1	3	1	12
Lindbergh White	0-2	0-0	0	0	0
Totals	26-56	13-21	32	19	65

Half time: Louisville 42-26. Officials: Hernjack and Grossman. Attendance: 10,000.

West First Round

at Pocatello, Idaho

Weber State	fg-fga	ft-fta	rb	pf	tp
Brady Small	6-11	9-10	5	1	21
Bob Davis	12-22	8-10	13	3	32
Jonnie Knoble	4-14	6-10	14	3	14
Richard Cooper	2- 5	4- 7	9	1	8
Wes VanDyke	2- 4	1- 3	3	4	5
Kelly McGarry	0- 0	0- 1	1	0	0
Ralph Williams	0- 0	1- 3	0	0	1
Greg Soter	1- 2	2- 3	0	1	4
Ken Gubler	0- 1	0- 0	0	0	0
Rick Camac	0- 1	2- 4	5	1	2
Riley Wimberley	1- 3	0- 1	2	1	2
Dave Muirbrook	1- 2	0- 0	1	1	2
Team			6		
Totals	29-65	33-52	59	16	91

Hawaii	fg-fga	ft-fta	rb	pf	tp
Dwight Holiday	6-13	2- 3	6	5	14
Jerome Freeman	3-13	5- 5	5	4	11
John Penebacker	3- 9	0- 4	7	5	6
Al Davis	5-13	4- 5	7	5	14
Bob Nash	3-16	1- 4	10	5	7
Mike Kendall	0- 1	2- 2	1	3	2
Mark Skillicorn	0- 1	0- 0	2	0	0
Artie Wilson	0- 2	0- 0	1	0	0
Tyrone Bradshaw	2- 3	0- 0	3	3	4
Mike Blackshire	0- 3	2- 2	1	1	2
Todd Huber	1- 1	0- 0	3	4	2
Charles Williams	1- 3	0- 0	2	0	2
Team			5		
Totals	24-78	16-25	53	35	64

Half time: Weber State 37-30. Officials: Bognaseo and Evans.

at Pocatello, Idaho

Long Beach State	fg-fga	ft-fta	rb	pf	tp
Eric McWilliams	8-14	0- 0	8	5	16
Glenn McDonald	7-14	1- 1	7	0	15
Chuck Terry	4-10	4- 5	4	3	12
Ed Ratleff	8-16	5- 6	5	2	21
Leonard Gray	2-16	3- 5	11	3	7
Lamont King	7- 8	2- 2	4	4	16
Nate Stephens	3-10	2- 4	10	4	8
Team			5		
Totals	39-88	17-23	54	21	95

Brigham Young	fg-fga	ft-fta	rb	pf	tp
Kresimir Cosic	9-20	9- 9	13	3	27
Doug Richards	9-10	6- 6	7	2	24
Brian Ambrozich	4-10	3- 4	13	3	11
Bernie Fryer	6-19	3- 5	3	2	15
Phil Tollestrup	6-15	1- 1	5	5	13
Belmont Anderson	0- 1	0- 0	1	0	0
Kalevi Sarkalahti	0- 0	0- 1	0	0	0
Team			4		
Totals	34-75	22-26	46	15	90

Half time: Brigham Young 49-39. Regulation Score: 79-79. Officials: Brown and Herrold. Attendance: 10,823.

West Regional

at Provo, Utah

Weber State	fg-fga	ft-fta	rb	pf	tp
Bob Davis	4-14	8-13	6	4	16
Wes VanDyke	2-11	0- 1	1	3	4
Richard Cooper	2-10	4- 6	12	4	8
Brady Small	1-12	2- 3	2	0	4
Jonnie Knoble	3- 8	3- 8	9	4	9
Riley Wimberley	7-15	0- 0	5	0	14
Ken Gubler	1- 2	0- 0	1	2	2
Greg Soter	0- 0	1- 2	0	0	1
Ralph Williams	0- 1	0- 0	0	0	0
Team			18		
Totals	20-73	18-33	54	17	58

UCLA	fg-fga	ft-fta	rb	pf	tp
Larry Farmer	7-15	1- 1	7	1	15
Keith Wilkes	4-12	2- 2	13	4	10
Bill Walton	1- 1	2- 5	12	4	4
Greg Lee	3- 8	0- 0	4	1	6
Henry Bibby	7-18	2- 2	3	2	16
Tommy Curtis	3- 7	1- 1	3	2	7
Larry Hollyfield	2- 9	0- 0	5	2	4
Swen Nater	5- 9	2- 4	8	2	12
Vince Carson	0- 3	0- 1	5	2	0
Jon Chapman	1- 1	0- 1	2	1	2
Andy Hill	3- 4	4- 4	1	2	10
Gary Franklin	2- 2	0- 0	2	0	4
Team			11		
Totals	38-89	14-21	76	23	90

Half time: UCLA 42-25. Officials: Copeland and Fouty.

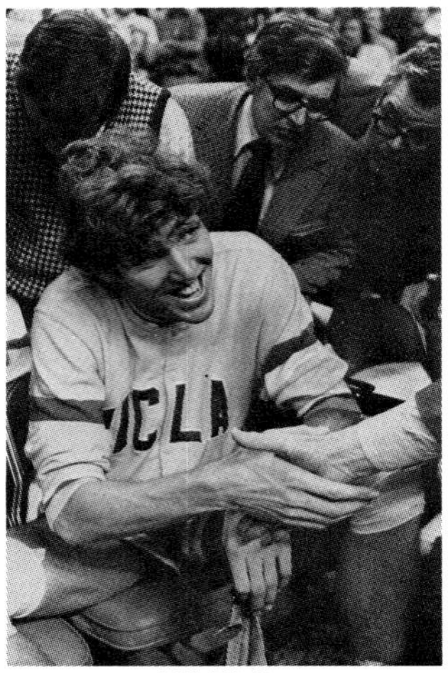

Bill Walton

at Provo, Utah

Long Beach State	fg-fga	ft-fta	rb	pf	tp
Chuck Terry	6-14	4- 4	4	1	16
Glenn McDonald	3-10	2- 3	5	2	8
Leonard Gray	3- 7	0- 0	4	3	6
Ed Ratleff	7-17	2- 3	5	0	16
Eric McWilliams	4-10	3- 5	12	4	11
Nate Stephens	2- 4	0- 1	3	1	4
Lamont King	2- 4	2- 4	1	3	6
Bob Lynn	4- 4	0- 0	5	0	8
Tom Motley	0- 0	0- 0	0	1	0
Roy Miller	0- 1	0- 0	0	0	0
Team			8		
Totals	31-71	13-20	47	15	75

San Francisco	fg-fga	ft-fta	rb	pf	tp
Johnny Burks	3-10	1- 1	9	3	7
Byron Jones	1- 6	2- 4	11	3	4
Kevin Restani	4-16	1- 5	17	4	9
Phil Smith	3-10	2- 2	9	2	8
Mike Quick	7-17	5- 6	0	2	19
John Boro	3- 9	0- 0	3	2	6
Anthony Lewis	0- 1	0- 0	2	1	0
John Hancock	0- 3	0- 0	0	0	0
Ron Centerall	1- 1	0- 0	1	0	2
Team			6		
Totals	22-73	11-18	58	17	55

Half time: Long Beach State 33-22. Officials: Wedge and Wortman. Attendance: 15,247.

at Provo, Utah

San Francisco	fg-fga	ft-fta	rb	pf	tp
Johnny Burks	4-11	2- 2	3	5	10
Byron Jones	5- 5	0- 1	7	4	10
Kevin Restani	1- 7	1- 2	4	3	3
Phil Smith	6-13	5- 7	0	2	17
Mike Quick	8-13	8-10	2	2	24
John Boro	3- 7	4- 7	7	2	10
Ron Centerall	0- 0	0- 0	0	2	0
Team			14		
Totals	27-56	20-29	37	20	74

Weber State	fg-fga	ft-fta	rb	pf	tp
Bob Davis	8-15	5- 7	11	3	21
Jonnie Knoble	6-13	2- 3	6	4	14
Richard Cooper	3-12	1- 2	10	4	7
Brady Small	4- 8	1- 1	3	2	9
Wes VanDyke	2- 4	3- 4	1	4	7
Riley Wimberly	2- 8	2- 3	5	1	6
Greg Soter	0- 2	0- 0	0	0	0
Team			6		
Totals	25-62	14-20	42	18	64

Half time: San Francisco 36-31. Officials: Wedge and Fouty.

at Provo, Utah

Long Beach State	fg-fga	ft-fta	rb	pf	tp
Chuck Terry	2- 6	2- 2	4	4	6
Leonard Gray	2- 5	3- 4	3	4	7
Eric McWilliams	2- 4	3- 3	5	4	7
Glenn McDonald	3- 3	2- 2	5	0	8
Ed Ratleff	7-19	3- 6	3	3	17
Bob Lynn	2- 6	2- 2	8	2	6
Nate Stephens	1- 5	0- 0	3	1	2
Lamont King	2- 2	0- 0	0	3	4
Team			2		
Totals	21-50	15-19	33	21	57

UCLA	fg-fga	ft-fta	rb	pf	tp
Keith Wilkes	4-10	6- 7	6	3	14
Larry Farmer	2- 7	1- 3	3	3	5
Bill Walton	7-10	5- 7	11	3	19
Greg Lee	2- 6	2- 3	3	0	6
Henry Bibby	10-17	3- 4	4	2	23
Larry Hollyfield	0- 1	0- 0	0	2	0
Swen Nater	2- 2	1- 2	1	0	5
Tommy Curtis	0- 0	0- 0	0	1	0
Vince Carson	0- 0	0- 0	1	1	0
Andy Hill	0- 0	1- 3	0	0	1
Team			7		
Totals	27-53	19-29	36	15	73

Half time: UCLA 34-23. Officials: Copeland and Wortman. Attendance: 15,152.

Semifinals

at Los Angeles, California

North Carolina	fg-fga	ft-fta	rb	pf	tp
Bobby Jones	4- 8	1- 1	9	3	9
Dennis Wuycik	7-16	6- 6	6	4	20
Robert McAdoo	10-19	4- 5	15	5	24
Steve Previs	1- 5	3- 6	3	4	5
George Karl	5-14	1- 3	6	3	11
Kim Huband	0- 1	0- 0	2	2	0
Bill Chamberlain	2- 5	2- 3	10	4	6
Don Johnston	0- 1	0- 0	0	1	0
Billy Chambers	0- 1	0- 1	0	1	0
Team			1		
Totals	29-70	17-25	52	27	75

Florida State	fg-fga	ft-fta	rb	pf	tp
Rowland Garrett	4- 8	3- 7	5	4	11
Ron King	6-17	10-10	5	1	22
Reggie Royals	6- 8	6- 7	10	5	18
Lawrence McCray	3- 6	3- 6	9	3	9
Greg Samuel	2- 4	1- 4	1	0	5
Ron Harris	1- 6	2- 2	4	2	4
Otto Petty	3- 5	4- 7	1	5	10
Larry Gay	0- 1	0- 0	0	0	0
Team			6		
Totals	25-55	29-43	41	20	79

Half time: Florida State 45-32. Officials: Scott and Brown.

at Los Angeles, California

Louisville	fg-fga	ft-fta	rb	pf	tp
Mike Lawhon	0- 7	1- 2	3	3	1
Ron Thomas	2- 4	0- 0	3	5	4
Al Vilcheck	3- 6	0- 0	1	5	6
Jim Price	11-23	8- 9	5	3	30
Henry Bacon	5-11	5- 7	4	0	15
Larry Carter	4- 8	0- 0	2	0	8
Bill Bunton	1- 5	1- 1	4	1	3
Ken Bradley	1- 3	0- 0	2	1	2
Ron Stallings	1- 2	0- 1	1	2	2
Tim Cooper	0- 1	2- 2	1	1	2
Paul Pry	2- 3	0- 0	1	1	4
Joe Meiman	0- 1	0- 0	1	0	0
Team			4		
Totals	30-74	17-22	32	22	77

UCLA	fg-fga	ft-fta	rb	pf	tp
Keith Wilkes	5-11	2- 2	6	0	12
Larry Farmer	6-12	3- 5	4	2	15
Bill Walton	11-13	11-12	21	2	33
Greg Lee	3- 6	4- 6	4	1	10
Henry Bibby	1- 5	0- 0	3	5	2
Tommy Curtis	4- 5	0- 0	2	2	8
Larry Hollyfield	3- 6	0- 0	4	1	6
Vince Carson	1- 1	0- 0	0	1	2
Swen Nater	0- 0	2- 4	1	1	2
Andy Hill	1- 1	4- 4	0	1	6
Jon Chapman	0- 0	0- 1	1	0	0
Gary Franklin	0- 1	0- 0	2	0	0
Team			3		
Totals	35-61	26-34	51	16	96

Half time: UCLA 39-31. Officials: Hernjack and Copeland. Attendance: 15,189.

National Third Place

at Los Angeles, California

North Carolina	fg-fga	ft-fta	rb	pf	tp
Bill Chamberlain	4- 6	1- 1	4	5	9
Dennis Wuycik	8-12	11-16	8	2	27
Robert McAdoo	12-20	6- 6	19	1	30
Steve Previs	2- 5	3- 5	4	4	7
George Karl	6- 8	4- 5	2	5	16
Kim Huband	0- 0	0- 0	2	1	0
Bobby Jones	4- 8	3- 4	4	5	11
Craig Carson	0- 0	0- 0	2	0	0
Ray Hite	0- 0	1- 3	1	1	1
Billy Chambers	0- 0	4- 4	0	0	4
Team			1		
Totals	36-59	33-44	47	24	105

Louisville	fg-fga	ft-fta	rb	pf	tp
Mike Lawhon	4-10	5- 6	2	3	13
Ron Thomas	5-11	4- 6	10	4	14
Al Vilcheck	3- 5	2- 3	5	3	8
Jim Price	9-17	5- 7	4	5	23
Henry Bacon	3- 8	6- 8	4	3	12
Bill Bunton	2- 4	1- 2	5	2	5
Larry Carter	1- 5	0- 0	0	0	2
Tim Cooper	2- 5	4- 5	0	4	8
Ken Bradley	1- 4	0- 0	4	2	2
Joe Meiman	0- 2	0- 0	1	3	0
Ron Stallings	1- 5	0- 0	2	2	2
Paul Pry	1- 2	0- 0	1	0	2
Team			5		
Totals	32-78	27-37	43	31	91

Half time: North Carolina 51-34. Officials: Hernjack and Copeland.

Championship

at Los Angeles, California

Florida State	fg-fga	ft-fta	rb	pf	tp
Rowland Garrett	1- 9	1- 1	5	1	3
Ron King	12-20	3- 3	6	1	27
Reggie Royals	5- 7	5- 6	10	5	15
Lawrence McCray	3- 6	2- 5	6	4	8
Greg Samuel	3-10	0- 0	1	1	6
Ron Harris	7-13	2- 3	6	1	16
Otto Petty	0- 0	1- 1	0	1	1
Otis Cole	0- 2	0- 0	2	1	0
Team			6		
Totals	31-67	14-19	42	15	76

UCLA	fg-fga	ft-fta	rb	pf	tp
Keith Wilkes	11-16	1- 2	10	4	23
Larry Farmer	2- 6	0- 0	6	2	4
Bill Walton	9-17	6-11	20	4	24
Greg Lee	0- 0	0- 0	2	0	0
Henry Bibby	8-17	2- 3	3	2	18
Tommy Curtis	4-14	0- 1	4	1	8
Larry Hollyfield	1- 6	0- 0	2	2	2
Swen Nater	1- 2	0- 1	1	0	2
Team			2		
Totals	36-78	9-18	50	15	81

Half time: UCLA 50-39. Officials: Brown and Scott. Attendance: 15,063.

1973

East First Round

at Philadelphia, Pennsylvania

Syracuse	fg-fga	ft-fta	rb	pf	tp
Mike Lee	9-16	4- 5	4	3	22
Bob Dooms	5-10	0- 4	9	5	10
Rudy Hackett	5-13	2- 4	18	1	12
Dennis DuVal	9-22	0- 0	3	4	18
Mark Wadach	3- 8	1- 2	3	3	7
Jim Lee	1- 4	4- 5	0	0	6
Tom Stundis	2- 2	4- 4	1	0	8
Team			5		
Totals	34-75	15-24	43	16	83

Furman	fg-fga	ft-fta	rb	pf	tp
Clyde Mayes	5-13	1-1	11	4	11
Roy Simpson	7-15	2-3	7	2	16
Fessor Leonard	5-14	0-0	11	4	10
Baron Hill	3-5	0-0	0	2	6
Rust Hunt	1-2	0-0	1	0	2
Craig Lynch	6-11	0-0	7	3	12
Ed Kelley	3-10	3-3	2	4	9
Gary Clark	1-3	2-3	2	0	4
Bud Bierly	3-4	2-2	5	1	8
Todd Brenizer	2-3	0-0	3	3	4
Team			3		
Totals	36-80	10-12	52	23	82

Half time: Syracuse 43-37. Officials: Honzo and Housman. Attendance: 3,006.

at Williamsburg, Virginia

St. John's, N.Y.	fg-fga	ft-fta	rb	pf	tp
Bill Schaeffer	8-19	0-0	8	3	16
Tony Prince	1-3	0-0	7	2	2
Ed Searcy	6-12	7-8	10	1	19
Mel Utley	2-9	2-4	5	5	6
Kevin Cluess	3-8	0-0	4	0	6
Larry Jenkins	0-0	0-0	0	0	0
Frank Alagia	4-10	4-6	0	3	12
Bill Smith	0-2	0-0	2	2	0
Team			5		
Totals	24-63	13-18	41	16	61

Pennsylvania	fg-fga	ft-fta	rb	pf	tp
Phil Hankinson	8-16	0-0	10	2	16
Ron Haigler	7-16	6-6	6	1	20
John Beecroft	3-8	2-3	3	2	8
Bob Bigelow	3-10	2-2	4	3	8
Craig Littlepage	0-1	0-0	4	5	0
Bill Finger	0-0	0-0	0	0	0
Zoltan Varga	0-0	0-0	1	0	0
Larry Lewis	1-2	0-0	1	1	2
John Jablonski	3-5	2-3	4	4	8
Team			5		
Totals	25-58	12-14	38	18	62

Half time: Pennsylvania 38-32. Officials: Saar and Grossman. Attendance: 3,250.

at Jamaica, New York

St. Joseph's, Pa.	fg-fga	ft-fta	rb	pf	tp
Mike Bantom	10-19	3-4	13	4	23
Kevin Furey	3-9	5-8	8	1	11
Craig Kelly	2-4	1-2	1	0	5
Pat McFarland	8-13	0-1	7	0	16
Jim O'Brien	3-8	1-2	2	1	7
Mike Moody	4-6	0-0	2	5	8
Bob Sabol	1-2	0-0	1	0	2
Lou Peltzer	1-4	0-0	1	0	2
Fran Rafferty	1-1	0-0	1	0	2
Totals	33-66	10-17	36	11	76

Providence	fg-fga	ft-fta	rb	pf	tp
Ernie DiGregorio	14-21	3-4	2	4	31
Charles Crawford	2-4	0-1	5	1	4
Marvin Barnes	10-21	1-2	17	4	21
Kevin Stacom	5-11	2-2	3	2	12
Fran Costello	4-8	1-2	11	2	9
Nehru King	4-8	4-4	2	0	12
Totals	39-73	11-15	40	13	89

Half time: Providence 36-29. Officials: Hernjak and Crowley. Attendance: 4,430.

East Regional

at Charlotte, North Carolina

Syracuse	fg-fga	ft-fta	rb	pf	tp
Dennis DuVal	11-17	0-0	2	0	22
Mark Wadach	3-6	2-2	3	4	8
Mike Lee	8-13	1-2	3	4	17
Rudy Hackett	4-10	1-3	5	3	9
Bob Dooms	3-5	0-0	4	2	6
Jim Lee	3-6	3-4	1	2	9
Tom Stundis	0-1	0-0	0	1	0
Bill Suprunowicz	1-1	0-0	0	0	2
Scott Stapleton	0-0	0-1	1	0	0
Steve Shaw	0-0	0-0	0	1	0
Don Begner	1-2	0-0	0	0	2
Chuck Wickman	0-0	0-0	1	0	0
Bruce Bartholomew	0-0	0-0	0	0	0
Team			3		
Totals	34-61	7-12	23	17	75

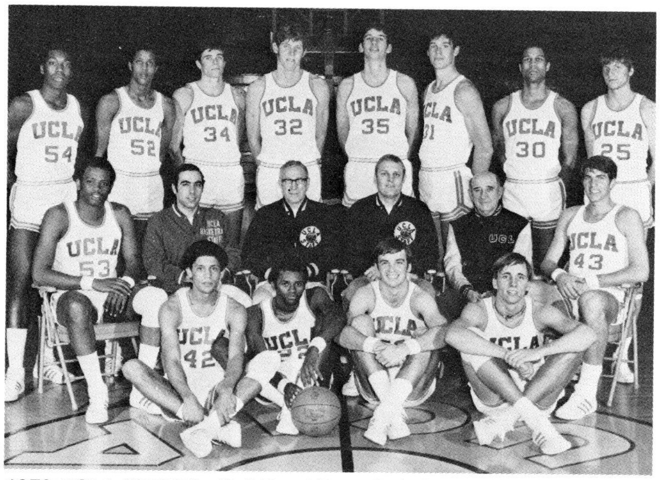

1973 UCLA BRUINS—(l-r) Front Row: Bob Webb, Tommy Curtis, Gary Franklin, Casey Corliss; Second Row: Larry Hollyfield, Les Friedman, John Wooden, Gary Cunningham, Ducky Drake, Greg Lee; Third Row: Larry Farmer, Keith Wilkes, Dave Meyers, Bill Walton, Ralph Drollinger, Swen Nater, Vince Carson, Pete Trgovich.

Maryland	fg-fga	ft-fta	rb	pf	tp
John Lucas	9-17	3-4	5	2	21
Bob Bodell	5-11	2-2	1	1	12
Len Elmore	5-10	0-0	14	2	10
Tom McMillen	8-10	2-2	6	2	18
Jim O'Brien	8-14	6-7	6	2	22
Darrell Brown	3-4	0-1	4	2	6
Howard White	0-0	0-0	1	1	0
Owen Brown	0-0	0-0	1	1	0
Tom Roy	0-0	0-0	1	1	0
Maurice Howard	1-1	0-0	0	0	2
Rich Porac	0-1	0-0	0	0	0
Bill Hahn	0-0	0-0	0	0	0
Team			3		
Totals	39-68	13-16	42	14	91

Half time: Maryland 35-34. Officials: Shosid and Bain. Attendance: 11,003.

at Charlotte, North Carolina

Pennsylvania	fg-fga	ft-fta	rb	pf	tp
John Beecroft	1-6	0-0	1	0	2
Ron Haigler	7-15	4-4	12	4	18
Phil Hankinson	9-29	1-3	9	1	19
Bob Bigelow	5-19	0-0	6	3	10
Craig Littlepage	1-1	0-0	0	3	2
John Jablonski	0-0	0-0	0	0	0
Bill Finger	0-0	0-0	0	0	0
Steve Batory	0-1	0-0	0	0	0
Zoltan Varga	5-9	0-0	2	1	10
Larry Lewis	1-6	0-0	5	1	2
Keith Hansen	1-1	0-0	0	1	2
Bruce Frank	0-1	0-0	0	0	0
Team			5		
Totals	30-88	5-7	40	14	65

Providence	fg-fga	ft-fta	rb	pf	tp
Ernie DiGregorio	9-21	0-0	3	2	18
Kevin Stacom	7-9	2-2	5	0	16
Marvin Barnes	10-10	0-0	13	3	20
Nehru King	7-11	4-4	6	2	18
Fran Costello	1-3	0-0	4	4	2
Gary Bello	0-0	0-0	0	0	0
Dave Modest	0-0	0-0	0	0	0
Mark Anderson	0-0	0-0	0	0	0
Charles Crawford	6-6	0-0	3	1	12
Al Baker	0-1	0-0	3	0	0
Rich Dunphy	0-0	1-2	1	0	1
Team			6		
Totals	40-61	7-8	44	12	87

Half time: Providence 36-29. Officials: Wilcoxen and Lawson. Attendance: 11,003.

at Charlotte, North Carolina

Pennsylvania	fg-fga	ft-fta	rb	pf	tp
John Beecroft	3-6	4-4	1	2	10
Craig Littlepage	1-2	2-3	5	2	4
Bob Bigelow	4-6	0-0	4	4	8
Ron Haigler	9-16	0-0	5	4	18
Phil Hankinson	6-12	5-5	6	1	17
John Jablonski	0-1	0-0	2	1	0
Larry Lewis	4-8	1-2	1	2	9
Zoltan Varga	0-2	0-0	1	0	0
Bill Finger	1-1	0-0	2	1	2
Steve Batory	0-2	0-0	0	0	0
Team			5		
Totals	28-56	12-14	32	17	68

Syracuse	fg-fga	ft-fta	rb	pf	tp
Mark Wadach	3-8	0-0	4	5	6
Dennis DuVal	10-24	0-0	7	2	20
Mike Lee	2-10	2-3	3	4	6
Rudy Hackett	9-17	2-3	15	0	20
Bob Dooms	6-8	0-0	9	4	12
James Lee	0-4	3-4	3	1	3
Tom Stundis	0-1	0-1	1	1	0
Scott Stapleton	1-5	0-0	2	1	2
Team			4		
Totals	31-77	7-11	48	18	69

Half time: Pennsylvania 35-29. Officials: Wilcoxen and Lawson. Attendance: 10,400.

at Charlotte, North Carolina

Providence	fg-fga	ft-fta	rb	pf	tp
Ernie DiGregorio	14-21	2-2	3	5	30
Kevin Stacom	10-17	4-5	2	3	24
Fran Costello	2-5	4-4	6	4	8
Charles Crawford	2-4	3-3	5	2	7
Marvin Barnes	8-18	3-5	15	2	19
Nehru King	7-9	1-3	7	1	15
Team			3		
Totals	43-74	17-22	41	17	103

Maryland	fg-fga	ft-fta	rb	pf	tp
John Lucas	9-20	2-2	6	5	20
Bob Bodell	2-8	0-0	7	3	4
Tom McMillen	10-16	5-5	6	4	25
Jim O'Brien	3-9	2-2	3	1	8
Len Elmore	7-11	0-1	10	5	14
Darrell Brown	1-3	0-0	1	0	2
Tom Roy	4-5	0-2	5	3	8
Maurice Howard	2-6	0-0	0	1	4
Owen Brown	2-4	0-0	1	0	4
Howard White	0-1	0-0	0	0	0
Team			3		
Totals	40-83	9-12	42	22	89

Half time: Maryland 51-50. Officials: Shosid and Bain. Attendance: 10,400.

Midwest First Round

at Wichita, Kansas

Texas Tech	fg-fga	ft-fta	rb	pf	tp
Phil Bailey	3-5	0-0	0	0	6
Rick Bullock	8-18	3-5	7	3	19
Jim Derkowski	0-0	0-0	0	0	0
William Johnson	2-5	2-2	5	1	6
Gene Kaberline	0-0	0-0	0	1	0
Richard Little	3-11	0-0	0	5	6
Bryan Mauk	0-0	0-0	0	C	0
Don Moore	0-2	0-0	0	2	0
Ron Richardson	8-11	1-2	6	3	17
Ed Wakefield	6-12	4-4	7	1	16
Totals	30-64	10-13	25	16	70

South Carolina	fg-fga	ft-fta	rb	pf	tp
Mike Dunleavy	5-10	1-2	1	0	11
Alex English	7-11	1-1	15	3	15
Brian Winters	4-5	1-1	3	5	9
Dan Traylor	8-13	0-0	16	5	16
Bob Mathias	0-0	0-0	2	0	0
Kevin Joyce	6-16	9-10	1	2	21
Casey Manning	1-2	0-0	1	0	2
Mark Greiner	2-3	0-1	4	1	4
Totals	33-60	12-15	43	16	78

Half Time: 30-30. Officials: Winters and Powell. Attendance: 6,389.

at Wichita, Kansas

Houston	fg-fga	ft-fta	rb	pf	tp
Donnell Hayes	5-11	0-0	0	4	10
Jerry Bonney	3-9	0-2	4	1	6
Dwight Jones	6-11	6-7	14	3	18
Maurice Presley	2-3	0-0	8	3	4
Louis Dunbar	11-26	5-7	4	4	27
Sidney Edwards	5-9	0-0	8	1	10
David Marrs	0-0	0-0	0	0	0
Steve Newsome	6-15	2-4	9	5	14
Team			6		
Totals	38-84	13-20	53	21	89

SW Louisiana	fg-fga	ft-fta	rb	pf	tp
Dwight Lamar	15-34	5-6	3	1	35
Percy Wells	1-1	0-0	0	1	2
Jerry Bisbano	4-9	3-3	4	3	11
Fred Saunders	2-7	0-0	8	5	4
Robert Wilson	3-11	4-4	7	2	10
Larry Fogle	5-9	7-10	9	1	17
Roy Ebron	10-15	3-4	11	4	23
Team			9		
Totals	40-86	22-27	51	17	102

Half time: Southwestern Louisiana 46-39. Officials: Dunn and Shosid. Attendance: 6,389.

Midwest Regional

at Houston, Texas

Memphis State	fg-fga	ft-fta	rb	pf	tp
Bill Laurie	0-1	6-7	1	4	6
Billy Buford	5-7	0-0	10	3	10
Larry Finch	8-17	9-10	1	4	25
Ronnie Robinson	5-16	1-4	17	2	11
Larry Kenon	16-30	2-6	20	4	34
Jim Liss	0-0	0-0	0	0	0
Doug McKinney	0-0	0-0	0	1	0
Wes Westfall	0-1	0-0	0	0	0
Bill Cook	2-5	0-0	0	1	4
Team			11		
Totals	36-77	18-27	60	19	90

South Carolina	fg-fga	ft-fta	rb	pf	tp
Mike Dunleavy	4-10	4-4	0	3	12
Alex English	9-15	1-1	8	5	19
Brian Winters	5-11	4-4	8	5	14
Dan Traylor	5-12	0-4	6	3	10
Kevin Joyce	8-21	2-2	2	2	18
Jim Walsh	0-0	0-0	0	0	0
Bob Mathias	1-1	0-0	1	0	2
Casey Manning	0-0	0-0	0	4	0
Mark Greiner	0-0	0-0	1	0	0
Tom Cox	0-0	1-2	1	0	1
Team			6		
Totals	32-70	12-17	33	22	76

Half time: Memphis State 39-24. Officials: Grossman and Hernjak. Attendance: 10,060.

at Houston, Texas

Kansas State	fg-fga	ft-fta	rb	pf	tp
Lon Kruger	6-11	4-6	2	2	16
Bob Chipman	4-6	3-5	2	1	11
Larry Williams	2-8	0-0	7	2	4
Ernie Kusnyer	7-15	1-3	7	4	15
Steve Mitchell	4-7	0-0	5	5	8
Danny Beard	0-1	0-0	1	0	0
Jerry Thruston	1-3	1-2	3	2	3
Gene McVey	4-5	1-4	3	2	9
Team			11		
Totals	28-56	10-20	41	18	66

SW Louisiana	fg-fga	ft-fta	rb	pf	tp
Dwight Lamar	8-21	2-2	4	2	18
Jerry Bisbano	2-7	0-0	2	5	4
Fred Saunders	4-8	0-0	7	4	8
Larry Fogle	4-14	2-3	7	3	10
Roy Ebron	5-15	6-7	12	4	16
Percy Wells	0-0	0-0	0	0	0
Andre Brown	0-0	0-0	1	1	0
Robert Wilson	3-7	1-2	6	2	7
Team			7		
Totals	26-72	11-14	46	21	63

Half time: Kansas State 38-26. Officials: Moreau and Howell. Attendance: 10,060.

at Houston, Texas

SW Louisiana	fg-fga	ft-fta	rb	pf	tp
Dwight Lamar	11-27	0-0	8	4	22
Jerry Bisbano	1-6	1-2	3	3	3
Fred Saunders	8-16	3-6	16	3	19
Larry Fogle	6-17	0-1	14	2	12
Roy Ebron	9-17	2-3	10	5	20
Andre Brown	1-3	1-2	2	1	3
Mike Haney	0-0	0-0	0	1	0
Robert Wilson	2-5	0-0	4	3	4
Dan Wright	1-3	0-0	1	1	2
Team			6		
Totals	39-94	7-14	64	23	85

South Carolina	fg-fga	ft-fta	rb	pf	tp
Mike Dunleavy	4-8	3-4	0	2	11
Alex English	9-18	4-4	10	3	22
Brian Winters	4-12	2-2	3	0	10
Dan Traylor	8-15	0-2	16	3	16
Kevin Joyce	1-13	10-13	6	1	12
Jim Walsh	0-0	0-0	0	0	0
Bob Mathias	0-0	0-0	1	1	0
Casey Manning	6-10	1-2	3	1	13
Mark Greiner	2-2	0-0	2	2	4
Tom Cox	1-2	0-0	1	0	2
Team			8		
Totals	35-80	20-27	50	13	90

Half time: Southwestern Louisiana 39-33. Officials: Grossman and Hernjak. Attendance: 10,060.

at Houston, Texas

Kansas State	fg-fga	ft-fta	rb	pf	tp
Lon Kruger	6-12	3-3	5	3	15
Bob Chipman	1-4	1-2	2	1	3
Larry Williams	2-8	0-0	5	2	4
Ernie Kusnyer	8-19	5-10	5	4	21
Steve Mitchell	6-14	0-1	6	3	12
Danny Beard	0-3	1-2	1	1	1
Doug Snider	0-3	0-0	0	2	0
Jerry Thruston	2-3	0-2	1	2	4
Gene McVey	4-7	4-4	4	1	12
Team			5		
Totals	29-73	14-24	34	19	72

Memphis State	fg-fga	ft-fta	rb	pf	tp
Bill Laurie	2-4	4-4	3	2	8
Billy Buford	2-5	0-0	3	4	4
Larry Finch	10-16	12-12	2	2	32
Ronnie Robinson	7-10	0-0	16	3	14
Larry Kenon	7-12	0-0	7	4	14
Jerry Tetzlaff	0-1	0-2	2	0	0
Jim Liss	1-1	0-0	0	0	2
Ken Andrews	0-0	0-0	0	1	0
Doug McKinney	0-1	0-0	0	0	0
Wes Westfall	5-6	0-0	6	5	10
Bill Cook	3-6	2-2	3	0	8
Clarence Jones	0-0	0-0	0	1	0
Team			5		
Totals	37-62	18-20	47	22	92

Half time: Memphis State 44-34. Officials: Howell and Moreau. Attendance: 10,060.

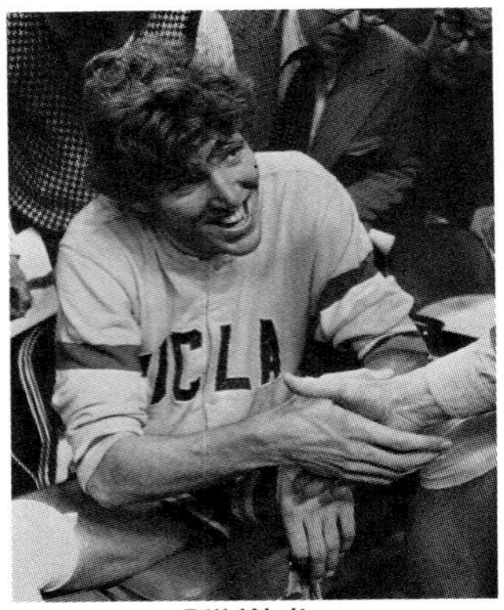

Bill Walton

Midwest First Round

at Dayton, Ohio

Marquette	fg-fga	ft-fta	rb	pf	tp
Allie McGuire	3-8	2-3	2	1	8
Maurice Lucas	8-16	8-9	12	3	24
Larry McNeill	5-11	1-2	5	5	11
George Frazier	9-12	2-3	8	2	20
Marcus Washington	2-5	0-0	2	0	4
Dave Delsman	1-1	2-2	0	1	4
Ed Daniels	1-2	0-0	0	5	2
Mike Mills	0-0	0-0	1	1	0
Paul Vollmer	0-1	0-0	0	0	0
William Tatum	2-3	0-0	2	0	4
Jerry Homan	0-0	0-0	0	0	0
Team			3		
Totals	31-59	15-19	35	18	77

Miami, Ohio	fg-fga	ft-fta	rb	pf	tp
Phil Lumpkin	4-12	0-0	0	2	8
Larry Garloch	2-7	0-0	8	5	4
Rich Hampton	9-18	3-3	6	2	21
Gary Dees	2-4	0-0	1	3	4
Dave Elmer	4-4	2-2	10	4	10
Steve Fields	3-5	0-0	2	2	6
Warren Dorsey	1-5	4-4	3	0	6
Kim Essenburg	0-1	0-0	0	1	0
Rod Dieringer	0-0	3-4	0	0	3
John Freytag	0-0	0-0	0	0	0
Gary DeMoss	0-0	0-0	0	0	0
Steve Handy	0-0	0-0	0	0	0
Team			2		
Totals	25-56	12-13	32	19	62

Half time: Marquette 38-31. Officials: Gyenes and Parry. Attendance: 13,458.

at Dayton, Ohio

Austin Peay St.	fg-fga	ft-fta	rb	pf	tp
Dan Odums	2-9	2-2	9	2	6
Percy Howard	4-11	2-4	5	5	10
Ed Childress	5-10	0-0	1	4	10
James Williams	12-26	2-2	5	3	26
Howard Jackson	4-6	0-2	4	3	8
Jerry Wanstrath	1-2	2-2	1	3	4
Robert Turner	2-4	1-2	6	2	5
Richard Jimmerson	4-7	0-1	5	3	8
Kemp Hampton	0-0	0-0	0	0	0
Team			5		
Totals	34-75	9-15	41	25	77

Jacksonville	fg-fga	ft-fta	rb	pf	tp
Henry Williams	6-17	3-4	6	2	15
Leon Benbow	6-13	6-8	3	3	18
Abe Steward	3-7	2-5	13	2	8
Jim Clark	4-6	0-0	3	3	8
Butch Taylor	6-9	8-10	16	3	20
Dave Stowers	0-0	0-0	0	3	0
Rick Coleman	2-6	0-0	1	1	4
Bob Nylin	1-1	0-0	1	2	2
Team			3		
Totals	28-59	19-27	46	19	75

Half time: Austin Peay 47-32. Officials: Pace and Stout. Attendance: 13,458.

Mideast Regional

at Nashville, Tennessee

Marquette	fg-fga	ft-fta	rb	pf	tp
Larry McNeill	5-9	2-2	12	4	12
George Frazier	4-7	0-0	2	5	8
Maurice Lucas	6-15	0-0	5	4	12
Allie McGuire	6-9	3-3	1	2	15
Marcus Washington	10-15	0-0	5	3	20
Dave Delsman	1-1	0-0	0	1	2
Ed Daniels	0-1	0-0	1	1	0
Mike Mills	0-0	0-0	0	0	0
William Tatum	0-1	0-0	0	0	0
Totals	32-58	5-5	26	20	69

Indiana	fg-fga	ft-fta	rb	pf	tp
Steve Green	8-15	0-1	6	3	16
John Ritter	5-9	4-4	6	2	14
Steve Downing	12-17	5-11	10	2	29
Jim Crews	3-4	0-0	1	1	6
Quinn Buckner	2-6	0-2	7	3	4
John Laskowski	1-2	4-4	1	1	6
Totals	31-53	13-22	31	12	75

Half time: Marquette 38-35. Officials: Brown and Evans. Attendance: 15,581.

at Nashville, Tennessee

Kentucky	fg-fga	ft-fta	rb	pf	tp
Ron Lyons	6-16	0-0	4	0	12
Jimmy Dan Conner	4-7	1-1	2	4	9
Mike Flynn	3-8	4-6	6	5	10
Kevin Grevey	10-24	1-2	13	4	21
Jim Andrews	15-19	0-0	14	1	30
Ray Edelman	1-3	0-0	0	0	2
Larry Stamper	5-9	0-0	7	0	10
Jerry Hale	0-0	0-0	1	0	0
Rich Drewitz	0-0	0-0	0	0	0
Steve Lochmueller	2-2	0-0	1	1	4
Bob Guyette	4-9	0-0	8	1	8
Totals	50-97	6-9	56	16	106

Austin Peay St.	fg-fga	ft-fta	rb	pf	tp
Dan Odums	5-10	1-1	2	2	11
Percy Howard	7-10	0-0	9	4	14
Ed Childress	10-19	2-2	5	3	22
James Williams	13-31	0-0	6	4	26
Howard Jackson	10-19	3-7	18	2	23
Richard Jimmerson	0-2	0-0	0	0	0
Robert Turner	0-2	0-0	1	0	0
Kemp Hampton	1-3	0-0	2	0	2
Jerry Wanstrath	0-3	2-2	4	0	2
Totals	46-99	8-12	47	15	100

Half time: Austin Peay 47-43. Regulation Score: 92-92. Officials: Soriano and Ditty. Attendance: 15,581.

at Nashville, Tennessee

Austin Peay St.	fg-fga	ft-fta	rb	pf	tp
Howard Jackson	8-15	6-7	17	3	22
James Williams	9-18	4-4	2	1	22
Percy Howard	0-1	2-4	7	2	2
Ed Childress	3-13	2-2	3	5	8
Dan Odums	2-3	0-0	3	2	4
Mickey Fisher	0-0	0-0	1	0	0
Richard Jimmerson	0-1	0-0	2	1	0
Luther Jackson	1-1	0-0	0	2	2
Gary Sewell	0-0	0-0	0	0	0
Robert Turner	1-3	2-3	2	1	4
Kemp Hampton	2-7	1-1	0	1	5
Tom Higdon	0-0	2-2	2	0	2
Jerry Wanstrath	1-2	0-0	3	5	2
Team			1		
Totals	27-64	19-23	43	23	73

Marquette	fg-fga	ft-fta	rb	pf	tp
George Frazier	1-4	2-3	5	5	4
Larry McNeill	12-17	3-4	15	5	27
Maurice Lucas	9-18	2-3	19	2	20
Allie McGuire	7-24	3-3	4	2	17
Marcus Washington	2-12	2-3	5	3	6
Ed Daniels	0-1	0-0	1	0	0
Mike Mills	0-0	0-0	0	0	0
William Tatum	2-3	2-2	2	0	6
Jerry Homan	0-0	0-0	0	0	0
Rick Campbell	3-8	0-1	4	3	6
Dave Delsman	0-2	2-2	1	1	2
Team			0		
Totals	36-89	16-21	56	21	88

Half time: Marquette 57-42. Officials: Soriano and Evans. Attendance: 15,581.

at Nashville, Tennessee

Indiana	fg-fga	ft-fta	rb	pf	tp
Quinn Buckner	8-21	0-1	11	3	16
Steve Downing	10-22	3-4	13	3	23
Steve Green	5-13	4-4	6	3	14
John Ritter	4-5	1-1	2	2	9
Jim Crews	0-2	0-0	2	0	0
John Laskowski	4-5	2-4	6	1	10
Totals	31-68	10-14	40	12	72

Kentucky	fg-fga	ft-fta	rb	pf	tp
Ron Lyons	3-7	2-2	2	0	8
Jimmy Dan Conner	1-6	0-0	10	2	2
Mike Flynn	4-10	0-0	2	4	8
Kevin Grevey	7-14	0-0	8	4	14
Jim Andrews	11-20	1-2	10	3	23
Ray Edelman	0-0	0-0	0	0	0
Larry Stamper	0-0	0-0	0	0	0
Jerry Hale	0-1	0-0	0	0	0
Steve Lochmueller	2-4	0-0	1	3	4
Bob Guyette	3-4	0-0	3	1	6
Totals	31-66	3-4	36	17	65

Half time: Indiana 45-32. Officials: Ditty and Brown. Attendance: 16,000.

West First Round

at Logan, Utah

Weber State	fg-fga	ft-fta	rb	pf	tp
Dan Dion	0-6	0-0	2	0	0
Brady Small	8-17	2-2	3	1	18
Ken Gubler	3-7	4-4	2	4	10
Steve Fleming	6-11	4-6	9	4	16
Richard Cooper	2-5	0-0	5	5	4
Jim Watts	5-5	1-2	3	4	11
Riley Wimberly	4-10	0-1	5	5	8
Wes Van Dyke	3-5	2-2	3	1	8
Brad Tausheck	0-0	0-0	1	1	0
Tom DeVita	0-2	0-0	1	0	0
Dave Muirbrook	0-0	0-1	1	0	0
Frank Childs	0-1	0-0	0	0	0
Team			5		
Totals	31-69	13-18	40	25	75

Long Beach State	fg-fga	ft-fta	rb	pf	tp
Rick Aberegg	1-6	2-2	2	3	4
Glenn McDonald	1-5	2-2	2	1	4
Ed Ratleff	9-13	7-7	6	2	25
Leonard Gray	11-18	3-3	7	3	25
Nate Stephens	5-9	2-4	5	5	12
Roscoe Pondexter	5-11	2-2	8	3	12
Ernie Douse	2-3	2-5	5	4	6
Lamont King	0-3	0-0	0	1	0
Team			7		
Totals	34-68	20-25	42	22	88

Half time: Long Beach State 41-39. Officials: Evans and Turner. Attendance: 6,706.

at Logan, Utah

Oklahoma City	fg-fga	ft-fta	rb	pf	tp
Ozie Edwards	13-28	5-5	9	4	31
James Washington	4-13	3-5	8	3	11
Ron Brown	1-8	3-6	8	3	5
Marvin Rich	6-22	4-6	9	5	16
Mike Tosee	3-6	0-1	2	2	6
Norm Russell	2-5	1-2	5	1	5
Lacy Lanier	0-1	4-5	1	3	4
Herb Gilkey	0-3	0-0	3	1	0
Mike Polansky	0-1	0-0	0	0	0
Jim Lackey	0-0	0-0	0	1	0
Team			10		
Totals	29-87	20-30	55	23	78

Arizona State	fg-fga	ft-fta	rb	pf	tp
Ken Gray	2-6	1-1	5	1	5
Mike Contreras	10-14	1-2	7	4	21
Jim Owens	8-16	0-0	2	3	16
Ron Kennedy	4-11	2-2	8	5	10
Mark Wasley	4-6	0-0	6	4	8
Rudy White	6-10	7-8	6	1	19
James Brown	3-5	1-4	6	1	7
Gary Jackson	2-5	3-6	3	5	7
Jack Schrader	4-4	2-4	4	4	10
Mike Moon	0-5	0-1	3	0	0
Team			13		
Totals	43-82	17-28	63	28	103

Half time: Arizona State 42-40. Officials: Skinner and Overby. Attendance: 6,706.

GAME-BY-GAME RESULTS

West Regional

at Los Angeles, California

Long Beach State	fg-fga	ft-fta	rb	pf	tp
Ed Ratleff	4-18	4- 4	7	3	12
Leonard Gray	4- 6	2- 2	8	2	10
Nate Stephens	9-20	0- 1	16	1	18
Glenn McDonald	2- 9	0- 0	2	1	4
Rick Aberegg	4-10	0- 0	1	5	8
Roscoe Pondexter	5-14	1- 2	6	3	11
Ernie Douse	2- 5	0- 0	4	2	4
Lamont King	0- 0	0- 0	0	2	0
Team			2		
Totals	30-82	7- 9	46	19	67

San Francisco	fg-fga	ft-fta	rb	pf	tp
Kevin Restani	8-15	2- 3	9	2	18
Snake Jones	0- 3	0- 0	4	1	0
Eric Fernsten	4-14	0- 0	17	2	8
Phil Smith	5-11	10-14	6	2	20
Mike Quick	12-18	1- 2	6	3	25
John Boro	2- 2	2- 3	2	0	6
Anthony Lewis	0- 1	0- 0	0	0	0
Team			4		
Totals	31-64	15-22	48	10	77

Half time: San Francisco 37-31. Officials: White and Wortman. Attendance: 12,632.

at Los Angeles, California

UCLA	fg-fga	ft-fta	rb	pf	tp
Keith Wilkes	6-14	0- 0	10	2	12
Larry Farmer	5-10	0- 0	4	2	10
Bill Walton	13-18	2- 2	14	3	28
Larry Hollyfield	9-16	2- 2	5	3	20
Greg Lee	1- 2	1- 1	0	0	3
Tommy Curtis	2- 3	3- 3	1	2	7
Dave Meyers	2- 3	2- 3	5	1	6
Swen Nater	2- 5	0- 2	2	2	4
Vince Carson	0- 0	0- 2	1	0	0
Gary Franklin	1- 2	0- 0	2	0	2
Pete Trgovich	2- 5	0- 0	2	0	4
Bob Webb	0- 2	0- 0	0	2	0
Casey Corliss	0- 0	2- 2	0	1	2
Ralph Drollinger	0- 0	0- 0	0	1	0
Team			5		
Totals	43-80	12-17	51	19	98

Arizona State	fg-fga	ft-fta	rb	pf	tp
Ken Gray	2- 4	0- 1	2	0	4
Mark Wasley	3- 8	0- 0	10	1	6
Ron Kennedy	2- 7	5- 6	8	5	9
Mike Contreras	9-20	0- 0	4	3	18
Jim Owens	8-20	6- 8	4	2	22
Rudy White	3- 6	0- 0	2	0	6
Gary Jackson	3- 8	4- 6	4	3	10
Jim Brown	2- 6	2- 3	6	2	6
Jack Schrader	0- 1	0- 0	3	1	0
Mike Moon	0- 2	0- 0	1	0	0
Team			4		
Totals	32-82	17-24	48	17	81

Half time: UCLA 51-37. Officials: Copeland and Fouty. Attendance: 12,671.

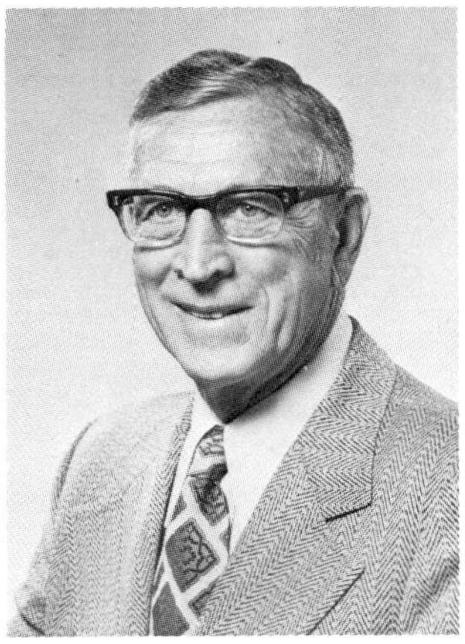

John Wooden

at Los Angeles, California

Arizona State	fg-fga	ft-fta	rb	pf	tp
Ken Gray	6-11	0- 0	14	3	12
Mark Wasley	5- 9	0- 1	4	3	10
Ron Kennedy	4- 9	1- 1	9	4	9
Mike Contreras	10-18	1- 1	1	3	21
Jim Owens	7-17	2- 2	3	3	16
Rudy White	2- 7	0- 0	3	2	4
Gary Jackson	2- 7	2- 2	2	2	6
Jack Schrader	1- 2	0- 0	2	2	2
James Brown	0- 3	0- 0	1	1	0
Team			4		
Totals	37-83	6- 7	43	23	80

Long Beach State	fg-fga	ft-fta	rb	pf	tp
Ed Ratleff	6-14	4- 5	13	3	16
Leonard Gray	3- 7	3- 4	2	4	9
Nate Stephens	7-15	3- 4	7	1	17
Glenn McDonald	1- 7	0- 0	8	1	2
Rick Aberegg	3- 5	6- 6	2	3	12
Ernie Douse	3- 8	3- 7	4	0	9
Roscoe Pondexter	7-11	3- 6	10	1	17
Lamont King	1- 1	0- 0	1	1	2
Team			4		
Totals	31-68	22-32	51	14	84

Half time: 42-42. Officials: Wortman and Fouty. Attendance: 12,705.

at Los Angeles, California

San Francisco	fg-fga	ft-fta	rb	pf	tp
Kevin Restani	4-11	0- 0	9	0	8
Phil Smith	8-13	1- 1	3	0	17
Eric Fernsten	2- 5	0- 0	8	3	4
Mike Quick	4- 9	0- 0	2	1	8
John Boro	0- 3	2- 2	0	3	2
Team			4		
Totals	18-41	3- 3	26	7	39

UCLA	fg-fga	ft-fta	rb	pf	tp
Keith Wilkes	6-13	0- 0	1	0	12
Larry Farmer	5-10	3- 3	4	0	13
Bill Walton	4- 7	1- 2	14	0	9
Larry Hollyfield	0- 3	0- 0	1	0	0
Greg Lee	1- 4	0- 0	1	0	2
Dave Meyers	1- 3	0- 0	3	3	2
Tommy Curtis	6- 9	0- 1	1	1	12
Swen Nater	0- 2	0- 0	1	0	0
Gary Franklin	1- 2	0- 0	2	0	2
Vince Carson	0- 0	0- 0	1	1	0
Bob Webb	0- 1	0- 0	0	1	0
Pete Trgovich	1- 2	0- 0	0	0	2
Team			1		
Totals	25-56	4- 6	30	6	54

Half time: UCLA 23-22. Officials: White and Copeland. Attendance: 12,705.

Semifinals

at St. Louis, Missouri

Memphis State	fg-fga	ft-fta	rb	pf	tp
Billy Buford	3- 7	0- 0	3	2	6
Larry Kenon	14-27	0- 4	22	1	28
Ron Robinson	11-17	2- 3	16	2	24
Bill Laurie	1- 3	2- 3	1	4	4
Larry Finch	7-16	7- 9	6	4	21
Bill Cook	3- 6	2- 3	1	2	8
Wes Westfall	2- 3	3- 4	2	0	7
Clarence Jones	0- 1	0- 0	0	0	0
Team			3		
Totals	41-80	16-26	54	15	98

Providence	fg-fga	ft-fta	rb	pf	tp
Charles Crawford	5-12	0- 0	15	3	10
Fran Costello	5- 5	1- 1	8	5	11
Marvin Barnes	5- 7	2- 3	3	4	12
Ernie DiGregorio	15-36	2- 2	2	4	32
Kevin Stacom	6-15	3- 3	5	5	15
Nehru King	2- 6	0- 0	1	1	4
Al Baker	0- 0	0- 0	1	0	0
Rich Dunphy	0- 1	1- 2	1	0	1
Gary Bello	0- 0	0- 0	0	0	0
Team			3		
Totals	38-82	9-11	39	22	85

Half time: Providence 49-40. Officials: Ditty and White. Attendance: 19,029.

at St. Louis, Missouri

UCLA	fg-fga	ft-fta	rb	pf	tp
Keith Wilkes	5-10	3- 4	6	3	13
Larry Farmer	3- 6	1- 2	3	4	7
Bill Walton	7-12	0- 0	17	4	14
Greg Lee	0- 1	0- 0	0	0	0
Larry Hollyfield	5- 6	0- 0	2	1	10
Tommy Curtis	9-15	4- 7	2	2	22
Dave Meyers	2- 3	0- 0	5	1	4
Swen Nater	0- 0	0- 0	0	1	0
Team			3		
Totals	31-53	8-13	38	16	70

Indiana	fg-fga	ft-fta	rb	pf	tp
Quinn Buckner	3-10	0- 1	5	2	6
Jim Crews	4-10	0- 0	2	3	8
Steve Downing	12-20	2- 4	5	5	26
Steve Green	1- 7	0- 0	5	2	2
John Ritter	6-10	1- 1	2	3	13
John Laskowski	1- 8	0- 0	4	0	2
Tom Abernethy	0- 1	0- 0	1	1	0
Trent Smock	0- 0	0- 0	0	0	0
Don Noort	0- 0	0- 0	1	0	0
Frank Wilson	0- 0	0- 0	0	0	0
Craig Morris	0- 0	0- 0	0	0	0
Steve Ahlfield	0- 0	0- 0	0	0	0
Doug Allen	1- 1	0- 0	0	0	2
Jerry Memering	0- 0	0- 0	0	0	0
Team			4		
Totals	28-67	3- 6	29	16	59

Half time: UCLA 40-22. Officials: Shosid and Howell. Attendance: 19,029.

National Third Place

at St. Louis, Missouri

Providence	fg-fga	ft-fta	rb	pf	tp
Charles Crawford	1- 4	2- 3	5	4	4
Nehru King	2-10	0- 0	5	3	4
Fran Costello	8-15	3- 4	4	3	19
Ernie DiGregorio	7-22	3- 4	7	4	17
Kevin Stacom	10-21	9-10	7	3	29
Al Baker	0- 2	2- 2	7	0	2
Rich Dunphy	0- 1	4- 4	1	3	4
Gary Bello	0- 1	0- 0	0	0	0
Mark McAndrew	0- 1	0- 0	1	0	0
Dave Modest	0- 1	0- 0	0	0	0
Team			2		
Totals	28-78	23-27	39	20	79

Indiana	fg-fga	ft-fta	rb	pf	tp
Steve Green	8-13	0- 1	7	4	16
John Ritter	8-15	5- 8	7	5	21
Steve Downing	10-17	1- 1	14	3	21
Quinn Buckner	5- 9	5- 5	8	3	15
Jim Crews	3-10	0- 1	4	3	6
John Laskowski	4- 7	0- 0	5	3	8
Tom Abernethy	1- 1	0- 0	1	1	2
Trent Smock	0- 0	0- 0	0	0	0
Jerry Memering	0- 0	0- 0	1	0	0
Steve Ahlfield	1- 2	4- 4	1	2	6
Frank Wilson	1- 1	0- 1	1	0	2
Doug Allen	0- 1	0- 0	0	0	0
Craig Morris	0- 0	0- 0	0	0	0
Don Noort	0- 0	0- 0	0	0	0
Team			2		
Totals	41-76	15-21	51	24	97

Half time: Indiana 51-42. Officials: Ditty and White. Attendance: 19,301.

Championship

at St. Louis, Missouri

UCLA	fg-fga	ft-fta	rb	pf	tp
Keith Wilkes	8-14	0- 0	7	2	16
Larry Farmer	1- 4	0- 0	2	2	2
Bill Walton	21-22	2- 5	13	4	44
Greg Lee	1- 1	3- 3	3	2	5
Larry Hollyfield	4- 7	0- 0	3	4	8
Tommy Curtis	1- 4	2- 2	3	1	4
Dave Meyers	2- 7	0- 0	3	1	4
Swen Nater	1- 1	0- 0	3	2	2
Gary Franklin	1- 2	0- 1	1	0	2
Vince Carson	0- 0	0- 0	0	0	0
Bob Webb	0- 0	0- 0	0	0	0
Team			2		
Totals	40-62	7-11	40	18	87

Memphis State	fg-fga	ft-fta	rb	pf	tp
Billy Buford	3- 7	1- 2	3	1	7
Larry Kenon	8-16	4- 4	8	3	20
Ron Robinson	3- 6	0- 1	7	4	6
Bill Laurie	0- 1	0- 0	0	0	0
Larry Finch	9-21	11-13	1	2	29
Wes Westfall	0- 1	0- 0	0	5	0
Bill Cook	1- 4	2- 2	0	1	4
Doug McKinney	0- 0	0- 0	0	0	0
Clarence Jones	0- 0	0- 0	0	0	0
Jerry Tetzlaff	0- 0	0- 2	0	1	0
Jim Liss	0- 1	0- 0	0	0	0
Ken Andrews	0- 0	0- 0	0	0	0
Team			2		
Totals	24-57	18-24	21	17	66

Half time: 39-39. Officials: Howell and Shosid. Attendance: 19,301.

1974

East First Round

at Jamaica, New York

Pennsylvania	fg-fga	ft-fta	rb	pf	tp
Whitey Varga	4- 7	0- 0	2	2	8
Ron Haigler	8-21	3- 4	9	2	19
John Engles	12-21	3- 4	10	4	27
Bob Bigelow	2- 5	0- 0	4	1	4
John Beecroft	1- 9	2- 2	1	1	4
Bill Finger	0- 1	0- 0	1	0	0
Ed Stesanski	1- 1	0- 0	0	2	2
John Jablonski	1- 2	0- 1	1	0	2
Henry Johnson	1- 2	0- 0	4	2	2
Ed Enoch	0- 0	0- 0	0	0	0
Bill Jones	0- 0	1- 2	1	0	1
Team			1		
Totals	30-69	9-13	34	14	69

Providence	fg-fga	ft-fta	rb	pf	tp
Gary Bello	6-11	5- 5	3	1	17
Mark McAndrew	1- 9	0- 0	14	3	2
Marvin Barnes	11-20	4- 4	17	3	26
Kevin Stacom	8-17	0- 0	2	1	16
Bob Cooper	7-11	0- 0	8	2	14
Al Baker	2- 3	2- 2	2	2	6
Joe Hassett	0- 5	0- 0	1	0	0
Rick Santos	1- 1	0- 0	2	1	2
Rich Dunphy	0- 1	1- 2	0	1	1
Team			2		
Totals	36-78	12-13	51	14	84

Half time: Providence 39-34. Officials: Crowley and Saar. Attendance: 5,683.

at Morgantown, West Virginia

St. Joseph's, Pa.	fg-fga	ft-fta	rb	pf	tp
Ron Righter	7-14	3- 5	10	3	17
Eugene Prybella	1- 7	0- 0	4	1	2
Kevin Furey	2- 3	2- 3	8	4	6
Michael Moody	2- 8	3- 5	7	3	7
James O'Brien	2- 7	1- 1	1	4	5
John Zipp	0- 0	0- 0	0	0	0
Francis Rafferty	1- 3	0- 0	0	1	2
Craig Kelly	1- 2	1- 1	1	1	3
Louis Peltzer	0- 0	0- 0	0	0	0
Stephen Maczinko	0- 0	0- 0	0	0	0
Edward Benson	0- 0	0- 0	0	0	0
Team			5		
Totals	16-44	10-15	36	17	42

Pittsburgh	fg-fga	ft-fta	rb	pf	tp
Bill Knight	5-16	1- 2	7	3	11
Martin Mickey	6-12	0- 2	5	3	12
Jim Bolla	1- 2	0- 2	2	2	2
Kirk Bruce	1- 6	1- 1	2	0	3
Tom Richards	2- 7	1- 2	3	1	5
Ken Wagoner	0- 0	0- 0	1	0	0
Lew Hill	4- 6	1- 2	4	3	9
Keith Starr	4- 8	2- 2	1	3	10
Willie Kelly	1- 1	0- 0	0	1	2
Marvin Abrams	0- 1	0- 0	0	0	0
George McBride	0- 0	0- 0	0	0	0
Sam Flemming	0- 0	0- 0	0	0	0
Team			5		
Totals	24-59	6-13	30	16	54

Half time: Pittsburgh 25-16. Officials: Folsom and Jacobs. Attendance: 6,663.

David Thompson

312

at Philadelphia, Pennsylvania

South Carolina	fg-fga	ft-fta	rb	pf	tp
Bob Mathias	2- 6	0- 1	8	4	4
Nate Davis	8-19	0- 0	13	4	16
Alex English	5-15	1- 2	11	4	11
Mike Dunleavy	5-14	2- 2	4	0	12
Brian Winters	11-27	0- 0	1	5	22
Mark Greiner	1- 2	0- 2	7	2	2
Jim Walsh	0- 1	0- 0	0	0	0
Team			5		
Totals	32-84	3- 7	49	19	67

Furman	fg-fga	ft-fta	rb	pf	tp
Bud Bierly	0- 4	0- 0	5	2	0
Craig Lynch	6-17	2- 2	8	1	14
Clyde Mayes	9-13	3- 3	16	1	21
Ed Kelly	4- 7	2- 3	4	2	10
Bruce Grimm	8-18	3- 5	2	2	19
Fessor Leonard	4- 9	3- 4	2	4	11
Gary Clark	0- 2	0- 0	2	0	0
Baron Hill	0- 0	0- 0	1	0	0
Team			10		
Totals	31-70	13-17	50	12	75

Half time: Furman 39-38. Officials: Hartman and Burch. Attendance: 1,042.

East Regional

at Raleigh, North Carolina

North Carolina St.	fg-fga	ft-fta	rb	pf	tp
Moe Rivers	3-16	5- 6	3	3	11
Tom Burleson	7-19	2- 5	24	3	16
Monte Towe	5-14	5- 6	4	3	15
Tim Stoddard	1- 6	0- 0	3	4	2
David Thomson	16-29	8-10	10	2	40
Phil Spence	1- 2	0- 0	2	2	2
Steve Nunce	1- 2	4- 4	4	2	6
Mark Moeller	0- 0	0- 0	2	0	0
Team			6		
Totals	34-88	24-31	58	19	92

Providence	fg-fga	ft-fta	rb	pf	tp
Gary Bello	4-10	1- 2	3	1	9
Mark McAndrew	2- 2	0- 0	0	2	4
Marvin Barnes	5-14	4- 7	13	5	14
Kevin Stacom	8-17	2- 2	4	5	18
Bob Cooper	7-13	3- 4	10	2	17
Al Baker	1- 3	0- 1	3	4	2
Rick Santos	3- 5	0- 0	3	5	6
Joe Hassett	4-11	0- 0	1	2	8
Rich Dunphy	0- 0	0- 0	0	0	0
Team			7		
Totals	34-75	10-16	44	26	78

Half time: North Carolina State 44-39. Officials: Richards and Goddard. Attendance: 12,400.

at Raleigh, North Carolina

Pittsburgh	fg-fga	ft-fta	rb	pf	tp
Tom Richards	3- 5	0- 0	1	3	6
Bill Knight	12-20	10-11	7	4	34
Kirk Bruce	6- 9	0- 0	6	2	12
Mickey Martin	5-14	0- 0	4	4	10
Jim Bolla	0- 1	0- 0	0	0	0
Lew Hill	6-13	0- 0	1	2	12
Keith Starr	1- 4	1- 3	4	3	3
Ken Wagoner	1- 1	0- 0	2	1	2
Willie Kelly	1- 2	0- 0	2	2	2
Team			8		
Totals	35-69	11-16	35	21	81

Furman	fg-fga	ft-fta	rb	pf	tp
Ed Kelly	3- 7	3- 4	0	4	9
Fessor Leonard	7-13	3- 3	5	5	17
Clyde Mayes	6-11	0- 1	8	2	12
Craig Lynch	3- 6	0- 0	4	2	6
Bruce Grimm	9-18	9-11	6	4	27
Bud Bierly	1- 3	1- 1	4	4	3
Baron Hill	1- 2	2- 2	1	1	4
Michael Hall	0- 0	0- 0	0	0	0
Gary Clark	0- 0	0- 0	0	0	0
Team			6		
Totals	30-60	18-22	34	22	78

Half time: Pittsburgh 38-34. Officials: Bain and Galvan. Attendance: 12,400.

at Raleigh, North Carolina

Providence	fg-fga	ft-fta	rb	pf	tp
Mark McAndrew	2- 3	0- 0	5	3	4
Bob Cooper	7-10	2- 4	6	3	16
Marvin Barnes	8-20	2- 2	21	4	18
Gary Bello	5- 8	0- 0	3	1	10
Kevin Stacom	8-22	2- 5	7	0	18
Al Baker	2- 3	3- 4	0	2	7
Rick Santos	5- 6	2- 2	2	1	12
Joe Hassett	4- 7	2- 2	2	0	10
Rich Dunphy	0- 0	0- 0	0	0	0
Bob Ollquist	0- 1	0- 0	1	0	0
Tom Walters	0- 1	0- 0	0	0	0
Team			2		
Totals	41-81	13-19	49	14	95

Furman	fg-fga	ft-fta	rb	pf	tp
Clyde Mayes	9-21	2- 4	13	2	20
Craig Lynch	7-10	1- 1	3	0	15
Fessor Leonard	4-16	3- 3	9	4	11
Ed Kelly	5-12	0- 0	6	1	10
Bruce Grimm	8-16	1- 2	2	3	17
Bud Bierly	1- 2	2- 2	2	1	4
Baron Hill	0- 3	0- 0	1	1	0
Michael Hall	2-11	0- 0	9	3	4
Gary Clark	1- 3	0- 1	1	2	2
Team			5		
Totals	37-94	9-13	51	18	83

Half time: Providence 47-37. Officials: Richards and Goddard. Attendance: 12,400.

at Raleigh, North Carolina

North Carolina St.	fg-fga	ft-fta	rb	pf	tp
Tim Stoddard	3- 9	1- 2	6	3	7
David Thompson	3- 4	2- 3	2	0	8
Tom Burleson	9-19	8- 8	12	4	26
Moe Rivers	8-12	1- 4	8	2	17
Monte Towe	6-17	7- 7	4	2	19
Phil Spence	4-10	2- 3	14	3	10
Steve Nunce	1- 4	2- 2	2	2	4
Mark Moeller	0- 0	0- 0	0	0	0
Greg Hawkins	1- 4	5- 6	1	2	7
Dwight Johnson	0- 0	0- 0	0	0	0
Craig Kuszmual	0- 0	0- 0	0	0	0
Mike Buurma	0- 0	0- 0	0	0	0
Bruce Dayhuff	0- 0	0- 0	0	0	0
Bill Lake	0- 0	2- 2	0	0	2
Team			11		
Totals	35-79	30-37	60	18	100

at Raleigh, North Carolina

Pittsburgh	fg-fga	ft-fta	rb	pf	tp
Bill Knight	9-19	1- 2	10	2	19
Mickey Martin	6-13	0- 0	2	3	12
Jim Bolla	2- 3	0- 0	0	2	4
Tom Richards	3- 7	4- 4	2	3	10
Kirk Bruce	0- 5	3- 4	1	3	3
Keith Starr	2- 7	0- 0	2	1	4
Lew Hill	5-12	0- 1	3	3	10
Ken Wagoner	0- 0	0- 0	5	0	0
Willie Kelly	1- 3	1- 2	2	4	3
Sam Flemming	1- 1	1- 3	1	1	3
Marvin Abrams	2- 3	0- 0	1	2	4
Bob Shrewsbury	0- 2	0- 0	0	1	0
George McBride	0- 1	0- 0	0	0	0
Mark Disco	0- 0	0- 0	2	1	0
Team			8		
Totals	31-76	10-16	34	31	72

Half time: North Carolina State 47-41. Officials: Bain and Galvin. Attendance: 12,400.

West First Round

at Pocatello, Idaho

New Mexico	fg-fga	ft-fta	rb	pf	tp
Gabe Nava	3-12	0- 0	2	2	6
Wendell Taylor	1- 4	0- 0	2	4	2
Bernard Hardin	8-22	3- 3	6	2	19
Pat King	2- 5	0- 1	1	1	4
Dan Davis	1- 1	0- 0	0	0	2
Bob Toppert	0- 1	0- 0	0	0	0
Bruce Battle	2- 6	0- 0	3	0	4
Mark Saiers	8-15	2- 2	14	1	18
Rich Pokorski	1- 1	0- 0	4	3	2
Bill Hagins	6- 8	2- 2	10	5	14
Paul Kruse	1- 1	0- 0	3	1	2
Team			5		
Totals	33-76	7- 8	50	19	73

Idaho State	fg-fga	ft-fta	rb	pf	tp
Kevin Hoyt	7-18	0- 0	5	0	14
Matt Stranningan	1- 5	2- 2	0	3	4
Dennis Green	0- 1	1- 2	1	0	1
Leroy Gibbons	3- 7	0- 0	10	4	6
Frank Krahn	0- 0	0- 0	0	1	0
Jim Anderson	6-14	1- 1	9	2	13
George Rodriguez	0- 3	2- 2	2	2	2
Dan Spindler	6- 9	2- 3	5	1	14
Ron Kruidhof	0- 2	0- 0	1	0	0
Steve Hayes	3- 5	3- 4	1	2	9
Paul Doos	1- 2	0- 0	2	0	2
Team			2		
Totals	27-66	11-14	38	17	65

Half time: New Mexico 39-34. Officials: Soloman and Harrold. Attendance: 9,400.

at Pocatello, Idaho

Dayton	fg-fga	ft-fta	rb	pf	tp
Don Smith	9-17	4- 4	3	3	22
John Davis	8-15	6- 6	4	4	22
Mike Sylvester	13-20	4- 4	11	2	30
John Von Lehman	1- 2	2- 4	5	2	4
Leighton Moulton	0- 0	0- 0	0	0	0
Joe Fisher	2- 2	2- 2	7	1	6
Jim Testerman	0- 0	0- 0	0	0	0
Allen Elijah	2- 4	0- 1	9	3	4
Team			1		
Totals	35-60	18-21	40	15	88

Los Angeles State	fg-fga	ft-fta	rb	pf	tp
Alfonso Brigham	6-16	0- 1	2	1	12
Bobby Taylor	4- 7	0- 0	2	2	8
Terry Tate	1- 4	0- 1	4	3	2
Tommie Lipsey	9-15	4- 4	8	2	22
Billy Mallory	7-14	0- 1	4	5	14
Willie Jackson	5- 8	2- 3	1	3	12
Dwight Slaughter	3- 6	0- 0	1	5	6
Darcy Bailey	2- 4	0- 0	3	2	4
Team			4		
Totals	37-74	6-10	29	23	80

Half time: Dayton 46-44. Officials: Sherwood and Korte. Attendance: 5,683.

West Regional

at Tucson, Arizona

New Mexico	fg-fga	ft-fta	rb	pf	tp
Bernard Hardin	7-14	2- 3	7	3	16
Mark Saiers	6- 7	0- 0	5	3	12
Bill Hagins	4- 6	1- 2	4	0	9
Gabe Nava	2- 8	0- 0	2	3	4
Wendell Taylor	4- 8	2- 2	2	0	10
Rich Pokorski	0- 1	0- 0	0	0	0
Bob Toppert	0- 1	0- 0	0	0	0
Pat King	3- 3	4- 4	1	2	10
Bruce Battle	0- 1	0- 0	1	0	0
Mike Patterson	0- 0	0- 0	1	1	0
Team			5		
Totals	26-49	9-11	28	12	61

San Francisco	fg-fga	ft-fta	rb	pf	tp
Jeff Randell	3- 9	2- 2	6	3	8
Kevin Restani	7-12	0- 0	4	2	14
Eric Fernsten	3- 5	1- 1	3	3	7
John Boro	1- 1	2- 2	3	2	4
Phil Smith	3-13	1- 2	1	2	7
Russ Coleman	2- 3	0- 0	1	5	4
Howard Smith	8-12	2- 2	3	0	18
Brad Quanstrom	1- 1	0- 0	1	1	2
Team			4		
Totals	28-56	8- 9	26	18	64

Half time: San Francisco 28-24. Officials: Wartman and Weiler. Attendance: 13,314.

at Tucson, Arizona

Dayton	fg-fga	ft-fta	rb	pf	tp
Mike Sylvester	12-21	12-13	13	4	36
Allen Elijah	1- 4	0- 0	4	4	2
John Von Lehman	1- 4	0- 0	0	1	2
Don Smith	12-23	2- 2	4	2	26
John Davis	7-13	3- 7	4	4	17
Joe Fisher	6- 6	3- 5	4	5	15
Jim Testerman	1- 3	0- 0	3	4	2
Team			5		
Totals	40-74	20-25	38	23	100

UCLA	fg-fga	ft-fta	rb	pf	tp
Dave Meyers	13-25	2- 4	14	5	28
Keith Wilkes	7-15	0- 0	7	5	14
Bill Walton	13-23	1- 3	19	2	27
Tommy Curtis	0- 0	0- 0	0	1	0
Greg Lee	6-10	0- 0	3	3	12
Andre McCarter	4- 8	2- 3	1	2	10
Marques Johnson	5- 8	4- 5	5	2	14
Pete Trgovich	2- 6	0- 0	0	2	4
Richard Washington	0- 1	0- 1	1	0	0
Gary Franklin	1- 1	0- 1	0	1	2
Team			5		
Totals	51-97	9-17	55	23	111

Half time: UCLA 48-36. Regulation Score: 80-80. First Overtime: 88-88, Second Overtime: 98-98. Officials: Copeland and Stout. Attendance: 13,314.

at Tucson, Arizona

Dayton	fg-fga	ft-fta	rb	pf	tp
Mike Sylvester	4-18	2- 5	6	4	10
Allen Elijah	6-10	0- 0	9	4	12
John Von Lehman	0- 0	0- 0	4	5	0
Don Smith	10-20	2- 2	4	4	22
John Davis	3-10	2- 2	4	4	8
Joe Fisher	1- 5	3- 4	3	1	5
Jim Testerman	0- 0	0- 0	1	0	0
Jerome Holland	2- 2	0- 0	1	0	4
Team			4		
Totals	26-66	9-13	33	23	61

Norman Sloan

New Mexico	fg-fga	ft-fta	rb	pf	tp
Bernard Hardin	7-14	0-2	12	3	14
Mark Saiers	4-7	3-4	6	1	11
Bill Hagins	1-2	1-2	4	2	3
Gabe Nava	5-7	0-1	3	0	10
Wendell Taylor	6-14	2-3	3	3	14
Bruce Battle	0-0	0-0	2	0	0
Rich Pokorski	2-3	3-7	1	3	7
Mike Petterson	2-4	2-3	6	3	6
Pat King	0-3	0-0	2	0	0
Bob Toppert	0-6	1-2	2	0	1
Dan Davis	0-1	0-0	3	0	0
Team			3		
Totals	27-61	12-24	47	15	66

Half time: New Mexico 26-22. Officials: Wortman and Stout. Attendance: 13,658.

at Tucson, Arizona

UCLA	fg-fga	ft-fta	rb	pf	tp
Tommy Curtis	3-7	0-0	2	0	6
Greg Lee	3-6	2-2	4	0	8
Bill Walton	7-12	3-5	9	3	17
Dave Meyers	6-11	0-0	2	3	12
Keith Wilkes	13-28	1-1	8	0	27
Andre McCarter	1-2	0-1	2	2	2
Marques Johnson	2-3	1-2	5	1	5
Pete Trgovich	0-0	0-0	1	0	0
Ralph Drollinger	0-2	0-0	2	0	0
Bob Webb	0-0	0-0	1	0	0
Richard Washington	2-2	0-0	1	1	4
Gary Franklin	1-1	0-0	0	0	2
Team			4		
Totals	38-74	7-11	41	10	83

San Francisco	fg-fga	ft-fta	rb	pf	tp
Jeff Randell	0-6	2-2	7	3	2
Kevin Restani	10-13	0-0	7	1	20
Eric Fernsten	1-3	1-2	5	5	3
Phil Smith	9-20	0-0	4	3	18
Howard Smith	3-4	3-3	3	5	9
Russ Coleman	0-2	0-0	1	1	0
John Boro	0-3	0-0	1	1	0
Brad Quanstrom	3-4	0-0	2	0	6
Marlon Redmond	1-3	0-0	0	0	2
Tony Styles	0-2	0-0	1	0	0
Team			2		
Totals	27-60	6-7	33	19	60

Half time: UCLA 35-23. Officials: Weiler and Copeland. Attendance: 13,314.

Midwest Regional

at Tulsa, Oklahoma

Creighton	fg-fga	ft-fta	rb	pf	tp
Gene Harmon	7-13	2-2	6	0	16
Doug Brookins	5-14	0-0	15	0	10
Mike Heck	2-3	0-0	1	2	4
Ralph Bobik	2-7	4-5	1	2	8
Charles Butler	2-2	0-0	2	1	4
Ted Weubben	3-7	0-1	3	5	6
Tom Anderson	2-2	0-0	1	0	4
Richie Smith	1-1	0-0	0	0	2
Team			6		
Totals	24-49	6-8	35	10	54

Kansas	fg-fga	ft-fta	rb	pf	tp
Norman Cook	4-7	3-4	7	1	11
Roger Morningstar	9-19	0-0	5	3	18
Danny Knight	1-4	0-0	1	0	2
Tom Kivisto	2-8	2-2	3	3	6
Dale Greenlee	2-8	0-1	4	1	4
Rick Suttle	5-13	0-0	6	2	10
Tommie Smith	2-3	0-0	1	1	4
Team			4		
Totals	25-62	5-7	31	11	55

Half time: Creighton 33-30. Officials: Crowley and Folsom. Attendance: 10,575.

at Tulsa, Oklahoma

Louisville	fg-fga	ft-fta	rb	pf	tp
Bill Butler	2-8	3-4	2	2	7
Junior Bridgeman	5-13	3-5	8	1	13
Wesley Cox	3-6	2-2	8	4	8
Allen Murphy	6-14	1-2	0	4	13
Terry Howard	3-4	3-3	1	3	9
Ike Whitfield	3-8	1-2	1	0	7
Danny Brown	5-6	2-2	1	1	12
Billy Harmon	0-0	0-0	0	1	0
Jim Protenic	1-1	0-0	1	1	2
Tony Kinnaird	0-1	0-0	0	0	0
Stan Bunton	0-1	0-0	2	4	0
Jeff Wayne	0-0	0-0	1	0	0
Team			7		
Totals	28-62	15-20	32	21	71

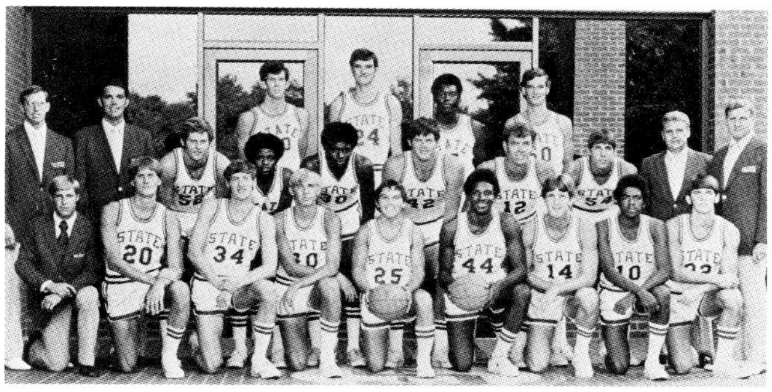

1974 NORTH CAROLINA STATE WOLFPACK—(l-r) Front Row: Mike Sloan, Steve Smoral, Craig Kuszmaul, Mark Moeller, Monte Towe, David Thompson, Greg Hawkins, Moe Rivers, Bruce Dayhuff; Second Row: Eddie Biedenbach, Art Musselman, Steve Nuce, Dwight Johnson, Jerry Hunt, Tim Stoddard, Steve Smith, Ken Gehring, Sam Esposito, Norman Sloan; Third Row: Bill Lake, Tommy Burleson, Phil Spence, Mike Buurma.

Creighton	fg-fga	ft-fta	rb	pf	tp
Gene Harmon	7-19	8-8	8	4	22
Doug Brookins	9-12	1-1	7	2	19
Mike Heck	4-7	0-0	7	3	8
Ralph Bobik	2-7	0-1	3	4	4
Charles Butler	2-5	0-0	3	1	4
Ted Weubben	5-6	4-6	3	2	14
Tom Anderson	2-3	1-2	2	1	5
Bimbo Pietro	1-1	0-0	0	0	2
Richie Smith	1-2	0-0	2	2	2
Team			5		
Totals	33-62	14-18	40	19	80

Half time: 38-38. Officials: Crowley and Folsom. Attendance: 10,575.

at Tulsa, Oklahoma

Oral Roberts	fg-fga	ft-fta	rb	pf	tp
Duane Fox	4-8	0-0	5	4	8
Greg McDougald	5-11	3-4	6	4	13
Eddie Woods	4-7	3-5	6	5	11
Sam McCants	8-24	8-11	10	2	24
Al Boswell	7-23	4-4	3	4	18
Anthony Roberts	6-9	0-0	6	0	12
Willis Collins	2-6	0-0	7	3	4
Team			9		
Totals	36-88	18-24	52	22	90

Kansas	fg-fga	ft-fta	rb	pf	tp
Norman Cook	5-7	0-1	7	2	10
Roger Morningstar	6-8	4-5	6	4	16
Danny Knight	9-16	1-2	8	4	19
Tom Kivisto	5-12	3-4	1	3	13
Dale Greenlee	8-14	2-2	2	3	18
Rick Suttle	5-10	2-2	6	4	12
Tommie Smith	2-6	1-2	5	1	5
Team			9		
Totals	40-73	13-18	44	21	93

Half time: Kansas 45-44. Officials: Howell and Nichols. Attendance. 10,575.

Semifinals

at Greensboro, North Carolina

UCLA	fg-fga	ft-fta	rb	pf	tp
Dave Meyers	6-9	0-1	8	4	12
Keith Wilkes	5-17	5-5	7	5	15
Bill Walton	13-21	3-3	18	2	29
Tommy Curtis	4-8	3-4	5	4	11
Greg Lee	4-11	0-0	4	2	8
Marques Johnson	0-3	0-0	0	0	0
Andre McCarter	1-2	0-0	0	0	2
Team			2		
Totals	33-71	11-13	44	18	77

North Carolina St.	fg-fga	ft-fta	rb	pf	tp
Tim Stoddard	4-11	1-2	9	5	9
David Thompson	12-25	4-6	10	3	28
Tom Burleson	9-20	2-6	14	4	20
Moe Rivers	3-8	1-2	2	3	7
Monte Towe	4-10	4-4	2	4	12
Phil Spence	2-3	0-0	5	0	4
Greg Hawkins	0-0	0-0	0	0	0
Team			2		
Totals	34-77	12-20	44	19	80

Half time: 35-35. Regulation Score: 65-65. First Overtime: 77-77. Officials: Weiler and Galvin. Attendance: 15,829.

at Greensboro, North Carolina

Kansas	fg-fga	ft-fta	rb	pf	tp
Norman Cook	1-3	2-4	5	5	4
Roger Morningstar	5-13	0-0	5	4	10
Danny Knight	0-5	0-0	5	3	0
Dale Greenlee	3-7	0-0	3	4	6
Tom Kivisto	2-7	2-5	2	4	6
Rick Suttle	8-13	3-4	9	2	19
Tommie Smith	3-4	0-0	4	3	6
Team			4		
Totals	22-52	7-13	37	25	51

Marquette	fg-fga	ft-fta	rb	pf	tp
Maurice Ellis	2-9	1-2	10	3	5
Earl Tatum	5-11	4-6	3	3	14
Maurice Lucas	7-11	4-4	14	2	18
Lloyd Walton	2-7	3-4	1	4	7
Marcus Washington	5-12	6-11	3	4	16
Ed Daniels	0-2	0-0	0	1	0
Rick Campbell	0-1	0-0	1	0	0
Jerry Homan	1-2	0-0	0	2	2
Dave Delsman	0-1	2-2	0	1	2
Barry Brennan	0-0	0-0	0	0	0
John Bryant	0-0	0-0	0	0	0
Paul Vollmer	0-0	0-0	0	0	0
Greg Johnson	0-0	0-0	0	0	0
Team			6		
Totals	22-56	20-29	38	20	64

Half time: Kansas 24-23. Officials: Brown and Howell. Attendance: 15,829.

National Third Place

at Greensboro, North Carolina

UCLA	fg-fga	ft-fta	rb	pf	tp
Dave Meyers	3-5	2-2	1	3	8
Keith Wilkes	6-10	0-0	5	0	12
Bill Walton	3-3	0-3	8	1	6
Tommy Curtis	0-0	0-0	0	0	0
Greg Lee	0-2	0-0	0	2	0
Pete Trgovich	6-9	2-2	2	1	14
Andre McCarter	1-4	2-2	4	1	4
Gary Franklin	1-2	0-0	3	1	2
Marques Johnson	2-3	0-2	2	0	4
Ralph Drollinger	1-6	5-8	6	4	7
Richard Washington	4-6	0-1	5	1	8
Bob Webb	4-7	2-2	0	1	10
Jim Spillane	0-1	1-2	1	2	1
Wilbert Olinde	1-1	0-0	2	0	2
Team			2		
Totals	32-59	14-24	41	17	78

Kansas	fg-fga	ft-fta	rb	pf	tp
Norman Cook	3-11	3-4	8	4	9
Roger Morningstar	1-7	1-2	6	4	3
Danny Knight	5-10	2-2	5	2	12
Dale Greenlee	7-12	3-3	3	2	17
Tom Kivisto	2-5	4-5	3	3	8
Tommie Smith	3-7	0-0	4	4	6
Rick Suttle	2-11	0-0	7	5	4
Donnie Von Moore	0-2	0-0	2	0	0
Dave Taynor	1-4	0-0	0	0	2
Team			3		
Totals	24-69	13-16	41	24	61

Half time: Kansas 38-31. Officials: Weiler and Galvin. Attendance: 15,742.

Championship

Marquette	fg-fga	ft-fta	rb	pf	tp
Maurice Ellis	6-16	0-0	11	5	12
Earl Tatum	2-7	0-0	3	4	4
Maurice Lucas	7-13	7-9	13	4	21
Lloyd Walton	4-10	0-0	2	2	8
Marcus Washington	3-13	5-8	4	3	11
Dave Delsman	0-0	0-0	0	2	0
Ed Daniels	1-3	1-2	0	3	3
Rick Campbell	2-3	0-0	1	3	4
Jerry Homan	0-4	1-2	6	2	1
Barry Brennan	0-0	0-0	0	1	0
Team			3		
Totals	25-69	14-21	43	29	64

North Carolina St.	fg-fga	ft-fta	rb	pf	tp
Tim Stoddard	3-4	2-2	7	5	8
David Thompson	7-12	7-8	7	3	21
Tom Burleson	6-9	2-6	11	4	14
Moe Rivers	4-9	6-9	2	2	14
Monte Towe	5-10	6-7	3	1	16
Phil Spence	1-2	1-2	3	2	3
Mark Moeller	0-0	0-0	0	0	0
Team			1		
Totals	26-46	24-34	34	17	76

Half time: North Carolina State 39-30. Officials: Howell and Brown. Attendance: 15,742.

1975

East First Round

at Philadelphia, Pennsylvania

Syracuse	fg-fga	ft-fta	rb	pf	tp
Rudy Hackett	11-19	8-10	12	2	30
Chris Sease	8-11	2-3	5	5	18
Earnie Seibert	1-4	0-0	3	3	2
Jim Lee	7-14	6-7	8	0	20
Jim Williams	3-9	0-0	0	3	6
Ross Kindel	0-4	3-4	2	1	3
Kevin King	4-9	0-0	6	2	8
Marty Byrnes	0-1	0-0	1	1	0
Steve Shaw	0-1	0-0	1	0	0
Totals	34-72	19-24	38	17	87

La Salle	fg-fga	ft-fta	rb	pf	tp
Donn Wilber	3-8	0-0	10	4	6
Bill Taylor	9-21	2-4	7	2	20
Joe Bryant	11-24	3-6	14	5	25
Charlie Wise	6-12	2-2	5	3	14
Glenn Collier	8-14	0-0	4	2	16
Gregg Metzinger	1-3	0-0	1	1	2
Barry Brodzinski	0-1	0-0	0	1	0
Varick Cutler	0-0	0-0	1	1	0
Totals	38-83	7-12	42	19	83

Half time: Syracuse 36-33. Regulation Score: 71-71. Officials: Grossman and Honzo.

at Charlotte, North Carolina

New Mexico State	fg-fga	ft-fta	rb	pf	tp
Bill Allen	7-11	0-0	3	1	14
Dexter Hawkins	2-6	3-3	0	5	7
Jim Bostic	11-15	0-0	12	4	22
Russell Letz	4-10	0-0	8	3	8
Richard Robinson	5-11	0-0	4	3	10
Alan Graham	0-4	4-4	5	4	4
Danny Lopez	1-4	0-1	0	2	2
George Pannell	0-1	0-0	0	0	0
Ricky Gibson	1-3	0-1	1	0	2
Jim Dove	0-0	0-0	0	0	0
John DiBiase	0-0	0-0	0	0	0
Team			5		
Totals	31-65	7-9	38	22	69

GAME-BY-GAME RESULTS

North Carolina	fg-fga	ft-fta	rb	pf	tp
Phil Ford	4- 9	4- 5	4	1	12
Brad Hoffman	7-12	2- 2	1	2	16
Mitch Kupchak	9-11	0- 2	8	4	18
Walter Davis	5-11	1- 2	2	1	11
Tommy LaGarde	5- 7	1- 1	4	5	11
Ed Stahl	2- 4	6- 6	3	2	10
Mickey Bell	1- 1	3- 4	1	1	5
John Kuester	1- 2	2- 2	0	0	4
Bill Chambers	1- 1	0- 0	1	0	2
Dave Hanners	1- 1	0- 0	0	1	2
Bruce Buckley	0- 1	0- 0	0	0	0
Tom Zaliagiris	1- 1	0- 0	0	0	2
Woody Coley	0- 0	0- 0	0	0	0
Eric Harry	0- 0	0- 0	0	0	0
Team			2		
Totals	37-61	19-24	26	17	93

Half time: North Carolina 39-37. Officials: Housman and Perry.

at Charlotte, North Carolina

Furman	fg-fga	ft-fta	rb	pf	tp
Ronnie Smith	1- 4	0- 0	2	5	2
Fessor Leonard	7-15	0- 0	14	4	14
Clyde Mayes	14-31	0- 2	19	4	28
Craig Lynch	4-16	0- 0	3	1	8
Michael Hall	7-16	0- 0	5	2	14
Steve Green	3- 3	0- 0	0	0	6
John Cottingham	0- 0	0- 0	4	2	0
Baron Hill	2- 4	0- 0	3	2	4
Team			5		
Totals	38-89	0- 2	55	20	76

Boston College	fg-fga	ft-fta	rb	pf	tp
Mel Weldon	1- 7	7- 8	2	0	9
Bob Carrington	8-19	1- 3	8	3	17
Wil Morrison	6-13	8-10	5	0	20
Bill Collins	7-11	4- 5	13	3	18
Jeff Bailey	8-15	0- 0	2	2	16
Mike Shirey	1- 1	0- 0	3	1	2
Team			4		
Totals	31-66	20-26	37	9	82

Half time: Boston College 37-34. Officials: Nichols and Spitter. Attendance: 11,666.

at Philadelphia, Pennsylvania

Kansas State	fg-fga	ft-fta	rb	pf	tp
Doug Snider	2- 6	1- 2	2	3	5
Dan Droge	3-10	3- 4	8	4	9
Carl Gerlach	8-13	4- 5	16	1	20
Chuckie Williams	10-22	0- 1	3	1	20
Mike Evans	4-10	5- 5	2	1	13
Bobby Noland	1- 5	0- 0	10	4	2
Jim Molinari	0- 1	0- 0	1	0	0
Totals	28-67	13-17	42	14	69

Pennsylvania	fg-fga	ft-fta	rb	pf	tp
Henry Johnson	5-12	2- 3	17	4	12
Bob Bigelow	7-16	1- 2	8	2	15
Ron Haigler	8-21	1- 3	9	3	17
Mark Lonetto	7-14	0- 0	2	4	14
John Beecroft	1- 4	0- 0	1	4	2
Ed Stefanski	1- 1	0- 0	1	3	2
Bill Jones	0- 2	0- 0	0	0	0
Totals	29-70	4- 8	38	20	62

Half time: Kansas State 40-28. Officials: Hernjak and Overby. Attendance: 9,233.

Richard Washington

East Regional

at Providence, Rhode Island

North Carolina	fg-fga	ft-fta	rb	pf	tp
Phil Ford	7-10	10-10	1	4	24
Brad Hoffman	10-12	0- 0	1	1	20
Dave Hanners	0- 0	0- 0	0	1	0
John Kuester	0- 1	0- 0	0	1	0
Mitch Kupchak	6-11	0- 0	8	3	12
Walter Davis	2- 4	0- 0	2	5	4
Mickey Bell	0- 0	0- 1	1	0	0
Tom Zaliagiris	0- 0	0- 0	0	0	0
Bruce Buckley	0- 0	0- 2	0	0	0
Bill Chambers	0- 1	0- 0	0	1	0
Ed Stahl	2- 4	0- 0	1	1	4
Tommy LaGarde	5- 6	2- 2	7	1	12
Team			6		
Totals	32-49	12-15	27	18	76

Syracuse	fg-fga	ft-fta	rb	pf	tp
Jim Lee	12-18	0- 0	0	3	24
Ross Kindel	0- 0	0- 0	0	0	0
Jim Williams	9-11	1- 2	0	4	19
Kevin King	4- 7	4- 6	2	5	12
Rudy Hackett	3- 7	0- 0	1	4	6
Earnie Seibert	3- 9	0- 0	9	2	6
Bob Parker	0- 0	1- 2	0	0	1
Chris Sease	4- 8	2- 4	6	2	10
Team			6		
Totals	35-60	8-14	24	20	78

Half time: North Carolina 42-41. Officials: Dreith and Overby.

at Providence, Rhode Island

Boston College	fg-fga	ft-fta	rb	pf	tp
Jeff Jurgens	0- 0	0- 0	0	0	0
Mel Weldon	2-10	2- 2	2	4	6
Mike Shirey	0- 0	0- 0	1	0	0
Bob Carrington	5-15	4- 5	4	5	14
Jeff Bailey	5-14	0- 0	3	1	10
Wil Morrison	7-20	3- 4	9	3	17
Bill Collins	8-16	2- 2	8	2	18
Team			7		
Totals	27-75	11-13	34	15	65

Kansas State	fg-fga	ft-fta	rb	pf	tp
Chuckie Williams	15-25	2- 2	3	3	32
Mike Evans	3- 6	1- 2	5	1	7
Doug Snider	3- 3	0- 0	4	3	6
Bobby Noland	1- 1	1- 1	0	1	3
Carl Gerlach	9-10	2- 4	13	3	20
Dan Droge	3- 9	0- 0	7	3	6
Team			7		
Totals	34-54	6- 9	39	14	74

Half time: Kansas State 39-36. Officials: Galvan and Lawson. Attendance: 10,981.

at Providence, Rhode Island

North Carolina	fg-fga	ft-fta	rb	pf	tp
Phil Ford	8-16	3- 3	1	2	19
Brad Hoffman	8-15	0- 0	3	3	16
Dave Hanners	0- 0	0- 0	1	0	0
John Kuester	1- 1	1- 1	0	0	3
Mitch Kupchak	14-18	8-13	13	4	36
Walter Davis	7-12	0- 1	5	5	14
Woody Coley	0- 0	0- 0	0	0	0
Mickey Bell	0- 3	0- 0	6	0	0
Tom Zaliagiris	0- 0	2- 2	0	0	2
Bruce Buckley	0- 0	0- 0	2	1	0
Bill Chambers	0- 1	0- 0	0	0	0
Ed Stahl	5- 9	6- 6	9	3	16
Eric Harry	0- 0	0- 0	0	0	0
Tommy LaGarde	1- 2	2- 2	2	0	4
Team			10		
Totals	44-77	22-28	52	18	110

Boston College	fg-fga	ft-fta	rb	pf	tp
John O'Brien	0- 0	0- 0	1	0	0
Jeff Jurgens	1- 1	0- 0	0	0	2
Mel Weldon	7-13	0- 0	4	5	14
Mitch Buonaguro	2- 2	0- 1	1	1	4
Frank Tracey	0- 1	0- 0	0	0	0
Mike Shirey	2- 6	0- 0	2	1	4
Bob Carrington	10-20	3- 3	2	3	23
Syd Sheppard	3- 6	2- 2	5	3	8
Jeff Bailey	2-13	7- 8	1	2	11
Wil Morrison	5- 8	0- 1	4	4	10
Bill Collins	5- 8	4- 4	6	4	14
Team			5		
Totals	37-78	16-19	31	23	90

Half time: North Carolina 54-37. Officials: Dreith and Overby.

John Wooden

at Providence, Rhode Island

Kansas State	fg-fga	ft-fta	rb	pf	tp
Chuckie Williams	14-27	7- 9	7	2	35
Mike Evans	6-21	8- 8	7	5	20
Jim Molinari	0- 0	0- 0	1	0	0
Doug Snider	5-10	1- 3	6	4	11
Bob Noland	0- 1	2- 2	5	5	2
Carl Gerlach	0- 4	0- 0	4	5	0
Dan Droge	5-15	1- 2	18	4	11
Darryl Winston	4- 6	0- 0	0	2	8
Team			7		
Totals	34-84	19-24	54	28	87

Syracuse	fg-fga	ft-fta	rb	pf	tp
Jim Lee	10-17	5- 7	3	5	25
Larry Arrington	0- 0	0- 0	0	0	0
Ross Kindel	3- 5	2- 2	4	3	8
Jim Williams	4- 8	2- 2	3	5	10
Kevin King	4- 7	2- 2	4	1	10
Steve Shaw	0- 0	0- 1	1	0	0
Rudy Hackett	10-21	8-16	16	3	28
Earnie Seibert	1- 4	0- 0	3	3	2
Chris Sease	5-12	2- 2	10	4	12
Team			5		
Totals	37-74	21-32	49	24	95

Half time: Kansas State 38-36. Regulation Score: 76-76. Officials: Galvan and Lawson. Attendance: 9,295.

Mideast First Round

at Tuscaloosa, Alabama

Georgetown	fg-fga	ft-fta	rb	pf	tp
Mike Riley	4- 9	1- 1	2	1	9
Bill Thomas	0- 3	0- 0	1	1	0
Merlin Wilson	4- 7	0- 0	4	5	8
Ed Hopkins	3- 8	2- 3	8	2	8
Larry Long	4-13	0- 0	5	3	8
Jonathan Smith	4- 8	0- 0	3	1	8
Bill Lynn	6-17	2- 2	11	2	14
Mike McDermott	1- 5	0- 0	4	0	2
Derrick Jackson	9-14	0- 1	6	4	18
Craig Esherick	0- 0	0- 0	0	0	0
Team			6		
Totals	35-84	5- 7	49	22	75

Central Michigan	fg-fga	ft-fta	rb	pf	tp
Dan Roundfield	8-10	3- 8	7	2	19
Jim Helmink	7-12	4- 4	7	2	18
Russ Davis	3- 9	3- 4	7	1	9
Leonard Drake	2- 8	2- 2	2	3	6
James McElroy	7-17	5- 6	4	2	19
Dennis Parks	0- 3	4- 4	3	2	4
Al Cicotte	0- 0	0- 0	0	0	0
Jerry McClain	1- 1	0- 0	3	0	2
Darryl Alexander	0- 1	0- 0	0	0	0
Kurt Kaeding	0- 0	0- 0	0	0	0
Team			5		
Totals	28-61	21-28	38	12	77

Half time: Central Michigan 38-37. Officials: Copeland and Maracich.

at Tuscaloosa, Alabama

Marquette	fg-fga	ft-fta	rb	pf	tp
Bo Ellis	7-13	5- 8	7	4	19
Earl Tatum	5-10	0- 0	5	5	10
Jerry Homan	0- 8	2- 2	3	3	2
Butch Lee	0- 3	0- 0	2	2	0
Lloyd Walton	5-17	3- 4	3	4	13
Dave Delsman	0- 2	0- 0	0	0	0
Rick Campbell	1- 5	0- 0	9	4	2
Craig Butrym	0- 0	0- 0	1	1	0
Gary Rosenberger	0- 2	0- 0	0	2	0
Bill Neary	2- 2	3- 5	4	0	7
Barry Brennan	0- 0	0- 0	0	0	0
Paul Vollmer	0- 0	1- 2	0	1	1
Team			6		
Totals	20-62	14-21	40	26	54

Kentucky	fg-fga	ft-fta	rb	pf	tp
Kevin Grevey	8-18	3- 8	3	3	19
Bob Guyette	2- 8	10-12	15	1	14
Rick Robey	2- 4	0- 0	3	5	4
Jimmy Dan Conner	5- 9	3- 4	3	4	13
Mike Flynn	3- 5	2- 3	3	4	8
Larry Johnson	2- 5	0- 0	7	2	4
Jack Givens	0- 0	0- 0	0	0	0
Mike Phillips	5- 9	1- 3	6	0	11
Jerry Hale	0- 3	4- 0	0	3	0
Dan Hall	0- 0	0- 0	0	1	0
James Lee	0- 0	0- 1	0	0	0
Merion Haskins	0- 0	0- 0	2	0	0
G. J. Smith	0- 0	0- 0	0	0	0
Joey Holland	0- 0	0- 0	1	1	0
Team			3		
Totals	27-58	22-34	47	21	76

Half time: Marquette 28-25. Officials: Wortman and DeBonis. Attendance: 9,825.

at Lexington, Kentucky

Texas-El Paso	fg-fga	ft-fta	rb	pf	tp
Ed Lynum	1- 3	2- 3	8	3	4
John Saffle	1- 3	4- 4	4	5	5
Gary Brewster	4-10	2- 2	5	5	10
Ron Jones	1- 6	0- 0	1	4	2
Rudy Alvarez	2- 2	0- 0	3	4	4
Charles Draper	3- 5	0- 0	4	4	6
Jake Poole	2- 6	0- 0	0	2	4
Tom Pauling	3- 8	0- 0	5	0	6
Calvin Hale	4- 6	2- 2	4	0	10
Ted Williams	0- 0	2- 2	0	0	2
James Edmonson	0- 1	0- 0	0	0	0
Clifford Russell	0- 1	0- 1	0	0	0
Team			3		
Totals	21-51	11-14	31	25	53

Indiana	fg-fga	ft-fta	rb	pf	tp
John Laskowski	5-12	5-6	6	1	15
Steve Green	5-7	4-6	2	4	14
Kent Benson	3-8	1-3	10	4	7
Bob Wilkerson	3-8	1-4	5	3	7
Quinn Buckner	5-15	2-4	9	3	12
Tom Abernethy	4-7	2-4	3	2	10
Wayne Radford	0-0	6-8	2	1	6
Steve Ahlfeld	1-1	0-0	0	0	2
John Kamstra	0-0	0-0	0	0	0
Mark Haymore	0-1	0-0	1	0	0
Jim Wisman	1-1	1-1	0	0	3
Don Noort	0-0	0-0	1	2	0
Jim Crews	1-1	0-0	0	0	2
Scott May	0-0	0-0	1	1	0
Team			1		
Totals	28-61	22-36	41	21	78

Half time: Indiana 31-24. Officials: Turner and Reed.

at Lexington, Kentucky

Oregon State	fg-fga	ft-fta	rb	pf	tp
Don Smith	7-10	1-2	7	0	15
Lonnie Shelton	11-20	1-2	11	4	23
Doug Oxsen	4-6	3-4	7	1	11
Charlie Neal	1-4	0-0	1	1	2
George Tucker	1-4	1-1	0	5	3
Paul Miller	4-7	2-2	3	4	10
Rickey Lee	1-5	0-1	4	5	2
Roosevelt Daniel	3-6	0-0	0	2	6
Leon Jordan	0-1	2-2	0	2	2
Steve Bakke	0-2	0-0	0	0	0
Carl Runyon	0-1	0-0	0	0	0
Tim Hennessey	1-2	0-2	1	1	2
Mark Gregg	0-1	0-0	0	0	0
Brad Woolrich	1-1	0-0	1	0	2
Team			5		
Totals	34-70	10-16	40	25	78

Middle Tenn. State	fg-fga	ft-fta	rb	pf	tp
George Sorrell	10-20	3-6	17	3	23
Steve Peeler	2-5	1-2	5	3	5
Tim Sisneros	4-7	2-5	8	3	10
Jimmy Martin	6-15	6-9	3	2	18
Claude Taylor	0-2	0-0	1	5	0
Fred Allen	0-6	0-0	3	1	0
Kim Malcom	0-2	0-0	0	0	0
Donnie Darcus	4-4	3-3	3	2	11
Ricky Collins	0-0	0-0	0	0	0
John Bonner	0-0	0-0	1	0	0
Team			3		
Totals	26-61	15-25	44	19	67

Half time: Oregon State 30-19. Officials: Perry and Barlow. Attendance: 11,500.

Mideast Regional

at Dayton, Ohio

Kentucky	fg-fga	ft-fta	rb	pf	tp
Jimmy Dan Conner	4-10	0-0	2	4	8
Mike Flynn	5-8	1-2	11	3	11
Rick Robey	5-9	1-2	7	4	11
Kevin Grevey	6-17	5-6	4	3	17
Bob Guyette	3-6	0-0	7	1	6
Jack Givens	6-12	0-0	6	2	12
Mike Phillips	7-12	1-3	7	3	15
Larry Johnson	2-5	2-3	2	3	6
Dan Hall	0-1	0-0	0	1	0
Jerry Hale	1-2	0-0	0	0	2
James Lee	0-0	0-0	1	2	0
G. J. Smith	1-1	0-0	0	0	2
Reggie Warford	0-0	0-0	0	0	0
Merion Haskins	0-0	0-0	0	0	0
Team			3		
Totals	40-83	10-16	50	26	90

Central Michigan	fg-fga	ft-fta	rb	pf	tp
Leonard Drake	3-9	3-5	12	1	9
James McElroy	8-20	1-3	5	4	17
Dan Roundfield	6-18	8-13	11	3	20
Russ Davis	4-6	2-2	5	5	10
Jim Helmink	4-13	2-2	6	3	10
Dennis Parks	1-1	0-0	0	0	2
Darryl Alexander	2-4	1-2	3	1	5
Kurt Kaeding	0-2	0-1	2	0	0
Jerry McClain	0-3	0-0	2	0	0
Al Cicotte	0-0	0-0	0	0	0
Team			7		
Totals	28-76	17-28	53	17	73

Half time: Kentucky 44-37. Officials: Filiberti and Soriano.

at Dayton, Ohio

Oregon State	fg-fga	ft-fta	rb	pf	tp
Charlie Neal	3-6	0-2	2	3	6
George Tucker	4-12	0-0	4	0	8
Doug Oxsen	2-4	0-0	4	0	4
Don Smith	6-11	2-3	2	4	14
Lonnie Shelton	3-5	1-1	6	5	7
Paul Miller	4-10	1-2	9	4	9
Rickey Lee	4-7	0-1	3	0	8
Roosevelt Daniel	3-4	2-2	1	1	8
Carl Runyon	2-5	0-0	1	0	4
Tim Hennessey	1-1	1-3	1	2	3
Team			1		
Totals	32-65	7-14	34	19	71

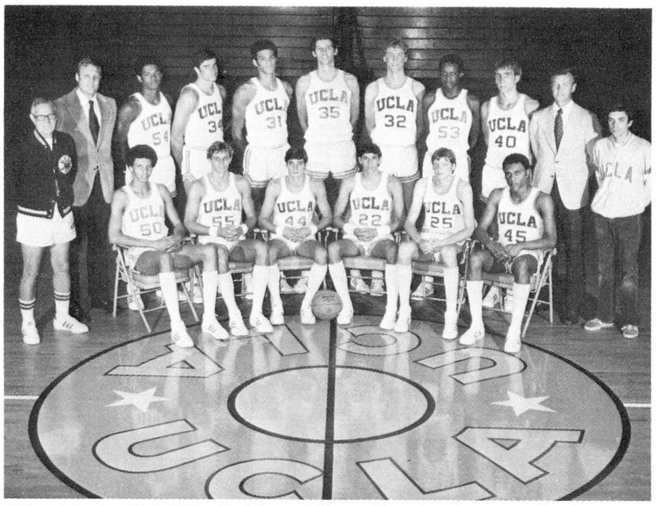

1975 UCLA BRUINS—(l-r) Front Row: Marvin Thomas, Gavin Smith, Jim Spillane, Raymond Townsend, Pete Trgovich, Andre McCarter; Second Row: John Wooden, Gary Cunningham, Marques Johnson, Dave Meyers, Richard Washington, Ralph Drollinger, Brett Vroman, Wilbert Olinde, Casey Corliss, Frank Arnold, Len Friedman.

Indiana	fg-fga	ft-fta	rb	pf	tp
Bob Wilkerson	4-8	2-2	5	4	10
Quinn Buckner	3-7	0-0	2	4	6
Kent Benson	11-18	1-2	9	3	23
John Laskowski	2-4	0-1	6	0	4
Steve Green	14-19	6-6	2	2	34
Wayne Radford	1-1	0-0	5	1	2
Tom Abernethy	0-0	0-0	1	1	0
Scott May	0-2	0-0	0	1	0
Steve Ahlfeld	0-0	0-0	0	0	0
Mark Haymore	0-0	0-0	0	1	0
Jim Wisman	0-0	0-0	0	0	0
Don Noort	0-0	0-0	0	0	0
Jim Crews	0-0	2-2	1	0	2
John Kamstra	0-0	0-1	0	0	0
Team			1		
Totals	35-59	11-14	32	17	81

Half time: Indiana 48-27. Officials: Korte and Sherwood. Attendance: 13,458.

at Dayton, Ohio

Central Michigan	fg-fga	ft-fta	rb	pf	tp
Russ Davis	3-8	0-0	3	5	6
Jim Helmink	4-10	1-2	4	0	9
Dan Roundfield	10-13	5-9	10	4	25
Leonard Drake	4-9	2-3	8	5	10
James McElroy	8-16	5-8	6	1	21
Dennis Parks	0-0	2-2	2	1	2
Jerry McClain	2-7	0-0	4	1	4
Kurt Kaeding	1-1	2-2	2	2	4
Darryl Alexander	3-3	1-2	3	2	7
Al Cicotte	0-0	0-0	0	0	0
Totals	35-67	18-28	42	21	88

Oregon State	fg-fga	ft-fta	rb	pf	tp
Don Smith	9-14	0-2	10	0	18
Lonnie Shelton	5-9	0-0	4	5	10
Doug Oxsen	3-9	2-2	0	2	8
Charlie Neal	4-6	2-2	4	4	10
George Tucker	6-13	1-2	7	3	13
Paul Miller	8-16	0-1	4	5	16
Rickey Lee	4-6	0-0	2	2	8
Roosevelt Daniel	1-3	2-5	4	2	4
Team			4		
Totals	40-76	7-14	39	23	87

Half time: Central Mich. 49-41. Officials: Filiberti and Muffick.

at Dayton, Ohio

Indiana	fg-fga	ft-fta	rb	pf	tp
Steve Green	10-17	1-1	4	4	21
Scott May	1-4	0-0	0	2	2
Kent Benson	13-18	7-9	23	3	33
Quinn Buckner	3-11	2-2	7	5	8
Bob Wilkerson	6-15	2-2	11	3	14
John Laskowski	4-13	4-6	3	3	12
Tom Abernethy	0-1	0-0	0	0	0
Wayne Radford	0-0	0-0	0	1	0
Steve Ahlfeld	0-0	0-0	0	0	0
Team			2		
Totals	37-79	16-20	50	21	90

Kentucky	fg-fga	ft-fta	rb	pf	tp
Kevin Grevey	6-19	5-6	3	4	17
Bob Guyette	0-1	2-4	7	4	2
Rick Robey	3-6	4-4	4	5	10
Jimmy Dan Conner	8-20	1-3	5	0	17
Mike Flynn	9-13	4-5	3	4	22
Jack Givens	4-7	0-0	6	0	8
Mike Phillips	4-4	2-2	4	5	10
Larry Johnson	3-5	0-1	1	0	6
Dan Hall	0-0	0-0	1	0	0
Merion Haskins	0-0	0-0	0	0	0
Team			3		
Totals	37-75	18-25	37	22	92

Half time: 44-44. Officials: Soriano and Korte. Attendance: 13,458.

Midwest First Round

at Lubbock, Texas

Cincinnati	fg-fga	ft-fta	rb	pf	tp
Brian Williams	7-13	4-4	10	4	18
Mike Franklin	3-7	0-0	20	5	6
Robert Miller	4-6	5-9	6	4	13
Steve Collier	7-16	6-6	1	1	20
Mike Jones	4-8	2-3	4	5	10
Hal Ward	3-8	2-2	3	2	8
Paul Fazekas	0-0	2-2	0	2	2
Mike Artis	1-4	0-0	3	0	2
Garry Kamstra	2-7	3-3	1	1	7
Bobby Sherlock	0-0	1-2	0	1	1
Team			5		
Totals	31-59	25-31	53	25	87

Texas A&M	fg-fga	ft-fta	rb	pf	tp
John Thornton	4-12	4-5	5	3	12
Barry Davis	5-17	6-7	15	1	16
Jerry Mercer	1-3	0-1	5	5	2
Mike Floyd	2-8	2-2	2	3	6
Sonny Parker	6-12	2-3	6	5	14
Cedric Joseph	1-2	0-1	2	1	2
Ray Roberts	5-14	5-6	2	3	15
Webb Williams	0-5	0-2	4	1	0
Gates Erwin	0-2	0-0	0	2	0
Mike Williams	0-1	0-0	0	0	0
Chuck Tone	6-9	0-1	2	0	12
Team			4		
Totals	30-85	19-28	47	24	79

Half time: Cincinnati 37-27. Officials: Howell and Snedeker.

at Tulsa, Oklahoma

Louisville	fg-fga	ft-fta	rb	pf	tp
Allen Murphy	6-14	4-5	0	4	16
Wesley Cox	3-4	0-0	7	4	6
William Bunton	6-11	1-1	11	1	13
Junior Bridgeman	15-18	6-7	11	3	36
Phillip Bond	0-3	0-0	0	4	0
Ike Whitfield	2-4	0-0	2	3	4
Rick Wilson	1-6	2-2	7	1	4
Billy Harmon	0-0	0-0	0	1	0
Stanley Bunton	0-0	0-0	1	0	0
Terry Howard	0-0	4-4	0	0	4
Ricky Gallon	2-2	0-0	1	1	4
Danny Brown	2-5	0-0	3	2	4
Team			2		
Totals	37-67	17-19	45	24	91

Rutgers	fg-fga	ft-fta	rb	pf	tp
Phil Sellers	12-17	5-8	4	4	29
Hollis Copeland	3-14	3-4	6	3	9
Mike Palko	0-1	0-0	2	0	0
Ed Jordan	8-13	3-8	4	5	19
Mike Dabney	4-14	0-0	5	4	8
Bruce Scherer	0-1	0-0	0	1	0
Jeff Kleinbaum	2-2	0-0	1	0	4
Steve Hefele	4-5	1-2	3	3	9
Team			3		
Totals	33-67	12-22	28	20	78

Half time: Rutgers 46-44. Officials: Menz and Cosby.

at Lubbock, Texas

Maryland	fg-fga	ft-fta	rb	pf	tp
Steve Sheppard	3-6	4-5	7	3	10
Owen Brown	8-11	0-3	11	3	16
Tom Roy	3-3	0-0	7	5	6
Brad Davis	6-9	2-2	0	5	14
John Lucas	9-15	1-2	3	2	19
Maurice Howard	7-11	2-3	2	5	16
Bill Hahn	0-0	0-2	1	0	0
Chris Patton	0-0	2-2	0	0	2
Team			2		
Totals	36-55	11-19	33	23	83

Creighton	fg-fga	ft-fta	rb	pf	tp
Daryl Heeke	6-11	2-3	2	5	14
Cornell Smith	1-5	1-4	10	5	3
Doug Brookins	9-20	7-8	5	3	25
Tom Anderson	6-9	1-2	2	4	13
Charles Butler	6-16	6-6	5	2	18
Rick Apke	1-4	2-2	2	1	4
Bob Scrutchens	0-1	0-0	0	1	0
Tim McConnell	1-1	0-0	0	0	2
Team			4		
Totals	30-67	19-25	30	21	79

Half time: Maryland 43-31. Officials: Calvan and Brown. Attendance: 7,100.

at Tulsa, Oklahoma

Kansas	fg-fga	ft-fta	rb	pf	tp
Donnie Von Moore	0-2	0-0	1	5	0
Norman Cook	3-7	2-2	10	5	8
Rick Suttle	7-10	3-5	10	3	17
Clint Johnson	4-7	0-0	1	5	8
Dale Greenlee	3-9	0-0	3	5	6
Danny Knight	7-13	1-1	2	2	15
Tommie Smith	2-6	0-0	2	5	4
Roger Morningstar	3-9	0-1	2	3	6
Milt Gibson	2-3	1-2	1	5	5
Ken Koenigs	0-0	2-2	2	0	2
Cris Barnthouse	0-1	0-0	1	1	0
Team			2		
Totals	31-67	9-13	37	39	71

GAME-BY-GAME RESULTS

316

Notre Dame	fg-fga	ft-fta	rb	pf	tp
Bill Paterno	3-8	3-4	3	3	9
Dave Batton	5-12	8-9	6	3	18
Toby Knight	1-5	4-4	6	4	6
Jeff Carpenter	0-0	2-3	2	3	2
Adrian Dantley	9-15	15-21	10	2	33
Dwight Clay	2-6	0-3	3	1	4
Peter Crotty	0-0	0-0	2	3	0
Ray Martin	0-2	1-3	3	0	1
Don Williams	1-1	2-3	0	0	4
Totals	21-49	35-50	35	19	77

Half time: Notre Dame 44-32. Officials: Wanamaker and Crowley. Attendance: 10,575.

Midwest Regional

at Las Cruces, New Mexico

Cincinnati	fg-fga	ft-fta	rb	pf	tp
Garry Kamstra	3-7	0-0	1	3	6
Hal Ward	3-7	0-0	0	4	6
Mike Jones	9-18	0-1	6	2	18
Mike Artis	1-4	0-1	1	0	2
Bobby Sherlock	0-0	0-0	0	1	0
Steve Collier	4-14	4-6	0	4	12
Mike Franklin	2-5	0-0	13	5	4
Robert Miller	5-8	1-2	7	3	11
Brian Williams	2-11	0-0	2	1	4
Team			3		
Totals	29-74	5-9	33	23	63

Louisville	fg-fga	ft-fta	rb	pf	tp
Junior Bridgeman	8-15	4-5	8	2	20
Danny Brown	2-2	0-0	0	0	4
Ricky Gallon	7-11	2-5	6	1	16
Allen Murphy	4-9	5-7	6	4	13
Terry Howard	0-1	2-2	1	0	2
Stanley Bunton	0-1	0-0	0	0	0
Phillip Bond	2-4	6-7	7	2	10
Billy Harmon	0-0	0-0	0	0	0
William Bunton	1-1	0-0	8	2	2
Ike Whitfield	4-4	0-0	4	0	8
Wesley Cox	1-5	1-2	2	0	3
Rick Wilson	0-1	0-0	1	1	0
Team			5		
Totals	29-54	20-28	48	12	78

Half time: Louisville 42-25. Officials: Hernjak and Nichols.

at Las Cruces, New Mexico

Maryland	fg-fga	ft-fta	rb	pf	tp
John Boyle	0-0	0-0	0	1	0
Steve Sheppard	4-8	1-1	4	3	9
John Lucas	8-12	8-8	0	3	24
John Newsome	0-0	0-1	0	0	0
Bill Hahn	0-0	0-0	1	0	0
Maurice Howard	5-9	0-0	4	4	10
Brad Davis	4-12	8-10	4	0	16
Owen Brown	7-13	4-5	9	4	18
Chris Patton	0-0	0-0	1	0	0
Tom Roy	3-4	0-0	6	4	6
Team			2		
Totals	31-58	21-25	31	19	83

Notre Dame	fg-fga	ft-fta	rb	pf	tp
Jeff Carpenter	1-3	2-2	3	4	4
Dwight Clay	0-1	0-0	1	1	0
Ray Martin	1-3	0-0	2	4	2
Dave Kuzmicz	0-1	0-0	0	0	0
Don Williams	0-7	0-1	3	2	0
Toby Knight	5-10	1-2	12	3	11
Adrian Dantley	10-18	5-8	11	5	25
Dave Batton	6-8	0-2	1	2	12
Bill Paterno	7-16	3-4	7	2	17
Team			2		
Totals	30-67	11-19	42	23	71

Half time: Maryland 38-36. Officials: Howell and Diehl. Attendance: 6,800.

at Las Cruces, New Mexico

Notre Dame	fg-fga	ft-fta	rb	pf	tp
Jeff Carpenter	1-5	2-2	5	5	4
Dwight Clay	1-4	0-0	2	2	2
Ray Martin	0-2	1-3	2	3	1
Randy Haefner	0-0	0-0	0	0	0
Dave Kuzmicz	2-2	0-0	1	1	4
Don Williams	1-3	0-0	1	4	2
Bill Drew	0-0	0-0	0	0	0
Peter Crotty	0-1	0-0	3	1	0
Toby Knight	7-19	2-6	15	5	16
Adrian Dantley	10-15	14-19	6	4	34
Dave Batton	2-8	0-1	5	2	4
Myron Schuckman	0-0	0-0	0	0	0
Bill Paterno	10-17	0-0	7	4	20
Team			6		
Totals	34-76	19-31	53	31	87

Cincinnati	fg-fga	ft-fta	rb	pf	tp
Garry Kamstra	5-11	10-12	0	1	20
Hal Ward	2-4	5-6	2	5	9
Mike Jones	8-15	1-2	7	5	17
Mike Artis	1-1	0-1	3	0	2
Bobby Sherlock	0-0	0-0	0	1	0
Steve Collier	0-9	0-0	3	2	0
Mike Franklin	2-10	1-2	16	3	5
Paul Fazekas	0-0	0-0	0	0	0
Robert Miller	12-17	2-4	10	2	26
Brian Williams	8-15	0-1	2	4	16
Team			7		
Totals	38-82	19-28	50	23	95

Half time: Cincinnati 47-38. Regulation Score: 76-76. Officials: Hernjak and Diehl.

at Las Cruces, New Mexico

Maryland	fg-fga	ft-fta	rb	pf	tp
Don Boyle	0-0	0-0	0	0	0
Steve Sheppard	2-6	6-6	5	2	10
John Lucas	11-19	5-6	6	4	27
John Newsome	0-0	0-0	0	0	0
Bill Hahn	0-0	0-0	0	0	0
Maurice Howard	1-6	0-1	0	5	2
Brad Davis	3-7	2-2	2	5	8
Owen Brown	8-22	3-4	2	4	19
Chris Patton	0-0	0-0	0	2	0
Tom Roy	5-9	6-6	20	3	16
Team			8		
Totals	30-69	22-25	43	25	82

Louisville	fg-fga	ft-fta	rb	pf	tp
Junior Bridgeman	3-11	7-10	3	4	13
Danny Brown	2-4	0-0	0	1	4
Ricky Gallon	1-2	0-1	6	0	2
Allen Murphy	10-18	0-0	4	5	20
Terry Howard	0-0	2-2	0	0	2
Stanley Bunton	0-0	0-0	0	0	0
Phillip Bond	9-17	5-6	4	2	23
Billy Harmon	0-0	0-0	0	0	0
William Bunton	6-8	1-3	12	4	13
Ike Whitfield	2-4	0-0	0	1	4
Wesley Cox	6-9	3-4	9	2	15
Rick Wilson	0-0	0-0	0	1	0
Team			2		
Totals	39-73	18-26	40	20	96

Half time: Louisville 42-37. Officials: Howell and Nichols. Attendance: 5,200.

West First Round

at Tempe, Arizona

Alabama	fg-fga	ft-fta	rb	pf	tp
T. R. Dunn	9-18	3-5	7	2	21
Charles Russell	5-13	0-0	2	5	10
Leon Douglas	12-21	5-14	21	3	29
Charles Cleveland	8-19	2-2	13	5	18
Anthony Murray	2-3	4-5	3	4	8
Rickey Brown	3-8	0-1	3	3	6
Johnny Dill	1-2	0-2	1	3	2
Team			3		
Totals	40-84	14-29	53	25	94

Arizona State	fg-fga	ft-fta	rb	pf	tp
Mike Moon	5-5	0-0	2	3	10
Lionel Hollins	6-14	5-6	3	5	17
Scott Lloyd	8-11	2-3	8	5	18
Rudy White	5-15	7-9	3	3	17
Jack Schrader	5-9	3-3	11	4	13
Gary Jackson	4-5	2-2	2	1	10
James Holliman	4-6	0-2	6	3	8
Nate Drayton	1-1	0-0	1	1	2
Ken Wright	1-3	0-0	3	4	2
Greg White	0-0	0-0	0	2	0
Rick Taylor	0-0	0-0	0	0	0
Team			2		
Totals	39-69	19-25	41	31	97

Half time: Arizona St. 55-36. Officials: Bagnasco and Tunney.

at Tempe, Arizona

San Diego State	fg-fga	ft-fta	rb	pf	tp
Steve Copp	5-10	6-11	17	4	16
Bob Kovach	5-11	0-2	5	3	10
Will Connelly	12-22	1-4	12	2	25
Allen Bunting	2-9	0-0	5	4	4
Ray Leary	5-9	0-0	1	5	10
Mark Delsman	2-3	2-5	2	0	6
Bob Green	3-4	1-2	3	1	7
Gary Earle	0-2	0-0	2	4	0
Raul Contreras	1-1	0-0	0	0	2
Jeff Welshans	0-0	0-1	2	1	0
Team			4		
Totals	35-71	10-25	53	24	80

Nevada-Las Vegas	fg-fga	ft-fta	rb	pf	tp
Jackie Robinson	4-11	1-3	8	2	9
Glen Gondrezick	4-11	0-0	4	5	8
Lewis Brown	9-14	0-1	12	4	18
Eddie Owens	10-15	1-4	8	2	21
Ricky Sobers	7-16	7-8	2	4	21
Boyd Batts	2-4	2-3	2	5	6
Robert Smith	3-6	1-2	1	1	7
Mike Milke	0-1	0-0	1	0	0
Matt Porter	0-1	0-1	1	0	0
John Freeman	0-0	0-0	1	1	0
Team			3		
Totals	39-79	12-22	43	24	90

Half time: Nevada Las Vegas 48-43. Officials: Brown and Crowell. Attendance: 14,733.

at Pullman, Washington

UCLA	fg-fga	ft-fta	rb	pf	tp
Rich Washington	11-14	0-1	17	4	22
Dave Myers	9-18	8-10	12	4	26
Jim Spillane	2-7	0-0	1	1	4
Andre McCarter	0-7	4-5	2	2	4
Wilbert Olinde	0-0	0-0	0	1	0
Raymond Townsend	0-1	0-0	1	0	0
Pete Trgovich	8-16	1-2	3	4	17
Ralph Drollinger	3-3	2-4	3	0	8
Marques Johnson	9-20	4-4	13	4	22
Team			7		
Totals	42-86	19-26	59	20	103

Michigan	fg-fga	ft-fta	rb	pf	tp
Joe Johnson	3-12	5-7	1	4	11
Dave Baxter	0-1	0-0	0	0	0
Steve Grote	7-15	0-0	9	5	14
Wayman Britt	3-6	2-2	5	5	8
Rick White	3-7	0-1	6	2	6
C. J. Kupec	13-25	2-4	5	3	28
John Robinson	9-16	6-6	7	4	24
Team			8		
Totals	38-82	15-20	41	23	91

Half time: Michigan 50-46. Regulation Score: 87-87. Officials: Sherwood and Stern.

at Pullman, Washington

Utah State	fg-fga	ft-fta	rb	pf	tp
Blair Martineau	2-3	0-0	1	3	4
Jimmy Moore	5-15	0-3	8	5	10
Rich Haws	10-18	6-8	12	3	26
Blair Reed	0-10	0-0	4	3	0
Oscar Williams	0-2	2-4	1	4	2
Mike Rock	4-6	0-0	1	2	8
Ed Gregg	5-14	3-6	7	2	13
Mike Santos	0-1	0-0	1	1	0
Team			5		
Totals	26-69	11-21	40	23	63

Montana	fg-fga	ft-fta	rb	pf	tp
Mark Nord	0-1	0-0	0	0	0
Mike R. Richardson	4-6	5-8	3	2	13
Larry Smedley	3-5	3-5	11	2	9
Ken McKenzie	4-19	2-2	13	4	10
Tim Stambaugh	0-1	0-0	1	5	0
Eric Hays	9-18	7-8	8	3	25
Ben DeMers	0-2	0-0	1	1	0
Tom Peck	5-8	2-2	3	4	12
Team			8		
Totals	25-60	19-25	48	21	69

Half time: Utah State 32-29. Officials: Soriano and Palesse. Attendance: 10,150.

West Regional

at Portland, Oregon

Arizona State	fg-fga	ft-fta	rb	pf	tp
James Holliman	2-5	2-3	3	1	6
Mike Moon	3-10	0-0	6	2	6
Rudy White	6-11	0-0	6	4	12
Lionel Hollins	6-16	0-3	3	3	12
Jack Schrader	5-9	3-4	15	4	13
Ken Wright	0-2	1-2	0	2	1
Scott Lloyd	8-13	1-1	3	4	17
Gary Jackson	8-11	1-2	6	0	17
Team			5		
Totals	38-77	8-15	47	20	84

Nevada-Las Vegas	fg-fga	ft-fta	rb	pf	tp
Robert Smith	5-11	3-3	1	1	13
Mike Milke	0-0	0-0	0	0	0
Lewis Brown	3-5	0-1	9	2	6
Eddie Owens	8-15	0-0	6	3	16
Glen Gondrezick	5-8	2-2	3	5	12
Jackie Robinson	4-9	0-0	7	0	8
Ricky Sobers	6-18	8-10	3	5	20
Boyd Batts	2-6	2-2	4	3	6
Team			6		
Totals	33-72	15-18	39	19	81

Half time: Nevada-Las Vegas 50-42. Officials: Pace and Weiler.

at Portland, Oregon

Montana	fg-fga	ft-fta	rb	pf	tp
Eric Hays	13-16	6-7	7	2	32
Mike R. Richardson	1-5	0-0	4	4	2
Ben DeMers	0-2	0-0	0	1	0
Tom Peck	0-1	0-0	4	1	0
Larry Smedley	5-12	0-0	5	2	10
Ken McKenzie	9-22	2-6	10	3	20
Tim Stambaugh	0-2	0-0	2	0	0
Team			4		
Totals	28-60	8-13	36	13	64

UCLA	fg-fga	ft-fta	rb	pf	tp
Raymond Townsend	1-1	0-0	1	0	2
Pete Trgovich	6-11	4-6	3	3	16
Rich Washington	7-17	2-2	11	3	16
Dave Meyers	6-14	0-0	5	1	12
Ralph Drollinger	3-5	2-4	9	3	8
Casey Corliss	0-1	0-0	0	1	0
Jim Spillane	0-1	0-0	0	2	0
Andre McCarter	3-8	0-2	1	1	6
Marques Johnson	3-7	1-2	6	1	7
Gavin Smith	0-0	0-0	0	0	0
Team			4		
Totals	29-65	9-16	40	15	67

Half time: UCLA 34-33. Officials: Workman and Fouty. Attendance: 9,797.

at Portland, Oregon

Montana	fg-fga	ft-fta	rb	pf	tp
Eric Hays	2-5	3-5	4	4	7
Mike R. Richardson	3-9	0-2	1	2	6
Mike J. Richardson	3-6	0-2	5	0	6
Ben DeMers	1-2	2-2	1	2	4
Tom Peck	4-7	2-2	1	2	10
Larry Smedley	6-10	3-4	8	1	15
Ken McKenzie	6-11	2-6	11	3	14
Tim Stambaugh	1-8	3-4	5	3	5
Team			3		
Totals	26-58	15-27	39	17	67

Nevada-Las Vegas	fg-fga	ft-fta	rb	pf	tp
Robert Smith	6-12	0-0	3	2	12
Eddie Owens	3-14	4-7	7	3	10
Lewis Brown	9-15	2-2	13	4	20
Glen Gondrezick	2-4	0-0	3	3	4
Jackie Robinson	2-5	2-4	5	0	6
Ricky Sobers	1-11	5-7	9	4	7
Boyd Batts	8-15	0-0	5	4	16
Team			5		
Totals	31-76	13-20	50	20	75

Half time: Montana 36-34. Officials: Weiler and Pace.

at Portland, Oregon

Arizona State	fg-fga	ft-fta	rb	pf	tp
James Holliman	1-5	1-2	7	3	3
Mike Moon	2-5	0-0	0	1	4
Rudy White	6-13	3-4	5	5	15
Lionel Hollins	8-22	0-1	0	4	16
Jack Schrader	4-12	1-2	12	4	9
Ken Wright	2-4	0-1	3	0	4
Scott Lloyd	8-13	4-8	9	4	20
Greg White	0-0	0-0	0	0	0
Gary Jackson	2-4	0-0	2	2	4
Team			2		
Totals	33-78	9-18	40	23	75

UCLA	fg-fga	ft-fta	rb	pf	tp
Pete Trgovich	4-14	0-1	4	3	8
Rich Washington	8-13	0-0	12	5	16
Dave Meyers	4-15	3-4	13	3	11
Ralph Drollinger	3-4	3-3	3	5	9
Andre McCarter	2-5	5-8	5	1	9
Wilbert Olinde	0-0	1-2	1	1	1
Marques Johnson	14-20	7-8	12	1	35
Team			3		
Totals	35-71	19-26	53	19	89

Half time: UCLA 46-36. Officials: Workman and Fouty. Attendance: 8,534.

Semifinals

at San Diego, California

Syracuse	fg-fga	ft-fta	rb	pf	tp
Rudy Hackett	4- 6	6- 9	5	5	14
Chris Sease	7-11	4- 4	10	4	18
Earnie Seibert	2- 3	0- 2	6	5	4
Jim Lee	10-17	3- 3	3	4	23
Jim Williams	2- 9	0- 1	2	5	4
Kevin King	2- 8	1- 3	5	1	5
Ross Kindel	1- 3	1- 2	1	1	3
Steve Shaw	0- 0	0- 0	2	2	0
Bob Parker	2- 3	4- 7	2	3	8
Marty Byrnes	0- 0	0- 1	1	0	0
Larry Kelley	0- 1	0- 0	0	0	0
Mark Meadors	0- 0	0- 0	1	0	0
Team			2		
Totals	30-61	19-32	40	30	79

Kentucky	fg-fga	ft-fta	rb	pf	tp
Kevin Grevey	5-13	4- 5	3	5	14
Bob Guyette	2- 3	3- 4	6	3	7
Rick Robey	3- 8	3- 7	11	4	9
Jimmy Dan Conner	5- 9	2- 4	5	4	12
Mike Flynn	4- 9	3- 5	3	4	11
Jack Givens	10-20	4- 8	11	2	24
Larry Johnson	2- 4	0- 0	1	3	4
Mike Phillips	5- 6	0- 2	4	4	10
James Lee	1- 4	0- 1	2	1	2
Merion Haskins	0- 0	2- 2	1	0	2
Jerry Hale	0- 1	0- 0	3	0	0
Dan Hall	0- 0	0- 0	1	1	0
Reggie Warford	0- 0	0- 0	0	0	0
G. J. Smith	0- 1	0- 0	0	0	0
Team			6		
Totals	37-78	21-38	57	31	95

Half time: Kentucky 44-32. Officials: Soriano and Galvan.

at San Diego, California

Louisville	fg-fga	ft-fta	rb	pf	tp
Allen Murphy	14-28	5- 7	2	2	33
Wesley Cox	5- 8	4-11	16	2	14
William Bunton	3- 4	1- 2	7	2	7
Junior Bridgeman	4-15	4- 4	15	4	12
Phillip Bond	2- 6	2- 2	3	1	6
Ike Whitfield	0- 0	0- 0	1	1	0
Ricky Gallon	0- 3	0- 0	2	2	0
Danny Brown	1- 1	0- 0	1	0	2
Rick Wilson	0- 0	0- 0	0	0	0
Terry Howard	0- 0	0- 1	0	0	0
Team			2		
Totals	29-65	16-27	49	14	74

UCLA	fg-fga	ft-fta	rb	pf	tp
Dave Meyers	6-16	4- 6	7	3	16
Marques Johnson	5-10	0- 0	11	2	10
Rich Washington	11-19	4- 6	8	4	26
Pete Trgovich	6-12	0- 0	2	5	12
Andre McCarter	3-12	0- 0	2	2	6
Ralph Drollinger	1- 2	1- 2	4	5	3
Wilbert Olinde	0- 0	0- 0	0	0	0
Jim Spillane	1- 2	0- 0	1	1	2
Team			1		
Totals	33-73	9-14	36	22	75

Half time: Louisville 37-33. Regulation Score: 65-65. Officials: Wortman and Nichols. Attendance: 15,151.

National Third Place

at San Diego, California

Louisville	fg-fga	ft-fta	rb	pf	tp
Allen Murphy	9-18	2- 2	8	5	20
Wesley Cox	1- 3	2- 4	12	3	4
William Bunton	10-16	4- 5	6	4	24
Junior Bridgeman	7-14	7- 8	11	2	21
Phillip Bond	5- 7	2- 3	4	1	12
Ricky Gallon	5- 7	1- 2	7	0	11
Danny Brown	2- 5	0- 1	1	2	4
Ike Whitfield	0- 0	0- 0	2	0	0
Rick Wilson	0- 0	0- 0	0	0	0
Billy Harmon	0- 2	0- 1	2	1	0
Terry Howard	0- 0	0- 0	0	0	0
Team			1		
Totals	39-72	18-26	54	18	96

Syracuse	fg-fga	ft-fta	rb	pf	tp
Rudy Hackett	12-22	4- 4	13	5	28
Chris Sease	3- 8	0- 0	3	5	6
Earnie Seibert	0- 1	1- 2	3	1	1
Jim Lee	12-29	3- 3	5	1	27
Jim Williams	4- 7	2- 3	1	5	10
Kevin King	3-12	4- 5	5	5	10
Bob Parker	3- 5	0- 0	3	3	6
Ross Kindel	0- 2	0- 0	0	1	0
Marty Byrnes	0- 0	0- 0	0	0	0
Steve Shaw	0- 0	0- 0	0	0	0
Mark Meadors	0- 0	0- 0	1	0	0
Team			3		
Totals	37-86	14-17	37	26	88

Half time: Louisville 42-26. Regulation Score: 78-78. Officials: Galvan and Soriano.

Championship

at San Diego, California

UCLA	fg-fga	ft-fta	rb	pf	tp
Dave Meyers	9-18	6- 7	11	4	24
Marques Johnson	3- 9	0- 1	7	2	6
Rich Washington	12-23	4- 5	12	4	28
Pete Trgovich	7-16	2- 4	5	4	16
Andre McCarter	3- 6	2- 3	2	1	8
Ralph Drollinger	4- 6	2- 5	13	4	10
Team			5		
Totals	38-78	16-25	55	19	92

Kentucky	fg-fga	ft-fta	rb	pf	tp
Kevin Grevey	13-30	8-10	5	4	34
Bob Guyette	7-11	2- 2	7	3	16
Rick Robey	1- 3	0- 0	9	5	2
Jimmy Dan Conner	4-12	1- 2	5	1	9
Mike Flynn	3- 9	4- 5	3	4	10
Jack Givens	3-10	2- 3	6	3	8
Larry Johnson	0- 3	0- 0	3	3	0
Mike Phillips	1- 7	2- 3	6	4	4
Dan Hall	1- 1	0- 0	1	0	2
James Lee	0- 0	0- 0	0	1	0
Team			4		
Totals	33-86	19-25	49	28	85

Half time: UCLA 43-40. Officials: Nichols and Workman. Attendance: 15,151.

1976

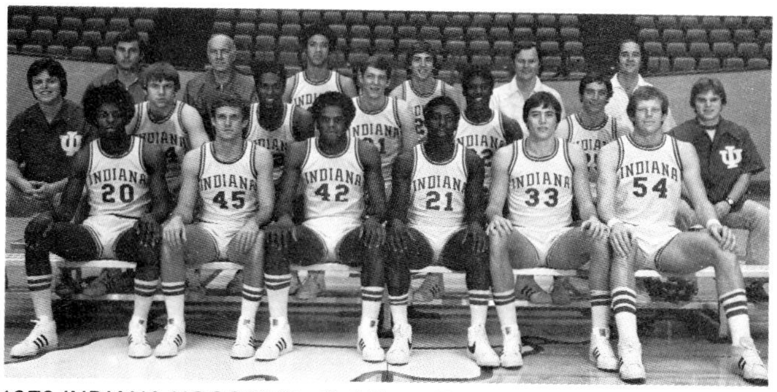

1976 INDIANA HOOSIERS—(l-r) Front Row: Bob Wilkerson, Jim Crews, Scott May, Quinn Buckner, Tom Abernethy, Kent Benson; Second Row: Tim Walker, Rich Valavicius, Mark Haymore, Scott Eells, Wayne Radford, Bob Bender, Chuck Swenson; Third Row: Bobby Knight, Harold Andreas, Jim Roberson, Jim Wisman, Bob Donewald, Bob Weltlich.

East First Round

at Charlotte, North Carolina

DePaul	fg-fga	ft-fta	rb	pf	tp
Ron Norwood	11-15	6- 7	2	3	28
Randy Ramsey	0- 1	2- 2	1	3	2
Curtis Watkins	3- 4	4- 6	8	2	10
Andy Pancratz	3- 5	1- 2	3	1	7
Dave Corzine	4-10	6- 6	4	5	14
Joe Ponsetto	3- 9	0- 1	12	2	6
Gary Garland	1- 2	0- 0	1	0	2
Randy Hook	0- 0	0- 0	0	0	0
Team			3		
Totals	25-46	19-24	34	16	69

Virginia	fg-fga	ft-fta	rb	pf	tp
Wally Walker	4-15	3- 3	7	5	11
Marc Iavaroni	4- 8	1- 2	2	2	9
Otis Fulton	5- 8	0- 0	8	1	10
Billy Langloh	5-14	4- 4	2	5	14
Dave Koesters	4-11	0- 0	1	3	8
Steve Castellan	1- 3	2- 2	3	1	4
Bob Stokes	2- 3	0- 0	0	1	4
Tom Briscoe	0- 0	0- 0	0	2	0
Team			2		
Totals	25-62	10-11	25	20	60

Half time: Virginia 37-31. Officials: Stockner and Sylvester.

at Charlotte, North Carolina

Tennessee	fg-fga	ft-fta	rb	pf	tp
Ernie Grunfeld	13-23	10-13	8	3	36
Mike Jackson	5-13	4- 5	1	5	14
Doug Ashworth	3- 6	0- 0	3	2	6
Austin Clark	3- 9	3- 3	8	5	9
Johnny Dardon	4- 8	0- 0	1	2	8
Terry Crosby	0- 2	0- 2	1	3	0
Mike Smithson	1- 1	0- 0	1	0	2
Team			2		
Totals	29-62	17-23	25	20	75

Virginia Military	fg-fga	ft-fta	rb	pf	tp
Ron Carter	8-11	3- 6	14	4	19
Curt Reppart	5- 7	1- 3	1	2	11
John Krovic	6- 9	5- 5	2	0	17
Will Bynum	8-14	4- 4	4	4	20
Dave Montgomery	4- 5	2- 4	6	4	10
George Borojevich	2- 4	0- 0	5	3	4
Kelly Lombard	0- 0	0- 0	0	1	0
Pat Kelley	0- 0	0- 0	0	1	0
Totals	33-50	15-22	32	19	81

Half time: Tennessee 38-37. Officials: Korte and Bain. Attendance: 11,666.

at Providence, Rhode Island

Princeton	fg-fga	ft-fta	rb	pf	tp
Pete Molloy	0- 0	0- 1	1	1	0
Mickey Steuerer	1- 2	2- 2	3	1	4
Bill Omeltchenko	1- 3	0- 0	2	4	2
Arnold Hill	7-14	0- 1	7	5	14
Frank Sowinski	4- 6	3- 3	4	4	11
Barnes Hauptfuhrer	5- 8	2- 2	3	1	12
Bob Slaughter	5- 8	0- 0	7	3	10
Lon Ramati	0- 0	0- 0	0	0	0
Team			3		
Totals	23-41	7- 9	30	19	53

Rutgers	fg-fga	ft-fta	rb	pf	tp
Phil Sellers	3-15	7- 9	8	3	13
Jim Bailey	1- 5	0- 0	3	2	2
Ed Jordan	7-11	2- 3	5	2	16
Mike Dabney	5-14	3- 4	4	2	13
Hollis Copeland	4- 7	0- 0	5	2	8
Mark Conlin	0- 0	0- 0	0	0	0
Steve Hefele	0- 1	0- 0	1	1	0
Abdel Anderson	1- 3	0- 0	2	4	2
Team			4		
Totals	21-56	12-16	32	16	54

Half time: Rutgers 33-25. Officials: White and Spitler.

at Providence, Rhode Island

Connecticut	fg-fga	ft-fta	rb	pf	tp
Jim Abromaitis	0- 2	0- 0	0	2	0
Jeff Carr	7-12	3- 8	9	3	17
Anthony Hanson	5-10	2- 3	8	5	12
Bill Harris	0- 0	0- 0	0	1	0
Lawrence Kelly	0- 0	0- 0	1	0	0
Randy LaVigne	2- 2	1- 1	3	0	5
John Thomas	1- 3	3- 4	10	2	5
Al Weston	6-12	6- 6	1	4	18
Joe Welton	11-20	1- 4	1	2	23
Team			9		
Totals	32-61	16-26	42	19	80

Hofstra	fg-fga	ft-fta	rb	pf	tp
Pat Kammerer	3- 7	2- 4	5	4	8
Rich Laurel	4- 9	3- 3	5	5	11
Ken Rood	8-18	2- 3	0	5	18
Willie Vickers	1- 1	1- 3	1	2	3
Bernard Tomlin	7-13	2- 2	2	2	16
John Irving	9-11	2- 5	12	4	20
Bob Bush	0- 0	0- 0	0	0	0
Mark Jenkins	1- 3	0- 0	6	2	2
Team			4		
Totals	33-62	12-20	35	24	78

Half time: Hofstra 43-30. Regulation Score: 75-75. Officials: Serriano and Savage. Attendance: 12,189.

East Regional

at Greensboro, North Carolina

DePaul	fg-fga	ft-fta	rb	pf	tp
Ron Norwood	9-20	5- 7	3	5	23
Randy Ramsey	4- 8	0- 0	1	2	8
Curtis Watkins	4-12	2- 4	8	5	10
Dave Corzine	6-15	2- 4	15	5	14
Joe Ponsetto	2- 3	1- 6	8	4	5
Greg Coehlo	0- 1	0- 0	0	0	0
Gary Garland	1- 3	0- 0	4	5	2
Randy Hook	1- 1	0- 1	0	2	2
Emmett McGovern	1- 6	0- 0	3	2	2
Andy Pancratz	0- 5	0- 0	4	5	0
Gary Wydra	0- 0	0- 0	0	0	0
Team			12		
Totals	28-74	10-22	58	35	66

Virginia Military	fg-fga	ft-fta	rb	pf	tp
Ron Carter	8-14	5-10	12	4	21
Curt Reppart	1- 3	3-10	3	4	5
John Krovic	4-12	0- 2	5	2	8
Will Bynum	7-12	8-10	6	4	22
Dave Montgomery	4-12	4- 7	14	3	12
Kelly Lombard	0- 0	0- 0	0	1	0
George Borojevich	1- 3	1- 3	1	4	3
Team			5		
Totals	25-56	21-42	46	22	71

Half time: DePaul 33-31. Regulation Score: 62-62. Officials: Sonano and Sylvester.

at Greensboro, North Carolina

Connecticut	fg-fga	ft-fta	rb	pf	tp
Joe Whelton	6-14	2- 3	0	3	14
Al Weston	8-17	8- 8	5	2	24
John Thomas	2- 8	2- 4	19	4	6
Tony Hanson	10-17	3- 3	9	4	23
Jeff Carr	1- 3	2- 2	1	1	4
Bill Harris	1- 4	2- 2	0	1	4
Larry Kelly	0- 3	0- 0	1	1	0
Randy LaVigne	0- 1	0- 0	0	0	0
Jim Abromaitis	2- 6	0- 0	9	3	4
Totals	30-73	19-22	44	19	79

Rutgers	fg-fga	ft-fta	rb	pf	tp
Phil Sellers	4-13	0- 2	5	3	8
Jim Bailey	0- 4	0- 2	2	4	0
Ed Jordan	6-10	6- 6	5	1	18
Mike Dabney	8-16	2- 4	6	2	18
Hollis Copeland	8-11	0- 0	4	5	16
Stan Nance	0- 1	0- 0	0	0	0
Mark Conlin	0- 0	0- 1	1	3	0
Jeff Kleinbaum	0- 2	0- 0	2	0	0
Steve Hefele	7- 9	0- 0	7	2	14
Abdel Anderson	6-16	7- 9	11	2	19
Team			7		
Totals	39-82	15-23	50	22	93

Half time: Rutgers 53-47. Officials: Bain and White. Attendance: 10,362.

at Greensboro, North Carolina

Rutgers	fg-fga	ft-fta	rb	pf	tp
Phil Sellers	6- 9	4- 5	12	4	16
Jim Bailey	3- 6	0- 0	5	4	6
Ed Jordan	7-11	9-10	4	3	23
Mike Dabney	9-17	5- 6	2	2	23
Hollis Copeland	4- 8	0- 0	5	4	8
Stan Nance	0- 0	0- 0	0	0	0
Bruce Scherer	0- 0	0- 0	1	0	0
Mark Conlin	0- 0	0- 0	1	0	0
Jeff Kleinbaum	0- 0	1- 2	0	0	1
Steve Hefele	2- 4	0- 3	1	2	4
Mike Palko	1- 1	0- 0	0	0	2
Abdel Anderson	3- 5	2- 6	9	4	8
Team			2		
Totals	35-61	21-32	42	23	91

Virginia Military	fg-fga	ft-fta	rb	pf	tp
Ron Carter	6-12	3- 4	7	4	15
Curt Reppart	2- 4	0- 1	2	5	4
John Krovic	5-19	0- 0	4	1	10
Will Bynum	12-20	10-12	7	5	34
Dave Montgomery	2- 3	1- 2	4	5	5
Dave Slomski	1- 2	0- 0	2	0	2
Saul Smith	0- 2	0- 0	3	3	0
Dan Stephens	0- 0	0- 0	0	0	0
Kelly Lombard	0- 0	0- 1	0	5	0
George Borojevich	2- 6	1- 2	6	2	5
Harland Niehaus	0- 0	0- 0	0	0	0
Pat Kelley	0- 2	0- 0	0	0	0
Team			2		
Totals	30-70	15-22	37	30	75

Half time: Rutgers 48-34. Officials: Bain and White. Attendance: 9,193.

Midwest First Round

at Denton, Texas

Wichita State	fg-fga	ft-fta	rb	pf	tp
Lynbert Johnson	5- 9	2- 4	7	3	12
Robert Gray	5-13	0- 0	7	3	10
Bob Elmore	5-10	8-10	7	4	18
Calvin Bruton	6-13	3- 4	3	2	15
Bob Trogele	1- 4	3- 4	4	2	5
Charles Brent	3- 5	0- 0	3	1	6
Steve Kalocinski	1- 3	0- 0	3	2	2
Doug Yoder	2- 2	1- 2	3	0	5
Jim McCullough	0- 0	0- 0	0	0	0
Sid Ford	0- 0	0- 0	0	0	0
Team			4		
Totals	28-59	17-24	41	17	73

Michigan	fg-fga	ft-fta	rb	pf	tp
Wayman Britt	2- 8	0- 0	5	2	4
John Robinson	4- 7	2- 2	4	3	10
Phil Hubbard	6-12	3- 5	9	5	15
Rickey Green	4-17	2- 3	7	3	10
Steve Grote	7-10	3- 4	4	3	17
Dave Baxter	3- 6	0- 0	0	4	6
Alan Hardy	0- 3	0- 0	3	0	0
Joel Thompson	1- 1	0- 0	1	0	2
Tom Staton	3- 5	0- 0	0	2	6
Tom Bergen	2- 5	0- 0	1	4	4
Team			7		
Totals	32-74	10-14	41	26	74

Half time: Wichita State 41-35. Officials: Moreau and Bellanti.

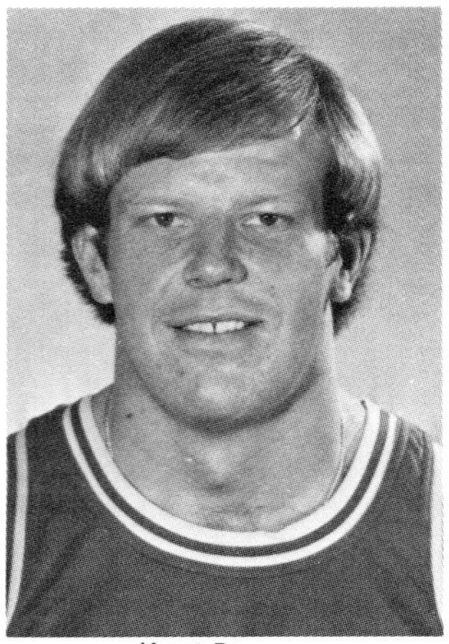

Kent Benson

at Lawrence, Kansas

Notre Dame	fg-fga	ft-fta	rb	pf	tp
Ray Martin	0- 1	0- 0	1	3	0
Bill Paterno	2- 8	0- 0	4	2	4
Dave Batton	1- 8	0- 0	6	1	2
Bruce Flowers	4- 5	0- 0	2	3	8
Adrian Dantley	10-18	7- 8	8	3	27
Don Williams	11-17	0- 0	2	2	22
Bernard Rencher	2- 6	0- 0	4	0	4
Toby Knight	6-10	0- 0	6	4	12
Team			5		
Totals	36-73	7- 8	38	18	79

Cincinnati	fg-fga	ft-fta	rb	pf	tp
Steve Collier	3- 7	0- 0	2	2	6
Brian Williams	9-19	1- 2	6	2	19
Bob Miller	4- 6	1- 3	7	1	9
Mike Jones	3- 5	0- 0	5	4	6
Pat Cummings	3- 7	2- 2	4	2	8
Gary Yoder	6- 8	2- 2	3	0	14
Hal Ward	3- 5	6- 6	1	1	12
Garry Kamstra	1- 2	0- 0	2	0	2
Mike Artis	1- 4	0- 0	0	0	2
Team			3		
Totals	33-63	12-15	33	12	78

Half time: Cincinnati 39-37. Officials: Wedge and Nichols.

at Lawrence, Kansas

Washington	fg-fga	ft-fta	rb	pf	tp
Lars Hansen	6-10	2- 2	10	5	14
Kim Stewart	6- 8	0- 2	6	4	12
James Edwards	4-12	4- 4	10	5	12
Chester Dorsey	3- 4	1- 2	5	5	7
Clarence Ramsey	7-16	0- 2	1	3	14
Ken Lombard	1- 4	0- 0	0	5	2
Mike Neill	2- 4	0- 0	1	1	4
Chris Parker	0- 0	0- 0	1	0	0
Greg Jack	1- 2	0- 1	4	0	2
Al Smith	0- 0	0- 0	1	0	0
Team			6		
Totals	30-60	7-13	45	28	67

Missouri	fg-fga	ft-fta	rb	pf	tp
Kim Anderson	6-11	0- 3	6	5	12
Jim Kennedy	5-11	10-13	4	1	20
James Clabon	4- 9	0- 1	10	3	8
Jeff Currie	1- 2	1- 2	5	4	3
Willie Smith	7-23	7-10	2	3	21
Stan Ray	2- 3	0- 0	2	2	4
Scott Sims	0- 0	1- 2	2	0	1
Mark Anderson	0- 0	0- 0	0	0	0
Team			6		
Totals	25-59	19-31	37	18	69

Half time: Washington 36-30. Officials: DeBonis and Folsom. Attendance: 11,130.

at Denton, Texas

Texas Tech	fg-fga	ft-fta	rb	pf	tp
Grady Newton	3- 6	0- 0	5	2	6
Mike Russell	8-13	5- 7	12	5	21
Rick Bullock	7- 9	5- 7	5	4	19
Keith Kitchens	3- 6	4- 4	5	2	10
Steve Dunn	2- 6	3- 4	2	2	7
Grant Dukes	1- 5	0- 0	3	3	2
Geoff Huston	1- 1	0- 0	1	0	2
Rudy Liggins	1- 1	0- 0	1	1	2
Mike Edwards	0- 0	0- 0	0	0	0
Stanley Lee	0- 1	0- 0	0	0	0
Danny Ivey	0- 0	0- 0	0	0	0
Team			5		
Totals	26-48	17-22	39	19	69

Syracuse	fg-fga	ft-fta	rb	pf	tp
Dale Shackleford	2- 8	0- 0	8	3	4
Chris Sease	2- 8	0- 1	2	1	4
Marty Byrnes	4- 7	4- 6	6	3	12
Ross Kindell	0- 3	1- 2	2	3	1
James Williams	9-20	3- 4	0	3	21
Earnie Seibert	0- 2	0- 0	0	1	0
Larry Kelley	7- 9	0- 0	1	4	14
Bill Keys	0- 1	0- 2	2	0	0
Kevin James	0- 1	0- 0	1	0	0
Kevin King	0- 0	0- 0	0	1	0
Larry Arrington	0- 2	0- 0	0	1	0
Team			6		
Totals	24-61	8-15	28	20	56

Half time: Texas Tech 39-28. Officials: Filiberti and Wortman. Attendance: 9,884.

Midwest Regional

at Louisville, Kentucky

Texas Tech	fg-fga	ft-fta	rb	pf	tp
Grady Newton	3- 6	0- 0	4	3	6
Mike Russell	6-15	2- 4	14	1	14
Rick Bullock	8-20	7-12	14	5	23
Keith Kitchens	0- 7	0- 0	0	1	0
Steve Dunn	2- 9	0- 2	2	1	4
Rudy Liggins	0- 3	0- 0	0	2	0
Geoff Huston	4-10	2- 2	1	2	10
Grant Dukes	4- 8	0- 0	3	1	8
Mike Edwards	4- 8	2- 5	4	4	10
Stanley Lee	0- 0	0- 0	0	0	0
Bob Rudolph	0- 1	0- 0	0	0	0
Team			4		
Totals	31-87	13-25	46	20	75

Missouri	fg-fga	ft-fta	rb	pf	tp
Jim Kennedy	7-14	1- 3	6	3	15
Kim Anderson	7-12	1- 2	11	4	15
James Clabon	4-10	0- 0	5	4	8
Jeff Currie	2- 4	2- 3	3	1	6
Willie Smith	13-21	4- 6	10	2	30
Stan Ray	4- 7	0- 0	6	3	8
Scott Sims	0- 1	4- 4	3	2	4
Danny Van Rheen	0- 0	0- 0	1	0	0
Brad Droy	0- 0	0- 0	0	0	0
Dave Stallman	0- 0	0- 0	0	1	0
Team			6		
Totals	37-69	12-18	51	20	86

Half time: Missouri 45-36. Officials: Nichols and Folsom.

at Louisville, Kentucky

Notre Dame	fg-fga	ft-fta	rb	pf	tp
Bruce Flowers	3- 6	0- 0	9	5	6
Adrian Dantley	12-19	7- 8	5	1	31
Toby Knight	1- 4	0- 0	5	4	2
Ray Martin	1- 2	0- 1	2	5	2
Don Williams	6-13	3- 4	2	3	15
Dave Batton	2- 8	2- 2	13	2	6
Bill Paterno	5- 9	0- 0	4	2	10
Bernard Rencher	1- 1	2- 3	0	0	4
Jeff Carpenter	0- 0	0- 0	0	1	0
Team			2		
Totals	31-62	14-18	42	23	76

Michigan	fg-fga	ft-fta	rb	pf	tp
Wayman Britt	6- 9	0- 0	3	5	12
John Robinson	5-13	5- 6	8	2	15
Phil Hubbard	5-13	1- 2	10	4	11
Rickey Green	8-16	4- 4	4	1	20
Steve Grote	4-10	6- 6	4	5	14
Tom Staton	3- 6	0- 1	2	3	6
Dave Baxter	1- 5	0- 0	1	0	2
Alan Hardy	0- 1	0- 0	1	0	0
Tom Bergen	0- 0	0- 0	0	0	0
Team			3		
Totals	32-73	16-19	36	20	80

Half time: Notre Dame 41-40. Officials: Morgan and Wortman. Attendance: 11,753.

at Louisville, Kentucky

Michigan	fg-fga	ft-fta	rb	pf	tp
Wayman Britt	3-10	1- 2	3	3	7
John Robinson	6-12	9-10	16	2	21
Phil Hubbard	8-10	4- 7	18	3	20
Rickey Green	9-25	5- 7	2	4	23
Steve Grote	2- 4	0- 0	1	5	4
Dave Baxter	6-12	6- 8	5	2	18
Tom Staton	1- 2	0- 0	2	0	2
Tom Bergen	0- 0	0- 0	0	0	0
Alan Hardy	0- 0	0- 0	0	2	0
Team			2		
Totals	35-75	25-34	49	21	95

Missouri	fg-fga	ft-fta	rb	pf	tp
Jim Kennedy	8-10	0- 1	8	5	16
Kim Anderson	2- 6	0- 3	7	5	4
James Clabon	0- 2	0- 0	2	1	0
Jeff Currie	3- 8	1- 3	2	5	7
Willie Smith	18-35	7-11	7	4	43
Stan Ray	6-12	1- 2	15	3	13
Scott Sims	1- 2	0- 0	2	2	2
Mark Anderson	1- 4	1- 2	0	4	3
Danny Van Rheen	0- 0	0- 0	0	0	0
Dave Stallman	0- 0	0- 0	0	0	0
Team			2		
Totals	39-79	10-22	45	29	88

Half time: Michigan 50-37. Officials: Nichols and Wortman. Attendance: 8,378.

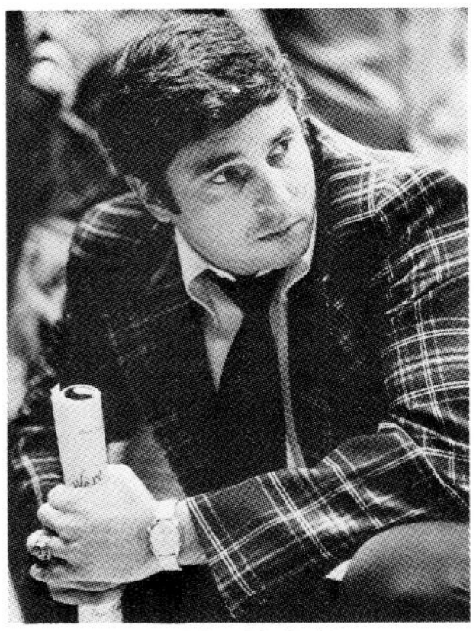

Bobby Knight

Mideast First Round

at Dayton, Ohio

North Carolina	fg-fga	ft-fta	rb	pf	tp
Walter Davis	6-17	4- 5	7	3	16
Tommy LaGarde	9-16	4- 4	11	3	22
Mitch Kupchak	3-11	2- 2	12	2	8
Phil Ford	1- 5	0- 0	2	1	2
John Kuester	3- 8	0- 0	1	4	6
Bruce Buckley	2- 4	0- 1	0	0	4
Dudley Bradley	1- 5	0- 0	0	1	2
Tom Zaliagiris	0- 2	0- 0	0	0	0
Dave Hanners	1- 2	0- 0	0	5	2
Woody Coley	0- 1	0- 0	1	0	0
Bill Chambers	1- 2	0- 0	0	1	2
Keith Valentine	0- 0	0- 0	0	1	0
Team			2		
Totals	27-73	10-12	36	21	64

Alabama	fg-fga	ft-fta	rb	pf	tp
Reginald King	6-11	1- 2	11	4	13
Rickey Brown	4-12	0- 0	7	3	8
Leon Douglas	16-23	3- 5	17	4	35
T. R. Dunn	3- 7	0- 0	6	1	6
Anthony Murray	3- 6	7-12	1	3	13
Keith McCord	1- 1	0- 0	0	2	2
Greg McElveen	0- 2	2- 2	1	0	2
Team			6		
Totals	33-62	13-21	49	17	79

Half time: Alabama 40-28. Officials: Ditty and Diehl.

at Notre Dame, Indiana

St. John's, N.Y.	fg-fga	ft-fta	rb	pf	tp
John Farmer	2- 6	0- 0	3	2	4
Beaver Smith	2- 9	1- 2	8	4	5
George Johnson	5-15	0- 0	7	2	10
Glen Williams	10-15	0- 1	3	4	20
Frank Alagia	7-13	3- 4	6	2	17
Cecil Rellford	5- 7	0- 0	2	4	10
Billy Clarke	0- 0	0- 0	0	1	0
Kevelin Winfree	1- 1	0- 0	1	1	2
Tom Weadock	0- 0	0- 0	0	0	0
Ralph Menar	0- 0	0- 0	0	0	0
Tom Calabrese	0- 1	0- 0	0	0	0
Hernel Robertson	1- 3	0- 0	2	0	2
Ron McGugins	0- 0	0- 0	0	0	0
Fred McRae	0- 1	0- 0	1	0	0
Team			3		
Totals	33-71	4- 7	36	20	70

Indiana	fg-fga	ft-fta	rb	pf	tp
Scott May	14-23	5- 5	7	3	33
Tom Abernethy	3- 5	1- 2	6	2	7
Kent Benson	8-18	4- 4	13	3	20
Bob Wilkerson	1- 5	4- 4	3	1	6
Quinn Buckner	7-13	1- 2	2	3	15
Wayne Radford	2- 2	1- 1	3	2	5
Jim Wisman	0- 1	0- 0	0	0	0
Jim Crews	1- 1	0- 0	2	0	2
Rich Valavicius	0- 1	0- 0	0	0	0
Bob Bender	0- 0	0- 0	0	0	0
Jim Roberson	0- 1	0- 0	0	0	0
Mark Haymore	1- 1	0- 0	1	0	2
Team			4		
Totals	37-71	16-18	41	14	90

Half time: Indiana 44-37. Officials: Turner and Herrold.

at Dayton, Ohio

Marquette	fg-fga	ft-fta	rb	pf	tp
Bo Ellis	5-14	1-1	14	3	11
Earl Tatum	8-14	2-2	6	1	18
Jerome Whitehead	6-9	0-0	7	3	12
Butch Lee	10-20	1-3	5	0	21
Lloyd Walton	3-12	3-4	3	3	9
Bernard Toone	1-1	0-0	0	2	2
Bill Neary	0-1	0-0	0	0	0
Gary Rosenberger	2-2	0-0	2	0	4
Ulice Payne	1-1	0-0	1	0	2
Craig Butrym	0-0	0-0	0	0	0
Barry Brennen	0-0	0-0	0	0	0
Team			2		
Totals	36-74	7-10	40	12	79

Western Kentucky	fg-fga	ft-fta	rb	pf	tp
Mike Warner	1-3	0-0	4	1	2
Wilson James	1-6	2-3	5	5	4
James Johnson	3-4	3-3	9	2	9
Chuck Rawlings	7-14	0-0	1	2	14
Johnny Britt	9-17	1-1	3	3	19
Bill Scillian	3-6	0-0	4	0	6
Steve Ashby	0-0	0-0	0	0	0
Lloyd Terry	1-2	2-2	1	2	4
Gary Gregory	1-1	0-0	0	0	2
Damon Grimes	0-0	0-0	0	0	0
Team			2		
Totals	26-53	8-9	29	15	60

Half time: Marquette 36-29. Officials: Brown and Grossman. Attendance: 13,458.

at Notre Dame, Indiana

Virginia Tech	fg-fga	ft-fta	rb	pf	tp
Russell Davis	7-18	2-4	11	4	16
Phil Thieneman	2-4	0-0	1	1	4
Ernest Wansley	2-3	0-0	3	4	4
Larry Cooke	5-20	1-1	6	4	11
Dave Sensibaugh	2-5	0-0	1	0	4
Duke Thorpe	7-9	5-7	9	4	19
Kyle McKee	4-8	1-3	10	5	9
Team			7		
Totals	29-67	9-15	48	22	67

Western Michigan	fg-fga	ft-fta	rb	pf	tp
Jeff Tyson	11-27	3-5	8	4	25
Paul Griffin	5-6	4-7	15	3	14
Tom Cutter	4-9	9-11	11	4	17
Jimmie Harvey	5-11	0-0	2	2	10
Jim Kurzen	1-5	0-0	1	1	2
Marty Murray	4-10	1-3	4	2	9
Dale DeBruin	0-1	0-2	1	1	0
S. L. Sales	0-0	0-2	0	1	0
Mike Reardon	0-3	0-0	1	0	0
Marc Throop	0-0	0-0	0	0	0
Team			8		
Totals	30-72	17-30	51	18	77

Half time: Virginia Tech 39-30. Regulation Score: 65-65. Officials: Honzo and Crowell. Attendance: 11,345.

Mideast Regional

at Baton Rouge, Louisiana

Indiana	fg-fga	ft-fta	rb	pf	tp
Tom Abernethy	2-6	4-5	6	1	8
Scott May	9-22	7-9	16	2	25
Kent Benson	7-11	1-2	5	4	15
Bob Wilkerson	6-12	2-2	12	1	14
Quinn Buckner	5-8	2-5	2	4	12
Wayne Radford	0-1	0-0	1	1	0
Jim Wisman	0-0	0-0	0	0	0
Rick Valavicius	0-0	0-1	0	0	0
Team			2		
Totals	29-60	16-24	44	13	74

Alabama	fg-fga	ft-fta	rb	pf	tp
Rickey Brown	3-7	1-2	5	4	7
Reginald King	2-6	0-0	6	5	4
Leon Douglas	5-16	2-6	7	4	12
Anthony Murray	7-11	1-2	7	1	15
T. R. Dunn	7-14	2-2	5	5	16
Keith McCord	5-9	1-2	3	2	11
Tommy Bonds	1-2	0-0	0	1	2
Greg McElveen	1-4	0-0	1	1	2
Team			1		
Totals	31-69	7-14	35	23	69

Half time: Indiana 37-29. Officials: Turner and Brown.

at Baton Rouge, Louisiana

Marquette	fg-fga	ft-fta	rb	pf	tp
Bo Ellis	3-7	2-2	7	4	8
Earl Tatum	5-12	0-0	8	4	10
Jerome Whitehead	5-10	0-0	7	1	10
Butch Lee	8-14	0-0	0	2	16
Lloyd Walton	6-12	0-0	1	4	12
Ulice Payne	0-1	0-0	1	0	0
Bernard Toone	1-1	0-0	0	0	2
Bill Neary	0-0	0-0	2	0	0
Gary Rosenberger	1-4	2-2	0	0	4
Team			1		
Totals	29-61	4-4	27	15	62

Western Michigan	fg-fga	ft-fta	rb	pf	tp
Paul Griffin	1-2	0-0	9	3	2
Jeff Tyson	8-16	2-4	5	5	18
Tom Cutter	8-12	5-5	17	1	21
Jim Kurzen	1-2	0-0	0	2	2
Jimmie Harvey	4-13	2-4	2	0	10
Marty Murray	2-9	0-0	2	2	4
Dale DeBruin	0-0	0-1	3	0	0
Totals	24-54	9-14	38	13	57

Half time: Marquette 28-25. Officials: Herrold and Ditty. Attendance: 14,150.

at Baton Rouge, Louisiana

Marquette	fg-fga	ft-fta	rb	pf	tp
Bo Ellis	4-6	1-2	7	3	9
Earl Tatum	10-15	2-2	6	5	22
Jerome Whitehead	3-10	1-2	9	4	7
Butch Lee	4-18	0-0	2	1	8
Lloyd Walton	1-9	0-0	2	3	2
Gary Rosenberger	1-2	0-1	1	2	2
Bernard Toone	2-5	2-2	4	0	6
Bill Neary	0-1	0-0	2	0	0
Team			1		
Totals	25-66	6-9	34	18	56

Indiana	fg-fga	ft-fta	rb	pf	tp
Tom Abernethy	4-7	4-5	5	2	12
Scott May	7-10	1-2	3	3	15
Kent Benson	8-12	2-2	9	2	18
Bob Wilkerson	2-3	2-2	3	1	6
Quinn Buckner	4-9	1-2	8	2	9
Wayne Radford	1-4	0-0	0	0	2
Rich Valavicius	0-0	1-2	2	0	1
Jim Crews	1-2	0-0	1	1	2
Team			2		
Totals	27-47	11-15	33	11	65

Half time: Indiana 36-35. Officials: Ditty and Brown. Attendance: 14,150.

West First Round

at Tempe, Arizona

Memphis State	fg-fga	ft-fta	rb	pf	tp
Alvin Wright	2-6	0-0	1	3	4
Dexter Reed	8-17	0-0	1	3	16
Bill Cook	3-11	7-8	4	4	13
Marion Hillard	4-8	3-4	8	4	11
John Washington	2-2	2-2	1	5	6
John Gunn	5-8	0-0	4	2	10
Buster Hancock	0-0	3-4	0	0	3
John Kilzer	0-0	0-0	0	0	0
Clarence Jones	3-6	2-2	4	3	8
Ed Wilson	3-6	0-0	9	5	6
Team			4		
Totals	30-64	17-20	36	29	77

Pepperdine	fg-fga	ft-fta	rb	pf	tp
Flintie Williams	6-9	2-2	7	2	14
Dennis Johnson	3-9	4-8	6	4	10
Marcos Leite	12-22	10-11	8	3	34
Dick Skophammer	3-7	2-3	10	4	8
Ollie Matson	7-16	5-9	11	3	19
Brian Goorjian	0-1	0-1	0	0	0
Howie Dallmar	1-1	0-0	0	1	2
Team			3		
Totals	32-65	23-34	45	17	87

Half time: Memphis State 41-38. Officials: Menz and Wooldridge.

at Eugene, Oregon

San Diego State	fg-fga	ft-fta	rb	pf	tp
Ray Leary	3-7	0-0	1	1	6
Gary Earle	0-2	0-0	1	1	0
Mark Delsman	2-4	0-0	2	3	4
Jerry Brown	0-0	0-0	1	0	0
Steve Copp	8-19	4-5	11	3	20
Mike Dodd	0-0	0-0	0	0	0
Bob Kovach	3-11	5-8	6	3	11
Will Connelly	5-14	1-2	9	3	11
Joel Kramer	1-3	0-0	0	0	2
Allen Bunting	3-13	4-4	5	3	10
Team			3		
Totals	25-73	14-19	39	17	64

UCLA	fg-fga	ft-fta	rb	pf	tp
Raymond Townsend	3-6	0-0	0	2	6
Richard Washington	10-15	5-5	8	3	25
Brett Vroman	0-0	0-0	2	2	0
David Greenwood	1-3	2-2	3	4	4
Ralph Drollinger	2-4	0-0	7	4	4
Jim Spillane	1-2	0-0	1	2	2
Andre McCarter	4-9	2-5	5	0	10
Wilbert Olinde	0-0	0-0	0	0	0
Marques Johnson	7-9	5-6	9	4	19
Gavin Smith	2-7	0-0	1	1	4
Team			7		
Totals	30-55	14-18	43	22	74

Half time: UCLA 35-32. Officials: Fouty and Dreith.

at Tempe, Arizona

Arizona	fg-fga	ft-fta	rb	pf	tp
Jim Rappis	8-13	4-5	3	4	20
Herman Harris	6-12	1-2	3	3	13
Bob Elliott	5-11	4-9	8	0	14
Al Fleming	3-7	6-10	12	3	12
Phil Taylor	6-7	3-5	11	5	15
Gilbert Myles	1-2	7-9	5	1	9
Gary Harrison	0-0	0-0	0	1	0
Len Gordy	0-0	0-0	0	1	0
Sylvester Maxey	0-0	0-0	0	0	0
Bob Aleksa	0-0	0-0	0	0	0
Jerome Gladney	0-0	0-0	1	0	0
Team			7		
Totals	29-52	25-40	50	18	83

Georgetown	fg-fga	ft-fta	rb	pf	tp
Mike Riley	0-0	2-2	4	3	2
Derrick Jackson	10-23	2-3	0	3	22
Merlin Wilson	1-4	2-2	4	5	4
Felix Yeoman	0-1	0-0	2	0	0
Al Dutch	2-8	2-2	5	2	6
Craig Esherick	0-2	0-0	0	0	0
Bill Lynn	1-7	0-0	2	1	2
Steve Martin	1-4	0-0	2	1	2
Bill Thomas	0-2	0-0	0	2	0
Jonathan Smith	9-17	2-3	4	5	20
Larry Long	3-8	4-4	7	1	10
Garry Wilson	0-0	0-0	1	4	0
Mike McDermott	1-3	0-0	1	0	2
Ed Hopkins	3-3	0-0	4	4	6
Team			4		
Totals	31-82	14-16	40	31	76

Half time: Arizona 41-32. Officials: Galvin and Copeland. Attendance: 8,185.

at Eugene, Oregon

Boise State	fg-fga	ft-fta	rb	pf	tp
Steve Connor	8-16	10-13	1	4	26
Dominic Trutanich	0-0	0-0	0	0	0
Terry Miller	1-3	3-5	1	2	5
Tommy Morgan	2-2	1-2	1	1	5
Trent Johnson	6-11	0-1	6	3	12
Marvin Stewart	0-1	2-2	0	0	2
Dan Jones	7-13	4-5	9	4	18
Kip Newell	0-1	0-0	0	0	0
Sean McKenna	1-1	2-2	1	2	4
Mark Christianson	0-2	0-0	3	3	0
Pat Hoke	3-5	0-4	3	5	6
Team			9		
Totals	28-55	22-34	34	24	78

Nevada-Las Vegas	fg-fga	ft-fta	rb	pf	tp
Robert Smith	2-5	1-1	0	5	5
Eddie Owens	11-18	2-3	4	5	24
Mike Milke	0-0	0-0	0	0	0
Reggie Theus	2-3	2-2	1	5	6
Lewis Brown	4-9	2-3	8	2	10
Glen Gondrezick	5-14	1-2	6	3	11
Matt Porter	0-0	0-0	0	1	0
Mickey Berkowitz	0-0	0-0	1	0	0
Jackie Robinson	9-13	2-3	13	3	20
Sam Smith	6-12	4-6	4	3	16
Boyd Batts	5-11	1-1	7	4	11
Phil Paramore	0-1	0-0	3	0	0
Don Weimer	0-1	0-3	2	0	0
Team			8		
Totals	44-87	15-24	57	31	103

Half time: Nevada-Las Vegas 48-39. Officials: Hannon and Hernjak. Attendance: 9,100.

West Regional

at Los Angeles, California

UCLA	fg-fga	ft-fta	rb	pf	tp
Richard Washington	7-18	2-5	6	2	16
Marques Johnson	6-14	6-6	10	3	18
David Greenwood	5-9	0-0	7	5	10
Andre McCarter	2-4	0-0	2	1	4
Raymond Townsend	4-6	0-0	4	2	8
Ralph Drollinger	4-7	0-0	6	5	8
Gavin Smith	3-4	0-2	0	0	6
Jim Spillane	0-0	0-0	0	0	0
Brett Vroman	0-0	0-0	1	1	0
Team			6		
Totals	31-62	8-13	42	19	70

Pepperdine	fg-fga	ft-fta	rb	pf	tp
Ollie Matson	4-9	2-3	5	5	10
Dick Skophammer	4-11	0-0	9	4	8
Marcos Leite	4-14	8-10	8	3	16
Flintie Williams	4-10	2-2	0	3	10
Dennis Johnson	7-14	2-5	6	2	16
Howie Dallmar	0-0	0-0	2	1	0
Brian Goorjian	0-0	0-0	0	0	0
Ray Ellis	0-0	1-2	2	0	1
Team			4		
Totals	23-58	15-22	36	18	61

Half time: UCLA 40-35. Officials Galvin and Fouty.

at Los Angeles, California

Arizona	fg-fga	ft-fta	rb	pf	tp
Phil Taylor	7-15	4-9	15	3	18
Al Fleming	3-7	0-2	11	5	6
Bob Elliott	7-11	6-9	12	4	20
Jim Rappis	10-14	4-4	1	5	24
Herman Harris	13-22	5-10	9	4	31
Len Gordy	2-5	1-3	6	5	5
Jerome Gladney	2-2	2-3	3	0	6
Gilbert Myles	0-0	3-4	0	2	3
Sylvester Maxey	0-0	0-0	0	1	0
Tim Marshall	0-0	0-0	0	0	0
Gary Harrison	0-0	1-2	0	0	1
Team			4		
Totals	44-76	26-46	61	29	114

Nevada-Las Vegas	fg-fga	ft-fta	rb	pf	tp
Eddie Owens	9-18	3-3	1	5	21
Jackie Robinson	1-3	0-1	4	5	2
Boyd Batts	4-12	0-2	9	3	8
Robert Smith	4-10	10-10	1	4	18
Glen Gondrezick	4-9	0-1	5	5	8
Lewis Brown	10-19	4-5	16	4	24
Sam Smith	9-20	8-10	5	5	26
Reggie Theus	1-5	0-1	4	2	2
Mike Milke	0-0	0-0	0	1	0
Team			1		
Totals	42-96	25-33	46	34	109

Half time: Arizona 51-47. Regulation Score: 103-103. Officials: Dreith and Menz. Attendance: 12,683.

GAME-BY-GAME RESULTS

320

at Los Angeles, California

UCLA	fg-fga	ft-fta	rb	pf	tp
Richard Washington	11-24	0-0	10	2	22
Marques Johnson	7-14	0-0	7	4	14
David Greenwood	4-8	2-2	4	2	10
Raymond Townsend	7-12	2-4	3	1	16
Andre McCarter	4-7	1-2	3	0	9
Gavin Smith	1-1	0-0	1	0	2
Ralph Drollinger	1-5	1-3	6	3	3
Jim Spillane	1-1	0-0	0	1	2
Brett Vroman	0-0	0-1	1	0	0
Brad Holland	2-2	0-0	0	0	4
Roy Hamilton	0-0	0-0	0	0	0
Wilbert Olinde	0-0	0-0	0	0	0
Team			6		
Totals	38-74	6-12	41	13	82

Arizona	fg-fga	ft-fta	rb	pf	tp
Phil Taylor	7-12	0-0	7	3	14
Al Fleming	6-17	2-3	16	4	14
Bob Elliott	4-9	2-3	6	2	10
Jim Rappis	1-8	2-2	2	3	4
Herman Harris	9-19	0-0	1	3	18
Jerome Gladney	1-2	0-0	1	1	2
Len Gordy	0-0	0-0	0	0	0
Gilbert Myles	0-0	0-0	1	0	0
Gary Harrison	0-0	0-0	0	1	0
Sylvester Maxey	0-1	2-2	0	0	2
Brian Jung	0-0	0-0	0	0	0
Tim Marshall	0-0	0-0	0	1	0
Larry Demic	1-1	0-0	1	0	2
Bob Aleksa	0-0	0-0	0	0	0
Team			6		
Totals	29-69	8-10	41	18	66

Half time: UCLA 38-35. Officials: Galvin and Fouty. Attendance: 12,459.

Semifinals

at Philadelphia, Pennsylvania

Michigan	fg-fga	ft-fta	rb	pf	tp
Wayman Britt	5-9	1-1	5	4	11
John Robinson	8-13	4-5	16	2	20
Phil Hubbard	8-13	0-3	13	4	16
Rickey Green	7-16	2-2	6	4	16
Steve Grote	4-13	6-6	4	4	14
Dave Baxter	2-5	1-2	3	0	5
Tom Staton	1-1	2-2	0	1	4
Tom Bergen	0-0	0-0	0	0	0
Joel Thompson	0-0	0-0	0	0	0
Lloyd Schinnerer	0-0	0-0	0	1	0
Alan Hardy	0-0	0-0	0	0	0
Bobby Jones	0-0	0-0	0	0	0
Len Lillard	0-0	0-0	0	0	0
Team			2		
Totals	35-70	16-21	50	20	86

Rutgers	fg-fga	ft-fta	rb	pf	tp
Phil Sellers	5-13	1-3	8	4	11
Hollis Copeland	7-12	1-1	5	3	15
Jim Bailey	1-3	4-6	6	0	6
Ed Jordan	6-20	4-4	4	4	16
Mike Dabney	5-17	0-1	5	4	10
Abdel Anderson	3-8	0-1	6	3	6
Mark Conlin	2-2	0-0	1	2	4
Steve Hefele	1-1	0-0	1	2	2
Team			2		
Totals	30-76	10-16	38	22	70

Half time: Michigan 46-29. Officials: Wortman and Fouty.

at Philadelphia, Pennsylvania

UCLA	fg-fga	ft-fta	rb	pf	tp
Richard Washington	6-15	3-4	8	3	15
Marques Johnson	6-10	0-1	6	2	12
David Greenwood	2-5	1-2	10	2	5
Ray Townsend	2-10	0-0	3	1	4
Andre McCarter	2-9	0-0	4	5	4
Ralph Drollinger	0-3	2-2	1	3	2
Brad Holland	0-2	0-0	0	0	0
Jim Spillane	0-2	0-0	1	0	0
Gavin Smith	3-4	0-0	0	3	6
Roy Hamilton	0-1	1-2	0	0	1
Brett Vroman	0-0	0-0	1	2	0
Chris Lippert	0-0	2-2	0	0	2
Wilbert Olinde	0-0	0-0	0	0	0
Team			3		
Totals	21-61	9-13	37	21	51

Indiana	fg-fga	ft-fta	rb	pf	tp
Tom Abernethy	7-8	0-1	6	3	14
Scott May	5-16	4-6	4	2	14
Kent Benson	6-15	4-6	9	4	16
Bobby Wilkerson	1-5	3-4	19	3	5
Quinn Buckner	6-14	0-1	3	3	12
Jim Crews	1-1	2-3	3	0	4
Team			1		
Totals	26-59	13-21	45	15	65

Half time: Indiana 34-26. Officials: Brown and Bain. Attendance: 17,540.

National Third Place

at Philadelphia, Pennsylvania

UCLA	fg-fga	ft-fta	rb	pf	tp
Richard Washington	5-8	1-2	0	4	11
David Greenwood	2-4	1-2	8	5	5
Ralph Drollinger	6-8	0-0	16	5	12
Andre McCarter	11-19	4-4	5	1	26
Marques Johnson	11-21	8-12	18	1	30
Ray Townsend	3-7	2-2	2	3	8
Brett Vroman	0-0	0-0	1	1	0
Gavin Smith	3-9	2-2	4	2	8
Jim Spillane	2-3	0-0	0	1	4
Wilbert Olinde	1-1	0-0	1	0	2
Team			2		
Totals	44-80	18-24	57	23	106

Rutgers	fg-fga	ft-fta	rb	pf	tp
Phil Sellers	8-21	7-10	12	3	23
Hollis Copeland	9-19	0-2	13	3	18
Jim Bailey	3-10	1-1	5	2	7
Ed Jordan	4-16	0-2	4	3	8
Mike Dabney	9-18	3-5	5	3	21
Abdel Anderson	4-13	5-6	4	2	13
Mark Conlin	0-0	0-0	0	0	0
Steve Hefele	1-3	0-1	5	4	2
Team			5		
Totals	38-100	16-27	53	20	92

Half time: UCLA 57-49. Officials: Fouty and Bain.

Championship

at Philadelphia, Pennsylvania

Michigan	fg-fga	ft-fta	rb	pf	tp
Wayman Britt	5-6	1-1	3	5	11
John Robinson	4-8	0-1	6	2	8
Phil Hubbard	4-8	2-2	11	5	10
Rickey Green	7-16	4-5	6	3	18
Steve Grote	4-9	4-6	1	4	12
Tom Bergen	0-1	0-0	0	1	0
Tom Staton	2-5	3-4	2	3	7
Dave Baxter	0-2	0-0	0	2	0
Joel Thompson	0-0	0-0	0	0	0
Alan Hardy	1-2	0-0	2	0	2
Team			1		
Totals	27-57	14-19	32	25	68

Indiana	fg-fga	ft-fta	rb	pf	tp
Tom Abernethy	4-8	3-3	4	2	11
Scott May	10-17	6-6	8	4	26
Kent Benson	11-20	3-5	9	3	25
Bobby Wilkerson	0-1	0-0	0	1	0
Quinn Buckner	5-10	6-9	8	4	16
Wayne Radford	0-1	0-0	1	0	0
Jim Crews	0-1	2-2	1	1	2
Jim Wisman	0-1	2-3	1	4	2
Rich Valavicius	1-1	0-0	0	0	2
Mark Haymore	1-1	0-0	1	0	2
Bob Bender	0-0	0-0	0	0	0
Team			3		
Totals	32-61	22-28	36	19	86

Half time: Michigan 35-29. Officials: Wortman and Brown. Attendance: 17,540.

1977

East First Round

at Raleigh, North Carolina

Virginia Military	fg-fga	ft-fta	rb	pf	tp
Ron Carter	9-18	0-0	6	2	18
Will Bynum	7-17	4-7	8	1	18
Dave Montgomery	6-11	5-6	5	3	17
John Krovic	3-12	2-3	4	2	8
Kelly Lombard	1-1	4-4	4	3	6
George Borojevich	3-4	0-0	6	0	6
Pat Kelley	0-1	0-0	0	0	0
Jeryl Salmond	0-1	0-0	1	0	0
Team			4		
Totals	29-65	15-20	38	11	73

Duquesne	fg-fga	ft-fta	rb	pf	tp
Don Maser	7-17	0-0	7	2	14
Rich Cotten	4-10	0-0	8	5	8
Don Gambridge	2-3	0-0	8	5	4
Norm Nixon	13-24	1-3	3	5	27
Lonnie McClain	3-12	0-0	3	2	6
Jesse Hubbard	1-3	1-2	7	2	3
John Moore	0-2	0-0	0	0	0
Jeff Baldwin	2-6	0-0	2	1	4
Pat Felix	0-0	0-0	0	0	0
Team			7		
Totals	32-77	2-5	45	22	66

Half time: 33-33. Officials: Dreith and Korte.

at Raleigh, North Carolina

North Carolina	fg-fga	ft-fta	rb	pf	tp
Mike O'Koren	3-8	5-9	5	3	11
Bruce Buckley	0-3	1-3	3	3	1
Rich Yonakor	3-5	0-0	5	1	6
Phil Ford	10-18	7-7	1	0	27
John Kuester	1-7	0-0	2	4	2
Dudley Bradley	4-6	0-0	8	2	8
Steve Krafcisin	2-5	0-0	5	1	4
Tom Zaliagiris	4-5	0-0	1	2	8
Jeff Wolf	1-1	0-0	1	0	2
Woody Coley	0-0	0-0	0	0	0
David Colescott	0-0	0-0	0	1	0
John Virgil	0-1	0-0	0	0	0
Team			2		
Totals	28-59	13-19	33	17	69

Purdue	fg-fga	ft-fta	rb	pf	tp
Walter Jordan	8-18	0-0	7	3	16
Wayne Walls	5-11	0-0	6	3	10
Tom Scheffler	2-2	2-2	1	3	6
Eugene Parker	5-9	2-2	2	4	12
Bruce Parkinson	3-4	4-4	1	2	10
Joe Barry Carroll	1-4	1-1	8	2	3
Jerry Sichting	1-3	2-2	1	2	4
Gerald Thomas	1-2	3-4	2	0	5
Team			1		
Totals	26-53	14-15	29	19	66

Half time: Purdue 44-42. Officials: Galvan and Turner. Attendance: 12,400.

at Philadelphia, Pennsylvania

Princeton	fg-fga	ft-fta	rb	pf	tp
Frank Sowinski	4-11	8-10	3	3	16
Bob Slaughter	2-6	2-2	3	1	6
Bob Roma	4-7	0-0	1	5	8
Bill Omeltchenko	2-4	6-6	4	4	10
Doug Snyder	3-6	0-0	3	1	6
Bob Kleinert	0-3	0-0	2	1	0
Rich Rizzuto	0-0	0-0	0	0	0
Tom Young	3-5	4-4	1	2	10
Rich Starsia	0-0	0-0	0	0	0
John Lewis	1-1	0-0	1	1	2
Tim Olah	0-0	0-0	0	1	0
Team			1		
Totals	19-43	20-22	19	19	58

Kentucky	fg-fga	ft-fta	rb	pf	tp
Jack Givens	3-9	1-3	5	1	7
Rick Robey	7-9	6-6	9	3	20
Mike Phillips	1-3	0-0	3	3	2
Larry Johnson	3-7	1-2	2	2	7
Jay Shidler	3-5	4-4	1	3	10
James Lee	3-4	0-1	1	4	6
Merion Haskins	2-4	0-0	2	2	4
Truman Claytor	6-8	0-1	3	0	12
Dwane Casey	0-0	0-0	1	0	0
LaVon Williams	1-1	2-2	1	2	4
Team			2		
Totals	29-50	14-19	30	20	72

Half time: Kentucky 29-22. Officials: Bain and Goddard.

at Philadelphia, Pennsylvania

Notre Dame	fg-fga	ft-fta	rb	pf	tp
Toby Knight	7-15	5-6	12	5	19
Dave Batton	2-4	2-2	5	3	6
Bruce Flowers	6-9	2-5	9	3	14
Rich Branning	3-10	1-3	3	3	7
Don Williams	10-19	5-6	4	2	25
Jeff Carpenter	1-1	0-0	0	1	2
Bill Paterno	5-6	4-5	2	4	14
Bill Hanzlik	1-2	1-2	2	1	3
Team			7		
Totals	35-66	20-29	44	22	90

Hofstra	fg-fga	ft-fta	rb	pf	tp
Pat Kammerer	2-6	0-1	5	5	4
Rich Laurel	15-35	5-9	6	4	35
John Irving	7-14	3-3	12	5	17
Ken Rood	7-19	2-3	6	2	16
Willie Vickers	1-5	1-2	4	2	3
Arnold Coleman	1-3	2-4	1	3	4
Mark Jerkins	0-3	0-0	7	2	0
Jack Barry	0-0	0-0	3	1	0
Brian Appel	2-2	0-0	1	2	4
Team			4		
Totals	35-87	13-22	49	26	83

Half time: Notre Dame 48-37. Officials: Herrold and Sanders. Attendance: 9,208.

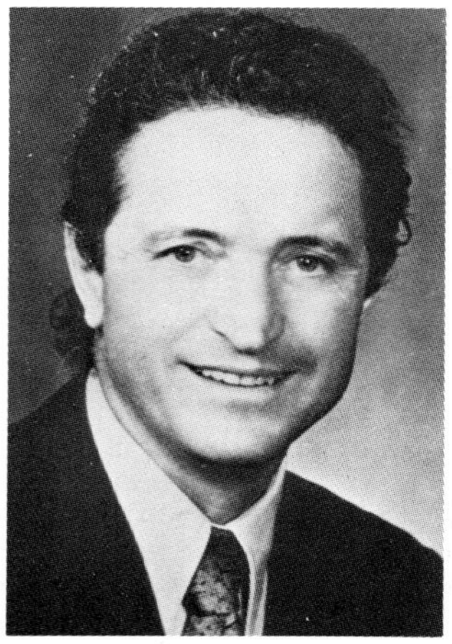

Al McGuire

East Regional

at College Park, Maryland

Virginia Military	fg-fga	ft-fta	rb	pf	tp
Will Bynum	6-13	0-0	5	3	12
Ron Carter	13-26	2-4	10	4	28
Dave Montgomery	7-12	4-5	11	4	18
John Krovic	4-16	0-1	4	0	8
Kelly Lombard	1-5	0-0	1	3	2
George Borojevich	2-4	2-2	2	2	6
Jeryl Salmond	1-1	0-0	3	0	2
Pat Kelley	0-2	0-0	0	0	0
Harlan Neihaus	1-2	0-0	2	0	2
Steve Wagner	0-0	0-0	0	0	0
Dave Slomski	0-0	0-0	0	0	0
Team			3		
Totals	35-81	8-12	41	16	78

Kentucky	fg-fga	ft-fta	rb	pf	tp
Jack Givens	9-16	8-9	9	1	26
James Lee	4-8	4-4	5	3	12
Rick Robey	4-7	0-1	7	2	8
Larry Johnson	0-4	0-0	2	3	0
Jay Shidler	2-3	0-0	1	1	4
Truman Claytor	13-15	3-4	4	3	29
Merion Haskins	2-2	0-0	0	0	4
Mike Phillips	5-8	0-0	4	3	10
Dwane Casey	0-0	0-0	2	0	0
LaVon Williams	0-2	0-0	1	1	0
Team			3		
Totals	39-65	15-18	38	17	93

Half time: Kentucky 44-41. Officials: Bain and Galvan.

GAME-BY-GAME RESULTS

at College Park, Maryland

Notre Dame	fg-fga	ft-fta	rb	pf	tp
Bruce Flowers	5-5	1-3	5	5	11
Dave Batton	3-5	0-0	4	3	6
Toby Knight	10-13	2-3	14	2	22
Don Williams	6-14	5-5	1	4	17
Rich Branning	5-7	8-9	2	2	18
Bill Paterno	1-1	1-2	3	2	3
Jeff Carpenter	0-0	0-0	0	0	0
Bill Hanzlik	0-0	0-0	1	1	0
Team			1		
Totals	30-45	17-22	31	19	77

North Carolina	fg-fga	ft-fta	rb	pf	tp
Walter Davis	4-12	0-0	8	2	8
Mike O'Koren	6-10	4-6	5	5	16
Rich Yonakor	1-6	0-0	4	2	2
Phil Ford	10-22	9-9	2	3	29
John Kuester	5-11	4-4	1	1	14
Steve Krafcisin	1-1	0-0	1	1	2
Bruce Buckley	1-1	0-0	1	2	2
Dudley Bradley	0-1	0-0	0	3	0
Jeff Wolf	0-0	0-0	0	0	0
Tom Zaliagiris	3-6	0-0	0	2	6
David Colescott	0-0	0-0	0	0	0
Team			5		
Totals	31-70	17-19	27	21	79

Half time: Notre Dame 40-30. Officials: Sanders and Turner. Attendance: 14,500.

at College Park, Maryland

North Carolina	fg-fga	ft-fta	rb	pf	tp
Walter Davis	7-11	7-9	6	2	21
Mike O'Koren	6-10	2-2	7	2	14
Rich Yonakor	4-7	0-0	5	5	8
Phil Ford	1-3	0-0	0	4	2
John Kuester	3-5	13-14	3	1	19
Bruce Buckley	0-0	0-0	0	2	0
Steve Krafcisin	0-0	8-8	3	2	8
Tom Zaliagiris	1-1	3-3	0	2	5
Dudley Bradley	1-1	0-1	1	0	2
Jeff Wolf	0-0	0-0	0	1	0
David Colescott	0-0	0-0	0	1	0
John Virgil	0-0	0-0	0	0	0
Team			1		
Totals	23-38	33-36	26	22	79

Kentucky	fg-fga	ft-fta	rb	pf	tp
Jack Givens	10-18	6-6	4	1	26
Rick Robey	5-6	5-5	3	5	15
Mike Phillips	6-7	0-0	3	3	12
Larry Johnson	3-11	3-4	6	5	9
Jay Shidler	0-4	0-0	0	2	0
Truman Claytor	2-6	0-0	2	5	4
James Lee	2-9	2-2	6	4	6
Merion Haskins	0-0	0-1	0	1	0
Dwane Casey	0-0	0-0	0	0	0
Team			3		
Totals	28-61	16-18	27	26	72

Half time: North Carolina 53-41. Officials: Bain and Galvan. Attendance: 14,500.

West First Round

at Pocatello, Idaho

Louisville	fg-fga	ft-fta	rb	pf	tp
Wesley Cox	8-14	7-11	12	3	23
Larry Williams	7-13	0-0	7	5	14
Ricky Gallon	1-5	2-2	5	1	4
Rick Wilson	3-10	0-0	1	5	6
Phillip Bond	4-10	2-2	5	3	10
Danny Brown	0-0	0-0	0	0	0
Tony Branch	0-1	0-0	0	1	0
Bobby Turner	3-5	2-3	1	0	8
Billy Harmon	0-0	0-0	0	0	0
Darrell Griffith	6-10	2-6	6	4	14
Team			9		
Totals	32-68	15-24	46	22	79

UCLA	fg-fga	ft-fta	rb	pf	tp
Marques Johnson	7-14	3-4	14	3	17
David Greenwood	2-8	4-4	7	3	8
Gig Sims	2-3	0-0	3	0	4
Roy Hamilton	4-6	3-3	2	1	11
Jim Spillane	4-12	8-10	4	2	16
Brad Holland	7-12	2-3	3	1	16
Raymond Townsend	1-6	0-0	0	1	2
Brett Vroman	2-3	5-5	2	4	9
Wilbert Olinde	0-0	0-0	1	0	0
Kiki Vandeweghe	2-4	0-1	2	1	4
Team			7		
Totals	31-68	25-30	45	16	87

Half time: UCLA 39-36. Officials: Bernjak and Palesse.

at Pocatello, Idaho

Idaho State	fg-fga	ft-fta	rb	pf	tp
Greg Griffin	6-19	2-3	15	2	14
Jeff Cook	5-10	8-11	16	3	18
Steve Hayes	13-23	3-7	11	3	29
Ed Thompson	1-2	0-0	2	4	2
Scott Goold	1-7	0-1	3	4	2
Kelly Gardner	0-1	0-0	0	0	0
Ernie Wheeler	4-7	3-5	3	2	11
Brian Bemis	1-1	0-0	0	0	2
Paul Wilson	0-0	1-2	1	0	1
Brand Robinson	1-2	2-3	2	2	4
Mark McQuaid	0-1	0-0	0	2	0
Stan Klos	0-0	0-0	1	0	0
Team			9		
Totals	32-73	19-32	63	22	83

Long Beach State	fg-fga	ft-fta	rb	pf	tp
Lloyd McMillian	8-11	4-5	8	4	20
Michael Wiley	6-15	2-7	10	2	14
Clarence Ruffen	3-8	0-0	7	5	6
Richard Johnson	3-11	7-9	6	4	13
Dale Dillon	2-7	0-0	1	4	4
Ron Austin	0-1	0-0	0	0	0
Danny Marques	1-1	0-0	0	0	2
Glen Gerke	1-4	0-0	0	2	2
Donnie Martin	0-5	0-0	1	2	0
Francois Wise	4-5	3-4	6	1	11
Tony McGee	0-2	0-2	0	1	0
James Dawson	0-2	0-2	1	4	0
Mark Stefl	0-0	0-0	0	1	0
Team			8		
Totals	28-72	16-29	48	30	72

Half time: Idaho State 33-30. Officials: Fouty and Crowley. Attendance: 10,897.

at Tucson, Arizona

St. John's, N.Y.	fg-fga	ft-fta	rb	pf	tp
George Johnson	11-20	2-2	14	4	24
Cecil Rellford	4-12	0-2	9	4	8
Rudy Wright	1-2	0-0	5	1	2
Tom Calabrese	4-7	0-0	0	4	8
Glen Williams	7-12	4-6	5	5	18
Tom Weadock	0-2	0-0	2	1	0
Kevelin Winfree	3-7	0-2	1	1	6
Gordon Thomas	1-1	0-0	0	0	2
Bill Clarke	0-0	0-0	0	1	0
Team			4		
Totals	31-63	6-12	40	21	68

Utah	fg-fga	ft-fta	rb	pf	tp
Jeff Judkins	8-17	2-2	4	1	18
Greg Deane	10-14	5-6	9	0	25
Buster Matheney	4-11	0-1	4	4	8
Jeff Jonas	3-10	5-6	5	1	11
Earl Williams	1-3	4-6	3	4	6
Donnie Rice	2-3	0-0	1	2	4
Coby Leavitt	0-1	0-1	3	1	0
Team			5		
Totals	28-59	16-22	34	13	72

Half time: Utah 36-29. Officials: Weiler and Wirtz.

at Tucson, Arizona

San Francisco	fg-fga	ft-fta	rb	pf	tp
Marlon Redmond	11-20	0-0	13	4	22
James Hardy	3-9	1-5	6	5	7
Bill Cartwright	5-10	5-8	8	4	15
John Cox	3-9	3-4	1	4	9
Winford Boynes	10-15	10-10	8	4	30
Jeff Randell	3-7	2-3	8	1	8
Rod Williams	1-4	0-0	0	2	2
Allen Thompson	0-1	0-0	0	1	0
Ray Hamilton	0-1	0-2	1	0	0
Erik Gilberg	0-0	2-2	1	0	2
Team			7		
Totals	36-76	23-36	53	25	95

Nevada-Las Vegas	fg-fga	ft-fta	rb	pf	tp
Eddie Owens	8-12	6-9	7	3	22
Sam Smith	5-7	4-4	2	0	14
Larry Moffett	2-4	0-0	4	5	4
Robert Smith	6-12	2-2	1	4	14
Glen Gondrezick	8-12	5-7	5	4	21
Reggie Theus	11-18	5-7	8	3	27
Lewis Brown	5-12	0-0	7	5	10
Tony Smith	3-7	0-0	2	1	6
Mike Milke	0-2	0-2	1	0	0
Matt Porter	0-0	1-2	2	0	1
Gary Wagner	0-1	0-0	1	0	0
John Rodriquez	1-2	0-0	2	3	2
Team			8		
Totals	49-89	23-33	50	28	121

Half time: Nevada-Las Vegas 63-44. Officials: Diehl and Nichols. Attendance: 13,451.

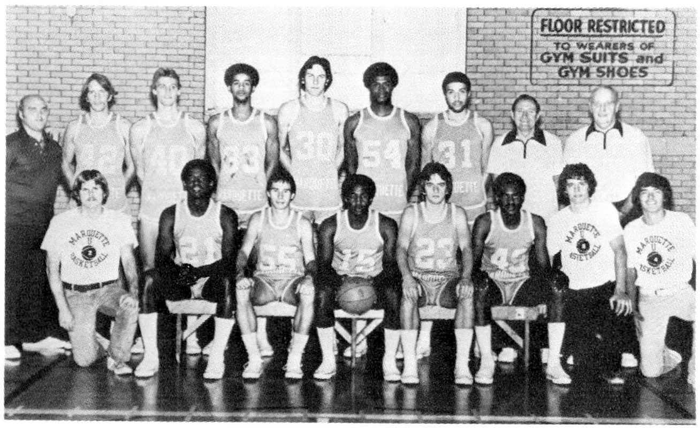

1977 MARQUETTE WARRIORS—(l-r) Front Row: Greg Stack, Ulice Payne, Gary Rosenberger, Butch Lee, Jim Boylan, Robert Byrd, Tom Hayden, David DuChateau; Second Row: Rick Majerus, Bill Neary, Jim Dudley, Bernard Toone, Craig Butrym, Jerome Whitehead, Bo Ellis, Hank Raymonds, Bob Weingart.

321

West Regional

at Provo, Utah

Idaho State	fg-fga	ft-fta	rb	pf	tp
Greg Griffin	4-14	4-4	8	4	12
Jeff Cook	4-10	0-0	14	4	8
Steve Hayes	11-20	5-7	12	3	27
Ed Thompson	4-10	6-8	4	3	14
Scott Goold	1-4	0-0	1	2	2
Ernie Wheeler	0-2	4-4	1	2	4
Brand Robinson	4-7	0-0	5	0	8
Paul Wilson	0-2	1-2	1	1	1
Team			9		
Totals	28-69	20-25	55	19	76

UCLA	fg-fga	ft-fta	rb	pf	tp
Roy Hamilton	5-14	1-3	6	5	11
Gig Sims	0-1	0-0	2	1	0
David Greenwood	10-23	0-2	14	4	20
Jim Spillane	2-8	0-0	1	5	4
Marques Johnson	7-14	7-8	13	3	21
Brett Vroman	1-2	0-0	0	1	2
Brad Holland	3-10	3-4	0	2	9
Kiki Vandeweghe	3-8	0-0	2	1	6
Raymond Townsend	1-2	0-0	0	1	2
Wilbert Olinde	0-1	0-0	1	0	0
James Wilkes	0-0	0-0	0	1	0
Team			9		
Totals	32-83	11-17	48	24	75

Half time: UCLA 38-32. Officials: Nichols and Wirtz.

at Provo, Utah

Utah	fg-fga	ft-fta	rb	pf	tp
Jeff Judkins	10-18	3-4	7	2	23
Greg Deane	4-7	2-2	0	5	10
Buster Matheney	6-10	2-5	13	5	14
Jeff Jonas	3-11	6-9	3	4	12
Earl Williams	6-11	6-6	8	2	18
Mike Dunn	1-1	0-1	2	1	2
Donnie Rice	1-2	0-0	0	0	2
Coby Leavitt	0-0	2-2	2	2	2
Team			7		
Totals	31-60	21-29	42	21	83

Nevada-Las Vegas	fg-fga	ft-fta	rb	pf	tp
Glen Gondrezick	6-12	1-2	5	5	13
Sam Smith	4-10	0-2	2	3	8
Larry Moffett	1-7	0-0	17	4	2
Robert Smith	8-14	5-5	3	3	21
Eddie Owens	8-20	0-5	3	3	16
Reggie Theus	3-8	8-9	3	2	14
Tony Smith	5-10	0-1	3	3	10
Lewis Brown	2-6	0-0	2	1	4
Team			10		
Totals	37-87	14-19	50	24	88

Half time: Nevada-Las Vegas 40-39. Officials: Fouty and Palesse. Attendance: 21,639.

at Provo, Utah

Idaho State	fg-fga	ft-fta	rb	pf	tp
Greg Griffin	5-13	7-7	7	4	17
Jeff Cook	5-10	0-0	10	1	10
Steve Hayes	7-10	2-3	13	2	16
Ed Thompson	8-16	11-15	3	3	27
Scott Goold	1-4	0-0	1	3	2
Brand Robinson	2-5	2-2	1	4	6
Ernie Wheeler	2-6	1-2	2	1	5
Paul Wilson	1-2	1-2	0	3	3
Brian Bemis	0-0	2-2	0	1	2
Mark McQuaid	1-1	0-0	3	0	2
Stan Klos	0-1	0-0	0	0	0
Kelly Gardner	0-0	0-0	0	1	0
Team			3		
Totals	32-68	26-33	43	23	90

Nevada-Las Vegas	fg-fga	ft-fta	rb	pf	tp
Glen Gondrezick	3-8	1-2	9	4	7
Sam Smith	6-16	4-4	2	3	16
Larry Moffett	4-8	0-1	16	5	8
Robert Smith	4-8	2-2	2	4	10
Eddie Owens	10-19	4-5	3	3	24
Reggie Theus	6-12	4-5	3	3	16
Tony Smith	7-10	4-4	2	1	18
Lewis Brown	4-8	0-0	4	3	8
Mike Milke	0-0	0-0	0	1	0
Matt Porter	0-0	0-0	0	0	0
John Rodriquez	0-0	0-0	0	0	0
Gary Wagner	0-1	0-0	0	0	0
Team			9		
Totals	44-90	19-23	50	27	107

Half time: Idaho State 52-51. Officials: Fouty and Palesse. Attendance: 19,298.

Mideast First Round

at Bloomington, Indiana

Michigan	fg-fga	ft-fta	rb	pf	tp
John Robinson	7-13	2-2	3	4	16
Tom Staton	0-1	0-0	2	3	0
Phil Hubbard	6-15	4-6	12	4	16
Steve Grote	3-7	2-2	3	3	8
Rickey Green	17-21	3-3	4	1	37
Dave Baxter	5-7	0-0	2	0	10
Joel Thompson	0-0	1-2	2	1	1
Alan Hardy	1-1	0-0	0	0	2
Tom Bergen	1-1	0-1	0	2	2
Team			5		
Totals	40-66	12-16	33	18	92

Holy Cross	fg-fga	ft-fta	rb	pf	tp
Michael Vicens	11-16	1-2	8	5	23
Bill Doran	6-9	2-3	3	2	14
Chris Potter	9-19	2-3	7	2	20
Kevin McAuley	2-6	4-4	5	2	8
Peter Beckenbach	3-8	0-2	2	2	6
Charlie Browne	3-9	0-0	6	3	6
Gregory Gaskins	2-2	0-0	1	0	4
Team			3		
Totals	36-69	9-14	35	16	81

Half time: Holy Cross 40-39. Officials: Moreau and Birk.

GAME-BY-GAME RESULTS

at Bloomington, Indiana

N.C.-Charlotte	fg-fga	ft-fta	rb	pf	tp
Lew Massey	6-13	2-2	4	3	14
Kevin King	4-7	1-3	2	4	9
Cedric Maxwell	11-15	10-12	18	4	32
Chad Kinch	6-19	2-2	1	2	14
Melvin Watkins	5-8	2-2	2	4	12
Phil Scott	1-3	2-2	2	1	4
Jeff Gruber	2-3	2-2	2	1	6
Lee Whitfield	0-0	0-0	0	1	0
Team			7		
Totals	35-68	21-25	38	20	91

Central Michigan	fg-fga	ft-fta	rb	pf	tp
Leonard Drake	5-12	3-4	2	5	13
Jeff Tropf	7-17	8-8	7	3	22
Ben Poquette	6-15	3-4	12	4	15
Dave Grauzer	1-5	0-0	1	1	2
Val Bracey	7-16	2-2	8	4	16
Leon Guydon	7-13	0-0	7	3	14
K. C. Janer	1-1	2-2	0	0	4
Kurt Kaeding	0-0	0-0	1	0	0
Tony Hosey	0-0	0-0	2	0	0
Team			6		
Totals	34-79	18-20	46	20	86

Half time: North Carolina-Charlotte 49-46. Regulation Score: 81-81. Officials: Jacob and Pavis. Attendance: 12,638.

at Baton Rouge, Louisiana

Middle Tenn. State	fg-fga	ft-fta	rb	pf	tp
Leroy Coleman	1-4	0-0	1	1	2
Greg Joyner	8-17	7-8	15	3	23
Bob Martin	13-23	2-3	4	4	28
Lewis Mack	1-8	0-0	4	5	2
Sleepy Taylor	4-13	1-3	11	5	9
Julius Brown	6-13	0-0	3	1	12
Sam Burrell	0-1	0-0	1	1	0
Derek Render	0-0	0-0	0	0	0
Gil Thompson	0-0	0-0	0	1	0
Team			3		
Totals	33-79	10-14	42	21	76

Detroit	fg-fga	ft-fta	rb	pf	tp
John Long	9-16	2-2	3	2	20
Ron Bostick	2-2	0-0	4	3	4
Terry Tyler	12-16	5-8	15	1	29
Dennis Boyd	6-14	2-2	3	3	14
Terry Duerod	4-5	2-3	4	0	10
Jeff Whitlow	3-4	0-0	1	2	6
Turono Anderson	2-4	0-0	0	2	4
Wilbert McCormick	1-1	0-0	0	0	2
Wilbur Ross	0-0	0-0	0	1	0
Keith Jackson	1-2	0-0	2	0	2
Dave Niles	0-0	2-3	0	0	2
Team			2		
Totals	40-64	13-18	34	14	93

Half time: Detroit 46-38. Officials: Brown and Hannah.

at Baton Rouge, Louisiana

Tennessee	fg-fga	ft-fta	rb	pf	tp
Ernie Grunfeld	10-16	6-11	12	5	26
Bernard King	8-19	7-8	12	5	23
Reggie Johnson	6-12	5-5	10	4	17
Johnny Darden	3-8	0-0	1	2	6
Mike Jackson	6-13	0-0	3	5	12
Terry Crosby	0-4	0-0	3	2	0
Chuck Threeths	0-0	0-0	2	1	0
Bert Bertelkamp	2-3	0-0	0	3	4
Team			1		
Totals	35-75	18-24	44	27	88

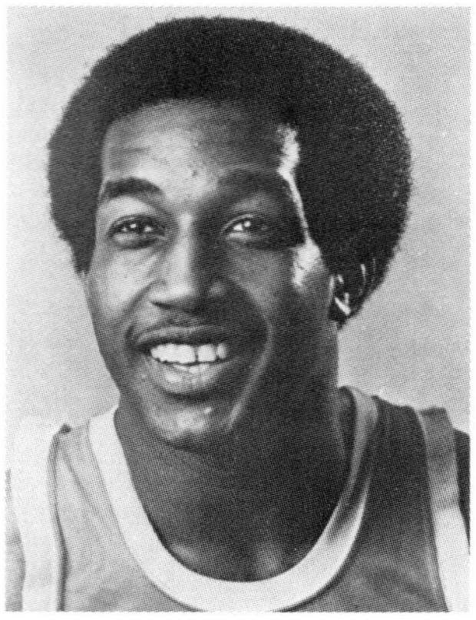

Butch Lee

Syracuse	fg-fga	ft-fta	rb	pf	tp
Dale Shackelford	3-4	1-5	9	4	7
Marty Byrnes	4-9	7-7	11	2	15
Roosevelt Bouie	3-8	2-2	4	5	8
Larry Kelley	9-15	4-4	2	1	22
James Williams	7-13	2-2	1	2	16
Ross Kindel	5-9	2-3	2	2	12
Louis Orr	2-6	2-4	9	5	6
Bill Drew	2-4	3-4	2	1	7
Robert Parker	0-0	0-0	0	1	0
Team			2		
Totals	35-68	23-31	42	23	93

Half time: Tennessee 38-35. Regulation Score: 78-78. Officials: Burch and Richard. Attendance: 5,965.

Mideast Regional

at Lexington, Kentucky

Michigan	fg-fga	ft-fta	rb	pf	tp
Tom Staton	4-8	0-1	3	4	8
John Robinson	12-18	1-2	7	2	25
Phil Hubbard	8-19	6-7	26	3	22
Rickey Green	4-13	3-5	5	1	11
Steve Grote	7-14	2-3	3	2	16
Joel Thompson	1-1	0-0	1	0	2
Dave Baxter	0-2	0-0	0	1	0
Alan Hardy	1-3	0-0	2	0	2
Team			4		
Totals	37-78	12-18	51	13	86

Detroit	fg-fga	ft-fta	rb	pf	tp
John Long	12-24	1-1	7	3	25
Ron Bostick	3-9	0-0	10	4	6
Terry Tyler	8-12	1-1	9	2	17
Dennis Boyd	8-16	0-0	1	2	16
Terry Duerod	5-12	1-2	0	3	11
Wilbert McCormick	1-2	0-0	1	0	2
Turono Anderson	1-3	0-0	0	0	2
Wilbur Ross	0-0	0-0	0	0	0
Jeff Whitlow	1-3	0-0	2	4	2
Team			3		
Totals	39-81	3-4	33	18	81

Half time: Michigan 48-44. Officials: Brown and Birk.

at Lexington, Kentucky

Syracuse	fg-fga	ft-fta	rb	pf	tp
Dale Shackleford	8-14	0-0	6	5	16
Marty Byrnes	7-7	2-3	3	4	16
Roosevelt Bouie	6-8	0-0	5	2	12
Larry Kelley	0-7	0-0	2	0	0
Jim Williams	2-8	0-0	1	3	4
Hal Cohen	0-0	0-0	0	0	0
Ross Kindel	0-3	1-2	0	1	1
Bill Drew	4-13	0-0	3	3	8
Kevin James	0-0	0-0	0	0	0
Louis Orr	1-5	0-0	1	3	2
Team			7		
Totals	28-65	3-5	28	21	59

N.C.-Charlotte	fg-fga	ft-fta	rb	pf	tp
Lew Massey	7-12	0-0	6	3	14
Kevin King	6-9	1-2	7	0	13
Cedric Maxwell	4-6	11-11	5	1	19
Chad Kinch	6-8	4-6	1	0	16
Melvin Watkins	6-8	1-2	1	2	13
Jeff Gruber	1-4	2-2	0	1	4
Todd Crowley	0-0	0-0	0	0	0
Lee Whitfield	0-0	0-1	1	0	0
Phil Scott	0-3	2-2	4	4	2
Ken Angel	0-1	0-0	0	0	0
Mike Hester	0-2	0-0	1	1	0
Team			7		
Totals	30-53	21-26	33	12	81

Half time: North Carolina-Charlotte 38-22. Officials: Jacob and Burke. Attendance: 22,286.

at Lexington, Kentucky

Michigan	fg-fga	ft-fta	rb	pf	tp
Tom Staton	0-4	0-0	3	5	0
John Robinson	5-9	1-2	4	4	11
Phil Hubbard	5-14	4-4	7	4	14
Rickey Green	9-19	2-6	2	1	20
Steve Grote	3-8	1-2	3	5	7
Joel Thompson	3-5	0-0	1	2	6
Dave Baxter	2-7	0-0	0	3	4
Alan Hardy	3-8	0-0	4	4	6
Tom Bergen	0-0	0-0	0	0	0
Team			8		
Totals	30-74	8-14	32	28	68

N.C.-Charlotte	fg-fga	ft-fta	rb	pf	tp
Lew Massey	6-13	7-9	11	4	19
Kevin King	2-3	2-3	3	2	6
Cedric Maxwell	10-16	5-8	13	4	25
Chad Kinch	3-10	5-5	3	2	11
Melvin Watkins	2-7	2-2	6	2	6
Jeff Gruber	3-3	0-0	0	2	6
Phil Scott	1-1	0-1	1	1	2
Mike Hester	0-0	0-0	0	0	0
Team			6		
Totals	27-53	21-28	43	17	75

Half time: North Carolina-Charlotte 40-27. Officials: Brown and Burke. Attendance: 22,301.

Midwest First Round

at Omaha, Nebraska

Cincinnati	fg-fga	ft-fta	rb	pf	tp
Mike Jones	2-4	2-2	4	5	6
Brian Williams	2-6	1-2	3	4	5
Bob Miller	9-13	2-2	10	4	20
Gary Yoder	3-11	0-0	2	0	6
Steve Collier	3-9	0-0	1	3	6
Eddie Lee	3-3	2-3	1	2	8
Keith Hemans	0-2	0-0	0	1	0
Mick Shoemaker	0-0	0-0	0	0	0
Paul Fazakas	0-0	0-0	0	0	0
Curtis Cabbel	0-0	0-0	0	0	0
Team			4		
Totals	22-48	7-9	25	19	51

Marquette	fg-fga	ft-fta	rb	pf	tp
Bo Ellis	8-13	1-2	5	3	17
Bill Neary	0-3	2-2	4	1	2
Jerome Whitehead	6-8	3-3	6	3	15
Butch Lee	6-14	1-1	5	2	13
Jim Boylan	2-5	5-5	0	3	9
Bernard Toone	0-2	4-5	6	2	4
Gary Rosenberger	3-9	0-1	4	1	6
Team			5		
Totals	25-54	16-19	35	15	66

Half time: Cincinnati 31-28. Officials: Grossman and Copeland.

at Omaha, Nebraska

Arizona	fg-fga	ft-fta	rb	pf	tp
Len Gordy	4-9	2-2	7	3	10
Bob Elliott	9-12	5-6	6	3	23
Phil Taylor	2-3	0-0	6	0	4
Herman Harris	8-20	0-0	7	3	16
Gary Harrison	1-3	0-0	1	3	2
Gilbert Myles	7-13	2-2	1	0	16
Tim Marshall	0-1	0-0	4	2	0
Larry Demic	0-0	0-0	0	0	0
Jerome Gladney	1-6	4-6	4	3	6
Kenny Davis	0-0	0-0	0	0	0
Team			6		
Totals	32-67	13-16	42	17	77

SIU-Carbondale	fg-fga	ft-fta	rb	pf	tp
Richard Ford	4-7	0-0	7	5	8
Gary Wilson	5-11	2-5	7	3	12
Corky Abrams	7-9	1-2	5	2	15
Mike Glenn	15-22	5-5	1	0	35
Wayne Abrams	0-4	1-4	2	3	1
Alfred Grant	1-2	0-0	1	2	2
Barry Smith	0-0	0-0	0	0	0
Al Williams	2-3	0-0	1	0	4
Mel Hughlett	2-6	0-0	2	1	4
Team			5		
Totals	36-64	9-16	31	16	81

Half time: Southern Illinois 45-40. Officials: Reed and White. Attendance: 9,821.

at Norman, Oklahoma

Kansas State	fg-fga	ft-fta	rb	pf	tp
Curtis Redding	14-18	4-4	9	3	32
Larry Dassie	4-11	0-0	11	2	8
Darryl Winston	1-5	4-6	9	2	6
Scott Langton	9-12	1-2	3	2	19
Mike Evans	9-19	2-2	4	3	20
Dan Droge	0-2	0-0	0	0	0
Tyrone Ladson	1-2	0-0	2	0	2
Jerry Black	0-1	0-0	1	0	0
Team			3		
Totals	38-70	11-14	42	12	87

Providence	fg-fga	ft-fta	rb	pf	tp
Bill Eason	6-9	0-0	2	2	12
Bruce Campbell	3-8	0-2	0	4	6
Robert Cooper	5-11	1-2	8	2	11
Joe Hassett	13-19	0-0	6	0	26
Dwight Williams	4-14	3-3	2	3	11
Robert Misevicius	7-15	0-0	8	2	14
Paul Oristaglio	0-1	0-0	1	0	0
Team			1		
Totals	38-77	4-7	28	13	80

Half time: Providence 40-37. Officials: Ditty and Kelley.

at Norman, Oklahoma

Wake Forest	fg-fga	ft-fta	rb	pf	tp
Rod Griffin	10-17	6-9	10	4	26
Jerry Schellenberg	6-12	5-6	3	2	17
Larry Harrison	0-1	0-0	5	4	0
Skip Brown	8-17	7-8	1	4	23
Frank Johnson	4-8	4-4	3	2	12
Leroy McDonald	2-6	2-2	3	2	6
Mike Palma	0-0	0-0	0	0	0
Mark Dale	0-0	0-0	1	1	0
Don Mulnix	1-2	0-0	1	1	2
John Hendler	0-0	0-0	1	1	0
Team			1		
Totals	31-63	24-29	29	21	86

Arkansas	fg-fga	ft-fta	rb	pf	tp
Jim Counce	3-4	6-6	3	4	12
Marvin Delph	7-14	4-6	8	2	18
Steve Stroud	3-5	0-0	3	4	6
Ron Brewer	9-11	2-4	2	3	20
Sidney Moncrief	6-8	0-2	10	5	12
Steve Schall	6-7	0-2	0	3	12
Ray Buckner	0-1	0-0	0	2	0
Troy Trumbo	0-0	0-0	0	1	0
Team			1		
Totals	34-50	12-20	27	24	80

Half time: Arkansas 46-33. Officials: Wortman and Buckiewicz. Attendance: 10,871.

Midwest Regional

at Oklahoma City, Oklahoma

Kansas State	fg-fga	ft-fta	rb	pf	tp
Curtis Redding	4-16	4-4	14	5	12
Larry Dassie	7-12	4-4	6	4	18
Darryl Winston	5-6	2-4	11	2	12
Scott Langton	3-5	2-2	5	3	8
Mike Evans	8-14	0-0	0	4	16
Dan Droge	0-1	0-0	0	1	0
Tyrone Ladson	0-0	0-0	0	0	0
Team			4		
Totals	27-54	12-14	40	19	66

Marquette	fg-fga	ft-fta	rb	pf	tp
Bill Neary	0-2	0-0	3	2	0
Bo Ellis	5-14	9-11	3	2	19
Jerome Whitehead	1-9	0-0	6	2	2
Butch Lee	12-23	2-2	4	1	26
Jim Boylan	4-4	0-0	2	1	8
Gary Rosenberger	0-4	0-0	1	0	0
Bernard Toone	2-4	4-5	5	4	8
Jim Dudley	2-3	0-0	3	3	4
Team			2		
Totals	26-63	15-18	29	15	67

Half time: Kansas State 36-28. Officials: Woltman and Buckiewicz.

at Oklahoma City, Oklahoma

Wake Forest	fg-fga	ft-fta	rb	pf	tp
Rod Griffin	8-9	6-8	5	3	22
Jerry Schellenberg	9-16	4-4	6	1	22
Larry Harrison	0-1	0-0	3	3	0
Skip Brown	7-15	11-12	2	1	25
Frank Johnson	4-10	0-0	0	3	8
Leroy McDonald	2-3	5-6	4	2	9
Don Mulnix	0-0	0-0	0	1	0
John Hendler	0-1	0-0	1	1	0
Team			3		
Totals	30-55	26-30	24	15	86

SIU-Carbondale	fg-fga	ft-fta	rb	pf	tp
Richard Ford	7-10	3- 4	6	5	17
Gary Wilson	6-13	0- 3	7	4	12
Corky Abrams	3- 4	2- 2	3	4	8
Mike Glenn	15-23	0- 0	4	3	30
Wayne Abrams	2- 5	3- 4	6	2	7
Alfred Grant	1- 7	1- 1	5	1	3
Barry Smith	2- 2	0- 1	3	1	4
Mel Hughlett	0- 0	0- 0	1	0	0
Tom Harris	0- 0	0- 0	0	2	0
Al Williams	0- 0	0- 0	0	0	0
Team			4		
Totals	36-64	9-15	39	22	81

Half time: Southern Illinois 35-34. Officials: Reed and Copeland. Attendance: 10,185.

at Oklahoma City, Oklahoma

Marquette	fg-fga	ft-fta	rb	pf	tp
Bill Neary	3- 5	1- 2	6	4	7
Bo Ellis	8-14	4- 6	7	3	20
Jerome Whitehead	1- 5	0- 0	5	4	2
Butch Lee	8-15	3- 4	2	2	19
Jim Boylan	3- 5	1- 2	5	2	7
Bernard Toone	6-11	6- 6	2	2	18
Gary Rosenberger	2- 4	5- 6	2	1	9
Jim Dudley	0- 1	0- 0	0	0	0
Team			3		
Totals	31-60	20-26	32	18	82

Wake Forest	fg-fga	ft-fta	rb	pf	tp
Rod Griffin	6-10	4- 4	4	4	16
Jerry Schellenberg	7-12	5- 8	5	2	19
Larry Harrison	4- 5	3- 4	4	4	11
Skip Brown	5-12	0- 1	5	4	10
Frank Johnson	3-13	0- 0	4	4	6
Don Mulnix	1- 2	0- 0	1	1	2
Leroy McDonald	0- 0	4- 4	5	3	4
John Hendler	0- 0	0- 0	0	1	0
Team			3		
Totals	26-54	16-21	31	23	68

Half time: Wake Forest 35-31. Officials: Copeland and Wortman. Attendance: 8,935.

Semifinals

at Atlanta, Georgia

North Carolina	fg-fga	ft-fta	rb	pf	tp
Walter Davis	7- 7	5- 6	5	3	19
Mike O'Koren	14-19	3- 5	8	1	31
Rich Yonakor	5- 7	1- 4	9	0	11
Phil Ford	4-10	4- 5	6	2	12
John Kuester	2- 5	5- 7	6	0	9
Tom Zaliagiris	0- 1	0- 0	0	0	0
Steve Krafcisin	0- 0	0- 1	2	1	0
Bruce Buckley	1- 5	0- 0	2	3	2
Dudley Bradley	0- 1	0- 0	1	0	0
Jeff Wolf	0- 1	0- 0	1	0	0
Dave Colescott	0- 0	0- 0	0	1	0
Team			1		
Totals	33-56	18-28	41	11	84

Nevada-Las Vegas	fg-fga	ft-fta	rb	pf	tp
Eddie Owens	7-15	0- 0	2	4	14
Glen Gondrezick	4- 8	0- 0	5	4	8
Larry Moffett	6- 9	1- 2	9	5	13
Robert Smith	4-11	0- 1	1	1	8
Sam Smith	10-18	0- 0	2	1	20
Tony Smith	6- 8	0- 2	1	3	12
Reggie Theus	4-11	0- 0	5	4	8
Lewis Brown	0- 0	0- 0	1	0	0
Team			3		
Totals	41-80	1- 5	29	22	83

Half time: Nevada-Las Vegas 49-43. Officials: Brown and Copeland.

at Atlanta, Georgia

N.C.-Charlotte	fg-fga	ft-fta	rb	pf	tp
Lew Massey	7-13	0- 0	8	1	14
Kevin King	2- 7	0- 0	5	2	4
Cedric Maxwell	5- 6	7- 9	12	2	17
Chad Kinch	1- 7	2- 2	4	2	4
Melvin Watkins	2- 4	2- 3	0	5	6
Jeff Gruber	2- 6	0- 0	0	0	4
Phil Scott	0- 0	0- 0	0	0	0
Team			1		
Totals	19-43	11-14	30	12	49

Marquette	fg-fga	ft-fta	rb	pf	tp
Bo Ellis	2- 8	0- 0	5	4	4
Bill Neary	0- 1	0- 0	2	3	0
Jerome Whitehead	10-16	1- 2	16	1	21
Butch Lee	5-18	1- 1	3	3	11
Jim Boylan	4- 9	0- 0	3	2	8
Bernard Toone	2- 6	2- 2	1	3	6
Gary Rosenberger	0- 0	1- 2	1	0	1
Team			2		
Totals	23-58	5- 7	33	16	51

Half time: Marquette 25-22. Officials: Fouty and Galvin. Attendance: 16,086.

National Third Place

at Atlanta, Georgia

Nevada-Las Vegas	fg-fga	ft-fta	rb	pf	tp
Eddie Owens	14-28	6- 8	8	2	34
Glen Gondrezick	3- 8	1- 2	7	4	7
Larry Moffett	6- 9	0- 0	6	4	12
Robert Smith	4- 7	2- 2	1	1	10
Sam Smith	5-10	0- 0	5	2	10
Reggie Theus	11-18	2- 5	5	4	24
Tony Smith	1- 6	0- 0	0	0	2
Lewis Brown	3- 9	1- 1	5	5	7
Team			3		
Totals	47-95	12-18	40	22	106

N.C.-Charlotte	fg-fga	ft-fta	rb	pf	tp
Lew Massey	11-19	0- 0	7	3	22
Kevin King	1- 4	0- 2	0	1	2
Cedric Maxwell	9-15	12-13	16	2	30
Chad Kinch	11-20	8- 8	12	5	30
Melvin Watkins	1- 5	0- 0	4	2	2
Phil Scott	2- 4	0- 0	6	3	4
Jeff Gruber	1- 1	0- 0	0	1	2
Ken Angel	0- 1	2- 3	2	1	2
Lee Whitfield	0- 0	0- 0	0	0	0
Todd Crowley	0- 0	0- 0	0	0	0
Mike Hester	0- 1	0- 0	3	0	0
Jerry Winston	0- 2	0- 0	0	0	0
Team			1		
Totals	36-72	22-26	51	18	94

Half time: North Carolina-Charlotte 55-50. Officials: Brown and Fouty.

Championship

at Atlanta, Georgia

North Carolina	fg-fga	ft-fta	rb	pf	tp
Walter Davis	6-13	8-10	8	4	20
Mike O'Koren	6-10	2- 4	11	5	14
Rich Yonakor	3- 5	0- 0	4	0	6
Phil Ford	3-10	0- 0	2	3	6
John Kuester	2- 6	1- 2	0	5	5
Steve Krafcisin	1- 1	0- 0	0	0	2
Tom Zaliagiris	2- 3	0- 0	0	3	4
Dudley Bradley	1- 1	0- 0	0	2	2
Bruce Buckley	0- 1	0- 0	0	1	0
Jeff Wolf	0- 1	0- 0	1	0	0
Dave Colescott	0- 0	0- 0	0	0	0
Woody Coley	0- 0	0- 0	0	0	0
Ged Doughton	0- 0	0- 0	0	0	0
John Virgil	0- 0	0- 0	0	1	0
Team			2		
Totals	24-51	11-16	28	24	59

Marquette	fg-fga	ft-fta	rb	pf	tp
Bo Ellis	5- 9	4- 5	9	4	14
Bill Neary	0- 2	0- 0	0	1	0
Jerome Whitehead	2- 8	4- 4	11	2	8
Butch Lee	6-14	7- 7	3	1	19
Jim Boylan	5- 7	4- 4	4	3	14
Gary Rosenberger	1- 1	4- 4	1	1	6
Bernard Toone	3- 6	0- 1	0	1	6
Team			1		
Totals	22-47	23-25	29	13	67

Half time: Marquette 39-27. Officials: Galvan and Copeland. Attendance: 16,086.

1978

Mideast First Round

at Indianapolis, Indiana

Michigan State	fg-fga	ft-fta	rb	pf	tp
Gregory Kelser	9-10	5- 7	11	2	23
Earvin Johnson	5- 9	4- 6	7	3	14
Jay Vincent	2- 3	2- 3	4	1	6
Terry Donnelly	6- 9	0- 0	3	2	12
Bob Chapman	7-12	0- 0	1	2	14
Mike Brkovich	0- 0	0- 0	0	1	0
Ronald Charles	3- 4	0- 2	3	4	6
Donald Flowers	0- 0	0- 0	0	0	0
Nate Phillips	0- 1	0- 0	0	0	0
Mike Longaker	0- 0	0- 0	0	0	0
Len Williams	0- 0	0- 0	0	0	0
Alfred Brown	0- 2	0- 0	1	0	0
Dan Riewald	0- 0	0- 0	1	0	0
Rick Kaye	0- 0	0- 0	0	1	0
Sten Feldreich	1- 2	0- 0	2	1	2
Team			2		
Totals	33-52	11-18	35	17	77

Providence	fg-fga	ft-fta	rb	pf	tp
Bill Eason	3-10	0- 2	6	4	6
Bruce Campbell	9-16	6- 6	8	4	24
Bob Misevicius	6-10	1- 1	6	4	13
Dwight Williams	1- 6	2- 4	1	5	4
Paul Cristaglio	0- 1	0- 0	0	1	0
Jerry Scott	2- 6	0- 1	1	0	4
David Frye	0- 1	2- 2	1	0	2
John Nolan	0- 1	2- 2	0	0	2
Ernie Delgatto	0- 0	0- 0	1	0	0
Rudy Williams	2- 6	2- 4	4	3	6
Rich Hunger	0- 2	2- 2	1	2	2
Team			5		
Totals	23-59	17-24	34	23	63

Half time: Michigan State 38-26. Officials: Overby and Kelley.

at Knoxville, Tennessee

Western Kentucky	fg-fga	ft-fta	rb	pf	tp
James Johnson	9-17	3- 4	12	1	21
Greg Jackson	4- 8	3- 6	6	4	11
Aaron Bryant	7-12	2- 4	9	5	16
Steve Ashby	5- 9	2- 3	4	4	12
Darryl Turner	5-13	2- 4	4	3	12
Mike Prince	4-11	0- 0	2	2	8
Greg Burbach	0- 0	1- 2	2	0	1
Mike Reese	3- 4	0- 0	2	0	6
Team			4		
Totals	37-74	13-23	45	19	87

Syracuse	fg-fga	ft-fta	rb	pf	tp
Marty Byrnes	8-19	5- 9	7	4	21
Louis Orr	6-12	2- 2	8	4	14
Roosevelt Bouie	7-14	2- 4	15	1	16
Ross Kindel	0- 1	0- 0	1	0	0
Dale Shackleford	2- 4	0- 0	0	5	4
Hal Cohen	11-16	1- 1	4	5	23
Eddie Moss	2- 3	0- 1	2	1	4
Marty Headd	1- 5	0- 0	1	0	2
Kevin James	1- 2	0- 0	1	1	2
Dan Schayes	0- 0	0- 0	0	0	0
Team			5		
Totals	38-76	10-17	44	21	86

Half time: 41-41. Regulation Score: 76-76. Officials: Weiler and Bishop.

at Indianapolis, Indiana

Marquette	fg-fga	ft-fta	rb	pf	tp
Ulice Payne	5-12	1- 2	4	4	11
Bernard Toone	6-10	0- 1	5	5	12
Jerome Whitehead	5- 8	0- 0	10	3	10
Butch Lee	10-16	7-10	3	3	27
Jim Boylan	5-10	5- 7	4	1	15
Oliver Lee	1- 1	0- 0	1	0	2
Gary Rosenberger	2- 5	0- 0	2	0	4
Team			3		
Totals	34-62	13-20	32	16	81

Miami, Ohio	fg-fga	ft-fta	rb	pf	tp
Randy Ayers	7-13	6- 7	10	3	20
Archie Aldridge	7-15	5- 6	8	3	19
Bill Lake	0- 2	2- 2	1	2	2
Rick Goins	9-13	0- 0	0	3	18
John Shoemaker	10-15	0- 0	4	2	20
Rich Babcock	0- 0	3- 4	0	0	3
Todd Jones	0- 1	0- 0	1	0	0
Tom Dunn	1- 3	0- 0	4	5	2
Team			6		
Totals	34-62	16-19	34	18	84

Half time: Marquette 38-33. Regulation Score: 75-75. Officials: Clymer and Pavia. Attendance: 16,519.

at Knoxville, Tennessee

Florida State	fg-fga	ft-fta	rb	pf	tp
David Thompson	6-14	3- 4	5	3	15
Harry Davis	5-10	1- 4	7	3	11
Kris Anderson	3- 5	0- 0	3	5	6
Tony Jackson	4- 7	2- 2	5	4	10
Eugene Harris	4-11	1- 3	3	2	9
Hank Mann	0- 0	0- 0	0	0	0
James Bozeman	0- 1	0- 0	0	1	0
Mickey Dillard	8-10	5- 5	1	5	21
James Smith	0- 0	0- 0	0	0	0
Murray Brown	2- 4	0- 3	3	0	4
Team			4		
Totals	32-62	12-21	31	23	76

Kentucky	fg-fga	ft-fta	rb	pf	tp
Jack Givens	4- 9	3- 3	4	5	11
Rick Robey	2- 2	8-10	4	5	12
Mike Phillips	6- 9	2- 2	6	1	14
Kyle Macy	6-10	2- 3	5	1	14
Truman Claytor	7-13	2- 2	1	1	16
Dwane Casey	0- 0	0- 0	0	2	0
Jay Shidler	1- 1	0- 0	0	1	2
James Lee	2- 5	6- 8	3	3	10
Fred Cowan	1- 2	0- 0	3	1	2
Lavon Williams	1- 2	2- 2	5	2	4
Team			1		
Totals	30-53	25-30	32	22	85

Half time: Florida State 39-32. Officials: Brown and Forte. Attendance: 12,700.

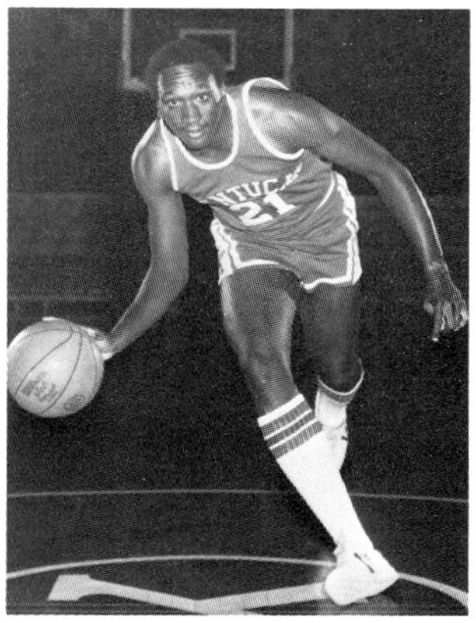

Jack Givens

West First Round

at Eugene, Oregon

Kansas	fg-fga	ft-fta	rb	pf	tp
Ken Koenigs	4- 6	0- 0	6	5	8
Paul Mokeski	9-15	0- 2	12	4	18
Clint Johnson	7-11	1- 3	1	5	15
John Douglas	5-17	4- 6	7	4	14
Darnell Valentine	5-14	1- 2	3	5	11
Wilmore Fowler	0- 4	0- 0	0	2	0
Milt Gibson	0- 0	0- 0	0	0	0
Donnie Von Moore	3- 8	2- 4	4	4	8
Brad Sanders	1- 1	0- 0	0	0	2
Scott Anderson	0- 0	0- 0	1	1	0
Team			4		
Totals	34-76	8-17	38	30	76

UCLA	fg-fga	ft-fta	rb	pf	tp
David Greenwood	7-15	0- 1	10	3	14
James Wilkes	0- 3	5- 6	3	0	5
Gig Sims	1- 2	0- 0	3	2	2
Roy Hamilton	6-16	11-18	7	3	23
Raymond Townsend	8-12	6- 6	5	2	22
Darrell Allums	2- 4	2- 2	11	3	6
Kiki Vandeweghe	4- 7	3- 6	6	1	11
Team			2		
Totals	28-59	27-39	47	14	83

Half time: Kansas 45-42. Officials: Copeland and Crowley.

at Eugene, Oregon

Arkansas	fg-fga	ft-fta	rb	pf	tp
Jim Counce	2- 3	0- 0	8	2	4
Marvin Delph	9-16	2- 2	8	1	20
Steve Schall	3- 5	0- 0	4	4	6
Ron Brewer	7-15	5- 7	3	2	19
Sidney Moncrief	5- 9	6- 6	5	4	16
Mike Watley	0- 2	0- 0	0	0	0
Alan Zahn	1- 1	0- 0	1	3	2
Ulysses Reed	1- 3	0- 0	0	1	2
James Crockett	2- 4	0- 0	1	0	4
Team			4		
Totals	30-58	13-15	34	17	73

Weber State	fg-fga	ft-fta	rb	pf	tp
David Johnson	4-17	1- 2	6	3	9
Kurt Moore	7- 9	0- 0	7	2	14
Richard Smith	3-11	2- 2	8	4	8
Mark Mattos	1- 5	0- 0	2	0	2
Bruce Collins	5-15	3- 5	5	2	13
Ben Howland	3- 6	0- 2	0	2	6
Darrell Brown	0- 0	0- 0	0	0	0
Jim Gibson	0- 0	0- 0	0	0	0
Rob McKone	0- 1	0- 0	1	1	0
Team			3		
Totals	23-64	6-11	32	14	52

Half time: Arkansas 32-26. Officials: Diehl and Bain. Attendance: 9,141.

at Tempe, Arizona

San Francisco	fg-fga	ft-fta	rb	pf	tp
Winford Boynes	10-14	0- 0	8	3	20
Doug Jemison	3- 9	2- 2	5	2	8
Bill Cartwright	9-12	5- 7	11	3	23
Rod Williams	1- 4	1- 2	5	2	3
John Cox	4-11	4- 4	5	1	12
Sam Williams	1- 4	0- 0	2	3	2
Team			3		
Totals	28-54	12-15	39	14	68

North Carolina	fg-fga	ft-fta	rb	pf	tp
Mike O'Koren	5-13	4- 5	5	2	14
Dudley Bradley	2- 3	0- 0	0	2	4
Jeff Wolf	2- 8	0- 0	2	2	4
Tom Zaliagiris	3- 3	0- 0	2	1	6
Phil Ford	7-21	0- 0	1	3	14
David Colescott	1- 1	0- 0	0	0	2
Ged Doughton	0- 0	0- 0	0	0	0
Al Wood	3- 9	0- 0	5	2	6
Pete Budko	0- 0	0- 0	0	0	0
Jeff Crompton	2- 5	0- 1	7	3	4
John Virgil	5- 8	0- 0	0	2	10
Team			5		
Totals	30-71	4- 6	27	17	64

Half time: 32-32. Officials: Cavatto and Fouty.

at Tempe, Arizona

Fullerton State	fg-fga	ft-fta	rb	pf	tp
Greg Bunch	8-10	2- 4	5	5	18
Kevin Heenan	10-17	2- 3	5	2	22
Steve Shaw	1- 1	0- 1	1	2	2
Keith Anderson	9-14	5- 7	1	1	23
Mike Linden	1- 3	4- 4	5	2	6
Mike Niles	7-13	5- 6	6	3	19
Team			1		
Totals	36-58	18-25	24	15	90

New Mexico	fg-fga	ft-fta	rb	pf	tp
Marvin Johnson	7-15	1- 2	1	3	15
Phil Abney	7- 9	2- 3	7	4	16
Jimmy Allen	3- 5	0- 0	10	2	6
Michael Cooper	6-15	0- 1	4	2	12
Russell Saunders	5-11	3- 3	2	2	13
Will Smiley	3- 5	3- 3	3	2	9
Willie Howard	5- 9	0- 1	5	4	10
Mark Felix	1- 3	2- 2	1	2	4
Mike Stewart	0- 0	0- 0	0	0	0
Team			2		
Totals	37-72	11-15	35	21	85

Half time: New Mexico 44-38. Officials: Savicga and Grossman. Attendance: 11,316.

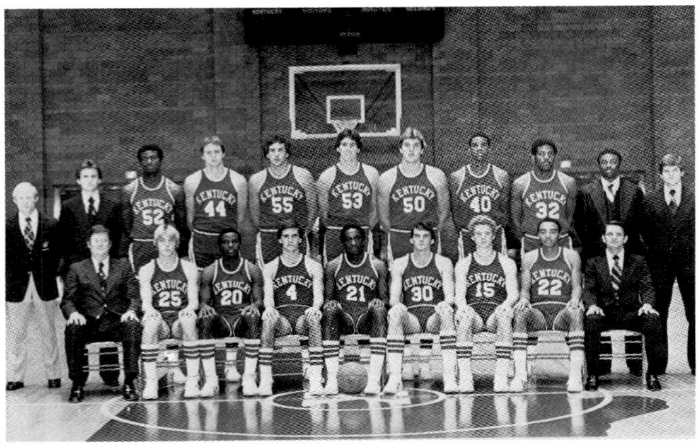

1978 KENTUCKY WILDCATS—(l-r) Front Row: Joe B. Hall, Jay Shidler, Dwane Casey, Kyle Macy, Jack Givens, Tim Stephens, Chris Gettelfinger, Truman Claytor, Dick Parsons; Second Row: Walt McCombs, Don Sullivan, LaVon Williams, Scott Courts, Mike Phillips, Rick Robey, Chuck Aleksinas, Fred Cowan, James Lee, Leonard Hamilton, Joe Dean Jr.

East First Round

at Charlotte, North Carolina

Rhode Island	fg-fga	ft-fta	rb	pf	tp
Sly Williams	12-18	3- 6	9	5	27
Stan Wright	4-11	0- 0	3	4	8
Irv Chatman	1- 6	1- 3	12	4	3
John Nelson	3-11	0- 1	4	2	6
Jiggy Williamson	6- 9	0- 0	2	2	12
Percy Davis	2- 3	0- 1	1	2	4
Jim Wright	1- 7	0- 0	3	2	2
Team			7		
Totals	29-65	4-11	41	21	62

Duke	fg-fga	ft-fta	rb	pf	tp
Eugene Banks	7-15	0- 1	10	3	14
Kenny Dennard	0- 3	0- 1	5	3	0
Mike Gminski	10-18	5- 5	10	3	25
John Harrell	0- 4	0- 0	1	2	0
Jim Spanarkel	8-13	2- 5	5	2	18
Bob Bender	0- 3	0- 0	0	3	0
Scott Goetsch	0- 1	0- 0	2	0	0
Harold Morrison	0- 0	0- 0	0	0	0
Steve Gray	0- 0	0- 0	0	0	0
Jim Suddath	1- 4	4- 4	4	0	6
Team			4		
Totals	26-61	11-16	41	16	63

Half time: Rhode Island 31-30. Officials: Turner and Winters.

at Philadelphia, Pennsylvania

Pennsylvania	fg-fga	ft-fta	rb	pf	tp
Tony Price	6-14	4- 4	12	5	16
Keven McDonald	16-25	5- 6	11	2	37
Matt White	0- 1	0- 0	2	5	0
Stan Greene	4- 8	0- 0	1	3	8
Bobby Willis	4- 9	0- 0	6	3	8
Tom Crowley	3- 4	4- 4	0	2	10
Tim Smith	3- 7	1- 5	2	2	7
James Salters	1- 2	2- 3	0	0	4
Ed Kuhl	1- 4	0- 0	3	0	2
Bruce Bergwall	0- 1	0- 0	0	1	0
Team			5		
Totals	38-75	16-22	42	23	92

St. Bonaventure	fg-fga	ft-fta	rb	pf	tp
Delmar Harrod	6- 9	1- 2	6	5	13
Greg Sanders	10-24	10-14	13	4	30
Tim Waterman	6-14	1- 3	16	2	13
Nick Urzetta	1- 6	0- 0	4	3	2
Glenn Hagan	6-19	7- 7	1	2	19
Mark Belcher	1- 2	2- 3	0	2	4
Dan Viglianco	0- 0	0- 0	0	0	0
Mark Spencer	0- 0	0- 0	0	3	0
Alfonza Jones	1- 1	0- 0	2	2	2
Team			4		
Totals	31-75	21-29	46	23	83

Half time: St. Bonaventure 42-37. Officials: Bosone and Wortman.

at Charlotte, North Carolina

Furman	fg-fga	ft-fta	rb	pf	tp
Rodney Arnold	5-16	0- 0	0	3	10
Al Daniel	9-18	3- 4	7	3	21
Jonathan Moore	7-13	5- 6	14	4	19
Bruce Grimm	2-13	2- 3	2	4	6
Ron Smith	1- 1	0- 0	1	3	2
Dale Crowe	1- 1	0- 0	1	1	2
Rick McKinney	1- 2	0- 0	2	0	2
Team			3		
Totals	26-64	10-13	30	18	62

Indiana	fg-fga	ft-fta	rb	pf	tp
Wayne Radford	8- 9	4- 4	6	5	20
Mike Woodson	13-24	0- 2	6	3	26
Ray Tolbert	1- 4	0- 0	9	4	2
Tommy Baker	2- 3	0- 1	6	2	4
Jim Wisman	3- 5	0- 2	2	1	6
Butch Carter	1- 1	3- 4	1	2	5
Steve Risley	0- 0	0- 0	1	0	0
Team			2		
Totals	28-46	7-13	33	17	63

Half time: Indiana 34-24. Officials: Galvan and Korte. Attendance: 11,666.

at Philadelphia, Pennsylvania

La Salle	fg-fga	ft-fta	rb	pf	tp
James Connolly	7-13	1- 2	9	5	15
Jim Wolkiewicz	8-12	2- 2	5	4	18
Michael Brooks	14-17	7- 9	14	2	35
Darryl Gladden	6-17	0- 0	3	5	12
Kurt Kanaskie	6-16	3- 4	0	4	15
Tony Plakis	1- 3	0- 0	4	5	2
Stan Williams	0- 0	0- 0	1	0	0
Joe Mihalich	0- 0	0- 0	0	2	0
Tony DiLeo	0- 0	0- 0	0	0	0
Team			6		
Totals	42-78	13-17	42	27	97

Villanova	fg-fga	ft-fta	rb	pf	tp
Reggie Robinson	10-16	2- 2	10	5	22
Keith Herron	10-16	4- 7	4	3	24
Alex Bradley	9-18	4- 4	8	3	22
Rory Sparrow	7-11	5- 6	2	4	19
Whitey Rigsby	5-10	4- 8	7	2	14
Steve Lincoln	1- 3	0- 0	0	0	2
Jay Underman	0- 0	0- 0	0	1	0
Tom Sienkiewicz	0- 1	0- 0	0	0	0
Marty Caron	0- 1	0- 1	1	1	0
Team			4		
Totals	42-76	19-28	36	19	103

Half time: LaSalle 49-46. Officials: Filliberti and Howell. Attendance: 9,208.

Midwest First Round

at Wichita, Kansas

Utah	fg-fga	ft-fta	rb	pf	tp
Jeff Judkins	4-13	3- 5	8	3	11
Danny Vranes	7-12	3- 7	10	4	17
Buster Matheney	17-28	2- 2	8	3	36
Earl Williams	1- 4	0- 0	7	4	2
Michael Grey	5-10	2- 5	2	3	12
Scott Martin	0- 0	2- 2	1	1	2
Mike Dunn	1- 1	0- 0	1	0	2
Greg Deane	1- 3	0- 0	2	3	2
Tom Chambers	0- 1	2- 2	0	1	2
Team			4		
Totals	36-72	14-23	43	22	86

Missouri	fg-fga	ft-fta	rb	pf	tp
Clay Johnson	13-23	4- 5	10	4	30
Curtis Berry	3- 3	0- 1	0	3	6
Stan Ray	2- 9	0- 1	12	2	4
Larry Drew	7-14	0- 0	1	1	14
Jeff Currie	7-12	4- 6	7	5	18
Ken Stoehner	0- 0	0- 0	0	1	0
Mike Foster	0- 0	0- 0	0	1	0
Brad Droy	2- 5	3- 4	8	4	7
Team			4		
Totals	34-66	11-17	42	21	79

Half time: Utah 44-38. Regulation Score: 64-64. First Overtime Score: 70-70. Officials: Crowel and Burson.

at Tulsa, Oklahoma

Houston	fg-fga	ft-fta	rb	pf	tp
Cecile Rose	4- 9	6- 7	2	3	14
Charles Thompson	5-10	0- 0	8	2	10
Mike Schultz	7- 9	1- 4	5	3	15
Kenneth Ciolli	0- 1	0- 0	0	3	0
Kenneth Williams	7-16	3- 4	2	2	17
Chuck O'Neall	0- 3	0- 0	0	0	0
Mark Trammell	2- 4	0- 0	1	1	4
Byron Gibson	1- 3	0- 0	1	1	2
Carl Byrd	0- 2	0- 0	0	1	0
Willie Porter	0- 0	0- 0	2	2	0
George Walker	4- 6	0- 0	4	0	8
Cedric Fears	2- 5	3- 4	3	2	7
Darnell Roper	0- 0	0- 0	0	2	0
Leonard Mitchell	0- 0	0- 0	1	1	0
Team			1		
Totals	32-68	13-19	30	23	77

Notre Dame	fg-fga	ft-fta	rb	pf	tp
Kelly Tripucka	4- 9	6- 8	4	0	14
Dave Batton	6- 8	0- 0	6	2	12
Bruce Flowers	2- 3	2- 2	2	4	6
Rich Branning	7-14	0- 0	0	2	14
Don Williams	8-14	3- 4	1	1	19
Tim Healy	0- 2	0- 0	0	0	0
Randy Haefner	0- 1	0- 2	1	0	0
Stan Wilcox	3- 4	0- 0	1	0	6
Orlando Woolridge	1- 2	0- 1	3	2	2
Bill Hanzlik	2- 4	0- 0	3	1	4
Gilbert Salinas	1- 1	1- 3	2	0	3
Bill Laimbeer	7- 9	6- 6	9	4	20
Team			5		
Totals	41-71	18-26	37	16	100

Half time: Notre Dame 47-32. Officials: Nichols and Herrold.

at Wichita, Kansas

Creighton	fg-fga	ft-fta	rb	pf	tp
Kevin McKenna	8- 9	2- 2	1	3	18
Rick Apke	7-16	0- 0	4	3	14
David Wesley	7-10	0- 0	8	3	14
Randy Eckcer	5- 8	3- 6	2	3	13
John C. Johnson	2- 3	1- 2	1	1	5
Kevin Kuehl	5- 7	0- 1	5	2	10
Tim McConnell	2- 3	0- 0	2	1	4
Team			7		
Totals	36-56	6-11	30	16	78

DePaul	fg-fga	ft-fta	rb	pf	tp
Joe Ponsetto	4- 9	2- 2	7	2	10
Curtis Watkins	7-10	0- 1	3	5	14
Dave Corzine	9-14	1- 2	11	2	19
Randy Ramsey	7-12	1- 1	3	3	15
Gary Garland	7-13	6- 7	2	3	20
Clyde Bradshaw	0- 2	0- 0	0	1	0
William Dise	0- 5	2- 4	3	0	2
Team			2		
Totals	34-65	12-17	31	17	80

Half time: Creighton 48-34. Officials: Jacob and MacArthur. Attendance: 10,582.

GAME-BY-GAME RESULTS

325

at Tulsa, Oklahoma

Louisville	fg-fga	ft-fta	rb	pf	tp
Bobby Turner	1- 4	1- 2	2	2	3
Larry Williams	8-13	5- 7	12	3	21
Rickey Gallon	3- 6	2- 2	7	3	8
Darrell Griffith	9-18	7- 7	4	2	25
Rick Wilson	4-11	7- 7	2	5	15
David Smith	0- 1	3- 4	6	0	3
Tony Branch	0- 2	1- 2	0	2	1
Team			8		
Totals	25-55	26-31	41	17	76

St. John's, N.Y.	fg-fga	ft-fta	rb	pf	tp
Kevelin Winfree	0- 2	0- 0	0	1	0
George Johnson	10-25	4- 4	20	4	24
Wayne McKoy	3-10	3- 6	5	5	9
Tom Calabrese	1- 3	0- 0	1	3	2
Reggie Carter	6-16	2- 2	6	5	14
Bernard Rencher	5-15	1- 1	2	2	11
Ron Plair	0- 0	0- 0	0	0	0
Gordon Thomas	3-10	1- 3	1	0	7
Paul Berwanger	0- 0	0- 0	2	3	0
Frank Gilroy	0- 1	0- 0	2	0	0
Rudy Wright	0- 2	1- 2	5	1	1
Team			3		
Totals	28-84	12-18	47	24	68

Half time: Louisville 39-34. Officials: Hernjak and White. Attendance: 10,075.

Mideast Regional

at Dayton, Ohio

Western Kentucky	fg-fga	ft-fta	rb	pf	tp
James Johnson	5- 8	2- 5	7	5	12
Greg Jackson	8-12	5-10	6	1	21
Aaron Bryant	5- 7	2- 2	7	5	12
Darryl Turner	6-19	0- 0	4	5	12
Steve Ashby	0- 1	0- 0	0	1	0
Mike Prince	2- 7	0- 0	1	0	4
Greg Burbach	0- 1	0- 0	0	2	0
Mike Reese	3- 6	0- 3	3	2	6
John Rahn	1- 4	0- 0	3	1	2
Don Thomas	0- 0	0- 0	0	0	0
Team			0		
Totals	30-65	9-20	31	22	69

Michigan State	fg-fga	ft-fta	rb	pf	tp
Earvin Johnson	3-17	7-11	9	2	13
Gregory Kelser	11-18	1- 2	13	5	23
Jay Vincent	6- 8	0- 0	6	4	12
Bob Chapman	10-12	3- 6	3	3	23
Terry Donnelly	0- 1	0- 0	1	0	0
Ronald Charles	4- 4	5- 6	8	3	13
Mike Brkovich	1- 1	0- 0	1	1	2
Sten Feldreich	0- 0	0- 0	1	3	0
Alfred Brown	1- 1	0- 0	1	0	2
Dan Riewald	0- 0	0- 0	0	0	0
Donald Flowers	1- 1	0- 0	0	0	2
Team			2		
Totals	37-63	16-25	45	21	90

Half time: Michigan State 39-29. Officials: MacArthur and Clymer.

at Dayton, Ohio

Kentucky	fg-fga	ft-fta	rb	pf	tp
Jack Givens	6-13	0- 1	9	4	12
Rick Robey	6- 8	2- 2	7	1	14
Mike Phillips	11-13	2- 3	4	2	24
Kyle Macy	1- 3	0- 0	0	1	2
Truman Claytor	6- 7	1- 1	1	3	13
James Lee	4- 9	4- 5	8	1	12
Jay Shidler	0- 1	0- 0	0	2	0
LaVon Williams	1- 1	0- 0	0	1	2
Fred Cowan	3- 5	0- 0	1	3	6
Chuck Aleksinas	1- 4	0- 0	3	1	2
Dwane Casey	1- 1	0- 0	0	0	2
Tim Stephens	0- 0	0- 0	2	1	0
Scott Courts	1- 1	0- 0	1	1	2
Team			1		
Totals	41-66	9-12	37	21	91

Miami, Ohio	fg-fga	ft-fta	rb	pf	tp
Randy Ayers	9-11	0- 0	8	5	18
Archie Aldridge	4-10	3- 4	3	2	11
Bill Lake	2- 4	2- 2	0	2	6
John Shoemaker	2- 8	6- 6	0	1	10
Rick Goins	6-10	0- 0	2	1	12
Tom Dunn	2- 3	0- 0	1	1	4
Terry Brady	1- 4	0- 0	4	1	2
Todd Jones	1- 1	0- 0	0	2	2
Todd Harkins	0- 0	2- 3	1	1	2
Rich Babcock	0- 2	0- 0	0	1	0
Brian Bays	0- 0	0- 1	0	0	0
Rick Lantz	1- 3	0- 2	2	0	2
Phil Griesinger	0- 1	0- 0	0	0	0
Team			2		
Totals	28-57	13-16	23	17	69

Half time: Kentucky 46-30. Officials: Jacob and Bishop. Attendance: 13,458.

at Dayton, Ohio

Michigan State	fg-fga	ft-fta	rb	pf	tp
Earvin Johnson	2-10	2- 2	4	4	6
Gregory Kelser	9-12	1- 3	13	3	19
Jay Vincent	4- 7	0- 0	1	1	8
Terry Donnelly	0- 0	2- 2	0	5	2
Bob Chapman	5- 9	0- 0	1	5	10
Ronald Charles	2- 3	0- 0	0	0	4
Mike Brkovich	0- 0	0- 0	0	0	0
Team			0		
Totals	22-41	5- 7	19	18	49

Kentucky	fg-fga	ft-fta	rb	pf	tp
Jack Givens	6-12	2- 3	7	3	14
Rick Robey	3- 4	0- 0	4	1	6
Mike Phillips	3- 5	4- 4	8	1	10
Kyle Macy	4-10	10-11	1	2	18
Truman Claytor	0- 5	0- 0	0	2	0
James Lee	1- 1	0- 0	1	4	2
Jay Shidler	1- 2	0- 0	1	2	2
LaVon Williams	0- 0	0- 0	1	1	0
Team			0		
Totals	18-39	16-18	23	16	52

Half time: Michigan State 27-22. Officials: Clymer and Bishop. Attendance: 13,458.

West Regional

at Albuquerque, New Mexico

UCLA	fg-fga	ft-fta	rb	pf	tp
David Greenwood	8-13	1- 4	4	5	17
James Wilkes	3- 5	0- 0	0	5	6
Gig Sims	0- 1	0- 0	4	2	0
Raymond Townsend	1-11	0- 0	2	2	2
Roy Hamilton	9-16	1- 2	1	4	19
Brad Holland	4- 9	0- 0	0	2	8
Darrell Allums	6- 7	0- 2	10	4	12
Marvin Thomas	1- 1	0- 0	2	0	2
Kiki Vandeweghe	2- 4	0- 0	4	0	4
Team			3		
Totals	34-67	2- 8	30	24	70

Arkansas	fg-fga	ft-fta	rb	pf	tp
Jim Counce	0- 1	2- 2	3	0	2
Marvin Delph	11-14	1- 1	10	2	23
Steve Schall	4- 7	0- 0	2	4	8
Ron Brewer	5-14	8-10	5	0	18
Sidney Moncrief	7-13	7-13	11	3	21
Alan Zahn	1- 1	0- 0	2	3	2
Ulysses Reed	0- 0	0- 2	0	0	0
Team			3		
Totals	28-50	18-28	36	12	74

Half time: Arkansas 42-29. Officials: Nichols and Fouty.

at Albuquerque, New Mexico

San Francisco	fg-fga	ft-fta	rb	pf	tp
Winford Boynes	8-14	1- 2	2	3	17
Doug Jemison	5-12	3- 4	11	3	13
Bill Cartwright	9-11	9-15	9	2	27
Rod Williams	0- 3	0- 0	3	4	0
John Cox	2- 9	0- 0	4	0	4
Sam Williams	2- 6	0- 0	2	4	4
James Hardy	3- 4	1- 2	4	0	7
Team			2		
Totals	29-59	14-23	37	16	72

Fullerton State	fg-fga	ft-fta	rb	pf	tp
Greg Bunch	11-15	2- 2	12	2	24
Kevin Heenan	7-13	1- 1	5	1	15
Steve Shaw	3- 7	0- 0	3	0	6
Keith Anderson	6-15	0- 2	4	3	12
Mike Linden	3- 9	1- 2	2	3	7
Mike Niles	3- 6	1- 3	3	5	7
Greg Palm	2- 4	0- 0	4	4	4
Team			5		
Totals	35-69	5-10	38	18	75

Half time: San Francisco 44-32. Officials: Weiler and Bain. Attendance: 17,750.

at Albuquerque, New Mexico

Fullerton State	fg-fga	ft-fta	rb	pf	tp
Greg Bunch	3- 9	3- 4	10	3	9
Kevin Heenan	5-14	1- 2	0	2	11
Steve Shaw	1- 4	0- 0	3	1	2
Keith Anderson	11-22	1- 1	9	1	23
Mike Linden	1- 7	0- 0	3	1	2
Mike Niles	4- 6	3- 4	3	4	11
Greg Palm	0- 0	0- 0	0	1	0
Team			6		
Totals	25-62	8-11	34	13	58

Arkansas	fg-fga	ft-fta	rb	pf	tp
Jim Counce	2- 2	0- 2	1	4	4
Marvin Delph	7-13	0- 0	5	2	14
Steve Schall	5- 6	0- 0	9	2	10
Ron Brewer	11-19	0- 0	3	4	22
Sidney Moncrief	4- 7	3- 4	4	4	11
Ulysses Reed	0- 0	0- 0	1	0	0
Team			2		
Totals	29-47	3- 6	25	16	61

Half time: Arkansas 39-24. Officials: Weiler and Bain. Attendance: 18,144.

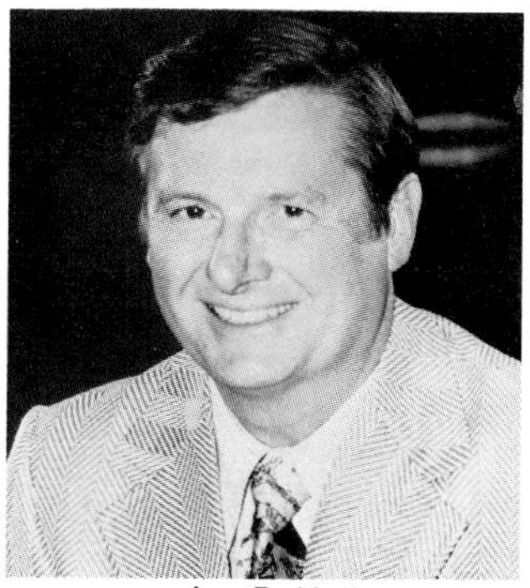

Joe B. Hall

East Regional

at Providence, Rhode Island

Duke	fg-fga	ft-fta	rb	pf	tp
Eugene Banks	8-17	5- 6	10	4	21
Kenny Dennard	4- 4	0- 1	5	4	8
Mike Gminski	6-14	2- 3	10	1	14
John Harrell	2- 4	2- 3	2	4	6
Jim Spanarkel	6-14	9- 9	6	1	21
Bob Bender	3- 5	2- 5	4	1	8
Steve Gray	0- 0	0- 0	0	0	0
Harold Morrison	0- 1	2- 2	0	0	2
Jim Suddath	1- 1	0- 0	1	1	2
Scott Goetsch	1- 2	0- 0	4	1	2
Team			4		
Totals	31-62	22-29	46	17	84

Pennsylvania	fg-fga	ft-fta	rb	pf	tp
Keven McDonald	5- 9	0- 1	5	4	10
Tony Price	6-16	5- 7	7	4	17
Matt White	3- 6	0- 2	11	4	6
Bobby Willis	7-14	2- 3	3	3	16
Stan Greene	2- 7	2- 2	1	5	6
Tom Crowley	5- 7	2- 4	3	3	12
James Salters	0- 0	0- 0	0	3	0
Tim Smith	6-10	1- 2	3	3	13
Team			2		
Totals	34-69	12-20	35	29	80

Half time: Duke 44-40. Officials: Herrold and Savidge.

at Providence, Rhode Island

Villanova	fg-fga	ft-fta	rb	pf	tp
Reggie Robinson	5-13	2- 2	7	3	12
Keith Herron	11-16	1- 2	5	2	23
Alex Bradley	1-11	4- 4	12	3	6
Rory Sparrow	5- 9	2- 4	2	4	12
Whitey Rigsby	2- 2	0- 1	3	4	4
Steve Lincoln	2- 3	0- 0	1	1	4
Marty Caron	0- 0	0- 0	0	1	0
Jay Underman	0- 0	0- 0	0	2	0
Team			7		
Totals	26-54	9-13	37	20	61

Indiana	fg-fga	ft-fta	rb	pf	tp
Wayne Radford	8-19	6- 8	6	3	22
Mike Woodson	11-19	2- 2	4	3	24
Ray Tolbert	4- 8	0- 2	4	5	8
Jim Wisman	1- 3	4- 4	1	0	6
Butch Carter	0- 0	0- 0	1	1	0
Tommy Baker	0- 0	0- 0	1	3	0
Steve Risley	0- 0	0- 1	2	1	0
Jim Roberson	0- 0	0- 0	1	1	0
Team			5		
Totals	24-49	12-17	25	17	60

Half time: Indiana 43-35. Officials: Kelley and Winters. Attendance: 10,689.

at Providence, Rhode Island

Villanova	fg-fga	ft-fta	rb	pf	tp
Reggie Robinson	8-17	0- 0	4	0	16
Keith Herron	8-19	4- 7	2	4	20
Alex Bradley	3- 7	4- 6	5	2	10
Rory Sparrow	1- 4	0- 0	2	4	2
Whitey Rigsby	3- 8	8-10	13	3	14
Bruce Anders	0- 0	0- 0	0	0	0
Steve Lincoln	2- 3	0- 0	1	2	4
Larry Sock	1- 2	0- 0	0	0	2
Tom Sienkiewicz	0- 3	0- 0	0	1	0
Ron Cowan	0- 1	0- 0	0	1	0
Marty Caron	0- 0	0- 0	0	1	0
Jay Underman	2- 3	0- 0	1	1	4
Team			2		
Totals	28-67	16-23	30	19	72

Duke	fg-fga	ft-fta	rb	pf	tp
Eugene Banks	6-10	5- 6	10	4	17
Kenny Dennard	8-12	0- 0	4	4	16
Mike Gminski	10-17	1- 1	10	3	21
John Harrell	3- 4	2- 2	1	1	8
Jim Spanarkel	9-11	4- 6	5	3	22
Rob Hardy	0- 0	0- 0	1	0	0
Bruce Bell	0- 0	0- 0	1	0	0
Bob Bender	0- 1	0- 0	2	2	0
Steve Gray	1- 1	0- 0	0	0	2
Harold Morrison	0- 0	0- 0	1	1	0
Jim Suddath	2- 3	0- 0	0	2	4
Scott Goetsch	0- 1	0- 0	1	1	0
Team			4		
Totals	39-60	12-15	40	21	90

Half time: Duke 46-32. Officials: Kelley and Winters. Attendance: 10,804.

Midwest Regional

at Lawrence, Kansas

Utah	fg-fga	ft-fta	rb	pf	tp
Jeff Judkins	7-17	2- 2	4	3	16
Danny Vranes	6-10	2- 3	11	4	14
Buster Matheney	4- 9	0- 0	4	5	8
Earl Williams	2- 2	0- 0	1	1	4
Michael Grey	1- 4	0- 0	1	5	2
Greg Deane	1- 3	6- 7	3	2	8
Tom Chambers	2- 5	0- 1	3	3	4
Scott Martin	0- 1	0- 0	0	2	0
Karl Bankowski	0- 2	0- 0	0	1	0
Jay Judkins	0- 0	0- 0	0	0	0
Coby Leavitt	0- 0	0- 0	0	0	0
Team			6		
Totals	23-53	10-13	33	26	56

Notre Dame	fg-fga	ft-fta	rb	pf	tp
Kelly Tripucka ...	8-11	4-5	4	3	20
Dave Batton	6-12	3-5	6	2	15
Bruce Flowers ...	0-1	0-1	3	5	0
Rich Branning....	3-7	5-7	0	3	11
Don Williams	5-14	0-1	2	2	10
Bill Laimbeer	1-3	2-5	5	2	4
Bill Hanzlik.....	2-3	3-3	2	4	7
Stan Wilcox	0-0	0-0	0	0	0
Tracy Jackson ...	1-1	0-0	2	0	2
Orlando Woolridge	0-0	0-0	0	0	0
Jeff Carpenter ...	0-0	0-0	0	0	0
Randy Haefner ...	0-0	0-0	0	0	0
Gilbert Salinas ...	0-0	0-0	1	0	0
Tim Healy	0-0	0-0	0	0	0
Team...........			11		
Totals	26-52	17-27	36	21	69

Half time: Notre Dame 28-26. Officials: Galvan and Diehl.

at Lawrence, Kansas

Louisville	fg-fga	ft-fta	rb	pf	tp
Bobby Turner	9-18	5-5	8	2	23
Larry Williams ...	6-12	1-2	9	4	13
Ricky Gallon.....	5-12	2-4	3	4	12
Darrell Griffith ..	9-15	1-3	3	5	19
Rick Wilson	9-20	2-3	6	3	20
David Smith	0-0	0-0	2	1	0
Tony Branch.....	1-2	0-0	0	1	2
Roger Burkman..	0-0	0-0	1	3	0
Team..........			6		
Totals	39-79	11-17	38	23	89

DePaul	fg-fga	ft-fta	rb	pf	tp
Curtis Watkins ...	6-10	4-5	8	2	16
Joe Ponsetto	4-4	0-0	4	3	8
Dave Corzine	18-28	10-10	9	3	46
Randy Ramsey ...	1-3	4-5	4	4	6
Gary Garland	3-11	4-4	2	1	10
Clyde Bradshaw ..	0-2	0-1	1	1	0
William Dise	2-3	0-0	1	2	4
Gary Wydra	0-0	0-0	0	0	0
Team..........			9		
Totals	34-61	22-25	38	16	90

Half time: DePaul 36-35. Regulation Score: 74-74. First Overtime Score: 82-82. Officials: Howell and Wortman. Attendance: 10,300.

at Lawrence, Kansas

DePaul	fg-fga	ft-fta	rb	pf	tp
Curtis Watkins ...	4-8	0-0	6	4	8
Joe Ponsetto	4-12	0-0	6	5	8
Dave Corzine	6-11	5-7	7	2	17
Randy Ramsey ...	1-5	0-0	4	1	2
Gary Garland	8-16	2-2	6	5	18
Clyde Bradshaw ..	3-8	0-0	0	2	6
William Dise	2-6	1-2	3	2	5
Randy Hook	0-0	0-0	0	0	0
Gary Wydra	0-0	0-0	0	0	0
Team..........			4		
Totals	28-66	8-11	36	21	64

Notre Dame	fg-fga	ft-fta	rb	pf	tp
Kelly Tripucka ...	9-22	0-0	11	2	18
Dave Batton.....	1-5	5-6	6	1	7
Bruce Flowers ...	2-2	3-3	1	4	7
Rich Branning....	6-12	3-3	4	0	15
Don Williams	5-12	4-4	3	2	14
Tracy Jackson ...	2-4	1-1	4	1	5
Bill Hanzlik......	2-3	0-0	3	2	4
Stan Wilcox	0-1	0-0	1	0	0
Bill Laimbeer	4-8	4-7	10	4	12
Jeff Carpenter ...	1-1	0-0	0	0	2
Randy Haefner ...	0-0	0-0	0	0	0
Gilbert Salinas ...	0-0	0-0	0	0	0
Orlando Woolridge	0-0	0-0	0	0	0
Team..........			4		
Totals	32-70	20-24	47	16	84

Half time: Notre Dame 37-33. Officials: Howell and Wortman. Attendance: 10,110.

Semifinals

at St. Louis, Missouri

Arkansas	fg-fga	ft-fta	rb	pf	tp
Jim Counce	2-2	2-3	2	4	6
Marvin Delph	5-13	5-6	8	3	15
Steve Schall.....	3-5	0-0	3	5	6
Ron Brewer	5-12	6-8	5	2	16
Sidney Moncrief ..	5-11	3-7	5	3	13
Alan Zahn	1-1	1-2	2	3	3
Ulysses Reed	0-0	0-0	0	2	0
Team..........			1		
Totals	21-44	17-26	26	22	59

Kentucky	fg-fga	ft-fta	rb	pf	tp
Jack Givens	10-16	3-4	9	2	23
Rick Robey......	3-6	2-2	8	2	8
Mike Phillips	1-6	3-4	2	4	5
Kyle Macy	2-8	3-4	3	4	7
Truman Claytor ..	1-2	0-1	0	4	2
Jay Shidley	3-5	0-0	2	4	6
James Lee	4-8	5-5	8	4	13
Dwane Casey	0-0	0-0	0	0	0
Tim Stephens	0-0	0-0	0	0	0
Fred Cowan	0-0	0-0	0	1	0
LaVon Williams..	0-0	0-0	0	1	0
Team...........			0		
Totals	24-51	16-20	32	26	64

Half time: Kentucky 32-30. Officials: Howell and Bain.

at St. Louis, Missouri

Duke	fg-fga	ft-fta	rb	pf	tp
Eugene Banks....	8-15	6-7	12	1	22
Kenny Dennard ...	2-3	3-5	7	5	7
Mike Gminski	13-17	3-4	5	2	29
John Harrell......	0-2	6-6	2	2	6
Jim Spanarkel ...	4-11	12-12	4	1	20
Bob Bender	0-1	2-3	2	2	2
Scott Goetsch....	1-1	0-0	0	0	2
Jim Suddath.....	1-3	0-0	0	2	2
Team...........			2		
Totals	29-53	32-37	34	15	90

Notre Dame	fg-fga	ft-fta	rb	pf	tp
Kelly Tripucka ...	5-17	2-2	9	3	12
Dave Batton.....	3-6	4-4	2	1	10
Bruce Flowers ...	5-8	0-0	6	3	10
Rich Branning....	4-10	0-0	1	3	8
Don Williams	8-15	0-1	2	2	16
Bill Laimbeer	1-5	5-6	10	5	7
Bill Hanzlik.....	3-8	2-2	6	5	8
Tracy Jackson ...	5-6	1-2	0	4	11
Stan Wilcox	2-2	0-0	0	0	4
Team...........			1		
Totals	36-77	14-17	37	26	86

Half time: Duke 43-29. Officials: Kelley and Clymer. Attendance: 18,721.

National Third Place

at St. Louis, Missouri

Arkansas	fg-fga	ft-fta	rb	pf	tp
Jim Counce	1-3	0-0	0	1	2
Marvin Delph	7-10	7-8	5	4	21
Steve Schall.....	3-9	0-0	11	3	6
Ron Brewer	7-16	6-6	6	3	20
Sidney Moncrief ..	3-6	4-6	4	4	10
Alan Zahn	4-6	2-3	2	2	10
Ulysses Reed	0-0	0-0	1	1	0
Chris Bennett	1-2	0-0	0	1	2
Team..........			1		
Totals	26-52	19-23	30	19	71

Notre Dame	fg-fga	ft-fta	rb	pf	tp
Kelly Tripucka ...	3-6	4-6	5	2	10
Dave Batton.....	6-12	3-3	7	3	15
Bruce Flowers ...	4-9	4-6	5	4	12
Rich Branning....	1-8	1-2	1	3	3
Don Williams	2-8	1-2	3	0	5
Bill Hanzlik......	4-5	0-0	2	4	8
Bill Laimbeer	1-1	0-0	3	2	2
Tracy Jackson ...	5-8	1-2	2	2	11
Stan Wilcox	1-2	0-0	1	1	2
Orlando Woolridge	0-0	1-2	1	1	1
Team..........			3		
Totals	27-59	15-23	33	22	69

Half time: Arkansas 40-36. Officials: Howell and Kelley.

Championship

at St. Louis, Missouri

Duke	fg-fga	ft-fta	rb	pf	tp
Eugene Banks....	6-12	10-12	8	2	22
Kenny Dennard...	5-7	0-0	8	5	10
Mike Gminski	6-16	8-8	12	3	20
John Harrell....	2-2	0-0	0	3	4
Jim Spanarkel ...	8-16	5-6	2	4	21
Jim Suddath.....	1-3	2-3	2	1	4
Bob Bender	1-2	5-5	1	3	7
Scott Goetsch....	0-1	0-0	1	1	0
Team..........			1		
Totals	29-59	30-34	35	22	88

Kentucky	fg-fga	ft-fta	rb	pf	tp
Jack Givens	18-27	5-8	8	4	41
Rick Robey......	8-11	4-6	11	2	20
Mike Phillips	1-4	2-2	5	4	4
Kyle Macy	3-3	3-4	0	1	9
Truman Claytor ..	3-5	2-4	0	2	8
James Lee	4-8	0-4	4	4	8
Jay Shidler	1-5	0-1	1	3	2
Chuck Aleksinas..	0-0	0-0	0	1	0
LaVon Williams..	1-3	0-0	4	2	2
Fred Cowan	0-2	0-0	2	1	0
Tim Stephens	0-0	0-0	0	0	0
Scott Courts	0-0	0-0	0	0	0
Chris Gettelfinger .	0-0	0-0	0	0	0
Dwane Casey	0-0	0-0	0	1	0
Team...........			0		
Totals	39-68	16-25	32	26	94

Half time: Kentucky 45-38. Officials: Bain and Clymer. Attendance: 18,721.

326